ローマ字	ひらがな	かたかな	ローマ字	ひらがな	かたかな	ローマ字	ひらがな	かたかな	ローマ字	ひらがな	かたかな
	お	オ									
	こ	コ	kya	きゃ	キャ	kyu	きゅ	キュ	kyo	きょ	キョ
so	そ	ソ	sha	しゃ	シャ	shu	しゅ	シュ	sho	しょ	ショ
to	と	ト	cha	ちゃ	チャ	chu	ちゅ	チュ	cho	ちょ	チョ
no	の	ノ	nya	にゃ	ニャ	nyu	にゅ	ニュ	nyo	にょ	ニョ
ho	ほ	ホ	hya	ひゃ	ヒャ	hyu	ひゅ	ヒュ	hyo	ひょ	ヒョ
mo	も	モ	mya	みゃ	ミャ	myu	みゅ	ミュ	myo	みょ	ミョ
yo	よ	ヨ									
ro	ろ	ロ	rya	りゃ	リャ	ryu	りゅ	リュ	ryo	りょ	リョ
o	を	ヲ									
go	ご	ゴ	gya	ぎゃ	ギャ	gyu	ぎゅ	ギュ	gyo	ぎょ	ギョ
zo	ぞ	ゾ	ja	じゃ	ジャ	ju	じゅ	ジュ	jo	じょ	ジョ
do	ど	ド									
bo	ぼ	ボ	bya	びゃ	ビャ	byu	びゅ	ビュ	byo	びょ	ビョ
po	ぽ	ポ	pya	ぴゃ	ピャ	pyu	ぴゅ	ピュ	pyo	ぴょ	ピョ

ローマ字つづりの注意事項

(1) はねる音はすべて "n" で表した。
新聞 *shinbun*　天気 *tenki*

(2) はねる音の "n" の次にすぐ母音字または "y" が続く場合には、"n" の次にアポストロフィー "'" を入れた。
原因 *gen'in*　金曜日 *kin'yōbi*

(3) つまる音は次に来る子音字を重ねて表した。ただし、子音字が "ch" の場合には "tch" とした。

学校 *gakkō*　マッチ *matchi*

(4) "あっ" のような感動詞の場合、つまる音はアポストロフィーをつけて表した。
あっ、たいへんだ。　*A'! Taihen da.*

(5) 長音は母音字の上に長音符号をつけて表した。ただし、"i" の場合には、"ii" とした。
セーター *sētā*　コーヒー *kōhii*

THE JAPAN FOUNDATION
BASIC
JAPANESE-ENGLISH
DICTIONARY

基礎日本語学習辞典

BONJINSHA

Copyright ©1986
by The Japan Foundation

ISBN 4-89358-004-3

First edition: December 1986

Published by Bonjinsha, Co. Ltd.
6-2, Kōjimachi, Chiyoda-ku, Tokyo 102, Japan

Printed in Japan

Preface

As international exchange deepens, the role of language as a means for mutual understanding becomes larger. The Japanese language is no exception, and for the past ten years the number of persons studying Japanese in foreign countries has been steadily on the rise.

However, at present there are next to no easy-to-use dictionaries in their own language for such foreigners starting their study of Japanese. Therefore most foreign students of Japanese are forced to make do with dictionaries—Japanese-English, Japanese-French, etc.—compiled for Japanese students of European languages. These dictionaries may be useful for intermediate and advanced students of Japanese who know such European languages well, but it seems that they are very difficult for beginning students to use. That is, the example sentences are written in *kanji* with no *furigana* or romanization and the lack of translations in their own language makes them difficult to understand for those whose native language is not English, French, or the like.

We at the Japan Foundation thus felt that there was a need for a dictionary easy to use by such beginning students of Japanese with editions in various foreign languages. Therefore we embarked on the compilation of this dictionary. A selection of basic vocabulary has been made from words in everyday use, an analysis of the different senses in which these words are used has been carried out, and those different senses shown through example phrases and sentences. *Furigana* and romanization have been included so that this work can be used by beginning students.

Since an English translation has been added on the right-hand side of each page, this edition should be easy for English speakers to understand. The study of language is in effect the attempt to understand by overcoming cultural differences, and in the translation when no exact equivalent exists the closest approximation has been chosen; cultural explanations have been added as necessary.

This dictionary will have served its purpose if through its use the student finds it even a little easier to understand this basic vocabulary and to use it in the actual speaking and writing of Japanese. We would be happy to receive comments and suggestions for use in later editions.

We would also like to express our thanks here to all the individuals who have participated in the planning, compilation, translation, and checking of this dictionary.

Japanese Studies Department
The Japan Foundation
September 1986

iii

About This Dictionary

1. This dictionary has been compiled for use by foreigners studying Japanese who are still at a relatively early stage in their studies.

2. There are 2,873 separate entries, chiefly centering around vocabulary used by Japanese language teaching institutions on the introductory level. The choice of entries was made based on Japanese language teaching materials, studies of vocabulary in common use, dictionaries, and consultations with persons involved in teaching Japanese as a foreign language.

3. For the convenience of the user, the entries are written in roman letters followed by the standard writing in *kanji* and/or *kana*. Romanization has also been provided for example expressions, compounds, and sentences; and *furigana* is provided for *kanji* in the entries and the example expressions, compounds, and sentences.

4. In order to clarify the meaning and usage of the entry words and to aid in the formation of one's own sentences, example sentences have been provided; compounds and idiomatic expressions using that word are also included. In addition, as necessary, different senses of the word have been shown and explanations of usage given. Indication has also been made of words of contrasting and similar meaning to be consulted.

5. An English translation accompanies the Japanese text so the student can compare the two.

6. The different senses given for the entries, in accordance with the nature of this dictionary, have been restricted to the basic ones but are at times quite detailed so that they will be useful at a relatively high level of study.

Using This Dictionary

This dictionary consists of a Japanese text on the left-hand side of the page with a corresponding English translation on the right-hand side of the page.

I. The entries

  (1) The form of the entry

    (a) The entry is written first in roman letters and then in the standard Japanese writing in *kanji* and/or *kana* followed by an abbreviation indicating part or parts of speech.

    (b) The entry is given in the dictionary or citation form. Adjective-verbs are given in the stem form.

    (c) The hyphens with prefixes and suffixes indicate where they are attached to other words.

      dai-　第-〖頭〗

      -bu　-部〖尾〗

    (d) In the case of compounds, the symbol ~ indicates the omission of some word or element.

      (~**te**) **ageru**　(~て) あげる〖連〗

    (e) More than one part of speech has been indicated where appropriate.

      taihen　たいへん〖副, 形動〗

    Nouns and adverbs that can be used with *suru* as Type III verbs have been indicated as such.

      benkyō　勉強〖名, ~する〗

      hakkiri　はっきり〖副, ~する〗

  (2) The arrangement of entries

    (a) The entries are in alphabetical order.

    (b) In the case of different entries with the same spelling, those written in *kanji* come before those written in *kana*.

      fuku　吹く〖動 I〗

      fuku　ふく〖動 I〗

    (c) Words with the same pronunciation usually differentiated by *kanji* are treated as separate entries. There is no particular rule of order in such a case.

      atataka　暖か〖形動〗　　**ateru**　当てる〖動 II〗

      atataka　温か〖形動〗　　**ateru**　充てる〖動 II〗

II. The form of writing in Japanese

(1) The use of *tōyō kanji*, *kana*, and inflectional *kana* follows standards established by the Japanese government.

(2) *Furigana* is included for all *kanji* in the entries, example compounds, example expressions, and example sentences. *Kanji* have been used as much as possible for words usually written in *kanji* while words generally written in *hiragana* have been written in *hiragana*. Thus in some cases a word may be written in both *kanji* and *hiragana* in the example sentences for a single entry.

> 絵を掛ける　　　　(e o *kakeru*)
> 心配をかける　　　(shinpai o *kakeru*)

(3) Numbers are written in *kanji* in the entries but, as the text is written in horizontal form, are generally in arabic numerals in the text itself.

(4) The romanization generally follows that of the second table in the Japanese government's *Rōmaji no tsuzurikata* (The Romanization of Japanese). See also the table at the front of this volume.

III. The example sentences

(1) Example sentences for the entry are indicated by the sign ¶.

> ¶はがきを5枚ください。　(*Hagaki* o gomai kudasai.)

(2) Sentences spoken by different speakers are indicated by 「　」 in the Japanese text.

> ¶「これは日本語の本ですか。」(Kore wa Nihongo no hon desu ka?)
>
> 「はい，そうです。」　(*Hai,* sō desu.)

(3) Within the example expressions and sentences, the entry word is indicated by boldface type in the Japanese and italics in the romanization.

> **ha ha**　**母**〖名〗
> ¶**母**は今年 60 歳です。　　(*Haha* wa kotoshi rokujissai desu).

IV. The explanations of meaning and usage

(1) When judged advisable, different senses of the entry are indicated by the numbers ①, ②, ③, etc.; the individual meanings appear within brackets.

(2) The senses are generally listed with those used most frequently appearing first.

(3) Where more than one part of speech is applicable, separate explanations have been provided if there is a significant difference in meaning.

jissai 実際〔名，副〕

1〔名〕

¶彼の話は**実際**とはだいぶ違います。

(Kare no hanashi wa *jissai* to wa daibu chigaimasu.)

2〔副〕

¶この問題には**実際**困っています。

(Kono mondai ni wa *jissai* komatte imasu.)

(4) Usage notes are indicated by a boldface asterisk (＊). Where the note only applies to that one particular sense of the word, a small asterisk (＊) has been used.

V. Words of contrasting meaning and other related words

(1) Words of contrasting meaning for an entry are indicated by ⇔. When the word applies for only one sense of the entry ↔ is used.

(2) A cross-reference to a word with a related meaning is indicated by ▷. A cross-reference to a related word applying to a single sense of the entry is indicated by →.

(3) When the entry appears under a different form the reader is referred to the correct entry by ☞.

VI. The abbreviations used for the parts of speech

The abbreviations used for the parts of speech in the entries are:

〔名〕	〖n〗	noun
〔代〕	〖pron〗	pronoun
〔動Ⅰ〕	〖v I〗	Type I verb (*godan* verb; *-u* verb)
〔動Ⅱ〕	〖v II〗	Type II verb (*-ru* verb)
〔動Ⅲ〕	〖v III〗	Type III verb
〔形〕	〖adj〗	adjective
〔形動〕	〖adj-v〗	adjective-verb
〔副〕	〖adv〗	adverb
〔連体〕	〖attrib〗	attributive
〔接〕	〖conj〗	conjunction
〔感〕	〖interj〗	interjection
〔助動〕	〖auxil〗	auxiliary
〔助〕	〖part〗	particle
〔頭〕	〖pref〗	prefix
〔尾〕	〖suf〗	suffix
〔連〕	〖compd〗	compound

Concerning the English-language Edition

I. The entries

(1) The form of the entry

    (a) To help beginning students, there are entries for verb endings (*-ba*, *-mashō*, *-masu*, *-nai*, *-nakereba naranai*, *-nasai*, *-rareru*, *-reru*, *-saseru*, *-seru*, *-ta*, *-tara*, *-te*, *-te mo*, *-te wa*, *-yō*, *-zu*, etc.) not usually found in other Japanese-English dictionaries. Entries for expressions with a verb in the *-te* form plus a helping verb are found under the helping verb ([*-te*] *ageru*, [*-te*] *ikenai*, [*-te*] *kuru*, [*-te*] *miru*, [*-te*] *oku*, [*-te*] *shimau*, etc.). Entries for expressions with a verb in the stem form plus a second verb are also found under the second verb (*-au*, *-dasu*, *-komu*, *-sugiru*, etc.).

    (b) Words often used with the prefix *o-* are generally found under the base form (*cha*, *rei*, *tagai*, *tearai*, etc.).

    (c) Idiomatic expressions can generally be found listed as separate senses under both of the key words. For example, *hara ga tatsu* can be found under both the entries for *hara* and for *tatsu*.

(2) The arrangement of entries

    (a) The alphabetical order is letter by letter, not word by word.

nan(-)	何 (-)
nana	七
naname	斜め
nanatsu	七つ
nan de mo	何でも
nani(-)	何 (-)
nani ka	何か

    (b) The alphabetical order is often affected by the system of romanization.

      ① " ん " is romanized as "n".

        新聞   shinbun

      ② Long vowels are transcribed with a macron except for "i", which is written "ii".

        セーター   sētā   ビール   biiru

      ③ Certain words have been transcribed with a doubled vowel in accordance with how they are written in Japanese: *baai*, *hoo*, *koori*, *kooru*, *kuu*, *nuu*, *oo-*, *ooi*, *ookii*, *ookina*, *ookisa*, *ooku*, *oozei*, *too*, *tooi*, *tooka*, *tooku*, *toori*, *-toori*, *tooru*, and *toosu*.

④ No distinction is made in the alphabetical order between short vowels and long vowels written with a macron, but the word with the short vowel comes first if the words are otherwise spelled the same.

yowai	弱い
yoyaku	予約
yōyaku	ようやく
yoyū	余裕
yu	湯
yū-	夕 -
yūbe	ゆうべ
yubi	指

⑤ Words written with a doubling of the vowel are alphabetized accordingly.

ba	ば	betsu ni	別に
baai	場合	biiru	ビール
(-) bai	(-) 倍	bijutsu	美術
baka	ばか	bikkuri suru	びっくりする

II. The English translation

(1) The definitions

   (a) Different senses of the word in the definition at the head of the entry are separated by semicolons.

   (b) The definitions for different senses found in brackets are often not a direct translation of the Japanese definition but rather the English equivalent of the word being defined.

chikaku ③[数量などがそれより少し足りないが

それとほとんど同じぐらいであること]

(literally, an amount, etc., being a little less but almost the same) →
[nearly, almost]

(2) The translations of the example phrases and sentences

   (a) The translations have been kept as close to the Japanese original as possible, and a literal translation is generally given if a natural English sentence close to the Japanese is not possible.

   (b) In some cases one Japanese sentence may become two sentences in English and vice versa. The part of speech may also change in the translation. For this reason, the reader will notice that the words in boldface type in the English translations may not correspond exactly to what is in boldface in the Japanese text.

(c) The choice of the singular or the plural or of the definite or indefinite article in the English translation is often arbitrary as this is not made definite in the Japanese original. Thus "*Kodomo ga niwa de asonde imasu*" could be "A child is playing in the yard," "The child is playing in the yard," "Children are playing in the yard," or "The children are playing in the yard." The most likely possibility has been chosen.

(d) An attempt has been made to indicate major alternative possibilities in sense, tense, and meaning of individual vocabulary items, but these are not exhaustive.

(e) The translations are in American English, and an effort has been made to make them easy to understand for non-native as well as native speakers of English.

(3) Symbols used in the English translation

(a) // separates different example compounds or phrases.

(b) [ ] indicates items specified in English but not in Japanese.

あ，あれは上田さんです。

Oh, that's [Mr.] Ueda.

(c) ( ) indicates items specified in Japanese but not in English.

姉は洗たく物にアイロンをかけています。

My (elder) sister is ironing the laundry.

お茶をどうぞ。

Please have some (green) tea.

(d) ⟦ ⟧ indicates alternative possibilities.

成績が上がる

one's grades ⟦business results⟧ improve

雨が降りだしました。

It has started to rain ⟦It started to rain⟧.

(e) * indicates incorrect or ungrammatical sentences.

(4) The reader is also referred to the "Introduction to Japanese Grammar" found at the back of this volume.

は　し　が　き

　国際間の交流が一層深まるに従って、意思疎通の手段として言語の果たす役
割は大きくなってきています。日本語もその例外ではなく、ここ10年来海外で
日本語を学ぶ人の数は増大の一途をたどっています。

　ところが、日本語の学習を始めようとする外国人にとって、自国語の訳がつ
いた使い易い辞書がほとんどないのが現状です。従って多くの外国人学習者は、
日本人の外国語学習用に編集された「和英辞典」や「和仏辞典」を代用してい
る場合が多いようです。これらの辞典は英語やフランス語が良くできる中・上
級の学習者には有益であったとしても、初級学習者にとっては非常に使いにく
いといわれています。というのは、文例中の漢字に振り仮名がなく、ローマ字
表記もついていないし、英語等以外の言語を母国語とする学習者にとって自国
語の対訳もなく、解りにくいからです。

　国際交流基金では、こうした初級の日本語学習者にとって使い易い辞典を各
国語版で刊行する必要があると考え、本「基礎日本語学習辞典」の編集を進め
てまいりました。日常使われる言葉から基礎語彙を選定し、その語のもつ意味
の分類を行い、それぞれの意味ごとに語の使われ方を語例や文例の中で明示し
ました。振り仮名およびローマ字表記も添えましたので、初めての学習者も利
用できるものと確信しております。

　ページの右側には対照に英語訳を付けましたので、英語を母国語とする学習
者にとって解り易いはずです。ことばの学習は文化の違いを超えて理解しよう
とする試みでもあるわけですが、英語訳を付けるに当っては、日本語の意味に
ぴったりとする訳語がない場合にはその近似値を選び、必要に応じて文化的説
明を加えて理解を助けました。

　本辞典を利用することにより基本語彙の理解が少しでも容易になり、また文
例の中でどう用いられるかを学ぶことによって、実際に話したり書いたりする
時に役立てられれば、本辞典の役割は果たされたことになります。本辞典につ
いてご意見・ご批判をお寄せいただければ、改訂の際に参考にさせていただき
ます。

　最後に、本辞典の企画・編集に参画された編集委員の先生方、翻訳、校閲の
諸先生および御協力頂いた方々に心より感謝の意を表したいと存じます。

　昭和　61 年 9 月

国際交流基金日本研究部

は じ め に

1. この辞典は、日本語を学習する外国人が、比較的初期の段階において使用することを目的として編集されたものです。

2. 見出し語として、2873語を収録しました。各日本語教育機関などにおいて初期の段階で多く取り扱われる語が中心になっています。

   見出し語は日本語の教材や語い調査、辞書などを参考にして、日本語教育に関係している方々の合議によって決めました。

3. 学習者が自習するのに便利なように見出し語はローマ字で示し、それに日本語の標準的な表記を併記しました。

   語例および用例には、すべてローマ字の表記を併記し、また漢字にはすべて振り仮名をつけました。

4. 見出し語の意味や用法がよく理解できるように、また、文章を書くときに役立つように、用例を挙げ、さらにその語に関連した複合語や慣用的な語句も挙げました。また、必要に応じて、意味分類をするとともに注を付してその用法について解説を加えました。

   なお、反対語や参照語なども示しました。

5. 学習者が日本語を英語と比較して学習できるように、日本語に対応する英語による翻訳を添えました。

6. 見出し語の意味分類は、この辞典の性格から基礎的なものに限りましたが、やや高い段階の学習にも利用できるように少し詳しい分類を行ったものもあります。

凡　　　例

　この辞典は、左側には日本語、右側にはそれに対応する英語による訳文が載せてあります。

I.　見出し語

(1)　書き表し方

　　(a)　初めにローマ字で示し、次に日本語の標準的な表記を示して、その品詞名などを略語で添えました。

　　(b)　活用語は「終止の形」で示しました。ただし、形容動詞は語幹の形で示しました。

　　(c)　見出し語のうち、接頭語・接尾語については、次のように、つく語の位置にハイフン「-」を置きました。

　　　　dai-　第-〖頭〗　　**-bu**　-部〖尾〗

　　(d)　連語については、前に語がつくものは、それを「～」で示し、次のようにしました。

　　　　(～te) ageru　（～て）**あげる**〖連〗

　　(e)　二つ以上の品詞にわたるものは、それを併記しました。

　　　　taihen　たいへん〖副, 形動〗

　　また、名詞、副詞などで動Ⅲの動詞として用いられるものは、〖名、～する〗〖副、～する〗などして示しました。

　　　　benkyō　勉強〖名, ～する〗

　　　　hakkiri　はっきり〖副, ～する〗

(2)　配　　列

　　(a)　見出し語はアルファベット順に配列しました。

　　(b)　見出し語に同音異義語が二つ以上ある場合は、漢字表記の語を先に仮名表記の語をあとに挙げました。

　　　　fuku　吹く〖動Ⅰ〗

　　　　fuku　ふく〖動Ⅰ〗

　　(c)　同音の語で普通漢字によって書き分けられているものについては、別の見出し語として取り扱いました。その先後については、特に問いませんでした。

　　　　atataka　暖か〖形動〗　　　**ateru**　当てる〖動Ⅱ〗

　　　　atataka　温か〖形動〗　　　**ateru**　充てる〖動Ⅱ〗

Ⅱ. 日本語の表記について

(1) 当用漢字（内閣告示の当用漢字表・同音訓表・同字体表）、現代かなづかい（内閣告示）、送り仮名の付け方（内閣告示）を基準としました。

(2) 見出し語および語例、用例の漢字にはすべて振り仮名をつけました。広く漢字による表記が行われているものは、できるだけ漢字による表記をとりましたが、一般的に平仮名で表記されることが多いと思われるものは平仮名にしました。したがって、同じ見出し語の中の用例でも漢字によって表記したものと平仮名によって表記したものとがある場合があります。

絵を掛ける　　　　　　　（e o *kakeru*）

心配をかける　　　　　　（shinpai o *kakeru*）

(3) 数詞については、見出し語は漢数字で示してありますが、本文が横書きなので、適宜、算用数字を使用しました。

(4) ローマ字の表記は、おおむね内閣告示「ローマ字のつづり方」の「第2表」によりました。

なお、表のとびらの「ローマ字・平仮名・片仮名対照表」を参照してください。

Ⅲ. 用例について

(1) 見出し語を実際に用いた語例、用例のうち、用例は ¶ で示しました。

¶はがきを5枚ください。　（*Hagaki* o gomai kudasai.）

(2) 会話文の用例は、「　」で示しました。

¶「これは日本語の本ですか。」　（Kore wa Nihongo no hon desu ka?）

「はい，そうです。」　（*Hai*, sō desu.）

(3) 語例、用例中の見出し語に当たる語は、ゴチック体で示し、ローマ字表記は、イタリック体で示しました。

haha 母《名》

¶母は今年60歳です。　（*Haha* wa kotoshi rokujissai desu.）

Ⅳ. 意味・用法の説明

(1) 見出し語の意味を分類したほうがよいと認めた場合は、①、②、③…と分類し、[　]の中にその意味の説明をしました。

(2) 意味分類の配列は、普通によく使われるものを先にしました。

(3) 二つ以上の品詞などにわたるもので、意味の上で必要な場合は、それぞれ品詞別の項目を立てて記述しました。

jissai 実際〖名，副〗

1〖名〗

¶彼の話は**実際**とはだいぶ違います。

(Kare no hanashi wa *jissai* to wa daibu chigaimasu.)

2〖副〗

¶この問題には**実際**困っています。

(Kono mondai ni wa *jissai* komatte imasu.)

(4) 見出し語の用法について説明する必要があると認めた場合は、＊をつけて説明しました。

また、意味分類の中の各項の用法について説明する場合は、＊をつけて説明しました。

Ⅴ．反対語・参照語など

(1) 見出し語に対する反対語がある場合は、⇔ で示しました。

また、意味分類の中の各項における反対語は ↔ で示しました。

(2) 見出し語に対して関係のある語を参照語として挙げましたが、見出し語全体に対する参照語は ⇨ で示しました。

また、意味分類の中の各項における参照語は → で示しました。

(3) 他の見出し語を参照する場合は、☞ で示しました。

Ⅵ．品詞名などの略語

〔名〕	名詞	〔副〕	副詞
〔代〕	代名詞	〔連体〕	連体詞
〔動Ⅰ〕	Ⅰ型の動詞（五段活用）	〔接〕	接続詞
〔動Ⅱ〕	Ⅱ型の動詞（上一段活用	〔感〕	感動詞
	・下一段活用）	〔助動〕	助動詞
〔動Ⅲ〕	Ⅲ型の動詞（カ行変格活用	〔助〕	助詞
	・サ行変格活用）	〔頭〕	接頭語
〔形〕	形容詞	〔尾〕	接尾語
〔形動〕	形容動詞	〔連〕	連語

Ⅶ．英語への翻訳について

(1) 定義

    (a) 見出しの初めに併記した定義のうち、意味に差異のある語については、; を用いて区分しました。

    (b) 意味分類をした定義のうち、[ ]の中には、日本語による定義の直訳

ではなく、英語における同義語を示しました。

chikaku ③[数量などがそれより少し足りないが

それとほとんど同じぐらいであること]

(literally, an amount, etc., being a little less but almost the same) →
[nearly, almost]

(2) 語例及び用例の翻訳

(a) 翻訳はできるだけ日本語の原文に近づけるように努めましたが、英文の表現として不自然になる場合には、通常、文字通りの訳文も別に記しました。

(b) 翻訳の際、一つの和文に対応する英文が2つになる場合や、その逆の場合、また、品詞が変わる場合があります。このため、英文中でボールド体で表記した語が、和文中のゴシック体で表記した語と一字一句そのまま対応しているとは限りません。

(c) 日本語の原文においては、単数・複数或いは、定冠詞・不定冠詞の区別がないので、英語に翻訳する際には適宜選択しました。

(d) 文意や時制、個々の語彙の意味等の点において言い換えが可能な表現を示すように試みましたが、すべてを網羅しているわけではありません。

(e) 翻訳にあたってはアメリカ英語を採用し、英語を母国語とする学習者はもちろん、それ以外の学習者にも理解し易いように努めました。

(3) 英語訳で用いた記号について

(a) // は語例を併記する際区分するのに用いました。

(b) [ ]の中には、英語においてのみ区別のある語彙を示しました。

あ、あれは上田さんです。

Oh, that's [Mr.] Ueda.

(c) ( )の中には日本語においてのみ区別のある語彙を示しました。

姉は洗たく物にアイロンをかけています。

My (elder) sister is ironing the laundry.

(d) ⟦ ⟧の中には言い換えが可能な表現を示しました。

成績が上がる

one's grades ⟦business results⟧ improve

(e) ＊は間違った或いは非文法的な文例を示しました。

(4) 学習者の参考となるよう巻末に "Introduction to Japanese Grammar" を編集しました。

A

a あ〖感〗
¶あ, 富士山が見えます。(A! Fujisan ga miemasu.)
¶あ, あれは上田さんです。 (A! Are wa Ueda san desu.)
¶あっ, 地震だ。(A'! Jishin da.)

ā ああ〖副〗
¶ああいう人は見たことがありません。(Āiu hito wa mita koto ga arimasen.)
¶ああ忙しくては, ゆっくり食事をする暇もないでしょう。(Ā isogashikute wa, yukkuri shokuji o suru hima mo nai deshō.)
* 話し手にとっても話し相手に対してもともに隔たりのあるものごとの様子をさし示すのに使う。
⇒kō こう　sō そう　dō どう

ā ああ〖感〗
¶ああ, うれしい。(Ā, ureshii.)
¶ああ, そうですか。わかりました。(Ā, sō desu ka. Wakarimashita.)

abiru 浴びる〖動Ⅱ〗
湯を浴びる (yu o abiru)　川で水を浴びる (kawa de mizu o abiru)　日光を浴びる (nikkō o abiru)
¶わたしは毎朝シャワーを浴びます。(Watashi wa maiasa shawā o abimasu.)

abunai 危ない〖形〗
¶危ないから, 道の真ん中を歩かないで

a [[interj]]　**Oh!**
¶ **Oh** look! You can see Mount Fuji.

¶ **Oh,** that's [Mr.] Ueda.

¶ **Oh!** It's an earthquake!

ā [[adv]]　**that, so**
¶ I've never seen **that** sort of person before.

¶ [They] look **so** busy [they] probably don't have time to eat leisurely.

* Used for something at a distance from both the speaker and the listener.

ā [[interj]]　**Oh!, Ah!**
¶ **Oh,** I'm so glad!
¶ **Oh,** is that so? I understand.

abiru [[v II]]　**pour on oneself; bathe in**
take a bath // **take** a dip in a river // **be bathed** in sunlight
¶ I **take** a shower every morning.

abunai [[adj]]　**dangerous**
¶ Don't walk in the middle of the

1

ください。(*Abunai* kara, michi no mannaka o arukanaide kudasai.)

¶ガソリンスタンドの近くでたばこを吸うのは危ないです。(Gasorin-sutando no chikaku de tabako o suu no wa *abunai* desu.)

street—**it's dangerous.**

¶ **It's dangerous** to smoke near a gasoline station.

abura 油〚名〛

¶機械に油をさしてください。(Kikai ni *abura* o sashite kudasai.)

¶機械を直したので、手が油で汚れました。(Kikai o naoshita node, te ga *abura* de yogoremashita.)

¶料理には油をよく使います。(Ryōri ni wa *abura* o yoku tsukaimasu.)

abura 〚n〛 oil, grease

¶ Please **oil** the machine.

¶ [My] hands are all **greasy** because [I] fixed the machine.

¶ One often uses **oil** in cooking.

achira あちら〚代〛

①[話し手にとっても話し相手に対してもともに隔たりのある関係にある方向をさし示す]

¶あちらに見えるのが富士山です。(*Achira* ni mieru no ga Fujisan desu.)

¶「新宿へ行く電車のホームはどちらですか。」(Shinjuku e iku densha no hōmu wa dochira desu ka?)

「あちらのホームです。」(*Achira* no hōmu desu.)

* 話し手・話し相手のどちらにも身近な関係にない方向をさし示すのに使う。

②[話し手にとっても話し相手に対してもともに隔たりのある関係にある方向に存在する所をさし示す]

¶ここは危ないですから、あちらで遊びなさい。(Koko wa abunai desu kara, *achira* de asobinasai.)

achira 〚pron〛 there; that

① [indicates a direction distant from both the speaker and the listener]

¶ The mountain you can see **over there** is Mount Fuji.

¶ "Which is the platform for the train going to Shinjuku?"

"It's **that** platform **over there.**"

* Used to indicate a direction not close physically to either the speaker or the listener.

② [indicates a place distant from both the speaker and the listener]

¶ Play **over there** because it's dangerous here.

¶北海道の山田さんからのお便りによると、**あちら**はまだときどき雪が降るそうです。(Hokkaidō no Yamada san kara no otayori ni yoru to, *achira* wa mada tokidoki yuki ga furu sō desu.)

* 話し手・話し相手のどちらにも身近な関係にない方向に存在する所をさし示す。東京にいる話し手が同じ東京にいる話し相手に対して北海道のことについて言う場合は「あちら (achira)」と言う。

③［話し手にとっても話し相手に対してともに隔たりのある関係にある方向に存在する人をさし示す］

¶こちらは山田さんで、**あちら**は田中さんです。(Kochira wa Yamada san de, *achira* wa Tanaka san desu.)

¶このことについては、**あちら**様では何とおっしゃっていますか。(Kono koto ni tsuite wa, *achira* sama de wa nan to osshatte imasu ka?)

* 話し手・話し相手のどちらにも身近な関係にない方向にいる人をさし示すのに使う。現に話題になっている先方の人も「あちら (achira)」または「あちら様 (achira sama)」と言う。

④［話し手にとっても話し相手に対してともに隔たりのある関係にある方向に存在するものをさし示す］

¶こちらは山田さんので、**あちら**は田中さんのです。(Kochira wa Yamada san no de, *achira* wa Tanaka san no desu.)

¶ According to what I hear from [Miss] Yamada in Hokkaido, it still snows **there** sometimes.

* Indicates a place not close physically to either the speaker or the listener. A speaker in Tokyo talking to someone who is also in Tokyo will refer to Hokkaido as *achira*.

③ [indicates a person distant from both the speaker and the listener]

¶ This is [Mrs.] Yamada and **that** is [Mr.] Tanaka.

¶ What do **they** have to say concerning this matter (very polite)?

* Used to indicate a person not close physically to either the speaker or the listener. A person not present whose identity is known to both the speaker and the listener can also be referred to as *achira* or *achira sama*.

④ [indicates something distant from both the speaker and the listener]

¶ This is [Mrs.] Yamada's and **that** is [Mr.] Tanaka's.

¶あちらのほうがおいしそうですから、**あちら**を5個ください。 (Achira no hō ga oishisō desu kara, *achira* o goko kudasai.)

＊「あっち (atchi)」とも言うが、「あちら (achira)」のほうが丁寧な言葉である。

⇨**kochira** こちら　**sochira** そちら　**dochira** どちら

¶ Those over there look better; give me five of **them.**

＊ *Atchi* is also used in conversation, but *achira* is more polite.

afureru　あふれる〖動Ⅱ〗

¶大雨が降って、池の水が**あふれまし**た。 (Ooame ga futte, ike no mizu ga *afuremashita*.)

¶ビールがコップから**あふれて**しまいました。 (Biiru ga koppu kara *afurete* shimaimashita.)

afureru 〚v II〛 overflow

¶ It rained heavily and the pond **overflowed** its banks.

¶ The beer **ran over** the top of the glass.

agaru　上がる〖動Ⅰ〗

①[上へ行く、高い所へ行く]
二階へ上がる (nikai e *agaru*) 階段を上がる (kaidan o *agaru*)

¶いすに上がって、たなの上の本を取ってください。 (Isu ni *agatte*, tana no ue no hon o totte kudasai.)

¶どうぞ、こちらへお上がりください。 (Dōzo, kochira e o*agari* kudasai.)

②[値段・価値・程度などが高くなる]
物価が上がる (bukka ga *agaru*) 温度が上がる (ondo ga *agaru*) 成績が上がる (seiseki ga *agaru*) 月給が上がる (gekkyū ga *agaru*)

¶来月から、バス代が 20 円上がるそうです。 (Raigetsu kara, basudai ga nijūen *agaru* sō desu.)

↔**sagaru** 下がる

agaru 〚v I〛 go up; rise; eat, drink

① [go up, climb]
go up to the second floor // **climb** the stairs

¶ Please **stand** on the chair and reach down the book on the shelf.

¶ Please **come in** (that is, up from the lowered entryway).

② [rise in price, value, degree, etc.]
prices **rise** // the temperature **rises** // one's grades 〚business results〛 **improve** // one's (monthly) salary **rises**

¶ I hear that bus fares are **going up** 20 yen from next month.

③[食べる，飲む]

¶どうぞ，お茶をおあがりください。
(Dōzo, ocha o oagari kudasai.)

＊「食べる (taberu)」「飲む (nomu)」
の尊敬語。

ageru　上げる〖動Ⅱ〗

①[下から上へ移す]

¶この荷物をたなに上げましょうか。
(Kono nimotsu o tana ni agemashō
ka?)

②[値段・価値・程度などを高める]

値段を上げる (nedan o ageru)
温度を上げる (ondo o ageru)　月給を
上げる (gekkyū o ageru)

¶政府は来年から税金を上げるそうで
す。(Seifu wa rainen kara zeikin o
ageru sō desu.)

↔sageru　下げる

③[やる，与える]

結婚のお祝いを上げる　(kekkon no
oiwai o ageru)

¶この本をあなたに上げましょう。
(Kono hon o anata ni agemashō.)

¶どれでも好きな物を上げるから，持っ
て行きなさい。(Dore demo suki na
mono o ageru kara, motte ikinasai.)

＊「やる (yaru)」「与える (ataeru)」
の謙譲語であるが，最近はむしろ上品
な言葉として使う。普通，対等または
目下の人にある物を与えるときに使う。
目上の人の場合も使うが，直接目上の
人に言う場合には使わない。直接目上
の人に向かって言うときには「差し上
げる (sashiageru)」を使う。「この本

③ [eat, drink]

¶ Please **have** some tea.

＊ *Agaru* is the honorific form of
taberu and *nomu*.

ageru〖v II〗　raise; give

① [raise something]

¶ **Shall I put** this bag **up** on the shelf
for you?

② [raise prices, value, degree, etc.]

raise prices // **raise** the temperature
// **raise** (monthly) wages

¶ I hear that the government is going
to **raise** taxes from next year.

③ [give]

give a wedding present

¶ **I'll give** you this book.

¶ **I want you to have** whichever you
like; please take it with you.

＊ *Ageru* is the humble form of *yaru*,
ataeru; recently used as refined language. Usually used when giving
something to someone of equal or
lower status. Also used in the case of
superiors but not in direct address.
When directly addressing a person of
higher status, such as one's teacher,

を先生に差し上げます。(Kono hon o sensei ni sashiagemasu.)」

→yaru やる　sashiageru 差し上げる

ageru　挙げる〖動Ⅱ〗

①[下から上へ持ち上げる]

¶答えがわかった人は手を挙げてください。(Kotae ga wakatta hito wa te o *agete* kudasai.)

②[並べて人に示す]

¶先生は例を挙げて説明してくださいました。(Sensei wa rei o *agete* setsumei shite kudasaimashita.)

③[式などを行う]

¶わたしたちは教会で結婚式を挙げました。(Watashitachi wa kyōkai de kekkonshiki o *agemashita*.)

(〜te) ageru　（〜て）あげる〖連〗

¶わたしはその人に駅へ行く道を教えてあげました。(Watashi wa sono hito ni eki e iku michi o oshiete *agemashita*.)

¶その荷物を持ってあげましょうか。(Sono nimotsu o motte *agemashō* ka?)

¶わたしは友達に漢字を教えてあげました。(Watashi wa tomodachi ni kanji o oshiete *agemashita*.)

＊「（〜て）やる（[〜te] yaru）」の謙譲の言い方であるが，むしろ上品な言い方として使われる。一般に，動作をする人が相手の人のためにある動作をするという意味を表す。動作をする人の側に立って言うときに使う。普通，

---

sashiageru is used: "*Kono hon o sensei ni sashiagemasu*" (This book is for you, sir).

ageru 〖v II〗 raise; give; hold
(a ceremony)

① [raise]

¶ Will those who know the answer please **raise** their hands.

② [give, offer]

¶ The teacher explained by **giving** an example.

③ [hold a ceremony, etc.]

¶ We **had** our wedding ceremony in a church.

(-te) ageru 〖compd〗 do someone the favor of -ing

¶ I **told** that person the way to the station.

¶ **Let me carry** that bag for you.

¶ I **taught** my friend *kanji*.

＊ The humble form of (-te) *yaru* but now often used as refined language. Generally expresses the meaning of the speaker performing some action for the benefit of the listener. It is not usually used when directly

目上の人に直接向かって言うときには
使わない。例えば、先生が大きな荷物
を持っているような場合に「そのお荷
物を持ってあげましょう。(Sono oni-
motsu o motte agemashō.)」とは言
わない。そのような場合には「そのお
荷物をお持ちしましょう。(Sono oni-
motsu o omochi shimashō.)」と言
う。
⇨(〜**te**) **yaru** (〜て) やる

ai 愛〖名, 〜する〗
母の愛 (haha no *ai*) 神の愛 (kami
no *ai*) 平和を愛する (heiwa o *ai*suru)
¶あの人は親切なので、みんなに愛さ
れています。(Ano hito wa shinsetsu
na node, minna ni *ai*sarete imasu.)

aida 間〖名〗
①[空間的な隔たり、二つの物にはさ
まれた所]
¶机と机の間をもう少し広くしてくだ
さい。(Tsukue to tsukue no *aida* o
mō sukoshi hiroku shite kudasai.)
¶銀行と郵便局の間の道をまっすぐ行
くと、学校の前に出ます。(Ginkō to
yūbinkyoku no *aida* no michi o
massugu iku to, gakkō no mae ni
demasu.)
②[限られた一続きの時間]
¶1時から2時までの間にここへ来て
ください。 (Ichiji kara niji made
no *aida* ni koko e kite kudasai.)
¶ずいぶん長い間お目にかかりません
でしたね。(Zuibun nagai *aida*

addressing a person of higher status.
For example, when one's teacher is
carrying a large bag or package, one
should not say * "*Sono onimotsu o
motte agemashō.*" In such a case one
would say "*Sono onimotsu o omochi
shimashō.*"

ai 〚n, 〜*suru*〛 **love, affection**
a mother's **love** // divine **love** // **to
love** peace

¶ Since that person is kind, [he] is
loved by all.

aida 〚n〛 **space; interval; relations**
① [physical space, the space between
two things]
¶ Please move the desks a little farther **apart.**

¶ When you go straight along the
street **between** the bank and the post
office, you come out in front of the
school.

② [a certain interval of time]
¶ Please come here **between** one
and two o'clock.

¶ I haven't seen you for such a long
time.

ome ni kakarimasen deshita ne.)

¶わたしが留守の間にだれか訪ねてきたようです。 (Watashi ga rusu no *aida* ni dare ka tazunete kita yō desu.)

③[間がら・関係など]

¶近ごろ，山田さんは奥さんとの間がうまくいっていないようです。 (Chikagoro, Yamada san wa okusan to no *aida* ga umaku itte inai yō desu.)

¶A国とB国との間についに戦争が起こりました。 (Ē-koku to Bii-koku to no *aida* ni tsuini sensō ga okorimashita.)

aijō 愛情〖名〗

¶子供に対する親の愛情はなによりも強いです。 (Kodomo ni taisuru oya no *aijō* wa nani yori mo tsuyoi desu.)

¶二人の愛情はますます深くなっていきました。 (Futari no *aijō* wa masumasu fukaku natte ikimashita.)

airon アイロン〖名〗

¶姉は洗たく物にアイロンをかけています。 (Ane wa sentakumono ni *airon* o kakete imasu.)

aisatsu あいさつ〖名, ～する〗

¶日本では，朝「お早うございます。」とあいさつをします。 (Nihon de wa, asa "Ohayō gozaimasu." to *aisatsu* o shimasu.)

¶わたしがあいさつしたのに，山田さんは返事をしませんでした。(Watashi

¶ It seems that someone came to visit **while** I was out.

③ [relations, etc.]

¶ It seems that Mr. Yamada and his wife aren't getting along well recently.

¶ In the end war broke out **between** Country A and Country B.

aijō 〖n〗 **love, affection**

¶ **The love** of parents for their children is stronger than anything else.

¶ **The affection** between the two deepened further.

airon 〖n〗 **iron**

¶ My (elder) sister is **ironing** the laundry.

aisatsu 〖n, ～*suru*〗 **greeting**

¶ In Japan, one **greets** people in the morning with *ohayō gozaimasu* 〖good morning〗.

¶ Although I **greeted** [her], [Mrs.] Yamada gave no response.

8

ga *aisatsu* shita noni, Yamada san wa henji o shimasen deshita.)

aisukuriimu アイスクリーム〖名〗
¶アイスクリームは牛乳と砂糖と卵で作ります。(*Aisukuriimu* wa gyūnyū to satō to tamago de tsukurimasu.)

aite 相手〖名〗
¶わたしは結婚の**相手**を探しています。(Watashi wa kekkon no *aite* o sagashite imasu.)
¶わたしには困ったときの相談**相手**がいません。(Watashi ni wa komatta toki no sōdan-*aite* ga imasen.)
¶この店は外国人を**相手**に商売をしています。(Kono mise wa gaikoku-jin o *aite* ni shōbai o shite imasu.)

aizu 合図〖名, ～する〗
¶ピストルの音を**合図**に子供たちは駆けだしました。(Pisutoru no oto o *aizu* ni kodomotachi wa kakedashi-mashita.)
¶手を挙げて**合図**しても，タクシーは止まりませんでした。(Te o agete *aizu* shite mo, takushii wa tomarimasen deshita.)

aji 味〖名〗
味がいい (*aji* ga ii) 味が濃い (*aji* ga koi) 味が薄い (*aji* ga usui) 味をみる (*aji* o miru)
¶このスープはとてもいい**味**ですね。(Kono sūpu wa totemo ii *aji* desu ne.)
¶この料理は砂糖やしょう油などで**味**をつけます。(Kono ryōri wa satō

aisukuriimu 〖n〗 ice cream
¶ **Ice cream** is made from milk, sugar, and eggs.

aite 〖n〗 the other party, the object of
¶ I am looking for **someone** to marry.

¶ I have **no one** to consult when I have a problem.

¶ This shop does most of its business with foreigners 〚This shop **caters to** foreigners〛.

aizu 〖n, ～*suru*〗 signal
¶ The children started to run at **the signal** of a pistol shot.

¶ The taxi didn't stop even though [I] **signaled** it by raising [my] hand.

aji 〖n〗 flavor, taste
taste good // be strongly **flavored** // be weakly **flavored** // to taste (something)
¶ This soup is delicious.

¶ This dish is mainly **flavored** with sugar and soy sauce.

ya shōyu nado de *aji* o tsukemasu.)

aka 赤〖名〗
赤鉛筆 (*aka*enpitsu)
¶信号が赤に変わりました。 (Shingō
ga *aka* ni kawarimashita.)

akachan 赤ちゃん〖名〗
男の赤ちゃん (otoko no *akachan*)
かわいい赤ちゃん (kawaii *akachan*)
＊「赤ん坊 (akanbō)」の丁寧な言い方。
⇨akanbō 赤ん坊

akai 赤い〖形〗
赤いシャツ (*akai* shatsu)　赤いりん
ご (*akai* ringo)
¶庭に赤い花が咲きました。(Niwa ni
akai hana ga sakimashita.)
¶山田さんはビールを飲むと，すぐ顔
が赤くなります。 (Yamada san wa
biiru o nomu to, sugu kao ga *akaku*
narimasu.)

akanbō 赤ん坊〖名〗
¶赤ん坊が泣いています。(*Akanbō* ga
naite imasu.)
¶赤ん坊のお守りをしてください。
(*Akanbō* no omori o shite kudasai.)
＊他人の赤ん坊は「赤ちゃん (aka-
chan)」と言うほうがよい。
⇨akachan 赤ちゃん

akari 明かり〖名〗
①[電燈などの光]
明かりをつける (*akari* o tsukeru)
明かりを消す (*akari* o kesu)
¶隣の部屋はまだ明かりがついていま
す。(Tonari no heya wa mada

aka 〖n〗 **red**
a **red** pencil
¶ The traffic light turned **red.**

akachan 〖n〗 **baby**
a **baby** boy // a cute **baby**

＊ The polite way of saying *akanbō*.

akai 〖adj〗 **red**
a **red** shirt 〚T-shirt, etc.〛// a **red** apple
¶ A **red** flower is in bloom in the garden.
¶ When [Mr.] Yamada drinks beer,
[his] face soon becomes **flushed.**

akanbō 〖n〗 **baby**
¶ **The baby** is crying.

¶ Please look after **the baby** for me.

＊ It is best to use *akachan* to refer to
a baby which is not one's own.

akari 〖n〗 **light**
① [electric light, etc.]
turn on **the light** // turn off **the light**

¶ **The lights** are still on in the next
room 〚in the next-door apartment〛.

akari ga tsuite imasu.)

¶丘の上から港の**明かり**が見えます。

(Oka no ue kara minato no *akari* ga miemasu.)

②[日や月の光]

¶月の**明かり**で波が光っています。

(Tsuki no *akari* de nami ga hikatte imasu.)

¶ From the top of the hill you can see the harbor **lights.**

② [sunlight, moonlight]

¶ The waves are glimmering in the moon**light.**

akarui 明るい〖形〗

¶この部屋はたいへん**明るい**ですね。

(Kono heya wa taihen *akarui* desu ne.)

¶この電球は暗いから，もっと**明るい**のに取り替えたほうがいいですよ。

(Kono denkyū wa kurai kara, motto *akarui* no ni torikaeta hō ga ii desu yo.)

¶雨がやんで，空が**明る**くなってきました。(Ame ga yande, sora ga *akaruku* natte kimashita.)

⇔**kurai** 暗い

akarui 〖adj〗 **bright**

¶ This room **is** very **sunny** 〖**well lighted; cheerful**〗.

¶ This light bulb is too weak. You should replace it with a **brighter** one.

¶ The rain has stopped and the sky is now **clear** 〖The rain stopped and the sky became **clear**〗.

akeru 開ける〖動Ⅱ〗

かばんを**開ける** (kaban o *akeru*) かぎを**開ける** (kagi o *akeru*) 口を**開ける** (kuchi o *akeru*) 本を**開ける** (hon o *akeru*)

¶暑いから窓を**開けて**ください。

(Atsui kara mado o *akete* kudasai.)

¶このびんのふたを**開けて**くださいませんか。(Kono bin no futa o *akete* kudasaimasen ka?)

¶ゆうべ，３時間しか寝なかったので，眠くて目を**開けて**いられません。

(Yūbe, sanjikan shika nenakatta

akeru 〖v Ⅱ〗 **open**

open a bag 〖suitcase, briefcase, etc.〗 // **open** a lock // **open** one's mouth // **open** a book

¶ It's hot—please **open** the window.

¶ Would you please **open** this bottle for me?

¶ Since I only slept three hours last night, I'm so sleepy I can hardly **keep** my eyes **open.**

node, nemukute me o *akete* irare-masen.)

⇔shimeru 閉める　tojiru 閉じる

akeru　空ける〖動Ⅱ〗

席を空ける (seki o *akeru*)　時間を
空ける (jikan o *akeru*)

¶今日の午後は家を空けます。(Kyō no
gogo wa ie o *akemasu.*)

akeru　明ける〖動Ⅱ〗

①[明るくなる，朝になる]

¶夜が明けて，辺りが明るくなってき
ました。(Yo ga *akete*, atari ga akaruku natte kimashita.)

②[一年が終わって新年になる]

¶明けましておめでとうございます。

(*Akemashite* omedetō gozaimasu.)

aki　秋〖名〗

¶日本では九月と十月と十一月は秋で
す。(Nihon de wa kugatsu to jūgatsu to jūichigatsu wa *aki* desu.)

aki　空き〖名〗

空き家 (*akiya*)　空き箱 (*aki*bako)
空きびん (*aki*bin)

akiraka　明らか〖形動〗

明らかな事実 (*akiraka* na jijitsu)

¶あの人がうそをついているのは明ら
かです。(Ano hito ga uso o tsuite
iru no wa *akiraka* desu.)

¶その考えは明らかに間違っています。
(Sono kangae wa *akiraka* ni machigatte imasu.)

¶この物語は，だれが作ったのか明ら
かではありません。(Kono monoga-
tari wa, dare ga tsukutta no ka

akeru 〖v II〗　leave vacant, keep
open

make room (for someone to sit
down) // **keep** a time **open** (for
someone)

¶ **I will not be** at home this afternoon.

akeru 〖v II〗　dawn; open, begin

① [become light, to dawn]

¶ **With the dawn** it has become ⟦it
became⟧ light all around.

② [one year ends and the new year
begins]

¶ Happy **New Year!**

aki 〖n〗　autumn

¶ In Japan **autumn** is September,
October, and November.

aki 〖n〗　being empty

a **vacant** house // an **empty** box //
an **empty** bottle

akiraka 〖adj-v〗　clear, plain, evi-
dent

an **obvious** fact

¶ **It is obvious** that [he] is lying.

¶ That notion is **plainly** mistaken.

¶ **It is not clear** who wrote this tale.

akiraka de wa arimasen.)

akirameru あきらめる〖動Ⅱ〗

¶なくした時計はもうあきらめなさい。(Nakushita tokei wa mō *akiramenasai.*)

¶わたしは日本への留学をあきらめました。(Watashi wa Nihon e no ryūgaku o *akiramemashita.*)

akiru 飽きる〖動Ⅱ〗

①[じゅうぶんに満足する]

飽きるほど食べる (*akiru* hodo taberu)

¶毎日、魚ばかり食べていたので、もう飽きました。(Mainichi, sakana bakari tabete ita node, mō *akimashita.*)

②[ものごとを続けて行うのがいやになる]

仕事にあきる (shigoto ni *akiru*)

¶この絵は何度見てもあきません。(Kono e wa nando mite mo *akimasen.*)

aku 開く〖動Ⅰ〗

¶窓が開いています。(Mado ga *aite* imasu.)

¶風で戸が開きました。(Kaze de to ga *akimashita.*)

¶かぎが掛かっていて、ドアが開きません。(Kagi ga kakatte ite, doa ga *akimasen.*)

¶朝早くて、まだ店が開いていません。(Asa hayakute, mada mise ga *aite* imasu.)

⇔shimaru 閉まる

akirameru 〖vⅡ〗 give up (doing something), resign oneself to

¶You'd better reconcile yourself to the loss of your watch.

¶I have given up on the idea of studying in Japan.

akiru 〖vⅡ〗 be satiated; tire of

① [be satiated, be completely satisfied]

eat to one's heart's content

¶Since I've eaten nothing but fish every day, I've had my fill of it.

② [tire of, lose interest in]

be tired of a job

¶I never tire of this picture no matter how many times I look at it.

aku 〖vⅠ〗 open, be opened

¶The window is open.

¶The wind blew the door open.

¶The door won't open because it's locked.

¶It's early in the morning and the stores aren't open yet.

aku 空く〖動Ⅰ〗

¶このアパートには，今空いた部屋はありません。(Kono apāto ni wa, ima *aita* heya wa arimasen.)

¶汽車がこんでいて，空いている席はありませんでした。(Kisha ga konde ite, *aite* iru seki wa arimasen deshita.)

akushu 握手〖名，〜する〗

友達と握手する (tomodachi to *akushu* suru)

amai 甘い〖形〗

¶このお菓子はとても甘いです。(Kono okashi wa totemo *amai* desu.)

¶わたしは甘い物より辛い物のほうが好きです。(Watashi wa *amai* mono yori karai mono no hō ga suki desu.)

⇔karai 辛い

amari 余り〖名〗

¶魚の余りをねこにやりました。(Sakana no *amari* o neko ni yarimashita.)

amari あまり〖副〗

①[そんなに，それほど]

¶このバナナはあまりおいしくありません。(Kono banana wa *amari* oishiku arimasen.)

¶わたしはあまりラジオを聞きません。(Watashi wa *amari* rajio o kikimasen.)

* あとに打ち消しの言葉が来る。「あまり〜ない(amari〜nai)」の形で使う。
②[とても，非常に]

aku 〚v I〛 **become empty, not be in use**

¶ There are no **vacant** apartments now in this apartment building.

¶ The train was crowded, and there were no **empty** seats.

akushu 〚n, ~*suru*〛 **a handshake** **shake hands** with a friend

amai 〚adj〛 **to be sweet**

¶ This candy 〚cake, etc.〛 **is** very **sweet.**

¶ I like salty 〚sharply flavored〛 foods better than **sweet** ones.

amari 〚n〛 **the remaining, the rest, surplus**

¶ I gave the **leftover** fish to the cat.

amari 〚adv〛 **(not) very; too much**

① [(not) very, (not) so]

¶ This banana does not taste **very** good.

¶ I don't listen to the radio **very much.**

* Used with the negative. Used in the pattern "*amari ~ -nai.*"
② [too much, very, extremely]

¶あまり急いだので、かぎを忘れてきました。(*Amari* isoida node, kagi o wasurete kimashita.)

¶あまり無理をすると、病気になりますよ。(*Amari* muri o suru to, byōki ni narimasu yo.)

¶この本はあまりおもしろかったので、途中でやめられませんでした。(Kono hon wa *amari* omoshirokatta node, tochū de yameraremasen deshita.)

* あとに肯定の言葉が来る。
* 「あんまり (anmari)」とも言う。

amaru 余る〖動Ⅰ〗

¶まだお金は余っています。(Mada okane wa *amatte* imasu.)

¶紙を配りますから、余ったら先生に返してください。(Kami o kubarimasu kara, *amattara* sensei ni kaeshite kudasai.)

ame 雨〖名〗

¶昨日は雨が降りました。(Kinō wa *ame* ga furimashita.)

¶今日も朝から雨です。(Kyō mo asa kara *ame* desu.)

¶午後になって、雨がやみました。(Gogo ni natte, *ame* ga yamimashita.)

¶雨に降られて、ぬれてしまいました。(*Ame* ni furarete, nurete shimaimashita.)

ami 網〖名〗

¶子供たちが網で魚を捕っています。(Kodomotachi ga *ami* de sakana o totte imasu.)

¶ I was in **such** a hurry that I forgot my key.

¶ You will become ill if you overdo **so much.**

¶ This book was **so** interesting that I couldn't stop reading until I had finished it.

* Used with the positive.
* Variant: *anmari*.

amaru 〖v I〗 remain, be in excess

¶ There is still some money **left over.**

¶ I am going to hand out paper; **if there is any extra,** please return it to the teacher.

ame 〖n〗 rain

¶ **It rained** yesterday.

¶ **It's been raining** from the morning today too.

¶ It stopped **raining** in the afternoon.

¶ I got wet when I was caught in **the rain.**

ami 〖n〗 net

¶ Children are catching fish in **a net.**

¶海岸で漁師が網を編んでいます。
(Kaigan de ryōshi ga *ami* o ande imasu.)

amu　編む〖動Ⅰ〗

¶お母さんが子供のセーターを編んでいます。(Okāsan ga kodomo no sētā o *ande* imasu.)

¶竹を編んで，かごを作ります。(Take o *ande,* kago o tsukurimasu.)

ana　穴〖名〗

①[物の表面からくぼんでいる空間]

¶穴を掘って，木を植えました。(*Ana* o hotte, ki o uemashita.)

②[物の向こう側までつきぬけている空間]

¶シャツに穴があきました。(Shatsu ni *ana* ga akimashita.)

¶くつの底に穴があいてしまいました。(Kutsu no soko ni *ana* ga aite shimaimashita.)

anata　あなた〖代〗

あなたがた (*anata*gata)　あなたたち (*anata*tachi)

¶あなたは田中さんですか。(*Anata* wa Tanaka san desu ka?)

¶あなたのお国はどちらですか。(*Anata* no okuni wa dochira desu ka?)

¶これをあなたに上げましょう。(Kore o *anata* ni agemashō.)

＊目上の人に対してはあまり言わない。例えば先生などに対しては「あなた (anata)」と言わないで，「先生 (sensei)」と言うほうがよい。「あな

¶ Along the shore fishermen are weaving **nets.**

amu 〚v I〛　knit, braid, weave

¶ The mother **is knitting** a sweater for her child.

¶ [They] **weave** bamboo to make baskets.

ana 〚n〛　hole

① [a depression in a surface]

¶ I dug **a hole** and planted a tree.

② [a hole in something]

¶ There is **a hole** in the shirt 〚undershirt〛.

¶ I have **a hole** in the bottom of my shoe.

anata 〚pron〛　you

you (plural) // **you** (plural)

¶ Are **you** [Miss] Tanaka?

¶ What country are **you** from?

¶ I am giving this to **you.**

＊ Not used so much toward persons of higher status. For example, one should address a teacher or doctor as *sensei* rather than *anata. Anata* is

た (anata)」は,自分と同じ程度の人,
または目下の人に対して使う。「-がた
(-gata)」「-たち (-tachi)」は複数を
表す。「-たち (tachi)」より「-がた
(-gata)」のほうが丁寧な言い方であ
る。

used toward those of the same or
lower status but is usually omitted if
understood from context. For the
plural, *-gata* and *-tachi* are used; the
former is more polite.

ane 姉〖名〗

¶わたしには姉が三人います。(Wata-
shi ni wa *ane* ga sannin imasu.)
¶いちばん上の姉は銀行に勤めていま
す。(Ichiban ue no *ane* wa ginkō
ni tsutomete imasu.)
＊自分の姉のことを他人に話す場合
に使う。直接,姉に呼びかける場合や,
他人の姉のことを言う場合は,「お姉
さん (onēsan)」と言う。
⇒imōto 妹 ⇒onēsan お姉さん

ane 〖n〗 elder sister

¶ I have three **older sisters.**

¶ My eldest **sister** works at a bank.

＊ Used to refer to one's own sister
when talking to others. When directly addressing one's elder sister or
when referring to someone else's
elder sister, *onēsan* is used.

angai 案外〖副,形動〗

案外に安い (*angai* ni yasui)
¶この本は案外安いですね。 (Kono
hon wa *angai* yasui desu ne.)
¶この計画は案外うまくいくかもしれ
ません。(Kono keikaku wa *angai*
umaku iku ka mo shiremasen.)

angai 〖adv, adj-v〗 contrary to ex-
pectation, unexpectedly
surprisingly inexpensive

¶ This book is cheaper **than one
would expect.**
¶ This plan might work out **surprisingly** well.

ani 兄〖名〗

¶わたしには兄が二人あります。
(Watashi ni wa *ani* ga futari arimasu.)
¶上の兄は医者で,二番めの兄は大学
の先生をしています。 (Ue no *ani*
wa isha de, nibanme no *ani* wa
daigaku no sensei o shite imasu.)
＊自分の兄のことを他人に話す場合
に使う。直接,兄に呼びかける場合や,

ani 〖n〗 elder brother

¶ I have two **older brothers.**

¶ My eldest **brother** is a doctor and
my next eldest **brother** is a university
professor.
＊ Used to refer to one's own brother
when talking with others. When
directly addressing one's elder

他人の兄のことを言う場合は，「お兄
さん (oniisan)」と言う。
⇔otōto 弟　⇨oniisan お兄さん

anna　あんな〖連体〗
①［話し手にとっても話し相手に対して
もともに隔たりのある関係にあるもの
ごとの状態をさし示す］
¶あんないい家に住んでみたいです。
(*Anna* ii ie ni sunde mitai desu.)
＊話し手・話し相手にともに身近な関
係にないものごとの状態をさし示すの
に使う。
②［文脈の上で前に述べたものごとの
状態を話し手にとっても話し相手に対
してもともに隔たりのある関係でさし
示す］
¶上田さんは田中さんにとてもひどい
ことを言うんです。上田さんがあんな
人だとは思いませんでした。　(Ueda
san wa Tanaka san ni totemo hidoi
koto o iu n desu. Ueda san ga
anna hito da to wa omoimasen
deshita.)
⇨konna こんな　sonna そんな
donna どんな

annai　案内〖名，〜する〗
案内人 (*annai*in)　案内所 (*annai*jo)
道を案内する (michi o *annai* suru)
¶京都を案内していただけませんか。
(Kyōto o *annai* shite itadakemasen
ka?)

anna ni　あんなに〖副〗
¶山田さんはあんなに金持ちなのに，

brother or referring to someone
else's elder brother, *oniisan* is used.

anmari ☞ **amari**

anna 〖attrib〗　**such, that sort of**
① [indicates something distant from
both the speaker and the listener]

¶ I would like to live in **that sort** of
nice house.
* Used to indicate a condition not
psychologically close for either the
speaker or the listener.
② [indicates something mentioned
earlier that is distant from both the
speaker and the listener]

¶ [Mr.] Ueda said some terrible
things to [Mr.] Tanaka. I didn't think
that [he] was **that sort** of person.

annai 〖n, 〜*suru*〗　**guidance; information**

a guide // an **information** office
〖desk, counter〗 // **show** (someone)
the way

¶ Won't you **show [us] around**
Kyoto?

anna ni 〖adv〗　**in that way, to that
extent**

¶ Even though [Mrs.] Yamada is **so**

18

とてもけちです。 (Yamada san wa *anna ni* kanemochi na noni, totemo kechi desu.)

¶あんなに驚いたのは初めてです。
(*Anna ni* odoroita no wa hajimete desu.)

¶あんなに謝っているのですから、今度だけは許してあげましょう。
(*Anna ni* ayamatte iru no desu kara, kondo dake wa yurushite agemashō.)

＊ 話し手にとっても話し相手に対してもともに隔たりのある関係にあるものごとの程度や状態をさし示すのに使う。

⇨**konna ni** こんなに　**sonna ni** そんなに　**donna ni** どんなに

ano　あの〚連体〛

①〔話し手にとっても話し相手に対してもともに隔たりのあるものごととの関係をさし示す〕
あの人 (*ano hito*)　　あの方 (*ano kata*)

¶「あの机の上に何がありますか。」
(*Ano* tsukue no ue ni nani ga arimasu ka?) 「かばんがあります。」
(Kaban ga arimasu.)

¶「あの人はだれですか。」 (*Ano* hito wa dare desu ka?)「あの人は中村さんです。」 (*Ano* hito wa Nakamura san desu.)

¶「あの方はどなたですか。」(*Ano* kata wa donata desu ka?) 「あの方は上田先生です。」 (*Ano* kata wa Ueda sensei desu.)

---

rich, [she] is very stingy.

¶ I've never been **so** surprised.

¶ Since [he] has apologized **so much,** let's forgive [him] this one time.

＊ Used to indicate the degree or condition of something at a distance from both the speaker and the listener.

ano 〚attrib〛　**that, those**

① [indicates something distant from both the speaker and the listener]
that person // **that** person (more polite)

¶ "What is on top of **that** desk?"
"A bag 〚briefcase, etc.〛 is."

¶ "Who is **that** person over there?"
"**That** is [Miss] Nakamura."

¶ "Who is **that** person over there?" (more polite).
"**That** is Professor Ueda."

* 話し手・話し相手にともに身近ではないものごととの関係をさし示すのに使う。

②[文脈の上で前に述べたものごとと話し手・話し相手との隔たりのある関係をさし示す]

¶「中村さんや田中さんもお金が足りなくて困っていますか。」(Nakamura san ya Tanaka san mo okane ga tarinakute komatte imasu ka?)「いいえ、あの人たちはお金には困っていません。」(Iie, *ano* hitotachi wa okane ni wa komatte imasen.)

¶戦争中は物がなくてずいぶん苦労しました。あの時のことは忘れられません。(Sensōchū wa mono ga nakute zuibun kurō shimashita. *Ano* toki no koto wa wasureraremasen.)

* 文脈的に前に述べたものごととの関係を話し手・話し相手ともに身近な関係にはないものとしてさし示すのに使う。

③[話し手にとっても話し相手に対してもともに隔たりのある関係にあって共通に了解されているものごととの関係をさし示す]

¶「あのことはどうなりましたか。」(*Ano* koto wa dō narimashita ka?)「ああ、あのことはもう解決しましたよ。」(Ā, *ano* koto wa mō kaiketsu shimashita yo.)

¶去年の夏、北海道で親切な人に会いましたね。あの方は今どうしていらっしゃるかしら。(Kyonen no natsu,

* Used for something not physically close to either the speaker or the listener.

② [indicates something mentioned earlier that is distant from both the speaker and the listener]

¶ "Are [Mr.] Nakamura and [Miss] Tanaka troubled by a lack of money?"

"No, **they** (literally, **those** people) have enough money."

¶ During the war we suffered greatly from the scarcity of goods. I will never forget **that** time.

* Used to indicate that something mentioned previously is not psychologically close to either the speaker or the listener.

③ [indicates something known to both the speaker and the listener that is distant from both of them]

¶ "What happened in regard to **that** matter?"

"Oh, **that** has already been resolved."

¶ Last summer we met that kind person in Hokkaido, didn't we? I wonder how [he] is now.

Hokkaidō de shinsetsu na hito ni aimashita ne. *Ano* kata wa ima dō shite irassharu kashira?)

⇨**kono** この　**sono** その　**dono** どの

anshin　安心〘名，〜する〙
¶あなたの元気な顔を見て安心しました。(Anata no genki na kao o mite *anshin* shimashita.)
¶合格の発表を見るまでは安心できません。(Gōkaku no happyō o miru made wa *anshin* dekimasen.)

antei　安定〘名，〜する〙
¶次第に物価が安定してきました。(Shidai ni bukka ga *antei* shite kimashita.)

anzen　安全〘名，形動〙
交通安全 (kōtsū-*anzen*)
¶公園で遊べば安全です。(Kōen de asobeba *anzen* desu.)
¶車の運転は安全を第一に考えなければなりません。(Kuruma no unten wa *anzen* o daiichi ni kangaenakereba narimasen.)
⇔**kiken** 危険

ao　青〘名〙
青色 (*ao*iro)
¶信号が青になったら，道を渡りましょう。(Shingō ga *ao* ni nattara, michi o watarimashō.)
＊「青信号 (*ao*shingō)」「青葉 (*ao*ba)」などのように，緑色も「青 (ao)」と言うことがある。

aoi　青い〘形〙

anshin〚n, ~*suru*〛 **peace of mind**
¶ **I am relieved** to see that you are well〚**I was relieved** to see that you were well〛.
¶ **I'll have no peace** until I've seen the announcement of those who have passed the examination.

antei〚n, ~*suru*〛 **stability, stabilization**
¶ Prices have gradually **stabilized**〚Prices gradually **stabilized**〛.

anzen〚n, adj-v〛 **safety**
traffic **safety**
¶ **It will be safe** if [they] play in the park.
¶ In driving one must consider **safety** first.

ao〚n〛 **blue, green**
the color **blue**
¶ Let's cross the street when the light turns **green**.
＊ Although it usually means "blue," *ao* is sometimes used for "green" as in *aoshingo* (a green light) and *aoba* (green leaves).

aoi〚adj〛 **blue, green; pale**

①[青の色をしている様子]
青い空 (*aoi* sora)　青い海 (*aoi* umi)
¶田中さんは青いセーターを着ています。 (Tanaka san wa *aoi* sētā o kite imasu.)
*「青い草 (aoi kusa)」「青いりんご (aoi ringo)」などのように緑色も「青い (aoi)」と言うことがある。
②[顔に血の気がなく元気のない様子]
¶山田さんは病気で青い顔をしています。(Yamada san wa byōki de *aoi* kao o shite imasu.)

apāto　アパート〖名〗
¶わたしはアパートに住んでいます。
(Watashi wa *apāto* ni sunde imasu.)

arai　荒い〖形〗
①[穏やかでない]
¶今日は波が荒いので泳げません。
(Kyō wa nami ga *arai* node oyogemasen.)
②[乱暴な様子]
¶上田さんは道具の使い方が荒いので，何でもすぐ壊してしまいます。(Ueda san wa dōgu no tsukaikata ga *arai* node, nan demo sugu kowashite shimaimasu.)

arasou　争う〖動Ⅰ〗
①[けんかをする，言い合いをする]
¶兄弟が互いに争うのはよくありません。(Kyōdai ga tagai ni *arasou* no wa yoku arimasen.)
②[競争する]
優勝を争う (yūshō o *arasou*)
¶田中さんと山田さんはクラスで一番

① [blue, green]
the **blue** sky // the **blue** sea
¶ [Mrs.] Tanaka is wearing a **blue** sweater.
* Although it usually means "blue," *aoi* is sometimes used for the color green as in *aoi kusa* (green grasses) and *aoi ringo* (green apple).
② [pale]
¶ [Mr.] Yamada is **pale** from [his] illness.

apāto 〖n〗 apartment, apartment building
¶ I am living in **an apartment**.

arai 〖adj〗 rough
① [rough; not calm, gentle, or soft]
¶ [We] cannot swim today because the waves **are rough**.

② [rough, rude]
¶ Because [Mr.] Ueda is so **rough**, everything [he] uses soon breaks.

arasou 〖v I〗 argue; compete
① [argue, quarrel]
¶ It is not good for brothers **to quarrel** with each other.

② [compete]
compete for victory
¶ [Mr.] Tanaka and [Miss] Yamada

を争っています。 (Tanaka san to Yamada san wa kurasu de ichiban o *arasotte* imasu.)

aratameru　改める〖動Ⅱ〗
規則を改める (kisoku o *aratameru*)
欠点を改める (ketten o *aratameru*)
¶今年から交通規則が改められました。
(Kotoshi kara kōtsū-kisoku ga *aratameraremashita*.)
¶その悪い癖は改めたほうがいいですよ。 (Sono warui kuse wa *aratameta* hō ga ii desu yo.)

arau　洗う〖動Ⅰ〗
¶わたしは朝起きて顔を洗います。
(Watashi wa asa okite kao o *araimasu*.)
¶シャツが汚れたから、洗ってください。 (Shatsu ga yogoreta kara, *aratte* kudasai.)

arawareru　現れる〖動Ⅱ〗
¶この辺には，ときどきくまが現れるそうです。 (Kono hen ni wa, toki-doki kuma ga *arawareru* sō desu.)
¶舞台の右の方から，一人の漁師が現れました。 (Butai no migi no hō kara, hitori no ryōshi ga *arawaremashita*.)

arawasu　現す〖動Ⅰ〗
¶雲の間から太陽が顔を現しました。
(Kumo no aida kara taiyō ga kao o *arawashimashita*.)
¶山田さんはその会議に最後まで姿を現しませんでした。 (Yamada san wa sono kaigi ni saigo made sugata

are competing for first place in the class.

aratameru 〖vⅡ〗 **change, reform revise** the regulations // **mend** one's faults
¶ Traffic regulations **are revised** from this year.

¶ You should **correct** that bad habit.

arau 〖vⅠ〗 **wash**
¶ I get up in the morning and **wash** my face.

¶ Please **wash** my shirt 〚undershirt〛 as it is dirty.

arawareru 〖vⅡ〗 **appear, emerge**
¶ I hear that sometimes bears **come out** in this area.

¶ A fisherman **appeared** from the right side of the stage.

arawasu 〖vⅠ〗 **show, reveal**
¶ The sun **is looking** 〚looked〛 **out** from between the clouds.

¶ [Mrs.] Yamada **never showed** [her]self at that meeting.

o *arawashimasen* deshita.)

arawasu 表す〘動Ⅰ〙

¶感謝の気持ちをどのように表したら
よいかわかりません。 (Kansha no
kimochi o dono yō ni *arawashitara*
yoi ka wakarimasen.)

¶この文章には，作者の気持ちがよく
表されています。 (Kono bunshō ni
wa, sakusha no kimochi ga yoku
arawasarete imasu.)

are あれ〘代〙

①[話し手からも話し相手からもとも
に隔っていると認められるものごとを
さし示す]

¶「あれは何ですか。」 (*Are* wa nan
desu ka?)「あれは郵便局です。」(*Are*
wa yūbinkyoku desu.)

¶「壁に掛けてあるのはだれの写真です
か。 (Kabe ni kakete aru no wa
dare no shashin desu ka?)「あれ
はわたしの両親の写真です。」 (*Are*
wa watashi no ryōshin no shashin
desu.)

＊ 話し手が「あれ（are）」でさし示す
ものは話し相手も「あれ（are）」でさ
し示す。

②[話題に上ったある人を対等以下の
人としてさし示すのに使う]

¶山田君，あれは信用ができない男で
すよ。(Yamada kun? *Are* wa shin'
yō ga dekinai otoko desu yo.)

＊ その場にいない人をさし示すことが
多い。

③[文脈の上で前に述べたものごとを

arawasu 〚vＩ〛 **show, express**

¶ I don't know how **to express** my
gratitude.

¶ The feelings of the author **are** fully
revealed in these sentences.

are 〚pron〛 **that, that one**

① [indicates something judged to be
physically distant from both the
speaker and the listener]

¶ "What is **that**?"

"**That** is the post office."

¶ "Whose photograph is that hanging
on the wall?"

"**That** is a photograph of my
parents."

＊ When the speaker refers to something as *are*, the listener also refers to
it as *are*.

② [used to indicate that someone
who comes up in conversation is a
person of equal or lower status]

¶ Yamada? **That**'s a man who can't
be trusted.

＊ Usually used to refer to someone
who is not present.

③ [used to indicate that something

心理的・時間的に隔たりのある関係に
あるものとして回想的にさし示す]

¶去年山に登った時、深い谷へ落ちそ
うになりました。**あれ**を思うと、もう
山へは登る気がしません。 (Kyonen
yama ni nobotta toki, fukai tani
e ochisō ni narimashita. *Are* o
omou to, mō yama e wa noboru
ki ga shimasen.)

④[文脈の上で前に述べた心理的・時
間的に隔たりのある過去のことがらの
成立した時をさし示す]

¶上田さんとは3年前に京都で別れま
した。**あれ**から一度も会っていません。
(Ueda san to wa sannen mae ni
Kyōto de wakaremashita. *Are*
kara ichido mo atte imasen.)

⑤[話し手にとっても話し相手に対し
てもともに隔たりのある関係にあって
共通に了解されているものごとをさし
示す]

¶「先日お願いした**あれ**はどうなりまし
たか。」 (Senjitsu onegai shita *are*
wa dō narimashita ka?)「あの本で
すか。**あれ**はまだ田中さんが返してく
れません。もう少し待ってください。」
(Ano hon desu ka? *Are* wa mada
Tanaka san ga kaeshite kuremasen.
Mō sukoshi matte kudasai.)

⇨kore これ sore それ dore どれ

areru 荒れる〘動Ⅱ〙

①[穏やかでなくなる]

¶台風が近づいたので、海が荒れてい
ます。 (Taifū ga chikazuita node,

mentioned earlier is distant psychologically or in terms of time]

¶ When I was mountain climbing last year I almost fell into a deep ravine. When I think about **that,** I don't feel like climbing mountains any more.

④ [indicates a certain time in the past referred to earlier that is distant psychologically or in terms of time]

¶ I parted from [Mr.] Ueda three years ago in Kyoto. I haven't met [him] at all since **that time.**

⑤ [indicates something known to both the listener and the speaker that is distant from them]

¶ "What happened in regard to **that matter** that I asked you to take care of the other day?"

  "That book? [Mrs.] Tanaka hasn't returned **it** to me yet. Please wait a little longer."

areru 〖v Ⅱ〗 become rough; fall into decay

① [become rough, cease being calm]

¶ The sea **is rough** because a

umi ga *arete* imasu.)

②[手入れなどをしなくてひどい状態になる]

手が荒れる (te ga *areru*) 肌が荒れる (hada ga *areru*)

¶この家はずいぶん荒れていますね。(Kono ie wa zuibun *arete* imasu ne.)

②[fall into decay, fall into a bad state from neglect, etc.]

get roughened ⟦chapped⟧ hands // **get roughened ⟦chapped⟧** skin

¶ This house **has** really **been neglected.**

arigatai ありがたい〖形〗

¶親切にしていただき，本当にありがたいと思っています。(Shinsetsu ni shite itadaki, hontō ni *arigatai* to omotte imasu.)

arigatai ⟦adj⟧ **grateful, thankful**

¶ You've been so kind to me; I'm really **grateful.**

arigatō ありがとう〖連〗

¶今日は，どうもありがとう。本当に楽しかったです。(Kyō wa, dōmo *arigatō*. Hontō ni tanoshikatta desu.)

¶「けっこうな物をいただきまして，ありがとうございました。」(Kekkō na mono o itadakimashite *arigatō* gozaimashita.)「いいえ，どういたしまして。」(Iie, dō itashimashite.)

⇨**arigatai ありがたい**

arigatō ⟦compd⟧ **Thank you**

¶ **Thank you** for today. It was really pleasant.

¶ "**Thank you** very much for this fine gift."

"No, not at all."

aru ある〖動Ⅰ〗

①[ものなどがある所に存在する]

¶机の上に本があります。(Tsukue no ue ni hon ga *arimasu*.)

¶どこかに貸家はありませんか。(Doko ka ni kashiya wa *arimasen* ka?)

②[ものなどがある所に位置する]

¶富士山は東京の西にあります。(Fujisan wa Tōkyō no nishi ni *arimasu*.)

aru ⟦v I⟧ **be, exist; be located; have, possess; take place**

①[there is, there are, exist, be found]

¶ **There is** a book on top of the desk.

¶ **Isn't there** a house to rent somewhere?

②[be located, stand, lie, etc.]

¶ Mount Fuji **lies** to the west of Tokyo.

¶家の後ろに川があります。 (Ie no ushiro ni kawa ga *arimasu*.)

¶ A river **runs** behind the house.

③[あるものがあるものに付属して存在する]

③ [have, possess, be equipped with]

¶その家には広い庭があります。 (Sono ie ni wa hiroi niwa ga *arimasu*.)

¶ That house **has** a large garden 〚yard〛.

¶この家にはふろ場がありません。 (Kono ie ni wa furoba ga *arimasen*.)

¶ This house **doesn't have** a Japanese bath.

④[あるものがあるものに含まれている]

④ [be contained in, be included in]

¶この本にはおもしろい話がたくさんあります。 (Kono hon ni wa omoshiroi hanashi ga takusan *arimasu*.)

¶ This book **contains** many interesting stories.

⑤[時間・距離・重さ・広さなどがどの程度あるかを表す]

⑤ [number, weigh, measure (in regard to time, distance, weight, width, etc.)]

¶時間がありませんから，急いでください。 (Jikan ga *arimasen* kara, isoide kudasai.)

¶ There **isn't** time to spare so please hurry.

¶夏休みはどのくらいありますか。 (Natsuyasumi wa dono kurai *arimasu* ka?)

¶ How long **is** summer vacation?

¶この荷物は何キロぐらいあるでしょうか。 (Kono nimotsu wa nankiro gurai *aru* deshō ka?)

¶ How many kilograms does this package **weigh?**

¶部屋の広さはどのくらいありますか。 (Heya no hirosa wa dono kurai *arimasu* ka?)

¶ How big **is** the room?

⑥[人があるものを持っている]

⑥ [possess, be blessed with]

¶わたしはお金がありません。 (Watashi wa okane ga *arimasen*.)

¶ I **don't have** any money.

¶田中さんは子供が3人あります。

¶ [Mrs.] Tanaka **has** three children.

(Tanaka san wa kodomo ga sannin *arimasu*.)

¶彼は音楽の才能があります。 (Kare wa ongaku no sainō ga *arimasu*.)

⑦[あることが行われる]

¶あしたは試験があります。 (Ashita wa shiken ga *arimasu*.)

¶学校は4時まであります。 (Gakkō wa yoji made *arimasu*.)

¶今日は、午前中に会議がありました。(Kyō wa, gozenchū ni kaigi ga *arimashita*.)

⑧[あることが発生する，ある事態などが起こる]

¶昨日，ここで交通事故がありました。(Kinō, koko de kōtsū-jiko ga *arimashita*.)

¶ゆうべ，大きな地震がありました。(Yūbe, ookina jishin ga *arimashita*.)

¶山田さんからさっき電話がありましたよ。 (Yamada san kara sakki denwa ga *arimashita* yo.)

⑨[ときどきあることをする，ときどきある状態になる]

¶おふろに入る前に御飯を食べることがあります。(Ofuro ni hairu mae ni gohan o taberu koto ga *arimasu*.)

¶外国に一人で住んでいると，寂しいことがあります。(Gaikoku ni hitori de sunde iru to, sabishii koto ga *arimasu*.)

* 「動詞・形容詞(連体の形)＋ことが(も)ある (koto ga[mo] aru)」の形

¶ He **is endowed with** musical talent.

⑦ [take place]

¶ [We] **have** a test tomorrow.

¶ [We] **have** school until four o'clock.

¶ [I] **had** a meeting during the morning today.

⑧ [happen, occur]

¶ A traffic accident **took place** here yesterday.

¶ **There was** a large earthquake last night.

¶ **There was** a telephone call from [Mr.] Yamada a little while ago.

⑨ [occasional occurrence]

¶ **There are times** when [I] eat before taking a bath.

¶ When one lives alone in a foreign country, **sometimes** one is lonely.

* Used in the pattern "verb or adjective (dictionary form) + *koto ga* [[*mo*]] *aru*."

で使う。

⑩［あることがらの経験がある］

¶あの人には，前に一度会ったことが
あります。(Ano hito ni wa, mae ni
ichido atta koto ga *arimasu*.)

¶わたしは日本へ行ったことがありま
せん。(Watashi wa Nihon e itta
koto ga *arimasen*.)

＊「動詞・形容詞（たの形）＋ことが（も）
ある (koto ga[mo] aru)」の形で使
う。

aru　ある〖連体〗

ある日 (*aru* hi)　ある人 (*aru* hito)

¶田中さんはある学校で数学を教えて
います。(Tanaka san wa *aru* gakkō
de sūgaku o oshiete imasu.)

(〜te) aru　(〜て) ある〖連〗

¶壁に絵が掛けてあります。(Kabe ni
e ga kakete *arimasu*.)

¶暑いので，戸が開けてあります。
(Atsui node, to ga akete *arimasu*.)

＊「他動詞（ての形）＋ある (aru)」の
形で使う。

⇨ **(〜te) iru　(〜て) いる**

aruku　歩く〖動Ⅰ〗

¶ここから駅まで歩いて10分かかりま
す。(Koko kara eki made, *aruite*
jippun kakarimasu.)

¶日本では，人は道の右側を歩きます。
(Nihon de wa, hito wa michi no
migigawa o *arukimasu*.)

asa　朝〖名〗

朝御飯 (*asa*gohan)　朝日 (*asa*hi)

毎朝 (mai*asa*)

⑩ [have the experience of]

¶ **I have** met [him] once before.

¶ **I have never** been to Japan.

＊ Used in the pattern "verb or adjective (*-ta* form) + *koto ga [mo] aru*."

aru 〖attrib〗　**a certain, some**
one day 〖a **certain** day〗 // **some**one 〖a **certain** person〗

¶ [Miss] Tanaka is teaching mathematics at a school **somewhere** 〖at a **certain** school〗.

(-te) aru 〖compd〗　**being in the state of -ing**

¶ There **is** a picture **hanging** on the wall.

¶ The door **is standing open** because it's so hot.

＊ Used in the pattern "transitive verb (*-te* form) + *aru*."

aruku 〖v Ⅰ〗　**walk**

¶ It takes 10 minutes **to walk** from here to the station.

¶ In Japan people **walk** on the right-hand side of the road.

asa 〖n〗　**morning**

breakfast // the **morning** sun; Asahi (proper noun) // every **morning**

¶あなたは朝何時に起きますか。

(Anata wa *asa* nanji ni okimasu ka?)

asai 浅い〖形〗

¶深い方へ行かないで，浅い所で遊びなさい。(Fukai hō e ikanaide, *asai* tokoro de asobinasai.)

¶この池は浅くて，底が見えます。(Kono ike wa *asakute*, soko ga miemasu.)

⇔fukai 深い

asanebō 朝寝坊〖名，～する〗

¶朝寝坊をして，学校に遅刻してしまいました。(*Asanebō* o shite, gakkō ni chikoku shite shimaimashita.)

asatte あさって〖名〗

¶あさっては何曜日ですか。 (*Asatte* wa naniyōbi desu ka?)

¶あさって，あなたのうちに行ってもいいですか。(*Asatte*, anata no uchi ni itte mo ii desu ka?)

ase 汗〖名〗

汗が出る (*ase* ga deru) ハンカチで汗をふく (hankachi de *ase* o fuku)

¶階段を急いで上ったら，汗をかきました。 (Kaidan o isoide nobottara, *ase* o kakimashita.)

ashi 足〖名〗

①〔歩くときに使う体の一部〕

足が強い (*ashi* ga tsuyoi) 足が弱い (*ashi* ga yowai)

¶少し歩くと，すぐ足が疲れます。

(Sukoshi aruku to, sugu *ashi* ga tsukaremasu.)

¶ What time do you get up **in the morning?**

asai 〚adj〛 **shallow**

¶ Don't go to the deep end but play where **it's shallow.**

¶ This pond 〚pool〛 **is shallow;** one can see the bottom.

asanebō 〚n, ~*suru*〛 **late riser, sleepyhead**

¶ **I overslept** and was late for school.

asatte 〚n〛 **the day after tomorrow**

¶ What day of the week is **the day after tomorrow?**

¶ Is it all right if I come to your home **the day after tomorrow?**

ase 〚n〛 **sweat, perspiration**

to sweat, perspire // wipe off **sweat** with a handkerchief

¶ I hurried up the stairs and got all **sweaty.**

ashi 〚n〛 **foot, leg; walking**

① [foot, leg; part of the body used when walking]

be a good **walker** // be a poor **walker**

¶ **My legs** soon tire after walking just a little.

¶だれかの足音が聞こえてきました。
(Dare ka no *ashi*oto ga kikoete kimashita.)

②［歩くこと］
足が遅い (*ashi* ga osoi)
¶山田さんは足が速いですね。もう，あんなに遠くへ行ってしまいました。
(Yamada san wa *ashi* ga hayai desu ne. Mō anna ni tooku e itte shimaimashita.)

ashi 脚〖名〗
¶机の脚が折れてしまいました。
(Tsukue no *ashi* ga orete shimaimashita.)

ashita あした〖名〗
¶あしたは何日ですか。 (*Ashita* wa nannichi desu ka?)
¶あした映画を見に行きませんか。
(*Ashita* eiga o mi ni ikimasen ka?)

asobu 遊ぶ〖動Ⅰ〗
¶子供が庭で遊んでいます。(Kodomo ga niwa de *asonde* imasu.)
¶ときどき，トランプをして遊びます。
(Tokidoki toranpu o shite *asobimasu*.)
¶昨日，新宿へ遊びに行きました。
(Kinō, Shinjuku e *asobi* ni ikimashita.)
¶わたしのうちへ遊びに来てください。
(Watashi no uchi e *asobi* ni kite kudasai.)

asoko あそこ〖代〗
①［話し手にとっても話し相手に対してもともに隔たりのある関係にある所

¶ [I] can 〖could〗 hear someone **coming** 〖someone's **footsteps**〗.

② [walking]
be a slow **walker**
¶ [Mr.] Yamada is a fast **walker.** [He] has already moved that far away.

ashi 〖n〗 **leg**
¶ The desk **leg** is broken.

ashita 〖n〗 **tomorrow**
¶ What is the date **tomorrow?**

¶ Won't you go with [me] to see a movie **tomorrow?**

asobu 〖v I〗 **play, amuse oneself**
¶ The children **are playing** in the garden 〖yard〗.
¶ Sometimes [we] play cards (literally, **enjoy ourselves** playing cards).

¶ Yesterday **I enjoyed myself** in Shinjuku.

¶ Please come and **visit** me.

asoko 〖pron〗 **there, over there**
① [indicates a place physically distant from both the speaker and the

をさし示す]

¶『あそこでテレビを見ている人はだれですか。』 (*Asoko* de terebi o mite iru hito wa dare desu ka?) 「あの人は上田さんです。」 (Ano hito wa Ueda san desu.)

¶『どこが玄関ですか。』 (Doko ga genkan desu ka?) 「あそこが玄関です。」 (*Asoko* ga genkan desu.)

②[話し手にとっても話し相手に対してもともに隔たりのある関係にあるものごとの状態や問題の点などをさし示す]

¶山田さんの病気があそこまで進んでいたとはだれも気づきませんでした。 (Yamada san no byōki ga *asoko* made susunde ita to wa dare mo kizukimasen deshita.)

¶中村さんがあそこまで知っているとは思いませんでした。 (Nakamura san ga *asoko* made shitte iru to wa omoimasen deshita.)

⇨**koko** ここ **soko** そこ **doko** どこ

asu 明日〖名〗⇨**ashita** あした

ataeru 与える〖動Ⅱ〗

①[あるものをほかの人にやってその人のものにする]

金を与える (kane o *ataeru*) ほうびを与える (hōbi o *ataeru*)

②[やるべきことを割り当てる]

¶先生は一人一人の学生に別々の問題を与えて答えさせました。 (Sensei wa hitorihitori no gakusei ni betsu-

listener]

¶ "Who is that person watching television **over there?**"

"That is [Mrs.] Ueda."

¶ "Where is the entryway?"

"The entryway is **over there.**"

② [indicates a condition, problem point, etc., psychologically distant from both the speaker and the listener]

¶ No one noticed that [Miss] Yamada's illness had advanced to **that point.**

¶ I didn't think that [Mr.] Nakamura knew **that much** about it.

asu ☞ **ashita**

ataeru 〖v Ⅱ〗 **give; assign; inflict**

① [give, bestow]

give away money // **give** a reward

② [assign]

¶ The teacher **gave** each of the students a different problem to answer.

betsu no mondai o *ataete* kotae-
sasemashita.)

¶わたしは<ruby>与<rt>あた</rt></ruby>えられた<ruby>仕事<rt>しごと</rt></ruby>をいつもき
ちんとします。 (Watashi wa *ata-
erareta* shigoto o itsu mo kichinto
shimasu.)

③[損害などを被らせる]

¶<ruby>今度<rt>こんど</rt></ruby>の<ruby>台風<rt>たいふう</rt></ruby>は<ruby>各地<rt>かくち</rt></ruby>に<ruby>大<rt>おお</rt></ruby>きな<ruby>被害<rt>ひがい</rt></ruby>を<ruby>与<rt>あた</rt></ruby>
えました。 (Kondo no taifū wa
kakuchi ni ookina higai o *ataemashita*.)

atama <ruby>頭<rt>あたま</rt></ruby>〘名〙

①[頭部]

<ruby>頭<rt>あたま</rt></ruby>を<ruby>洗<rt>あら</rt></ruby>う (*atama* o arau) <ruby>頭<rt>あたま</rt></ruby>を<ruby>下<rt>さ</rt></ruby>げ
る (*atama* o sageru)

¶<ruby>頭<rt>あたま</rt></ruby>が<ruby>痛<rt>いた</rt></ruby>いので，学校を<ruby>休<rt>やす</rt></ruby>みました。
(*Atama* ga itai node, gakkō o yasu-
mimashita.)

②[頭脳，頭の働き]

<ruby>頭<rt>あたま</rt></ruby>が<ruby>悪<rt>わる</rt></ruby>い (*atama* ga warui) <ruby>頭<rt>あたま</rt></ruby>を<ruby>使<rt>つか</rt></ruby>
う (*atama* o tsukau)

¶あの<ruby>学生<rt>がくせい</rt></ruby>はとても<ruby>頭<rt>あたま</rt></ruby>がいいですよ。
(Ano gakusei wa totemo *atama* ga
ii desu yo.)

atarashii <ruby>新<rt>あたら</rt></ruby>しい〘形〙

①[ものごとができたり始まったりし
てから間のない様子]

<ruby>新<rt>あたら</rt></ruby>しい<ruby>家<rt>いえ</rt></ruby> (*atarashii* ie)

¶このくつは<ruby>買<rt>か</rt></ruby>ったばかりで，まだ<ruby>新<rt>あたら</rt></ruby>
しいです。(Kono kutsu wa katta
bakari de, mada *atarashii* desu.)

②[新鮮ないきいきしている様子]

<ruby>新<rt>あたら</rt></ruby>しい<ruby>魚<rt>さかな</rt></ruby> (*atarashii* sakana)

¶<ruby>新<rt>あたら</rt></ruby>しい<ruby>野菜<rt>やさい</rt></ruby>を<ruby>生<rt>なま</rt></ruby>で<ruby>食<rt>た</rt></ruby>べるのは，<ruby>体<rt>からだ</rt></ruby>にた

¶ I always do carefully the work I am
assigned to do.

③ [inflict, suffer (damage, etc.)]

¶ Each area **suffered** much damage
in the last typhoon.

atama 〚n〛 **head; brains**

① [head]

wash **one's hair** // lower 〚bow〛
one's head

¶ I stayed home from school because
I have a **head**ache.

② [brains, intelligence]

be slow **witted** // use **one's head,**
think

¶ That student is very **intelligent.**

atarashii 〚adj〛 **new; fresh**

① [brand-new]

a **new** house

¶ These shoes are still **new**—I just
bought them.

② [fresh]

fresh fish

¶ They say it's very good for one's

いへんいいそうです。　(*Atarashii
yasai o nama de taberu no wa,
karada ni taihen ii sō desu.*)
③[今までにないものが初めてできあがる様子]
新しい型の自動車　(*atarashii* kata
no jidōsha)

¶山田さんは新しく家を建てました。
(Yamada san wa *atarashiku* ie o
tatemashita.)

⇔**furui** 古い

atari 辺り〖名〗

¶この辺りは夜になると，寂しくなります。(Kono *atari* wa yoru ni naru
to, sabishiku narimasu.)

¶学校の辺りに貸間はないでしょうか。
(Gakkō no *atari* ni kashima wa
nai deshō ka?)

＊いつも「この辺り (kono atari)」「その辺り (sono atari)」「あの辺り」
(ano atari)」「どの辺り (dono atari)」
「名詞＋の(no)＋辺り(atari)」の形で
使う。

-atari -あたり〖尾〗

①[時・所などを表す言葉のあとにつけてだいたいを言うときに使う]

¶次の日曜あたりはどうですか。

(Tsugi no nichiyō *atari* wa dō desu
ka?)

¶去年あたりは野菜が安かったのですが，今年は高くなりました。(Kyonen
atari wa yasai ga yasukatta no
desu ga, kotoshi wa takaku narimashita.)

health to eat **fresh,** raw vegetables.

③ [novel, the latest thing]

a **new**-model car

¶ [Mr.] Yamada built a **new** house.

atari 〖n〗　vicinity

¶ It is lonely **around** here after dark.

¶ Might there not be a room for rent
near the school?

＊ Always used in the patterns "noun
+ *no* + *atari*", "*kono atari*" (around
here), "*sono atari*" (around there),
"*ano atari*" (around there), and
"*dono atari*" (whereabouts).

-atari 〖suf〗　**about, around; per**

① [about, around, approximately
(after words expressing time, place,
etc.)]

¶ How about next Sunday **or there-
abouts** (when making an appointment, etc.)?

¶ Last year **or so** vegetables were
cheap, but this year they've become
expensive.

¶今度，新宿あたりでいっしょに食事をしましょう。(Kondo, Shinjuku *atari de* issho ni shokuji o shimashō.)

②[数や単位などを表す言葉につけて割合や平均を言うときに使う]

¶会費は一人あたり 3,000 円です。(Kaihi wa hitori *atari* sanzen'en desu.)

¶このひもは 1 メートルあたりいくらですか。(Kono himo wa ichimētoru *atari* ikura desu ka?)

atarimae　あたりまえ〖形動，〜の〗

あたりまえのこと (*atarimae* no koto)

¶借りた物を返すのはあたりまえです。(Karita mono o kaesu no wa *atarimae* desu.)

⇨**tōzen** 当然

ataru　当たる〖動Ⅰ〗

①[ぶつかる，触れる]

¶ボールが頭に当たりました。(Bōru ga atama ni *atarimashita*.)

②[日の光がそこまで及ぶ]

¶この部屋はよく日が当たって暖かいです。(Kono heya wa yoku hi ga *atatte* atatakai desu.)

③[日・光・熱・風などを体に受ける]

¶寒いから，火に当たりましょう。(Samui kara, hi ni *atarimashō*.)

④[予想などがそのとおりになる]

¶今日の天気予報は当たりました。(Kyō no tenki-yohō wa *atarimashita*.)

↔**hazureru** 外れる

¶ Let's have dinner together next time **somewhere in the** Shinjuku **area.**

② [per (when added to numbers, units, etc.)]

¶ The dues 〚fee for a group party or outing〛 are three thousand yen **per** person.

¶ How much is this cord 〚string, lace, tape, thong, ribbon, etc.〛 **per** meter?

atarimae 〚adj-v, ~*no*〛 **matter of course; proper**

a matter of course

¶ **It goes without saying** that one should return borrowed articles.

ataru 〚v Ⅰ〛 **hit, touch; hit the mark**

① [hit, touch]

¶ The ball **hit** [his] head.

② [sunlight reaches a certain point]

¶ This room is warm as it **gets** much sun.

③ [be in the path of sunlight, light, heat, wind, etc.]

¶ As it's cold **let's warm ourselves** at the fire.

④ [a prediction, etc., is proven right]

¶ Today's weather report **was correct.**

⑤［的中する］
¶ピストルの弾がちょうど真ん中に当たりました。(Pisutoru no tama ga chōdo mannaka ni *atarimashita*.)
↔hazureru 外れる

⑥［くじで金や賞品などをもらえることになる］
¶くじで100万円当たりました。(Kuji de hyakuman'en *atarimashita*.)
↔hazureru 外れる

atataka 暖か〚形動〛
暖かな毛布 (*atataka* na mōfu)
¶昨日は穏やかで暖かな日でした。
(Kinō wa odayaka de *atataka* na hi deshita.)
¶風邪を引いたので，暖かにして寝ました。(Kaze o hiita node, *atataka* ni shite nemashita.)
⇨atatakai 暖かい

atataka 温か〚形動〛
温かな心 (*atataka* na kokoro) 温かな家庭 (*atataka* na katei) 温かなコーヒー (*atataka* na kōhii)
⇨atatakai 温かい

atatakai 暖かい〚形〛
暖かい日 (*atatakai* hi) 暖かい毛布 (*atatakai* mōfu)
¶春が来て，暖かくなりました。
(Haru ga kite, *atatakaku* narimashita.)
⇨atataka 暖か

atatakai 温かい〚形〛
温かいスープ (*atatakai* sūpu)

⑤ [hit the mark]
¶ The pistol bullet **hit** exactly in the middle.

⑥ [win money, a prize, etc., in a lottery]
¶ [I] **won** 1 million yen in a lottery.

atataka [[adj-v]] **warm**
a **warm** blanket
¶ Yesterday was a mild, **warm** day.

¶ Since I caught ⟦had caught⟧ a cold, I bundled up **warmly** and went to bed.

atataka [[adj-v]] **warm; kindly**
a **warm** ⟦**kindly**⟧ heart // a **happy** home // **hot** coffee

atatakai [[adj]] **warm**
a **warm** day // a **warm** blanket
¶ Spring has come and it has become **warmer.**

atatakai [[adj]] **warm; kindly**
hot soup // a **happy** home, a **happy**

温かい家庭 (*atatakai* katei)

¶このプールの水は温かいですね。
(Kono pūru no mizu wa *atatakai* desu ne.)

¶一郎さんは心の温かい人です。
(Ichirō san wa kokoro no *atatakai* hito desu.)

⇒atataka 温か

atatameru 暖める〖動Ⅱ〗

¶ストーブをたいて，部屋を暖めました。(Sutōbu o taite, heya o *atata-memashita.*)

atatameru 温める〖動Ⅱ〗

¶牛乳を温めて飲みました。(Gyūnyū o *atatamete* nomimashita.)

atena あて名〖名〗

手紙にあて名を書く (tegami ni *ate-na* o kaku)

ateru 当てる〖動Ⅱ〗

①[あるものをほかの ものに触れさせる]

額に手を当てる (hitai ni te o *ateru*)

②[言い当てる]

¶この箱の中に何が入っているか，当ててごらんなさい。(Kono hako no naka ni nani ga haitte iru ka, *atete* goran nasai.)

③[割り当てる]

¶先生は一人一人に当てて本を読ませました。 (Sensei wa hitorihitori ni *atete* hon o yomasemashita.)

④[日や風などに触れさせる]

布団を日に当てる (futon o hi ni *ateru*) 風に当てて乾かす (kaze ni

family

¶ The water in this pool **is warm,** isn't it?

¶ Ichirō is a **warmhearted** person.

atatameru 〖v Ⅱ〗 **heat, warm**

¶ [I] lighted the (wood or coal) heater and **warmed up** the room.

atatameru 〖v Ⅱ〗 **warm, heat up**

¶ [I] **heated** some milk and drank it.

atchi ☞ achira

atena 〖n〗 **recipient's name** (on an envelope or postcard)

to address a letter (that is, write **the recipient's name**)

ateru 〖v Ⅱ〗 **apply, strike; guess; call on; expose to**

① [apply, strike; touch something to something]

lay one's hand on one's 〚someone else's〛 forehead

② [guess]

¶ Try **to guess** what's in this box!

③ [call on]

¶ The teacher **called on** them to read the book one by one.

④ [expose to the sun, wind, etc.]

air out bedding in the sun // **dry** (something) in the breeze

37

atete kawakasu)

¶フィルムは日に当てないようにして
ください。(Firumu wa hi ni *atenai*
yō ni shite kudasai.)

ateru 充てる〖動Ⅱ〗

¶夜は勉強の時間に充てています。
(Yoru wa benkyō no jikan ni *atete*
imasu.)

¶月給の2割を家賃に充てています。
(Gekkyū no niwari o yachin ni
atete imasu.)

あと ato〖名〗

①[後ろ]
あとを振り返る (*ato* o furikaeru)
¶わたしのあとから犬がついてきまし
た。(Watashi no *ato* kara inu ga
tsuite kimashita.)
→ushiro 後ろ

②[のち]
¶わたしはあとで行きます。(Watashi
wa *ato* de ikimasu.)
¶四、五日あとにまた来てください。
(Shi-gonichi *ato* ni mata kite kudasai.)

③[残り、し残したこと]
¶あとはまたあしたやりましょう。
(*Ato* wa mata ashita yarimashō.)
¶必要な物だけ残して、あとは捨てて
ください。(Hitsuyō na mono dake
nokoshite, *ato* wa sutete kudasai.)

atsui 暑い〖形〗

¶今日は暑いですね。(Kyō wa *atsui*
desu ne.)
¶昼間は暑かったが、夕方から涼しく

ateru 〖v II〗 **assign, allocate**

¶ [My] evenings **are set aside** for
study.

¶ Twenty percent of [my] (monthly)
wages **is allocated** to rent.

ato 〖n〗 **back, rear; after, later; the
rest**

① [back, rear]
look **back**
¶ A dog **followed** me.

② [after, later]
¶ I'll come **later.**

¶ Please come again **in** four or five
days.

③ [the rest]
¶ Let's do **the rest** tomorrow.

¶ Please set aside only what you need
and throw away **the rest.**

atsui 〖adj〗 **hot, warm**

¶ **It's hot** today, isn't it?

¶ **It was hot** during the day, but it's

なりました。(Hiruma wa *atsukatta ga, yūgata kara suzushiku nari-mashita.*)

⇔samui 寒い

atsui 熱い〖形〗

¶熱いお茶を一杯ください。(*Atsui ocha o ippai kudasai.*)

¶おふろが熱かったら，水を入れてください。(*Ofuro ga atsukattara, mizu o irete kudasai.*)

⇔tsumetai 冷たい

atsui 厚い〖形〗

厚い本 (*atsui* hon) 厚い壁 (*atsui* kabe)

¶この辞書はずいぶん厚いですね。(*Kono jisho wa zuibun atsui desu ne.*)

¶冬は厚いセーターを着ます。(*Fuyu wa atsui sētā o kimasu.*)

⇔usui 薄い

atsukau 扱う〖動Ⅰ〗

①[受け付ける，仕事としてそれをする]

¶郵便局では貯金も扱っています。(*Yūbinkyoku de wa chokin mo atsukatte imasu.*)

②[操作する，取り扱う]

¶わたしはこの機械の扱い方がわかりません。(*Watashi wa kono kikai no atsukaikata ga wakarimasen.*)

③[待遇する]

客を丁寧に扱う (kyaku o teinei ni *atsukau*) 扱いにくい人 (*atsukai-nikui hito*)

cooled off this evening 〖it cooled off during the evening〗.

atsui 〖adj〗 **hot, heated**

¶ Please give me a cup of **hot** (green) tea.

¶ If the bath **is too hot,** please add some cold water.

atsui 〖adj〗 **thick**

a **thick** book // a **thick** wall; a **major** obstacle

¶ This dictionary **is** very **thick.**

¶ In the winter everyone wears 〖I wear〗 **heavy** sweaters.

atsukau 〖v Ⅰ〗 **handle; deal with**

① [handle, accept, transact (business)]

¶ Post offices **handle** savings accounts too.

② [handle, work (something)]

¶ I don't know how **to work** this machine.

③ [treat, deal with]

treat a customer 〖guest〗 politely // a person hard **to deal with,** a difficult person

atsumaru　集まる〘動Ⅰ〙

¶あした10時に駅前に**集**まってくださ
い。(Ashita jūji ni ekimae ni *atsumatte* kudasai.)

¶ここは夏になると、人がたくさん**集**
まってきます。(Koko wa natsu ni
naru to, hito ga takusan *atsumatte*
kimasu.)

¶会費は全部**集**まりました。　(Kaihi
wa zenbu *atsumarimashita*.)

atsumeru　集める〘動Ⅱ〙

お金を**集**める (okane o *atsumeru*)

¶わたしは切手を**集**めています。
(Watashi wa kitte o *atsumete* imasu.)

¶友達を**集**めて、パーティーを開きまし
た。(Tomodachi o *atsumete,* pātii
o hirakimashita.)

au　会う〘動Ⅰ〙

¶またあした**会**いましょう。　(Mata
ashita *aimashō*.)

¶昨日、わたしは山田さんに**会**いまし
た。(Kinō, watashi wa Yamada san
ni *aimashita*.)

＊目上の人には、丁寧な言い方「お
目にかかる (ome ni kakaru)」を使
う。

⇨wakareru 別れる

au　遭う〘動Ⅰ〙

¶田中さんは交通事故に**遭**ったそうで
す。(Tanaka san wa kōtsū-jiko ni
atta sō desu.)

¶雨に降られて、ひどい目に**あ**いまし
た。(Ame ni furarete, hidoi me

atsumaru 〚v Ⅰ〛 **gather together,
be collected**

¶ Please **assemble** in front of the
station at ten o'clock tomorrow.

¶ In summer lots of people **flock to**
this place.

¶ The dues 〚fees〛 have all **been collected.**

atsumeru 〚v Ⅱ〛 **gather, collect
collect 〚raise〛 money**

¶ I **collect** stamps.

¶ [We] **got** [our] friends **together**
and had a party.

au 〚v Ⅰ〛 **meet**

¶ **Let's meet** again tomorrow.

¶ I **met** [Miss] Yamada yesterday.

＊ When referring to persons of
higher status, a more polite expression, *ome ni kakaru,* is used.

au 〚v Ⅰ〛 **encounter, be subjected
to**

¶ I hear that [Mrs.] Tanaka **was in** a
traffic accident.

¶ I was caught in the rain and **had** an
awful time.

ni *aimashita*.)

au 合う〔動Ⅰ〕

①〔適合する，適当である〕

¶このくつは大きすぎて，わたしには合いません。(Kono kutsu wa ooki-sugite, watashi ni wa *aimasen*.)

¶この眼鏡は，わたしに合っていません。(Kono megane wa, watashi ni *atte* imasen.)

②〔合致する，同じである〕

¶わたしは，山田さんとはよく意見が合います。(Watashi wa, Yamada san to wa yoku iken ga *aimasu*.)

③〔調和する〕

¶ネクタイと服が合っていません。(Nekutai to fuku ga *atte* imasen.)

¶あの壁にはこの色のカーテンが合います。(Ano kabe ni wa kono iro no kāten ga *aimasu*.)

④〔正しいものと一致する〕

¶あなたの時計は合っていますか。(Anata no tokei wa *atte* imasu ka?)

¶この計算は合っています。 (Kono keisan wa *atte* imasu.)

¶答えが合っている人は，手を挙げてください。(Kotae ga *atte* iru hito wa, te o agete kudasai.)

⑤〔いくつかのものが互いに同じことをする〕

話し合う (hanashi*au*)　　愛し合う (aishi*au*)

¶困ったときは，お互いに助け合いましょう。(Komatta toki wa, otagai ni tasuke*aimashō*.)

(-)au 〚v I〛 **fit; coincide; match; be correct**

① [fit]

¶ These shoes **do not fit** me; they are too big.

¶ These glasses **are not right** for me (that is, the lenses are incorrect).

② [agree with, coincide with]

¶ [Mr.] Yamada and I often **have the same** opinions.

③ [match, go together, be in harmony]

¶ [His] necktie and suit **do not go together.**

¶ This color curtain **goes well** 〚**would go well**〛 with those walls.

④ [be correct, match something that is correct]

¶ Is your watch **correct?**

¶ These calculations **are correct.**

¶ Would those with the **correct** answer please raise their hands.

⑤ [do something together with someone]

talk **with** // love **each other**

¶ **Let's help each other** when we have a problem.

* 「動詞(基幹の形)+合う(au)」の形
で使う。

awaseru　合わせる〖動Ⅱ〗

①[二つ以上のものを一つにする]
手を合わせる (te o *awaseru*)　声を
合わせる (koe o *awaseru*)　心を合
わせる (kokoro o *awaseru*)

¶橋を架けるために，みんなが力を合
わせて働きました。(Hashi o kakeru
tame ni, minna ga chikara o *awasete* hatarakimashita.)

②[あるものに適合させる，一致させ
る]

¶時計の針を駅の時計に合わせました。
(Tokei no hari o eki no tokei ni
awasemashita.)

¶ピアノに合わせて歌いましょう。
(Piano ni *awasete* utaimashō.)

③[二つのものを比べる，照らし合わ
せる]

¶答えを合わせてみました。(Kotae o
awasete mimashita.)

awateru　あわてる〖動Ⅱ〗

¶どろぼうはあわてて逃げました。
(Dorobō wa *awatete* nigemashita.)

¶あまりあわてたので，財布を忘れまし
た。(Amari *awateta* node, saifu o
wasuremashita.)

¶そんなにあわてなくても，時間はじ
ゅうぶんあります。(Sonna ni *awate-
nakute* mo, jikan wa jūbun arimasu.)

ayamaru　謝る〖動Ⅰ〗

¶田中さんは「わたしが悪かった。」と

---

* Used in the pattern "verb (stem
form) + -*au*."

awaseru 〚v II〛 **combine; adjust;
compare**

① [combine; put together two or
more things]

put one's hands **together** (in
worship, etc.) // speak **as one**; sing
in chorus // **cooperate** warmly, **be
united**

¶ Everyone **combined** their strength
to raise the bridge.

② [adjust, set, adapt]

¶ [I] **set** [my] watch by the station
clock (past action).

¶ Let's sing **accompanied by** the
piano.

③ [compare two things]

¶ [They] **checked** [their] answers
〚**compared** their answers among
themselves〛.

awateru 〚v II〛 **be flustered, be
hurried**

¶ The thief **panicked** and ran.

¶ **I was in** such **a hurry** 〚I was so
flustered〛 that I forgot my wallet.

¶ There is plenty of time so you don't
need to be **in** such **a hurry.**

ayamaru 〚v I〛 **apologize**

¶ [Mr.] Tanaka **apologized** by

言って謝りました。 (Tanaka san wa "Watashi ga warukatta." to itte *ayamarimashita*.)

¶いくら謝っても，山田さんは許してくれませんでした。 (Ikura *ayamatte* mo, Yamada san wa yurushite kuremasen deshita.)

ayashii 怪しい〖形〗

¶この辺で怪しい男を見ませんでしたか。 (Kono hen de *ayashii* otoko o mimasen deshita ka?)

azukaru 預かる〖動Ⅰ〗

¶この荷物を預かってくれる所はないでしょうか。 (Kono nimotsu o *azukatte* kureru tokoro wa nai deshō ka?)

¶銀行では1円以上のお金を預かります。 (Ginkō de wa ichien ijō no okane o *azukarimasu*.)

azukeru 預ける〖動Ⅱ〗

¶友達に荷物を預けてきました。 (Tomodachi ni nimotsu o *azukete* kimashita.)

¶銀行に10万円預けてあります。 (Ginkō ni jūman'en *azukete* arimasu.)

¶わたしは近所の人に赤ん坊を預けて，働きに行っています。 (Watashi wa kinjo no hito ni akanbō o *azukete*, hataraki ni itte imasu.)

saying, "I was at fault."

¶ No matter how much **I apologized,** [Miss] Yamada wouldn't forgive me.

ayashii 〖adj〗 questionable, suspicious

¶ Didn't you see a **suspicious-looking** man around here?

azukaru 〖v I〗 take charge of, be entrusted with

¶ Isn't there somewhere that **will look after** this package 〖bag, etc.〗 for me?

¶ Banks **will receive on deposit** money from one yen up.

azukeru 〖v II〗 place in someone's charge, entrust to

¶ **I left** my bag 〖luggage, package, etc.〗 **with** a friend.

¶ **I have** a hundred thousand yen **deposited** in the bank.

¶ I go to work **leaving** my baby **in the care of** a neighbor.

B

ba　場〖名〗

¶その場にいなかったので，詳しいことはわかりません。　(Sono *ba* ni inakatta node, kuwashii koto wa wakarimasen.)

¶皆が集まっているから，この場で決めましょう。(Mina ga atsumatte iru kara, kono *ba* de kimemashō.)

ba　ば〖助〗

①〔前件が成立する場合には後件が成立するという関係を表す〕

¶春になれば，花が咲きます。　(Haru ni nare*ba*, hana ga sakimasu.)

¶2に3を足せば，5になります。(Ni ni san o tase*ba*, go ni narimasu.)

¶天気がよければ，汽車の窓から富士山が見えます。(Tenki ga yokere*ba*, kisha no mado kara Fujisan ga miemasu.)

¶「あした雨が降れば，旅行には行きませんか。」　(Ashita ame ga fure*ba*, ryokō ni wa ikimasen ka?)　「いいえ，雨が降っても行きます。」　(Iie, ame ga futte mo ikimasu.)

¶安ければ，りんごを五つ買ってきてください。　(Yasukere*ba*, ringo o itsutsu katte kite kudasai.)

¶父はお酒を飲めば，歌を歌いました。(Chichi wa osake o nome*ba*, uta o utaimashita.)

＊普通，前件と後件の主語が同じで，

ba 〚n〛 **place; occasion**

¶ I wasn't **there** so I don't know any details.

¶ Since everyone is present, let's decide it **here and now.**

-ba 〚part〛 **if, when**

① [indicates something happens when another thing happens]

¶ **When** spring comes, flowers will bloom.

¶ Two plus three is five (literally, **If** you add three to two it is five).

¶ **When** the weather is good, one can see Mount Fuji from the train window.

¶ "Will you give up (literally, not go on) your trip **if** it rains tomorrow?"
   "No, I will go even if it rains."

¶ **If** they are cheap, please buy five apples.

¶ My father used to sing **when** he drank *sake*.

＊ Usually when the subjects of both

しかも前件が動作を表す動詞の場合は，後件には「〜う[よう]（〜u [yō]）」などの意志，「〜なさい（〜nasai）」などの命令，「〜てください（〜te kudasai）」などの依頼，「〜てはいけない（〜te wa ikenai）」などの禁止などの言い方は来ない。「安ければ，りんごを五つ買ってきてください。(Yasukereba, ringo o itsutsu katte kite kudasai.)」という文は前件が状態を表す形容詞であるから言えるが，「お酒を飲めば，歌を歌いなさい。(Osake o nomeba, uta o utainasai.)」とは言えない。また，後件が動詞の過去・完了を表す「たの形」のときは過去の習慣を表す。

→to と　tara たら　te mo ても
②[前件が もし成立していた場合には後件も成立するという関係を表す]
¶父が病気にならなければ，大学をやめなくてもよかったのですが。(Chichi ga byōki ni naranakere*ba*, daigaku o yamenakute mo yokatta no desu ga.)
¶背がもう少し高ければ，バレーボールの選手になっていたと思います。(Sei ga mō sukoshi takakere*ba*, barēbōru no senshu ni natte ita to omoimasu.)
* 前件には実際には成立しなかったことがらが来る。

→tara たら　nara なら
③[願望や示唆などの意味を表す]
¶学生の時にもっと勉強していればと

clauses are the same and the verb of the -ba clause indicates an action, the -ba clause is *not* followed by an expression of desire (-ō [-yō], etc.), an order (-nasai, etc.), a request (-te kudasai, etc.), or a prohibition (-te wa ikenai, etc.). "Yasukereba, ringo o itsutsu katte kite kudasai" is possible because the -ba clause is an adjective indicating a condition, but a sentence like *"Osake o nomeba, uta o utainasai" is not possible. Further, when the second clause is in the -ta form expressing past or completed action, then the -ba clause indicates habitual action in the past.

② [indicates something would have happened if another thing had happened]
¶ If my father hadn't become ill, I wouldn't have had to leave the university.

¶ I think [I] would have become a volleyball player if [I] had been a little taller.

* In this case, the -ba clause expresses something that didn't actually happen.

③ [indicates desire, a suggestion, etc.]

思いました。 (Gakusei no toki ni motto benkyō shite ire*ba* to omoimashita.)

¶料理はまだたくさんあるから，もっとめしあがれば。 (Ryōri wa mada takusan aru kara, motto meshiagare*ba*?)

→tara たら

④[評価などを導くことを表す]

¶どんなカメラを選べばいいか教えてください。 (Donna kamera o erabe*ba* ii ka oshiete kudasai.)

¶大学に入るためには，もっと勉強しなければいけませんよ。 (Daigaku ni hairu tame ni wa, motto benkyō shinakere*ba* ikemasen yo.)

*「～ばいい（～ba ii）」「～ばいけない（～ba ikenai）」などの形で使う。

⑤[前件に既に成立していることを述べてその条件のもとで後件が成立するという関係を表す]

¶ここまで送っていただけば，あとは一人で帰れます。 (Koko made okutte itadake*ba*, ato wa hitori de kaeremasu.)

¶あなたにそう言われれば，そんな気がします。 (Anata ni sō iwarere*ba*, sonna ki ga shimasu.)

⑥[前件のことがらが成立する場合それに比例して後件のことがらの程度も進むという関係を表す]

¶物価が上がれば上がるほど生活が苦しくなります。 (Bukka ga agare*ba* agaru hodo seikatsu ga kurushiku

¶ **I wished** then that **I had** studied more in my student days.

¶ Since there is still lots of food left, **won't you** have some more?

④ [introduces or invites a judgment, evaluation, etc.]

¶ Please tell me what camera I **should** choose.

¶ You **must** study harder in order to be able to enter a university.

* Used in the patterns "-*ba ii*," "-*ba ikenai*," etc.

⑤ [indicates something happens based on something that has already happened]

¶ **Now that you have** come with me up to here, I can go the rest of the way by myself.

¶ **When** you say that, I feel that it is so.

⑥ [indicates something happens in proportion to something else]

¶ **The more** prices rise, the harder it is to make ends meet.

narimasu.)

¶アパートは部屋が広ければ広いほど高くなります。(Apāto wa heya ga hiroke*ba* hiroi hodo takaku narimasu.)

*「〜ば〜ほど (〜ba〜hodo)」の形で使う。

⑦[類似したものごとを列挙するときに使う]

¶上田さんの部屋にはラジオもあればテレビもあります。 (Ueda san no heya ni wa rajio mo are*ba* terebi mo arimasu.)

¶中村さんは英語も話せばフランス語も話します。 (Nakamura san wa Eigo mo hanase*ba* Furansugo mo hanashimasu.)

→shi し

⑧[前件が後件のことがらの出どころとなっているという関係を表す]

¶ラジオの天気予報によれば，午後からは雨が降るそうです。 (Rajio no tenki-yohō ni yore*ba*, gogo kara wa ame ga furu sō desu.)

*「〜によれば (〜ni yoreba)」の形で使う。

→to と

baai 場合［名］

①[ものごとの起こるとき，ある状態になったとき]

¶雨が降った場合にはピクニックに行きません。(Ame ga futta *baai* ni wa pikunikku ni ikimasen.)

¶困った場合には，わたしに相談して

¶ Apartments are more expensive **the larger** the rooms are.

* Used in the pattern "verb or adjective (-*ba* form) + verb or adjective (dictionary form) + *hodo*."

⑦ [used when citing similar things]

¶ There's a television in [Miss] Ueda's room **as well as** a radio.

¶ [Mr.] Nakamura speaks **not only** English **but** French as well.

⑧ [indicates that something is the source for another thing]

¶ **According to** the weather report on the radio, it's going to rain in the afternoon.

* Used in the pattern "~ *ni yoreba*."

baai ⟦n⟧ **case, occasion, time; situation, circumstances**

① [occasion, time]

¶ **In the case** of rain, [we] won't go on the picnic.

¶ Please consult me **when** you are

ください。 (Komatta *baai* ni wa, watashi ni sōdan shite kudasai.)

②[その時の事情]

¶場合によっては、あした来られないかもしれません。(*Baai* ni yotte wa, ashita korarenai ka mo shiremasen.)

(-)**bai** (-)倍〘名, 尾〙

1〘名〙

¶2の倍は4です。(Ni no *bai* wa yon desu.)

2〘尾〙

¶物価が以前の3倍になりました。(Bukka ga izen no san*bai* ni narimashita.)

baka ばか〘名, 形動〙

ばか者(*baka*mono) ばかにする(*baka* ni suru)

¶あの人はクラスのみんなにばかにされています。 (Ano hito wa kurasu no minna ni *baka* ni sarete imasu.)

bakari ばかり〘助〙

①[数量を表す言葉についてだいたいの分量・程度などを表す]

¶すみませんが、5分ばかり待ってください。 (Sumimasen ga, gofun *bakari* matte kudasai.)

¶1万円ばかり貸していただけないでしょうか。(Ichiman'en *bakari* kashite itadakenai deshō ka?)

②[ものごとがそれだけであるという限定の意味を表す]

¶田中さんは自分の意見ばかり言って、人の意見を聞きません。 (Tanaka san

troubled.

② [circumstances, situation]

¶ I might not be able to come tomorrow depending on **circumstances.**

(-)**bai** 〖n, suf〗 **double; times**

1 〖n〗 double

¶ **Twice** two is four.

2 〖suf〗 times, -fold

¶ Prices are three **times** what they were formerly.

baka 〖n, adj-v〗 **fool; stupidity**

a fool // look down on, make fun of, hold in contempt

¶ That person **is looked down upon** by the whole class.

bakari 〖part〗 **about; only; just**

① [about, approximately (following expressions of quantity)]

¶ I'm sorry, but could you please wait **around** five minutes?

¶ Could you lend me ten thousand yen **or so?**

② [only]

¶ [Miss] Tanaka **only** gives [her] own opinions and won't listen to those of

wa jibun no iken *bakari* itte, hito
no iken o kikimasen.)

¶山田さんは英語ばかりでなく，フラ
ンス語も話せます。(Yamada san wa
Eigo *bakari* de naku, Furansugo
mo hanasemasu.)

¶あの人は遊んでばかりいて勉強しま
せん。(Ano hito wa asonde *bakari*
ite benkyō shimasen.)

* 「名詞＋ばかり (bakari)」「動詞(連
体の形)＋ばかり (bakari)」「動詞（て
の形)＋ばかり (bakari)＋いる (iru)」
の形で使う。

③[ある動作がいつでも行われるよう
な状態にあることを表す]

¶夕食はもういつでも食べられるばか
りになっています。 (Yūshoku wa
mō itsu demo taberareru *bakari* ni
natte imasu.)

* 「動詞(連体の形)＋ばかり (bakari)」
などの形で使う。

④[ある動作が行われて間もない状態
にあることを表す]

¶父は今帰ってきたばかりです。(Chi-
chi wa ima kaette kita *bakari*
desu.)

¶わたしは日本語を習い始めたばかり
で，まだ上手に話せません。
(Watashi wa Nihongo o naraihaji-
meta *bakari* de, mada jōzu ni hanasemasen.)

* 「動詞(たの形)＋ばかり (bakari)」
の形で使う。

bakuhatsu　爆発〖名，〜する〗

---

others.

¶ [Mrs.] Yamada speaks **not only**
English but also French.

¶ [He] **only** plays and never studies.

* Used in the patterns "noun +
bakari," "verb (dictionary form) +
bakari," "verb (-*te* form) + *bakari* +
iru."

③ [indicates that one can start doing
something at any time]

¶ Dinner **is ready;** we can start eating at any time.

* Used in the pattern "verb (dictionary form) + *bakari*," etc.

④ [just, just now, only, only now]

¶ Father has **just now** come home.

¶ I have **just** started to learn Japanese and cannot speak it well yet.

* Used in the pattern "verb (-*ta*
form) + *bakari*."

bakuhatsu 〚n, ~*suru*〛 **explosion**

①［物質の体積が急激に増大して飛び
散り破壊力を出すこと］
¶工場で爆発が起こりました。 (Kōjō
de *bakuhatsu* ga okorimashita.)
¶ガス爆発で，家が壊れました。
(Gasu-*bakuhatsu* de, ie ga kowaremashita.)
②［不満などが急に表に現れること］
¶ついに国民の不満が爆発しました。
(Tsuini kokumin no fuman ga
bakuhatsu shimashita.)

ban 晩〘名〙
朝から晩まで (asa kara *ban* made)
晩御飯 (*ban*gohan)　前の晩 (mae
no *ban*)　毎晩 (mai*ban*)
¶あしたの晩，中村さんがうちに来ま
す。(Ashita no *ban,* Nakamura san
ga uchi ni kimasu.)
¶一晩じゅう寝ないで起きていました。
(Hito*ban*jū nenaide okite imashita.)

(-)ban　(-)番〘名，尾〙
1〘名〙
①［見張りなどをすること］
番人 (*ban*nin)　番犬 (*ban*ken)
留守番 (rusu*ban*)
¶あの店は，いつも子供が番をしてい
ます。(Ano mise wa, itsu mo kodomo ga *ban* o shite imasu.)
②［順序や順番を表す］
¶次は田中さんの読む番です。(Tsugi
wa Tanaka san no yomu *ban*
desu.)

2〘尾〙
1番 (ichi*ban*)　2番 (ni*ban*)

① [physical explosion]

¶ **An explosion** occurred at the factory.

¶ The house was destroyed in a gas
explosion.

② [explosion of discontent, etc.]
¶ Finally the discontent of the people
exploded.

ban 〖n〗　evening, night
from morning to **night** // supper //
the **night** before // every **night**

¶ [Mr.] Nakamura is coming to [our]
house tomorrow **evening.**

¶ I was up all **night** without getting
any sleep at all.

(-)ban 〖n, suf〗　watch, guard;
　　order, one's turn; number, place
1 〖n〗
① [watch over, guard]
a **watch**man, **guard** // a **watch**dog //
guarding an empty house against
theft, fire, etc.
¶ That shop is always **tended** by children.
② [order, one's turn]
¶ Next it is [Miss] Tanaka's **turn** to
read.

2 〖suf〗　number, place
Number 1 // **Number** 2

¶3番めの妹は今年 15 歳です。

(Sanbanme no imōto wa kotoshi jūgosai desu.)

bangō 番号〖名〗

電話番号 (denwa-*bangō*) 番号をつける (*bangō* o tsukeru)

¶あなたの部屋の番号は何番ですか。

(Anata no heya no *bangō* wa nanban desu ka?)

bangumi 番組〖名〗

ラジオ番組 (rajio-*bangumi*)

¶今夜は, おもしろいテレビ番組がありますか。 (Kon'ya wa, omoshiroi terebi-*bangumi* ga arimasu ka?)

basho 場所〖名〗

①〔所, 位置〕

¶ここが事故のあった場所です。

(Koko ga jiko no atta *basho* desu.)

¶わたしのうちは買い物に便利な場所にあります。 (Watashi no uchi wa kaimono ni benri na *basho* ni arimasu.)

②〔人などのいる所, 席〕

¶会場へ早く行って, 場所を取っておいてください。 (Kaijō e hayaku itte, *basho* o totte oite kudasai.)

basu バス〖名〗

バスに乗る (*basu* ni noru) バスを降りる (*basu* o oriru)

¶バスの停留所はどこですか。 (*Basu* no teiryūjo wa doko desu ka?)

¶このバスはどこ行きですか。

(Kono *basu* wa doko yuki desu ka?)

¶ My **third** younger sister is ⟦will be⟧ 15 years old this year.

bangō 〖n〗 number

a telephone **number** // assign **a number** to

¶ What is **the number** of your room?

bangumi 〖n〗 program

a radio **program**

¶ Are there any interesting television **programs** on this evening?

basho 〖n〗 place

① [place, location, position]

¶ This is **the place** where the accident was.

¶ My home is in **a location** convenient for shopping.

② [place, seat]

¶ Please go to the auditorium ⟦theater, hall, etc.⟧ early and save **seats** for [us].

basu 〖n〗 bus

take **a bus** // get off **a bus**

¶ Where is the **bus** stop?

¶ Where does this **bus** go (that is, its final destination)?

batā バター〖名〗

¶パンにバターをつけて食べます。

(Pan ni *batā* o tsukete tabemasu.)

batā 〚n〛 **butter**

¶ [I] **butter** bread and eat it.

beddo ベッド〖名〗

¶あの部屋にはベッドが二つ置いてあります。(Ano heya ni wa *beddo* ga futatsu oite arimasu.)

¶わたしはいつもベッドで寝ています。(Watashi wa itsu mo *beddo* de nete imasu.)

⇨shindai 寝台

beddo 〚n〛 **bed**

¶ There are two **beds** in that room.

¶ I always sleep in **a bed.**

benjo 便所〖名〗

便所に行く (*benjo* ni iku)

¶すみませんが、便所はどこでしょうか。(Sumimasen ga, *benjo* wa doko deshō ka?)

＊「便所 (benjo)」と言うより「手洗い (tearai)」、「お手洗い (otearai)」、「トイレ (toire)」と言ったほうが感じがいい。

⇨tearai 手洗い　toire トイレ

benjo 〚n〛 **toilet, bathroom**

go to **the bathroom**

¶ Excuse me. Where is **the lavatory** 〚**Men's Room, Ladies' Room**, etc.〛?

＊ *Tearai, otearai,* or *toire* sound better than *benjo.*

benkyō 勉強〖名, 〜する〗

¶あなたは何の勉強をしているのですか。(Anata wa nan no *benkyō* o shite iru no desu ka?)

¶日本語の勉強は難しいですか。(Nihongo no *benkyō* wa muzukashii desu ka?)

¶わたしは日本語を勉強しています。(Watashi wa Nihongo o *benkyō* shite imasu.)

benkyō 〚n, ~*suru*〛 **study**

¶ What are you **studying?**

¶ Is it hard **to learn** Japanese?

¶ I **am studying** Japanese.

benri 便利〖名, 形動〗

¶わたしの家は駅の近くですから便利です。(Watashi no ie wa eki no

benri 〚n, adj-v〛 **convenience, convenient**

¶ My house **is convenient** as it is

52

chikaku desu kara *benri* desu.)

¶これは小さくて,持って歩くのに便利な辞書です。 (Kore wa chiisakute, motte aruku no ni *benri* na jisho desu.)

¶鉄道ができてから, この町は便利になりました。 (Tetsudō ga dekite kara, kono machi wa *benri* ni narimashita.)

⇔fuben 不便

bentō 弁当〖名〗

弁当箱 (*bentō*bako)

¶わたしは, 毎日学校へお弁当を持って行きます。 (Watashi wa, mainichi gakkō e o*bentō* o motte ikimasu.)

beru ベル〖名〗

¶御用の方はこのベルを押してください。 (Goyō no kata wa kono *beru* o oshite kudasai.)

¶授業の終わりのベルが鳴りました。 (Jugyō no owari no *beru* ga narimashita.)

betsu 別〖名, 形動〗

①[分けること, 区別]

¶この学校へは男女の別なく入学できます。 (Kono gakkō e wa danjo no *betsu* naku nyūgaku dekimasu.)

¶あなたの物は別にしてあります。 (Anata no mono wa *betsu* ni shite arimasu.)

②[ほか, 同じでない]

¶今日は忙しいので, また別の日に来てください。 (Kyō wa isogashii node, mata *betsu* no hi ni kite

near the station.

¶ This is a small dictionary **handy** to carry around with one.

¶ This town has become **easier to get to** since the opening of the railway.

bentō 〚n〛 **box lunch**

a **lunch** box

¶ I take **my lunch** to school with me every day.

beru 〚n〛 **bell**

¶ Please ring this **bell** for service (a written notice).

¶ The end-of-class **bell** has rung.

betsu 〚n, adj-v〛 **distinction; different, another**

① [distinction, classification]

¶ One can enter this school with no **distinction** by sex.

¶ The things for you 〚your things〛 are set aside **separately.**

② [different, another, separate]

¶ [I]'m busy today so please come again **another** day.

kudasai.)

¶この紙ではなく，別の紙に書いてください。(Kono kami de wa naku, *betsu* no kami ni kaite kudasai.)

betsu ni 別に〖副〗

¶「何か御用ですか。」(Nani ka goyō desu ka?) 「いいえ，別に用事はありません。」(Iie, *betsu ni* yōji wa arimasen.)

¶「なにか欲しい物がありますか。」(Nani ka hoshii mono ga arimasu ka?)「いいえ，別に。」(Iie, *betsu ni.*)

＊ あとに打ち消しの言葉が来る。

biiru ビール〖名〗

ビールびん (*biiru*bin)

ビールを飲む (*biiru* o nomu)

¶ビールを1本ください。(*Biiru* o ippon kudasai.)

bijutsu 美術〖名〗

美術品 (*bijutsu*hin) 美術館 (*bijutsu*kan)

¶わたしは日本の美術について研究したいと思っています。(Watashi wa Nihon no *bijutsu* ni tsuite kenkyū shitai to omotte imasu.)

bikkuri suru びっくりする〖動Ⅲ〗

¶急に犬がほえだしたので，どろぼうはびっくりして逃げました。(Kyū ni inu ga hoedashita node, dorobō wa *bikkuri shite* nigemashita.)

¶あまり値段が高いので，びっくりしました。(Amari nedan ga takai node, *bikkuri shimashita.*)

bin びん〖名〗

¶ Please don't write it on this paper but on a **separate** piece of paper.

betsu ni 〚adv〛 (not) **particularly**

¶ "Was there something you wanted to see me about?"

"No, **not particularly.**"

¶ "Is there something you would like?"

"No, **nothing in particular.**"

＊ Used with the negative.

biiru 〚n〛 beer

a **beer** bottle // drink **beer**

¶ A bottle of **beer,** please.

bijutsu 〚n〛 art

a work of **art** // an **art** museum

¶ I would like to do research concerning Japanese **art.**

bikkuri suru 〚v Ⅲ〛 be surprised, amazed, frightened

¶ The thief **was frightened** by the sudden barking of the dog and fled.

¶ **I was surprised** the price was so high.

bin 〚n〛 bottle

ビールびん (biiru*bin*)　インクびん (inku*bin*)　しょう油びん (shōyu*bin*)　空きびん (aki*bin*)

a beer **bottle** // an ink **bottle** // a soy sauce **bottle** // an empty **bottle**

binbō　貧乏〖名，形動，〜する〗
貧乏な人 (*binbō* na hito)　貧乏になる (*binbō* ni naru)
¶家が貧乏だったので，わたしは大学へ行けませんでした。　(Ie ga *binbō* datta node, watashi wa daigaku e ikemasen deshita.)
⇨ mazushii 貧しい

binbō 〚n, adj-v, 〜*suru*〛　**poverty, poor**
a **poor** person // become **poor**
¶ Since my family **was poor,** I was not able to go to college.

binsen　便せん〖名〗
¶文房具屋で便せんと封筒を買ってきてください。(Bunbōguya de *binsen* to fūtō o katte kite kudasai.)

binsen 〚n〛　**letter paper**
¶ Please go buy me **letter paper** and envelopes at a stationery store.

biru　ビル〖名〗
¶50階建ての高いビルが建ちました。(Gojikkaidate no takai *biru* ga tachimashita.)

biru 〚n〛　**building, office building**
¶ A tall **building** 50 stories high has been built.

biza　ビザ〖名〗
¶アメリカへ行くのにビザを取りました。(Amerika e iku no ni *biza* o torimashita.)

biza 〚n〛　**visa**
¶ I obtained **a visa** to go to the United States.

bōeki　貿易〖名，〜する〗
貿易商 (*bōeki*shō)　貿易港 (*bōeki*kō)
¶最近，日本とアジアの国々との貿易が盛んになりました。(Saikin, Nihon to Ajia no kuniguni to no *bōeki* ga sakan ni narimashita.)

bōeki 〚n, 〜*suru*〛　**trade, commerce**
a trader 〚importer, exporter〛 // a **trade** port
¶ **Trade** has been flourishing between Japan and other Asian countries recently.

boku　ぼく〖代〗
君とぼく (kimi to *boku*)　ぼくの家 (*boku* no ie)
¶ぼくはまだ学生です。　(*Boku* wa mada gakusei desu.)

boku 〚pron〛　**I**
you and **me** // **my** house
¶ **I** am still a student.

＊親しい相手に対して男性が使う。

bon'yari　ぽんやり〖副，～と，～する〗

①［ものごとのはっきりしない様子］

¶遠くの山がぽんやり見えます。

(Tooku no yama ga *bon'yari* miemasu.)

¶眠くて頭がぽんやりしています。

(Nemukute atama ga *bon'yari* shite imasu.)

②［意識が集中しない様子，不注意な様子］

¶ぽんやりしていて，かさをバスの中に忘れてしまいました。　(*Bon'yari* shite ite, kasa o basu no naka ni wasurete shimaimashita.)

¶ぽんやりしていて，簡単な計算を間違えました。　(*Bon'yari* shite ite, kantan na keisan o machigaemashita.)

bōshi　帽子〖名〗

帽子をかぶる　(*bōshi* o kaburu)

帽子をとる　(*bōshi* o toru)

botan　ボタン〖名〗

①［洋服などの合わせる部分につけるもの］

ボタンをはめる　(*botan* o hameru)

ボタンをかける　(*botan* o kakeru)

ボタンを外す　(*botan* o hazusu)

¶シャツのボタンがとれそうです。

(Shatsu no *botan* ga toresō desu.)

②［機械などを作動させるために押すもの］

¶エレベーターに乗って，7階のボタ

＊ Used by men in conversation with close acquaintances.

bon'yari 〖adv, ~*to*, ~*suru*〗　**vague, unclear; abstracted, absent-minded**

① [vague, obscure, unclear, foggy, etc.]

¶ A distant mountain 〚mountain range〛 can be seen **dimly.**

¶ I'm so sleepy **I can't think straight.**

② [abstracted, absentminded, careless]

¶ I **absentmindedly** left my umbrella on the bus.

¶ I **carelessly** made a mistake in a simple calculation.

bōshi 〖n〗　**hat, cap**

put on **a hat** // take off **a hat**

botan 〖n〗　**button**

① [button (clothing)]

fasten **a button** // fasten **a button** // un**button** (something)

¶ **A button** on [my] shirt is loose.

② [button (mechanical)]

¶ [I] got in the elevator and pressed

ンを押しました。(Erebētā ni notte, nanakai no *botan* o oshimashita.)

-bu　-部〖尾〗

①［全体をいくつかに分けたもの］
¶この本は1部と2部に分かれています。(Kono hon wa ichi*bu* to ni*bu* ni wakarete imasu.)

②［組織の上での区分］
¶山田さんはＡ新聞社の写真部に勤めています。(Yamada san wa Ē-shinbunsha no shashin*bu* ni tsutomete imasu.)

③［スポーツ・文化活動などのグループ］
野球部 (yakyū*bu*)　山岳部 (sangaku*bu*)　スキー部 (sukii*bu*)　演劇部 (engeki*bu*)

④［本や雑誌や新聞などを数えるのに使う］
¶この新聞は一部いくらですか。(Kono shinbun wa ichi*bu* ikura desu ka?)

-bu　-分〖尾〗

①［温度の1度の10分の1の単位］
¶熱が 38 度5分あります。(Netsu ga sanjūhachido go*bu* arimasu.)

②［利率などの1割の10分の1の単位］
¶この預金の利息は1年に8分です。(Kono yokin no risoku wa ichinen ni hachi*bu* desu.)

bubun　部分〖名〗
一部分 (ichi*bubun*)　大部分 (dai*bubun*)　部分品 (*bubun*hin)
¶このくつは底の部分がゴムでできて

the button for the seventh floor.

-bu 〖suf〗 part, section; division, department; club; copy

① [part, section]
¶ This book is divided into a **Part** I and a **Part** II.

② [organizational unit (department, division, section, etc.)]
¶ [Mrs.] Yamada works in the photography **department** of Newspaper A.

③ [school or company club (sports, cultural, etc.)]
a baseball **club** // a mountaineering **club** // a ski **club** // a drama **club**

④ [copy; the counter for copies of books, magazines, newspapers, etc.]
¶ How much is a **copy** of this newspaper?

-bu 〖suf〗 *bu*

① [one *bu* (= one-tenth of one degree of temperature)]
¶ [He] has a fever of 38.**5 degrees.**
② [one *bu* (=1% of interest, etc.)]
¶ These savings have a yearly interest of 8 **percent.**

bubun 〖n〗 part, portion
a **part** ⟦portion, section, installment, etc.⟧ // a large **part**; the majority // **parts, components**

います。(Kono kutsu wa soko no *bubun* ga gomu de dekite imasu.)

¶火事で建物の一部分が焼けました。(Kaji de tatemono no ichi*bubun* ga yakemashita.)

bubunteki 部分的〚形動〛

¶この建物は，部分的に直せばまだ使えます。(Kono tatemono wa, *bubunteki* ni naoseba mada tsukaemasu.)

buhin 部品〚名〛

ラジオの部品 (rajio no *buhin*) 自動車の部品 (jidōsha no *buhin*) 部品を取り替える (*buhin* o torikaeru)

＊「部分品 (bubunhin)」とも言う。

buji 無事〚名，形動〛

¶無事に日本に着きましたから，御安心ください。(*Buji* ni Nihon ni tsukimashita kara, goanshin kudasai.)

¶車はひどく壊れましたが，運転していた人は無事でした。(Kuruma wa hidoku kowaremashita ga, unten shite ita hito wa *buji* deshita.)

bukka 物価〚名〛

物価が高い (*bukka* ga takai) 物価が安い (*bukka* ga yasui) 物価が下がる (*bukka* ga sagaru)

¶また物価が上がって，生活が苦しくなりました。(Mata *bukka* ga agatte, seikatsu ga kurushiku narimashita.)

bukkyō 仏教〚名〛

仏教を信じる (*bukkyō* o shinjiru) 仏教徒 (*bukkyō*to) 仏教美術 (*bukkyō*-bijutsu)

¶ **The sole** of these shoes is made of rubber.

¶ A **part** of the building was destroyed by fire.

bubunteki 〚adj-v〛 **partly, partially**

¶ This building can still be used if it is repaired **here and there.**

buhin 〚n〛 **parts, components**

radio **parts** // automobile **parts** // to replace **a part**

＊ Variant: *bubunhin*.

buji 〚n, adj-v〛 **safe, well**

¶ Please don't worry as 〚I am happy to inform you that〛 I have arrived **safely** in Japan.

¶ The car was severely damaged, but the driver **escaped injury.**

bukka 〚n〛 **prices** (of goods)

prices are high // **prices** are low // **prices** are falling

¶ **Prices** have gone up again, and it is hard to make ends meet.

bukkyō 〚n〛 **Buddhism**

to believe in **Buddhism** // a **Buddhist** // **Buddhist** art

bun 文〔名〕

¶この言葉を使って短い文を作りなさい。(Kono kotoba o tsukatte mijikai *bun* o tsukurinasai.)

¶わたしは文が下手ですから，手紙を書くのがきらいです。(Watashi wa *bun* ga heta desu kara, tegami o kaku no ga kirai desu.)

(-) bun (-) 分〔名，尾〕

1 〔名〕

①〔割り当てられたもの，持ち分〕

¶電車の切符は，あなたの分も買ってあります。(Densha no kippu wa, anata no *bun* mo katte arimasu.)

②〔ある数に分けた中のいくつか〕

3分の2 (san*bun* no ni)

2 〔尾〕

3人分の料理 (sannin*bun* no ryōri)

¶今日，わたしは今月分の月給をもらいました。(Kyō, watashi wa kongetsu*bun* no gekkyū o moraimashita.)

bunbōgu 文房具〔名〕

¶文房具屋ではノートや鉛筆などを売っています。(*Bunbōgu*ya de wa nōto ya enpitsu nado o utte imasu.)

bungaku 文学〔名〕

文学者 (*bungaku*sha)　日本文学 (Nihon-*bungaku*)

¶わたしは日本へ文学の勉強に来ました。(Watashi wa Nihon e *bungaku* no benkyō ni kimashita.)

bunka 文化〔名〕

¶わたしは日本文化について勉強した

bun 〚n〛 sentence; text; writing style

¶ Make up a short **sentence** using this word.

¶ I don't like writing letters since I am not a good **writer.**

(-)bun 〚n, suf〛 share, portion; amount; division, part, segment

1 〚n〛

① [share, portion]

¶ **Your** train ticket is bought too.

② [amount, percentage, number of shares of the whole]

two-**thirds**

2 〚suf〛 division, part, segment

three **servings** of food

¶ I received my pay **for this month** today.

bunbōgu 〚n〛 stationery, writing materials

¶ **Stationery** stores sell notebooks, pencils, etc.

bungaku 〚n〛 literature

a person **of letters** // Japanese **literature**

¶ I came to Japan to study **literature.**

bunka 〚n〛 culture, civilization

¶ I want to study Japanese **culture.**

いと思っています。 (Watashi wa Nihon-*bunka* ni tsuite benkyō shitai to omotte imasu.)

bunpō 文法〖名〗

¶日本語の**文法**はそんなに難しくありません。 (Nihongo no *bunpō* wa sonna ni muzukashiku arimasen.)
¶この文は**文法**的に間違っています。 (Kono bun wa *bunpō*teki ni machigatte imasu.)

bunshō 文章〖名〗

文章を作る (*bunshō* o tsukuru)
¶山田さんは**文章**がたいへん上手です。 (Yamada san wa *bunshō* ga taihen jōzu desu.)

busshitsu 物質〖名〗

①[物体の実質]
¶ダイヤモンドは非常に硬い**物質**です。 (Daiyamondo wa hijō ni katai *busshitsu* desu.)

②[精神に対するもの，金や品物など]
¶現代の社会は，**物質**的には豊かになったが，精神的には貧しくなったと言う人がいます。 (Gendai no shakai wa, *busshitsu*teki ni wa yutaka ni natta ga, seishinteki ni wa mazushiku natta to iu hito ga imasu.)

buta 豚〖名〗

butai 舞台〖名〗

①[音楽や劇などをする所]
¶**舞台**ではちょうど日本の踊りをやっていました。 (*Butai* de wa chōdo Nihon no odori o yatte imashita.)
②[活躍する場]

bunpō 〖n〗 **grammar**

¶ Japanese **grammar** is not so difficult.

¶ This sentence is **grammatically** wrong.

bunshō 〖n〗 **composition; writing style; sentence**

write **a composition**
¶ [Mr.] Yamada is a very good **writer.**

busshitsu 〖n〗 **substance, matter; the material**

① [substance, matter]
¶ A diamond is an extremely hard **substance.**

② [the material (vs. the spiritual)]
¶ Some people say that contemporary society has become **materially** affluent but spiritually poor.

buta 〖n〗 **pig, hog**

butai 〖n〗 **stage**

① [theatrical stage]
¶ They were just then doing Japanese dancing on **the stage.**

② [stage of operations]

¶この小説の舞台は京都です。(Kono shōsetsu no *butai* wa Kyōto desu.)

¶ **The setting** of this novel is Kyoto.

butaniku 豚肉〖名〗
¶わたしは牛肉より豚肉のほうが好きです。(Watashi wa gyūniku yori *butaniku* no hō ga suki desu.)

butaniku 〚n〛 **pork**
¶ I like **pork** better than beef.

butsukaru ぶつかる〖動Ⅰ〗
①[当たる，突き当たる]
¶自動車が電車にぶつかって，けが人が出ました。(Jidōsha ga densha ni *butsukatte,* keganin ga demashita.)
②[出会う]
¶今，大きな問題にぶつかって困っています。(Ima, ookina mondai ni *butsukatte* komatte imasu.)

butsukaru 〚v I〛 **strike, hit, run into; come across, encounter**
① [strike, hit, run into]
¶ A car **ran into** a train; some persons were injured.
② [come across, encounter]
¶ [I] am now **confronted by** a large problem and don't know what to do.

butsukeru ぶつける〖動Ⅱ〗
¶頭をドアにぶつけてしまいました。(Atama o doa ni *butsukete* shimaimashita.)
¶ボールをぶつけて，ガラスを壊してしまいました。(Bōru o *butsukete,* garasu o kowashite shimaimashita.)

butsukeru 〚v II〛 **strike, hit**
¶ [I] **hit** [my] head on the door.
¶ [My] ball **struck** the window and broke it.

-byō -秒〖尾〗
¶1分は 60 秒です。(Ippun wa rokujū*byō* desu.)

-byō 〚suf〛 **a second** (of time)
¶ One minute is 60 **seconds.**

byōin 病院〖名〗
¶田中さんは三日に一度病院に通っているそうです。(Tanaka san wa mikka ni ichido *byōin* ni kayotte iru sō desu.)
¶その病気は，大きな病院で診てもらったほうがいいですよ。(Sono byōki wa, ookina *byōin* de mite moratta hō ga ii desu yo.)

byōin 〚n〛 **hospital, clinic**
¶ I hear that [Miss] Tanaka is being treated at **the hospital** once every three days.
¶ With that illness, you had better be treated at a large **hospital.**

byōki 病気〔名〕

病気になる (*byōki* ni naru)　病気に
かかる (*byōki* ni kakaru)　病気が治
る (*byōki* ga naoru)　病気を治す
(*byōki* o naosu)　重い病気 (omoi
byōki)　軽い病気 (karui *byōki*)

¶山田さんの病気はもうよくなりまし
たか。(Yamada san no *byōki* wa
mō yoku narimashita ka?)

¶お父さんの御病気はいかがですか。
(Otōsan no go*byōki* wa ikaga desu
ka?)

¶病気で学校を 1 週間休みました。
(*Byōki* de gakkō o isshūkan yasumimashita.)

byōki 〚n〛　illness, disease

become **ill** 〚**sick**〛 // become **ill** 〚**sick**〛
// get well, recover from **an illness**
〚**disease**〛 // cure **a disease** // a serious **illness** 〚**disease**〛 // a slight **illness**

¶ Has [Mrs.] Yamada's **illness** become better yet?

¶ How is your (**sick**) father?

¶ [I] was absent from school for one
week due to **illness.**

C

cha 茶〖名〗

お茶を飲む (ocha o nomu) お茶を入れる (ocha o ireru) 濃いお茶 (koi ocha)

¶お茶をどうぞ。(Ocha o dōzo.)

¶お茶でも飲みに行きませんか。

(Ocha demo nomi ni ikimasen ka?)

¶秋子さんのうちでお茶とお菓子をごちそうになりました。(Akiko san no uchi de ocha to okashi o gochisō ni narimashita.)

chairo 茶色〖名〗

¶山田さんは茶色のズボンをはいています。 (Yamada san wa chairo no zubon o haite imasu.)

chanto ちゃんと〖副, ～する〗

①[きちんと, きれいに]

¶上田さんの部屋はいつもちゃんとかたづけてあります。 (Ueda san no heya wa itsu mo chanto katazukete arimasu.)

¶田中さんはいつもちゃんとネクタイを締めています。 (Tanaka san wa itsu mo chanto nekutai o shimete imasu.)

②[すっかり, 完全に]

¶出発の用意はちゃんとできています。(Shuppatsu no yōi wa chanto dekite imasu.)

¶部屋代は, 毎月ちゃんと払っていま

cha 〖n〗 (green) **tea**

drink **tea** // fix **tea** // strong **tea**

¶ Please have **some tea** (said when handing a cup of tea to someone).

¶ How about going somewhere for **some tea** (or other light refreshment)?

¶ I was treated to **tea** and a sweet at Akiko's.

chairo 〖n〗 **brown, light brown**

¶ [Mr.] Yamada is wearing **brown** trousers.

chanto 〖adv, ～*suru*〗 **properly, exactly; perfectly, duly**

① [properly, exactly, neatly, in good order]

¶ [Miss] Ueda's room is always **neat.**

¶ [Mr.] Tanaka always **neatly** wears a tie.

② [perfectly, duly]

¶ **Everything is ready** for [our] departure.

¶ [I] pay [my] rent **punctually**

す。(Heyadai wa, maitsuki *chanto* haratte imasu.)

⇨kichinto きちんと

chawan 茶わん〖名〗

湯飲み茶わん (yunomi-*jawan*) コーヒー茶わん (kōhii-*jawan*) 茶わんを割る (*chawan* o waru) 御飯を茶わんに盛る (gohan o *chawan* ni moru) ¶茶わんにお茶をついで飲みました。(*Chawan* ni ocha o tsuide nomimashita.)

chi 血〖名〗

血が出る (*chi* ga deru) 血が止まる (*chi* ga tomaru) 鼻血 (hana*ji*)

chichi 父〖名〗

¶わたしは父に手紙を書きました。(Watashi wa *chichi* ni tegami o kakimashita.)

＊ 自分の父親のことを他人に話す場合に使う。直接，父親に呼びかける場合や，他人の父親のことを言う場合は，「お父さん (otōsan)」「お父様 (otōsama)」と言う。

⇔haha 母 ⇨otōsan お父さん

chigai 違い〖名〗

①〔違うこと，差があること〕
¶兄弟でもこんなに性格の違いがあります。(Kyōdai demo konna ni seikaku no *chigai* ga arimasu.)
¶姉とわたしは三つ違いです。(Ane to watashi wa mittsu *chigai* desu.)
②〔間違えること〕
計算違い (keisan*chigai*) 思い違い (omoi*chigai*)

[regularly] every month.

chawan 〚n〛 (rice) **bowl**, (tea)**cup**

a tea**cup** // a coffee **cup** // break **a cup** [**bowl**] // dish rice out into **a bowl**

¶ [I] poured (green) tea into **the cup** and drank it.

chi 〚n〛 **blood**

bleed // stop **bleeding** // a nose-**bleed**

chichi 〚n〛 **father**

¶ I wrote a letter to **my father.**

＊ Used to refer to one's own father when speaking with others. When directly addressing one's father or referring to someone else's father, *otōsan* or *otōsama* is used instead.

chigai 〚n〛 **difference; mistake**

① [difference, discrepancy]

¶ Even though they are brothers, they have such **different** personalities.

¶ There is a three-year **difference** in age between my elder sister and myself.

② [mistake]

miscalculation // a **mis**understanding, **mis**apprehension

¶それはわたしの考え違いでした。

(Sore wa watashi no kangae*chigai* deshita.)

¶ I was **mistaken.**

chigai nai　違いない〖連〗

¶あ，あれは山田さんに**違い**ありません。　(A! Are wa Yamada san ni *chigai arimasen*.)

¶田中さんは必ず来るに**違い**ありません。　(Tanaka san wa kanarazu kuru ni *chigai arimasen*.)

chigai nai 〖compd〗　**certainly, un-doubtedly; it is certain that, there is no doubt that**

¶ Oh, look! **Surely** that's [Mrs.] Yamada.

¶ **There's no doubt** that [Mr.] Tanaka will come.

chigau　違う〖動Ⅰ〗

①[同じでなくなる，相違する]

大きさが**違う** (ookisa ga *chigau*)

重さが**違う** (omosa ga *chigau*)

意見が**違う** (iken ga *chigau*)

¶習慣は国によって**違い**ます。　(Shūkan wa kuni ni yotte *chigaimasu*.)

②[間違う]

¶この字は**違**っていますよ。 (Kono ji wa *chigatte* imasu yo.)

¶電話番号が**違**っています。 (Denwabangō ga *chigatte* imasu.)

③[あることがらを否定するのに使う]

¶「これはあなたのですか。」(Kore wa anata no desu ka?)「いいえ，**違い**ます。」(Iie, *chigaimasu*.)

chigau 〖v I〗　**differ; be wrong; no, not**

① [differ, vary]

be different in size // **be different** in weight // have **differing** opinions

¶ Customs **differ** from country to country.

② [be wrong, mistaken]

¶ This (written) character 〖letter, *kanji*, etc.〗 **is wrong.**

¶ You have the **wrong** number (said on the telephone).

③ [no, not; used to deny something]

¶ "Is this yours?"
"No, **it's not.**"

chihō　地方〖名〗

①[ある広がりをもつ地域]

¶この**地方**は，夏は雨があまり降りません。　(Kono *chihō* wa, natsu wa ame ga amari furimasen.)

②[田舎]

¶**地方**へ行くと，空気がきれいです。(*Chihō* e iku to, kūki ga kirei

chihō 〖n〗　**district, region; the provinces, the country**

① [district, region, area]

¶ It doesn't rain very much in the summer in this **area** 〖**around** here, in these **parts**〗.

② [the provinces, the country]

¶ The air is clean in **the country.**

desu.)

chiisai　小さい〖形〗

①〔形などが大きくない様子〕

小さい花 (*chiisai* hana)

¶このくつはわたしには小さいです。
(Kono kutsu wa watashi ni wa *chiisai* desu.)

②〔程度などが低い様子〕

小さい声 (*chiisai* koe)

¶ラジオの音をもう少し小さくしてください。(Rajio no oto o mō sukoshi *chiisaku* shite kudasai.)

③〔年齢が少ない〕

¶小さい時のことはよく覚えていません。(*Chiisai* toki no koto wa yoku oboete imasen.)

⇔ookii　大きい　⇒chiisana　小さな

chiisana　小さな〖連体〗

小さな花 (*chiisana* hana)　小さな手 (*chiisana* te)　小さな家 (*chiisana* ie)

⇔ookina　大きな　⇒chiisai　小さい

chijimeru　縮める〖動Ⅱ〗

¶このズボンは長すぎますから，少し縮めてください。(Kono zubon wa nagasugimasu kara, sukoshi *chijimete* kudasai.)

¶お金が足りなくなったので，日本にいる期間を縮めなければなりません。
(Okane ga tarinaku natta node, Nihon ni iru kikan o *chijimenakereba* narimasen.)

chijimu　縮む〖動Ⅰ〗

¶このシャツはナイロン製ですから，洗っても縮みません。(Kono shatsu wa

chiisai 〖adj〗　**small, little; young**

① [small (in size); too small]

a **small** flower

¶ These shoes **are too small** for me.

② [small (in degree, etc.)]

a **low** voice

¶ Please **turn** the radio **down** a little bit.

③ [low in age, young]

¶ [I] don't remember things from when [I] **was little** very well.

chiisana 〖attrib〗　**small, little**

a **small** flower // a **small** hand // a **small** house

chijimeru 〖v II〗　**shorten, contract, reduce**

¶ Please **shorten** these trousers a little as they are too long.

¶ **I must reduce** my stay in Japan since I am running out of money.

chijimu 〖v I〗　**shrink, contract, be shortened**

¶ As this shirt is made of nylon, **it**

naironsei desu kara, aratte mo
chijimimasen.)

chijō 地上〖名〗

¶地下鉄を降りて, エスカレーターで地
上に出ました。 (Chikatetsu o orite,
esukarētā de *chijō* ni demashita.)

⇔chika 地下

chika 地下〖名〗

地下水 (*chika*sui) 地下道 (*chika*dō)
地下室 (*chika*shitsu) 地下街 (*chika*gai) 地下鉄 (*chika*tetsu) 地下
2階 (*chika* nikai)

¶ここは地下 150 メートルぐらい掘
らないと, 水が出ません。 (Koko wa
chika hyakugojūmētoru gurai ho-
ranai to, mizu ga demasen.)

¶地下で働く人もいます。 (*Chika* de
hataraku hito mo imasu.)

⇔chijō 地上

chikagoro 近ごろ〖名〗

¶近ごろ, 山田さんから手紙が来ませ
んね。 (*Chikagoro*, Yamada san
kara tegami ga kimasen ne.)

¶近ごろの学生はあまり勉強しません。
(*Chikagoro* no gakusei wa amari
benkyō shimasen.)

chikai 近い〖形〗

①[距離的に離れていない]

¶あなたのうちは学校から近いですか。
(Anata no uchi wa gakkō kara
chikai desu ka?)

↔tooi 遠い

②[時間的にあまり離れていない, 間も
ない]

---

won't shrink when washed.

chijō 〖n〗 aboveground, ground
level

¶ [I] got off the subway and took the
escalator up to **the surface.**

chika 〖n〗 underground, subterra-
nean

underground water, groundwater //
an **under**pass, an **underground** passage // **a basement** // an **underground** shopping center // a **sub**way
// a second **basement**

¶ You have to drill **down** about 150
meters here to hit water.

¶ There are people who work **underground.**

chikagoro 〖n〗 recently, nowadays

¶ There haven't been any letters **recently** from [Miss] Yamada.

¶ Students don't study very hard
nowadays.

chikai 〖adj〗 near, close to; nearly,
soon; almost

① [near, close to]

¶ Is your home **near** the school?

② [nearly, soon, in a short time]

¶近いうちにまた会いましょう。
(*Chikai* uchi ni mata aimashō.)
¶もう12時に近いです。　(Mō jūniji
ni *chikai* desu.)
¶あの人は、日本へ来てからもう2年
近くなります。(Ano hito wa, Nihon
e kite kara mō ninen *chikaku*
narimasu.)
③[数量などがそれより少し足りない
が それとほとんど同じぐらいである]
¶会場に千人近い人が集まってきまし
た。(Kaijō ni sennin *chikai* hito ga
atsumatte kimashita.)

chikaku　近く〖名〗
①[距離的に離れていない所]
¶わたしは学校の近くに住んでいます。
(Watashi wa gakkō no *chikaku* ni
sunde imasu.)
¶この近くに郵便局はありませんか。
(Kono *chikaku* ni yūbinkyoku wa
arimasen ka?)
↔tooku　遠く　→fukin　付近
②[時間的にあまり離れていないこと]
¶もう12時近くです。　(Mō jūniji
chikaku desu.)
¶1時間近く待ったのに，山田さんは
まだ来ません。　(Ichijikan *chikaku*
matta noni, Yamada san wa mada
kimasen.)
③[数量などがそれより少し足りない
が それとほとんど同じぐらいである
こと]
¶千人近くの人が会場に集まりました。
(Sennin *chikaku* no hito ga kaijō

¶ Let's meet again **soon.**

¶ It's **almost** twelve o'clock.

¶ It's **nearly** two years since [he]
came to Japan.

③ [almost, nearly, close to (the same
amount)]
¶ **Close to** a thousand persons came
to the auditorium 〖theater, hall, etc.〗.

chikaku 〖n〗 **close, nearby; shortly, before long; nearly, almost**
① [close, nearby]
¶ I live **near** the school.

¶ Isn't there a post office **nearby?**

② [shortly, before long]
¶ It's **nearly** twelve o'clock.

¶ Even though I've waited **nearly** an
hour, [Mrs.] Yamada still hasn't
come.

③ [nearly, almost]

¶ **Nearly** a thousand people came to
the auditorium 〖hall, theater, etc.〗.

ni atsumarimashita.)

¶この時計は10万円近くしました。
(Kono tokei wa jūman'en *chikaku* shimashita.)

¶食費と部屋代で，1か月8万円近くかかります。(Shokuhi to heyadai de, ikkagetsu hachiman'en *chikaku* kakarimasu.)

chikara 力〖名〗

①[体力]

力がない (*chikara* ga nai) 力が強い (*chikara* ga tsuyoi) 力が弱い (*chikara* ga yowai)

¶あの人は体が小さいのに，力があります。(Ano hito wa karada ga chiisai noni, *chikara* ga arimasu.)

②[能力・学力など]

力がある (*chikara* ga aru) 力がない (*chikara* ga nai)

¶わたしは日本語を話す力がまだ弱いです。(Watashi wa Nihongo o hanasu *chikara* ga mada yowai desu.)

chikatetsu 地下鉄〖名〗

¶わたしは地下鉄で東京駅へ行きました。(Watashi wa *chikatetsu* de Tōkyō-eki e ikimashita.)

chikazuku 近づく〖動Ⅰ〗

¶船がこちらへ近づいてきました。(Fune ga kochira e *chikazuite* kimashita.)

¶試験の日が近づいてきました。(Shiken no hi ga *chikazuite* kimashita.)

chikoku 遅刻〖名，〜する〗

¶朝寝坊して，学校に遅刻しました。

¶ This watch cost **almost** a hundred thousand yen.

¶ Room and board take **close to** eighty thousand yen a month.

chikara 〚n〛 strength, force; ability, proficiency

① [strength, force]
weak // strong // weak

¶ Even though small, [he] **is strong.**

② [ability, proficiency]
be able // be incapable; be powerless

¶ I **can't speak** Japanese **well** yet.

chikatetsu 〚n〛 subway

¶ I went to Tokyo Station on **the subway.**

chikazuku 〚v I〛 approach, come near

¶ The ship **is 〚was〛 approaching.**

¶ The day of the examination **has 〚had〛 drawn near.**

chikoku 〚n, ~*suru*〛 lateness, being late

(Asanebō shite, gakkō ni *chikoku* shimashita.)

¶ [I] overslept and **was late** for school.

chikyū 地球〖名〗
¶地球は太陽の周りを回っています。
(*Chikyū* wa taiyō no mawari o mawatte imasu.)

chikyū 〖n〗 **the earth, the globe**
¶ **The earth** revolves around the sun.

chiri 地理〖名〗
①[世界の地形・気候・生物・都市・産業・交通などの様子]
地理学 (*chiri*gaku)
¶上田さんは中学校の**地理**の先生です。
(Ueda san wa chūgakkō no *chiri* no sensei desu.)
②[ある土地の様子]
¶兄は東京の**地理**に詳しいです。(Ani wa Tōkyō no *chiri* ni kuwashii desu.)

chiri 〖n〗 **geography; topography, geographical features**
① [geography]
(the science of) **geography**
¶ [Mr.] Ueda teaches **geography** in junior high school.
② [topography, geographical features (of a certain area)]
¶ My older brother **knows his way around** Tokyo (physically).

chiru 散る〖動Ⅰ〗
①[花や葉が落ちる]
¶桜はもう**散って**しまいました。(Sakura wa mō *chitte* shimaimashita.)
②[集中しない、心が落ち着かない]
¶隣がうるさいので、気が**散って**勉強ができません。(Tonari ga urusai node, ki ga *chitte* benkyō ga dekimasen.)
*「気が散る (ki ga chiru)」の形で使う。

chiru 〖vⅠ〗 **fall, scatter**
① [(flowers, leaves) fall, scatter]
¶ The cherry blossoms have all **fallen.**
② [be distracted]
¶ **I can't concentrate** on my studies because they are so noisy next door.
* Used in the pattern "*ki ga chiru.*"

chishiki 知識〖名〗
¶大学で専門的な**知識**を身につけたいと思っています。(Daigaku de senmonteki na *chishiki* o mi ni tsuketai to omotte imasu.)
¶わたしは、日本文学についての**知識**

chishiki 〖n〗 **knowledge**
¶ I want to obtain a specialized **education** at a university.
¶ I have hardly any **knowledge** at all

はほとんどありません。(Watashi wa, Nihon-bungaku ni tsuite no *chishiki* wa hotondo arimasen.)

of Japanese literature.

chizu 地図〖名〗

日本地図 (Nihon-*chizu*)　世界地図 (sekai-*chizu*)

¶地図で探しましたが，その町は載っていませんでした。(*Chizu* de saga-shimashita ga, sono machi wa notte imasen deshita.)

¶駅からあなたのうちまでの地図をかいてください。(Eki kara anata no uchi made no *chizu* o kaite kudasai.)

chizu 〖n〗 **map**

a map of Japan // a world **map**

¶ [I] looked for that town on **the map,** but it wasn't there.

¶ Please draw me **a map** of the way from the station to your place.

-chō -長〖尾〗

校長 (kō*chō*)　課長 (ka*chō*)　社長 (sha*chō*)　会長 (kai*chō*)　議長 (gi*chō*)

-chō 〖suf〗 **head, director,** etc.

a (school) **principal** // a (section) **chief** // a (company) **president** // a (committee) **chairman**; a (society) **president** // **a chairman** (of a representative assembly); **a leader** of a meeting

chōdo ちょうど〖副〗

① [過不足のない様子]

¶今，ちょうど6時です。(Ima, *chōdo* rokuji desu.)

¶「その本はいくらでしたか。」(Sono hon wa ikura deshita ka?) 「ちょうど千円でした。」(*Chōdo* sen'en deshita.)

② [ぐあいよく，都合よく，折よく]

¶「おふろのお湯はぬるくないですか。」(Ofuro no oyu wa nuruku nai desu ka?) 「ちょうどいいです。」(*Chōdo* ii desu.)

¶この洋服はわたしにちょうどよく合っています。(Kono yōfuku wa watashi ni *chōdo* yoku atte imasu.)

¶ちょうどよいところへ来てくれまし

chōdo 〖adv〗 **exactly, precisely; just right**

① [exactly, precisely]

¶ It's **exactly** six o'clock now.

¶ "How much was that book?"

"**Exactly** a thousand yen."

② [just right]

¶ "Isn't the bathwater a little too cool?"

"No, it's **just** right."

¶ This piece of clothing is a **perfect** fit on me.

¶ You couldn't have come at a **better**

た。(*Chōdo* yoi tokoro e kite kure-mashita.)

time 《You have come at **exactly** the right time》.

chokin 貯金〖名, 〜する〗

¶郵便局から貯金を下ろしてきました。(Yūbinkyoku kara *chokin* o oroshite kimashita.)

¶わたしは毎月1万円ずつ貯金しています。(Watashi wa maitsuki ichiman'en zutsu *chokin* shite imasu.)

chokin 〖n, 〜*suru*〗 **savings**

¶ [I] withdrew **[my] savings** from the post office.

¶ **I save** ten thousand yen every month.

chōku チョーク〖名〗

¶チョークで黒板に漢字を書いてください。(*Chōku* de kokuban ni kanji o kaite kudasai.)

¶白いチョークを1本取ってください。(Shiroi *chōku* o ippon totte kudasai.)

chōku 〖n〗 **chalk**

¶ Please write the *kanji* on the blackboard with **chalk.**

¶ Please hand me a piece of white **chalk.**

chokusen 直線〖名〗

¶ものさしを使って、直線を引きました。(Monosashi o tsukatte, *chokusen* o hikimashita.)

⇔**kyokusen** 曲線

chokusen 〖n〗 **straight line**

¶ I drew **a straight line** using a ruler 《measuring stick》.

chokusetsu 直接〖名〗

¶わたしが上田さんに直接きいてみます。(Watashi ga Ueda san ni *chokusetsu* kiite mimasu.)

¶このガラスのなべは、直接火にかけても大丈夫です。(Kono garasu no nabe wa, *chokusetsu* hi ni kakete mo daijōbu desu.)

⇔**kansetsu** 間接

chokusetsu 〖n〗 **direct, immediate, personal**

¶ I will **personally** ask [Miss] Ueda.

¶ It is safe to put this glass pot **directly** on the burner.

chōmen 帳面 ☞**nōto** ノート

chōmen ☞ **nōto**

chōsa 調査〖名, 〜する〗

人口調査 (jinkō-*chōsa*) 調査用紙 (*chōsa*-yōshi)

chōsa 〖n, 〜*suru*〗 **investigation, research**

a census // a questionnaire

¶警察が今，この事故の原因を**調査**しています。 (Keisatsu ga ima, kono jiko no gen'in o *chōsa* shite imasu.)

¶ The police are now **investigating** the cause of this accident.

¶**調査**の結果，事故の原因がわかりました。 (*Chōsa* no kekka, jiko no gen'in ga wakarimashita.)

¶ **Investigation** revealed the cause of the accident 〚Upon **investigation,** the cause of the accident was identified〛.

chōshi 調子〚名〛

chōshi 〚n〛 tone, pitch; condition

①［音の高低］
声の**調子**が高い (koe no *chōshi* ga takai)

① [tone, pitch (of sound)]
a voice is high-**pitched**

¶山田さんの歌はいつも**調子**が外れています。 (Yamada san no uta wa itsu mo *chōshi* ga hazurete imasu.)

¶ [Mrs.] Yamada always sings **off key.**

¶このピアノは音の**調子**がおかしいです。 (Kono piano wa oto no *chōshi* ga okashii desu.)

¶ This piano is **out of tune.**

②［状態，ぐあい］
¶今日は体の**調子**がいいです。 (Kyō wa karada no *chōshi* ga ii desu.)

② [condition, state]
¶ I feel very **well** today.

¶この機械は**調子**が悪いですね。 (Kono kikai wa *chōshi* ga warui desu ne.)

¶ Something **is wrong** with this machine.

chōsho 長所〚名〛

chōsho 〚n〛 strong point, advantage

¶だれにも**長所**と短所があります。 (Dare ni mo *chōsho* to tansho ga arimasu.)

¶ Everyone has their **strong points** and weak points.

¶この機械の**長所**は取り扱いが簡単だということです。 (Kono kikai no *chōsho* wa toriatsukai ga kantan da to iu koto desu.)

¶ **The strong point** of this machine is its ease of handling.

⇔tansho 短所　⇒ketten 欠点

chotto ちょっと〚副〛

chotto 〚adv〛 for a moment; a little bit

①［時間が短い様子］
¶疲れたから，**ちょっと**休みましょう。

① [for a moment, a short time]

(Tsukareta kara, *chotto* yasumimashō.)

¶ちょっと待ってください。 (*Chotto* matte kudasai.)

②[ものごとの程度などがわずかな様子]

¶もうちょっとゆっくり話してください。(Mō *chotto* yukkuri hanashite kudasai.)

¶ちょっと値段が高すぎます。もう少し安いのはありませんか。 (*Chotto* nedan ga takasugimasu. Mō sukoshi yasui no wa arimasen ka?)

-chū -中〖尾〗

①[あるものの中]
空気中 (kūki*chū*) 血液中 (ketsueki*chū*)

②[ある時間の間]
午前中 (gozen*chū*) 今週中 (kon-shū*chū*)

¶今月中には日本へ行きたいと思っています。(Kongetsu*chū* ni wa Nihon e ikitai to omotte imasu.)

③[あることをしている間]
勉強中 (benkyō*chū*) 仕事中(shigoto*chū*) 食事中 (shokuji*chū*) 使用中 (shiyō*chū*)

¶先生は今、授業中です。(Sensei wa ima, jugyō*chū* desu.)

¶山田さんに電話をかけましたが、話し中でした。(Yamada san ni denwa o kakemashita ga, hanashi*chū* deshita.)

chūgakkō 中学校〖名〗

¶ [I'm] tired; let's rest **a little while.**

¶ Please wait **a moment.**

② [a little bit, slightly]

¶ Please speak **a little bit** more slowly.

¶ That is **a little** too expensive. Don't you have anything a little cheaper?

-chū 〖suf〗 in, within; during

① [in, within (something)]
in the air // **in** the blood

② [during, while]
in the morning; **all through** the morning // **during** this week; **all this** week

¶ I want to go to Japan **sometime** this month.

③ [during, under, in progress]
to be studying; **while** studying // to be at work; **while** at work // to be dining; **while** dining // **in** use

¶ The professor is **in** class now.

¶ I telephoned [Mr.] Yamada, but the line was **busy.**

chūgakkō 〖n〗 junior high school, lower secondary school

¶弟は**中学校**へ通っています。 (Otōto wa *chūgakkō* e kayotte imasu.)

＊「中学校 (chūgakkō)」を略して「中学 (chūgaku)」とも言う。

chūgakusei 中学生〖名〗

¶弟は**中学生**です。 (Otōto wa *chūgakusei* desu.)

chūi 注意〖名, ～する〗

①[何かをするときなどに それが順調にいくように いろいろな点によく気をつけること]

注意深い (*chūi*bukai) 不注意 (fu-*chūi*)

¶交通信号に**注意**しながら, 道を渡りました。 (Kōtsū-shingō ni *chūi* shinagara, michi o watarimashita.)

¶これから話すことは大事ですから,**注意**して聞いてください。 (Kore kara hanasu koto wa daiji desu kara, *chūi* shite kiite kudasai.)

②[悪いことなどが起こらないように前もってじゅうぶんに気をつけること]

¶寒くなりましたから, 風邪を引かないように**注意**してください。 (Samuku narimashita kara, kaze o hikanai yō ni *chūi* shite kudasai.)

¶冬の山は危ないですから, **注意**してください。(Fuyu no yama wa abunai desu kara, *chūi* shite kudasai.)

③[言動などについてその人に気をつけるように言うこと]

注意を与える (*chūi* o ataeru)

¶成績が下がったので, 先生に**注意**されました。 (Seiseki ga sagatta node,

¶ My younger brother is in **junior high school.**

＊ *Chūgakkō* is sometimes abbreviated to *chūgaku*.

chūgakusei 〖n〗 **junior high school student**

¶ My younger brother is **a junior high school student.**

chūi 〖n, ~*suru*〗 **attention; caution; warning**

① [attention; pay attention, be careful (when doing something)]
careful; attentive // careless; inattentive

¶ [They] crossed the street **paying heed** to the traffic signal.

¶ What I am going to say now is important so please listen **carefully.**

② [caution; be careful, keep watch (to prevent something bad from happening)]

¶ It has gotten colder so please **be careful** not to catch a cold.

¶ Mountains are dangerous in the winter so please **take care.**

③ [warning; to advise, to warn]
give **advice**; give **a warning**

¶ [I] **was warned** by my teacher as [my] grades had fallen.

sensei ni *chūi* saremashita.)

¶バスの運転手さんが，「窓から手を出さないでください。」とお客に注意しました。(Basu no untenshusan ga, "Mado kara te o dasanaide kudasai." to okyaku ni *chūi* shimashita.)

¶ The bus driver **warned** the passenger, saying "Please don't put your hand out of the window."

chūjun 中旬〖名〗

¶わたしは9月の中旬に旅行する予定です。(Watashi wa kugatsu no *chūjun* ni ryokō suru yotei desu.)

⇨jōjun 上旬 gejun 下旬

chūjun 〖n〗 **the middle third of the month**

¶ I plan to take a trip in **mid-September.**

chūmoku 注目〖名，～する〗

¶彼の研究は世界じゅうから注目されています。(Kare no kenkyū wa sekaijū kara *chūmoku* sarete imasu.)

¶日本の経済的な発展は，他の国々から注目されています。(Nihon no keizaiteki na hatten wa, ta no kuniguni kara *chūmoku* sarete imasu.)

chūmoku 〖n，～*suru*〗 **attention, notice**

¶ His research **has attracted attention** throughout the world.

¶ Other nations **are watching** Japan's economic growth **with interest.**

chūmon 注文〖名，～する〗

¶どんな料理を注文しましょうか。(Donna ryōri o *chūmon* shimashō ka?)

¶電話でも注文できますか。(Denwa de mo *chūmon* dekimasu ka?)

¶手紙で注文すれば，すぐ送ってくれます。(Tegami de *chūmon* sureba, sugu okutte kuremasu.)

chūmon 〖n，～*suru*〗 **order; request**

¶ What dishes **shall we order?**

¶ Can one **place an order** by telephone?

¶ **If you order** by mail, they will send it right away.

chūō 中央〖名〗

¶町の中央から四方に道が延びています。(Machi no *chūō* kara shihō ni

chūō 〖n〗 **center, middle, heart**

¶ Streets extend in all directions from **the center** of the town.

michi ga nobite imasu.)

chūsha 注射〖名，〜する〗

予防注射 (yobō-*chūsha*)　注射を打つ
(*chūsha* o utsu)

¶看護婦さんは腕に注射をしてくれま
した。 (Kangofusan wa ude ni
chūsha o shite kuremashita.)

chūsha 駐車〖名，〜する〗

駐車場 (*chūsha*jō)　駐車禁止 *chūsha*-kinshi)

¶ここに駐車しないでください。 (Ko-
ko ni *chūsha* shinaide kudasai.)

chūshi 中止〖名，〜する〗

¶試合は雨のため中止になりました。
(Shiai wa ame no tame *chūshi* ni
narimashita.)

¶わたしは忙しくなったので，外国へ
行くのを中止しました。(Watashi wa
isogashiku natta node, gaikoku e
iku no o *chūshi* shimashita.)

chūshin 中心〖名〗

①〔物・所などの真ん中〕
円の中心 (en no *chūshin*)　台風の
中心 (taifū no *chūshin*)
¶町の中心に住んでいますから便利で
す。 (Machi no *chūshin* ni sunde
imasu kara benri desu.) ·

②〔最も重要な点，重要な役割をする
人〕
問題の中心 (mondai no *chūshin*)
¶上田さんが中心となって，この研究
会を作りました。 (Ueda san ga
chūshin to natte, kono kenkyūkai
o tsukurimashita.)

chūsha 〖n, ~*suru*〗 injection, shot

a preventive **injection**, an inocula-
tion // give **an injection** 〖shot〗

¶ The nurse gave me **an injection** in
the arm.

chūsha 〖n, ~*suru*〗 (automobile)
parking

a **parking** zone, a **parking** lot // No
Parking

¶ Please **don't park** here.

chūshi 〖n, ~*suru*〗 discontinue,
suspend, stop, call off

¶ The game **was called off** because
of rain.

¶ I **called off** my trip abroad because
I am 〖was〗 so busy.

chūshin 〖n〗 center, core; heart,
crux, nucleus

① [center, core, middle]

the **middle** of a circle // the **center**
of a typhoon

¶ It's convenient for me living in the
center of the town.

② [heart, crux, nucleus]

the **heart** of the problem

¶ This study group was formed
centering around [Mr.] Ueda.

D

da だ〖助動〗

①[あるものがある類に属するものであるという関係を表すのに使う]

¶それは日本語の本だ。(Sore wa Nihongo no hon *da*.)

¶田中さんは学生だ。 (Tanaka san wa gakusei *da*.)

¶山田さんは学生ではない。(Yamada san wa gakusei *de* wa nai.)

¶この建物は病院で, あの建物は学校だ。(Kono tatemono wa byōin *de*, ano tatemono wa gakko *da*.)

②[あるものがあるものと一致するものであるという関係を表すのに使う]

¶ここは銀座だ。 (Koko wa Ginza *da*.)

¶このクラスでいちばん背の高い人は山田さんだ。(Kono kurasu de ichiban se no takai hito wa Yamada san *da*.)

¶この小説の作者は中村さんだ。(Kono shōsetsu no sakusha wa Nakamura san *da*.)

③[あるものがある空間に存在するという関係を表するのに使う]

¶「お母さんは今どこにいる。」(Okāsan wa ima doko ni iru?) 「お母さんは台所だ。」 (Okāsan wa daidokoro *da*.)

¶山田先生の研究室はあの建物の2階だ。 (Yamada sensei no kenkyū-

da [[auxil]] **is, are**

① [indicates something is in a particular category]

¶ That **is** a book written in Japanese.

¶ [Mr.] Tanaka **is** a student.

¶ [Miss] Yamada **is not** a student.

¶ This building **is** a hospital, and that one **is** a school.

② [indicates that one thing equals another]

¶ This **is** the Ginza.

¶ The tallest person in this class **is** [Mr.] Yamada.

¶ The author of this novel **is** [Miss] Nakamura.

③ [indicates a person or thing exists in a certain space]

¶ "Where is your mother now?"
  "**She's** in the kitchen."

¶ Professor Yamada's office 〘study room, laboratory〙 **is** on the second

78

shitsu wa ano tatemono no nikai *da*.)

¶郵便局は駅の前だ。(Yūbinkyoku wa eki no mae *da*.)

④〔人などがある動作を続けていると いう時間的な関係を表すのに使う〕

¶「先生は。」(Sensei wa?)「先生は今 授業中だ。」(Sensei wa ima jugyō-chū *da*.)

¶「お父さんはいる。」 (Otōsan wa iru?) 「父は今旅行中だ。」(Chichi wa ima ryokōchū *da*.)

¶上田さんは今食事中だと思います。 (Ueda san wa ima shokujichū *da* to omoimasu.)

*「先生は今授業だ。(Sensei wa ima jugyō da.)」「父は今旅行だ。(Chichi wa ima ryokō da.)」「上田さんは今 食事だと思います。(Ueda san wa ima shokuji da to omoimasu.)」と も言う。

⑤〔ものごとのある事態やものごとが ある状態にあることなどを表すのに使 う〕

¶昨日は一日じゅう雨だった。 (Kinō wa ichinichijū ame *datta*.)

¶あした雨なら，旅行には行きません。 (Ashita ame *nara*, ryokō ni wa ikimasen.)

¶田中さんは病気だから今日は来ない よ。(Tanaka san wa byōki *da*kara kyō wa konai yo.)

¶今日は学校が休みなので，映画を見 に行こうと思っています。(Kyō wa

floor of that building.

¶ The post office **is** in front of the station.

④ [indicates a person or thing is in the course of doing some action]

¶ The professor 〖teacher〗? [He] **is** in class now.

¶ "Is your father there?"
"No, **he's** away on a trip now."

¶ I believe that [Mrs.] Ueda **is** at lunch 〖dinner〗 now.

* One can also omit -*chū* and say "*Sensei wa ima jugyō da*," "*Chichi wa ima ryokō da*," or "*Ueda san wa ima shokuji da to omoimasu*."

⑤ [indicates the situation or condition of someone or something]

¶ **It rained** all day yesterday.

¶ **If it rains** tomorrow [we] won't go on [our] trip.

¶ [Mr.] Tanaka won't be coming today as [he] **is** sick.

¶ As there **is** no school today, I think I'll go to see a movie.

gakkō ga yasumi *na* node, eiga o mi ni ikō to omotte imasu.)

＊ ものごとの関係や状態などについての確定的な判断を表すのに使う。丁寧に言う場合には、「です (desu)」となる。

＊「だ (da)」は「終止の形」、「で (de)」「なら (ば) (nara [ba])」「なので (na node)」は「接続の形」、「だった (datta)」は「たの形」、「で (は) ない (de [wa] nai)」は「ないの形」である。

⇨desu です　darō だろう　nara なら

＊ Used to express definite conclusions about a condition, situation, or relationship. When one speaks politely, *da* becomes *desu*.

＊ The sentence-final form is *da*; continuative forms are *de*, *nara[ba]*, and *na node*; the *-ta* form is *datta*; and the negative form is *de [wa] nai*.

dai 題〖名〗

¶あの本の題は何でしたか。(Ano hon no *dai* wa nan deshita ka?)

¶「日本」という題で作文を書きました。("Nihon" to iu *dai* de sakubun o kakimashita.)

dai 〖n〗 title; subject, theme

¶ What is 〖was〗 **the title** of that book?

¶ [I] wrote a composition on **the theme**, "Japan."

dai- 大-〖頭〗

①[大きい]
大会社 (*dai*gaisha)　大企業 (*dai*kigyō)　大事件 (*dai*jiken)　大劇場 (*dai*gekijō)

②[優れた, 立派な]
大音楽家 (*dai*ongakka)　大学者 (*dai*gakusha)　大人物 (*dai*jinbutsu)

③[程度がはなはだしい]
大きらい (*dai*kirai)　大成功 (*dai*seikō)　大賛成 (*dai*sansei)

¶わたしは魚が大好きです。(Watashi wa sakana ga *dai*suki desu.)

dai- 〖pref〗 large; great; extreme

① [large, big, great]
a **large** company // a **large** enterprise 〖corporation, company〗 // a **major** incident // a **large** theater

② [great, outstanding]
a **great** musician // an **eminent** scholar // a **great** person, an **outstanding** personality

③ [extreme degree]
hate, detest // a **great** success // **fully** approve of something

¶ I **love** fish.

dai- 第-〖頭〗

¶今日は第3課を勉強しました。
(Kyō wa *dai*sanka o benkyō shimashita.)

dai- 〖pref〗 Number~

¶ Today [we] studied Lesson 3.

(-) dai (-) 台〖名, 尾〗

1〖名〗

¶この台に乗って，たなの上の物を取ってください。(Kono *dai* ni notte, tana no ue no mono o totte kudasai.)

2〖尾〗

¶東京の自動車は全部で何台ぐらいありますか。(Tōkyō no jidōsha wa zenbu de nan*dai* gurai arimasu ka?)

¶わたしの家にはテレビが一台もありません。(Watashi no ie ni wa terebi ga ichi*dai* mo arimasen.)

(-)dai 〖n, suf〗 stand, pedestal, dais, platform; units, sets

1 〖n〗 stand, pedestal, base, table, platform, bench, block

¶ Please stand on this **footstool** and take down something 〚everything〛 on the shelf for me.

2 〖suf〗 units, sets; the counter for relatively large manufactured items such as cars, bicycles, television sets, radios, and sewing machines

¶ About **how many** automobiles are there in Tokyo?

¶ There isn't even one television **set** in my house.

-dai -代〖尾〗

部屋代 (heya*dai*)　下宿代 (geshuku*dai*)　本代 (hon*dai*)　洗たく代 (sentaku*dai*)　バス代 (basu*dai*)　タクシー代 (takushii*dai*)

¶食事代は一か月いくらかかりますか。(Shokuji*dai* wa ikkagetsu ikura kakarimasu ka?)

-dai 〖suf〗 charge, fee

room **rent** // a boardinghouse **charge** // a book **bill** // a laundry **charge** // a bus **fare** // a taxi **fare**

¶ How much do you **pay for meals** a month 〚How much will **meals cost** a month〛?

daibu だいぶ〖副〗

¶病気はもうだいぶよくなりました。(Byōki wa mō *daibu* yoku narimashita.)

¶田中さんとはだいぶ長い間会っていません。(Tanaka san to wa *daibu* nagai aida atte imasen.)

daibu 〖adv〗 greatly, much, very
¶ [My] illness is **much** better.

¶ [I] haven't met [Miss] Tanaka in **quite** a long time.

daibubun 大部分〖名〗

daibubun 〖n〗 most of, majority of

¶宿題は**大部分**終わりました。 (Shukudai wa *daibubun* owarimashita.)

¶**大部分**の学生はもう帰りました。

(*Daibubun* no gakusei wa mō kaerimashita.)

⇒**ichibubun** 一部分

daidokoro 台所〚名〛

台所用品 (*daidokoro*yōhin)

¶母は**台所**で夕食の支度をしています。

(Haha wa *daidokoro* de yūshoku no shitaku o shite imasu.)

daigaku 大学〚名〛

大学生 (*daigaku*sei) 大学に入る

(*daigaku* ni hairu) 大学を出る

(*daigaku* o deru) 国立大学 (kokuritsu-*daigaku*) 私立大学 (shiritsu-*daigaku*) 大学院 (*daigaku*in)

¶わたしはA**大学**の学生です。

(Watashi wa Ē-*daigaku* no gakusei desu.)

¶わたしは１９７５年に**大学**を卒業しました。(Watashi wa senkyū-hyaku-nanajūgonen ni *daigaku* o sotsugyō shimashita.)

daihyō 代表〚名，〜する〛

①［多くの人に代わって意見などを述べること，またその人］

代表者 (*daihyō*sha) 学生の意見を代表する (gakusei no iken o *daihyō* suru)

¶山田さんがクラスの**代表**に選ばれました。(Yamada san ga kurasu no *daihyō* ni erabaremashita.)

②［一つまたは一部分によってその全

¶ [I] have finished **most** of the homework.

¶ **Most** of the students have already left.

daidokoro 〚n〛 kitchen

kitchenware

¶ My mother is in **the kitchen** fixing dinner.

daigaku 〚n〛 college, university

a **college** 〚**university**〛 student, an undergraduate // enter **college** // graduate from **college** // a national **university** // a private **university** 〚**college**〛 // graduate **school**

¶ I am a student at **University** A 〚**College** A〛.

¶ I graduated from **college** in 1975.

daihyō 〚n, ~*suru*〛 representative

① [representative, delegate]

a representative, a delegate // **represent** student opinion

¶ [Miss] Yamada was elected as the class **representative.**

② [representative, typical]

体を表すこと，またそのもの]

代表的な作品 (*daihyō*teki na saku-hin)

¶ラジオや自動車は日本の代表的な輸出品です。 (Rajio ya jidōsha wa Nihon no *daihyō*teki na yushutsu-hin desu.)

a **representative** work (of art, litera-ture, etc.)

¶ Radios and automobiles are **repre-sentative** Japanese exports.

daiichi ni 第一に〚副〛

¶日本へ行ったら，まず第一に京都へ行きたいと思っています。 (Nihon e ittara, mazu *daiichi ni* Kyōto e ikitai to omotte imasu.)

¶まず第一に健康に気をつけなければなりません。(Mazu *daiichi ni* kenkō ni ki o tsukenakereba narimasen.)

daiichi ni 〚adv〛 **first, first of all**

¶ When I go to Japan, I want to go to Kyoto **first of all.**

¶ One should take care of one's health **above all else.**

daiji 大事〚名，形動〛

大事な用事 (*daiji* na yōji)

¶どうぞ，体を大事にしてください。 (Dōzo, karada o *daiji* ni shite kudasai.)

¶これは父の大事にしている花びんです。 (Kore wa chichi no *daiji* ni shite iru kabin desu.)

daiji 〚n, adj-v〛 **important, precious**

important business, an **important** engagement

¶ Please **take good care** of yourself.

¶ This is a vase **treasured** by my father.

daijin 大臣〚名〛

総理大臣 (sōri*daijin*) 文部大臣 (monbu*daijin*) 大蔵大臣 (ookura-*daijin*) 外務大臣 (gaimu*daijin*)

daijin 〚n〛 (government) **minister**

the prime **minister** // the **minister** of education // the **minister** of finance // the **minister** of foreign affairs

daijōbu 大丈夫〚形動〛

①[心配する必要のない様子]

¶この水を飲んでも大丈夫ですか。 (Kono mizu o nonde mo *daijōbu* desu ka?)

¶お体はもう大丈夫ですか。 (Okarada wa mō *daijōbu* desu ka?)

daijōbu 〚adj-v〛 **safe; certain**

① [safe, free from danger, all right]

¶ **Is it safe** to drink this water?

¶ **Are you recovered** now (literally, Is your body **all right** now)?

②[間違いのない確かな様子]

¶**大丈夫**,あしたは天気ですよ。(*Daijōbu*, ashita wa tenki desu yo.)

＊ 語幹だけで副詞的にも使う。

daikin 代金〖名〗

¶わたしはまだ本の**代金**を払っていません。 (Watashi wa mada hon no *daikin* o haratte imasen.)

¶**代金**を先にいただきます。(*Daikin* o saki ni itadakimasu.)

＊ 普通,物を買って払う金のことをいう。

daitai だいたい〖名〗

¶だいたいのことはわかりました。 (*Daitai* no koto wa wakarimashita.)

¶仕事は**だいたい**終わりました。 (Shigoto wa *daitai* owarimashita.)

¶わたしも,あなたと**だいたい**同じ意見です。 (Watashi mo, anata to *daitai* onaji iken desu.)

＊ 副詞的に使われることが多い。

daitōryō 大統領〖名〗

副**大統領** (fuku-*daitōryō*) **大統領**夫人 (*daitōryō* fujin)

dakara だから〖接〗

¶昨日はひどい雨でした。だから, どこへも行きませんでした。 (Kinō wa hidoi ame deshita. *Dakara*, doko e mo ikimasen deshita.)

¶彼は毎晩酒を飲んでいました。だから, 病気になったのです。(Kare wa maiban sake o nonde imashita. *Dakara*, byōki ni natta no desu.)

② [certain, sure]

¶ **Don't worry.** The weather will be fine tomorrow.

＊ Sometimes *daijōbu* alone is used adverbially.

daikin 〚n〛 **price, charge, bill**

¶ I haven't paid my book **bill** yet.

¶ Please **pay** in advance 〚now〛.

＊ Usually refers to the money used to pay for something.

daitai 〚n〛 **outline, gist; generally, on the whole**

¶ **For the most part** I understand.

¶ The work is **practically** finished.

¶ I have **substantially** the same opinion as you.

＊ Often used adverbially.

daitōryō 〚n〛 **president** (of a country)

a vice-**president** // the First Lady

dakara 〚conj〛 **accordingly, therefore**

¶ It was raining heavily yesterday. **Therefore** [I] didn't go anywhere.

¶ He drank every night. **Therefore** he became ill.

＊ 前に述べた理由を受けて,その帰結をあとに続けるときに使う。丁寧に言う場合には「ですから (desukara)」を使う。

dake だけ〔助〕

①[それ以外にはないという限定の意味を表す]

¶その問題が できなかった のはわたしだけでした。 (Sono mondai ga dekinakatta no wa watashi *dake* deshita.)

¶旅行にはクラスの学生の半分だけが参加しました。(Ryokō ni wa kurasu no gakusei no hanbun *dake* ga sanka shimashita.)

¶たくさんのりんごの中から、おいしそうなのだけを選んで買いました。

(Takusan no ringo no naka kara, oishisō na no *dake* o erande kaimashita.)

＊「～だけが (～dake ga)」「～だけを (～dake o)」は「が (ga)」「を (o)」を省略して使うことが多い。「学生の半分だけ参加しました。(Gakusei no hanbun dake sanka shimashita.)」「おいしそうなのだけ選んで買いました。(Oishisō na no dake erande kaimashita.)」

＊ 少ないということを強調したいときは、「だけ (dake)」よりも「～しか～ない (～shika ～nai)」を使う。「鉛筆は一本だけあります。(Enpitsu wa ippon dake arimasu.)」と言うより,鉛筆は一本しかありません。(Enpi-

＊ Used when stating the result or conclusion for a cause given earlier. When speaking more politely, *desukara* is used instead.

dake 〖part〗 only, no more than; as much as

① [only, no more than]

¶ I was the **only** one who couldn't do that problem.

¶ **Only** half of the students in the class went on the trip.

¶ Among many apples, [I] picked out and bought **only** the ones that looked good.

＊ The particles *ga* and *o* of "~ *dake ga*" and "~ *dake o*" are often omitted: "*Gakusei no hanbun dake sanka shimashita*"; "*Oishisō na no dake erande kaimashita.*"

＊ When one wants to emphasize the smallness of the quantity, the pattern "~ *shika -nai*" is used rather than *dake*. For example, "*Enpitsu wa ippon shika arimasen*" (I have only one pencil) is more emphatic than

85

tsu wa ippon shika arimasen.)」と
言う。

②［ものごとの程度の限界を表す］

¶成功するかどうかわかりませんが，できるだけ努力してみます。 (Seikō
suru ka dō ka wakarimasen ga,
dekiru *dake* doryoku shite mimasu.)

¶この花を欲しいだけ持って行ってもいいですよ。 (Kono hana o hoshii
dake motte itte mo ii desu yo.)

daku 抱く〖動Ⅰ〗

¶女の子が人形を抱いています。

(Onna no ko ga ningyō o *daite*
imasu.)

¶ちょっと赤ちゃんを抱かせてください。 (Chotto akachan o *dakasete*
kudasai.)

damaru 黙る〖動Ⅰ〗

①［何も言わない，話さない］

¶わたしがあいさつしたのに，あの人は黙って行ってしまいました。 (Watashi ga aisatsu shita noni, ano
hito wa *damatte* itte shimaimashita.)

¶このことは，ほかの人には黙っていてください。 (Kono koto wa, hoka
no hito ni wa *damatte* ite kudasai.)

②［前もって何も言わない，断らない］

¶あの人は黙って学校を休みました。

(Ano hito wa *damatte* gakkō o
yasumimashita.)

¶タイプライターを黙って持って行かないでください。 (Taipuraitā o *damatte* motte ikanaide kudasai.)

"*Enpitsu wa ippon dake arimasu.*"

② [as much as]

¶ I don't know if I'll succeed or not,
but I'll try **as hard as** I can.

¶ You may take **as many** of these
flowers as you'd like.

daku 〚v I〛 embrace, hold in one's
arms

¶ The little girl **is holding** a doll.

¶ Please **let me hold** the baby for a
moment.

damaru 〚v I〛 be silent, don't
speak; without notice, without permission

① [be silent, don't speak]

¶ Even though I greeted [her], [she]
left **without a word.**

¶ Please **don't say anything** about
this matter to anyone else.

② [without prior notice, without permission]

¶ [He] stayed home from school
without any explanation.

¶ Please don't move the typewriter
without getting permission.

dame　だめ〘形動〙

①[むだ，効果がない様子]

¶やってみましたが，だめでした。
(Yatte mimashita ga, *dame* deshita.)

¶いくらあの人に注意してもだめです。
(Ikura ano hito ni chūi shite mo *dame* desu.)

②[役に立たない様子]

¶このラジオは古くてもうだめです。
(Kono rajio wa furukute mō *dame* desu.)

③[望みがない様子]

¶中村さんはA大学を受けましたが，だめらしいです。 (Nakamura san wa Ē-daigaku o ukemashita ga, *dame* rashii desu.)

④[それをしてはいけないという意味を表す]

¶「あした休んでもいいですか。」
(Ashita yasunde mo ii desu ka?)
「だめです。」(*Dame* desu.)

¶約束を守らなくてはだめですよ。
(Yakusoku o mamoranakute wa *dame* desu yo.)

¶もっと早起きしなければだめですよ。
(Motto hayaoki shinakereba *dame* desu yo.)

(-) dan　(-) 段〘名，尾〙

1〘名〙

本箱の上の段，下の段 (honbako no ue no *dan*, shita no *dan*)　寝台車の上の段(shindaisha no ue no *dan*)

2〘尾〙

dame 〚adj-v〛　**useless; no good; hopeless, impossible; must, must not**

① [useless, vain, unavailing]

¶ I tried to do it but **it was no good.**

¶ **It's no use** no matter how much one admonishes [him].

② [no good]

¶ This radio is old and **not good for anything.**

③ [hopeless, impossible]

¶ [Mr.] Nakamura took the entrance examination for University A, but it seems [he] **was unsuccessful.**

④ [must, must not (do something)]

¶ "Is it all right if I take the day off tomorrow?"
　 "No, it isn't."

¶ **One must** keep one's promises.

¶ **You must** get up earlier.

(-)dan 〚n, suf〛　**step, rung; grade, rank**

1 〚n〛　step, rung, deck, tier
the upper **shelf**, lower **shelf** of a bookcase // the upper **berth** in a train sleeping car

2 〚suf〛

①［階段などを数えるときに使う］

¶危ないから，階段は1段ずつ降りなさい。 (Abunai kara, kaidan wa ichi*dan* zutsu orinasai.)

②［柔道や碁などで強さの程度によって与えられる資格］

¶山田さんは柔道2段です。(Yamada san wa jūdō ni*dan* desu.)

-dan -団〖尾〗

選手団 (senshu*dan*)

¶その事故については，調査団を作って調べています。 (Sono jiko ni tsuite wa, chōsa*dan* o tsukutte shirabete imasu.)

danbō 暖房〖名，〜する〗

暖房のある部屋 (*danbō* no aru heya)

暖房がきく (*danbō* ga kiku) 暖房をつける (*danbō* o tsukeru)

¶うちには暖房設備が何もありません。 (Uchi ni wa *danbō*-setsubi ga nani mo arimasen.)

¶この部屋は，暖房しているから暖かいです。(Kono heya wa, *danbō* shite iru kara atatakai desu.)

⇔reibō 冷房

dandan だんだん〖副〗

¶だんだん寒くなってきました。 (*Dandan* samuku natte kimashita.)

¶日本語の勉強がだんだん難しくなってきました。 (Nihongo no benkyō ga *dandan* muzukashiku natte kimashita.)

danjo 男女〖名〗

男女平等 (*danjo*-byōdō) 男女共学

① [the counter for stairs, steps]

¶ That's dangerous; go down the stairs one **step** at a time.

② [the counter for grades or ranks as in judo, *go*, etc.]

¶ [Miss] Yamada holds a *nidan* ⟦the second **rank**⟧ in judo.

-dan ⟦suf⟧ body, group, organization

sports **team** ⟦squad, group⟧

¶ A study **group** ⟦inquiry **commission**⟧ has been formed and is investigating that accident.

danbō ⟦n, ~*suru*⟧ heating

a room with **heat** // can be **heated**; is well **heated** // turn on **the heat**

¶ There is no **heating** system in my home.

¶ This room is warm because **the heat is on.**

dandan ⟦adv⟧ increasingly; step by step, gradually

¶ It has **gradually** gotten colder and colder.

¶ [My] Japanese studies have **gradually** gotten more difficult.

danjo ⟦n⟧ man and woman, male and female, both sexes

equality of **the sexes** // **co**education

(*danjo*-kyōgaku) 男女同権 (*danjo*-dōken)

¶学生は男女合わせて 20 名です。(Gakusei wa *danjo* awasete nijūmei desu.)

¶この会社は，男女で給料の差がありません。(Kono kaisha wa, *danjo* de kyūryō no sa ga arimasen.)

// equal rights **for men and women**

¶ **Male and female,** there are 20 students in all.

¶ There is no difference in pay **according to sex** in this company.

dansei 男性〖名〗

¶今の社会は男性中心です。(Ima no shakai wa *dansei* chūshin desu.)

¶これは男性用のシャツです。(Kore wa *dansei*yō no shatsu desu.)

⇔josei 女性

dansei 〖n〗 male

¶ Present-day society is **male** oriented.

¶ This is a **men's** shirt.

danshi 男子〖名〗

¶このクラスは男子ばかりです。(Kono kurasu wa *danshi* bakari desu.)

¶男子の学生より女子学生のほうが，よく勉強するようです。(*Danshi* no gakusei yori joshi-gakusei no hō ga, yoku benkyō suru yō desu.)

⇔joshi 女子

danshi 〖n〗 boy, man, male

¶ This class is all **male.**

¶ It seems that female students study harder than **male** students.

dansu ダンス〖名〗

社交ダンス (shakō-*dansu*) フォークダンス (fōku-*dansu*) ダンスパーティー (*dansu*-pātii) ダンス音楽 (*dansu*-ongaku) ダンスをする (*dansu* o suru)

dansu 〖n〗 dance, dancing

social 〖ballroom〗 **dancing** // a folk **dance,** folk **dancing** // a **dance** party // **dance** music // to **dance**

dantai 団体〖名〗

政治団体 (seiji-*dantai*) 宗教団体 (shūkyō-*dantai*) 団体旅行 (*dantai*-ryokō)

¶団体で旅行するのはとても楽しいです。(*Dantai* de ryokō suru no wa

dantai 〖n〗 group, party; organization, association

a political **organization** // a religious **body** // a **group** tour, traveling **in a party**

¶ It is very pleasant to travel **with**

totemo tanoshii desu.)

-darake -だらけ〖尾〗

どろだらけ (doro*darake*) 傷だらけ
(kizu*darake*) 血だらけ (chi*darake*)
ごみだらけ (gomi*darake*)

¶この計算は間違いだらけです。(Ko-
no keisan wa machigai*darake* desu.)

¶本がほこりだらけになってしまいま
した。(Hon ga hokori*darake* ni
natte shimaimashita.)

dare だれ〖代〗

¶あの人はだれですか。(Ano hito wa
dare desu ka?)

¶これはだれの本ですか。 (Kore wa
dare no hon desu ka?)

¶これはだれが書きましたか。(Kore
wa *dare* ga kakimashita ka?)

¶あなたはだれに会いたいのですか。
(Anata wa *dare* ni aitai no desu
ka?)

¶「教室の中にだれかいますか。」(Kyō-
shitsu no naka ni *dare* ka imasu
ka?)「いいえ、だれもいません。」(Iie,
dare mo imasen.)

¶この図書館は、だれでも入ることが
できます。(Kono toshokan wa, *dare*
demo hairu koto ga dekimasu.)

¶このことは、だれにも言わないでく
ださい。(Kono koto wa, *dare* ni mo
iwanaide kudasai.)

darō だろう〖助動〗

¶あしたはたぶん雨だろう。 (Ashita
wa tabun ame *darō*.)

¶わたしが行かなくても、田中さんは

others.

-darake 〚suf〛 **filled with ~,
covered with ~**

covered with mud // **covered with**
injuries; **covered with** scars // **covered with** blood, blood**stained** //
full of trash, littered

¶ These figures are **full of** mistakes.

¶ The books have gotten **all** dusty.

dare 〚pron〛 **who, whom, whose;
no one, someone, anyone, everyone**

¶ **Who** is that person?

¶ **Whose** book is this?

¶ **Who** wrote this?

¶ **Who** do you want to see?

¶ "Is there **anyone** in the classroom?"

  "No, there's **nobody** there."

¶ **Anyone** can enter this library.

¶ Please don't say anything about
this matter to **anyone.**

darō 〚auxil〛 **perhaps, will probably, I think**

¶ It **will probably** rain tomorrow.

¶ [Mrs.] Tanaka **will probably** go

行くだろう。(Watashi ga ikanakute mo, Tanaka san wa iku *darō*.)

even if I don't.

¶母はもうすぐ帰ってくるだろうと思います。(Haha wa mō sugu kaette kuru *darō* to omoimasu.)

¶ My mother **should** be back soon.

＊名詞・動詞・形容詞・形容動詞・ある種の助動詞・助詞「の」などについて，推測の意味を表す。

＊ Used after nouns, verbs, adjectives, adjective-verbs, certain auxiliaries, and the particle *no* to express conjecture or supposition.

⇒**deshō** でしょう **da** だ

dasu 出す〔動Ⅰ〕

dasu 〚v Ⅰ〛 **put out, put forth; present, submit; produce, yield**

①〔何かを中から外に移す〕
ポケットから財布を出す (poketto kara saifu o *dasu*) 本棚なから本を出す (hondana kara hon o *dasu*)
¶あまりうるさいので，ねこを外へ出しました。(Amari urusai node, neko o soto e *dashimashita*.)

① [put out, take out, bring out]
take one's wallet **out** of one's pocket // **take** a book **from** the bookshelf

¶ **I put** the cat **out** because it was so noisy 〚such a nuisance〛.

↔**ireru** 入れる

②〔前の方などへ伸ばす，突き出す〕
足を前に出す (ashi o mae ni *dasu*)
¶電車の窓から手を出すと危ないですよ。(Densha no mado kara te o *dasu* to abunai desu yo.)

② [stretch out, stick out]
stretch one's legs **out**
¶ It is dangerous to **put** one's hand **out** of a train window.

③〔ほかの所へ行かせる〕
子供を使いに出す (kodomo o tsukai ni *dasu*)

③ [send somewhere]
send a child on an errand

④〔車や船などをその仕事に就かせる〕
舟を海に出す (fune o umi ni *dasu*)
臨時列車を出す (rinji-ressha o *dasu*)

④ [run, put out (a train, boat, etc.)]
put a ship **out** to sea // **run** a special train

⑤〔手紙や荷物などを目的の所に向けて送る〕
小包を出す (kozutsumi o *dasu*) 野菜を市場に出す (yasai o ichiba ni *dasu*)

⑤ [send, post, forward letters, freight, etc.]
send a parcel // **send** vegetables to market

¶今朝，お母さんに手紙を出しました。
(Kesa, okāsan ni tegami o *dashimashita.*)

¶ **I mailed** a letter to my mother this morning.

¶冬服をクリーニングに出しました。
(Fuyufuku o kuriiningu ni *dashimashita.*)

¶ [I] **sent** the winter clothing to the cleaners.

⑥[出版する，掲載する]
経済学の本を出す　(keizaigaku no hon o *dasu*)　雑誌を出す (zasshi o *dasu*)　新聞に広告を出す (shinbun ni kōkoku o *dasu*)

⑥ [publish, print, insert]
publish ⟦**have published**⟧ an economics book // **publish** a magazine // **insert** an ad in the newspaper

¶今度，日本文化についての論文を雑誌に出しました。(Kondo, Nihon-bunka ni tsuite no ronbun o zasshi ni *dashimashita.*)

¶ Recently [I] had an article of [mine] about Japanese culture **appear** in a magazine.

⑦[広く人の目に触れるようにする]
掲示を出す (keiji o *dasu*)　看板を出す (kanban o *dasu*)

⑦ [put up, hang out, hoist]
put up a notice // **put up** a signboard ⟦**shingle**⟧

⑧[渡す，提出する]
願書を出す (gansho o *dasu*)　欠席届を出す (kessekitodoke o *dasu*)

⑧ [present, submit, hand in]
make an application in writing // **give** written notice of one's absence

¶書き終わった人は出してください。
(Kakiowatta hito wa *dashite* kudasai.)

¶ Will those who have finished writing please **hand in** their papers ⟦forms, etc.⟧.

⑨[問題などを課する]
¶先生はいつも宿題をたくさん出します。(Sensei wa itsu mo shukudai o takusan *dashimasu.*)

⑨ [assign, set (someone a problem, etc.)]

¶ Our teacher always **assigns** us lots of homework.

⑩[発生させる，発する]
火事を出す (kaji o *dasu*)

⑩ [issue, give forth, produce]
start a fire

¶そんなに大きな声を出さないでください。(Sonna ni ookina koe o *dasanaide* kudasai.)

¶ Please **don't speak** in such a loud voice.

¶父は熱を出して寝ています。(Chichi

¶ My father is in bed **with** a fever.

wa netsu o *dashite* nete imasu.)

⑪[更に増加させる]

¶あまりスピードを出しては危ないですよ。(Amari supiido o *dashite* wa abunai desu yo.)

¶もっと元気を出して歩いてください。(Motto genki o *dashite* aruite kudasai.)

⑫[提供してもてなす]

お茶を出す (ocha o *dasu*) お菓子を出す (okashi o *dasu*) ビールを出す (biiru o *dasu*)

-dasu -だす〖尾〗

¶雨が降りだしました。(Ame ga furi-*dashimashita*.)

¶汽車が動きだしました。 (Kisha ga ugoki*dashimashita*.)

¶赤ん坊が急に泣きだしました。(Akanbō ga kyū ni naki*dashimashita*.)

＊「動詞（基幹の形）＋だす (dasu)」の形で使う。

de で〖助〗

①[動作などの行われる場所を表す]

¶昼御飯はどこで食べましょうか。(Hirugohan wa doko *de* tabemashō ka?)

¶日本では，車は道の左側を走ります。(Nihon *de* wa, kuruma wa michi no hidarigawa o hashirimasu.)

②[ある限定的な時間・空間などの範囲を表す]

¶世界でいちばん高い山はエベレストです。(Sekai *de* ichiban takai yama

⑪ [put forth, increase]

¶ It's dangerous **to go too fast.**

¶ Please walk **putting more spirit into it.**

⑫ [put out, offer, serve]

offer (green) tea // **serve** a sweet // **serve** beer

-dasu 〖suf〗 start -ing

¶ It **has started** to rain 〚It **started** to rain〛.

¶ The train **started** to move.

¶ The baby suddenly **started** to cry 〚**burst out** crying〛.

＊ Used in the pattern "verb (stem form) + -*dasu.*"

de 〖part〗 in, at, by

① [indicates the place where an action occurs]

¶ **Where** shall we eat lunch?

¶ **In** Japan automobiles run on the left-hand side of the road.

② [pinpoints a time period or physical space]

¶ The highest mountain **in** the world is Mount Everest.

wa Eberesuto desu.)

¶一年じゅうでいちばん寒い月 はいつ
ですか。(Ichinenjū *de* ichiban samui
tsuki wa itsu desu ka?)

③[手段・方法・材料などを表す]
タクシーで行く (takushii *de* iku)
鉛筆で書く (enpitsu *de* kaku) 日
本語で話す (Nihongo *de* hanasu)

¶あなたの国まで航空便で何日ぐらい
かかりますか。   (Anata no kuni
made kōkūbin *de* nannichi gurai
kakarimasu ka?)

¶この花は紙でできています。(Kono
hana wa kami *de* dekite imasu.)

④[原因・理由などを表す]
¶わたしは病気で学校を休みました。
(Watashi wa byōki *de* gakkō o
yasumimashita.)

¶今、外国へ行く準備でとても忙しいで
す。(Ima, gaikoku e iku junbi *de*
totemo isogashii desu.)

⑤[限定的な状態を表す]
¶みんなで先生の家へ行きましょう。
(Minna *de* sensei no ie e ikimashō.)

¶わたしはゆうべ寂しい道を一人で帰
ってきました。   (Watashi wa yūbe
sabishii michi o hitori *de* kaette
kimashita.)

⑥[時間・値段・数量などの限定を表
す]
¶この仕事は1日でできます。(Kono
shigoto wa ichinichi *de* dekimasu.)

¶もう1週間で夏休みが来ます。(Mō
isshūkan *de* natsuyasumi ga kima-

¶ Which is the coldest month **in** the
year?

③ [indicates means, method, mate-
rial]
go **by** taxi // write **with** a pencil //
speak **in** Japanese

¶ How many days does it take things
sent airmail to get to your country?

¶ This flower is made **out of** paper.

④ [indicates cause, reason]
¶ I stayed home from school **due to**
illness.

¶ [I] am very busy now **with** preparations for going abroad.

⑤ [indicates an exclusive agent]
¶ Let's **all** go to [our] teacher's house
together.

¶ Last night I came home **alone**
through the deserted streets.

⑥ [indicates boundaries of time,
value, quantity]
¶ This job can be done **in** one day.

¶ **In** one week summer vacation will
be here.

su.)

¶この時計は１万円で買いました。
(Kono tokei wa ichiman'en *de* kai-mashita.)

¶この鉛筆は２本で 50 円です。(Kono enpitsu wa nihon *de* gojūen desu.)

＊「こちらは銀行で,あちらは病院です。(Kochira wa ginkō de, achira wa byōin desu.)」の「で (de)」は,助動詞「だ (da)」の「接続の形」である。

deguchi 出口〖名〗

¶出口はどちらですか。 (*Deguchi* wa dochira desu ka?)

⇔iriguchi 入り口

dekakeru 出かける〖動Ⅱ〗

旅行に出かける (ryokō ni *dekakeru*)
散歩に出かける (sanpo ni *dekakeru*)
買い物に出かける (kaimono ni *dekakeru*)

¶今, 父は仕事で出かけています。
(Ima, chichi wa shigoto de *dekakete* imasu.)

¶そろそろ出かけましょうか。 (Soro-soro *dekakemashō* ka?)

dekiru できる〖動Ⅱ〗

①[あることをする能力がある, あることをすることが可能である]
運転ができる (unten ga *dekiru*) 泳ぎができる (oyogi ga *dekiru*) 運転できる (unten *dekiru*)

¶あなたは日本語を話すことができますか。(Anata wa Nihongo o hana-su koto ga *dekimasu* ka?)

¶ [I] bought this watch 〚clock〛 **for** ten thousand yen.

¶ These pencils are **2 for** 50 yen.

＊ The *de* in a sentence like "*Kochira wa ginkō de, achira wa byōin desu*" (This is a bank and that is a hospital) is the *-te* form of *da*.

deguchi 〚n〛 exit

¶ Which way is **the exit?**

dekakeru 〚v Ⅱ〛 go out, start out
set out on a journey // **go out** for a walk // **go out** shopping

¶ My father **is out** at work now.

¶ Let's **be off.**

dekiru 〚v Ⅱ〛 can, be able to; be made; be ready; be made of; grow, produce; be skilled

① [can, be able to, be possible]
be able to drive // **be able** to swim // **be able** to drive

¶ **Can** you speak Japanese?

¶あの人はフランス語ができるそうで
す。(Ano hito wa Furansugo ga
dekiru sō desu.)

¶I hear that [he] **knows** French.

¶今日は波が荒いから，泳ぐことができ
ません。(Kyō wa nami ga arai
kara, oyogu koto ga *dekimasen*.)

¶[We] **cannot** go swimming today as
the sea is rough.

②[ものごとが生じる，発生する]
家ができる (ie ga *dekiru*) 赤ん坊が
できる (akanbō ga *dekiru*)

② [be made, be produced, come into
existence]
build a house // **have** a baby

¶用事ができたので，遊びに行けなく
なりました。(Yōji ga *dekita* node,
asobi ni ikenaku narimashita.)

¶Something **has come up** so I can't
visit you.

¶近くに新しい駅ができました。
(Chikaku ni atarashii eki ga *dekimashita*.)

¶A new station **has been built**
nearby.

③[準備が終わる，完成する]
¶食事の用意ができました。(Shokuji
no yōi ga *dekimashita*.)

③ [be ready, be completed]
¶The meal **is ready.**

¶立派な論文ができましたね。(Rippa
na ronbun ga *dekimashita* ne.)

¶**You've written** a fine paper ⟦essay,
article, thesis⟧ here.

④[作られる]
¶このテーブルは木でできています。
(Kono tēburu wa ki de *dekite* imasu.)

④ [be made of]
¶This table **is made of** wood.

⑤[生産される]
米ができる (kome ga *dekiru*)
¶寒い地方ではみかんができません。
(Samui chihō de wa mikan ga
dekimasen.)

⑤ [grow, produce]
to grow rice
¶Mandarin oranges **can't be grown**
in cold regions.

⑥[学問・才能などが優れている，成績
がいい]
よくできる子供 (yoku *dekiru* kodomo) できない生徒 (*dekinai* seito)
¶あの学生はたいへんよくできます。

⑥ [be skilled, be proficient, be good
at]
an **able** ⟦**bright**⟧ child // a **poor** student
¶That is an **excellent** student.

(Ano gakusei wa taihen yoku *dekimasu*.)

¶試験はよくできましたか。 (Shiken wa yoku *dekimashita* ka?)

⑦[可能なかぎり]

¶できるだけ早く来てください。 (*Dekiru* dake hayaku kite kudasai.)

*「できるだけ (dekiru dake)」「できるかぎり (dekiru kagiri)」の形で使う。

demo でも〖助〗

①[特別な例を挙げて他の場合ももちろんであるという意味を表す]

¶それは子供でもできます。 (Sore wa kodomo *demo* dekimasu.)

¶高い山の上には夏でも雪があります。 (Takai yama no ue ni wa natsu *demo* yuki ga arimasu.)

②[前のことがらに関係なくあとのことがらが実現することを表す]

¶試合は雨でも行われます。 (Shiai wa ame *demo* okonawaremasu.)

¶今からでも遅くはありません。 (Ima kara *demo* osoku wa arimasen.)

③[軽く一例として挙げる場合に使う]

¶コーヒーでも飲みませんか。 (Kōhii *demo* nomimasen ka?)

¶日曜日にでも見に行きましょうか。 (Nichiyōbi ni *demo* mi ni ikimashō ka?)

④[すべての]

いつでも (itsu *demo*)　どこでも (doko *demo*)　何でも (nan *demo*)　何年でも (nannen *demo*)

---

demo

¶ **Did you do well** on the exam?

⑦ [to the extent possible, as ~ as possible]

¶ Please come as soon **as possible** 〚as soon **as you can**〛.

* Used in the patterns "*dekiru dake*" and "*dekiru kagiri.*"

demo 〚part〛 **even; even if, even though; or the like; all**

① [even; indicates that a condition is true in exceptional circumstances and so is of course true at other times]

¶ **Even** a child can do that.

¶ There is snow on the top of high mountains **even** in the summer.

② [even, even if, even though; indicates something will be realized regardless of something else]

¶ The game will take place **even in the case** of rain.

¶ It isn't too late **even** now.

③ [or the like, maybe; used to lightly suggest something]

¶ How about some coffee **or something?**

¶ Why don't we go to see it on, **say,** Sunday?

④ [all]

at **any** time, always // **any**where, **every**where // **any**thing, **every**thing // for **however many** years, forever

¶そんなことはだれでも知っています。
(Sonna koto wa dare *demo* shitte
imasu.)

¶どんな難しいことでもわかります。
(Donna muzukashii koto *demo* wakarimasu.)

* 疑問の言葉といっしょに使う。

denchi 電池〖名〗

電池が切れる (*denchi* ga kireru)

電池を新しいのと取り替える (*denchi*
o atarashii no to torikaeru)

denki 電気〖名〗

①[電燈]

¶暗くなったので, 電気をつけました。
(Kuraku natta node, *denki* o tsukemashita.)

¶最後に部屋を出る人は電気を消して
ください。 (Saigo ni heya o deru
hito wa *denki* o keshite kudasai.)

②[電燈をつけたり物を動かしたりす
るエネルギーの一つ]

電気製品 (*denki*-seihin) 電気洗たく
機 (*denki*-sentakuki) 電気冷蔵庫
(*denki*-reizōko) 電気スタンド
(*denki*-sutando)

¶アイロンに電気が通じません。 (Ai-
ron ni *denki* ga tsūjimasen.)

denpō 電報〖名〗

電報を打つ (*denpō* o utsu)

電報で知らせる (*denpō* de shiraseru)

¶日本に着いたら, すぐ電報を打ちま
す。 (Nihon ni tsuitara, sugu *denpō*
o uchimasu.)

densen 伝染〖名, ～する〗

¶ **Everyone** knows that.

¶ [He] knows **everything**, no matter
how difficult.

* Used with interrogatives.

denchi 〖n〗 electric battery

a battery goes dead // replace **a battery** with a new one

denki 〖n〗 electric light; electricity

① [electric light]

¶ [I] turned on **the lights** as it had
gotten dark.

¶ Will the last person to leave the
room please turn off **the lights.**

② [electricity]

an **electrical** appliance // an **electric**
washing machine // an **electric** refrigerator // an **electric** lamp

¶ This iron is broken; **the electricity**
doesn't flow through it.

denpō 〖n〗 telegram

send **a telegram** // inform by **telegram**

¶ [I] will send [you] **a telegram** without delay upon arrival in Japan.

densen 〖n, ～*suru*〗 contagious, in-
fectious

¶各地に伝染病が流行しています。
(Kakuchi ni *densen*byō ga ryūkō shite imasu.)

¶この病気は伝染するので，注意してください。(Kono byōki wa *densen* suru node, chūi shite kudasai.)

¶ **Epidemics** have broken out in various districts.

¶ This disease **is contagious** so please take care.

densha 電車〖名〗

電車に乗る (*densha* ni noru) 電車を降りる (*densha* o oriru) 電車で行く (*densha* de iku) 電車賃 (*densha*chin)

¶東京の電車はいつもこんでいます。
(Tōkyō no *densha* wa itsu mo konde imasu.)

densha 〚n〛 **train** (run by electricity), **streetcar**

get on **a train** // get off **a train** // go by **train** // a **train** fare

¶ **The trains** in Tokyo are always crowded.

dentō 電燈〖名〗

電燈をつける (*dentō* o tsukeru)
電燈を消す (*dentō* o kesu)

¶部屋に電燈がついているから，だれかいると思います。(Heya ni *dentō* ga tsuite iru kara, dare ka iru to omoimasu.)

dentō 〚n〛 **electric light, electric lamp**

turn on **an electric light** // turn off **an electric light**

¶ Since **a light** is on in the room, I think someone is there.

denwa 電話〖名，〜する〗

電話料金 (*denwa*-ryōkin) 公衆電話 (kōshū-*denwa*) 電話帳 (*denwa*chō) 国際電話 (kokusai*denwa*) 電話で話す (*denwa* de hanasu) 電話をかける (*denwa* o kakeru) 電話を切る (*denwa* o kiru) 電話口へ呼び出す (*denwa*guchi e yobidasu)

¶あなたのうちの電話番号を教えてください。(Anata no uchi no *denwa*-bangō o oshiete kudasai.)

¶上田さん，田中さんから電話です。
(Ueda san, Tanaka san kara *denwa*

denwa 〚n, ~*suru*〛 **telephone**

a **telephone** bill, a **telephone** charge // a public **telephone,** a pay **phone** // a **telephone** book, a **telephone** directory // an overseas **telephone call** // talk on **the telephone** // make **a telephone call, telephone** someone // hang up **the phone** // call someone to **the telephone**

¶ Please tell me your home **telephone** number.

¶ [Mr.] Ueda, there's **a telephone call** for you from [Miss] Tanaka.

desu.)

¶もしもし，上田さんは今ほかの電話に出ていますから，ちょっとお待ちください。 (Moshi moshi, Ueda san wa ima hoka no *denwa* ni dete imasu kara, chotto omachi kudasai.)

¶ Hello, [Mr.] Ueda is now on another **line.** Please wait a moment.

¶電話を切らずにおいてください。
(*Denwa* o kirazu ni oite kudasai.)

¶ Please **hold the line.**

¶さきほど，田中さんから電話がありました。 (Sakihodo, Tanaka san kara *denwa* ga arimashita.)

¶ There was **a telephone call** [for you] a little while ago from [Mrs.] Tanaka.

¶今，話し中で電話が通じません。
(Ima, hanashichū de *denwa* ga tsūjimasen.)

¶ **I can't get through** to [him] now; the line is busy.

¶何か用があったら，わたしに電話をください。 (Nani ka yō ga attara, watashi ni *denwa* o kudasai.)

¶ Give me **a call** if there's anything I can do for you.

¶またあとで電話します。 (Mata ato de *denwa* shimasu.)

¶ **I will call** again later.

depāto デパート〖名〗

¶母はデパートへ買い物に行きました。
(Haha wa *depāto* e kaimono ni ikimashita.)

depāto 〖n〗 department store

¶ My mother went shopping at **a department store.**

¶デパートではいろいろな物を売っています。 (*Depāto* de wa iroiro na mono o utte imasu.)

¶ They sell various things in **a department store.**

deru 出る〖動Ⅱ〗

①[家の中などから外に行く]
部屋を出る (heya o *deru*)　学校の門を出る (gakkō no mon o *deru*)　会社を4時に出る (kaisha o yoji ni *deru*)　外に出る (soto ni *deru*)　庭に出る (niwa ni *deru*)

deru 〖vⅡ〗 go out, come out; leave; appear

① [go, out, come out]
go out of a room // **come through** the school gate // **leave** the office at four o'clock // **go outside** // **go out** into the garden 〖yard〗

¶父は3時にうちを出ました。(Chichi wa sanji ni uchi o *demashita*.)

↔hairu 入る

②[学校を卒業する・家を去る・会社を辞めるなどの意味を表す]
¶わたしは2年前に大学を出ました。(Watashi wa ninen mae ni daigaku o *demashita*.)

③[出発する]
旅行に出る (ryokō ni *deru*)
¶この汽車は何時に出ますか。(Kono kisha wa nanji ni *demasu* ka?)
¶もう船が出る時間です。(Mō fune ga *deru* jikan desu.)

④[現れる]
木の芽が出る (ki no me ga *deru*)
¶山の上に月が出ました。(Yama no ue ni tsuki ga *demashita*.)

⑤[出席する, 出勤する]
¶わたしは今日の会議には出られません。(Watashi wa kyō no kaigi ni wa *deraremasen*.)
¶わたしはあしたの日曜日にも会社へ出ます。(Watashi wa ashita no nichiyōbi ni mo kaisha e *demasu*.)

⑥[出版される, 掲載される]
新刊本が出る (shinkanbon ga *deru*)
¶この言葉は辞書に出ていません。(Kono kotoba wa jisho ni *dete* imasen.)
¶今日の新聞にA国の大地震のことが出ていました。(Kyō no shinbun ni Ē-koku no oojishin no koto ga *dete* imashita.)

¶ My father **left** the house at three o'clock.

② [graduate (from school), leave (home), quit (work)]
¶ I **graduated** from college two years ago.

③ [start, leave, depart]
leave on a trip
¶ What time does this train **leave?**
¶ It's time for the ship **to depart.**

④ [appear, come out]
a tree **buds**
¶ The moon **has appeared** ⟦The moon **appeared**⟧ over the mountain.

⑤ [be present, attend]
¶ I **can't attend** today's meeting.

¶ I **will go to work** even tomorrow, Sunday.

⑥ [be published, be issued]
a new book **will be published**
¶ This word **isn't listed** in the dictionary.

¶ News of a large earthquake in Country A **appeared** in today's newspaper.

deshō

⑦[生じる，発生する，流れ出る]
¶風邪を引いて，熱が出ました。(Kaze o hiite, netsu ga *demashita*.)
¶どうしたんですか。足から血が出ていますよ。(Dō shita n desu ka? Ashi kara chi ga *dete* imasu yo.)

⑧[ある所に到達する]
¶この道をまっすぐ行くと，駅の前に出ます。(Kono michi o massugu iku to, eki no mae ni *demasu*.)

deshō　でしょう〖助動〗
¶あしたは雨が降るでしょう。(Ashita wa ame ga furu *deshō*.)
¶田中さんは間もなく来るでしょう。(Tanaka san wa mamonaku kuru *deshō*.)
＊「だろう (darō)」の丁寧な言葉。
⇒**darō　だろう**

desu　です〖助動〗
¶これは本です。(Kore wa hon *desu*.)
¶わたしは田中です。(Watashi wa Tanaka *desu*.)
¶昨日はいい天気でした。(Kinō wa ii tenki *deshita*.)
¶この鉛筆はだれのですか。(Kono enpitsu wa dare no *desu* ka?)
＊「だ (da)」の丁寧な言葉。
⇒**da　だ**

detarame　でたらめ〖名，形動〗
でたらめな答え (*detarame* na kotae)
¶あの人の言うことはでたらめで信用できません。(Ano hito no iu koto wa *detarame* de shin'yō dekimasen.)

⑦ [occur, break out, arise]
¶ I caught a cold and **had** ⟦**have**⟧ a **fever.**
¶ What happened? Your leg ⟦foot⟧ **is bleeding!**

⑧ [lead to, come out]
¶ If you go straight along this street, **you'll come out** in front of the station.

deshō ⟦auxil⟧ **perhaps, will probably, I think**
¶ It **will probably** rain tomorrow.
¶ **I think** [Mr.] Tanaka will come soon.

＊ *Deshō* is a more polite form of *darō*.

desu ⟦auxil⟧ **is, are**
¶ This **is** a book.
¶ I **am** [Miss] Tanaka ⟦My name **is** Tanaka⟧.
¶ The weather **was** fine yesterday.
¶ Whose pencil **is** this?

＊ *Desu* is a more polite form of *da*.

detarame ⟦n, adj-v⟧ **random, irresponsible, hit-or-miss, nonsense**
a **random** answer
¶ That person talks **irresponsibly.** You can't trust anything [he] says.

¶でたらめを言っては困ります。(De-
tarame o itte wa komarimasu.)
¶このたなの本はでたらめに並べてあ
ります。(Kono tana no hon wa
detarame ni narabete arimasu.)

dewa　では〖接〗

①［相手の話を受けてそれを根拠とし
て自分の考え・判断などを述べるとき
に使う］
¶「いつ旅行に行きましょうか。」(Itsu
ryokō ni ikimashō ka?)「わたし
はいつでもいいですよ。」(Watashi
wa itsu demo ii desu yo.)「では,
今度の日曜日にしましょう。」(Dewa,
kondo no nichiyōbi ni shimashō.)
¶「何をお飲みになりますか。」(Nani o
onomi ni narimasu ka?)「わたしは
コーヒーを飲みます。」(Watashi wa
kōhii o nomimasu.)「では, わたしも
コーヒーにしましょう。」(Dewa,
watashi mo kōhii ni shimashō.)
②［何かを始めたり終えたりまたは別
れたりするときに使う言葉］
¶では, これから会議を開きます。
(Dewa, kore kara kaigi o hirakimasu.)
¶では, 本日はこれで終わります。
(Dewa, honjitsu wa kore de owarimasu.)
¶では, お先に失礼します。(Dewa,
osaki ni shitsurei shimasu.)
＊「わたしは日本人ではありません。
(Watashi wa Nihonjin de wa arimasen.)」の「で (de)」は助動詞であ

¶ It won't do for you to talk **so
carelessly.**
¶ The books on this shelf are
arranged **haphazardly.**

dewa 〖conj〗　well, well then

① [well then, in that case; used to
state a conclusion or judgment of the
speaker based on what the other has
said]
¶ "When shall we leave on our trip?"
　"Anytime is fine with me."
　"Well then, let's make it next Sunday."

¶ "What will you have to drink?"
　"I'll have coffee."
　"Then I'll have coffee too."

② [well, so, now; used at a time of
transition or parting]
¶ **Well,** let's start the meeting now.

¶ **Well,** this will be all for today.

¶ **Well,** I'll be leaving now ⟦**Well,**
good-bye now⟧.
＊ In a sentence like "Watashi wa
Nihonjin de wa arimasen" (I am not a
Japanese), de is part of the copula.

り、「日本では、車は道の左側を走ります。(Nihon de wa, kuruma wa michi no hidarigawa o hashirimasu.)」の「で (de)」は助詞である。
＊「じゃ (ja)」とも言う。

⇨**soredewa** それでは

-do　-度〚尾〛
①[回数などを表すのに使う]
¶もう一度言ってください。(Mō ichi-do itte kudasai.)

②[温度などの程度を表す]
¶ここでは夏の気温は普通 30 度ぐらいになります。(Koko de wa natsu no kion wa futsū sanjūdo gurai ni narimasu.)

dō　どう〚副〛
①[話し手にとってものごとの不明な内容・状態などを表す]
¶「あしたの天気はどうでしょうか。」(Ashita no tenki wa dō deshō ka?)「たぶんいい天気でしょう。」(Tabun ii tenki deshō.)
¶「あしたの音楽会にいらっしゃいますか。」(Ashita no ongakkai ni irasshaimasu ka?)「まだどうするか決めていません。」(Mada dō suru ka kimete imasen.)
¶「上田さん、今日はどうかしたのですか。元気がありませんね。」(Ueda san, kyō wa dō ka shita no desu ka? Genki ga arimasen ne.)「体のぐあいが悪いのです。」(Karada no guai ga warui no desu.)
¶この言葉はどういう意味ですか。

In a sentence like "*Nihon de wa, kuruma wa michi no hidarigawa o hashirimasu*" (Cars run on the left-hand side of the road in Japan), *de* is a particle.
＊ Variant: *ja*.

-do 〚suf〛 **times; degrees**
① [the counter for number of times]
¶ Please say it **once** again.

② [the counter for degrees of temperature, etc.]
¶ The temperature here in the summer is usually around 30 **degrees.**

dō 〚adv〛 **how, what**
① [how, what]

¶ "I wonder **what** the weather **will be like** tomorrow."
"It will probably be fine."

¶ "Are you going to the concert 〚recital〛 tomorrow?"
"I haven't decided yet **what** I'll do."

¶ "Is **something the matter** today, [Mr.] Ueda? You seem to be a little low."
"Yes, I don't feel well."

¶ **What** is the meaning of this word?

(Kono kotoba wa *dō* iu imi desu ka?)

¶山田さんは来るかどうかわかりません。(Yamada san wa kuru ka *dō* ka wakarimasen.)

¶ I don't know **whether** [Miss] Yamada will come or not.

②［話し相手の意向や状態などを尋ねるのに使う］

② [what, how; used to inquire into the intentions or situation of the listener]

¶わたしはこの夏に北海道へ行きます。どうですか。いっしょに行きませんか。(Watashi wa kono natsu ni Hokkaidō e ikimasu. *Dō* desu ka? Issho ni ikimasen ka?)

¶ I'm going to Hokkaido this summer. **How about it?** Won't you go with me?

¶「上田さん、あなたはテニスはどうですか。」(Ueda san, anata wa tenisu wa *dō* desu ka?)「見るのは好きですが、自分ではやりません。」(Miru no wa suki desu ga, jibun de wa yarimasen.)

¶ "Do you play tennis, [Mrs.] Ueda?"

"I like to watch, but I don't play it myself."

¶「けがをしたそうですが、どうですか。」(Kega o shita sō desu ga, *dō* desu ka?)「おかげさまで、だいぶよくなりました。」(Okagesama de, daibu yoku narimashita.)

¶ "I heard you were hurt. **How are you?**"

"Much better, thank you."

＊普通「どうですか（dō desu ka）」の形で使う。

＊ Usually used in the pattern "*dō desu ka.*"

→ikaga いかが

⇒kō こう sō そう ā ああ

doa ドア［名］

doa [[n]] door

ドアを開ける (*doa* o akeru) ドアを閉める (*doa* o shimeru)

open **the door** // close **the door**

¶ドアにかぎを掛けました。(*Doa* ni kagi o kakemashita.)

¶ [I] locked **the door.**

dōbutsu 動物［名］

dōbutsu [[n]] animal

動物園 (*dōbutsu*en) 動物学 (*dō-*

a zoo // zoology

dochira

*butsu*gaku)

dochira　どちら〖代〗

①［話し手にとって不明な方向を表す〕
¶「病院はどちらでしょうか。」(Byōin
wa *dochira* deshō ka?)「病院はあ
ちらです。」(Byōin wa achira desu.)
¶「東京はどちらですか。」(Tōkyō wa
dochira desu ka?)「東京はこちらで
す。」(Tōkyō wa kochira desu.)
＊「どっち (dotchi)」とも言うが,「ど
ちら (dochira)」のほうが丁寧な言葉
である。
②［話し手にとって不明な方向にある
所を表す〕
¶「あなたのおうちはどちらですか。」
(Anata no ouchi wa *dochira* desu
ka?)「わたしのうちは新宿です。」
(Watashi no uchi wa Shinjuku
desu.)
¶「あなたはどちらの国からおいでにな
りましたか。」(Anata wa *dochira* no
kuni kara oide ni narimashita ka?)
「わたしは日本から来ました。」(Wa-
tashi wa Nihon kara kimashita.)
＊「どこ (doko)」よりも丁寧な言葉。
③［話し手にとって不明な人を表す〕
¶失礼ですが,どちら様ですか。
(Shitsurei desu ga, *dochira* sama
desu ka?)
＊いつも「どちら様 (dochira sama)」
の形で使う。
＊「だれ (dare)」と言うよりも丁寧な
言い方である。「どなた(donata)」「ど
なた様 (donata sama)」などとも言

dochira 〚pron〛 **where; who; which**

① [which way, where]

¶ **"Which way** is the hospital?"
"It's that way."

¶ **"Which direction** is Tokyo?"
"It's this direction."

＊ *Dotchi* is also used, but *dochira* is
more polite.

② [where]

¶ **"Where** do you live?"
"I live in Shinjuku."

¶ **"What** country are you from?"
"I am from Japan."

＊ *Dochira* is more polite than *doko*.
③ [who]
¶ Might I ask **your name,** please
(literally, **Who** are you)?

＊ Always used in the pattern *dochira
sama*.
＊ *Dochira* is more polite than *dare*.
Donata and *donata sama* are also
used as polite forms of *dare*.

106

う。

④[二つのものごとの中から一つのものを選ぶときに使う]

¶「上田さんと中村さんとどちらが背が高いですか。」 (Ueda san to Nakamura san to *dochira* ga sei ga takai desu ka?)「上田さんのほうが、中村さんより背が高いです。」 (Ueda san no hō ga, Nakamura san yori sei ga takai desu.)

¶「あなたは魚と肉とどちらが好きですか。」 (Anata wa sakana to niku to *dochira* ga suki desu ka?)「わたしはどちらも好きです。」 (Watashi wa *dochira* mo suki desu.)

¶「作文を書くのに題は書かなくてもいいですか。」 (Sakubun o kaku no ni dai wa kakanakute mo ii desu ka?)「書いても書かなくてもいいです。どちらでもいいです。」 (Kaite mo kakanakute mo ii desu. *Dochira* demo ii desu.)

* 助詞「でも (demo)」がつくと、全面的な肯定を表す。助詞「も (mo)」がつくと、全面的な肯定または全面的な否定を表す。

*「どっち (dotchi)」とも言うが、「どちら (dochira)」のほうが丁寧な言葉である。

⇨kochira こちら　sochira そちら　achira あちら

dōgu 道具〚名〛
台所道具 (daidokoro-*dōgu*)
¶テーブルの上の勉強道具をかたづけ

④ [which, which one]

¶ "**Who** is taller, [Mr.] Ueda or [Mr.] Nakamura?"

"[Mr.] Ueda is taller than [Mr.] Nakamura."

¶ "**Which** do you like better, fish or meat?"

"I like **both of them**."

¶ "Is it all right not to write down the title when writing a composition?"

"You may write it down or not write it down. **Either** will be fine."

* *Dochira demo* (either, whichever) is affirmative in meaning. *Dochira mo* (both, either; neither) can be affirmative or negative depending on the context.

* *Dotchi* is also used, but *dochira* is more polite.

dōgu 〚n〛 instrument, implement, utensil, tool
kitchen**ware**

てください。 (Tēburu no ue no benkyō-*dōgu* o katazukete kudasai.)

¶道具があれば、自分でラジオが直せます。 (*Dōgu* ga areba, jibun de rajio ga naosemasu.)

dō itashimashite　どういたしまして〚連〛

¶「どうもありがとうございました。」(Dōmo arigatō gozaimashita.)

「いいえ，どういたしまして。」 (Iie, *dō itashimashite*.)

dōji　同時〚名〛

①〔同じ時〕

¶二人が着いたのは，ほとんど同時でした。 (Futari ga tsuita no wa, hotondo *dōji* deshita.)

¶発車のベルが鳴り終わると同時に，ドアが閉まりました。(Hassha no beru ga nariowaru to *dōji* ni, doa ga shimarimashita.)

②〔あることがらと共に〕

¶この本はおもしろいと同時にためになります。(Kono hon wa omoshiroi to *dōji* ni tame ni narimasu.)

¶この計画には，よい点もあると同時に悪い点もあります。(Kono keikaku ni wa, yoi ten mo aru to *dōji* ni warui ten mo arimasu.)

dōjō　同情〚名，～する〛

¶わたしたちは、地震で被害を受けた人たちに同情して，お金を集めて送りました。 (Watashitachi wa, jishin de higai o uketa hitotachi ni *dōjō* shite, okane o atsumete okurima-

¶ Please clear away the study **things** on the table.

¶ If I had **the tools,** I could repair the radio myself.

dō itashimashite 〚compd〛 **not at all, don't mention it, you're welcome**

¶ "Thank you very much."

"Oh no, **not at all.**"

dōji 〚n〛 **at the same time; while**

① [at the same time, simultaneously]

¶ The two arrived almost **simultaneously.**

¶ The doors closed **the moment** the departure bell stopped ringing.

② [while, along with]

¶ This book is **both** interesting and instructive.

¶ This plan has bad points **as well as** good points.

dōjō 〚n, ～*suru*〛 **sympathy, compassion**

¶ **Sympathizing** with those who had suffered in the earthquake, we collected and sent off money to them.

shita.)

doko　どこ〖代〗

①[話し手にとって不明な所を表す]

¶「どこが玄関ですか。」(*Doko* ga gen-kan desu ka?)「あそこが玄関です。」(Asoko ga genkan desu.)

¶「あなたの学校はどこにありますか。」(Anata no gakkō wa *doko* ni ari-masu ka?)「わたしの学校は京都にあります。」(Watashi no gakkō wa Kyōto ni arimasu.)

¶「あなたの国はどこですか。」(Anata no kuni wa *doko* desu ka?)「わたしの国は日本です。」 (Watashi no kuni wa Nihon desu.)

¶「あなたはどこの大学に行っていますか。」 (Anata wa *doko* no daigaku ni itte imasu ka?)「わたしはA大学に行っています。」 (Watashi wa Ē-daigaku ni itte imasu.)

¶どこでもいいから，遊びに行きましょう。(*Doko* demo ii kara, asobi ni ikimashō.)

¶わたしは，今日は，どこへも行かずに一日じゅう勉強しようと思っています。(Watashi wa kyō wa, *doko* e mo ikazu ni ichinichijū benkyō shiyō to omotte imasu.)

*助詞「でも (demo)」がつくと全面的な肯定を表す。また，助詞「も (mo)」がつくと，全面的な肯定または全面的な否定を表す。

②[話し手にとって当面するものごとの不明な点・部分・範囲・状態などを

doko 〖pron〗 **where; what place, whereabouts**

① [where]

¶ "**Where** is the entryway?"
"It's over there."

¶ "**Where** is your school?"
"It's in Kyoto."

¶ "**What** country are you from?"
"I am from Japan."

¶ "**What** university do you go to?"
"I go to University A."

¶ Let's go out somewhere, **anywhere.**

¶ I'm planning to study all day today without going **anywhere.**

* *Doko demo* (anywhere, every-where) is affirmative in meaning. *Doko mo* (anywhere, everywhere; nowhere) can be affirmative or nega-tive depending on the context.

② [what place, whereabouts]

表す]

¶「昨日はどこまで勉強しましたか。」(Kinō wa *doko* made benkyō shimashita ka?)「50ページまで勉強しました。」Gojippēji made benkyō shimashita.)

¶「顔色がよくありませんね。どこか悪いのですか。」(Kaoiro ga yoku arimasen ne. *Doko* ka warui no desu ka?)「今朝から胃が痛いのです。」(Kesa kara i ga itai no desu.)

¶あなたの研究はどこまで進んでいますか。(Anata no kenkyū wa *doko* made susunde imasu ka?)

⇨**koko** ここ **soko** そこ **asoko** あそこ

doku 毒〖名〗

毒虫 (*doku*mushi) 毒へび (*doku*hebi) 毒ガス (*doku*gasu)

¶このきのこには毒があります。(Kono kinoko ni wa *doku* ga arimasu.)

dokuritsu 独立〖名, ～する〗

独立国 (*dokuritsu*koku) 独立運動 (*dokuritsu*-undō) 独立戦争 (*dokuritsu*-sensō)

¶わたしたちは民族独立のために戦いました。(Watashitachi wa minzoku-*dokuritsu* no tame ni tatakaimashita.)

¶あの人は独立心が強いです。(Ano hito wa *dokuritsu*shin ga tsuyoi desu.)

dōmo どうも〖副〗

①[どうしても, どのようにやってみ

¶ "**How far** did [you] study yesterday?"

"[We] studied up to page 50."

¶ "You look pale. Is **anything** the matter?"

"My stomach has been hurting since this morning."

¶ **How far** have you progressed in your research?

doku 〚n〛 poison

a **poisonous** insect // a **poisonous** snake // a **toxic** gas

¶ This mushroom **is poisonous.**

dokuritsu 〚n, ~*suru*〛 independence, freedom

a **sovereign** nation, an **independent** state // an **independence** movement // the American **Revolution;** a war for **independence**

¶ We fought for **self-determination.**

¶ [He] has a strong spirit of **independence** 〚He is a very **independent** person〛.

dōmo 〚adv〛 no matter how hard one tries; somehow; very, quite

① [no matter how hard one tries, no

110

ても]

¶どうもうまく発音できません。

(*Dōmo* umaku hatsuon dekimasen.)

¶この文の意味はどうもよくわかりません。 (Kono bun no imi wa *dōmo* yoku wakarimasen.)

* あとに打ち消しまたは否定的な意味の言葉が来る。

②[どう考えてもはっきりしないが]

¶あの人には, どうもどこかで会ったような気がします。 (Ano hito ni wa, *dōmo* doko ka de atta yō na ki ga shimasu.)

③[たいへん, ほんとうに]

¶どうもありがとうございます。

(*Dōmo* arigatō gozaimasu.)

¶どうも失礼しました。 (*Dōmo* shitsurei shimashita.)

donata どなた〘代〙

¶あの方はどなたですか。 (Ano kata wa *donata* desu ka?)

¶失礼ですが, どなた様でいらっしゃいますか。(Shitsurei desu ga, *donata* sama de irasshaimasu ka?)

* 「だれ (dare)」の丁寧な言い方。

dondon どんどん〘副〙

¶物価がどんどん上がっています。

(Bukka ga *dondon* agatte imasu.)

¶どんどん進むので, 予習がたいへんです。(*Dondon* susumu node, yoshū ga taihen desu.)

* 「どんどんと(dondon to)」とも言う。

donna どんな〘連体〙

matter what one does]

¶ I **just** can't pronounce it right.

¶ I **just** can't seem to understand the meaning of this sentence.

* Followed by a negative or words having a negative sense.

② [somehow]

¶ **Somehow** I feel I've met that person before somewhere.

③ [very, quite, really]

¶ Thank you **very much.**

¶ I beg your pardon 〘I'm **very** sorry; Thank you for your time, etc.〙.

donata 〚pron〛 **who, whom**

¶ **Who** is that person?

¶ Excuse me, but may I ask **your name** please (literally, **who** are you)?

* *Donata* is a more polite form of *dare*.

dondon 〚adv〛 **rapidly, steadily**

¶ Prices are rising **rapidly.**

¶ As [we] are moving ahead so **rapidly,** preparing [our] lessons is a real task.

* *Dondon to* is also used.

donna 〚attrib〛 **what, what sort of, what kind of**

111

¶「あなたは**どんな**スポーツが好きですか。」(Anata wa *donna* supōtsu ga suki desu ka?)「わたしはテニスがいちばん好きです。」(Watashi wa tenisu ga ichiban suki desu.)

¶「山田さんは山でけがをしたそうです。」(Yamada san wa yama de kega o shita sō desu.)「**どんな**ぐあいなのでしょうか。」(*Donna* guai na no deshō ka?)

¶おいしそうですね。**どんな**材料で作りましたか。(Oishisō desu ne. *Donna* zairyō de tsukurimashita ka?)

¶「**どんな**質問でもいいですか。」(*Donna* shitsumon demo ii desu ka?)「はい, **どんな**質問でもいいです。」(Hai, *donna* shitsumon demo ii desu.)

¶あの人にきけば, **どんな**ことでもわかります。(Ano hito ni kikeba, *donna* koto demo wakarimasu.)

＊ 話し手にとって不明なものごとの内容・状態などを表す。「どんな(donna)＋名詞＋でも(demo)」の形で全面的な肯定を表す。

⇒konna こんな　sonna そんな　anna あんな

donna ni　どんなに〘副〙

①[ものごとの状態・数量などの程度を強調して表すときに使う]

¶外国語が自由に話せたら**どんなに**いいでしょう。(Gaikokugo ga jiyū ni hanasetara, *donna ni* ii deshō.)

¶ "**What** sports do you like?"
"I like tennis best."

¶ "I hear that [Mr.] Yamada was hurt in the mountains."
"I wonder **how** [he] is."

¶ That dish looks very good. **What** ingredients is it made from?

¶ "Is **whatever** question all right?"
"Yes, please ask **any** question at all."

¶ That person knows the answer to **anything** you might ask.

＊ The pattern "*donna* + noun + *demo*" (any ～, every ～) is affirmative in meaning. It indicates something incompletely known to the speaker.

donna ni 〚adv〛　**how, to what extent; however, no matter how**

① [how, to what extent, how much]

¶ **How** nice it would be to be able to speak a foreign language fluently!

¶戦争中みんながどんなに苦労したか，今のあなたがたにはわからないでしょう。(Sensōchū minna ga *donna ni* kurō shita ka, ima no anata gata ni wa wakaranai deshō.)

②[ものごとの状態・数量などの限りない程度を仮定して表すときに使う]

¶どんなにお金があっても，テレビは買いませんか。(*Donna ni* okane ga atte mo, terebi wa kaimasen ka?)

¶どんなに急いでも，汽車には間に合いません。(*Donna ni* isoide mo, kisha ni wa maniaimasen.)

* いつも「どんなに〜ても (donna ni〜te mo)」の形で使い，あとに否定的な言葉が来る。

→**ikura** いくら

⇨**konna ni** こんなに　**sonna ni** そんなに　**anna ni** あんなに

dono どの〚連体〛

どの人 (*dono* hito)　どの方 (*dono* kata)

¶「中村さんのはどのかばんですか。」(Nakamura san no wa *dono* kaban desu ka?)「あの大きなかばんです。」(Ano ookina kaban desu.)

¶お金はどのくらい持って行けばいいでしょうか。(Okane wa *dono* kurai motte ikeba ii deshō ka?)

¶「どのくらい日本語を習っていますか。」(*Dono* kurai Nihongo o naratte imasu ka?)「約1年です。」(Yaku ichinen desu.)

¶どの本でもいいですから，読みたい

¶ You people today cannot imagine **how much** everyone suffered during the war.

② [however, no matter how]

¶ You wouldn't buy a television set **no matter how much** money you had?

¶ **However much** [you] hurry, [you] won't be able to catch the train.

* Always used in the pattern "*donna ni ~-te mo*." Followed by words or expressions having a negative sense.

dono 〚attrib〛 which, what

who, **which** one // who, **which** one (polite)

¶ "**Which** suitcase 〚briefcase, bag, etc.〛 is yours, [Miss] Nakamura 〚**Which** suitcase is Miss Nakamura's〛?"

"It's that large one over there."

¶ **How much** money should [I] take with [me]?

¶ "**How long** have you been studying Japanese?"

"About one year."

¶ Take a book you would like to

113

本をお持ちなさい。(*Dono* hon demo
ii desu kara, yomitai hon o omo-
chinasai.)

¶どの問題もみんな難しかったです。
(*Dono* mondai mo minna muzukashikatta desu.)

＊ 話し手にとって不明なものごと・
数量・程度などを表すのに使う。「どの
(dono)＋名詞＋でも (demo)」の形
は全面的な肯定を表す。「どの (dono)
＋名詞＋も (mo)」の形は，全面的な
肯定または全面的な否定を表す。

⇨kono この　sono その　ano あの

dore どれ〚代〛

¶「あなたの本はどれですか。」(Anata
no hon wa *dore* desu ka?)「わたし
の本はこれです。」(Watashi no hon
wa kore desu.)

¶「東京の地図はどれですか。」(Tōkyō
no chizu wa *dore* desu ka?)「東京
の地図はあれです。」(Tōkyō no chizu
wa are desu.)

¶どれでもあなたの好きなものを取り
なさい。(*Dore* demo anata no suki
na mono o torinasai.)

¶どれもみんな好きです。(*Dore* mo
minna suki desu.)

¶どれもあまり好きではありません。
(*Dore* mo amari suki de wa arimasen.)

＊ 普通，三つ以上のものごとの中か
ら一つを選ぶときに使う。助詞「も
(mo)」がつくと全面的な肯定または
全面的な否定を表す。助詞「でも

read, **any one** of them.

¶ **All** of the problems were difficult.

＊ The pattern "*dono* + noun +
demo" (whichever, any, every) is
affirmative in meaning. The pattern
"*dono* + noun + *mo*" (every; no,
none) can be affirmative or negative
depending on the context.

dore 〚pron〛 which

¶ "**Which** is your book?"
"It's this one."

¶ "**Which** is a map of Tokyo?"
"It's that one."

¶ Take **whichever** you like.

¶ I like **all of them.**

¶ I don't like **any of them** very well.

＊ Usually used when choosing one
out of three or more items. *Dore mo*
(any, all, every; none, no) can be
affirmative or negative in meaning
depending on the context. *Dore*

(demo)」がつくと全面的な肯定を表し，選択が自由であることを表す。

⇨kore これ　sore それ　are あれ

dore　どれ〔感〕

¶どれ，見せてごらん。(*Dore*, misete goran.)

＊何かを見せてもらうときなどに相手に言う言葉。

dōro　道路〔名〕

広い**道路** (hiroi *dōro*)　　狭い**道路** (semai *dōro*)

¶今の時間は，**道路**がたいへんこんでいます。(Ima no jikan wa, *dōro* ga taihen konde imasu.)

dorobō　どろぼう〔名〕

¶留守中にどろぼうに入られました。(Rusuchū ni *dorobō* ni hairaremashita.)

doryoku　努力〔名，〜する〕

努力家 (*doryoku*ka)

¶**努力**すれば，だれでも上手になれます。(*Doryoku* sureba, dare demo jōzu ni naremasu.)

¶**努力**したので，いい成績がもらえました。(*Doryoku* shita node, ii seiseki ga moraemashita.)

dōsa　動作〔名〕

¶年を取ると，だんだん**動作**が鈍くなります。(Toshi o toru to, dandan *dōsa* ga nibuku narimasu.)

dōshite　どうして〔副〕

①〔なぜ〕

¶昨日はどうして学校を休んだのですか。(Kinō wa *dōshite* gakkō o ya-

demo (any, any one, whichever) is affirmative in meaning; it indicates a freedom of choice.

dore [[interj]]　**well, come, now**

¶ Let me see it, **will you?**

＊ Said when wanting to be shown something or the like.

dōro [[n]]　**road, street, highway**

a wide **street** // a narrow **street**

¶ **The roads** are very crowded at this time of the day.

dorobō [[n]]　**thief**

¶ My home **was broken into** when no one was there.

doryoku [[n, ~*suru*]]　**effort, endeavor; strive**

a hard worker, an industrious person

¶ Anyone can become good at it if they really **apply themselves.**

¶ [He] was able to receive good grades because [he] **worked hard.**

dōsa [[n]]　**action, movement, bearing**

¶ As one ages, one becomes progressively slower **in movement.**

dōshite [[adv]]　**why; how**

① [why]

¶ **Why** did you stay home from school yesterday?

sunda no desu ka?)

¶あの人が来ないのは，どうしてでしょう。 (Ano hito ga konai no wa, *dōshite* deshō?)

* 理由などをたずねるときに使う言葉。

→**naze** なぜ

②[どのようにして，どういう方法で]
¶夏休みをどうして過ごそうかと考えています。 (Natsuyasumi o *dōshite* sugosō ka to kangaete imasu.)

dōshite mo　どうしても〚連〛

①[どういうふうにしても，どのように考えても]
¶この問題はどうしてもわかりません。 (Kono mondai wa *dōshite mo* wakarimasen.)

¶あの人と結婚するのはどうしてもいやです。 (Ano hito to kekkon suru no wa *dōshite mo* iya desu.)

* あとに打ち消しまたは否定的な意味の言葉が来る。

②[必ず，どんなことがあっても]
¶この試合には，どうしても勝ちたいんです。 (Kono shiai ni wa, *dōshite mo* kachitai n desu.)

¶昨日は学校を休んだので，今日はどうしても行かなければなりません。
(Kinō wa gakkō o yasunda node, kyō wa *dōshite mo* ikanakereba narimasen.)

doyō(bi)　土曜（日）〚名〛
dōzo　どうぞ〚副〛

¶どうぞお入りください。 (*Dōzo* ohairi kudasai.)

¶ I wonder **why** [he] doesn't 〚hasn't〛 come.

* Used when asking the reason for something.

② [how, by what means, in what way]

¶ I am thinking about **how** to spend summer vacation.

dōshite mo 〚compd〛 **whatever one may do; no matter what, at any cost**

① [whatever one may do, by no means]

¶ I can't understand this problem **no matter what I do.**

¶ **I hate the very thought of** marrying that person.

* Followed by a negative or words having a negative sense.

② [no matter what, at any cost, must]

¶ I am determined to win this match 〚game〛 **no matter what.**

¶ Since I stayed home from school yesterday, I must **by all means** go today.

dotchi ☞ **dochira**

doyō(bi) 〚n〛 **Saturday**
dōzo 〚adv〛 **please, kindly**

¶ **Please** come in.

116

¶わたしは山田です。どうぞよろしく。
(Watashi wa Yamada desu. *Dōzo* yoroshiku.)

¶ My name is Yamada. **I'm pleased to make your acquaintance.**

E

e 絵〔名〕
絵はがき (ehagaki)　絵本 (ehon)
絵の具 (enogu)　絵をかく (e o kaku)
¶田中さんは絵が上手です。 (Tanaka san wa e ga jōzu desu.)
¶どんな絵が好きですか。 (Donna e ga suki desu ka?)

e え〔感〕
¶え、何ですか。(E! Nan desu ka?)
¶えっ、それは本当ですか。(E'! Sore wa hontō desu ka?)

e へ〔助〕
¶昨日、銀行へ行きました。(Kinō, ginkō e ikimashita.)
¶道の真ん中へ出ないでください。(Michi no mannaka e denaide kudasai.)

ebi えび〔名〕

eda 枝〔名〕
木の枝 (ki no eda)　枝を折る (eda o oru)

ee ええ〔感〕
¶「この本を貸してください。」 (Kono hon o kashite kudasai.)　「ええ、いいですよ。」(Ee, ii desu yo.)
¶「お元気ですか。」(Ogenki desu ka?)　「ええ、おかげさまで。」(Ee, okage-sama de.)
＊「はい (hai)」のほうが丁寧な言葉である。

e [[n]]　picture, painting, drawing
a **picture** postcard // a **picture** book // pigments, paints // draw [[paint]] a **picture**
¶ [Mrs.] Tanaka can **draw** [[paint]] well.
¶ What sort of **pictures** [[paintings]] do you like?

e [[interj]]　Oh!, What!; eh?, what?
¶ What did you say?
¶ **What!** Is that really so?

e [[part]]　to, toward, into
¶ [I] went **to** the bank yesterday.

¶ Please don't go out **into** the middle of the street.

ebi [[n]]　shrimp, lobster, prawn

eda [[n]]　branch, bough, twig
a tree **branch** [[twig]] // break off a **branch** [[twig]]

ee [[interj]]　yes, yeah
¶ "Please lend me this book [Please let me use this book for a while]."　"**Yes,** certainly."
¶ "How are you?"　"Fine, thank you."
(More literally, "Are you healthy?"　"**Yes,** thanks to you.")
＊ *Hai* is more polite than *ee*.

⇨hai はい

eiga 映画〖名〗

映画館 (*eiga*kan) ニュース映画 (nyūsu-*eiga*)

¶今晩、映画を見に行きましょう。(Konban, *eiga* o mi ni ikimashō.)

¶あの映画はおもしろいですか。(Ano *eiga* wa omoshiroi desu ka?)

eiga 〚n〛 movie, motion picture

a **movie** theater // a news**reel,** news **film**

¶ Let's go to see **a movie** tonight.

¶ Is that **movie** interesting?

eigo 英語〖名〗

¶英語の本を買いました。(*Eigo* no hon o kaimashita.)

¶英語で手紙を書きました。(*Eigo* de tegami o kakimashita.)

eigo 〚n〛 English, the English language

¶ [I] bought a book written in **English.**

¶ [I] wrote a letter in **English.**

eikyō 影響〖名、〜する〗

¶子供は友達の影響を受けやすいです。(Kodomo wa tomodachi no *eikyō* o ukeyasui desu.)

¶仏教は日本の文化に大きな影響を与えました。(Bukkyō wa Nihon no bunka ni ookina *eikyō* o ataemashita.)

eikyō 〚n, 〜*suru*〛 influence, effect

¶ Children are easily **influenced** by their friends.

¶ Buddhism exerted a great **influence** on Japanese culture.

eisei 衛生〖名〗

公衆衛生 (kōshū-*eisei*) 衛生的 (*eisei*teki)

¶あの店の衛生状態はたいへんいいです。(Ano mise no *eisei*-jōtai wa taihen ii desu.)

eisei 〚n〛 hygiene, sanitation

public **health** // **sanitary, hygienic**

¶ The **sanitary** conditions in that store 〚restaurant, bar, etc.〛 are very good.

eiyō 栄養〖名〗

栄養が足りない (*eiyō* ga tarinai)

¶この食べ物はたいへん栄養があります。(Kono tabemono wa taihen *eiyō* ga arimasu.)

¶じゅうぶんに栄養を取ってください。(Jūbun ni *eiyō* o totte kudasai.)

eiyō 〚n〛 nutrition, nourishment

be under**nourished**

¶ This food is very **nutritious.**

¶ Please be sure to get adequate **nutrition.**

eki 駅〘名〙

駅長 (ekichō)　駅員 (ekiin)

¶駅から家まで歩いて5分です。(Eki kara ie made aruite gofun desu.)

¶駅のそばに銀行があります。(Eki no soba ni ginkō ga arimasu.)

ekitai 液体〘名〙

¶あのびんの中の液体は何ですか。(Ano bin no naka no ekitai wa nan desu ka?)

¶危険な液体には色がつけてあります。(Kiken na ekitai ni wa iro ga tsukete arimasu.)

⇒kitai 気体　kotai 固体

(-) en (-) 円〘名, 尾〙

1〘名〙

円をかく (en o kaku)　円形の建物 (enkei no tatemono)

2〘尾〙

100円 (hyakuen)　1万円 (ichiman'en)

enchō 延長〘名, ～する〙

¶ビザを延長しました。(Biza o enchō shimashita.)

¶留学の期間を1年間延長したいです。(Ryūgaku no kikan o ichinenkan enchō shitai desu.)

enjin エンジン〘名〙

¶あの車のエンジンはたいへんいいです。(Ano kuruma no enjin wa taihen ii desu.)

¶新しいエンジンの調子はどうですか。(Atarashii enjin no chōshi wa dō desu ka?)

eki 〚n〛 station

a **station**master // a **station** employee

¶ It is a five-minute walk from **the station** to the house.

¶ There is a bank near **the station**.

ekitai 〚n〛 liquid (state), fluid

¶ What is **the liquid** in that bottle?

¶ Dangerous **liquids** have had coloring added.

(-)en 〚n, suf〛 circle; yen

1 〚n〛 a circle

draw **a circle** // a **round** building

2 〚suf〛 the counter for yen

one hundred **yen** // ten thousand **yen**

enchō 〚n, ～suru〛 continuation, extension

¶ [I] **extended** [my] visa.

¶ I want **to extend** my studies abroad for a year.

enjin 〚n〛 engine

¶ That car's **engine** is very good.

¶ How is the new **engine** running?

enjo 援助〖名, ～する〗

¶この計画を実現するには, 政府の援助が必要です。 (Kono keikaku o jitsugen suru ni wa, seifu no *enjo* ga hitsuyō desu.)

¶たくさんの学生が経済的な援助を希望しています。 (Takusan no gakusei ga keizaiteki na *enjo* o kibō shite imasu.)

enjo 〚n, ~*suru*〛 **assistance, aid**

¶ Government **assistance** will be necessary to realize this project.

¶ Many students are hoping for financial **aid**.

enki 延期〖名, ～する〗

¶試験は延期になりました。 (Shiken wa *enki* ni narimashita.)

¶雨のために旅行を延期しました。 (Ame no tame ni ryokō o *enki* shimashita.)

enki 〚n, ~*suru*〛 **postponement**

¶ The exam **has been postponed.**

¶ [They] **postponed** [their] trip because of rain.

enpitsu 鉛筆〖名〗

赤鉛筆 (aka*enpitsu*) 色鉛筆 (iro-*enpitsu*) 鉛筆削り (*enpitsu*kezuri)

¶この鉛筆は一本いくらですか。 (Kono *enpitsu* wa ippon ikura desu ka?)

¶ここは鉛筆で書いてください。 (Koko wa *enpitsu* de kaite kudasai.)

enpitsu 〚n〛 **pencil**

a red **pencil** // a colored **pencil** // a **pencil** sharpener

¶ How much are these **pencils** apiece?

¶ Please write this part here in **pencil.**

enryo 遠慮〖名, ～する〗

¶どうぞ遠慮しないでください。 (Dōzo *enryo* shinaide kudasai.)

¶彼はたいへん遠慮深いです。 (Kare wa taihen *enryo*bukai desu.)

enryo 〚n, ~*suru*〛 **reserve, diffidence**

¶ Please **don't hold back** 〚Please **don't stand on ceremony;** Please **don't be shy**〛.

¶ He is a very **reserved** person.

enshi 遠視〖名〗

¶遠視の眼鏡を作りました。 (*Enshi* no megane o tsukurimashita.)

⇔kinshi 近視

enshi 〚n〛 **farsightedness, long-sightedness**

¶ I had glasses made for my **farsightedness.**

ensō 演奏〖名, ～する〗

ensō 〚n, ~*suru*〛 **musical performance, recital**

ギターを演奏する (gitā o *ensō* suru)
ピアノ曲を演奏する (pianokyoku o *ensō* suru)

¶今晩，ピアノの演奏会があります。(Konban, piano no *ensō*kai ga arimasu.)

entotsu 煙突〖名〗
¶あの工場には煙突が何本も立っています。(Ano kōjō ni wa *entotsu* ga nanbon mo tatte imasu.)
¶煙突から煙がたくさん出ています。(*Entotsu* kara kemuri ga takusan dete imasu.)

erabu 選ぶ〖動Ⅰ〗
¶好きな飲み物を選んでください。(Suki na nomimono o *erande* kudasai.)
¶田中さんは社長に選ばれました。(Tanaka san wa shachō ni *erabaremashita*.)

erai 偉い〖形〗
①〔人物・能力などが優れている〕
¶上田博士は偉い学者です。(Ueda hakushi wa *erai* gakusha desu.)
¶あの学生は将来偉くなるでしょう。(Ano gakusei wa shōrai *eraku* naru deshō.)
②〔地位などが上である〕
¶会社の偉い人に会いました。(Kaisha no *erai* hito ni aimashita.)
¶彼は偉くないのに、いばっています。(Kare wa *eraku* nai noni, ibatte imasu.)

erebētā エレベーター〖名〗

perform on the guitar // perform a piece on the piano

¶ There is a piano **recital** tonight.

entotsu 〖n〗 chimney, smokestack
¶ There are many **smokestacks** at that factory.

¶ A lot of smoke is coming out of **the chimney.**

erabu 〖v I〗 choose, select
¶ Please **choose** what you would like to drink.

¶ [Mr.] Tanaka **was chosen** president of the company.

erai 〖adj〗 great, excellent; eminent
① [great, excellent, outstanding]
¶ Dr. Ueda is a **great** scholar.

¶ That student should **make [his] mark** in the future.

② [eminent, celebrated, famous, of high position]
¶ [I] met a person **high up** in the company.
¶ He puts on airs even though **he's nobody important.**

erebētā 〖n〗 elevator

¶エレベーターで5階まで行きました。(*Erebētā* de gokai made ikimashita.)

¶階段よりエレベーターのほうが楽です。(Kaidan yori *erebētā* no hō ga raku desu.)

esukarētā　エスカレーター〚名〛

¶1階から3階までエスカレーターで行きました。(Ikkai kara sangai made *esukarētā* de ikimashita.)

¶ [I] went up to the fifth floor in **the elevator.**

¶ Taking **the elevator** is easier than walking up the stairs.

esukarētā 〚n〛　escalator

¶ [I] went from the first to the third floor on **the escalator.**

F

firumu　フィルム〖名〗

¶このカメラに**フィルム**を入れてください。(Kono kamera ni *firumu* o irete kudasai.)

¶カラー**フィルム**で写真を写しました。(Karā-*firumu* de shashin o utsushimashita.)

fōku　フォーク〖名〗

¶ナイフと**フォーク**を買いました。(Naifu to *fōku* o kaimashita.)

¶食事のとき，はしと**フォーク**とどちらを使いますか。(Shokuji no toki, hashi to *fōku* to dochira o tsukaimasu ka?)

fu-　不-〖頭〗

不衛生 (*fu*eisei)　不合格 (*fu*gōkaku)　不可能 (*fu*kanō)　不完全 (*fu*kanzen)　不健康 (*fu*kenkō)　不規則 (*fu*kisoku)　不公平 (*fu*kōhei)　不満 (*fu*man)　不都合 (*fu*tsugō)　不運 (*fu*un)

¶この村は，まだ電気も水道もなくてたいへん**不便**です。(Kono mura wa, mada denki mo suidō mo nakute taihen *fu*ben desu.)

¶あの人は知っているのに，教えてくれませんでした。**不親切**な人です。(Ano hito wa shitte iru noni, oshiete kuremasen deshita. *Fu*-shinsetsu na hito desu.)

＊ 多くの場合，次に来る言葉を反対

firumu 〚n〛 **film**

¶ Please put **film** in this camera.

¶ [I] took the photograph with color **film.**

fōku 〚n〛 **fork**

¶ [I] bought knives and **forks.**

¶ Which do you use when you eat, chopsticks or **a fork?**

fu- 〚pref〛 **non-, un-**

insanitary conditions // **dis**qualification, failure, rejection // **im**possibility // **in**completeness, **im**perfection // poor health, **un**healthiness // **ir**regularity // **in**justice, **un**fairness // **dis**satisfaction, **dis**content // **in**convenience; **im**propriety // **mis**fortune

¶ This village is very **inconvenient;** it doesn't have electricity or running water yet.

¶ Even though [he] knew that, [he] didn't tell me. [He]'s a very **inconsiderate** person.

＊ In most cases, adding *fu*- to a

の意味にする。

fuan 不安〖名, 形動〗

¶試験に合格するかどうか不安です。

(Shiken ni gōkaku suru ka dō ka *fuan* desu.)

¶入試の結果がわかるまで不安な気持ちです。 (Nyūshi no kekka ga wakaru made *fuan* na kimochi desu.)

fuben 不便〖名, 形動〗

¶わたしの家は, 駅から遠くて不便です。 (Watashi no ie wa, eki kara tookute *fuben* desu.)

¶この辺は, 店がなくて買い物に不便な所です。 (Kono hen wa, mise ga nakute kaimono ni *fuben* na tokoro desu.)

⇔benri 便利

fuda 札〖名〗

①[文字などを書いて何かにつけたり何かの印としたりする小さな紙や板など]

名札 (na*fuda*) 荷札 (ni*fuda*)

¶受付で番号札を受け取ってください。 (Uketsuke de bangō*fuda* o uketotte kudasai.)

②[災難などを受けないようにと神社や寺などが出してくれるもの, お守り]

¶神社で交通安全のお札をもらってきました。 (Jinja de kōtsū-anzen no o*fuda* o moratte kimashita.)

fudan ふだん〖名〗

ふだん着 (*fudan*gi)

¶今朝は, ふだんより1時間早く起き

word gives it the opposite meaning.

fuan 〖n, adj-v〗 **anxiety, uncertainty, uneasiness**

¶ **I am worried** over whether [I] will pass the exam or not.

¶ **I will be anxious** until we find out the results of the entrance exam.

fuben 〖n, adj-v〗 **inconvenience**

¶ My house **is inconvenient** as it is so far from the station.

¶ This area **is inconvenient** for shopping as there are few shops.

fuda 〖n〗 **label, tag, nameplate; charm, talisman**

① [label, tag, nameplate, ticket; small piece of paper or wood with something written upon it]

a name**plate,** place **card,** identification **tag** // a baggage **tag**

¶ Please receive **a number** at the reception desk.

② [charm or talisman obtained at a shrine or temple for protection against misfortune]

¶ [I] obtained **a charm** for traffic safety at a shrine.

fudan 〖n〗 **usual, ordinary everyday** clothing

¶ [I] got up an hour earlier than

ました。 (Kesa wa, *fudan* yori ichijikan hayaku okimashita.)

¶ふだん勉強しないと、試験のときに困りますよ。(*Fudan* benkyō shinai to, shiken no toki ni komarimasu yo.)

usual this morning.

¶ If you don't study **ordinarily,** you will have a hard time when you have an exam.

fude 筆〖名〗

¶筆で名前を書いてください。 (*Fude* de namae o kaite kudasai.)

¶あしたは，すみと筆を持って来てください。(Ashita wa, sumi to *fude* o motte kite kudasai.)

fude 〖n〗 writing brush, brush

¶ Please write your name with **a brush.**

¶ Please bring ink and **brushes** tomorrow.

fueru 増える〖動Ⅱ〗

¶体重が5キロ増えました。(Taijū ga gokiro *fuemashita*.)

¶このごろ，交通事故が増えています。(Konogoro, kōtsū-jiko ga *fuete* imasu.)

⇔heru 減る ⇨zōka 増加, masu 増す

fueru 〖v Ⅱ〗 increase

¶ [I] **gained** five kilos.

¶ Traffic accidents **are increasing** these days.

fūfu 夫婦〖名〗

夫婦げんか (*fūfu*-genka) 新婚夫婦 (shinkon-*fūfu*)

¶あの二人は結婚して夫婦になりました。 (Ano futari wa kekkon shite *fūfu* ni narimashita.)

¶夫婦そろって旅行しました。 (*Fūfu* sorotte ryokō shimashita.)

fūfu 〖n〗 husband and wife, a married couple

a **marital** quarrel // newly**weds**

¶ Those two have married and formed **a couple.**

¶ Both **husband and wife** ⟦My husband/wife and I⟧ went on a trip together.

fujin 婦人〖名〗

婦人服 (*fujin*fuku) 婦人ぐつ (*fujin*gutsu) 婦人物 (*fujin*mono) 婦人用 (*fujin*yō)

¶婦人問題の研究をしています。 (*Fujin*-mondai no kenkyū o shite

fujin 〖n〗 woman, lady, female

women's clothes // **women's** shoes // an item for use by **women** // for **women,** for use by **women**

¶ [I] am studying **women's** problems.

imasu.)

fujin 夫人〖名〗

首相夫人 (shushō *fujin*)

¶山田夫人と田中夫人が委員に選ばれました。(Yamada *fujin* to Tanaka *fujin* ga iin ni erabaremashita.)

fukai 深い〖形〗

①[表面から底までの距離が長い]

深い海 (*fukai* umi) 深い井戸 (*fukai* ido)

¶日本の周りの海でいちばん深い所はどこですか。(Nihon no mawari no umi de ichiban *fukai* tokoro wa doko desu ka?)

¶深い所では泳がないでください。(*Fukai* tokoro de wa oyoganaide kudasai.)

↔asai 浅い

②[入り口から奥までの距離が長い]

山が深い (yama ga *fukai*)

¶一匹のしかが深い森の中に住んでいました。(Ippiki no shika ga *fukai* mori no naka ni sunde imashita.)

③[学問や知識などがじゅうぶんにある様子]

¶彼はこの問題について深い知識を持っています。(Kare wa kono mondai ni tsuite *fukai* chishiki o motte imasu.)

④[霧などが濃い]

深い霧 (*fukai* kiri)

⑤[程度などが大きい]

注意深い (chūi*bukai*) 遠慮深い (enryo*bukai*) 用心深い (yōjin*bukai*)

fujin 〖n〗 wife, Mrs. ~

the **wife** of the prime minister

¶ **Mrs.** Yamada and **Mrs.** Tanaka were chosen to be on the committee.

fukai 〖adj〗 deep; dense; profound

① [deep; far from top to bottom]

a **deep** sea // a **deep** well

¶ Where is the **deepest** point in the seas around Japan?

¶ Please don't swim where the water **is deep.**

② [deep, dense; far from front to back]

deep in the mountains

¶ A deer lived **deep** in the forest.

③ [deep, profound (knowledge, learning, etc.)]

¶ He possesses a **profound** knowledge concerning this problem.

④ [heavy, dense (fog, etc.)]

a **heavy** fog

⑤ [deep, profound, intense, strong] careful, attentive // reserved, modest, shy // careful, cautious

127

¶御親切を深く感謝します。(Goshin-setsu o *fukaku* kansha shimasu.)

¶ I am **profoundly** grateful for your kindness to me.

fukasa 深さ〖名〗

¶この湖の深さは200メートルあります。(Kono mizuumi no *fukasa* wa nihyakumētoru arimasu.)

⇨-sa -さ

fukasa 〚n〛 **depth**

¶ This lake is two hundred meters **deep.**

fukin 付近〖名〗

¶この付近に病院がありますか。(Kono *fukin* ni byōin ga arimasu ka?)

¶駅の付近には店がたくさんあります。(Eki no *fukin* ni wa mise ga takusan arimasu.)

⇨chikaku 近く

fukin 〚n〛 **vicinity, neighborhood**

¶ Is there a hospital **near** here?

¶ There are many shops **around** the station.

fukō 不幸〖名, 形動〗

不幸な一生 (*fukō* na isshō)

¶彼は不幸にも交通事故に遭って, ひどいけがをしました。(Kare wa *fukō* ni mo kōtsū-jiko ni atte, hidoi kega o shimashita.)

⇔kōfuku 幸福

fukō 〚n, adj-v〛 **unhappiness, sorrow; misfortune**

a life of **misery,** an **unhappy** lifetime

¶ He **had the misfortune** to be seriously injured in a traffic accident.

fuku 服〖名〗

婦人服 (fujin*fuku*)　子供服 (kodomo*fuku*)　和服 (wa*fuku*)　洋服 (yō*fuku*)

¶母が新しい服を作ってくれました。(Haha ga atarashii *fuku* o tsukutte kuremashita.)

¶冬の服をクリーニングに出しました。(Fuyu no *fuku* o kuriiningu ni dashimashita.)

fuku 〚n〛 **dress, clothing, clothes**

women's **clothing** // children's **clothing** // Japanese-style **clothing** // Western-style **clothing**

¶ My mother made me some new **clothes.**

¶ [I] sent the winter **clothing** to the cleaners.

fuku- 副-〖頭〗

副大統領 (*fuku*-daitōryō)　副社長

fuku- 〚pref〛 **assistant, deputy, acting, vice-, secondary, auxiliary**

the **vice**-president (of a nation) //

(*fuku*-shachō)　　副読本 (*fuku*-dokuhon)

the **vice**-president (of a company) // a **supplementary** reader

fuku　吹く〖動Ⅰ〗

①［風などが動いて通りすぎる］
¶昨日は一日じゅう強い風が吹いていました。(Kinō wa ichinichijū tsuyoi kaze ga *fuite* imashita.)

②［口から息を勢いよく出す］
¶ろうそくの火を吹いて消しました。(Rōsoku no hi o *fuite* keshimashita.)

③［息で楽器などを鳴らす］
ハーモニカを吹く (hāmonika o *fuku*) トランペットを吹く (toranpetto o *fuku*)

fuku　ふく〖動Ⅰ〗
¶ハンカチで汗をふきました。 (Hankachi de ase o *fukimashita*.)
¶机の上が汚れているから，ふいてください。(Tsukue no ue ga yogorete iru kara, *fuite* kudasai.)

fukumeru　含める〖動Ⅱ〗
¶お客は子供を含めて 15 人です。(Okyaku wa kodomo o *fukumete* jūgonin desu.)
¶税金も含めて月給はいくらですか。(Zeikin mo *fukumete* gekkyū wa ikura desu ka?)

fukumu　含む〖動Ⅰ〗
¶海の水は塩分を含んでいます。(Umi no mizu wa enbun o *fukunde* imasu.)
¶このソースには何が含まれていますか。 (Kono sōsu ni wa nani ga

fuku 〖vⅠ〗 blow

① [blow (the wind, etc.)]
¶ A strong wind **was blowing** all day yesterday.

② [blow, breathe out]
¶ [I] **blew** out the candle.

③ [play a wind instrument]
play on a harmonica // **blow** a trumpet

fuku 〖vⅠ〗 wipe, mop
¶ [I] **wiped** the sweat **off** with a handkerchief.
¶ The desk top is dirty—please **wipe it off**.

fukumeru 〖vⅡ〗 include
¶ **Including** children, the guests 〖customers〗 number 15 persons.
¶ How much is the monthly wage **including** tax?

fukumu 〖vⅠ〗 contain
¶ Seawater **contains** salt.

¶ What **is in** this sauce?

fukumarete imasu ka?)

fukuramu　ふくらむ〚動Ⅰ〛
風船がふくらむ (fūsen ga *fukuramu*)
¶春になって、木の芽がふくらんできました。 (Haru ni natte, ki no me ga *fukurande* kimashita.)

fukureru　ふくれる〚動Ⅱ〛
¶ビールをたくさん飲んだので、おなかがふくれました。 (Biiru o takusan nonda node, onaka ga *fukuremashita*.)

(-) fukuro　(-)袋〚名, 尾〛
1〚名〛
ビニール袋 (biniiru-*bukuro*)　紙袋 (kami*bukuro*)
¶これを袋に入れてください。 (Kore o *fukuro* ni irete kudasai.)
2〚尾〛
¶お菓子を一袋買いました。 (Okashi o hito*fukuro* kaimashita.)

fukushū　復習〚名, ～する〛
¶予習も復習も大切です。 (Yoshū mo *fukushū* mo taisetsu desu.)
¶家でよく復習してください。 (Ie de yoku *fukushū* shite kudasai.)
⇔**yoshū** 予習

fukusū　複数〚名〛
¶日本語には、単数と複数の区別はあまりありません。 (Nihongo ni wa, tansū to *fukusū* no kubetsu wa amari arimasen.)
¶あなたの国の言葉では、複数の形はどう表しますか。 (Anata no kuni

fukuramu 〚v Ⅰ〛　swell, expand, bulge out

the balloon **is being inflated**
¶ Spring has come and the buds on the trees **are swelling.**

fukureru 〚v Ⅱ〛　swell out, expand
¶ My stomach **is bloated** 〚full〛 as I drank a lot of beer.

(-)fukuro 〚n, suf〛　bag, sack; bagful, sackful
1 〚n〛　bag, sack
a plastic **bag**, vinyl **bag** // a paper **bag**
¶ Please put this in **a bag.**

2 〚suf〛　bagful, sackful; the counter for bags or sacks of something
¶ [I] bought **a bag** of candy.

fukushū 〚n, ～*suru*〛　review (of lessons)
¶ Both preparation and **review** of lessons are important.
¶ Please **review** this well at home.

fukusū 〚n〛　plural
¶ The distinction between singular and **plural** isn't made very often in the Japanese language.

¶ How is the **plural** form expressed in your native language?

no kotoba de wa, *fukusū* no katachi wa dō arawashimasu ka?)
⇔tansū 単数

fukuzatsu 複雑〖形動〗

¶複雑な漢字はまだ書けません。
(*Fukuzatsu* na kanji wa mada
kakemasen.)

¶あの人の話は複雑で，よくわかりま
せん。(Ano hito no hanashi wa
fukuzatsu de, yoku wakarimasen.)
⇨kantan 簡単

fumu 踏む〖動Ⅰ〗

¶花を踏まないように気をつけてくだ
さい。(Hana o *fumanai* yō ni ki o
tsukete kudasai.)

¶電車の中で足を踏まれました。
(Densha no naka de ashi o *fuma-
remashita.*)

- fun - 分〖尾〗

1分 (ip*pun*)　2分 (ni*fun*)　3分
(san*pun*)　4分 (yon*pun*)　5分
(go*fun*)　6分 (rop*pun*)　7分 (nana*fun*)　8分 (hap*pun*)　9分 (kyū-
fun)　10分 (jip*pun*)

¶今，1時15分です。 (Ima, ichiji
jūgo*fun* desu.)

¶家から駅まで歩いて10分です。
(Ie kara eki made aruite jip*pun*
desu.)

funabin 船便〖名〗

¶これを船便でお願いします。 (Kore
o *funabin* de onegai shimasu.)

¶船便のほうが航空便より安いです。
(*Funabin* no hō ga kōkūbin yori

fukuzatsu 〖adj-v〗 **complicated, involved**

¶ [I] can't write **complex** *kanji* yet.

¶ [His] stories 〚lectures〛 **are complicated,** and I don't understand them
very well.

fumu 〖vⅠ〗 **step on, tread on**

¶ Please be careful **not to step on**
the flowers.

¶ Someone **stepped on** my foot in
the train.

-fun 〖suf〗 the counter for minutes
one **minute** // two **minutes** // three
minutes // four **minutes** // five **min-
utes** // six **minutes** // seven **min-
utes** // eight **minutes** // nine **min-
utes** // ten **minutes**

¶ It's now 1:**15.**

¶ It's a 10-**minute** walk from the
house to the station.

funabin 〖n〗 **sea mail, shipping
service**

¶ Please send this by **sea mail.**

¶ **Sea mail** is cheaper than airmail.

yasui desu.)

⇨**kōkūbin** 航空便

fune 船〖名〗

船で旅行する (*fune* de ryokō suru)

¶大きな船が港に着きました。 (Ookina *fune* ga minato ni tsukimashita.)

fureru 触れる〖動Ⅱ〗

①[さわる]

¶この作品に手を触れないでください。 (Kono sakuhin ni te o *furenaide* kudasai.)

②[ついでに問題にする，言及する]

¶先生は講義の中で公害の問題に触れました。 (Sensei wa kōgi no naka de kōgai no mondai ni *furemashita*.)

furikaeru 振り返る〖動Ⅰ〗

①[後ろを見る]

¶秋子さんは何度も振り返って手を振りました。 (Akiko san wa nando mo *furikaette* te o furimashita.)

②[昔のことを思い出してみる]

¶子供のころを振り返ると，とても懐かしいです。 (Kodomo no koro o *furikaeru* to, totemo natsukashii desu.)

furo ふろ〖名〗

ふろ場 (*furo*ba) ふろ屋 (*furo*ya)

¶おふろが沸きました。 (O*furo* ga wakimashita.)

¶おふろに入りました。 (O*furo* ni hairimashita.)

furu 降る〖動Ⅰ〗

fune 〚n〛 **boat, ship**

travel by **boat**

¶ A large **ship** has arrived in port 〚A large **ship** arrived in port〛.

fureru 〚v Ⅱ〛 **touch, feel; touch on, mention**

① [touch, feel]

¶ Please **don't touch** this work of art.

② [touch on, mention, allude to]

¶ The teacher 〚professor〛 **touched upon** the problem of pollution in the lecture.

furikaeru 〚v Ⅰ〛 **look back, turn around; look back at, review**

① [look back, turn one's head, turn around]

¶ Akiko **looked back** 〚**turned around**〛 many times and waved.

② [look back at, review past events]

¶ **Thinking back over** my childhood, I feel very nostalgic.

furo 〚n〛 **bath**

bathroom (for taking a bath only) // public **bath**

¶ **The bath** is heated 〚is ready〛.

¶ I had **a bath**.

furu 〚v Ⅰ〛 **fall** (rain, snow, etc.)

¶雨が降ってきました。 (Ame ga
futte kimashita.)

¶あなたの国では雪が降りますか。
(Anata no kuni de wa yuki ga
furimasu ka?)

furu 振る〖動Ⅰ〗

①[ゆり動かす]

ハンカチを振る (hankachi o *furu*)
¶子供が電車の窓から手を振っていま
す。 (Kodomo ga densha no mado
kara te o *futte* imasu.)

②[漢字に読み方をつける]
¶次の漢字に仮名を振りなさい。
(Tsugi no kanji ni kana o *furi-
nasai*.)

furueru 震える〖動Ⅱ〗

¶寒いので子供が震えています。
(Samui node kodomo ga *furuete-
imasu*.)

¶恐ろしくて，ひざが震えました。
(Osoroshikute, hiza ga *furuemashita*.)

furui 古い〖形〗

¶あの人の考えはもう古いです。 (Ano
hito no kangae wa mō *furui* desu.)
¶この建物はずいぶん古くなりました
ね。 (Kono tatemono wa zuibun
furuku narimashita ne.)
⇔atarashii 新しい

fushigi 不思議〖形動〗

¶日本ではなぜ牛肉がこんなに高いの
か不思議です。 (Nihon de wa naze
gyūniku ga konna ni takai no ka
fushigi desu.)

furu 〖v I〗 **wave; give, attach**

① [wave]

wave one's handkerchief
¶ The children **are waving** their
hands out of the window of the train.

② [write the reading alongside *kanji*]
¶ **Write** the readings in *kana* **alongside** the following *kanji*.

furueru 〖v II〗 **tremble, shiver,
shake**

¶ The children **are shivering** because of the cold.

¶ My knees **were trembling** with
fright.

furui 〖adj〗 **old; dated**

¶ [His] way of thinking **is behind
the times.**

¶ This building **is** really **old** now,
isn't it?

fushigi 〖adj-v〗 **wonderful, strange,
mysterious, curious**

¶ **It's strange** that beef should be so
expensive in Japan.

¶こんな簡単な問題がなぜ解決できないのか，それが**不思議**です。(Konna kantan na mondai ga naze kaiketsu dekinai no ka, sore ga *fushigi* desu.)

¶ **It's curious** that such a simple problem hasn't been solved.

¶ひどい事故でしたが，**不思議**に彼は無事でした。(Hidoi jiko deshita ga, *fushigi* ni kare wa buji deshita.)

¶ It was a terrible accident, but **miraculously enough** he escaped injury.

fusoku 不足〖名，～する〗

fusoku 〖n, ~*suru*〗 **insufficiency, deficiency**

¶料金が 50 円**不足**していますから，そこで切手を買ってはってください。(Ryōkin ga gojūen *fusoku* shite imasu kara, soko de kitte o katte hatte kudasai.)

¶ It's 50 yen **short**; please buy a stamp for it over there (literally, buy a stamp over there and put it on).

¶栄養が**不足**すると，病気になります。(Eiyō ga *fusoku* suru to, byōki ni narimasu.)

¶ **Malnutrition** leads to illness.

futa ふた〖名〗

futa 〖n〗 **cover, lid**

¶おふろの**ふた**をしてください。(Ofuro no *futa* o shite kudasai.)

¶ Please put **the cover** back on the bathtub.

¶びんの**ふた**がなかなか開きません。(Bin no *futa* ga nakanaka akimasen.)

¶ **The lid** of this bottle is difficult to open.

futari 二人〖名〗

futari 〖n〗 **two persons, a couple**

¶**二人**でいっしょに来てください。(*Futari* de issho ni kite kudasai.)

¶ Please come together, **the two of you.**

¶あの夫婦は子供が**二人**あります。(Ano fūfu wa kodomo ga *futari* arimasu.)

¶ That couple has **two** children.

futatabi 再び〖副〗

futatabi 〖adv〗 **again, a second time**

¶**再び**お目にかかれるかどうかわかりませんね。(*Futatabi* ome ni kakareru ka dō ka wakarimasen ne.)

¶ I don't know if we will ever be able to meet **again.**

¶**再び**同じ間違いを繰り返したくあり

¶ I don't want to make the same mis-

ません。(*Futatabi* onaji machigai o
kurikaeshitaku arimasen.)

futatsu 二つ〖名〗

①[2個]

¶りんごを二つください。 (Ringo o
futatsu kudasai.)

②[2歳]

¶この子は今年二つになります。
(Kono ko wa kotoshi *futatsu* ni
narimasu.)

futo ふと〖副〗

¶駅に向かって歩いているうちに, ふと
忘れ物をしたことに気がつきました。
(Eki ni mukatte aruite iru uchi ni,
futo wasuremono o shita koto ni
ki ga tsukimashita.)

¶ふと見ると, もう桜が咲いていまし
た。 (*Futo* miru to, mō sakura ga
saite imashita.)

fūtō 封筒〖名〗

¶この手紙を封筒に入れて出してくだ
さい。(Kono tegami o *fūtō* ni irete
dashite kudasai.)

¶封筒と便せんをください。(*Fūtō* to
binsen o kudasai.)

futoi 太い〖形〗

太い木 (*futoi* ki) 太い腕 (*futoi* ude)

¶もっと太いひもはありませんか。
(Motto *futoi* himo wa arimasen
ka?)

⇔hosoi 細い

futon 布団〖名〗

掛け布団 (kake*buton*)　　敷き布団
(shiki*buton*) 座布団 (za*buton*)

take **twice.**

futatsu 〚n〛 **two**

① [two items]

¶ Please give me **two** apples.

② [two years old]

¶ This child will be **two years old**
this year.

futo 〚adv〛 **suddenly, accidentally**

¶ As I was walking toward the station, I **suddenly** realized that I had
forgotten something.

¶ When I **happened to** look that
way, I saw that the cherry blossoms
were in bloom.

fūtō 〚n〛 **envelope**

¶ Please put this letter in **an envelope** and mail it.

¶ **Envelopes** and letter paper,
please.

futoi 〚adj〛 **thick, broad**

a **thick** tree // a **big** arm

¶ Don't you have any **thicker** cord
〚rope, string, ribbon, etc.〛 than this?

futon 〚n〛 **futon, Japanese-style
bedding**

top **futon,** coverlet // bottom **futon,**
sleeping mat // *zabuton*, Japanese

布団を敷く (*futon* o shiku)

¶寒いから，布団をもう一枚掛けてください。(Samui kara, *futon* o mō ichimai kakete kudasai.)

futoru 太る〖動Ⅰ〗

¶最近，少し太りました。 (Saikin, sukoshi *futorimashita*.)

¶太ったので，洋服が合わなくなりました。(*Futotta* node, yōfuku ga awanaku narimashita.)

⇔**yaseru** やせる

futsū 普通〖名，形動〗

普通列車 (*futsū*-ressha)

¶朝御飯は普通7時ごろ食べます。

(Asagohan wa *futsū* shichiji goro tabemasu.)

¶ここから駅までは普通に歩いて5分です。 (Koko kara eki made wa *futsū* ni aruite gofun desu.)

futsuka 二日〖名〗

①[日付]

¶今日は五月二日です。(Kyō wa go-gatsu *futsuka* desu.)

②[日数]

¶風邪を引いて，二日間休みました。

(Kaze o hiite, *futsuka*kan yasumi-mashita.)

⇨**-ka** -日

fuyu 冬〖名〗

¶ここの冬はとても寒いです。 (Koko no *fuyu* wa totemo samui desu.)

¶冬休みには京都へ旅行します。

(*Fuyu*yasumi ni wa Kyōto e ryokō shimasu.)

floor **cushion** // lay out the **bedding**

¶ It's cold so please put on one more **coverlet.**

futoru 〖v I〗 put on weight, grow stout

¶ [I]'ve **put on** some **weight** lately.

¶ [I]'ve **put on weight** so that [my] clothes don't fit anymore.

futsū 〖n, adj-v〗 usual, ordinary, regular

regular train; **local** train

¶ [I] **usually** eat breakfast around seven o'clock.

¶ At an **ordinary** pace it's a five-minute walk from here to the station.

futsuka 〖n〗 the second day of the month; two days

① [the second day of the month]

¶ Today is **the second** of May.

② [two days]

¶ [I] caught a cold and stayed home for **two days.**

fuyu 〖n〗 winter

¶ **The winters** are very cold here.

¶ [I] am going to travel to Kyoto during **winter** vacation.

G

ga　が〖助〗

①〔動作や存在や状態などの主体を表す〕

¶「そこに何がありますか。」(Soko ni nani *ga* arimasu ka?) 「ここに本があります。」(Koko ni hon *ga* arimasu.)

¶丘の上には桜の花がきれいに咲いていました。(Oka no ue ni wa sakura no hana *ga* kirei ni saite imashita.)

¶昨日は一日じゅう雨が降っていました。(Kinō wa ichinichijū ame *ga* futte imashita.)

¶だれが窓ガラスを割ったのですか。(Dare *ga* madogarasu o watta no desu ka?)

¶公園の桜の花がとてもきれいです。(Kōen no sakura no hana *ga* totemo kirei desu.)

¶海は波が静かでした。(Umi wa nami *ga* shizuka deshita.)

¶どれがあなたの万年筆ですか。(Dore *ga* anata no mannenhitsu desu ka?)

②〔希望や好ききらいなどの感情の対象を表す〕

¶わたしは山登りが好きです。(Watashi wa yamanobori *ga* suki desu.)

¶兄は運動がきらいです。(Ani wa undō *ga* kirai desu.)

ga 〖part〗　a particle acting as a subject marker

① [indicates the subject of an action, state, condition, etc.]

¶ "What is there?"
　"There is a book here."

¶ Beautiful cherry blossoms were in bloom on the hilltop.

¶ It rained all day yesterday.

¶ Who broke the window?

¶ The cherry blossoms in the park are very pretty.

¶ The ocean waves were gentle.

¶ Which one is your fountain pen?

② [indicates the object of feelings of desire, like, dislike, etc.]

¶ I like mountain climbing.

¶ My (elder) brother dislikes exercise.

¶「あなたは何が欲しいですか。」(Anata wa nani *ga* hoshii desu ka?)「わたしはカメラが欲しいです。」(Watashi wa kamera *ga* hoshii desu.)

¶わたしは水が飲みたいです。(Watashi wa mizu *ga* nomitai desu.)

¶わたしは頭が痛いです。(Watashi wa atama *ga* itai desu.)

*「動詞(基幹の形)+たい(tai)」の形で希望を表す場合には「を(o)」も使われる。「わたしは田舎に家を建てたいです。(Watashi wa inaka ni ie o tatetai desu.)」

③[能力・可能不可能・上手下手などの対象を表す]

¶中村さんは上手に英語が話せます。(Nakamura san wa jōzu ni Eigo *ga* hanasemasu.)

¶わたしは中国語がよくわかりません。(Watashi wa Chūgokugo *ga* yoku wakarimasen.)

¶わたしはまだ泳ぐことができません。(Watashi wa mada oyogu koto *ga* dekimasen.)

¶中村さんはスキーがとても上手です。(Nakamura san wa sukii *ga* totemo jōzu desu.)

ga が〚助〛

①[前件から当然予想される結果が後件において成立しないという関係を表す]

¶種をまきましたが、とうとう芽が出ませんでした。(Tane o makimashita *ga*, tōtō me ga demasen deshita.)

¶ "What do you want?"

"I want a camera."

¶ I want a drink of water.

¶ I have a headache.

* The particle *o* can also be used in the pattern "verb (stem form) + *-tai*": "*Watashi wa inaka ni ie o tatetai desu*" (I want to build a house in the country).

③ [indicates the object of ability, possibility, impossibility, skill, lack of skill, etc.]

¶ [Mr.] Nakamura can speak English well.

¶ I can't understand Chinese very well.

¶ I still can't swim.

¶ [Miss] Nakamura can ski very well.

ga 〚part〛 **but, and**

① [but, and yet; indicates that what would naturally follow the first clause is lacking]

¶ [I] planted 〚sowed〛 some seeds, **but** in the end they did not come up.

¶頭が痛いので薬を飲みましたが，少しもよくなりません。(Atama ga itai node kusuri o nomimashita *ga*, sukoshi mo yoku narimasen.)

② [前件が後件に対して対比的・対立的な関係にあることを表す]

¶ペンはありますが，インクがありません。 (Pen wa arimasu *ga*, inku ga arimasen.)

¶わたしは海は好きですが，山はあまり好きではありません。(Watashi wa umi wa suki desu *ga*, yama wa amari suki de wa arimasen.)

¶わたしは約束どおり早く行きましたが，山田さんはずいぶん遅れて来ました。 (Watashi wa yakusokudōri hayaku ikimashita *ga*, Yamada san wa zuibun okurete kimashita.)

¶去年の冬はずいぶん寒かったですが，今年は暖かでたいへん楽です。(Kyonen no fuyu wa zuibun samukatta desu *ga*, kotoshi wa atataka de taihen raku desu.)

③ [前件が後件に対する前置きなどの関係にあることを表す]

¶すみませんが，水を一杯ください。 (Sumimasen *ga*, mizu o ippai kudasai.)

¶こちらは山田でございますが，中村さんでしょうか。 (Kochira wa Yamada de gozaimasu *ga*, Nakamura san deshō ka?)

¶駅へ行きたいのですが，どう行ったらよいでしょうか。 (Eki e ikitai no

¶ I took some medicine for my headache, **but** it hasn't gotten any better at all.

② [but; indicates that the second clause is in contrast or opposition to the first clause]

¶ There's a pen, **but** there isn't any ink.

¶ I like the ocean, **but** I don't particularly like the mountains.

¶ I came on time, **but** [Mrs.] Yamada came very late.

¶ It was a very severe winter last year, **but** this year it's a very warm and easy one.

③ [but, and; indicates that the first clause is preliminary or introductory to the second clause]

¶ Excuse me, **but** could I have a glass of water please?

¶ This is [Mr.] Yamada calling. Is this [Mr.] Nakamura?

¶ I want to go to the station. Could you please tell me the way?

---

desu *ga*, dō ittara yoi deshō ka?)

④［前件のことがらが後件のことがらに対して共存的な関係にあることを表す］

¶山田さんは体も大きいが、力もあります。(Yamada san wa karada mo ookii *ga*, chikara mo arimasu.)

¶去年の冬も寒かったですが、今年もやはり寒いですね。(Kyonen no fuyu mo samukatta desu *ga*, kotoshi mo yahari samui desu ne.)

¶山田さんは医者ですが、息子さんもやはり医者になりました。(Yamada san wa isha desu *ga*, musukosan mo yahari isha ni narimashita.)

⇒keredomo けれども

ga が〖助〗

①［ものごとをはっきり断定的に言うのを避けて柔らかく言い、相手の反応を待つ気持ちを表す］

¶実はお金を少しお借りしたいのですが。(Jitsu wa okane o sukoshi okari shitai no desu *ga*.)

¶父は今外出しておりますが。(Chichi wa ima gaishutsu shite orimasu *ga*.)

②［望ましいことがらの成立を願う気持ちや実現しなかったことがらを回想してそれが成立していればどんなによかったかというような気持ちなどを表す］

¶今日じゅうにあの峠を越えることができればよいが。(Kyōjū ni ano tōge o koeru koto ga dekireba yoi *ga*.)

④ [and; indicates the coexistence of the first and second clauses]

¶ [Mr.] Yamada is large, **and** [he] is strong too.

¶ Last winter was cold, **and** it's cold this winter too.

¶ [Mrs.] Yamada is a doctor, **and** [her] son became a doctor too.

ga 〖part〗 **but, and**

① [used to soften a statement and to indicate that one is waiting for the listener's response]

¶ Actually I would like to borrow a little money....

¶ My father is out now....

② [expresses a desire for something to happen or regret that something didn't happen]

¶ It would be nice if we could get over that ridge sometime today ⟦If only we could get over that ridge sometime today⟧....

¶学生の時に海外旅行をしておけばよかったのだが。(Gakusei no toki ni kaigai-ryokō o shite okeba yokatta no da *ga*.)

⇨ **keredomo** けれども

gai 害〖名 〜する〗
害虫 (*gai*chū) 公害 (kō*gai*) 水害 (sui*gai*)
¶たばこは健康に**害**があります。
(Tabako wa kenkō ni *gai* ga arimasu.)

gaijin 外人〖名〗
¶あの**外人**は日本語が上手ですね。
(Ano *gaijin* wa Nihongo ga jōzu desu ne.)
¶観光のため，たくさんの**外人**が京都へ行きます。 (Kankō no tame, takusan no *gaijin* ga Kyōto e ikimasu.)
＊「外国人 (gaikokujin)」とも言う。

gaikō 外交〖名〗
外交官 (*gaikō*kan) 外交問題 (*gaikō*-mondai) 外交政策 (*gaikō*-seisaku)
¶それは**外交**上の秘密です。(Sore wa *gaikō*jō no himitsu desu.)
¶A国とB国との間には現在**外交**関係がありません。(Ē-koku to Bii-koku to no aida ni wa genzai *gaikō*-kankei ga arimasen.)

gaikoku 外国〖名〗
外国人 (*gaikoku*jin) 外国語 (*gai-koku*go)
¶わたしはまだ**外国**へ行ったことがありません。(Watashi wa mada *gai-*

¶ If only I had traveled abroad when I was a student....

gai 〚n, 〜*suru*〛 **injury, harm**
a **harmful** insect // pollution // flood **damage**
¶ Smoking is **bad for** one's health.

gaijin 〚n〛 **foreigner, alien**
¶ That **foreigner** speaks Japanese well.
¶ Many **foreigners** go to Kyoto to sightsee.

＊ Variant: *gaikokujin*.

gaikō 〚n〛 **diplomacy**
a **diplomat,** the **diplomatic** service // a **diplomatic** question // a **diplomatic** policy
¶ That is a **diplomatic** secret.
¶ At present, Country A does not have **diplomatic** relations with Country B.

gaikoku 〚n〛 **foreign country**
a **foreigner** // a **foreign** language
¶ I've never been to **a foreign country.**

koku e itta koto ga arimasen.)

gakkari suru がっかりする〖動Ⅲ〗
¶入学試験に落ちてがっかりしました。　(Nyūgaku-shiken ni ochite *gakkari shimashita*.)
¶失敗してもがっかりしないでください。　(Shippai shite mo *gakkari shinaide* kudasai.)

gakki 楽器〖名〗
¶あなたは何か楽器が弾けますか。
(Anata wa nani ka *gakki* ga hikemasu ka?)
¶あの店にはいろいろな楽器があります。　(Ano mise ni wa iroiro na *gakki* ga arimasu.)

gakki 学期〖名〗
¶学期の終わりには試験があります。
(*Gakki* no owari ni wa shiken ga arimasu.)
¶1学期に漢字を400勉強しました。
(Ichi*gakki* ni kanji o yonhyaku benkyō shimashita.)

gakkō 学校〖名〗
小学校 (shō*gakkō*)　中学校 (chū*gakkō*)　高等学校 (kōtō*gakkō*)　専門学校 (senmon-*gakkō*)　公立学校 (kōritsu-*gakkō*)　私立学校 (shiritsu-*gakkō*)
¶病気で学校を休みました。　(Byōki de *gakkō* o yasumimashita.)
¶どこの学校を卒業しましたか。
(Doko no *gakkō* o sotsugyō shimashita ka?)

-gaku -学〖尾〗

gakkari suru 〚v III〛 be discouraged, be disappointed
¶ I am 〚was〛 **disheartened** over failing the school entrance exam.
¶ **Don't lose heart** even if you should suffer a failure.

gakki 〚n〛 musical instrument
¶ Can you play **a musical instrument?**
¶ That shop has various **musical instruments.**

gakki 〚n〛 academic term, school term, semester
¶ There's an exam at the end of **the term.**
¶ [I] learned four hundred *kanji* in one **semester.**

gakkō 〚n〛 school
elementary **school** // junior high **school,** lower secondary **school** // high **school,** upper secondary **school** // technical **school,** professional **school** // public **school** // private **school**
¶ [I] stayed home from **school** due to illness.
¶ What **school** did you graduate from?

-gaku 〚suf〛 study, science, learning

物理学 (butsuri*gaku*) 地理学 (chiri-*gaku*) 言語学 (gengo*gaku*) 語学 (go*gaku*) 法律学 (hōritsu*gaku*) 人類学 (jinrui*gaku*) 化学 (ka*gaku*) 経済学 (keizai*gaku*) 農学 (nō*gaku*) 歴史学 (rekishi*gaku*) 生物学 (sei-butsu*gaku*) 政治学 (seiji*gaku*) 社会学 (shakai*gaku*) 宗教学 (shū-kyō*gaku*) 水産学 (suisan*gaku*) 薬学 (yaku*gaku*)

gakubu 学部〖名〗
学部長 (*gakubu*chō) 文学部 (bun-*gakubu*) 法学部 (hō*gakubu*) 医学部 (i*gakubu*) 工学部 (kō*gakubu*) 理学部 (ri*gakubu*) 政治経済学部 (seijikeizai-*gakubu*) 商学部 (shō-*gakubu*)

gakumon 学問〖名, 〜する〗
¶ずっと学問を続けていきたいと思っています。 (Zutto *gakumon* o tsuzukete ikitai to omotte imasu.)
¶これは学問的にも立派な研究です。 (Kore wa *gakumon*teki ni mo rippa na kenkyū desu.)

gakunen 学年〖名〗
¶あなたの大学は一学年何人ぐらいですか。 (Anata no daigaku wa ichi-*gakunen* nannin gurai desu ka?)
¶学年末試験はいつですか。(*Gakunen*-matsu-shiken wa itsu desu ka?)

gakusei 学生〖名〗
学生服 (*gakusei*fuku) 学生運動 (*gakusei*-undō)
¶わたしは学生です。 (Watashi wa

physics, physical **science** // geography // linguistics, philology // foreign language **study** // jurisprudence, // anthropology // chemistry // economics, // (the **science** of) agriculture // history, // biology // political **science** // sociology, social **studies** // the **science** of religion // fishery **science** // pharmacy, pharmacology

gakubu 〚n〛 (university or college) **department, faculty**
dean, head of a **department** or **faculty** // **faculty** of letters // law **school,** law **faculty** // medical **school** // **school** of engineering // **department** of science and mathematics // **department** of political science and economics // **department** of commercial science

gakumon 〚n, *~suru*〛 **learning, scholarship**
¶ I would like to keep **studying** as long as possible.
¶ This is a fine piece of research **academically** speaking as well.

gakunen 〚n〛 **school year, academic year; class**
¶ How many students are there **in each year** at your university?
¶ When are the **final** exams?

gakusei 〚n〛 **student**
a **student** uniform // the **student** movement
¶ I am **a student.**

gakusei desu.)

¶この大学には何人学生がいますか。
(Kono daigaku ni wa nannin *gakusei* ga imasu ka?)

＊高等学校の生徒は「高校生 (kōkō-sei)」と言う。

＊普通「学生 (gakusei)」は「大学生 (daigakusei)」を指し、「高校生 (kō-kōsei)」「中学生 (chūgakusei)」は「生徒 (seito)」、「小学生 (shōgakusei)」は「児童 (jidō)」と言う。

¶ How many **students** are there at this university?

＊ High-school students are called *kōkōsei*.

＊ *Gakusei* usually refers to college students (*daigakusei*). High-school students (*kōkōsei*) and junior-high students (*chūgakusei*) are called *seito*, and elementary school students (*shōgakusei*) are called *jidō*.

gakusha 学者〖名〗

¶あの人は有名な学者です。 (Ano hito wa yūmei na *gakusha* desu.)
¶おおぜいの学者がこの問題を研究しています。(Oozei no *gakusha* ga kono mondai o kenkyū shite imasu.)

gakusha 〖n〗 scholar

¶ [He] is a celebrated **scholar.**

¶ A great number of **scholars** are studying this problem.

gakushū 学習〖名, ～する〗

¶語学の学習には辞書が必要です。
(Gogaku no *gakushū* ni wa jisho ga hitsuyō desu.)
¶この本を使って日本語を学習しました。 (Kono hon o tsukatte Nihongo o *gakushū* shimashita.)

gakushū 〖n, ～*suru*〗 learning, study

¶ Dictionaries are necessary in language **study.**

¶ [I] **studied** Japanese using this book.

gaman 我慢〖名, ～する〗

¶あの人の態度にはもう我慢ができません。 (Ano hito no taido ni wa mō *gaman* ga dekimasen.)
¶もう少し我慢してください。 (Mō sukoshi *gaman* shite kudasai.)

gaman 〖n, ～*suru*〗 patience, endurance

¶ I've run out of patience with [his] attitude.

¶ Please be patient a little longer.

ganbaru がんばる〖動I〗

¶試験が近いので，夜遅くまでがんばって勉強しています。 (Shiken ga chikai node, yoru osoku made

ganbaru 〖v I〗 persist, hold firm

¶ The exam is close so [I]'m **staying up** and studying until late at night.

ganbatte benkyō shite imasu.)

¶がんばってください。　(*Ganbatte kudasai.*)

¶ **Don't give up** [**Never say die; Keep on fighting; etc.**].

garasu　ガラス〖名〗

ガラスのコップ (*garasu* no koppu)
¶子供が窓ガラスを割りました。
(Kodomo ga mado*garasu* o warimashita.)

garasu 〚n〛 **glass**

a glass, a **glass** tumbler

¶ The children broke the window [[the window **glass**]].

-garu　-がる〖尾〗

行きたがる (ikita*garu*)　うれしがる (ureshi*garu*)　いやがる (iya*garu*)
¶子供がお菓子を欲しがっています。
(Kodomo ga okashi o hoshi*gatte* imasu.)
¶暖房がないので，みんな寒がっています。(Danbō ga nai node, minna samu*gatte* imasu.)

＊「-がる (-garu)」は形容詞・形容動詞の語幹および「たい (tai)」の「た (ta)」に続き，そのように感じる，またはそのような様子にみせるなどの意味を表す。普通は話し手や聞き手以外の人について言う場合に使う。

⇨**tagaru**　たがる

-garu 〚suf〛 **feel ～, want to ～, be apt to ～**

want to go, **be anxious** to go // be glad // dislike, be unwilling to

¶ Children **crave** sweets.

¶ There's no heating so everyone **is feeling** the cold.

＊ The suffix *-garu* is added to the stem form of adjectives and adjective-verbs or to the *-ta-* of *-tai*. It expresses how someone feels or appears to feel. It is usually used to refer to someone other than the speaker or the listener.

gasorin　ガソリン〖名〗

ガソリンスタンド (*gasorin*-sutando)
¶車にガソリンを入れました。(Kuruma ni *gasorin* o iremashita.)

gasorin 〚n〛 **gasoline**

a **gas** station, service station

¶ [I] had **gas** put in the car.

gasu　ガス〖名〗

ガス爆発 (*gasu*-bakuhatsu)　ガス中毒 (*gasu*-chūdoku)，　ガスストーブ (*gasu*-sutōbu)　プロパンガス (puropan-*gasu*)

¶ガスのにおいがしたので，窓を開け

gasu 〚n〛 **a gas**

a **gas** explosion // **gas** poisoning // a **gas** heater // propane **gas**

¶ There was a smell of **gas** so [I]

ました。 (*Gasu* no nioi ga shita node, mado o akemashita.)

opened the window.

-gatsu -月〖尾〗

1月 (ichi*gatsu*) 2月 (ni*gatsu*)
3月 (san*gatsu*) 4月 (shi*gatsu*)
5月 (go*gatsu*) 6月 (roku*gatsu*)
7月 (shichi*gatsu*) 8月 (hachi*gatsu*)
9月 (ku*gatsu*) 10月 (jū*gatsu*)
11月 (jūichi*gatsu*) 12月 (jūni*gatsu*)

-gatsu 〖suf〗 **month**

January // February // March // April // May // June // July // August // September // October // November // December

-gawa -側〖尾〗

こちら側 (kochira*gawa*) 向こう側 (mukō*gawa*) 中側 (naka*gawa*) 外側 (soto*gawa*)

¶道の両側に木が植えてあります。 (Michi no ryō*gawa* ni ki ga uete arimasu.)

¶日本では人は右側を，車は左側を通ります。 (Nihon de wa hito wa migi*gawa* o, kuruma wa hidari*gawa* o toorimasu.)

-gawa 〖suf〗 **side; part**

this **side** // the other **side,** the opposite **side** // the in**side** // the out**side**

¶ There are trees planted on both **sides** of the street.

¶ In Japan people walk on the right-hand **side** and cars run on the left-hand **side** of the road.

geijutsu 芸術〖名〗

芸術品 (*geijutsu*hin) 芸術家 (*geijutsu*ka)

¶わたしは日本の芸術に興味を持っています。 (Watashi wa Nihon no *geijutsu* ni kyōmi o motte imasu.)

geijutsu 〖n〗 (fine) **art, an art, the arts**

a work of **art,** an **art** object // **an artist**

¶ I am interested in **the fine arts and performing arts** of Japan.

gejun 下旬〖名〗

¶今月の下旬に引っ越します。 (Kongetsu no *gejun* ni hikkoshimasu.)

¶3月の下旬から4月の上旬にかけて旅行します。 (Sangatsu no *gejun* kara shigatsu no jōjun ni kakete ryokō shimasu.)

⇒**jōjun** 上旬 **chūjun** 中旬

gejun 〖n〗 **the last third of the month**

¶ [I]'m going to move **late** this month 〖**towards the end** of this month〗.

¶ [I] will be traveling from **late** March through early April 〖from **the last part** of March through the early part of April〗.

gēmu　ゲーム〚名〛

¶みんなでゲームをしましょう。
(Minna de *gēmu* o shimashō.)
¶日本の子供はどんなゲームをして遊びますか。(Nihon no kodomo wa donna *gēmu* o shite asobimasu ka?)

geki　劇〚名〛

悲劇 (hi*geki*)　喜劇 (ki*geki*)
¶外国人の学生が日本語で劇をしました。(Gaikokujin no gakusei ga Nihongo de *geki* o shimashita.)
¶あなたも劇に出ますか。(Anata mo *geki* ni demasu ka?)

gekijō　劇場〚名〛

¶あの劇場では今何をやっていますか。(Ano *gekijō* de wa ima nani o yatte imasu ka?)
¶劇場は満員で入れませんでした。(*Gekijō* wa man'in de hairemasen deshita.)

gekkyū　月給〚名〛

¶今度月給をもらったら、レコードを買うつもりです。(Kondo *gekkyū* o morattara, rekōdo o kau tsumori desu.)

gendai　現代〚名〛

現代的 (*gendai*teki)　現代日本文学
(*gendai*-Nihonbungaku)
¶現代は科学の時代です。(*Gendai* wa kagaku no jidai desu.)

gen'in　原因〚名〛

¶今、事故の原因を調べています。
(Ima, jiko no *gen'in* o shirabete imasu.)

gēmu 〚n〛　a game

¶ Let's all play **a game.**

¶ What sort of **games** do Japanese children play for fun?

geki 〚n〛　drama, play, theatrical performance

tragedy // comedy

¶ The foreign students performed **a play** in Japanese.

¶ Are you going to be in **the play?**

gekijō 〚n〛　theater

¶ What's on now at that **theater?**

¶ **The theater** was full and [we] weren't able to get in.

gekkyū 〚n〛　monthly salary, wages

¶ I plan to buy some records when I **get paid** next.

gendai 〚n〛　the present age, today modern, up-to-date // contemporary Japanese literature

¶ **This** is the age of science.

gen'in 〚n〛　cause, source, origin

¶ **The cause** of the accident is presently under investigation.

¶火事の原因はたばこの火でした。

(Kaji no *gen'in* wa tabako no hi deshita.)

⇔**kekka** 結果

genjitsu 現実〖名〗

¶理想と現実は違います。　(Risō to *genjitsu* wa chigaimasu.)

¶現実は厳しいですよ。(*Genjitsu* wa kibishii desu yo.)

genkan 玄関〖名〗

¶玄関にだれか来たようです。

(*Genkan* ni dare ka kita yō desu.)

¶日本では玄関でくつを脱いで上がります。　(Nihon de wa *genkan* de kutsu o nuide agarimasu.)

genki 元気〖名, 形動〗

①[活動力があっていきいきしていること]

元気がある (*genki* ga aru)　元気がいい (*genki* ga ii)　元気な子供 (*genki* na kodomo)

②[体の状態がよくて健康であること]

¶「お元気ですか。」(O*genki* desu ka?)「はい, おかげさまで元気です。」(Hai, okagesama de *genki* desu.)

¶彼はもうすぐ元気になって退院するでしょう。　(Kare wa mō sugu *genki* ni natte taiin suru deshō.)

genkin 現金〖名〗

現金で払う (*genkin* de harau)

¶今, 現金でいくら持っていますか。

(Ima, *genkin* de ikura motte imasu ka?)

¶現金を持っていると, すぐ使ってし

¶ **The cause** of the fire was a cigarette butt.

genjitsu 〖n〗 actuality, reality

¶ The ideal and **the real** 〖**actual**〗 are two different things.

¶ **Reality** is a harsh taskmaster 〖**Life** is hard〗.

genkan 〖n〗 vestibule, entryway, entrance hall

¶ It looks like someone has come **to the door.**

¶ In Japan one takes off one's shoes **inside the front door.**

genki 〖n, adj-v〗 energy, vitality; health

① [energy, vitality]

be **in good spirits,** be **in good vigor** // be **in high spirits,** be **in good vigor** // an **active** child

② [health, vigor]

¶ "How are you?"

"Fine, thank you." (Literally, "Are you **in good health?**" "Yes, **I am** thanks to you.")

¶ He should soon **be up and about** and able to leave the hospital.

genkin 〖n〗 cash

pay in **cash**

¶ How much **money** do you have with you now?

¶ When [I] carry **cash** with [me], [I]

まいます。(*Genkin* o motte iru to, sugu tsukatte shimaimasu.)

soon spend it all.

genryō 原料〖名〗
¶日本の酒の原料は米です。 (Nihon no sake no *genryō* wa kome desu.)
¶石油を原料にして，いろいろな物ができます。(Sekiyu o *genryō* ni shite, iroiro na mono ga dekimasu.)

genryō 〚n〛 **raw material(s)**
¶ **The raw material** of Japanese *sake* is rice.
¶ Various products are made from **the raw material** petroleum.

genshō 現象〖名〗
不思議な現象 (fushigi na *genshō*)
¶それは世界的な現象です。 (Sore wa sekaiteki na *genshō* desu.)
¶高い山では珍しい自然現象が見られます。(Takai yama de wa mezurashii shizen-*genshō* ga miraremasu.)

genshō 〚n〛 **phenomenon**
a strange **phenomenon** 〚**happening**〛
¶ That is a worldwide **phenomenon.**
¶ Rare natural **phenomena** can be observed on high mountains.

genshō 減少〖名，〜する〗
¶この国の人口は次第に減少しています。(Kono kuni no jinkō wa shidai ni *genshō* shite imasu.)
¶今年の夏は天気が悪かったので，米の生産が減少しました。(Kotoshi no natsu wa tenki ga warukatta node, kome no seisan ga *genshō* shimashita.)
⇔zōka 増加 ⇒heru 減る

genshō 〚n, 〜*suru*〛 **decrease, decline**
¶ The population of this country **is** gradually **declining.**
¶ Rice production **has dropped** due to the bad weather this past summer.

genzai 現在〖名〗
¶現在，わたしは東京に住んでいます。(*Genzai*, watashi wa Tōkyō ni sunde imasu.)
¶現在でも電気のない村があります。(*Genzai* demo denki no nai mura ga arimasu.)
⇒kako 過去 mirai 未来

genzai 〚n〛 **now, presently**
¶ I am **presently** living in Tokyo.
¶ Even **now** there are villages which are not electrified.

geshuku 下宿〖名，〜する〗

geshuku 〚n, 〜*suru*〛 **lodging, a boardinghouse, a rooming house**

¶いい下宿を探しています。　(Ii *ge-shuku* o sagashite imasu.)

¶わたしは学校のそばに下宿しています。　(Watashi wa gakkō no soba ni *geshuku* shite imasu.)

getsuyō(bi)　月曜(日)〖名〗

gijutsu　技術〖名〗
技術者 (*gijutsu*sha)　工業技術 (kōgyō-*gijutsu*)　技術の進歩 (*gijutsu* no shinpo)

¶この国の農業技術はたいへん進んでいます。　(Kono kuni no nōgyō-*gijutsu* wa taihen susunde imasu.)

gimon　疑問〖名〗
¶疑問があったら，おっしゃってください。　(*Gimon* ga attara, osshatte kudasai.)

¶彼が成功するかどうかは疑問です。　(Kare ga seikō suru ka dō ka wa *gimon* desu.)

gimu　義務〖名〗
義務を果たす (*gimu* o hatasu)
¶国民は税金を払う義務があります。　(Kokumin wa zeikin o harau *gimu* ga arimasu.)

¶日本の義務教育は 9 年間です。　(Nihon no *gimu*-kyōiku wa kyū-nenkan desu.)
⇔kenri 権利

gin　銀〖名〗
銀色 (*gin*iro)　銀貨 (*gin*ka)

ginkō　銀行〖名〗
銀行員 (*ginkō*in)
¶銀行にお金を預けておきます。(Gin-

¶ [I] am looking for a good **room.**

¶ I am living in **a rooming house** near school.

getsuyō(bi) 〚n〛　Monday

gijutsu 〚n〛　technique, skill, technology

a technical expert, technician, engineer // industrial **technology** // the advance of **technology**

¶ The agricultural **techniques** of this country are very advanced.

gimon 〚n〛　doubt, question

¶ If you have **any doubts,** please tell [us] about them.

¶ **It's doubtful** whether he will succeed or not.

gimu 〚n〛　duty, obligation

fulfill **one's obligations,** discharge **one's duties**

¶ Citizens have **an obligation** to pay taxes.

¶ **Compulsory** education is for nine years in Japan.

gin 〚n〛　silver (the metal)

silver, silver colored // **silver** coins

ginkō 〚n〛　bank

bank employee

¶ I put my money in **the bank** for

kō ni okane o azukete okimasu.)

¶銀行からお金を下ろします。(*Ginkō kara okane o oroshimasu.*)

giron　議論〖名, 〜する〗

¶それについては、いろいろ議論があります。(*Sore ni tsuite wa, iroiro giron ga arimasu.*)

¶わたしたちはゆうべ遅くまで日本の政治について議論しました。(*Watashitachi wa yūbe osoku made Nihon no seiji ni tsuite giron shimashita.*)

gitā　ギター〖名〗

ギターを弾く (*gitā o hiku*)

¶彼はギターが上手です。(*Kare wa gitā ga jōzu desu.*)

¶ギターに合わせて、みんなで歌いました。(*Gitā ni awasete, minna de utaimashita.*)

go　五〖名〗

go-　御-〖頭〗

①〔尊敬の意味を表す〕

¶御両親はお元気ですか。(*Goryōshin wa ogenki desu ka?*)

¶御旅行はいかがでしたか。(*Goryokō wa ikaga deshita ka?*)

②〔謙譲の意味を表す〕

¶あした御連絡します。(*Ashita gorenraku shimasu.*)

¶あとで御説明します。(*Ato de gosetsumei shimasu.*)

⇨**o-　お-**

(-)go　(-)語〖名, 尾〗

1〖名〗

safekeeping.

¶ [I] withdraw money from **the bank.**

giron 〚n, ~*suru*〛 **argument, discussion, debate**

¶ There is much that is **debatable** concerning that matter.

¶ We **discussed** Japanese politics until late last night.

gitā 〚n〛 **guitar**

play **the guitar**

¶ He plays **the guitar** well.

¶ All sang accompanied by **a guitar.**

go 〚n〛 **five**

go- 〚pref〛 **an honorific prefix**

① [indicates respect toward the listener]

¶ How are your parents 〖Are your parents in good health〗?

¶ How was your trip?

② [indicates humility on the part of the speaker]

¶ I'll be in touch with you tomorrow.

¶ I'll explain later.

(-)go 〚n, suf〛 **word; language**

1 〚n〛 word

151

¶次の語は何と読みますか。　(Tsugi no go wa nan to yomimasu ka?)

¶ How is the next **word** read?

2〚尾〛

中国語 (Chūgoku*go*)　　ドイツ語 (Doitsu*go*)　英語 (Ei*go*)　フランス語 (Furansu*go*)　日本語 (Nihon*go*)　スペイン語 (Supein*go*)　　現代語 (gendai*go*)　近代語 (kindai*go*)

2〚suf〛　language

Chinese (**language**) // German (**language**) // English (**language**) // French (**language**) // Japanese (**language**) // Spanish (**language**) // the present-day **language** // the modern **language**

-go　-後〚尾〛

1時間後 (ichijikan*go*)　数日後 (sūjitsu*go*)　戦後 (sen*go*)　帰国後 (kikoku*go*)

¶母の死後，父は寂しそうです。(Haha no shi*go*, chichi wa sabishisō desu.)

¶数年後に日本へ行く予定です。(Sūnen*go* ni Nihon e iku yotei desu.)

-go〚suf〛　after, later, since

after one hour, one hour **later** // **after** several days, several days **later** // **after** the war, **post**war // **after** returning to one's native country

¶ My father seems lonely **since** my mother's death.

¶ I plan to go to Japan **in** a few years.

-gō　-号〚尾〛

1号車 (ichi*gō*sha)　2月号 (ni-gatsu*gō*)

-gō〚suf〛　**number, issue**

Car **No.** 1 (of a train) // the February **issue** (of a magazine or journal)

gobusata　ごぶさた〚名，～する〛

¶長い間ごぶさたしました。(Nagai aida *gobusata* shimashita.)

¶ごぶさたしていますが，皆さんお元気ですか。(*Gobusata* shite imasu ga, minasan ogenki desu ka?)

gobusata〚n, ~*suru*〛　an expression used in apology when one has been out of contact with the other person for some time

¶ Please excuse me **for my** long **silence**.

¶ Sorry to **have been out of touch.** I hope everyone is well.

gochisō　ごちそう〚名，～する〛

¶テーブルの上には，ごちそうがたくさん並んでいました。(Tēburu no ue ni wa, *gochisō* ga takusan narande imashita.)

¶先生のお宅で夕食をごちそうになりました。(Sensei no otaku de yūshoku o *gochisō* ni narimashita.)

gochisō〚n, ~*suru*〛　**hospitality, treat, delicacies;** an expression used to express gratitude for food or drink served or paid for by the listener

¶ Many **delicacies** were laid out on the table.

¶ I **was invited** to dinner at the home of my teacher 〚professor〛.

¶先日はごちそうさまでした。(Senjitsu wa *gochisō*sama deshita.)

gogatsu 五月〖名〗

gogo 午後〖名〗

¶あしたの午後，デパートへ買い物に行きます。(Ashita no *gogo*, depāto e kaimono ni ikimasu.)

¶午後から雨が降るでしょう。(*Gogo* kara ame ga furu deshō.)

⇔gozen 午前

gohan 御飯〖名〗

①[食事]
朝御飯 (asa*gohan*)　昼御飯 (hiru*gohan*)　晩御飯 (ban*gohan*)　夕御飯 (yū*gohan*)

②[米を炊いた食べ物]
御飯を炊く (*gohan* o taku)

¶朝は御飯とパンとどちらがいいですか。(Asa wa *gohan* to pan to dochira ga ii desu ka?)

gokai 誤解〖名，〜する〗

¶それは誤解です。(Sore wa *gokai* desu.)

¶つまらない誤解のため，あの二人はけんかしてしまいました。(Tsumaranai *gokai* no tame, ano futari wa kenka shite shimaimashita.)

gōkaku 合格〖名，〜する〗
不合格 (fu*gōkaku*)

¶彼は入学試験に合格しました。(Kare wa nyūgaku-shiken ni *gōkaku* shimashita.)

¶この製品は検査に合格しています。(Kono seihin wa kensa ni *gōkaku*

¶ Thank you for **your hospitality** 〖kindness in **treating me** to a meal, etc.〗 the other day.

gogatsu 〚n〛 the month of May

gogo 〚n〛 afternoon, PM

¶ [I]'m going to go shopping at a department store tomorrow **afternoon.**

¶ It will probably rain from **midday.**

gohan 〚n〛 a meal; boiled rice

① [a meal]

breakfast // lunch // dinner, supper // dinner, supper

② [boiled rice]

to cook **rice**

¶ Which would you prefer for breakfast, **rice** or bread 〖toast, a croissant, etc.〗?

gokai 〚n, ~*suru*〛 misunderstanding, misapprehension

¶ That is **a misunderstanding.**

¶ Those two quarreled because of a trifling 〖foolish〗 **misunderstanding.**

gōkaku 〚n, ~*suru*〛 passing an examination, being declared eligible, passing an inspection

failure, disqualification, elimination, rejection

¶ He **passed** the school entrance examination.

¶ This product **has passed** inspection.

gōkei 合計〖名, ～する〗

¶「参加者は合計何人ですか。」(Sanka-sha wa *gōkei* nannin desu ka?)「合計３５人です。」(*Gōkei* sanjū-gonin desu.)

¶食事代と交通費を合計するといくらになりますか。(Shokujidai to kōtsūhi o *gōkei* suru to ikura ni narimasu ka?)

gokurōsama 御苦労さま〖連〗

¶御苦労さまでした。(*Gokurōsama* deshita.)

＊目上の人に対しては使わない。

gomen kudasai ごめんください〖連〗

¶玄関で「ごめんください。」と言う声がしました。(Genkan de "*Gomen kudasai*." to iu koe ga shimashita.)

¶奥さんは、「では、ごめんください。」と言って電話を切りました。(Okusan wa, "Dewa, *gomen kudasai*." to itte denwa o kirimashita.)

gomen nasai ごめんなさい〖連〗

¶遅くなって、ごめんなさい。(Osoku natte, *gomen nasai*.)

¶わたしが悪かったです。ごめんなさい。(Watashi ga warukatta desu. *Gomen nasai*.)

⇒sumimasen すみません

gomi ごみ〖名〗

ごみ箱 (*gomibako*) ごみ袋 (*gomibukuro*) ごみ捨て場 (*gomisuteba*)

¶ここにごみを捨てないでください。

gōkei 〚n, ~*suru*〛 total, sum total

¶ "How many participants are there **all together?**"

"There are **a total** of 35 participants."

¶ How much do meal and travel expenses **come to?**

gokigen ☞ **kigen**

gokurōsama 〚compd〛 an expression used to someone who is doing or has just finished some task for the speaker

¶ **Thank you very much** 〚Thank you for your trouble; Good-bye〛.

＊ Not used toward persons of higher status.

gomen kudasai 〚compd〛 an expression used to call attention to oneself if no one is in sight or when parting from or ending a telephone conversation with a person of higher status

¶ Someone at the door called out, "*Gomen kudasai*."

¶ The wife ended the telephone conversation with the words, "*Dewa, gomen kudasai*."

gomen nasai 〚compd〛 I'm sorry; excuse me

¶ **I'm sorry** to be late.

¶ It was my fault. **I'm very sorry.**

gomi 〚n〛 dust, litter, garbage, trash

a **trash** container // a **trash** bag // a **garbage** dump

(Koko ni *gomi* o sutenaide kudasai.)

¶東京では、一日にどのぐらいごみが出ますか。(Tōkyō de wa, ichinichi ni dono gurai *gomi* ga demasu ka?)

gomu ゴム〔名〕

消しゴム (keshi*gomu*)　ゴムひも (*gomu*himo)　輪ゴム (wa*gomu*)

¶このひもはゴムのように伸びますね。(Kono himo wa *gomu* no yō ni nobimasu ne.)

(〜te) goran nasai (〜て)ごらんなさい〔連〕

¶ちょっと食べてごらんなさい。(Chotto tabete *goran nasai*.)

¶来てごらんなさい。きれいな鳥がいますよ。(Kite *goran nasai*. Kirei na tori ga imasu yo.)

-goro -ごろ〔尾〕

¶毎朝6時ごろ起きます。(Maiasa rokuji *goro* okimasu.)

¶わたしたちは今年の10月ごろ結婚します。(Watashitachi wa kotoshi no jūgatsu *goro* kekkon shimasu.)

-goto -ごと〔尾〕

¶日曜ごとにつりに行きます。(Nichiyō *goto* ni tsuri ni ikimasu.)

¶1メートルごとに木を植えました。(Ichimētoru *goto* ni ki o uemashita.)

gozaimasu ございます〔連〕

¶何か御用がございますか。(Nani ka goyō ga *gozaimasu* ka?)

¶お変わりございませんか。(Okawari

¶ Please don't throw away **trash** here 〚No littering; No dumping〛.

¶ How much **garbage** is produced in Tokyo a day?

gomu 〚n〛 rubber, gum (elastic)
(rubber) eraser // **elastic** band // **rubber** band

¶ This string stretches like **elastic.**

(-te) goran nasai 〚compd〛 **try and** ~ (cannot be used toward those of higher status)

¶ **Have a taste** of it.

¶ **Come** here a minute! There's a pretty bird.

-goro 〚suf〛 about, around

¶ [I] get up every morning **around** six o'clock.

¶ We are going to get married this year **around** October.

-goto 〚suf〛 every ~, at an interval of ~

¶ [He] goes fishing **every** Sunday.

¶ [I] planted trees at one-meter **intervals.**

gozaimasu 〚compd〛 there is, there are, be, have

¶ **Is there** something I can do for you 〚Did you want to see me about something〛?

¶ How have you been doing (literal-

155

gozaimasen ka?)

¶遅くなりまして，申し訳ございません。(Osoku narimashite, mōshiwake *gozaimasen.*)

¶ありがとうございます。 (Arigatō *gozaimasu.*)

¶お早うございます。 (Ohayō *gozaimasu.*)

¶御結婚，おめでとうございます。 (Gokekkon, omedetō *gozaimasu.*)

¶あれが博物館でございます。 (Are ga hakubutsukan de *gozaimasu.*)

✻「ある (aru)」の丁寧語。

ly, **Aren't** there any changes)?

¶ I'm very sorry to be late.

¶ Thank you very much.

¶ Good morning.

¶ Congratulations on your wedding.

¶ That **is** the museum.

✻ *Gozaimasu* is the polite form of *aru.*

gozen 午前〚名〛

¶学校は午前9時に始まります。 (Gakkō wa *gozen* kuji ni hajimarimasu.)

¶土曜の午前中は家にいます。 (Doyō no *gozen*chū wa ie ni imasu.)

⇔gogo 午後

gozen 〚n〛 morning, AM

¶ School starts at 9 AM.

¶ I will be at home Saturday **morning** 〚I am at home Saturday **mornings**〛.

guai ぐあい〚名〛

①〔体などの調子・状態〕

¶お体のぐあいはいかがですか。 (Okarada no *guai* wa ikaga desu ka?)

②〔ものごとのありさま・やり方〕

¶おはしはこういうぐあいに使います。 (Ohashi wa kōiu *guai* ni tsukaimasu.)

guai 〚n〛 physical condition, health; condition, state

① [physical condition, health]

¶ How are you feeling?

② [condition, state]

¶ Chopsticks are used in this **manner.**

gunjin 軍人〚名〛

¶父は軍人でした。(Chichi wa *gunjin* deshita.)

gunjin 〚n〛 soldier, serviceman, member of the armed forces

¶ My father was **in the military.**

guntai 軍隊〚名〛

¶この国では，若い男の人はみんな軍

guntai 〚n〛 troops, army, the military

隊に入ります。（Kono kuni de wa, wakai otoko no hito wa minna *guntai* ni hairimasu.）

¶軍隊での経験は役に立ちますか。
（*Guntai* de no keiken wa yaku ni tachimasu ka?）

gurai　ぐらい〚助〛☞**kurai** くらい

-guramu　-グラム〚尾〛
¶牛肉を500グラム買いました。（Gyū-niku o gohyaku*guramu* kaimashi-ta.）

¶これは100グラムいくらですか。
（Kore wa hyaku*guramu* ikura desu ka?）

gūsū　偶数〚名〛
¶2,4,6は偶数で、1,3,5は奇数です。
（Ni, shi, roku wa *gūsū* de, ichi, san, go wa kisū desu.）
¶偶数の札を持っている人は、こちら側に座ってください。（*Gūsū* no fuda o motte iru hito wa, kochiragawa ni suwatte kudasai.）
⇔**kisū** 奇数

gūzen　偶然〚名, 副, 形動〛
¶デパートで偶然田中さんに会いました。（Depāto de *gūzen* Tanaka san ni aimashita.）
¶それは本当に偶然の一致です。（Sore wa hontō ni *gūzen* no itchi desu.）

gyaku　逆〚名, 形動〛
¶時計の針を逆に回さないでください。
（Tokei no hari o *gyaku* ni mawa-sanaide kudasai.）
¶あの人の考えはその逆です。　（Ano

gyaku

¶ In this country all young men have to serve in **the military.**

¶ Is one's **military** experience of any use 〚Will my **military** experience be of any use〛?

gurai ☞ **kurai**

-guramu 〚suf〛 **gram(s)**
¶ [I] bought five hundred **grams** of beef.

¶ How much is one hundred **grams** of this?

gūsū 〚n〛 **an even number, the even numbers**
¶ Two, four, and six are **even num-bers;** and one, three, and five are odd numbers.
¶ Will those having **even-numbered** tickets 〚tags〛 please sit on this side.

gūzen 〚n, adv, adj-v〛 **chance, acci-dent**
¶ **I happened** to meet [Mrs.] Tanaka at a department store.
¶ That is really **a coincidence.**

gyaku 〚n, adj-v〛 **reverse, inverse, the contrary**
¶ Please don't move the hands of the watch 〚clock〛 **backwards.**
¶ [His] opinion is **the complete op-**

157

hito no kangae wa sono *gyaku* desu.)

(-)**gyō** (-)行〖名, 尾〗

1〖名〗
行をかえる (*gyō* o kaeru)

2〖尾〗
¶1行ずつ読んでください。 (Ichi*gyō* zutsu yonde kudasai.)
¶下から3行めの漢字が読めません。
(Shita kara san*gyō*me no kanji ga yomemasen.)

gyogyō 漁業〖名〗
漁業組合 (*gyogyō*-kumiai)
¶日本は漁業がたいへん盛んです。
(Nihon wa *gyogyō* ga taihen sakan desu.)

gyōji 行事〖名〗
¶2学期の行事の予定を教えてください。 (Nigakki no *gyōji* no yotei o oshiete kudasai.)
¶日本の年中行事についてレポートを書きます。(Nihon no nenjū-*gyōji* ni tsuite repōto o kakimasu.)

gyūniku 牛肉〖名〗
¶牛肉を買って, すきやきをしました。
(*Gyūniku* o katte, sukiyaki o shimashita.)
¶牛肉と豚肉とどちらが好きですか。
(*Gyūniku* to butaniku to dochira ga suki desu ka?)

gyūnyū 牛乳〖名〗
牛乳びん (*gyūnyū*bin) 牛乳配達 (*gyūnyū*-haitatsu) 牛乳屋 (*gyūnyū*ya)

posite of that.

(-)**gyō** 〚n, suf〛 line of type, row of type

1 〚n〛 a line of type
begin a new **line** (on a page)

2 〚suf〛 the counter for lines of type
¶ Please read aloud one **line** each.
¶ I can't read the *kanji* in the third **line** from the bottom.

gyogyō 〚n〛 fishing industry
fishermen's union
¶ The **fishing industry** is very active in Japan.

gyōji 〚n〛 event, function
¶ Please inform me of **the events** scheduled for the second term.
¶ [I] am writing a report on annual **events** ⌈rites⌉ in Japan.

gyūniku 〚n〛 beef
¶ [I] bought **beef** and fixed *sukiyaki*.
¶ Which do you like better, **beef** or pork?

gyūnyū 〚n〛 (cow's) **milk**
a **milk** bottle // a **milk** delivery // a **dairy**man, **milk**man, **milk** shop

¶朝御飯はいつもパンと牛乳です。
(Asagohan wa itsu mo pan to *gyūnyū* desu.)
⇨**miruku** ミルク

¶ [I] always have bread 〚toast, a croissant, a pastry, etc.〛 and **milk** for breakfast.

H

ha 歯〔名〕

歯ブラシ (haburashi) 歯医者 (ha-isha) 歯みがき (hamigaki) 虫歯 (mushiba) 練り歯みがき (neri-hamigaki) 歯が生える (ha ga hae-ru) 歯が抜ける (ha ga nukeru)

¶毎朝歯をみがきます。 (Maiasa ha o migakimasu.)

¶急に歯が痛くなりました。 (Kyū ni ha ga itaku narimashita.)

ha 葉〔名〕

¶秋には木の葉が散ります。 (Aki ni wa ko no ha ga chirimasu.)

haba 幅〔名〕

¶この川の幅は何メートルぐらいありますか。 (Kono kawa no haba wa nanmētoru gurai arimasu ka?)

¶この道の幅は狭いですね。 (Kono michi no haba wa semai desu ne.)

habuku 省く〔動Ⅰ〕

¶ここでは詳しい説明は省きます。 (Koko de wa kuwashii setsumei wa habukimasu.)

¶重要でないところは省いてください。 (Jūyō de nai tokoro wa habuite kudasai.)

hachi 八〔名〕

hachigatsu 八月〔名〕

hadaka 裸〔名〕

①[着物などを着ないで全身を出している姿]

ha [[n]] tooth, teeth

a **tooth**brush // a dentist // **tooth**paste, **tooth** powder // a decayed **tooth, tooth** with a cavity // **tooth**paste // cut **a tooth,** teethe // lose **a tooth,** lose **one's teeth**

¶ [I] brush **[my] teeth** every morning.

¶ I suddenly got a **tooth**ache 〖**My teeth** suddenly started to hurt〗.

ha [[n]] leaf

¶ Tree **leaves** fall in the autumn.

haba [[n]] width, breadth, range

¶ How many meters **wide** is this river?

¶ This street is narrow, isn't it?

habuku [[v I]] omit, leave out, skip

¶ At this time **I will dispense with** a detailed explanation.

¶ Please **skip over** unimportant parts.

hachi [[n]] eight

hachigatsu [[n]] August

hadaka [[n]] nude; denuded, uncovered

① [nude, naked body]

¶男の子が裸で遊んでいます。(Otoko no ko ga *hadaka* de asonde imasu.)

②[覆いなどのない様子，またその姿]
裸馬 (*hadaka*uma)

¶裸の電燈に触ると熱いです。

(*Hadaka* no dentō ni sawaru to atsui desu.)

hadashi はだし〖名〗

¶砂浜をはだしで走りました。(Sunahama o *hadashi* de hashirimashita.)

¶くつ下を脱いで，はだしになりました。(Kutsushita o nuide, *hadashi* ni narimashita.)

hade 派手〖形動〗

¶彼はいつも派手なシャツを着ています。 (Kare wa itsu mo *hade* na shatsu o kite imasu.)

¶この服はわたしには派手ですか，地味ですか。(Kono fuku wa watashi ni wa *hade* desu ka, jimi desu ka?)
⇔jimi 地味

hae はえ〖名〗

¶はえが1匹飛んでいます。(*Hae* ga ippiki tonde imasu.)

¶この町にはあまりはえがいません。(Kono machi ni wa amari *hae* ga imasen.)

＊「はい (hai)」とも言う。

haeru 生える〖動Ⅱ〗

¶庭に草がたくさん生えてきました。(Niwa ni kusa ga takusan *haete* kimashita.)

¶赤ん坊の歯が生えました。(Akanbō no ha ga *haemashita*.)

¶ A boy is playing **without any clothes on.**

② [denuded, uncovered]
a **barebacked** horse

¶ A **naked** electric bulb is hot to the touch.

hadashi 〚n〛 **bare feet, barefooted**

¶ [I] ran **barefoot** along the sandy beach.

¶ I took off [my] socks and went **barefoot.**

hade 〚adj-v〛 **showy, gaudy, flashy**

¶ He always wears a rather **loud 〖bright, splashy〗** shirt.

¶ Is this outfit **too young 〖gay〗** or too old 〖subdued〗 for me?

hae 〚n〛 **fly**

¶ **A fly** is buzzing around.

¶ There aren't very many **flies** in this town.

＊ Variant: *hai.*

haeru 〚v II〛 **grow, sprout**

¶ A lot of weeds **have appeared** in the yard.

¶ The baby **has cut** its first teeth.

hagaki はがき〖名〗

絵はがき (ehagaki)　年賀はがき (nenga-hagaki)　往復はがき (ōfuku-hagaki)　郵便はがき (yūbin-hagaki)

¶はがきを5枚ください。 (Hagaki o gomai kudasai.)

¶友達にはがきを出しました。(Tomodachi ni hagaki o dashimashita.)

hagemasu 励ます〖動Ⅰ〗

¶先生は試験に落ちた学生を励ましました。 (Sensei wa shiken ni ochita gakusei o hagemashimashita.)

¶「がんばりなさい。」と友達に励まされました。 ("Ganbarinasai." to tomodachi ni hagemasaremashita.)

hageshii 激しい〖形〗

激しい風 (hageshii kaze)

¶雨が激しく降ってきました。 (Ame ga hageshiku futte kimashita.)

¶ここは交通が激しいから気をつけてください。(Koko wa kōtsū ga hageshii kara ki o tsukete kudasai.)

haha 母〖名〗

¶母は今年60歳です。 (Haha wa kotoshi rokujissai desu.)

¶母の料理が懐かしいです。(Haha no ryōri ga natsukashii desu.)

＊自分の母親のことを他人に話す場合に使う。直接、母親に呼びかける場合や、他人の母親のことを言う場合は、「お母さん (okāsan)」「お母様 (okāsama)」と言う。

⇔chichi 父　⇒ okāsan お母さん

hai はい〖感〗

hagaki 〖n〗 postcard

a picture **postcard** // a New Year's **(post)card** // a double **postcard** with a card for replying // **a postcard**

¶ Five **postcards,** please.

¶ [I] sent **a postcard** to a friend.

hagemasu 〖v Ⅰ〗 encourage, cheer up

¶ The teacher **tried to cheer up** the students who had failed the exam.

¶ **I was encouraged** by my friends with the word "Ganbarinasai."

hageshii 〖adj〗 strong, intense, severe

a **strong** wind

¶ It has started to rain **heavily** 〖It started to rain **heavily**〗.

¶ Please be careful as the traffic **is heavy** here.

haha 〖n〗 mother

¶ **My mother** is 60 years old this year.

¶ I am homesick for **my mother's** cooking.

＊ Used to refer to one's own mother when talking with others. When directly addressing one's own mother or referring to someone else's mother, okāsan or okāsama is used.

hai 〖interj〗 yes

162

¶「これは日本語の本ですか。」(Kore wa Nihongo no hon desu ka?)「はい，そうです。」(*Hai,* sō desu.)

¶「そこに辞書がありますか。」(Soko ni jisho ga arimasu ka?)「はい，あります。」(*Hai,* arimasu.)

＊「ええ (ee)」より丁寧な言葉。

⇔iie いいえ　⇨ee ええ

¶ "Is this book written in Japanese?" "**Yes,** it is."

¶ "Is there a dictionary over there?" "**Yes,** there is."

＊ *Hai* is more polite than *ee*.

hai　灰〘名〙

¶たばこの灰はここに入れてください。(Tabako no *hai* wa koko ni irete kudasai.)

¶ストーブの灰を掃除してください。(Sutōbu no *hai* o sōji shite kudasai.)

hai 〚n〛 **ash, ashes**

¶ Please put your cigarette **ashes** in this.

¶ Please clean **the ashes** from the stove.

hai ☞ hae

-hai　-杯〘尾〙

1杯 (ip*pai*)　2杯 (ni*hai*)　3杯 (san*bai*)　4杯 (yon*hai*)　5杯 (go*hai*)　6杯 (rop*pai*)　7杯 (nana*hai*)　8杯 (hap*pai*)　9杯 (kyū*hai*)　10杯 (jip*pai*)

¶「お砂糖を何杯入れましょうか。」(Osatō o nan*bai* iremashō ka?)「2杯入れてください。」(Ni*hai* irete kudasai.)

-hai 〚suf〛 the counter for cups, glasses, or spoonfuls of something

1 **glassful** 〚**cupful, spoonful**〛 // 2 **glassfuls** // 3 **glassfuls** // 4 **glassfuls** // 5 **glassfuls** // 6 **glassfuls** // 7 **glassfuls** // 8 **glassfuls** // 9 **glassfuls** // 10 **glassfuls**

¶ "How many **spoonfuls** 〚**cups**〛 of sugar should I put in?"

"Please put in two **spoonfuls** 〚**cups**〛."

haiiro　灰色〘名〙

¶灰色のズボンを買いました。(*Haiiro* no zubon o kaimashita.)

¶空が曇って灰色になりました。(Sora ga kumotte *haiiro* ni narimashita.)

haiiro 〚n〛 **gray, ash colored**

¶ [I] bought a pair of **gray** slacks.

¶ The sky has clouded over 〚The sky clouded over〛 and turned **a gray color.**

hairu　入る〘動Ⅰ〙

①[外から中に移る]

家の中に入る (ie no naka ni *hairu*)　玄関を入る (genkan o *hairu*)　門を入

hairu 〚v I〛 **enter, come in; contain; join; receive; begin**

① [enter, come in]

come inside the house // **come into**

る (mon o *hairu*)

¶夕方おふろに入ります。 (Yūgata ofuro ni *hairimasu*.)

↔**deru** 出る

②[あるものが区切られた所に入れてある]

¶この箱の中に何が入っていますか。 (Kono hako no naka ni nani ga *haitte* imasu ka?)

③[組織や団体などに加わる]

大学に入る (daigaku ni *hairu*) 会社に入る (kaisha ni *hairu*) 仲間に入る (nakama ni *hairu*)

¶わたしはテニス部に入りました。 (Watashi wa tenisubu ni *hairimashita*.)

④[あるものが自分のものになる]

手に入る (te ni *hairu*) お金が入る (okane ga *hairu*)

¶今日はボーナスが入りました。(Kyō wa bōnasu ga *hairimashita*.)

⑤[ある時刻・時期になる]

梅雨に入る (tsuyu ni *hairu*) 夜に入る (yoru ni *hairu*)

¶8月に入って急に暑くなりました。 (Hachigatsu ni *haitte* kyū ni atsuku narimashita.)

haitatsu 配達〖名、〜する〗

牛乳配達 (gyūnyū-*haitatsu*) 新聞配達 (shinbun-*haitatsu*) 郵便配達 (yūbin-*haitatsu*)

¶このテーブルをあした配達してください。 (Kono tēburu o ashita *haitatsu* shite kudasai.)

the entryway // **come in** the gate

¶ [I] **take** a bath in the evenings.

② [contain, hold]

¶ What's **in** this box?

③ [join, enter]

enter a university // **join** a company, **go to work** for a company // **join** others in something, **mix** with others

¶ I **joined** the tennis club.

④ [get, receive]

obtain, be obtained, **come into** one's possession // **come into** money, be paid

¶ [I] **received** [my] bonus today.

⑤ [begin, set in]

enter the rainy season // **become** evening, night **falls**

¶ It has suddenly gotten hot **since the beginning** of August 〖It suddenly got hot **from the beginning** of August〗.

haitatsu 〖n, ~*suru*〗 **delivery**

milk **delivery** // newspaper **delivery** // mail **delivery**

¶ Please **deliver** this table tomorrow.

¶郵便は一日に何回配達されますか。

(Yūbin wa ichinichi ni nankai *haitatsu* saremasu ka?)

¶ How many times **is** the mail **delivered** a day?

haiyū 俳優〖名〗

映画俳優 (eiga-*haiyū*)　かぶき俳優 (kabuki-*haiyū*)

¶あの俳優の名前を知っていますか。

(Ano *haiyū* no namae o shitte imasu ka?)

¶あの俳優はたいへん人気があります。

(Ano *haiyū* wa taihen ninki ga arimasu.)

haiyū 〖n〗 **actor, actress**

a film **actor,** film **actress** // a kabuki **player**

¶ Do you know the name of that **actor** 〖**actress**〗?

¶ That **actor** 〖**actress**〗 is very popular.

haizara 灰ざら〖名〗

¶灰ざらはどこですか。(*Haizara* wa doko desu ka?)

haizara 〖n〗 **ashtray**

¶ Where is **the ashtray?**

haji 恥〖名〗

¶みんなの前で恥をかきました。

(Minna no mae de *haji* o kakimashita.)

¶子供が悪いことをすれば，親の恥になります。(Kodomo ga warui koto o sureba, oya no *haji* ni narimasu.)

haji 〖n〗 **shame, disgrace, humiliation**

¶ [I] **disgraced** [myself] in front of everyone.

¶ If a child does something bad, it **brings shame** to its parents.

hajimaru 始まる〖動Ⅰ〗

¶次の授業は3時に始まります。

(Tsugi no jugyō wa sanji ni *hajimarimasu.*)

¶会議はいつ始まりましたか。(Kaigi wa itsu *hajimarimashita* ka?)

⇔owaru 終わる

hajimaru 〖vⅠ〗 **begin, commence**

¶ The next class **starts** at three o'clock.

¶ When did the meeting **start?**

hajime 初め〖名〗

¶3月の初めに試験があります。

(Sangatsu no *hajime* ni shiken ga arimasu.)

¶夏の初めに旅行します。(Natsu no

hajime 〖n〗 **the beginning, the start**

¶ There's an exam **early** in March.

¶ [I] will go on a trip at **the begin-**

hajime ni ryokō shimasu.)

⇔**owari** 終わり

hajime 始め〖名〗

¶始めから終わりまで，みんな熱心に彼の話を聞きました。(*Hajime* kara owari made, minna nesshin ni kare no hanashi o kikimashita.)

¶あの映画の始めのほうはあまりおもしろくありません。(Ano eiga no *hajime* no hō wa amari omoshiroku arimasen.)

⇔**owari** 終わり

hajimemashite 初めまして〖連〗

¶初めまして，どうぞよろしく。

(*Hajimemashite*, dōzo yoroshiku.)

hajimeru 始める〖動Ⅱ〗

①[ものごとを開始する]

¶さあ，勉強を始めましょう。(Sā, benkyō o *hajimemashō*.)

¶今日は10ページから始めます。

(Kyō wa jippēji kara *hajimemasu*.)

②[ある動作・作用が始まることを表す]

¶桜の花が咲き始めました。(Sakura no hana ga saki*hajimemashita*.)

¶9月から日本語を習い始めました。

(Kugatsu kara Nihongo o narai-*hajimemashita*.)

＊「動詞（基幹の形）＋始める(hajimeru)」の形で使う。

⇔**oeru** 終える

hajimete 初めて〖副〗

¶今年の夏，初めて富士山に登りました。(Kotoshi no natsu, *hajimete*

---

ning of the summer.

hajime 〚n〛 **beginning, outset**

¶ Everyone listened to his talk 〚story〛 intently from **beginning** to end.

¶ **The first part** of that movie isn't very interesting.

hajimemashite 〚compd〛 an expression used when meeting someone for the first time

¶ **How do you do?** I'm pleased to make your acquaintance.

(-)hajimeru 〚v Ⅱ〛 **start** (something); **start ~ing**

① [start (something)]

¶ Well, **let's start** class.

¶ Today [we] **will be starting** from page 10.

② [start ~ing, start to ~]

¶ The cherry blossoms **have started** to bloom.

¶ [I] **started** studying Japanese in September.

＊ Used in the pattern "verb (stem form) + *-hajimeru*."

hajimete 〚adv〛 **for the first time**

¶ This summer [I] climbed Mount Fuji **for the first time.**

Fujisan ni noborimashita.)

¶今日、初めて日本語で電話しました。
(Kyō, *hajimete* Nihongo de denwa shimashita.)

haka 墓〖名〗

墓場 (*haka*ba)　墓参り (*haka*mairi)

¶お寺の後ろにお墓があります。
(Otera no ushiro ni o*haka* ga arimasu.)

¶先祖のお墓にお参りしました。
(Senzo no o*haka* ni omairi shimashita.)

hakari はかり〖名〗

はかりで量る (*hakari* de hakaru)

¶牛肉をはかりにかけて、100グラムずつに分けてください。 (Gyūniku o *hakari* ni kakete, hyakuguramu zutsu ni wakete kudasai.)

hakaru 計る〖動Ⅰ〗

身長を計る (shinchō o *hakaru*)

¶熱を計ったら 39 度ありました。
(Netsu o *hakattara* sanjūkudo arimashita.)

hakaru 測る〖動Ⅰ〗

面積を測る (menseki o *hakaru*)

¶池の深さを測ってみました。 (Ike no fukasa o *hakatte* mimashita.)

hakaru 量る〖動Ⅰ〗

目方を量る (mekata o *hakaru*)

¶体重を量ったら、60 キログラムありました。 (Taijū o *hakattara*, rokujikkiroguramu arimashita.)

hakken 発見〖名, ～する〗

¶アメリカ大陸はだれが発見しました

haka 〖n〗 **grave, tomb**

graveyard, cemetery // visit to **a grave**

¶ There are **graves** behind the temple.

¶ [I] visited the family **tombs.**

hakari 〖n〗 **scales, balance**

weigh on **a scale**

¶ Please weigh the beef on **the scale** and divide it into hundred-gram portions.

hakaru 〖v I〗 **measure**

measure someone's height

¶ When **I took** [my] temperature, it was 39 degrees.

hakaru 〖v I〗 **measure**

measure the area

¶ [I] **measured** the depth of the pond.

hakaru 〖v I〗 **measure**

weigh something 〚someone〛

¶ When **I weighed** myself 〚him, her〛, my 〚his, her〛 weight was 60 kilos.

hakase ☞ **hakushi**

hakken 〖n, ～*suru*〗 **discovery**

¶ Who **discovered** the American

¶ Today [I] made [my] **first** telephone call in Japanese.

か。 (Amerika-tairiku wa dare ga *hakken* shimashita ka?)

¶早くがんの薬が発見されるといいですね。 (Hayaku gan no kusuri ga *hakken* sareru to ii desu ne.)

hakkiri はっきり〖副, 〜する〗
¶名前ははっきり書いてください。
(Namae wa *hakkiri* kaite kudasai.)
¶今日は富士山がはっきり見えます。
(Kyō wa Fujisan ga *hakkiri* mie-masu.)
¶ゆうべあまり寝なかったので、今日は頭がはっきりしません。 (Yūbe amari nenakatta node, kyō wa atama ga *hakkiri* shimasen.)
＊「はっきりと (hakkiri to)」とも言う。

hakkō 発行〖名, 〜する〗
発行所 (*hakkō*jo) 発行者 (*hakkō*-sha)
¶その本は来月発行される予定です。
(Sono hon wa raigetsu *hakkō* sareru yotei desu.)
¶この雑誌は毎週発行されます。
(Kono zasshi wa maishū *hakkō* saremasu.)

(-) hako (-)箱〖名, 尾〗

1〖名〗
本箱 (hon*bako*)
¶その箱の中に何が入っていますか。
(Sono *hako* no naka ni nani ga haitte imasu ka?)

2〖尾〗
¶たばこを二箱買ってきてください。

continent?

¶ I hope that a drug for cancer **will be discovered** soon.

hakkiri 〚adv, ~*suru*〛 **clearly, distinctly**

¶ Please write your name **clearly.**

¶ Mount Fuji can be seen **clearly** today.

¶ My head **is fuzzy** today as I didn't get much sleep last night.

＊ Variant: *hakkiri to.*

hakkō 〚n, ~*suru*〛 **publish, issue publisher** (company) // **publisher** (person within a publishing company in charge of the publication of a given book)

¶ That book is scheduled **to be published** next month.

¶ This magazine **comes out** monthly.

(-)hako 〚n, suf〛 **box, case, package, container**

1 〚n〛 box, case, package
a book**case**
¶ What is in that **box?**

2 〚suf〛 the counter for packages or cases of something

(Tabako o futa*hako* katte kite kudasai.)

¶ Please buy me two **packs** of cigarettes.

hakobu 運ぶ〖動Ⅰ〗
¶重い物は車で運びましょう。 (Omoi mono wa kuruma de *hakobimashō*.)
¶この荷物をわたしの部屋へ運んでください。 (Kono nimotsu o watashi no heya e *hakonde* kudasai.)

hakobu 〖v I〗 carry, transport
¶ **Let's take** the heavy things by car 〚taxi, van, truck, etc.〛.
¶ Please **take** this luggage 〚these bags, boxes, etc.〛 to my room.

haku 掃く〖動Ⅰ〗
ほうきで庭を掃く (hōki de niwa o *haku*)
¶神社の周りは，いつも きれいに 掃いてあります。 (Jinja no mawari wa, itsu mo kirei ni *haite* arimasu.)

haku 〖v I〗 sweep
sweep the garden 〚yard〛 with a broom
¶ The grounds of a shrine are always nicely **swept.**

haku はく〖動Ⅰ〗
¶くつ下をはかないで，くつをはきました。 (Kutsushita o *hakanaide*, kutsu o *hakimashita*.)
¶彼女はいつもズボンをはいています。 (Kanojo wa itsu mo zubon o *haite* imasu.)
⇔nugu 脱ぐ

haku 〖v I〗 put on, wear (something below the waist)
¶ [I] **put on** shoes **without putting on** socks.
¶ She always **has on** slacks.

hakubutsukan 博物館〖名〗
¶国立博物館はどこですか。 (Kokuritsu-*hakubutsukan* wa doko desu ka?)
¶日曜日に博物館へ見学に行きました。 (Nichiyōbi ni *hakubutsukan* e kengaku ni ikimashita.)

hakubutsukan 〖n〗 museum
¶ Where is the National **Museum?**
¶ [We] went to **the museum** on Sunday.

hakushi 博士〖名〗
¶田中教授は文学博士です。 (Tanaka kyōju wa bungaku-*hakushi* desu.)
¶田中博士の講義はたいへん おもしろいです。 (Tanaka *hakushi* no kōgi

hakushi 〖n〗 doctor, holder of a doctorate
¶ Professor Tanaka **has a doctorate** in literature.
¶ **Dr.** Tanaka's lectures are very interesting.

wa taihen omoshiroi desu.)

＊「博士(hakase)」とも言う。

hameru　はめる〖動Ⅱ〗

指輪をはめる (yubiwa o *hameru*)

¶秋子さんは革の手袋をはめています。
(Akiko san wa kawa no tebukuro o *hamete* imasu.)

han　判〖名〗

¶ここに判を押してください。 (Koko ni *han* o oshite kudasai.)

¶この領収書には判がありません。
(Kono ryōshūsho ni wa *han* ga arimasen.)

＊「判こ(hanko)」とも言う。

-han　-半〖尾〗

¶今，9時半です。 (Ima, kuji *han* desu.)

¶もう2時間半働きました。 (Mō nijikan *han* hatarakimashita.)

hana　花〖名〗

花見 (*hana*mi)

¶春になって，庭に花が咲きだしました。 (Haru ni natte, niwa ni *hana* ga sakidashimashita.)

¶花びんの花が枯れました。 (Kabin no *hana* ga karemashita.)

hana　鼻〖名〗

¶子供が転んで，鼻にけがをしました。
(Kodomo ga koronde, *hana* ni kega o shimashita.)

¶あの子はよく鼻血を出します。(Ano ko wa yoku *hana*ji o dashimasu.)

hana　はな〖名〗

¶風邪を引いたので，はなが出て困り

＊ Variant: *hakase*.

hameru 〚v II〛 **put on, pull on, wear** (ring, gloves, etc.)

put on a ring

¶ Akiko **is wearing** leather gloves.

han 〚n〛 **stamp, seal, seal impression**

¶ Please stamp **your seal** here.

¶ This receipt does not bear **a seal**.

＊ Variant: *hanko*.

-han 〚suf〛 **half**

¶ It's now 9:**30**.

¶ [I]'ve already worked for two and **a half** hours.

hana 〚n〛 **flower, blossom**

cherry-blossom viewing

¶ With the coming of spring, **flowers** started to bloom in the garden.

¶ **The flowers** in the vase have withered.

hana 〚n〛 **nose**

¶ The child fell and injured **[his] nose.**

¶ That child often has **nose**bleeds.

hana 〚n〛 **nasal mucus**

¶ I caught a cold and am now trou-

ます。(Kaze o hiita node, *hana* ga dete komarimasu.)

¶はなをかみなさい。(*Hana* o kaminasai.)

hanareru 離れる〖動Ⅱ〗

①[二つのものの間の距離が開く]

¶ここから5キロほど離れた所に池があります。(Koko kara gokiro hodo *hanareta* tokoro ni ike ga arimasu.)

②[ある場所から遠ざかる]
東京を離れる (Tōkyō o *hanareru*)
席を離れる (seki o *hanareru*)

③[いっしょであったものの間に距離ができる]

¶あの学生たちは親と離れて生活しています。(Ano gakuseitachi wa oya to *hanarete* seikatsu shite imasu.)

hanashi 話〖名〗

①[自分の感じていることや考えていることなどを人に言うこと]

¶今，父はお客さんと話をしています。(Ima, chichi wa okyakusan to *hanashi* o shite imasu.)

②[相談・交渉など]
話がまとまる (*hanashi* ga matomaru)

¶ちょっと話があるんですが…。(Chotto *hanashi* ga aru n desu ga…)

③[物語など]
昔話 (mukashi*banashi*)

hanasu 話す〖動Ⅰ〗

¶留学のことをお父さんに話しましたか。(Ryūgaku no koto o otōsan ni

bled by **a runny nose.**

¶ Blow **your nose.**

hanareru 〚v II〛 **be apart from; leave, depart; separate from**

① [be apart from, be at a distance from]

¶ There is a pond five kilometers **away** ⟦**at a distance of** five kilometers from here⟧.

② [leave, depart]

leave Tokyo // **step away from** one's seat ⟦desk⟧

③ [separate from, part from]

¶ Those students are living **away from** home (literally, **away from** their parents).

hanashi 〚n〛 **talk; consultation; story**

① [talk, conversation, speech]

¶ My father is now **talking** with a guest ⟦customer⟧.

② [consultation, negotiations]
come to an agreement

¶ There is **something I would like to talk with you about.**

③ [story, tale]
a legend, folk**tale**

hanasu 〚v I〛 **talk, speak, discuss, tell**

¶ Did you **talk with** your father

hanashimashita ka?)

¶日本語を話すことができますか。

(Nihongo o *hanasu* koto ga dekimasu ka?)

hanasu 放す〖動Ⅰ〗

小鳥を放す (kotori o *hanasu*)

¶池に魚を放しました。 (Ike ni sakana o *hanashimashita*.)

hanasu 離す〖動Ⅰ〗

①[二つのものの間をあける]

ハンドルから手を離す (handoru kara te o *hanasu*) 間を離す (aida o *hanasu*) 机と机を離す (tsukue to tsukue o *hanasu*)

②[視線を外してほかの方を見る]

¶赤ん坊から目を離さないでください。

(Akanbō kara me o *hanasanaide* kudasai.)

hanbai 販売〖名, ～する〗

販売店 (*hanbai*ten) 自動販売機 (jidō*hanbai*ki)

¶あの薬屋では化粧品の販売もしています。 (Ano kusuriya de wa keshōhin no *hanbai* mo shite imasu.)

¶汽車の中でもお弁当を販売していますか。 (Kisha no naka de mo obentō o *hanbai* shite imasu ka?)

hanbun 半分〖名〗

¶りんごを半分ずつ食べましょう。

(Ringo o *hanbun* zutsu tabemashō.)

¶これを半分に分けてください。(Kore o *hanbun* ni wakete kudasai.)

handan 判断〖名, ～する〗

about studying abroad?

¶ Can you **speak** Japanese?

hanasu 〖v I〗 **let go, release**

set a small bird **free**

¶ [I] **let** the fish **loose** in the pond 〚pool〛.

hanasu 〖v I〗 **separate, divide; remove one's eyes from**

① [separate, divide two things]

take one's hand(s) **off** the handle 〚steering wheel, handlebar, doorknob, etc.〛 // **move** two things **apart** 〚**further apart**〛 // **move** the desks **apart**

② [remove one's eyes from]

¶ Please **don't take your eyes off** the baby 〚Please **keep your eyes on** the baby〛.

hanbai 〖n, ～*suru*〗 **sales, selling**

a shop, store // a **vending** machine

¶ That drugstore also **sells** cosmetics.

¶ Are box lunches **on sale** on the train?

hanbun 〖n〗 **half**

¶ Let's each have **half** of the apple.

¶ Please divide this **in half**.

handan 〖n, ～*suru*〗 **judgment, decision**

¶どちらがいいか判断に迷っています。(Dochira ga ii ka *handan* ni mayotte imasu.)

¶I am having trouble **deciding** which would be better.

¶それがいいか悪いかは，自分で判断してください。(Sore ga ii ka warui ka wa, jibun de *handan* shite kudasai.)

¶Please **judge** for yourself whether that is good or bad.

handobaggu ハンドバッグ〖名〗
ハンドバッグを開ける (*handobaggu* o akeru)

handobaggu 〚n〛 handbag, purse, pocketbook
open **a handbag**

¶新しいハンドバッグを買いました。(Atarashii *handobaggu* o kaimashita.)

¶[I] bought a new **handbag**.

＊「ハンドバック (handobakku)」とも言う。

＊Variant: *handobakku*.

handoru ハンドル〖名〗

①〔ドアの取っ手〕
¶ハンドルを回してドアを開けました。(*Handoru* o mawashite doa o akemashita.)

handoru 〚n〛 doorknob, door handle; steering wheel

① [doorknob, door handle]
¶[I] turned **the doorknob** and opened the door.

②〔自動車などの手で握って回す部分〕
¶ハンドルを左に切って，前から来る車をよけました。(*Handoru* o hidari ni kitte, mae kara kuru kuruma o yokemashita.)

② [steering wheel, handlebar]
¶Turning **the wheel** to the left, [I] avoided hitting the oncoming car.

hane 羽〖名〗
¶鳥は羽を広げて飛びます。(Tori wa *hane* o hirogete tobimasu.)

hane 〚n〛 wing
¶Birds spread **their wings** and fly.

¶つるは羽にけがをしていました。(Tsuru wa *hane* ni kega o shite imashita.)

¶The crane had an injured **wing**.

hane 羽根〖名〗
赤い羽根 (akai *hane*)　　羽根つき (*hane*tsuki)

hane 〚n〛 feather, down
a red **feather** // battledore and shuttlecock

173

¶羽根布団を買いました。(*Hane*buton o kaimashita.)

haneru 跳ねる〚動Ⅱ〛

①［飛び上がる，おどり上がる］
馬が跳ねる (uma ga *haneru*)

②［水やどろなどが飛び散る］
¶どろ水が跳ねてズボンが汚れました。(Doromizu ga *hanete* zubon ga yogoremashita.)

han'i 範囲〚名〛

¶試験の範囲を教えてください。(Shiken no *han'i* o oshiete kudasai.)

¶地震で広い範囲に被害が出ました。(Jishin de hiroi *han'i* ni higai ga demashita.)

hankachi ハンカチ〚名〛

ハンカチで手をふく (*hankachi* de te o fuku)

¶いつもハンカチを2枚持っています。(Itsu mo *hankachi* o nimai motte imasu.)

hannichi 半日〚名〛

¶仕事は半日で終わりました。(Shigoto wa *hannichi* de owarimashita.)

¶土曜には半日だけ働きます。(Doyō ni wa *hannichi* dake hatarakimasu.)

hansei 反省〚名，～する〛

¶あの人は悪いことをしても，少しも反省しません。(Ano hito wa warui koto o shite mo, sukoshi mo *hansei* shimasen.)

hansha 反射〚名，～する〛

haneru 〚v II〛 **leap, jump; spatter, splash**

① [leap, jump, spring, prance]
a horse **bucks**

② [spatter, splash]
¶ Muddy water **spattered** [my] trousers and dirtied them.

han'i 〚n〛 **extent, scope, bounds, limits**

¶ Please tell us what the exam **will cover.**

¶ The earthquake caused damage over a wide **area.**

hankachi 〚n〛 **handkerchief**

wipe one's hands on **a handkerchief**

¶ [I] always carry two **handkerchiefs** with [me].

hanko ☞ **han**

hannichi 〚n〛 **half a day, a half day**

¶ The work was finished in **half a day.**

¶ [I] only work **half a day** on Saturday.

hansei 〚n, ~*suru*〛 **self-examination, reflection, reconsideration**

¶ Even when [he] does something bad, [he] **has no second thoughts** whatsoever.

hansha 〚n, ~*suru*〛 (physical) **reflection**

0

¶鏡は光を反射します。(Kagami wa hikari o *hansha* shimasu.)

¶月は太陽の光を反射して光っています。(Tsuki wa taiyō no hikari o *hansha* shite hikatte imasu.)

hantai 反対〖名, 〜する〗

①[あることに対して逆の関係にあること]
反対の方向 (*hantai* no hōkō) 駅の反対側 (eki no *hantai*gawa)

②[ある意見や立場などに逆らうこと]
¶わたしはその考えに反対です。(Watashi wa sono kangae ni *hantai* desu.)

¶父に反対されて留学をあきらめました。(Chichi ni *hantai* sarete ryūgaku o akiramemashita.)

↔**sansei** 賛成

hantō 半島〖名〗

¶あの半島の周りを船で回りました。(Ano *hantō* no mawari o fune de mawarimashita.)

¶日本でいちばん大きい半島は紀伊半島です。(Nihon de ichiban ookii *hantō* wa Kii-*hantō* desu.)

hantoshi 半年〖名〗

¶日本に来てからもう半年になります。(Nihon ni kite kara mō *hantoshi* ni narimasu.)

¶半年後に結婚します。(*Hantoshi*go ni kekkon shimasu.)

hantsuki 半月〖名〗

¶日本へ来るのが予定より半月遅れました。(Nihon e kuru no ga yotei

¶ Mirrors **reflect** light.

¶ The moon shines **reflecting** the rays of the sun.

hantai 〚n, ~*suru*〛 reverse, opposite; opposition, objection

① [the reverse, opposite, contrary]
the **opposite** direction // the **other** side of the station

② [opposition, objection]
¶ I **am opposed** to that idea.

¶ I gave up studying abroad as my father **was against it.**

hantō 〚n〛 peninsula

¶ [I] went around that **peninsula** by boat.

¶ The biggest **peninsula** in Japan is the Kii **Peninsula.**

hantoshi 〚n〛 half a year, a half year

¶ **Half a year** has already passed since [I] came to Japan.

¶ I will get married in **half a year.**

hantsuki 〚n〛 half a month, a half month

¶ [My] coming to Japan was **a half**

yori *hantsuki* okuremashita.)

¶この半月の間に病気がずいぶんよく
なりました。　(Kono *hantsuki* no
aida ni byōki ga zuibun yoku narimashita.)

happyō　発表〖名, ～する〗

¶みんなの前で自分の意見を発表しま
した。(Minna no mae de jibun no
iken o *happyō* shimashita.)

¶あした，試験の結果が発表されます。
(Ashita, shiken no kekka ga *happyō*
saremasu.)

hara　腹〖名〗

①[胃や腸の部分]

腹が痛い (*hara* ga itai)　腹が減る
(*hara* ga heru)　腹がすく (*hara* ga
suku)　腹をこわす (*hara* o kowasu)

* 丁寧に言うときは，普通「おなか
(onaka)」と言う。

②[気持ち・感情などを表す]

腹が立つ (*hara* ga tatsu)

¶上田さんはそれを聞いて，たいへん
腹を立てました。(Ueda san wa sore
o kiite, taihen *hara* o tatemashita.)

harau　払う〖動Ⅰ〗

①[代金などを相手に渡す]

¶食事代はわたしが払います。　(Sho-
kujidai wa watashi ga *haraimasu*.)

¶もう授業料を払いましたか。　(Mō
jugyōryō o *haraimashita* ka?)

②[たたいたりして取り除く]

¶ブラシで洋服のほこりを払いました。
(Burashi de yōfuku no hokori o
haraimashita.)

month later than planned.

¶ In the past **half month** [my] illness
has greatly improved.

happyō 〚n, ～*suru*〛 announcement, making public

¶ [I] **set forth** my opinion in front of
everyone.

¶ The results of the exam **will be
announced** tomorrow.

hara 〚n〛 stomach; spirit

① [stomach, abdomen]

have a **stomach**ache, have a pain in
one's stomach // be hungry // be
hungry // upset **one's stomach**

* *Onaka* is more polite than *hara*.

② [spirit, heart, mind, intention]

lose **one's temper,** be angry

¶ When [Mr.] Ueda heard that, [he]
became very **angry.**

harau 〚v Ⅰ〛 pay; clear away, brush
off

① [pay]

¶ I'll **pay** the restaurant bill.

¶ **Have you paid** your tuition yet?

② [clear away, sweep away, brush
off]

¶ [I] **removed** lint from [my] suit
〚dress, etc.〛 with a brush.

¶オーバーの雪を払って家に入りました。 (Ōbā no yuki o *haratte* ie ni hairimashita.)

¶ [I] **brushed** the snow off of [my] overcoat and came into the house.

hare 晴れ〖名〗

¶あしたは晴れ後曇りでしょう。 (Ashita wa *hare* nochi kumori deshō.)

¶晴れの日には，ここから富士山が見えます。 (*Hare* no hi ni wa, koko kara Fujisan ga miemasu.)

⇨**kumori** 曇り

hare 〖n〗 **fair weather**

¶ Tomorrow will probably be **fair,** later cloudy.

¶ On a **clear** day one can see Mount Fuji from here.

hareru 晴れる〖動Ⅱ〗

¶午後はたぶん晴れるでしょう。 (Gogo wa tabun *hareru* deshō.)

¶今日はよく晴れて，いいお天気になりました。 (Kyō wa yoku *harete,* ii otenki ni narimashita.)

⇨**kumoru** 曇る

hareru 〖v Ⅱ〗 **become clear, clear up**

¶ **It will** probably **become clear** in the afternoon.

¶ **It's cleared up** nicely and become a fine day today.

hari 針〖名〗

¶この針に糸を通してください。 (Kono *hari* ni ito o tooshite kudasai.)

¶時計の針が5時を指しています。 (Tokei no *hari* ga goji o sashite imasu.)

hari 〖n〗 **needle, pin,** (clock) **hands, indicator**

¶ Please thread this **needle** for me.

¶ **The hands** of the clock 〖watch〗 show five o'clock.

haru 春〖名〗

¶冬が過ぎて，春が来ました。 (Fuyu ga sugite, *haru* ga kimashita.)

¶春と秋とどちらが好きですか。 (*Haru* to aki to dochira ga suki desu ka?)

haru 〖n〗 **spring, springtime**

¶ Winter is over and **spring** has come.

¶ Which do you like better, **spring** or fall?

haru 張る〖動Ⅰ〗

①[伸び広がる，伸ばし広げる]
幕を張る (maku o *haru*) 帆を張る (ho o *haru*) 木が根を張る (ki ga

haru 〖v Ⅰ〗 **stretch out, spread out; cover; stretch, extend**

① [stretch out, spread out]

stretch out a curtain // **unfurl** a sail

ne o *haru*)

¶川のそばにテントを張りました。

(Kawa no soba ni tento o *harima-shita*.)

②[一面に覆う]

¶池に氷が張りました。(Ike ni koori ga *harimashita*.)

③[綱や糸などを引き渡す]

糸を張る (ito o *haru*)

¶そこは綱を張って人が入れないようにしてあります。(Soko wa tsuna o *hatte* hito ga hairenai yō ni shite arimasu.)

haru はる〖動Ⅰ〗

¶この手紙に切手をはって出してください。 (Kono tegami ni kitte o *hatte* dashite kudasai.)

¶壁にきれいな紙をはりましょう。

(Kabe ni kirei na kami o *hari-mashō*.)

hasami はさみ〖名〗

¶はさみで紙を切ります。(*Hasami* de kami o kirimasu.)

¶このはさみはよく切れます。 (Kono *hasami* wa yoku kiremasu.)

hasamu はさむ〖動Ⅰ〗

¶料理をはしではさんで食べます。

(Ryōri o hashi de *hasande* tabe-masu.)

¶写真を本の間にはさんでおきました。(Shashin o hon no aida ni *hasande* okimashita.)

hashi 橋〖名〗

橋を架ける (*hashi* o kakeru)

// a tree is **deep-rooted**

¶ [I] **pitched** a tent beside the river.

② [cover]

¶ The pond **is 〚was〛 covered** with ice.

③ [stretch, extend]

stretch a thread between two points

¶ That area **is roped off** so no one can enter.

haru 〖v I〗 stick, paste, affix

¶ Please **put** a stamp on this letter and mail it.

¶ **Let's put** some pretty wallpaper **up** on the walls.

hasami 〖n〗 scissors, shears

¶ One cuts paper with **scissors.**

¶ These **scissors** cut well.

hasamu 〖v I〗 put between, insert

¶ [We] **pick up** food **between** [our] two chopsticks and eat it.

¶ [I] **put** the photo away **between** the leaves of a book.

hashi 〖n〗 bridge

build **a bridge**

¶この橋を渡って，向こう側に行きましょう。 (Kono *hashi* o watatte, mukōgawa ni ikimashō.)

¶ Let's cross this **bridge** to the other side.

hashi 端〖名〗

¶危ないから，道の端を歩きましょう。 (Abunai kara, michi no *hashi* o arukimashō.)

¶このひもの端を持ってください。 (Kono himo no *hashi* o motte kudasai.)

hashi 〖n〗 **end, tip, edge**

¶ Let's walk along **the edge** of the road to be safe (literally, because it's dangerous).

¶ Please hold **the end** of this string 〖cord, band, ribbon, etc.〗.

hashi はし〖名〗

¶あなたははしで食べることができますか。 (Anata wa *hashi* de taberu koto ga dekimasu ka?)

¶はしが使えませんから，フォークをください。 (*Hashi* ga tsukaemasen kara, fōku o kudasai.)

hashi 〖n〗 **chopsticks**

¶ Can you eat with **chopsticks?**

¶ Please give me a fork—I can't use **chopsticks.**

hashira 柱〖名〗

電信柱 (denshin*bashira*)

¶暗かったので柱に頭をぶつけました。 (Kurakatta node *hashira* ni atama o butsukemashita.)

¶子供が柱の周りを回って遊んでいます。 (Kodomo ga *hashira* no mawari o mawatte asonde imasu.)

hashira 〖n〗 **pillar, column, post, pole**

a telephone **pole,** electric **pole**

¶ As it was dark, [I] bumped my head on **a pillar.**

¶ The children are playing running around **the pole** 〖pillar〗.

hashiru 走る〖動Ⅰ〗

①[人や動物などが足を速く動かして行く]

犬が走る (inu ga *hashiru*)　馬が走る (uma ga *hashiru*)

¶遅くなったので，駅へ走っていきました。 (Osoku natta node, eki e *hashitte* ikimashita.)

②[船や車などが速い速度で進む.

hashiru 〖vⅠ〗 **run**

① [(animals and people) run]

a dog **runs** // a horse **gallops**

¶ As [I] was late, [I] **ran** to the station.

② [(vehicles) run, proceed at speed]

ヨットが水の上を走る (yotto ga mizu no ue o *hashiru*) 急行列車が走る (kyūkō-ressha ga *hashiru*)

¶町の中を車がたくさん走っています。 (Machi no naka o kuruma ga takusan *hashitte* imasu.)

a yacht **sails through** the water // an express train **runs**

¶ There **is** much **traffic** in the city.

hata 旗〖名〗

¶祭日には家の前に旗を立てます。 (Saijitsu ni wa ie no mae ni *hata* o tatemasu.)

¶子供が旗を振っています。(Kodomo ga *hata* o futte imasu.)

hata 〚n〛 **flag, banner**

¶ [We] fly **a flag** in front of the house on holidays.

¶ The children are waving **flags**.

hatachi 二十歳〖名〗

¶弟は今年二十歳になりました。 (Otōto wa kotoshi *hatachi* ni narimashita.)

¶日本の法律では二十歳から大人です。 (Nihon no hōritsu de wa *hatachi* kara otona desu.)

hatachi 〚n〛 **20 years of age**

¶ My younger brother became **20 years old** this year.

¶ In Japanese law one becomes an adult at **20.**

hatake 畑〖名〗

麦畑 (mugi*batake*) 野菜畑 (yasai-*batake*)

¶この畑では何を作っていますか。 (Kono *hatake* de wa nani o tsukutte imasu ka?)

¶この村では田より畑のほうが多いです。 (Kono mura de wa ta yori *hatake* no hō ga ooi desu.)

hatake 〚n〛 **cultivated field, dry field**

a wheat 〚barley〛 **field** // a vegetable **field**

¶ What are you growing in this **field?**

¶ This village has more **dry fields** than paddy fields.

hataraki 働き〖名〗

①[働いて仕事をすること]

働き者 (*hataraki*mono)

¶働きが過ぎると，病気になってしまいますよ。(*Hataraki* ga sugiru to, byōki ni natte shimaimasu yo.)

hataraki 〚n〛 **work; working, action; ability**

① [work, labor]

a good **worker,** a hard**working** person

¶ If you **work** too much, you will become ill.

②[あるものの機能・作用など]
胃の働き (i no *hataraki*)　薬の働き (kusuri no *hataraki*)
¶あの人は頭の働きが鋭いです。(Ano hito wa atama no *hataraki* ga surudoi desu.)

③[仕事をする才能，仕事をして収入などを得る能力]
働きのある人 (*hataraki* no aru hito)
¶中村さんはあまり働きがないので，生活が苦しいです。(Nakamura san wa amari *hataraki* ga nai node, seikatsu ga kurushii desu.)

hataraku 働く〖動Ⅰ〗

①[仕事をする，収入を得るために労働する]
¶母は毎日よく働きます。(Haha wa mainichi yoku *hatarakimasu*.)
¶兄は銀行で働いています。(Ani wa ginkō de *hataraite* imasu.)

②[あるものが機能する]
頭がよく働かない (atama ga yoku *hatarakanai*)　引力が働く (inryoku ga *hataraku*)

hatasu 果たす〖動Ⅰ〗
約束を果たす (yakusoku o *hatasu*)
使命を果たす (shimei o *hatasu*)
¶彼はやっと目的を果たしました。(Kare wa yatto mokuteki o *hatashimashita*.)
¶責任を果たして安心しました。(Sekinin o *hatashite* anshin shimashita.)

-hatsu -発〖尾〗

② [working, function, operation, action]
the function [[working]] of the stomach // the action of a medicine
¶ [He] is sharp-**witted** [[has a keen **intelligence**]].

③ [ability (to do a job), capability (of getting a good income)]
an able [[resourceful]] person, a good provider
¶ Because [Mr.] Nakamura **is a poor provider,** they have trouble making ends meet.

hataraku [[v I]]　to work, labor; to work, function

① [to work, labor]

¶ My mother **works** hard every day.

¶ My older brother **works** at a bank.

② [to work, function, operate]
one's head **is sluggish** // gravity **comes into play** [[operation]]

hatasu [[v I]]　achieve, accomplish, realize, discharge, fulfill
carry out one's promises // **accomplish** one's mission
¶ He finally **achieved** his objective.

¶ I am relieved **to have fulfilled** my responsibility [[**discharged** my obligation]].

-hatsu [[suf]]　departing (from ~, at ~)

¶東京発の電車に乗りました。(Tōkyō *hatsu* no densha ni norimashita.)

¶5時発の急行で行きましょう。

(Goji *hatsu* no kyūkō de ikimashō.)

hatsuka 二十日〖名〗

①[日付を表す]

¶わたしの誕生日は五月二十日です。

(Watashi no tanjōbi wa gogatsu *hatsuka* desu.)

②[日数を表す]

¶病気で二十日も学校を休みました。

(Byōki de *hatsuka* mo gakkō o yasumimashita.)

hatsumei 発明〖名, 〜する〗

発明家 (*hatsumei*ka)

¶だれがラジオを発明しましたか。

(Dare ga rajio o *hatsumei* shimashita ka?)

¶電話が発明されて, たいへん便利になりました。 (Denwa ga *hatsumei* sarete, taihen benri ni narimashita.)

hatsuon 発音〖名, 〜する〗

¶あの人はたいへん発音がいいです。

(Ano hito wa taihen *hatsuon* ga ii desu.)

¶先生, もう一度発音してください。

(Sensei, mō ichido *hatsuon* shite kudasai.)

hattatsu 発達〖名, 〜する〗

¶この国は工業が発達しています。

(Kono kuni wa kōgyō ga *hattatsu* shite imasu.)

¶この辺も交通が発達して便利になりました。 (Kono hen mo kotsū ga

¶ [I] took the train **leaving from** Tokyo.

¶ Let's go on the five o'clock express.

hatsuka 〚n〛 **the 20th of the month; 20 days**

① [the 20th of the month]

¶ My birthday is May **20.**

② [20 days]

¶ [I] stayed home from school **20 days** due to illness.

hatsumei 〚n, ~*suru*〛 **invention an inventor**

¶ Who **invented** the radio?

¶ **The invention** of the telephone has made life very convenient.

hatsuon 〚n, ~*suru*〛 **pronunciation**

¶ [He] has very good **pronunciation** 〚has hardly any accent〛.

¶ Please **pronounce** it again (said to one's teacher or professor).

hattatsu 〚n, ~*suru*〛 **development, advance, progress**

¶ This country has an **advanced** industry.

¶ Transportation **has advanced** in this area and it has become more *hattatsu* shite benri ni narimashita.)

hatten 発展〖名, ～する〗

¶駅ができてからこの辺は急に発展しました。 (Eki ga dekite kara kono hen wa kyū ni *hatten* shimashita.)

¶この会社は海外へも発展しています。 (Kono kaisha wa kaigai e mo *hatten* shite imasu.)

hayai 早い〖形〗

①〔ある基準・比較の時間より前である〕

¶わたしは毎日早く寝て、早く起きます。 (Watashi wa mainichi *hayaku* nete, *hayaku* okimasu.)

¶上田さんは中村さんよりいつも早く学校へ来ます。 (Ueda san wa Nakamura san yori itsu mo *hayaku* gakkō e kimasu.)

②〔ある基準の時間までには間がある〕

¶出発にはまだ早いから、コーヒーでも飲みましょう。 (Shuppatsu ni wa mada *hayai* kara, kōhii demo nomimashō.)

¶9時ですから，寝るにはまだ早いです。 (Kuji desu kara, neru ni wa mada *hayai* desu.)

⇔**osoi** 遅い

hayai 速い〖形〗

足が速い (ashi ga *hayai*) 流れが速い (nagare ga *hayai*)

¶船より飛行機のほうが速いです。 (Fune yori hikōki no hō ga *hayai* desu.)

¶もっと速く歩きましょう。 (Motto

convenient to live here.

hatten 〚n, ～*suru*〛 **expansion, growth**

¶ This area suddenly **developed** after the building of the station.

¶ This company **is expanding** overseas as well.

hayai 〚adj〛 **early**

① [early; be earlier than a set time]

¶ I go to bed **early** and get up **early** every day.

¶ [Miss] Ueda always comes to school **earlier** than [Mrs.] Nakamura.

② [early, too early, too soon; there is still time before a set time]

¶ **There's** still **some time left** before departure so let's have some coffee or something.

¶ As it's nine o'clock, it's still **too early** to go to bed.

hayai 〚adj〛 **fast, quick**

be a **fast** walker 〚runner〛 // a **rapid** stream, a **fast** current

¶ Airplanes **are faster** than ships.

¶ Let's walk **faster**.

hayaku arukimashō.)

⇔**osoi** 遅い

hayaru はやる〖動Ⅰ〗

¶悪い風邪がはやっています。(Warui kaze ga *hayatte* imasu.)

¶今，若い人の間ではどんな歌がはやっていますか。(Ima, wakai hito no aida de wa donna uta ga *hayatte* imasu ka?)

hayasa 速さ〖名〗

¶新幹線の速さはどのくらいですか。(Shinkansen no *hayasa* wa dono kurai desu ka?)

⇨**-sa -さ**

hayashi 林〖名〗

¶林の中で鳥が鳴いています。(*Hayashi* no naka de tori ga naite imasu.)

¶山や林の写真を写しました。(Yama ya *hayashi* no shashin o utsushimashita.)

hazu はず〖名〗

①〖ものごとの経過などから言って当然そうなる事情にあるということを表す〗

¶この漢字はもう習ったのだから，読めるはずですよ。(Kono kanji wa mō naratta no da kara, yomeru *hazu* desu yo.)

¶この道をまっすぐ行けば，大通りに出るはずです。(Kono michi o massugu ikeba, oodoori ni deru *hazu* desu.)

¶「飛行機は何時にここを出発するこ

hayaru 〚v I〛 be prevalent; be popular, be in fashion

¶ There's a bad flu virus **going around** now.

¶ What sorts of songs **are popular** among young people now?

hayasa 〚n〛 speed, rapidity

¶ What is **the speed** of the Shinkansen 〚bullet train〛?

hayashi 〚n〛 wood, woods, grove

¶ A bird is singing in **the woods.**

¶ [I] took pictures of mountains and **woods.**

hazu 〚n〛 ought to, should, be supposed to, be expected to

① [ought to, should; indicates that something ought to be or is expected to be so]

¶ Since you've already studied this *kanji*, you **should** be able to read it.

¶ If you go straight along this street, you **ought to** come out at a major thoroughfare.

とになっていますか。」 (Hikōki wa nanji ni koko o shuppatsu suru koto ni natte imasu ka?) 「ちょうど 12 時に出発するはずです。」(Chōdo jūniji ni shuppatsu suru *hazu* desu.)

②［当然なこととして予定されていることなどが実現に至らなかったような場合に使う］

¶上田さんは今年の4月に大学を卒業するはずだったが，都合で1年延ばしたそうです。(Ueda san wa kotoshi no shigatsu ni daigaku o sotsugyō suru *hazu* datta ga, tsugō de ichinen nobashita sō desu.)

¶飛行機は 12 時にここに到着するはずでしたが，霧のため遅れるそうです。(Hikōki wa jūniji ni koko ni tōchaku suru *hazu* deshita ga, kiri no tame okureru sō desu.)

* 「はずだった (hazu datta)」の形で使うことが多い。

③［常識的に考えてとてもそういうことはありえないということを表す］

¶子供にそんな重い物が持てるはずはありません。 (Kodomo ni sonna omoi mono ga moteru *hazu* wa arimasen.)

¶2か月日本語を習っただけで，こんな難しい本が読めるはずはありません。(Nikagetsu Nihongo o naratta dake de, konna muzukashii hon ga yomeru *hazu* wa arimasen.)

* 普通「はずはない (hazu wa nai)」

¶ "What time is the plane scheduled to depart?"

"It **is due to** take off at twelve o'clock sharp."

② [ought to have, should have; indicates that something that was expected to take place didn't]

¶ [Mr.] Ueda **was supposed to** graduate from college this April, but I hear that's been postponed one year due to personal circumstances.

¶ The plane **was supposed to** land here at twelve o'clock, but I hear it's been delayed due to fog.

* Usually used in the pattern "~ *hazu datta*."

③ [cannot be, hardly be possible that; indicates that something cannot be so according to common sense, etc.]

¶ A child **can hardly be expected** to be able to carry something that heavy.

¶ **No one can** read such a difficult book after having studied Japanese for only two months.

* Usually used in the pattern "~ *hazu wa nai*."

185

の形で使う。

hazukashii　恥ずかしい〖形〗

¶こんなに易しい質問に答えられなくては，恥ずかしいです。　(Konna ni yasashii shitsumon ni kotaerarenakute wa, *hazukashii* desu.)

¶恥ずかしくて，顔が赤くなりました。 (*Hazukashikute*, kao ga akaku narimashita.)

¶少女は恥ずかしそうに下を向きました。 (Shōjo wa *hazukashisō* ni, shita o mukimashita.)

hazureru　外れる〖動Ⅱ〗

①[取れて離れる]

¶ボタンが外れました。　(Botan ga *hazuremashita*.)

¶戸が外れてしまいました。　(To ga *hazurete* shimaimashita.)

②[予想やくじなどが当たらない]

くじが外れる (kuji ga *hazureru*)

¶今日の天気予報は外れました。(Kyō no tenki-yohō wa *hazuremashita*.)

¶彼の予想はよく外れます。(Kare no yosō wa yoku *hazuremasu*.)

↔ataru 当たる

③[正しいものごとからそれる]

歌の調子が外れる (uta no chōshi ga *hazureru*)

¶規則に外れたことをしてはいけません。 (Kisoku ni *hazureta* koto o shite wa ikemasen.)

hazusu　外す〖動Ⅰ〗

¶時計を外して，机の上に置きました。 (Tokei o *hazushite*, tsukue no ue

---

hazukashii 〚adj〛 **be ashamed, be embarrassed, be shy; be shameful, be disgraceful**

¶ [I] **am ashamed 〚embarrassed〛** not to be able to answer such a simple question.

¶ [I] **blushed out of shame 〚embarrassment〛**.

¶ The young girl looked **shyly** downward.

hazureru 〚v II〛 **come off, get loose; miss, go wide; depart from**

① [come off, get loose, get out of place, be dislocated]

¶ The button **has come undone.**

¶ The door **has come off its hinges.**

② [miss, go wide, be beside the point]

hold a **losing** ticket in a lottery

¶ Today's weather report **was off the mark.**

¶ He is often **disappointed in** his expectations.

③ [depart from, be contrary to, be out of line]

to sing **out of** tune

¶ One mustn't do anything **against** the rules.

hazusu 〚v I〛 **take off**

¶ [I] **took off** [my] watch and placed it on the desk.

ni okimashita.)

¶ちょっと眼鏡を外してください。

(Chotto megane o *hazushite* kudasai.)

heiki 平気〚形動〛

¶彼は冬でもシャツだけで平気です。

(Kare wa fuyu demo shatsu dake de *heiki* desu.)

¶あの子は平気な顔でうそをつきました。 (Ano ko wa *heiki* na kao de uso o tsukimashita.)

heikin 平均〚名，〜する〛

¶クラスの平均点は何点ですか。

(Kurasu no *heikin*ten wa nanten desu ka?)

¶平均して一日に何時間勉強しますか。

(*Heikin* shite ichinichi ni nanjikan benkyō shimasu ka?)

heitai 兵隊〚名〛

¶村の若い人はみんな兵隊に行ってしまいました。 (Mura no wakai hito wa minna *heitai* ni itte shimaimashita.)

¶戦争が終わって，兵隊はみんな帰ってきました。 (Sensō ga owatte, *heitai* wa minna kaette kimashita.)

heiwa 平和〚名，形動〛

平和運動 (*heiwa*-undō)　世界平和 (sekai-*heiwa*)

¶戦争が終わって，平和がもどってきました。 (Sensō ga owatte, *heiwa* ga modotte kimashita.)

¶平和な家庭をつくりたいです。

(*Heiwa* na katei o tsukuritai desu.)

heiki 〚adj-v〛 **calmness, unconcern, self-possession**

¶ He **thinks nothing of** going about in his shirt-sleeves even in the winter.

¶ That child **nonchalantly** 〚**boldfacedly, shamelessly**〛 told a lie.

heikin 〚n, ~*suru*〛 **average**

¶ What was the **average** mark 〚grade **average**〛 of the class?

¶ How many hours a day do you study **on the average?**

heitai 〚n〛 **soldier, sailor**

¶ The young people of the village have all gone away into **the military.**

¶ With the end of the war, all of **the soldiers** returned 〚have returned〛 home.

heiwa 〚n, adj-v〛 **peace, harmony**

the **peace** movement // world **peace**

¶ **Peace** was 〚has been〛 restored with the ending of the war.

¶ I want to create a **tranquil** home.

hen

hen 辺〖名〗

¶彼のうちはどの辺ですか。(Kare no uchi wa dono *hen* desu ka?)

¶この辺に電話がありますか。(Kono *hen* ni denwa ga arimasu ka?)

hen 変〖形動〗

¶門の前に変な人がいます。(Mon no mae ni *hen* na hito ga imasu.)

¶あの人は泣いたり笑ったりして、今日は少し変です。(Ano hito wa naitari warattari shite, kyō wa sukoshi *hen* desu.)

henji 返事〖名, ～する〗

①[呼びかけなどに対して答えること]

¶名前を呼んだら、返事をしてください。(Namae o yondara, *henji* o shite kudasai.)

②[受けた手紙に対する答えの手紙]

¶家から手紙が来たので、すぐ返事を出しました。(Ie kara tegami ga kita node, sugu *henji* o dashimashita.)

henka 変化〖名, ～する〗

¶日本語の動詞の変化を習いました。(Nihongo no dōshi no *henka* o naraimashita.)

¶この国では、一年じゅう気温があまり変化しません。(Kono kuni de wa, ichinenjū kion ga amari *henka* shimasen.)

henkō 変更〖名, ～する〗

¶スケジュールに変更があったら、すぐ連絡してください。(Sukejūru ni *henkō* ga attara, sugu renraku

---

hen 〖n〗 locality, region, neighborhood, vicinity

¶ In what **general vicinity** is his house?

¶ Is there a telephone **around** here 〖**near** here〗?

hen 〖adj-v〗 strange, odd

¶ There's a **strange-looking** person in front of the gate.

¶ [She] is acting a little **oddly** today, laughing and crying and the like.

henji 〖n, ～*suru*〗 answer, response, reply

① [verbal response, answer]

¶ Please **answer** when your name is called.

② [written reply]

¶ A letter came from home and [I] soon **answered** it.

henka 〖n, ～*suru*〗 change, variation; inflection, conjugation

¶ [I] studied **the conjugations** of Japanese verbs.

¶ The temperature **doesn't change** very much throughout the year in this country.

henkō 〖n, ～*suru*〗 change, alteration, modification

¶ If there should be **any change** in the schedule, please notify me with-shite kudasai.)

¶出発の予定を変更しました。(Shuppatsu no yotei o *henkō* shimashita.)

¶ [I] **changed** [my] scheduled time 〖day〗 of departure.

heru 減る〖動Ⅰ〗

人口が減る (jinkō ga *heru*)

¶病気で体重が5キロ減りました。(Byōki de taijū ga gokiro *herimashita*.)

¶これ以上収入が減ると困ります。(Kore ijō shūnyū ga *heru* to komarimasu.)

⇔**fueru** 増える ⇨**masu** 増す
genshō 減少

heru 〖vⅠ〗 decrease

the population **decreases**

¶ [I] **lost** five kilos due to illness.

¶ I don't know what I'll do if my income **decreases** any more than this.

heta 下手〖形動〗

¶上手な人も下手な人もみんないっしょに歌いました。(Jōzu na hito mo *heta* na hito mo minna issho ni utaimashita.)

¶日本語がまだ下手なので、早く上手になりたいです。(Nihongo ga mada *heta* na node, hayaku jōzu ni naritai desu.)

⇔**jōzu** 上手 ⇨**mazui** まずい
umai うまい

heta 〖adj-v〗 unskillful, poor at, awkward

¶ They all sang together, good singers and **bad** singers.

¶ As I'm still **poor at** Japanese, I want to become good at it as quickly as possible.

heya 部屋〖名〗

部屋代 (*heya*dai)

¶学校のそばに部屋を借りました。(Gakkō no soba ni *heya* o karimashita.)

¶わたしの部屋は2階にあります。(Watashi no *heya* wa nikai ni arimasu.)

heya 〖n〗 room, apartment

room rent, rent

¶ [I] rented **a room** 〖apartment〗 near the school.

¶ My **room** 〖apartment〗 is on the second floor.

hi 日〖名〗

hi 〖n〗 sun; sunlight; daytime; day

189

①〔太陽〕

¶日は東から昇って，西に沈みます。

(*Hi* wa higashi kara nobotte, nishi ni shizumimasu.)

②〔日光〕

日当たりがいい (*hi*atari ga ii)

¶ぬれた服を日に干しましょう。

(Nureta fuku o *hi* ni hoshimashō.)

¶海に行ったので，日に焼けました。

(Umi ni itta node, *hi* ni yakemashita.)

¶ここはよく日が当たります。 (Koko wa yoku *hi* ga atarimasu.)

③〔昼間の時間〕

¶だんだん日が短くなりました。

(Dandan *hi* ga mijikaku narimashita.)

¶夏は日が長くなります。 (Natsu wa *hi* ga nagaku narimasu.)

④〔1日，24時間〕

ある日 (aru *hi*)　その日 (sono *hi*)

次の日 (tsugi no *hi*)　天気のよい日 (tenki no yoi *hi*)

hi　火〔名〕

¶たばこの火を貸してください。

(Tabako no *hi* o kashite kudasai.)

¶ガスの火を消してください。 (Gasu no *hi* o keshite kudasai.)

¶ストーブの火をつけました。(Sutōbu no *hi* o tsukemashita.)

-hi　-費〔尾〕

交通費 (kōtsū*hi*)　生活費 (seikatsu-*hi*)　会費 (kai*hi*)　旅費 (ryo*hi*)

¶食費は一か月いくらぐらいかかりま

① [sun]

¶ **The sun** rises in the east and sets in the west.

② [sunlight]

be **sunny,** get much **sunlight**

¶ Let's dry the wet clothes in **the sun.**

¶ [I] got **sun**burned ⟦tanned⟧ at the ocean.

¶ It's nice and **sunny** here ⟦This spot gets lots of **sunshine**⟧.

③ [day, daytime]

¶ The days gradually got shorter.

¶ **The days** are longer in the summer.

④ [day, 24 hours]

one **day,** a certain **day** // that **day** // the next **day** // a nice **day,** a clear **day**

hi ⟦n⟧　fire, flame

¶ Please give me **a light.**

¶ Please turn off the gas **burner.**

¶ [I] **lighted** the stove ⟦heater⟧.

-hi ⟦suf⟧　expenses, cost

car**fare,** transportation **expenses** // living **expenses** // a **fee** (for a party, outing, etc.), membership **fee,** membership **dues** // travel **expenses**

すか。(Shoku*hi* wa ikkagetsu ikura gurai kakarimasu ka?)

hibiku 響く〖動Ⅰ〗

①［音などが辺りに伝わる］
滝の音が響く (taki no oto ga *hibiku*)

¶工事の音が響いてきてうるさいです。(Kōji no oto ga *hibiite* kite urusai desu.)

②［音などが反響する］
¶トンネルの中では声が響きます。(Tonneru no naka de wa koe ga *hibikimasu*.)

hidari 左〖名〗

左足 (*hidari*ashi) 左手 (*hidari*te)
¶日本では車は左側を通ります。(Nihon de wa kuruma wa *hidari*gawa o toorimasu.)

¶あの銀行の左の建物は何ですか。(Ano ginkō no *hidari* no tatemono wa nan desu ka?)

⇔**migi** 右

hidoi ひどい〖形〗

①［程度が激しい，はなはだしい］
¶ひどい風でかさがこわれました。(*Hidoi* kaze de kasa ga kowaremashita.)

¶バスがひどくこんでいました。(Basu ga *hidoku* konde imashita.)

②［残酷な，情けがない，被害などがはなはだしい］
¶人を自動車でひいて逃げてしまうようなひどい人がいます。(Hito o jidōsha de hiite nigete shimau yō

hibiku 〚v I〛 sound, resound, reverberate; echo

① [sound, resound, reverberate]
the waterfall makes a **booming** sound

¶ The construction sounds are very **loud and jarring.**

② [echo]
¶ Voices **echo** in the tunnel.

hidari 〚n〛 left

the **left** foot 〚leg〛 // the **left** hand 〚arm〛; **left**-hand
¶ In Japan traffic runs on **the left.**

¶ What is the building to **the left** of that bank?

hidoi 〚adj〛 severe, intense; cruel, harsh

① [severe, intense, heavy, terrible]
¶ [My] umbrella broke in the **strong** wind.

¶ The bus was **terribly** crowded.

② [cruel, harsh, hard]

¶ There are people **terrible** enough to run away after hitting someone with their car.

na *hidoi* hito ga imasu.)

¶台風のためにひどい目に遭いました。
(Taifū no tame ni *hidoi* me ni aimashita.)

hieru　冷える〖動Ⅱ〗

①[寒くなる，寒く感じる]
体が冷える (karada ga *hieru*)

¶今晩はずいぶん冷えますね。 (Konban wa zuibun *hiemasu* ne.)

②[冷たくなる]
¶冷えたビールがありますか。 (*Hieta* biiru ga arimasu ka?)

hifu　皮膚〖名〗

皮膚病 (*hifu*byō)　皮膚科 (*hifu*ka)

¶この子は皮膚が弱いので困ります。
(Kono ko wa *hifu* ga yowai node komarimasu.)

¶日に焼けて皮膚が赤くなりました。
(Hi ni yakete *hifu* ga akaku narimashita.)

higai　被害〖名〗

被害地 (*higai*chi)

¶台風のため，各地に大きな被害がありました。 (Taifū no tame, kakuchi ni ookina *higai* ga arimashita.)

¶昨日の交通事故の被害者は30歳ぐらいの男の人でした。 (Kinō no kōtsū-jiko no *higai*sha wa sanjissai gurai no otoko no hito deshita.)

higashi　東〖名〗

東側 (*higashi*gawa)　東風 (*higashi*-kaze)

¶太陽は東から出て，西に沈みます。
(Taiyō wa *higashi* kara dete, nishi

¶ [I] suffered **greatly** 〖had a **terrible** experience〗 because of the typhoon.

hieru 〖v II〗　**grow cold, become chilled**

① [it becomes cold or chilly, one feels cold or chilly]

one's body **is chilled**

¶ **It's** very **chilly** this evening, isn't it?

② [something becomes cold, chilled]

¶ Is there any **cold** beer?

hifu 〖n〗　**skin**

a **skin** disease // **dermatology, dermatology** department

¶ This child has a delicate **skin** and we don't know what to do.

¶ [I] burned in the sun and **[my] skin** turned red.

higai 〖n〗　**damage, harm, injury**

the **afflicted** region, the **affected** area

¶ The typhoon caused great **damage** in many places.

¶ **The victim** of yesterday's traffic accident was a male of about 30 years.

higashi 〖n〗　**east**

the **eastern** side // an **easterly** wind, a wind from **the east**

¶ The sun rises in **the east** and sets in the west.

ni shizumimasu.)

¶風が東から西に吹いています。

(Kaze ga *higashi* kara nishi ni fuite imasu.)

⇔nishi 西

hige　ひげ〖名〗

ひげが伸びる (*hige* ga nobiru)　ひげを伸ばす (*hige* o nobasu)

¶田中さんのひげは立派ですね。

(Tanaka san no *hige* wa rippa desu ne.)

¶忙しくて二、三日ひげをそりませんでした。 (Isogashikute ni-sannichi *hige* o sorimasen deshita.)

hihyō　批評〖名, ～する〗

¶新しい本の批評が新聞に出ています。

(Atarashii hon no *hihyō* ga shinbun ni dete imasu.)

¶彼はその小説を厳しく批評しました。

(Kare wa sono shōsetsu o kibishiku *hihyō* shimashita.)

hijō　非常〖名〗

非常口 (*hijō*guchi)　非常時 (*hijō*ji)

¶非常の場合には、ここから出てください。 (*Hijō* no baai ni wa, koko kara dete kudasai.)

hijō ni　非常に〖副〗

¶試験は非常に難しかったです。

(Shiken wa *hijō ni* muzukashikatta desu.)

¶今日は非常に寒いです。 (Kyō wa *hijō ni* samui desu.)

hikaku　比較〖名, ～する〗

ＡとＢを比較する (ē to bii o *hikaku*

hige 〚n〛 **moustache, beard, whiskers**

one's beard 〚moustache〛 grows longer // to let **one's beard 〚moustache〛** grow

¶ Mr. Tanaka has a fine **beard 〚moustache; beard and moustache〛**.

¶ [I] was so busy [I] didn't **shave** for two or three days.

hihyō 〚n, ～*suru*〛 **criticism, review**

¶ **Reviews** of new books appear in the newspaper.

¶ He severely **criticized** that novel.

hijō 〚n〛 **emergency, extraordinary situation**

emergency exit // **an emergency, crisis**

¶ In case of **emergency,** please go out this way 〚from here〛.

hijō ni 〚adv〛 **extremely, greatly**

¶ The exam was **extremely** difficult.

¶ It's **terribly** cold today.

hikaku 〚n, ～*suru*〛 **comparison to compare** A with B

suru)

¶いろいろな店の値段を比較して，い
ちばん安い店で買い物をしました。

(Iroiro na mise no nedan o *hikaku*
shite, ichiban yasui mise de kaimono o shimashita.)

⇒**kuraberu** 比べる

hikari 光〚名〛

¶月の光が明るく照っていました。

(Tsuki no *hikari* ga akaruku tette
imashita.)

¶電気が消えたので，ろうそくの光で
勉強しました。　　(Denki ga kieta
node, rōsoku no *hikari* de benkyō
shimashita.)

hikaru 光る〚動Ⅰ〛

ダイヤモンドが光る (daiyamondo ga
hikaru)

¶空には星が光っています。 (Sora ni
wa hoshi ga *hikatte* imasu.)

¶遠くで何か光りましたが，何でしょ
うか。 (Tooku de nani ka *hikari-
mashita* ga, nan deshō ka?)

-hiki -匹〚尾〛

1匹 (ip*piki*)　2匹 (ni*hiki*)　3匹
(san*biki*)　4匹 (yon*hiki*)　5匹 (go-
hiki)　6匹 (rop*piki*)　7匹 (nana*hiki*)
8匹 (hap*piki*)　9匹 (kyū*hiki*)　10
匹 (jip*piki*)

¶この池には魚が何匹ぐらいいますか。

(Kono ike ni wa sakana ga nan*biki*
gurai imasu ka?)

hikidashi 引き出し〚名〛

¶机の左の引き出しの中からはさみを

¶ [I] **compared** the prices at various
shops and did [my] shopping at the
cheapest one.

hikari 〚n〛 **light, illumination, glow**
¶ The moon **was shining** brightly.

¶ The electricity went out so [I] studied by **the light** of a candle.

hikaru 〚v I〛 **shine, be luminous**
a diamond **sparkles**

¶ A star **is** 〚Stars **are**〛 **shining** in the
sky.
¶ Something **flashed** in the distance.
I wonder what it could be.

-hiki 〚suf〛 the counter for animals,
fish, insects

one cat 〚dog, goldfish, ant, etc.〛 //
two cats // three cats // four cats //
five cats // six cats // seven cats //
eight cats // nine cats // ten cats
¶ **How many** fish are there in this
pond 〚pool〛?

hikidashi 〚n〛 **drawer, chest of
drawers**

194

出してください。(Tsukue no hidari no *hikidashi* no naka kara hasami o dashite kudasai.)

¶ Please fetch the scissors from the left **drawer** of the desk.

¶引き出しを開けたら，ちゃんと閉めてください。(*Hikidashi* o aketara, chanto shimete kudasai.)

¶ If you pull out **a drawer** then please close it again.

hikiukeru 引き受ける〖動Ⅱ〗

¶案内係は，わたしが引き受けます。(Annaigakari wa, watashi ga *hikiukemasu*.)

¶そんな難しいことを引き受けて大丈夫ですか。(Sonna muzukashii koto o *hikiukete* daijōbu desu ka?)

hikiukeru 〖v Ⅱ〗 undertake, take charge of

¶ I'll **take on** the job of handling the information desk.

¶ **You've taken** that **on,** but are you sure you can handle such a difficult task?

hikkoshi 引っ越し〖名，～する〗

¶中村さんの引っ越しの手伝いをしました。(Nakamura san no *hikkoshi* no tetsudai o shimashita.)

¶引っ越しの荷物はどのくらいありますか。(*Hikkoshi* no nimotsu wa dono kurai arimasu ka?)

hikkoshi 〖n, ～*suru*〗 moving, house moving

¶ [I] helped [Miss] Nakamura **move.**

¶ How much property do you have **to be moved?**

hikkosu 引っ越す〖動Ⅰ〗

¶来月，大学の近くに引っ越します。(Raigetsu, daigaku no chikaku ni *hikkoshimasu*.)

¶あの人はよく引っ越しますね。(Ano hito wa yoku *hikkoshimasu* ne.)

hikkosu 〖v Ⅰ〗 move (house)

¶ Next month [I] **will move** near to the university.

¶ [He] **moves** a lot.

hikōjō 飛行場〖名〗

¶今日，羽田飛行場に着きました。(Kyō, Haneda-*hikōjō* ni tsukimashita.)

¶中村さんは飛行場へ友達を迎えに行きました。(Nakamura san wa *hikōjō* e tomodachi o mukae ni ikimashita.)

hikōjō 〖n〗 airport, airfield

¶ [I] arrived at Haneda **Airport** today.

¶ [Mrs.] Nakamura went to **the airport** to meet a friend.

⇒kūkō 空港〈くうこう〉

hikōki 飛行機〈ひこうき〉〖名〗

¶飛行機に乗ったことがありますか。
(*Hikōki* ni notta koto ga arimasu ka?)

¶飛行機は西の方へ飛んでいきました。
(*Hikōki* wa nishi no hō e tonde ikimashita.)

hiku 引く〈ひく〉〖動Ⅰ〗

①[物などを自分の手もとに引き寄せる]
ドアの取っ手を引く (doa no totte o *hiku*)

¶このひもを引くと，電気がつきます。
(Kono himo o *hiku* to, denki ga tsukimasu.)

↔osu 押す〈おす〉

②[車などを引っ張る]
馬がそりを引く (uma ga sori o *hiku*)

¶重い荷物を積んだ車を引いたので，腕が痛くなりました。(Omoi nimotsu o tsunda kuruma o *hiita* node, ude ga itaku narimashita.)

③[導く]
¶お年寄りの手を引いて，会場を案内しました。(Otoshiyori no te o *hiite*, kaijō o annai shimashita.)

④[減らす]
¶5から3を引くと，2になります。
(Go kara san o *hiku* to, ni ni narimasu.)

¶あの店では，どの品物も1割引いて売っています。(Ano mise de wa, dono shinamono mo ichiwari *hiite* utte

hikōki 〖n〗 airplane, aircraft

¶ Have you ever ridden in **an airplane?**

¶ **The airplane** flew away toward the west.

hiku 〖v Ⅰ〗 pull; lead; subtract; look up; cite; install

① [pull by hand, draw]
pull on the door handle

¶ If **you pull on** this cord, the light will come on.

② [pull, haul, tow]
a horse **pulls** a sleigh

¶ [My] arms are sore because [I] **pulled** a cart piled with a heavy load.

③ [lead]

¶ **Taking** the elderly person by the hand, [I] showed [him] around the grounds 〚convention area, exhibition hall, auditorium, etc.〛.

④ [subtract, deduct, discount]

¶ Three **from** five is two.

¶ At that shop they sell everything at a 10 percent **discount.**

imasu.)

↔**tasu** 足す

⑤[風邪などにかかる]
¶風邪を引いて寝ています。 (Kaze o *hiite* nete imasu.)

⑥[辞書などから探しだす]
¶辞書を引いて，言葉の意味を調べました。(Jisho o *hiite*, kotoba no imi o shirabemashita.)

⑦[引用する]
¶先生は例を引いて説明しました。(Sensei wa rei o *hiite* setsumei shimashita.)

⑧[電燈・ガスなどを家の中に導き入れる]
電話を引く (denwa o *hiku*) 水道を引く (suidō o *hiku*) ガスを引く (gasu o *hiku*)

⑨[線などを長くかく]
線を引く (sen o *hiku*)

hiku 弾く〚動Ⅰ〛
¶彼はギターを弾いて歌いました。(Kare wa gitā o *hiite* utaimashita.)
¶子供が上手にピアノを弾きました。(Kodomo ga jōzu ni piano o *hikimashita*.)

hikui 低い〚形〛
①[下から上までの長さが小さい，ものの位置が地面などからあまり上の方にない様子]
低い木 (*hikui* ki) 背が低い (se ga *hikui*)
¶あの低い山は何と言いますか。(Ano *hikui* yama wa nan to iimasu ka?)

⑤ [catch a cold, the flu, etc.]
¶ [I] am in bed **with** a cold 〚the flu〛.

⑥ [look up in a dictionary, etc.]
¶ [I] **looked up** the meaning of a word in the dictionary.

⑦ [cite, quote, refer to]
¶ The teacher explained **with** an example.

⑧ [install electricity, gas, etc.]
install a telephone // **have** water pipes **laid** // **lay on** gas

⑨ [draw a line, sketch, etc.]
draw a line

hiku 〚vⅠ〛 **play** (a stringed instrument)
¶ He **played** the guitar and sang.
¶ The child **played** the piano well.

hikui 〚adj〛 **short; low**
① [short, low]
a **short** tree // **be short** of stature

¶ What is that **low** mountain called?

¶白い鳥が低く飛んでいきました。
(Shiroi tori ga *hikuku* tonde ikimashita.)

②[声・音が小さく聞こえる様子，音
階が下である様子]
低い音 (*hikui* oto)
¶二人は低い声で話しているので，何
を話しているかわかりません。(Futari
wa *hikui* koe de hanashite iru node,
nani o hanashite iru no ka wakarimasen.)
¶田中さんの声は低いです。 (Tanaka
san no koe wa *hikui* desu.)

③[温度や熱などの数値が小さい]
気圧が低い (kiatsu ga *hikui*)
¶ここは一年じゅう温度が低いから，植
物の生長が遅いです。 (Koko wa
ichinenjū ondo ga *hikui* kara, shokubutsu no seichō ga osoi desu.)

④[身分などが下である様子]
地位が低い (chii ga *hikui*)
⇔**takai** 高い

hima 暇〖名，形動〗
①[何かをする時間]
¶忙しくて本を読む暇もありません。
(Isogashikute hon o yomu *hima* mo
arimasen.)
②[何もしなくてもいい時間，あいて
いる時間]
¶今度の日曜はお暇ですか。 (Kondo
no nichiyō wa o*hima* desu ka?)
¶暇なときは何をしていますか。
(*Hima* na toki wa nani o shite
imasu ka?)

¶ The white bird flew away **close to
the ground.**

② [low volume, low pitch]
a **low** sound; a **low-pitched** sound

¶ As the two are speaking in **low**
voices, I can't hear what they're talking about.

¶ [Mr.] Tanaka has a **low-pitched**
voice.

③ [be low on a scale]
low atmospheric pressure

¶ The temperatures **are low** here the
year round so plant growth is slow.

④ [low, humble]
be low in position, **be low** in social
standing

hima 〖n, adj-v〗 time; leisure, leisure time
① [time (to do something)]

¶ [I]'m so busy [I] don't have **the
time** to read books.

② [leisure, leisure time, free time]

¶ **Are you free** this Sunday?

¶ What do you do in **your spare
time?**

¶お暇でしたら，遊びにいらっしゃってください。 (*Ohima* deshitara asobi ni irasshatte kudasai.)

¶ **If you aren't doing anything,** please come and visit me.

himitsu 秘密〖名，形動〗

¶これはまだ秘密ですから，ほかの人には話さないでください。 (Kore wa mada *himitsu* desu kara, hoka no hito ni wa hanasanaide kudasai.)

¶会社の秘密は守ってください。 (Kaisha no *himitsu* wa mamotte kudasai.)

himitsu 〖n, adj-v〗 **secret**

¶ This is still **a secret** so please don't tell anyone else.

¶ Please keep our business **secrets** safe.

himo ひも〖名〗

¶くつのひもが切れてしまいました。 (Kutsu no *himo* ga kirete shimaimashita.)

¶この小包をひもで縛ってください。 (Kono kozutsumi o *himo* de shibatte kudasai.)

himo 〖n〗 **string, cord, braid, band, ribbon, tape, strap, lace,** etc.

¶ [My] shoe**laces** broke.

¶ Please tie up this parcel with **string** 〖**cord, twine,** etc.〗.

hineru ひねる〖動Ⅰ〗

①[物を手などでねじって回す]

¶水道のせんをひねっても水が出ません。 (Suidō no sen o *hinette* mo mizu ga demasen.)

②[よい工夫をするためにいろいろと考えをめぐらす]

¶頭をひねって考えましたが，いい考えが浮かびません。 (Atama o *hinette* kangaemashita ga, ii kangae ga ukabimasen.)

hineru 〖v I〗 **twist, bend**

① [twist, turn]

¶ No water comes out when **you turn** the faucet **on.**

② [twist, turn, bend, incline (one's head), rack (one's brains)]

¶ [I] **racked** [my] brains but didn't have any good ideas.

hinichi 日にち〖名〗

①[ものごとを行う日，期日]

¶旅行の日にちを決めましょう。 (Ryokō no *hinichi* o kimemashō.)

¶会議の日にちと場所をメモしておい

hinichi 〖n〗 **day, date; days, time**

① [day, date, set date]

¶ Let's set **a date** for the trip.

¶ Please make a note of **the day(s)**

¶桜の花が**開き**ました。 (Sakura no hana ga *hirakimashita*.)

¶ The cherry blossoms **have opened** 〚The cherry blossoms **opened**〛.

②[閉じてあったものをあける]
小包を**開く** (kozutsumi o *hiraku*)

② [open, undo]
open a parcel

¶では，本を**開いて**勉強を始めましょう。 (Dewa, hon o *hiraite* benkyō o hajimemashō.)

¶ Well, let's **open** our books and start the lesson.

③[店などを新しく始める]
¶上田さんは駅のそばに果物屋を**開き**ました。(Ueda san wa eki no soba ni kudamonoya o *hirakimashita*.)

③ [open, start (a shop, etc.)]
¶ [Miss] Ueda **opened** a fruit store near the station.

④[会などを行う]
¶今晩7時から研究会を**開き**ます。(Konban shichiji kara kenkyūkai o *hirakimasu*.)

④ [hold (a meeting, party, etc.)]
¶ The study meeting **will be held** this evening from seven o'clock.

⇒tojiru 閉じる

hiroba 広場〚名〛
¶駅の前に広場があります。 (Eki no mae ni *hiroba* ga arimasu.)
¶広場に人がたくさん集まっています。(*Hiroba* ni hito ga takusan atsumatte imasu.)

hiroba 〚n〛 **open space, plaza, square**
¶ There is **a plaza** in front of the station.
¶ A lot of people are gathered in **the plaza**.

hirogaru 広がる〚動Ⅰ〛
①[空間的に大きくなる，広くなる]
¶学校の前の道が**広がり**ました。(Gakkō no mae no michi ga *hirogarimashita*.)
¶木の枝が四方に**広がって**います。(Ki no eda ga shihō ni *hirogatte* imasu.)

hirogaru 〚vⅠ〛 **spread, expand; spread, be disseminated**
① [spread, expand]
¶ The road **has been widened** in front of the school.
¶ The branches of the tree **are spreading out** in all directions.

②[ものごとがいろいろな人・場所などに及ぶ]
伝染病が**広がる** (densenbyō ga *hirogaru*)

② [spread, be disseminated]
a contagious disease **spreads**

201

¶うわさが町じゅうに広がっています。
(Uwasa ga machijū ni *hirogatte* imasu)

¶ The rumor **is spreading** throughout the town.

hirogeru 広げる〔動Ⅱ〕

①[空間的に大きくする，広くする]
道の幅を広げる (michi no haba o *hirogeru*)

¶店を広げて，きれいにしました。
(Mise o *hirogete*, kirei ni shimashita.)

②[開ける]
¶地図を広げて，旅行の相談をしました。 (Chizu o *hirogete*, ryokō no sōdan o shimashita.)

¶本を広げたまま眠ってしまいました。
(Hon o *hirogeta* mama nemutte shimaimashita.)

hirogeru 〖v II〗 extend, expand; open, spread out

① [extend, expand, enlarge]
widen the road

¶ [They] **enlarged** and fixed up the shop 〖restaurant, etc.〗.

② [open, spread out, unfold]
¶ **Spreading out** a map, [we] consulted about the trip.

¶ [I] fell asleep with [my] book still **open.**

hiroi 広い〔形〕
¶あの家の庭は広いです。(Ano ie no niwa wa *hiroi* desu.)
¶この部屋はあまり広くありません。
(Kono heya wa amari *hiroku* arimasen.)
⇔semai 狭い

hiroi 〖adj〗 wide, broad, spacious
¶ That house has a **large** garden 〖**extensive** yard〗.
¶ This room **isn't** very **big.**

hirosa 広さ〔名〕
¶この家の広さはどのくらいですか。
(Kono ie no *hirosa* wa dono kurai desu ka?)
⇨-sa -さ

hirosa 〖n〗 area, dimensions
¶ What is **the floor space** of this house?

hirou 拾う〔動Ⅰ〕
①[落ちているものなどを取り上げる]
¶道でお金を拾いました。 (Michi de okane o *hiroimashita*.)
¶紙くずを拾って，この箱に入れてく

hirou 〖v I〗 pick up; find
① [pick up, gather, find]
¶ [I] **found** some money in the street.
¶ Please **pick up** the wastepaper and

ださい。(Kamikuzu o *hirotte*, kono hako ni irete kudasai.)

↔suteru 捨てる

②[タクシーなどを呼び止めて乗る]
¶雨が降ってきたから，タクシーを拾いましょう。(Ame ga futte kita kara, takushii o *hiroimashō*.)

put it in this box.

② [find, catch (a taxi, etc.)]
¶ It's started to rain—**let's take** a taxi.

hiru 昼〚名〛

①[昼間]
¶昼も夜も休まずに働きました。
(*Hiru* mo yoru mo yasumazu ni hatarakimashita.)
¶今日は昼寝をしました。(Kyō wa *hiru*ne o shimashita.)

↔yoru 夜

②[正午]
昼休み (*hiru*yasumi)
¶彼はいつもお昼ごろ会社へ来ます。
(Kare wa itsu mo o*hiru* goro kaisha e kimasu.)
¶もう昼御飯を食べましたか。(Mō *hiru*gohan o tabemashita ka?)

③[昼御飯]
¶お昼は何にしますか。(O*hiru* wa nani ni shimasu ka?)
¶お昼はおそばにしましょう。(O*hiru* wa osoba ni shimashō.)

hiruma 昼間〚名〛
¶彼は昼間働いて，夜学校へ行きます。
(Kare wa *hiruma* hataraite, yoru gakkō e ikimasu.)
¶昼間からそんなにお酒を飲まないでください。(*Hiruma* kara sonna ni osake o nomanaide kudasai.)

hiru 〚n〛 daytime; noon, noontime; lunch

① [daytime]
¶ [I] worked nonstop **day** and night.

¶ [I] took **a nap** today.

② [noon, noontime, midday]
noon recess, **lunch** hour
¶ He always comes to the office around **noon**.

¶ Have you eaten **lunch** yet?

③ [lunch, noon meal]
¶ What do you want to eat for **lunch?**

¶ Let's have *soba* for **lunch.**

hiruma 〚n〛 day, daytime, during the daytime

¶ He works **during the day** and goes to school at night.

¶ Please don't drink so much so **early in the day** 〚**during the daytime**〛.

⇔yoru 夜

hisashiburi 久しぶり〖名〗

¶久しぶりに昔の友達に会いました。

(*Hisashiburi* ni mukashi no tomo-dachi ni aimashita.)

¶久しぶりですね。お元気ですか。

(*Hisashiburi* desu ne. Ogenki desu ka?)

hitai 額〖名〗

¶ハンカチで額の汗をふきました。

(Hankachi de *hitai* no ase o fuki-mashita.)

¶子供の時，額にけがをしました。

(Kodomo no toki, *hitai* ni kega o shimashita.)

hitei 否定〖名, 〜する〗

否定的な意見 (*hitei*teki na iken)

¶それは事実ですから否定しません。

(Sore wa jijitsu desu kara *hitei* shimasen.)

⇔kōtei 肯定

hito 人〖名〗

①〖人間〗

男の人 (otoko no *hito*)　女の人 (onna no *hito*)　いい人 (ii *hito*)　悪い人 (warui *hito*)

¶あそこに人が何人いますか。(Asoko ni *hito* ga nannin imasu ka?)

②〖ほかの人，他人〗

¶田中さんは人のことを全然考えません。 (Tanaka san wa *hito* no koto o zenzen kangaemasen.)

¶人をばかにしてはいけません。(*Hito* o baka ni shite wa ikemasen.)

hisashiburi 〖n〗 **after a long time;** an expression used when meeting someone after some time has passed

¶ [I] met an old friend **after a long separation.**

¶ It's been **a long time**, hasn't it? How are you doing?

hitai 〖n〗 **forehead, brow**

¶ [I] wiped the sweat from [my] **forehead** with a handkerchief.

¶ [I] hurt [my]self on **the forehead** when [I] was a child.

hitei 〖n, ~*suru*〗 **denial**

a **dissenting** view

¶ [I] **don't deny** that that is so.

hito 〖n〗 **person, people; other people, others**

① [person, people, human beings]

a man // a woman // a good **person** // a bad **person**

¶ How many **people** are there over there?

② [other people, others]

¶ [Mrs.] Tanaka doesn't think of **other people** at all 〖show any consideration for **others**〗.

¶ One mustn't make fun of **others.**

hitori 一人〚名〛

¶あの人は子供が一人しかありません。
(Ano hito wa kodomo ga *hitori*
shika arimasen.)
¶費用は一人千円です。　(Hiyō wa
hitori sen'en desu.)
¶今年の夏は一人で旅行しました。
(Kotoshi no natsu wa *hitori* de
ryokō shimashita.)
¶一人で荷物を全部運びました。
(*Hitori* de nimotsu o zenbu hako-
bimashita.)

hitori 独り〚名〛

独り者 (*hitori*mono)　独りぼっち
(*hitori*botchi)
¶あの人はまだ独りです。　(Ano hito
wa mada *hitori* desu.)

hitoshii 等しい〚形〛

¶AとBは長さが等しいです。　(Ē to
bii wa nagasa ga *hitoshii* desu.)
¶そんなやり方はどろぼうに等しいで
す。(Sonna yarikata wa dorobō ni
hitoshii desu.)

hitotsu 一つ〚名〛

①[1個]
¶このりんごは一ついくらですか。
(Kono ringo wa *hitotsu* ikura desu
ka?)
②[1歳]
¶この子は一つになったばかりです。
(Kono ko wa *hitotsu* ni natta
bakari desu.)

hitotsuki 一月〚名〛

¶部屋代は一月いくらですか。(Heya-

hitori 〚n〛 one person

¶ [He] has only **one** child.

¶ The cost is a thousand yen **per person.**

¶ [I] went on a trip **by [my]self** this
summer.

¶ [I] transferred all of the load
〚baggage, bags〛 **by [my]self.**

hitori 〚n〛 alone, single

an **unmarried** person // all **by oneself,** all **alone**
¶ [He] is still **single.**

hitoshii 〚adj〛 equal, identical,
equivalent, similar, like

¶ A and B **are equal** in length.

¶ That's **tantamount to** thievery
〚That **amounts to** thievery〛.

hitotsu 〚n〛 one, one item; one
year of age

① [one item]
¶ How much are these apples
apiece?

② [one year of age]
¶ This child has just turned **one year
old.**

hitotsuki 〚n〛 one month

¶ How much is **one month's** rent?

dai wa *hitotsuki* ikura desu ka?)
¶胃の手術をして，一月以上入院しました。(I no shujutsu o shite, *hitotsuki* ijō nyūin shimashita.)

¶ [I] had a stomach operation and was hospitalized for over **a month.**

hitsuji　羊〖名〗
羊を飼う (*hitsuji* o kau)
¶羊はたいへんおとなしい動物です。(*Hitsuji* wa taihen otonashii dōbutsu desu.)

hitsuji　〖n〗　sheep
raise **sheep**
¶ **Sheep** are very docile animals.

hitsuyō　必要〖名，形動〗
¶そんなことをする必要はありません。(Sonna koto o suru *hitsuyō* wa arimasen.)
¶このお金で必要な物を買ってください。(Kono okane de *hitsuyō* na mono o katte kudasai.)
¶研究のために日本語が必要です。(Kenkyū no tame ni Nihongo ga *hitsuyō* desu.)

hitsuyō　〖n, adj-v〗　need, necessity; necessary, essential
¶ There is no **need** to do such a thing.
¶ Please buy something you **need** with this money.
¶ Japanese **is essential** to [my] research.

hiyasu　冷やす〖動Ⅰ〗
¶ビールを冷やしておいてください。(Biiru o *hiyashite* oite kudasai.)
¶熱があるから，氷で頭を冷やしてください。(Netsu ga aru kara, koori de atama o *hiyashite* kudasai.)

hiyasu　〖vⅠ〗　cool, ice, refrigerate
¶ Please put the beer in the refrigerator ⟦cooler⟧ to **get cold.**
¶ Since [she] has a fever, please **cool** [her] head with an ice pack.

hiyō　費用〖名〗
¶旅行の費用はいくらぐらいかかりますか。(Ryokō no *hiyō* wa ikura gurai kakarimasu ka?)
¶費用を計算してみましょう。(*Hiyō* o keisan shite mimashō.)

hiyō　〖n〗　expense, cost
¶ How much will **the expenses** for the trip be?
¶ Let's calculate **the expenses.**

hiza　ひざ〖名〗
¶ひざを曲げて座りました。(*Hiza* o magete suwarimashita.)

hiza　〖n〗　knee, lap
¶ [I] bent **[my] knees** and sat down.

¶ひざにちょっとけがをしました。
(*Hiza* ni chotto kega o shimashita.)

¶ [I] injured **my knee** slightly.

-ho -歩〔尾〕

1歩 (ip*po*)　2歩 (ni*ho*)　3歩
(san*po*)　4歩 (yon*ho*)　5歩 (go*ho*)
6歩 (rop*po*)　7歩 (nana*ho*)　8歩
(hap*po*)　9歩 (kyū*ho*)　10歩
(jip*po*)

-ho 〖suf〗　**a step, a pace**

one **step** // two **steps** // three **steps**
// four **steps** // five **steps** // six
steps // seven **steps** // eight **steps**
// nine **steps** // ten **steps**

¶ここからあそこまで何歩ありますか。
(Koko kara asoko made nan*po*
arimasu ka?)

¶ How many **steps** is it from here to
there?

¶1歩前に出てください。 (Ip*po* mae
ni dete kudasai.)

¶ Please take one **step** forward.

hō 方〔名〕

¶黒板の方を見てください。 (Koku-
ban no *hō* o mite kudasai.)

¶鳥が北の方へ飛んでいきます。(Tori
ga kita no *hō* e tonde ikimasu.)

hō 〖n〗　**direction, way**

¶ Please look **toward** at the blackboard.

¶ The bird is flying **toward** the
north.

hō ほう〔名〕

①[ものごとを比べてそのうちの一つ
を取り上げて表すのに使う]

¶わたしはみかんよりりんごのほうが
好きです。(Watashi wa mikan yori
ringo no *hō* ga suki desu.)

¶ビールは冷たいほうがおいしいです
よ。(Biiru wa tsumetai *hō* ga oishii
desu yo.)

②[いくつかのものごとのうちで適当
で望ましいものごとを取り上げて表
すのに使う]

¶あなたはもっと運動をしたほうがい
いですよ。 (Anata wa motto undō
o shita *hō* ga ii desu yo.)

¶ああいう危険な所へはあまり行かな

hō 〖n〗　**side, part; class, category**

① [side; indicates something singled
out from two or more alternatives]

¶ I like apples better than oranges
(literally, mandarin oranges).

¶ Beer tastes best cold.

② [used to indicate something singled out as desirable to do]

¶ You should exercise more.

¶ It would be best not to go very

いほうがいいですよ。　(Āiu kiken na tokoro e wa amari ikanai *hō ga ii desu yo.*)

* 普通「ほうがいい（hō ga ii）」の形で使う。

③［ものごとを二つの部類に分けて考える場合どちらかといえばその一方に属するということを表すのに使う］

¶中村さんはどちらかといえばまじめなほうです。　(Nakamura san wa dochira ka to ieba majime na *hō desu.*)

¶この店の料理はおいしいほうですよ。　(Kono mise no ryōri wa oishii *hō desu yo.*)

hōbō　ほうぼう〖名〗

¶ほうぼう捜しましたが，時計は見つかりませんでした。　(*Hōbō* sagashimashita ga, tokei wa mitsukarimasen deshita.)

¶日本へ行ったら，ほうぼうを旅行したいと思います。　(Nihon e ittara, *hōbō* o ryokō shitai to omoimasu.)

hodo　ほど〖助〗

①［だいたいの量や程度を表す］

¶病気で1年ほど会社を休みました。　(Byōki de ichinen *hodo* kaisha o yasumimashita.)

¶牛肉を300グラムほどください。　(Gyūniku o sanbyakuguramu *hodo* kudasai.)

②［比較の基準のものごとを例に挙げてものごとの程度を表す］

¶今年は去年ほど寒くありません。

---

much to such dangerous places.

* Usually used in the pattern "~ *hō ga ii.*"

③ [class, category; used when assigning someone or something to one of two categories]

¶ [Mr.] Nakamura is on the serious side.

¶ The food at this restaurant 〚bar, etc.〛 is quite good.

hōbō 〚n〛 every direction, everywhere, here and there

¶ [I] searched **everywhere** for [my] watch, but [I] couldn't find it.

¶ When I go to Japan, I want to travel **all around.**

hodo 〚part〛 about, around; as ~ as; the more ~ the more ~
① [about, around]

¶ [I] stayed home from work for **about** a year due to illness.

¶ Please give me three hundred grams **or so** of beef.

② [as ~ as]

¶ This year is not **as** cold **as** last year.

(Kotoshi wa kyonen *hodo* samuku arimasen.)

¶平仮名は漢字ほど複雑ではありません。 (Hiragana wa kanji *hodo* fukuzatsu de wa arimasen.)

¶上田さんほど熱心な学生はいません。 (Ueda san *hodo* nesshin na gakusei wa imasen.)

* 普通 「～ほど ～ない (～hodo ～nai)」 の形で使う。

③ [二つのことがらのうち一方の程度の変化に応じて他方の程度も変化するという関係を表すのに使う]

¶早ければ早いほどいいです。 (Hayakereba hayai *hodo* ii desu.)

¶勉強すればするほどおもしろくなります。 (Benkyō sureba suru *hodo* omoshiroku narimasu.)

* 「～ば ～ほど (～ba ～hodo)」 の形で使う。

hogaraka 朗らか 〖形動〗

¶彼女はいつも朗らかです。 (Kanojo wa itsu mo *hogaraka* desu.)

¶子供たちは大きな声で朗らかに笑いました。 (Kodomotachi wa ookina koe de *hogaraka* ni waraimashita.)

hōhō 方法 〖名〗

¶わたしはいろいろな方法で実験をやってみました。 (Watashi wa iroiro na *hōhō* de jikken o yatte mimashita.)

¶どの方法がいちばんいいですか。 (Dono *hōhō* ga ichiban ii desu ka?)

¶ *Hiragana* aren't **as** complex **as** *kanji*.

¶ No one is **as** hardworking a student **as** [Mr.] Ueda 〖You couldn't find another student **as** hardworking **as** Mr. Ueda〗.

* Usually used in the pattern "~ *hodo* ~ *nai*."

③ [the more ~ the more ~]

¶ The **sooner** the **better**.

¶ **The more** you study **the more** interesting it is.

* Used in the pattern "-*ba* ~ *hodo*."

hogaraka 〖adj-v〗 **cheerful, bright**
¶ She is always **cheerful**.

¶ The children laughed **merrily**.

hoho ☞ **hoo**

hōhō 〖n〗 **method, way**
¶ [I] conducted experiments using various **methods**.

¶ Which **method** is best 〖What is the best **way to do it**〗?

hoka 〖ほか〗〖名〗

①[別の人・物・時・所などを表す]

¶この問題について, ほかの人はどう思っていますか。 (Kono mondai ni tsuite, *hoka* no hito wa dō omotte imasu ka?)

¶この店は高いから, ほかの店で買いましょう。 (Kono mise wa takai kara, *hoka* no mise de kaimashō.)

②[あるものごとを除いて]

¶東京にはあなたのほかに知っている人はいません。(Tōkyō ni wa anata no *hoka* ni shitte iru hito wa imasen.)

¶雨がひどかったので, 上田さんとわたしのほかにはだれも来ませんでした。(Ame ga hidokatta node, Ueda san to watashi no *hoka* ni wa dare mo kimasen deshita.)

*普通「～ほかに (～hoka ni)」の形で使い, あとに打ち消しの言葉が来る。

③[あるものごとだけでなくそれ以外に]

¶そのほかに質問はありませんか。(Sono *hoka* ni shitsumon wa arimasen ka?)

¶このクラスには, 中国人のほかにアメリカ人もいます。 (Kono kurasu ni wa, Chūgokujin no *hoka* ni Amerikajin mo imasu.)

*普通「～ほかに (～hoka ni)」の形で使う。

hoken 保険〖名〗

保険会社 (*hoken*-gaisha)　保険金

hoka 〖n〗 other, another; except for, other than; besides, in addition to

① [other, another]

¶ What do **the rest** of you think about this problem?

¶ This shop is expensive so let's buy it **somewhere else.**

② [except for, other than, but]

¶ I don't know anyone in Tokyo **but** you.

¶ As it was raining heavily, no one came **except** [Miss] Ueda and me.

* Usually used in the pattern "~ *hoka ni*" followed by a negative.

③ [besides, in addition to]

¶ Are there **any other** questions?

¶ There are Americans **as well as** Chinese in this class.

* Usually used in the pattern "~ *hoka ni.*"

hoken 〖n〗 insurance

insurance company // **insurance,**

(*hoken*kin) 健康保険 (kenkō-
hoken) 生命保険 (seimei-*hoken*)
火災保険 (kasai-*hoken*)
¶どんな保険に入っていますか。
(Donna *hoken* ni haitte imasu
ka?)
¶この車に保険を掛けましたか。
(Kono kuruma ni *hoken* o kakemashita ka?)

hōkō　方向〖名〗
①[進んでいく向き，方角]
風の方向 (kaze no *hōkō*)
¶駅はどちらの方向ですか。 (Eki wa
dochira no *hōkō* desu ka?)
¶東はこちらの方向だと思います。
(Higashi wa kochira no *hōkō* da to
omoimasu.)
②[目標・目的・方針など]
¶将来の方向はまだわかりません。
(Shōrai no *hōkō* wa mada wakarimasu.)

hōkoku　報告〖名，〜する〗
報告書 (*hōkoku*sho) 調査報告 (chōsa-
hōkoku) 研究報告 (kenkyū-*hōkoku*)
¶わたしは，そのことについてまだ報
告を受けていません。 (Watashi wa,
sono koto ni tsuite mada *hōkoku*
o ukete imasen.)
¶そのことについては，社長に詳しく
報告しました。 (Sono koto ni tsuite
wa, shachō ni kuwashiku *hōkoku*
shimashita.)

hokori　ほこり〖名〗
ほこりを払う (*hokori* o harau)

insurance money (that is, money
paid to one by an insurance company) // health **insurance** // life in-
surance // fire **insurance**
¶ What kinds of **insurance** do you
have?
¶ Have you taken out **insurance** on
〚**insured**〛 this car?

hōkō 〚n〛　direction, course;
course, aim, object
① [direction, course]
the direction of the wind
¶ In which **direction** is the station?
¶ I think that east is this **way.**

② [course, aim, object]
¶ I haven't decided on my future
course yet.

hōkoku 〚n, 〜*suru*〛　report
a written **report,** paper, transactions,
record // **a report** of an investigation, surveyor's **report,** findings // **a
report** of research, research paper
¶ I haven't yet received **a report** concerning that matter.
¶ [I] made a full **report** concerning
that matter to the president of the
company.

hokori 〚n〛　dust, lint
brush off **dust** 〚**lint**〛

¶あの部屋には，だいぶほこりがたまっています。(Ano heya ni wa, daibu *hokori* ga tamatte imasu.)

hōmen　方面〖名〗

①[その方向に当たる地域]

¶東京方面へ行く人は，ここで乗り換えてください。(Tōkyō *hōmen* e iku hito wa, koko de norikaete kudasai.)

②[領域・分野など]

¶中村さんは文学の方面に詳しいです。(Nakamura san wa bungaku no *hōmen* ni kuwashii desu.)

¶その計画は各方面から注目されています。　(Sono keikaku wa kaku-*hōmen* kara chūmoku sarete imasu.)

homeru　ほめる〖動Ⅱ〗

¶お母さんは子供をほめました。(Okāsan wa kodomo o *homemashita*.)

¶学生は先生にほめられました。(Gakusei wa sensei ni *homeraremashita*.)

hōmon　訪問〖名，～する〗

¶みんなで先生の家を訪問しました。(Minna de sensei no ie o *hōmon* shimashita.)

¶午後，社長を訪問する予定です。(Gogo, shachō o *hōmon* suru yotei desu.)

hon　本〖名〗

¶机の上に本が何冊ありますか。(Tsukue no ue ni *hon* ga nansatsu

¶ That room has gotten 〖is〗 very **dusty.**

hōmen 〖n〗　direction, district; field, aspect

① [direction, district]

¶ Persons going in **the direction** of Tokyo should transfer here.

② [field, aspect, sphere]

¶ [Mrs.] Nakamura is well acquainted with **the field** of literature.

¶ That project is attracting attention from all **sides.**

homeru 〖v II〗　praise

¶ The mother **praised** the child.

¶ The student **was praised** by the teacher.

hōmon 〖n, ～*suru*〗　call, visit, interview

¶ We all **visited** our teacher's home together.

¶ [I] intend to **pay a call** on the president of the company in the afternoon.

hon 〖n〗　book

¶ How many **books** are there on the desk?

arimasu ka?)

¶この本の5ページを開けてください。
(Kono *hon* no gopēji o akete kuda-sai.)

-hon -本〖尾〗
1本 (ip*pon*) 2本 (ni*hon*) 3本
(san*bon*) 4本 (yon*hon*) 5本
(go*hon*) 6本 (rop*pon*)
7本 (nana*hon*) 8本 (hap*pon*)
9 本 (kyū*hon*) 10本 (jip*pon*)

¶そこに鉛筆が何本ありますか。(Soko
ni enpitsu ga nan*bon* arimasu ka?)

hone 骨〖名〗

①[人・動物の体を支える堅い組織]
¶転んで足の骨を折りました。(Koron-
de ashi no *hone* o orimashita.)

¶この魚は骨がたくさんあります。
(Kono sakana wa *hone* ga takusan
arimasu.)

②[苦労をする，世話をする]
¶漢字の勉強はなかなか骨が折れます。
(Kanji no benkyō wa nakanaka
hone ga oremasu.)

¶彼が骨を折ってくれたので成功しま
した。(Kare ga *hone* o otte kureta
node seikō shimashita.)

＊「骨が折れる (hone ga oreru)」「骨
を折る (hone o oru)」の形で使うこ
とが多い。

hontō 本当〖名〗

¶それは本当ですか。(Sore wa *hontō*
desu ka?)

¶これは本当の話です。 (Kore wa
hontō no hanashi desu.)

-hon 〚suf〛 the counter for long,
cylindrical objects

one pen 〚pencil, piece of chalk,
cigarette, bottle, etc.〛 // two pens //
three pens // four pens // five pens //
six pens // seven pens // eight pens //
nine pens // ten pens

¶ **How many** pencils are there there?

hone 〚n〛 bones, skeleton; trouble,
pains, effort

① [bones, skeleton]

¶ [I] fell down and broke **a bone** in
[my] leg 〚foot〛.

¶ This fish has many **bones.**

② [trouble, pains, effort]

¶ Studying *kanji* **takes much effort**
〚*Kanji* are hard to learn〛.

¶ [We] succeeded because he **did so
much** for [us].

＊ Usually used in the patterns "*hone
ga oreru*" and "*hone o oru.*"

hontō 〚n〛 true, really, authentic

¶ Is that **true** 〚Is that **really so**〛?

¶ This is a **true** story 〚This is something that **really** happened〛.

⇨uso うそ

hontō ni 本当に〖副〗

¶今日は本当に暑いです。　(Kyō wa *hontō ni* atsui desu.)

¶本当にありがとうございました。(*Hontō ni* arigatō gozaimashita.)

⇨makoto ni まことに

hon'yaku 翻訳〖名, ～する〗

¶わたしは将来翻訳の仕事がしたいです。　(Watashi wa shōrai *hon'yaku* no shigoto ga shitai desu.)

¶英語の小説を日本語に翻訳しました。(Eigo no shōsetsu o Nihongo ni *hon'yaku* shimashita.)

¶この劇はフランス語から日本語に翻訳されたものです。　(Kono geki wa Furansugo kara Nihongo ni *hon'yaku* sareta mono desu.)

⇨yakusu 訳す

hoo 〖ほお〖名〗

¶子供がほおを赤くして走っています。(Kodomo ga *hoo* o akaku shite hashitte imasu.)

¶病気でだんだんほおがやせてきました。　(Byōki de dandan *hoo* ga yasete kimashita.)

＊「ほほ(hoho)」とも言う。

hōritsu 法律〖名〗

法律を守る (*hōritsu* o mamoru)

¶それは法律で禁止されています。(Sore wa *hōritsu* de kinshi sarete imasu.)

¶その法律を破ると、どうなりますか。(Sono *hōritsu* o yaburu to, dō nari-

---

hontō ni 〖adv〗 **really, very**

¶ It's **really** hot today.

¶ Thank you **very much indeed.**

hon'yaku 〖n, ~*suru*〗 **translation**

¶ In the future I want to do **translation** work.

¶ [I] **translated** a novel from English into Japanese.

¶ This play **has been translated** into Japanese from French.

hoo 〖n〗 **cheek(s)**

¶ The running children have rosy 〖reddened〗 **cheeks.**

¶ Due to illness [I] have gradually become quite hollow-**cheeked.**

＊ Variant: *hoho*.

hōritsu 〖n〗 **law**

observe **the law**

¶ That is prohibited by **law.**

¶ What will happen to [me] if [I] break that **law?**

214

masu ka?)

horobiru 滅びる〚動Ⅱ〛

国が滅びる (kuni ga *horobiru*)

¶その動物は日本ではもう滅びてしまいました。(Sono dōbutsu wa Nihon de wa mō *horobite* shimaimashita.)

horu 掘る〚動Ⅰ〛

¶庭に穴を掘って木を植えました。(Niwa ni ana o *hotte* ki o uemashita.)

¶山を掘ってトンネルを作りました。(Yama o *hotte* tonneru o tsukurimashita.)

hoshi 星〚名〛

星が出る (*hoshi* ga deru)　流れ星 (nagare*boshi*)

¶今夜は星がきれいです。(Kon'ya wa *hoshi* ga kirei desu.)

¶あの星はよく光っていますね。(Ano *hoshi* wa yoku hikatte imasu ne.)

hoshii 欲しい〚形〛

¶新しいくつが欲しいです。(Atarashii kutsu ga *hoshii* desu.)

¶今は何も欲しくありません。(Ima wa nani mo *hoshiku* arimasen.)

(～te) hoshii (～て)ほしい〚連〛

¶わたしの悪いところをはっきり言ってほしいんです。(Watashi no warui tokoro o hakkiri itte *hoshii* n desu.)

¶日曜にわたしの家に来てほしいのですが…。(Nichiyō ni watashi no ie ni kite *hoshii* no desu ga…)

hōshin 方針〚名〛

教育方針 (kyōiku-*hōshin*)

horobiru 〚v Ⅱ〛 **be ruined, perish**

a country **falls**

¶ That animal **has become extinct** in Japan.

horu 〚v Ⅰ〛 **dig, bore, drill**

¶ [I] **dug** a hole in the garden 〚yard〛 and planted a tree.

¶ **They cut** a tunnel through the mountain.

hoshi 〚n〛 **star**

the stars come out // a shooting **star,** meteor

¶ **The stars** are pretty tonight.

¶ That **star** is shining brightly, isn't it?

hoshii 〚adj〛 (I) **want, desire**

¶ **I want** some new shoes.

¶ **I don't want** anything right now.

(-te) hoshii 〚compd〛 **I want someone to ～**

¶ **I would like** you to frankly tell me my bad points.

¶ **I would like** you to come to my house on Sunday if you can.

hōshin 〚n〛 **course, policy**

educational **policy**

¶来年度の**方針**を立てましょう。
(Rainendo no *hōshin* o tatemashō.)
¶政府の外交**方針**が発表されました。
(Seifu no gaikō-*hōshin* ga happyō saremashita.)

hoshō 保証〖名, 〜する〗
¶この時計には１年間の**保証**がついています。(Kono tokei ni wa ichinen-kan no *hoshō* ga tsuite imasu.)
¶彼の正直なことはわたしが**保証**します。 (Kare no shōjiki na koto wa watashi ga *hoshō* shimasu.)
¶入学には**保証**人が必要です。(Nyūgaku ni wa *hoshō*nin ga hitsuyō desu.)

hoshō 保障〖名, 〜する〗
安全**保障** (anzen-*hoshō*) 老後の生活を**保障**する (rōgo no seikatsu o *hoshō* suru)
¶社会**保障**は現在大きな社会問題の一つになっています。 (Shakai-*hoshō* wa genzai ookina shakai-mondai no hitotsu ni natte imasu.)

hōsō 放送〖名, 〜する〗
放送番組 (*hōsō*-bangumi) **放送**局 (*hōsō*kyoku) 海外**放送** (kaigai-*hōsō*)
¶午後１時からテレビで首相の**放送**があります。 (Gogo ichiji kara terebi de shushō no *hōsō* ga arimasu.)
¶その事件はニュースで**放送**されました。(Sono jiken wa nyūsu de *hōsō* saremashita.)

hosoi 細い〖形〗
¶**細い**ひもで縛ると切れてしまいます。

¶ Let's formulate **our policy** 〚map out **our course**〛 for next year.
¶ The government's foreign **policy** has been announced.

hoshō 〚n, 〜*suru*〛 **guarantee**
¶ This watch 〚clock〛 has a one-year **guarantee.**

¶ I **will vouch for** his honesty.

¶ **A sponsor** 〚reference, guarantor〛 is necessary for admission to the school 〚college〛.

hoshō 〚n, 〜*suru*〛 **security, guarantee**
(national) **security** // **guarantee** the livelihood of the elderly

¶ Social **security** is presently a major social problem.

hōsō 〚n, 〜*suru*〛 (radio, television) **broadcasting**
a **radio** program, **television** program // a **broadcasting** station, **radio** or **television** station // overseas **broadcasting**, an overseas **broadcast**
¶ There will be a television **broadcast** by the prime minister at 1 PM.
¶ That incident **was broadcast** on the news.

hosoi 〚adj〛 **thin, fine, slender, narrow**
¶ It will break if you tie it with a thin

(*Hosoi* himo de shibaru to kirete shimaimasu.)

¶彼のズボンは細くて長いですね。

(Kare no zubon wa *hosokute* nagai desu ne.)

⇔futoi 太い

hosu 干す〖動Ⅰ〗

¶庭に洗たく物を干しました。 (Niwa ni sentakumono o *hoshimashita*.)

¶この干した魚を食べてみますか。

(Kono *hoshita* sakana o tabete mimasu ka?)

hoteru ホテル〖名〗

¶駅のそばのホテルに泊まりました。

(Eki no soba no *hoteru* ni tomarimashita.)

¶ホテルに部屋を予約しました。

(*Hoteru* ni heya o yoyaku shimashita.)

hotondo ほとんど〖名, 副〗

1〖名〗

¶出席者のほとんどがそれに賛成しました。 (Shussekisha no *hotondo* ga sore ni sansei shimashita.)

¶ほとんどの学生がその会に出席しました。(*Hotondo* no gakusei ga sono kai ni shusseki shimashita.)

2〖副〗

¶病気はほとんどよくなりました。

(Byōki wa *hotondo* yoku narimashita.)

¶その仕事はほとんど終わりました。

(Sono shigoto wa *hotondo* owarimashita.)

string 〖cord〗.

¶ His trousers are long and **slender-legged.**

hosu 〖v I〗 **dry**

¶ [I] **dried** the laundry in the yard.

¶ Will you try a taste of this **dried** fish?

hoteru 〖n〗 **hotel**

¶ [I] stayed at **a hotel** near the station.

¶ [I] reserved a room at **a hotel.**

hotondo 〖n, adv〗 **almost all; almost, nearly**

1 〖n〗 almost all

¶ **Almost all** of those present were in favor of that.

¶ **Almost all** of the students attended that meeting 〖assembly, party〗.

2 〖adv〗 almost, nearly

¶ [I] am **almost completely** recovered from [my] illness.

¶ That work is **nearly** finished.

hyaku 百〖名〗

hyō 表〖名〗

時間表 (jikan*hyō*)　時刻表 (jikoku-*hyō*)　予定表 (yotei*hyō*)　動詞の活用表 (dōshi no katsuyō*hyō*)

¶1か月の予定を表にしました。

(Ikkagetsu no yotei o *hyō* ni shimashita.)

¶調査の結果を表にまとめてください。

(Chōsa no kekka o *hyō* ni matomete kudasai.)

hyōban 評判〖名〗

¶あの先生はたいへん評判がいいです。

(Ano sensei wa taihen *hyōban* ga ii desu.)

¶新しい社長の評判はどうですか。

(Atarashii shachō no *hyōban* wa dō desu ka?)

hyōgen 表現〖名，〜する〗

表現の自由 (*hyōgen* no jiyū)

¶自分の考えを正確に表現するのは難しいことです。(Jibun no kangae o seikaku ni *hyōgen* suru no wa muzukashii koto desu.)

hyōjun 標準〖名〗

標準語 (*hyōjun*go)

¶田中さんのうちの赤ちゃんは標準よりかなり大きいそうです。(Tanaka san no uchi no akachan wa *hyōjun* yori kanari ookii sō desu.)

¶彼の成績は標準以下です。(Kare no seiseki wa *hyōjun* ika desu.)

hyōmen 表面〖名〗

①〔物の外側の部分〕

hyaku 〚n〛 one hundred

hyō 〚n〛 table, schedule, chart, list, diagram

schedule // **schedule** of arrivals and departures // **program, schedule** // **table** of verb conjugations

¶ [I] made a one-month **schedule** (in tabular form).

¶ Please put the results of the survey into **tabular form.**

hyōban 〚n〛 reputation, public estimation, popularity

¶ That teacher **is highly spoken of** 〖That teacher **is very popular**〗.

¶ What does everyone **think of** the new president of the company?

hyōgen 〚n, ~*suru*〛 expression

freedom of **expression**

¶ It is difficult **to** precisely **express** one's thoughts.

hyōjun 〚n〛 standard, norm

the **standard** language

¶ I hear that the Tanaka baby is considerably larger than **the norm.**

¶ His grades are 〖business record is〗 **substandard.**

hyōmen 〚n〛 surface; exterior

① [surface]

¶月の表面には穴がたくさんあります。
(Tsuki no *hyōmen* ni wa ana ga takusan arimasu.)

¶ There are many holes in **the surface** of the moon.

②[外に現れたところ，うわべ]

¶彼は表面は穏やかですが，心の中では怒っているでしょう。 (Kare wa *hyōmen* wa odayaka desu ga, kokoro no naka de wa okotte iru deshō.)

② [exterior, outward appearance]

¶ He is **outwardly** calm, but inwardly he's probably angry 〔He is calm **on the outside,** but I bet he's angry on the inside〕.

I

i 胃〖名〗
胃腸 (ichō)
¶最近, 少し胃の調子が悪いです。
(Saikin, sukoshi *i* no chōshi ga warui desu.)
¶あの子は胃が丈夫です。(Ano ko wa *i* ga jōbu desu.)

ichi 一〖名〗

ichi 位置〖名, 〜する〗
¶この部屋の家具の位置を変えましょう。(Kono heya no kagu no *ichi* o kaemashō.)
¶わたしの学校は東京の東に位置しています。(Watashi no gakkō wa Tōkyō no higashi ni *ichi* shite imasu.)

ichiba 市場〖名〗
¶母は市場へ買い物に行きました。
(Haha wa *ichiba* e kaimono ni ikimashita.)
¶市場はいつもこんでいます。(*Ichiba* wa itsu mo konde imasu.)

ichiban いちばん〖副〗
¶いちばん好きな食べ物は何ですか。
(*Ichiban* suki na tabemono wa nan desu ka?)
¶東京は日本でいちばん大きい都会です。(Tōkyō wa Nihon de *ichiban* ookii tokai desu.)

ichibu 一部〖名〗
¶一部の人はその計画に反対です。

i 〚n〛 **stomach**
stomach and intestines
¶ [I] have recently been having some **stomach** trouble.

¶ That child has a strong **stomach** 〚good **digestion**〛.

ichi 〚n〛 **one**

ichi 〚n, ~*suru*〛 **location, position**
¶ Let's change **the position** of the furniture in this room.

¶ My school **is located** to the east of Tokyo 〚in east Tokyo〛.

ichiba 〚n〛 **market, marketplace**
¶ My mother went to **the market** to shop.

¶ **The market** is always crowded.

ichiban 〚adv〛 **most, best, number one, first**
¶ What foods do you like **the best?**

¶ Tokyo is the **largest** city in Japan.

ichibu 〚n〛 **part, section**
¶ **Some** are opposed to that plan.

220

(*Ichibu* no hito wa sono keikaku ni hantai desu.)

¶台風で村の一部に被害が出ました。

(Taifū de mura no *ichibu* ni higai ga demashita.)

⇨zenbu 全部

ichibubun 一部分〖名〗

¶宿題はまだ一部分しか終わっていません。(Shukudai wa mada *ichibubun* shika owatte imasen.)

¶昨夜の火事で,町は一部分を残してほとんど焼けてしまいました。(Sakuya no kaji de, machi wa *ichibubun* o nokoshite hotondo yakete shimaimashita.)

⇨daibubun 大部分

ichido ni 一度に〖副〗

¶電車のドアが開くと,一度にたくさんの人が降りてきました。 (Densha no doa ga aku to, *ichido ni* takusan no hito ga orite kimashita.)

¶こんなにたくさんの仕事を一度にやろうと思っても無理です。(Konna ni takusan no shigoto o *ichido ni* yarō to omotte mo muri desu.)

⇨ichiji ni 一時に

ichigatsu 一月〖名〗

ichigo いちご〖名〗

ichiji 一時〖名〗

①[短い時間,しばらくの間]

一時停止 (*ichiji*-teishi)

¶工事のため一時店を閉めます。(Kōji no tame *ichiji* mise o shimemasu.)

¶子供が病気で,一時はとても心配で

¶ **Part** of the village was damaged in the typhoon.

ichibubun 〚n〛 **part, section**

¶ Only **part** of the homework is done.

¶ Almost all of the town burned down in the fire last night; only **a part** of it remains.

ichido ni 〚adv〛 **at once, at one time, simultaneously**

¶ When the train doors opened, lots of people poured out **all at once.**

¶ It is impossible to think of doing this much work **at one time.**

ichigatsu 〚n〛 **January**

ichigo 〚n〛 **strawberries**

ichiji 〚n〛 **for a time, temporarily; once, at one time; one o'clock**

① [for a time, temporarily]

momentary stop (of a train, car, etc.)

¶ The shop will be closed **temporarily** due to construction.

した。(Kodomo ga byōki de, *ichiji* wa totemo shinpai deshita.)

②〔過去のある時，その当時〕

¶あの歌は一時たいへんはやりました。(Ano uta wa *ichiji* taihen hayarimashita.)

ichiji ni 一時に〘副〙

¶一時にそんなにたくさんのことはできません。(*Ichiji ni* sonna ni takusan no koto wa dekimasen.)

⇨**ichido ni** 一度に

ichinichi 一日〘名〙

¶雨が降っていたので，今日は一日じゅう家にいました。(Ame ga futte ita node, kyō wa *ichinichi*jū ie ni imashita.)

¶これでやっと一日の仕事が終わりました。(Kore de yatto *ichinichi* no shigoto ga owarimashita.)

⇨**-nichi** -日

ichiō 一応〘副〙

¶できるかどうかわかりませんが，一応やってみましょう。(Dekiru ka dō ka wakarimasen ga, *ichiō* yatte mimashō.)

¶決める前に一応あの人に相談してください。(Kimeru mae ni *ichiō* ano hito ni sōdan shite kudasai.)

¶上田さんは旅行には行かないと思いますが，一応話してみましょう。(Ueda san wa ryokō ni wa ikanai to omoimasu ga, *ichiō* hanashite mimashō.)

ido 井戸〘名〙

¶ **For a time** [we] were very worried by [our] child's illness.

② [once, at one time]

¶ **At one time** that song was very popular.

ichiji ni 〖adv〗 at once, at one time, all together

¶ [I] cannot do that much 〚that many things〛 **all at one time.**

ichinichi 〖n〗 one day, all day

¶ As it was raining, [I] stayed at home **all day** today.

¶ With this the **day's** work is finally finished.

ichiō 〖adv〗 once, in outline, in general, tentatively, for the time being

¶ I'm not sure whether it can be done or not but I'll just give it a try **anyway.**

¶ Before deciding please consult with [him] **once** about it.

¶ I don't think [Mr.] Ueda will be going on the trip but let's talk to him about it **just in case.**

ido 〖n〗 a well

井戸を掘る (*ido o horu*)

¶この地方では井戸の水を使っています。　(Kono chihō de wa *ido* no mizu o tsukatte imasu.)

dig **a well**

¶ In this region **well**-water is used.

ie　家〔名〕

①〔住居〕

¶あの人の家はこの近くです。　(Ano hito no *ie* wa kono chikaku desu.)

¶彼は最近立派な家を建てました。　(Kare wa saikin rippa na *ie* o tatemashita.)

②〔家庭〕

¶田中さんの家にはピアノがあります。　(Tanaka san no *ie* ni wa piano ga arimasu.)

¶彼は貧しい家に生まれました。　(Kare wa mazushii *ie* ni umaremashita.)

⇒**uchi** うち

ie 〚n〛 **house, home; household, family**

① [house, home, residence]

¶ [His] **home** is near here.

¶ He recently built a lovely **house.**

② [household, family]

¶ **The Tanakas** have a piano.

¶ He was born into a poor **family.**

igai　意外〔形動〕

意外な事件 (*igai* na jiken)　意外な結果 (*igai* na kekka)

¶試験は意外に易しかったです。　(Shiken wa *igai* ni yasashikatta desu.)

¶試験に失敗したと思っていたら，意外なことにいい成績でした。 (Shiken ni shippai shita to omotte itara, *igai* na koto ni ii seiseki deshita.)

igai 〚adj-v〛 **unexpected, surprising**

a **surprising** incident // an **unexpected** outcome

¶ The test was **surprisingly** easy.

¶ I thought I had failed the test, but **to my surprise** I got a good grade on it.

igai　以外〔名〕

¶生の魚以外は何でも食べます。　(Nama no sakana *igai* wa nan demo tabemasu.)

¶そこへ行くには歩く以外に方法があ

igai 〚n〛 **except for, other than**

¶ I eat everything **with the exception** of raw fish.

¶ One can **only** go there on foot

りません。(Soko e iku ni wa aruku *igai* ni hōhō ga arimasen.)

igaku 医学〔名〕

医学博士 (*igaku*-hakushi)

¶わたしは医学の勉強をしたいと思っています。 (Watashi wa *igaku* no benkyō o shitai to omotte imasu.)

¶あの国の医学はたいへん進んでいます。(Ano kuni no *igaku* wa taihen susunde imasu.)

igo 以後〔名〕

①[その時からのち]

¶午後5時以後はうちにいます。

(Gogo goji *igo* wa uchi ni imasu.)

↔izen 以前

②[今からのち, 今後]

¶すみません。以後じゅうぶん気をつけます。 (Sumimasen. *Igo* jūbun ki o tsukemasu.)

ihan 違反〔名, ～する〕

規則違反 (kisoku-*ihan*) 交通違反 (kōtsū-*ihan*) 選挙違反 (senkyo-*ihan*) スピード違反 (supiido-*ihan*) 契約に違反する (keiyaku ni *ihan* suru)

¶そんなことをすると法律に違反します。(Sonna koto o suru to hōritsu ni *ihan* shimasu.)

ii いい〔形〕

①[正しい立派な様子]

¶困っている人を助けることはいいことですよ。 (Komatte iru hito o tasukeru koto wa *ii* koto desu yo.)

¶いいと思ったことは, 勇気を出して

[There is no way to get there **other than** on foot].

igaku 〚n〛 **medicine, medical science**

a doctor **of medicine,** an MD

¶ I want to study **medicine.**

¶ **Medicine** is very advanced in that country.

igo 〚n〛 **after that, afterward; after this, from now on**

① [after that, afterward, thereafter]

¶ I will be at home **after** 5 PM.

② [after this, from now on, hereafter, in the future]

¶ I'm sorry. I'll be very careful **from now on.**

ihan 〚n, ～*suru*〛 **violation, infraction**

a violation of regulations, **an infraction** of the rules // a traffic **violation** // an election law **violation** // a speeding **violation,** speeding // **violate** a contract

¶ That sort of thing **is against** the law.

ii 〚adj〛 **good, right; excellent, fine; suitable**

① [good, right]

¶ **It is good** to help those who are in trouble.

¶ Be brave and do what you think is

right.

②[善良である様子]
¶上田さんは親切ないい人です。
(Ueda san wa shinsetsu na *ii* hito desu.)

↔warui 悪い →yoi よい

②[good, good-natured]
¶[Mrs.] Ueda is a kind and **good** person.

③[親しい様子]
¶山田さんと中村さんは仲がいいです。
(Yamada san to Nakamura san wa naka ga *ii* desu.)
* 普通「仲がいい (naka ga ii)」の形で使う。

↔warui 悪い →yoi よい

③[good, close, intimate]
¶[Mr.] Yamada and [Mr.] Nakamura are on **good** terms with each other.
* Usually used in the pattern "*naka ga ii.*"

④[ものごとの優れている様子]
いい声 (*ii* koe) いい品物 (*ii* shinamono) いい習慣 (*ii* shūkan)
¶あの子はたいへん頭がいいです。
(Ano ko wa taihen atama ga *ii* desu.)
¶中村さんは2学期はたいへんいい成績でした。 (Nakamura san wa nigakki wa taihen *ii* seiseki deshita.)

↔warui 悪い →yoi よい

④[good, excellent, fine]
a **fine** voice // **good** merchandise // a **good** custom 〔habit〕
¶That child is very **bright**.
¶[Miss] Nakamura got very **good** grades the second semester.

⑤[好ましい様子, 気持ちのよい様子]
景色がいい (keshiki ga *ii*) 気分がいい (kibun ga *ii*)
¶今日はいい天気です。 (Kyō wa *ii* tenki desu.)
¶この店は感じのいい店ですね。
(Kono mise wa kanji no *ii* mise desu ne.)
¶少しお酒を飲んで, いい気持ちにな

⑤[good, fine, pleasing, nice]
a **nice** view // be in a **good** mood, feel **good**
¶It's a **beautiful** day today.
¶This shop 〔restaurant, bar, etc.〕 has a **nice** feel about it.
¶[I] drank a little and felt **good**.

225

りました。(Sukoshi osake o nonde, *ii* kimochi ni narimashita.)

↔**warui 悪い** →**yoi よい**

⑥［感情的に望ましい様子］

¶お母さんの病気が早くよくなるといいですね。 (Okāsan no byōki ga hayaku yoku naru to *ii* desu ne.)

⑦［適当で望ましいと思う様子］

¶あんな所へは二度と行かないほうがいいですよ。 (Anna tokoro e wa nido to ikanai hō ga *ii* desu yo.)

¶わたしはこちらのほうがいいです。 (Watashi wa kochira no hō ga *ii* desu.)

＊普通「ほうがいい (hō ga ii)」の形で使う。

⑧［好都合な様子，ほどよい様子］

¶この辞書は小さくて，持って歩くのにはちょうどいいです。 (Kono jisho wa chiisakute, motte aruku no ni wa chōdo *ii* desu.)

¶このシャツはあなたにちょうどいい大きさです。 (Kono shatsu wa anata ni chōdo *ii* ookisa desu.)

⑨［じゅうぶんである様子］

¶今度の旅行には，どのぐらいお金を持って行けばいいでしょう。 (Kondo no ryokō ni wa, dono gurai okane o motte ikeba *ii* deshō?)

→**yoi よい**

⑩［あるものごとに対して効果がある様子］

健康にいい体操 (kenkō ni *ii* taisō)

¶この薬は風邪にたいへんいいですよ。

⑥ [it would be good if ~, I hope, I wish]

¶ **I hope** your mother recovers quickly from her illness.

⑦ [be better, prefer]

¶ **It would be best** not to go to that sort of place a second time.

¶ I **prefer** this one.

＊ Usually used in the pattern "~ *hō ga ii*."

⑧ [good, proper, suitable]

¶ This dictionary is small and just **right** for carrying about with one.

¶ This shirt is exactly the **right** size for you.

⑨ [will do, be enough, serve the purpose]

¶ How much money **should** one bring on the trip?

⑩ [good for, efficacious]

exercise **that is good** for one's health

¶ This medicine **is** very **good** for a

(Kono kusuri wa kaze ni taihen *ii* desu yo.)

↔**warui** 悪い

＊「いい (ii)」は「終止の形」「連体の形」が 使われる。「ないの形」は「よくない (yoku nai)」「たの形」は「よかった (yokatta)」などと「よい yoi」が使われる。

＊ *Ii* is the sentence-final and dictionary form. *Yoi* is used for other forms: the negative form is *yoku nai* and the -*ta* form is *yokatta*.

（〜te mo）ii　（〜ても）いい〘連〙

①［許可の意味を表す］

¶試験はボールペンで書いてもいいです。 (Shiken wa bōrupen de kaite mo *ii* desu.)

¶「ここでたばこを吸ってもいいですか。」 (Koko de tabako o sutte mo *ii* desu ka?) 「いいえ，吸ってはいけません。」 (Iie, sutte wa ikemasen.)

②［不必要の意味を表す］

¶そんなに急がなくてもいいです。 (Sonna ni isoganakute mo *ii* desu.)

¶「薬を飲まなくてもいいですか。」 (Kusuri o nomanakute mo *ii* desu ka?)「いいえ，飲まなくてはいけません。」 (Iie, nomanakute wa ikemasen.)

＊「〜なくてもいい (〜 nakute mo ii)」の形で使う。

⇔**（〜te wa）ikenai　（〜ては）いけない**　⇒**（〜te mo）kamawanai （〜ても）かまわない**

（-te mo）ii 〘compd〙 **may 〜, be all right to 〜; do not have to 〜**

① [may 〜, be all right to 〜]

¶ **One may** use a ball-point pen for the test.

¶ "**Is it all right** to smoke here?"
"No, it isn't."

② [do not have to 〜, need not 〜]

¶ [You] **don't have to** hurry so.

¶ "**Is it all right** not to take any medicine?"
"No, you have to take some."

＊ Used in the pattern "-*nakute mo ii*."

iie　いいえ〘感〙

¶「あれはあなたの本ですか。」 (Are wa anata no hon desu ka?)
「いいえ，違います。」(*Iie*, chigaima-

iie 〘interj〙 **no**

¶ "Is that your book?"
"**No,** it's not."

cold 〚the flu〛.

su.)

¶「あなたは日本語が話せますか。」

(Anata wa Nihongo ga hanase-

masu ka?) 「いいえ，話せません。」

(*Iie*, hanasemasen.)

⇔**hai** はい

iin 委員〖名〗

委員長 (*iin*chō) 委員会 (*iin*kai)

¶クラスの新しい委員を選びました。

(Kurasu no atarashii *iin* o erabi-

mashita.)

¶その問題について委員の報告を聞き

ました。 (Sono mondai ni tsuite *iin*

no hōkoku o kikimashita.)

iiwake 言い訳〖名〗

¶彼はいつもいろいろと言い訳をしま

す。 (Kare wa itsu mo iroiro to

iiwake o shimasu.)

¶そんな言い訳は聞きたくありません。

(Sonna *iiwake* wa kikitaku ari-

masen.)

ijimeru いじめる〖動Ⅱ〗

¶動物をいじめてはいけません。

(Dōbutsu o *ijimete* wa ikemasen.)

¶男の子が女の子をいじめています。

(Otoko no ko ga onna no ko o

ijimete imasu.)

ijō 以上〖名〗

①〔ある数量・時間などよりも多いこ

と〕

¶毎日 8 時間以上働きます。(Mainichi

hachijikan *ijō* hatarakimasu.)

¶この地方では一年間に千ミリ以上の

雨が降ります。 (Kono chihō de wa

¶ "Can you speak Japanese?"

"**No,** I can't."

iin 〚n〛 **committee member, delegate**

the **committee** chairman // a committee, commission, board, panel

¶ [We] chose a new class **representative.**

¶ [I] listened to **the commissioner's**
report concerning that problem.

iiwake 〚n〛 **explanation, excuse,
apology**

¶ He always has various **excuses.**

¶ I don't want to hear that kind of
excuse.

ijimeru 〚v II〛 **tease, annoy, ill-
treat, torment, persecute**

¶ One mustn't **tease** 〚**torment**〛
animals.

¶ A boy is **teasing** 〚**annoying**〛 a
girl.

ijō 〚n〛 **or more, more than;
beyond, above; the above-
mentioned; since, seeing that**

① [or more, more than, not less
than]

¶ [I] work **more than** eight hours
〚eight hours **or more**〛 every day.

¶ One thousand millimeters **or more**
of rain falls a year in this area.

ichinenkan ni senmiri *ijō* no ame ga furimasu.)

*「8時間以上 (hachijikan ijō)」という場合は8時間を含む。

↔**ika** 以下

②［ある状態などよりも程度が高いこと］

平均以上 (heikin *ijo*)

¶試験は予想以上に難しかったです。(Shiken wa yosō *ijō* ni muzukashikatta desu.)

¶もうこれ以上我慢できません。(Mō kore *ijō* gaman dekimasen.)

↔**ika** 以下

③［これまでに言ったことなど］

¶私の言いたいことは以上です。(Watakushi no iitai koto wa *ijō* desu.)

¶以上，どうぞよろしくお願いします。(*Ijō*, dōzo yoroshiku onegai shimasu.)

↔**ika** 以下

④［前のことがらによってあとのことがらが当然成立するという関係を表す］

¶約束した以上，守らなければなりません。(Yakusoku shita *ijō*, mamoranakereba narimasen.)

¶お世話になった以上，お礼を言うのは当然です。(Osewa ni natta *ijō*, orei o iu no wa tōzen desu.)

ijō 異常〖名，形動〗

¶機械を調べてみましたが，何も異常はありません。(Kikai o shirabete

* When *ijō* is used with a figure, it means that figure and more. Thus, strictly speaking, *hachijikan ijō* means "eight hours or more" and not simply "more than eight hours."

② [beyond, above, past]

above average

¶ The exam was **more** difficult than expected.

¶ I can't stand **any more** than this 〖This is all I can take〗.

③ [the above-mentioned, the foregoing]

¶ **That** is all I had to say.

¶ I now commend **this matter** to you 〖I hereby ask for your cooperation in **the above matter**〗.

④ [since, so long as, seeing that]

¶ You must keep a promise **once** you have made it.

¶ It is only fitting to thank people **after** being helped by them.

ijō 〖n, adj-v〗 **unusual, abnormal**

¶ [I] have examined the machinery but there is nothing **wrong** with it.

mimashita ga, nani mo *ijō* wa arimasen.)

¶今年の夏は**異常**に暑かったです。

(Kotoshi no natsu wa *ijō* ni atsukatta desu.)

ika　以下〖名〗

①[ある数量・時間などよりも少ないこと]

¶今朝は零度**以下**まで気温が下がりました。　(Kesa wa reido *ika* made kion ga sagarimashita.)

¶１９歳**以下**の人はたばこを吸ってはいけません。(Jūkyūsai *ika* no hito wa tabako o sutte wa ikemasen.)

＊「１９歳**以下** (jūkyūsai ika)」という場合は１９歳も含む。

②[ある状態などよりも程度が低いこと]

平均**以下** (heikin *ika*)

¶今年の米の収穫は予想**以下**でした。

(Kotoshi no kome no shūkaku wa yosō *ika* deshita.)

③[これまでに言ったことよりあとのこと]

¶**以下**は彼の言葉です。(*Ika* wa kare no kotoba desu.)

¶**以下**は省略します。(*Ika* wa shōryaku shimasu.)

⇔**ijō** 以上

ikaga　いかが〖副〗

¶お体のぐあいはいかがですか。

(Okarada no guai wa *ikaga* desu ka?)

¶コーヒーをもう一杯いかがですか。

¶ Summer was **abnormally** hot this year.

ika 〚n〛 **and less, less than; under, below; the following**

① [and less, less than, under, below]

¶ Temperatures fell to zero **and below** this morning.

¶ Those 19 years of age **and below** aren't allowed to smoke.

＊ When used with a figure, *ika* means that figure and less. Thus, strictly speaking, *jūkyūsai ika* means "19 years and below" and not simply "less than 19 years."

② [under, below]

below average

¶ The rice harvest this year was **smaller** than expected.

③ [the following, the hereafter, mentioned below]

¶ **The following** is in his own words.

¶ **The rest** is omitted.

ikaga 〚adv〛 **how, what**

¶ **How** do you feel (literally, **What** is the condition of your body)?

¶ Would you like another cup of cof-

(Kōhii o mō ippai *ikaga* desu ka?)

＊「どう (dō)」より丁寧な言葉。

⇨**dō** どう

ikasu　生かす〖動Ⅰ〗

¶川で捕った魚は,あの池の中で生かしておきましょう。 (Kawa de totta sakana wa, ano ike no naka de *ikashite* okimashō.)

ike　池〖名〗

¶庭に池があって，金魚が泳いでいます。 (Niwa ni *ike* ga atte, kingyo ga oyoide imasu.)

¶今朝は池の水が凍りました。

(Kesa wa *ike* no mizu ga koorimashita.)

ikebana　生け花〖名〗

¶生け花を習っていますか。 (*Ikebana* o naratte imasu ka?)

¶田中さんは生け花の歴史を研究しています。 (Tanaka san wa *ikebana* no rekishi o kenkyū shite imasu.)

iken　意見〖名，〜する〗

①［あるものごとについての考え］

意見を言う (*iken* o iu)　意見を述べる (*iken* o noberu)

¶わたしもあなたと同じ意見です。

(Watashi mo anata to onaji *iken* desu.)

¶あなたとはよく意見が合いますね。

(Anata to wa yoku *iken* ga aimasu ne.)

¶みんなその意見に従いました。(Minna sono *iken* ni shitagaimashita.)

②［教えるように言って聞かせること］

---

fee?

＊ *Ikaga* is more polite than *dō*.

ikasu 〚v I〛　revive, keep alive

¶ Let's put the fish [we] caught in the river into the pond 〚pool〛 (literally, Let's put the fish we caught in the river into the pond and **keep them alive**).

ike 〚n〛　pond, pool, basin

¶ There's **a pool** in the garden where goldfish are swimming.

¶ **The pond** froze this morning.

ikebana 〚n〛　Japanese flower arrangement, *ikebana*

¶ Are you studying *ikebana?*

¶ [Mrs.] Tanaka is researching the history of *ikebana.*

iken 〚n, ~*suru*〛　opinion, view; advice, admonition

① [opinion, view, idea]

give 〚express〛 **one's opinion** // give 〚express〛 **one's opinion**

¶ I agree with your **opinion.**

¶ We often hold the same **opinion,** don't we?

¶ Everyone accepted that **opinion.**

② [advice, admonition]

231

¶勉強しないので，子供に意見しました。(Benkyō shinai node, kodomo ni *iken* shimashita.)

¶ [I] **scolded** the children for not studying.

ikenai いけない〖連〗

¶あなたの言い方がいけなかったので，あの人は怒ったのです。 (Anata no iikata ga *ikenakatta* node, ano hito wa okotta no desu.)

¶風邪を引くといけないから，もう一枚シャツを着ました。(Kaze o hiku to *ikenai* kara, mō ichimai shatsu o kimashita.)

ikenai 〖compd〗 **bad, wrong, to blame**

¶ [He] got angry because the way you talked to [him] **was out of line.**

¶ [I] wore one more shirt as [I] **didn't want to** catch a cold.

(～te wa) ikenai （～ては）いけない〖連〗

¶この中へ入ってはいけません。(Kono naka e haitte wa *ikemasen*.)

¶ここでたばこを吸ってはいけません。(Koko de tabako o sutte wa *ikemasen*.)

⇔(～te mo) ii （～ても）いい
⇔(～te mo) kamawanai （～ても）かまわない

(-te wa) ikenai 〖compd〗 **must not, should not, be forbidden**

¶ **No** admittance 〖Keep out; **Don't** come into this place; etc.〗.
¶ This is a **no**-smoking area.

iki 息〖名〗

息をする (*iki* o suru) 息をはく (*iki* o haku)

¶走ったので息が切れました。(Hashitta node *iki* ga kiremashita.)

¶深く息を吸ってください。(Fukaku *iki* o sutte kudasai.)

iki 〖n〗 **a breath, breathing**

to breathe // breathe out, exhale
¶ [I] am **out of breath** as [I] have been running 〖I was **out of breath** as I had been running〗.
¶ Please take a deep **breath.**

iki 行き〖名〗

行き帰り (*iki*kaeri) 行き先 (*iki*-saki)

¶行きの切符は買えましたが，帰りの切符は買えませんでした。(*Iki* no kippu

iki 〖n〗 **going, bound for**

going and returning, coming and **going** // destination
¶ [I] was able to buy a ticket **for the trip there** but couldn't get a return

wa kaemashita ga, kaeri no kippu
wa kaemasen deshita.)

¶東京行きの電車に乗りました。

(Tōkyō *iki* no densha ni norimashita.)

⇨yuki 行き

ikinari　いきなり〚副〛

¶道路にいきなり子供が飛び出してき
ました。　(Dōro ni *ikinari* kodomo
ga tobidashite kimashita.)

¶いきなり質問されても答えられませ
ん。　(*Ikinari* shitsumon sarete mo
kotaeraremasen.)

ikioi　勢い〚名〛

¶この村の農業は非常な勢いで発展し
ました。(Kono mura no nōgyō wa
hijō na *ikioi* de hatten shimashita.)

¶子供は勢いよく走っていきました。

(Kodomo wa *ikioi* yoku hashitte
ikimashita.)

ikiru　生きる〚動Ⅱ〛

¶百歳まで生きる人は少ないです。

(Hyakusai made *ikiru* hito wa
sukunai desu.)

¶この虫は何を食べて生きていますか。

(Kono mushi wa nani o tabete
ikite imasu ka?)

ikka　一家〚名〛

¶田中さん一家は音楽がたいへん好き
です。(Tanaka san *ikka* wa ongaku
ga taihen suki desu.)

¶昨日は一家そろって買い物に出かけ
ました。(Kinō wa *ikka* sorotte kaimono ni dekakemashita.)

ticket.

¶ [I] got on the train **for** Tokyo.

ikinari 〚adv〛　**suddenly, abruptly,
all of a sudden, without notice**

¶ A child **suddenly** ran out into the
road 〚A child has **suddenly** run out
into the road〛.

¶ [I] can't answer when **suddenly**
asked something.

ikioi 〚n〛　**vigor, energy, power,
force**

¶ Agriculture has advanced **in a
spurt** in this village.

¶ The children ran off **energetically.**

ikiru 〚v Ⅱ〛　**live, be alive**

¶ Few people **live** to the age of one
hundred.

¶ What does this insect **subsist** on?

ikka 〚n〛　**a family, a household**

¶ The Tanaka **family** is very fond of
music.

¶ Yesterday the whole **family** went
out shopping together.

iku 行く〖動Ⅰ〗

①[ある目的の所へ向かって進む]

¶昨日はどこへ**行きました**か。 (Kinō wa doko e *ikimashita* ka?)

¶このバスは飛行場へ**行きます**か。 (Kono basu wa hikōjō e *ikimasu* ka?)

↔kuru 来る

②[ものごとが行われる]

¶今度の計画はうまく**いき**そうです。 (Kondo no keikaku wa umaku *ikisō* desu.)

¶この仕事はあなたが考えているようにはいかないと思いますよ。 (Kono shigoto wa anata ga kangaete iru yō ni wa *ikanai* to omoimasu yo.)

③[結婚して他家に入る]

¶春子さんは去年の春お嫁に**いきまし た**。 (Haruko san wa kyonen no haru oyome ni *ikimashita*.)

＊「行く (yuku)」とも言う。

(〜te) iku (〜て)いく〖連〗

①[動作がある方向へ進むことを表す]

¶鳥が北の方へ飛んで**いきます**。 (Tori ga kita no hō e tonde *iki-masu*.)

¶子供はお弁当を持って**いきました**。 (Kodomo wa obentō o motte *ikima-shita*.)

②[ある動作・状態などが継続する様子を表す]

¶この本は読んで**いく**うちに，だんだんおもしろくなるでしょう。 (Kono hon wa yonde *iku* uchi ni, dandan

iku〚vⅠ〛 go, come; proceed

① [go, come, advance toward a particular target]

¶ Where **did you go** yesterday?

¶ Does this bus **go** to the airport?

② [proceed]

¶ **It looks like** this project **will turn out** well.

¶ I don't think this work **will pro-ceed** in the way you think.

③ [marry and enter another house-hold]

¶ Haruko **married** last spring.

＊ Variant: *yuku*.

(-te) iku〚compd〛 an expression in-dicating movement, progression, change, etc.

① [indicates movement]

¶ Some birds **are flying off** to the north.

¶ The children **took** their lunches with them.

② [indicates the continuation of an action or state]

¶ You will probably find this book more and more interesting **as you read** it.

omoshiroku naru deshō.)

¶これからは親と離れて一人で生活していかなければなりません。 (Kore kara wa oya to hanarete hitori de seikatsu shite *ikanakereba* narimasen.)

③[ある状態に変化する様子を表す]

¶これからますます寒くなっていきますから，風邪を引かないように気をつけてください。 (Kore kara masumasu samuku natte *ikimasu* kara, kaze o hikanai yō ni ki o tsukete kudasai.)

¶みんなの努力で町がだんだんきれいになっていきます。 (Minna no doryoku de machi ga dandan kirei ni natte *ikimasu*.)

⇔(〜**te**) **kuru** (〜て) くる

iku- 幾-〚頭〛

幾度 (*iku*do) 幾日 (*iku*nichi) 幾人 (*iku*nin)

＊「何- (nan-)」より少しかたい感じで，いっしょに使われる語もあまり多くない。

⇨**nan-** 何-

ikura いくら〚名，副〛

1〚名〛

①[不明な数量・値段などを表す]

¶これはいくらですか。 (Kore wa *ikura* desu ka?)

¶そのくつはいくらで買いましたか。 (Sono kutsu wa *ikura* de kaimashita ka?)

¶この荷物の目方はいくらぐらいあり

¶ [I] **must** leave home and live alone from now on.

③ [indicates change in a state of affairs]

¶ As it **will get** colder and colder from now on please be careful not to catch a cold.

¶ The town is gradually **becoming** cleaner due to everyone's efforts.

iku- 〚pref〛 **how many; several**

how many times; **several** times // **how many** days; **what** day of the month; **several** days // **how many** people; **several** people

＊ The prefex *iku-* is somewhat more formal than *nan-* and can only be used with a restricted set of words.

ikura 〚n, adv〛 **how much, how many; hardly any, not much; however 〜, no matter how 〜**

1 〚n〛

① [how much, how many]

¶ **How much** is this?

¶ **How much** did you pay for those shoes?

¶ **How much** does this luggage

ますか。(Kono nimotsu no mekata wa *ikura* gurai arimasu ka?)

②[ものごとのわずかであることを表す]

¶今月はもうお金はいくらも残っていません。(Kongetsu wa mō okane wa *ikura* mo nokotte imasen.)

¶費用はいくらもかかりませんから, 今度の旅行に参加しませんか。(Hiyō wa *ikura* mo kakarimasen kara, kondo no ryokō ni sanka shimasen ka?)

*「いくらも ～ ない (ikura mo ～ nai)」の形で使う。

2〖副〗

¶いくら高くても買います。(*Ikura* takakute mo kaimasu.)

¶いくら呼んでも返事がありません。(*Ikura* yonde mo henji ga arimasen.)

＊「いくら～ても (ikura ～ te mo)」の形で使うことが多い。

ikutsu 幾つ〖名〗

①[何歳]

¶お子さんはお幾つですか。(Okosan wa o*ikutsu* desu ka?)

②[何個]

¶そこに卵が幾つありますか。(Soko ni tamago ga *ikutsu* arimasu ka?)

¶兄は時計を幾つも持っています。(Ani wa tokei o *ikutsu* mo motte imasu.)

ima 今〖名〗

①[現在]

〚freight, load, cargo, etc.〛 weigh?

② [not much, not many, very few]

¶ [I] have **hardly any** money left for this month.

¶ Won't you come on the trip? It won't cost **very much.**

* Used in the pattern "*ikura mo ～ -nai*."

2 〚adv〛 however ～, no matter how ～

¶ [I] will buy it **no matter how** expensive it may be.

¶ There is no response **no matter how much** one calls.

＊ Usually used in the pattern "*ikura ～ -te mo.*"

ikutsu 〚n〛 **how old; how many**

① [how old]

¶ **How old** is your child?

② [how many; several]

¶ **How many** eggs are there there?

¶ My older brother owns **several** watches.

ima 〚n〛 **now, at present; just now, soon**

① [now, at present]

¶今, 何時ですか。(*Ima,* nanji desu ka?)

¶ What time is it **now?**

¶この本は今から50年ぐらい前に書かれました。 (Kono hon wa *ima* kara gojūnen gurai mae ni kakaremashita.)

¶ This book was written about 50 years **ago.**

②[現在を中心にごく近い前後の時]

② [just now, soon]

¶わたしは今来たばかりです。(Watashi wa *ima* kita bakari desu.)

¶ I have **just now** arrived.

¶今行きますから, ちょっと待ってください。(*Ima* ikimasu kara, chotto matte kudasai.)

¶ I will come **right away** so please wait for me.

imi 意味〖名, ～する〗

imi 〖n, ～*suru*〗 **meaning, sense; significance**

①[言葉などの表しているものごと・内容]

① [meaning, sense (of a word, etc.)]

¶この言葉の意味がわかりません。(Kono kotoba no *imi* ga wakarimasen.)

¶ [I] don't know **the meaning** of this word.

¶この印は何を意味していますか。(Kono shirushi wa nani o *imi* shite imasu ka?)

¶ What is **the meaning** of this mark?

②[ねうち・ためになることなど]

② [significance, meaning, value]

¶この仕事はたいへん意味があると思います。 (Kono shigoto wa taihen *imi* ga aru to omoimasu.)

¶ I think this job is very **meaningful.**

imo 芋〖名〗

imo 〖n〗 **potato**

じゃが芋 (jaga*imo*) 里芋 (sato*imo*) さつま芋 (satsuma*imo*) 山芋 (yama*imo*)

potato, white **potato** // taro // sweet **potato** // yam

imōto 妹〖名〗

imōto 〖n〗 **younger sister**

¶わたしには妹が二人います。(Watashi ni wa *imōto* ga futari imasu.)

¶ I have two **younger sisters.**

¶妹さんはお元気ですか。 (*Imōto-san wa ogenki desu ka?*)
⇔ane 姉

inai 以内〖名〗
¶この本は1週間以内に返してください。 (Kono hon wa isshūkan *inai* ni kaeshite kudasai.)
¶この建物の10メートル以内で火を使ってはいけません。 (Kono tatemono no jūmētoru *inai* de hi o tsukatte wa ikemasen.)

inaka 田舎〖名〗
¶たくさんの人が田舎から都会へ出て働いています。 (Takusan no hito ga *inaka* kara tokai e dete hataraite imasu.)
¶冬休みには田舎へ帰ります。 (Fuyuyasumi ni wa *inaka* e kaerimasu.)
⇨tokai 都会

ine 稲〖名〗
稲刈り (*inekari*)
¶稲がよく実っています。 (*Ine* ga yoku minotte imasu.)

inku インク〖名〗
¶ペンとインクをください。 (Pen to *inku* o kudasai.)
¶万年筆にインクを入れました。 (Mannenhitsu ni *inku* o iremashita.)

inochi 命〖名〗
命を助ける (*inochi* o tasukeru) 命が助かる (*inochi* ga tasukaru)
¶ひどいけがですが，命は大丈夫です。 (Hidoi kega desu ga, *inochi* wa

inai 〚n〛 within, no more than
¶ Please return this book **within** one week.

¶ It is forbidden to have a fire 〚to smoke, etc.〛 **within** 10 meters of this building.

inaka 〚n〛 country, countryside; one's native place
¶ Many people have left **the country** and gone to the city to work.

¶ [I] will return **home to the countryside** during winter vacation.

ine 〚n〛 rice plant
rice reaping, harvesting **rice**
¶ **The rice plants** are doing well.

inku 〚n〛 ink
¶ A pen and **ink,** please.

¶ [I] put **ink** in the fountain pen.

inochi 〚n〛 life
save 〚spare〛 **someone's life,** save 〚spare〛 **a creature's life** // escape death, survive
¶ It's a bad injury but not a **mortal**

How is your **sister** (literally, Is your **younger sister** well)?

inu

daijōbu desu.)

¶毎年たくさんの人が交通事故で命を落としています。 (Mainen takusan no hito ga kōtsū-jiko de *inochi* o otoshite imasu.)

inoru 祈る〖動Ⅰ〗

¶御健康を祈ります。 (Gokenkō o *inorimasu*.)

¶神に平和を祈りました。 (Kami ni heiwa o *inorimashita*.)

insatsu 印刷〖名, ～する〗

印刷物 (*insatsu*butsu)　印刷所 (*insatsu*jo)

¶この本は印刷が悪くて読みにくいです。 (Kono hon wa *insatsu* ga warukute yominikui desu.)

¶この本は日本で印刷されました。 (Kono hon wa Nihon de *insatsu* saremashita.)

inshō 印象〖名〗

第一印象 (daiichi-*inshō*)　印象的 (*inshō*teki)

¶新しい先生はみんなにいい印象を与えました。 (Atarashii sensei wa minna ni ii *inshō* o ataemashita.)

¶あのレストランはサービスが悪くて, たいへん印象が悪かったです。(Ano resutoran wa sābisu ga warukute, taihen *inshō* ga warukatta desu.)

¶あの人はあまり印象に残っていません。 (Ano hito wa amari *inshō* ni nokotte imasen.)

inu 犬〖名〗

¶門の前に犬がいます。 (Mon no mae

one.

¶ Every year a great many people lose **their lives** in traffic accidents.

inoru 〖v I〗 **pray; wish**

¶ [I] **hope** for your continued good health.

¶ [I] **prayed** to God for peace.

insatsu 〖n, ～*suru*〗 **printing, press-work**

printed matter // a press, a **print** shop

¶ **The printing** in this book is poor so it is hard to read.

¶ This book **was printed** in Japan.

inshō 〖n〗 **impression**

one's first **impression** // **impressive, memorable, striking, dramatic**

¶ The new teacher **impressed** everyone favorably.

¶ The service was bad in that restaurant, giving a very poor **impression**.

¶ [He] didn't make a very strong **impression** on me.

inu 〖n〗 **dog**

¶ There is **a dog** in front of the gate.

ni *inu* ga imasu.)

¶彼は犬を2匹飼っています。 (Kare wa *inu* o nihiki katte imasu.)

¶ He keeps two **dogs.**

ippai いっぱい〚副, 形動〛

①[満ちている様子, あるものの中に何かが限度まである様子]

腹いっぱい食べる (hara *ippai* taberu)

¶もうおなかがいっぱいです。 (Mō onaka ga *ippai* desu.)

¶デパートは人でいっぱいでした。 (Depāto wa hito de *ippai* deshita.)

②[全部, 限りを尽くす様子]

時間いっぱい (jikan *ippai*) 精いっぱい (sei *ippai*)

¶今月いっぱい東京にいます。 (Kongetsu *ippai* Tōkyō ni imasu.)

ippan 一般〚名〛

一般的 (*ippan*teki)

¶そんな専門的なことは一般の人にはわからないでしょう。 (Sonna senmonteki na koto wa *ippan* no hito ni wa wakaranai deshō.)

¶この本は一般の本屋にはありません。 (Kono hon wa *ippan* no hon'ya ni wa arimasen.)

¶この商品はまだ一般には売られていません。 (Kono shōhin wa mada *ippan* ni wa urarete imasen.)

ippan ni 一般に〚副〛

¶今度の試験は一般に難しかったです。 (Kondo no shiken wa *ippan ni* muzukashikatta desu.)

¶最近の映画は一般にあまりおもしろ

ippai 〚adv, adj-v〛 full; all, the whole of

① [full]

to eat until **full**

¶ [I]'m **full.**

¶ The department store **was filled** with people.

② [all, the whole of]

until one's time **is up,** using **all** the time available for some task // with **all** one's might, **to the best of** one's abilities

¶ [I] will be in Tokyo **all** this month.

ippan 〚n〛 general, common general, in general

¶ The **average** person probably can't understand such a specialized matter.

¶ This book will not be found in the **average** bookstore.

¶ This product is not yet on **general** sale.

ippan ni 〚adv〛 generally, in general, on the whole, commonly, usually

¶ **On the whole,** the exam this time was difficult.

¶ **Generally speaking,** recent

くありません。 (Saikin no eiga wa *ippan ni* amari omoshiroku arimasen.)

movies haven't been very interesting.

ippō 一方〖名〗

①[片方, 一つの方面]
一方通行 (*ippō*-tsūkō)

¶一方の言うことだけで判断するのは危険です。 (*Ippō* no iu koto dake de handan suru no wa kiken desu.)

¶もう一方の人たちは, この問題についてどう言っていますか。 (Mō *ippō* no hitotachi wa kono mondai ni tsuite dō itte imasu ka?)

②[一つの傾向が強くなるばかりであること]

¶収入は減る一方です。 (Shūnyū wa heru *ippō* desu.)

¶交通事故は増える一方です。(Kōtsū-jiko wa fueru *ippō* desu.)

irai 以来〖名〗

¶日本に来て以来, ずっと東京に住んでいます。 (Nihon ni kite *irai*, zutto Tōkyō ni sunde imasu.)

¶先月以来田中さんに会っていません。 (Sengetsu *irai* Tanaka san ni atte imasen.)

irassharu いらっしゃる〖動Ⅰ〗

①[来る]

¶よくいらっしゃいました。 (Yoku *irasshaimashita*.)

¶こちらにいらっしゃい。 (Kochira ni *irasshai*.)

* 「来る (kuru)」の尊敬語。

②[行く]

ippō 〖n〗 one side; one-way, only

① [one side]

one-way traffic

¶ It is risky to make judgments based on just **one side** of the story.

¶ What do **others** have to say about this problem?

② [one-way, only]

¶ Income **goes on** declining (that is, it never increases).

¶ Traffic accidents **steadily** increase (that is, they never decrease).

irai 〖n〗 since, after that

¶ [I] have lived in Tokyo **ever since** coming to Japan.

¶ [I] haven't seen [Miss] Tanaka **since** last month.

irassharu 〖v I〗 come; go; be

① [come]

¶ Welcome. [I'm] glad **you could come.**

¶ **Come** over here please.

* This *irassharu* is the honorific form of *kuru*.

② [go]

¶これから会議にいらっしゃいますか。(Kore kara kaigi ni *irasshaimasu* ka?)

¶先生は旅行にいらっしゃいました。(Sensei wa ryokō ni *irasshaimashita*.)

* 「行く (iku)」の尊敬語。

③[いる]

¶「先生は研究室にいらっしゃいますか。」(Sensei wa kenkyūshitsu ni *irasshaimasu* ka?)「はい、いらっしゃいます。」(Hai, *irasshaimasu*.)

¶あそこで新聞を読んでいらっしゃる方はどなたですか。(Asoko de shinbun o yonde *irassharu* kata wa donata desu ka?)

* 「いる (iru)」の尊敬語。

④[である]

¶あの方は上田さんの奥さんでいらっしゃいます。(Ano kata wa Ueda san no okusan de *irasshaimasu*.)

¶その後お元気でいらっしゃいますか。(Sono go ogenki de *irasshaimasu* ka?)

* 「である (de aru)」の尊敬語。

* 「ますの形」は「いらっしゃいます (irasshaimasu)」となる。

ireru　入れる〖動Ⅱ〗

①[ものを何かの中に移す]

¶コーヒーに砂糖を入れますか。(Kōhii ni satō o *iremasu* ka?)

¶窓を開けて、新しい空気を入れましょう。(Mado o akete, atarashii kūki o *iremashō*.)

¶ **Are you going** to the meeting 〚conference〛 now?

¶ The professor 〚teacher, doctor, etc.〛 **has left** on a trip.

* This *irassharu* is the honorific form of *iku*.

③ [be, exist, be present]

¶ "**Is** the professor in the office 〚laboratory〛?"　"Yes, [he] **is**."

¶ Who is that gentleman 〚lady〛 reading a newspaper over there?

* This *irassharu* is the honorific form of *iru*.

④ [be]

¶ That lady **is** Mr. Ueda's wife.

¶ How **have you been** since then?

* This *irassharu* is the honorific form of *de aru*.

* The *-masu* form of *irassharu* is *irasshaimasu*.

ireru 〚v II〛 **put in, add; send; include; prepare** (hot drinks)

① [put in, add, insert]

¶ Do you **take** sugar **in** your coffee?

¶ Let's open the window to **let in** some fresh air.

↔**dasu** 出す

②[学校や病院などに入らせる]

¶今年，子供を小学校に**入れ**ました。

(Kotoshi, kodomo o shōgakkō ni *iremashita*.)

¶母が病気になったので，駅の前の病院に**入れ**ました。(Haha ga byōki ni natta node, eki no mae no byōin ni *iremashita*.)

③[含める，いっしょに計算する]

¶結婚した兄も**入れ**て兄弟は5人です。(Kekkon shita ani mo *irete* kyōdai wa gonin desu.)

④[お茶やコーヒーなどが飲めるように用意する]

¶お茶を**入れ**ましょう。　(Ocha o *iremashō*.)

iriguchi　入り口〖名〗

¶この建物の**入り口**はどこですか。

(Kono tatemono no *iriguchi* wa doko desu ka?)

¶**入り口**はあちらです。(*Iriguchi* wa achira desu.)

⇔**deguchi**　出口

iro　色〖名〗

茶色 (cha*iro*)　灰色 (hai*iro*)　黄色 (ki*iro*)　緑色 (midori*iro*)　桃色 (momo*iro*)

¶あなたはどんな**色**が好きですか。

(Anata wa donna *iro* ga suki desu ka?)

¶濃い**色**がいいですか，薄い**色**がいいですか。　(Koi *iro* ga ii desu ka, usui *iro* ga ii desu ka?)

② [be admitted to a hospital, school, etc.]

¶ My child **started** elementary school this year.

¶ My mother is sick and **was admitted** to the hospital in front of the station.

③ [include]

¶ **Counting** my married (elder) brother, there are five of us children.

④ [prepare (coffee, tea, etc.)]

¶ I'll **fix** some tea now.

iriguchi 〖n〗 entrance

¶ Where is **the entrance** of this building?

¶ **The entrance** is over there.

iro 〖n〗 color

light brown, brown // gray // yellow // green // pink

¶ What **colors** do you like?

¶ Do you want a dark **color** or a light **color**?

iroiro

iroiro いろいろ〖副，形動，〜の〗

¶この問題についていろいろ考えてみましたが，どうしたらよいかわかりません。(Kono mondai ni tsuite *iroiro* kangaete mimashita ga, dō shitara yoi ka wakarimasen.)

¶デパートではいろいろな物を売っています。 (Depāto de wa *iroiro* na mono o utte imasu.)

¶学生の意見はいろいろです。 (Gakusei no iken wa *iroiro* desu.)

＊ 副詞は「いろいろと (iroiro to)」の形でも使う。また，「いろいろな (iroiro na)」は「いろんな (ironna)」とも言う。

⇨samazama さまざま

iru 要る〖動I〗

¶この計画を実現するにはいくらぐらいお金が要りますか。(Kono keikaku o jitsugen suru ni wa ikura gurai okane ga *irimasu* ka?)

¶この雑誌はもう要りませんから捨ててください。 (Kono zasshi wa mō *irimasen* kara sutete kudasai.)

iru いる〖動II〗

①〔人や動物などがある所に存在する〕
¶父は今部屋にいます。 (Chichi wa ima heya ni *imasu*.)

¶今そこにはだれもいません。 (Ima soko ni wa dare mo *imasen*.)

②〔滞在する，住んでいる〕
¶あの外国人はもう5年も日本にいます。(Ano gaikokujin wa mō gonen mo Nihon ni *imasu*.)

iroiro 〚adv, adj-v, ~*no*〛 **various, several**

¶ [I] have thought about this problem **from various angles,** but [I] don't know what to do.

¶ Department stores sell **a variety** of items.

¶ Student opinion **is divided.**

＊ The adverbial *iroiro* is also used in the form *iroiro to*. *Iroiro na* sometimes becomes *ironna*.

iru 〚v I〛 **need, be necessary**

¶ How much money **will be needed** to carry out this project?

¶ [I] **don't need** these magazines any longer; please throw them out.

iru 〚v II〛 **be, exist; live, reside**

① [be, exist]

¶ My father **is** now in his room.

¶ No one **is** there now.

② [live, reside, dwell]

¶ That foreigner **has** already **been** in Japan for five years.

244

(~te) iru

ishi

(**~te**) **iru** （～て）いる〘連〙

①［動作・作用の進行の状態を表す〕

¶子供が庭で遊んでいます。(Kodomo ga niwa de asonde *imasu*.)

¶兄は部屋で本を読んでいます。(Ani wa heya de hon o yonde *imasu*.)

②［職業などに従事している状態を表す〕

¶姉は銀行で働いています。(Ane wa ginkō de hataraite *imasu*.)

¶弟は大学で教えています。(Otōto wa daigaku de oshiete *imasu*.)

③［ある動作の結果の状態を表す〕

¶窓が開いています。(Mado ga aite *imasu*.)

¶この時計は壊れています。(Kono tokei wa kowarete *imasu*.)

¶彼は帽子をかぶっています。(Kare wa bōshi o kabutte *imasu*.)

→(**~te**) **aru** （～て）ある

isha 医者〘名〙

医者に診てもらう (*isha* ni mite morau)

¶早く医者を呼んでください。

(Hayaku *isha* o yonde kudasai.)

¶どこの医者にかかっていますか。

(Doko no *isha* ni kakatte imasu ka?)

＊丁寧に言うときは「お医者さん (oishasan)」と言う。

ishi 意思〘名〙

¶彼にわたしの意思をはっきり伝えてください。(Kare ni watashi no *ishi* o hakkiri tsutaete kudasai.)

(-te) **iru** 〚compd〛 an expression indicating continuing action or a resultant state

① [be ~ing, keep ~ing; indicates continuing action]

¶ The children **are playing** in the garden 〚yard〛.

¶ My (older) brother **is reading** a book in his room.

② [indicates the state of being engaged in an occupation, etc.]

¶ My older sister **works** at a bank.

¶ My younger brother **is teaching** at a college.

③ [be ~; indicates a state resulting from an action]

¶ The window **is open.**

¶ This watch 〚clock〛 **is broken.**

¶ He **is wearing** a hat.

isha 〚n〛 doctor, physician, surgeon

see **a doctor**

¶ Please call **a doctor** right away.

¶ Who is **your doctor?**

＊ When one has to be polite one should use *oishasan* to refer to a doctor. In direct address a doctor is called *sensei*.

ishi 〚n〛 intent, purpose, intention

¶ Please clearly convey my **intentions** to him.

245

¶手縦ではなかなか**意思**が通じません。
(Tegami de wa nakanaka *ishi* ga tsūjimasen.)

ishi 意志〖名〗

意志が弱い (*ishi* ga yowai) **意志**が堅い (*ishi* ga katai) 自由**意志** (jiyū-*ishi*)

¶彼は**意志**が強いですね。 (Kare wa *ishi* ga tsuyoi desu ne.)

ishi 石〖名〗

¶この橋は**石**でできています。 (Kono hashi wa *ishi* de dekite imasu.)

¶池に**石**を投げないでください。 (Ike ni *ishi* o nagenaide kudasai.)

isogashii 忙しい〖形〗

¶今日は**忙しい**日でした。 (Kyō wa *isogashii* hi deshita.)

¶勉強が**忙しくて**, 遊ぶ暇がありません。 (Benkyō ga *isogashikute*, asobu hima ga arimasen.)

isogu 急ぐ〖動Ⅰ〗

¶時間がないから**急ぎ**ましょう。 (Jikan ga nai kara *isogimashō*.)

¶遅刻しそうなので, **急いで**出かけました。 (Chikoku shisō na node, *isoide* dekakemashita.)

¶**急がない**と遅れますよ。 (*Isoganai* to okuremasu yo.)

¶**急げば**まだ 12 時の汽車に間に合うでしょう。 (*Isogeba* mada jūniji no kisha ni maniau deshō.)

issho ni いっしょに〖副〗

¶みんなで**いっしょに**言ってください。 (Minna de *issho ni* itte kudasai.)

¶ It is difficult to communicate **one's intentions** in a letter.

ishi 〚n〛 **will**

be weak **willed** // be firm **willed** // of one's own free **will**

¶ He is a man **of strong character, isn't he?**

ishi 〚n〛 **stone, rock, pebble**

¶ This bridge is made of **stone.**

¶ Please don't throw **stones** 〚**pebbles**〛 into the pond 〚pool〛.

isogashii 〚adj〛 **be busy, be engaged**

¶ Today has been a **busy** day.

¶ [I]'m **busy** with studying and have no time for play.

isogu 〚v I〛 **hurry, be in a hurry, make haste**

¶ **Let's hurry** as time is getting short.

¶ [I] left **in a hurry** as it looked like [I] would be late.

¶ You'll be late if **you don't hurry.**

¶ If [you] hurry [you] can probably still make the twelve o'clock train.

issho ni 〚adv〛 **together**

¶ Will everyone please say it **together.**

¶友達といっしょに映画へ行きます。

(Tomodachi to *issho ni* eiga e ikimasu.)

¶ [I] am going to go to a movie **with** a friend.

isshō 一生〖名〗

¶彼は一生結婚しませんでした。

(Kare wa *isshō* kekkon shimasen deshita.)

¶人の一生は短いものです。(Hito no *isshō* wa mijikai mono desu.)

isshō 〖n〗 lifetime, one's whole life

¶ He remained single **all his life.**

¶ **Human life** is short.

isshōkenmei 一生懸命〖副, 形動〗

¶一生懸命働いても,生活が楽になりません。(*Isshōkenmei* hataraite mo, seikatsu ga raku ni narimasen.)

¶あの学生は一生懸命に勉強しています。(Ano gakusei wa *isshōkenmei* ni benkyō shite imasu.)

¶早く日本語が上手になろうと,みんな一生懸命です。(Hayaku Nihongo ga jōzu ni narō to, minna *isshōkenmei* desu.)

isshōkenmei 〖adv, adj-v〗 as hard as one can, wholeheartedly, with all one's might

¶ Even if one works **as hard as one can,** it's still difficult to make a good living.

¶ That student is studying **hard.**

¶ All **are intent** on becoming good in Japanese quickly.

issō いっそう〖副〗

¶8月は今よりいっそう暑くなります。(Hachigatsu wa ima yori *issō* atsuku narimasu.)

¶勉強が前よりいっそうおもしろくなりました。(Benkyō ga mae yori *issō* omoshiroku narimashita.)

issō 〖adv〗 more, much more, still more

¶ It becomes **much** hotter in August than it is now.

¶ [My] studies have become **much more** interesting now than before.

isu いす〖名〗

いすに腰掛ける (*isu* ni koshikakeru)

いすに座る (*isu* ni suwaru)

¶どうぞ,そのいすにお掛けください。(Dōzo, sono *isu* ni okake kudasai.)

isu 〖n〗 chair, sofa

sit down on **a chair** // sit down on **a chair**

¶ Please take **a chair** 〖**a seat**〗 there.

ita 板〖名〗

ita 〖n〗 board, plank

またいた (man*ait*a)

¶板を組み立てて、本箱を作りました。
(*Ita* o kumitatete, honbako o tsu-kurimashita.)

a chopping **board** ⟦**block**⟧

¶ [I] built a bookcase out of **boards.**

itadaku いただく〘動Ⅰ〙

①[もらう]

¶先生に本をいただきました。(Sensei ni hon o *itadakimashita*.)

¶お見舞いにきれいな花をいただきました。(Omimai ni kirei na hana o *itadakimashita*.)

*「もらう (morau)」の謙譲語。ある人が目上の人から与えられたものを受け取るという意味を表す。受け取る人の側に立って言うときに使う。与える人が対等か目下の人などである場合には「もらう (morau)」を使う。

→morau もらう

②[食べる，飲む]

¶「どうぞ、おあがりください。」(Dōzo, oagari kudasai.)「では、いただきます。」(Dewa, *itadakimasu*.)

¶「もう少しお召し上がりになりませんか。」(Mō sukoshi omeshiagari ni narimasen ka?)「ありがとうございます。もうじゅうぶんにいただきました。」(Arigatō gozaimasu. Mō jūbun ni *itadakimashita*.)

*「食べる (taberu)」「飲む (nomu)」の謙譲語。

③[食事の前のあいさつの言葉]

¶いただきます。(*Itadakimasu*.)

(〜te) itadaku　(〜て) いただく〘連〙

itadaku 〘v I〙　receive; eat, drink

① [receive]

¶ **I received** a book from my teacher ⟦My teacher gave me a book⟧.

¶ **I received** some pretty flowers as a get-well present.

* *Itadaku* is the humble form for *morau*; it expresses the meaning of someone receiving something from someone of higher status. It is used from the point of view of the recipient. When the giver is of equal or lower status, *morau* is used.

② [eat, drink]

¶ "Please go ahead and eat."
"Thank you, **I will.**"

¶ "Won't you have some more?"
"No, thank you. I couldn't **eat** another thing."

* This *itadaku* is the humble form for *taberu, nomu.*

③ [set expression used before a meal]

¶ Thank you for this food I am about **to eat.**

(-te) itadaku 〘compd〙　receive the favor of something being done

¶わたしは田中先生に日本語を教えていただきました。 (Watashi wa Tanaka sensei ni Nihongo o oshiete *itadakimashita*.)

¶旅行の写真を見せていただきたいんですが。 (Ryokō no shashin o misete *itadakitai* n desu ga.)

＊ 普通ある人が動作をする人の動作によって利益や恩恵などを受けたり，または依頼してある動作をさせるようにしたりする意味を表す。利益を受けたり，依頼したりする人の側に立って言うときに使う。動作をする人が利益などを受ける人より目上の人であるときに使う。動作をする人が対等か目下の人などである場合には「（〜て）もらう（[〜te] morau）」を使う。

⇨（〜**te**) morau （〜て）もらう

itai 痛い〚形〛

¶少し頭が痛いです。 (Sukoshi atama ga *itai* desu.)

¶急に歯が痛くなりました。 (Kyū ni ha ga *itaku* narimashita.)

¶昨日はおなかが痛かったので，学校を休みました。 (Kinō wa onaka ga *itakatta* node, gakkō o yasumimashita.)

itazura いたずら〚名，形動，〜する〛

¶うちの子はいたずらで困ります。 (Uchi no ko wa *itazura* de komarimasu.)

¶子供がいたずらして，時計を壊しました。 (Kodomo ga *itazura* shite,

¶ Professor Tanaka **kindly** taught me Japanese ⟦**was kind enough** to teach me Japanese⟧.

¶ **Could I please** see the photographs of the trip?

＊ Usually (*-te*) *itadaku* expresses the meaning of receiving some benefit from the actions of another or of requesting and having some action done for one. It is used from the standpoint of the person receiving the benefit or making the request and when the person doing the action is of higher status than the recipient. When the person doing the favor is of equal or lower status, (*-te*) *morau* is used.

itai ⟦adj⟧ **be painful, be sore, hurts**

¶ I have a slight head**ache**.

¶ My teeth suddenly started **to ache.**

¶ I stayed home from school yesterday as I had a stomach**ache.**

itazura ⟦n, adj-v, ~*suru*⟧ **mischief, trick, prank**

¶ Our child **is always up to mischief** and we don't know what to do.

¶ The children **were fooling around** and broke the clock ⟦watch⟧.

249

itchi

tokei o kowashimashita.)

itchi 一致〖名, ～する〗

¶二人の意見が一致しました。(Futari no iken ga *itchi* shimashita.)

¶彼は言うこととすることが一致していません。 (Kare wa iu koto to suru koto ga *itchi* shite imasen.)

ito 糸〖名〗

毛糸 (ke*ito*) 絹糸 (kinu*ito*) 木綿糸 (momen*ito*)

¶この糸はとても丈夫です。 (Kono *ito* wa totemo jōbu desu.)

¶針と糸を貸してください。 (Hari to *ito* o kashite kudasai.)

itoko いとこ〖名〗

¶彼はわたしのいとこです。(Kare wa watashi no *itoko* desu.)

¶わたしにはいとこがたくさんいます。 (Watashi ni wa *itoko* ga takusan imasu.)

itsu いつ〖名〗

¶いつ日本へ来ましたか。(*Itsu* Nihon e kimashita ka?)

¶この宿題はいつまでですか。 (Kono shukudai wa *itsu* made desu ka?)

¶彼はいつ行っても留守です。 (Kare wa *itsu* itte mo rusu desu.)

¶夜はいつでも家にいます。 (Yoru wa *itsu* demo ie ni imasu.)

itsuka 五日〖名〗

①[日付を表す]

¶五月五日は子供の日です。(Gogatsu *itsuka* wa kodomo no hi desu.)

②[日数を表す]

itchi 〚n, ～*suru*〛 be in accord, be consistent, correspond with

¶ The views of the two **are** ⟦**were**⟧ in **accord.**

¶ His acts **are not in accordance** with his words.

ito 〚n〛 thread, yarn, string, line, **filament,** etc.

yarn, wool **yarn** // silk **thread** // cotton **thread,** cotton **yarn**

¶ This **thread** ⟦**string, line**⟧ is very strong.

¶ Please lend me a needle and **thread.**

itoko 〚n〛 cousin

¶ He is my **cousin.**

¶ I have many **cousins.**

itsu 〚n〛 when

¶ **When** did you come to Japan?

¶ **When** is this homework due?

¶ **Whenever** [I] go to his home he is out.

¶ I am at home **anytime** in the evenings.

itsuka 〚n〛 the fifth of the month; five days

① [the fifth of the month]

¶ The **fifth** of May is Children's Day.

② [five days]

250

五日間 (*itsuka*kan)

¶風邪で五日も学校を休みました。

(Kaze de *itsuka* mo gakkō o yasu-mimashita.)

⇨ **-ka** -日

itsu ka いつか〖副〗

¶いつかうちへ遊びに来てください。

(*Itsu ka* uchi e asobi ni kite kudasai.)

¶彼にはいつか会ったことがあります。

(Kare ni wa *itsu ka* atta koto ga arimasu.)

itsu mo いつも〖副〗

¶妹の電話はいつも長いです。 (Imōto no denwa wa *itsu mo* nagai desu.)

¶彼はいつも本を読んでいます。

(Kare wa *itsu mo* hon o yonde imasu.)

itsutsu 五つ〖名〗

①[5個]

¶みかんを五つください。 (Mikan o *itsutsu* kudasai.)

②[5歳]

¶この子は五つです。 (Kono ko wa *itsutsu* desu.)

ittai いったい〖副〗

¶そんなにあわてて，いったいどうしたのですか。 (Sonna ni awatete, *ittai* dō shita no desu ka?)

¶彼はいったい何を考えているのかわたしにはわかりません。 (Kare wa *ittai* nani o kangaete iru no ka watashi ni wa wakarimasen.)

iu 言う〖動Ⅰ〗

for **five days,** a period of **five days**

¶ [I] stayed home from school **for five days** with a cold 〚the flu〛.

itsu ka 〚adv〛 **sometime, at one time**

¶ Please come and visit me **some-time.**

¶ [I] have met him **at some time or other.**

itsu mo 〚adv〛 **always**

¶ My younger sister **always** talks for a long time on the telephone.

¶ He is **always** reading a book.

itsutsu 〚n〛 **five items; five years of age**

① [five items]

¶ Please give me **five** mandarin oranges.

② [five years of age]

¶ This child is **five years old.**

ittai 〚adv〛 **what 〚how, why〛 in the world, what 〚how, why〛 on earth**

¶ **What on earth** is the matter that you are so flustered?

¶ I don't know **what in the world** he can be thinking of.

iu 〚v I〛 **say, state, express; be said; be called, named**

①[思ったことや考えたことなどを言葉で表す]

¶中村さんは「今度の旅行には行きたくない。」と**言って**いました。(Nakamura san wa "Kondo no ryokō ni wa ikitaku nai." to *itte* imashita.)

¶あの人はその問題について何と**言って**いましたか。(Ano hito wa sono mondai ni tsuite nan to *itte* imashita ka?)

②[ものごとの評価を表すときに使う]

¶山田さんは中村さんのことをあまりよく**言いません**。(Yamada san wa Nakamura san no koto o amari yoku *iimasen*.)

* 普通「よく言う (yoku iu)」「悪く言う (waruku iu)」の形で使う。

③[おおぜいの人がそう称する]

¶彼は学生時代は秀才と**言われて**いました。(Kare wa gakusei-jidai wa shūsai to *iwarete* imashita.)

④[そう呼ばれる，そう称される]

¶さっき田中さんという人が来ましたよ。(Sakki Tanaka san to *iu* hito ga kimashita yo.)

¶これは何という花ですか。(Kore wa nan to *iu* hana desu ka?)

*「～という (～ to iu)」の形で使う。

⑤[ものごとの様子などを例示するのに使う]

¶こういうぐあいにすると，うまくいきますよ。(Kō*iu* guai ni suru to, umaku ikimasu yo.)

¶そういう問題はわたしにはよくわか

---

① [say, speak, state, remark, express]

¶ [Miss] Nakamura **said,** "I don't want to go on the trip this time."

¶ What did [he] **say** concerning that problem?

② [expresses an evaluation]

¶ [Mrs.] Yamada doesn't have much good **to say** about [Mrs.] Nakamura.

* Usually used in the patterns "*yoku iu*" and "*waruku iu*."

③ [be said, be called, be talked about, people say]

¶ He **was said to be** ⟦**known as**⟧ a bright boy in his student days.

④ [be called, be named, be termed]

¶ **A** [Mr.] Tanaka was here earlier.

¶ What is this flower **called?**

* Used in the pattern "～ *to iu*."

⑤ [used to describe a condition]

¶ It will go better if you do it **like** this.

¶ I don't understand that **sort of**

ありません。 (Sō*iu* mondai wa watashi ni wa yoku wakarimasen.)

¶ああいう人はどうしても好きになれ
ません。 (Ā*iu* hito wa dōshite mo
suki ni naremasen.)

¶これはどういう意味ですか。 (Kore
wa dō*iu* imi desu ka?)

*「こう (kō)」「そう (sō)」「ああ
(ā)」「どう (dō)」などの言葉につく。
「こういうふうに (kōiu fū ni)」「こ
ういったふうに (kōitta fū ni)」な
どの形でも使う。

iwa 岩〔名〕

¶山で岩から落ちてけがをしました。
(Yama de *iwa* kara ochite kega o
shimashita.)

¶あの岩の上に鳥がいます。 (Ano *iwa*
no ue ni tori ga imasu.)

iwau 祝う〔動Ⅰ〕

¶みんなで友達の誕生日を祝いました。
(Minna de tomodachi no tanjōbi o
iwaimashita.)

¶友達の結婚を祝って、プレゼントしま
した。 (Tomodachi no kekkon o
iwatte, purezento shimashita.)

iya いや〔形動〕

¶あの人はいつも不満ばかり言ってい
て、いやな人です。 (Ano hito wa
itsu mo fuman bakari itte ite, *iya*
na hito desu.)

¶都会の生活はもういやになりました。
(Tokai no seikatsu wa mō *iya* ni
narimashita.)

iyoiyo いよいよ〔副〕

---

problem well.

¶ Somehow I just can't like that **sort
of** person.

¶ **What** does this mean?

* Used with the words *kō, sō, ā, dō,*
etc. Used in the patterns "*kō iu fū
ni,*" "*kō itta fū ni,*" etc.

iwa 〖n〗 **rock, crag**

¶ [I] fell from **some rocks** in the
mountains and hurt [my]self.

¶ There is a bird on that **rock** over
there.

iwau 〖v I〗 **congratulate, celebrate**

¶ [We] all **celebrated** a friend's
birthday together.

¶ [I] gave my friend a wedding present.

iya 〖adj-v〗 **disagreeable, unpleasant, distasteful, offensive**

¶ [He] is a **disagreeable** person who
is always complaining.

¶ I have gotten **fed up** with city life.

iyoiyo 〖adv〗 **ever more, more and
more; at last**

① [ますます，よりいっそう]

¶台風が近づいて，風はいよいよ激しくなりました。(Taifū ga chikazuite, kaze wa *iyoiyo* hageshiku narimashita.)

¶問題はいよいよ複雑になってきました。 (Mondai wa *iyoiyo* fukuzatsu ni natte kimashita.)

② [予定されていたことなどがついに起こる様子，とうとう]

¶いよいよ出発の日が来ました。
(*Iyoiyo* shuppatsu no hi ga kimashita.)

¶いよいよ今日が卒業式ですね。
(*Iyoiyo* kyō ga sotsugyōshiki desu ne.)

izen 以前〖名〗

① [ある時より前]
¶出発は2月10日以前にしましょう。
(Shuppatsu wa nigatsu tooka *izen* ni shimashō.)
↔以後 **igo**

② [今からしばらく前，昔]
¶この辺は以前とても静かでした。
(Kono hen wa *izen* totemo shizuka deshita.)

---

① [ever more, more and more, increasingly]

¶ With the approaching typhoon, the winds have become ⟦the winds became⟧ **increasingly** violent.

¶ The problem has gotten **more and more** complicated.

② [at last, finally]

¶ Well, the day of departure has arrived.

¶ Well, today is **finally** graduation day, isn't it?

izen 〖n〗 in advance, before; ago, formerly

① [in advance, before a certain time]
¶ Let's make the departure **prior to** February 10.

② [ago, formerly]
¶ **It used to be** very quiet around here.

J

ja　じゃ〖接〗　☞dewa では

jama　邪魔〖名, 形動, ～する〗
仕事の邪魔をする (shigoto no *jama* o suru)

¶ラジオの音が邪魔になって，勉強ができません。(Rajio no oto ga *jama* ni natte, benkyō ga dekimasen.)

¶午後，お邪魔してもよろしいでしょうか。 (Gogo, o*jama* shite mo yoroshii deshō ka?)

ji-　次-〖頭〗
次回 (*ji*kai)　次週 (*ji*shū)

(-)ji　(-)字〖名, 尾〗

1〖名〗
漢字 (kan*ji*)　ローマ字 (rōma*ji*)　文字 (mo*ji*)
¶田中先生は字が上手です。 (Tanaka sensei wa *ji* ga jōzu desu.)

2〖尾〗
¶漢字を三百字ぐらい習いました。 (Kanji o sanbyaku*ji* gurai naraimashita.)

-ji　-次〖尾〗
第一次世界大戦 (daiichi*ji*-sekai-taisen)　二次試験 (ni*ji*-shiken)

-ji　-時〖尾〗
¶今，何時ですか。 (Ima, nan*ji* desu ka?)

¶授業は4時に終わります。 (Jugyō wa yo*ji* ni owarimasu.)

jibiki　字引〖名〗　☞jisho 辞書

---

ja ☞ dewa

jama 〚n, adj-v, ～*suru*〛 **hindrance, obstruction, intrusion**
hinder someone's work

¶ The sound of the radio **is interfering** with my studying.

¶ May I **intrude on you** 〚**come and see you**〛 this afternoon?

ji- 〚pref〛 **next, the following**
next time // **next** week

(-)ji 〚n, suf〛 **written character, letter, ideograph, handwriting**

1 〚n〛
a Chinese **character,** *kanji* // roman **letters** // written **characters**
¶ Professor Tanaka has good **handwriting.**

2 〚suf〛
¶ [I] learned 〚have learned〛 about three hundred ***kanji.***

-ji 〚suf〛 a suffix indicating order
World War **I** // the **second** examination

-ji 〚suf〛 **o'clock;** the counter for the hour
¶ What **time** is it now?

¶ Class ends at four **o'clock.**

jibiki ☞ **jisho**

255

jibun 自分〖名〗

自分自身 (*jibun*-jishin)

¶彼はいつも自分のことしか考えません。 (Kare wa itsu mo *jibun* no koto shika kangaemasen.)

¶自分の物は自分でかたづけてください。 (*Jibun* no mono wa *jibun* de katazukete kudasai.)

¶自分かってなことはしないでください。 (*Jibun*katte na koto wa shinaide kudasai.)

jidai 時代〖名〗

時代劇 (*jidai*geki) 時代遅れ (*jidai*-okure) 学生時代 (gakusei-*jidai*) 明治時代 (Meiji-*jidai*) 大正時代 (Taishō-*jidai*)

¶この物語の時代はいつごろですか。 (Kono monogatari no *jidai* wa itsu goro desu ka?)

¶あの人のおじいさんの時代には，あの店はたいへん有名でした。 (Ano hito no ojiisan no *jidai* ni wa, ano mise wa taihen yūmei deshita.)

jidōsha 自動車〖名〗

自動車事故 (*jidōsha*-jiko) 自動車旅行 (*jidōsha*-ryokō) 自動車に乗る (*jidōsha* ni noru) 自動車を運転する (*jidōsha* o unten suru)

¶自動車の運転ができますか。 (*Jidōsha* no unten ga dekimasu ka?)

¶道の真ん中で自動車が故障しました。 (Michi no mannaka de *jidōsha* ga koshō shimashita.)

jibun 〚n〛 self, oneself oneself, by oneself

¶ He never thinks of anyone 〚anything〛 but **himself.**

¶ Please put away your things **yourself.**

¶ Please don't do anything on **your own** authority 〚without consulting others〛.

jidai 〚n〛 period, age

a **costume** play, **historical** drama // out-of-**date**, behind **the times** // student **days** // the Meiji **era** // the Taishō **era**

¶ What is **the period** of this story?

¶ In **the time** of [his] grandfather, that shop 〚restaurant, etc.〛 was very famous.

jidōsha 〚n〛 automobile, car, motorcar

an **auto** accident // a **car** trip // ride in **a car** // drive **a car**

¶ Can you drive?

¶ **A car** broke down 〚has broken down〛 in the middle of the road.

jigyō 事業〖名〗
事業団 (*jigyō*dan)　事業家 (*jigyō*-ka)
¶彼は新しい事業を始めました。
(Kare wa atarashii *jigyō* o hajime-mashita.)
¶彼はその事業に成功しましたか。
(Kare wa sono *jigyō* ni seikō shimashita ka?)

jijitsu 事実〖名〗
事実を話す (*jijitsu* o hanasu)　事実を伝える (*jijitsu* o tsutaeru)
¶その物語は事実を基にして書かれています。　(Sono monogatari wa *jijitsu* o moto ni shite kakarete imasu.)

jijō 事情〖名〗
日本事情 (Nihon-*jijō*)
¶彼は家庭の事情で学校をやめました。
(Kare wa katei no *jijō* de gakkō o yamemashita.)
¶それには何か事情があるらしいです。
(Sore ni wa nani ka *jijō* ga aru rashii desu.)

(-)jikan (-)時間〖名, 尾〗
1〖名〗
①[ある一定の時の長さ]
時間がない (*jikan* ga nai)
¶この仕事は時間がかかりそうです。
(Kono shigoto wa *jikan* ga kaka-risō desu.)
¶食事までにはまだじゅうぶん時間があります。　(Shokuji made ni wa mada jūbun *jikan* ga arimasu.)

jigyō 〖n〗 enterprise, undertaking; business, industry
a **business** association // an entre-preneur, industrialist
¶ He has embarked upon a new en-terprise ⸢He embarked upon a new enterprise⸥.
¶ Did he succeed in that under-taking?

jijitsu 〖n〗 fact, actuality, the truth
tell **the truth** // report **the facts**

¶ That story is based on **fact.**

jijō 〖n〗 circumstances, condi-tions, situation, state of things
the state of affairs in Japan
¶ He quit school for family **reasons.**

¶ It seems that there is some **reason** for that.

(-)jikan 〖n, suf〗 time; an hour
1 〖n〗
① [time, period]
have no **time,** be pressed for **time**
¶ It looks like this job will take **time.**

¶ There is still lots of **time** until mealtime.

¶その放送の時間は午後8時から9時までです。(Sono hōsō no *jikan* wa gogo hachiji kara kuji made desu.)

② [時刻]
時間に間に合う (*jikan* ni maniau)
時間に遅れる (*jikan* ni okureru)
時間を守る (*jikan* o mamoru)

→**jikoku** 時刻

③ [何かをするために区切った一定の時の長さ]
時間割り (*jikan*wari)
自由時間 (jiyū-*jikan*)

¶理科の時間に実験をしました。(Rika no *jikan* ni jikken o shimashita.)

2 〖尾〗
¶毎日5時間ぐらい勉強します。(Mainichi go*jikan* gurai benkyō shimasu.)

jiken 事件〖名〗
¶今日，銀行の前で人が殺されるという事件が起こりました。(Kyō, ginkō no mae de hito ga korosareru to iu *jiken* ga okorimashita.)
¶わたしはその事件には関係がありません。(Watashi wa sono *jiken* ni wa kankei ga arimasen.)

jiki 時期〖名〗
¶もう桜の時期は過ぎました。 (Mō sakura no *jiki* wa sugimashita.)
¶勉強には秋が最も良い時期でしょう。(Benkyō ni wa aki ga mottomo yoi *jiki* deshō.)

jikken 実験〖名, ～する〗
実験室 (*jikken*shitsu) 実験に成功す

¶ **The time** of that broadcast is 8–9 PM.

② [time, the hour]
be in **time** for // be late // be on **time,** be punctual

③ [time, a set time for something]

a **time**table, schedule // free **time**

¶ [We] performed an experiment during science **class.**

2 〖suf〗 the counter for hours
¶ [I] study about five **hours** daily.

jiken 〖n〗 matter, affair, incident, event
¶ Today there was **an incident** in front of the bank in which a person was killed.

¶ I don't have anything to do with that **matter.**

jiki 〖n〗 time, season
¶ The cherry **season** is already over.

¶ Autumn is probably the best **season of the year** for studying.

jikken 〖n, ~*suru*〗 experiment, test
a laboratory // succeed in **an ex-**

る (*jikken* ni seikō suru)

¶化学の実験で石けんを作りました。
(Kagaku no *jikken* de sekken o tsukurimashita.)

¶[I] made soap in a laboratory **experiment** for chemistry class.

¶その理論が正しいかどうか**実験して**みました。 (Sono riron ga tadashii ka dō ka *jikken* shite mimashita.)

¶[I] tried **to test** whether that theory was correct or not.

jikkō 実行〖名, ～する〗

¶その計画は**実行**が難しいです。(Sono keikaku wa *jikkō* ga muzukashii desu.)

¶あの人は言ったことは必ず**実行**します。 (Ano hito wa itta koto wa kanarazu *jikkō* shimasu.)

jikkō 〖n, ～*suru*〗 carry out, put into practice, execute, realize

¶That plan will be difficult **to implement**.

¶[He] always **delivers on** what [he] says 〚**does** what he says he will〛.

jiko 自己〖名〗

自己中心 (*jiko*-chūshin) 自己批判 (*jiko*-hihan) 自己満足 (*jiko*-manzoku) 自己宣伝 (*jiko*-senden) 自己紹介 (*jiko*-shōkai) 自己主張 (*jiko*-shuchō)

¶**自己**を知ることは難しいです。(*Jiko* o shiru koto wa muzukashii desu.)

jiko 〖n〗 oneself, self, ego

self-centeredness, selfishness // **self**-criticism // **self**-satisfaction // **self**-advertisement // **self**-introduction // **self**-assertion

¶It is difficult to know **oneself**.

jiko 事故〖名〗

自動車**事故** (jidōsha-*jiko*) 交通**事故** (kōtsū-*jiko*)

¶電車の**事故**で学校に遅れました。(Densha no *jiko* de gakkō ni okuremashita.)

¶彼は車を運転していて, まだ一度も**事故**を起こしていません。 (Kare wa kuruma o unten shite ite, mada ichido mo *jiko* o okoshite imasen.)

jiko 〖n〗 accident

an auto **accident** // a traffic **accident**

¶[I] was late for school because of a train **accident**.

¶He hasn't had a single **accident** in all the time he's been driving.

jikoku 時刻〖名〗

時刻表 (*jikoku*hyō)

jikoku 〖n〗 time, hour

a **time**table, schedule

¶ただ今の時刻は9時5分です。

(Tadaima no *jikoku* wa kuji gofun desu.)

¶急げば約束の時刻に間に合います。

(Isogeba yakusoku no *jikoku* ni maniaimasu.)

⇒(-)**jikan** (-)時間

jiman 自慢〖名, 〜する〗

¶これが父の自慢の花びんです。(Kore ga chichi no *jiman* no kabin desu.)

¶彼はいつも自分の娘を自慢しています。 (Kare wa itsu mo jibun no musume o *jiman* shite imasu.)

jimi 地味〖形動〗

¶この着物は若い娘には少し地味でしょう。 (Kono kimono wa wakai musume ni wa sukoshi *jimi* deshō.)

¶わたしは地味な色のほうが好きです。 (Watashi wa *jimi* na iro no hō ga suki desu.)

⇔**hade** 派手

jimu 事務〖名〗

事務員 (*jimu*in) 事務室 (*jimu*-shitsu) 事務所 (*jimu*sho)

¶わたしは事務関係の仕事を探しています。 (Watashi wa *jimu*-kankei no shigoto o sagashite imasu.)

¶彼は事務の能力があります。 (Kare wa *jimu* no nōryoku ga arimasu.)

-jin -人〖尾〗

アメリカ人 (Amerika*jin*) 中国人 (Chūgoku*jin*) ドイツ人 (Doitsu*jin*) フランス人 (Furansu*jin*) イギリス人 (Igirisu*jin*) インド人 (Indo*jin*)

¶ **The time** is now 9:05.

¶ If [you] hurry, [you] can get there by the appointed **time.**

jiman 〖n, ~*suru*〗 **boast, be proud of**

¶ This vase is my father's **pride and joy.**

¶ He is always **boasting about** his daughter.

jimi 〖adj-v〗 **plain, quiet, sober, restrained, conservative**

¶ This *kimono* is a little **on the conservative side** for a young lady.

¶ I like **subdued** colors.

jimu 〖n〗 **business matters, office work, desk work**

a clerk, **clerical** worker // a **clerical** office, **administrative** office // an office, **business** premises

¶ I am looking for an **office** job 〚**administrative** position〛.

¶ With his eye for detail he is good at **office work.**

-jin 〖suf〗 **person, persons**

American(s), // 〚the〛 Chinese // German(s) // a Frenchman 〚Frenchwoman〛, the French // an Englishman 〚Englishwoman〛, the

日本人 (Nihon*jin*) スペイン人 (Supein*jin*) タイ人 (Tai*jin*) 外人 (gai*jin*) 外国人 (gaikoku*jin*) 知識人 (chishiki*jin*) 現代人 (gendai*jin*)

¶あの人は何人ですか。(Ano hito wa nani*jin* desu ka?)

English // Indian(s) (from India) // a [the] Japanese // a Spaniard, the Spanish // a Thai, the Thais // a foreigner // a foreigner // an intellectual // a contemporary, a modern **person**

¶ What **nationality** is that person?

jinja 神社〖名〗

¶今度の旅行では古い神社やお寺を見て歩きました。(Kondo no ryokō de wa furui *jinja* ya otera o mite arukimashita.)

¶毎年, お正月には神社へお参りに行きます。(Mainen, oshōgatsu ni wa *jinja* e omairi ni ikimasu.)

jinja 〖n〗 **Shinto shrine**

¶ On [my] trip this time [I] visited ancient **shrines** and temples.

¶ Every year [I] make a **shrine** visit during the New Year holiday season.

jinkō 人口〖名〗

人口調査 (*jinkō*-chōsa) 人口問題 (*jinkō*-mondai)

¶あなたの国の人口はどのくらいですか。(Anata no kuni no *jinkō* wa dono kurai desu ka?)

¶この町の人口は今も増え続けています。(Kono machi no *jinkō* wa ima mo fuetsuzukete imasu.)

jinkō 〖n〗 **population**

a census // the **population** problem

¶ What is **the population** of your country?

¶ **The population** of this city continues to increase.

jinsei 人生〖名〗

人生観 (*jinsei*kan) 人生相談 (*jinsei*-sōdan)

¶人生の目的は何ですか。(*Jinsei* no mokuteki wa nan desu ka?)

jinsei 〖n〗 **human life**

view of **life,** one's attitude toward **life** // counseling, seeking advice about **personal** problems

¶ What is the purpose of **life?**

jishin 自信〖名〗

自信がつく (*jishin* ga tsuku) 自信を失う (*jishin* o ushinau)

¶試験に合格する自信がありません。(Shiken ni gōkaku suru *jishin* ga

jishin 〖n〗 **(self-)confidence**

gain **confidence** // lose **confidence**

¶ **I am not sure** I will pass the exam.

arimasen.)

¶もっと自信を持って，がんばってく
ださい。 (Motto *jishin* o motte,
ganbatte kudasai.)

jishin 地震〖名〗

地震が起こる (*jishin* ga okoru) 地
震が起きる (*jishin* ga okiru)

¶今朝，大きい地震がありました。
(Kesa, ookii *jishin* ga arimashita.)

¶今度の地震で大きな被害が出ました。
(Kondo no *jishin* de ookina higai
ga demashita.)

jisho 辞書〖名〗

¶言葉の意味がわからないときは辞書
を引きます。 (Kotoba no imi ga
wakaranai toki wa *jisho* o hikimasu.)

¶この言葉は辞書に出ていません。
(Kono kotoba wa *jisho* ni dete
imasen.)

⇨**jiten** 辞典

jishū 自習〖名，〜する〗

自習時間 (*jishū*-jikan)

¶先生が御病気でお休みですから，静
かに自習してください。 (Sensei ga
gobyōki de oyasumi desu kara,
shizuka ni *jishū* shite kudasai.)

jissai 実際〖名，副〗

1〖名〗

¶彼の話は実際とはだいぶ違います。
(Kare no hanashi wa *jissai* to wa
daibu chigaimasu.)

¶彼はああ言っていますが，実際はど
うでしたか。(Kare wa ā itte imasu

¶ Keep going—**you can do it** (literally, Have **confidence** and hang on
in there)!

jishin 〚n〛 **earthquake**

an earthquake takes place // **an
earthquake** takes place

¶ There was a large **earthquake** this
morning.

¶ The last **earthquake** caused extensive damage.

jisho 〚n〛 **dictionary**

¶ When [I] come across words whose
meaning [I] don't know, [I] look
them up in **the dictionary.**

¶ This word doesn't appear in **the
dictionary.**

jishū 〚n, ~*suru*〛 **study, independent study, teaching oneself**

study hours

¶ As the teacher is absent today due
to illness, please **study** quietly **by
yourselves.**

jissai 〚n, adv〛 **truth, actuality; really, actually**

1 〚n〛

¶ His story is quite different from **the
actual facts of the matter.**

¶ That's what he says, but what's **the
real story?**

ga, *jissai* wa dō deshita ka?)

¶習った日本語を**実際**に話す機会がなくて残念です。(Naratta Nihongo o *jissai* ni hanasu kikai ga nakute zannen desu.)

2〖副〗

¶この問題には**実際**困っています。(Kono mondai ni wa *jissai* komatte imasu.)

jisshū 実習〖名, 〜する〗
実習生 (*jisshū*sei) 教育実習 (kyōiku-*jisshū*) 実習費 (*jisshū*hi)
¶**実習**の経験はたいへん役に立ちます。(*Jisshū* no keiken wa taihen yaku ni tachimasu.)
¶今、病院で**実習**しています。(Ima, byōin de *jisshū* shite imasu.)

jiten 辞典〖名〗
国語辞典 (kokugo-*jiten*) 漢和辞典 (kanwa-*jiten*) 英和辞典 (eiwa-*jiten*) 和英辞典 (waei-*jiten*)
⇨jisho 辞書

jiten 事典〖名〗
百科事典 (hyakka-*jiten*) 医学事典 (igaku-*jiten*)

jitensha 自転車〖名〗
¶**自転車**に乗れますか。(*Jitensha* ni noremasu ka?)
¶**自転車**で学校へ通っています。(*Jitensha* de gakkō e kayotte imasu.)

jitsugen 実現〖名, 〜する〗
¶この計画の**実現**には、たいへんなお金がかかります。(Kono keikaku no

¶ It's a shame I don't have any opportunity to **actually** speak Japanese after having studied it.

2 〖adv〗

¶ [I] **really** don't know what to do about this problem 〖I am **really** in a fix due to this problem〗.

jisshū 〖n, ～*suru*〗 **practice, practical training, on-the-job training**
a trainee, apprentice, intern // **practice** teaching, **student** teaching // a **practice** fee, **training** fee
¶ **On-the-job training** is very useful.

¶ [I] an now **an intern** at a hospital.

jiten 〖n〗 **dictionary**
a Japanese-language **dictionary** // a Japanese-language Chinese character **dictionary** // an English-Japanese **dictionary** // a Japanese-English **dictionary**

jiten 〖n〗 **encyclopedia**
an encyclopedia // a medical **encyclopedia**

jitensha 〖n〗 **bicycle**
¶ Can you ride **a bicycle**?

¶ [I] go to school by **bicycle.**

jitsugen 〖n, ～*suru*〗 **realize, actualize, materialize, come true**
¶ It will cost a lot **to implement** this

263

jitsugen ni wa, taihen na okane ga kakarimasu.)

¶日本に留学できて，やっと長い間の夢が**実現**しました。 (Nihon ni ryūgaku dekite, yatto nagai aida no yume ga *jitsugen* shimashita.)

¶いつ月旅行が**実現**するでしょうか。

(Itsu tsukiryokō ga *jitsugen* suru deshō ka?)

jitsu ni 実に〖副〗

¶あの人は**実に**きれいですね。 (Ano hito wa *jitsu ni* kirei desu ne.)

¶あの映画は**実に**おもしろいです。

(Ano eiga wa *jitsu ni* omoshiroi desu.)

jitsu wa 実は〖副〗

¶**実は**，お願いがあるのですが…。

(*Jitsu wa*, onegai ga aru no desu ga...)

¶「どうして学校をやめるのですか。」

(Dōshite gakkō o yameru no desu ka?) 「**実は**，父が亡くなって働かなければならなくなったからです。」

(*Jitsu wa*, chichi ga nakunatte hatarakanakereba naranaku natta kara desu.)

jitto じっと〖副，〜する〗

①[体を動かさないで静かにしている様子]

¶あの子は少しも**じっと**していません。 (Ano ko wa sukoshi mo *jitto* shite imasen.)

②[苦しいこと・痛いことなどに耐える様子]

plan.

¶ [I] was finally **able to realize** my long-held dream and go to school in Japan.

¶ When do you suppose travel to the moon **will become a reality?**

jitsu ni 〖adv〗 truly, really, indeed, very, awfully

¶ She is **really** beautiful.

¶ That movie is **really** interesting.

jitsu wa 〖adv〗 really, actually, in fact, as a matter of fact, to tell the truth

¶ **Actually,** I have a favor to ask of you....

¶ "Why are you quitting school?" "**The fact is** my father has died and I have to go to work."

jitto 〖adv, ~*suru*〗 quietly; patiently, stoically; steadily, fixedly

① [quietly, without moving]

¶ That child is never **still** for a moment.

② [patiently, stoically]

¶手術は痛かったが, **じっと我慢**しました。(Shujutsu wa itakatta ga, *jitto gaman shimashita*.)

③[視線や考えなどをほかに向けない様子]

¶彼は**じっと**その絵を見ていました。(Kare wa *jitto* sono e o mite imashita.)

¶彼女は**じっと**何かを考えているようでした。(Kanojo wa *jitto* nani ka o kangaete iru yō deshita.)

jiyū　自由〖名, 形動〗

①[何の統制・制限も受けない様子]
自由時間 (*jiyū*-jikan)　　**自由**行動 (*jiyū*-kōdō)　**自由**経済 (*jiyū*-keizai)　**自由**主義 (*jiyū*-shugi)　出版の**自由** (shuppan no *jiyū*)　　表現の**自由** (hyōgen no *jiyū*)

¶作文の題は**自由**ですから, あしたまでに書いてきてください。(Sakubun no dai wa *jiyū* desu kara, ashita made ni kaite kite kudasai.)

②[思うとおりに行動する様子]

¶田中さんは英語もフランス語も**自由**に話せます。(Tanaka san wa Eigo mo Furansugo mo *jiyū* ni hanasemasu.)

jōbu　丈夫〖形動〗

①[体が健康な様子]

¶体を**丈夫**にするために毎日運動をしています。(Karada o *jōbu* ni suru tame ni mainichi undō o shite imasu.)

②[物などがしっかりしている様子]

¶ The operation was painful but I **stoically** bore the pain.

③ [steadily, fixedly, intently, concentratedly]

¶ He **was staring** at that painting.

¶ It looked like she was **intently** thinking about something.

jiyū 〖n, adj-v〗　**freedom; freely**

① [freedom, liberty]

free time // **freedom** of movement; having a **free** hand // a **free** economy // **liberal**ism // **freedom** of the press // **freedom** of expression

¶ Please write a composition by tomorrow on **any** topic **you desire.**

② [freely, as one likes, without restraint]

¶ [Mrs.] Tanaka speaks both English and French **fluently.**

jōbu 〖adj-v〗　**healthy, hardy; strong, substantial, tough**

① [healthy, hardy, robust]

¶ [I] exercise every day in order to **build up** [my] health.

② [strong, substantial, tough]

丈夫なくつ下 (*jōbu* na kutsushita)
¶このかばんはとても丈夫です。
(Kono kaban wa totemo *jōbu* desu.)

durable socks

¶ This suitcase 〖bag, briefcase, etc.〗 is very **solidly built.**

jōdan 冗談〖名〗
¶あの人はよく冗談を言って，人を笑わせます。(Ano hito wa yoku *jōdan* o itte, hito o warawasemasu.)
¶今の話は冗談ではなく，本当のことです。(Ima no hanashi wa *jōdan* de wa naku, hontō no koto desu.)

jōdan 〖n〗 **joke, pleasantry**

¶ [He] is often **joking** and making people laugh.

¶ That wasn't **a joke,** it's the truth.

jōjun 上旬〖名〗
¶わたしは8月の上旬に旅行に出かけます。(Watashi wa hachigatsu no *jōjun* ni ryokō ni dekakemasu.)
⇨chūjun 中旬 gejun 下旬

jōjun 〖n〗 **the first third of the month**

¶ I will be leaving on a trip in **early** August.

jōken 条件〖名〗
¶条件が悪いので，あの仕事はやめました。(*Jōken* ga warui node, ano shigoto wa yamemashita.)
¶どんな条件であのアパートを借りましたか。(Donna *jōken* de ano apāto o karimashita ka?)

jōken 〖n〗 **term, condition, stipulation**

¶ I quit that job because **the terms of employment** were poor.

¶ On what **terms** did you rent that apartment?

josei 女性〖名〗
¶この店では女性の物しか売っていません。(Kono mise de wa *josei* no mono shika utte imasen.)
¶働く女性はだんだん多くなっています。(Hataraku *josei* wa dandan ooku natte imasu.)
⇔dansei 男性

josei 〖n〗 **woman, women**

¶ This shop sells only **women's** goods.

¶ The number of working **women** is gradually increasing.

joshi 女子〖名〗
女子大 (*joshi*dai) 女子学生 (*joshi*-gakusei) 女子用 (*joshi*yō) 女子寮

joshi 〖n〗 **girl, woman, female**
a **women's** college // a **female** student, a co-ed // **women's,** for use by

(*joshi*ryō)

¶このクラスは男子４名，女子３名です。(Kono kurasu wa danshi yonmei, *joshi* sanmei desu.)

¶体育の時間は男子と女子に分かれます。(Taiiku no jikan wa danshi to *joshi* ni wakaremasu.)

⇔**danshi** 男子

jōshiki 常識〖名〗

常識外れ (*jōshiki*hazure) 非常識 (hi*jōshiki*)

¶こんなことは常識です。(Konna koto wa *jōshiki* desu.)

¶あの人は常識がありません。(Ano hito wa *jōshiki* ga arimasen.)

jōtai 状態〖名〗

経済状態 (keizai-*jōtai*) 健康状態 (kenkō-*jōtai*) 精神状態 (seishin-*jōtai*)

¶この建物はたいへん古くて危険な状態です。(Kono tatemono wa taihen furukute kiken na *jōtai* desu.)

¶あんな状態では試験に合格しないでしょう。(Anna *jōtai* de wa shiken ni gōkaku shinai deshō.)

jōzu 上手〖形動〗

¶日本語が上手になりたいです。(Nihongo ga *jōzu* ni naritai desu.)

¶あの子はピアノが上手ですね。(Ano ko wa piano ga *jōzu* desu ne.)

⇔**heta** 下手 ⇨**umai** うまい

jū 十〖名〗

women // a **women's** 〚**girls'**〛 dormitory

¶ There are four boys 〚**men**〛 and three **girls** 〚**women**〛 in this class.

¶ Physical education classes are divided into male and **female** sections.

jōshiki 〚n〛 **common sense**

contrary to **common sense**, absurd // senseless, absurd, preposterous

¶ This sort of thing is **a matter of common sense** 〚is **common knowledge**〛.

¶ [He] doesn't have **good sense**.

jōtai 〚n〛 state, condition, situation, state of affairs

economic **conditions**, financial **situation** // **state** of health // mental **state, state** of mind

¶ This building is very old and in a hazardous **condition**.

¶ Considering **that** (i.e., his illness, his lack of preparation, etc.), [he] probably won't pass the exam.

jōzu 〚adj-v〛 skill, proficiency

¶ I want to become **good at** Japanese.

¶ That child plays the piano **well**, doesn't it?

jū 〚n〛 ten

-jū -じゅう〖尾〗

① [その期間ずっと]

¶昨日は一日じゅう本を読んでいました。 (Kinō wa ichinichi*jū* hon o yonde imashita.)

¶子供の病気が心配で、一晩じゅう起きていました。 (Kodomo no byōki ga shinpai de, hitoban*jū* okite imashita.)

¶この島は一年じゅういい天気です。 (Kono shima wa ichinen*jū* ii tenki desu.)

② [ある場所全体、どこでも]

¶日本じゅうの人がそのテレビ番組を見ました。 (Nihon*jū* no hito ga sono terebi-bangumi o mimashita.)

¶世界じゅうの人々が平和を願っています。 (Sekai*jū* no hitobito ga heiwa o negatte imasu.)

jūbun じゅうぶん〖副、形動〗

¶旅行の費用は五万円でじゅうぶんでしょう。 (Ryokō no hiyō wa goman'en de *jūbun* deshō.)

¶冬の登山にはじゅうぶんな準備が必要です。 (Fuyu no tozan ni wa *jūbun* na junbi ga hitsuyō desu.)

¶お体にじゅうぶん気をつけてください。 (Okarada ni *jūbun* ki o tsukete kudasai.)

jūdō 柔道〖名〗

柔道初段 (*jūdō* shodan)

¶柔道を習っています。 (*Jūdō* o naratte imasu.)

¶柔道の先生を紹介してください。

-jū 〖suf〗 **through, throughout; everywhere**

① [through, throughout, in the course of]

¶ [I] was reading books **all** day yesterday.

¶ [I] was up **all** night with worry over [my] sick child.

¶ This island has good weather **throughout** the year.

② [everywhere, throughout]

¶ People **all over** Japan watched that television program.

¶ People **everywhere** in the world want peace.

jūbun 〖adv, adj-v〗 **enough, sufficient**

¶ Fifty thousand yen **should be enough** to cover the cost of the trip.

¶ It is necessary to make **thorough** preparations for mountain climbing in the winter.

¶ Please take **good** care of yourself.

jūdō 〖n〗 **judo**

shodan, the first grade of black belt in **judo**

¶ [I] am studying **judo**.

¶ Could you please give me the name

(*Jūdō* no sensei o shōkai shite
kudasai.) | of a **judo** teacher?

jūgatsu 十月〘名〙

jugyō 授業〘名, ～する〙
授業中 (*jugyō*chū) 授業時間
(*jugyō*-jikan) 授業料 (*jugyō*-
ryō)
¶土曜にも授業がありますか。(Doyō
ni mo *jugyō* ga arimasu ka?)
¶日本語の授業は9時に始まります。
(Nihongo no *jugyō* wa kuji ni
hajimarimasu.)

jūichigatsu 十一月〘名〙
(-)**jun** (-)順〘名, 尾〙
1〘名〙
¶背の高い順に並んでください。 (Se
no takai *jun* ni narande kudasai.)
2〘尾〙
番号順 (bangō*jun*) 年齢順 (nenrei*jun*) 成績順 (seiseki*jun*)

junban 順番〘名〙
¶順番に並んでください。 (*Junban*
ni narande kudasai.)
¶タクシー乗り場でおおぜいの人が順
番を待っています。(Takushii-noriba
de oozei no hito ga *junban* o matte
imasu.)

junbi 準備〘名, ～する〙
¶じゅうぶんな準備をして，山に登り
ました。 (Jūbun na *junbi* o shite,
yama ni noborimashita.)
¶今,試験の準備で忙しいです。(Ima,
shiken no *junbi* de isogashii desu.)

jūnigatsu 十二月〘名〙

jūgatsu 〚n〛 October

jugyō 〚n, ～*suru*〛 teaching, a class
during **school** hours; during **class** //
school hours; **class** periods // tuition
¶ Are there **classes** on Saturday
too?
¶ Japanese **class** starts at nine
o'clock.

jūichigatsu 〚n〛 November
(-)**jun** 〚n, suf〛 order, sequence
1 〚n〛
¶ Please line up **in order** by height,
from tallest to shortest.
2 〚suf〛
numerical **order** // **in order** of age //
in order of grades achieved

junban 〚n〛 turn, order
¶ Please line up **in order.**

¶ Many people are waiting **their turn**
at the taxi stand.

junbi 〚n, ～*suru*〛 preparations
¶ [I] climbed the mountain after **preparing** fully.

¶ [I]'m busy now **preparing** for exams.

jūnigatsu 〚n〛 December

269

junjo 順序〖名〗

¶みんなにわかるように**順序**よく話してください。(Minna ni wakaru yō ni *junjo* yoku hanashite kudasai.)

¶漢字を書くときは、正しい**順序**で書きなさい。(Kanji o kaku toki wa, tadashii *junjo* de kakinasai.)

jūsho 住所〖名〗

¶ここに**住所**と名前を書いてください。(Koko ni *jūsho* to namae o kaite kudasai.)

¶すみませんが、**住所**を教えていただけませんか。(Sumimasen ga, *jūsho* o oshiete itadakemasen ka?)

jūsu ジュース〖名〗

いちご**ジュース** (ichigo-*jūsu*) みかん**ジュース** (mikan-*jūsu*) りんご**ジュース** (ringo-*jūsu*) 野菜**ジュース** (yasai-*jūsu*)

jūtaku 住宅〖名〗

住宅地 (*jūtaku*chi) **住宅**街 (*jūtaku*gai) **住宅**問題 (*jūtaku*-mondai) **住宅**難 (*jūtaku*nan)

¶都会では**住宅**がたいへん不足しています。 (Tokai de wa *jūtaku* ga taihen fusoku shite imasu.)

¶あの建物は1階が店で、2階から上が**住宅**です。 (Ano tatemono wa ikkai ga mise de, nikai kara ue ga *jūtaku* desu.)

jūyō 重要〖形動〗

重要書類 (*jūyō*-shorui)

¶これは非常に**重要**な問題です。

junjo 〖n〗 order, sequence, procedure

¶ Please talk **systematically** so everyone will understand.

¶ When writing *kanji*, write the strokes in the correct **order**.

jūsho 〖n〗 address

¶ Please write your name and **address** here.

¶ Excuse me, but could you give me **your address** please?

jūsu 〖n〗 juice, fruit drinks

strawberry **juice** // mandarin orange **juice** // apple **juice** // vegetable **juice**

jūtaku 〖n〗 house, residence

a **residential** area // a **residential** street, **residential** block // the **housing** problem // a **housing** shortage

¶ There is a severe shortage of **housing** in the cities.

¶ That building has shops on the first floor and **living quarters** from the second floor upward.

jūyō 〖adj-v〗 important

important documents; **classified** papers

(Kore wa hijō ni *jūyō* na mondai desu.)

¶彼の実験はこの研究にとってたいへん**重要**です。 (Kare no jikken wa kono kenkyū ni totte taihen *jūyō* desu.)

¶ This is a matter of great **importance**.

¶ His experiment **is crucial** for this research.

K

ka 蚊〖名〗

蚊に食われる (*ka* ni kuwareru) 蚊帳 (*kaya*)

¶この辺は夏になると，蚊が多いです。(Kono hen wa natsu ni naru to, *ka* ga ooi desu.)

ka か〖助〗

¶あなたはあしたどこかへ行きますか。(Anata wa ashita doko *ka* e ikimasu ka?)

¶何か欲しいものがありますか。(Nani *ka* hoshii mono ga arimasu ka?)

¶山田さんの誕生日はいつか知っていますか。(Yamada san no tanjōbi wa itsu *ka* shitte imasu ka?)

¶隣の部屋にだれかいますか。(Tonari no heya ni dare *ka* imasu ka?)

¶ゆうべ食べた魚が悪かったためか，おなかが痛いです。(Yūbe tabeta sakana ga warukatta tame *ka*, onaka ga itai desu.)

ka か〖助〗

①[いくつかあるもののうち一つを選ぶときに使う]

¶来週の土曜日か日曜日に海へ泳ぎに行きます。(Raishū no doyōbi *ka* nichiyōbi ni umi e oyogi ni ikimasu.)

¶正しい答えはAかBかわかりますか。(Tadashii kotae wa ē *ka* bii *ka*

ka 〚n〛 mosquito

be bitten by **a mosquito** // a **mosquito** net

¶ There are many **mosquitoes** in this area in the summer.

ka 〚part〛 the interrogative particle

¶ Are you going **anywhere** tomorrow?

¶ Is there **something** you want 〚you'd like〛?

¶ Do you know **when** [Mrs.] Yamada's birthday is?

¶ Is there **anyone** in the room next door?

¶ My stomach aches, **probably** because the fish I ate last night was bad.

ka 〚part〛 or

① [or; used when two different alternatives are possible]

¶ I will go to the ocean to swim next Saturday **or** Sunday.

¶ Do you know if the correct answer is A **or** B?

wakarimasu ka?)

¶大学に進むか社会に出て働くか，まだ決めていません。　(Daigaku ni susumu *ka* shakai ni dete hataraku *ka*, mada kimete imasen.)

②[二つの可能性のうちどちらかはっきりしないときに使う]

¶あしたハイキングに行くか行かないか早く決めてください。(Ashita haikingu ni iku *ka* ikanai *ka* hayaku kimete kudasai.)

¶あの人は今日来るかどうかわかりません。　(Ano hito wa kyō kuru *ka* dō *ka* wakarimasen.)

¶学校があした休みかどうかきいてください。　(Gakkō ga ashita yasumi *ka* dō *ka* kiite kudasai.)

¶このりんごはおいしいかどうか食べてみましょう。(Kono ringo wa oishii *ka* dō *ka* tabete mimashō.)

③[あるものごとを例として挙げる]

¶のどが渇いたから，コーヒーか何かを飲みましょう。(Nodo ga kawaita kara, kōhii *ka* nani ka o nomimashō.)

¶この仕事は山田さんかだれかに頼みましょう。(Kono shigoto wa Yamada san *ka* dare ka ni tanomimashō.)

¶それはデパートかどこかで売っていると思います。(Sore wa depāto *ka* doko ka de utte iru to omoimasu.)

*「～か何か（～ka nani ka）」「～かだれか（～ka dare ka）」「～かどこか（～ka doko ka）」の形で使う。ま

¶ [I] haven't decided yet whether to go to college **or** to go out into the world and get a job.

② [or; used when one alternative and its opposite are possible]

¶ Please hurry up and make up your mind whether you are going hiking tomorrow **or** not.

¶ I don't know if [he] is coming today **or** not.

¶ Please inquire whether there is school tomorrow **or** not.

¶ Let's try these apples and see if they're good tasting **or** not.

③ [or; used when offering something as one possibility]

¶ I'm thirsty. Let's have some coffee **or** something.

¶ Let's ask [Mr.] Yamada **or** someone to do this work.

¶ I think that's on sale 〚one can buy that〛 at a department store **or** the like.

* Used in the patterns "～ *ka nani ka*," "～ *ka dare ka*," and "～ *ka doko ka*." After the second *ka*, the

273

た，あとのほうの「か (ka)」につく
助詞の「が (ga)」「を (o)」は省略
することができる。

ka　か〚助〛

①[質問の意味を表す]

¶あれは何ですか。(Are wa nan desu
ka?)

¶あなたは学生ですか。　(Anata wa
gakusei desu *ka*?)

¶ここはどこですか。(Koko wa doko
desu *ka*?)

②[勧誘・依頼などを表す]

¶映画を見に行きませんか。　(Eiga o
mi ni ikimasen *ka*?)

¶ちょっと，その本を見せてください
ませんか。　　　(Chotto, sono hon o
misete kudasaimasen *ka*?)

③[相手の意向をうかがうのに使う]

¶私がその本を買ってきましょうか。
(Watakushi ga sono hon o katte
kimashō *ka*?)

¶この仕事はわたしがいたしましょう
か。(Kono shigoto wa watashi ga
itashimashō *ka*?)

④[疑念の意味を表す]

¶あれは何だろうか。　(Are wa nan
darō *ka*?)

¶こんな難しい問題がわたしにできる
だろうか。(Konna muzukashii mondai ga watashi ni dekiru darō *ka*?)

¶こんな小さな舟に5人も乗って大丈
夫だろうか。(Konna chiisana fune ni
gonin mo notte daijōbu darō *ka*?)

⑤[自問自答の形で事実を確かめるの

particles *ga* and *o* are sometimes
omitted.

ka 〚part〛　the sentence-final interrogative particle

① [indicates a question]

¶ What's that?

¶ Are you a student?

¶ Where is this 〖Where am I〗?

② [indicates an invitation or request]

¶ Won't you come to a movie with
[me]?

¶ Would you let me see that book for
a moment, please?

③ [used to inquire about the desires
of the listener]

¶ Would you like me to buy that
book?

¶ Shall I do this job 〖How about my
doing this work〗?

④ [indicates doubt]

¶ What do you suppose that is 〖I
wonder what that is〗?

¶ I'm not sure I can do such a difficult problem.

¶ Can five people fit into this small
boat all right?

⑤ [used to confirm something in the

に使う]

¶「山田さんは試験に失敗したそうです。」(Yamada san wa shiken ni shippai shita sō desu.)「やはりそうでしたか。全然勉強しませんでしたからね。」(Yahari sō deshita *ka*. Zenzen benkyō shimasen deshita kara ne.)

(-)ka (-)課〚名, 尾〛

1〚名〛

①[役所・会社などの事務組織の区別の一つ]

課長 (*ka*chō) 学生課 (gakusei*ka*)

＊普通, 局・部の下, 係の上に位置する。

②[教科書などの一区切りを表す]

¶昨日習った課を復習してください。

(Kinō naratta *ka* o fukushū shite kudasai.)

2〚尾〛

¶今日は第5課から始めましょう。

(Kyō wa daigo*ka* kara hajime-mashō.)

(-)ka (-)科〚名, 尾〛

1〚名〛

科目 (*ka*moku)

¶あなたは文学部のどの科に進むつもりですか。(Anata wa bungakubu no dono *ka* ni susumu tsumori desu ka?)

2〚尾〛

学科 (gak*ka*) 文科 (bun*ka*) 理科 (ri*ka*) 内科 (nai*ka*) 外科 (ge*ka*) 眼科 (gan*ka*) 歯科 (shi*ka*)

-ka -日〚尾〛

---

form of a rhetorical question]

¶ "I hear [Miss] Yamada failed [her] exam."

"Really? That's just what I expected. [She] didn't study at all."

(-)ka 〚n, suf〛 **division, section; lesson**

1 〚n〛

① [division, section]

a **section** chief // the student **division**

＊ A *ka* is generally below a *kyoku* or a *bu* and above a *kakari*.

② [lesson (in a textbook)]

¶ Please review the **chapter(s)** [we] studied yesterday.

2 〚suf〛 lesson, section

¶ Let's start today with **Lesson** 5.

(-)ka 〚n, suf〛 **course; branch, department, faculty**

1 〚n〛 course

subject, course (in school)

¶ What **course** do you plan to major in within the faculty of literature?

2 〚suf〛 branch, department, faculty

school **subject; course** of study, curriculum // **dept.** of liberal arts // science; the science **course** // internal medicine, internal **dept.** (of a hospital) // surgery, **dept.** of surgery // ophthalmology, **dept.** of opthalmology // dentistry

-ka 〚suf〛 **days**

①[日付を表す]
二日 (futsu*ka*) 三日 (mik*ka*) 四
日 (yok*ka*) 五日 (itsu*ka*) 六日
(mui*ka*) 七日 (nano*ka*) 八日
(yō*ka*) 九日 (kokono*ka*) 十日
(too*ka*) 十四日 (jūyok*ka*) 二十日
(hatsu*ka*) 二十四日 (nijūyok*ka*)
¶三月三日は女の子のお祭りの日です。
(Sangatsu mik*ka* wa onna no ko
no omatsuri no hi desu.)

②[日数を表す]
¶あと三日で夏休みです。(Ato mik*ka*
de natsuyasumi desu.)
¶上田さんは十日間も学校を休んでい
ます。(Ueda san wa too*ka*kan mo
gakkō o yasunde imasu.)
＊「一日」は，日付を表すときは普通
「ついたち (tsuitachi)」と言い，日数
を表すときは「いちにち (ichinichi)」
と言う。
⇨-nichi -日

-ka -家〔尾〕
政治家 (seiji*ka*) 小説家 (shōsetsu-
ka) 芸術家 (geijutsu*ka*) 専門家
(senmon*ka*) 音楽家 (ongak*ka*) 作
曲家 (sakkyoku*ka*) 画家 (ga*ka*)
評論家 (hyōron*ka*)

-ka -化〔尾〕
電化 (den*ka*) 自動化 (jidō*ka*) オ
ートメーション化 (ōtomēshon*ka*)
具体化 (gutai*ka*) 映画化 (eiga*ka*)
合理化 (gōri*ka*) 近代化 (kindai*ka*)
民主化 (minshu*ka*)
¶最近の日本の農業は機械化されてい

① [the counter for days of the month]

the second (of the month) // the third // the fourth // the fifth // the sixth // the seventh // the eighth // the ninth // the tenth // the fourteenth // the twentieth // the twenty-fourth
¶ The **third** of March is Girls' Day.

② [the counter for number of days]
¶ In three **days** it will be summer vacation.
¶ [Mr.] Ueda has been absent from school for 10 **days.**

＊ The compound "一日" is read *tsuitachi* when referring to the first of the month and *ichinichi* when referring to one day.

-ka 〔suf〕 the suffix for a person carrying on a given profession
a politic**ian** // a novel**ist** // an art**ist** // a special**ist,** expert // a music**ian** // a compos**er** // a paint**er** // a critic, commentat**or**

-ka 〔suf〕 -ize, -zation
electrifica**tion** // automa**tion,** automati**zation** // automa**tion,** automati**zation** // embodiment, actuali**zation,** giving concrete form to // **making into** a film // rationali**zation** // moderni**zation** // democrati**zation**

ます。 (Saikin no Nihon no nōgyō wa kikai*ka* sarete imasu.)

¶ In recent times Japanese agriculture is becoming **mechanized.**

-ka- -か〖尾〗

1か所 (ik*ka*sho)　3か月 (san*ka*getsu)　5か国 (go*ka*koku)

¶ 1年は 12 か月です。 (Ichinen wa jūni*ka*getsu desu.)

＊ 数字のあとにつけて年月・所などを数えるのに使う。

-ka- 〖suf〗 the suffix used for counting

one place // three months // five countries

¶ One year is 12 months.

＊ Used between the numeral and the unit when counting units of time, places, etc.

kabā カバー〖名〗

まくらカバー (makura-*kabā*) 本にカバーを掛ける (hon ni *kabā* o kakeru)

kabā 〖n〗 **a cover**

a pillow**case** // put a book **cover** on a book

kaban かばん〖名〗

¶山田さんはいつも黒いかばんを提げて歩いています。 (Yamada san wa itsu mo kuroi *kaban* o sagete aruite imasu.)

kaban 〖n〗 **bag, briefcase, satchel, suitcase, trunk**

¶ [Mr.] Yamada always carries a black **briefcase.**

kabe 壁〖名〗

¶壁に絵が掛けてあります。 (*Kabe* ni e ga kakete arimasu.)

¶壁を白く塗りました。 (*Kabe* o shiroku nurimashita.)

kabe 〖n〗 **wall**

¶ There is a painting hanging on **the wall.**

¶ [I] painted **the wall(s)** white.

kabin 花びん〖名〗

¶花びんに花が生けてあります。 (*Kabin* ni hana ga ikete arimasu.)

kabin 〖n〗 **vase, flower vase**

¶ There is an arrangement of flowers in **the vase.**

kaburu かぶる〖動Ⅰ〗

①〔ある物で頭・顔などをおおう〕

¶赤い帽子をかぶっている人はだれですか。 (Akai bōshi o *kabutte* iru hito wa dare desu ka?)

¶寒いので，毛布を頭からかぶって寝ました。 (Samui node, mōfu o atama kara *kabutte* nemashita.)

kaburu 〖v I〗 **wear** (on the head); **pour over; cover**

① [wear or put something on the head or face]

¶ Who is the person **wearing** a red hat 〖ski cap, etc.〗?

¶ As it was cold [I] slept with the covers **up over** [my] head.

②[頭の上から浴びる]
波を**かぶる** (nami o *kaburu*)
¶あまり暑いので，水を**かぶり**ました。
(Amari atsui node, mizu o *kaburi-mashita*.)
③[物の表面をおおう]
¶1週間も掃除をしなかったので，机はほこりを**かぶって**います。 (Isshū-kan mo sōji o shinakatta node, tsukue wa hokori o *kabutte* imasu.)

②[pour over the head or top of something]
covered with waves
¶ As it was so hot **I poured** cool water **over myself.**
③[cover something]
¶ As [I] haven't cleaned for a week, the desk **is covered** with dust.

kachi 価値〖名〗
価値がある (*kachi* ga aru) 価値がない (*kachi* ga nai) 価値が高い (*kachi* ga takai) 価値が低い (*kachi* ga hikui)
¶あの人にこの絵の価値がわかるでしょうか。 (Ano hito ni kono e no *kachi* ga wakaru deshō ka?)
¶あの映画は見る価値があります。 (Ano eiga wa miru *kachi* ga arimasu.)

kachi 〖n〗 value, worth
valuable, worthy, of **value** // worthless, of no **value** // of great **value**, invaluable // of little **value**

¶ Does [he] comprehend **the value** 〖**true worth**〗 of this painting?

¶ That movie **is worth** seeing.

kado 角〖名〗
①[とがったところ]
¶子供が机の角に頭をぶつけて，けがをしました。(Kodomo ga tsukue no *kado* ni atama o butsukete, kega o shimashita.)
②[道の折れ曲がったところ]
角の店 (*kado* no mise)
¶その角を右に曲がった所に交番があります。 (Sono *kado* o migi ni magatta tokoro ni kōban ga arimasu.)

kado 〖n〗 corner, edge; corner, turning
①[corner, edge]
¶ The child hit [his] head on **the corner** of the desk and hurt [him]self.

②[corner, turning]
a **corner** shop
¶ If you turn right at that **corner**, you will find a police box.

kaeru 変える〖動Ⅱ〗

kaeru 〖v Ⅱ〗 change, alter

¶熱は氷を水に変えます。 (Netsu wa koori o mizu ni *kaemasu.*)

¶ Heat **converts** ice to water.

¶都合が悪くなったので，出発の日を変えました。 (Tsugō ga waruku natta node, shuppatsu no hi o *kaemashita.*)

¶ [I] **changed** the departure date as it had become inconvenient.

¶飛行機は方向を変えて，南に向かいました。 (Hikōki wa hōkō o *kaete*, minami ni mukaimashita.)

¶ The plane **altered** direction and headed south.

kaeru 代える〖動II〗

kaeru 〖v II〗 **change, substitute**

¶今度の試合には田中選手に代えて上田選手を出すことにしました。 (Kondo no shiai ni wa Tanaka senshu ni *kaete* Ueda senshu o dasu koto ni shimashita.)

¶ [I] have decided **to substitute** Ueda for Tanaka in the next game.

¶わたしの命に代えても，子供の命を助けたいと思います。 (Watashi no inochi ni *kaete* mo, kodomo no inochi o tasuketai to omoimasu.)

¶ I want to save the life of my child even **at the expense** of my own.

kaeru 換える〖動II〗

kaeru 〖v II〗 **change, exchange**

¶窓を開けて，部屋の空気を換えましょう。 (Mado o akete, heya no kūki o *kaemashō.*)

¶ Let's open the window and **get some fresh** air in the room.

¶電車を降りて，バスに乗り換えました。 (Densha o orite, basu ni nori-*kaemashita.*)

¶ [I] got off the train and **transferred** to a bus.

kaeru 替える〖動II〗

kaeru 〖v II〗 **change, exchange, substitute**

¶池の水が汚れたので替えました。 (Ike no mizu ga yogoreta node *kaemashita.*)

¶ [I] **changed** the water in the pool as it was dirty.

¶パーティーがあるので，洋服を替えて出かけました。 (Pātii ga aru node, yōfuku o *kaete* dekakemashita.)

¶ [I] **changed** my clothes and left for the party.

kaeru 帰る〖動I〗

kaeru 〖v I〗 **return, go 〖come〗 back home**

279

¶山田さんは昨日外国から帰ってきました。 (Yamada san wa kinō gaikoku kara *kaette* kimashita.)

¶ [Miss] Yamada **returned home** from abroad yesterday.

¶わたしは8時までにうちへ帰らなければなりません。 (Watashi wa hachiji made ni uchi e *kaeranakereba* narimasen.)

¶ I **must return home** by eight o'clock.

¶お母さんは何時ごろお帰りになりますか。 (Okāsan wa nanji goro *okaeri* ni narimasu ka?)

¶ What time will your mother **arrive home?**

kaeru 返る〖動 I 〗

kaeru 〚v I〛 **return to, be returned to**

¶時計が無事に持ち主に返りました。 (Tokei ga buji ni mochinushi ni *kaerimashita.*)

¶ The watch 〚clock〛 **was returned** to its owner all right.

kaesu 返す〖動 I 〗

kaesu 〚v I〛 **return, give back**

¶この前借りたお金はあした返します。 (Kono mae karita okane wa ashita *kaeshimasu.*)

¶ Tomorrow [I] **will pay back** the money [I] borrowed from [you].

¶今,図書館へ本を返しに行くところです。 (Ima, toshokan e hon o *kaeshi* ni iku tokoro desu.)

¶ [I]'m now on my way to the library **to return** a book.

kagaku 科学〖名〗

kagaku 〚n〛 **science**

科学者 (*kagaku*sha) 人文科学 (jinbun-*kagaku*) 自然科学 (shizen-*kagaku*) 社会科学 (shakai-*kagaku*) 科学的 (*kagaku*teki) 科学博物館 (*kagaku*-hakubutsukan)

a scientist // cultural **sciences,** humanities // natural **science(s)** // social **science(s)** // **scientific** // a **science** museum

¶20世紀になって,科学は非常に進歩しました。 (Nijisseiki ni natte, *kagaku* wa hijō ni shinpo shimashita.)

¶ **Science** has advanced greatly since the beginning of the 20th century.

¶その考えは非科学的だと思います。 (Sono kangae wa hi*kagaku*teki da to omoimasu.)

¶ [I] think that way of thinking 〚idea〛 is **unscientific.**

kagaku 化学〖名〗

応用化学 (ōyō-*kagaku*) 化学肥料 (*kagaku*-hiryō) 化学変化 (*kagaku*-henka) 化学作用 (*kagaku*-sayō) 化学反応 (*kagaku*-hannō) 化学記号 (*kagaku*-kigō)

kagaku 〚n〛 chemistry

applied **chemistry** // **artificial** 〚**chemical**〛 fertilizer // a **chemical** change // **chemical** action // **chemical** reaction // a **chemical** symbol

kagami 鏡〖名〗

鏡を見る (*kagami* o miru)

¶あなたの姿が鏡に映っています。 (Anata no sugata ga *kagami* ni utsutte imasu.)

¶鏡がないと、ネクタイが締められません。 (*Kagami* ga nai to, nekutai ga shimeraremasen.)

kagami 〚n〛 mirror

look in **a mirror**

¶ Your image is reflected in **a mirror.**

¶ [I] can't tie [my] necktie without **a mirror.**

kagayaku 輝く〖動Ⅰ〗

①[明るく光る]

¶空には星が輝いています。 (Sora ni wa hoshi ga *kagayaite* imasu.)

¶山の上の雪が朝日を受けて輝いています。 (Yama no ue no yuki ga asahi o ukete *kagayaite* imasu.)

②[明るく晴れやかに見える]

目が輝く (me ga *kagayaku*)

¶上田さんの顔は喜びに輝いています。 (Ueda san no kao wa yorokobi ni *kagayaite* imasu.)

kagayaku 〚v Ⅰ〛 shine; sparkle, light up

① [shine, sparkle, gleam, etc.]

¶ Stars **are shining** in the sky.

¶ The snow on top of the mountain **is glittering** in the morning sun.

② [sparkle, light up]

one's eyes **sparkle**

¶ [Miss] Ueda's face **is lit up** 〚**beaming**〛 with joy.

kage 影〖名〗

①[水や鏡などに映って見える人や物の形]

¶湖に富士山の影が映っています。 (Mizuumi ni Fujisan no *kage* ga utsutte imasu.)

②[光をさえぎったときにできる暗い部分の形]

kage 〚n〛 reflection; shadow

① [reflection (in a mirror, water, etc.)]

¶ Mount Fuji **is reflected** in the lake.

② [shadow, silhouette]

¶ガラス戸に人の影が映っています。

(Garasudo ni hito no *kage* ga utsu-tte imasu.)

kage 陰〚名〛

①[光線の当たらない所]

¶この家はビルの陰になっているので,日当たりが悪いです。 (Kono ie wa biru no *kage* ni natte iru node, hiatari ga warui desu.)

¶暑いから日陰で休みましょう。

(Atsui kara hi*kage* de yasumi-mashō.)

②[物にさえぎられて直接見えない所]

電柱の陰に隠れる (denchū no *kage* ni kakureru)

¶船が島の陰に隠れて見えなくなりました。 (Fune ga shima no *kage* ni kakurete mienaku narimashita.)

kagi かぎ〚名〛

かぎを掛ける (*kagi* o kakeru) かぎを閉める (*kagi* o shimeru) かぎを開ける (*kagi* o akeru) 合いかぎ (ai*kagi*)

¶部屋の戸には必ずかぎを掛けてから,出かけてください。 (Heya no to ni wa kanarazu *kagi* o kakete kara, dekakete kudasai.)

kagiri 限り〚名〛

①[ものごとの限界を表す]

¶人の力には限りがあります。 (Hito no chikara ni wa *kagiri* ga ari-masu.)

¶船は限りなく広い海を進んでいきました。 (Fune wa *kagiri* naku hiroi

¶ Someone's **silhouette** can be seen behind the glass door.

kage 〚n〛 **shade; the back, the other side**

① [shade, shadows]

¶ As this house is in **the shade** of an office building it doesn't get much sun.

¶ It's hot—let's go rest in **the shade**.

② [the back, the other side]

hide **behind** a telephone pole

¶ The ship can't be seen now as it is hidden **behind** the island.

kagi 〚n〛 **key, lock**

lock up // lock up // unlock // a duplicate **key,** pass**key**

¶ Please be sure to always **lock** your door when going out.

kagiri 〚n〛 **limits, bounds; as far as; as long as, unless**

① [limits, bounds]

¶ There's **a limit** to human strength.

¶ The ship moved over the **boundlessly** vast ocean.

umi o susunde ikimashita.)

¶申し込みは3月10日限りで締め切り
ます。 (Mōshikomi wa sangatsu
tooka *kagiri* de shimekirimasu.)

②[ものごとの範囲を表す]
¶わたしの知っている限りのことを話
しましょう。(Watashi no shitte iru
kagiri no koto o hanashimashō.)
¶この辺りは見渡す限り畑が広がって
います。 (Kono atari wa miwatasu
kagiri hatake ga hirogatte imasu.)

③[ある条件の限界を表す]
¶あの人が謝らない限り，わたしは許
しません。(Ano hito ga ayamaranai
kagiri, watashi wa yurushimasen.)

kagiru 限る〖動 I〗

①[範囲を限定する]
¶この劇場は小さいので，入場者は100
名以内に限られています。 (Kono
gekijō wa chiisai node, nyūjōsha
wa hyakumei inai ni *kagirarete*
imasu.)
¶わたしは毎日復習の時間を2時間と
限っています。 (Watashi wa mai-
nichi fukushū no jikan o nijikan
to *kagitte* imasu.)

②[それだけはほかと違って特別であ
ると限定する]
¶あの人に限って，そんなことはしな
いでしょう。 (Ano hito ni *kagitte*,
sonna koto wa shinai deshō.)
¶この店は土曜日に限り，一割引きで
売っています。 (Kono mise wa
doyōbi ni *kagiri*, ichiwaribiki de

¶ Applications will not be accepted
after March 10 〖after the **cut-off**
date, March 10〗.

② [as far as, as much as; indicates
the furthermost extent of something]
¶ I will tell you **as much as** I know
about it.

¶ Fields stretch out here **as far as**
the eye can see.

③ [as long as, unless; indicates the
bounds of a condition on something]
¶ I won't forgive [him] **unless** [he]
apologizes to me.

kagiru 〖v I〗 limit, restrict

① [limit, restrict]
¶ As this theater is small, admittance
is limited to a hundred persons.

¶ I **restrict** my time spent reviewing
lessons each day to two hours.

② [used to define one thing as special and different from others]
¶ [He], **at least,** wouldn't do such a
thing 〖He would be the last person in
the world to do such a thing〗.

¶ This shop is offering a 10 percent
discount on Saturday **alone.**

utte imasu.)

* いつも「〜に限って (ni kagitte)」「〜に限り (〜ni kagiri)」の形で使う。

* Always used in the patterns "~ *ni kagitte*" and "~ *ni kagiri*."

kago かご〖名〗

かごを編む (*kago* o amu)　くずかご (kuzu*kago*)　虫かご (mushi*kago*)

¶鳥かごの中で小鳥が鳴いています。

(Tori*kago* no naka de kotori ga naite imasu.)

¶そのかごの中に果物がありますよ。

(Sono *kago* no naka ni kudamono ga arimasu yo.)

kago [[n]] **cage; basket**

weave **a basket** // a wastepaper **basket,** waste**basket,** trash **basket** // an insect **cage**

¶ A bird is singing in **its cage.**

¶ There's fruit in that **basket.**

kagu 家具〖名〗

¶テーブルは家具の一つです。

(Tēburu wa *kagu* no hitotsu desu.)

kagu [[n]] **furniture, household furnishings**

¶ A table is a piece of **furniture.**

kai 貝〖名〗

貝がら (*kai*gara)

¶海岸で珍しい貝を拾いました。

(Kaigan de mezurashii *kai* o hiroimashita.)

¶昔，中国では貝がお金の役目をしていました。 (Mukashi, Chūgoku de wa *kai* ga okane no yakume o shite imashita.)

kai [[n]] **shellfish, shell**

a shell

¶ [I] found a rare **seashell** at the shore.

¶ **Shells** were used for money in the past in China.

(-)kai (-)階〖名，尾〗

1〖名〗

¶おもちゃは，この上の階で売っています。 (Omocha wa, kono ue no *kai* de utte imasu.)

(-)kai [[n, suf]] **floor, story**

1 [[n]]

¶ Toys are sold on the next **floor** up.

2〖尾〗

1階 (ik*kai*)　3階 (san*gai*)　6階 (rok*kai*)　8階 (hak*kai*[hachi*kai*])　10階 (jik*kai*)　何階 (nan*gai*)　2階建ての家 (ni*kai*date no ie)

2 [[suf]]

the first **floor** // the third **floor** // the sixth **floor** // the eighth **floor** // the tenth **floor** // which **floor,** how many **floors** // a two-**story** house

¶わたしはこの建物の5階に住んでいます。(Watashi wa kono tatemono no go*kai* ni sunde imasu.)

¶ I live on the fifth **floor** of this building.

(-)**kai**　(-)会〖名，尾〗

(-)kai 〚n, suf〛 **meeting, assembly; society, association**

1〖名〗

1 〚n〛 meeting, assembly, gathering

会を開く (*kai* o hiraku)　会を閉じる (*kai* o tojiru)　会に出席する (*kai* ni shusseki suru)　会合 (*kai*gō)

open **a meeting** 〚party〛 // close **a meeting** 〚party〛 // attend **a meeting** 〚party〛 // **a meeting**, **a gathering**

¶今日は3時からお茶の会があります。(Kyō wa sanji kara ocha no *kai* ga arimasu.)

¶ There's a tea ceremony **meeting** 〚tea **party**〛 from three o'clock today.

2〖尾〗

2 〚suf〛

①[ある目的のために人々が集まること]

① [a gathering of persons for a certain purpose]

送別会 (sōbetsu*kai*)　委員会 (iin*kai*)

a farewell **party** // a committee, a commission; a committee **meeting**

¶あした，上田先生の歓迎会をします。(Ashita, Ueda sensei no kangei*kai* o shimasu.)

¶ A welcome **party** 〚welcoming **reception**〛 will be held tomorrow for [Mr.] Ueda.

¶音楽会は7時から始まります。(Ongak*kai* wa shichiji kara hajimarimasu.)

¶ **The concert** 〚recital〛 starts at seven o'clock.

②[関係のある人々の作った団体]

② [society, association, group]

¶わたしたちは日本文化研究会を作りました。(Watashitachi wa Nihon-bunka-kenkyū*kai* o tsukurimashita.)

¶ We formed a Japanese culture study **group.**

(-)**kai**　(-)回〖名，尾〗

(-)kai 〚n, suf〛 **time, round, game, inning**

1〖名〗

1 〚n〛

回を重ねる (*kai* o kasaneru)

do many **times**

¶今回は出席できませんが，次回は必ず出席します。(Kon*kai* wa shusseki dekimasen ga, ji*kai* wa kanarazu shusseki shimasu.)

¶ I can't attend this **time,** but I'll be there without fail next **time.**

2〖尾〗

2 〚suf〛

¶「日本へ何回行きましたか。」(Nihon e nan*kai* ikimashita ka?)「一回も行ったことがありません。」(Ik*kai* mo itta koto ga arimasen.)

¶委員会は1か月に2回開かれます。(Iinkai wa ikkagetsu ni ni*kai* hirakaremasu.)

¶ "How many **times** have you been to Japan?"

"I've never been there even **once.**"

¶ The committee 〚commission, council〛 meets **twice** a month.

kaidan 階段〚名〛

階段を上る (*kaidan* o noboru) 階段を降りる (*kaidan* o oriru)

¶階段が急だから、気をつけてください。(*Kaidan* ga kyū da kara, ki o tsukete kudasai.)

kaidan 〚n〛 stairs, stairway, flight of stairs

go up **the stairs,** go upstairs // go down **the stairs,** go downstairs

¶ Please be careful as **the stairs** are very steep.

kaifuku 回復〚名, ～する〛

¶天候の回復を待って、出発しましょう。(Tenkō no *kaifuku* o matte, shuppatsu shimashō.)

¶上田さんは1か月休んで、ようやく健康を回復しました。(Ueda san wa ikkagetsu yasunde, yōyaku kenkō o *kaifuku* shimashita.)

¶一度失った信用を回復するのはたいへんです。(Ichido ushinatta shin'yō o *kaifuku* suru no wa taihen desu.)

kaifuku 〚n, ～*suru*〛 recovery

¶ Let's wait for the weather **to improve** before setting out.

¶ After staying at home a month, [Mr.] Ueda has finally **regained** [his] health.

¶ It is difficult **to restore** trust once it has been lost.

kaigai 海外〚名〛

¶来年、海外旅行をするつもりです。(Rainen, *kaigai*-ryokō o suru tsumori desu.)

¶新聞で国内のニュースはもちろん、海外のニュースもよく読んでいます。(Shinbun de kokunai no nyūsu wa mochiron, *kaigai* no nyūsu mo yoku yonde imasu.)

kaigai 〚n〛 overseas, abroad

¶ I plan to travel **abroad** next year.

¶ [I] often read the **international** news in the newspaper; of course [I] read the domestic news, too.

kaigan 海岸〚名〛

kaigan 〚n〛 seashore, coast, beach

¶今朝, 海岸を散歩しました。(Kesa, *kaigan* o sanpo shimashita.)

¶汽車は海岸に沿って走っています。(Kisha wa *kaigan* ni sotte hashitte imasu.)

kaigi 会議〖名〗

会議室 (*kaigi*shitsu) 会議場 (*kaigi*-jō) 国際会議 (kokusai*kaigi*) 会議を開く (*kaigi* o hiraku) 会議に出席する (*kaigi* ni shusseki suru) 会議に欠席する (*kaigi* ni kesseki suru)

¶今日, 2時から会議があります。(Kyō, niji kara *kaigi* ga arimasu.)

¶今, 社長は会議中です。(Ima, shachō wa *kaigi*chū desu.)

kaikei 会計〖名〗

①[お金の出し入れを計算・管理すること]

会計検査 (*kaikei*-kensa) 会計簿 (*kaikei*bo)

¶会計課の窓口へ行って, お金を払ってください。(*Kaikei*ka no madoguchi e itte, okane o haratte kudasai.)

②[レストランなどでの代金の勘定・支払い]

¶今日の会計はわたしがします。(Kyō no *kaikei* wa watashi ga shimasu.)

¶会計をお願いします。(*Kaikei* o onegai shimasu.)

→kanjō 勘定

kaiketsu 解決〖名, ～する〗

未解決の問題 (mi*kaiketsu* no mon-

kaigi 〖n〗 meeting, conference

a **conference** room, **assembly** room // a **conference** hall // an international **conference** 〖congress〗 // hold a **conference** 〖meeting〗 // attend **a meeting** 〖conference〗 // be absent from **a meeting** 〖conference〗

¶ There is **a meeting** 〖conference〗 today at two o'clock.

¶ The president (of the company) is now **in conference**.

kaikei 〖n〗 accounts; bill

① [accounts]

an audit, auditing // an **account** book

¶ Please proceed to the **accounts** window 〖cashier〗 and pay.

② [bill (at a restaurant, etc.)]

¶ I'll **pay** today.

¶ **The bill,** please.

kaiketsu 〖n, ～*suru*〗 solution, settlement

an un**solved** problem, a pending

dai)

¶わたしたちは問題の解決に努力しています。 (Watashitachi wa mondai no *kaiketsu* ni doryoku shite imasu.)

¶この問題の解決がつくまでには時間がかかりそうです。 (Kono mondai no *kaiketsu* ga tsuku made ni wa jikan ga kakarisō desu.)

¶あの事件はまだ解決していません。 (Ano jiken wa mada *kaiketsu* shite imasen.)

question

¶ We are working **to solve** the problem.

¶ It looks like it will be some time before this matter **is settled.**

¶ That case **hasn't been solved** yet.

kaikyō 回教〖名〗

回教国 (*kaikyō*koku)   回教徒 (*kaikyō*to)

kaikyō 〚n〛 Mohammedanism, Islam

a **Moslem** land // a **Moslem**

kaimono 買い物〖名〗

¶わたしは毎週日曜日に買い物をします。 (Watashi wa maishū nichiyōbi ni *kaimono* o shimasu.)

¶母はデパートへ買い物に行きました。 (Haha wa depāto e *kaimono* ni ikimashita.)

¶買い物をしてから，映画を見ました。 (*Kaimono* o shite kara, eiga o mimashita.)

kaimono 〚n〛 shopping, a purchase

¶ I go **shopping** every week on Sunday.

¶ My mother has gone to a department store **to shop.**

¶ After **shopping,** [I] went to a movie.

kaisha 会社〖名〗

会社員 (*kaisha*in)   株式会社 (kabushiki-*gaisha*)

¶大学を卒業して，貿易会社に入りました。 (Daigaku o sotsugyō shite, bōeki-*gaisha* ni hairimashita.)

¶わたしの弟は建築会社に勤めています。 (Watashi no otōto wa kenchiku-*gaisha* ni tsutomete imasu.)

¶先月，上田さんは会社を辞めました。

kaisha 〚n〛 company, business firm

a **company** employee, an **office** worker // a joint-stock **company,** a corporation

¶ [I] graduated from college and went to work for a trading **company.**

¶ My younger brother works for a construction **firm.**

¶ [Mrs.] Ueda quit [her] **job** last

(Sengetsu, Ueda san wa *kaisha* o yamemashita.)

month.

kaiwa 会話〖名, 〜する〗
英会話 (eikaiwa)
¶学校では,文法だけでなく会話も習っています。 (Gakkō de wa, bunpō dake de naku *kaiwa* mo naratte imasu.)
¶わたしは日本人と初めて日本語で会話してみました。 (Watashi wa Nihonjin to hajimete Nihongo de *kaiwa* shite mimashita.)

kaiwa 〖n, 〜*suru*〗 conversation, talk

English **conversation, conversation** in English

¶ In school [we] are studying not only grammar but **conversational skills** as well.

¶ I tried for the first time **to converse** with a Japanese in Japanese.

kaji 火事〖名〗
火事になる (*kaji* ni naru) 火事が起きる (*kaji* ga okiru) 火事を消す (*kaji* o kesu)
¶昨日の火事はたばこの火が原因だそうです。 (Kinō no *kaji* wa tabako no hi ga gen'in da sō desu.)
¶上田さんの家は火事で焼けました。 (Ueda san no ie wa *kaji* de yakemashita.)

kaji 〖n〗 fire

a fire takes place // **a fire** takes place // put out **a fire**

¶ I hear the cause of **the fire** yesterday was a cigarette butt.

¶ [Mrs.] Ueda's house **burned down.**

kakaeru 抱える〖動Ⅱ〗
①[腕で支えてわきの下・胸の前などで物を持つ]
¶上田さんは研究室からたくさんの本を抱えて出てきました。 (Ueda san wa kenkyūshitsu kara takusan no hon o *kakaete* dete kimashita.)
②[負担になるものを持っている]
¶田中さんは5人の子供を抱えて,苦しい生活をしています。 (Tanaka san wa gonin no kodomo o *kakaete*, kurushii seikatsu o shite imasu.)

kakaeru 〖v Ⅱ〗 carry; bear a burden

① [carry in or under one's arms]
¶ [Miss] Ueda came out of the professor's office **carrying** many books.

② [bear a burden]
¶ [Mr.] Tanaka has a hard time making ends meet with five children **to feed.**

¶山田さんはたくさんの仕事を抱えて忙しそうです。 (Yamada san wa takusan no shigoto o *kakaete* isogashisō desu.)

kakaku 価格〖名〗

¶米の価格が 20 パーセント上がりました。 (Kome no *kakaku* ga nijippāsento agarimashita.)

¶上田さんは家を 500 万円の価格で売りました。 (Ueda san wa ie o gohyakuman'en no *kakaku* de urimashita.)

(-)kakari (-)係〖名, 尾〗

1〖名〗

係長 (*kakari*chō) 係員 (*kakari*in)

¶係の者がいないので, よくわかりません。 (*Kakari* no mono ga inai node, yoku wakarimasen.)

2〖尾〗

案内係 (annai*gakari*)

kakaru 掛かる〖動Ⅰ〗

①〖壁などに下がる〗

¶壁にきれいな絵が掛かっています。 (Kabe ni kirei na e ga *kakatte* imasu.)

¶この部屋の窓にはカーテンが掛かっていません。 (Kono heya no mado ni wa kāten ga *kakatte* imasen.)

②〖かぎがしてある〗

¶この部屋にはかぎが掛かっていて入れません。 (Kono heya ni wa kagi ga *kakatte* ite hairemasen.)

③〖時間・費用などが必要である〗

¶学校まで何分ぐらいかかりますか。

¶ [Miss] Yamada seems very busy with the many jobs [she] **has to do.**

kakaku 〖n〗 **price, value, cost**

¶ **The price** of rice rose 20 percent.

¶ [Mr.] Ueda sold [his] house **for** 5 million yen.

(-)kakari 〖n, suf〗 **charge, duty, subsection, person in charge**

1 〖n〗

an **assistant section** chief, chief **clerk** // the clerk **in charge,** an attendant

¶ The person **in charge** of that isn't here right now, and I'm not familiar with that 〚and I'm afraid I can't help you〛.

2 〖suf〗

a **clerk** at an information desk, desk **clerk,** usher

kakaru 〖v Ⅰ〗 **hang, be suspended; require, take; be placed on something; be covered; catch, work**

① [hang, be suspended]

¶ There is a pretty picture **hanging** on the wall.

¶ The windows in this room **have not been hung** with curtains.

② [be locked]

¶ This room **is locked** so [we] can't enter.

③ [require (time, money, etc.)]

¶ How many minutes **does it take** to

(Gakkō made nanpun gurai *kakarimasu* ka?)

¶交通費は一か月いくらぐらい**かかり**ますか。 (Kōtsūhi wa ikkagetsu ikura gurai *kakarimasu* ka?)

④［電話が通じる］

¶さっき山田さんから電話が**かかって**きましたよ。 (Sakki Yamada san kara denwa ga *kakatte* kimashita yo.)

⑤［会う］

¶いつかまたお目に**かかり**たいと思います。(Itsu ka mata ome ni *kakaritai* to omoimasu.)

* いつも「お目にかかる（ome ni kakaru）」の形で使う。

⑥［医者に診てもらう］

¶わたしは丈夫なので，今まで医者に**かかった**ことがありません。 (Watashi wa jōbu na node, ima made isha ni *kakatta* koto ga arimasen.)

⑦［水などがふりかかる］

¶自動車がすぐそばを通ったので，ズボンにどろ水が**かかって**汚れました。(Jidōsha ga sugu soba o tootta node, zubon ni doromizu ga *kakatte* yogoremashita.)

⑧［税金が加わる］

¶この品物には税金が**かかって**いません。(Kono shinamono ni wa zeikin ga *kakatte* imasen.)

⑨［心配になる］

¶試験の結果が気に**かかって**，何も食べられません。 (Shiken no kekka ga

go to school from here 〖**take you** to go to school〗?

¶ How much **is** carfare a month?

④ [be telephoned]

¶ **There was** a call from [Miss] Yamada earlier.

⑤ [meet]

¶ **I hope we can meet** again sometime.

* Always used in the pattern "*ome ni kakaru*."

⑥ [consult a doctor]

¶ I'm robust so that I've never **been to see** a doctor.

⑦ [be splashed by water, etc.]

¶ The car went by right next to me so that my trousers **were splattered** with dirty water.

⑧ [be taxed]

¶ This merchandise is tax-**free.**

⑨ [worry, be anxious]

¶ [I]'m **so nervous** about the results of the test that [I] can't eat.

ki ni *kakatte*, nani mo taberaremasen.)

* いつも「気にかかる (ki ni kakaru)」の形で使う。

⑩[こんろなどの上に置かれたりしている]

¶ガスこんろになべが**かかって**います。(Gasu-konro ni nabe ga *kakatte* imasu.)

⑪[霧などが立ちこめる]

¶霧が**かかって**，周りの景色がよく見えません。(Kiri ga *kakatte*, mawari no keshiki ga yoku miemasen.)

⑫[悪いこと・好ましくないことなどが人に及ぶ]

手数が**かかる** (tesū ga *kakaru*)

¶先生に御迷惑が**かかって**は申し訳ありません。(Sensei ni gomeiwaku ga *kakatte* wa mōshiwake arimasen.)

⑬[機械が働き始める]

ブレーキが**かかる** (burēki ga *kakaru*)

¶寒いので，自動車のエンジンがなかなか**かかりません**。(Samui node, jidōsha no enjin ga nakanaka *kakarimasen.*)

¶目覚まし時計が**かかって**いなかったので，起きられませんでした。(Mezamashidokei ga *kakatte* inakatta node, okiraremasen deshita.)

kakaru 架かる〖動Ⅰ〗

¶この川には木の橋が**架かって**います。(Kono kawa ni wa ki no hashi ga *kakatte* imasu.)

kakeru 欠ける〖動Ⅱ〗

* Always used in the pattern "*ki ni kakaru.*"

⑩ [be placed on top of a burner, etc.]

¶ There **is** a pot on the gas burner.

⑪ [covered with fog, etc.]

¶ The surrounding area can't be seen very well as it **is enveloped** in fog 〚mist〛.

⑫ [have something bad befall one]

(a task) **is** bothersome

¶ I'm sorry **to trouble** you, sir 〚ma'am〛 (said to one's teacher or professor).

⑬ [catch, work]

brakes **work**

¶ As it's cold, the engine **doesn't start** right away.

¶ [I] overslept as the alarm clock **wasn't set.**

kakaru 〖v I〗 be built across, be constructed over

¶ There **is** a wooden bridge across this river.

kakeru 〖v II〗 be broken off; lack

①[物の一部分が壊れる]

¶このさらは少し欠けています。
(Kono sara wa sukoshi *kakete* imasu.)

① [be broken off, chipped]

¶ This dish **is** a little **chipped.**

¶硬い物を切ったので，ナイフの刃が欠けてしまいました。(Katai mono o kitta node, naifu no ha ga *kakete* shimaimashita.)

¶ As I cut something hard, the blade of the knife **got nicked.**

②[不足する]

¶あの人は常識に欠けていますね。
(Ano hito wa jōshiki ni *kakete* imasu ne.)

② [lack, be short, be missing]

¶ [He] **is lacking** in common sense.

¶今日の会議はメンバーが二人欠けていますね。(Kyō no kaigi wa menbā ga futari *kakete* imasu ne.)

¶ Today's meeting **is missing** two members.

kakeru 掛ける〖動Ⅱ〗

①[いすなどに腰を下ろす]

ベンチに腰を掛ける (benchi ni koshi o *kakeru*)

kakeru 〖v Ⅱ〗 sit down; hang up; put on; multiply; spend; place on; turn on; sprinkle on; extending over

① [sit down]

sit down on a bench

¶どうぞ，このいすにお掛けください。
(Dōzo, kono isu ni o*kake* kudasai.)

¶ Please **sit down** here in this chair.

②[壁などに下げる]

¶壁にきれいな絵が掛けてあります。
(Kabe ni kirei na e ga *kakete* arimasu.)

② [hang up, suspend]

¶ A pretty picture **has been hung** on the wall.

③[かぎをする]

¶わたしはいつも ドアにかぎを掛けておきます。(Watashi wa itsu mo doa ni kagi o *kakete* okimasu.)

③ [lock]

¶ I always **lock** my door.

④[物の上にかぶせる]

¶寒いから布団をたくさん掛けて寝ました。(Samui kara futon o takusan *kakete* nemashita.)

④ [put on, cover with]

¶ As it was cold I slept with many covers **on.**

⑤[ある数を何倍かする]

⑤ [multiply]

¶2に3を掛けると6になります。

(Ni ni san o *kakeru* to roku ni narimasu.)

¶ Two **times** three (literally, three **times** two) is six.

⑥［費用・時間などを費やす］

時間をかける (jikan o *kakeru*) お金をかける (okane o *kakeru*)

⑥ [spend time, money, etc.]

spend time (on something) // **spend** money (on something)

⑦［電話をする］

¶友達に電話をかけました。 (Tomodachi ni denwa o *kakemashita*.)

⑦ [make a telephone call]

¶ [I] **telephoned** a friend.

⑧［眼鏡をつける］

¶あの眼鏡をかけた女の人はだれですか。 (Ano megane o *kaketa* onna no hito wa dare desu ka?)

⑧ [wear glasses]

¶ Who is that woman **wearing** glasses?

⑨［こんろなどの上にのせる］

¶ガスこんろになべがかけてあります。 (Gasu-konro ni nabe ga *kakete* arimasu.)

⑨ [place on a burner, etc.]

¶ A pot **has been placed** on ⟦**is on**⟧ the gas burner.

⑩［機械などを働かせる］

ブレーキをかける (burēki o *kakeru*)

レコードをかける (rekōdo o *kakeru*)

¶ラジオをかけてもいいですか。

(Rajio o *kakete* mo ii desu ka?)

⑩ [turn on, start]

put on the brakes // **play** a record

¶ Is it all right if **I turn on** the radio?

⑪［目方を量る］

はかりにかける (hakari ni *kakeru*)

⑪ [weigh]

weigh on a scale

⑫［ふりかける］

¶味が薄いですから，塩をかけて食べてください。(Aji ga usui desu kara, shio o *kakete* tabete kudasai.)

⑫ [sprinkle, pour on, dash]

¶ It's lightly seasoned ⟦It may be on the bland side⟧ so please **add** salt if you like.

⑬［心配させる］

¶両親に心配をかけないようにしなさい。 (Ryōshin ni shinpai o *kakenai* yō ni shinasai.)

⑬ [cause worry]

¶ Don't do anything **to worry** your parents (literally, Act so as **not to worry** your parents).

⑭［ある時・場所からある時・場所に及ぶ］

⑭ [extending over, from ～ to ～]

¶わたしは先週の土曜日から日曜日にかけて旅行しました。(Watashi wa senshū no doyōbi kara nichiyōbi ni *kakete* ryokō shimashita.)

¶わたしは奈良から京都にかけて，お寺を見て歩きました。(Watashi wa Nara kara Kyōto ni *kakete*, otera o mite arukimashita.)

* いつも「～から～にかけて (～kara ～ni kakete)」の形で使う。

kakeru 架ける〖動Ⅱ〗

¶この川には木の橋が架けてあります。(Kono kawa ni wa ki no hashi ga *kakete* arimasu.)

kakeru 駆ける〖動Ⅱ〗

¶遅刻しそうなので，学校まで駆けていきました。(Chikoku shisō na node, gakkō made *kakete* ikimashita.)

⇨hashiru 走る

kakitome 書留〖名〗

書留郵便 (*kakitome*-yūbin) 現金書留 (genkin-*kakitome*)

¶この手紙を書留で出してください。(Kono tegami o *kakitome* de dashite kudasai.)

¶この手紙を書留にしてください。(Kono tegami o *kakitome* ni shite kudasai.)

kakkō かっこう〖名〗

¶この自動車はスマートで，かっこうがいいですね。(Kono jidōsha wa sumāto de, *kakkō* ga ii desu ne.)

kako 過去〖名〗

¶ I took a trip on Saturday **and** Sunday last week.

¶ I visited temples from Nara **to** Kyoto.

* Always used in the pattern "～ *kara* ～ *ni kakete*."

kakeru 〖v II〗 build, construct

¶ A wooden bridge **has been built** over this river.

kakeru 〖v II〗 run

¶ [I] **ran** to school as it looked like [I] would be late.

kakitome 〖n〗 registered (mail)

registered mail // sending cash by **registered mail**

¶ Please have this letter sent by **registered mail.**

¶ I'd like to send this letter by **registered mail.**

kakkō 〖n〗 appearance, shape

¶ This car is smart and stylish **looking.**

kako 〖n〗 the past

¶彼はできるだけ**過去**のことを思い出さないようにしています。(Kare wa dekiru dake *kako* no koto o omoidasanai yō ni shite imasu.)

¶わたしは**過去**3年間、外国で生活をしていました。(Watashi wa *kako* sannenkan, gaikoku de seikatsu o shite imashita.)

¶次の動詞の**過去**形は何ですか。(Tsugi no dōshi no *kako*kei wa nan desu ka?)

⇨genzai 現在　mirai 未来

kakomu　囲む〖動Ⅰ〗

¶先生を**囲んで**、一晩楽しく話しました。(Sensei o *kakonde*, hitoban tanoshiku hanashimashita.)

¶日本は海に**囲まれた**国です。(Nihon wa umi ni *kakomareta* kuni desu.)

¶次の言葉のうち正しいものを○で**囲みなさい**。(Tsugi no kotoba no uchi tadashii mono o maru de *kakominasai*.)

kaku-　各-〖頭〗

各国 (*kak*koku)　各人 (*kaku*jin)

¶わたしはこの夏日本の**各**地を旅行しました。(Watashi wa kono natsu Nihon no *kaku*chi o ryokō shimashita.)

¶**各**クラス2名の委員を選びました。(*Kaku*kurasu nimei no iin o erabimashita.)

kaku　書く〖動Ⅰ〗

¶わたしは友達に手紙を**書きました**。(Watashi wa tomodachi ni tegami

¶ He makes it a practice to forget **the past** as much as possible.

¶ **In the past** I lived abroad for three years.

¶ What is the **past** tense of the next verb?

kakomu 〖vⅠ〗 enclose, surround, ring, encircle

¶ **Sitting around** our teacher, we passed a pleasant evening in conversation.

¶ Japan is a country **surrounded** by the sea.

¶ **Circle** the correct choice(s) among the following words.

kaku- 〖pref〗 each, every

each country, **various** countries, **all** countries // **each** person, **every**body

¶ This summer I traveled in **various** districts throughout Japan.

¶ **Each** class chose two representatives.

kaku 〖vⅠ〗 write, compose

¶ I **wrote** a letter to a friend.

o *kakimashita.*)

¶ここに名前を書いてください。

(Koko ni namae o *kaite* kudasai.)

¶この万年筆はとても書きやすいです。

(Kono mannenhitsu wa totemo *kakiyasui* desu.)

kaku かく〖動Ⅰ〗

地図をかく (chizu o *kaku*)

¶子供たちが花の絵をかいています。

(Kodomotachi ga hana no e o *kaite* imasu.)

kaku かく〖動Ⅰ〗

①〔ひっかく〕

¶背中がかゆいからかいてください。

(Senaka ga kayui kara *kaite* kudasai.)

¶あの人は頭をかく癖があります。

(Ano hito wa atama o *kaku* kuse ga arimasu.)

②〔汗を出す〕

¶急いで来たので，汗をかきました。

(Isoide kita node, ase o *kaki-mashita.*)

kakudo 角度〖名〗

①〔角の度数〕

角度を測る (*kakudo* o hakaru)

¶正三角形のそれぞれの角度は 60 度です。 (Seisankakkei no sorezore no *kakudo* wa rokujūdo desu.)

②〔ものごとを見たり考えたりする立場〕

¶その問題をいろいろな角度から考えてみました。(Sono mondai o iroiro na *kakudo* kara kangaete mima-

¶ Please **write** your name here.

¶ This fountain pen **is** very **easy to write with.**

kaku 〚v I〛 draw, paint

draw a map

¶ The children **are drawing** 〚**painting**〛 pictures of flowers.

kaku 〚v I〛 scratch; sweat

① [scratch]

¶ My back itches; please **scratch it** for me.

¶ [He] has a habit of **scratching** [his] head.

② [sweat, perspire]

¶ **I am sweaty** as I hurried here.

kakudo 〚n〛 angle; viewpoint

① [angle, degrees of an angle]

compute **an angle**

¶ Each **angle** of an equilateral triangle is 60 degrees.

② [viewpoint, angle]

¶ I considered that problem from various **angles.**

shita.)

kakureru 隠れる〔動Ⅱ〕

①[物にさえぎられて直接見えなくなる]

¶太陽が雲に**隠れて**しまいました。
(Taiyō ga kumo ni *kakurete* shimaimashita.)

¶船が島の陰に**隠れて**見えなくなりました。 (Fune ga shima no kage ni *kakurete* mienaku narimashita.)

②[人目につかないように身を隠しておく]

隠れ家 (*kakure*ga)

¶危険が過ぎるまで, **隠れて**いるほうがいいですよ。 (Kiken ga sugiru made, *kakurete* iru hō ga ii desu yo.)

kakusu 隠す〔動Ⅰ〕

①[人の目につかないようにする]

¶どろぼうは盗んだ財布を木の下に**隠しました**。 (Dorobō wa nusunda saifu o ki no shita ni *kakushimashita*.)

¶**隠して**おいた手紙を母に読まれてしまいました。 (*Kakushite* oita tegami o haha ni yomarete shimaimashita.)

②[人に知られないようにする, 秘密にする]

欠点を**隠す** (ketten o *kakusu*)

¶山田さんはそのことを**隠さないで**みんな話してくれました。 (Yamada san wa sono koto o *kakusanaide* minna hanashite kuremashita.)

¶彼は真実をわたしたちに**隠そう**とし

kakureru [[v II]] **be lost to sight; hide**

① [be lost to sight, disappear from view]

¶ The sun **is** [**was**] **hidden** behind some clouds.

¶ The ship **has become** [**became**] **lost to sight** behind the island.

② [hide, conceal onself]

a **hide**out, a **hide**away, a retreat

¶ You had better **hide** until the danger is past.

kakusu [[v I]] **hide, conceal**

① [hide, conceal, keep from sight]

¶ The thief **hid** the stolen wallet beneath a tree.

¶ My mother read the letter **I had hidden**.

② [hide, conceal, keep secret]

hide weak points

¶ [Miss] Yamada **didn't hide** that but told [us] everything about it.

¶ He **tried to keep** the truth from us.

ました。 (Kare wa shinjitsu o watashitachi ni *kakusō* to shimashita.)

(〜te mo) kamawanai （〜ても）かまわない〚連〛

①[許可の意味を表す]

¶「ボールペンで書いてもかまいませんか。」(Bōrupen de kaite mo *kamaimasen* ka?)「ええどうぞ。」(Ee, dōzo.)

¶「ここでたばこを吸ってもかまいませんか。」(Koko de tabako o sutte mo *kamaimasen* ka?)「いいえ、吸ってはいけません。」(Iie, sutte wa ikemasen.)

②[不必要の意味を表す]

¶お金は今すぐ払わなくてもかまいません。(Okane wa ima sugu harawanakute mo *kamaimasen*.)

¶「あした、買い物に行かなくてもかまいませんか。」(Ashita, kaimono ni ikanakute mo *kamaimasen* ka?)「いいえ、行かなくてはいけません。」(Iie, ikanakute wa ikemasen.)

*「〜なくてもかまわない（〜nakute mo kamawanai）」の形で使う。

⇔（〜te wa) ikenai （〜ては）いけない

⇨（〜te mo) ii （〜ても）いい

kamera カメラ〚名〛

¶これは日本製のカメラです。 (Kore wa Nihonsei no *kamera* desu.)

kami 神〚名〛

¶あなたは神を信じますか。 (Anata

(-te mo) kamawanai 〚compd〛 **don't mind, don't care, it's all right**

① [indicates permission]

¶ "**Is it all right** to write it with a ball-point pen?"

 "Yes, that will be fine."

¶ "**Is it all right** to smoke here?"

 "No, it's not."

② [indicates something is unnecessary]

¶ **It's all right** if you don't pay right away.

¶ "**Is it all right** if [I] don't go shopping tomorrow?"

 "No, [you] must go."

* Used in the pattern "*-nakute mo kamawanai.*"

kamera 〚n〛 **camera**

¶ This **camera** was made in Japan.

kami 〚n〛 **God, a god, a deity**

¶ Do you believe in **God**?

wa *kami* o shinjimasu ka?)

¶あなたの無事を神に祈っています。

(Anata no buji o *kami* ni inotte
imasu.)

＊「神様 (kamisama)」とも言う。

¶ [I] will pray for your safety.

＊ Variant: *kamisama*.

kami　紙〖名〗

紙くず (*kamikuzu*)　紙包み (*kami-zutsumi*)　紙袋 (*kamibukuro*)　紙
芝居 (*kamishibai*)

¶その紙を1枚ください。(Sono *kami*
o ichimai kudasai.)

kami 〚n〛 paper

waste**paper, paper** scraps // a
paper-wrapped parcel // a **paper** bag
// a **picture-card** show

¶ Please give me a sheet of that
paper.

kami　髪〖名〗

髪をとかす (*kami* o tokasu)　髪を
分ける (*kami* o wakeru)　髪を刈る
(*kami* o karu)　髪を伸ばす (*kami*
o nobasu)　髪を洗う (*kami* o arau)

¶髪が伸びたので, 床屋へ行きました。
(*Kami* ga nobita node, tokoya e
ikimashita.)

¶髪の毛をもう少し短くしてください。
(*Kami*noke o mō sukoshi mijikaku
shite kudasai.)

kami 〚n〛 hair

comb **one's hair** // part **one's hair**
// cut **someone's hair**, have **one's
hair** cut // let **one's hair** grow //
wash **one's hair**

¶ [I] went to the barber as **[my] hair**
had grown out.

¶ Please cut **it** a little shorter (said to
someone cutting one's hair).

kaminari　雷〖名〗

¶雷が鳴って, 強い雨が降ってきまし
た。　(*Kaminari* ga natte, tsuyoi
ame ga futte kimashita.)

¶どこかに雷が落ちたらしいです。
(Doko ka ni *kaminari* ga ochita
rashii desu.)

kaminari 〚n〛 thunder, thunder-bolt

¶ It **thundered** and started ⟦has
started⟧ raining heavily.

¶ It seems that **lightning** struck
somewhere.

kamisama ☞ kami

kamisori　かみそり〖名〗

安全かみそり (*anzen-kamisori*)

¶毎朝, 電気かみそりでひげをそりま
す。　(Maiasa, denki-*kamisori* de
hige o sorimasu.)

kamisori 〚n〛 razor

a safety **razor**

¶ [I] shave every morning with an
electric **shaver**.

¶このかみそりはあまりよく切れませんね。(Kono *kamisori* wa amari yoku kiremasen ne.)

¶ This **razor** doesn't shave very well.

kamoku 科目〖名〗

選択科目 (sentaku-*kamoku*) 必修科目 (hisshū-*kamoku*)

¶大学の入学試験には, どんな科目がありますか。(Daigaku no nyūgaku-shiken ni wa, donna *kamoku* ga arimasu ka?)

kamoku 〖n〗 subject, course, curriculum

an elective, an optional **course** // a required **course**

¶ What sort of **subjects** are covered in the university entrance examination?

ka mo shirenai かもしれない〖連〗

¶雨が降るかもしれないから, かさを持って行ったほうがいいですよ。

(Ame ga furu *ka mo shirenai* kara, kasa o motte itta hō ga ii desu yo.)

¶彼は時間に遅れるかもしれません。

(Kare wa jikan ni okureru *ka mo shiremasen*.)

¶彼の話は本当かもしれません。

(Kare no hanashi wa hontō *ka mo shiremasen*.)

ka mo shirenai 〖compd〗 maybe, perhaps

¶ You'd better take an umbrella as it **may** rain.

¶ He **might** be late.

¶ His story **might** be true.

kamu かむ〖動I〗

¶御飯をよくかんで食べなさい。

(Gohan o yoku *kande* tabenasai.)

¶わたしは犬にかまれて, けがをしました。(Watashi wa inu ni *kamarete*, kega o shimashita.)

kamu 〖v I〗 bite, chew

¶ **Chew** your food 〚rice〛 well.

¶ I was injured when a dog **bit** me.

-kan -間〖尾〗

①[ある一定の長さ]

1時間 (ichi*kan*) 1週間 (isshū-*kan*) 短期間 (tanki*kan*)

¶疲れましたから, 10分間休憩しませんか。(Tsukaremashita kara, ji-

-kan 〖suf〗 interval, period; between

① [interval, period]

one hour // one week // a short **period** of time

¶ [I]'m tired. Let's take a **10-minute**

ppun*kan* kyūkei shimasen ka?)

¶わたしは高校の3年間, 1日も休みませんでした。(Watashi wa kōkō no sannen*kan*, ichinichi mo yasumimasen deshita.)

② [ある地点からある地点までの隔たり]

¶東京・大阪間の距離は550キロメートルです。(Tōkyō-Oosaka*kan* no kyori wa gohyaku-gojikkiromētoru desu.)

③ [間がら, 関係]

¶夫婦間の問題はほかの人にはわかりにくいです。(Fūfu*kan* no mondai wa hoka no hito ni wa wakarinikui desu.)

¶A, Bの両国間には今貿易上の問題がいろいろあります。(Ē, Bii no ryōkoku*kan* ni wa ima bōekijō no mondai ga iroiro arimasu.)

kana 仮名〖名〗

平仮名 (hira*gana*) 片仮名 (kata*kana*) 振り仮名 (furi*gana*) 仮名遣い (*kana*zukai)

¶外国人の名前は片仮名で書きます。(Gaikokujin no namae wa kata*kana* de kakimasu.)

¶次の漢字に仮名をつけなさい。(Tsugi no kanji ni *kana* o tsukenasai.)

⇒**hiragana** 平仮名 **katakana** 片仮名

kanai 家内〖名〗

¶これは家内が作った料理です。

break.

¶ I wasn't absent even a single day in the **three years** of high school.

② [between two points, from ~ to ~]

¶ The distance **between** Tokyo and Osaka is 550 kilometers.

③ [between, among]

¶ Problems **between** husbands and wives are difficult for outsiders to understand.

¶ There are presently various trade problems **between** countries A and B.

kana 〚n〛 the Japanese syllabary alphabets

hiragana // kata**kana** // *furigana* (**kana** printed to the side of *kanji* giving the reading) // **kana** orthography, rules for the use of **kana**

¶ The names of foreigners are written in *kata***kana.**

¶ Write down the pronunciation of the following *kanji* in **kana.**

kanai 〚n〛 **one's wife**

¶ This dish was cooked by **my wife.**

(Kore wa *kanai* ga tsukutta ryōri desu.)

¶これがわたしの家内です。どうぞ，よろしく。(Kore ga watashi no *kanai* desu. Dōzo, yoroshiku.)

＊他人に自分の妻のことを話す場合に使う。

⇨tsuma 妻　okusan 奥さん

kanarazu　必ず〖副〗

¶あしたの朝6時に必ず来てください。(Ashita no asa rokuji ni *kanarazu* kite kudasai.)

¶約束は必ず守ります。(Yakusoku wa *kanarazu* mamorimasu.)

kanari　かなり〖副，形動，〜の〗

¶上田さんの病気はかなり重いようです。(Ueda san no byōki wa *kanari* omoi yō desu.)

¶わたしは日本語を読むことはかなりできますが，話すことはまだ下手です。(Watashi wa Nihongo o yomu koto wa *kanari* dekimasu ga, hanasu koto wa mada heta desu.)

¶田中さんはかなりの収入があります。(Tanaka san wa *kanari* no shūnyū ga arimasu.)

kanashii　悲しい〖形〗

¶去年死んだ母のことを思うと悲しくなります。(Kyonen shinda haha no koto o omou to *kanashiku* narimasu.)

¶あの少女は悲しそうな顔をしていますね。(Ano shōjo wa *kanashisō* na kao o shite imasu ne.)

¶ This is **my wife.** I'd like you to meet her.

＊ *Kanai* is used when talking about one's own wife with others.

kanarazu 〚adv〛　**certainly, without fail**

¶ Please **be sure** to come tomorrow morning at six o'clock.

¶ [I] **never fail** to keep [my] promises.

kanari 〚adv, adj-v, ~*no*〛　**fairly, quite, considerably**

¶ [Mr.] Ueda's illness seems to be **quite** serious.

¶ I can read Japanese **fairly** well, but I'm still poor at speaking.

¶ [Mr.] Tanaka has a **handsome** income.

kanashii 〚adj〛　**sad, unhappy, sorrowful, mournful**

¶ I become **sad** when I think about my mother who died last year.

¶ That young girl looks **sad,** doesn't she?

⇔ureshii うれしい

kanban 看板〖名〗
酒屋の看板 (sakaya no *kanban*)

¶映画館の看板はほかの看板と比べて大きいです。 (Eigakan no *kanban* wa hoka no *kanban* to kurabete ookii desu.)

kanban 〚n〛 **signboard, sign**
a liquor shop **sign**

¶ **The signboards** for movie theaters are large compared to other **signboards.**

kane 金〖名〗
金を払う (*kane* o harau) 金がない (*kane* ga nai) 金をなくす (*kane* o nakusu)

¶今度の旅行には，ずいぶんお金がかりました。 (Kondo no ryokō ni wa zuibun o*kane* ga kakarimashita.)

¶お金を千円貸してください。(O*kane* o sen'en kashite kudasai.)

kane 〚n〛 **money**
to pay **money** // have no **money**, have little **money** // lose **some money**

¶ The last trip was very **expensive.**

¶ Please loan me a thousand yen.

kane 鐘〖名〗
鐘を鳴らす (*kane* o narasu)

¶お寺の鐘が鳴りました。 (Otera no *kane* ga narimashita.)

¶教会の鐘の音が聞こえてきました。 (Kyōkai no *kane* no ne ga kikoete kimashita.)

kane 〚n〛 **bell, gong**
ring **a bell**

¶ The temple **bell** sounded.

¶ One can 〚could〛 hear the sound of church **bells.**

kanemochi 金持ち〖名〗
¶彼は一生懸命に働いて金持ちになりました。 (Kare wa isshōkenmei ni hataraite *kanemochi* ni narimashita.)

¶上田さんは金持ちの家に生まれました。(Ueda san wa *kanemochi* no ie ni umaremashita.)

kanemochi 〚n〛 **a rich person**
¶ He worked very hard and **made his fortune.**

¶ [Miss] Ueda was born into a **wealthy** family.

kangae 考え〖名〗
¶わたしにいい考えがあります。 (Watashi ni ii *kangae* ga arimasu.)

kangae 〚n〛 **thought, thinking, idea, opinion, way of thinking**
¶ I have a good **idea.**

¶あの人の考えには賛成できません。
(Ano hito no *kangae* ni wa sansei dekimasen.)

kangaeru 考える〖動Ⅱ〗
¶あなたは今，何を考えているのですか。(Anata wa ima, nani o *kangaete* iru no desu ka?)
¶この計画についてどう考えますか。
(Kono keikaku ni tsuite dō *kangaemasu* ka?)
¶よく考えてから返事をします。
(Yoku *kangaete* kara henji o shimasu.)

kangei 歓迎〖名，～する〗
¶あなたを心から歓迎します。(Anata o kokoro kara *kangei* shimasu.)
¶山田さんのために歓迎会を開きました。(Yamada san no tame ni *kangei*kai o hirakimashita.)

kangofu 看護婦〖名〗
¶わたしの姉は看護婦をしています。
(Watashi no ane wa *kangofu* o shite imasu.)
¶看護婦さん，頭が痛いんですが…。
(*Kangofu* san, atama ga itai n desu ga...)

kani かに〖名〗
kanji 漢字〖名〗
当用漢字 (tōyō*kanji*)
¶あした，漢字の試験があります。
(Ashita, *kanji* no shiken ga arimasu.)
¶日本人の名前はほとんど漢字で書かれています。(Nihonjin no namae

¶ I can't agree with [his] **way of thinking.**

kangaeru 〚v II〛 **think, consider**
¶ What are you **thinking about?**

¶ What **do you think** of this project?

¶ I'd like **to think** about it before giving you my answer.

kangei 〚n, ~*suru*〛 **welcome**
¶ **I welcome** you from the bottom of my heart.
¶ [We] held a **welcoming** party 〚reception〛 for [Mrs.] Yamada.

kangofu 〚n〛 **nurse**
¶ My elder sister is **a nurse.**

¶ **Nurse,** my head aches.

kani 〚n〛 **crab**
kanji 〚n〛 **Chinese characters**
the *tōyō **kanji*** (the Chinese characters designated for daily use)
¶ There's a ***kanji*** test tomorrow.

¶ Almost all Japanese personal names are written in ***kanji.***

wa hotondo *kanji* de kakarete imasu.)

kanji 感じ〖名〗

①[感覚]

¶氷を長い間持っていると，冷たくて指の感じがなくなってきます。(Koori o nagai aida motte iru to, tsumetakute yubi no *kanji* ga nakunatte kimasu.)

②[ものごとから受ける感情・印象]

¶あの人はとても感じのいい人です。(Ano hito wa totemo *kanji* no ii hito desu.)

¶この絵は明るい感じの絵ですね。(Kono e wa akarui *kanji* no e desu ne.)

kanjiru 感じる〖動Ⅱ〗

①[感覚を生じる]

¶手術をしましたが，あまり痛みは感じませんでした。(Shujutsu o shimashita ga, amari itami wa *kanjimasen* deshita.)

②[ものごとに対してある気持ちを抱く]

¶外国語の必要を感じて，勉強を始めました。(Gaikokugo no hitsuyō o *kanjite*, benkyō o hajimemashita.)

kanjō 感情〖名〗

¶あの人は，あまり感情を顔に表しません。(Ano hito wa, amari *kanjō* o kao ni arawashimasen.)

¶人間は感情の動物です。(Ningen wa *kanjō* no dōbutsu desu.)

kanjō 勘定〖名，～する〗

kanji 〚n〛 **feeling, sensation; impression, feeling**

① [feeling, sensation]

¶ When one holds ice for a long time, the cold makes one lose **the sensation** in one's fingers.

② [impression, feeling, effect]

¶ [He] is a very **nice** person.

¶ This is a **cheerful** picture 〚painting〛, isn't it?

kanjiru 〚v II〛 **feel, experience; feel, be struck by**

① [feel, experience]

¶ I had an operation but **I didn't feel** much pain.

② [feel, be struck by, be affected by]

¶ **I realized** the necessity of knowing foreign languages and started studying one.

kanjō 〚n〛 **feeling, emotion**

¶ [He] doesn't show [his] feelings very much in [his] face.

¶ Humans are **emotional** creatures.

kanjō 〚n, ～*suru*〛 **counting, calculation, computation; payment, settlement of accounts**

①〔計算〕

お金を勘定する　(okane o *kanjō* suru)

¶箱の中にりんごがいくつあるか勘定してください。　(Hako no naka ni ringo ga ikutsu aru ka *kanjō* shite kudasai.)

②〔支払い〕

¶お勘定をお願いします。　(Okanjō o onegai shimasu.)

¶今日の勘定はわたしが払います。　(Kyō no *kanjō* wa watashi ga haraimasu.)

¶勘定を済ませて, ホテルを出ました。　(*Kanjō* o sumasete, hoteru o demashita.)

→**kaikei** 会計

kankei 関係〘名, ～する〙

¶あなたと上田さんとは, どういう関係ですか。　(Anata to Ueda san to wa, dōiu *kankei* desu ka?)

¶A国とB国との関係が悪化しました。　(Ē-koku to Bii-koku to no *kankei* ga akka shimashita.)

¶わたしはその会には関係していません。　(Watashi wa sono kai ni wa *kankei* shite imasen.)

kankō 観光〘名〙

観光地 (*kankō*chi)　観光バス (*kankō*-basu)　観光客 (*kankō*kyaku)

観光旅行 (*kankō*-ryokō)

¶京都は観光都市として有名です。　(Kyōto wa *kankō*-toshi to shite yūmei desu.)

① [counting, calculation, computation]

count money

¶ Please **count** how many apples are in the box.

② [payment, settlement of accounts]

¶ **The bill,** please.

¶ I'll pay today (for dinner, etc.).

¶ [I] paid **the bill** and checked out of the hotel.

kankei 〚n, ~*suru*〛 relation, relationship

¶ What is your **connection** with [Mr.] Ueda?

¶ **Relations** worsened between countries A and B.

¶ I **have nothing to do** with that association 〚club, etc.〛.

kankō 〚n〛 sightseeing

a **resort** area, a **sightseeing** place // a **sightseeing** bus // **a tourist** // a **sightseeing** trip

¶ Kyoto is famous as a **tourist** city.

kankyō 環境〖名〗
社会環境 (shakai-*kankyō*)　家庭環境 (katei-*kankyō*)　環境衛生 (*kankyō*-eisei)
¶子供はよい環境で育てなければなりません。 (Kodomo wa yoi *kankyō* de sodatenakereba narimasen.)

kankyō 〚n〛 environment, surroundings
social **environment** // home **environment** // **environmental** hygiene 〚sanitation〛
¶ Children should be raised in a good home **environment**.

kanō 可能〖名, 形動〗
不可能 (fu*kanō*)
¶日本語がわからなくても, 日本の大学に入ることは可能でしょうか。
(Nihongo ga wakaranakute mo, Nihon no daigaku ni hairu koto wa *kanō* deshō ka?)
¶火星に生物が住んでいる可能性はほとんどないでしょう。 (Kasei ni seibutsu ga sunde iru *kanō*sei wa hotondo nai deshō.)

kanō 〚n, adj-v〛 possibility, possible
impossible, impossibility
¶ **Is it possible** to become a student at a Japanese university even if one doesn't know Japanese?

¶ There is little **chance** of life on Mars.

kanojo 彼女〖代〗
¶彼女はどこへ行きましたか。 (*Kanojo* wa doko e ikimashita ka?)
⇒kare 彼

kanojo 〚pron〛 she, her
¶ Where did **she** go?

kansatsu 観察〖名, ～する〗
¶わたしの子供は虫の観察に興味を持っています。 (Watashi no kodomo wa mushi no *kansatsu* ni kyōmi o motte imasu.)
¶植物の生長を観察しています。
(Shokubutsu no seichō o *kansatsu* shite imasu.)

kansatsu 〚n, ～*suru*〛 observation
¶ My children are interested in **observing** insects.

¶ [He] **is studying** the growth of plants.

kansei 完成〖名, ～する〗
¶わたしの研究も完成に近づいてきました。 (Watashi no kenkyū mo *kansei* ni chikazuite kimashita.)

kansei 〚n, ～*suru*〛 completion
¶ My research is nearing **completion**.

¶この建物は去年の10月に完成しました。(Kono tatemono wa kyonen no jūgatsu ni *kansei* shimashita.)

¶ This building **was completed** in October of last year.

kansetsu 間接〚名〛

間接税 (*kansetsuzei*) 間接話法 (*kansetsu*-wahō) 間接的な影響 (*kansetsu*teki na eikyō)

¶上田さんとは直接話したことはありませんが、友人を通して間接に知っています。(Ueda san to wa chokusetsu hanashita koto wa arimasen ga, yūjin o tooshite *kansetsu* ni shitte imasu.)

⇔chokusetsu 直接

kansetsu 〚n〛 **indirectness, indirect** an **indirect** tax, **indirect** taxation // **indirect** narration // an **indirect** influence

¶ I've never spoken directly with [Mr.] Ueda but I know of [him] **at second hand** through friends.

kansha 感謝〚名, ～する〛

¶クラスを代表して、先生に感謝の言葉を述べたいと思います。(Kurasu o daihyō shite, sensei ni *kansha* no kotoba o nobetai to omoimasu.)

¶御親切を心から感謝します。(Goshinsetsu o kokoro kara *kansha* shimasu.)

kansha 〚n, ～*suru*〛 **thanks, gratitude**

¶ Representing the class, I would like to express **our gratitude** to you, sir 〚ma'am〛 (said to one's teacher or professor).

¶ **I am** deeply **grateful** for your kindness to me.

kanshin 感心〚名, 形動, ～する〛

¶まだ子供なのに、よく働いて感心ですね。(Mada kodomo na noni, yoku hataraite *kanshin* desu ne.)

¶あの犬は、どろぼうを捕まえた感心な犬です。(Ano inu wa, dorobō o tsukamaeta *kanshin* na inu desu.)

¶上田さんは山田さんの上手な話し方にたいへん感心したようです。(Ueda san wa Yamada san no jōzu na hanashikata ni taihen *kanshin* shita yō desu.)

kanshin 〚n, adj-v, ～*suru*〛 **admiration, wonder**

¶ **I'm impressed** at how hard [he] works even though still a child.

¶ That's **some** dog! It caught a thief.

¶ [Mr.] Ueda seems **to have been** very **impressed** by [Mr.] Yamada's skillful way of talking.

kantan 簡単〖形動〗

①[ものごとが単純・簡略である様子]

¶時間がないので，簡単に説明します。
(Jikan ga nai node, *kantan* ni setsu-mei shimasu.)

¶これは簡単な機械ですから，だれにでも動かせますよ。 (Kore wa *kantan* na kikai desu kara, dare ni demo ugokasemasu yo.)

→**fukuzatsu** 複雑

②[ものごとが平易でわかりやすい様子]

¶こんな簡単な問題がわからないのですか。 (Konna *kantan* na mondai ga wakaranai no desu ka?)

¶試験は意外に簡単でした。 (Shiken wa igai ni *kantan* deshita.)

kanzen 完全〖名，形動〗

完全無欠 (*kanzen*-muketsu) 不完全 (fu*kanzen*)

¶今度の実験は完全に失敗しました。
(Kondo no jikken wa *kanzen* ni shippai shimashita.)

¶この建物はまだ完全にでき上がっていません。 (Kono tatemono wa mada *kanzen* ni dekiagatte imasen.)

kanzume かん詰め〖名〗

¶これは牛肉のかん詰めです。 (Kore wa gyūniku no *kanzume* desu.)

⇨-**zume** -詰め

kao 顔〖名〗

顔つき (*kao*tsuki) 顔を洗う (*kao* o arau) 悲しそうな顔をする (kana-shisō na *kao* o suru)

kantan 〚adj-v〛 **simple**

① [simple, uncomplicated, brief]

¶ Since there isn't much time, [I]'ll explain **briefly.**

¶ This is a **simple** machine that anyone can operate.

② [simple, easy]

¶ You mean you don't understand this sort of **simple** problem?

¶ The test was surprisingly **easy.**

kanzen 〚n, adj-v〛 **perfection, perfect, completeness, complete**

absolute perfection // im**perfect,** in**complete**

¶ This experiment was a **complete** failure.

¶ This building is not yet **completely** finished.

kanzume 〚n〛 **canned goods, canned food**

¶ This is **a can** of beef.

kao 〚n〛 **face**

look, expression (on one's face) // wash **one's face** // **look** sad

¶恥ずかしくて顔が真っ赤になりました。(Hazukashikute *kao* ga makka ni narimashita.)

¶上田さんはびっくりした顔でわたしを見ました。(Ueda san wa bikkuri shita *kao* de watashi o mimashita.)

¶顔色が悪いですね。どこかぐあいが悪いのですか。 (*Kao*iro ga warui desu ne. Doko ka guai ga warui no desu ka?)

¶ **My face** turned bright red from embarrassment 〚shame〛.

¶ [Miss] Ueda looked at me with a surprised expression on **[her] face.**

¶ You **look** pale. Do you feel ill?

kara 空〚名〛

空びん (*kara*bin) 空箱 (*kara*bako)
¶この箱は空です。 (Kono hako wa *kara* desu.)

kara 〚n〛 **empty, vacant**

an **empty** bottle // an **empty** box
¶ This box is **empty.**

kara から〚助〛

①[時・所などの起点を表す]
¶学校は8時から始まります。(Gakkō wa hachiji *kara* hajimarimasu.)

¶うちから駅まで歩いて10分です。(Uchi *kara* eki made aruite jippun desu.)

¶父は昨日外国から帰ってきました。(Chichi wa kinō gaikoku *kara* kaette kimashita.)

②[経由する所を表す]
¶わたしの部屋の窓から港が見えます。(Watashi no heya no mado *kara* minato ga miemasu.)

¶戸のすき間から冷たい風が入ってきます。(To no sukima *kara* tsumetai kaze ga haitte kimasu.)

③[動作の出どころなどを表す]
¶友達からお祝いの品物をもらいました。 (Tomodachi *kara* oiwai no

kara 〚part〛 **from; after**

① [from, at (a given time or place)]
¶ School starts **at** eight o'clock.

¶ It's a 10-minute walk **from** my home to the station.

¶ My father returned home **from** overseas yesterday.

② [from, out of (an intermediary place)]
¶ You can see the harbor **from** the window of my room.

¶ A cold draft is coming in **from** around the door.

③ [from (a source of an action, etc.)]
¶ [I] received a present **from** a friend.

shinamono o moraimashita.)

¶わたしは山田先生から日本語を教えていただきました。　(Watashi wa Yamada sensei *kara* Nihongo o oshiete itadakimashita.)

¶図書館から借りた本をなくしてしまいました。 (Toshokan *kara* karita hon o nakushite shimaimashita.)

④[原料・材料などを表す]

¶日本の酒は米から作ります。(Nihon no sake wa kome *kara* tsukurimasu.)

¶石油からいろいろな物が作られます。 (Sekiyu *kara* iroiro na mono ga tsukuraremasu.)

⑤[原因・理由・根拠となるものごとを表す]

¶この事故は運転手の不注意から起ったものです。　(Kono jiko wa untenshu no fuchūi *kara* okotta mono desu.)

⑥[順序・順番の初めを表す]

¶このページの1番から順に読んでください。(Kono pēji no ichiban *kara* jun ni yonde kudasai.)

¶あなたから始めてください。(Anata *kara* hajimete kudasai.)

⑦[ある動作・作用が終わったあとに他の動作・作用が行われることを表す]

¶あなたはうちへ帰ってから何をしますか。　(Anata wa uchi e kaette *kara* nani o shimasu ka?)

¶御飯を食べてからテレビを見ます。 (Gohan o tabete *kara* terebi o

¶ I was taught Japanese **by** Professor Yamada.

¶ [I] lost a library book.

④ [from, out of (some raw material)]

¶ Japanese *sake* is made **from** rice.

¶ Various things can be made **from** petroleum.

⑤ [from, out of, due to (some cause or reason)]

¶ This accident was caused **by** careless driving.

⑥ [from (the beginning or the first one)]

¶ Start reading this page **from** number one.

¶ We'll start **with** you.

⑦ [after (doing something)]

¶ What do you do 〚will you do〛 **after** returning home?

¶ [I] watch television **after** eating dinner.

mimasu.)

¶学校を卒業してから10年たちました。(Gakkō o sotsugyō shite *kara* jūnen tachimashita.)

*「動詞（ての形）＋から（kara）」の形で使う。

kara　から〖助〗

①[前件が理由・根拠をなし後件がその帰結となっているという関係を表す]

¶暑いから，窓を開けてください。(Atsui *kara,* mado o akete kudasai.)

¶遅くなったから，タクシーで帰りましょう。(Osoku natta *kara,* takushii de kaerimashō.)

¶危ないから，道路で遊んではいけません。(Abunai *kara,* dōro de ason-de wa ikemasen.)

¶ゆっくりしていては汽車に乗り遅れるから，早く行きなさい。(Yukkuri shite ite wa kisha ni noriokureru *kara,* hayaku ikinasai.)

* 後件には，「～でしょう（deshō）」などの推量，「～う［よう］（～u［yō]）」などの意志，「～なさい（nasai）」などの命令，「～てください（～te kudasai）」などの依頼，「～てはいけない（～te wa ikenai）」などの禁止などの主観的な言い方も来る。

→node　ので

②[前件の成立する理由や根拠などを後件によって説明するのに使う]

¶山田さんが休んだのは風邪を引いたからです。(Yamada san ga yasunda

¶ Ten years have ⟦had⟧ passed **since** [I] graduated from school.

* Used in the pattern "verb (*-te* form) + *kara.*"

kara ⟦part⟧ **because**

① [because; indicates the second clause is a consequence of the first one]

¶ It's hot. Please open the window.

¶ **As** it's late, let's take a taxi home.

¶ One mustn't play in the street **because** it's dangerous.

¶ Go quickly **as** you will miss the train if you don't.

* Subjective expressions can also be used in the second clause such as inferences with *deshō*, expressions of intent or will with *-ō* ⟦*-yō*⟧, imperatives with *-nasai*, requests with *-te kudasai*, and prohibitions with *-te wa ikenai.*

② [because; indicates the first clause is explained by the second clause]

¶ [Mrs.] Yamada was absent **because** [she] caught a cold.

no wa kaze o hiita *kara* desu.)

¶みんな夜遅くまで勉強しています。試験が近づいた**から**です。 (Minna yoru osoku made benkyō shite imasu. Shiken ga chikazuita *kara* desu.)

* 「〜からだ (〜kara da)」「〜からです (〜kara desu)」の形で使う。

¶ Everyone is studying until late at night. That's **because** exams are approaching.

* Used in the patterns "〜 *kara da*" and "〜 *kara desu*."

karā　カラー〚名〛

カラーテレビ (*karā*-terebi)　カラー写真 (*karā*-shashin)　カラーフィルム (*karā*-firumu)

¶あなたのテレビは**カラー**ですか，白黒ですか。 (Anata no terebi wa *karā* desu ka, shirokuro desu ka?)

karā 〚n〛 **color**

color television // a **color** photo // **color** film

¶ Is your television set **color** or black and white?

karada　体〚名〛

①[身体]
¶上田さんはずいぶん**体**の大きい人ですね。 (Ueda san wa zuibun *karada* no ookii hito desu ne.)

¶柔道の練習で**体**じゅうが痛くなりました。 (Jūdō no renshū de *karada*jū ga itaku narimashita.)

②[健康の状態]
¶**体**のぐあいが悪いので，学校を休みました。 (*Karada* no guai ga warui node, gakkō o yasumimashita.)

¶**体**にはじゅうぶん気をつけてください。 (*Karada* ni wa jūbun ki o tsukete kudasai.)

karada 〚n〛 **body; health**

① [body]
¶ [Mr.] Ueda is **a big man,** isn't he?

¶ I ache 〚ached〛 all over **my body** from practicing judo.

② [health]
¶ [I] **didn't feel well** so [I] stayed home from school.

¶ Please take good care of **yourself.**

karai　辛い〚形〛

①[香辛料の味]
¶そんなに**からし**をつけたら**辛い**ですよ。 (Sonna ni karashi o tsuketara

karai 〚adj〛 **hot** (taste); **salty**

① [hot, sharp]
¶ It will be **very hot** if you put on so much mustard.

karai desu yo.)

¶あの店のカレーは辛かったですね。
(Ano mise no karē wa *karakatta* desu ne.)

②[塩味が強い]
¶この魚料理は塩辛いですね。(Kono sakanaryōri wa shio*karai* desu ne.)

↔amai 甘い

kare 彼〖代〗
¶彼の名前は上田です。 (*Kare* no namae wa Ueda desu.)

⇨kanojo 彼女

karendā カレンダー〖名〗
カレンダーをめくる (*karendā* o mekuru)
¶来月の15日は何曜日か,カレンダーで調べてください。 (Raigetsu no jūgonichi wa naniyōbi ka, *karendā* de shirabete kudasai.)

kareru 枯れる〖動Ⅱ〗
枯れ木 (*kare*ki) 枯れ葉 (*kare*ha)
¶水をやらなかったので,木が枯れてしまいました。(Mizu o yaranakatta node, ki ga *karete* shimaimashita.)

kariru 借りる〖動Ⅱ〗
金を借りる (kane o *kariru*) 部屋を借りる (heya o *kariru*)
¶わたしは上田さんから1万円借りました。(Watashi wa Ueda san kara ichiman'en *karimashita*.)
¶借りた本はあした返します。(*Karita* hon wa ashita kaeshimasu.)
¶電話をお借りできますか。(Denwa o o*kari* dekimasu ka?)

¶ That restaurant's curry **was really hot,** wasn't it?

② [salty]
¶ This fish is **very salty,** isn't it?

kare 〖pron〗 he, his
¶ **His** name is Ueda.

karendā 〖n〗 calendar
turn over **a calendar,** tear a sheet off **a calendar**
¶ Please look at **the calendar** and see what day of the week the fifteenth is next month.

kareru 〖v Ⅱ〗 wither, die
a **dead** tree // a **dead** leaf
¶ The tree **died** because it hadn't been watered.

kariru 〖v Ⅱ〗 borrow; hire, rent
borrow money // **rent** a room
¶ I **borrowed** ten thousand yen from [Miss] Ueda.
¶ Tomorrow I will return the book I **borrowed.**
¶ Do you have a telephone I **could use?**

⇔kasu 貸す

karui 軽い〖形〗

①[目方が少ない]

¶この荷物は軽いから，片手で持てます。
(Kono nimotsu wa *karui* kara, katate de motemasu.)

②[たいした程度ではない]

¶上田さんの病気は軽いそうです。
(Ueda san no byōki wa *karui* sō desu.)

¶子供が大学を卒業したので，わたしの責任も軽くなりました。(Kodomo ga daigaku o sotsugyō shita node, watashi no sekinin mo *karuku* narimashita.)

⇔omoi 重い

kasa かさ〖名〗

雨がさ (ama*gasa*) 日がさ (hi*gasa*) かさをさす (*kasa* o sasu) かさをひろげる (*kasa* o hirogeru) かさをつぼめる (*kasa* o tsubomeru)

¶電車の中にかさを忘れてきました。
(Densha no naka ni *kasa* o wasurete kimashita.)

kasanaru 重なる〖動 I〗

①[物の上に物がのる]

¶机の上にたくさんの本が重なっています。(Tsukue no ue ni takusan no hon ga *kasanatte* imasu.)

¶電車が急に止まったので，乗客が重なって倒れました。(Densha ga kyū ni tomatta node, jōkyaku ga *kasanatte* taoremashita.)

②[ものごとが次々に起こる]

karui 〖adj〗 light; trifling

① [light, not heavy]

¶ As this package 〖luggage, bag〗 **is light** it can be carried in one hand.

② [trifling, slight]

¶ I hear that [Mrs.] Ueda's illness **isn't serious.**

¶ As my children have graduated from college, my responsibility has become **lighter.**

kasa 〖n〗 umbrella

a (rain) **umbrella** // a parasol // put up **an umbrella** // open **an umbrella** // close **an umbrella**

¶ I left **my umbrella** in the train.

kasanaru 〖v I〗 be piled up; occur one after another

① [(things are) piled up]

¶ Many books **are piled up** on the desk.

¶ The train stopped abruptly and the passengers fell over **on top of each other.**

② [(events) occur one after another]

¶あの人は不幸が重なってお気の毒ですね。(Ano hito wa fukō ga *kasanatte* okinodoku desu ne.)

¶ Isn't it unfortunate how [he] has suffered **one** misfortune **after another!**

kasaneru 重ねる〔動Ⅱ〕

①[物の上に物をのせる]

¶寒いからシャツを重ねて着ました。(Samui kara shatsu o *kasanete* kimashita.)

②[ものごとを繰り返す]

¶失敗を重ねましたが、やっと成功しました。 (Shippai o *kasanemashita* ga, yatto seikō shimashita.)

kasaneru 〚v Ⅱ〛 pile up, lay one on top of another; repeat

① [pile up, lay one on top of another]

¶ It's cold so [I]'m wearing **two layers** of shirts.

② [repeat]

¶ After **a series** of failures at last [I]'ve succeeded 〚I succeeded〛.

kashi 菓子〔名〕

菓子屋 (*kashi*ya)

¶このお菓子はとてもおいしいです。(Kono *okashi* wa totemo oishii desu.)

kashi 〚n〛 sweets, confectionary, cake, pastry

a **confectionary** store, **candy** store

¶ This **candy** 〚**sweet**〛 is very good.

kashikomarimashita かしこまりました〔連〕

¶「この品物を包んでください。」(Kono shinamono o tsutsunde kudasai.) 「はい、かしこまりました。」(Hai, *kashikomarimashita*.)

kashikomarimashita 〚compd〛 a set expression of understanding or agreement usually used by an employee toward a customer

¶ "Please wrap this merchandise."

"**Certainly,** sir 〚ma'am〛."

kasu 貸す〔動Ⅰ〕

本を貸す (hon o *kasu*)

¶千円ほど貸してくださいませんか。(Sen'en hodo *kashite* kudasaimasen ka?)

¶わたしは田中さんにお金を貸してあげました。 (Watashi wa Tanaka san ni okane o *kashite* agemashita.)

⇔kariru 借りる

kasu 〚v Ⅰ〛 lend, loan, rent out

lend a book

¶ Could you please **lend** me a thousand yen?

¶ I **loaned** [Mr.] Tanaka some money.

kata 肩〔名〕

肩がこる (*kata* ga koru)　肩に担ぐ

kata 〚n〛 shoulder(s)

have a stiff **shoulder(s)** // carry on

(*kata* ni katsugu)

¶わたしはおばあさんの肩をたたいて
あげました。 (Watashi wa obāsan
no *kata* o tataite agemashita.)
¶上田さんは胸が厚く，肩幅が広いで
す。(Ueda san wa mune ga atsuku,
*kata*haba ga hiroi desu.)

kata 型〖名〗
大型 (oo*gata*) 小型 (ko*gata*)
¶この自動車は１９８０年型です。
(Kono jidōsha wa senkyūhyaku-
hachijūnen*gata* desu.)
¶この洋服は型が古いですね。(Kono
yōfuku wa *kata* ga furui desu ne.)

(-)kata (-)方〖名，尾〗
1〖名〗
¶あの方はどなたですか。 (Ano *kata*
wa donata desu ka?)
¶上田さんという方がいらっしゃいま
した。 (Ueda san to iu *kata* ga
irasshaimashita.)
* 人を丁寧に呼ぶときの言葉。

2〖尾〗
話し方 (hanashi*kata*) 泳ぎ方 (oyogi*kata*) 教え方 (oshie*kata*)
¶この漢字の読み方がわかりません。
(Kono kanji no yomi*kata* ga wakarimasen.)

katachi 形〖名〗
四角い形をした入れ物 (shikakui *ka-
tachi* o shita iremono)
¶あの山は富士山のような形をしてい
ます。 (Ano yama wa Fujisan no
yō na *katachi* o shite imasu.)

one's shoulder

¶ I massaged my grandmother's
shoulders by hitting them lightly
with my fists.

¶ Mr. Ueda is thick-chested and
broad-**shouldered.**

kata 〚n〛 model, pattern, make,
style
large-**size,** king-**size,** over**size** //
small-**size,** pocket-**size,** miniature
¶ This is a **1980** car.

¶ **The cut** of this piece of clothing is
old-fashioned.

(-)kata 〚n, suf〛 person; method,
way of doing something

1 〚n〛 person
¶ Who is that **gentleman** 〚**lady**〛?
¶ **A** [Mr.] Ueda is here 〚came〛.

* Used to refer to persons politely;
the polite form of *hito*.

2 〚suf〛 method, way of doing something
way of speaking // **way** of swimming, **how to** swim // **method** of
teaching, **how to** teach
¶ [I] don't know **the reading** for this
kanji.

katachi 〚n〛 shape, form
a square container

¶ That mountain is similar **in shape**
to Mount Fuji.

¶上田さんはいろいろな形の石を集めています。(Ueda san wa iroiro na *katachi* no ishi o atsumete imasu.)

katai 堅い〚形〛

①［材質などがしっかりしている様子］
¶この机は堅い木で作ってあります。
(Kono tsukue wa *katai* ki de tsukutte arimasu.)
¶このくつの革は堅いですね。(Kono kutsu no kawa wa *katai* desu ne.)
②［まじめである様子，まちがいなどない様子］
堅い人 (*katai* hito)
¶パーティーですから，堅い話ではなくおもしろい話をしてください。
(Pātii desu kara, *katai* hanashi de wa naku omoshiroi hanashi o shite kudasai.)

katai 固い〚形〛

①［しっかりとして変わらない様子］
¶わたしは上田さんと固い約束をしました。(Watashi wa Ueda san to *katai* yakusoku o shimashita.)
¶もう，お酒を飲まないと固く決心しました。(Mō, osake o nomanai to *kataku* kesshin shimashita.)
②［力が入ってゆるみのない様子］
固い握手 (*katai* akushu) 固く結ぶ (*kataku* musubu)
¶この荷物のひもを固くしばってください。(Kono nimotsu no himo o *kataku* shibatte kudasai.)
③［融通のきかない様子，がんこな様子］

¶ [Mrs.] Ueda collects rocks of various **shapes.**

katai 〚adj〛 hard, stiff; steady, reliable, upright

① [hard, stiff, tough]
¶ This desk is made of **hard** wood.

¶ The leather of these shoes **is stiff.**

② [steady, reliable, upright, serious, dry]
a **reliable** 〚upright, unbending, straitlaced〛 person
¶ This is a party so please talk about something interesting and less **dry** 〚**serious**〛.

katai 〚adj〛 firm, steady; tight; stubborn; hard

① [firm, steady, strong]
¶ I made a **firm** promise to [Mr.] Ueda.

¶ I have made a **firm** resolution not to drink anymore.

② [tight, with no looseness]
a **firm** handshake // tie **tightly**
¶ Please tie up this parcel **tightly.**

③ [stubborn, obstinate]

¶山田さんは頭の固い人です。 (Yamada san wa atama no *katai* hito desu.)

④［やわらかくない様子］

¶パンがかたくなってしまいました。 (Pan ga *kataku* natte shimaimashita.)

katai 硬い〚形〛

¶ダイヤモンドは非常に硬い物質です。 (Daiyamondo wa hijō ni *katai* busshitsu desu.)

katakana 片仮名〚名〛

¶外国語を日本語で書き表す場合は、片仮名で書きます。 (Gaikokugo o Nihongo de kakiarawasu baai wa, *katakana* de kakimasu.)

⇒kana 仮名 hiragana 平仮名

katamaru 固まる〚動Ⅰ〛

¶このセメントはすぐ固まります。 (Kono semento wa sugu *katamarimasu*.)

katameru 固める〚動Ⅱ〛

①［粉や土などをかたくする］

¶この人形は土を固めて作ったものです。 (Kono ningyō wa tsuchi o *katamete* tsukutta mono desu.)

②［しっかりとしたものにする］

¶わたしは国へ帰る決心を固めました。 (Watashi wa kuni e kaeru kesshin o *katamemashita*.)

katamichi 片道〚名〛

片道切符 (*katamichi*-kippu)

¶小学生のころ片道5キロの道を毎日歩いて通いました。 (Shōgakusei no

¶ [Mr.] Yamada is quite **stubborn.**

④ [hard, not soft]

¶ The bread has gotten **hard.**

katai 〚adj〛 **hard**

¶ A diamond is an extremely **hard** substance.

katakana 〚n〛 the *katakana* syllabary for writing Japanese

¶ In the Japanese language foreign words are written with *katakana*.

katamaru 〚v I〛 become hard, harden, solidify, congeal

¶ This cement **hardens** quickly.

katameru 〚v II〛 harden, make hard; strengthen

① [harden, make hard]

¶ This doll is made of **hardened** earth.

② [strengthen]

¶ I am 〚was〛 **firmly** resolved to return to my native country.

katamichi 〚n〛 one-way

a **one-way** ticket

¶ When in elementary school, [I] walked to school every day, a trip

koro *katamichi* gokiro no michi o mainichi aruite kayoimashita.)
⇔ōfuku 往復

katamuku　傾く〖動Ⅰ〗

①[斜めになる]
¶地震で家が傾いてしまいました。
(Jishin de ie ga *katamuite* shimaimashita.)
¶この柱は10度も傾いています。
(Kono hashira wa jūdo mo *katamuite* imasu.)

②[太陽や月が地平線に近づく]
¶太陽が西に傾いてきました。 (Taiyō ga nishi ni *katamuite* kimashita.)

katazukeru　かたづける〖動Ⅱ〗

①[整理してきちんとする]
¶机の上をかたづけなさい。 (Tsukue no ue o *katazukenasai*.)

②[処理すべきものごとをやってしまう]
¶わたしはこの仕事をかたづけてから帰ります。 (Watashi wa kono shigoto o *katazukete* kara kaerimasu.)

katei　家庭〖名〗

家庭を持つ (*katei* o motsu)　　家庭教師 (*katei*-kyōshi)　　家庭教育 (*katei*-kyōiku)
¶上田さんのうちはたいへん明るい家庭です。 (Ueda san no uchi wa taihen akarui *katei* desu.)
¶上田さんの奥さんはとても家庭的な方です。 (Ueda san no okusan wa totemo *katei*teki na kata desu.)

kāten　カーテン〖名〗

katamuku 〖vI〗　tilt, slant; sink, set

① [tilt, slant, incline]

¶ The house **is tilting** as a result of the earthquake.

¶ This pillar **is slanting** at an angle of 10 degrees.

② [sink, set]
¶ The sun **is** 〚**was**〛 **low** in the west.

katazukeru 〖vII〗　put in order, straighten up; dispose of, finish up

① [put in order, straighten up, put away, clear off]
¶ **Tidy up** your desk.

② [dispose of, finish up]
¶ I will go home after I **finish up** this piece of work.

katei 〖n〗　home, family, household

be married and settled down // a tutor, private teacher // **home** training

¶ [Mr.] Ueda has a very happy **home.**

¶ Mr. Ueda's wife is a very **domestic** woman.

kāten 〖n〗　curtains

of five kilometers **each way.**

カーテンを掛ける *(kāten o kakeru)*
カーテンを引く *(kāten o hiku)*
¶窓に白いレースの**カーテン**が掛かっています。 *(Mado ni shiroi rēsu no kāten ga kakatte imasu.)*

hang up **curtains** // pull **a curtain** closed
¶ There are white lace **curtains** hanging at the window(s).

katsu 勝つ〖動Ⅰ〗
¶わたしたちはその試合に4対3で**勝**ちました。 *(Watashitachi wa sono shiai ni yon tai san de kachimashita.)*
⇔makeru 負ける

katsu 〖v Ⅰ〗 **win**
¶ We **won** that match by a score of 4 to 3.

katsudō 活動〖名, ～する〗
政治**活動** *(seiji-katsudō)* 活動的な人 *(katsudōteki na hito)*
¶この学校は課外**活動**が盛んです。 *(Kono gakkō wa kagai-katsudō ga sakan desu.)*
¶休火山が再び**活動**し始めました。 *(Kyūkazan ga futatabi katsudō shihajimemashita.)*

katsudō 〖n, ～suru〗 **activity, activities**
political **activity** // an **active** ⸤energetic⸥ person
¶ Extracurricular **activities** are popular at this school.
¶ A dormant volcano has become **active** once again.

katte 勝手〖名〗
¶母は今お**勝手**にいます。 *(Haha wa ima okatte ni imasu.)*
⇒daidokoro 台所

katte 〖n〗 **kitchen**
¶ My mother is in **the kitchen** now.

katte かって〖形動〗
¶あの人は自分**かって**なことばかりします。 *(Ano hito wa jibunkatte na koto bakari shimasu.)*
¶人の物を**かって**に使っては困ります。 *(Hito no mono o katte ni tsukatte wa komarimasu.)*

katte 〖adj-v〗 **one's own convenience, selfishness, willfulness**
¶ [He] only acts **to please [him]self** ⸤He never thinks of others⸥.
¶ It will not do to help yourself to the possessions of others **as if they were your own.**

kau 買う〖動Ⅰ〗
¶わたしは八百屋で野菜を**買**いました。 *(Watashi wa yaoya de yasai o*

kau 〖v Ⅰ〗 **buy**
¶ I **bought** vegetables at the vegetable store.

kaimashita.)

¶わたしはデパートへ服を買いに行きます。 (Watashi wa depāto e fuku o *kai* ni ikimasu.)

¶ I am going to the department store **to buy** some clothes.

¶ノートを買いたいのですが，どこで売っていますか。 (Nōto o *kaitai* no desu ga, doko de utte imasu ka?)

¶ **I want to buy** a notebook—where are they sold?

⇔**uru** 売る

kau 飼う〖動 I 〗

¶わたしのうちでは，ねこを飼っています。(Watashi no uchi de wa, neko o *katte* imasu.)

kau 〖v I〗 raise, rear

¶ We **keep** a cat 〚cats〛 at my home.

kawa 川〖名〗

ナイル川 (Nairu*gawa*) 川幅 (*kawahaba*)

¶家の前に川が流れています。(Ie no mae ni *kawa* ga nagarete imasu.)

¶川岸にホテルが1軒建っています。(*Kawa*gishi ni hoteru ga ikken tatte imasu.)

kawa 〖n〗 river, stream

the Nile **River** // the width of **a river**

¶ There is **a river** 〚stream〛 running in front of the house.

¶ There is a single hotel standing on the **river**bank.

kawa 皮〖名〗

毛皮 (ke*gawa*)

¶みかんは皮をむいて食べます。(Mikan wa *kawa* o muite tabemasu.)

kawa 〖n〗 skin, hide, fur, peel, shell

fur

¶ **One peels** a mandarin orange before eating it.

kawa 革〖名〗

革ぐつ (*kawa*gutsu) 革のカバン (*kawa* no kaban)

¶このベルトは革でできています。(Kono beruto wa *kawa* de dekite imasu.)

kawa 〖n〗 leather

leather shoes // a **leather** bag 〚briefcase, suitcase, etc.〛

¶ This belt is made of **leather**.

kawaigaru かわいがる〖動 I 〗

¶おじいさんはわたしをとてもかわいがってくれました。 (Ojiisan wa

kawaigaru 〖v I〗 love, pet, show affection to, be attached to

¶ I **was a special favorite** of my

watashi o totemo *kawaigatte* kuremashita.)

¶上田さんは犬をたいへんかわいがっています。 (Ueda san wa inu o taihen *kawaigatte* imasu.)

¶ [Mr.] Ueda **is very fond** of [his] grandfather. dog.

kawaii かわいい〖形〗

¶とてもかわいい人形ですね。 (Totemo *kawaii* ningyō desu ne.)

¶田中さんからかわいい子犬をもらいました。 (Tanaka san kara *kawaii* koinu o moraimashita.)

kawaii 〖adj〗 **cute, sweet, charming**

¶ This is a very **cute** doll, isn't it?

¶ I received a **cute** little puppy from [Mrs.] Tanaka.

kawaisō かわいそう〖形動〗

¶両親のいない子供はかわいそうです。 (Ryōshin no inai kodomo wa *kawaisō* desu.)

¶あの子はかわいそうに目が見えないのです。 (Ano ko wa *kawaisō* ni me ga mienai no desu.)

kawaisō 〖adj-v〗 **poor, pitiful, pathetic**

¶ Children without parents **are to be pitied.**

¶ **Sadly enough** that child is blind.

kawakasu 乾かす〖動Ⅰ〗

¶ぬれた服を火で乾かしました。 (Nureta fuku o hi de *kawakashimashita*.)

kawakasu 〖v Ⅰ〗 **dry, dry out**

¶ [I] **dried** the wet clothes at the fire.

kawaku 乾く〖動Ⅰ〗

¶天気がいいので、洗たく物がすぐ乾きます。 (Tenki ga ii node, sentakumono ga sugu *kawakimasu*.)

kawaku 〖v Ⅰ〗 **dry, become dry**

¶ As it's a nice day laundry 〖the laundry〗 will soon **dry.**

kawaku 渇く〖動Ⅰ〗

¶のどが渇いたから、水を一杯ください。 (Nodo ga *kawaita* kara, mizu o ippai kudasai.)

kawaku 〖v Ⅰ〗 **be thirsty**

¶ **I'm thirsty**—please give me a glass of water.

kawari 代わり〖名〗

¶父の代わりにわたしが来ました。 (Chichi no *kawari* ni watashi ga kimashita.)

kawari 〖n〗 **substitute, in place of**

¶ I've come **in place of** my father.

¶上田先生が病気なので，代わりに山田先生が教えてくださいました。

(Ueda sensei ga byōki na node, *kawari* ni Yamada sensei ga oshiete kudasaimashita.)

¶ Professor Ueda was sick so Professor Yamada taught **in [his] place.**

kawari 替わり〖名〗

¶あまりおいしかったので，コーヒーのお替わりをしました。 (Amari oishikatta node, kōhii no o*kawari* o shimashita.)

kawari 〖n〗 **another helping, a refill**

¶ As it was so good, I had **another cup** of coffee.

¶御飯のお替わりはいかがですか。

(Gohan no o*kawari* wa ikaga desu ka?)

¶ Would you like **another helping** 〖**serving**〗 of rice?

kawaru 代わる〖動Ⅰ〗

¶これからのエネルギーは，石油に代わって原子力になるでしょう。(Kore kara no enerugii wa, sekiyu ni *kawatte* genshiryoku ni naru deshō.)

＊別の人や物が，その役割をする場合に使う。

kawaru 〖v I〗 **take the place of, replace, substitute for**

¶ In the future nuclear power will probably **replace** oil as our principal source of energy.

＊ This *kawaru* is used when a different person or thing substitutes in or fulfills a given function or role.

kawaru 替わる〖動Ⅰ〗

¶最近，あの会社は経営者が替わりました。(Saikin, ano kaisha wa keieisha ga *kawarimashita*.)

＊ある地位や役割を占めていた人がほかの人と交替する場合に使う。

kawaru 〖v I〗 **change**

¶ The manager 〖chief executive〗 of that company **has changed** recently.

＊ This *kawaru* is used when a person holding a certain position or role is replaced by someone else.

kawaru 変わる〖動Ⅰ〗

¶信号が赤から青に変わりました。

(Shingō ga aka kara ao ni *kawarimashita*.)

¶このごろのお天気は変わりやすいです。(Konogoro no otenki wa *kawari-yasui* desu.)

kawaru 〖v I〗 **change**

¶ The light **changed** from red to green.

¶ The weather **is very changeable** lately.

＊前の状態とは違った状態になる場合に使う。

kawase 為替〖名〗

¶お金を為替にして送りました。

(Okane o *kawase* ni shite okurimashita.)

kayō(bi) 火曜(日)〖名〗

kayou 通う〖動Ⅰ〗

①[何度も同じ所を通る]

¶わたしは自転車で学校に**通って**います。(Watashi wa jitensha de gakkō ni *kayotte* imasu.)

¶わたしの生まれた所は，バスも**通わ ない**ほどの田舎です。 (Watashi no umareta tokoro wa, basu mo *kayowanai* hodo no inaka desu.)

②[心が通じる]

¶お互いの心が**通い**合っていなければ，いっしょに生活できません。 (Otagai no kokoro ga *kayoi*atte inakereba, issho ni seikatsu dekimasen.)

kayui かゆい〖形〗

¶虫に刺された所が**かゆい**ので，薬をつけました。 (Mushi ni sasareta tokoro ga *kayui* node, kusuri o tsukemashita.)

¶夏は汗をかくので，体が**かゆく**なります。(Natsu wa ase o kaku node, karada ga *kayuku* narimasu.)

kazan 火山〖名〗

¶日本には**火山**がたくさんあります。(Nihon ni wa *kazan* ga takusan arimasu.)

kazari 飾り〖名〗

＊ This *kawaru* is used when the existing situation or condition has changed to a new one.

kawase 〚n〛 **money order,** (currency) **exchange**

¶ [I] sent the money by **money order.**

kayō(bi) 〚n〛 **Tuesday**

kayou 〚v I〛 **commute, run** (between); **be conveyed**

① [commute, visit frequently, go to and from, run (between)]

¶ I **commute** to school by bicycle.

¶ My birthplace is in such an out-of-the-way place that it **isn't** even **served by** a bus.

② [be conveyed, be communicated]

¶ People can't live together if they can't **understand** each other's feelings.

kayui 〚adj〛 **itchy**

¶ As the spot where I had been bitten 〚stung〛 by an insect **itched,** I put on some medicine.

¶ One's body becomes **itchy** in the summer when one sweats a lot.

kazan 〚n〛 **volcano**

¶ There are many **volcanoes** in Japan.

kazari 〚n〛 **ornament, decoration**

首飾り (kubi*kazari*)

¶町はお祭りのための飾りでいっぱいです。(Machi wa omatsuri no tame no *kazari* de ippai desu.)

a necklace

¶ There are **decorations** up all over town for the festival.

kazaru 飾る〘動Ⅰ〙

¶客が来るので，部屋に花を飾りました。(Kyaku ga kuru node, heya ni hana o *kazarimashita*.)

¶部屋をきれいに飾って，ダンス・パーティーをしました。(Heya o kirei ni *kazatte*, dansu-pātii o shimashita.)

kazaru 〖v I〗 **decorate, ornament**

¶ [I] **put** flowers **out** in the room because a guest was coming.

¶ [We] **decorated** the room nicely and had a dance party.

kaze 風〘名〙

風が吹く (*kaze* ga fuku) 風がやむ (*kaze* ga yamu)

¶午前中は風が強かったが，午後からは弱くなりました。(Gozenchū wa *kaze* ga tsuyokatta ga, gogo kara wa yowaku narimashita.)

kaze 〖n〗 **wind, breeze, draft**

the wind blows // **the wind** dies down

¶ **The wind** was strong during the morning but fell off in the afternoon.

kaze 風邪〘名〙

風邪薬 (*kaze*gusuri)

¶ゆうべ寒かったので，風邪を引いてしまいました。(Yūbe samukatta node, *kaze* o hiite shimaimashita.)

kaze 〖n〗 **a cold, the flu**

cold medicine

¶ It was cold last night and [I] caught **a cold.**

kazoeru 数える〘動Ⅱ〙

数を数える (kazu o *kazoeru*)

¶日本語で1から10まで数えてください。(Nihongo de ichi kara jū made *kazoete* kudasai.)

¶本は1冊，2冊と数えます。(Hon wa issatsu, nisatsu to *kazoemasu*.)

kazoeru 〖v II〗 **count**

to count

¶ Please **count** from one to ten in Japanese.

¶ Books **are counted** *issatsu*, *nisatsu*, and so on in Japanese.

kazoku 家族〘名〙

家族制度 (*kazoku*-seido) 大家族 (dai*kazoku*) 核家族 (kaku*kazoku*)

kazoku 〖n〗 **family**

the **family** system // an extended **family** // a nuclear **family**

¶御家族の皆さんはお元気ですか。
(Go*kazoku* no minasan wa ogenki
desu ka?)

¶ How is **your family?**

¶夏休みには家族そろって旅行するつ
もりです。　(Natsuyasumi ni wa
kazoku sorotte ryokō suru tsumori
desu.)

¶ I plan to take a trip with the whole
family during summer vacation.

kazu 数〖名〗

kazu 〚n〛　number

数を数える (*kazu* o kazoeru)

to count

¶自動車の数が年ごとに増えています。
(Jidōsha no *kazu* ga toshigoto ni
fuete imasu.)

¶ **The number** of cars on the roads
increases each year.

¶数多くの人がその意見に賛成してい
ます。(*Kazu* ooku no hito ga sono
iken ni sansei shite imasu.)

¶ **A great many** people have expressed their agreement with that
view.

ke 毛〖名〗

ke 〚n〛　hair, feather, fur; wool

①〔動物の体や頭などに生える細かい
糸のような物〕

① [hair, feather, fur, down]

髪の毛 (kamino*ke*)　毛が生える (*ke*
ga haeru)　毛が抜ける (*ke* ga nukeru)　毛深い (*ke*bukai)

(human) **hair** // **hair** grows in // **hair**
falls out, lose **one's hair** // be **hairy**

¶このブラシは豚の毛でできています。
(Kono burashi wa buta no *ke* de
dekite imasu.)

¶ This brush is made from hog **bris-
tles.**

②〔織物などの原料としての羊毛，ま
たそれで作ったもの〕

② [wool]

毛織物 (*ke*orimono)　　毛糸 (*ke*ito)

woolen cloth, **woolen** goods //
woolen yarn, knitting yarn

¶毛のシャツはとても暖かいです。
(*Ke* no shatsu wa totemo atatakai
desu.)

¶ **Wool** shirts are very warm.

kechi けち〖形動〗

kechi 〚adj-v〛　stingy, miserly

¶あの人はけちだから，お金を貸して
くれないと思います。(Ano hito wa
kechi da kara, okane o kashite

¶ I don't think [he] will loan [us] any
money because [he]'s **so stingy.**

kurenai to omoimasu.)

¶人間は，お金がたまるとますますけ
ちになると言われています。(Ningen
wa, okane ga tamaru to masumasu *kechi* ni naru to iwarete
imasu.)

kega けが〖名，〜する〗
けが人 (*kega*nin)　大けが (ookega)
¶転んで足にけがをしました。
(Koronde ashi ni *kega* o shimashita.)
¶彼はけがが原因で死にました。
(Kare wa *kega* ga gen'in de shini-
mashita.)

-kei -系〖尾〗
文科系 (bunka*kei*)　理科系 (rika*kei*)
太陽系 (taiyō*kei*)　日系人 (nik*kei*-
jin)

keiei 経営〖名，〜する〗
経営者 (*keiei*sha)　個人経営 (kojin-
keiei)　多角経営 (takaku*keiei*)　経
営学 (*keiei*gaku)
¶この町には中国人経営のレストラン
が3軒あります。　(Kono machi ni
wa Chūgokujin *keiei* no resutoran
ga sangen arimasu.)
¶上田さんはホテルを経営しています。
(Ueda san wa hoteru o *keiei* shite
imasu.)

keikaku 計画〖名，〜する〗
計画経済 (*keikaku*-keizai)　計画者
(*keikaku*sha)　都市計画 (toshi-*keikaku*)
¶政府は経済5か年計画を立てました。

¶ It's said that people become **stin-
gier** the more money they have.

kedo ☞ **keredomo**

kega 〖n, ~*suru*〗　**injury, wound**
an **injured** person, the wounded // a
serious **injury**
¶ [I] fell and **hurt** [my] leg 〖foot〗.
¶ He died of **his wound(s)**.

-kei 〖suf〗　**system; descent; fac-
tion, clique**
of 〖a graduate of〗 the department of
liberal arts // of 〖a graduate of〗 the
science department // the solar **system** // a person of Japanese **descent**
(and born outside of Japan)

keiei 〖n, ~*suru*〗　**management,
administration, operation**
a **manager, executive, operator,
proprietor** // private **management**
// multiple **operation** // business
administration
¶ There are three restaurants under
Chinese **management** in this town.
¶ [Mr.] Ueda **runs** a hotel.

keikaku 〖n, ~*suru*〗　**plan, project,
scheme**
a **planned** economy // **a promoter,
planner** // city **planning**
¶ The government drew up a five-

(Seifu wa keizai gokanen *keikaku* o tatemashita.)

¶研究は計画どおりに進んでいます。 (Kenkyū wa *keikaku* doori ni susunde imasu.)

¶この犯罪は計画的に行われたようですね。 (Kono hanzai wa *keikaku*teki ni okonawareta yō desu ne.)

keikan 警官〖名〗
婦人警官 (fujin-*keikan*) 警官隊 (*keikan*tai)

¶どろぼうは警官に捕まりました。 (Dorobō wa *keikan* ni tsukamarimashita.)

¶道がわからないときは警官に尋ねます。 (Michi ga wakaranai toki wa *keikan* ni tazunemasu.)

⇒omawarisan お巡りさん

keiken 経験〖名, ～する〗
経験がある (*keiken* ga aru) 経験がない (*keiken* ga nai) 経験が深い (*keiken* ga fukai) 経験を積む (*keiken* o tsumu)

¶わたしはまだ日本で生活した経験はありません。 (Watashi wa mada Nihon de seikatsu shita *keiken* wa arimasen.)

¶わたしは外国に行った時、言葉がわからなくてつらい経験をしました。 (Watashi wa gaikoku ni itta toki, kotoba ga wakaranakute tsurai *keiken* o shimashita.)

keikō 傾向〖名〗
¶都市の人口は次第に増える傾向にあ

year economic **plan.**

¶ Research is proceeding according to **plan** ⟦**schedule**⟧.

¶ It appears that this was a **premeditated** crime.

keikan ⟦n⟧ police officer, policeman, the police
policewoman // **police** force ⟦squad⟧

¶ The thief was caught by **the police.**

¶ [I] ask **a policeman** when [I] don't know the way.

keiken ⟦n, ~*suru*⟧ experience
have **experience,** be experienced // have no **experience,** be inexperienced // have much ⟦extensive⟧ **experience** // gain **experience,** add to **one's experience**

¶ I don't yet have **any experience** of life in Japan.

¶ Not knowing the language(s), I had painful **experiences** when I went abroad.

keikō ⟦n⟧ tendency, inclination
¶ There is **a tendency** for the

ります。(Toshi no jinkō wa shidai ni fueru *keikō* ni arimasu.)

¶あの人は何でも大げさに言う傾向があります。(Ano hito wa nan demo oogesa ni iu *keikō* ga arimasu.)

keikōtō　けい光燈〖名〗

¶最近では，どの家庭でもけい光燈を使っています。(Saikin de wa, dono katei demo *keikōtō* o tsukatte imasu.)

keisan　計算〖名，～する〗

計算が合う (*keisan* ga au)　計算を間違える (*keisan* o machigaeru)　計算が早い (*keisan* ga hayai)

¶山田さんはこんな易しい計算もできません。 (Yamada san wa konna yasashii *keisan* mo dekimasen.)

¶一か月の食費がどのくらいになるか計算してください。 (Ikkagetsu no shokuhi ga dono kurai ni naru ka *keisan* shite kudasai.)

keisatsu　警察〖名〗

警察官 (*keisatsu*kan)　警察署 (*keisatsu*sho)　警察犬 (*keisatsu*ken)

¶お金を拾ったので，警察に届けました。(Okane o hirotta node, *keisatsu* ni todokemashita.)

keishiki　形式〖名〗

①〔ものごとを行うときの一定の型〕

¶この小説は手紙の形式で書かれています。 (Kono shōsetsu wa tegami no *keishiki* de kakarete imasu.)

②〔ものごとの内容の伴わない表面的なあり方〕

population of cities to gradually increase.

¶ [He] **tends** to exaggerate everything.

keikōtō 〘n〙 a fluorescent light

¶ Recently all households have come to use **fluorescent lights.**

keisan 〘n, ~*suru*〙 calculation, computation, accounts

the figures add up, **the figures** prove to be correct // miscalculate, do **a sum** wrong // be quick at **figures**

¶ [Mr.] Yamada can't do even a simple **calculation** like this one.

¶ Please **calculate** how much one month's food expenses come to.

keisatsu 〘n〙 the police

a **police** officer // a **police** station // a **police** dog

¶ [I] found some money and turned it over to **the police.**

keishiki 〘n〙 form, formalities; external form

① [form, formalities]

¶ This novel is written in **the form** of a series of letters.

② [external form]

形式的 (*keishiki*teki)

¶形式よりも内容が大切です。 (*Keishiki* yori mo naiyō ga taisetsu desu.)

keito 毛糸〖名〗

¶毛糸で編んだくつ下は暖かいですね。(*Keito* de anda kutsushita wa atatakai desu ne.)

keiyaku 契約〖名, ～する〗

契約書 (*keiyaku*sho) 契約を結ぶ

(*keiyaku* o musubu) 契約を守る

(*keiyaku* o mamoru) 契約を破る

(*keiyaku* o yaburu)

¶一か月二万円で家を借りる契約をしました。(Ikkagetsu niman'en de ie o kariru *keiyaku* o shimashita.)

¶来年の３月で契約が切れます。(Rainen no sangatsu de *keiyaku* ga kiremasu.)

keizai 経済〖名〗

①〔社会生活に必要なものを生産したり分配したり消費したりする活動〕

¶第二次大戦後, 日本の経済は大きく発展しました。 (Dainiji-taisengo, Nihon no *keizai* wa ookiku hatten shimashita.)

②〔お金のやりくり, 財政状態〕

¶田中さんは今仕事がないので, 経済的に苦しいようです。(Tanaka san wa ima shigoto ga nai node, *keizai*teki ni kurushii yō desu.)

③〔お金などがあまりかからないこと〕

¶タクシーよりも電車のほうが経済的です。 (Takushii yori mo densha

formal, a matter of **form**

¶ Content is more important than **external form** 〖Substance is more important than **form**〗.

keito 〖n〗 woolen yarn, knitting wool

¶ Knitted **wool** socks are warm, aren't they?

keiyaku 〖n, ～*suru*〗 contract, agreement

a (written) **contract** // conclude a **contract** // abide by **a contract** // break **a contract**

¶ [I] signed **a contract** to rent a house for twenty thousand yen a month.

¶ **The contract** expires in March of next year.

keizai 〖n〗 economy, economics; finance; saving, economy

① [economy, economics]

¶ Japan's **economy** made great strides after World War II.

② [finance]

¶ As [Mr.] Tanaka is presently out of work, it seems [he]'s having a hard time **financially**.

③ [saving, economy]

¶ The train is more **economical** than a taxi.

no hō ga *keizai*teki desu.)

kekka 結果〘名〙

¶試験の結果はいつ発表されますか。
(Shiken no *kekka* wa itsu happyō
saremasu ka?)

¶長い間努力した結果，ついに実験に
成功しました。(Nagai aida doryoku
shita *kekka*, tsuini jikken ni seikō
shimashita.)

⇔gen'in 原因

kekkō けっこう〘副，形動〙

1〘副〙

¶このカメラは古いが，けっこうよく
撮れます。(Kono kamera wa furui
ga, *kekkō* yoku toremasu.)

2〘形動〙

①[よい，立派だ]

¶けっこうな贈り物をありがとうござ
いました。(*Kekkō* na okurimono o
arigatō gozaimashita.)

②[じゅうぶんだ]

¶「お茶をもう一杯いかがですか。」
(Ocha o mō ippai ikaga desu ka?)
「もう，けっこうです。」(Mō *kekkō*
desu.)

kekkon 結婚〘名，〜する〙

結婚式 (*kekkon*shiki)　結婚生活 (*kekkon*-seikatsu)　結婚届 (*kekkon*-
todoke)　国際結婚 (kokusai*kekkon*)

¶上田さんは秋子さんに結婚を申し込
みました。(Ueda san wa Akiko san
ni *kekkon* o mōshikomimashita.)

¶上田さんと秋子さんは来月結婚しま
す。(Ueda san to Akiko san wa

kekka 〚n〛 **result, outcome**

¶ When will **the results** of the exam
be annouced?

¶ Long-term efforts at last **resulted**
in the success of the experiment.

kekkō 〚adv, adj-v〛 **quite, fairly
well; good, fine; well enough, fine
as is**

1 〚adv〛 quite, fairly well

¶ This camera is old but works **quite**
well.

2 〚adj-v〛

① [good, fine, nice, excellent]

¶ Thank you for the **lovely** present.

② [well enough, fine as is]

¶ "Would you like another cup of
(green) tea?"

"No, this is **fine** 〚No, thank you〛."

kekkon 〚n, ~*suru*〛 **marriage**

a **marriage** ceremony, wedding //
married life // registration of **one's
marriage** // **marriage** between those
of different nationalities

¶ Mr. Ueda **proposed** to Akiko.

¶ Mr. Ueda and Akiko **are going to
get married** next month.

raigetsu *kekkon* shimasu.)

¶御結婚おめでとうございます。

(Go*kekkon* omedetō gozaimasu.)

kekkyoku 結局〚副〛

¶いろいろ話し合いましたが，結局いい考えは出てきませんでした。(Iroiro hanashiaimashita ga, *kekkyoku* ii kangae wa dete kimasen deshita.)

¶このフットボールの試合は，結局Aチームが勝ちました。(Kono futtobōru no shiai wa, *kekkyoku* Ē-chiimu ga kachimashita.)

kemono 獣〚名〛

¶あの森にはいろいろな獣がいます。

(Ano mori ni wa iroiro na *kemono* ga imasu.)

kemuri 煙〚名〛

たばこの煙 (tabako no *kemuri*)

¶工場の煙突から煙が出ています。

(Kōjō no entotsu kara *kemuri* ga dete imasu.)

ken 券〚名〛

乗車券 (jōsha*ken*) 定期券 (teiki*ken*) 急行券 (kyūkō*ken*) 入場券 (nyūjō*ken*) 前売り券 (maeuri*ken*) 診察券 (shinsatsu*ken*) 招待券 (shōtai*ken*) 割引券 (waribiki*ken*) 食券 (shok*ken*) 旅券 (ryo*ken*) 株券 (kabu*ken*)

¶券を買わなければ入場できません。

(*Ken* o kawanakereba nyūjō dekimasen.)

¶音楽会の券が2枚ありますから，いっしょに行きませんか。(Ongakkai no

¶ Congratulations on **your marriage.**

kekkyoku 〚adv〛 **finally, ultimately, in the end**

¶ We talked about various possibilities but **in the end** had no good ideas.

¶ **Ultimately** Team A won this football 〚soccer〛 match.

kemono 〚n〛 **beast, animal, wild animal**

¶ There are various **wild animals** in that forest.

kemuri 〚n〛 **smoke, fumes**

cigarette **smoke,** tobacco **fumes**

¶ **Smoke** is being emitted from the factory smokestack(s).

ken 〚n〛 **ticket, coupon, bond**

a passenger **ticket** // a commuting **pass,** season **pass** // an express **ticket** // an admission **ticket,** platform **ticket** // an advance **ticket** // a clinic registration **card** // a complimentary **ticket,** invitation **card** (for an exhibition, etc.) // a discount **coupon** // a meal **ticket,** food **coupon** // a passport // a stock **certificate**

¶ You cannot enter without **a ticket.**

¶ I have two **tickets** to a concert 〚recital〛. Won't you come with me?

ken ga nimai arimasu kara, issho
ni ikimasen ka?)

ken 県〖名〗
広島県 (Hiroshima-*ken*) 県庁 (*ken-*
chō) 県知事 (*ken*chiji)

-ken -軒〖尾〗
1軒 (ik*ken*) 3軒 (san*gen*) 6軒
(rok*ken*) 8軒 (hak*ken*) 何軒
(nan*gen*)
¶川の向こうに家が二, 三軒見えます。
(Kawa no mukō ni ie ga ni-san*gen*
miemasu.)

kenbutsu 見物〖名, 〜する〗
¶来週, わたしたちは京都見物に行き
ます。 (Raishū, watashitachi wa
Kyōto-*kenbutsu* ni ikimasu.)
¶今晩, 歌舞伎を見物するつもりです。
(Konban, kabuki o *kenbutsu* suru
tsumori desu.)

kenchiku 建築〖名, 〜する〗
建築家 (*kenchiku*ka) 建築様式
(*kenchiku*-yōshiki) 建築材料 (*ken-*
chiku-zairyō) 建築工事 (*kenchiku-*
kōji) 建築技術 (*kenchiku*-gijutsu)
建築学 (*kenchiku*gaku) 木造建築
(mokuzō-*kenchiku*) コンクリート建
築 (konkuriito-*kenchiku*)
¶古い時代の日本の建築は たいへん美
しいです。 (Furui jidai no Nihon no
kenchiku wa taihen utsukushii
desu.)
¶このお寺は百年前に建築されたそう
です。 (Kono otera wa hyakunen
mae ni *kenchiku* sareta sō desu.)

ken 〚n〛 **prefecture**
Hiroshima **Prefecture** // **prefectural**
office // **prefectural** governor

-ken 〚suf〛 the counter for houses
one **house** // three **houses** // six
houses // eight **houses** // how
many **houses**
¶ Two or three **houses** can be seen
on the other side of the river.

kenbutsu 〚n, ~*suru*〛 **sightseeing,
visit**
¶ We are going to go **see the sights**
in Kyoto next week.

¶ I plan to **go see** *kabuki* tonight.

kenchiku 〚n, ~*suru*〛 **construction,
building, architecture**
an architect // style of **building,
architectural** style // **construction**
materials // **construction** work //
construction techniques // **architecture** // a wooden **building** // a
concrete **building**

¶ Ancient Japanese **architecture** is
〚Ancient Japanese **buildings** are〛
very beautiful.

¶ This temple is said to **have been
constructed** a hundred years ago.

kengaku 見学〖名, 〜する〗

見学旅行 (*kengaku*-ryokō)

¶学校から工場見学に行きました。

(Gakkō kara kōjō-*kengaku* ni iki-mashita.)

kenka けんか〖名, 〜する〗

兄弟げんか (kyōdai-*genka*)　夫婦げんか (fūfu-*genka*)

¶子供たちがけんかをしています。

(Kodomotachi ga *kenka* o shite imasu.)

¶わたしは上田さんとけんかしてしまいました。(Watashi wa Ueda san to *kenka* shite shimaimashita.)

kenkō 健康〖名, 形動〗

健康診断 (*kenkō*-shindan)　健康状態 (*kenkō*-jōtai)　健康保険 (*kenkō*-ho-ken)　健康を害する (*kenkō* o gai-suru)

¶健康にじゅうぶん注意してください。

(*Kenkō* ni jūbun chūi shite kuda-sai.)

¶たばこの吸いすぎは健康に悪いです。

(Tabako no suisugi wa *kenkō* ni warui desu.)

¶父はもうすっかり健康を回復しました。(Chichi wa mō sukkari *kenkō* o kaifuku shimashita.)

¶健康な人なら, 一日 30 キロは歩けますよ。(*Kenkō* na hito nara, ichinichi sanjikkiro wa arukemasu yo.)

kenkyū 研究〖名, 〜する〗

研究室 (*kenkyū*shitsu)　研究所 (*kenkyū*jo)　研究会 (*kenkyū*kai)

kengaku 〖n, 〜*suru*〗 study by inspection, field trip

an **inspection** trip, a **study** tour, a **school** trip

¶ [I] went on **a school trip** to a factory.

kenka 〖n, 〜*suru*〗 quarrel, argument, fight, coming to blows

a quarrel between brothers // **a quarrel** between husband and wife, domestic **strife**

¶ The children **are arguing** ⟦**fighting**⟧.

¶ I **quarreled** ⟦**had a fight**⟧ with [Mrs.] Ueda.

kenkō 〖n, adj-v〗 health

a **physical** checkup, a **medical** examination // the condition of **one's health** // **health** insurance // injure **one's health**

¶ Please take good care **of yourself.**

¶ Smoking too much is bad for **one's health.**

¶ My father is completely **recovered** now.

¶ A person **in good health** should be able to walk 30 kilometers in one day.

kenkyū 〖n, 〜*suru*〗 study, research, investigation

a study, office, laboratory // a re-

研究費 (*kenkyū*hi)　研究活動 (*kenkyū*-katsudō)

¶最近，わたしたちの国でも日本研究が盛んになってきました。　(Saikin, watashitachi no kuni de mo Nihon-*kenkyū* ga sakan ni natte kimashita.)

¶あなたは日本で何を研究するつもりですか。(Anata wa Nihon de nani o *kenkyū* suru tsumori desu ka?)

kenpō　憲法〖名〗

憲法を制定する (*kenpō* o seitei suru)　憲法を改正する (*kenpō* o kaisei suru)

¶5月3日は日本の憲法記念日です。(Gogatsu mikka wa Nihon no *kenpō*-kinenbi desu.)

kenri　権利〖名〗

¶第二次大戦後，女性にも男性と同じ権利が与えられました。(Dainiji-taisengo, josei ni mo dansei to onaji *kenri* ga ataeraremashita.)

¶国民は教育を受ける権利と義務があります。(Kokumin wa kyōiku o ukeru *kenri* to gimu ga arimasu.)
⇔gimu　義務

kensa　検査〖名，〜する〗

検査を受ける (*kensa* o ukeru)　身体検査 (shintai-*kensa*)

¶この機械は検査に合格しています。(Kono kikai wa *kensa* ni gōkaku shite imasu.)

¶わたしは空港で荷物を厳しく検査されました。(Watashi wa kūkō de

search laboratory, **research** institute // a **study** group, society for the **study** of a certain subject // **research** funds, **research** expenses // **research** activities

¶ Recently **the study** of Japan has become popular in our country.

¶ What do you plan **to study** in Japan?

kenpō 〖n〗 a constitution

establish **a constitution** // revise **a constitution**

¶ The third of May is **Constitution** Day in Japan.

kenri 〖n〗 a right, a claim

¶ After World War II women were granted the same **rights** as men.

¶ Citizens have **the right** and obligation of receiving an education.

kensa 〖n, ~*suru*〗 inspection, examination, test

be **examined** // a physical **examination**, a checkup, a physical

¶ This machine has passed **inspection**.

¶ My bags were subjected to a rigorous **inspection** at the airport.

nimotsu o kibishiku *kensa* saremashita.)

kensetsu 建設〖名，〜する〗
建設工事 (*kensetsu*-kōji)　建設費
(*kensetsu*hi)　建設会社 (*kensetsu*-
gaisha)
¶政府は高速道路の建設を計画してい
ます。　(Seifu wa kōsoku-dōro no
kensetsu o keikaku shite imasu.)
¶今年じゅうに10万戸の住宅を建設
する予定です。(Kotoshijū ni jūman-
ko no jūtaku o *kensetsu* suru yotei
desu.)

kenshū 研修〖名，〜する〗
研修生 (*kenshū*sei)　研修所 (*kenshū*jo)　研修期間 (*kenshū*-kikan)
¶あしたから技術研修が始まります。
(Ashita kara gijutsu-*kenshū* ga
hajimarimasu.)
¶学校を卒業して，すぐ工場で研修
するつもりです。(Gakkō o sotsugyō
shite, sugu kōjō de *kenshū* suru
tsumori desu.)

keredomo けれども〖助〗
①[前件から当然予想される結果が後
件において成立しないという関係を表
す]
¶やっと家を建てたのですけれども，ま
た引っ越さなければならなくなりまし
た。　(Yatto ie o tateta no desu
keredomo, mata hikkosanakereba
naranaku narimashita.)
¶一生懸命勉強したけれども，試験
には受かりませんでした。(Isshōken-

kensetsu 〚n, 〜*suru*〛 **construction,
erection, building, establishment
construction** work // the cost of
construction, construction expenses // a **construction** firm
¶ The government is planning **the
construction** of an expressway.

¶ One hundred thousand houses are
scheduled **to be built** before the year
is out.

kenshū 〚n, 〜*suru*〛 **training, study
and training, on-the-job training
a trainee** // an **in-service training**
institute // a term of **training**
¶ Technical **training** starts from
tomorrow.

¶ I plan to enter **on-the-job training**
at a factory soon after graduating
from school.

keredomo 〚part〛 **but, although;
however, nevertheless**
① [but, although, even though; indicates the disappointment in the
second clause of what would be expected as a natural result of the first
clause]
¶ [We] were finally able to build a
house, **but** then [we] had to move
again.
¶ **Although** I studied very hard, I

mei benkyō shita *keredomo*, shiken ni wa ukarimasen deshita.)

②[前件が後件に対して対比的・対立的な関係にあることを表す]

¶車を買いたい**けれども**，お金がないので買えません。 (Kuruma o kaitai *keredomo*, okane ga nai node kaemasen.)

¶わたしは田中さんを知っています**けれども**，田中さんはわたしを知らないでしょう。 (Watashi wa Tanaka san o shitte imasu *keredomo*, Tanaka san wa watashi o shiranai deshō.)

③[前件が後件に対する前置きなどの関係にあることを表す]

¶もしもし，上田です**けれども**，田中さんはいらっしゃいますか。

(Moshi moshi, Ueda desu *keredomo*, Tanaka san wa irasshaimasu ka?)

¶すみません**けれど**，上田さんのお宅はどの辺でしょうか。 (Sumimasen *keredo*, Ueda san no otaku wa dono hen deshō ka?)

¶時計を買いたいのです**けれど**，どこの店で買ったらいいでしょうか。

(Tokei o kaitai no desu *keredo*, doko no mise de kattara ii deshō ka?)

¶バスで行こうと思いました**けれども**，あまり天気がいいので，歩いていくことにしました。 (Basu de ikō to omoimashita *keredomo*, amari tenki ga ii node, aruite iku koto ni shi-

failed the exam.

② [but, however, nevertheless; indicates that the first clause is in contrast or opposition to the second clause]

¶ I want to buy a car **but** can't because I don't have the money.

¶ I know [Miss] Tanaka. **However,** [Miss] Tanaka probably doesn't know me.

③ [but, and; indicates the first clause introduces the second one]

¶ Hello, this [Mr.] Ueda. Is [Mr.] Tanaka there?

¶ Excuse me. Whereabouts is the Ueda residence?

¶ I want to buy a watch 〚clock〛. Where is a good store to buy it?

¶ I thought I would go by bus, **but** it was such a nice day that I decided to walk instead.

mashita.)

④[前件のことがらが後件のことがらに対して共存的な関係にあることを表す]

¶わたしはテレビも欲しいけれど, ラジオもやはり欲しいです。(Watashi wa terebi mo hoshii *keredo*, rajio mo yahari hoshii desu.)

¶北海道へも行きたいけれど, 沖縄へも行ってみたいです。 (Hokkaidō e mo ikitai *keredo*, Okinawa e mo itte mitai desu.)

＊「けれど (keredo)」「けども (kedomo)」「けど (kedo)」とも言う。

⇨ga が

keredomo けれども〖助〗

①[ものごとをはっきり断定的に言うのを避けて柔らかく言い相手の反応を待つ気持ちを表す]

¶あなたがどういう意味でおっしゃっているのかわからないんですけれども。 (Anata ga dōiu imi de osshatte iru no ka wakaranai n desu *keredomo*.)

¶あの方のお名前が思い出せないんですけれども。 (Ano kata no onamae ga omoidasenai n desu *keredomo*.)

②[望ましいことがらの成立を願う気持ちや実現しなかったことがらを回想してそれが成立していればどんなによかったかというような気持ちを表す]

¶父が生きていたら, 大学へも行けたんですけれども。 (Chichi ga ikite itara, daigaku e mo iketa n desu *keredomo*.)

④ [but, however; indicates the coexistence of the first and second clauses]

¶ I want a television **but** I also want a radio.

¶ I want to go to Hokkaido **but** I'd also like to go to Okinawa.

＊ Variants: *keredo*, *kedomo*, and *kedo*.

keredomo 〖part〗 **but**

① [but; employed to soften one's speech and avoid saying something directly and conclusively and also to indicate that one is awaiting the listener's response]

¶ I'm not sure what you mean by that... (omitted: please make it clearer, etc.).

¶ I can't remember that person's name... (omitted: could you tell me what it is?).

② [but; used to express the wish that something could happen or to express how nice it would have been if something could have been realized]

¶ If my father had lived I could have gone to college... (omitted: **but** he died and I couldn't).

kesa

¶試験に合格していればいいのですけれども。 (Shiken ni gōkaku shite ireba ii no desu *keredomo*.)

＊「けれど (keredo)」「けども (kedomo)」「けど (kedo)」とも言う。

⇨ga が

keredomo けれども〖接〗

¶わたしは田中さんを知っています。けれども、田中さんはわたしを知らないでしょう。 (Watashi wa Tanaka san o shitte imasu. *Keredomo*, Tanaka san wa watashi o shiranai deshō.)

¶わたしは大学へ行きたいんです。けれども、お金がないんです。 (Watashi wa daigaku e ikitai n desu. *Keredomo*, okane ga nai n desu.)

＊ 前のことがらを受けて、それから予想される結果に合わないことや対比的・対立的なことなどをあとに言うときに使う。「けれど (keredo)」「けども (kedomo)」「けど (kedo)」とも言う。

⇨shikashi しかし

keru ける〖動Ⅰ〗

¶ボールをけって遊びましょう。 (Bōru o *kette* asobimashō.)

¶上田さんは馬にけられて、けがをしました。 (Ueda san wa uma ni *kerarete*, kega o shimashita.)

kesa 今朝〖名〗

¶わたしは今朝6時に起きました。 (Watashi wa *kesa* rokuji ni okimashita.)

¶ [I] hope [I] passed the exam (omitted: **but** I'm not sure I did).

＊ Variants: *keredo*, *kedomo*, and *kedo*.

keredomo 〖conj〗 **however, but**

¶ I know [Mr.] Tanaka. **However,** [Mr.] Tanaka probably doesn't know me.

¶ I want to go to college. **However,** I don't have the money for it.

＊ *Keredomo* is used when the second sentence doesn't agree with what would be expected to follow the first sentence or when it is in contrast or opposition to it. Variants are *keredo*, *kedomo*, and *kedo*.

keru 〖v Ⅰ〗 **kick**

¶ Let's play **kicking** the ball.

¶ [Mr.] Ueda was injured when [he] **was kicked** by a horse.

kesa 〖n〗 **this morning**

¶ I got up at six o'clock **this morning.**

keshigomu 消しゴム〖名〗

¶間違えた字を消しゴムで消しました。
(Machigaeta ji o *keshigomu* de keshimashita.)

keshiki 景色〖名〗

¶北海道には景色のいい所がたくさんあります。(Hokkaidō ni wa *keshiki* no ii tokoro ga takusan arimasu.)

¶ここから見る富士山の景色は本当にすばらしいです。(Koko kara miru Fujisan no *keshiki* wa hontō ni subarashii desu.)

keshō 化粧〖名, ～する〗

化粧品 (*keshō*hin)

¶姉は今お化粧をしています。(Ane wa ima o*keshō* o shite imasu.)

¶あの人は化粧しなくてもきれいです。(Ano hito wa *keshō* shinakute mo kirei desu.)

kesseki 欠席〖名, ～する〗

欠席者 (*kesseki*sha) 欠席届 (*kesseki*todoke)

¶試験が終わると，急に欠席者が多くなります。(Shiken ga owaru to, kyū ni *kesseki*sha ga ooku narimasu.)

¶上田さんは病気で今日は欠席です。(Ueda san wa byōki de kyō wa *kesseki* desu.)

¶急用ができましたので，今日の会議は欠席します。(Kyūyō ga dekimashita node, kyō no kaigi wa *kesseki* shimasu.)

⇔shusseki 出席

keshigomu 〖n〗 (rubber) **eraser**

¶ [I] erased the mistaken letter with **an eraser.**

keshiki 〖n〗 **scenery, view**

¶ There is much beautiful **scenery** in Hokkaido.

¶ **The view** of Mount Fuji from here is really wonderful.

keshō 〖n, ～*suru*〗 **makeup,** (one's) **toiletry**

cosmetics

¶ My (elder) sister is now putting on **her makeup.**

¶ She is beautiful even without **makeup.**

kesseki 〖n, ～*suru*〗 **absence, non-attendance**

an absentee // a report of **absence**

¶ After exams are over, the number of students **missing class** suddenly goes up.

¶ [Miss] Ueda **is absent** today due to illness.

¶ As some urgent business has arisen, [I] **will be absent** from today's meeting.

kesshin 決心〖名, 〜する〗

¶わたしは今日からたばこをやめる決心をしました。 (Watashi wa kyō kara tabako o yameru *kesshin* o shimashita.)

¶行こうかどうしようか，まだ決心がつきません。 (Ikō ka dō shiyō ka, mada *kesshin* ga tsukimasen.)

kesshin 〖n, 〜*suru*〗 **determination, resolution**

¶ I **have resolved** to quit smoking from today on.

¶ [I] haven't **made up my mind** yet whether to go or not.

kesshite 決して〖副〗

¶御親切は決して忘れません。 (Go-shinsetsu wa *kesshite* wasuremasen.)

¶その問題の解決は決して簡単ではありません。 (Sono mondai no kaiketsu wa *kesshite* kantan de wa arimasen.)

＊ あとに打ち消しの言葉が来る。

kesshite 〖adv〗 **never, by no means**

¶ I will **never** forget your kindness.

¶ Solving that problem will **by no means** be easy.

＊ *Kesshite* is used with the negative.

kesu 消す〖動 I〗

①［明かりや火などをなくす］

火を消す (hi o *kesu*)

¶ゆうべは電気を消さないで寝てしまいました。 (Yūbe wa denki o *kesanaide* nete shimaimashita.)

②［スイッチを切って音などをなくす］

ラジオを消す (rajio o *kesu*)

¶見ないときは，テレビを消しなさい。 (Minai toki wa, terebi o *keshinasai*.)

③［物の形などを見えなくする］

¶黒板の字を消してください。 (Kokuban no ji o *keshite* kudasai.)

¶間違ったところを消しゴムで消して書き直しました。(Machigatta tokoro o keshigomu de *keshite* kakinaoshimashita.)

kesu 〖v I〗 **put out, extinguish; turn off; erase; disappear, vanish**

① [put out, extinguish (lights, fire, etc.)]

put out a fire

¶ [I] fell asleep last night **without turning off** the lights.

② [turn off (a switch, etc.)]

turn off the radio

¶ **Turn off** the television when you are not watching it.

③ [erase, rub out, delete]

¶ Please **erase** the words on the blackboard.

¶ I corrected it, **erasing** the mistaken parts with an eraser.

④〔姿などが見られなくなる〕
¶この動物は昔はたくさんいたんですが、最近はすっかり姿を消してしまいました。(Kono dōbutsu wa mukashi wa takusan ita n desu ga, saikin wa sukkari sugata o *keshite* shimaimashita.)

ketsuron 結論〖名〗
¶何回も話し合いましたが、なかなか結論が出ませんでした。(Nankai mo hanashiaimashita ga, nakanaka *ketsuron* ga demasen deshita.)
¶この工事を今年じゅうに完成するのは無理だという結論に達しました。(Kono kōji o kotoshijū ni kansei suru no wa muri da to iu *ketsuron* ni tasshimashita.)

kettei 決定〖名, 〜する〗
¶わたしは皆さんの決定に従います。(Watashi wa minasan no *kettei* ni shitagaimasu.)
¶出発の日はもう決定しましたか。(Shuppatsu no hi wa mō *kettei* shimashita ka?)

ketten 欠点〖名〗
¶上田さんの欠点は約束を守らないことです。(Ueda san no *ketten* wa yakusoku o mamoranai koto desu.)
¶このレストランは、料理はおいしいのですが、いつもこんでいるのが欠点です。(Kono resutoran wa, ryōri wa oishii no desu ga, itsu mo konde iru no ga *ketten* desu.)
⇨tansho 短所

ketsuron 〖n〗 conclusion
¶ [We] talked together many times but couldn't arrive at **any conclusion**.
¶ [They] came to **the conclusion** that it was impossible to complete this construction work before the end of the year.

kettei 〖n, ~*suru*〗 a decision, a determination, a conclusion
¶ I will abide by **the decision** of all.
¶ **Have you set** the departure date yet?

ketten 〖n〗 fault, defect, flaw, weak point
¶ [Mr.] Ueda's **major weak point** is not keeping [his] promises.
¶ The food is good at this restaurant, but its always being crowded is **a drawback**.

④ [disappear, vanish]
¶ This animal was plentiful in the past but recently has completely **disappeared**.

kezuru 削る〖動Ⅰ〗

①[物の表面を薄くそぎとる]
¶ナイフで鉛筆を削ります。 (Naifu de enpitsu o *kezurimasu.*)

②[必要でない部分を取り除く]
¶余分なところを削って，文章を短くしました。 (Yobun na tokoro o *kezutte*, bunshō o mijikaku shimashita.)

ki 木〖名〗

¶庭に桜の木を植えました。 (Niwa ni sakura no *ki* o uemashita.)
¶都会には木が少ないです。 (Tokai ni wa *ki* ga sukunai desu.)
¶日本には木でできた家が多いです。 (Nihon ni wa *ki* de dekita ie ga ooi desu.)

ki 気〖名〗

①[注意する]
¶病気にならないように気をつけてください。 (Byōki ni naranai yō ni *ki* o tsukete kudasai.)
¶気をつけないと，自動車にひかれますよ。 (*Ki* o tsukenai to, jidōsha ni hikaremasu yo.)
* いつも「気をつける (ki o tsukeru)」「気をつけない (ki o tsukenai)」の形で使う。

②[あることがらを意識するようになる]
¶電車を降りてから，かばんがないのに気がつきました。 (Densha o orite kara, kaban ga nai no ni *ki* ga tsukimashita.)

kezuru 〖vⅠ〗 shave, sharpen, whittle; cut down, reduce

① [shave, sharpen, whittle; remove the surface of an object]
¶ One **sharpens** a pencil with a knife.

② [cut down, reduce, cross out, delete; remove an unnecessary part]
¶ [I] shortened the text by **taking out** the unnecessary parts.

ki 〖n〗 tree, shrub, wood

¶ [I] planted a cherry **tree** in the garden 〖yard〗.
¶ There are few **trees** 〖is little **foliage**〗 in the city.
¶ There are many houses made of **wood** in Japan.

ki 〖n〗 spirit, mood, feeling, mind

① [be careful, take care, pay attention to]
¶ Please **take care** not to become ill.

¶ **Look out** or you will be hit by a car!

* Always used in the patterns "*ki o tsukeru*" and "*ki o tsukenai*."

② [notice, become aware of, perceive]
¶ After getting off the train **I noticed** that I didn't have my bag 〖suitcase, briefcase, etc.〗.

¶わたしがあいさつをしたのに，上田さんは気がつきませんでした。
(Watashi ga aisatsu o shita noni, Ueda san wa *ki* ga tsukimasen deshita.)

* いつも「気がつく (ki ga tsuku)」「気がつかない (ki ga tsukanai)」の形で使う。

→kizuku 気づく

③[ものごとに対してある感じを持つ]
¶日本に来てまだ2週間しかたっていませんが，もう2か月もたったような気がします。 (Nihon ni kite mada nishūkan shika tatte imasen ga, mō nikagetsu mo tatta yō na *ki* ga shimasu.)

¶そのうち大きな地震が来そうな気がします。(Sonouchi ookina jishin ga kisō na *ki* ga shimasu.)

¶ここにいると，外国にいるような気がしません。 (Koko ni iru to, gaikoku ni iru yō na *ki* ga shimasen.)

* いつも「気がする (ki ga suru)」「気がしない (ki ga shinai)」の形で使う。

④[あることをいつも考えて心配したり心を煩わしたりする]
¶中村さんは試験の点ばかり気にしています。(Nakamura san wa shiken no ten bakari *ki* ni shite imasu.)

¶お金のことは気にしないで勉強だけしなさい。 (Okane no koto wa *ki* ni shinaide benkyō dake shinasai.)

*いつも「気にする (ki ni suru)」「気

¶ Although I greeted [him], [Mr.] Ueda **didn't notice** me.

* Always used in the patterns "*ki ga tsuku*" and "*ki ga tsukanai.*"

③ [feel, think, have the feeling that ~]

¶ It has only been two weeks since I came to Japan but **it feels like** two months.

¶ **I have the feeling** that a big earthquake is coming one of these days.

¶ When I'm here **I don't feel like** I'm in a foreign country.

* Always used in the patterns "*ki ga suru*" and "*ki ga shinai.*"

④ [mind, be concerned about, worry about]

¶ [Mr.] Nakamura **is** only **concerned** about test marks.

¶ Just study and **don't concern yourself** with money matters.

* Always used in the patterns "*ki ni*

にしない (ki ni shinai)」の形で使う。

⑤［あることが頭から離れないで落ち着かない］

¶試験のことが気になって，眠れませんでした。 (Shiken no koto ga *ki* ni natte, nemuremasen deshita.)

¶隣の部屋の音が気になって勉強できません。 (Tonari no heya no oto ga *ki* ni natte benkyō dekimasen.)

¶わたしは周りがうるさくても気になりません。(Watashi wa mawari ga urusakute mo *ki* ni narimasen.)

¶隣に座った美人が気になって，落ち着いて本が読めませんでした。 (Tonari ni suwatta bijin ga *ki* ni natte, ochitsuite hon ga yomemasen deshita.)

* いつも「気になる (ki ni naru)」「気にならない (ki ni naranai)」の形で使う。

⑥［安全や健康などが心配になる］

¶病気で寝ている母のことがいつも気にかかっています。 (Byōki de nete iru haha no koto ga itsu mo *ki* ni kakatte imasu.)

¶飛行機が予定の時間を過ぎても到着しないので，気にかかります。 (Hikōki ga yotei no jikan o sugite mo tōchaku shinai node, *ki* ni kakarimasu.)

*いつも「気にかかる (ki ni kakaru)」の形で使う。

⑦［満足する，好きになる］

¶この部屋が気に入ったので，借りる

suru" and "*ki ni shinai*."

⑤ [be bothered about, weigh on one's mind, get on one's nerves]

¶ I couldn't sleep for **worrying** about the exam.

¶ **I'm bothered** by the noise ⟦sounds⟧ next door so that I can't study ⟦I can't study with those sounds going on next door⟧.

¶ **It doesn't bother me** if it's noisy around me.

¶ **I was so conscious** of the beautiful woman sitting next to me that I couldn't concentrate on my book.

* Always used in the patterns "*ki ni naru*" and "*ki ni naranai*."

⑥ [worry about, be anxious about]

¶ **I am** always **anxious** about my mother who is ill in bed.

¶ **I am worried** because the plane hasn't arrived yet even though it's past its scheduled time of arrival.

* Always used in the pattern "*ki ni kakaru*."

⑦ [be pleased with, like, take a liking to]

ことにしました。(Kono heya ga *ki* ni itta node, kariru koto ni shimashita.)

¶壁の色が気に入らないので，塗り替えることにしました。(Kabe no iro ga *ki* ni iranai node, nurikaeru koto ni shimashita.)

* いつも「気に入る (ki ni iru)」「気に入らない (ki ni iranai)」の形で使う。

⑧[何かをしようと思う]

¶この会社で働く気があるなら，社長に紹介してあげましょう。(Kono kaisha de hataraku *ki* ga aru nara, shachō ni shōkai shite agemashō.)

¶勉強する気がないのに，大学へ行ってもむだです。(Benkyō suru *ki* ga nai noni, daigaku e itte mo muda desu.)

¶あまり暑いので，仕事をする気がしません。(Amari atsui node, shigoto o suru *ki* ga shimasen.)

¶日本に一度行ってみたい気がします。(Nihon ni ichido itte mitai *ki* ga shimasu.)

* いつも「〜する気がある (〜suru ki ga aru)」「〜する気がない (〜suru ki ga nai)」「〜する気がする (〜suru ki ga suru)」「〜する気がしない (〜suru ki ga shinai)」の形で使う。

-ki -器〖尾〗

①[器具]

食器 (shok*ki*)　洗面器 (senmen*ki*)

電熱器 (dennetsu*ki*)　消火器 (shō-

¶ I've decided to rent this room 〚apartment〛 as **it's to my liking.**

¶ I decided to repaint the walls 〚have the walls repainted〛 as **I don't like** the present color.

* Always used in the patterns "*ki ni iru*" and "*ki ni iranai.*"

⑧ [feel like ~ing, be disposed to]

¶ If you think **you'd like** to work at this company, I'll introduce you to the president.

¶ It's useless to go to college if **you don't want** to study.

¶ **I don't feel like** working as it's so hot.

¶ **I'd like** to go to Japan at least once.

* Always used in the patterns "*~ suru ki ga aru,*" "*~ suru ki ga nai,*" "*~ suru ki ga suru,*" and "*~ suru ki ga shinai.*"

-ki 〖suf〗 utensil, tool, apparatus; bodily organ

① [utensil, tool, apparatus]

table**ware**, a dinner **set** // a wash**basin**, wash**bowl** // an electric hot **plate** // a fire **extinguisher** // a telekaki 受話器 (juwaki) 楽器 (gakki)

②[器官]

消化器 (shōkaki) 呼吸器 (kokyūki)

-ki -機〖尾〗

①[機械]

写真機 (shashinki) 印刷機 (insatsu-ki) 扇風機 (senpūki) 洗たく機 (sentakuki)

②[飛行機]

ジェット機 (jettoki) 旅客機 (ryo-kakki)

③[飛行機などの数を表す]

1機 (ikki) 2機 (niki) 3機 (sanki) 6機 (rokki) 何機 (nanki)

kibishii 厳しい〖形〗

①[厳格な]

¶あの先生はとても厳しいです。(Ano sensei wa totemo *kibishii* desu.)

¶わたしは子供を厳しく育てました。(Watashi wa kodomo o *kibishiku* sodatemashita.)

②[激しい，程度がはなはだしい]

¶二月になってから，寒さが厳しくなりました。(Nigatsu ni natte kara, samusa ga *kibishiku* narimashita.)

kibō 希望〖名，～する〗

¶わたしの希望は，将来医者になることです。(Watashi no *kibō* wa, shōrai isha ni naru koto desu.)

¶あの人は日本留学を希望しています。(Ano hito wa Nihon-ryūgaku o *kibō* shite imasu.)

kibun 気分〖名〗

①[心の状態，気持ち]

phone **receiver** // a musical **instrument**

② [bodily organ]

digestive **organs** // respiratory **organs**

-ki 〚suf〛 **machine; aircraft**

① [machine, mechanism]

a camera // a printing **machine, press** // an electric fan // a washing **machine**

② [aircraft]

a jet **plane** // a passenger **plane,** an airliner

③ [the counter for aircraft]

one **plane** 〚helicopter, etc.〛 // two **planes** // three **planes** // six **planes** // how many **planes**

kibishii 〚adj〛 **severe, strict; intense, severe**

① [severe, strict, rigorous, harsh]

¶ That teacher is very **strict.**

¶ I raised my children **strictly.**

② [intense, severe, hard]

¶ The cold became **much more severe** from February.

kibō 〚n, ～*suru*〛 **hope, desire, wish, aspiration**

¶ My **aspiration** is to become a doctor someday.

¶ [He] **hopes** to study in Japan.

kibun 〚n〛 **mood, feeling; atmosphere**

① [mood, feeling, frame of mind]

¶元気がありませんね。気分が悪いのではありませんか。 (Genki ga arimasen ne. *Kibun* ga warui no de wa arimasen ka?)

¶シャワーを浴びたあとはとてもいい気分です。 (Shawā o abita ato wa totemo ii *kibun* desu.)

②[ふんいき]
¶町はお祭りで楽しい気分にあふれています。 (Machi wa omatsuri de tanoshii *kibun* ni afurete imasu.)

kichinto きちんと〖副〗

①[正確な様子]
¶上田さんは、約束どおりきちんと3時に来ました。 (Ueda san wa, yakusoku doori *kichinto* sanji ni kimashita.)

②[整っている様子]
¶部屋の中をきちんと整理してください。 (Heya no naka o *kichinto* seiri shite kudasai.)

¶田中さんはいつもきちんとしたかっこうをしています。 (Tanaka san wa itsu mo *kichinto* shita kakkō o shite imasu.)

⇨**chanto ちゃんと**

kieru 消える〖動Ⅱ〗

①[明かりや火などがなくなる]
¶風でろうそくの火が消えました。 (Kaze de rōsoku no hi ga *kiemashita*.)

¶電気が突然消えました。 (Denki ga totsuzen *kiemashita*.)

②[ものの形や姿などが見えなくなる]

¶ You don't seem well. Do you **feel** ill?

¶ **One feels** really good after taking a shower.

② [atmosphere]
¶ The city has a merry festival **air.**

kichinto 〖adv〗 **exactly; neatly**

① [exactly, accurately, carefully, regularly]
¶ [Miss] Ueda came **punctually** at three o'clock **sharp.**

② [neatly, tidily]
¶ Please **tidy up** the room.

¶ [Mr.] Tanaka is always **neatly dressed** 〖well-groomed〗.

kieru 〖v Ⅱ〗 **go out, be extinguished; vanish, disappear**

① [go out, be extinguished]
¶ The candle **went out** in the wind 〖draft〗.

¶ The lights suddenly **went out.**

② [vanish, disappear]

350

¶飛行機が夜空に消えていきました。

(Hikōki ga yozora ni *kiete* ikimashita.)

¶ The airplane **disappeared** in the night sky.

kigaeru ☞ **kikaeru**

kigen 期限〖名〗

¶このキップは期限が切れていますよ。

(Kono kippu wa *kigen* ga kirete imasu yo.)

kigen 〖n〗 term, period, time limit

¶ This ticket has **expired.**

¶借りた本は期限内に返してください。

(Karita hon wa *kigen*nai ni kaeshite kudasai.)

¶ Please return borrowed books within **the time limit.**

¶2年の期限つきで家を借りました。

(Ninen no *kigen*tsuki de ie o karimashita.)

¶ [I] rented a house for **a term** of two years.

kigen きげん〖名〗

①〔快・不快などの心の状態〕

¶山田さんは試験で100点を取ったので，とてもきげんがいいです。

(Yamada san wa shiken de hyakuten o totta node, totemo *kigen* ga ii desu.)

kigen 〖n〗 humor, temper, mood; state of health or mind

① [humor, temper, mood]

¶ [Miss] Yamada is in a very good **mood** as [she] scored 100 on the test.

¶わたしが遅れてきたので，田中さんはきげんが悪いです。 (Watashi ga okurete kita node, Tanaka san wa *kigen* ga warui desu.)

¶ [Mr.] Tanaka is in a bad **mood** as I came late.

¶上田さんは，わたしにきげんよく会ってくれました。 (Ueda san wa, watashi ni *kigen* yoku atte kuremashita.)

¶ [Mrs.] Ueda met me in a good **mood.**

②〔他人の健康・気分の状態〕

¶ごきげんいかがですか。 (Go*kigen* ikaga desu ka?)

② [state of health or mind]

¶ How are you?

＊あいさつの言葉として「ごきげん (gokigen)」の形で使う。

＊ Used in the form *gokigen* in greetings.

kigyō 企業〖名〗

kigyō 〖n〗 business, enterprise, undertaking

中小企業 (chūshō-*kigyō*)

¶大企業で働いている人は労働条件がいいです。 (Dai*kigyō* de hataraite iru hito wa rōdō-jōken ga ii desu.)

¶個人企業の経営はなかなかたいへんです。 (Kojin-*kigyō* no keiei wa nakanaka taihen desu.)

kihon 基本〔名〕

基本的人権 (*kihon*teki-jinken)

¶何をするのにも基本が大事です。 (Nani o suru no ni mo *kihon* ga daiji desu.)

¶何をするのにも基本を学ばなければなりません。 (Nani o suru no ni mo *kihon* o manabanakereba narimasen.)

¶首相は外交についての基本的な考えを述べました。 (Shushō wa gaikō ni tsuite no *kihon*teki na kangae o nobemashita.)

kiiro 黄色〔名〕

¶田中さんは黄色のシャツを着ています。 (Tanaka san wa *kiiro* no shatsu o kite imasu.)

kiiroi 黄色い〔形〕

¶秋になると、木の葉が黄色くなります。 (Aki ni naru to, ko no ha ga *kiiroku* narimasu.)

kiji 記事〔名〕

新聞記事 (shinbun-*kiji*)

¶今朝の新聞におもしろい記事が出ていました。 (Kesa no shinbun ni omoshiroi *kiji* ga dete imashita.)

kiji 生地〔名〕

small and medium **enterprises,** minor **enterprises**

¶ Working conditions are good for those working for big **business.**

¶ Private **enterprises** 〖One-man **businesses**〗 are quite difficult to run.

kihon 〖n〗 foundation, basis, standard

fundamental human rights

¶ **The fundamentals** 〖**basics**〗 are important no matter what one does.

¶ One must learn **the fundamentals** 〖**basics**〗 no matter what one does.

¶ The prime minister talked about [his] **fundamental** views on international relations.

kiiro 〖n〗 yellow

¶ [Mr.] Tanaka is wearing a **yellow** shirt 〖knit shirt, T-shirt, etc.〗.

kiiroi 〖adj〗 yellow

¶ Leaves turn **yellow** in the fall.

kiji 〖n〗 news story, article (in a newspaper or magazine)

newspaper **article** 〖**account**〗

¶ There was an interesting **item** in this morning's newspaper.

kiji 〖n〗 cloth

¶このワイシャツの**生地**は木綿です。
(Kono waishatsu no *kiji* wa momen desu.)

kikaeru 着替える〖動Ⅱ〗
¶雨にぬれたので，洋服を**着替えました**。 (Ame ni nureta node, yōfuku o *kikaemashita*.)
＊「着替える (kigaeru)」とも言う。

kikai 機会〖名〗
¶わたしの国には日本人がほとんどいないので，日本語を話す**機会**がありません。 (Watashi no kuni ni wa Nihonjin ga hotondo inai node, Nihongo o hanasu *kikai* ga arimasen.)
¶わたしは**機会**があれば，日本へ行きたいと思います。 (Watashi wa *kikai* ga areba, Nihon e ikitai to omoimasu.)

kikai 機械〖名〗
¶この**機械**は日本製です。(Kono *kikai* wa Nihonsei desu.)
¶わたしはこの**機械**の動かし方がわかりません。 (Watashi wa kono *kikai* no ugokashikata ga wakarimasen.)

kikan 機関〖名〗
①[エンジン]
蒸気**機関**車 (jōki-*kikan*sha) 電気**機関**車 (denki-*kikan*sha)
②[ある目的を持った組織]
教育**機関** (kyōiku-*kikan*)
¶都市は交通**機関**が発達しています。
(Toshi wa kōtsū-*kikan* ga hattatsu shite imasu.)

kikaeru 〖v Ⅱ〗 change clothes
¶ [I] **changed** the clothes that had gotten wet in the rain.

＊ Variant: *kigaeru*.

kikai 〖n〗 opportunity, chance, occasion
¶ As there are hardly any Japanese in my country, there are no **opportunities** for me to speak Japanese.

¶ I'd like to go to Japan if I had **the chance**.

kikai 〖n〗 machine, machinery, mechanism, device, apparatus
¶ This **machinery** was made in Japan.

¶ I don't know how to operate this **machine**.

kikan 〖n〗 engine; institution
① [engine]
a steam **locomotive** // an electric **locomotive**
② [institution, facilities, system; an organization with a set purpose]
an educational **institution**
¶ Transportation **facilities** are advanced in the city.

kikan 期間〔名〕

¶あなたが外国にいた期間はどのくらいですか。(Anata ga gaikoku ni ita *kikan* wa dono kurai desu ka?)

¶東京での滞在期間は1週間の予定です。(Tōkyō de no taizai-*kikan* wa isshūkan no yotei desu.)

kiken 危険〔名, 形動〕

¶危険だから，触らないでください。(*Kiken* da kara, sawaranaide kudasai.)

¶危険な所へ行ってはいけません。(*Kiken* na tokoro e itte wa ikemasen.)

¶大水のために，この辺は危険になってきました。(Oomizu no tame ni, kono hen wa *kiken* ni natte kimashita.)
⇔anzen 安全

kikō 気候〔名〕

¶わたしの国は，一年じゅうあまり気候の変化がありません。(Watashi no kuni wa, ichinenjū amari *kikō* no henka ga arimasen.)

kikoeru 聞こえる〔動Ⅱ〕

①〔音や声が耳に入る〕
¶聞こえませんから，もっと大きい声で話してください。(*Kikoemasen* kara, motto ookii koe de hanashite kudasai.)

②〔そのように思える，そのように理解される〕
¶上田さんの話は本当らしく聞こえますが，ほとんどうそです。(Ueda

kikan 〚n〛 term, period of time

¶ How long was **your stay** abroad?

¶ The scheduled **time** of stay in Tokyo is one week.

kiken 〚n, adj-v〛 danger, risk, hazard

¶ Don't touch it—**it's dangerous.**

¶ You shouldn't go to **dangerous** places.

¶ Flooding has made this area **unsafe.**

kikō 〚n〛 climate, weather

¶ In my country there is little variation in **climate** throughout the year.

kikoeru 〚v Ⅱ〛 hear, be heard; sound ~, seem ~

① [hear, be heard, be audible]
¶ [I] **can't hear** you. Please speak up.

② [sound ~, seem ~]

¶ What [Mr.] Ueda says **sounds** true but is almost all false.

san no hanashi wa, hontō rashiku
kikoemasu ga, hotondo uso desu.)

kikoku 帰国〖名, 〜する〗

¶だんだん帰国の日が近づいてきまし
たね。 (Dandan *kikoku* no hi ga
chikazuite kimashita ne.)

¶1年間の留学が終わって，間もなく
帰国します。 (Ichinenkan no ryūgaku ga owatte, mamonaku *kikoku*
shimasu.)

kiku 菊〖名〗

¶日本では，秋になると菊の花が咲き
ます。 (Nihon de wa, aki ni naru
to *kiku* no hana ga sakimasu.)

kiku 効く〖動Ⅰ〗

¶この薬は風邪にとてもよく効きます。
(Kono kusuri wa kaze ni totemo
yoku *kikimasu*.)

kiku 利く〖動Ⅰ〗

¶この車はブレーキが利きません。
(Kono kuruma wa burēki ga *kikimasen*.)

kiku 聞く〖動Ⅰ〗

①［音や声を耳に入れて理解する］
話を聞く (hanashi o *kiku*)
¶山田さんは今部屋で音楽を聞いてい
ます。 (Yamada san wa ima heya
de ongaku o *kiite* imasu.)

¶あなたは上田さんが病気だというこ
とをだれから聞きましたか。 (Anata
wa Ueda san ga byōki da to iu
koto o dare kara *kikimashita* ka?)

②［要求・注意などを受け入れる］
¶あの子は両親の言うことをよく聞き

kikoku 〖n, ~*suru*〗 **return to one's
country**

¶ The day of **[your] return home** is
getting closer and closer, isn't it?

¶ [My] year of study abroad is ending
and soon [I] **will be returning to
[my] own country.**

kiku 〖n〗 **chrysanthemum**

¶ **Chrysanthemums** bloom in the
autumn in Japan.

kiku 〖v Ⅰ〗 **be effective, be good for**

¶ This medicine **is** very **effective** for
colds.

kiku 〖v Ⅰ〗 **work, act**

¶ This car's 〖cart's, etc.〗 brakes **don't
work.**

kiku 〖v Ⅰ〗 **hear, listen to; obey**

① [hear, listen to]
listen to a story, **listen to** someone
talking

¶ [Miss] Yamada **is listening to**
music in [her] room now.

¶ Who **did you hear** about [Mr.]
Ueda's illness from 〖Who told you
about Mr. Ueda's illness〗?

② [obey, comply]
¶ That child **minds** its parents.

ます。 (Ano ko wa ryōshin no iu koto o yoku *kikimasu*.)

kiku きく〖動Ⅰ〗

¶交番で駅へ行く道をききました。 (Kōban de eki e iku michi o *kikimashita*.)

¶わからないことは何でも先生にききなさい。 (Wakaranai koto wa nan demo sensei ni *kikinasai*.)

kimari 決まり〖名〗

① [決められていることがら，規則]

¶学校の決まりは守らなければなりません。 (Gakkō no *kimari* wa mamoranakereba narimasen.)

② [ものごとのしめくくり]

¶わたしはこの仕事に決まりをつけてから帰ります。 (Watashi wa kono shigoto ni *kimari* o tsukete kara kaerimasu.)

* 「決まりがつく (kimari ga tsuku)」「決まりをつける (kimari o tsukeru)」の形で使う。

kimaru 決まる〖動Ⅰ〗

¶会は来週開かれることに決まりました。 (Kai wa raishū hirakareru koto ni *kimarimashita*.)

¶出発の日が決まったら，知らせてください。 (Shuppatsu no hi ga *kimattara*, shirasete kudasai.)

¶田中さんには決まった仕事がありません。 (Tanaka san ni wa *kimatta* shigoto ga arimasen.)

kimeru 決める〖動Ⅱ〗

¶今度の大会に参加することに決めま

kiku 〖v I�〗 ask, inquire

¶ [I] **asked** for directions to the station at a police box.

¶ **Ask** your teacher about anything at all that you don't understand.

kimari 〖n〗 rule, regulation; settlement, conclusion

① [rule, regulation]

¶ One must obey the school **rules.**

② [settlement, conclusion]

¶ I will go home after **concluding** this piece of work.

* Used in the patterns "*kimari ga tsuku*" and "*kimari o tsukeru*."

kimaru 〖v I〗 be decided, be settled, be fixed, be arranged

¶ **It has been decided** to hold the party 〚meeting, conference〛 next week.

¶ Please inform me when the date of departure **has been fixed.**

¶ [Mr.] Tanaka doesn't have a **regular job.**

kimeru 〖v II〗 decide, settle, fix, arrange, determine

¶ [I] **decided** to participate in the

した。 (Kondo no taikai ni sanka suru koto ni *kimemashita*.)

¶飛行機の手荷物は 20 キロ以下と決められています。 (Hikōki no tenimotsu wa nijikkiro ika to *kimerarete imasu*.)

next convention 〔rally, tournament, meet, etc.〕.

¶ Airplane baggage **is set** at no more than 20 kilograms.

kimi 君〖代〗

¶君はぼくの本がどこにあるか知らない。 (*Kimi* wa boku no hon ga doko ni aru ka shiranai?)

¶君，いっしょに映画を見に行こう。 (*Kimi*, issho ni eiga o mi ni ikō.)

＊ 普通，親しい男どうしの間で使う。

kimi 〖pron〗 **you**

¶ Do **you** know where my book is?

¶ Let's go to a movie together.
＊ *Kimi* is generally used among males who know each other well.

kimochi 気持ち〖名〗

①［心の感じ方］

¶この部屋は明るくて，気持ちがいいですね。 (Kono heya wa akarukute, *kimochi* ga ii desu ne.)

¶あなたは子供を亡くしたお母さんの気持ちがわかりますか。 (Anata wa kodomo o nakushita okāsan no *kimochi* ga wakarimasu ka?)

②［体のぐあいによって感じる気分］

¶田中さんは気持ちが悪くなったので，家に帰りました。 (Tanaka san wa *kimochi* ga waruku natta node, ie ni kaerimashita.)

kimochi 〖n〗 **feeling, sensation**

① [feeling, sensation, mood]

¶ This room is bright and **pleasant**, isn't it?

¶ Can you understand how a mother **feels** when she has lost a child?

② [feeling or sensation caused by one's physical condition]

¶ [Mr.] Tanaka went home as [he] **was feeling sick.**

kimono 着物〖名〗

¶あのきれいな着物を着ている女の人はだれですか。 (Ano kirei na *kimono* o kite iru onna no hito wa dare desu ka?)

kimono 〖n〗 *kimono*, **clothes, clothing**

¶ Who is that woman wearing a beautiful *kimono*?

kin 金〖名〗

金ペン (*kin*pen) 金時計 (*kin*dokei)

kin 〖n〗 **gold**

a **gold** pen // a **gold** watch // a **gold**

金貨 (*kin*ka) 金色 (*kin*'iro) 金髪 (*kin*patsu)

¶秋子さんは金の指輪をはめています。(Akiko san wa *kin* no yubiwa o hamete imasu.)

¶父は金縁の眼鏡をかけています。(Chichi wa *kin*buchi no megane o kakete imasu.)

coin, **gold** currency // **gold, golden, gold** color // **fair** hair

¶ Akiko is wearing a **gold** ring.

¶ My father wears a pair of **gold**-rimmed glasses.

kindai 近代〚名〛

近代化 (*kindai*ka) 近代史 (*kindai*-shi) 近代思想 (*kindai*-shisō)

¶近代的な建物が次々と建築されています。(*Kindai*teki na tatemono ga tsugitsugi to kenchiku sarete imasu.)

kindai 〚n〛 **modern ages, recent times**

modernization // **modern** history // **modern** thought

¶ **Modern** buildings are being put up one after another.

kin'en 禁煙〚名, 〜する〛

¶上映中は禁煙です。(Jōeichū wa *kin'en* desu.)

¶体の調子が悪いので, 禁煙しています。(Karada no chōshi ga warui node, *kin'en* shite imasu.)

kin'en 〚n, 〜*suru*〛 **prohibition of smoking, No Smoking** (sign)

¶ **Smoking is prohibited** during the showing of the film.

¶ [I] **am refraining from smoking** because [I] don't feel in very good shape 〚quite up to par〛.

kinen 記念〚名, 〜する〛

記念日 (*kinen*bi) 記念品 (*kinen*hin) 記念写真 (*kinen*-shashin)

¶わたしたちは卒業を記念して, 木を植えました。(Watashitachi wa sotsugyō o *kinen* shite, ki o uemashita.)

kinen 〚n, 〜*suru*〛 **commemoration**

a **memorial** day, an anniversary // a souvenir, memento, keepsake // a **souvenir** photograph

¶ We planted a tree **in commemoration** of our graduation.

kingan ☞ **kinshi**

kinjo 近所〚名〛

¶この近所に交番はありませんか。(Kono *kinjo* ni kōban wa arimasen ka?)

¶上田さんは学校の近所に住んでいます。(Ueda san wa gakkō no *kinjo* ni sunde imasu.)

kinjo 〚n〛 **neighborhood, vicinity**

¶ Is there a police box **near** here?

¶ [Mrs.] Ueda lives **near** the school.

⇨chikaku 近く

kinō 昨日〖名〗

¶昨日は何曜日でしたか。 (*Kinō* wa naniyōbi deshita ka?)

¶これは昨日の新聞です。 (Kore wa *kinō* no shinbun desu.)

kinodoku 気の毒〖形動〗

①［他人の不幸などに同情する様子］

¶あの人は火事で家が焼けて気の毒ですね。 (Ano hito wa kaji de ie ga yakete *kinodoku* desu ne.)

②［迷惑をかけてすまないと思う様子］

¶昨日山田さんがわざわざ来てくれたのに，留守で気の毒なことをしました。 (Kinō Yamada san ga wazawaza kite kureta noni, rusu de *kinodoku* na koto o shimashita.)

kinshi 禁止〖名，〜する〗

通行禁止 (tsūkō-*kinshi*)　駐車禁止 (chūsha-*kinshi*)　立ち入り禁止 (tachiiri-*kinshi*)

¶夜は外出禁止です。 (Yoru wa gaishutsu-*kinshi* desu.)

¶政府は米の輸出を禁止しました。 (Seifu wa kome no yushutsu o *kinshi* shimashita.)

kinshi 近視〖名〗

¶上田さんは近視なので，眼鏡をかけています。 (Ueda san wa *kinshi* na node, megane o kakete imasu.)

＊「近眼 (kingan)」とも言う。

⇔enshi 遠視

kinu 絹〖名〗

絹のネクタイ (*kinu* no nekutai)

kinō 〖n〗 **yesterday**

¶ What day of the week was it **yesterday?**

¶ This is **yesterday's** newspaper.

kinodoku 〖adj-v〗 **pitiful, poor, unfortunate, regrettable, too bad**

① [used in sympathy toward the misfortune of others]

¶ **What a pity it is** that [he] lost [his] house in a fire.

② [used to express one's regret at having inconvenienced others]

¶ **I feel bad** that I wasn't at home yesterday when [Miss] Yamada came to see me.

kinshi 〖n, ~*suru*〗 **prohibition**

No Passage // **No** Parking // Keep Out, **No** Admittance, **No** Trespassing

¶ There's an evening **curfew** in effect.

¶ The government **has prohibited** the exporting of rice.

kinshi 〖n〗 **nearsightedness, shortsightedness**

¶ [Mr.] Ueda wears glasses because [he] is **nearsighted.**

＊ Variant: *kingan*.

kinu 〖n〗 **silk**

a **silk** necktie

kin'yō(bi) 金曜(日)〖名〗

kinzoku 金属〖名〗
¶木の机より金属製の机のほうが丈夫です。(Ki no tsukue yori *kinzoku*-sei no tsukue no hō ga jōbu desu.)

kioku 記憶〖名, 〜する〗
記憶力 (*kioku*ryoku)
¶わたしは一度あの人に会った記憶があります。(Watashi wa ichido ano hito ni atta *kioku* ga arimasu.)
¶小さい時のことはほとんど記憶していません。(Chiisai toki no koto wa hotondo *kioku* shite imasen.)

kion 気温〖名〗
気温が上がる (*kion* ga agaru) 気温が下がる (*kion* ga sagaru)
¶一日のうちで気温がいちばん高くなるのは午後の2時ごろです。(Ichinichi no uchi de *kion* ga ichiban takaku naru no wa gogo no niji goro desu.)

kippu 切符〖名〗
¶東京までの切符を買いました。(Tōkyō made no *kippu* o kaimashita.)
¶音楽会の切符はもう売り切れました。(Ongakkai no *kippu* wa mō urikiremashita.)

kirai きらい〖形動〗
¶食べ物できらいな物はありません。(Tabemono de *kirai* na mono wa arimasen.)
¶わたしはうそをつく人が大きらいです。(Watashi wa uso o tsuku hito

kin'yō(bi) 〚n〛 Friday

kinzoku 〚n〛 metal
¶ **Metal** desks are more durable than wooden ones.

kioku 〚n, ~*suru*〛 memory, recollection
memory, one's powers of **memory**
¶ I have **a memory** of once meeting [him].
¶ [I] **remember** hardly anything of when [I] was small.

kion 〚n〛 (atmospheric) **temperature**
the temperature rises // **the temperature** falls
¶ The highest **temperature** of the day comes at around two o'clock in the afternoon.

kippu 〚n〛 ticket
¶ [I] bought **a ticket** to Tokyo.

¶ **The tickets** for the concert are already sold out.

kirai 〚adj-v〛 dislike, aversion, hatred
¶ There are no foods that I **dislike** 〚I like all foods〛.

¶ I **hate** people who lie.

ga dai*kirai* desu.)

⇔**suki** 好き

kirau きらう〚動Ⅰ〛

¶あなたは，なぜあの人をそんなにきらうのですか。 (Anata wa, naze ano hito o sonna ni *kirau* no desu ka?)

¶あの人はみんなにきらわれています。 (Ano hito wa minna ni *kirawarete* imasu.)

kirau 〚vⅠ〛 **to dislike, hate**

¶ Why do you **dislike** [him] so?

¶ [He] **is disliked** by all.

kire きれ〚名〛

¶この本の表紙にはきれがはってあります。 (Kono hon no hyōshi ni wa *kire* ga hatte arimasu.)

kire 〚n〛 **cloth**

¶ This is a **cloth**bound book.

kirei きれい〚形動〛

①［美しい］

¶このきれいな花を一本ください。 (Kono *kirei* na hana o ippon kudasai.)

¶あの女の人は本当にきれいですね。 (Ano onna no hito wa hontō ni *kirei* desu ne.)

②［よごれていない，清潔だ］

きれいな水 (*kirei* na mizu)

¶窓を開けてきれいな空気を入れましょう。 (Mado o akete *kirei* na kūki o iremashō.)

③［きちんとしている様子］

¶あなたの部屋はいつもきれいですね。 (Anata no heya wa itsu mo *kirei* desu ne.)

④［すっかり，完全に］

¶たくさんあった料理をきれいに食べてしまいました。 (Takusan atta

kirei 〚adj-v〛 **beautiful; clean; tidy, neat; completely, thoroughly**

① [beautiful, pretty, good-looking]

¶ Please give me one of these **pretty** flowers.

¶ That woman is really **beautiful,** isn't she?

② [clean, pure, clear]

clear water, **pure** water

¶ Let's open the window and let in some **fresh** air.

③ [tidy, neat, in good order]

¶ Your room is always **nice and neat,** isn't it?

④ [completely, thoroughly]

¶ [We] finished off **all** of the many dishes of food.

ryōri o *kirei* ni tabete shimaima-shita.)

* 「きれいに (kirei ni)」の形で副詞的に使う。

* Used adverbially in the form *kirei ni*.

kireru 切れる〖動Ⅱ〗

kireru 〖v Ⅱ〗 break; split; rip; break off, be cut off; run out, be exhausted, be sold out; expire, run out; cut well, be sharp

①[一つながりのものが途中でいくつかに分かれてしまう]

¶つり糸が切れて、魚が逃げてしまいました。(Tsuriito ga *kirete*, sakana ga nigete shimaimashita.)

① [break, give way]

¶ The fishing line **snapped** and the fish got away.

②[裂ける、傷がつく]

¶ズボンの後ろが切れていますよ。(Zubon no ushiro ga *kirete* imasu yo.)

② [split, rip]

¶ There's **a rip** in the seat of your trousers.

¶ガラスで手が切れました。(Garasu de te ga *kiremashita*.)

¶ [I] **cut** [my] hand on some glass.

③[続いていたものが一時終わる]

¶話をしている途中で、電話が切れてしまいました。(Hanashi o shite iru tochū de, denwa ga *kirete* shimaimashita.)

③ [break off, be cut off, be disconnected]

¶ We were **cut off** in the middle of our telephone conversation.

④[使ったり売ったりして品物が一時なくなる]

¶油が切れたらしく、機械が動かなくなりました。(Abura ga *kireta* rashiku, kikai ga ugokanaku narimashita.)

④ [run out, be exhausted, be sold out]

¶ The machine seems to have stopped running because it **ran out** of oil.

¶紙が切れていますから、買っておいてください。(Kami ga *kirete* imasu kara, katte oite kudasai.)

¶ We've **run out** of paper. Please buy some more.

⑤[ある期間が過ぎる]

期限が切れる (kigen ga *kireru*)

¶この定期券は、もう切れていますよ。(Kono teikiken wa, mō *kirete* ima-

⑤ [expire, run out]

a time limit **expires**

¶ This pass 〖train pass〗 **has expired.**

su yo.)

⑥[よく切ることができる]

¶このナイフはよく切れます。 (Kono naifu wa yoku *kiremasu*.)

-kireru -きれる〖尾〗

①[最後まですることができる]

¶隣のラジオがあまりうるさいので、我慢しきれないで文句を言いに行きました。 (Tonari no rajio ga amari urusai node, gaman shi*kirenaide* monku o ii ni ikimashita.)

＊ あとに打ち消しの言葉を伴って，不可能の意味を表す。

②[完全にすることができる，すっかりすることができる]

¶こんなにたくさんの料理はとても食べきれません。 (Konna ni takusan no ryōri wa totemo tabe*kiremasen*.)

¶明日までにはこの本は読み切れません。 (Asu made ni wa kono hon wa yomi*kiremasen*.)

kiri 霧〖名〗

夜霧 (yo*giri*) 霧が深い (*kiri* ga fukai) 霧がかかる (*kiri* ga kakaru) 霧が晴れる (*kiri* ga hareru)

kirisutokyō キリスト教〖名〗

キリスト教を信じる (*kirisutokyō* o shinjiru) キリスト教徒 (*kirisuto-kyō*to)

-kiro -キロ〖尾〗

5キログラム (go*kiro*guramu) 6キロメートル (rok*kiro*mētoru)

kiroku 記録〖名，〜する〗

①[書いておくこと，またその文書]

⑥ [cut well, be sharp]

¶ This knife **cuts** well 〚**is sharp**〛.

-kireru 〚suf〛 **be able to do to the end; be able to do all**

① [be able to do to the end]

¶ The radio was so loud next door that I **couldn't stand it any longer** and went to complain.

＊ This *-kireru* is used in the negative and expresses impossibility.

② [be able to finish, be able to do all of something]

¶ [I] **can't possibly eat** this much food.

¶ [I] **can't read all** of this book by tomorrow.

kiri 〚n〛 **fog, mist, spray**

a night **fog,** a night **mist** // be **foggy,** be **misty** // **a fog** 〚**mist**〛 gathers // **a fog** lifts, **a mist** clears

kirisutokyō 〚n〛 **Christianity**

believe in **Christianity** // a **Christian**

-kiro 〚suf〛 **a kilo, kilometer, kilogram, kilowatt, kilocycle, kiloliter,** etc.

five **kilograms** // six **kilometers**

kiroku 〚n, ~*suru*〛 **record, document; record, record time**

① [record, document]

kiru

¶図書館には、この町についての古い記録が残っています。(Toshokan ni wa, kono machi ni tsuite no furui *kiroku* ga nokotte imasu.)
¶ Ancient **documents** concerning this city are preserved in the library.

¶会議でみんなが言ったことを記録してください。(Kaigi de minna ga itta koto o *kiroku* shite kudasai.)
¶ Please keep **a record** of what everyone says at the meeting.

②[競技などの成績]　② [record, record time]
¶上田さんは水泳で世界記録をつくりました。(Ueda san wa suiei de sekai-*kiroku* o tsukurimashita.)
¶ [Mr.] Ueda set a world **record** in swimming.

kiru 着る〖動Ⅱ〗　**kiru** 〚v II〛 put on, wear
¶寒いので、セーターを着ました。(Samui node, sētā o *kimashita*.)
¶ [I] **wore** a sweater because it was cold.
¶暑いから、上着を着ないで会社へ行きます。(Atsui kara, uwagi o *kinaide* kaisha e ikimasu.)
¶ [I] go to work **without** a suit coat because it's so hot.
¶あなたの着ている洋服はどこで買ったのですか。(Anata no *kite* iru yōfuku wa doko de katta no desu ka?)
¶ Where did you buy the clothes you're **wearing?**
⇔nugu 脱ぐ

kiru 切る〖動Ⅰ〗　**kiru** 〚v I〛 cut; switch off; break off, cut off
①[ナイフなどで物を傷つけたりいくつかの部分に分けたりする]　① [cut, chop, carve]
¶大きなりんごを四つに切って食べました。(Ookina ringo o yottsu ni *kitte* tabemashita.)
¶ [I] **cut** a large apple into four pieces and ate it.
¶ナイフで手を切ってしまいました。(Naifu de te o *kitte* shimaimashita.)
¶ [I] **cut** [my] hand on a knife.
②[電気などを止める]　② [switch off, turn off]
¶テレビのスイッチを切ってください。(Terebi no suitchi o *kitte* kudasai.)
¶ Please **turn off** the television.
③[続いている行為・関係などをやめ　③ [break off, cut off, break with sever connections]

364

る]

¶電話を切らないで, そのまま待って いてください。(Denwa o *kiranaide*, sono mama matte ite kudasai.)

-kiru   -きる〔尾〕

①[あることを全部終える, 最後まで あることをやる]

¶この小説を一晩で読み**きって**しまい ました。(Kono shōsetsu o hitoban de yomi*kitte* shimaimashita.)

¶一つの料理を食べ**きらない**うちに, もう次の料理が出てきました。 (Hitotsu no ryōri o tabe*kiranai* uchi ni, mō tsugi no ryōri ga dete kimashita.)

②[完全にその状態になる] 枯れ**きった**木 (kare*kitta* ki)

¶食べすぎたり飲みすぎたりするのが 体によくないことはわかり**きっていま** す。(Tabesugitari nomisugitari suru no ga karada ni yoku nai koto wa wakari*kitte* imasu.)

③[それ以上のひどい状態はない] 困り**きる** (komari*kiru*) 弱り**きる** (yowari*kiru*)

¶疲れ**きって**, もう一歩も歩けません。 (Tsukare*kitte*, mō ippo mo aruke-masen.)

④[勇気を出してあることをする, は っきりあることをする]

¶高い所から思い**きって**飛び降りまし た。(Takai tokoro kara omoi*kitte* tobiorimashita.)

¶いやなことはいやだと言い**きる**勇気

¶ Please **hold the line** (said on the telephone).

-kiru 〖suf〗 **finish; completely ~; dare to**

① [finish, end]

¶ [I] **finished** reading this book in one evening.

¶ The next dish came **before [I] could finish** eating the previous one.

② [completely reach a certain state] a **completely** dead tree

¶ [I] am **fully** aware that eating and drinking too much are bad for the health.

③ [a completely bad condition] be **greatly** embarrassed, be at one's wit's ends, be at a loss // be run down, break down; be at a loss, be floored

¶ [I]'m **completely** exhausted; [I] can't take another step.

④ [dare to, be able to]

¶ [I] **summoned [my] courage** and leaped down from that high place.

¶ You must have the courage to

を持たなければいけません。(Iya na koto wa iya da to ii*kiru* yūki o motanakereba ikemasen.)

kisetsu 季節〖名〗

¶桜の咲く**季節**になりました。(Sakura no saku *kisetsu* ni narimashita.)

¶日本では四つの**季節**がはっきりしています。(Nihon de wa yottsu no *kisetsu* ga hakkiri shite imasu.)

kisha 汽車〖名〗

汽車に乗る (*kisha* ni noru) 汽車を降りる (*kisha* o oriru) 東京行きの汽車 (Tōkyō yuki no *kisha*) 東京発の汽車 (Tōkyō hatsu no *kisha*) 汽車賃 (*kisha*chin)

kisha 記者〖名〗

新聞**記者** (shinbun-*kisha*) 雑誌**記者** (zasshi-*kisha*)

kishi 岸〖名〗

¶船が**岸**に近づいてきました。(Fune ga *kishi* ni chikazuite kimashita.)

¶川岸で子供が遊んでいます。(Kawa-*gishi* de kodomo ga asonde imasu.)

kiso 基礎〖名〗

①[建物の土台]

¶この家は**基礎**がしっかりしています。(Kono ie wa *kiso* ga shikkari shite imasu.)

②[学問などのもとになるたいせつな部分]

¶どんな勉強でも**基礎**が大切です。(Donna benkyō demo *kiso* ga taisetsu desu.)

kisoku 規則〖名〗

kisetsu 〚n〛 season, time of the year

¶ The cherry blossom **season** has 〚had〛 started.

¶ Japan has four distinct **seasons.**

kisha 〚n〛 train

take **a train,** ride in **a train,** board **a train** // get off **a train** // **a train** bound for Tokyo, the Tokyo **train** // **the train** from Tokyo, **a train** starting in Tokyo // a **railroad** fare

kisha 〚n〛 reporter, journalist

a newspaper **reporter** // a magazine **writer,** journalist

kishi 〚n〛 banks, shore, coast

¶ The boat is nearing 〚neared〛 **the shore.**

¶ Children are playing along the river**bank.**

kiso 〚n〛 foundation, base

① [foundation (of a building)]

¶ This house has a solid **foundation.**

② [base, foundation (of learning, etc.)]

¶ A firm grounding in **the basics** is important in any field of study.

kisoku 〚n〛 rule, regulations

come out and say so when you don't want to do something.

交通規則 (kōtsū-*kisoku*) 規則を守る (*kisoku* o mamoru) 規則を破る (*kisoku* o yaburu)

¶学生は学校の規則に従わなければなりません。 (Gakusei wa gakkō no *kisoku* ni shitagawanakereba narimasen.)

traffic **regulations** // obey **the rules** // break **the rules**

¶ Students must observe school **regulations.**

¶わたしは毎日規則正しい生活をしています。 (Watashi wa mainichi *kisoku* tadashii seikatsu o shite imasu.)

¶ I live a **regular** life 〚keep **regular** hours〛.

¶中村さんは不規則な生活をしたので, 病気になってしまいました。 (Nakamura san wa fu*kisoku* na seikatsu o shita node, byōki ni natte shimaimashita.)

¶ [Mr.] Nakamura became ill because [he] led an **irregular** life.

¶会は1か月に2回, 規則的に開かれています。 (Kai wa ikkagetsu ni nikai, *kisoku*teki ni hirakarete imasu.)

¶ The club 〚association, group〛 meets **regularly** twice a month.

kissaten 喫茶店〚名〛

¶わたしたちは喫茶店でコーヒーを飲みました。 (Watashitachi wa *kissaten* de kōhii o nomimashita.)

kissaten 〚n〛 tearoom, coffee shop, cafe

¶ We drank coffee in **a coffee shop.**

kisū 奇数〚名〛

¶1, 3, 5という数は奇数と言い, 2, 4, 6は偶数と言います。 (Ichi, san, go to iu sū wa *kisū* to ii, ni, shi, roku wa gūsū to iimasu.)

⇔gūsū 偶数

kisū 〚n〛 odd number, uneven number

¶ One, three, and five are called **odd numbers,** and two, four, and six are called even numbers.

kita 北〚名〛

北風 (*kita*kaze) 北側 (*kita*gawa) 北向き (*kita*muki)

¶北国ではもう雪が降っています。

kita 〚n〛 north

north wind, **northerly** wind // the **north** side // **northern** exposure, facing **north**

367

(*Kita*guni de wa mō yuki ga futte imasu.)

⇔minami 南

kitai 期待〖名, ～する〗

¶あの青年は将来を期待されています。 (Ano seinen wa shōrai o *kitai* sarete imasu.)

¶その音楽会は期待していたとおりすばらしいものでした。 (Sono ongakkai wa *kitai* shite ita toori subarashii mono deshita.)

kitai 気体〖名〗

¶空気は気体です。 (Kūki wa *kitai* desu.)

⇒ekitai 液体 kotai 固体

kitanai 汚い〖形〗

¶汚い手で触らないでください。 (*Kitanai* te de sawaranaide kudasai.)

¶掃除をしないので, 部屋が汚くなっています。 (Sōji o shinai node, heya ga *kitanaku* natte imasu.)

kitte 切手〖名〗

記念切手 (kinen-*kitte*) 切手をはる (*kitte* o haru)

kitto きっと〖副〗

¶あの人はきっと来ますよ。 (Ano hito wa *kitto* kimasu yo.)

¶いくら呼んでも返事がないから, きっと留守ですよ。 (Ikura yonde mo henji ga nai kara, *kitto* rusu desu yo.)

kiwamete 極めて〖副〗

¶この問題の解決は極めて難しいです。

Snow is already falling in **the North.**

kitai 〖n, ～*suru*〗 expectation, anticipation, hope

¶ **Much is expected** of that youth in the future.

¶ That concert 〚recital〛 was as marvelous **as expected.**

kitai 〖n〗 a gaseous body, gas, vapor

¶ The air is **gaseous.**

kitanai 〖adj〗 dirty

¶ Please don't touch it 〚me〛 with **dirty** hands.

¶ The room has gotten **dirty** as [I] haven't been cleaning it.

kitte 〖n〗 (postage) **stamp**

a commemorative **stamp** // paste **a stamp** on

kitto 〖adv〗 certainly, undoubtedly

¶ [He]'ll come **for sure.**

¶ [She] **must** not be at home as there's no reply no matter how much one calls to [her].

kiwamete 〖adv〗 extremely, very

¶ This problem will be **extremely**

(Kono mondai no kaiketsu wa *ki-wamete* muzukashii desu.)

¶この計画に反対する人は極めて少な
いです。 (Kono keikaku ni hantai
suru hito wa *kiwamete* sukunai
desu.)

¶ **Very** few are opposed to this plan.

kizu 傷〖名〗

①[けがなどをして体についたあと]
¶その足の傷はどうしたのですか。
(Sono ashi no *kizu* wa dō shita no
desu ka?)
¶わたしは医者へ行って，傷の手当て
をしてもらいました。 (Watashi wa
isha e itte, *kizu* no teate o shite
moraimashita.)
②[品物が傷んでいること]
¶このりんごにはきずがありますよ。
(Kono ringo ni wa *kizu* ga arimasu
yo.)
¶この花びんはきずがついているから
安いです。(Kono kabin wa *kizu* ga
tsuite iru kara yasui desu.)

kizu [[n]] **wound, injury; flaw, dis-
figuration**

① [wound, injury, cut, scratch,
bruise, scar; refers to living crea-
tures]

¶ How did you get that leg [[foot]] **injury** [[scar]]?

¶ I went to the doctor and had my
injury treated.

② [flaw, disfigurement, defect, crack,
scratch, bruise; refers to objects]

¶ This apple **is bruised.**

¶ This vase is cheap because it **is de-
fective** [[is scratched]].

kizuku 気づく〖動Ⅰ〗

¶田中さんは自分が悪かったというこ
とに気づきました。(Tanaka san wa
jibun ga warukatta to iu koto ni
kizukimashita.)
¶山田さんはわたしに気づかないで，
通り過ぎていきました。 (Yamada
san wa watashi ni *kizukanaide*,
toorisugite ikimashita.)

＊ 普通「〜に気づく （〜ni kizuku)」
の形で使う。
⇨ki 気

kizuku [[v Ⅰ]] **notice, perceive, realize**

¶ [Mr.] Tanaka later **realized** that
[he] had been at fault.

¶ [Miss] Yamada went by **without
noticing** that I was there.

＊ Generally used in the pattern
"*~ ni kizuku.*"

ko 子〖名〗

①[親から生まれたもの]

¶うちの子は今年小学校に入学します。 (Uchi no *ko* wa kotoshi shō-gakkō ni nyūgaku shimasu.)

¶ねこが子を産みました。 (Neko ga *ko* o umimashita.)

↔oya 親

②[幼い者]

¶あの子の名前は何と言いますか。 (Ano *ko* no namae wa nan to iimasu ka?)

¶庭で男の子と女の子が遊んでいます。 (Niwa de otoko no *ko* to onna no *ko* ga asonde imasu.)

↔otona 大人

⇒kodomo 子供

-ko -個〖尾〗

¶1個50円のりんごを5個買いました。 (Ik*ko* gojūen no ringo o go*ko* kaimashita.)

¶この卵は10個でいくらですか。 (Kono tamago wa jik*ko* de ikura desu ka?)

kō こう〖副〗

①[話し手に身近な関係にあるものごとの様子をさし示す]

¶その漢字はこう書くんです。 (Sono kanji wa *kō* kaku n desu.)

¶こう忙しくては、ゆっくり新聞も読めません。 (*Kō* isogashikute wa, yukkuri shinbun mo yomemasen.)

②[文脈の上で前に述べたものごとの状態などを話し手に身近な関係にある

ko 〚n〛 one's child(ren), offspring; children, the young

① [one's child(ren), offspring]

¶ Our **child** enters elementary school this year.

¶ The cat had **kittens.**

② [children, the young]

¶ What is the name of that **child?**

¶ A **boy** and **girl** are playing in the yard.

-ko 〚suf〛 a piece, an item; the counter for small objects

¶ I bought **five** apples at fifty yen **each.**

¶ How much are **10** of these eggs?

kō 〚adv〛 like this, this way

① [like this, this way; indicates something close to the speaker]

¶ That *kanji* is written **like this.**

¶ When [I] am **this** busy [I] can't read a newspaper leisurely.

② [like this, this way; indicates that something already mentioned is close

ものとしてさし示したりまたあとから
述べる話し手の考えなどを前もってさ
し示したりする]

¶人々は板の上で木の棒をもんで，火
を出すことを発明しました。その後，
石と石とを打ち合わせて火を出すこと
を考えました。こうして，火が発明さ
れてから世界はどんどん開けてきまし
た。 (Hitobito wa ita no ue de ki
no bō o monde, hi o dasu koto o
hatsumei shimashita. Sono go, ishi
to ishi to o uchiawasete hi o dasu
koto o kangaemashita. *Kō* shite,
hi ga hatsumei sarete kara sekai
wa dondon hirakete kimashita.)

¶わたしはこう思います。いくら学問
があっても，人に対する思いやりがな
くてはいけません。(Watashi wa *kō*
omoimasu. Ikura gakumon ga atte
mo, hito ni taisuru omoiyari ga
nakute wa ikemasen.)

⇨**sō** そう **ā** ああ **dō** どう

kōba 工場〖名〗
工場で働く (kōba de hataraku)
＊「工場 (kōba)」は小さい個人経営
の作業場を主として言う。
⇨**kōjō** 工場

kōban 交番〖名〗
¶交番のお巡りさんが丁寧に道を教え
てくれました。(Kōban no omawari-
san ga teinei ni michi o oshiete
kuremashita.)

kobosu こぼす〖動Ⅰ〗
¶机の上に水をこぼしてしまいました。

to the speaker or introduces an opinion, etc., of the speaker]

¶ Humans discovered producing fire
by rubbing a stick on top of a board.
After that they thought of striking
rocks together to start a fire. **In this
way** their world was rapidly opened
up after the discovery of fire.

¶ **This** is what I think. However
learned someone may be, he or she
should still show consideration toward others.

kōba 〚n〛 factory, workshop
work in **a factory**
＊ *Kōba* chiefly refers to a small, pri-
vately managed workplace.

kōban 〚n〛 police box
¶ The policeman at **the police box**
gave me careful directions.

kobosu 〚v Ⅰ〛 spill, shed, drop
¶ [I] **spilled** water on the top of the

(Tsukue no ue ni mizu o *koboshite* shimaimashita.)

¶あの映画を見て，涙を こぼさない 人はいないでしょう。 (Ano eiga o mite, namida o *kobosanai* hito wa inai deshō.)

kōcha 紅茶〚名〛

¶紅茶がいいですか。コーヒーがいいですか。 (*Kōcha* ga ii desu ka? Kōhii ga ii desu ka?)

kochira こちら〚代〛

①〔話し手に身近な関係にある方向をさし示す〕

¶どうぞ，こちらへ。 (Dōzo, *kochira* e.)

¶皆さん，写真を撮りますから，こちらを見てください。 (Minasan, shashin o torimasu kara, *kochira* o mite kudasai.)

②〔話し手に身近な関係にある方向に存在する所などをさし示す〕

¶わたしがこちらへ来てから 10 年になります。 (Watashi ga *kochira* e kite kara jūnen ni narimasu.)

¶「トイレはどこにありますか。」(Toire wa doko ni arimasu ka?) 「トイレはこちらです。」 (Toire wa *kochira* desu.)

③〔話し手に身近な関係にある方向にいる人をさし示す〕

¶御紹介します。こちらは山田さんです。 (Goshōkai shimasu. *Kochira* wa Yamada san desu.)

* 話し手にとって対等または目上の人

desk.

¶ No one can see that movie **without shedding** some tears 〖The person doesn't exist who can see that movie **without crying**〗.

kōcha 〚n〛 (black) tea

¶ Which would you like—**tea** or coffee?

kochira 〚pron〛 **this way, here; this place; this person; this one; this side, I, we**

① [this way, here; indicates a direction physically close to the speaker]

¶ **This way,** please.

¶ Will everyone please look **this way** so that I can take the photograph.

② [this place, here; indicates a place, etc., physically close to the speaker]

¶ Ten years have passed since I came **here.**

¶ "Where are the rest rooms?" "The rest rooms are **here.**"

③ [this person; indicates a person physically close to the speaker]

¶ Let me introduce you. **This** is [Mrs.] Yamada.

* *Kochira* is used to refer to someone of equal or higher status than the

に対して使う。「こちらの方 (kochira no kata)」とも言う。

④[話し手に身近な関係にある方向に存在するものをさし示す]

¶「どちらの時計になさいますか。」(Dochira no tokei ni nasaimasu ka?)「そうですね。こちらのほうにしましょう。(Sō desu ne. *Kochira no hō ni shimashō.*)

¶そちらよりこちらのほうがいいです。こちらをください。 (Sochira yori *kochira* no hō ga ii desu. *Kochira* o kudasai.)

⑤[話し手自身や話し手側の者を表す、わたし、わたしたち]

¶もしもし、上田さんですか。こちらは中村です。 (Moshimoshi, Ueda san desu ka? *Kochira* wa Nakamura desu.)

¶おかげさまで、こちらはみんな元気に暮らしております。 (Okagesama de, *kochira* wa minna genki ni kurashite orimasu.)

＊「こっち (kotchi)」とも言うが、「こちら (kochira)」のほうが丁寧な言葉である。

⇨sochira そちら　achira あちら　dochira どちら

kōchō　校長〖名〗
¶上田さんのお父さんは小学校の校長です。 (Ueda san no otōsan wa shōgakkō no *kōchō* desu.)

kōdō　行動〖名、〜する〗
¶団体で行動しているとき自分勝手な

speaker. *Kochira no kata* is also used.

④ [this one; indicates something physically close to the speaker]

¶ "Which watch ⟦clock⟧ would you like?"

　"Well, let's see. I'll take **this one.**"

¶ I like **this one** better than that one. Please give me **this one.**

⑤ [this side, I, we; indicates the speaker or those on the speaker's side]

¶ Hello. Is that [Mr.] Ueda? **This** is [Mr.] Nakamura calling.

¶ **I and my family** are all well, thank you.

＊ *Kotchi* is also used, but *kochira* is more polite.

kōchō 〖n〗　**principal, headmaster**
¶ [Miss] Ueda's father is an elementary school **principal.**

kōdō 〖n, ~*suru*〗　**action, movement, behavior**
¶ When **acting** together with others

行動をすると, 他人に迷惑をかけます。
(Dantai de *kōdō* shite iru toki jibunkatte na *kōdō* o suru to, tanin ni meiwaku o kakemasu.)

¶上田さんはたいへん行動的な人です。
(Ueda san wa taihen *kōdō*teki na hito desu.)

in a group, **acting** only to please oneself will inconvenience others.

¶ [Mr.] Ueda is a **take-charge** person 〚Mr. Ueda never hesitates to **take action**〛.

kodomo 子供〚名〛

①[親から生まれたもの]
¶わたしの子供は3人とも女です。
(Watashi no *kodomo* wa sannin tomo onna desu.)

↔**oya** 親

②[幼い者]
¶公園で子供たちが遊んでいます。
(Kōen de *kodomo*tachi ga asonde imasu.)

↔**otona** 大人

⇨**ko** 子

kodomo 〚n〛 one's child(ren); children, the young

① [one's child(ren), offspring]
¶ My three **children** are all girls.

② [children, the young]
¶ **Children** are playing in the park.

koe 声〚名〛

¶声が小さくて聞こえません。 (*Koe* ga chiisakute kikoemasen.)

¶田中先生はいつも大きい声で話します。 (Tanaka sensei wa itsu mo ookii *koe* de hanashimasu.)

koe 〚n〛 voice

¶ **[Your] voice** is low and I can't hear what [you]'re saying.

¶ Professor 〚Doctor〛 Tanaka always speaks in a loud **voice**.

kōen 公園〚名〛

¶公園へ散歩に行きましょう。 (*Kōen* e sanpo ni ikimashō.)

kōen 〚n〛 park, public garden
¶ Let's go for a walk in **the park**.

koeru 越える〚動Ⅱ〛

¶この山を越えた所にわたしの村があります。 (Kono yama o *koeta* tokoro ni watashi no mura ga arimasu.)

koeru 〚v Ⅱ〛 cross, go across
¶ My village lies **on the other side** of this mountain.

koeru 超える〚動Ⅱ〛

¶昨日は40度を超える暑さでした。

koeru 〚v Ⅱ〛 exceed, be over
¶ Yesterday the heat **exceeded** 40

(Kinō wa yonjūdo o *koeru* atsusa deshita.)

¶この狭い国に一億を超える人が住んでいます。 (Kono semai kuni ni ichioku o *koeru* hito ga sunde imasu.)

¶ **Over** 100 million people live in this small country.

kōfuku 幸福〖名, 形動〗

¶わたしは今とても幸福です。 (Watashi wa ima totemo *kōfuku* desu.)

¶幸福な家庭に育って幸せですね。 (*Kōfuku* na katei ni sodatte shiawase desu ne.)

¶田中さんは結婚して幸福に暮らしています。 (Tanaka san wa kekkon shite *kōfuku* ni kurashite imasu.)

⇔**fukō** 不幸

kōfuku 〚n, adj-v〛 **happiness, good fortune**

¶ I am very **happy** now.

¶ You are fortunate to have grown up in a **happy** home.

¶ [Mr.] Tanaka is living in wedded **bliss.**

kōfun 興奮〖名, ～する〗

¶山田さんは会議で田中さんと大声で議論していましたが、その時の興奮がまだ続いているようです。 (Yamada san wa kaigi de Tanaka san to oogoe de giron shite imashita ga, sono toki no *kōfun* ga mada tsuzuite iru yō desu.)

¶試合を見ていた人たちは興奮して立ち上がりました。 (Shiai o mite ita hitotachi wa *kōfun* shite tachiagarimashita.)

kōfun 〚n, ～*suru*〛 **excitement, agitation**

¶ [Mr.] Yamada raised [his] voice and argued with [Mr.] Tanaka at the meeting, and **the aroused emotions** of that time seem to still be alive.

¶ The people watching the game 〚match〛 came to their feet **in their excitement.**

kōgai 郊外〖名〗

¶わたしは東京の郊外に住んでいます。 (Watashi wa Tōkyō no *kōgai* ni sunde imasu.)

kōgai 〚n〛 **suburbs, environs, outskirts**

¶ I live in **the suburbs** of Tokyo.

kōgai 公害〖名〗

kōgai 〚n〛 **environmental pollution**

375

¶飛行機や汽車の騒音は公害の一種です。 (Hikōki ya kisha no sōon wa *kōgai* no isshu desu.)

¶この町の人々は，工場から出る煙の公害で苦しんでいます。 (Kono machi no hitobito wa, kōjō kara deru kemuri no *kōgai* de kurushinde imasu.)

¶ The noise of planes and trains is one form of **pollution.**

¶ The people of this city suffer **air pollution** caused by factory emissions.

kōgeki 攻撃〚名，～する〛
敵から攻撃を受ける (teki kara *kōgeki* o ukeru)　敵を攻撃する (teki o *kōgeki* suru)

kōgeki 〚n, ~*suru*〛 **attack**
be attacked by an enemy, be under enemy **attack** // **attack** an enemy, **make an attack** on the enemy

kogeru 焦げる〚動Ⅱ〛
¶魚が真っ黒に焦げてしまいました。 (Sakana ga makkuro ni *kogete* shimaimashita.)

¶パンを焼くとき，焦げないように気をつけてください。 (Pan o yaku toki, *kogenai* yō ni ki o tsukete kudasai.)

kogeru 〚v Ⅱ〛 **burn, scorch**
¶ The fish **is 〚was〛 burnt** to a cinder.

¶ When toasting bread, please be careful **not to burn it.**

kōgi 講義〚名，～する〛
¶今日は日本語の助詞についての講義があります。 (Kyō wa Nihongo no joshi ni tsuite no *kōgi* ga arimasu.)

¶あしたは田中先生が上田先生の代わりに講義します。 (Ashita wa Tanaka sensei ga Ueda sensei no kawari ni *kōgi* shimasu.)

kōgi 〚n, ~*suru*〛 **lecture**
¶ There is **a lecture** today about the use of particles in Japanese.

¶ Tomorrow Professor Tanaka **will lecture** in place of Professor Ueda.

kogitte 小切手〚名〛
¶現金ではなく，小切手で支払います。 (Genkin de wa naku, *kogitte* de shiharaimasu.)

kogitte 〚n〛 (bank) **check**
¶ [I] will pay by **check** rather than in cash.

kōgyō 工業〚名〛

kōgyō 〚n〛 **an industry, the manufacturing industry**

376

重工業 (jūkōgyō) 軽工業 (keikō-
gyō) 工業専門学校 (kōgyō-sen-
mongakkō) 工業地帯 (kōgyō-
chitai)

¶この国は工業が発達しています。
(Kono kuni wa kōgyō ga hattatsu
shite imasu.)

heavy **industry** // light **industry** // a
technical school // an **industrial**
area, a **manufacturing** district

¶ This country is advanced **indus-
trially.**

kōhei 公平〖名, 形動〗

¶上田先生はすべての学生に公平です。
(Ueda sensei wa subete no gakusei
ni kōhei desu.)

¶このお菓子を公平に分けてください。
(Kono okashi o kōhei ni wakete
kudasai.)

kōhei 〖n, adj-v〗 impartiality, fairness, justice

¶ Professor Ueda **is impartial** toward all students.

¶ Please divide this candy 〚sweet〛
evenly.

kōhii コーヒー〖名〗

¶コーヒーを飲みに行きましょう。
(Kōhii o nomi ni ikimashō.)

¶コーヒーに砂糖とミルクを入れてく
ださい。(Kōhii ni satō to miruku
o irete kudasai.)

kōhii 〖n〗 coffee

¶ Let's go have **a cup of coffee.**

¶ Please put sugar and milk in **my
coffee.**

koi 濃い〖形〗

①[色の程度が強い様子]
¶あの濃い茶色の服を着ているのが, わ
たしの兄です。(Ano koi chairo no
fuku o kite iru no ga, watashi no
ani desu.)

¶ここの部分だけ濃く塗ってください。
(Koko no bubun dake koku nutte
kudasai.)

②[味の程度が強い様子]
濃いお茶 (koi ocha)
¶わたしは料理は濃い味のほうが好き
です。(Watashi wa ryōri wa koi
aji no hō ga suki desu.)

koi 〖adj〗 dark in color, deep in
color; strong in taste; thick, heavy
(in density)

① [dark in color, deep in color]
¶ The man in the **dark** brown suit is
my older brother.

¶ Please paint just this part **dark.**

② [strong in taste, strong in flavor]
strong green tea
¶ I prefer **strongly** flavored dishes.

¶わたしは濃いコーヒーは飲めませんから、薄くしてください。(Watashi wa *koi* kōhii wa nomemasen kara, usuku shite kudasai.)

③[密度が高い様子]

ひげが濃い (hige ga *koi*)

¶濃い霧のため、電車が遅れました。(*Koi* kiri no tame, densha ga okuremashita.)

⇨usui 薄い

koi 恋〖名, 〜する〗

初恋 (hatsu*koi*) 恋人 (*koi*bito)

¶恋は人間を美しくします。(*Koi* wa ningen o utsukushiku shimasu.)

¶上田さんは田中さんの妹に恋をしています。(Ueda san wa Tanaka san no imōto ni *koi* o shite imasu.)

⇨ren'ai 恋愛

kōji 工事〖名, 〜する〗

工事中 (*kōji*chū)

¶この道は道路工事のため通れません。(Kono michi wa dōro-*kōji* no tame tooremasen.)

¶この工事はいつ完成しますか。(Kono *kōji* wa itsu kansei shimasu ka?)

kojin 個人〖名〗

個人主義 (*kojin*-shugi)

¶個人の権利を守らなければなりません。(*Kojin* no kenri o mamoranakereba narimasen.)

¶これはわたしの個人的な意見です。(Kore wa watashi no *kojin*teki na iken desu.)

¶ I can't drink **strong** coffee so please make mine on the weak side.

③ [thick, heavy (in density)]

a **heavy** moustache 〚beard〛

¶ The train was late due to **heavy** fog.

koi 〚n, 〜*suru*〛 love

one's first **love**, puppy **love** // a lover, boyfriend, girlfriend

¶ **Love** makes people beautiful.

¶ Mr. Ueda **is in love** with [Mr.] Tanaka's younger sister.

kōji 〚n, 〜*suru*〛 construction, construction work

under **construction**

¶ This street is closed to traffic due to road **repairs.**

¶ When will this **construction work** be completed?

kojin 〚n〛 individual, persons in their private capacity

individualism

¶ The rights of **the individual** must be protected.

¶ This is my **personal** opinion.

kōjō 工場〖名〗
自動車工場 (jidōsha-kōjō)
¶この工場では，何人の工員が働いていますか。(Kono kōjō de wa, nannin no kōin ga hataraite imasu ka?)
¶工場の煙突から出る煙が空気を汚しています。(Kōjō no entotsu kara deru kemuri ga kūki o yogoshite imasu.)
⇨kōba 工場

kōka 効果〖名〗
¶この方法で勉強すれば，効果が上がりますよ。(Kono hōhō de benkyō sureba, kōka ga agarimasu yo.)
¶漢字の効果的な勉強法を教えてください。(Kanji no kōkateki na benkyōhō o oshiete kudasai.)

kōkai 後悔〖名，〜する〗
¶学生時代にもっと勉強しておけばよかったと後悔しています。(Gakuseijidai ni motto benkyō shite okeba yokatta to kōkai shite imasu.)
¶今になって後悔しても遅いですよ。(Ima ni natte kōkai shite mo osoi desu yo.)

kōkan 交換〖名，〜する〗
¶お金と交換に品物を渡します。(Okane to kōkan ni shinamono o watashimasu.)
¶わたしたちは留学生を招いて意見の交換をしました。(Watashitachi wa ryūgakusei o maneite iken no kōkan o shimashita.)

kōjō 〚n〛 **factory, plant**
an automobile **manufacturing plant**
¶ How many workers are employed at this **factory?**

¶ The smoke coming out of the **factory** smokestacks is dirtying the air.

kōka 〚n〛 **effect, effectiveness, efficiency, result**
¶ You will have better **results** if you study with this method.

¶ Please teach [us] an **efficient** 〖**effective, good**〗 way to study kanji.

kōkai 〚n, ～suru〛 **regret, remorse, repentance**
¶ **I regret** that I didn't study harder in my student days.

¶ It's too late for **regrets** now.

kōkan 〚n, ～suru〛 **exchange, interchange, barter**
¶ One hands over merchandise **in exchange** for money.

¶ We invited foreign students and **had an exchange** of views.

kokka 国家〖名〗

¶第二次大戦後，世界に新しい国家が次々に誕生しました。 (Dainiji-taisengo, sekai ni atarashii *kokka* ga tsugitsugi ni tanjō shimashita.)

¶国家の安全を守るために条約を結びます。 (*Kokka* no anzen o mamoru tame ni jōyaku o musubimasu.)

kokka 国歌〖名〗

kokki 国旗〖名〗

¶オリンピック会場には世界各国の国旗が飾られます。 (Orinpikku-kaijō ni wa sekai-kakkoku no *kokki* ga kazararemasu.)

koko ここ〖代〗

①[空間的に話し手に身近な関係にある所などをさし示す]

¶「鉛筆はどこにありますか。」 (Enpitsu wa doko ni arimasu ka?) 「ここにあります。」 (*Koko* ni arimasu.)

¶「ここは銀座ですか。」 (*Koko* wa Ginza desu ka?) 「いいえ、ここは銀座ではありません。銀座はこの次です。」 (Iie, *koko* wa Ginza de wa arimasen. Ginza wa kono tsugi desu.)

¶「あなたはいつからこの寮に住んでいますか。」 (Anata wa itsu kara kono ryō ni sunde imasu ka?) 「去年の四月に日本に来てから、ずっとここに住んでいます。」 (Kyonen no shigatsu ni Nihon ni kite kara, zutto *koko* ni sunde imasu.)

＊話し手と話し相手が同じ所にいる場

kokka 〖n〗 **state, country, nation**

¶ After World War II new **nations** entered the world community one after the other.

¶ Treaties are concluded in order to protect the security of **the state.**

kokka 〖n〗 **national anthem**

kokki 〖n〗 **national flag**

¶ When the Olympics are held, **the national flags** of countries around the world are on display.

koko 〖pron〗 **here, this place; this**

① [here, this place; indicates a place physically close to the speaker]

¶ "Where is my pencil?"
"**Here** it is."

¶ "Is **this** Ginza?"
"No, **this** isn't Ginza. Ginza is the next stop."

¶ "How long have you been living in this dormitory?"
"I've been living **here** ever since I came to Japan last April (that is, last year in April)."

＊ When the speaker and listener are

合には, 話し手が「ここ (koko)」で
さし示す所は, 話し相手も「ここ(ko-
ko)」でさし示す。

②[話し手が指さして説明する場合な
どにそのさし示している所などを表
す]

¶「名前はどこに書いたらいいですか。」
(Namae wa doko ni kaitara ii
desu ka?)「ここに書いてください。」
(*Koko* ni kaite kudasai.)

¶この地図を見てください。ここが東
京で, ここが大阪です。(Kono chizu
o mite kudasai. *Koko* ga Tōkyō de,
koko ga Oosaka desu.)

③[話し手が現に取り上げているもの
ごとの範囲・部分・点などをさし示
す]

¶今日の勉強はここまでです。(Kyō
no benkyō wa *koko* made desu.)

¶ここが特に大切なところです。(*Koko*
ga tokuni taisetsu na tokoro desu.)

④[話し手の当面する時間を基準とし
てその前後の時間のある範囲をさし示
す]

¶ここ二, 三日はまだ雨が降り続くそ
うです。(*Koko* ni-sannichi wa mada
ame ga furitsuzuku sō desu.)

¶ここ一週間はずっと風邪で寝ていま
した。(*Koko* isshūkan wa zutto
kaze de nete imashita.)

⇒soko そこ　asoko あそこ　doko
どこ

kōkoku 広告〖名, 〜する〗
新聞広告 (shinbun-*kōkoku*)

both in the same place, the listener
will also use *koko* for a place the
speaker refers to as *koko*.

② [here, this place; a place indicated
by the speaker when pointing while
explaining, etc.]

¶ "Where should I write my name?"
"Please write it **here**."

¶ Please look at this map. Tokyo is
here and Osaka is **here** 〖This is
Tokyo and **this** is Osaka〗.

③ [here, this; indicates a section, a
point, the environment, etc., of
whatever the speaker is talking about
at the time]

¶ **This** concludes our studies for today 〖That's all for today〗.

¶ **This** is an especially important
part.

④ [this; takes the present time of the
speaker as the standard and indicates
a period before or after that]

¶ It looks like the rain will continue
for **the next** two or three days.

¶ [I] have been in bed **this past**
week with a cold 〖the flu〗.

kōkō ☞ **kōtōgakkō**

kōkoku 〖n, 〜*suru*〗 **advertisement,
notice, announcement, publicity**

a newspaper **advertisement**, classified **ad** in the newspaper

¶新聞に新しい自動車の広告が出ています。(Shinbun ni atarashii jidōsha no *kōkoku* ga dete imasu.)

kokonoka 九日〖名〗

①[日付を表す]
一月九日 (ichigatsu *kokonoka*)

②[日数を表す]
¶病気で九日も学校を休みました。(Byōki de *kokonoka* mo gakkō o yasumimashita.)

⇨ -ka -日

kokonotsu 九つ〖名〗

①[9個]
¶ここにみかんが九つあります。(Koko ni mikan ga *kokonotsu* arimasu.)

②[9歳]
¶今年，この子は九つです。(Kotoshi, kono ko wa *kokonotsu* desu.)

kokoro 心〖名〗

心細い (*kokoro*bosoi)
¶あの人は心の優しい人です。(Ano hito wa *kokoro* no yasashii hito desu.)
¶御親切を心から感謝いたします。(Goshinsetsu o *kokoro* kara kansha itashimasu.)
¶心をこめてお礼の手紙を書きました。(*Kokoro* o komete orei no tegami o kakimashita.)

kokuban 黒板〖名〗

¶黒板に今習った漢字を書きなさい。(*Kokuban* ni ima naratta kanji o kakinasai.)

kokonoka 〚n〛 the ninth of the month; nine days

① [the ninth of the month]
January **9**

② [nine days]
¶ [I] was absent from school for **nine days** due to illness.

kokonotsu 〚n〛 nine; nine years old

① [nine, nine items]
¶ There are **nine** mandarin oranges here.

② [nine years old]
¶ This child is **nine years old** this year.

kokoro 〚n〛 heart, mind, spirit, feeling

forlorn, down**hearted,** lonely, discouraging
¶ [He] is a **kindhearted** person.

¶ I thank you for your kindness from the bottom of **my heart.**

¶ [I] wrote a **heartfelt** letter of thanks.

kokuban 〚n〛 blackboard
¶ Write the *kanji* we've just studied on **the blackboard.**

kōkūbin 航空便〖名〗

¶ジャカルタから東京まで**航空便**なら三日で届きます。 (Jakaruta kara Tōkyō made *kōkūbin* nara mikka de todokimasu.)

⇒funabin 船便

kokugai 国外〖名〗

¶上田さんは主に**国外**で活躍しています。(Ueda san wa omo ni *kokugai* de katsuyaku shite imasu.)

⇔kokunai 国内

kokugo 国語〖名〗

①[日本語]

国語辞典 (*kokugo*-jiten)　**国語**学 (*kokugo*gaku)

¶上田先生は中学校で**国語**を教えています。 (Ueda sensei wa chūgakkō de *kokugo* o oshiete imasu.)

②[国の公的言語]

¶オーストラリアの**国語**は英語です。 (Ōsutoraria no *kokugo* wa Eigo desu.)

kokumin 国民〖名〗

国民感情 (*kokumin*-kanjō)　**国民**生活 (*kokumin*-seikatsu)　**国民**性 (*kokumin*sei)

¶**国民**は税金を納める義務があります。 (*Kokumin* wa zeikin o osameru gimu ga arimasu.)

kokunai 国内〖名〗

¶郵便料金は**国内**どこでも同じです。 (Yūbin-ryōkin wa *kokunai* doko demo onaji desu.)

⇔kokugai 国外

kōkūbin 〚n〛 **airmail**

¶ Mail sent **airmail** from Jakarta takes three days to get to Tokyo.

kokugai 〚n〛 **overseas, outside the country**

¶ [Mr.] Ueda's activities are predominantly conducted **overseas.**

kokugo 〚n〛 **the Japanese language; the language of a nation**

① [the Japanese language]

a **Japanese-language** dictionary // the linguistic study of **Japanese**

¶ [Miss] Ueda teaches **Japanese** in middle school.

② [the language of a nation]

¶ **The national language** of Australia is English.

kokumin 〚n〛 **a nation, a people, a citizen**

national sentiment // **national** life // the **national** character, **national** traits

¶ **Citizens** have a duty to pay taxes.

kokunai 〚n〛 **interior, domestic, inside a country**

¶ Postage rates are the same anywhere **in the country.**

kokuritsu 国立〖名〗
国立大学 (*kokuritsu*-daigaku) 国立公園 (*kokuritsu*-kōen) 国立劇場 (*kokuritsu*-gekijō) 国立病院 (*kokuritsu*-byōin)

¶この建物は国立博物館です。(Kono tatemono wa *kokuritsu*-hakubutsu-kan desu.)

⇒**kōritsu** 公立 **shiritsu** 私立

kokusai 国際〖名〗
国際関係 (*kokusai*kankei) 国際連合 (*kokusai*rengō) 国際協力 (*kokusai*kyōryoku) 国際問題 (*kokusai*-mondai) 国際電話 (*kokusai*denwa) 国際結婚 (*kokusai*kekkon)

¶東京で漁業についての国際会議が開かれました。(Tōkyō de gyogyō ni tsuite no *kokusai*kaigi ga hiraka-remashita.)

¶英語は国際的な言葉です。(Eigo wa *kokusai*teki na kotoba desu.)

＊ いつも他の言葉といっしょに使う。

kokuseki 国籍〖名〗
¶国籍と名前をこのカードに書いてください。(*Kokuseki* to namae o kono kādo ni kaite kudasai.)

¶わたしの国籍は日本です。(Watashi no *kokuseki* wa Nihon desu.)

kokyū 呼吸〖名, ～する〗
¶高い山に登ると, 呼吸が苦しくなります。(Takai yama ni noboru to, *kokyū* ga kurushiku narimasu.)

¶マラソンをしたあとで, 何回も深呼吸をしました。(Marason o shita ato

kokuritsu 〖n〗 **national, state-run**
a **national** university // a **national** park // a **national** theater, the **National** Theater // a **national** hospital

¶ This building is the **National** Museum.

kokusai 〖n〗 **international, international intercourse**
international relations // the United **Nations** // **international** cooperation // an **international** problem, a **diplomatic** issue // an **overseas** telephone call // marriage between persons **of differing nationality**

¶ An **international** conference on fishing has opened 〚was held〛 in Tokyo.

¶ English is an **international** language.

＊ *Kokusai* is always used in compounds with other words.

kokuseki 〖n〗 **nationality, citizenship**
¶ Please write **your nationality** and name on these cards.

¶ I am a Japanese **national**.

kokyū 〖n, ～*suru*〗 **breath, breathing, respiration**
¶ One experiences difficulty **in breathing** when climbing a high mountain.

¶ [He] **breathed** deeply in and out

de, nankai mo shin*kokyū* o shimashita.)

komakai 細かい〖形〗

①［形や金額が小さい］

¶目が悪いので、細かい字は読めませ
ん。(Me ga warui node, *komakai* ji
wa yomemasen.)

¶1万円を細かくしてください。
(Ichiman'en o *komakaku* shite kudasai.)

②［内容が詳しい］

¶このことについて、もっと細かく説
明しましょう。(Kono koto ni tsuite,
motto *komakaku* setsumei shimashō.)

＊「細か (komaka)」（形動）という
言葉もある。「細かな字 (komaka na
ji)」

komaru 困る〖動Ⅰ〗

¶この国の人たちは食糧に困っていま
す。(Kono kuni no hitotachi wa
shokuryō ni *komatte* imasu.)

¶工場がうるさくて、近所の人が困っ
ています。(Kōjō ga urusakute,
kinjo no hito ga *komatte* imasu.)

¶難しい質問をされて、返事に困りまし
た。(Muzukashii shitsumon o
sarete, henji ni *komarimashita*.)

kome 米〖名〗

¶日本では米が主食です。(Nihon de
wa *kome* ga shushoku desu.)

komu こむ〖動Ⅰ〗

¶日曜日なので、映画館はたいへんこ
んでいました。(Nichiyōbi na node,

several times after completing the
marathon.

komakai 〖adj〗 small, fine; de-
tailed

① [small, fine, minute]

¶ [My] eyes are bad so [I] can't read
small print.

¶ Please give me **change** for this ten-
thousand-yen bill.

② [detailed, minute]

¶ Let me explain **in** more **detail**
about this matter.

＊ The word *komaka* (an adjective-
verb) can also be used, as in *komaka
na ji* (small print).

komaru 〖v Ⅰ〗 be in difficulties; be
badly off; be at a loss, be bothered

¶ The people in this country **are
short** of food.

¶ The neighborhood people **are inconvenienced** by the noise of the
factory.

¶ [I] was asked a difficult question
and **was hard put** for an answer.

kome 〖n〗 rice

¶ **Rice** is the staple food of Japan.

komu 〖v Ⅰ〗 be crowded

¶ The movie theater **was** very
crowded as it was Sunday.

eigakan wa taihen *konde* imashita.)

-komu -込む〔尾〕

①[中に入る，入れる]

プールに飛び込む（pūru ni tobi*komu*）

¶雨が降ってきたので，軒下に駆け込みました。 (Ame ga futte kita node, nokishita ni kake*komimashita*.)

¶この欄に国籍と名前を書き込んでください。(Kono ran ni kokuseki to namae o kaki*konde* kudasai.)

②[すっかりそういう状態になる]

¶あの人は何を考え込んでいるのでしょう。(Ano hito wa nani o kangae-*konde* iru no deshō.)

¶中村さんはお酒を飲んで，眠り込んでしまいました。 (Nakamura san wa osake o nonde, nemuri*konde* shimaimashita.)

* 動詞のあとについて，その動詞の意味を強める。

komugi 小麦〔名〕

¶小麦粉でパンを作ります。(*Komugi-ko* de pan o tsukurimasu.)

kona 粉〔名〕

粉ミルク (*kona*miruku) 粉薬 (*kona*gusuri) 粉石けん (*kona*sekken)

¶この菓子は米の粉で作ります。

(Kono kashi wa kome no *kona* de tsukurimasu.)

konban 今晩〔名〕

¶今晩6時から音楽会があります。

(*Konban* rokuji kara ongakkai ga arimasu.)

-komu 〔suf〕 **come in, put in; completely ~**

① [come in, put in]

jump 〖**dive**, **plunge**〗 into the pool

¶ It started raining so [I] **ran under** the eaves.

¶ Please **fill in** this column with your nationality and name.

② [completely ~]

¶ I wonder what [he] **is so lost in thought** about.

¶ [Mr.] Nakamura was drinking and **fell fast asleep.**

* *-komu* intensifies the meaning of the verb it is added to.

komugi 〖n〗 **wheat**

¶ Bread is made from (**wheat**) flour.

kona 〖n〗 **flour, meal, powder, dust**

powdered milk, **dry** milk // **powdered** medicine // soap **powder,** soap **flakes,** washing **powder**

¶ This sweet is made from rice **flour.**

konaida ☞ **konoaida**

konban 〖n〗 **this evening, tonight**

¶ There is a concert 〖recital〗 **tonight** at six o'clock.

⇒kon'ya 今夜

konban wa 今晩は〖連〗

¶今晩は。(*Konban wa!*)

kondo 今度〖名〗

①[この次, 近い将来]

¶今度の日曜日に映画を見に行きましょう。(*Kondo no nichiyōbi ni eiga o mi ni ikimashō.*)

¶今度日本に行くときは, 両親も連れていくつもりです。(*Kondo Nihon ni iku toki wa, ryōshin mo tsurete iku tsumori desu.*)

②[今回]

¶今度の実験は成功しました。(*Kondo no jikken wa seikō shimashita.*)

¶入学試験のため一生懸命勉強しましたが, 今度もだめでした。(*Nyūgaku-shiken no tame isshōkenmei benkyō shimashita ga, kondo mo dame deshita.*)

* 何回か繰り返されるものごとのうち, いちばん最近のことについて言うときに使う。

③[最近]

¶今度, 新しく来た先生のお名前は何と言いますか。(*Kondo, atarashiku kita sensei no onamae wa nan to iimasu ka?*)

¶わたしは今度初めて日本へ来ました。(*Watashi wa kondo hajimete Nihon e kimashita.*)

* 新しく起こったものごとについて言うときに使う。

kongetsu 今月〖名〗

konban wa 〖compd〗 a greeting used in the evening

¶ Good evening.

kondo 〖n〗 next time; this time; recently

① [next time, soon]

¶ Let's go to see a movie **next** Sunday.

¶ I plan to take my parents with me **the next time** I go to Japan.

② [this time, now]

¶ The experiment succeeded **this time.**

¶ [I] studied hard for the school entrance exam but failed **this time** too.

* Used for the most recent of a series of repeated events.

③ [recently]

¶ What is the name of the **new** teacher?

¶ I **recently** came to Japan for the first time.

* Used for something taking place not long before.

kongetsu 〖n〗 this month

387

¶わたしは今月の末に京都へ行きます。
(Watashi wa *kongetsu* no sue ni Kyōto e ikimasu.)

¶田中さんは今月アメリカから帰ってきます。 (Tanaka san wa *kongetsu* Amerika kara kaette kimasu.)

kongo 今後〖名〗

¶同じ間違いをしないように，今後は気をつけます。 (Onaji machigai o shinai yō ni, *kongo* wa ki o tsukemasu.)

¶今後ともよろしくお願いします。
(*Kongo* tomo yoroshiku onegai shimasu.)

konkuriito コンクリート〖名〗

¶この建物はコンクリート建築です。
(Kono tatemono wa *konkuriito*-kenchiku desu.)

konna こんな〖連体〗

①［話し手にとって身近な関係にあるものごとの様子をさし示す］

¶こんなひどい雨でも行くのですか。
(*Konna* hidoi ame demo iku no desu ka?)

¶難しい試験に通って，こんなうれしいことはありません。 (Muzukashii shiken ni tootte, *konna* ureshii koto wa arimasen.)

¶こんなふうにすると，うまくいきますよ。(*Konna* fū ni suru to, umaku ikimasu yo.)

②［文脈の上で前に述べたことがらの内容・状態などを話し手に身近な関係にあるものとしてさし示したりまたあ

¶ I am going to go to Kyoto at the end of **this month.**

¶ [Miss] Tanaka returns from the United States **this month.**

kongo 〚n〛 after this, from now on, hereafter, in the future

¶ I will be careful **from now on** not to make the same mistake again.

¶ I hope I can **continue** to receive your good offices.

konkuriito 〚n〛 concrete

¶ This is a **concrete** building.

konna 〚attrib〛 such, this, like this

① [such, this, like this; indicates something close to the speaker]

¶ Are you going even in **such** a heavy rain?

¶ Nothing could afford greater happiness than this passing of a difficult exam.

¶ It will work better if you do it **like this.**

② [this, like this; indicates that something mentioned earlier is close to the speaker or introduces an opin-

とから述べる話し手の考えなどを前もってさし示したりする〕

¶「もうあんな所へは二度と行きたくない。」と，子供は**こんな**ことを言うのです。("Mō anna tokoro e wa nido to ikitaku nai." to, kodomo wa *konna* koto o iu no desu.)

¶わたしは**こんな**ふうに考えます。子供にはあまりきびしくしても自由にさせてもよくないと思うのです。(Watashi wa *konna* fū ni kangaemasu. Kodomo ni wa amari kibishiku shite mo jiyū ni sasete mo yoku nai to omou no desu.)

⇨sonna そんな　　anna あんな
donna どんな

konna 困難〚名，形動〛

¶今月中に論文を完成するのは**困難**です。(Kongetsuchū ni ronbun o kansei suru no wa *konnan* desu.)
¶上田さんは**困難**な仕事をとうとうやり遂げました。(Ueda san wa *konnan* na shigoto o tōtō yaritogemashita.)
¶物価が上がって，生活が**困難**になってきました。(Bukka ga agatte, seikatsu ga *konnan* ni natte kimashita.)

konna ni こんなに〚副〛

¶この問題が**こんなに**複雑だとは思いませんでした。(Kono mondai ga *konna ni* fukuzatsu da to wa omoimasen deshita.)
¶**こんなに**楽しいパーティーは初めてです。(*Konna ni* tanoshii pātii wa

ion, etc., of the speaker]

¶ The child had **this** to say: "I never want to go to that sort of place again."

¶ **This** is what I think. I think it's bad to be either too strict or too easy-going with one's children.

konnan 〚n, adj-v〛 difficulty, trouble, suffering, distress, hardship

¶ **It will be difficult** to finish the thesis by the end of the month.

¶ [Mr.] Ueda finally finished that **difficult** task.

¶ With the rise in prices it has become 〚it became〛 **difficult** to make ends meet.

konna ni 〚adv〛 so, so much, like this

¶ I didn't think that this problem was **so** complicated.

¶ I have never before been to **such** an enjoyable party.

hajimete desu.)

¶こんなにたくさんいただいて，ありがとうございます。(*Konna ni* takusan itadaite, arigatō gozaimasu.)

✳ 話し手が身近に認めるものごとの状態・程度・数量などをさし示すのに使う。強調的にさし示すこともある。

⇒**sonna ni** そんなに　**anna ni** あんなに　**donna ni** どんなに

konnichi 今日〖名〗

¶今日の日本は民主国家として発展しています。(*Konnichi* no Nihon wa minshukokka to shite hatten shite imasu.)

konnichi wa 今日は〖連〗

¶今日は。(*Konnichi wa!*)

kono この〖連体〗

①[話し手とものごととの身近な関係をさし示す]

この人 (*kono* hito)　この方 (*kono* kata)

¶「このかばんはだれのですか。」(*Kono* kaban wa dare no desu ka?)「そのかばんは山田さんのです。」(Sono kaban wa Yamada san no desu.)

¶「この建物の中には教室がいくつありますか。」(*Kono* tatemono no naka ni wa kyōshitsu ga ikutsu arimasu ka?)「この建物の中には教室が 20 あります。」(*Kono* tatemono no naka ni wa kyōshitsu ga nijū arimasu.)

✳ 話し手と話し相手とが同じ所にいて，話し手にとっても話し相手にとっても身近な範囲の所にあるものごとは，話

¶ Thank you for giving me **all this.**

✳ *Konna ni* is used to indicate the condition, extent, amount, etc., of things recognized as close by the speaker. It is sometimes used as an intensifier.

konnichi 〖n〗 **today, these days, nowadays, at present**

¶ **Present-day** Japan is an advanced democracy.

konnichi wa 〖compd〗 a greeting used during the day

¶ **Good day** 〖**Good morning; Good afternoon; Hello**〗.

kono 〖attrib〗 **this, these**

① [this, these; indicates that someone or something is physically close to the speaker]

this person // **this** lady 〖gentleman〗

¶ "Whose bag 〖suitcase, briefcase, etc.〗 is **this?**"

"That bag is [Mr.] Yamada's."

¶ "How many classrooms are there in **this** building?"

"There are 20 classrooms in **this** building."

✳ The speaker and listener both use *kono* when they are in the same location and when the object or person is

し手も話し相手も「この (kono)」で
さし示す。

②[文脈の上で前に述べたものごとを
話し手にとって身近な関係にあるもの
としてさし示す]

¶昨日，ホテルに着きました。このホ
テルは林の中にあるので，たいへん涼
しいです。 (Kinō hoteru ni tsukimashita. *Kono* hoteru wa hayashi
no naka ni aru node, taihen suzushii desu.)

¶試験の成績が 60 点以上でなければ，
上のクラスには進めません。このこと
は，あなたも知っていたはずです。
(Shiken no seiseki ga rokujitten
ijō de nakereba, ue no kurasu ni
wa susumemasen. *Kono* koto wa,
anata mo shitte ita hazu desu.)

③[話し手の当面する時間を基準とし
てその前後の時間のある範囲をさし示
す]

¶山田さんはこの二，三日元気がない
です。 (Yamada san wa *kono* ni-
sannichi genki ga nai desu.)

⇨sono その ano あの dono どの

konoaida この間〖名〗

¶わたしはこの間，上田さんに会いま
した。(Watashi wa *konoaida*, Ueda
san ni aimashita.)

＊「こないだ (konaida)」とも言う。

⇨senjitsu 先日

konogoro このごろ〖名〗

¶このごろは忙しくて，新聞も読めま
せん。(*Konogoro* wa isogashikute,

---

physically close to both of them.

② [this, these; refers to something
mentioned earlier as something that
is close to the speaker]

¶ [I] arrived at the hotel yesterday.
As **this** hotel is in the middle of the
woods, it is very cool here.

¶ One cannot advance to the next
class unless one has a grade of 60 or
better on the exam. You must have
known **this**.

③ [this, these, past, next; indicates a
time before or after the present time
of the speaker, which is taken as the
standard]

¶ [Miss] Yamada has been in low
spirits **these past** two or three days.

konoaida 〚n〛 the other day, recently

¶ I met [Mr.] Ueda **the other day**.

＊ Variant: *konaida*.

konogoro 〚n〛 now, nowadays, recently, lately

¶ I'm so busy **these days** I can't

shinbun mo yomemasen.)

¶このごろの若者は髪の毛を長く伸ばしています。　(Konogoro no wakamono wa kaminoke o nagaku nobashite imasu.)

¶ Young people wear their hair long **these days.**

kono mae　この前〖連〗

¶この前，日本へ行った時は春でした。 (Kono mae, Nihon e itta toki wa haru deshita.)

¶この前の日曜日は家族と銀座へ行きました。(Kono mae no nichiyōbi wa kazoku to Ginza e ikimashita.)

⇨mae　前

kono mae 〖compd〗 **last, last time, before this, previously**

¶ It was spring when [I] went to Japan **the last time.**

¶ **Last** Sunday [I] went with my family to Ginza.

kono tsugi　この次〖連〗

¶この次の日曜日にテニスをしませんか。　(Kono tsugi no nichiyōbi ni tenisu o shimasen ka?)

¶この次は20ページから始めます。

(Kono tsugi wa nijippēji kara hajimemasu.)

kono tsugi 〖compd〗 **next, next time, another time**

¶ Won't you play tennis with me **next** Sunday?

¶ **Next time** we will start from page 20.

konshū　今週〖名〗

¶今週の土曜日にうちに来てください。 (Konshū no doyōbi ni uchi ni kite kudasai.)

¶今週，わたしは京都へ行くつもりです。　(Konshū, watashi wa Kyōto e iku tsumori desu.)

konshū 〖n〗 **this week**

¶ Please come to visit me **this** Saturday.

¶ I plan to go to Kyoto **this week.**

kon'ya　今夜〖名〗

¶今夜はこのホテルに泊まりましょう。 (Kon'ya wa kono hoteru ni tomarimashō.)

¶今夜，わたしのうちに来てください。 (Kon'ya, watashi no uchi ni kite kudasai.)

kon'ya 〖n〗 **this evening, tonight**

¶ Let's stay at this hotel **tonight.**

¶ Please come to visit me **this evening.**

⇒konban 今晩
こんばん

kon'yaku　婚約〖名, 〜する〗
こんやく

婚約指環 (kon'yaku-yubiwa)　　婚約
こんやくゆびわ　　　　　　　　　　こんやく

期間 (kon'yaku-kikan)　　　婚約者
きかん　　　　　　　　　　　　こんやくしゃ

(kon'yakusha)

¶一郎さんと春子さんは昨日婚約しま
いちろう　　はるこ　　　　きのう こんやく
した。 (Ichirō san to Haruko san
wa kinō kon'yaku shimashita.)

kon'yaku　〖n, 〜suru〗　engagement, betrothal

an **engagement** ring // an **engagement** period // a **fiancé, fiancée**

¶ Ichirō and Haruko **became engaged** yesterday.

koori　氷〖名〗
こおり

¶池に氷が張っています。 (Ike ni
いけ こおり　は
koori ga hatte imasu.)

¶暑いから、ジュースに氷を入れてく
あつ　　　　　　　　　こおり　い
ださい。 (Atsui kara, jūsu ni koori
o irete kudasai.)

koori　〖n〗　ice

¶ The pool 〖pond〗 **is frozen over.**

¶ Could you please put **ice** in the juice? It's such a hot day!

kooru　凍る〖動Ⅰ〗
こお

¶冬の間は池の水が凍ります。 (Fuyu
ふゆ あいだ いけ みず こお
no aida wa ike no mizu ga koori-
masu.)

¶夏は物が腐りやすいので, 凍らせて
なつ もの くさ　　　　　　こお
保存します。 (Natsu wa mono ga
ほぞん
kusariyasui node, koorasete hozon
shimasu.)

kooru　〖v I〗　freeze, be frozen over

¶ The pond **freezes** during the winter.

¶ Food goes bad easily during the summer so it is preserved **by freezing.**

koppu　コップ〖名〗

¶そのコップに水を一杯ください。
みず いっぱい
(Sono koppu ni mizu o ippai kudasai.)

koppu　〖n〗　glass, tumbler

¶ Please give me water in that **glass.**

kore　これ〖代〗

①[話し手に身近な関係にあるものご
とをさし示す]

¶「これはだれの本ですか。」(Kore wa
ほん
dare no hon desu ka?) 「それは上
うえ
田さんの本です。」 (Sore wa Ueda
だ　　　ほん
san no hon desu.)

¶「そのりんごはおいしいですよ。」

kore　〖pron〗　this, these; now; this person

① [this, these, this one; indicates something physically close to the speaker]

¶ "Whose book is **this**?"

　"That is [Mr.] Ueda's book."

(Sono ringo wa oishii desu yo.)「で
は，**これ**を五つください。」 (Dewa,
kore o itsutsu kudasai.)

¶「東京の地図は**これ**ですか。」(Tōkyō
no chizu wa *kore* desu ka?)「いい
え，東京の地図はそれではありませ
ん。」(Iie, Tōkyō no chizu wa sore
de wa arimasen.)

②[話し手が当面している時間をさし
示す，今]

¶「あなたは**これ**からどこへ行きます
か。」(Anata wa *kore* kara doko e
ikimasu ka?)「わたしは**これ**からデ
パートへ行きます。」 (Watashi wa
kore kara depāto e ikimasu.)

¶「あなたは**これ**から何をしますか。」
(Anata wa *kore* kara nani o shimasu ka?)「わたしは**これ**から図書館
で勉強します。」(Watashi wa *kore*
kara toshokan de benkyō shimasu.)

¶この前の試験は，**これ**までででいちば
んいい成績でした。(Kono mae no
shiken wa, *kore* made de ichiban
ii seiseki deshita.)

*「これから (kore kara)」「これまで
(kore made)」などの形で使う。

③[話し手の家族や友人などで話し手
の身近にいる者をさし示す]

¶**これ**が今年大学に入った弟です。
(*Kore* ga kotoshi daigaku ni haitta
otōto desu.)

¶**これ**がわたしの家内です。どうぞよ
ろしく。(*Kore* ga watashi no kanai
desu. Dōzo yoroshiku.)

¶ "Those apples are good."
"Well then, give me five of **them**."

¶ "Is **this** a map of Tokyo?"
"No, that isn't a map of Tokyo."

② [this, now; indicates the present
time of the speaker]

¶ "Where are you going **now?**"
"I'm going to the department store
now."

¶ "What are you going to do **now?**"
"I'm going to study at the library
now."

¶ [My] mark on the last exam was
the highest [I]'ve had up to **now.**

* Used in the patterns "*kore kara*,"
"*kore made*," etc.

③ [this, this person; indicates a person close to the speaker such as a
family member or friend]

¶ **This** is my younger brother, who
has started college this year.

¶ **This** is my wife. Let me introduce
you.

④［文脈の上で前に述べたものごとを話し手に身近な関係にあるものとしてさし示す］

¶わたしのうちでは犬を飼っています。これはどろぼうが入るのを防ぐためです。(Watashi no uchi de wa inu o katte imasu. *Kore* wa dorobō ga hairu no o fusegu tame desu.)

¶工場の煙突から出る煙は炭のような粒が集まったものです。石油が燃えるときに出る煙もこれと同じです。(Kōjō no entotsu kara deru kemuri wa sumi no yō na tsubu ga atsumatta mono desu. Sekiyu ga moeru toki ni deru kemuri mo *kore* to onaji desu.)

⑤［話し手が当面している今の状態をさし示す］

¶今日の勉強はこれまでにします。(Kyō no benkyō wa *kore* made ni shimasu.)

¶これで今日の授業は終わります。(*Kore* de kyō no jugyō wa owarimasu.)

¶これからが大切ですから，よく聞いていてください。(*Kore* kara ga taisetsu desu kara, yoku kiite ite kudasai.)

¶では，これで失礼します。(Dewa, *kore* de shitsurei shimasu.)

*「これまで (kore made)」「これで (kore de)」「これから (kore kara)」などの形で使う。

⇨sore それ　are あれ　dore どれ

④ [this; refers to something mentioned earlier as something that is close to the speaker]

¶ We keep a dog at my house. **This** is to prevent thieves from breaking in.

¶ The smoke coming from the factory smokestack is like charcoal soot. The smoke produced when oil burns is the same as **this.**

⑤ [this, now; indicates the present situation of the speaker]

¶ **This** ends the lesson for today.

¶ **This** concludes today's class.

¶ The **next** part is especially important so please listen carefully.

¶ Well, **with this** I'll take my leave 〚Well, I'll say good-bye **now**〛.

* Used in the patterns "*kore made*," "*kore de*," "*kore kara*," etc.

kore kara これから〖連〗

¶これからだんだん寒くなります。
(*Kore kara* dandan samuku nari-masu.)

¶これから気をつけます。(*Kore kara* ki o tsukemasu.)

¶わたしはこれから学校へ行くところ
です。(Watashi wa *kore kara* gakkō e iku tokoro desu.)

kōritsu 公立〖名〗

¶田中さんの子供は公立の小学校に通っています。 (Tanaka san no kodomo wa *kōritsu* no shōgakkō ni kayotte imasu.)

⇒kokuritsu 国立 shiritsu 私立

koro ころ〖名〗

¶子供のころ，よく川へ魚を捕りに行きました。(Kodomo no *koro*, yoku kawa e sakana o tori ni ikimashita.)

¶父はもう帰ってくるころだと思います。 (Chichi wa mō kaette kuru *koro* da to omoimasu.)

korobu 転ぶ〖動 I 〗

¶転んで足にけがをしました。
(*Koronde* ashi ni kega o shimashita.)

¶道が悪いから，転ばないように注意してください。 (Michi ga warui kara, *korobanai* yō ni chūi shite kudasai.)

korogaru 転がる〖動 I 〗

①[回りながら進む]
¶山の上から石が転がってきました。

kore kara 〖compd〗 **from now on, after this, in future**

¶ **From now on** it will become colder and colder.

¶ I'll be careful **in future.**

¶ I am on the point of leaving for school **now.**

kōritsu 〖n〗 **public, public institution**

¶ [Mrs.] Tanaka's children go to a **public** elementary school.

koro 〖n〗 **time, about, around**

¶ **When** [I] was a child [I] often went fishing in the river.

¶ I think it's **about time** for my father to come home.

korobu 〖v I〗 **fall down, have a fall**

¶ [I] **fell down** and injured [my] leg 〖foot〗.

¶ The road is bad so please be careful **not to fall.**

(-)korogaru 〖v I〗 **roll, roll over, tumble, fall; lie down**

① [roll, roll over, tumble, fall]

396

(Yama no ue kara ishi ga *korogatte* kimashita.)

¶卵がテーブルの上から転がり落ちました。 (Tamago ga tēburu no ue kara *korogari*ochimashita.)

②[横たわる]

¶わたしたちは草の上に寝転がって休みました。 (Watashitachi wa kusa no ue ni ne*korogatte* yasumimashita.)

korosu 殺す〖動Ⅰ〗

¶これはねずみを殺す薬です。 (Kore wa nezumi o *korosu* kusuri desu.)

¶その人は自分の部屋で殺されていました。(Sono hito wa jibun no heya de *korosarete* imashita.)

kōsai 交際〖名, ～する〗

¶山田さんは交際範囲が広いので, 友達がおおぜいいます。 (Yamada san wa *kōsai*-han'i ga hiroi node, tomodachi ga oozei imasu.)

¶外国人と交際したいのですが, 紹介していただけませんか。 (Gaikokujin to *kōsai* shitai no desu ga, shōkai shite itadakemasen ka?)

kōsaten 交差点〖名〗

¶交差点に立って, 信号が変わるのを待ちました。 (*Kōsaten* ni tatte, shingō ga kawaru no o machimashita.)

¶この交差点で, 交通事故がよく起こります。 (Kono *kōsaten* de, kōtsū-jiko ga yoku okorimasu.)

koshi 腰〖名〗

¶ A rock **came tumbling down** from the mountaintop.

¶ An egg **fell off** the table.

② [lie down]

¶ We **lay down** on the grass and rested.

korosu 〖v I〗 **kill, murder**

¶ This is a chemical for **killing** rats.

¶ [He] was found **murdered** in [his] room.

kōsai 〖n, ～*suru*〗 **associating with, keeping company with, having social relations with, mixing with, dating**

¶ [Mr.] Yamada has a wide **circle of acquaintances** and many friends.

¶ I would like **to become friends** with a foreigner. Could you introduce me to someone?

kōsaten 〖n〗 **intersection, crossroads, crossing**

¶ [I] stood at **the crossing** waiting for the light to change.

¶ Accidents are frequent at this **intersection.**

koshi 〖n〗 **waist, hip, small of the back**

腰を下ろす (*koshi* o orosu)　腰を
掛ける (*koshi* o kakeru)

¶わたしの おばあさんは年を取ってい
るので、腰が曲がっています。
(Watashi no obāsan wa toshi o
totte iru node, *koshi* ga magatte
imasu.)

sit down // sit down

¶ My grandmother is elderly and
bent with age.

koshikakeru 腰掛ける〖動Ⅱ〗
¶わたしは山田さんと並んで腰掛けま
した。(Watashi wa Yamada san to
narande *koshikakemashita*.)

koshikakeru 〖v II〗 **sit down, take a seat**

¶ I **sat down** next to [Mrs.] Yamada.

koshō 故障〖名、〜する〗
¶電車の故障で学校に遅れました。
(Densha no *koshō* de gakkō ni
okuremashita.)
¶この機械は故障しています。(Kono
kikai wa *koshō* shite imasu.)

koshō 〖n, ～*suru*〗 **trouble, breakdown, malfunction, defect, accident**

¶ [I] was late for school because of a
train **breakdown** 〚**accident**〛.

¶ This machine **is out of order.**

koshō こしょう〖名〗
¶肉料理にこしょうをかけると、味が
もっとよくなります。(Nikuryōri ni
koshō o kakeru to, aji ga motto
yoku narimasu.)

koshō 〖n〗 **pepper**

¶ Meat dishes taste better if one adds
pepper.

kōshō 交渉〖名、〜する〗
団体交渉 (dantai-*kōshō*)
¶交渉がなかなかまとまりません。
(*Kōshō* ga nakanaka matomarimasen.)
¶労働条件について会社と交渉した
結果、少しよくなりました。(Rōdō-
jōken ni tsuite kaisha to *kōshō*
shita kekka, sukoshi yoku narimashita.)

kōshō 〖n, ～*suru*〗 **negotiations, bargaining, talks**

collective **bargaining**

¶ **The negotiations** aren't near a
conclusion.

¶ Working conditions have improved
somewhat as a result of **talks** with
the management.

kotae 答え〖名〗

①[返事]

kotae 〖n〗 **answer, reply; answer, solution, result**

① [answer, reply, response]

¶部屋の外からいくら呼んでも答えがありませんでした。 (Heya no soto kara ikura yonde mo *kotae* ga arimasen deshita.)

② [解答]

¶その答えは間違っています。 (Sono *kotae* wa machigatte imasu.)

kotaeru 答える〖動Ⅱ〗

① [返事する]

¶わたしが名前を呼んだら、「はい。」と答えてください。(Watashi ga namae o yondara, "Hai." to *kotaete* kudasai.)

② [解答する]

¶次の質問に答えなさい。 (Tsugi no shitsumon ni *kotaenasai*.)

kotai 固体〖名〗

¶氷は水が固体になったものです。

(Koori wa mizu ga *kotai* ni natta mono desu.)

⇒ekitai 液体 kitai 気体

kōtai 交替〖名, ～する〗

¶あのスーパーマーケットの店員は8時間ずつ交替で働いています。 (Ano sūpāmāketto no ten'in wa hachijikan zutsu *kōtai* de hataraite imasu.)

¶フットボールの試合で山田さんがけがをしたので、田中さんと交替しました。(Futtobōru no shiai de Yamada san ga kega o shita node, Tanaka san to *kōtai* shimashita.)

kōtei 肯定〖名, ～する〗

¶山田さんはその質問に対して否定も肯定もしませんでした。 (Yamada

¶ There was no **response** from inside the room no matter how much [we] called from outside.

② [answer, solution, result (for a question or problem)]

¶ That **answer** is wrong.

kotaeru 〖v II〗 **answer, reply; answer, solve**

① [answer, reply, respond]

¶ Please **reply** *hai* 〖Here!〗 when I call your name.

② [answer, solve, do (a problem)]

¶ **Answer** the following questions.

kotai 〖n〗 **solid, solid body**

¶ Ice is **the solid form** of water.

kōtai 〖n, ～*suru*〗 **alternative, change, shift, relief, relay**

¶ The employees at that supermarket work in eight-hour **shifts.**

¶ Since Yamada was injured in the football 〖soccer〗 match, he **was relieved** by Tanaka.

kotchi ☞ **kochira**

kōtei 〖n, ～*suru*〗 **affirmative, affirmation**

¶ [Mr.] Yamada didn't give any defisan wa sono shitsumon ni taishite hitei mo *kōtei* mo shimasen deshita.)

⇔hitei 否定

koto こと〖名〗

①[ことがら，事実，問題]

¶わたしのことは心配しないでください。 (Watashi no *koto* wa shinpai shinaide kudasai.)

¶日本のことが新聞に出ています。 (Nihon no *koto* ga shinbun ni dete imasu.)

¶そんなことは知りませんでした。 (Sonna *koto* wa shirimasen deshita.)

②[可能を表す]

¶あなたは日本語を話すことができますか。 (Anata wa Nihongo o hanasu *koto* ga dekimasu ka?)

¶お金がないので買うことができません。 (Okane ga nai .node kau *koto* ga dekimasen.)

*「動詞（連体の形）＋ことができる (koto ga dekiru)」の形で使う。

③[場合を表す]

¶わたしは朝御飯を食べないで学校へ行くことがあります。 (Watashi wa asagohan o tabenaide gakkō e iku *koto* ga arimasu.)

*「動詞（連体の形）＋ことがある (koto ga aru)」の形で使う。

④[経験を表す]

¶あなたは京都へ行ったことがありますか。 (Anata wa Kyōto e itta *koto* ga arimasu ka?)

nite answer to that question (literally, didn't say no or **yes**).

koto 〖n〗 **matter, affair**

① [matter, affair, fact, question]

¶ Please don't worry **on my account.**

¶ There is **something** about Japan in the newspaper.

¶ I had no knowledge of that **matter.**

② [can, cannot; expresses ability]

¶ **Can** you speak Japanese?

¶ [I] **can't** buy it since [I] don't have the money for it.

* Used in the pattern "verb (dictionary form) + *koto ga dekiru.*"

③ [expresses circumstances or a case]

¶ **There are times** when I go to school without eating breakfast.

* Used in the pattern "verb (dictionary form) + *koto ga aru.*"

④ [expresses experience]

¶ **Have you ever** been to Kyoto?

*「動詞（たの形）＋ことがある（koto ga aru）」の形で使う。

⑤［決定を表す］

¶わたしは今日からたばこを吸わないことにしました。（Watashi wa kyō kara tabako o suwanai *koto* ni shimashita.）

*「動詞（連体の形）＋ことにする（koto ni suru）」の形で使う。

⑥［習慣を表す］

¶わたしは毎晩10時に寝ることにしています。（Watashi wa maiban jūji ni neru *koto* ni shite imasu.）

*「動詞（連体の形）＋ことにしている（koto ni shite iru）」の形で使う。

⑦［結果を表す］

¶わたしは来年、日本へ行くことになりました。（Watashi wa rainen, Nihon e iku *koto* ni narimashita.）

*「動詞（連体の形）＋ことになる（koto ni naru）」の形で使う。

⑧［必要を表す］

¶そんなに急ぐことはないですよ。（Sonna ni isogu *koto* wa nai desu yo.）

*「動詞（連体の形）＋ことはない（koto wa nai）」の形で使う。

⑨［命令を表す］

¶図書館の本は1週間以内に返すこと。（Toshokan no hon wa isshū-kan inai ni kaesu *koto*.）

*「動詞（連体の形）＋こと（koto）」の形で文末に使う。

kotoba 言葉〖名〗

---

* Used in the pattern "verb (*-ta* form) + *koto ga aru*."

⑤ [expresses decision]

¶ I **have decided** to stop smoking from today on.

* Used in the pattern "verb (dictionary form) + *koto ni suru*."

⑥ [make it a rule to ~; expresses habitual action]

¶ I **make it a practice** to go to bed every night at ten o'clock.

* Used in the pattern "verb (dictionary form) + *koto ni shite iru*."

⑦ [expresses a result]

¶ I **am going to** go to Japan next year.

* Used in the pattern "verb (dictionary form) + *koto ni naru*."

⑧ [expresses necessity]

¶ **There is no need** to be in such a hurry.

* Used in the pattern "verb (dictionary form) + *koto wa nai*."

⑨ [expresses an order]

¶ Library books **are to be** returned within one week.

* Used in the pattern "verb (dictionary form) + *koto*."

kotoba 〖n〗 **speech, language, word, phrase, expression**

¶あなたの国の言葉で本は何と言いますか。　(Anata no kuni no *kotoba* de hon wa nan to iimasu ka?)

¶今日は，あいさつの言葉を勉強しましょう。　(Kyō wa, aisatsu no *kotoba* o benkyō shimashō.)

kōtōgakkō　高等学校〚名〛

¶日本の高等学校は3年です。(Nihon no *kōtōgakkō* wa sannen desu.)

＊略して「高校 (kōkō)」とも言う。

kotoshi　今年〚名〛

¶今年は雨が多いですね。(*Kotoshi* wa ame ga ooi desu ne.)

¶わたしは今年じゅうにこの仕事を終わらせるつもりです。　(Watashi wa *kotoshi*jū ni kono shigoto o owaraseru tsumori desu.)

¶わたしは今年大学を卒業します。(Watashi wa *kotoshi* daigaku o sotsugyō shimasu.)

kotowaru　断る〚動Ⅰ〛

①［相手の願いを受け付けない］

¶仕事を頼まれましたが，忙しいので断りました。　(Shigoto o tanomaremashita ga, isogashii node *kotowarimashita*.)

②［前もって了解を求める］

¶用事があったので，課長に断って会社を休みました。(Yōji ga atta node, kachō ni *kotowatte* kaisha o yasumimashita.)

kōtsū　交通〚名〛

交通事故 (*kōtsū*-jiko)　交通信号 (*kōtsū*-shingō)　交通費 (*kōtsū*hi)

¶ What is **the word** for "book" in your native language?

¶ Today we will study **greetings.**

kōtōgakkō 〚n〛 high school, senior high school, upper secondary school

¶ **High school** is three years long in Japan.

＊ The abbreviated form *kōkō* is also used.

kotoshi 〚n〛 this year

¶ It's rained a lot **this year,** hasn't it?

¶ I plan to finish up this work before **the year** is out.

¶ I graduate from college **this year.**

kotowaru 〚v Ⅰ〛 decline, refuse; tell, give notice, ask permission

① [decline, refuse]

¶ I was asked to do a job but **refused** because I'm too busy.

② [tell, give notice, ask permission, apologize]

¶ I had something to attend to so I took some time off work **after informing** my section chief.

kōtsū 〚n〛 traffic, transport, transportation

a **traffic** accident // a **traffic** signal // **travel** expenses, **car**fare

¶この道は**交通**が激しいから注意してください。 (Kono michi wa *kōtsū* ga hageshii kara chūi shite kudasai.)

¶この辺は**交通**の便がいいですね。 (Kono hen wa *kōtsū* no ben ga ii desu ne.)

¶ Please be careful as **the traffic** is very heavy on this street.

¶ **Public transportation** is convenient in this area.

kowai 怖い〖形〗

①[厳しい]

¶山田先生はとても**怖い**先生です。 (Yamada sensei wa totemo *kowai* sensei desu.)

¶父が**怖い**顔でしかりました。 (Chichi ga *kowai* kao de shikarimashita.)

②[恐ろしい]

¶ゆうべ近所で火事があり，とても**怖かった**です。 (Yūbe kinjo de kaji ga ari, totemo *kowakatta* desu.)

¶この辺は昔からお化けが出るといわれているので，夜は**怖くて**通れません。 (Kono hen wa mukashi kara obake ga deru to iwarete iru node, yoru wa *kowakute* tooremasen.)

kowai 〖adj〗 terrible, dreadful; frightened, fearful

① [terrible, dreadful, grim]

¶ Professor Yamada **is** very **forbidding.**

¶ My father scolded me with a **terrible** expression on his face.

② [frightened, fearful]

¶ There was a fire nearby last night; **I was** quite **frightened.**

¶ It has long been said that this area is haunted by ghosts so that **I'm afraid** to walk through it at night.

kowareru 壊れる〖動Ⅱ〗

①[もとの形がなくなる]

¶地震で家がたくさん**壊れました**。 (Jishin de ie ga takusan *kowaremashita*.)

②[機械などが働かなくなる]

¶このラジオは**壊れて**います。 (Kono rajio wa *kowarete* imasu.)

kowasu 壊す〖動Ⅰ〗

①[破壊する]

¶この箱を**壊した**のはだれですか。

kowareru 〖v Ⅱ〗 be broken, be wrecked; be broken, be out of order

① [be broken, be wrecked, come to pieces]

¶ Many houses **were destroyed** in the earthquake.

② [be broken, be out of order]

¶ This radio **is broken.**

kowasu 〖v Ⅰ〗 break, destroy; injure

① [break, destroy, demolish]

(Kono hako o *kowashita* no wa dare desu ka?)

②[体を悪くする]

¶わたしはおなかをこわしているので，何も食べられません。(Watashi wa onaka o *kowashite* iru node, nani mo taberaremasen.)

¶上田さんは働きすぎて，体をこわしてしまいました。 (Ueda san wa hatarakisugite, karada o *kowashite* shimaimashita.)

koyomi 暦〖名〗

☞**karendā** カレンダー

kōzō 構造〖名〗

¶この機械は構造が簡単です。 (Kono kikai wa *kōzō* ga kantan desu.)

¶日本の社会構造は複雑です。(Nihon no shakai-*kōzō* wa fukuzatsu desu.)

kozukai 小遣い〖名〗

¶あなたの小遣いは一か月いくらですか。(Anata no *kozukai* wa ikkagetsu ikura desu ka?)

kozutsumi 小包〖名〗

¶これは小包にして送りましょう。

(Kore wa *kozutsumi* ni shite okurimashō.)

ku 九〖名〗

九人 (*ku*nin) 九時 (*ku*ji)

⇒**kyū** 九

kubaru 配る〖動Ⅰ〗

新聞を配る (shinbun o *kubaru*)

¶そのパンフレットを皆さんに配ってください。 (Sono panfuretto o minasan ni *kubatte* kudasai.)

¶ Who **broke** this box?

② [injure, damage (one's health)]

¶ I'm **having stomach trouble** and can't eat anything.

¶ [Mr.] Ueda **ruined [his] health** through overwork.

koyomi ☞ **karendā**

kōzō 〖n〗 **structure, framework, constitution, organization**

¶ This machine is simple **in design**.

¶ The social **structure** of Japan is complex.

kozukai 〖n〗 **pocket money, spending money, allowance**

¶ How much is your **allowance** each month?

kozutsumi 〖n〗 **parcel, package**

¶ Let's do this up in **a parcel** and mail it.

ku 〖n〗 **nine**

nine people // **nine** o'clock

kubaru 〖v Ⅰ〗 **distribute, pass out, deliver**

deliver newspapers

¶ Please **give** everyone one of those pamphlets.

kubetsu 区別〖名, 〜する〗

¶子供にはよいことと悪いことの区別をはっきり教えなければなりません。(Kodomo ni wa yoi koto to warui koto no *kubetsu* o hakkiri oshie-nakereba narimasen.)

¶あの兄弟は区別できないほどよく似ています。(Ano kyōdai wa *kubetsu* dekinai hodo yoku nite imasu.)

kubi 首〖名〗

kuchi 口〖名〗

kuchibiru くちびる〖名〗

kudamono 果物〖名〗

¶あなたはどんな果物が好きですか。(Anata wa donna *kudamono* ga suki desu ka?)

¶果物屋でみかんとりんごを買いました。(*Kudamono*ya de mikan to ringo o kaimashita.)

kudari 下り〖名〗

①[上から下に移ること，下り坂]
上り下りの船 (nobori *kudari* no fune)

¶山道の上りはたいへんですが，下りは楽です。(Yamamichi no nobori wa taihen desu ga, *kudari* wa raku desu.)

¶あそこからは坂が下りになりますから楽です。(Asoko kara wa saka ga *kudari* ni narimasu kara raku desu.)

②[中心からその他の所へ行く汽車・電車]
¶上りの電車はこんでいましたが，下

kubetsu 〖n, 〜*suru*〗 **distinction, difference**

¶ One must clearly teach children **the difference** between good and bad〖right and wrong〗.

¶ Those brothers look so much alike that it's hard **to tell them apart.**

kubi 〖n〗 **neck, head**

kuchi 〖n〗 **mouth**

kuchibiru 〖n〗 **lip(s)**

kudamono 〖n〗 **fruit**

¶ What **fruits** do you like?

¶ [I] bought some mandarin oranges and apples at a **fruit** store.

kudari 〖n〗 **descent, going down; outbound**

① [descent, going down]
downstream and upstream boats

¶ Going up mountain trails is arduous but **coming down** is easy.

¶ From over there it **slopes down-hill** and so is easier going.

② [outbound trains]

¶ The train going in was crowded but

りの電車はすいていました。(Nobori no densha wa konde imashita ga, *kudari* no densha wa suite imashita.)

⇔nobori 上り

kudaru 下る〖動Ⅰ〗

¶雨になったので，わたしたちは急いで山を下りました。 (Ame ni natta node, watashitachi wa isoide yama o *kudarimashita*.)

¶この坂を下った所に本屋があります。 (Kono saka o *kudatta* tokoro ni hon'ya ga arimasu.)

⇔noboru 上る

kudasai ください〖動Ⅰ〗

¶うちに着いたら，すぐ電話をください。(Uchi ni tsuitara, sugu denwa o *kudasai*.)

¶何か飲み物をくださいませんか。 (Nani ka nomimono o *kudasaimasen* ka?)

(go~) kudasai （御~）ください〖連〗

¶その問題は山田先生に御相談ください。 (Sono mondai wa Yamada sensei ni gosōdan *kudasai*.)

＊普通「御 (go)」のあとには「研究 (kenkyū)」「紹介 (shōkai)」などの漢語が来る。

(o~) kudasai （お~）ください〖連〗

¶もっとゆっくりお話しください。 (Motto yukkuri ohanashi *kudasai*.)

(~te) kudasai （~て）ください

coming out there was plenty of room.

kudaru 〚v I〛 descend, come down, go down

¶ It started raining so we hurriedly **descended** the mountain.

¶ There is a bookstore **at the bottom** of this hill.

kudasai 〚v I〛 give

¶ **Please call me** as soon as you arrive home.

¶ Could you **please give me** something to drink?

(go- ~) kudasai 〚compd〛 please ~

¶ **Please** consult Professor Yamada concerning that problem.

＊ Generally a Sino-Japanese compound such as *kenkyū* or *shōkai* follows *go-*.

(o- ~) kudasai 〚compd〛 please ~

¶ **Please** speak more slowly.

＊ Used in the pattern "*o-* + verb (stem form) + *kudasai*."

(-te) kudasai 〚compd〛 please ~

〖連〗

¶もっとゆっくり話してください。
(Motto yukkuri hanashite *kudasai*.)

¶第３課をみんなで読んでください。
(Daisanka o minna de yonde *kudasai*.)

¶寒いから、窓を開けないでください。
(Samui kara, mado o akenaide *kudasai*.)

kudasaru　くださる〖動Ⅰ〗

¶先生はわたしに本をくださいました。
(Sensei wa watashi ni hon o *kudasaimashita*.)

¶これは田中先生がくださったペンです。　(Kore wa Tanaka sensei ga *kudasatta* pen desu.)

＊「くれる (kureru)」「与える (ataeru)」の尊敬語。「ますの形」は「くださいます (kudasaimasu)」となる。ある人が話し手や話し手側の者にある物を与えるという意味を表す。その物を受け取る人の側に立って言うときに使う。一般に、与える人が受け取る人より目上の人であるときに使う。同等か目下の人である場合には「くれる (kureru)」を使う。

⇒kureru　くれる

(～te) kudasaru　（～て）くださる〖連〗

¶上田先生がわたしたちに日本語を教えてくださいました。　(Ueda sensei ga watashitachi ni Nihongo o oshiete *kudasaimashita*.)

¶病気で寝ていたら、先生がお見舞い

¶ **Please** speak more slowly.

¶ **Please** read Lesson 3 aloud, everyone.

¶ **Please** don't open the window: it's too cold.

kudasaru 〖vⅠ〗 **give**

¶ My teacher 〖professor〗 **gave** me a book.

¶ This is the pen that Professor 〖Doctor〗 Tanaka **gave** me.

＊ *Kudasaru* is the honorific form of *kureru* and *ataeru*. The -*masu* form is *kudasaimasu*. This verb expresses the meaning of someone giving something to the speaker or to someone close to the speaker. It is used from the standpoint of the recipient and is generally used when the donor is of higher status than the recipient. When the donor is of equal or lesser status, *kureru* is used instead.

(-te) kudasaru 〖compd〗 **do someone the favor of ~ing, be kind enough to ~**

¶ Professor Ueda taught us 〖**was kind enough** to teach us〗 Japanese.

¶ My teacher **was kind enough** to

に来てくださいました。 (Byōki de
nete itara, sensei ga omimai ni kite
kudasaimashita.)

＊「ますの形」は「(〜て)くださいま
す([〜te] kudasaimasu)」となる。
ある人が話し手や話し手側の者のため
にある動作をするという意味を表す。
話し手の側に立って言うときに使う。
一般に，動作をする人が話し手などよ
りも目上の人であるときに使う。同等
か目下の人である場合には「(〜て)く
れる([〜te] kureru)」を使う。

⇨ (〜te) **kureru** (〜て) **くれる**

kufū　工夫〚名，〜する〛

¶工夫に工夫を重ねて，ついに新製品
を完成しました。 (*Kufū* ni *kufū* o
kasanete, tsuini shinseihin o kansei shimashita.)

¶いろいろ工夫しながらお菓子を作る
のは楽しいです。 (Iroiro *kufū* shinagara okashi o tsukuru no wa
tanoshii desu.)

kugatsu　九月〚名〛

kugi　くぎ〚名〛

くぎを打つ (*kugi* o utsu)　くぎを
抜く (*kugi* o nuku)

kūki　空気〚名〛

¶都会は空気が汚れています。 (Tokai
wa *kūki* ga yogorete imasu.)

¶タイヤの空気が抜けていますよ。
(Taiya no *kūki* ga nukete imasu
yo.)

kūkō　空港〚名〛

¶空港から飛行機が次々に飛び立って

---

pay me a get-well visit when I was
sick in bed.

＊ The *-masu* form is (*-te*) *kudasaimasu*. This pattern is used to express the meaning of someone doing
something for the speaker or for
someone close to the speaker. It is
used from the standpoint of the
speaker, generally when the performer of the action is of higher status
than the recipient of that action.
When the performer is of equal or
lesser status, (*-te*) *kureru* is used instead.

kufū 〚n, ~*suru*〛 **device, invention,
plan, means, expedient**

¶ [We] **worked and worked** and
finally invented a new product.

¶ It is fun to make candy 〚sweets,
cakes, etc.〛 trying out different **ideas**
as one goes along.

kugatsu 〚n〛 **September**

kugi 〚n〛 **a nail, tack, rivet**

nail, drive in **a nail** // extract **a nail**

kūki 〚n〛 **air, atmosphere**

¶ **The air** is dirty in the city.

¶ Hey, your tire is going flat (literally, is losing **air**)!

kūkō 〚n〛 **airport**

¶ Airplanes are taking off from the

いきます。 (*Kūkō* kara hikōki ga tsugitsugi ni tobitatte ikimasu.)
⇨**hikōjō** 飛行場

airport one after the other.

(-) kumi (-) 組〖名, 尾〗

1〖名〗
¶わたしたちの組は全部で 15 名です。 (Watashitachi no *kumi* wa zenbu de jūgomei desu.)

2〖尾〗
¶3 年生はA組からE組まであります。 (Sannensei wa Ē-*gumi* kara Ii-*gumi* made arimasu.)

(-) kumi 〖n, suf〗 **class, band, squad, team, pair, group**

1 〖n〗
¶ There are 15 in all in our **squad** 〖**group**〗.

2 〖suf〗
¶ The third-year students are divided into five **squads,** from A to E.

---

kumiai 組合〖名〗
労働組合 (rōdō-*kumiai*) 協同組合 (kyōdō-*kumiai*)
¶この会社には組合があります。 (Kono kaisha ni wa *kumiai* ga arimasu.)
¶この売店は組合員だけが利用できます。 (Kono baiten wa *kumiai*in dake ga riyō dekimasu.)

kumiai 〖n〗 **association, league**
a labor **union** // a cooperative **association,** a cooperative
¶ This company **is unionized.**

¶ Only **co-op members** can use this store.

---

kumitateru 組み立てる〖動Ⅱ〗
¶このラジオは自分で組み立てました。 (Kono rajio wa jibun de *kumitatemashita*.)
¶材料を組み立てて, 本だなを作りました。(Zairyō o *kumitatete*, hondana o tsukurimashita.)

kumitateru 〖v Ⅱ〗 **put together, construct, assemble**
¶ **I put together** this radio myself.

¶ [I] **made** a bookcase from scratch.

---

kumo 雲〖名〗
¶今日は雲一つない, いい天気です。 (Kyō wa *kumo* hitotsu nai, ii tenki desu.)

kumo 〖n〗 **cloud(s)**
¶ It's a nice day today without a single **cloud** in sight.

---

kumori 曇り〖名〗
¶あしたは曇りで, 風も強いそうです。

kumori 〖n〗 **cloudiness, cloudy weather**
¶ They say that tomorrow it will be

(Ashita wa *kumori* de, kaze mo tsuyoi sō desu.)

⇒hare 晴れ

kumoru 曇る〖動Ⅰ〗

¶今日は朝から曇っています。 (Kyō wa asa kara *kumotte* imasu.)

⇒hareru 晴れる

kumu 組む〖動Ⅰ〗

①[からみ合わせる]

¶田中さんは腕を組んで考え込んでいます。(Tanaka san wa ude o *kunde* kangaekonde imasu.)

②[あることをするために仲間になる]

¶わたしは田中さんと組んでテニスの試合に勝ちました。 (Watashi wa Tanaka san to *kunde* tenisu no shiai ni kachimashita.)

kumu くむ〖動Ⅰ〗

¶バケツに水をくんで持って来てください。 (Baketsu ni mizu o *kunde* motte kite kudasai.)

¶川から水をくんできて、畑にまきます。(Kawa kara mizu o *kunde* kite, hatake ni makimasu.)

-kun -君〖尾〗

田中君 (Tanaka *kun*)

＊普通、男の人が男の友達や目下の男の人を呼ぶときに名前のあとにつけて使う。

kuni 国〖名〗

①[国家]

¶わたしのクラスの学生は、いろいろな国から来ています。 (Watashi no kurasu no gakusei wa, iroiro na

cloudy with strong winds.

kumoru 〚v I〛 become cloudy, become overcast

¶ Today **has been overcast** from the morning on.

kumu 〚v I〛 cross, braid, fold; unite, band together, join forces

① [cross, braid, fold]

¶ [Mr.] Tanaka is deep in thought with [his] arms **folded** across [his] chest.

② [unite, band together, join forces]

¶ [Miss] Tanaka and I **teamed up** and won the tennis match.

kumu 〚v I〛 draw, ladle, pump

¶ Please **fill** a bucket with water and bring it here.

¶ [They] **take** water from the river and water the fields with it.

-kun 〚suf〛 a suffix added to names **Mr.** Tanaka

＊ Generally added to names when men address their male friends or men lower in status than themselves.

kuni 〚n〛 country, nation; one's native place

① [country, nation]

¶ The students in my class are from many different **countries.**

kuni kara kite imasu.)

②[自分の生まれた所]

¶わたしはお正月には国へ帰ります。
(Watashi wa oshōgatsu ni wa *kuni*
e kaerimasu.)

kūrā　クーラー〖名〗

¶暑いときにはクーラーがあるといい
ですね。(Atsui toki ni wa *kūrā* ga
aru to ii desu ne.)

kuraberu　比べる〖動Ⅱ〗

¶この紙とその紙を比べると、この紙
のほうが質がいいです。(Kono kami
to sono kami o *kuraberu* to, kono
kami no hō ga shitsu ga ii desu.)

¶今年は去年に比べて雨が少ないです。
(Kotoshi wa kyonen ni *kurabete*
ame ga sukunai desu.)

⇒hikaku 比較

kurai　暗い〖形〗

¶この部屋は昼間でも暗いです。
(Kono heya wa hiruma demo *kurai*
desu.)

¶暗くなったから、家へ帰りましょう。
(*Kuraku* natta kara, ie e kaerimashō.)

⇔akarui 明るい

kurai　くらい〖助〗

①[だいたいの数量や程度などを表す]

¶「ここからあなたの家まで歩いてどの
くらいかかりますか。」(Koko kara
anata no ie made aruite dono *kurai*
kakarimasu ka?)　「15分ぐらい
です。」(Jūgofun *gurai* desu.)

¶「あなたのうちは駅からどのくらいあ

②[one's native place, one's hometown, one's birthplace]

¶ I always go back to **my hometown**
during the New Year's holidays.

kūrā 〚n〛 air conditioner

¶ It would be nice 〚It's nice〛 to have
an air conditioner when it's hot.

kuraberu 〚v II〛 compare, contrast

¶ If [we] **compare** this type of paper
with that one, this one is of better
quality.

¶ There has been less rain this year
than last year.

kurai 〚adj〛 dark, dim, gloomy

¶ This room **is dark** even during the
daytime.

¶ It's gotten **dark**—let's go home.

kurai 〚part〛 about; as ~ as ~; at
least; nothing as ~ as ~

① [about, ~ or so; expresses an
approximate amount or degree]

¶ **"How long** does it take to walk to
your house from here?"

　"About 15 minutes."

りますか。」(Anata no uchi wa eki kara dono *kurai* arimasu ka?) 「10 キロぐらいあります。」(Jikkiro *gurai* arimasu.)

¶「本代は一か月いくらぐらいかかりますか。」(Hondai wa ikkagetsu ikura *gurai* kakarimasu ka?)「三千円ぐらいかかります。」(Sanzen'en *gurai* kakarimasu.)

②[ある例を挙げてそれとだいたい同じ程度であることを表す]

¶上田さんの部屋は、ちょうどこれくらいの広さです。(Ueda san no heya wa, chōdo kore *kurai* no hirosa desu.)

¶山田さんくらい英語が上手に話せればいいのですが…。(Yamada san *kurai* Eigo ga jōzu ni hanasereba ii no desu ga...)

¶もう一歩も歩けないくらい疲れてしまいました。(Mō ippo mo arukenai *kurai* tsukarete shimaimashita.)

③[あるものごとを簡単なもの・やさしいもの・程度の低いものなどの例として示す]

¶子供でもこのくらいのことは知っていますよ。(Kodomo demo kono *kurai* no koto wa shitte imasu yo.)

¶こんな易しい漢字くらいだれだって書けますよ。(Konna yasashii kanji *kurai* dare datte kakemasu yo.)

¶日本語を半年も勉強しているのですから、もう平仮名ぐらいは書けるでしょう。(Nihongo o hantoshi mo

¶ "**How far** is your home from the station?"

"**About** 10 kilometers."

¶ "**How much** will be required for books per month?"

"**About** three thousand yen."

② [as ~ as ~, like ~, so ~ that; indicates that something is of approximately the same degree as something else being cited]

¶ [Mr.] Ueda's room ⟦apartment⟧ is just **about** the same size **as** this one.

¶ I wish I could speak English **as** well **as** [Miss] Yamada does.

¶ I was **so** tired **that** I couldn't take another step ⟦I am **so** tired **that** I can't take another step⟧.

③ [at least, at any rate; cites something as being simple, easy, of low degree, etc.]

¶ Even a child knows **that**.

¶ Anyone can write a *kanji* **as** easy **as** this one.

¶ [He] has been studying Japanese for half a year so [he] should be able to write *hiragana* **at least**.

benkyō shite iru no desu kara, mō
hiragana *gurai* kakeru deshō.)

¶お金がないといっても，百円くらい
は持っているでしょう。 (Okane ga
nai to itte mo, hyakuen *kurai* wa
motte iru deshō.)

④[ほかに同じ程度のものがなくそれ
がいちばんであるということを表す]
¶あの人くらい親切な人はいません。
(Ano hito *kurai* shinsetsu na hito
wa imasen.)

¶山に登ったとき飲む水くらいおいし
いものはありません。 (Yama ni no-
botta toki nomu mizu *kurai* oishii
mono wa arimasen.)

* 「〜くらい〜はない (〜kurai 〜 wa
nai)」の形で使う。

* 「ぐらい (gurai)」とも言う。

kurasu 暮らす〖動Ⅰ〗
¶1か月5万円で暮らすのは無理です。
(Ikkagetsu goman'en de *kurasu* no
wa muri desu.)
¶家族は皆元気に暮らしていますから，
御安心ください。(Kazoku wa mina
genki ni *kurashite* imasu kara,
goanshin kudasai.)

kurasu クラス〖名〗
¶わたしのクラスでは，上田さんがい
ちばん背が高いです。 (Watashi no
kurasu de wa, Ueda san ga ichiban
sei ga takai desu.)

kureru 暮れる〖動Ⅱ〗
①[日が沈んで暗くなる]
¶日が暮れる前に仕事を終えましょう。

¶ You say you don't have any
money, but you must have **at least**
one hundred yen.

④ [nothing as ~ as ~; indicates that
something is number one, that nothing else is of the same degree]

¶ You couldn't find anyone **kinder
than** [him] (literally, There is no one
as kind as him).

¶ Nothing tastes **better than** cold
water drunk while mountain climbing.

* Used in the pattern "~ *kurai* ~ *wa
nai*."

* Variant: *gurai*.

kurasu 〚v I〛 **live, make a living,
get along**

¶ It is impossible **to live** on fifty
thousand yen a month.

¶ **We are** all in fine health so please
don't worry about us 〚I am glad to
assure you that **we are** all in good
health〛.

kurasu 〚n〛 **class**

¶ [Mr.] Ueda is the tallest person in
my **class.**

kureru 〚v II〛 **get dark; end, come
to a close**

① [get dark]

¶ Let's finish this job before **it gets**

(Hi ga *kureru* mae ni shigoto o oemashō.)

②［時が経過して年や季節などが終わりになる］

¶あと数日で今年も暮れますね。(Ato sūjitsu de kotoshi mo *kuremasu* ne.)

kureru　くれる〖動Ⅱ〗

¶父がわたしにお金をくれました。

(Chichi ga watashi ni okane o *kuremashita.*)

¶上田さんが弟に誕生日のお祝いをくれました。(Ueda san ga otōto ni tanjōbi no oiwai o *kuremashita.*)

＊普通，ある人が話し手や話し手側の者にある物を与えるという意味を表す。その物を受け取る人の側に立って言うときに使う。一般に，与える人が受け取る人と同等か目下の人または身内の人であるときに使う。目上の人である場合には「くださる(kudasaru)」を使う。「先生がこの本をくださいました。(Sensei ga kono hon o kudasaimashita.)」

⇨kudasaru　くださる

(～**te**) **kureru**　(～て)くれる〖連〗

¶母がわたしにシャツを買ってくれました。(Haha ga watashi ni shatsu o katte *kuremashita.*)

¶このことについては上田さんにきけば，詳しく教えてくれると思います。

(Kono koto ni tsuite wa Ueda san ni kikeba kuwashiku oshiete *kureru* to omoimasu.)

＊ある人が話し手のためにある動作

dark.

② [end, (years, days, etc.) come to a close]

¶ In a few days this year **will draw to a close.**

kureru 〚v II〛 give

¶ My father **gave** me some money.

¶ [Mrs.] Ueda **gave** my younger brother a birthday present.

＊ *Kureru* usually expresses the meaning of someone giving something to the speaker or to someone close to the speaker. It is used from the standpoint of the recipient, generally when the donor is of equal or lesser status than the recipient or is within the recipient's inner circle. When the donor is of higher status, *kudasaru* is used instead, as in "*Sensei ga kono hon o kudasaimashita*" (My teacher gave me this book).

(-te) **kureru** 〚compd〛 **do someone the favor of ~, be kind enough to ~**

¶ My mother bought me a shirt.

¶ If you ask [Mr.] Ueda about this matter, I'm sure that [he] **will be kind enough** to tell you about it in some detail.

＊ This pattern expresses the meaning of someone doing something for

をするという意味を表す。話し手の側に立って言うときに使う。一般に，動作をする人が，話し手などと同等か目下の人であるときに使う。動作をする人が話し手などより目上である場合には，「(〜て) くださる ([〜te] kudasaru)」を使う。「先生に伺えば，詳しく教えてくださると思います。(Sensei ni ukagaeba, kuwashiku oshiete kudasaru to omoimasu.)」

⇨(〜**te**) **kudasaru** (〜て) くださる

kuriiningu クリーニング〚名〛
洋服をクリーニングに出す (yōfuku o *kuriiningu* ni dasu.)
¶ワイシャツが汚れたので，クリーニング屋へ持っていきました。(Waishatsu ga yogoreta node, *kuriininguya* e motte ikimashita.)

kurikaesu 繰り返す〚動Ⅰ〛
¶教科書を繰り返して読みましたが，わかりませんでした。(Kyōkasho o *kurikaeshite* yomimashita ga, wakarimasen deshita.)
¶その発音を何度も繰り返して練習しましたが，うまく言えませんでした。(Sono hatsuon o nando mo *kurikaeshite* renshū shimashita ga, umaku iemasen deshita.)

kurisumasu クリスマス〚名〛
¶12 月 24 日の夜にクリスマスパーティーを開きました。(Jūnigatsu nijūyokka no yoru ni *kurisumasu* pātii o hirakimashita.)

kuro 黒〚名〛

the speaker. It is used from the standpoint of the speaker, generally when the performer of the action is of equal or lesser status than the recipient. When the performer of the action is of higher status, (*-te*) *kudasaru* is used instead, as in "*Sensei ni ukagaeba, kuwashiku oshiete kudasaru to omoimasu*" (If you ask your teacher about that, I think she will give you a detailed explanation).

kuriiningu 〚n〛 **cleaning, dry cleaning, laundry**
send clothing to **the cleaners**
¶ [My] shirts were dirty so I took them to **the cleaners.**

kurikaesu 〚v Ⅰ〛 **repeat, do over again**
¶ [I] read about it in the textbook **many times** but [I] still didn't understand it.
¶ [I] practiced that pronunciation **over and over again** but still couldn't say it exactly right.

kurisumasu 〚n〛 **Christmas**
¶ [We] had a **Christmas** party on the evening of December 24.

kuro 〚n〛 **black**

415

kurō

黒インク (*kuro*inku)　白黒フィルム
(shiro*kuro*-firumu)　黒髪 (*kuro-*
kami)　黒砂糖 (*kuro*zatō)　黒ビー
ル (*kuro*biiru)

black ink // **black-** and -white film //
black hair // **brown** sugar, **unre-**
fined sugar // **dark** beer, **black** beer

kurō　苦労〖名, 〜する〗

¶御苦労さまでした。　(Gokurōsama
deshita.)

¶よい辞書がないので，勉強するのに
苦労しました。　(Yoi jisho ga nai
node, benkyō suru no ni *kurō*
shimashita.)

¶父が早く死んだので，母は苦労して
わたしたちを育てました。(Chichi ga
hayaku shinda node, haha wa *kurō*
shite watashitachi o sodatemashita.)

＊「御苦労さま。(Gokurōsama.)」
「御苦労さまでした。(Gokurōsama
deshita.)」というあいさつの言葉は目
上の者が目下の者に対して使う。

kurō 〖n, ~*suru*〗 **trouble, hardship,**
suffering, toil, labor, pains, cares,
worry, anxiety

¶ **Thank you very much** 〖Many
thanks **for your trouble**〗.

¶ I **had a hard time** studying that as
there isn't any good dictionary for it
〖as I didn't have a good dictionary〗.

¶ Since my father died young, my
mother **had a hard time of it** raising
us.

＊ The set expressions *Gokurōsama*
and *Gokurōsama deshita* are used by
persons of higher status towards
those of lower status.

kuroi　黒い〖形〗

¶田中さんは黒いくつをはいています。
(Tanaka san wa *kuroi* kutsu o
haite imasu.)

¶日に焼けて顔が黒くなりました。
(Hi ni yakete kao ga *kuroku* narimashita.)

kuroi 〖adj〗 **black, dark**

¶ [Mr.] Tanaka is wearing **black**
shoes.

¶ [My] face has 〖had〗 gotten **brown**
in the sun.

kuru　来る〖動Ⅲ〗

¶もうすぐ春が来ます。　(Mō sugu
haru ga *kimasu*.)

¶山田さんはまだ来ませんか。(Yama-
da san wa mada *kimasen* ka?)

¶今度日本へ来るときには，奥さんも連
れてきてください。(Kondo Nihon e

kuru 〖v Ⅲ〗 **come, arrive**

¶ Spring **will** soon **be here.**

¶ **Hasn't** [Miss] Yamada **arrived** yet?

¶ The next time **you come** to Japan
please bring your wife along with

kite kudasai.)

⇔iku 行く

(〜te) kuru （〜て）くる〚連〛

①［こちらへ近づく，あることをして
からこちらにもどる］

¶向こうから大きなトラックが走って
きました。 (Mukō kara ookina to-
rakku ga hashitte *kimashita*.)

¶すみません。今日は宿題をしてきま
せんでした。 (Sumimasen. Kyō wa
shukudai o shite *kimasen deshita*.)

¶その問題について，昨日図書館へ行
って調べてきました。(Sono mondai
ni tsuite, kinō toshokan e itte
shirabete *kimashita*.)

↔（〜te) iku （〜て）いく

②［動作・作用が継続してある時点に
至る］

¶この1年間毎日日本語を勉強してき
ました。(Kono ichinenkan mainichi
Nihongo o benkyō shite *kimashita*.)

¶今までこの会社に20年間勤めてき
ました。 (Ima made kono kaisha
ni nijūnenkan tsutomete *kimashita*.)

↔（〜te) iku （〜て）いく

③［動作・作用が始まる］

¶あっ，雨が降ってきた。 (A'! Ame
ga futte *kita*.)

¶急におなかが痛くなってきました。
(Kyū ni onaka ga itaku natte *kimashita*.)

④［だんだんにある状態に変わる］

¶大雨が降って，川の水が増えてきま

(-te) kuru 〚compd〛 an expression
indicating various conditions

① [approach; come having done
something]

¶ A large truck **came** 〚**is coming**〛
from the opposite direction.

¶ I'm sorry. I haven't done the
homework (literally, **I haven't come**
today with the homework done; **I've
come** today **without** having done the
homework).

¶ [I] **went** to the library yesterday
and did some research on that question.

② [indicates that an action or operation has continued and has reached a
certain point]

¶ This past year **I've studied**
Japanese every day.

¶ **I've worked** for this company 20
years now.

③ [indicates that an action or operation has begun]

¶ Oh, **it's started** to rain!

¶ My stomach **has** suddenly **started**
to ache 〚My stomach suddenly
started to ache〛.

④ [indicates that something gradually changes to a certain condition]

417

した。 (Ooame ga futte, kawa no mizu ga fuete *kimashita*.)

¶最近, 物価が高くなってきて, 人々は困っています。 (Saikin, bukka ga takaku natte *kite*, hitobito wa komatte imasu.)

¶霧がはれて, 星がはっきり見えてきました。 (Kiri ga harete, hoshi ga hakkiri miete *kimashita*.)

↔(~**te**) **iku** (~て) いく

⑤[ものごとが出現する]

¶いい考えが頭に浮かんできました。 (Ii kangae ga atama ni ukande *kimashita*.)

¶うちからの手紙を読んでいたら, 妹の顔が浮かんできました。 (Uchi kara no tegami o yonde itara, imōto no kao ga ukande *kimashita*.)

kuruma 車〖名〗

①[車輪]

¶この旅行かばんには車がついています。 (Kono ryokō-kaban ni wa *kuruma* ga tsuite imasu)

¶馬車の車が壊れてしまったから, 直してください。 (Basha no *kuruma* ga kowarete shimatta kara, naoshite kudasai.)

②[乗り物, 自動車]

車に乗る (*kuruma* ni noru)　車を降りる (*kuruma* o oriru)

¶ここから駅まで車で10分です。 (Koko kara eki made *kuruma* de jippun desu.)

kurushii 苦しい〖形〗

¶ With the heavy rains, the river **has risen** 〖**rose**〗.

¶ Recently prices **have gone up**, and people are having a hard time.

¶ With the lifting of the fog, the stars **have become** clearly visible 〖**became** clearly visible〗.

⑤ [indicates that something makes an appearance]

¶ A good idea **has come** to me 〖I hit upon a good idea〗.

¶ As I read a letter from home the face of my younger sister **flitted** across my mind.

kuruma 〖n〗 **wheel(s)**; (wheeled) **vehicle, car**

① [wheels, castors]

¶ This suitcase has attached **wheels**.

¶ One of **the wheels** of the cart 〖carriage, coach〗 is broken. Please fix it.

② [(wheeled) vehicle, car, taxi]
ride in **a car** 〖**taxi, carriage, wagon,** etc.〗 // get out of **a car** 〖**taxi, carriage, wagon,** etc.〗

¶ It is 10 minutes by **car** from here to the station.

kurushii 〖adj〗 **painful; trying, taxing, hard, difficult**

418

①[体のぐあいが悪くて我慢できない様子]

¶病人はとても苦しそうです。 (Byō-nin wa totemo *kurushisō* desu.)

②[お金や物などがなくて困っている様子]

¶月給が安いから生活が苦しいです。(Gekkyū ga yasui kara seikatsu ga *kurushii* desu.)

kurushimu 苦しむ〖動Ⅰ〗

①[体のぐあいが悪くて我慢できない]

¶田中さんは長い間病気で苦しんでいます。 (Tanaka san wa nagai aida byōki de *kurushinde* imasu.)

②[お金や物などがなくて困る]

¶世界には食べ物がなくて苦しんでいる人がおおぜいいます。(Sekai ni wa tabemono ga nakute *kurushinde* iru hito ga oozei imasu.)

¶都会の人たちは住宅の不足に苦しんでいます。 (Tokai no hitotachi wa jūtaku no fusoku ni *kurushinde* imasu.)

kusa 草〖名〗

草を刈る (*kusa* o karu) 枯草 (ka-re*kusa*) 草原 (*kusa*hara) 草花 (*kusa*bana)

¶庭に草が生えたので, 草取りをしました。 (Niwa ni *kusa* ga haeta node, *kusa*tori o shimashita.)

kusai 臭い〖形〗

汗臭い (ase*kusai*) 酒臭い (sake*kusai*)

¶この川はみんながごみを捨てるので,

① [painful, tormenting, (physically) trying]

¶ The patient **seems to be in** much **pain** 〚very **uncomfortable**〛.

② [trying, taxing, hard, difficult (financially, etc.)]

¶ As [my] wages are low [I] **have a hard time** making ends meet.

kurushimu 〚v I〛 **suffer, be in pain; be troubled, be distressed**

① [suffer, be in pain, be afflicted (physically)]

¶ [Mr.] Tanaka **has** long **been ill** (literally, **has** long **been suffering** with an illness, disease, etc.).

② [be troubled, be distressed (financially, etc.)]

¶ Many people in the world don't have enough to eat (literally, don't have enough to eat and **are suffering**).

¶ Urban dwellers **suffer** from the shortage of housing.

kusa 〚n〛 **grass, herb, weed**

cut **the grass** // dried **grass**, dry **herbs** // a **grassy** plain, a meadow // a flowering **plant,** a flower

¶ I **weeded** the garden because it needed it (literally, because **weeds** had grown in).

kusai 〚adj〛 **bad-smelling, stinking, smelly, smell of ~**

smell of sweat // **smell of** liquor, **have** liquor **on one's breath**

419

とても臭いです。 (Kono kawa wa minna ga gomi o suteru node, totemo *kusai* desu.)

¶ As everyone throws garbage in this river **it smells** very **bad**.

kusaru 腐る〖動 I 〗

kusaru 〚v I〛 **rot; go bad**

①[腐敗する]

① [rot, go bad, decay]

¶腐った魚を食べて，おなかをこわしました。 (*Kusatta* sakana o tabete, onaka o kowashimashita.)

¶ [I] ate some fish that **had gone bad** and got an upset stomach.

¶夏は食べ物が腐りやすいです。
(Natsu wa tabemono ga *kusari*-yasui desu.)

¶ Food **spoils** very easily in the summer.

¶腐らないようにこれを冷蔵庫に入れておきましょう。 (*Kusaranai* yō ni kore o reizōko ni irete okimashō.)

¶ Let's put this in the refrigerator so **it won't spoil.**

②[木などが悪くなって役に立たなくなる]

② [become bad and no longer useful]

¶この家はたいへん古くて，柱が腐っています。 (Kono ie wa taihen furukute, hashira ga *kusatte* imasu.)

¶ This house is very old, and the pillars 〚posts〛 **are rotten.**

kuse 癖〖名〗

kuse 〚n〛 **personal habit, mannerism, quirk, foible, weakness, vice**

¶あの人はうそをつく癖があります。
(Ano hito wa uso o tsuku *kuse* ga arimasu.)

¶ [He] is a **habitual** liar.

¶寝る前に本を読むのが癖になってしまいました。 (Neru mae ni hon o yomu no ga *kuse* ni natte shimai-mashita.)

¶ [I] have 〚had〛 fallen into **the habit** of reading before going to sleep.

kushami くしゃみ〖名〗

kushami 〚n〛 **a sneeze**
to sneeze

くしゃみをする (*kushami* o suru)
¶風邪を引いているので，くしゃみが出て困ります。(Kaze o hiite iru node, *kushami* ga dete komarimasu.)

¶ [I] have caught a cold and have an annoying **sneeze.**

kushi くし〖名〗

kushi 〚n〛 **comb**

¶わたしは毎朝くしで髪の毛をとかし

¶ I comb my hair every morning

420

ます。 (Watashi wa maiasa *kushi* de kaminoke o tokashimasu.)

kushin 苦心〖名, ～する〗

¶苦心の末, ようやく論文を書き終えました。 (*Kushin* no sue, yōyaku ronbun o kakioemashita.)

¶彼はたいへん苦心して, その詩を書きました。 (Kare wa taihen *kushin* shite, sono shi o kakimashita.)

kusuri 薬〖名〗

薬屋 (*kusuri*ya) 風邪薬 (kaze-*gusuri*) 薬代 (*kusuri*dai) 薬びん (*kusuri*bin)

¶今夜は薬を飲んで早く寝たほうがいいですよ。 (Kon'ya wa *kusuri* o nonde hayaku neta hō ga ii desu yo.)

¶この薬はあまり効きませんね。 (Kono *kusuri* wa amari kikimasen ne.)

kutsu くつ〖名〗

くつ屋 (*kutsu*ya) 長ぐつ (naga-*gutsu*) 運動ぐつ (undō*gutsu*) くつみがき (*kutsu*migaki) くつをはく (*kutsu* o haku) くつを脱ぐ (*kutsu* o nugu)

kutsushita くつ下〖名〗

ナイロンのくつ下 (nairon no *kutsushita*) 毛のくつ下 (ke no *kutsushita*)

¶このくつ下は婦人用です。 (Kono *kutsushita* wa fujin'yō desu.)

kuu 食う〖動 I〗

①[食べる]

kushin 〖n, ~*suru*〗 pains, efforts, labor, hard work

¶ After **much hard labor** [I] have finally finished 〚I finally finished〛 writing [my] thesis.

¶ He **put a lot** into the writing of that poem.

kusuri 〚n〛 medicine, drug, medication, chemical

a **drug**store, a pharmacy // cold **medicine** // a charge for **medicine** // a **medicine** bottle, a vial, a phial

¶ You'd better take **some medicine** and go to bed early tonight.

¶ This **medicine** doesn't seem to be very effective.

kutsu 〚n〛 shoes, boots

a **shoe** store, a **shoe**maker // **boots**, high **boots** // basketball 〚tennis, running〛 **shoes**, // **shoe** polishing, a **shoe**shine man // wear 〚put on〛 **shoes**, // take off **one's shoes**

kutsushita 〚n〛 socks, stockings

nylon **stockings**, nylon **socks** // wool **socks**

¶ These are women's **socks**.

kuu 〚v I〛 eat; bite; consume

① [eat]

えさを食う (esa o *kuu*)

¶木の葉がこんなに虫に食われています。(Ki no ha ga konna ni mushi ni *kuwarete* imasu.)

*「食べる (taberu)」に比べて，あまり丁寧な言葉ではない。

②[虫などがかんだり刺したりする]

¶蚊に食われて，手がかゆくてたまりません。(Ka ni *kuwarete*, te ga kayukute tamarimasen.)

③[消費する]

¶この車はずいぶんガソリンを食いますね。(Kono kuruma wa zuibun gasorin o *kuimasu* ne.)

kuwaeru 加える〖動Ⅱ〗

①[数量を増やす，足す]

¶2に3を加えると，5になります。(Ni ni san o *kuwaeru* to, go ni narimasu.)

¶この料理にはもう少し塩を加えてください。(Kono ryōri ni wa mō sukoshi shio o *kuwaete* kudasai.)

②[程度を大きくする]

¶汽車はだんだんスピードを加えていき，とうとう見えなくなってしまいました。(Kisha wa dandan supiido o *kuwaete* iki, tōtō mienaku natte shimaimashita.)

③[仲間に入れる]

仲間に加える (nakama ni *kuwaeru*)

¶その研究会にわたしも加えてください。(Sono kenkyūkai ni watashi mo *kuwaete* kudasai.)

④[ある動作・作用を与える]

(an animal) **eats** its food, (a fish) **takes** the bait

¶ The tree leaves are all **eaten up** by insects!

* *Kuu* is less polite than *taberu*.

② [(insects, etc.) bite]

¶ [My] hand is all itchy now from a mosquito **bite.**

③ [consume, eat up]

¶ This car **uses** a lot of gas ⟦is a real gas **guzzler**⟧.

kuwaeru 〚v II〛 **add, add up; increase; include; inflict, apply**

① [add, add up, add to]

¶ Two **plus** three is five.

¶ Please **add** a little more salt to this dish.

② [increase]

¶ The train gradually **speeded up** and disappeared into the distance.

③ [include, count in, incorporate] **take** into one's circle, **let join**

¶ Please **add** me to that study group.

④ [inflict, apply, give]

力を加える (chikara o *kuwaeru*)
¶ナイロンに熱を加えると，解けてしまいます。 (Nairon ni netsu o *kuwaeru* to, tokete shimaimasu.)

kuwashii 詳しい〖形〗
①〔詳細な〕
¶もっと詳しく話してください。 (Motto *kuwashiku* hanashite kudasai.)
¶その辞書よりもこの辞書の説明のほうが詳しいです。 (Sono jisho yori mo kono jisho no setsumei no hō ga *kuwashii* desu.)
②〔よく知っている〕
¶あの人は日本の歴史に詳しいですね。 (Ano hito wa Nihon no rekishi ni *kuwashii* desu ne.)
¶彼はこの辺の地理に詳しいです。 (Kare wa kono hen no chiri ni *kuwashii* desu.)
＊普通「〜に詳しい (〜ni kuwashii)」の形で使う。

kuzu くず〖名〗
紙くず (kami*kuzu*)　くずかご (*kuzu*kago)
¶くずを散らかさないようにしてください。 (*Kuzu* o chirakasanai yō ni shite kudasai.)

kuzureru 崩れる〖動Ⅱ〗
①〔形のある物が壊れて下に落ちる〕
¶大雨で山が崩れました。 (Ooame de yama ga *kuzuremashita*.)
②〔整っているもの・安定しているものなどが乱れる〕

apply force
¶ Nylon melts when **heated.**

kuwashii 〖adj〗 **detailed, minute; know well, be well versed**
① [detailed, minute, full]
¶ Please **elaborate.**
¶ This dictionary gives **fuller** explanations than that one.
② [know well, be well versed]
¶ [He] **knows a lot** about Japanese history.
¶ He **is well acquainted** with this neighborhood.
＊ Generally used in the pattern "~ *ni kuwashii.*"

kuzu 〖n〗 **rubbish, waste, garbage, trash, junk, rags,** etc.
wastepaper // a **waste**basket, **trash** can
¶ Please don't **litter.**

kuzureru 〖v Ⅱ〗 **crumble, collapse, fall down; break down, get out of shape, decline; can change money**
① [crumble, collapse, fall down]
¶ **There were landslides** due to the heavy rains.
② [break down, get out of shape, decline]

¶この帽子は形がくずれていますね。
(Kono bōshi wa katachi ga *kuzurete* imasu ne.)

¶今晩から天気がくずれそうです。
(Konban kara tenki ga *kuzuresō* desu.)

③[小銭に替えることができる]

¶一万円札がくずれますか。　(Ichiman'ensatsu ga *kuzuremasu* ka?)

kuzusu 崩す〚動Ⅰ〛

①[形あるものを壊す]

¶山を崩して道路を作っています。
(Yama o *kuzushite* dōro o tsukutte imasu.)

②[字画などを省いたり続けたりして書く]

¶くずした字は読みにくいです。
(*Kuzushita* ji wa yominikui desu.)

③[小銭にする]

¶千円札を百円玉にくずしてください。　(Sen'ensatsu o hyakuendama ni *kuzushite* kudasai.)

kyakkanteki 客観的〚形動〛

¶ものごとは客観的に見なければいけません。(Monogoto wa *kyakkanteki* ni minakereba ikemasen.)

⇔shukanteki 主観的

kyaku 客〚名〛

①[招かれて来る人，訪ねて来る人]
観光客 (kankō*kyaku*)　お客を呼ぶ
(o*kyaku* o yobu)

¶あしたはお客さんが3人来ます。
(Ashita wa o*kyaku*san ga sannin kimasu.)

¶ This hat **has lost** its shape.

¶ **It looks like** the weather **will deteriorate** from this evening.

③ [can break or change money]
¶ **Can you give me change** for a ten-thousand-yen bill?

kuzusu 〚v Ⅰ〛 **destroy, demolish; simplify; change money**

① [destroy, demolish, pull down, level]
¶ They **are leveling** a hill in building the road.

② [simplify (a written character, etc.)]
¶ Characters **written in a cursive style** are hard to read.

③ [break or change money]
¶ Please **give me** hundred-yen **coins** for this thousand-yen bill.

kyakkanteki 〚adj-v〛 **be objective**
¶ One must take an **objective** view of things.

kyaku 〚n〛 **guest; customer**
① [guest, caller, visitor, company]
a tourist, sightseer // invite **a guest**

¶ Three **visitors** 〚**guests**〛 will be coming tomorrow.

¶部屋が汚れているのに，お客が突然訪ねてきてあわてました。 (Heya ga yogorete iru noni, okyaku ga totsuzen tazunete kite awatemashita.)

¶ [My] apartment 〚room〛 was dirty so [I] was flustered when **someone** unexpectedly **came to visit.**

②〔物を買ったり食べたりしてお金を払う人〕

② [customer, client, passenger]

¶あの店はいつも客が多いです。 (Ano mise wa itsu mo kyaku ga ooi desu.)

¶ That shop 〚restaurant, bar, etc.〛 is always filled with **customers.**

¶デパートの店員は，客に対してたいへん丁寧な言葉を使います。(Depāto no ten'in wa, kyaku ni taishite taihen teinei na kotoba o tsukaimasu.)

¶ Department store employees use very polite language toward **customers.**

kyō 今日〖名〗

kyō 〚n〛 today

¶今日は何曜日ですか。 (Kyō wa naniyōbi desu ka?)

¶ What day of the week is it **today?**

¶今日から夏休みです。 (Kyō kara natsuyasumi desu.)

¶ Summer vacation starts **today.**

¶今日，銀行へ行くつもりです。(Kyō, ginkō e iku tsumori desu.)

¶ I plan to go to the bank **today.**

kyōdai 兄弟〖名〗

kyōdai 〚n〛 brothers, brothers and sisters, siblings

¶あなたは兄弟が何人ありますか。 (Anata wa kyōdai ga nannin arimasu ka?)

¶ How many **brothers and sisters** do you have?

¶兄弟は五人です。兄が二人，姉が二人，わたしはいちばん下です。(Kyōdai wa gonin desu. Ani ga futari, ane ga futari, watashi wa ichiban shita desu.)

¶ There are five of **us children**—my two older brothers, my two older sisters, and me, the youngest.

⇨shimai 姉妹

kyōdō 共同〖名〗

kyōdō 〚n〛 common, communal, joint, united, public

共同生活 (kyōdō-seikatsu)　共同便

collective life, **co**habitation // a

所 (*kyōdō*-benjo) 共同経営 (*kyōdō*-keiei) 共同墓地 (*kyōdō*-bochi)

¶わたしたちはこの部屋を共同で使っています。 (Watashitachi wa kono heya o *kyōdō* de tsukatte imasu.)

kyōgi 競技〚名〛

競技会 (*kyōgi*kai) 競技場 (*kyōgi*-jō)

¶水泳競技が間もなく始まります。 (Suiei-*kyōgi* ga mamonaku hajimarimasu.)

kyōiku 教育〚名, ～する〛

義務教育 (gimu-*kyōiku*) 職業教育 (shokugyō-*kyōiku*) 家庭教育 (katei-*kyōiku*) 教育費 (*kyōiku*hi) 教育映画 (*kyōiku*-eiga) 教育者 (*kyōiku*sha)

¶この国の教育程度はかなり高いです。 (Kono kuni no *kyōiku*-teido wa kanari takai desu.)

¶国の発展のためには教育が最も大切です。 (Kuni no hatten no tame ni wa *kyōiku* ga mottomo taisetsu desu.)

kyōju 教授〚名, ～する〛

①[教えること]

¶あの人はピアノの個人教授をしています。 (Ano hito wa piano no kojin-*kyōju* o shite imasu.)

②[大学の先生]

¶あの方は東京大学の教授です。 (Ano kata wa Tōkyō-daigaku no *kyōju* desu.)

kyoka 許可〚名, ～か〛

public 〚shared〛 toilet // joint management // a public cemetery

¶ We are sharing this room.

kyōgi 〚n〛 **match, contest, competition, game, sport, sports event**

an **athletic** meet, **track-and-field** meet; **a contest, competition** // a **sports** ground, stadium

¶ The swimming **events** will start momentarily.

kyōiku 〚n, ~*suru*〛 **education, instruction, training**

compulsory **education** // vocational **training** // home **training** // **educational** expenses // an **educational** film, **instructional** film // **an educator, a schoolteacher**

¶ The level of **education** in this country is quite high.

¶ **Education** is the most important element in the development of a nation.

kyōju 〚n, ~*suru*〛 **teaching, instruction; professor**

① [teaching, instruction]

¶ [He] **gives** private piano **lessons.**

② [professor]

¶ [He] is **a professor** at Tokyo University.

kyoka 〚n, ~*suru*〛 **permission, approval, authorization**

入学許可 (nyūgaku-*kyoka*)

¶出国許可がもらえないので，まだ出発できません。(Shukkoku-*kyoka* ga moraenai node, mada shuppatsu dekimasen.)

¶社長は山田さんの外国旅行を許可しました。(Shachō wa Yamada san no gaikoku-ryokō o *kyoka* shimashita.)

kyōkai 教会〘名〙

¶日曜日の朝は教会へ行くことにしています。(Nichiyōbi no asa wa *kyōkai* e iku koto ni shite imasu.)

kyōkasho 教科書〘名〙

¶教科書の10ページを開いてください。(*Kyōkasho* no jippēji o hiraite kudasai.)

¶あなたの学校では，どんな日本語の教科書を使っていますか。(Anata no gakkō de wa, donna Nihongo no *kyōkasho* o tsukatte imasu ka?)

(-)kyoku (-)曲〘名，尾〙

1〘名〙

¶わたしはこの曲が大好きです。
(Watashi wa kono *kyoku* ga daisuki desu.)

¶この曲は上田さんが作りました。
(Kono *kyoku* wa Ueda san ga tsukurimashita.)

2〘尾〙

¶あなたの国の歌を一曲歌ってください。 (Anata no kuni no uta o ik*kyoku* utatte kudasai.)

-kyoku -局〘尾〙

admission (to a school)

¶ [I] can't leave yet because [I] haven't been able to obtain a departure **permit.**

¶ The company president **approved** [Mr.] Yamada's overseas trip.

kyōkai ⟦n⟧ **church**

¶ I make it a practice to go to **church** on Sunday morning.

kyōkasho ⟦n⟧ **textbook, schoolbook, manual**

¶ Please open **your books** to page 10.

¶ What Japanese-language **textbooks** do they use at your school?

(-)kyoku ⟦n, suf⟧ **tune, melody, piece of music, musical composition**

1 ⟦n⟧

¶ I love this **piece** ⟦**song, tune**⟧.

¶ [Mr.] Ueda wrote this **piece.**

2 ⟦suf⟧

¶ Please sing **a song** from your country for us.

-kyoku ⟦suf⟧ **department, bureau**

427

郵便局 (yūbin*kyoku*) 電話局 (den-wa*kyoku*) 放送局 (hōsō*kyoku*)

a post **office** // a telephone **office** // a broadcasting ⟦radio, TV⟧ **station**

kyokusen 曲線〖名〗
⇔chokusen 直線

kyokusen ⟦n⟧ **curved line, curve**

kyōmi 興味〖名〗

kyōmi ⟦n⟧ **interest**

¶日本の茶道に興味を持っている外国人が多いです。 (Nihon no sadō ni *kyōmi* o motte iru gaikokujin ga ooi desu.)

¶ Many foreigners have **an interest** in the Japanese tea ceremony.

¶わたしは日本文学に興味があります。 (Watashi wa Nihon-bungaku ni *kyōmi* ga arimasu.)

¶ I'm **interested** in Japanese literature.

kyonen 去年〖名〗

kyonen ⟦n⟧ **last year**

¶わたしは去年の10月に日本へ行ってきました。 (Watashi wa *kyonen* no jūgatsu ni Nihon e itte kimashita.)

¶ I took a trip to Japan in October of **last year.**

¶わたしは去年大学を卒業しました。 (Watashi wa *kyonen* daigaku o sotsugyō shimashita.)

¶ I graduated from college **last year.**

kyori 距離〖名〗

kyori ⟦n⟧ **distance, interval, gap**

¶わたしの家から駅までの距離は約3キロです。 (Watashi no ie kara eki made no *kyori* wa yaku sankiro desu.)

¶ **The distance** from my house to the station is approximately three kilometers.

¶タクシーの料金は距離によって計算されます。 (Takushii no ryōkin wa *kyori* ni yotte keisan saremasu.)

¶ Taxi fares are calculated according to **distance.**

kyōryoku 協力〖名、～する〗

kyōryoku ⟦n, ~*suru*⟧ **cooperation, collaboration**

¶多くの人の協力によってダムは完成しました。 (Ooku no hito no *kyōryoku* ni yotte damu wa kansei shimashita.)

¶ The dam was ⟦has been⟧ completed through **the united efforts** of a great many people.

¶兄と協力して事業を始めました。 (Ani to *kyōryoku* shite jigyō o

¶ [I]'ve started a business **in collaboration** with my elder brother.

hajimemashita.)

kyōsanshugi 共産主義〖名〗

kyōshi 教師〖名〗
¶兄は数学の教師をしています。
(Ani wa sūgaku no *kyōshi* o shite imasu.)
⇨sensei 先生

kyōshitsu 教室〖名〗
¶教室の中では静かにしてください。
(*Kyōshitsu* no naka de wa shizuka ni shite kudasai.)

kyōsō 競争〖名, ～する〗
競争に勝つ (*kyōsō* ni katsu) 競争に負ける (*kyōsō* ni makeru)
¶田中さんと山田さんはいつも競争で勉強しています。 (Tanaka san to Yamada san wa itsu mo *kyōsō* de benkyō shite imasu.)
¶この辺は店が多いので，どの店も競争して安く売っています。 (Kono hen wa mise ga ooi node, dono mise mo *kyōsō* shite yasuku utte imasu.)

kyōtsū 共通〖名, ～する〗
共通点 (*kyōtsū*ten) 留学生にとって共通の問題 (ryūgakusei ni totte *kyōtsū* no mondai)
¶中国語と日本語は，漢字を使うという点で共通しています。(Chūgokugo to Nihongo wa, kanji o tsukau to iu ten de *kyōtsū* shite imasu.)

kyū 九〖名〗
十九世紀 (ju*kyū*seiki) 九階 (*kyū*kai)

kyōsanshugi 〚n〛 communism

kyōshi 〚n〛 teacher, instructor, schoolteacher
¶ My older brother **teaches** mathematics.

kyōshitsu 〚n〛 classroom, schoolroom
¶ Please be quiet while in **the classroom.**

kyōsō 〚n, ～*suru*〛 competition, contest, rivalry
win **a race,** be victorious in **a competition** // lose **a race,** be defeated in **a competition**
¶ [Mr.] Tanaka and [Mr.] Yamada are always **competing** with each other in their studies.
¶ There are many stores around here so they all sell cheaply **in competition with each other.**

kyōtsū 〚n, ～*suru*〛 common, shared
something **in common,** a **shared** similarity // a problem **in common** of foreign students
¶ The Chinese and Japanese languages have the use of Chinese characters **in common.**

kyū 〚n〛 nine
the 19th century // the **ninth** floor

⇨ku 九

kyū 急〖名, 形動〗

①［緊急な様子］

救急車 (kyū*kyū*sha)

¶急な用事ができたので, すぐ帰らなければなりません。(*Kyū* na yōji ga dekita node, sugu kaeranakereba narimasen.)

②［ものごとが突然に起こる様子］

¶電車が急に止まりました。(Densha ga *kyū* ni tomarimashita.)

③［傾斜が大きい様子］

¶この階段はずいぶん急ですね。(Kono kaidan wa zuibun *kyū* desu ne.)

④［ものごとの速い様子］

急行列車 (kyūkō-ressha)

¶この川の流れは急です。(Kono kawa no nagare wa *kyū* desu.)

kyū- 旧-〖頭〗

旧暦 (kyūreki) 旧正月 (kyūshō-gatsu) 旧市内 (kyūshinai) 旧漢字 (kyūkanji) 旧式 (kyūshiki)

⇨shin- 新-

kyūbyō 急病〖名〗

急病人 (kyūbyōnin)

¶上田さんは急病で来られなくなりました。(Ueda san wa kyūbyō de korarenaku narimashita.)

kyūgyō 休業〖名, ～する〗

臨時休業 (rinji-*kyūgyō*) 夏期休業 (kaki-*kyūgyō*)

¶このデパートは毎週木曜日が休業日です。(Kono depāto wa maishū

kyū 〖n, adj-v〗 **emergency, urgent; sudden; steep, sharp; rapid**

① [emergency, urgent, pressing]

an ambulance

¶ [I] must go home right away as something **urgent** has come up.

② [sudden, abrupt]

¶ The train stopped **suddenly.**

③ [steep, sharp]

¶ These are very **steep** stairs 〚steps〛, aren't they?

④ [rapid, swift]

an **express** train

¶ This river has a **swift** current.

kyū- 〖pref〗 **old, former, ex-**
the **old** calendar, the lunar calendar // the New Year according to the **old** calendar, the lunar New Year // within the **old** city // the **older** kanji, the **old** forms of kanji // **old**-style, out-of-date, **old**-fashioned

kyūbyō 〖n〗 **sudden illness, a sudden attack**
an **emergency** patient
¶ [Mr.] Ueda can't 〚couldn't〛 come because [he] **was suddenly taken ill.**

kyūgyō 〖n, ~suru〗 **suspension of business, being closed, a day off**
a special **holiday; Closed** Today (sign) // summer **holidays**
¶ This department store **is closed**

mokuyōbi ga *kyūgyō*bi desu.)

¶あの床屋には「本日休業」の札が出
ています。　(Ano tokoya ni wa
"honjitsu *kyūgyō*" no fuda ga dete
imasu.)

kyūjitsu　休日〖名〗

¶今度の休日には家族で旅行します。
(Kondo no *kyūjitsu* ni wa kazoku
de ryokō shimasu.)

kyūka　休暇〖名〗

¶休暇をとって旅行に出ます。(*Kyūka*
o totte ryokō ni demasu.)

¶休暇中は仕事のことはあまり考えま
せん。　(*Kyūka*chū wa shigoto no
koto wa amari kangaemasen.)

kyūkei　休憩〖名，〜する〗

¶10分間の休憩をしてから，また始め
ましょう。(Jippunkan no *kyūkei* o
shite kara, mata hajimemashō.)

¶会議は休憩しないで続けられまし
た。(Kaigi wa *kyūkei* shinaide tsu-
zukeraremashita.)

kyūkō　急行〖名〗

急行列車 (*kyūkō*-ressha)　急行券
(*kyūkō*ken)

¶午後7時に京都特別急行が発車
します。　(Gogo shichiji ni Kyōto
yuki tokubetsu-*kyūkō* ga hassha
shimasu.)

kyūryō　給料〖名〗

¶わたしの会社の給料日は毎月25日
です。(Watashi no kaisha no *kyūryō*bi wa maitsuki nijūgonichi
desu.)

every Thursday.

¶ That barbershop has a sign out
reading "**Closed** Today."

kyūjitsu　〚n〛　holiday, day off

¶ I am going on a trip with my family
over the coming **holiday.**

kyūka　〚n〛　holiday(s), vacation,
time off

¶ [I] am taking **some time off** and
going on a trip.

¶ While on **vacation** [I] rarely think
about work.

kyūkei　〚n, ~*suru*〛　rest, recess,
break, intermission

¶ Let's take a 10-minute **break** and
then start again.

¶ The meeting continued without a
break.

kyūkō　〚n〛　an express, express
train

an **express** train // an **express** ticket

¶ The limited **express** for Kyoto
leaves at 7 PM.

kyūryō　〚n〛　pay, wages, salary

¶ **Payday** at my company is the
twenty-fifth of the month.

¶給料には月給，週給，日給の3種類があります。(*Kyūryō* ni wa gekkyū, shūkyū, nikkyū no sanshurui ga arimasu.)

¶ There are three types of **wages**—monthly, weekly, and daily.

kyūyō　急用〖名〗

¶上田さんは急用ができたので，今朝早く国へ帰りました。(Ueda san wa *kyūyō* ga dekita node, kesa hayaku kuni e kaerimashita.)

¶田中さん，急用ですからすぐ来てください。(Tanaka san, *kyūyō* desu kara sugu kite kudasai.)

kyūyō 〚n〛　urgent matter, pressing business

¶ **Something urgent** came up so [Mr.] Ueda left for his hometown early this morning.

¶ [Mr.] Tanaka, please come here immediately; **it's urgent.**

M

ma-　真-〖頭〗

①［まことの，真実の］
真顔 (*ma*gao)
¶山田さんから真心のこもった贈り物をいただきました。　(Yamada san kara *ma*gokoro no komotta okurimono o itadakimashita.)

②［純粋な，正確な，ちょうど］
真水 (*ma*mizu)　　真冬 (*ma*fuyu)
真夜中 (*ma*yonaka)　真新しい (*ma*-atarashii)　真上 (*ma*ue)　真っ赤な花 (*ma*kka na hana)　真っ白な紙 (*ma*sshiro na kami)　部屋の真ん中 (heya no *ma*nnaka)　真ん丸い月 (*ma*nmarui tsuki)
¶真正面に見える建物が郵便局です。(*Ma*shōmen ni mieru tatemono ga yūbinkyoku desu.)

(-)ma　(-)間〖名，尾〗

1〖名〗

①［物と物との間］
¶3メートルずつ間を置いて木を植えました。　(Sanmētoru zutsu *ma* o oite ki o uemashita.)

②［時間，ひま］
¶約束の時間までには，まだちょっと間があります。(Yakusoku no jikan made ni wa, mada chotto *ma* ga arimasu.)

¶夢中で本を読んでいたら，いつの間にか朝になってしまいました。

ma- 〖pref〗　**true, genuine; just, exactly**

① [true, genuine, pure]
serious look, a **straight** face
¶ I received a gift from [Mrs.] Yamada with [her] **best** wishes.

② [just, exactly]
fresh water // **the dead** of winter, **midwinter** // **the middle** of the night, **the small hours** of the morning // **brand**-new // **right** above, **directly** overhead // crimson flower(s) // **snow**-white paper; blank paper // **the center** of the room // a **full** moon
¶ The building you can see **straight** ahead of you is the post office.

(-)ma 〖n, suf〗　**space, interval; time, spare time; a room**

1 〖n〗

① [space, interval; the area between two things]
¶ [I] planted trees three meters **apart.**

② [time, spare time, free time]
¶ There's still a little **time left** before the appointment.

¶ I was absorbed in a book and it was morning **before I knew it.**

(Muchū de hon o yonde itara, itsu no *ma* ni ka asa ni natte shimaimashita.)

③[部屋]
客間 (kyaku*ma*)　応接間 (ōsetsu*ma*)
茶の間 (chano*ma*)　居間 (i*ma*)　六畳間 (rokujō*ma*)

2〖尾〗
¶わたしのアパートは二間しかありません。 (Watashi no apāto wa futa-*ma* shika arimasen.)

mā　まあ〖副, 感〗

1〖副〗
¶まあ, ゆっくりしてください。 (*Mā*, yukkuri shite kudasai.)

¶おいしいかどうかわかりませんが, まあ食べてみてください。 (Oishii ka dō ka wakarimasen ga, *mā* tabete mite kudasai.)

2〖感〗
¶まあ, びっくりした。 (*Mā*, bikkuri shita.)

＊ 普通, 女の人が使う。

mabushii　まぶしい〖形〗
¶まぶしくて目を開けていられません。 (*Mabushikute* me o akete iraremasen.)

¶その部屋はまぶしいほど明るかった。 (Sono heya wa *mabushii* hodo akarukatta.)

machi　町〖名〗
①[人家が多く集まった所]
¶わたしは田舎を出て町で働きたいです。 (Watashi wa inaka o dete

---

③ [room, chamber]
drawing **room,** parlor // reception **room,** parlor // living **room,** sitting **room** // sitting **room,** living **room** // a six-*tatami*-mat **room**

2 〖suf〗　room, chamber
¶ My apartment is made up of only two **rooms.**

mā 〖adv, interj〗　**well, just; Oh!**
1 〖adv〗　well, just
¶ Please make yourself at home 〖Don't hurry off so soon〗.

¶ It may not be any good, but please try some.

2 〖interj〗　Oh!
¶ **What** a surprise!

＊ *Mā* is usually used by women.

mabushii 〖adj〗　**dazzling, glaring, blinding**
¶ **It's so bright** one can't keep one's eyes open.

¶ That room was very bright, **almost too bright.**

machi 〖n〗　**town, city; street, quarter**
① [town, city; densely populated area]
¶ I want to leave the country and

machi de hatarakitai desu.)

¶昨日は<ruby>町<rt>まち</rt></ruby>まで<ruby>買<rt>か</rt></ruby>い<ruby>物<rt>もの</rt></ruby>に<ruby>行<rt>い</rt></ruby>きました。
(Kinō wa *machi* made kaimono ni ikimashita.)

②[<ruby>家<rt></rt></ruby>がたくさん<ruby>並<rt>なら</rt></ruby>んでいてにぎやかな<ruby>通<rt>とお</rt></ruby>り]

¶<ruby>町<rt>まち</rt></ruby>を<ruby>歩<rt>ある</rt></ruby>いていたら，<ruby>山田<rt>やまだ</rt></ruby>さんに<ruby>会<rt>あ</rt></ruby>いました。 (*Machi* o aruite itara, Yamada san ni aimashita.)

¶<ruby>夕方<rt>ゆうがた</rt></ruby>の<ruby>町<rt>まち</rt></ruby>は<ruby>買<rt>か</rt></ruby>い<ruby>物<rt>もの</rt></ruby>をする<ruby>人<rt>ひと</rt></ruby>でたいへんにぎやかでした。 (Yūgata no *machi* wa kaimono o suru hito de taihen nigiyaka deshita.)

⇨mura <ruby>村<rt>むら</rt></ruby>

machiawaseru <ruby>待<rt>ま</rt></ruby>ち<ruby>合<rt>あ</rt></ruby>わせる〖<ruby>動<rt>どう</rt></ruby>Ⅱ〗

¶<ruby>山田<rt>やまだ</rt></ruby>さんと6<ruby>時<rt>じ</rt></ruby>に<ruby>東京<rt>とうきょう</rt></ruby><ruby>駅<rt>えき</rt></ruby>で<ruby>待<rt>ま</rt></ruby>ち<ruby>合<rt>あ</rt></ruby>わせました。 (Yamada san to rokuji ni Tōkyō-eki de *machiawasemashita*.)

machigaeru <ruby>間違<rt>まちが</rt></ruby>える〖<ruby>動<rt>どう</rt></ruby>Ⅱ〗

①[<ruby>誤<rt>あやま</rt></ruby>る，<ruby>違<rt>ちが</rt></ruby>える]

¶どうも<ruby>計算<rt>けいさん</rt></ruby>を<ruby>間違<rt>まちが</rt></ruby>えたようです。
(Dōmo keisan o *machigaeta* yō desu.)

②[とりちがえる]

¶ホテルで<ruby>部屋<rt>へや</rt></ruby>を<ruby>間違<rt>まちが</rt></ruby>えて，<ruby>隣<rt>となり</rt></ruby>の<ruby>部屋<rt>へや</rt></ruby>へ<ruby>入<rt>はい</rt></ruby>ってしまいました。 (Hoteru de heya o *machigaete*, tonari no heya e haitte shimaimashita.)

machigai <ruby>間違<rt>まちが</rt></ruby>い〖<ruby>名<rt>めい</rt></ruby>〗

①[<ruby>誤<rt>あやま</rt></ruby>り，<ruby>正<rt>ただ</rt></ruby>しくないこと]

¶<ruby>次<rt>つぎ</rt></ruby>の<ruby>文章<rt>ぶんしょう</rt></ruby>の<ruby>間違<rt>まちが</rt></ruby>いを<ruby>直<rt>なお</rt></ruby>しなさい。

(Tsugi no bunshō no *machigai* o

go to **the city** to work.

¶ [I] went to **town** 〚**downtown**〛 yesterday to shop.

② [street, quarter; lively street(s) with many houses]

¶ I met [Mrs.] Yamada while walking along **the street.**

¶ The night **streets** were bustling with shoppers.

machiawaseru 〚v II〛 **meet, arrange to meet, wait for**

¶ [Miss] Yamada and [I] **met** at Tokyo Station at six o'clock.

machigaeru 〚v II〛 **make a mistake, err; mistake, confuse**

① [make a mistake, err]

¶ There seems **to be a mistake** in these figures.

② [mistake, confuse]

¶ **I mistook** the room next door for mine at the hotel and entered it by mistake.

machigai 〚n〛 **mistake, error; accident, mishap**

① [mistake, error]

¶ Correct **the mistakes** in the next

naoshinasai.)

②[異常なこと「事故など」]

¶子供の帰りが遅いが，何か**間違い**が
あったのではないでしょうか。 (Ko-
domo no kaeri ga osoi ga, nani ka
machigai ga atta no de wa nai
deshō ka?)

machigai nai 間違いない〖連〗

¶あの学校が優勝するのは**間違いな
い**。 (Ano gakkō ga yūshō suru no
wa *machigai nai*.)

¶お金はあしたまでに**間違いなく**返し
ます。 (Okane wa ashita made ni
machigai naku kaeshimasu.)

machigau 間違う〖動Ⅰ〗

①[違う，誤る]

¶この漢字は**間違って**いますよ。
(Kono kanji wa *machigatte* imasu
yo.)

②[とりちがえる]

¶山田さんは，**間違って**わたしの本を
持って行ってしまいました。 (Yama-
da san wa, *machigatte* watashi no
hon o motte itte shimaimashita.)

mada まだ〖副〗

①[その状態が続いている様子]

¶**まだ**雨が降っています。(*Mada* ame
ga futte imasu.)

¶母は**まだ**帰ってきません。 (Haha
wa *mada* kaette kimasen.)

¶わたしは日本語が**まだ**下手です。
(Watashi wa Nihongo ga *mada*
heta desu.)

→**mō** もう

sentence.

② [accident, mishap, trouble]

¶ The children are late coming home.
Could **something have happened?**

machigai nai 〖compd〗 **without fail, certainly, surely**

¶ That school **is sure** to win.

¶ [I] will repay the money by tomorrow **without fail.**

machigau 〖v I〗 **make a mistake, err; mistake, confuse**

① [make a mistake, err]

¶ This *kanji* **is wrong.**

② [mistake, confuse]

¶ [Mr.] Yamada **mistakenly** went off
with my book.

mada 〖adv〗 **still, yet; only; more, still**

① [still, yet; a certain condition is
still in effect]

¶ It's **still** raining.

¶ My mother hasn't returned home
yet.

¶ My Japanese **still** isn't very good.

②［あまり時間がたっていない様子，わずかに］

¶汽車が走り出してから，**まだ**10分しかたっていません。(Kisha ga hashiri-dashite kara, *mada* jippun shika tatte imasen.)

¶わたしは日本へ来て**まだ**1年です。(Watashi wa Nihon e kite *mada* ichinen desu.)

→**mō もう**

③［もっと，ほかにも］

¶仕事は**まだ**たくさん残っています。(Shigoto wa *mada* takusan nokotte imasu.)

¶**まだ**見たい所はたくさんあります。(*Mada* mitai tokoro wa takusan arimasu.)

made　まで〖助〗

朝から晩**まで** (asa kara ban *made*)

¶午前9時から午後5時**まで**会社にいます。(Gozen kuji kara gogo goji *made* kaisha ni imasu.)

¶今週の土曜日**まで**学校は休みです。(Konshū no doyōbi *made* gakkō wa yasumi desu.)

¶ゆうべは遅く**まで**起きていました。(Yūbe wa osoku *made* okite imashita.)

¶ここから駅**まで**何分ぐらいですか。(Koko kara eki *made* nanpun gurai desu ka?)

¶東京から大阪**まで**は何キロぐらいありますか。(Tōkyō kara Oosaka *made* wa nankiro gurai arimasu ka?)

② [only, barely]

¶ **Only** 10 minutes have passed since the departure of the train.

¶ It's **only** been one year since I came to Japan.

③ [more, still]

¶ There's **still** a lot of work to do.

¶ There are **still** a lot of places I want to go to see.

made 〚part〛 **until, to, up to, as far as**

from morning **until** night

¶ I am at the office from 9 AM **to** 5 PM.

¶ School is off **through** this Saturday.

¶ [I] was up **until** late last night.

¶ How many minutes is it from here **to** the station?

¶ How many kilometers is it from Tokyo **to** Osaka?

made ni

made ni　までに〖連〗

¶来月の十日までに，この仕事を終えなければなりません。 (Raigetsu no tooka *made ni*, kono shigoto o oenakereba narimasen.)

¶レポートは来週の土曜日までに出してください。 (Repōto wa raishū no doyōbi *made ni* dashite kudasai.)

mado　窓〖名〗

窓を開ける (*mado* o akeru)　窓を閉める (*mado* o shimeru)

¶バスの窓から手を出さないでください。 (Basu no *mado* kara te o dasanaide kudasai.)

(-)mae　(-)前〖名，尾〗

1〖名〗

①[顔や目の向いている方，ものの正面]

駅前 (eki*mae*)

¶まっすぐ前の方を見てください。 (Massugu *mae* no hō o mite kudasai.)

¶前から3番めの人，立ってください。 (*Mae* kara sanbanme no hito, tatte kudasai.)

¶郵便局は銀行の前にあります。 (Yūbinkyoku wa ginkō no *mae* ni arimasu.)

→ushiro 後ろ

②[あるものごとの初めの部分]

¶この映画は前のほうはあまりおもしろくありません。 (Kono eiga wa *mae* no hō wa amari omoshiroku arimasen.)

made ni 〖compd〗　by, not later than, before

¶ This job must be finished **by** the tenth of next month.

¶ Please submit your report **by** Saturday next week.

mado 〖n〗　window

open **the window** // close **the window**

¶ Please don't put your hands out **the windows** of the bus.

(-)mae 〖n, suf〗　front; first part; before; ago; serving, portion

1 〖n〗

① [front]

in front of the station

¶ Please look straight **ahead.**

¶ Will the person third from **the front** please stand up.

¶ The post office is **in front of** the bank.

② [the first part]

¶ The **first** part of this movie isn't very interesting.

438

¶前の部分を理解してから先に進んでください。(*Mae* no bubun o rikai shite kara saki ni susunde kudasai.)

→ato あと

③[ある時点を基にしてそれより早い時]
¶今9時5分前です。(Ima kuji gofun *mae* desu.)

¶わたしは日本へ来る前に、少し日本語を勉強したことがあります。(Watashi wa Nihon e kuru *mae* ni, sukoshi Nihongo o benkyō shita koto ga arimasu.)

④[現在の時点より以前]
¶あなたは前に上田さんに会ったことがありますか。(Anata wa *mae* ni Ueda san ni atta koto ga arimasu ka?)

¶この前の日曜日にわたしは映画を見に行きました。(Kono *mae* no nichiyōbi ni watashi wa eiga o mi ni ikimashita.)

2〚尾〛
一人前の料理 (ichinin*mae* no ryōri)

magaru 曲がる〚動Ⅰ〛

①[ものがまっすぐでなくなる]
腰が曲がる (koshi ga *magaru*)
¶この木は枝が曲がるほどたくさんの実がなっています。(Kono ki wa eda ga *magaru* hodo takusan no mi ga natte imasu.)

②[進む向きを変える]
¶その角を右へ曲がると,交番があります。(Sono kado o migi e *magaru*

¶ Please move on to the rest after full comprehension of the **first** part.

③ [before, previous; earlier than a given time]
¶ It is now five **to** nine.

¶ I studied Japanese a little **before** coming to Japan.

④ [before, ago; earlier than the present time]
¶ Have you met [Mrs.] Ueda **before**?

¶ I went to see a movie **last** Sunday.

2 〚suf〛 serving, portion
a single **serving** (of a dish or meal)

magaru 〚v I〛 curve, be bent; turn; be crooked, bend

① [curve, be bent]
have a **bent** back
¶ This tree is so laden with fruit that its branches **are bent down**.

② [to turn]
¶ If you **turn** right at that corner, you'll find a police box.

to, kōban ga arimasu.)

③[道などが折れている]

¶川の所で道が曲がっています。

(Kawa no tokoro de michi ga *magatte* imasu.)

mageru 曲げる〖動Ⅱ〗

¶けがをして、足を曲げることができなくなりました。(Kega o shite, ashi o *mageru* koto ga dekinaku narimashita.)

¶いくら力があっても、この鉄棒を曲げることはできないでしょう。(Ikura chikara ga atte mo, kono tetsubō o *mageru* koto wa dekinai deshō.)

mago 孫〖名〗

¶山田さんは孫が3人あります。

(Yamada san wa *mago* ga sannin arimasu.)

mai- 毎-〖頭〗

毎週 (*mai*shū) 毎月 (*mai*tsuki) 毎年 (*mai*nen) 毎年 (*mai*toshi) 毎回 (*mai*kai) 毎日曜日 (*mai*nichiyōbi)

¶毎度ありがとうございます。(*Mai*do arigatō gozaimasu.)

-mai -枚〖尾〗

シャツ1枚 (shatsu ichi*mai*) はがき2枚 (hagaki ni*mai*)

¶このおさらは1枚500円です。

(Kono osara wa ichi*mai* gohyaku-en desu.)

maiasa 毎朝〖名〗

¶わたしは毎朝6時に起きます。

(Watashi wa *maiasa* rokuji ni okimasu.)

③ [be crooked, bend]

¶ There is **a bend** in the road at the river.

mageru 〖v II〗 to bend, curve, twist

¶ I hurt myself and can't 〖couldn't〗 **bend** my leg.

¶ No matter how strong [he] may be, I bet [he] can't **bend** this iron bar.

mago 〖n〗 grandchild, grandson, granddaughter

¶ [Mr.] Yamada has three **grandchildren.**

mai- 〖pref〗 every, each, apiece

every week, weekly // **every** month, monthly // **every** year, yearly // **every** year, yearly // **every** time, **each** time // **every** Sunday, **each** Sunday

¶ Thank you for your **continued** patronage (said to regular customers in stores, restaurants, etc.).

-mai 〖suf〗 sheet, piece, page, etc.; the counter for thin, flat objects

one shirt // **two** postcards

¶ These plates are five hundred yen **each.**

maiasa 〖n〗 every morning, each morning

¶ I get up at six o'clock **each morning.**

maiban 毎晩〖名〗

¶上田さんは毎晩遅くまで起きています。 (Ueda san wa *maiban* osoku made okite imasu.)

mainichi 毎日〖名〗

¶わたしは毎日ピアノの練習をします。 (Watashi wa *mainichi* piano no renshū o shimasu.)

mairu 参る〖動Ⅰ〗

①[行く，来る]

¶「いつこちらへいらっしゃいますか。」 (Itsu kochira e irasshaimasu ka?) 「明日参ります。」(Asu *mairimasu*.)

¶先月こちらに参りました。(Sengetsu kochira ni *mairimashita*.)

¶行って参ります。(Itte *mairimasu*.)

*「行く (iku)」「来る (kuru)」の謙譲語。

②[行く，来る]

¶すぐ車が参りますから，しばらくお待ちください。 (Sugu kuruma ga *mairimasu* kara, shibaraku omachi kudasai.)

¶雨が降って参りました。 (Ame ga futte *mairimashita*.)

*「行く (iku)」「来る (kuru)」の丁寧語。

③[神社や寺に行って参拝する]

¶お正月には神社にお参りします。 (Oshōgatsu ni wa jinja ni o*mairi* shimasu.)

majime まじめ〖形動〗

①[誠実である，一生懸命に何かをする]

maiban 〚n〛 every night, each evening, nightly

¶ [Mr.] Ueda stays up late **every night.**

mainichi 〚n〛 every day, each day, daily

¶ I practice the piano **every day.**

mairu 〚v I〛 go, come; visit a temple or shrine

① [go, come]

¶ "When will you be coming here?" "**I will come** tomorrow."

¶ **I came** here last month.

¶ **I'm going** now (set expression used when going out from a place one is going to return to the same day).

* *Mairu* is the humble form of *iku* and of *kuru*.

② [go, come]

¶ Please wait a moment. The car 〚taxi〛 **will be here** shortly.

¶ It **has started** to rain.

* *Mairu* is the polite form of *iku* and of *kuru*.

③ [visit a shrine or temple]

¶ [We] **visit** a shrine at New Year's.

majime 〚adj-v〛 steady, faithful, honest; serious, grave, earnest

① [steady, faithful, honest, sober]

¶あの学生はとてもまじめです。(Ano gakusei wa totemo *majime* desu.)
¶今度入ってきた人は、**まじめによく働きます**。(Kondo haitte kita hito wa, *majime* ni yoku hatarakimasu.)
②[本気である]
まじめな顔をする (*majime* na kao o suru)
¶わたしが**まじめに話しているのに、あの人は笑いました**。(Watashi ga *majime* ni hanashite iru noni, ano hito wa waraimashita.)

¶ That student is very **serious** 〚**diligent**〛.
¶ [Our] new colleague is **serious** and a hard worker.
② [serious, grave, earnest]
have a **serious** look on one's face; keep a **straight** face
¶ [He] laughed even though I was talking **seriously.**

majiru 交じる〚動Ⅰ〛
¶男の子の中に女の子が一人**交じって遊んでいます**。(Otoko no ko no naka ni onna no ko ga hitori *majitte* asonde imasu.)
¶この本は漢字と仮名の**交じった文で書いてあります**。(Kono hon wa kanji to kana no *majitta* bun de kaite arimasu.)

majiru 〚v Ⅰ〛 mix, mingle, be mixed, be blended
¶ The children are playing, with one girl **joining** several boys.
¶ This book is written in **a mixture** of *kanji* and *kana.*

majiru 混じる〚動Ⅰ〛
¶この米には石が**混じっています**。(Kono kome ni wa ishi ga *majitte* imasu.)
¶あの人には西洋人の血が**混じっています**。(Ano hito ni wa seiyōjin no chi ga *majitte* imasu.)

majiru 〚v Ⅰ〛 mix, mingle, be mixed, be blended
¶ There are stones **mixed in** with this rice.
¶ [He] **has some** Western 〚Occidental, European〛 blood **in [him].**

makaseru 任せる〚動Ⅱ〛
¶この仕事はあなたに**任せます**。(Kono shigoto wa anata ni *makasemasu.*)
¶どうしたらよいかは、あなたの判断に**任せます**。(Dō shitara yoi ka wa,

makaseru 〚v Ⅱ〛 entrust to, leave to
¶ **I'll leave** this job **up to** you to do.
¶ **I'll leave it to you** to decide what is best to do.

anata no handan ni *makasemasu*.)

makeru 負ける〖動Ⅱ〗

①〔相手が強くて勝つことができない〕

戦争に負ける (sensō ni *makeru*) 敵に負ける (teki ni *makeru*)

¶この次の試合には負けないようにがんばりましょう。 (Kono tsugi no shiai ni wa *makenai* yō ni ganbarimashō.)

↔katsu 勝つ →yabureru 敗れる

②〔値段を安くする〕

¶高すぎますね。もう少し負けてください。 (Takasugimasu ne. Mō sukoshi *makete* kudasai.)

¶あの本屋では1割負けてくれるそうです。(Ano hon'ya de wa ichiwari *makete* kureru sō desu.)

makka 真っ赤〖形動〗

真っ赤な太陽 (*makka* na taiyō) 真っ赤な口紅 (*makka* na kuchibeni)

¶恥ずかしくて、顔が真っ赤になりました。 (Hazukashikute, kao ga *makka* ni narimashita.)

makkura 真っ暗〖形動〗

¶電気が消えて，部屋の中が真っ暗になりました。(Denki ga kiete, heya no naka ga *makkura* ni narimashita.)

¶遅くなって，真っ暗な道を一人で帰りました。 (Osoku natte, *makkura* na michi o hitori de kaerimashita.)

makkuro 真っ黒〖形動〗

¶中村さんの髪の毛は真っ黒です。

makeru 〖v Ⅱ〗 be defeated, lose; give a price reduction

① [be defeated, lose]

lose a war // **be defeated** by the enemy, **lose** to one's opponent

¶ Let's stick in there and **win** the next game 〚match〛.

② [give a price reduction]

¶ It's too expensive. Please **come down** a little.

¶ I hear that bookstore **gives a** 10 percent **price reduction.**

makka 〖adj-v〗 very red, bright red, crimson

a **blood-red** sun // **crimson** lipstick

¶ [My] face turned **bright red** from embarrassment 〚shame〛.

makkura 〖adj-v〗 total darkness, pitch dark

¶ The electricity went off and the room turned **pitch dark.**

¶ It was late and [I] went home alone through the **pitch-dark** streets 〚along the **pitch-black** road〛.

makkuro 〖adj-v〗 deep black, jet black

¶ [Miss] Nakamura's hair is **jet**

(Nakamura san no kaminoke wa *makkuro* desu.)

¶日に焼けて，顔が真っ黒になりました。(Hi ni yakete, kao ga *makkuro* ni narimashita.)

black 〖raven black〗.

¶ [His] face is 〖was〗 **deeply tanned**.

makoto ni まことに〖副〗

¶遅くなって，まことに申し訳ありません。(Osoku natte, *makoto ni* mōshiwake arimasen.)

¶山田さんはまことに立派な方です。(Yamada san wa *makoto ni* rippa na kata desu.)

⇨hontō ni 本当に

makoto ni 〖adv〗 **really, truly, sincerely**

¶ I'm **very** sorry to be late.

¶ [Mr.] Yamada is **really** a fine person.

(-)maku (-)幕〖名, 尾〗

1〖名〗
幕が開く (*maku* ga aku) 幕が下りる (*maku* ga oriru) 幕を引く (*maku* o hiku)

¶壁に幕を張って映画を映しました。(Kabe ni *maku* o hatte eiga o utsushimashita.)

2〖尾〗
¶この芝居は5幕からなっています。(Kono shibai wa go*maku* kara natte imasu.)

(-)maku 〖n, suf〗 (stage) **curtain; act** (of a play)

1 〖n〗 (stage) curtain
the curtain rises 〖opens〗 // **the curtain** falls 〖closes〗 // draw 〖raise〗 **the curtain**

¶ [We] put **a makeshift screen** across the wall and showed a movie.

2 〖suf〗 act (of a play)
¶ This play is composed of five **acts**.

maku 巻く〖動 I〗

①[ねじって回す]
ねじを巻く (neji o *maku*)
¶時計を巻くのを忘れたので，止まってしまいました。(Tokei o *maku* no o wasureta node, tomatte shimaimashita.)

②[周りに長いものをからみつける]
¶ナイフで手を切ったので，包帯を巻

maku 〖v I〗 **turn, wind, roll up; wind around**

① [turn, wind, roll up]
turn a screw

¶ The clock 〖watch〗 stopped 〖has stopped〗 because [I] forgot **to wind** it.

② [wind around]
¶ [I] cut [my] hand with a knife and

きました。 (Naifu de te o kitta node, hōtai o *makimashita*.)

maku まく〖動Ⅰ〗

①[種などを土の上におく]

¶種をまきましたが，まだ芽が出ませ
ん。(Tane o *makimashita* ga, mada me ga demasen.)

②[広い範囲に散らす]

¶ほこりがひどいので，道に水をまき
ました。(Hokori ga hidoi node, michi ni mizu o *makimashita*.)

makura まくら〖名〗

まくらをする (*makura* o suru)

¶まくらが高すぎて，よく眠れません
でした。 (*Makura* ga takasugite, yoku nemuremasen deshita.)

mama まま〖名〗

¶くつをはいたまま部屋へ入ってはい
けません。 (Kutsu o haita *mama* heya e haitte wa ikemasen.)

¶あの人は家を出たまま帰ってきませ
ん。(Ano hito wa ie o deta *mama* kaette kimasen.)

¶この魚は生のまま食べられますか。
(Kono sakana wa nama no *mama* taberaremasu ka?)

¶テーブルの上は，かたづけないでその
ままにしておいてください。(Tēburu no ue wa, katazukenaide sono *mama* ni shite oite kudasai.)

＊「まま (mama)」の前に来る動詞は
「たの形」を使うことが多い。

mame 豆〖名〗

¶今晩は豆を煮て食べましょう。

wrapped a bandage **around it.**

maku [[v I]] **sow** (seed); **scatter, sprinkle**

① [sow (seed)]

¶ [I] **seeded** it but nothing has come up yet.

② [scatter, sprinkle]

¶ [I] **sprinkled** the road with water as it was so dusty.

makura [[n]] **pillow**

use **a pillow,** rest one's head on **a pillow**

¶ [I] couldn't sleep well as [my] **pillow** was too thick.

mama [[n]] **as is, as it stands**

¶ One mustn't enter the room with one's shoes **still on.**

¶ [He] left home and has **never** come back.

¶ Can this fish be eaten **raw?**

¶ Please don't put away the things on the table but leave them **as they are.**

＊ Verbs before *mama* are usually in the *-ta* form.

mame [[n]] **beans, peas, soybeans**

¶ Let's have boiled [[cooked]] **beans**

445

(Konban wa *mame* o nite tabe-mashō.)

¶しょう油は豆から造ります。

(Shōyu wa *mame* kara tsukuri-masu.)

¶ Soy sauce is made from **soy-beans.**

mamonaku　間もなく〖副〗

¶父は間もなく帰ると思います。

(Chichi wa *mamonaku* kaeru to omoimasu.)

¶試験が終わると間もなく夏休みです。

(Shiken ga owaru to *mamonaku* natsuyasumi desu.)

mamonaku 〖adv〗 **soon, presently, before long**

¶ My father should be home **shortly.**

¶ Summer vacation starts **soon** after the exams are over.

mamoru　守る〖動Ⅰ〗

①[害を受けないように防ぐ]

¶国を守るのは国民の義務です。

(Kuni o *mamoru* no wa kokumin no gimu desu.)

②[決めたことに従う]

規則を守る　(kisoku o *mamoru*)

¶約束は必ず守ります。　(Yakusoku wa kanarazu *mamorimasu*.)

¶あの人は，いつも時間を守らないで遅れてきます。(Ano hito wa, itsu mo jikan o *mamoranaide* okurete ki-masu.)

mamoru 〖v I〗 **protect; obey, observe**

① [protect, guard]

¶ It is the duty of citizens **to defend** their country.

② [obey, observe, fulfill]

keep to regulations, **observe** the rules

¶ [I] always **keep** [my] promises.

¶ [He] **is unpunctual** and always comes late.

man　万〖名〗

1万 (ichi*man*)　10万 (jū*man*) 100万 (hyaku*man*)　1000万 (sen*man*, [issen*man*])

man 〖n〗 **ten thousand**

10,000　//　100,000　//　1,000,000　// 10,000,000

mane　まね〖名，～する〗

人のまねをする　(hito no *mane* o suru)

¶上田さんは鳥の鳴き声のまねをするのが上手です。　(Ueda san wa tori

mane 〖n, ~*suru*〗 **imitation, mimicry**

imitate another; **follow suit**

¶ [Mr.] Ueda is skilled at **imitating** bird calls.

no nakigoe no *mane* o suru no ga jōzu desu.)

¶先生の発音をよく聞いて**まね**してください。(Sensei no hatsuon o yoku kiite *mane* shite kudasai.)

maneku 招く〖動Ⅰ〗

客を招く (kyaku o *maneku*)

¶友達を**招**いて，いっしょに食事をしました。 (Tomodachi o *maneite*, issho ni shokuji o shimashita.)

¶わたしたちは友達の結婚式に**招かれ**ました。 (Watashitachi wa tomodachi no kekkonshiki ni *manekaremashita*.)

¶わたしは日本政府に**招かれて**日本へ来ました。(Watashi wa Nihon-seifu ni *manekarete* Nihon e kimashita.)

⇨shōtai 招待

maneru まねる〖動Ⅱ〗

¶この建物はフランスの建築を**まねて**造ったものです。 (Kono tatemono wa Furansu no kenchiku o *manete* tsukutta mono desu.)

manga 漫画〖名〗

¶中村さんは漫画が大好きです。(Nakamura san wa *manga* ga daisuki desu.)

maniau 間に合う〖動Ⅰ〗

¶急げば，まだ9時15分発の汽車に間に合います。(Isogeba, mada kuji jūgofun hatsu no kisha ni *maniaimasu*.)

¶今度の旅行は，1万円あればじゅうぶん間に合います。(Kondo no ryokō

¶ Please listen carefully to the teacher's pronunciation and **copy it.**

maneku 〚v I〛 invite

invite a guest

¶ [I] **invited** a friend and we had a meal together.

¶ We **were invited** to a friend's wedding.

¶ I came to Japan **on the invitation** of the Japanese government.

maneru 〚v II〛 imitate, copy

¶ This building **is modeled** after the style of French architecture.

manga 〚n〛 cartoon, comics, comic book, caricature

¶ [Mr.] Nakamura is very fond of **comic magazines** 〚adult comic books〛.

maniau 〚v I〛 be in time for; meet the purpose, be enough, do

¶ If [you] hurry, **[you] can** still **make** the 9:15 train.

¶ Ten thousand yen **will be** quite **enough** for the coming trip.

wa, ichiman'en areba jūbun *ma-niaimasu.*)

man'in 満員〚名〛
満員電車 (*man'in*-densha)
¶バスが満員で乗れませんでした。
(Basu ga *man'in* de noremasen deshita.)
¶どこのホテルも満員でした。 (Doko no hoteru mo *man'in* deshita.)

mannaka 真ん中〚名〛
①［中心の辺り］
¶町の真ん中に公園があります。
(Machi no *mannaka* ni kōen ga arimasu.)
②［上下・左右の両端からみてちょうど中間のところ］
¶このひもを真ん中から切ってください。 (Kono himo o *mannaka* kara kitte kudasai.)
¶上の子は中学2年生で真ん中は小学校の6年生，下のは4年生です。
(Ue no ko wa chūgaku ninensei de *mannaka* wa shōgakkō no rokunensei, shita no wa yonensei desu.)

mannenhitsu 万年筆〚名〛
¶この万年筆は使いやすいです。
(Kono *mannenhitsu* wa tsukaiyasui desu.)

manzoku 満足〚名，形動，〜する〛
①［自分の思うとおりになってこれでじゅうぶんだと思うこと］
¶わたしは今の生活でじゅうぶん満足です。(Watashi wa ima no seikatsu de jūbun *manzoku* desu.)

man'in 〚n〛 **full, no vacancy, sold out, capacity**

a **crowded** train, a **jam-packed** train
¶ The bus **was full** and I couldn't get on.

¶ Every hotel **was full up.**

mannaka 〚n〛 **center; middle, halfway**

① [center]
¶ There is a park in **the center** of town 〚in **the heart** of the city〛.

② [middle, halfway]

¶ Please cut this string **in the middle.**

¶ [Our] oldest child is in the second year of junior high school, **the middle child** in the sixth year of elementary school, and the youngest child in the fourth year of elementary school.

mannenhitsu 〚n〛 **fountain pen**
¶ This **fountain pen** is easy to use.

manzoku 〚n, adj-v, ~*suru*〛 **satisfied, contented; perfect, complete, adequate**

① [satisfied, contented]
¶ I **am** fully **satisfied** with my present life.

¶こんな安い給料では満足できません。 (Konna yasui kyūryō de wa *manzoku* dekimasen.)

②[じゅうぶんである様子，完全である様子]

¶1か月5万円では満足な生活はできません。 (Ikkagetsu goman'en de wa *manzoku* na seikatsu wa dekimasen.)

¶あの人は易しい質問にも満足に答えられません。 (Ano hito wa yasashii shitsumon ni mo *manzoku* ni kotaeraremasen.)

maru 丸〖名〗

¶次の文のうち正しいものに丸をつけなさい。 (Tsugi no bun no uchi tadashii mono ni *maru* o tsukenasai.)

marude まるで〖副〗

①[ちょうどそのとおり，似ている]

¶こんなぜいたくな生活はまるで夢のようです。 (Konna zeitaku na seikatsu wa *marude* yume no yō desu.)

¶あの人は，犬をまるで自分の子供のようにかわいがっています。 (Ano hito wa, inu o *marude* jibun no kodomo no yō ni kawaigatte imasu.)

＊あとに「ようだ (yō da)」が来ることが多い。

②[全く，ぜんぜん]

¶あの兄弟はまるで性格が違います。 (Ano kyōdai wa *marude* seikaku ga chigaimasu.)

¶ [I] **cannot be satisfied** with such low wages.

② [perfect, complete, adequate, proper]

¶ One cannot live **adequately** on fifty thousand yen a month.

¶ [He] cannot answer even easy questions **satisfactorily.**

maru 〖n〗 circle

¶ Choose the correct sentences among the following and mark them with **a circle.**

marude 〖adv〗 **just like, exactly; completely, perfectly, entirely**

① [just like, exactly, as if]

¶ Such a life of luxury is **just like** a dream.

¶ [He] dotes on [his] dog **as if** it were [his] child.

＊ Often used with *yō da*.

② [completely, perfectly, entirely]

¶ Those brothers have **completely** different personalities.

¶わたしはそのことを**まるで**知りませんでした。(Watashi wa sono koto o *marude* shirimasen deshita.)

* あとに打ち消しの言葉や否定的な意味の言葉が来る。

marui 丸い〔形〕

丸い石 (*marui* ishi)

¶東の空に丸い月が出ました。

(Higashi no sora ni *marui* tsuki ga demashita.)

marui 円い〔形〕

円い窓 (*marui* mado) 円いテーブル (*marui* tēburu)

¶わたしたちは先生の周りに円く輪になって座りました。 (Watashitachi wa sensei no mawari ni *maruku* wa ni natte suwarimashita.)

mashō ましょう〔助動〕

①〔話し手の意志を表す〕

¶重そうなかばんですね。お持ちしましょう。(Omosō na kaban desu ne. Omochi shi*mashō*.)

¶あなたの切符も買っておきましょう。(Anata no kippu mo katte oki*mashō*.)

②〔勧誘を表す〕

¶今夜，映画を見に行きましょう。(Kon'ya, eiga o mi ni iki*mashō*.)

¶疲れましたね。お茶でも飲みましょうか。(Tsukaremashita ne. Ocha demo nomi*mashō* ka?)

⇨masu ます

massao 真っ青〔形動〕

①〔本当に青い様子〕

¶ I had **no** idea of that.

* Followed by the negative or words or expressions having a negative sense.

marui 〚adj〛 **round, circular, spherical**

a **round** stone 〚pebble, rock〛

¶ A **rounded** moon appeared in the eastern sky.

marui 〚adj〛 **round, circular, spherical**

a **round** window // a **round** table

¶ We sat **in a circle** around our teacher.

-mashō 〚auxil〛 a verb ending expressing the speaker's intent or an invitation

① [expresses the speaker's intent]

¶ That bag 〚suitcase, briefcase〛 looks heavy. **Let me** carry it for you.

¶ **Let me** buy your ticket too.

② [expresses an invitation or persuasion]

¶ **Let's go** to a movie tonight.

¶ That was tiring. **Why don't we have** some tea or something?

massao 〚adj-v〛 **deep blue; deadly pale**

① [deep blue]

真っ青な海 (*massao* na umi)

¶真っ青な空に白い雲が一つ浮かんでいます。(*Massao* na sora ni shiroi kumo ga hitotsu ukande imasu.)

②[顔色が悪く血の気のない様子]

¶山田さんは恐ろしさで真っ青になりました。(Yamada san wa osoroshi-sa de *massao* ni narimashita.)

masshiro 真っ白〖形動〗

¶山は雪で真っ白です。(Yama wa yuki de *masshiro* desu.)

¶庭に真っ白な菊の花が咲いています。(Niwa ni *masshiro* na kiku no hana ga saite imasu.)

massugu まっすぐ〖副, 形動〗

¶駅はこの道をまっすぐ行ったところにあります。(Eki wa kono michi o *massugu* itta tokoro ni arimasu.)

¶曲がった線でなく, まっすぐな線を引いてください。(Magatta sen de naku, *massugu* na sen o hiite kudasai.)

masu 増す〖動Ⅰ〗

①[増える, 多くなる]

¶昨日の雨で川の水が増しました。(Kinō no ame de kawa no mizu ga *mashimashita*.)

¶人口が増すと, ますます食糧が不足してきます。(Jinkō ga *masu* to, masumasu shokuryō ga fusoku shite kimasu.)

→fueru 増える

②[増やす, 多くする]

¶電報は5字増すごとに, 料金が高く

a **deep blue** sea

¶ There is a single white cloud floating in the **deep blue** sky.

② [deadly pale]

¶ [Mr.] Yamada **blanched** from fear.

masshiro 〚adj-v〛 **pure white**

¶ The mountain is **white** with snow.

¶ A **pure white** chrysanthemum is blooming in the garden 〚yard〛.

massugu 〚adv, adj-v〛 **straight, direct, upright**

¶ The station is **straight** along this street.

¶ Please draw a **straight** line, not a curved one.

masu 〚v I〛 **increase, rise; increase, raise**

① [increase, rise, grow]

¶ The river **has risen** due to the rain yesterday.

¶ As the population **increases,** the shortage of food deepens.

② [increase, raise, add to]

¶ The charge for a telegram goes up

なります。 (Denpō wa goji *masu* goto ni, ryōkin ga takaku narimasu.)

-masu ます〖助動〗

¶よく雨が降りますね。 (Yoku ame ga furi*masu* ne.)

¶机の上に本があります。 (Tsukue no ue ni hon ga ari*masu*.)

¶机の上には何もありません。 (Tsukue no ue ni wa nani mo ari*masen*.)

¶いっしょに遊びに行きませんか。 (Issho ni asobi ni iki*masen* ka.)

¶あしたは暇だから，わたしが行きます。 (Ashita wa hima da kara, watashi ga iki*masu*.)

¶昨日，わたしはデパートへ行きました。 (Kinō, watashi wa depāto e iki*mashita*.)

¶わたしは中国語が話せます。 (Watashi wa Chūgokugo ga hanase*masu*.)

¶わたしは日本語は話せません。 (Watashi wa Nihongo wa hanase*masen*.)

¶わたしは日本人ではありません。 (Watashi wa Nihonjin de wa ari*masen*.)

＊「ます (masu)」は，話し手の聞き手に対する丁寧な気持ちを表す。「よく雨が降るね。 (Yoku ame ga furu ne.)」と言うよりは，「よく雨が降りますね。 (Yoku ame ga furimasu ne.)」と言うほうが，丁寧な言い方で

with each **additional** five characters.

-masu 〚auxil〛 a verb ending expressing politeness

¶ **It's been raining** a lot lately, hasn't it? 〚How it **rains!**〛

¶ **There is** a book on the desk.

¶ **There is nothing** at all on the desk.

¶ **Won't you go** out with [us]?

¶ Since I'm free tomorrow, I **will go.**

¶ Yesterday I **went** to a department store.

¶ I **can speak** Chinese.

¶ I **can't speak** Japanese.

¶ I **am not** Japanese.

＊ *-masu* indicates the politeness of the speaker toward the listener. "*Yoku ame ga furimasu ne*" is more polite than "*Yoku ame ga furu ne*." "*Watashi wa Nihonjin de wa arimasen*" is the negative of "*Watashi*

ある。また「わたしは日本人ではありません。(Watashi wa Nihonjin de wa arimasen.)」は、「わたしは日本人です。(Watashi wa Nihonjin desu.)」の打ち消しの言い方である。

⇨**mashō** ましょう

masumasu ますます〖副〗

¶雨が**ますます**強く降ってきました。(Ame ga *masumasu* tsuyoku futte kimashita.)

¶2学期になったら，勉強が**ますます**難しくなってきました。(Nigakki ni nattara, benkyō ga *masumasu* muzukashiku natte kimashita.)

¶わたしも**ますます**元気ですから御安心ください。(Watashi mo *masumasu* genki desu kara goanshin kudasai.)

mata また〖副，接〗

1〖副〗

①[もう一度，再び]

¶どうぞ**また**おいでください。(Dōzo *mata* oide kudasai.)

¶山田さんはさっき食べたばかりなのに，**また**食べています。(Yamada san wa sakki tabeta bakari na noni, *mata* tabete imasu.)

②[同じく，やはり]

¶今日も**また**雨です。(Kyō mo *mata* ame desu.)

¶今度の試験も**また**だめでした。(Kondo no shiken mo *mata* dame deshita.)

＊「〜もまた（〜mo mata）」の形で

---

mata

wa Nihonjin desu."

masumasu 〖adv〗 **more and more, still more, still less**

¶ The rain has become 〖became〗 **still** stronger.

¶ The studies have become 〖became〗 **more** difficult **still** in the second semester.

¶ Don't worry about me as I am **still** going strong.

mata 〖adv, conj〗 **again, once more; also, as well, likewise; and, moreover, while**

1 〖adv〗

① [again, once more]

¶ Please come **again** sometime.

¶ Even though [he] ate just a little while ago, [Mr.] Yamada is eating **again** now.

② [also, as well, likewise]

¶ It's rainy **again** today.

¶ [I] didn't do well on the exam this time **either**.

＊ Used in the pattern "〜 *mo mata*."

453

使う。

2〚接〛
山また山が続く (yama *mata* yama ga tsuzuku)

¶あの人は医者でもあり，また小説家でもあります。 (Ano hito wa isha de mo ari, *mata* shōsetsuka de mo arimasu.)

＊ ものごとを列挙したり，また別のことをつけ加えたりするときに使う。

mata wa または〚接〛
2または3で割りきれる数 (ni *mata wa* san de warikireru kazu)

¶大学を卒業するまでに，日本語または中国語のどちらか一つを学ばなければなりません。 (Daigaku o sotsugyō suru made ni, Nihongo *mata wa* Chūgokugo no dochira ka hitotsu o manabanakereba narimasen.)

¶この建物の完成は今月中には無理で，来月または再来月になるでしょう。

(Kono tatemono no kansei wa kongetsuchū ni wa muri de, raigetsu *mata wa* saraigetsu ni naru deshō.)

＊ 二つのものごとのうち，どちらかであるときに使う。話すときには普通「2か3 (ni ka san)」「日本語か中国語 (Nihongo ka Chūgokugo)」「来月か再来月 (raigetsu ka saraigetsu)」などの言い方をする。

matchi マッチ〚名〛
マッチ箱 (*matchi*bako) マッチでたばこに火をつける (*matchi* de tabako ni hi o tsukeru)

2 〚conj〛 and, moreover, besides; while, on the other hand

mountains rise up **one after the other**

¶ [He] is **both** a doctor and a novelist.

＊ Used when listing items or when adding something else.

mata wa 〚conj〛 or, either ～ or ～
numbers that can be divided evenly by **either** two **or** three

¶ Before graduation from college one must study **either** Japanese **or** Chinese.

¶ It will be impossible to complete this building this month; it will probably be done next month **or** the month after that.

＊ Used for one of two possibilities. In speech *ka* is usually used, as in "*ni ka san*," "*Nihongo ka Chūgokugo*," "*raigetsu ka saraigetsu*," etc.

matchi 〚n〛 **match(es)**
a **match**box // light a cigarette 〚cigar〛 with **a match**

matomaru　まとまる〖動Ⅰ〗

①[集まって一つになる]
¶組ごとに**まとまって**電車に乗ってください。 (Kumi goto ni *matomatte* densha ni notte kudasai.)

②[決まりがつく，解決がつく]
¶みんなの意見がようやく**まとまりました**。 (Minna no iken ga yōyaku *matomarimashita*.)

③[整理がつく，できあがる]
¶論文が**まとまった**ので，発表したいと思っています。 (Ronbun ga *matomatta* node, happyō shitai to omotte imasu.)

matomeru　まとめる〖動Ⅱ〗

①[集めて一つにする]
¶紙くずを**まとめて**，ごみ箱に捨ててください。 (Kamikuzu o *matomete*, gomibako ni sutete kudasai.)

②[決まりをつける，解決する]
¶この話し合いを**まとめる**のは，とても難しいです。 (Kono hanashiai o *matomeru* no wa, totemo muzukashii desu.)

③[整理する，完成する]
¶卒業までに論文を**まとめ**なければなりません。 (Sotsugyō made ni ronbun o *matomenakereba* narimasen.)

matsu　待つ〖動Ⅰ〗

¶ちょっと**待って**ください。 (Chotto *matte* kudasai.)
¶わたしは毎日母からの手紙を**待って**います。 (Watashi wa mainichi haha kara no tegami o *matte*

matomaru 〖v I〗 be united; be settled, be concluded; be in order, take shape

① [be united, be collected]
¶ Please **gather** in your groups〖squads〗and then board the train.

② [be settled, be concluded, come to an agreement]
¶ **A uniformity** of opinion **was achieved** at last.

③ [be in order, take shape]
¶ My thesis has finally **taken shape** and I'd like to make some sort of public presentation of it.

matomeru 〖v II〗 unite, unify; settle, conclude; put in order

① [unite, unify, collect]
¶ Please **collect** the scrap paper and discard it in the trash can.

② [settle, conclude, bring to a conclusion]
¶ It will be very difficult **to bring** these negotiations **to a successful conclusion**.

③ [put in order, arrange]
¶ [I] **must finish** my thesis by graduation.

matsu 〖v I〗 wait, look for

¶ Please **wait** a moment.

¶ I **am looking for** a letter from my mother every day.

imasu.)

¶車を待たせてありますから，急いでください。 (Kuruma o *matasete* arimasu kara, isoide kudasai.)

-matsu -末〖尾〗

今月末 (kongetsu*matsu*) 週末 (shū-*matsu*) 年末 (nen*matsu*) 学期末 (gakki*matsu*)

matsuri 祭り〖名〗

¶町は祭りでたいへんにぎやかです。 (Machi wa *matsuri* de taihen nigi-yaka desu.)

¶日本にはいろいろな祭りがあります。 (Nihon ni wa iroiro na *matsuri* ga arimasu.)

mattaku 全く〖副〗

①〔全然，完全に〕

¶あなたが病気だったことは，全く知りませんでした。 (Anata ga byōki datta koto wa, *mattaku* shirimasen deshita.)

¶わたしの意見は田中さんの意見と全く同じです。 (Watashi no iken wa Tanaka san no iken to *mattaku* onaji desu.)

②〔実に，本当に〕

¶毎日雨ばかり降って，全くいやになります。(Mainichi ame bakari futte, *mattaku* iya ni narimasu.)

¶全くあなたの言うとおりです。 (*Mattaku* anata no iu toori desu.)

mawari 周り〖名〗

①〔周囲〕

¶池の周りに木がたくさん植えてあり

¶ Please hurry as the car ⟦taxi⟧ **is waiting.**

-matsu ⟦suf⟧ **the end of**

the end of this month // the week**end** // the year-**end** // **the end** of the semester

matsuri ⟦n⟧ **festival**

¶ The town is very gay and lively because of **the festival.**

¶ Japan has many different **festivals.**

mattaku ⟦adv⟧ **entirely, utterly; truly, indeed**

① [entirely, utterly, totally]

¶ I had **no idea whatsoever** that you were ill.

¶ I **completely** agree with [Mrs.] Tanaka.

② [truly, indeed, really]

¶ This rain every day is **really** depressing.

¶ You're **absolutely** right.

mawari ⟦n⟧ **circumference, surroundings; vicinity**

① [circumference, surroundings]

¶ There are numerous trees planted

ます。 (Ike no *mawari* ni ki ga takusan uete arimasu.)

② [あたり，付近]
¶駅の周りはとてもにぎやかです。
(Eki no *mawari* wa totemo nigiyaka desu.)

mawaru 回る〘動Ⅰ〙

① [回転する]
¶月は地球の周りを回ります。(Tsuki wa chikyū no mawari o *mawarimasu*.)

② [順に行く，ものごとが次々に移る]
¶病院で診察の順番が回ってくるまで座って待っていました。 (Byōin de shinsatsu no junban ga *mawatte* kuru made suwatte matte imashita.)
¶ほうぼうの図書館を回って探しましたが，その本は見つかりませんでした。(Hōbō no toshokan o *mawatte* sagashimashita ga, sono hon wa mitsukarimasen deshita.)

mawasu 回す〘動Ⅰ〙

① [回転させる]
¶時計の針を逆に回してはいけません。(Tokei no hari o gyaku ni *mawashite* wa ikemasen.)

② [順におくる]
¶この本を回しますから，順番に読んでください。(Kono hon o *mawashimasu* kara, junban ni yonde kudasai.)

mayou 迷う〘動Ⅰ〙

① [道がわからなくなる]

around the pond.

② [vicinity, neighborhood]
¶ It's very lively **around** the station.

mawaru 〖v I〗 revolve, rotate; make a round

① [revolve, rotate, turn round]
¶ The moon **revolves** around the earth.

② [make a round, make a tour]
¶ [I] sat at the hospital and waited **for [my] turn** to be examined.

¶ [I] **went around to** several libraries but [I] couldn't find that book.

mawasu 〖v I〗 turn, whirl; send on, pass round

① [turn, whirl, spin]
¶ One mustn't **turn** the hands of a clock 〖watch〗 backwards.

② [send on, pass round, transfer]
¶ Please read this book and **pass it on** to the next person.

mayou 〖v I〗 be lost, lose one's way; be in doubt, be bewildered

① [be lost, lose one's way]

¶わたしは山の中で道に迷ってしまいました。 (Watashi wa yama no naka de michi ni *mayotte* shimaimashita.)

② [はっきり決心できない]

¶どちらの本を買ったらよいか迷っています。 (Dochira no hon o kattara yoi ka *mayotte* imasu.)

¶日本にいようか、国へ帰ろうかと迷っています。 (Nihon ni iyō ka, kuni e kaerō ka to *mayotte* imasu.)

mazeru 混ぜる〚動Ⅱ〛

¶砂糖に塩を混ぜないでください。 (Satō ni shio o *mazenaide* kudasai.)

¶日本語に英語を混ぜて話すと、おかしいです。 (Nihongo ni Eigo o *mazete* hanasu to, okashii desu.)

mazu まず〚副〛

¶まず、あなたから意見を言ってください。 (*Mazu*, anata kara iken o itte kudasai.)

¶まず、初めに自己紹介をしましょう。 (*Mazu*, hajime ni jiko-shōkai o shimashō.)

mazui まずい〚形〛

① [おいしくない]

¶この料理はまずいですね。 (Kono ryōri wa *mazui* desu ne.)

↔oishii おいしい umai うまい

② [下手だ]

¶これはたいへんまずい字ですね。 (Kore wa taihen *mazui* ji desu ne.)

↔umai うまい →heta 下手

mazushii 貧しい〚形〛

¶ I **lost my way** on the mountain ⟦in the mountains⟧.

② [be in doubt, be bewildered, waver, vacillate]

¶ I **am not sure** which book to buy.

¶ I **am debating** ⟦trying to decide⟧ whether to stay in Japan or return to my native country.

mazeru 〚v II〛 **mix, blend**

¶ Please **don't mix** salt in with the sugar.

¶ It's strange when one **sprinkles** Japanese **with** English words.

mazu 〚adv〛 **first, first of all**

¶ Please state your opinions, starting with you **first.**

¶ **First,** let's start with self-introductions.

mazui 〚adj〛 **unpalatable, unappetizing; poor, unskillful**

① [unpalatable, unappetizing, unsavory]

¶ This dish **tastes awful.**

② [poor, unskillful]

¶ This is a very **poorly written** character.

mazushii 〚adj〛 **poor, impoverished**

¶あの子の家はとても貧しいです。
(Ano ko no ie wa totemo *mazushii* desu.)
¶世界にはまだ貧しい生活をしている人がおおぜいいます。 (Sekai ni wa mada *mazushii* seikatsu o shite iru hito ga oozei imasu.)
⇒**binbō** 貧乏

me 芽〖名〗
¶春になって，木や草が芽を出しました。(Haru ni natte, ki ya kusa ga *me* o dashimashita.)

(-)me (-)目〖名，尾〗
1〖名〗
①[ものを見る働きをする器官]
目を開ける (*me* o akeru) 目を閉じる (*me* o tojiru) 目薬 (*me*gusuri)
¶目にごみが入って痛いです。(*Me* ni gomi ga haitte itai desu.)
②[目の働き，目でものを見ること]
¶ねこは暗いところでもよく目が見えます。 (Neko wa kurai tokoro de mo yoku *me* ga miemasu.)
¶わたしは今朝6時に目を覚ましました。 (Watashi wa kesa rokuji ni *me* o samashimashita.)
③[思いがけないこと，好ましくないようなこと]
悲しい目にあう (kanashii *me* ni au)
つらい目にあう (tsurai *me* ni au)
いやな目にあう (iya na *me* ni au)
¶昨日はお金を盗まれて，ひどい目にあいました。 (Kinō wa okane o nusumarete, hidoi *me* ni aimashita.)

¶ That child's family **is** very **poor.**

¶ There are still a great number of people in the world who are living **in poverty.**

me 〖n〗 sprout, bud
¶ With the coming of spring, trees **budded** and grass **sprouted.**

(-)me 〖n, suf〗 eye(s); eyesight, vision; **-th,** the counter for indicating order
1 〖n〗
① [eye(s)]
open **one's eyes** // close **one's eyes** // **eye** medicine
¶ **[My]** eye hurts as there's some dirt in it.
② [eyesight, vision, look, glance]
¶ Cats **can see** well even in the dark.
¶ I **woke up** at six o'clock this morning.
③ [experience, bad experience]
suffer great sorrow, come to grief // have a bitter **experience,** suffer severely // have a humiliating **experience**
¶ I had a terrible **experience** yesterday—my money was stolen.

* 「〜目にあう（〜me ni au)」の形で使う。

④〔会う〕

¶先日、お父様にお目にかかりました。 (Senjitsu, otōsama ni ome ni kakarimashita.)

¶このことについては、お目にかかって直接申し上げます。 (Kono koto ni tsuite wa, ome ni kakatte chokusetsu mōshiagemasu.)

* 「会う (au)」の謙譲語。いつも「お目にかかる (ome ni kakaru)」の形で使う。

2 〔尾〕

1 番め (ichiban*me*) 10 番め (jūban-*me*) 一つめ (hitotsu*me*) 二つめ (futatsu*me*)

¶右から 3 番めの人が上田さんです。 (Migi kara sanban*me* no hito ga Ueda san desu.)

¶その駅はここから三つめです。(Sono eki wa koko kara mittsu*me* desu.)

medatsu 目立つ〖動 I 〗

¶上田さんは背が高いので、おおぜいの中でもよく目立ちます。 (Ueda san wa se ga takai node, oozei no naka de mo yoku *medachimasu.*)

¶このクラスには目立ってよくできる人はいません。(Kono kurasu ni wa *medatte* yokú dekiru hito wa imasen.)

medetai めでたい〖形〗

¶今日は娘が結婚するめでたい日です。 (Kyō wa musume ga kekkon suru

---

* Used in the pattern "~*me ni au.*"

④ [see, meet]

¶ **I met** your father the other day.

¶ I will tell you about this matter **face-to-face.**

* The humble form for *au.* Always used in the pattern "*ome ni kakaru.*"

2 〖suf〗 -th

first // ten**th** // first // second

¶ The person **third** from the right is [Miss] Ueda.

¶ That station is the **third** one from here.

medatsu 〖v I〗 **be conspicuous, stand out**

¶ As [Mr.] Ueda is tall, [he] **stands out** even in a crowd.

¶ There is no **conspicuously** outstanding student in this class.

medetai 〖adj〗 **happy, auspicious**

¶ Today is the **happy** day of my daughter's wedding.

medetai hi desu.)

¶上田さんはめでたく試験に合格しました。 (Ueda san wa *medetaku* shiken ni gōkaku shimashita.)

megane 眼鏡〖名〗
眼鏡をかける (*megane* o kakeru)
眼鏡を外す (*megane* o hazusu)
¶あの眼鏡をかけた人が田中さんです。 (Ano *megane* o kaketa hito ga Tanaka san desu.)

mei めい〖名〗
⇔oi おい

mei- 名-〖頭〗
名人 (*meijin*) 名演奏家 (*meiensō-ka*) 名画 (*meiga*) 名曲 (*meikyoku*) 名案 (*meian*)

-mei -名〖尾〗
①〔名前〕
学校名 (gakkō*mei*) 会社名 (kaisha-*mei*)
②〔人数を数えるときの言葉〕
数名 (sū*mei*) 15名 (jūgo*mei*)

meibo 名簿〖名〗
¶新しい学生の名簿を作りました。 (Atarashii gakusei no *meibo* o tsukurimashita.)

meiji 明治〖名〗
明治30年 (*Meiji* sanjūnen) 明治時代 (*Meiji*-jidai)

meirei 命令〖名, ～する〗
¶父の命令でおじの家へ行きました。 (Chichi no *meirei* de oji no ie e ikimashita.)
¶社長から外国へ行くように命令され

¶ **Happily,** [Miss] Ueda passed the exam.

megane 〖n〗 glasses, eyeglasses
wear **glasses** // take off **one's glasses**
¶ That person wearing **glasses** is [Mrs.] Tanaka.

mei 〖n〗 niece

mei- 〖pref〗 noted, celebrated, distinguished
a **master**, an **expert** // a **master** musician // a **famous** painting; an **excellent** film // a **famous** musical piece 〖tune〗 // an **excellent** idea

-mei 〖suf〗 name; the counter for persons
① [name]
a school **name** // a company **name**
② [the counter for persons]
several **persons** // 15 **persons**

meibo 〖n〗 list of names, register, roll
¶ [I] made up **a register** of new students.

meiji 〖n〗 Meiji; the name of a Japanese emperor and of the era of his reign (1868–1912)
Meiji 30 (1897) // the **Meiji** period

meirei 〖n, ～suru〗 order, command, instructions
¶ [I] went to my uncle's at **the instruction** of my father.
¶ [I] **was directed** to go abroad by

ました。 (Shachō kara gaikoku e iku yō ni *meirei* saremashita.)

meishi 名刺〖名〗

meiwaku 迷惑〖名，形動，〜する〗

¶テレビの音が大きいと，近所の迷惑になります。 (Terebi no oto ga ookii to, kinjo no *meiwaku* ni narimasu.)

¶御迷惑でしょうが，田中さんに会った時この本を返してください。

(Gomeiwaku deshō ga, Tanaka san ni atta toki kono hon o kaeshite kudasai.)

mekata 目方〖名〗

目方を量る (*mekata* o hakaru) 目方が増える (*mekata* ga fueru) 目方が減る (*mekata* ga heru)

¶病気のため，目方が10キロも減りました。 (Byōki no tame, *mekata* ga jikkiro mo herimashita.)

¶この荷物の目方はどのくらいですか。 (Kono nimotsu no *mekata* wa dono kurai desu ka?)

men 綿〖名〗

綿のシャツ (*men* no shatsu)

⇨momen 木綿

(-)men (-)面〖名，尾〗

1〖名〗

¶子供たちが動物の面をかぶって劇をしました。 (Kodomotachi ga dōbutsu no *men* o kabutte geki o shimashita.)

2〖尾〗

¶今朝の新聞の第1面には飛行機事故

the president of the company.

meishi 〖n〗 name card, business card

meiwaku 〖n, adj-v, 〜*suru*〗 trouble, inconvenience, annoyance, nuisance

¶ Playing the television loud **inconveniences** one's neighbors.

¶ **I'm sorry to inconvenience you,** but would you please return this book to [Mr.] Tanaka when you see [him]?

mekata 〖n〗 weight

weigh something, weigh oneself // gain **weight** // lose **weight**

¶ Due to illness [I] lost 10 kilos.

¶ How much does this load 〖luggage, freight〗 **weigh?**

men 〖n〗 cotton

a **cotton** shirt

(-)men 〖n, suf〗 mask; page

1 〖n〗 mask

¶ The children put on a play wearing animal **masks.**

2 〖suf〗 page

¶ There was a story about an airplane

のことが出ていました。 (Kesa no shinbun no daiichi*men* ni wa hikōki-jiko no koto ga dete imashita.)

crash on the front **page** of the newspaper this morning.

mendō めんどう〚名, 形動〛
①〔手数がかかる〕
¶辞書を引くのがめんどうだから, 友達に教えてもらいました。 (Jisho o hiku no ga *mendō* da kara, tomodachi ni oshiete moraimashita.)
¶自分で料理を作るのは, とてもめんどうです。 (Jibun de ryōri o tsukuru no wa, totemo *mendō* desu.)
②〔世話をする〕
¶あの子は妹のめんどうをよくみます。 (Ano ko wa imōto no *mendō* o yoku mimasu.)

mendō 〚n, adj-v〛 **difficulty, bother; attention, care**
① 〔difficulty, bother, trouble, nuisance〕
¶ I asked a friend about it as **it's a bother** to consult a dictionary.
¶ Doing one's own cooking **is a nuisance.**
② 〔attention, care〕
¶ That child **takes** good **care of** [his] younger sister.

menkyo 免許〚名〛
自動車の運転免許 (jidōsha no unten-*menkyo*)

menkyo 〚n〛 **license, permit**
a **license** to drive a car, a driver's **license**

menseki 面積〚名〛
¶日本の面積は, 37万平方キロメートルです。 (Nihon no *menseki* wa, sanjūnanaman-heihōkiromētoru desu.)

menseki 〚n〛 **area**
¶ **The area** of Japan is 370,000 square kilometers.

mesu 雌〚名〛
⇔**osu 雄**

mesu 〚n〛 **female** (animal)

-mētoru -メートル〚尾〛
3メートル (san*mētoru*)

-mētoru 〚suf〛 **meter(s)**
three **meters**

metta ni めったに〚副〛
¶あの学生はめったに間違いをしません。 (Ano gakusei wa *metta ni* machigai o shimasen.)
¶この地方ではめったに地震は起こり

metta ni 〚adv〛 **rarely, seldom**
¶ That student is **seldom** wrong.
¶ Earthquakes **are rare** in this area.

463

ません。(Kono chihō de wa *metta ni* jishin wa okorimasen.)

∴ あとに打ち消しの言葉が来る。

* *Metta ni* is used with the negative.

mezurashii 珍しい〖形〗

①[たまにしかない]

¶東京で12月に雪が降るのは珍しいです。(Tōkyō de jūnigatsu ni yuki ga furu no wa *mezurashii* desu.)

¶今朝は珍しく早く起きました。(Kesa wa *mezurashiku* hayaku okimashita.)

②[目新しい]

¶動物園には珍しい動物がたくさんいます。(Dōbutsuen ni wa *mezurashii* dōbutsu ga takusan imasu.)

¶珍しい物をいただいてありがとうございました。(*Mezurashii* mono o itadaite arigatō gozaimashita.)

mezurashii 〚adj〛 **rare, infrequent; rare, unusual**

① [rare, infrequent]

¶ **It is rare** for snow to fall in Tokyo in December.

¶ [I] got up early today **for a change.**

② [rare, unusual, novel]

¶ There are many **rare** animals in the zoo.

¶ Thank you for the **lovely** (literally, **uncommon**) present.

mi 実〖名〗

①[草や木の果実]

¶庭の木に実がなりました。(Niwa no ki ni *mi* ga narimashita.)

②[努力の結果]

¶上田さんの努力は、立派に実を結びました。(Ueda san no doryoku wa, rippa ni *mi* o musubimashita.)

*「実を結ぶ (mi o musubu)」の形で使う。

mi 〚n〛 **fruit; result**

① [fruit, nut, berry, seed]

¶ The trees in the yard 〚garden〛 are 〚were〛 **in fruit.**

② [result, fruit of one's labors]

¶ [Mr.] Ueda's efforts **paid off** 〚**have paid off**〛 handsomely.

* Used in the pattern "*mi o musubu.*"

mibun 身分〖名〗

身分証明書 (*mibun*-shōmeisho) 身分が高い (*mibun* ga takai) 身分が低い (*mibun* ga hikui)

mibun 〚n〛 **social standing, rank, identity**

identification, **identification** card 〚**papers**〛 // have a high **social standing** // have a low **social standing**

michi 道〖名〗

道を間違える (*michi* o machigaeru)

michi 〚n〛 **road, street, way**

take the wrong **way** 〚**turning**〛 //

道が悪い (*michi* ga warui) 道を尋ねる (*michi* o tazuneru)

¶交番で道をききました。 (Kōban de *michi* o kikimashita.)

¶学校へ行く道で，おじさんに会いました。 (Gakkō e iku *michi* de, oji-san ni aimashita.)

the roads are bad // ask **the way**, ask for **directions**

¶ [I] asked **the way** at a police box.

¶ **On [my] way** to school, [I] happened to meet my uncle.

midori 緑〖名〗

緑色 (*midori*iro)

¶5月は木や草の緑がきれいです。

(Gogatsu wa ki ya kusa no *midori* ga kirei desu.)

midori 〖n〗 **green**

green, the color **green**

¶ **The green** of the trees and grass is pretty in May.

mieru 見える〖動Ⅱ〗

①[目にうつる]

¶わたしの部屋から山が見えます。

(Watashi no heya kara yama ga *miemasu*.)

¶向こうに見えるのが，わたしたちの学校です。 (Mukō ni *mieru* no ga, watashitachi no gakkō desu.)

②[見ることができる]

¶ねこは夜でも目が見えます。 (Neko wa yoru demo me ga *miemasu*.)

③[そのように感じられる]

¶あの人は若く見えます。 (Ano hito wa wakaku *miemasu*.)

mieru 〖v Ⅱ〗 **see, be visible; be able to see; look, appear, seem**

① [see, be visible]

¶ **You can see** the mountains from my room 〚apartment〛.

¶ What **you see** over there is our school.

② [be able to see]

¶ Cats **can see** even at night.

③ [look, appear, seem]

¶ [She] **looks** younger than [she] is.

migaku みがく〖動Ⅰ〗

¶わたしは毎朝歯をみがきます。

(Watashi wa maiasa ha o *migakimasu*.)

¶くつをみがいてください。 (Kutsu o *migaite* kudasai.)

migaku 〖v Ⅰ〗 **polish, clean**

¶ I **brush** my teeth every morning.

¶ Please **polish** my shoes.

migi 右〖名〗

右手 (*migi*te) 右足 (*migi*ashi)

migi 〖n〗 **the right**

one's **right** hand 〚arm〛 // one's **right** foot 〚leg〛

¶日本では人は道の右側を歩きます。
(Nihon de wa hito wa michi no *migi*gawa o arukimasu.)
⇔hidari 左

migoto　みごと〖形動〗

¶これはみごとなりんごですね。
(Kore wa *migoto* na ringo desu ne.)

¶公園の桜がみごとに咲きました。
(Kōen no sakura ga *migoto* ni sakimashita.)

¶今度の計画はみごとに成功しました。
(Kondo no keikaku wa *migoto* ni seikō shimashita.)

mihon　見本〖名〗
見本市 (*mihon*'ichi)

¶見本を見て，買うか買わないか決めます。 (*Mihon* o mite, kau ka kawanai ka kimemasu.)

mijikai　短い〖形〗

①[もののある点からある点までの間隔が小さい]

¶このひもは短いです。 (Kono himo wa *mijikai* desu.)

¶あの女の子は短いスカートをはいています。(Ano onna no ko wa *mijikai* sukāto o haite imasu.)

②[時間の間隔が小さい]

¶授業と授業の間に短い休みがあります。 (Jugyō to jugyō no aida ni *mijikai* yasumi ga arimasu.)

③[忍耐力がない]

¶あの人は気が短くてすぐ怒ります。
(Ano hito wa ki ga *mijikakute*

migoto 〖adj-v〗 fine, excellent, superb, splendid, beautiful

¶ This is a **superb** apple.

¶ The cherry blossoms in the park were 〖are〗 **in their full splendor.**

¶ The plan this time succeeded **beautifully.**

mihon 〖n〗 sample, specimen, model, example

trade fair

¶ [I] will look at **a sample one** and decide whether or not to buy it.

mijikai 〖adj〗 short; brief

① [short, too short]

¶ This string 〖cord, lace, band, ribbon, etc.〗 **is short** 〖**too short**〗.

¶ That girl is wearing a **short** skirt.

② [brief]

¶ There is a **short** break between classes.

③ [short-tempered]

¶ [He] **is short-tempered** and angers very easily.

sugu okorimasu.)

* 「気が短い (ki ga mijikai)」の形で使う。

⇔nagai 長い

mikan みかん〔名〕

mikka 三日〔名〕

①〔日付を表す〕
三月三日 (sangatsu *mikka*)

②〔日数を表す〕
¶わたしは三日間の旅行をしました。
(Watashi wa *mikka*kan no ryokō o shimashita.)

⇨-ka -日

mimai 見舞い〔名〕

¶昨日，病気の友達のお見舞いに行きました。(Kinō, byōki no tomodachi no o*mimai* ni ikimashita.)

mimi 耳〔名〕

耳が遠い (*mimi* ga tooi)
¶あの人は耳が聞こえません。(Ano hito wa *mimi* ga kikoemasen.)

mina 皆〔名，副〕

1〔名〕
¶皆の意見が一致しました。(*Mina* no iken ga itchi shimashita.)
¶皆さん，お元気ですか。(*Mina*san, ogenki desu ka?)

2〔副〕
¶冷蔵庫の中の食べ物は皆食べてしまいました。(Reizōko no naka no tabemono wa *mina* tabete shimaimashita.)

⇨minna みんな

minami 南〔名〕

---

mikan 〚n〛 mandarin orange, tangerine

mikka 〚n〛 the third of the month; three days

① [the third of the month]
March **3**

② [three days]
¶ I went on a **three-day** trip.

mimai 〚n〛 an expression of sympathy, a condolence call or visit

¶ Yesterday [I] paid **a call** on a sick friend.

mimi 〚n〛 ear(s), hearing

be hard of **hearing,** have difficulty in **hearing**

¶ [He] **is deaf.**

mina 〚n, adv〛 all, everyone; everything

1 〚n〛 everyone

¶ **Everyone** held the same view.

¶ Are **you and your family all** well? 〚And how is **everyone** today?; Hello ladies and gentlemen〛.

2 〚adv〛 everything

¶ [We] ate **everything** that was in the refrigerator.

minami 〚n〛 south

467

南の風 (*minami* no kaze)

¶バナナは南の国の果物です。(Banana wa *minami* no kuni no kudamono desu.)

⇔kita 北

minato 港〖名〗

¶船が港に入ってきました。(Fune ga *minato* ni haitte kimashita.)

¶荷物が港に着いたので、取りに行きました。(Nimotsu ga *minato* ni tsuita node, tori ni ikimashita.)

minna みんな〖名, 副〗

1〖名〗

¶みんなでいっしょに歌いましょう。(*Minna* de issho ni utaimashō.)

＊「皆さん (minasan)」とは言うが、「みんなさん (minnasan)」とは言わない。

2〖副〗

¶宿題はみんな終わりました。(Shukudai wa *minna* owarimashita.)

⇒mina 皆

minoru 実る〖動Ⅰ〗

①[実がつく]

¶秋になると、果物が実ります。(Aki ni naru to, kudamono ga *minorimasu*.)

¶天気がよかったので、稲がよく実りました。(Tenki ga yokatta node, ine ga yoku *minorimashita*.)

②[成果が上がる]

¶長い間の研究がやっと実りました。(Nagai aida no kenkyū ga yatto

minato 〚n〛 harbor, port

¶ A ship has entered **the harbor** 〚A ship came into **the harbor**〛.

¶ The freight 〚luggage〛 had arrived at **the harbor** so [I] went to pick it up.

minna 〚n, adv〛 all, everyone; everything

1 〚n〛 everyone

¶ Let's **all** sing together.

＊ *Minasan* is possible but *minnasan is not.

2 〚adv〛 everything

¶ [I] have finished **all** the homework.

minoru 〚v I〛 bear fruit, ripen; produce results

① [bear fruit, ripen]

¶ Fruit **ripens** in the fall.

¶ There **is** 〚was〛 a good rice **crop** because of the favorable weather.

② [produce results, bear fruit]

¶ The long months 〚years〛 of research finally **paid off** 〚have finall

miru

minorimashita.)

minshushugi 民主主義〖名〗

minzoku 民族〖名〗
少数民族 (shōsū-*minzoku*)　民族学
(*minzoku*gaku)　民族主義 (*minzoku*-
shugi)　民族性 (*minzoku*sei)

miokuru 見送る〖動Ⅰ〗
¶友達を見送りに空港へ行きました。
(Tomodachi o *miokuri* ni kūkō e
ikimashita.)

mirai 未来〖名〗
¶未来の乗り物はどうなるでしょうか。
(*Mirai* no norimono wa dō naru
deshō ka?)
⇒genzai 現在　kako 過去

-miri -ミリ〖尾〗
1ミリ (ichi*miri*)　10ミリ (jū*miri*)

miru 見る〖動Ⅱ〗
①[目で見る]
¶山田さんは部屋でテレビを見ています。　(Yamada san wa heya de
terebi o *mite* imasu.)
¶昨日，わたしは映画を見に行きました。 (Kinō, watashi wa eiga o *mi*
ni ikimashita.)
②[読む]
¶毎朝，わたしは新聞を見てから，会
社へ行きます。(Maiasa, watashi wa
shinbun o *mite* kara, kaisha e
ikimasu.)
③[調べる]
¶この言葉は，辞書を見ても意味がよ
くわかりません。(Kono kotoba wa,
jisho o *mite* mo imi ga yoku wa-

minshushugi 〖n〗 **democracy**

minzoku 〖n〗 **people, race, nation**
a minority, a minority **race** // ethnol-
ogy // **national**ism, **racial**ism // the
character of **a people, racial** charac-
teristics

miokuru 〖v I〗 **see off**
¶ [I] went to the airport **to see off** a
friend.

mirai 〖n〗 **future**
¶ What do you suppose the vehicles
of **the future** will be like?

-miri 〖suf〗 **millimeter(s)**
one **millimeter** // 10 **millimeters**

miru 〖v II〗 **see, look at; read, look
through; examine, look up, try**
① [see, look at]
¶ [Miss] Yamada **is watching** television in [her] room.

¶ I went **to see** a movie yesterday.

② [read, look through]
¶ I go to work every morning after
taking a look at the newspaper.

③ [examine, look over, look up,
consult, test, try]
¶ I don't really understand the meaning of this word even after **looking it**

469

karimasen.)

¶ちょっと料理の味を見てください。

(Chotto ryōri no aji o *mite* kudasai.)

miru 診る〖動Ⅱ〗

¶風邪がなかなか治らないので，医者に診てもらいました。(Kaze ga nakanaka naoranai node, isha ni *mite* moraimashita.)

(〜te) miru （〜て）みる〖連〗

¶おいしいかどうか，食べてみてください。 (Oishii ka dō ka, tabete *mite* kudasai.)

¶その人がいい人かどうか，会ってみなければわかりません。(Sono hito ga ii hito ka dō ka, atte *minakereba* wakarimasen.)

miruku ミルク〖名〗

¶コーヒーにミルクを入れて飲みます。 (Kōhii ni *miruku* o irete nomimasu.)

⇨gyūnyū 牛乳

mise 店〖名〗

店が開いている (*mise* ga aite iru)

店が閉まっている (*mise* ga shimatte iru)

¶あなたはどの店でその品物を買いましたか。 (Anata wa dono *mise* de sono shinamono o kaimashita ka ?)

miseru 見せる〖動Ⅱ〗

¶ちょっと，その新聞を見せてください。(Chotto, sono shinbun o *misete* kudasai.)

¶本がないので，隣の人に見せてもら

---

up in the dictionary.

¶ Please **see what you think** of the flavoring of this dish.

miru 〖v II〗 **see, consult**

¶ [I] **went to see** a doctor since [my] cold 〖case of the flu〗 didn't seem to be getting any better.

(-te) miru 〖compd〗 **try, have a try at, test**

¶ Please taste it **and see** if it's any good.

¶ You can't know what [he]'s like **unless you go ahead** and meet [him].

miruku 〖n〗 (cow's) **milk**

¶ [I] take my coffee with **milk.**

mise 〖n〗 **store, office, firm, place of business, restaurant, coffee shop, bar,** etc.

be open, be open for business // be closed

¶ **Where** did you buy that merchandise?

miseru 〖v II〗 **show, let see**

¶ Please **let me see** that newspaper a moment.

¶ As I didn't have a copy of that

いました。(Hon ga nai node, tonari no hito ni *misete* moraimashita.)

mishin　ミシン〖名〗

ミシンで縫う (*mishin* de nuu)

miso　みそ〖名〗

みそしる (*miso*shiru)

¶みそは豆から造ります。 (*Miso* wa mame kara tsukurimasu.)

mitai da　みたい だ〖助動〗

①[外観がほかのものに似ているという意味を表す]

¶あの岩は人の顔みたいです。(Ano iwa wa hito no kao *mitai desu.*)

¶マッチ箱みたいに小さな家ですね。 (Matchibako *mitai ni* chiisana ie desu ne.)

②[そのように感じられる]

¶熱があって、風邪を引いたみたいです。(Netsu ga atte, kaze o hiita *mitai desu.*)

¶弟のほうが頭がいいみたいです。 (Otōto no hō ga atama ga ii *mitai desu.*)

③[あるものごとを例として示す]

¶あしたも今日みたいにいい天気だといいですね。 (Ashita mo kyō *mitai ni* ii tenki da to ii desu ne.)

¶あの人みたいに上手に日本語が話したいです。(Ano hito *mitai ni* jōzu ni Nihongo ga hanashitai desu.)

mitomeru　認める〖動Ⅱ〗

①[そうであると判断する]

¶田中さんは、自分の間違いをなかなか認めません。 (Tanaka san wa,

book, **I looked at** the one of the person sitting next to me.

mishin 〖n〗 **sewing machine**

sew on **a sewing machine**, sew by **machine**

miso 〖n〗 *miso*

miso shiru, **miso** soup

¶ *Miso* is made from soybeans.

mitai da 〖auxil〗 **like, similar to; seems, looks like; like, the same way**

① [like, similar to]

¶ That rock 〖crag〗 **looks like** a human face.

¶ It is a small, matchbox-**like** house.

② [seems, looks like]

¶ [I] have a fever; **it seems** [I]'ve caught a cold.

¶ **It seems** that the younger brother is smarter 〖smartest〗.

③ [like, the same way; used when citing something as an example]

¶ I hope that tomorrow will be another nice day **like** today.

¶ I would like to be able to speak Japanese well **like** [she] does.

mitomeru 〖v II〗 **recognize, admit; approve, grant**

① [recognize, admit]

¶ [Mr.] Tanaka **doesn't** readily

jibun no machigai o nakanaka *mitomemasen*.)

②［許す］

¶父はわたしの日本への留学を認めてくれませんでした。　(Chichi wa watashi no Nihon e no ryūgaku o *mitomete* kuremasen deshita.)

mitsukaru　見つかる〖動Ⅰ〗

¶なくした万年筆が見つかりました。(Nakushita mannenhitsu ga *mitsukarimashita*.)

¶いいアパートを探していますが、なかなか見つかりません。　(Ii apāto o sagashite imasu ga, nakanaka *mitsukarimasen*.)

mitsukeru　見つける〖動Ⅱ〗

¶友達の家を見つけるのに苦労しました。(Tomodachi no ie o *mitsukeru* no ni kurō shimashita.)

¶先日、本屋で珍しい本を見つけました。(Senjitsu, hon'ya de mezurashii hon o *mitsukemashita*.)

mittsu　三つ〖名〗

①［3個］

¶ここにりんごが三つあります。(Koko ni ringo ga *mittsu* arimasu.)

②［3歳］

¶うちの子はまだ三つです。(Uchi no ko wa mada *mittsu* desu.)

miyage　土産〖名〗

¶父が外国旅行の土産に時計を買ってきてくれました。(Chichi ga gaikoku ryokō no *miyage* ni tokei o katte kite kuremashita.)

admit [his] own mistakes.

② [approve, grant]

¶ My father **didn't approve** of my going to Japan to study.

mitsukaru 〚v I〛　**be found, be discovered**

¶ The lost fountain pen **has been found.**

¶ [I] am looking for a nice apartment but **am having a hard time finding one.**

mitsukeru 〚v II〛　**find, discover**

¶ [I] had a hard time **finding** [my] friend's house.

¶ [I] **discovered** a rare [unusual] book at the bookstore the other day.

mittsu 〚n〛　**three, three items; three years old**

① [three, three items]

¶ There are **three** apples here.

② [three years old]

¶ Our child is only **three years old.**

miyage 〚n〛　**souvenir, gift from one's travels**

¶ My father brought me a watch from his trip abroad.

¶友達のうちへお土産を持って行きました。 (Tomodachi no uchi e o*miyage* o motte ikimashita.)

¶ [I] took **a present** to my friend's home.

mizu 水〖名〗

水を飲む (*mizu* o nomu)

¶冷たい水を一杯ください。 (Tsumetai *mizu* o ippai kudasai.)

¶のどが渇いて、水が飲みたくなりました。 (Nodo ga kawaite, *mizu* ga nomitaku narimashita.)

mizu 〚n〛 (cold) **water**

drink **water**

¶ Please give me a glass of cold **water.**

¶ [I] became thirsty and wanted **some water** to drink 〚I am thirsty and want **some water** to drink〛.

mizuumi 湖〖名〗

¶琵琶湖は日本でいちばん大きい湖です。 (Biwako wa Nihon de ichiban ookii *mizuumi* desu.)

¶この湖はとても深いです。 (Kono *mizuumi* wa totemo fukai desu.)

mizuumi 〚n〛 **lake**

¶ Lake Biwa is the largest **lake** in Japan.

¶ This **lake** is very deep.

mo も〖助〗

①〔前に述べたものごとと同類のものごとであることを表す〕

¶山田さんは先生です。上田さんも先生です。 (Yamada san wa sensei desu. Ueda san *mo* sensei desu.)

¶あなたが行けば、わたしも行きます。 (Anata ga ikeba, watashi *mo* ikimasu.)

¶「これはいくらですか。」 (Kore wa ikura desu ka?) 「それは100円です。」 (Sore wa hyakuen desu.) 「じゃ、これは。」 (Ja, kore wa?) 「それも100円です。」 (Sore *mo* hyakuen desu.)

¶「昨日、これをデパートで買いました。」 (Kinō, kore o depāto de kaimashita.) 「その品物なら、スーパーマ

mo 〚part〛 **also; both; as much as that; even; neither ～ nor ～**

① [also, too; indicates someone or something is the same sort as one previously mentioned]

¶ [Mr.] Yamada is a teacher. [Mrs.] Ueda is **also** a teacher.

¶ If you go, I'll go **too.**

¶ "How much is this?"
  "That's a hundred yen."
  "And this one?"
  "That's **also** a hundred yen."

¶ "[I] bought this at a department store yesterday."
  "Oh, you can buy that at the super-

ーケットでも売っていますよ。」(Sono
shinamono nara, sūpāmāketto de
mo utte imasu yo.)

②[同類と認めるようなものごとを並
列するときに使う]

¶山田さんも中村さんも，もう帰りま
した。(Yamada san *mo* Nakamura
san *mo*, mō kaerimashita.)

¶わたしは平仮名も漢字も読めません。
(Watashi wa hiragana *mo* kanji *mo*
yomemasen.)

¶雨も降ってきたし，風も強くなって
きました。(Ame *mo* futte kita shi,
kaze *mo* tsuyoku natte kimashita.)

¶わたしはヨーロッパへもアメリカへ
も行ったことがありません。(Watashi
wa Yōroppa e *mo* Amerika e *mo*
itta koto ga arimasen.)

*「〜も〜も (〜mo〜mo)」の形で使
う。

③[全面的な肯定または全面的な否定
を表す]

¶山田さんは日曜日はいつもうちにい
ます。(Yamada san wa nichiyōbi
wa itsu *mo* uchi ni imasu.)

¶わたしはみかんもりんごもどちらも
好きです。(Watashi wa mikan mo
ringo mo dochira *mo* suki desu.)

¶部屋にはだれもいません。(Heya ni
wa dare *mo* imasen.)

¶食べる物が何もありません。(Tabe-
ru mono ga nani *mo* arimasen.)

¶この字引はどれも役に立ちません。
(Kono jibiki wa dore *mo* yaku ni

market **too.**"

② [both, either, neither; used when
citing items recognized as being
alike]

¶ **Both** [Mr.] Yamada **and** [Miss]
Nakamura have already gone home.

¶ I can read **neither** *hiragana* **nor**
kanji.

¶ It has started to rain and the wind
has gotten stronger ⟦It started to rain
and the wind picked up⟧.

¶ I've never been to **either** Europe
or the United States.

* Used in the pattern "*~ mo ~ mo*."

③ [indicates total affirmation or total
negation]

¶ [Mr.] Yamada is **always** at home
on Sunday.

¶ I like **both** mandarin oranges and
apples.

¶ **Nobody** is in the room.

¶ There is **nothing** to eat.

¶ **None** ⟦**Neither**⟧ of these dictionaries
is of any use.

tachimasen.)

¶先月はだれからも手紙が来ませんでした。(Sengetsu wa dare kara *mo* tegami ga kimasen deshita.)

¶かぎはどこにもありません。 (Kagi wa doko ni *mo* arimasen.)

¶国からは何の知らせも来ませんでした。(Kuni kara wa nan no shirase *mo* kimasen deshita.)

* 「何 (nani)」「だれ (dare)」「どれ (dore)」「どちら (dochira)」「どこ (doko)」「いつ (itsu)」などの疑問の言葉につく。「どこにも (doko ni mo)」「だれからも (dare kara mo)」「どこからも (doko kara mo)」などのように間に助詞が入ることもある。また「何の (nan no)＋名詞＋も (mo)」の形でも使う。

④［主題としてものごとを提示するのに使う］

¶長かった夏休みも終わって，あしたからまた学校が始まります。(Nagakatta natuyasumi *mo* owatte, ashita kara mata gakkō ga hajimarimasu.)

¶春が来て，富士山の雪も解け始めました。(Haru ga kite, Fujisan no yuki *mo* tokehajimemashita.)

¶さっきまであんなに泣いていた赤ん坊もようやく寝ました。(Sakki made anna ni naite ita akanbō *mo* yōyaku nemashita.)

* 時の経過に伴って生起するような動作・作用が起こる場合に，そのものご

¶ There weren't any letters from **anyone** last month.

¶ The keys are **nowhere** to be found.

¶ There was **no** word of that from [my] native country ⟦hometown⟧.

* *Mo* is added to interrogatives such as *nani*, *dare*, *dore*, *dochira*, *doko*, *itsu*, etc. It is sometimes used with other particles in between as in *doko ni mo*, *dare kara mo*, *doko kara mo*, etc. Also used in the pattern "*nan no* + noun + *mo*."

④ [used to indicate the subject matter]

¶ The long summer vacation has come to an end, and school starts again tomorrow.

¶ Spring has ⟦had⟧ come and the snow on Mount Fuji has ⟦had⟧ started to melt.

¶ The baby, crying so until a little while ago, has finally fallen asleep.

* This *mo* is used when taking up with some deep emotion acts or events which happen naturally in the

とをある感慨をこめて取り上げるとき
に使う。夏休みもいつか終わり，春に
なると雪が解けるのは，時の経過に伴
って起こる動作・作用である。そうし
たことが特に関心の深いものごとにつ
いて起こる場合に，例えば，終わるの
はまだまだと思っていた夏休みもつい
にとか，なかなか解けそうもない富士
山の雪もついにとかいうように，その
ものごとを感慨をこめて取り上げると
きに使う。

→wa は

⑤[時間や数量などを表す言葉につい
てその時間や数量が予想外であるとい
う気持ちを表す]

¶雨はもう3日も降っています。(Ame
wa mō mikka *mo* futte imasu.)

¶駅から学校まで歩いて20分もかかり
ます。(Eki kara gakkō made aruite
nijippun *mo* kakarimasu.)

¶おじさんはわたしに1万円もくれま
した。(Ojisan wa watashi ni ichiman'en *mo* kuremashita.)

* 予想外に多いという気持ちなどを表
す。あとに肯定の言い方が来る。

⑥[時間や数量などの範囲や限界を表
す]

¶それを買うのには1万円もあればじ
ゅうぶんでしょう。(Sore o kau no
ni wa ichiman'en *mo* areba jūbun
deshō.)

¶もうしばらく待ってください。10分
もすれば彼は来ると思います。(Mō
shibaraku matte kudasai. Jippun

course of time: summer vacation ending and snow melting in the spring
are things that come about in the
course of time. *Mo* is used to cite
such events when one is particularly
impressed or affected, for example
when the end of summer vacation is
suddenly upon one when one wasn't
expecting it or when the snow on
Mount Fuji which had shown no
signs of melting has suddenly started
to melt.

⑤ [as much as, as long as, as far as,
etc.; used with words indicating time
or amount when the total is larger
than expected]

¶ It has been raining for three **whole**
days now.

¶ It takes **all of** 20 minutes to walk
from the station to school.

¶ My uncle gave me ten thousand
yen!

* Used to express the feeling of
something being unexpectedly large,
etc. Followed by affirmative words or
expressions.

⑥ [used to express the limits or pa-
rameters of a time or amount]

¶ Ten thousand yen should be enough
to buy that.

¶ Please wait a little longer. He should
be here in 10 minutes, I think.

mo sureba kare wa kuru to omoimasu.)

* 時間や数量などを表す言葉について，
ある条件を述べるときに使う。

⑦［ある極端な場合を取り上げてその
ほかの場合も事情は同じであるという
意味を表す］

¶立っていることもできないほど疲れ
ました。(Tatte iru koto *mo* dekinai
hodo tsukaremashita.)

¶恐ろしくて，声も出ませんでした。
(Osoroshikute, koe *mo* demasen
deshita.)

¶もう半年も日本語を勉強したのに，
まだ平仮名も読めません。(Mō han-
toshi mo Nihongo o benkyō shita
noni, mada hiragana *mo* yomemasen.)

* あとに打ち消しの言葉が来る。

→**sae** さえ

⑧［あることがらを強調的に否定する
のに使う］

¶外国へは一度も行ったことがありま
せん。(Gaikoku e wa ichido *mo*
itta koto ga arimasen.)

¶お金は今一円も持っていません。
(Okane wa ima ichien *mo* motte
imasen.)

¶学生はまだ一人も来ていません。
(Gakusei wa mada hitori *mo* kite
imasen.)

* 最小の意味を表す言葉につく。あと
に打ち消しの言葉が来る。

⑨［あるものごとについて否定的な判

* Used when stating some condition
relating to words expressing time,
amount, etc.

⑦ [even; used when citing an extreme case and indicating that something else is the same]

¶ [I]'m so tired [I] can't stand up
much longer.

¶ [I] was so frightened [I] couldn't
even speak.

¶ Even though [I]'ve been studying
Japanese for half a year now, [I]
can't read **even** *hiragana* yet.

* Used with the negative.

⑧ [used to emphatically deny some-
thing]

¶ [I]'ve never been abroad **even** a
single time.

¶ [I] don't have a **single** cent on me
right now.

¶ Not a **single** student is here yet.

* Added to words expressing the
lowest possible amount. Used with
the negative.

⑨ [neither ~ nor ~ ; used to express

mō

断を続けて述べるのに使う]

¶日本語は易しくも難しくもありません。 (Nihongo wa yasashiku *mo* muzukashiku *mo* arimasen.)

¶今日は暑くも寒くもありません。 (Kyō wa atsuku *mo* samuku *mo* arimasen.)

¶映画は好きでもきらいでもありません。 (Eiga wa suki de *mo* kirai de *mo* arimasen.)

¶この言葉は英語でもドイツ語でもありません。 (Kono kotoba wa Eigo de *mo* Doitsugo de *mo* arimasen.)

¶この本は田中さんのでも山田さんのでもありません。 (Kono hon wa Tanaka san no de *mo* Yamada san no de *mo* arimasen.)

* あとに打ち消しの言葉が来る。「～も～も～ない（～mo ～mo ～nai)」の形で使う。

mō　もう〖副〗

①[既に]

¶もう6時です。(*Mō* rokuji desu.)

¶上田さんはもう帰りました。 (Ueda san wa *mō* kaerimashita.)

¶日本へ来てから，もう10年になります。(Nihon e kite kara, *mō* jūnen ni narimasu.)

→**mada まだ**

②[間もなく]

¶弟はもう来ると思います。 (Otōto wa *mō* kuru to omoimasu.)

¶もうすぐ試験が始まります。 (*Mō* sugu shiken ga hajimarimasu.)

a negative judgment about a series of items]

¶ The Japanese language is **neither** easy **nor** difficult.

¶ Today is **neither especially** hot **nor** cold.

¶ I don't **especially** like **or** dislike movies.

¶ This language is **neither** English **nor** German.

¶ This book doesn't belong to **either** [Miss] Tanaka **or** [Miss] Yamada.

* Used with the negative. Used in the pattern "~ *mo* ~ *mo -nai*."

mō 〖adv〗 already, yet; soon; again

① [already, yet]

¶ It's six o'clock **already.**

¶ [Mrs.] Ueda has **already** left for home.

¶ I've **already** been in Japan for 10 years (literally, It's **already** 10 years since I came to Japan).

② [soon, before long]

¶ I think my (younger) brother will be here **soon.**

¶ The exam will **soon** start.

→**mada** まだ

③[更に]

¶もう一度言ってください。(*Mō* ichido itte kudasai.)

¶お茶をもう一杯いかがですか。

(Ocha o *mō* ippai ikaga desu ka?)

mochiiru 用いる〖動Ⅱ〗

¶この機械には，新しい電池が用いられています。(Kono kikai ni wa, atarashii denchi ga *mochiirarete* imasu.)

⇒**tsukau** 使う

mochiron もちろん〖副〗

¶銀行は日曜日はもちろん休みです。

(Ginkō wa nichiyōbi wa *mochiron* yasumi desu.)

¶山田さんは，英語はもちろんフランス語も話せます。(Yamada san wa, Eigo wa *mochiron* Furansugo mo hanasemasu.)

modoru もどる〖動Ⅰ〗

①[元の所へ帰る]

¶自分の席にもどってください。

(Jibun no seki ni *modotte* kudasai.)

¶弟は忘れ物を取りにもどってきました。(Otōto wa wasuremono o tori ni *modotte* kimashita.)

②[失ったものが返ってくる]

¶落とした財布がもどってきました。

(Otoshita saifu ga *modotte* kimashita.)

¶若い時は二度ともどってこないのです。(Wakai toki wa nido to *modotte* konai no desu.)

③ [again, another, more]

¶ Please say it once **again**.

¶ Would you like **another** cup of (green) tea?

mochiiru 〖v Ⅱ〗 **use**

¶ A new type of battery **is used** in this machine.

mochiron 〖adv〗 **of course, needless to say**

¶ **Of course** banks are closed on Sunday.

¶ [Miss] Yamada speaks French, **not to mention** English.

modoru 〖v Ⅰ〗 **return, get back; return, revert**

① [return, get back; return to where one was originally]

¶ Please **return** to your seats.

¶ My (younger) brother **came back** to get something he had forgotten.

② [return, revert; something lost returns]

¶ [I] **got back** the wallet [I] had lost.

¶ The days of our youth can never **be retrieved** 〖We are only young once〗.

479

moeru 燃える〖動Ⅱ〗

①[火が燃える]

¶火事でたくさんの家が燃えてしまいました。(Kaji de takusan no ie ga *moete* shimaimashita.)

②[盛んな気持ちが起こる]

¶希望に燃えて大学に入学しました。(Kibō ni *moete* daigaku ni nyūgaku shimashita.)

mōfu 毛布〖名〗

¶寒いので，毛布を2枚掛けて寝ました。(Samui node, *mōfu* o nimai kakete nemashita.)

moguru 潜る〖動Ⅰ〗

¶あの人たちは海に潜って，魚を捕っているのです。(Ano hitotachi wa umi ni *mogutte*, sakana o totte iru no desu.)

¶かえるは冬の間土の中に潜って過ごします。(Kaeru wa fuyu no aida tsuchi no naka ni *mogutte* sugoshimasu.)

moji 文字〖名〗

仮名文字 (kana*moji*)

¶世界には文字を持っていない民族もいます。(Sekai ni wa *moji* o motte inai minzoku mo imasu.)

mōkeru もうける〖動Ⅱ〗

お金をもうける (okane o *mōkeru*)

¶あの人は商売でずいぶんもうけたらしいです。(Ano hito wa shōbai de zuibun *mōketa* rashii desu.)

mokuhyō 目標〖名〗

目標を立てる (*mokuhyō* o tateru)

moeru 〚v Ⅱ〛 **burn; burn** (with emotion)

① [burn]

¶ Many houses **burned down** in the fire.

② [burn, be aglow, be ablaze (with some emotion)]

¶ [He] entered college **full of** hope.

mōfu 〚n〛 **blanket**

¶ As it was cold [I] slept with two **blankets.**

moguru 〚v Ⅰ〛 **dive in, go in, go under, hole up in**

¶ Those men are **diving into** the ocean and catching fish.

¶ Frogs spend the winter **under** the ground.

moji 〚n〛 **letter, character**

the *kana* **characters**

¶ There are peoples in the world without any **written language.**

mōkeru 〚v Ⅱ〛 **profit, make money**

make money, make a profit

¶ It seems [he] **has done** very well in business.

mokuhyō 〚n〛 **goal, target, objective, aim, mark**

set **a goal**

¶わたしの家は、大きな木を目標にして来ればすぐわかります。 (Watashi no ie wa, ookina ki o *mokuhyō* ni shite kureba sugu wakarimasu.)

¶わたしは医学部へ入ることを目標に勉強しています。 (Watashi wa igakubu e hairu koto o *mokuhyō* ni benkyō shite imasu.)

mokuteki 目的〚名〛

目的地 (*mokuteki*chi) 目的を果たす (*mokuteki* o hatasu)

¶わたしは日本文学を研究する目的で日本に来ました。 (Watashi wa Nihon-bungaku o kenkyū suru *mokuteki* de Nihon ni kimashita.)

¶何の目的も持たないで大学へ入る人もいます。 (Nan no *mokuteki* mo motanaide daigaku e hairu hito mo imasu.)

mokuyō(bi) 木曜(日)〚名〛

momen 木綿〚名〛

木綿のシャツ (*momen* no shatsu) 木綿のくつ下 (*momen* no kutsu-shita) 木綿糸 (*momen*'ito)

⇨men 綿

momo 桃〚名〛

桃の木 (*momo* no ki) 桃の花 (*mo-mo* no hana)

mon 門〚名〛

表門 (omote*mon*) 裏門 (ura*mon*) 門が開く (*mon* ga aku) 門を開ける (*mon* o akeru) 門を閉める (*mon* o shimeru)

¶学校の門はもう閉まっていました。

mokuteki 〚n〛 **purpose, aim, objective**

one's destination // achieve **one's aim,** realize **one's objective**

¶ I came to Japan **for the purpose** of studying Japanese literature.

¶ There are those who enter college without any **purpose** whatsoever.

mokuyō(bi) 〚n〛 **Thursday**

momen 〚n〛 **cotton, cotton cloth**

a **cotton** shirt 〚undershirt〛 // **cotton** socks // **cotton** thread, **cotton** yarn

momo 〚n〛 **a peach, a peach tree**

a **peach** tree // a **peach** blossom

mon 〚n〛 **gate**

the front **gate,** main **entrance** // the rear **gate** // **a gate** opens // open **a gate** // close **a gate**

¶ The school **gate** was already

¶ You will soon find my house if you **look out for** a large tree.

¶ I am studying **with the goal** of getting into medical school.

(Gakkō no *mon* wa mō shimatte imashita.)

closed.

mondai　問題〖名〗

①〔質問〕

問題を解く (*mondai* o toku)

¶次の問題に答えなさい。 (Tsugi no *mondai* ni kotaenasai.)

¶今度の試験問題はとても難しかったです。 (Kondo no shiken-*mondai* wa totemo muzukashikatta desu.)

②〔解決すべきことがら〕

¶都会では交通事故が大きな問題になっています。 (Tokai de wa kōtsū-jiko ga ookina *mondai* ni natte imasu.)

¶人口問題の解決はたいへん難しいです。(Jinkō-*mondai* no kaiketsu wa taihen muzukashii desu.)

mono　物〖名〗

①〔物体，品物〕

¶物を大切にしましょう。 (*Mono* o taisetsu ni shimashō.)

¶袋の中にはいろいろな物が入っています。(Fukuro no naka ni wa iro-iro na *mono* ga haitte imasu.)

②〔品質〕

¶少しは高くても，物のいいほうが得です。 (Sukoshi wa takakute mo, *mono* no ii hō ga toku desu.)

＊ 普通「物がいい (mono ga ii)」「物が悪い (mono ga warui)」の形で使う。

③〔人・団体などに所属している物〕

¶これはあなたの物ですか。(Kore wa

mondai 〖n〗 question, problem; problem, issue

① [question, problem (exam, homework, etc.)]

solve **a problem**

¶ Answer the following **questions.**

¶ The exam **questions** were very difficult this time.

② [problem, issue, matter]

¶ Traffic accidents have become a major urban **problem.**

¶ The population **problem** is very difficult to solve.

mono 〖n〗 thing, physical object; quality; property

① [thing, physical object, article]

¶ One should not be wasteful.

¶ Inside the bag are various **objects.**

② [quality]

¶ It pays to buy **things** of good quality even though they may be a little more expensive.

＊ Usually used in the patterns "*mono ga ii*" and "*mono ga warui.*"

③ [property of a person, organization, etc.]

anata no *mono* desu ka?)

¶あの建物はわたしの会社の物になりました。 (Ano tatemono wa watashi no kaisha no *mono* ni narimashita.)

④[ある対象を具体的にささないで一般的にとらえて表すときに使う]

¶疲れているので, ものを言うのがめんどうです。 (Tsukarete iru node, *mono* o iu no ga mendō desu.)

¶あの人はものも食べないで, 一日じゅうラジオを作っています。 (Ano hito wa *mono* mo tabenaide, ichinichijū rajio o tsukutte imasu.)

* その対象が具体的に何であるかは文脈によって表される。

⑤[ものごとの特性などについて言うときに使う]

¶いい音楽というものは, 人の心を楽しくさせてくれます。 (Ii ongaku to iu *mono* wa, hito no kokoro o tanoshiku sasete kuremasu.)

¶この世界から戦争というものをなくしたいです。 (Kono sekai kara sensō to iu *mono* o nakushitai desu.)

* 「～というもの (～to iu mono)」の形で使う。「もの (mono)」は前の言葉の本来の性格などを広く示す。

⑥[そうするのが当然でありそうなるのが自然であるという意味を表す]

¶わからないときには人に聞くものですよ。 (Wakaranai toki ni wa hito ni kiku *mono* desu yo.)

¶ Is this **yours?**

¶ That building has come **into the possession** of my company.

④ [used when referring to something in general terms]

¶ Because I'm tired, it's a nuisance **to talk.**

¶ [He] makes radios all day without even **eating.**

* What is being referred to is made clear by the context.

⑤ [used when stressing the essential nature of something]

¶ **Good music** gladdens the human heart.

¶ I would like to see **such a thing** as war eliminated from this world.

* Used in the pattern " ~ *to iu mono*." In this case *mono* broadly indicates the essence of what precedes it.

⑥ [indicates that something is natural or a matter of course]

¶ You **should ask** someone when you don't understand something.

¶行けないとなると，いっそう行きたくなる**もの**です。(Ikenai to naru to, issō ikitaku naru *mono* desu.)

¶ When one can't go somewhere, **one wants** to go there all the more.

*「～ものだ（～mono da)」「～ものです（～mono desu)」などの形で使う。

* Used in the patterns "~ *mono da*" and "~ *mono desu.*"

⑦［感慨・感嘆などの意味を表す］

⑦ [used when expressing admiration, deep emotion, etc.]

¶よくこれまで我慢してきた**もの**だ。(Yoku kore made gaman shite kita *mono* da.)

¶ **[You]'ve done well** to stand it this long [You've been very patient about it].

¶漢字を覚えるのは難しい**もの**ですね。(Kanji o oboeru no wa muzukashii *mono* desu ne.)

¶ **It is difficult** to learn *kanji*, isn't it?

¶子供なのに，こんな難しい本がよく読める**もの**ですね。(Kodomo na noni, konna muzukashii hon ga yoku yomeru *mono* desu ne.)

¶ **What a** clever child that is to be able to read such a difficult book!

*「～ものだ（mono da)」「～ものです（mono desu)」などの形で使う。

* Used in the patterns "~ *mono da*" and "~ *mono desu.*"

⑧［過去にしばしば起こったことを回想するときに使う］

⑧ [used when referring to habitual action in the past]

¶子供のころ，よくこの川で泳いだ**もの**です。(Kodomo no koro, yoku kono kawa de oyoida *mono* desu.)

¶ **I used** to swim in this river often when I was young.

¶学生時代，友達とよく飲みに行った**もの**です。(Gakusei-jidai, tomodachi to yoku nomi ni itta *mono* desu.)

¶ In my student days **I often** went drinking with friends.

*「～たものだ（～ta mono da)」「～たものです（～ta mono desu)」の形で使う。「昔（mukashi)」「以前（izen)」「～のころ（～no koro)」のような過去を表す言葉といっしょに使うことが多い。

* Used in the patterns "*-ta mono da,*" "*-ta mono desu.*" It is often used with words indicating the past such as *mukashi*, *izen*, or ~ *no koro*.

mono 者〖名〗

mono 〚n〛 **person, somebody**

怠け者 (namake*mono*)

¶わたしは山田という者ですが、御主人はいらっしゃいますか。 (Watashi wa Yamada to iu *mono* desu ga, goshujin wa irasshaimasu ka?)

¶名前を呼ばれた者は、前へ出なさい。 (Namae o yobareta *mono* wa, mae e denasai.)

monogatari 物語〘名〙

源氏物語 (Genji*monogatari*)

¶おじいさんが昔の物語を話してくれました。 (Ojiisan ga mukashi no *monogatari* o hanashite kuremashita.)

monosashi ものさし〘名〙

¶どのくらいの長さか、ものさしで測ってごらんなさい。 (Dono kurai no nagasa ka, *monosashi* de hakatte goran nasai.)

morau もらう〘動 I〙

¶わたしは兄にお金をもらいました。 (Watashi wa ani ni okane o *moraimashita*.)

¶わたしは友達から手紙をもらいました。 (Watashi wa tomodachi kara tegami o *moraimashita*.)

＊普通、ある人が対等または目下の人などから与えられたものを受け取るという意味を表す。受け取る人の側に立って言うときに使う。与える人が目上の人である場合には「いただく (itadaku)」を使う。「わたしは先生から日本語の本をいただきました。 (Watashi wa sensei kara Nihongo

a lazy **person,** a lazybones

¶ I'm [Mr.] Yamada [This is Mr. Yamada speaking]. Is your husband at home?

¶ Will **those** whose names are called please step forward.

monogatari [[n]]   tale, story, novel

The Tale of Genji

¶ My grandfather told me ancient **tales.**

monosashi [[n]]   ruler, rule, a measure

¶ Now you try to measure its length with **a ruler** [yardstick, etc.].

morau [[v I]]   receive, accept, get

¶ I **got** some money from my older brother [My older brother gave me some money].

¶ I **received** a letter from a friend.

＊ Usually expresses the meaning of someone receiving something from a person of equal or lower status; used from the standpoint of the recipient. When the donor is of higher status, *itadaku* is used instead, as in *"Watashi wa sensei kara Nihongo no hon o itadakimashita"* (I received a no hon o itadakimashita.)」

⇒**itadaku** いただく

（～te) morau （～て）もらう〖連〗

¶わたしは父にくつを買ってもらいました。(Watashi wa chichi ni kutsu o katte *moraimashita*.)

¶わたしは山田さんに日本語を教えてもらいました。(Watashi wa Yamada san ni Nihongo o oshiete *moraimashita*.)

¶熱が高いから，医者に診てもらったほうがいいでしょう。(Netsu ga takai kara, isha ni mite *moratta* hō ga ii deshō.)

＊普通，ある人の動作によって，利益や恩恵を受けたり，または依頼してある動作をさせるようにしたりする意味を表す。利益を受けたり，依頼したりする人の側に立って言うときに使う。動作をする人が利益などを受ける人と同等か目下の人であるときに使う。動作をする人が目上の人である場合には「（～て）いただく（[～te] itadaku)」を使う。「わたしは先生に本を貸していただきました。(Watashi wa sensei ni hon o kashite itadakimashita.)」

⇒**（～te) itadaku** （～て）いただく

mori 森〖名〗

¶この町は森に囲まれています。(Kono machi wa *mori* ni kakomarete imasu.)

¶森の中の道を通っていくと，きれいな湖が見えてきました。(*Mori* no

Japanese book from my teacher; My teacher gave me a Japanese book).

(-te) morau 〖compd〗 **receive the favor of something being done; have someone do something, have something done**

¶ My father **bought me** a pair of shoes.

¶ [Miss] Yamada **taught me** Japanese 〖Miss Yamada **was kind enough to teach me** Japanese〗.

¶ You have a high fever; you should **have** a doctor **look you over.**

＊ Usually expresses the meaning of receiving some benefit through the actions of another, or of requesting that something be done for one; used from the standpoint of the person receiving the benefit or of the person making the request. The person performing the act is of equal or lower status than the one receiving the benefit of that act. When the person performing the act is of higher status, (*-te) itadaku* is used instead, as in "*Watashi wa sensei ni hon o kashite itadakimashita*" (My teacher lent me a book; I borrowed a book from my teacher).

mori 〖n〗 **forest, woods**

¶ This town is encircled by **woodlands.**

¶ As [we] went along the road through **the forest,** a lovely lake naka no michi o tootte iku to, kirei na mizuumi ga miete kimashita.)

moru 漏る〖動Ⅰ〗

¶この家は古いので，雨が降ると漏ってきます。(Kono ie wa furui node, ame ga furu to *motte* kimasu.)

¶車からガソリンが漏っていますよ。(Kuruma kara gasorin ga *motte* imasu yo.)

moshi もし〖副〗

¶もしあした雨が降ったら，テニスの試合はありません。(*Moshi* ashita ame ga futtara, tenisu no shiai wa arimasen.)

¶今度の日曜日にもし天気がよければ，山に行きます。(Kondo no nichiyōbi ni *moshi* tenki ga yokereba, yama ni ikimasu.)

¶もし食べたくないなら，食べなくてもいいですよ。(*Moshi* tabetaku nai nara, tabenakute mo ii desu yo.)

¶もしあの人が行かなくても，あなたは行きますか。(*Moshi* ano hito ga ikanakute mo, anata wa ikimasu ka?)

＊「もし (moshi)」は条件を表す「たら (tara)」「ば (ba)」「なら (nara)」「ても (te mo)」などとともに使う。

mōshikomu 申し込む〖動Ⅰ〗

①[自分の希望などを相手に伝える]

¶社長に面会を申し込んだら，断られました。(Shachō ni menkai o *mōshikondara*, kotowararemashita.)

¶山田さんは春子さんに結婚を申し込

came into view.

moru 〖vⅠ〗 leak, escape

¶ This house is old so that the roof **leaks** when it rains.

¶ Hey, your car **is leaking** gasoline!

moshi 〖adv〗 if, provided that, in case of

¶ There will be no tennis match tomorrow **if** it rains.

¶ [We] will go to the mountains next Sunday **if** the weather is nice.

¶ You don't have to eat **if** you don't want to.

¶ Are you going to go even **if** [he] doesn't?

＊ *Moshi* is used together with expressions of condition such as *-tara*, *-ba*, *nara*, and *-te mo*.

mōshikomu 〖vⅠ〗 request, propose; apply for

① [request, propose]

¶ **My request** for an interview with the company president was refused.

¶ It seems that Mr. Yamada **has**

んだらしいです。(Yamada san wa Haruko san ni kekkon o *mōshi-konda* rashii desu.)

②[募集などに応じる]

¶あなたはもう研究会への参加を申し込みましたか。(Anata wa mō kenkyūkai e no sanka o *mōshi-komimashita* ka?)

moshi moshi もしもし〖感〗

①[電話で相手に話しかけるときの言葉]

¶もしもし，山田さんですか。わたしは田中ですが…。(*Moshi moshi,* Yamada san desu ka? Watashi wa Tanaka desu ga...)

②[知らない人などに対する呼びかけの言葉]

¶もしもし，ハンカチが落ちましたよ。(*Moshi moshi,* hankachi ga ochi-mashita yo.)

mōshiwake nai 申し訳ない〖連〗

¶遅くなって申し訳ありません。

(Osoku natte *mōshiwake arimasen.*)

¶申し訳ないのですが，あしたの会議には出席できません。(*Mōshiwake nai* no desu ga, ashita no kaigi ni wa shusseki dekimasen.)

mosu 燃す〖動Ⅰ〗

¶古い手紙や日記を燃しました。

(Furui tegami ya nikki o *moshi-mashita.*)

¶マッチで火をつけて，紙を燃しました。(Matchi de hi o tsukete, kami o *moshimashita.*)

proposed to Haruko.

② [apply for]

¶ **Have you asked** if you could participate in the study meeting 〚**applied for** membership in the study group〛?

moshi moshi 〚interj〛 **Hello; Excuse me**

① [Hello; used when addressing someone on the telephone]

¶ **Hello,** is that [Mr.] Yamada? This is [Mr.] Tanaka.

② [Excuse me; used to address a stranger]

¶ **Excuse me!** You've dropped your handkerchief.

mōshiwake nai 〚compd〛 a set expression of apology (literally, there's no excuse)

¶ **I'm terribly sorry** to be late.

¶ **I'm very sorry,** but I won't be able to attend the meeting tomorrow.

mosu 〚vⅠ〛 **burn, put to the flame, ignite**

¶ [I] **burned** [my] old letters and diaries.

¶ [I] lit the paper with a match and **burned** it.

⇨moyasu 燃やす

mōsu〖申す〖動Ⅰ〗
¶わたしは上田と申します。(Watashi wa Ueda to *mōshimasu*.)
¶皆様の御親切に対してお礼を申し上げます。(Minasama no goshinsetsu ni taishite orei o *mōshi*agemasu.)
＊「言う (iu)」の謙譲語。

moto 元〖名〗
元首相 (*moto*-shushō)
¶あの人は元小学校の先生でした。(Ano hito wa *moto* shōgakkō no sensei deshita.)
¶本を読み終わったら，元にもどしてください。(Hon o yomiowattara, *moto* ni modoshite kudasai.)
¶久しぶりに行った町は，元のままでした。(Hisashiburi ni itta machi wa, *moto* no mama deshita.)

motomeru 求める〖動Ⅱ〗
①[要求する，相手に望む]
¶山田さんに意見を求めたら，黙っていました。(Yamada san ni iken o *motometara*, damatte imashita.)
¶あしたの会に出席を求められたのですが，都合が悪くて行けません。(Ashita no kai ni shusseki o *motomerareta* no desu ga, tsugō ga warukute ikemasen.)
②[欲しいものや人を探す]
¶二人は幸福を求めて旅に出ました。(Futari wa kōfuku o *motomete* tabi ni demashita.)
¶わたしの学校で，今英語の先生を求

mōsu 〖v I〗 say, call
¶ **My name is** Ueda.

¶ **I would like to thank** all of you for your kindness.

＊ *Mōsu* is the humble form of *iu*.

moto 〖n〗 former; source, origin
a **former** prime minister
¶ [He] was **formerly** 〖**originally**〗 an elementary school teacher.

¶ Please put the book **back** when you are finished with it.

¶ When [I] went back to the town after a long absence, it was exactly the same **as before.**

motomeru 〖v II〗 desire, request, demand; pursue, seek; buy
① [desire, request, demand, ask for]
¶ [Mrs.] Yamada remained silent **when asked** for [her] opinion.

¶ [I] **was requested** to attend tomorrow's meeting 〖session〗 but circumstances will not permit my going.

② [pursue, seek, search for]
¶ The two took to the road **in search** of happiness.

¶ My school is now **looking for** an

めています。(Watashi no gakkō de, ima Eigo no sensei o *motomete* imasu.)

③[買う]

¶「それはどこでお求めになりましたか。」(Sore wa doko de o*motome* ni narimashita ka?)「Ａデパートで買いました。」(Ē-depāto de kaimashita.)

motsu 持つ〖動Ⅰ〗

①[手に取る]

¶この荷物は重くて、一人では持つことができません。(Kono nimotsu wa omokute, hitori de wa *motsu* koto ga dekimasen.)

¶すみませんが、この荷物を持ってください。(Sumimasen ga, kono nimotsu o *motte* kudasai.)

②[身につける, 所有する]

¶あなたは時計を持っていますか。(Anata wa tokei o *motte* imasu ka?)

¶今、わたしはお金を持っていません。(Ima, watashi wa okane o *motte* imasen.)

③[心にいだく]

¶わたしは日本文化に興味を持っています。(Watashi wa Nihon-bunka ni kyōmi o *motte* imasu.)

④[負担する, 受け持つ]

¶山田先生はＡクラスを持っています。(Yamada sensei wa Ē-kurasu o *motte* imasu.)

¶今度の旅行の費用は会社が持ってく

English teacher.

③ [buy, purchase]

¶ "Where did you **purchase** that?" "I got it at Department Store A."

motsu 〖v I〗 **hold, carry; have with one, own, possess; have, harbor; be in charge of, pay**

① [hold, carry, take]

¶ These bags 〖packages, etc.〗 are too heavy for one person **to carry.**

¶ Could you please **carry** this bag 〖package, load, etc.〗 for me?

② [have with one, own, possess]

¶ **Are you wearing** a watch 〖**Do you own** a watch〗?

¶ I **don't have** any 〖that much〗 money on me at the moment.

③ [have, harbor, cherish, be endowed with]

¶ I'm interested (literally, **have** an interest) in Japanese culture.

④ [be in charge of, pay, stand]

¶ Professor Yamada **is in charge of** Class A.

¶ The company **will bear** the ex

れます。(Kondo no ryokō no hiyō wa kaisha ga *motte* kuremasu.)

penses of the coming trip.

mottainai もったいない〖形〗

¶その鉛筆はまだ書けますから、捨てるのはもったいないです。 (Sono enpitsu wa mada kakemasu kara, suteru no wa *mottainai* desu.)

¶待っている時間がもったいないので、本を読んでいました。 (Matte iru jikan ga *mottainai* node, hon o yonde imashita.)

mottainai 〖adj〗 **wasteful**

¶ That pencil can still be used; **it's a shame** to throw it away.

¶ [I] read a book so as **not to waste** the time [I] spent waiting.

motte iku 持って行く〖連〗

¶学校へ行くときは、このかばんを持って行きます。(Gakkō e iku toki wa, kono kaban o *motte ikimasu*.)

¶これを山田さんのところへ持って行ってください。(Kore o Yamada san no tokoro e *motte itte* kudasai.)

motte iku 〖compd〗 **take, take along**

¶ [I] **take** this bag [briefcase, etc.] when [I] go to school.

¶ Please **take** this to [Mr.] Yamada.

motte kuru 持って来る〖連〗

¶その本をここに持って来てください。(Sono hon o koko ni *motte kite* kudasai.)

¶あなたに借りた本は、あした持って来ます。(Anata ni karita hon wa, ashita *motte kimasu*.)

motte kuru 〖compd〗 **bring, fetch**

¶ Please **bring** that book to me.

¶ Tomorrow **I'll bring back** the book I borrowed from you.

motto もっと〖副〗

¶もっと一生懸命勉強しなさい。 (*Motto* isshōkenmei benkyō shinasai.)

¶もっと右の方へ寄ってください。 (*Motto* migi no hō e yotte kudasai.)

¶上田さんは英語が上手ですが、山田さんはもっと上手です。 (Ueda san wa Eigo ga jōzu desu ga, Yamada

motto 〖adv〗 **more, further, longer**

¶ Please study **harder.**

¶ Please move **more** to the right.

¶ [Miss] Ueda speaks English well, but [Miss] Yamada speaks it **still better.**

san wa *motto* jōzu desu.)

mottomo 最も〖副〗

¶富士山は日本で最も高い山です。

(Fujisan wa Nihon de *mottomo* takai yama desu.)

¶あなたの最も好きな食べ物は何ですか。 (Anata no *mottomo* suki na tabemono wa nan desu ka?)

mottomo もっとも〖形動〗

¶2時間も待たされたんですから，あの人が怒るのももっともです。

(Nijikan mo matasareta n desu kara, ano hito ga okoru no mo *mottomo* desu.)

¶朝から何も食べていないのなら，おなかがすくのはもっともです。 (Asa kara nani mo tabete inai no nara, onaka ga suku no wa *mottomo* desu.)

mottomo もっとも〖接〗

¶わたしは日本料理が好きです。もっとも，生の魚は食べられませんが。

(Watashi wa Nihon-ryōri ga suki desu. *Mottomo*, nama no sakana wa taberaremasen ga.)

¶私の兄弟はみんな頭がいいです。もっとも，私だけは例外です。

(Watakushi no kyōdai wa minna atama ga ii desu. *Mottomo* watakushi dake wa reigai desu.)

＊前のことがらを受けて，それに対する例外や条件をつけ加えたりするときに使う。

moyasu 燃やす〖動Ⅰ〗

mottomo 〚adv〛 **most, extremely**

¶ Mount Fuji is **the highest** mountain in Japan.

¶ What is your **favorite** food?

mottomo 〚adj-v〛 **reasonable, understandable, natural, justifiable**

¶ **It is only natural** that [he] was angry as [he] had been kept waiting for two hours.

¶ **Of course** you are hungry if you haven't eaten anything all day.

mottomo 〚conj〛 **however, though, indeed, of course**

¶ I like Japanese food. **However,** I can't eat raw fish.

¶ My brothers and sisters are all smart. **Of course,** I am the exception.

＊ Used when adding some exception or condition to the previous statement.

moyasu 〚v Ⅰ〛 **burn, put to the flame, ignite**

¶マッチで火をつけて，手紙を燃やしてしまいました。 (Matchi de hi o tsukete, tegami o *moyashite* shimaimashita.)

¶木をたくさん燃やしながら，その周りでみんなで歌を歌いました。 (Ki o takusan *moyashinagara*, sono mawari de minna de uta o utaimashita.)

⇨**mosu** 燃す

moyō 模様〖名〗

¶この花びんの模様はとてもきれいですね。 (Kono kabin no *moyō* wa totemo kirei desu ne.)

¶あの花の模様の着物を着ている人はだれですか。 (Ano hana no *moyō* no kimono o kite iru hito wa dare desu ka?)

mu(-) 無(-)〖名，頭〗

1〖名〗

¶長い間の努力が無になってしまいました。 (Nagai aida no doryoku ga *mu* ni natte shimaimashita.)

2〖頭〗

無意味 (*mu*imi) 無関係 (*mu*kankei)

muchū 夢中〖形動〗

¶このごろ，中村さんはカメラに夢中です。 (Konogoro, Nakamura san wa kamera ni *muchū* desu.)

¶山田さんは夢中でテレビを見ています。 (Yamada san wa *muchū* de terebi o mite imasu.)

muda むだ〖名，形動〗

①[効果がない]

¶ [I] lit the letter with a match and **burned** it.

¶ We sat and sang around the fire where **we burned** lots of wood.

moyō 〚n〛 **pattern, design**

¶ **The design** on this vase is very pretty.

¶ Who is that woman wearing the **flowered** kimono?

mu(-) 〚n, pref〛 **nothing, nil, zero**

1 〚n〛

¶ [Our] work for so long a time was all **in vain** 〚has all been **in vain**〛.

2 〚pref〛

meaning**less** // **un**related; **un**concerned; **ir**relevant

muchū 〚adj-v〛 **absorbed in, crazy about, abstracted**

¶ [Mr.] Nakamura is camera-**crazy** these days.

¶ [Mr.] Yamada **is absorbed** in a television program.

muda 〚n, adj-v〛 **useless, futile; wasteful**

① [useless, futile, fruitless]

¶あの人にはいくら注意してもむだです。 (Ano hito ni wa ikura chūi shite mo *muda* desu.)

¶ **It's no use** no matter how many times one warns [reprimands] [him].

¶試験に落ちて，山田さんの努力もむだになりました。 (Shiken ni ochite, Yamada san no doryoku mo *muda* ni narimashita.)

¶ All of [Mr.] Yamada's efforts **were in vain**—[he] failed [his] exam.

②[役に立たない使い方をする]
¶食べ物をむだにしてはいけません。 (Tabemono o *muda* ni shite wa ikemasen.)

② [wasteful]
¶ One shouldn't **waste** food.

¶一日じゅう何もしないで，時間をむだに過ごしてしまいました。 (Ichinichijū nani mo shinaide, jikan o *muda* ni sugoshite shimaimashita.)

¶ [I] **wasted** my time doing nothing all day.

mudan 無断〖名〗
¶あなたがいなかったので，無断で本を借りました。 (Anata ga inakatta node, *mudan* de hon o karimashita.)
¶この池の魚を無断で捕ってはいけません。 (Kono ike no sakana o *mudan* de totte wa ikemasen.)

mudan 〖n〗 **without permission, without notice**
¶ You weren't here so I borrowed a book **without asking.**
¶ One mustn't fish in this pond **without permission.**

mugi 麦〖名〗
大麦 (oo*mugi*) 小麦 (ko*mugi*)
¶ビールは麦から造ります。 (Biiru wa *mugi* kara tsukurimasu.)

mugi 〖n〗 **wheat, barley**
barley // wheat
¶ Beer is made from **barley.**

muika 六日〖名〗
①[日付を表す]
一月六日 (ichigatsu *muika*)
②[日数を表す]
¶病気で六日入院しました。 (Byōki de *muika* nyūin shimashita.)
⇨ -ka -日

muika 〖n〗 **the sixth day of the month; six days**
① [the sixth day of the month]
January **6**
② [six days]
¶ [I] was hospitalized **for six days** due to illness.

mukaeru 迎える〖動Ⅱ〗

mukaeru 〖v Ⅱ〗 **meet, welcome; greet**

494

①[人の来るのを待ち受ける]

¶父は田中さんを迎えに駅に行きました。 (Chichi wa Tanaka san o *mukae* ni eki ni ikimashita.)

¶友達はわたしを喜んで迎えてくれました。 (Tomodachi wa watashi o yorokonde *mukaete* kuremashita.)

②[その時の来るのを待つ]

¶母はお正月を迎える準備で忙しいです。 (Haha wa oshōgatsu o *mukaeru* junbi de isogashii desu.)

mukashi 昔〚名〛

¶おじいさんは, わたしに昔のことを話してくれました。 (Ojiisan wa, watashi ni *mukashi* no koto o hanashite kuremashita.)

¶昔々, ある所におじいさんとおばあさんがいました。 (*Mukashi mukashi*, aru tokoro ni ojiisan to obāsan ga imashita.)

mukau 向かう〚動Ⅰ〛

①[何かをするときにそのものを正面に見ることができる姿勢をとる]

鏡に向かう (kagami ni *mukau*) 壁に向かう (kabe ni *mukau*)

¶試験があるので, 毎日3時間机に向かうことにしています。 (Shiken ga aru node, mainichi sanjikan tsukue ni *mukau* koto ni shite imasu.)

* 普通, 「~に向かう (~ni mukau)」の形で使う。

②[相手とする, 対する]

¶その子は歩いてくる父親に向かって手を振りました。 (Sono ko wa aruite

① [meet, welcome, receive]

¶ My father went to the station **to meet** [Mr.] Tanaka.

¶ My friends **greeted** me happily.

② [greet; await a certain time]

¶ My mother is busy with preparations **for** the New Year's holidays.

mukashi 〚n〛 ancient times, former days, the past

¶ My grandfather told me about **past times**.

¶ **Once upon a time** there was an old man and an old woman.

mukau 〚v Ⅰ〛 face; meet, confront; facing one; proceed, head toward

① [face, be opposite to]

look in the mirror // **face** the wall

¶ I make it a rule to spend three hours a day **at** my desk preparing for my examinations.

* Usually used in the pattern "~ *ni mukau*."

② [meet, confront]

¶ The child waved **to** [his] approaching father.

kuru chichioya ni *mukatte* te o furimashita.)

* 普通,「～に向かう (～ni mukau)」の形で使う。

③[自分の方から見て]

¶向かって右が銀行です。 (*Mukatte migi ga ginkō desu.*)

* 普通,「向かって右 (mukatte migi)」「向かって左 (mukatte hidari)」の形で使う。

④[ある方向へ進む, ある状態に近づく]

¶田中さんは今大阪へ向かっているところです。 (*Tanaka san wa ima Oosaka e mukatte iru tokoro desu.*)

¶山田さんの病気はいいほうに向かっているそうです。 (*Yamada san no byōki wa ii hō ni mukatte iru sō desu.*)

* 普通,「～へ向かう (～e mukau)」「～に向かう (～ni mukau)」の形で使う。

mukeru 向ける〔動Ⅱ〕

¶恥ずかしいので, 顔を下に向けたまま黙っていました。 (*Hazukashii node, kao o shita ni muketa mama damatte imashita.*)

¶大きな音がしたので, 皆その方に目を向けました。 (*Ookina oto ga shita node, mina sono hō ni me o mukemashita.*)

¶山田さんは秋子さんにカメラを向けて, 写真を撮りました。 (*Yamada san wa Akiko san ni kamera o*

---

* Usually used in the pattern "~ *ni mukau*."

③ [facing one, opposite one]

¶ The bank is **on your** right.

* Usually used in the patterns "*mukatte migi*" and "*mukatte hidari*."

④ [proceed, head toward, tend toward]

¶ [Mr.] Tanaka **is** now **on [his] way to** Osaka.

¶ I hear that [Mrs.] Yamada's illness **has taken a turn for** the better.

* Usually used in the patterns "~ *e mukau*" and "~ *ni mukau*."

mukeru 〚v Ⅱ〛 turn toward, point at

¶ Embarrassed 〚Ashamed〛, **I kept** my head **down** and remained silent.

¶ Everyone turned and looked **in the direction** of the loud noise.

¶ [Mr.] Yamada **aimed** the camera **at** Akiko and took her picture.

mukete, shashin o torimashita.)

(-)**muki**　(-)向き〖名, 尾〗

1〖名〗

¶机の向きを変えましょう。 (Tsukue no *muki* o kaemashō.)

2〖尾〗

①[方向]

¶南向きの部屋は，日がよく当たります。(Minami *muki* no heya wa, hi ga yoku atarimasu.)

②[適していること]

¶この料理は子供向きですね。 (Kono ryōri wa kodomo *muki* desu ne.)

¶若い女の人向きの仕事がありますよ。 (Wakai onna no hito *muki* no shigoto ga arimasu yo.)

mukō　向こう〖名〗

①[ある物を隔てた反対の側]

¶あの山の向こう側に湖があります。 (Ano yama no *mukō*gawa ni mizuumi ga arimasu.)

¶敵は川の向こうまで来ています。 (Teki wa kawa no *mukō* made kite imasu.)

②[先の方，前の方，正面]

¶向こうから来るのは山田さんのようです。 (*Mukō* kara kuru no wa Yamada san no yō desu.)

¶向こうに見えるのが富士山です。 (*Mukō* ni mieru no ga Fujisan desu.)

③[少し離れている所]

¶子供は向こうへ行って遊んでいなさい。 (Kodomo wa *mukō* e itte

(-)**muki** 〖n, suf〗 direction; suitability

1 〖n〗 direction, position

¶ Let's change **the position** of the desks.

2 〖suf〗

① [direction, exposure]

¶ Rooms with a southern **exposure** are sunny.

② [suitability]

¶ This meal 〖dish〗 is **for** children.

¶ There is a job available **for** a young woman.

mukō 〖n〗 the other side; in front of one; beyond; one's destination, over there

① [the other side, the opposite side]

¶ There is a lake on **the other side** of that mountain.

¶ The enemy has advanced up to **the opposite side** of the river.

② [in front of one, the opposite direction]

¶ That seems to be [Mr.] Yamada coming towards us.

¶ **Over there** you can see Mount Fuji.

③ [beyond, over there; somewhat distant]

¶ Children, go play **over there.**

asonde inasai.)

④[行く先，話題になっている遠方の場所]

¶向こうに着いたら，手紙をください。(*Mukō* ni tsuitara, tegami o kudasai.)

¶「昨日，アメリカから帰ってきました。」(Kinō, Amerika kara kaette kimashita.)「向こうの生活はいかがでしたか。」(*Mukō* no seikatsu wa ikaga deshita ka?)

muku 向く〚動Ⅰ〛

①[その方向に面する]

¶わたしの部屋は南に向いています。(Watashi no heya wa minami ni *muite* imasu.)

②[体または顔をその方向へ回す]

下を向く (shita o *muku*)

¶写真を撮りますから，こちらを向いてください。(Shashin o torimasu kara, kochira o *muite* kudasai.)

③[適する]

¶この仕事は老人に向いています。(Kono shigoto wa rōjin ni *muite* imasu.)

¶この服は若い人には向きません。(Kono fuku wa wakai hito ni wa *mukimasen*.)

muku むく〚動Ⅰ〛

¶みかんの皮をむきました。(Mikan no kawa o *mukimashita*.)

¶わたしはりんごの皮をむかないで食べます。(Watashi wa ringo no kawa o *mukanaide* tabemasu.)

④ [one's destination, over there; a distant place that is being talked about]

¶ Please write [us] after you arrive **there.**

¶ "I arrived back from the United States yesterday."

"What was it like living **there?**"

muku 〚vI〛 face; turn toward, look toward; suit, be geared for

① [face, front on]

¶ My room **faces** south.

② [turn toward, look toward]

look down, lower **one's gaze**

¶ Please **look** this way; I'm going to take the photo now.

③ [suit, be geared for]

¶ This job **is suitable** for an elderly person.

¶ This outfit **is too old** for someone young.

muku 〚vI〛 peel, pare, skin

¶ [I] **peeled** a mandarin orange.

¶ I eat apples **without paring** them.

mune 胸〔名〕

¶先生はいつも胸のポケットにハンカ
チを入れています。(Sensei wa itsu
mo *mune* no poketto ni hankachi
o irete imasu.)

mura 村〔名〕

¶ここがわたしの生まれた村です。
(Koko ga watashi no umareta
mura desu.)

¶若い人は都会へ行ってしまい，村に
は年寄りと子供しかいません。
(Wakai hito wa tokai e itte shimai,
mura ni wa toshiyori to kodomo
shika imasen.)

⇨machi 町

murasaki 紫〔名〕

¶あの紫の花は何という名前ですか。
(Ano *murasaki* no hana wa nan to
iu namae desu ka?)

¶長い時間泳いでいたので，くちびる
が紫色になりました。(Nagai jikan
oyoide ita node, kuchibiru ga
*murasaki*iro ni narimashita.)

muri 無理〔名，形動〕

①〔筋道が通らないこと，道理に合わ
ないこと〕

¶2時間も待たされたんですから，あ
の人が怒るのも無理はありません。
(Nijikan mo matasareta n desu
kara, ano hito ga okoru no mo
muri wa arimasen.)

¶あまり働かないで，お金をたくさん
欲しいというのは無理です。(Amari
hatarakanaide, okane o takusan

mune 〚n〛 **breast, chest, lungs,
heart**

¶ [My] teacher 〚doctor〛 always has a
handkerchief in his **breast** pocket.

mura 〚n〛 **village**

¶ This is **the village** where I was
born.

¶ The young people all leave for the
city so that **the villages** are populated by the old and the very young.

murasaki 〚n〛 **purple**

¶ What is the name of that **purple**
flower?

¶ As [he] was swimming for a long
time, [his] lips turned 〚have turned〛
blue (literally, **purple**).

muri 〚n, adj-v〛 **unreasonable; impossible**

① [unreasonable, unwarrantable, un-
natural]

¶ As [he] was kept waiting for two
hours, **it's only natural** that [he] became angry.

¶ **It's asking too much** to want a lot
of money while not working much.

hoshii to iu no wa *muri* desu.)

②[適当だと思われる程度を超えること，それを押し切ってすること]

¶病気のあとは無理をしないほうがいいです。 (Byōki no ato wa *muri* o shinai hō ga ii desu.)

¶お酒がきらいな人に無理にすすめてはいけません。 (Osake ga kirai na hito ni *muri* ni susumete wa ikemasen.)

muryō 無料〖名〗

¶6歳以下の子供はバスが無料です。 (Rokusai ika no kodomo wa basu ga *muryō* desu.)

¶500名に無料でせっけんを配りました。 (Gohyakumei ni *muryō* de sekken o kubarimashita.)

⇔**yūryō** 有料 ⇒**tada** ただ

mushi 虫〖名〗

¶虫に刺されてかゆいので，薬をつけました。 (*Mushi* ni sasarete kayui node, kusuri o tsukemashita.)

¶庭で虫が鳴いています。 (Niwa de *mushi* ga naite imasu.)

mushiba 虫歯〖名〗

¶甘いものをたくさん食べると，虫歯になります。(Amai mono o takusan taberu to, *mushiba* ni narimasu.)

¶虫歯が痛くて，ものが食べられません。 (*Mushiba* ga itakute, mono ga taberaremasen.)

mushiro むしろ〖副〗

¶わたしは甘い物よりむしろ辛い物のほうが好きです。(Watashi wa amai

② [impossible, forced, excessive, immoderate, too difficult]

¶ It's best not **to overstrain oneself** after being ill.

¶ One shouldn't **force** liquor on those who don't like to drink.

muryō [[n]] free of charge

¶ The bus **is free** for children aged six and under.

¶ **Free** soap was distributed to five hundred persons.

mushi [[n]] insect, bug

¶ I put some medication on an **insect** bite that was itching.

¶ **Insects** are singing in the garden [[yard]].

mushiba [[n]] decayed tooth

¶ One will get **cavities** if one eats a lot of sweets.

¶ **My bad tooth** aches so much that I can't eat.

mushiro [[adv]] **rather** (than), **better, sooner**

¶ I like nonsweet [[salty]] foods **better**

mono yori *mushiro* karai mono no
hō ga suki desu.)

¶自分で木を買って作るより**むしろこ**
の箱を買ったほうが安いです。(Jibun
de ki o katte tsukuru yori, *mushiro*
kono hako o katta hō ga yasui
desu.)

musubu 結ぶ〖動Ⅰ〗

①[糸・ひも などをつなぎ合わせる，
ひもなどで締める]

糸を結ぶ (ito o *musubu*)　ひもを結
ぶ (himo o *musubu*)

¶ネクタイはどのように結ぶのですか。
(Nekutai wa dono yō ni *musubu*
no desu ka?)

¶荷物をひもで結びましょう。　(Ni-
motsu o himo de *musubimashō*.)

②[二つ以上の ものの 間に関係をつけ
る]

¶二人はようやく結ばれて，来月結婚
することになりました。 (Futari wa
yōyaku *musubarete*, raigetsu kekkon suru koto ni narimashita.)

③[離れている所の間に連絡をつける]

¶この島と東京を結ぶ船は，毎週土曜
日に来ます。(Kono shima to Tōkyō
o *musubu* fune wa, maishū doyōbi
ni kimasu.)

musuko 息子〖名〗

¶うちの息子は来年の3月に大学を卒
業します。　(Uchi no *musuko* wa
rainen no sangatsu ni daigaku o
sotsugyō shimasu.)

¶山田さんは息子さんが一人と娘さん

---

than sweet ones.

¶ It will be cheaper to buy this box
〚chest, casket, case, etc.〛 **than** to buy
the wood and make it oneself.

musubu 〚v I〛 tie, tie up; enter into relations with, contract; connect, link

① [tie, tie up, fasten, bind, knot]

tie threads 〚lines〛 **together** // **tie**
shoelaces, **tie** a package with string,
etc.

¶ How does one **tie** a necktie?

¶ **Let's tie up** the package with cord
〚string, a strap, etc.〛.

② [enter into relations with, con-
tract]

¶ The two have finally **gotten
together** and will be married next
month.

③ [connect, link]

¶ The ship **linking** this island with
Tokyo comes every Saturday.

musuko 〚n〛 son, boy

¶ Our **son** graduates from college in
March of next year.

¶ [Mr.] Yamada has one **son** and

が二人あります。　(Yamada san wa *musuko*san ga hitori to musume-san ga futari arimasu.)

⇔musume 娘

musume 娘〖名〗

①[自分の女の子供]

¶いちばん上の娘は今年 18 です。

(Ichiban ue no *musume* wa kotoshi jūhachi desu.)

↔musuko 息子

②[若い未婚の女性]

¶道できれいな娘さんにあいさつされたが、だれだかわかりませんでした。

(Michi de kirei na *musume*san ni aisatsu sareta ga, dare da ka wakarimasen deshita.)

muttsu 六つ〖名〗

①[6 個]

¶ここにみかんが六つあります。

(Koko ni mikan ga *muttsu* arimasu.)

②[6 歳]

¶日本では六つで小学校に入学します。　(Nihon de wa *muttsu* de shōgakkō ni nyūgaku shimasu.)

muyami ni むやみに〖副〗

¶むやみに食べると，おなかをこわしますよ。　(*Muyami ni* taberu to, onaka o kowashimasu yo.)

¶むやみにお金を使ってはいけません。 (*Muyami ni* okane o tsukatte wa ikemasen.)

muzukashii 難しい〖形〗

¶この本は難しくてわかりません。

musume 〚n〛 **daughter; young unmarried girl or woman**

① [daughter]

¶ My eldest **daughter** is 18 this year.

② [young unmarried girl or woman]

¶ A pretty **young lady** greeted me in the street but I don't know who she was.

muttsu 〚n〛 **six, six items; six years old**

① [six, six items]

¶ There are **six** mandarin oranges here.

② [six years old]

¶ In Japan one enters elementary school at **six years of age.**

muyami ni 〚adv〛 **immoderately, excessively, recklessly, indiscriminately**

¶ Eating **to excess** invites stomach trouble.

¶ You shouldn't **throw away** your money.

muzukashii 〚adj〛 **difficult, hard**

¶ This book **is so hard** that I can't

(Kono hon wa *muzukashikute* wakarimasen.)

¶日本語は難しいですか。 (Nihongo
wa *muzukashii* desu ka?)

¶この事件の解決はなかなか難しそう
です。(Kono jiken no kaiketsu wa
nakanaka *muzukashisō* desu.)

⇔yasashii 易しい

myō- 明-〖頭〗

明日 (*myō*nichi) 明後日 (*myō*go-
nichi) 明朝 (*myō*chō) 明晩
(*myō*ban)

myō 妙〖形動〗

¶山田さんが妙な顔をしてこちらを見
ていました。(Yamada san ga *myō*
na kao o shite kochira o mite
imashita.)

¶辺りが妙に静かになりました。
(Atari ga *myō* ni shizuka ni narimashita.)

myōji 名字〖名〗

¶わたしの名字は田中で，名前は太郎
です。 (Watashi no *myōji* wa Tanaka de, namae wa Tarō desu.)

¶日本の名字で多いのは，鈴木，山田
などです。(Nihon no *myōji* de ooi
no wa, Suzuki, Yamada nado desu.)

understand it.

¶ Is Japanese **difficult?**

¶ **It looks like** this incident **will be**
quite **difficult** to resolve.

myō- 〖pref〗 **tomorrow, the next
tomorrow** // the day after **tomorrow**
// **tomorrow** morning // **tomorrow**
evening, **tomorrow** night

myō 〖adj-v〗 **strange, odd, singular**
¶ [Miss] Yamada looked over here
with a **strange** look on [her] face.

¶ It fell **strangely** quiet.

myōji 〖n〗 **family name, surname**
¶ My **family name** is Tanaka and my
given name is Tarō.

¶ **Surnames** frequent in Japan are
Suzuki, Yamada, etc.

N

n　ん〖助〗☞no の

na　な〖助〗

①〔感動などの気持ちを表す〕

¶ああ，いい天気だな。（Ā ii tenki da *na*.）

¶あの花はきれいだな。　（Ano hana wa kirei da *na*.）

＊「なあ（nā）」とも言う。

②〔禁止の気持ちを表す〕

¶かぎを忘れるな。　（Kagi o wasureru*na*.）

¶部屋に入るな。（Heya ni hairu*na*.）

＊動詞（終止の形）に続く。

nado　など〖助〗

①〔同じようなものごとを列挙するときに使う〕

¶この店では本やノートや鉛筆などを売っています。　（Kono mise de wa hon ya nōto ya enpitsu *nado* o utte imasu.）

¶わたしは映画や芝居などはあまり好きではありません。　（Watashi wa eiga ya shibai *nado* wa amari suki de wa arimasen.）

＊普通「～や～や～など（～ya ～ya ～nado)」の形で使い，列挙するものがそれだけに限らないことを表す。

②〔ものごとを一例として挙げるときに使う〕

¶「日本語を勉強するのに何かいい本はありませんか。」(Nihongo o ben-

n ☞ no

na 〚part〛 a sentence-final particle used as an intensifier or to express prohibition

① [acts as an intensifier]

¶ **What a** nice day!

¶ **What a** lovely flower 〖**How** lovely that flower is〗!

＊ Variant: *nā*.

② [expresses prohibition]

¶ **Don't** forget your key 〖**Don't** forget to lock up〗.

¶ **Don't** go 〖come〗 in the room.

＊ Used immediately after a verb in the dictionary form.

nado 〚part〛 **and the like, etc.; or the like**

① [and the like, etc.; used when citing things of the same sort]

¶ This shop sells books, notebooks, pencils, **and so forth.**

¶ I am not very fond of movies, plays, **and the like.**

＊ Usually used in the pattern "~ *ya* ~ *ya* ~ *nado*"; indicates that there are other items in addition to those cited.

② [or the like; used when citing something as an example]

kyō suru no ni nani ka ii hon wa arimasen ka?)「そうですね。この本 **など**いかがですか。」 (Sō desu ne. Kono hon *nado* ikaga desu ka?)

¶お疲れになったでしょう。お茶**など** いかがですか。 (Otsukare ni natta deshō. Ocha *nado* ikaga desu ka?)

③［否定的な気持ちを込めてあるもの ごとを取り上げて言うときに使う］

¶山田さんはうそ**など**つく人ではあり ません。 (Yamada san wa uso *nado* tsuku hito de wa arimasen.)

¶こんなまずい料理**など**, とても食べ られません。 (Konna mazui ryōri *nado*, totemo taberaremasen.)

* 普通, あとに打ち消しの言葉や否定 的な意味の言葉が来る。

＊「なんか (nan ka)」とも言う。

nagai 長い〖形〗

①［もののある点からある点までの間 隔が大きい］

¶長い鉛筆と短い鉛筆が2本ずつあり ます。 (*Nagai* enpitsu to mijikai enpitsu ga nihon zutsu arimasu.)

②［時間の間隔が大きい］

¶わたしは長い間アメリカに住んでい ました。 (Watashi wa *nagai* aida Amerika ni sunde imashita.)

⇔mijikai 短い

nagameru ながめる〖動Ⅱ〗

①［見つめる］

¶その人は同じ絵を30分も**ながめて** いました。 (Sono hito wa onaji e o sanjippun mo *nagamete* imashita.)

¶ "Can you tell me some good books for studying Japanese?"

"Well, how about **something like this** book?"

¶ You must be tired. How about some tea **or something?**

③ [or the like, such a thing as; used when citing something in a denial]

¶ [Mr.] Yamada isn't a liar.

¶ There's no way anyone could eat **such** terrible food.

* Usually followed by words negative in form or sense.

＊ Variant: *nan ka*.

nagai 〖adj〗 **long; prolonged**

① [long (spatial), too long]

¶ There are two **long** pencils and two short pencils.

② [long (temporal), prolonged]

¶ I lived in the United States for a **long** time.

nagameru 〖v Ⅱ〗 **look at, watch; look out over, overlook**

① [look at, watch, see]

¶ That person **was looking at** the same picture for 30 minutes.

②[見渡す]

¶山の上から下の町を**ながめ**ました。
(Yama no ue kara shita no machi o *nagamemashita*.)

nagara　ながら〖助〗

①[ある動作を行う一方で他の動作も行うという意味を表す]

¶わたしはいつも音楽を聞き**ながら**仕事をします。(Watashi wa itsu mo ongaku o kiki*nagara* shigoto o shimasu.)

¶テレビを見**ながら**勉強してはいけません。(Terebi o mi*nagara* benkyō shite wa ikemasen.)

¶山田さんは働き**ながら**大学を卒業しました。(Yamada san wa hataraki-*nagara* daigaku o sotsugyō shimashita.)

* 二つの動作の主体は同じである。

②[ある動作・状態とそれと相いれない他の動作・状態とがともに成立するという関係を表す]

¶あの人はそのことを知ってい**ながら**教えてくれませんでした。(Ano hito wa sono koto o shitte i*nagara* oshiete kuremasen deshita.)

¶あの人は「はい，はい。」と言い**ながら**，いつも頼んだことをしてくれません。(Ano hito wa "Hai, hai." to ii*nagara*, itsu mo tanonda koto o shite kuremasen.)

* 普通，二つの動作・状態の主体は同じである。

③[断りや前置きなどを表すのに使う]

② [look out over, overlook]

¶ [I] **surveyed** the town below from the top of the mountain.

-nagara 〖part〗　while, as; though

① [while, as, at the same time that]

¶ I always listen to music while I work (literally, I always work **while** listening to music).

¶ One shouldn't watch television while studying (literally, One shouldn't study **while** watching television).

¶ [Mr.] Yamada worked [his] way through college.

* The subject of the two clauses is the same.

② [though, yet, in spite of]

¶ **Even though** [he] knew that, [he] didn't tell [me] about it.

¶ **In spite of** agreeing to it, [he] never does what [he]'s asked to do.

* Usually the subject of the two clauses is the same.

③ [used when refusing or in a preliminary remark]

¶残念ながら、用事があって、あしたのパーティーには出席できません。
(Zannen*nagara*, yōji ga atte, ashita no pātii ni wa shusseki dekimasen.)

¶失礼ながら、ラジオの音をもう少し小さくしていただけませんか。 (Shitsurei*nagara*, rajio no oto o mō sukoshi chiisaku shite itadakemasen ka?)

nagare 流れ〚名〛
¶この川はずいぶん流れが急ですね。
(Kono kawa wa zuibun *nagare* ga kyū desu ne.)
¶車の流れが激しくて、道の向こう側へ渡れません。 (Kuruma no *nagare* ga hageshikute, michi no mukō-gawa e wataremasen.)

nagareru 流れる〚動Ⅱ〛
①〔液体が低い方へ行く〕
¶町の中を川が流れています。(Machi no naka o kawa ga *nagarete* imasu.)
②〔水に浮いて行く〕
¶川に木の葉が落ちて、流れていきました。(Kawa ni ki no ha ga ochite, *nagarete* ikimashita.)

nagasa 長さ〚名〛
¶その橋の長さはどのくらいですか。
(Sono hashi no *nagasa* wa dono kurai desu ka?)
⇨**-sa** -さ

nagasu 流す〚動Ⅰ〛
¶ここに水を流さないでください。
(Koko ni mizu o *nagasanaide* ku-

¶ I'm sorry (literally, **although** it's a shame) but something has come up so that I will be unable to attend the party tomorrow.

¶ Excuse me (literally, **although** it's rude) but could you please turn your radio down a little bit?

nagare 〚n〛 flow, stream, current
¶ This is a very rapidly **running** river.

¶ **Traffic** is so heavy that one can't cross to the other side of the road.

nagareru 〚v Ⅱ〛 stream, flow, run; float, be carried away
① [stream, flow, run, drain]
¶ A river **runs** through the town 〚city〛.
② [float, be carried away]
¶ Tree leaves fell into the river and **were carried away.**

nagasa 〚n〛 length
¶ **How long** is that bridge 〚What is **the length** of that bridge〛?

nagasu 〚v Ⅰ〛 pour, let flow
¶ Please **don't run** the water here 〚Please don't get this place wet〛.

dasai.)

¶わたしは悲しい映画を見て，涙を流しました。 (Watashi wa kanashii eiga o mite, namida o *nagashimashita*.)

¶ I **cried** at the sad movie.

nageru 投げる〖動Ⅱ〗

¶子供がボールを投げています。

(Kodomo ga bōru o *nagete* imasu.)

¶池の中に石を投げないでください。

(Ike no naka ni ishi o *nagenaide* kudasai.)

nageru 〖v Ⅱ〗 throw, pitch, fling

¶ The children **are playing catch.**

¶ Please **don't throw** stones 〖pebbles〗 into the pond 〖pool〗.

nagusameru 慰める〖動Ⅱ〗

①[人を勇気づける]

¶試験に落ちた友達を慰めてあげました。 (Shiken ni ochita tomodachi o *nagusamete* agemashita.)

②[心をやわらげる]

¶音楽はわたしたちの心を慰めてくれます。 (Ongaku wa watashitachi no kokoro o *nagusamete* kuremasu.)

nagusameru 〖v Ⅱ〗 comfort, console, cheer up; soothe

① [comfort, console, cheer up]

¶ I tried **to cheer up** a friend who had failed an exam.

② [soothe]

¶ Music **soothes** our souls.

nai ない〖形〗

①[存在しない]

¶机の上には何もない。 (Tsukue no ue ni wa nani mo *nai*.)

¶その本が図書館にあるかないかわかりません。(Sono hon ga toshokan ni aru ka *nai* ka wakarimasen.)

↔**aru** ある

②[所有しない]

¶今お金がないから，あとで払います。 (Ima okane ga *nai* kara, ato de haraimasu.)

¶うちに電話がないので，不便です。 (Uchi ni denwa ga *nai* node, fuben

nai 〖adj〗 do not exist; do not have; not

① [do not exist]

¶ There **is nothing** on the desk.

¶ [I] do not know if that book is in the library or **not.**

② [do not have]

¶ [I] will pay later because [I] **don't have** the money for it now.

¶ [My] **not having** a telephone is inconvenient.

desu.)

↔**aru　ある**

③[状態を表す言葉などを打ち消す]

¶今日はあまり寒くないです。　(Kyō wa amari samuku *nai* desu.)

¶その映画はおもしろくなかったです。 (Sono eiga wa omoshiroku *nakatta* desu.)

¶たぶんあの人は日本人ではないでしょう。(Tabun ano hito wa Nihonjin de wa *nai* deshō.)

*「それは日本語の本ではない。(Sore wa Nihongo no hon de wa nai.)」を丁寧に言うときには「それは日本語の本ではありません。(Sore wa Nihongo no hon de wa arimasen.)」と言う。

nai　ない〘助動〙

¶本を見ないで, もう一度言ってください。(Hon o mi*naide*, mō ichido itte kudasai.)

¶今度の旅行にあなたがいっしょに行けなくて残念です。(Kondo no ryokō ni anata ga issho ni ike*nakute* zannen desu.)

¶勉強しなければ, 日本語が上手になりません。　(Benkyō shi*nakereba*, Nihongo ga jōzu ni narimasen.)

¶あした雨が降らなかったら, テニスをしに行きましょう。　(Ashita ame ga fura*nakattara*, tenisu o shi ni ikimashō.)

-nai　-内〘尾〙

学校内 (gakkō*nai*)　時間内 (jikan-

③ [not]

¶ **It's not** so cold today.

¶ That movie **wasn't** interesting.

¶ [He] probably **isn't** Japanese.

* The polite way of saying "*Sore wa Nihongo no hon de wa nai*" (That book is not written in Japanese) is "*Sore wa Nihongo no hon de wa arimasen.*"

-nai 〚auxil〛 a negative ending added to the stem of verbs

¶ Please say it once again **without** looking at your book.

¶ It's too bad that you **can't** go along with [us] on the coming trip.

¶ You will not become good at Japanese **if you don't** study.

¶ Let's go play tennis tomorrow **if it doesn't** rain.

-nai 〚suf〛 **within**

within the school // **within** the

naifu

nai) 東京都内 (Tōkyōto*nai*)　日本国内 (Nihonkoku*nai*)

allotted time // **within** Tokyo, **inside** Tokyo // **within** Japan, **inside** Japan

naifu ナイフ〚名〛

naifu 〚n〛 knife

naikaku 内閣〚名〛

内閣総理大臣 (*naikaku*-sōridaijin)
内閣が倒れる (*naikaku* ga taoreru)
内閣が替わる (*naikaku* ga kawaru)
¶昨日, 新しい内閣が誕生しました。
(Kinō, atarashii *naikaku* ga tanjō shimashita.)

naikaku 〚n〛 (government) **cabinet**

the prime minister, the premier // **a cabinet** falls // **the cabinet** changes

¶ A new **cabinet** came into being yesterday.

nairon ナイロン〚名〛

ナイロン製のくつ下 (*nairon*sei no kutsushita)

nairon 〚n〛 nylon

nylon socks

naiyō 内容〚名〛

①〔話や文章などの中身〕
書類の内容 (shorui no *naiyō*)
¶その手紙の内容を教えてください。
(Sono tegami no *naiyō* o oshiete kudasai.)
②〔価値のある中身〕
¶形式だけで内容のない会議でした。
(Keishiki dake de *naiyō* no nai kaigi deshita.)
¶この論文は題名は立派ですが, 内容がありません。 (Kono ronbun wa daimei wa rippa desu ga, *naiyō* ga arimasen.)

naiyō 〚n〛 **content(s), import; substance, depth**

① [content(s), import]
the contents of a document 〚of paperwork〛
¶ Please tell me **what** that letter **says.**
② [substance, depth]
¶ It was a meeting for show alone without any **real substance.**

¶ This thesis 〚paper, dissertation〛 has a fine-sounding title but has no **depth** to it.

naka 中〚名〛

①〔あるものの内部〕
¶寒いから, 家の中に入りましょう。
(Samui kara, ie no *naka* ni hairimashō.)
¶この袋の中には, 何が入っていますか。 (Kono fukuro no *naka* ni wa,

naka 〚n〛 **inside; among, of**
① [inside, interior]
¶ As it's cold let's go on **inside** the house.

¶ What's **inside** this bag?

510

nani ga haitte imasu ka?)

↔**soto** 外^{そと}

②[ある範囲のうち]

¶わたしは果物^{くだもの}の中^{なか}でりんごがいちばん好きです。　(Watashi wa kudamono no *naka* de ringo ga ichiban suki desu.)

② [among, of]

¶ **Of** fruits, I like apples best ⟦My favorite fruit is the apple⟧.

naka 仲^{なか}〖名〗

仲^{なか}が悪^{わる}い (*naka* ga warui)

¶あの二人^{ふたり}はとても仲^{なか}がいいです。　(Ano futari wa totemo *naka* ga ii desu.)

¶先週^{せんしゅう}, 仲^{なか}のいい友達^{ともだち}と音楽会^{おんがっかい}に行^いきました。(Senshū, *naka* no ii tomodachi to ongakkai ni ikimashita.)

naka 〖n〗 relations, relationship

be on bad **terms** with someone

¶ Those two **are very close.**

¶ Last week [I] went to a concert ⟦recital⟧ with a **good** friend.

nakama 仲間^{なかま}〖名〗

¶その子^こには仲間^{なかま}がおおぜいいます。　(Sono ko ni wa *nakama* ga oozei imasu.)

¶先週^{せんしゅう}, 会社^{かいしゃ}の仲間^{なかま}と旅行^{りょこう}しました。　(Senshū, kaisha no *nakama* to ryokō shimashita.)

nakama 〖n〗 colleagues, associates, set, circle

¶ That child has a wide **circle of acquaintances.**

¶ Last week [I] went on a trip with **people** from work.

nakanaka なかなか〖副〗

①[かなり, 相当^{そうとう}に]

¶この本^{ほん}はなかなかおもしろいです。　(Kono hon wa *nakanaka* omoshiroi desu.)

¶この問題^{もんだい}はなかなか難^{むずか}しいです。　(Kono mondai wa *nakanaka* muzukashii desu.)

②[容易^{ようい}でない, 期待^{きたい}どおりにならない]

¶この問題^{もんだい}は難^{むずか}しくて, なかなかできません。　(Kono mondai wa muzu-

nakanaka 〖adv〗 considerably, quite; not easily, not readily

① [considerably, quite, rather, very]

¶ This book is **quite** interesting.

¶ This problem is **quite** difficult.

② [not easily, not readily]

¶ This (test or homework) problem is difficult and **not easily** answered.

kashikute, *nakanaka* dekimasen.)

¶バスがなかなか来ません。(Basu ga *nakanaka* kimasen.)

¶ The bus **is long** in coming.

* あとに打ち消しの言葉が来る。

* Used with the negative.

nakereba naranai なければならない〖連〗

-nakereba naranai 〚compd〛 **must**

¶友達と約束したから，10時までに駅へ行かなければなりません。(Tomodachi to yakusoku shita kara, jūji made ni eki e ika*nakereba narimasen*.)

¶ [I] **must** go to the station by ten o'clock as [I] have an appointment with a friend.

¶日本の大学に入るためには，まず日本語を勉強しなければなりません。(Nihon no daigaku ni hairu tame ni wa, mazu Nihongo o benkyō shi*nakereba narimasen*.)

¶ In order to enter a Japanese university one **must** first learn Japanese.

＊「〜なくてはならない (〜nakute wa naranai)」とも言う。

＊ Variant: *-nakute wa naranai*.

⇨naranai ならない

naku 泣く〖動Ⅰ〗

naku 〚v Ⅰ〛 **cry**

¶赤ちゃんが泣いていますよ。(Akachan ga *naite* imasu yo.)

¶ The baby **is crying!**

¶母が死んだ時，わたしは一日じゅう泣きました。(Haha ga shinda toki, watashi wa ichinichijū *nakimashita*.)

¶ I **cried** all day long when my mother died.

naku 鳴く〖動Ⅰ〗

naku 〚v Ⅰ〛 (birds, insects) **cry, sing;** (animals) **bark, roar, mew,** etc.

¶庭で鳥が鳴いています。(Niwa de tori ga *naite* imasu.)

¶ A bird **is singing** in the yard 〚garden〛.

¶秋になると，虫が盛んに鳴きます。(Aki ni naru to, mushi ga sakan ni *nakimasu*.)

¶ When autumn comes one hears **the sound** of many insects.

nakunaru 亡くなる〖動Ⅰ〗

nakunaru 〚v Ⅰ〛 **pass away, die**

¶上田さんは，昨日病気で亡くなりま

¶ [Mr.] Ueda **passed away** yester-

した。 (Ueda san wa, kinō byōki de *nakunarimashita*.)

＊「死ぬ (shinu)」の丁寧な言葉。人間以外の動物には使わない。

⇨shinu 死ぬ

nakunaru なくなる〖動Ⅰ〗

①[尽きる，使い果たす]

¶時間が**なくなりました**から，今日の講義はこれで終わります。 (Jikan ga *nakunarimashita* kara, kyō no kōgi wa kore de owarimasu.)

¶たばこが**なくなった**から，買ってきてください。 (Tabako ga *nakunatta* kara, katte kite kudasai.)

②[見当たらなくなる]

¶わたしのかさが**なくなりました**。 (Watashi no kasa ga *nakunarimashita*.)

nakusu なくす〖動Ⅰ〗

①[紛失する]

¶友達から借りた本を**なくして**しまいました。 (Tomodachi kara karita hon o *nakushite* shimaimashita.)

¶昨日**なくした**財布がまだ見つかりません。 (Kinō *nakushita* saifu ga mada mitsukarimasen.)

②[ない状態にする]

¶交通事故を**なくす**ように，みんなで注意しましょう。 (Kōtsū-jiko o *nakusu* yō ni, minna de chūi shimashō.)

¶こんな悪い規則は**なくした**ほうがいいです。 (Konna warui kisoku wa *nakushita* hō ga ii desu.)

day due to illness.

＊ *Nakunaru* is the polite form of *shinu*. It is used only for human beings.

nakunaru 〚v I〛 run low, run out, be used up; be lost, be gone, be missing

① [run low, run out, be used up]

¶ Today's lecture will end here as we have **run out** of time.

¶ I have **run out** of cigarettes— please go buy me some.

② [be lost, be gone, be missing]

¶ My umbrella **is missing.**

nakusu 〚v I〛 lose; get rid of

① [lose, be deprived of]

¶ [I] **lost** 〚have **lost**〛 the book [I] borrowed from a friend.

¶ The wallet [I] **lost** yesterday still hasn't been found.

② [get rid of, do away with]

¶ Everyone should work **to eliminate** traffic accidents.

¶ It would be best **to get rid of** such a bad rule.

-nakute wa naranai ☞ -nakereba naranai

nama 生〔名〕

生魚 (*namazakana*) 生卵 (*nama-tamago*) 生野菜 (*nama*yasai)

¶あなたは魚を生で食べることができますか。 (Anata wa sakana o *nama* de taberu koto ga dekimasu ka?)

¶生の野菜をもっとたくさん食べなさい。 (*Nama* no yasai o motto takusan tabenasai.)

namae 名前〔名〕

¶わたしの名前は中村です。(Watashi no *namae* wa Nakamura desu.)

¶わたしは犬に「コロ」という名前をつけました。 (Watashi wa inu ni "Koro" to iu *namae* o tsukemashita.)

namakeru 怠ける〔動Ⅱ〕

¶一郎は勉強を怠けて，遊んでばかりいます。 (Ichirō wa benkyō o *namakete*, asonde bakari imasu.)

¶仕事を怠けてはいけません。 (Shigoto o *namakete* wa ikemasen.)

nami 波〔名〕

波が高い (*nami* ga takai) 波が荒い (*nami* ga arai)

¶この海岸は波が静かです。 (Kono kaigan wa *nami* ga shizuka desu.)

namida 涙〔名〕

涙を流す (*namida* o nagasu) 涙をこぼす (*namida* o kobosu) 涙が出る (*namida* ga deru)

¶その人は目に涙を浮かべて，別れのあいさつをしました。(Sono hito wa me ni *namida* o ukabete, wakare

nama 〚n〛 **raw, uncooked**

raw fish // a **raw** egg // **raw** vegetables; a salad

¶ Can you eat **raw** fish?

¶ Eat more **raw** vegetables!

namae 〚n〛 **name; given name**

¶ My **name** is Nakamura.

¶ I **named** my dog Koro.

namakeru 〚v II〛 **be idle, be lazy, neglect**

¶ Ichirō **is neglecting** his studies and doing nothing but playing around.

¶ You mustn't **slight** your work.

nami 〚n〛 **wave, surf**

the waves are high, **the sea** is rough // **the waves** are high, **the sea** is rough

¶ **The sea** is calm at this beach.

namida 〚n〛 **a tear**

shed **tears,** weep // shed **tears** // **tears** fall, **tears** come to one's eyes

¶ [He] said [his] farewell with **tears** in [his] eyes.

no aisatsu o shimashita.)

nan(-) 何(-)〖代，頭〗

1〖代〗

¶あれは何ですか。(Are wa *nan* desu
ka?)

¶これは何の薬ですか。(Kore wa *nan*
no kusuri desu ka?)

¶あの方は何というお名前ですか。
(Ano kata wa *nan* to iu onamae
desu ka?)

2〖頭〗

何匹 (*nan*biki) 何本 (*nan*bon) 何
秒 (*nan*byō) 何台 (*nan*dai) 何月
(*nan*gatsu) 何時 (*nan*ji) 何時間
(*nan*jikan) 何か月 (*nan*kagetsu)
何回 (*nan*kai) 何年 (*nan*nen) 何
日 (*nan*nichi) 何人 (*nan*nin) 何
十人 (*nan*jūnin) 十何人 (jū*nan*-
nin) 何千人 (*nan*zennin) 何分
(*nan*pun) 何週間 (*nan*shūkan) 何
足 (*nan*zoku)

⇒nani(-) 何(-)

nana 七〖名〗 ☞shichi 七

naname 斜め〖名〗

¶道路を斜めに渡るのは危険です。
(Dōro o *naname* ni wataru no wa
kiken desu.)

¶船が風で斜めに傾きました。(Fune
ga kaze de *naname* ni katamuki-
mashita.)

nanatsu 七つ〖名〗

① [7 個]

¶卵はあと七つ残っています。(Tama-
go wa ato *nanatsu* nokotte imasu.)

nan(-) 〚pron, pref〛 **what; what,
how many**

1 〚pron〛 **what**

¶ **What** is that?

¶ **What** is this medicine?

¶ **What** is that gentleman's 〚lady's〛
name?

2 〚pref〛 **what, how many**

how many (cats, dogs, etc.) // **how
many** (cigarettes, bottles, etc.) //
how many seconds // **how many**
(cars, machines, etc.) // **what** month
// **what** time, when // **how many**
hours // **how many** months // **how
many** times // **how many** years;
what year // **how many** days; **what
day** // **how many** people // **how
many** tens of persons // 10-**odd** people // **how many** thousands of persons // **how many** minutes // **how
many** weeks // **how many** pairs (of
socks, shoes, etc.)

nana ☞ shichi

naname 〚n〛 **oblique, slanting, di-
agonal**

¶ It is dangerous **not to take the
shortest path** when crossing the
street.

¶ The boat **listed** in the wind.

nanatsu 〚n〛 **seven; seven years of
age**

① [seven (items)]

¶ There are **seven** eggs left.

515

②[7歳]

¶娘は今年七つになります。(Musume wa kotoshi *nanatsu* ni narimasu.)

nan demo 何でも〔連〕

¶何でも好きな物を買ってあげましょう。 (*Nan demo* suki na mono o katte agemashō.)

¶何でもいいから，質問してください。 (*Nan demo* ii kara, shitsumon shite kudasai.)

nani(-) 何(-)〔代，頭〕

1〔代〕

¶そこに何がありますか。 (Soko ni *nani* ga arimasu ka?)

¶あなたは食べ物では何が好きですか。 (Anata wa tabemono de wa *nani* ga suki desu ka?)

¶朝，起きてから何をしますか。(Asa, okite kara *nani* o shimasu ka?)

2〔頭〕

何語 (*nani*go) 何色 (*nani*iro) 何人 (*nani*jin) 何曜日 (*nani*yōbi)
⇒nan(-) 何(-)

nani ka 何か〔連〕

¶そこに何かありますか。 (Soko ni *nani ka* arimasu ka?)

¶何か欲しい物がありますか。 (*Nani ka* hoshii mono ga arimasu ka?)

¶台所にパンか何かがあると思います。(Daidokoro ni pan ka *nani ka* ga aru to omoimasu.)

nani mo 何も〔連〕

¶ここには何もありません。(Koko ni wa *nani mo* arimasen.)

② [seven years of age]

¶ My daughter will be **seven** this year.

nan demo 〖compd〗 **anything, whatever**

¶ I will buy you **whatever** you want.

¶ Please ask **whatever** questions you may have.

nani(-) 〖pron, pref〗 **what**

1 〖pron〗

¶ **What** is that there?

¶ **What** foods do you like?

¶ **What** do you do in the morning after you get up?

2 〖pref〗

what language // **what** color // **what** nationality // **what** day of the week

nani ka 〖compd〗 **something, anything**

¶ Is there **anything** there?

¶ Is there **anything** you'd like?

¶ I think there is bread 〚rolls, etc.〛 or **something** in the kitchen.

nani mo 〖compd〗 **nothing, not anything**

¶ There is **nothing** here.

¶デパートで何も買いませんでした。
(Depāto de *nani mo* kaimasen deshita.)

＊あとに打ち消しの言葉が来る。

nanoka 七日〖名〗

①[日付を表す]
七月七日 (shichigatsu *nanoka*)

②[日数を表す]
¶一週間は七日です。 (Isshūkan wa *nanoka* desu.)

＊「なぬか (nanuka)」と言うこともある。

⇨-ka -日

nao なお〖副〗

①[更に，いっそう]
¶この本も難しいが，その本は**なお**難しいです。 (Kono hon mo muzukashii ga, sono hon wa *nao* muzukashii desu.)

¶わたしも背が高いが，兄のほうが**なお**高いです。 (Watashi mo se ga takai ga, ani no hō ga *nao* takai desu.)

②[やはり，依然，引き続いて]
¶母は 90 歳ですが，今も**なお**元気です。 (Haha wa kyūjissai desu ga, ima mo *nao* genki desu.)

naoru 直る〖動Ⅰ〗

①[正しくなる]
¶悪い習慣はなかなか**直り**ません。 (Warui shūkan wa nakanaka *naorimasen*.)

②[修繕してよくなる]
¶壊れていたテレビが**直り**ました。

¶ [I] didn't buy **anything** at the department store.

＊ Used with the negative.

nanka ☞ **nado**

nanoka 〚n〛 **the seventh of the month; seven days**

① [the seventh of the month]
July **7**

② [seven days]
¶ One week is **seven days.**

＊ Variant: *nanuka.*

nao 〚adv〛 **more, further, still more, less, still less; still, yet**

① [more, further, still more, less, still less]
¶ This book is difficult but that one is **even more** difficult.

¶ I am tall but my older brother is **still** taller.

② [still, yet]
¶ My mother is 90 years old but she **still** enjoys good health.

naoru 〚v I〛 **be corrected, be reformed; be repaired**

① [be corrected, be reformed]
¶ Bad habits are hard **to break.**

② [be repaired, be set to rights, be restored]

(Kowarete ita terebi ga *naorima-shita*.)

naoru 治る〖動Ⅰ〗

病気が治る (byōki ga *naoru*)

¶風邪はもう治りましたか。　(Kaze wa mō *naorimashita* ka?)

naosu 直す〖動Ⅰ〗

①[正しくする]

¶先生は学生の間違いを直します。

(Sensei wa gakusei no machigai o *naoshimasu*.)

②[修繕する]

¶ラジオが壊れたので，電気屋さんに直してもらいました。　(Rajio ga kowareta node, denkiyasan ni *naoshite* moraimashita.)

③[改めて何かをする]

¶この文章はもう一度書き直してください。(Kono bunshō wa mō ichido kaki*naoshite* kudasai.)

naosu 治す〖動Ⅰ〗

病気を治す (byōki o *naosu*)

¶虫歯は早く治したほうがいいですよ。(Mushiba wa hayaku *naoshita* hō ga ii desu yo.)

nara なら〖助動〗

①[前件が成立することを想定して現在の話し手の立場や判断などを後件で述べるという関係を表す]

¶あなたが行くなら，わたしも行くことにします。　(Anata ga iku *nara* watashi mo iku koto ni shimasu.)

¶この本をお読みになるなら，お貸ししましょう。(Kono hon o oyomi ni

¶ The broken television set **has been fixed.**

naoru 〚v I〛 recover, get well, get better, heal

recover from an illness

¶ **Are you over** your cold 〚case of the flu〛 now?

(-)naosu 〚v I〛 correct; repair, mend; do over again

① [correct]

¶ The teacher **corrects** the students' mistakes.

② [repair, mend]

¶ As the radio was broken, I had it **fixed** at the electric appliance shop.

③ [do over again]

¶ Please **re**write this sentence.

naosu 〚v I〛 cure, heal

cure an illness

¶ It is best to have cavities **cared for** early.

nara 〚auxil〛 if; as for

① [if, provided that; used when the speaker states a conclusion, etc., based on a stipulation in the first clause]

¶ **If** you are going, I will go too.

¶ I will lend you this book **if** you are interested in reading it.

naru *nara*, okashi shimashō.)

¶あしたお暇なら，わたしの家へ来てください。 (Ashita ohima *nara*, watashi no ie e kite kudasai.)

¶頭が痛いなら，早く帰って休んだほうがいいですよ。 (Atama ga itai *nara*, hayaku kaette yasunda hō ga ii desu yo.)

* 後件には普通，話し手の「〜う［よう］（〜u［yō]）」などの意志，「〜なさい（〜nasai）」などの命令，「〜てください（〜te kudasai）」などの依頼，「〜ほうがいい（〜hō ga ii）」などの勧告などの言い方が来る。また，後件のことがらの成立のほうが前件のことがらの成立より時間的に早い。「山田さんが来たら，わたしは帰ります。(Yamada san ga kitara, watashi wa kaerimasu.)」の場合には，山田さんが来てからわたしが帰るという意味であるが，「山田さんが来るなら，わたしは帰ります。(Yamada san ga kuru nara, watashi wa kaerimasu.)」の場合には，山田さんが来る前にわたしが帰るという意味になる。

②［前件がもし成立していた場合には後件も成立するという関係を表す］

¶もう少し背が高かったなら，どんなによかったでしょう。 (Mō sukoshi sei ga takakatta *nara*, donna ni yokatta deshō.)

¶お医者さんがもう少し早く来てくれたなら，父は助かったのに。 (Oishasan ga mō sukoshi hayaku kite

¶ Please come visit me tomorrow **if** you are free.

¶ **If** you have a headache you had better go home early and rest.

* In the second clause the speaker usually expresses an intention with *-ō* 〚*-yō*〛, a command with *-nasai*, a request with *-te kudasai*, a recommendation with ~ *hō ga ii*, etc. Also, the time of the second clause is earlier than that of the first, *nara*-clause. Thus "*Yamada san ga kitara, watashi wa kaerimasu*" (I will leave when Mr. Yamada comes) means that I will go after [Mr.] Yamada comes, but "*Yamada san ga kuru nara, watashi wa kaerimasu*" (If Mr. Yamada is coming, I will leave) means that I will leave before [Mr.] Yamada comes.

② [if; indicates that the second clause would have been realized if the first clause had been realized]

¶ How nice it would have been **if** [I] were a little taller.

¶ **If only** the doctor had come sooner, my father's life could have been saved.

kureta *nara,* chichi wa tasukatta noni.)

* 前件は実際には成立しなかったことがらが来る。「～たなら（～ta nara）」の形で使う。

* The first clause wasn't actually realized. Used in the pattern "*-ta nara.*"

→**ba** ば　**tara** たら

③〔話題とすることがらを提示するのに使う〕

③ [as for; used to indicate the topic]

¶その問題なら，もう解決しました。(Sono mondai *nara,* mō kaiketsu shimashita.)

¶ Oh, that problem has already been resolved.

¶「お兄さんはいらっしゃいますか。」(Oniisan wa irasshaimasu ka?)「兄なら今床屋へ行っていますよ。」(Ani *nara* ima tokoya e itte imasu yo.)

¶ "Is your older brother there?"
"Oh, he's gone to the barbershop."

→**tara** たら

* 助動詞「だ（da）」の「接続の形」である。「ならば（naraba）」とも言うが，普通「なら（nara）」の形で使う。

* *Nara* is the connective form of the auxiliary *da. Naraba* is also used but *nara* is the more usual form.

naraba ☞ **nara**

naraberu 並べる〖動Ⅱ〗

naraberu 〖v II〗 **arrange, place side by side, display**

¶机を１列に並べてください。(Tsukue o ichiretsu ni *narabete* kudasai.)

¶ Please **arrange** the desks in one row.

¶本だなには本がきちんと並べてあります。(Hondana ni wa hon ga kichinto *narabete* arimasu.)

¶ The books **are in** good **order** 〖**are arranged** nicely〗 in the bookcase.

narabu 並ぶ〖動Ⅰ〗

narabu 〖v I〗 **be in a row, stand in line**

¶わたしは田中さんと並んで座りました。(Watashi wa Tanaka san to *narande* suwarimashita.)

¶ I sat down **next to** [Mrs.] Tanaka.

¶道の両側にはいろいろな店が並んでいます。(Michi no ryōgawa ni wa

¶ Various shops **line** both sides of the street.

iroiro na mise ga *narande* imasu.)

naranai ならない〖連〗

①〔禁止の意味を表す〕
¶酒を飲んではならない。　(Sake o
nonde wa *naranai*.)

¶うそをついてはなりません。(Uso o
tsuite wa *narimasen*.)

*「動詞（ての形）＋は（wa）＋ならな
い（naranai）」の形で使う。

②〔義務や当然の意味を表す〕
¶友達と約束したから、10時までに駅
へ行かなければなりません。(Tomo-
dachi to yakusoku shita kara, jūji
made ni eki e ikanakereba *narimasen*.)

¶あしたまでに宿題を出さなくてはな
りません。(Ashita made ni shukudai o dasanakute wa *narimasen*.)

*「～なければならない（～nakereba
naranai）」「～なくてはならない（～
nakute wa naranai)」の形で使う。

⇨nakereba naranai　なければなら
ない

narau 習う〖動Ⅰ〗
¶わたしは今ピアノを習っています。
(Watashi wa ima piano o *naratte*
imasu.)

¶日本語を習うのはたいへんですか。
(Nihongo o *narau* no wa taihen
desu ka?)

nareru 慣れる〖動Ⅱ〗
¶わたしは日本の生活にもう慣れまし
た。　(Watashi wa Nihon no seikatsu ni mō *naremashita*.)

naranai 〚compd〛 **must not, should not; must, should, ought**

① [must not, should not]
¶ You **shouldn't** drink.

¶ One **shouldn't** tell lies.

* Used in the pattern "verb (*-te*
form) + *wa* + *naranai*."

② [must, should, ought, have to]
¶ [I] **have to** be at the station by ten
o'clock as [I] have an appointment
with a friend.

¶ The homework **has to** be handed
in by tomorrow.

* Used in the patterns "*-nakereba
naranai*" and "*-nakute wa naranai*."

narau 〚v I〛 **learn, study, be taught**
¶ I am presently **taking** piano **lessons.**

¶ Is Japanese hard **to learn?**

nareru 〚v II〛 **get used to, be
accustomed to, become experienced in**

¶ I am now **acclimated** to life in
Japan.

¶慣れれば，この仕事も楽になるでしょう。(*Narereba*, kono shigoto mo raku ni naru deshō.)

¶ [You] will find this job easier once [you] **get more used to it.**

nareru なれる〖動Ⅱ〗

¶この犬はわたしによくなれています。(Kono inu wa watashi ni yoku *narete* imasu.)

nareru 〚v Ⅱ〛 **become tame, be domesticated**

¶ This dog **is** quite **good with me.**

naru 鳴る〖動Ⅰ〗

¶電話のベルが鳴っています。(Denwa no beru ga *natte* imasu.)

¶ベルが鳴って授業が終わりました。(Beru ga *natte* jugyō ga owarimashita.)

naru 〚v Ⅰ〛 **sound, ring, peal, strike, boom,** etc.

¶ The telephone **is ringing.**

¶ Class ended with **the ringing** of the bell.

naru なる〖動Ⅰ〗

¶春になると，桜が咲きます。(Haru ni *naru* to, sakura ga sakimasu.)

¶３時になったら，少し休みましょう。(Sanji ni *nattara*, sukoshi yasumimashō.)

¶上田さんは将来医者になりたいそうです。(Ueda san wa shōrai isha ni *naritai* sō desu.)

¶太陽が昇って，辺りが急に明るくなりました。(Taiyō ga nobotte, atari ga kyū ni akaruku *narimashita*.)

¶この辺は夜になると，静かになります。(Kono hen wa yoru ni *naru* to, shizuka ni *narimasu*.)

¶一生懸命練習したので，だいぶ上手に日本語が話せるようになりました。(Isshōkenmei renshū shita node, daibu jōzu ni Nihongo ga hanaseru yō ni *narimashita*.)

＊ 名詞の場合は助詞「に (ni)」のあ

naru 〚v Ⅰ〛 **become, grow, turn**

¶ When spring **comes,** the cherry blossoms will come out 〚Cherry trees blossom in the spring〛.

¶ Let's take a break **at three o'clock.**

¶ I understand that [Miss] Ueda **wants to become** a doctor.

¶ It suddenly **became** light with the rising of the sun.

¶ It's quiet here **at** night.

¶ As [he] practiced hard, [he] **can now** speak Japanese quite well.

＊ *Naru* is used with the particle *ni* after nouns and adjective-verbs and

522

とに続き，形容詞・形容動詞の場合は
「連用の形」に続く。また動詞の場合
には「動詞（連体の形）＋ように（yō
ni）＋なる（naru）」の形になる。

naru　なる〖動Ⅰ〗
¶このみかんの木には，あまり実がな
りません。（Kono mikan no ki ni
wa, amari mi ga *narimasen*.)

narubeku　なるべく〖副〗
¶なるべく早く来てください。(*Naru-
beku* hayaku kite kudasai.)
¶なるべくゆっくり話してください。
(*Narubeku* yukkuri hanashite kudasai.)

nasai　なさい〖動Ⅰ〗
¶もう遅いから，うちへ帰りなさい。
(Mō osoi kara, uchi e kaeri*nasai*.)
¶もっと一生懸命勉強しなさい。
(Motto isshōkenmei benkyō shi*nasai*.)
＊「なさる（nasaru）」の「命令の形」。
命令するときには普通この形を使う。

nasaru　なさる〖動Ⅰ〗
¶夏休みはどうなさいますか。(Natsu-
yasumi wa dō *nasaimasu* ka?)
¶お食事は何になさいますか。(Osho-
kuji wa nan ni *nasaimasu* ka?)
¶どうぞ，御心配なさらないでくださ
い。(Dōzo, goshinpai *nasaranaide*
kudasai.)
＊「する（suru）」の尊敬語。「ますの
形」は「なさいます（nasaimasu）」と
なる。
⇨**suru　する**

naru 〚v I〛 bear fruit, be in fruit
¶ This mandarin orange tree **isn't
bearing** very well.

narubeku 〚adv〛 as ~ as possible
¶ Please come **as** quickly **as possible.**
¶ Please speak **as** slowly **as possible.**

(-)nasai 〚v I〛 an imperative form
¶ It's late; **you'd better** go home.

¶ **You'd better** study harder.

＊ *Nasai* is the imperative form of
nasaru; this is the form usually used
for imperatives.

nasaru 〚v I〛 do
¶ What are you going **to do** during
summer vacation?
¶ What would **you like** for dinner
〚lunch, breakfast〛?
¶ Please **don't** worry about it.

＊ *Nasaru* is the honorific form of
suru. The -*masu* form is *nasaimasu*.

nashi なし〚名〛

natsu 夏〚名〛
夏休み (*natsu*yasumi)

natsukashii 懐かしい〚形〛
¶学校時代のことを懐かしく思い出します。 (Gakkō-jidai no koto o *natsukashiku* omoidashimasu.)
¶中村さんは留学した時のことを懐かしそうに話してくれました。 (Nakamura san wa ryūgaku shita toki no koto o *natsukashisō* ni hanashite kuremashita.)

nawa なわ〚名〛
なわ飛び (*nawa*tobi)

naze なぜ〚副〛
¶あなたはなぜ昨日学校を休んだのですか。 (Anata wa *naze* kinō gakkō o yasunda no desu ka?)
¶「なぜ，大学へ行かなかったのですか。」 (*Naze*, daigaku e ikanakatta no desu ka?) 「奨学金がもらえなかったからです。」 (Shōgakukin ga moraenakatta kara desu.)
⇒**dōshite** どうして

nazenara なぜなら〚接〛
¶「わたしは大学へは行けませんでした。 なぜなら，うちが貧乏だったからです。 (Watashi wa daigaku e wa ikemasen deshita. *Nazenara*, uchi ga binbō datta kara desu.)」
¶今年は米があまり取れませんでした。 なぜなら，夏の間気温が低かったからです。 (Kotoshi wa kome ga amari toremasen deshita. *Nazenara*,

nashi 〚n〛 pear, pear tree

natsu 〚n〛 summer
summer vacation

natsukashii 〚adj〛 dear, beloved, feel a yearning for, feel nostalgic about
¶ I have **fond** memories of my student days.
¶ [Miss] Nakamura spoke **nostalgically** about the time [she] was studying abroad.

nawa 〚n〛 rope (made of straw or hemp)
to be jumping **rope**

naze 〚adv〛 why, for what reason
¶ **Why** were you absent from school yesterday?

¶ "**Why** didn't [you] go to college?" "Because [I] couldn't get any financial aid."

nazenara 〚conj〛 because, for, the reason is
¶ I couldn't go to college. **That's because** I came from a poor family.

¶ The rice crop was poor this year. **The reason is that** temperatures were low during the summer.

natsu no aida kion ga hikukatta kara desu.)

＊前のことがらを受けて，あとにその理由や根拠などを言うときに使う。「なぜならば（nazenaraba）」とも言う。また「なぜかと言えば（naze ka to ieba）」「どうしてかと言うと（dōshite ka to iu to）」という言い方もある。

＊普通「なぜなら，〜からです（nazenara, 〜kara desu）」の形で使う。

＊ Used when giving the reason for or background behind something previously stated. *Nazenaraba* is also used, as are *naze ka to ieba* and *dōshite ka to iu to*.

＊ Usually used in the pattern "*Nazenara, 〜 kara desu.*"

ne 根〘名〙

木の根（ki no *ne*）　草の根（kusa no *ne*）　根が出る（*ne* ga deru）　根が生える（*ne* ga haeru）　根が伸びる（*ne* ga nobiru）

ne 〚n〛　root(s)

the **roots** of a tree 〚shrub〛 // the **roots** of grass 〚an herb, a weed〛 // take **root; the roots** are exposed // take **root** // **the roots** spread

ne ね〘助〙

①［相手に同意を求めたり念を押したりする意味を表す］

¶あしたはきっと来てくださいね。（Ashita wa kitto kite kudasai *ne*.）
¶あなたが田中さんですね。（Anata ga Tanaka san desu *ne*.）

②［感嘆したり驚いたりする気持ちなどを表す］

¶このりんごは高いですね。（Kono ringo wa takai desu *ne*.）
¶秋子さんはきれいな人ですね。（Akiko san wa kirei na hito desu *ne*.）

③［自分はそう思うという軽い主張の気持ちを表す］

¶空がこんなに暗いから，夕方は雨になると思いますね。（Sora ga konna

ne 〚part〛　isn't it, doesn't it, don't you; I suppose, I believe; you see, you know

① [used to invite the concurrence of the listener or for emphasis]

¶ Now you will come tomorrow, **won't you?**
¶ You **must be** [Mr.] Tanaka.

② [used to express one's admiration, wonder, surprise, etc.]

¶ **My,** these apples are expensive!

¶ Isn't Akiko pretty!

③ [used to lightly stress that something is the speaker's opinion]

¶ I believe it will rain this evening— the skies are so dark now.

ni kurai kara, yūgata wa ame ni naru to omoimasu *ne*.)

¶この魚は腐っているようですから、食べないほうがいいですね。 (Kono sakana wa kussatte iru yō desu kara, tabenai hō ga ii desu *ne*.)

¶夕食のため豚肉を買います。牛肉は高いですからね。 (Yūshoku no tame butaniku o kaimasu. Gyūniku wa takai desu kara *ne*.)

④[ちょっと考える気持ちを表す]

¶「映画を見に行きませんか。」(Eiga o mi ni ikimasen ka?)「そうですね。今度の日曜日なら大丈夫です。」 (Sō desu *ne*. Kondo no nichiyōbi nara daijōbu desu.)

* 質問に答える場合、「そうね (sō ne)」「そうですね (sō desu ne)」の形で使うことが多い。

✻「ねえ (nē)」と言う場合もある。

¶ This fish seems to have gone bad. [We]'d better not eat it.

¶ I'm going to buy pork for dinner— beef is so expensive, **you know.**

④ [used when thinking something over]

¶ "Won't you come see a movie?" "**Let's see.** I could go next Sunday."

* *Ne* is often used in the patterns "*Sō ne*," "*Sō desu ne*" when answering a question.

✻ Variant: *nē*.

nedan 値段〖名〗

¶このくつの値段はいくらですか。 (Kono kutsu no *nedan* wa ikura desu ka?)

¶この品物には値段がついていませんね。 (Kono shinamono ni wa *nedan* ga tsuite imasen ne.)

nedan 〖n〗 **price, cost**

¶ What is **the price** of these shoes?

¶ There's no **price** on this merchandise.

negai 願い〖名〗

①[希望]

平和の願い (heiwa no *negai*)

②[依頼]

¶これからもよろしくお願いします。 (Kore kara mo yoroshiku o*negai* shimasu.)

negai 〖n〗 **desire, wish; request**

① [desire, wish, hope]

hopes for peace, **a desire** for peace

② [request]

¶ **I hope** to continue to receive your kind offices on my behalf (a set polite expression).

negau 願う〖動Ⅰ〗

①〔希望する〕

¶みんなが世界の平和を願っています。
(Minna ga sekai no heiwa o *negatte* imasu.)

②〔頼む〕

¶絵に手を触れないように願います。
(E ni te o furenai yō ni *negaimasu*.)

neji ねじ〖名〗

ねじを締める (*neji* o shimeru) ねじを外す (*neji* o hazusu)

¶機械のねじが外れました。 (Kikai no *neji* ga hazuremashita.)

¶毎晩、寝る前に時計のねじを巻きます。(Maiban, neru mae ni tokei no *neji* o makimasu.)

nejiru ねじる〖動Ⅰ〗

¶そんなにねじったら，腕が折れます。
(Sonna ni *nejittara*, ude ga oremasu.)

neko ねこ〖名〗

nekutai ネクタイ〖名〗

ネクタイを締める (*nekutai* o shimeru) ネクタイを外す (*nekutai* o hazusu)

¶いいネクタイをしていますね。 (Ii *nekutai* o shite imasu ne.)

nemui 眠い〖形〗

眠くなる (*nemuku* naru)

¶ゆうべはあまりよく眠れなかったので，今日は眠いです。 (Yūbe wa amari yoku nemurenakatta node, kyō wa *nemui* desu.)

negau 〖vⅠ〗 **desire, wish, hope for; request, implore**

① [desire, wish, hope for]

¶ All **hope** 〖**pray**〗 for world peace.

② [request, implore]

¶ **Kindly refrain** from touching the paintings.

neji 〖n〗 **screw**

turn **a screw,** screw // unscrew

¶ **A screw** has come off 〖is coming off〗 the machine.

¶ [I] **wind** [my] watch 〖clock〗 every night at bedtime.

nejiru 〖vⅠ〗 **twist, wrench, wring**

¶ **If you twist** [my] arm like that, you'll break it.

neko 〖n〗 **cat**

nekutai 〖n〗 **necktie, tie**

tie **a necktie** // unite **a necktie,** take off **a tie**

¶ That's a nice **tie** you have on.

nemui 〖adj〗 **be sleepy**

become **sleepy**

¶ **I'm sleepy** today because I didn't sleep very well last night.

¶田中さんは眠そうな顔をしています。
(Tanaka san wa *nemusō* na kao o shite imasu.)

¶ [Mrs.] Tanaka **looks sleepy.**

nemuru 眠る〖動Ⅰ〗

nemuru 〚v I〛 **sleep, fall asleep**

¶赤ちゃんはよく眠っています。
(Akachan wa yoku *nemutte* imasu.)

¶ The baby **is sleeping** soundly.

¶一晩じゅう, 眠らないで勉強しました。 (Hitobanjū, *nemuranaide* benkyō shimashita.)

¶ [I] **stayed up** all night studying.

¶ゆうべはよく眠れましたか。 (Yūbe wa yoku *nemuremashita* ka?)

¶ **Did you sleep** well last night?

-nen -年〖尾〗

-nen 〚suf〛 **year**

¶わたしは1930年に生まれました。 (Watashi wa senkyūhyakusanjū*nen* ni umaremashita.)

¶ I was born in 1930.

¶弟は小学校3年です。 (Otōto wa shōgakkō san*nen* desu.)

¶ My younger brother is in the third **year** of elementary school.

nendo 年度〖名〗

nendo 〚n〛 **year, term, fiscal year, school year**

昨年度 (saku*nendo*) 来年度 (rai*nendo*) 新年度 (shin*nendo*) 年度末 (*nendo*matsu)

last **year**, the previous **fiscal year** // next **year**, the coming **fiscal year** // the new **year** 〚fiscal year〛 // the end of **the year** 〚fiscal year〛

¶日本では, 4月に新しい年度が始まります。 (Nihon de wa, shigatsu ni atarashii *nendo* ga hajimarimasu.)

¶ In Japan the new **fiscal** 〚**academic**〛 **year** begins in April.

¶今年度の予算はどのくらいですか。 (Kon*nendo* no yosan wa dono kurai desu ka?)

¶ What is the budget for the current **fiscal year?**

nenrei 年齢〖名〗

nenrei 〚n〛 **age, years**

¶ここに住所, 氏名, 年齢を書いてください。 (Koko ni jūsho, shimei, *nenrei* o kaite kudasai.)

¶ Please write your name, address, and **age** here.

⇒toshi 年

nenryō 燃料〖名〗

nenryō 〚n〛 **fuel**

¶自動車の燃料は普通はガソリンで

¶ Gasoline is **the fuel** usually used in

す。　(Jidōsha no *nenryō* wa futsū
wa gasorin desu.)

nerau　ねらう〚動Ⅰ〛

¶ねこがねずみをねらっています。

(Neko ga nezumi o *neratte* imasu.)

neru　寝る〚動Ⅱ〛

①[眠る]

¶あなたはいつも何時ごろ寝ますか。

(Anata wa itsu mo nanji goro
nemasu ka?)

¶わたしは夜寝る前に歯をみがきます。

(Watashi wa yoru *neru* mae ni ha
o migakimasu.)

②[病気で休む]

¶父は風邪を引いて寝ています。(Chi-
chi wa kaze o hiite *nete* imasu.)

③[体を横にする]

¶山田さんは寝ながら本を読んでいま
す。　(Yamada san wa *nenagara*
hon o yonde imasu.)

nesshin　熱心〚形動〛

¶あした試験があるので，学生はみん
な熱心に勉強しています。　(Ashita
shiken ga aru node, gakusei wa
minna *nesshin* ni benkyō shite imasu.)

¶中村さんは仕事に熱心な人です。

(Nakamura san wa shigoto ni
nesshin na hito desu.)

netsu　熱〚名〛

①[熱さを感じさせるもとになるもの]
¶太陽の熱で水が温かくなりました。

(Taiyō no *netsu* de mizu ga atatakaku narimashita.)

automobiles.

nerau 〚v I〛　**aim at, set one's
sights on, stalk**

¶ The cat **is stalking** a mouse.

neru 〚v II〛　**sleep, go to sleep; be
ill in bed; lie down**

① [sleep, go to sleep, go to bed]

¶ What time do you **go to bed** each
night?

¶ I brush my teeth before **going to
bed** at night.

② [be ill in bed, be confined to bed]

¶ My father **is in bed** with a cold.

③ [lie down, be lying down]

¶ [Mr.] Yamada **is lying down** and
reading a book.

nesshin 〚adj-v〛　**enthusiastic, eager, earnest, dedicated**

¶ All the students are studying **hard**
as they have an exam tomorrow.

¶ [Mr.] Nakamura is a **hard** worker.

netsu 〚n〛　**heat; temperature, fever**

① [heat]

¶ The water was warmed by **the sun.**

¶ナイロンは熱に弱いです。 (Nairon wa *netsu* ni yowai desu.)

②[体の温度]

熱がある (*netsu* ga aru)　熱が下がる (*netsu* ga sagaru)　熱を計る (*netsu* o hakaru)

¶子供が風邪を引いて熱を出しました。 (Kodomo ga kaze o hiite *netsu* o dashimashita.)

nezumi ねずみ〖名〗

ni 二〖名〗

二階 (*ni*kai)　二番め (*ni*banme)

ni に〖助〗

①[ものごとが存在しているところまたある状態で存在しているところなどを表す]

¶机の上に日本語の本があります。 (Tsukue no ue *ni* Nihongo no hon ga arimasu.)

¶わたしは東京に住んでいます。 (Watashi wa Tōkyō *ni* sunde imasu.)

¶空に白い雲が浮かんでいます。 (Sora *ni* shiroi kumo ga ukande imasu.)

¶この道をまっすぐ行くと，左手に海が見えます。 (Kono michi o massugu iku to, hidarite *ni* umi ga miemasu.)

¶りんごにはいろいろな種類があります。 (Ringo *ni* wa iroiro na shurui ga arimasu.)

②[移動などの方向や到達するところまた移動したものの存在するところなどを表す]

¶ Nylon has a low **heat** tolerance.

② [temperature, fever]

run **a temperature,** have **a fever** // **one's fever** goes down // take **one's temperature**

¶ The child has caught a cold and is running **a temperature** 〚The child caught a cold and had **a fever**〛.

nezumi 〚n〛 mouse, rat

ni 〚n〛 two

the **second** floor // the **second** one, **second**

ni 〚part〛 in, on, at, to, into, by, from, with, for

① [in, on; indicates where something exists or where it exists in a certain condition, etc.]

¶ There is a Japanese book **on** the desk.

¶ I live **in** Tokyo.

¶ A white cloud is floating **in** the sky.

¶ If you go straight along this road, you will be able to see the ocean **on** the left.

¶ There are various types **of** apples.

② [in, at; indicates the direction or stopping place of a movement, the present location of something that had been moving, etc.]

バスに乗る (basu *ni* noru) 山に登る (yama *ni* noboru)

¶わたしは毎朝8時に学校に来ます。(Watashi wa maiasa hachiji ni gakkō *ni* kimasu.)

¶この道をまっすぐ行って，二つめの角を左に曲がると，駅の前に出ます。(Kono michi o massugu itte, futatsume no kado o hidari *ni* magaru to, eki no mae *ni* demasu.)

¶わたしはゆうべ10時に東京駅に着きました。(Watashi wa yūbe jūji ni Tōkyō-eki *ni* tsukimashita.)

* 移動の方向を特に意識して言う場合には「へ (e)」を使うこともある。

→**e** へ

③[ある動作の成立の結果の存在するところなどを表す]

¶庭にすみれの花を植えました。(Niwa *ni* sumire no hana o uemashita.)

¶この紙にあなたの名前と生年月日を書いてください。(Kono kami *ni* anata no namae to seinengappi o kaite kudasai.)

¶壁に日本の地図がはってあります。(Kabe *ni* Nihon no chizu ga hatte arimasu.)

④[ものごとの成り行き・変化などの結果を表す]

¶夕方から雨は雪になりました。(Yūgata kara ame wa yuki *ni* narimashita.)

¶みかんは11月ごろになると，黄色になっておいしくなります。(Mikan

ride a bus; get **on** a bus // climb a mountain

¶ I come **to** school every day at eight o'clock.

¶ If you go straight along this street and turn left at the second corner, you will come out **in** front of the station.

¶ I arrived **at** Tokyo Station last night at ten o'clock.

* Sometimes *e* is used rather than *ni* when one is particularly conscious of the direction of the movement.

③ [in, on; indicates the location of the result of an action]

¶ [I] planted violets **in** the garden 〚yard〛.

¶ Please write your name and date of birth **on** this paper.

¶ There is a map of Japan fastened **on** the wall.

④ [to, into; indicates the result of a course of events, a change, etc.]

¶ In the evening the rain changed **into** snow.

¶ Mandarin oranges turn orange and become better-tasting around No-

wa jūichigatsu goro *ni* naru to,
kiiro *ni* natte oishiku narimasu.)

¶わたしは将来医者になるつもりです。
(Watashi wa shōrai isha *ni* naru
tsumori desu.)

¶交通信号が青から赤に変わりました。
(Kōtsū-shingō ga ao kara aka *ni*
kawarimashita.)

→to と

⑤[ものごとを決めたり選んだり変化
させたりするその結果を表す]

¶今日はこれで終わりにします。(Kyō
wa kore de owari *ni* shimasu.)

¶わたしは来月京都に行くことにしま
した。(Watashi wa raigetsu Kyōto
ni iku koto *ni* shimashita.)

¶わたしはコーヒーにします。(Watashi
wa kōhii *ni* shimasu.)

¶子供は人形を患者にして，注射をし
たり，薬を飲ませたりして遊んでいま
す。 (Kodomo wa ningyō o kanja
ni shite, chūsha o shitari, kusuri
o nomasetari shite asonde imasu.)

⑥[動作・作用の行われる時や場合な
どを表す]

¶わたしは毎朝7時に起きます。
(Watashi wa maiasa shichiji *ni*
okimasu.)

¶あなたは夏休みにどこかへ行きます
か。(Anata wa natsuyasumi *ni* doko ka e ikimasu ka?)

¶この地方では春の初めによく強い風
が吹きます。(Kono chihō de wa
haru no hajime *ni* yoku tsuyoi

vember.

¶ My future plan is to become a doctor.

¶ The traffic light turned from green
to red.

⑤ [indicates the result of deciding,
choosing, changing something, etc.]
¶ Let's stop here today.

¶ I've decided to go to Kyoto next
month.

¶ Coffee for me, please.

¶ The children are playing, pretend-
ing a doll is a patient and giving it
shots, making it take medicine, and
so forth.

⑥ [at, in, on; indicates the time or
occasion when an action or process
takes place]

¶ I get up **at** seven o'clock each
morning.

¶ Are you going to go somewhere
during summer vacation?

¶ There are often strong winds in this
region **in** early spring.

kaze ga fukimasu.)

¶お金は物を売ったり買ったりすると きにいつも使うものです。(Okane wa mono o uttari kattari suru toki *ni* itsu mo tsukau mono desu.)

⑦［動作などの向けられる相手・対象 などを表す］

¶わたしは昨日国の母に手紙を書きま した。 (Watashi wa kinō kuni no haha *ni* tegami o kakimashita.)

¶わたしは今日山田さんに会います。 (Watashi wa kyō Yamada san *ni* aimasu.)

¶漢字は、今から千七百年ぐらい前に 日本に伝えられたものです。 (Kanji wa, ima kara sennanahyakunen gurai mae ni Nihon *ni* tsutaerareta mono desu.)

¶わたしは上田さんには本当に親しみ を感じます。(Watashi wa Ueda san *ni* wa hontō ni shitashimi o kanjimasu.)

⑧［動作や状態の根拠・よりどころな どを表す］

¶雨にぬれた木の葉が、朝日にきらき ら光っています。 (Ame *ni* nureta konoha ga, asahi *ni* kirakira hikatte imasu.)

¶旗が風に静かに揺れています。(Hata ga kaze *ni* shizuka ni yurete imasu.)

¶今朝の天気予報によると，午後は晴 れるそうです。(Kesa no tenki-yohō *ni* yoru to, gogo wa hareru sō

¶ Money is something that is always used **when** buying and selling.

⑦ [to, toward, for; indicates the object of an action, etc.]

¶ Yesterday I wrote a letter **to** my mother back home.

¶ I am meeting [Miss] Yamada today.

¶ *Kanji* were introduced **to** Japan about 1,700 years ago.

¶ I really feel close **to** [Mrs.] Ueda.

⑧ [by, from, with; indicates the source of an action, condition, etc.]

¶ The leaves wet **by** the rain are shining **in** the morning sun.

¶ The flag [banner, pennant] is gently fluttering **in** the wind.

¶ **According to** this morning's weather report, it will be clear [will clear up, will stop raining] this after-

desu.)

⑨[ほかのものが影響を受ける動作・
作用の主体や動作の出所を表す]

¶わたしは先生にほめられました。
(Watashi wa sensei *ni* homeraremashita.)

¶昨日，雨に降られて風邪を引いてし
まいました。(Kinō, ame *ni* furarete
kaze o hiite shimaimashita.)

¶わたしは小学校の時，山田先生に教
わりました。(Watashi wa shōgakkō
no toki, Yamada sensei *ni* osowari-
mashita.)

¶旅行先でお金が足りなくなって，友
達に借りました。(Ryokō saki de
okane ga tarinaku natte, tomodachi *ni* karimashita.)

⑩[ほかの者から影響を受けて行う動
作の主体を表す]

¶先生は正しく言えるようになるまで，
何度も同じことを学生に言わせます。
(Sensei wa tadashiku ieru yō ni
naru made, nando mo onaji koto
o gakusei *ni* iwasemasu.)

¶母は今赤ん坊にミルクを飲ませてい
ます。(Haha wa ima akanbō *ni*
miruku o nomasete imasu.)

⑪[行く・来るなどの動作の目的を表
す]

¶姉は八百屋へりんごを買いに行きま
した。 (Ane wa yaoya e ringo o
kai *ni* ikimashita.)

¶母はデパートへ買い物に行きました。
(Haha wa depāto e kaimono *ni*

noon.

⑨ [by, from, with; indicates the
source or performer of an action or
operation that affects another]

¶ I received a compliment **from** my
teacher.

¶ Yesterday I got wet **in** the rain and
caught a cold.

¶ When I was in elementary school, I
was taught **by** [Mr.] Yamada.

¶ I ran out of money while traveling
and borrowed some **from** a friend.

⑩ [indicates the performer of an act
caused by someone else]

¶ The teacher makes the students say
the same thing over and over until
they can say it correctly.

¶ My mother is now nursing the
baby.

⑪ [for, to; indicates the purpose of
an act such as going or coming some-
where]

¶ My elder sister went 〚has gone〛 to
the fruit and vegetable store **to** buy
apples.

¶ My mother went 〚has gone〛 shop-ikimashita.)

¶わたしは日本へ文学の勉強に来ました。(Watashi wa Nihon e bungaku no benkyō *ni* kimashita.)

¶わたしはこれから新宿にいる友達の所へ遊びに行きます。(Watashi wa kore kara Shinjuku ni iru tomodachi no tokoro e asobi *ni* ikimasu.)

* 「動詞（基幹の形)＋に (ni)」の形と「名詞＋に (ni)」の形とがある。

⑫[動作の行われる目的などを表す]

¶「この機械は何に使いますか。」(Kono kikai wa nan *ni* tsukaimasu ka?)
「この機械は紙を切るのに使います。」(Kono kikai wa kami o kiru no *ni* tsukaimasu.)

¶大学に入るためにはもっと勉強しなければなりません。(Daigaku ni hairu tame *ni* wa motto benkyō shinakereba narimasen.)

¶外国の文化を正しく理解するには,その国に住むのがいちばんです。(Gaikoku no bunka o tadashiku rikai suru *ni* wa, sono kuni ni sumu no ga ichiban desu.)

* 「動詞（連体の形) ＋ に(ni)」の形や「動詞（連体の形) ＋ の (no)＋に (ni)」の形や「名詞 ＋ に(ni)」の形などがある。

⑬[比較・異同・評価などの基準を表す]

¶わたしのうちは駅に近いです。(Watashi no uchi wa eki *ni* chikai desu.)

ping at the department store.

¶ I came to Japan **to** study literature.

¶ I am now going **to** visit a friend at [his] place in Shinjuku.

* Used in the patterns "verb (stem form) + *ni*" and "noun + *ni*."

⑫ [for, to; indicates the purpose or objective of an act]

¶ "What is this device ⟦machine⟧ used **for?**"
"It is **for** cutting paper."

¶ **To** get into college, [you] must study harder.

¶ The best course **for** correctly understanding a foreign culture is to go and live in that country.

* Used in the patterns "verb (dictionary form) + *ni*," "verb (dictionary form) + *no* + *ni*," "noun + *ni*," etc.

⑬ [to, for; indicates the criterion of a comparison, difference, evaluation, etc.]

¶ My home is near the station.

¶山田さんはお母さんによく似ています。 (Yamada san wa okāsan *ni* yoku nite imasu.)

¶たばこは体に悪いです。 (Tabako wa karada *ni* warui desu.)

⑭［割合・割り当てなどの基準を表す］
¶紙は一人に二枚ずつ渡してください。 (Kami wa hitori *ni* nimai zutsu watashite kudasai.)

¶わたしは一か月に一度床屋へ行きます。 (Watashi wa ikkagetsu *ni* ichido tokoya e ikimasu.)

¶わたしは一日おきにおふろに入ります。 (Watashi wa ichinichi oki *ni* ofuro ni hairimasu.)

⑮［動作・作用・状態などの様子を表す］
¶本は横に一列に並べてください。 (Hon wa yoko *ni* ichiretsu *ni* narabete kudasai.)

¶わたしは辞書を引かずに日本語の新聞が読めるようになりました。 (Watashi wa jisho o hikazu *ni* Nihongo no shinbun ga yomeru yō ni narimashita.)

¶仕事は予定どおりにうまくいっています。 (Shigoto wa yotei doori *ni* umaku itte imasu.)

⑯［ある能力をもっている主体を表す］
¶この問題はわたしにはわかりません。 (Kono mondai wa watashi *ni* wa wakarimasen.)

¶わたしにはとてもあんな難しい本は読めません。 (Watashi *ni* wa totemo anna muzukashii hon wa yome-

¶ [Miss] Yamada looks a lot like [her] mother.

¶ Smoking is bad **for** the health.

⑭ [per, at, for; indicates the basic unit of a rate, apportioning, etc.]

¶ Please give **each** person two sheets of paper.

¶ I go to the barber **once** a month.

¶ I take a bath **every other** day.

⑮ [indicates the condition of an action, operation, state, etc.]

¶ Please lay the books down **in** a single row.

¶ I have become 〚became〛 able to read a Japanese newspaper **without** consulting a dictionary.

¶ The work is progressing well and **on** schedule.

⑯ [indicates a person having a certain ability]

¶ I don't understand this problem.

¶ I could never read such a difficult book.

masen.)

¶あの人にできることなら，わたしにもできると思います。 (Ano hito *ni* dekiru koto nara, watashi *ni* mo dekiru to omoimasu.)

¶ If **[he]** can do it, I think that **I** can, too.

niau 似合う〖動Ⅰ〗

¶その洋服はあなたによく似合いますよ。 (Sono yōfuku wa anata ni yoku *niaimasu* yo.)

niau 〚v I〛 **become, suit, match well**

¶ That outfit **looks** very **nice** on you.

-nichi -日〖尾〗

①[日付を表す]

¶今日は２月11日です。 (Kyō wa nigatsu jūichi*nichi* desu.)

*「11日(jūichinichi)」以降は「14日 (jūyokka)」，「20日 (hatsuka)」，「24日 (nijūyokka)」を除いて，すべて「～にち (～nichi)」と言う。

②[日数を表す]

¶今日は一日じゅう忙しかったです。 (Kyō wa ichi*nichi*jū isogashikatta desu.)

¶もう四，五日待ってください。 (Mō shi-go*nichi* matte kudasai.)

⇨-ka -日

-nichi 〚suf〛 the counter used for days of the month and for days

① [the counter for days of the month]

¶ Today is February **11.**

* -*nichi* is added to all the days of the month above 10 with the exception of the 14th (*jūyokka*), the 20th (*hatsuka*), and the 24th (*nijūyokka*).

② [the counter for days]

¶ [I] was busy all **day** today.

¶ Please wait four or five **days** longer.

nichiyō (bi) 日曜(日)〖名〗

nichiyō(bi) 〚n〛 **Sunday**

nigai 苦い〖形〗

¶この薬は苦いですね。 (Kono kusuri wa *nigai* desu ne.)

¶濃いコーヒーは苦くて飲めません。 (Koi kōhii wa *nigakute* nomemasen.)

nigai 〚adj〛 **bitter**

¶ This medicine **is bitter,** isn't it?

¶ Strong coffee **is too bitter** for [me] to drink.

nigatsu 二月〖名〗

nigeru 逃げる〖動Ⅱ〗

¶ねこが魚を取って逃げました。

nigatsu 〚n〛 **February**

nigeru 〚v II〛 **run away, flee, escape**

¶ The cat took the fish and **ran off**

(Neko ga sakana o totte *nige-mashita*.)

¶警官は逃げるどろぼうを追いかけました。(Keikan wa *nigeru* dorobō o oikakemashita.)

nigiyaka　にぎやか〖形動〗
¶市場はいつもにぎやかです。(Ichiba wa itsu mo *nigiyaka* desu.)
¶ここはずいぶんにぎやかな所ですね。(Koko wa zuibun *nigiyaka* na tokoro desu ne.)

nigoru　濁る〖動Ⅰ〗
¶雨で川の水が濁っています。 (Ame de kawa no mizu ga *nigotte* imasu.)

nihon　日本〖名〗
日本人 (*Nihon*jin)　日本語 (*Nihon*go)　日本料理 (*Nihon*-ryōri)
＊「にっぽん (Nippon)」とも言う。

nikki　日記〖名〗
¶わたしは毎日日記をつけています。(Watashi wa mainichi *nikki* o tsukete imasu.)

niku　肉〖名〗
肉屋 (*niku*ya)　牛肉 (gyū*niku*)　鳥肉 (tori*niku*)
¶豚肉を100グラムください。(Buta*niku* o hyakuguramu kudasai.)
¶この肉は柔らかくておいしいです。(Kono *niku* wa yawarakakute oishii desu.)

-nikui　-にくい〖尾〗
¶この字はたいへん書きにくいです。(Kono ji wa taihen kaki*nikui* de-

with it.

¶ The policeman chased after the **fleeing** thief.

nigiyaka 〖adj-v〗 **lively, bustling, flourishing, noisy**
¶ The market is always **crowded and bustling.**
¶ This is a very **lively** place.

nigoru 〖v Ⅰ〗 **become muddy, impure, cloudy**
¶ The river **is muddy** after the rain.

Nihon 〖n〗 **Japan**
a **Japanese**, the **Japanese** // the **Japanese** language // **Japanese** cooking, **Japanese** food
＊ Variant: Nippon.

nikki 〖n〗 **diary, journal**
¶ I make a **diary** entry every day.

niku 〖n〗 **meat, flesh**
a **meat** shop, a butcher's, a butcher // beef // (dressed) chicken, fowl
¶ Please give me one hundred grams of **pork.**
¶ This **meat** is nice and tender.

-nikui 〖suf〗 **hard to ～, difficult to ～**
¶ This character is very **difficult** to write.

su.)

¶その本の題は長くて覚えにくいです。 (Sono hon no dai wa nagakute oboe*nikui* desu.)

⇔-yasui -やすい

nimotsu 荷物〖名〗

¶わたしの荷物はこのかばんとかさだけです。 (Watashi no *nimotsu* wa kono kaban to kasa dake desu.)

¶ホテルに着くと、ボーイが荷物を部屋まで運んでくれました。 (Hoteru ni tsuku to, bōi ga *nimotsu* o heya made hakonde kuremashita.)

-nin -人〖尾〗

①［その仕事をする人，その状態にある人を表す］
病人 (byō*nin*)　けが人 (kega*nin*)
保証人 (hoshō*nin*)

②［人数を表す］

¶「御兄弟は何人ですか。」 (Gokyōdai wa nan*nin* desu ka?) 「兄が一人と姉が二人，わたしを入れて四人です。」 (Ani ga hitori to ane ga futari, watashi o irete yo*nin* desu.)

＊「一人 (ichinin)」「二人 (ninin)」とは言わないで，「一人 (hitori)」「二人 (futari)」と言う。「四人 (shinin)」と言わないで「四人 (yonin)」と言う。

ningen 人間〖名〗

①［ひと］
¶人間は考える動物です。 (*Ningen* wa kangaeru dōbutsu desu.)

②［人柄］

nimotsu 〖n〗 **load, burden, baggage, goods, freight, cargo, one's belongings,** etc.

¶ I have only this bag〚suitcase, briefcase, etc.〛and umbrella **with me.**

¶ When [we] arrived at the hotel, the bellboy took **[our] luggage** up to the room.

-nin 〖suf〗 a suffix indicating a person; the counter for people

① [indicates a person doing a particular job or action or a person in a particular state]
a sick **person,** a patient, an invalid // an injured **person,** the wounded // a guarantor, a sponsor, a reference

② [the counter for people]

¶ "**How many** brothers and sisters do you have?"

"I have one older brother and two older sisters so there are **four of us** in all."

＊ Irregular forms are *hitori* (one person) and *futari* (two persons). Also, "four persons" is *yonin*, not ＊ *shinin*.

ningen 〖n〗 **a human being, humanity; character, personality**

① [a human being, humanity]

¶ **Humans** are thinking creatures 〚animals with the power of reason〛.

② [character, personality]

¶あの人は正直な人間です。　(Ano hito wa shōjiki na *ningen* desu.)

¶ [He] is naturally honest.

ningyō　人形〖名〗

¶妹は人形を欲しがっています。 (Imōto wa *ningyō* o hoshigatte imasu.)

ningyō 〚n〛　doll, puppet

¶ My younger sister wants **a doll.**

ninki　人気〖名〗

¶山田先生は学生に人気があります。 (Yamada sensei wa gakusei ni *ninki* ga arimasu.)

¶あなたの国でいちばん人気のあるスポーツは何ですか。 (Anata no kuni de ichiban *ninki* no aru supōtsu wa nan desu ka?)

ninki 〚n〛　popularity; popular

¶ Professor Yamada **is popular** with students.

¶ What sport is most **popular** in your country?

ninzū　人数〖名〗

¶このクラスの人数は何人ですか。 (Kono kurasu no *ninzū* wa nannin desu ka?)

ninzū 〚n〛　the number of persons

¶ **How many are there** in this class?

nioi　におい〖名〗

いいにおい (ii *nioi*)　いやなにおい (iya na *nioi*)　臭いにおい (kusai *nioi*)　においをかぐ (*nioi* o kagu)

¶台所からおいしそうなにおいがしてきました。 (Daidokoro kara oishisō na *nioi* ga shite kimashita.)

nioi 〚n〛　smell, odor, scent

a nice **odor** // an unpleasant **smell** // an offensive **smell** // smell something

¶ **The aroma** of something good drifted out 〚is drifting out〛 from the kitchen.

niou　におう〖動Ⅰ〗

¶この花はあまりにおいませんね。 (Kono hana wa amari *nioimasen* ne.)

¶ガスがもれていませんか。においますよ。 (Gasu ga morete imasen ka? *Nioimasu* yo.)

niou 〚v I〛　smell, give off a smell, be fragrant, stink

¶ This flower **doesn't have** much **smell.**

¶ Is that gas leaking? **It smells** like it.

Nippon ☞ **Nihon**

niru　煮る〖動Ⅱ〗

¶今晩は野菜を煮て食べましょう。

niru 〚v II〛　boil, cook

¶ Let's have **boiled** 〚cooked〛 vege-

(Konban wa yasai o *nite* tabema-shō.)

¶この魚は煮るより焼いたほうがおいしいです。 (Kono sakana wa *niru* yori yaita hō ga oishii desu.)

niru 似る〖動Ⅱ〗

¶あなたはお母さんに顔がよく似ていますね。 (Anata wa okāsan ni kao ga yoku *nite* imasu ne.)

¶兄弟だから，声がとても似ています。 (Kyōdai da kara, koe ga totemo *nite* imasu.)

nishi 西〖名〗

西側 (*nishi*gawa) 西の風 (*nishi* no kaze)

¶太陽は東から出て，西に沈みます。 (Taiyō wa higashi kara dete, *nishi* ni shizumimasu.)

⇔**higashi** 東

niwa 庭〖名〗

¶庭に花が咲いています。 (*Niwa* ni hana ga saite imasu.)

¶わたしの家の庭は狭いです。 (Watashi no ie no *niwa* wa semai desu.)

niwatori 鶏〖名〗

no の〖助〗

①[前の名詞などがあとに来る名詞などをいろいろな意味で修飾限定する]

東京の地図 (Tōkyō *no* chizu) 子供のくつ (kodomo *no* kutsu) 日本語の先生 (Nihongo *no* sensei)

¶これはわたしの本です。 (Kore wa watashi *no* hon desu.)

¶あれは木の机です。 (Are wa ki *no*

tables tonight.

¶ This fish is better grilled than **boiled** 〚**poached**〛.

niru 〚v Ⅱ〛 resemble, look like, sound like

¶ Your face **looks** a lot **like** your mother's.

¶ As [they] are brothers, [their] voices **are** a lot **alike**.

nishi 〚n〛 west

the **western** side // a **west** wind, a wind from **the west**

¶ The sun rises in the east and sets in **the west.**

niwa 〚n〛 garden, yard

¶ Flowers are blooming in **the garden.**

¶ **The yard** at my house is small.

niwatori 〚n〛 chicken(s)

no 〚part〛 of, for, by, in, on

① [indicates that the noun or other words preceding it modifies or restricts in some way the noun following it]

a map **of** Tokyo // children**'s** shoes // a teacher **of** Japanese

¶ This is **my** book.

¶ That is a **wooden** desk.

tsukue desu.)

¶母からの手紙が今日着きました。

(Haha kara *no* tegami ga kyō tsu-kimashita.)

* 普通「名詞＋の (no)＋名詞」の形で使うが、「名詞＋助詞＋の (no)＋名詞」の形で使うこともある。「母からの手紙 (haha kara no tegami)」は「母から来た手紙 (haha kara kita tegami)」の意味である。

②〔前の名詞があとに来る動作や状態などを表す名詞に対してその主体や目的である関係を表す〕

¶子供がお父さんの帰りを待っています。 (Kodomo ga otōsan *no* kaeri o matte imasu.)

¶学校に着いた時，授業の始まりのベルが鳴っていました。(Gakkō ni tsu-ita toki, jugyō *no* hajimari no beru ga natte imashita.)

¶ようやく日本語の読み書きができるようになりました。(Yōyaku Nihongo *no* yomikaki ga dekiru yō ni nari-mashita.)

¶南の海の水の青さはすばらしかった。 (Minami no umi no mizu *no* aosa wa subarashikatta.)

*「お父さんの帰り (otōsan no ka-eri)」は「お父さんが帰る (otōsan ga kaeru)」，「授業の始まり (jugyō no hajimari)」は「授業が始まる (jugyō ga hajimaru)」，「日本語の読み書き (Nihongo no yomikaki)」は「日本語を読んだり書いたりする (Nihongo

¶ A letter **from** my mother arrived today.

* Usually used in the pattern "noun + *no* + noun" but can also be used in the pattern "noun + particle + *no* + noun." *Haha kara no tegami* (a letter from my mother) is equivalent to *haha kara kita tegami* (a letter coming from my mother).

② [indicates that the noun preceding it is the subject or object of the action, state, etc., expressed in the noun following it]

¶ The children are waiting for ⟦looking forward to⟧ the return **of** their father.

¶ When [I] arrived at school, the bell for the beginning **of** class was ring-ing.

¶ [I] have finally become ⟦I finally became⟧ able to read and write Japanese.

¶ The blue **of** the water of the south-ern sea was wonderful ⟦The southern sea was a marvelous blue⟧.

* In the above sentences *otōsan no kaeri* (the father's return) = *otōsan ga kaeru* (the father returns), *jugyō no hajimari* (the start of class) = *jugyō ga hajimaru* (class starts), *Nihongo no yomikaki* (the reading and writing of Japanese) =

o yondari kaitari suru)」、「南の海の
水の青さ (minami no umi no mizu
no aosa)」 は 「南の海の水が青い
(minami no umi no mizu ga aoi)」
という意味を表す。

③[動詞や形容詞・形容動詞などが名
詞を修飾する形で使われる場合その動
作や状態の主体や対象などを表す]

¶上田さんの乗っていた車が事故を起
こしました。 (Ueda san *no* notte
ita kuruma ga jiko o okoshima-
shita.)

¶天気のいい日にはよく散歩します。
(Tenki *no* ii hi ni wa yoku sanpo
shimasu.)

¶おすしのきらいな人はいませんか。
(Osushi *no* kirai na hito wa imasen ka?)

* この場合の「の (no)」は「が (ga)」
と置き換えられる。

no の〖助〗

①[所属その他いろいろな意味で関係
のあるものごとを表す]

¶「このペンはだれのですか。」 (Kono
pen wa dare *no* desu ka?) 「わたし
のです。」 (Watashi *no* desu.)

¶「大きいりんごは100円で、小さいの
は70円です。」 (Ookii ringo wa
hyakuen de, chiisai *no* wa nanajū-
en desu.) 「では、その100円のを5
個ください。」 (Dewa, sono hyakuen
no o goko kudasai.)

* 前の名詞に関係のあるものごとが場
面や文脈によってわかっているときに

Nihongo o yondari kaitari suru (to
read and write Japanese), and *minami no umi no mizu no aosa* (the blue
of the water of southern seas) =
minami no umi no mizu ga aoi (the
water of southern seas is blue).

③ [indicates the subject or object of
a verb, adjective, or adjective-verb in
a noun phrase]

¶ The car that [Mr.] Ueda was riding
in caused an accident.

¶ [I] often take a walk on days when
the weather is nice.

¶ Is there anyone here who doesn't
like *sushi*?

* This particular *no* can be replaced
by *ga*.

no 〚part〛 **one; that, those; thing,
matter**

① [one; stands in for something previously mentioned]

¶ "**Whose** pen is this?"
　 "It's **mine.**"

¶ "The large apples are a hundred
yen and the small **ones** are seventy
yen."

　 "Well, please give me five of the
hundred yen **ones.**"

* Used when the thing related to a
previous noun is understood from the
situation or context. In the above

使う。「だれの (dare no)」は「だれのペン (dare no pen)」、「わたしの (watashi no)」は「わたしのペン (watashi no pen)」、「100円の (hyakuen no)」は「100円のりんご (hyakuen no ringo)」の意味である。

②〔前に来る動詞や形容詞・形容動詞の表すことがらに関係のあるものごとを表す〕

¶あそこに並んでいるのは、バスに乗る人たちです。(Asoko ni narande iru *no* wa, basu ni noru hitotachi desu.)

¶本がたくさん並んでいますが、いちばんおもしろいのはどれですか。(Hon ga takusan narande imasu ga, ichiban omoshiroi *no* wa dore desu ka?)

* 前に来る動詞や形容詞・形容動詞の表すことがらに関係のあるものごとが場面や文脈によってわかっているときに使う。「あそこに並んでいるの (asoko ni narande iru no)」は「あそこに並んでいる人たち (asoko ni narande iru hitotachi)」、「おもしろいの (omoshiroi no)」は「おもしろい本 (omoshiroi hon)」の意味である。

③〔前に来る動詞や形容詞・形容動詞の表すことがらを名詞のような働きにするときに使う〕

¶寒い日に外へ出るのはいやです。(Samui hi ni soto e deru *no* wa iya desu.)

¶山田さんが向こうから急いで来るの

sentences *dare no* (whose) = *dare no pen* (whose pen), *watashi no* (mine) = *watashi no pen* (my pen), and *hyakuen no* (the hundred yen ones) = *hyakuen no ringo* (the hundred yen apples).

② [that, those; stands for something related to the verb, adjective, adjective-verb, or phrase preceding it]

¶ **The people** lined up over there are waiting for the bus (literally, **What** is lined up over there is people who are to board the bus).

¶ There are lots of books here. Which is the most interesting **one?**

* Used when the thing related to the verb, adjective, adjective-verb, or phrase coming before is understood from the situation or context. In the above sentences *asoko ni narande iru no* (that which is lined up over there) = *asoko ni narande iru hitotachi* (the people who are lined up over there), and *omoshiroi no* (the interesting one) = *omoshiroi hon* (an interesting book).

③ [thing, matter, the fact that; used to make the preceding verb, adjective, adjective-verb, or phrase into a noun]

¶ I dislike **going out** on cold days 〖**Going out** on cold days is unpleasant〗.

が見えました。 (Yamada san ga mukō kara isoide kuru *no* ga mie-mashita.)

¶このアパートは狭いのが欠点です。 (Kono apāto wa semai *no* ga ketten desu.)

④[見聞きしたことに対する事情や根拠などを尋ねるときに使う]

¶「どうかしたのですか。顔色が悪いですね。」 (Dō ka shita *no* desu ka? Kaoiro ga warui desu ne.) 「ええ、頭が痛いのです。」 (Ee, atama ga itai no desu.)

¶「テレビを買わないのですか。」 (Terebi o kawanai *no* desu ka?) 「ええ、お金がないのです。」 (Ee, okane ga nai no desu.)

*「ん (n)」とも言う。「～の [ん] か (～no [n] ka)」「～の [ん] ですか (～no [n] desu ka)」の形で使う。

⑤[ものごとに対する事情や根拠などを説明するのに使う]

¶「田中さんは今度の旅行には行かないそうですね。」(Tanaka san wa kondo no ryokō ni wa ikanai sō desu ne.) 「田中さんは病気なのだそうです。」 (Tanaka san wa byōki na *no* da sō desu.)

¶テレビを買いたいのですが、お金がありません。 (Terebi o kaitai *no* desu ga, okane ga arimasen.)

*「ん (n)」とも言う。「～の [ん] だ (～no [n] da)」「～の [ん] です (～no [n] desu)」の形で使う。

¶ [I] saw [Miss] Yamada **come hurrying** in my direction.

¶ **The smallness** of this apartment is a drawback [One disadvantage of this apartment is **its smallness**].

④ [used when inquiring about something one has observed]

¶ "Is something wrong? You look pale."

"Yes, I have a headache."

¶ "You aren't going to buy a television?"

"That's right. [I] don't have the money for it."

* This *no* is sometimes shortened to *n*. Used in the patterns "~ *no* ⟦*n*⟧ *ka*" and "~ *no* ⟦*n*⟧ *desu ka*."

⑤ [used when explaining about something]

¶ "I hear that [Mr.] Tanaka isn't coming on the next trip."

"They say [he]'s ill."

¶ I want to buy a television set but I don't have the money for it.

* This *no* is sometimes shortened to *n*. Used in the patterns "~ *no* ⟦*n*⟧ *da*" and "~ *no* ⟦*n*⟧ *desu*.

no の〖助〗

① [質問するときに使う]

¶その映画、どこで見たの。　(Sono eiga, doko de mita *no*?)

¶昨日はどこへ行ったの。　(Kinō wa doko e itta *no*?)

¶今日は忙しいの。(Kyō wa isogashii *no*?)

* 文末のイントネーションが上がる。

② [あることがらの事情や根拠などを説明するのに使う]

¶今日はおなかが痛いの。だから、あまり食べたくないわ。(Kyō wa onaka ga itai *no*. Dakara, amari tabeta-kunai wa.)

¶「今度の旅行には行かないの。」(Kondo no ryokō ni wa ikanai *no*?) 「ええ、来週から試験が始まるの。」(Ee, raishū kara shiken ga hajimaru *no*.)

* 文末のイントネーションが下がる。

*「のよ (no yo)」とも言う。

* 主に女性や子供が使うが、男性もかなり使うようになった。普通、目上の人には使わない。

nobasu 延ばす〖動Ⅰ〗

¶試験の時間を少し延ばしてください。(Shiken no jikan o sukoshi *noba-shite* kudasai.)

¶用事ができたので、旅行の出発を1日延ばしました。(Yōji ga dekita node, ryokō no shuppatsu o ichi-nichi *nobashimashita*.)

nobasu 伸ばす〖動Ⅰ〗

no 〚part〛 a sentence-ending particle

① [used when asking a question]

¶ Where did [you] see that movie?

¶ Where did [you] go yesterday?

¶ Are [you] busy today?

* With this use of *no*, there is a rise in intonation at the end of the sentence.

② [used when explaining about something]

¶ I have a stomachache today. That's why I don't feel much like eating.

¶ "You aren't going on the coming trip?"

"That's right. Exams start next week."

* With this use of *no*, there is a falling intonation at the end of the sentence.

* Variant: *no yo*.

* Mainly used by women and children but also used by men quite a bit now. Usually not used towards those of higher status.

nobasu 〚v I〛 postpone, delay, extend, prolong

¶ Please **give** us a little **more time** for the exam.

¶ Something came up so [I] **postponed** [my] departure date a day.

nobasu 〚v I〛 lengthen, extend, stretch, spread out, unbend

546

背中を伸ばす (senaka o *nobasu*)
才能を伸ばす (sainō o *nobasu*)
¶本はたなの上の方にあるので，手を伸ばしても届きません。 (Hon wa tana no ue no hō ni aru node, te o *nobashite* mo todokimasen.)

nobiru 延びる〖動Ⅱ〗
¶昼休みの時間が 15 分延びました。 (Hiruyasumi no jikan ga jūgofun *nobimashita*.)
¶会議が延びて夕方までかかってしまいました。 (Kaigi ga *nobite* yūgata made kakatte shimaimashita.)

nobiru 伸びる〖動Ⅱ〗
①[長くなる]
¶髪が伸びたので，床屋へ行きました。 (Kami ga *nobita* node, tokoya e ikimashita.)
¶中学生になって，子供の背が急に伸びました。 (Chūgakusei ni natte, kodomo no se ga kyū ni *nobimashita*.)
¶この木は1年に5センチぐらい伸びます。 (Kono ki wa ichinen ni gosenchi gurai *nobimasu*.)
②[能力などが発達する]
¶去年に比べて今年は成績がずいぶん伸びました。 (Kyonen ni kurabete kotoshi wa seiseki ga zuibun *nobimashita*.)

nobori 上り〖名〗
①[下から上へ移ること，上り坂]
¶この道はあの木の所から上りになります。 (Kono michi wa ano ki no

stretch, straighten up // **develop** one's abilities, **cultivate** one's talent
¶ Since the book is towards the top of the bookcase [I] can't reach it.

nobiru 〚v II〛 be postponed, be delayed, be prolonged
¶ The noon break **has been extended** by 15 minutes.

¶ The meeting **stretched out** into the evening.

nobiru 〚v II〛 extend, lengthen, increase, grow; advance, make progress
① [extend, lengthen, increase, grow]
¶ [My] hair **grew out** and [I] went to the barber's.

¶ The child's height suddenly **shot up** after [he] entered middle school.

¶ This tree **grows** about five centimeters a year.

② [advance, make progress]
¶ Compared to last year, this year's record **has improved** considerably.

nobori 〚n〛 ascent, rise, going up; train bound for a major city
① [ascent, rise, going up]
¶ This road starts **going uphill** from

tokoro kara *nobori* ni narimasu.)

②〔地方から中心的な所へ行く汽車・電車〕

上り列車 (*nobori*ressha)

⇔kudari 下り

noboru 上る〔動Ⅰ〕

¶その階段は上るのがたいへんです。

(Sono kaidan wa *noboru* no ga taihen desu.)

⇔kudaru 下る

noboru 登る〔動Ⅰ〕

¶わたしはまだその山に登ったことがありません。 (Watashi wa mada sono yama ni *nobotta* koto ga arimasen.)

¶子供が木に登って遊んでいます。

(Kodomo ga ki ni *nobotte* asonde imasu.)

noboru 昇る〔動Ⅰ〕

¶東の空に太陽が昇りました。

(Higashi no sora ni taiyō ga *noborimashita.*)

nochi 後〔名〕

¶今日の天気は晴れ後曇りです。

(Kyō no tenki wa hare *nochi* kumori desu.)

¶また後ほどお電話します。 (Mata *nochi* hodo odenwa shimasu.)

node ので〔助〕

¶雨が降っているので，今日はテニスができません。 (Ame ga futte iru *node*, kyō wa tenisu ga dekimasen.)

¶ゆうべ遅くまで起きていたので，今日はとても眠いです。 (Yūbe osoku

that tree over there.

② [train going from the country into a major city]

the **ingoing** train, the **up** train

noboru 〚v I〛 climb, go up, mount, ascend

¶ **Climbing** those stairs is hard work.

noboru 〚v I〛 climb

¶ I haven't **climbed** that mountain yet.

¶ The children are playing, **climbing** trees.

noboru 〚v I〛 rise

¶ The sun **rose** in the eastern skies.

nochi 〚n〛 after, afterwards, later, in future

¶ The weather for today will be clear, **later** cloudy.

¶ I will call again **later** (polite, spoken on the telephone).

node 〚part〛 as, because, on account of, owing to

¶ [We] can't play tennis today—it's raining.

¶ [I] was up until late last night **so** [I] am very sleepy today.

made okite ita *node*, kyō wa totemo nemui desu.)

¶暑いので，上着を脱いで仕事をしました。 (Atsui *node,* uwagi o nuide shigoto o shimashita.)

¶部屋が静かなので，落着いて勉強ができました。 (Heya ga shizuka na *node,* ochitsuite benkyō ga dekimashita.)

¶日曜日なので，今日は電車がすいています。 (Nichiyōbi na *node,* kyō wa densha ga suite imasu.)

＊ 前件が原因となり，後件がその結果として成立するという原因結果の関係を表す。普通，後件には結果としての客観的な言い方が来る。

⇨**kara** から

nodo のど〖名〗

¶風邪を引いて，のどが痛いです。 (Kaze o hiite, *nodo* ga itai desu.)

¶のどが渇いたから，お茶が飲みたいです。 (*Nodo* ga kawaita kara, ocha ga nomitai desu.)

nōgyō 農業〖名〗

農業高校 (*nōgyō*-kōkō) 農業技術者 (*nōgyō*-gijutsusha)

¶この国の農業技術はかなり進んでいます。 (Kono kuni no *nōgyō*-gijutsu wa kanari susunde imasu.)

nohara 野原〖名〗

¶山を越えると，広い野原があります。 (Yama o koeru to, hiroi *nohara* ga arimasu.)

nōka 農家〖名〗

¶ **It was so hot that** [I] took off [my] suit jacket and worked in [my] shirt-sleeves.

¶ [I] was able to settle down and study **as** the room was quiet.

¶ The trains aren't crowded today **because** it's Sunday.

＊ Expresses a cause-and-effect relationship, with the cause stated in the first, *node*-clause and the effect in the second clause. Usually this result or effect is stated objectively.

nodo 〖n〗 throat, voice

¶ I have a sore **throat** from a cold.

¶ I'm **thirsty** and would like some (green) tea to drink.

nōgyō 〖n〗 agriculture, farming
an **agricultural** high school // an **agricultural** expert

¶ **Farming** methods are quite advanced in this country.

nohara 〖n〗 field, plain, plains
¶ There is a broad **plain** on the other side of the mountain.

nōka 〖n〗 farmhouse; farm family, farmer

①[農民の住んでいる家]

¶畑の向こうに農家が1軒見えます。
(Hatake no mukō ni *nōka* ga ikken miemasu.)

②[農業で生活している家庭]

¶わたしは農家に生まれました。
(Watashi wa *nōka* ni umaremashita.)

nokoru 残る〖動Ⅰ〗

①[余る]

¶昨日のごちそうがまだたくさん残っています。 (Kinō no gochisō ga mada takusan *nokotte* imasu.)

¶残った御飯を捨てないでください。
(*Nokotta* gohan o sutenaide kudasai.)

②[後までその場所にいる]

¶中村さんはまだ会社に残って仕事をしています。 (Nakamura san wa mada kaisha ni *nokotte* shigoto o shite imasu.)

nokosu 残す〖動Ⅰ〗

①[余らせる]

¶食べ物は残さないで全部食べなさい。
(Tabemono wa *nokosanaide* zenbu tabenasai.)

②[後にとどめる]

¶田中さんは家族を残して，一人で外国へ行きました。 (Tanaka san wa kazoku o *nokoshite*, hitori de gaikoku e ikimashita.)

nomimono 飲み物〖名〗

¶飲み物は何がいいですか。 (*Nomimono* wa nani ga ii desu ka?)

nokoru 〚v I〛 remain, be left; remain, stay

① [remain, be left, be left over]
¶ There **is** still a lot of food **left** from yesterday's party 〚dinner, etc.〛.

¶ Please don't throw out the **leftover** rice 〚**the leftovers**〛.

② [remain, stay, stay on]
¶ [Mr.] Nakamura is **still** at the office working.

nokosu 〚v I〛 leave, set aside; leave, leave behind

① [leave, set aside]
¶ Clean up your plate(s).

② [leave, leave behind]
¶ [Mr.] Tanaka **left** [his] family **behind** and went abroad alone.

nomimono 〚n〛 a drink, a beverage
¶ What would you like **to drink?**

① [farmhouse]
¶ **A farmhouse** is in sight across the field.

② [farm family, farmer]
¶ I was born into **a farm family.**

⇨**tabemono** 食べ物

nomu 飲む〖動Ⅰ〗

水を飲む (mizu o *nomu*)　酒を飲む
(sake o *nomu*)　薬を飲む (kusuri
o *nomu*)

¶ビールを飲みに行きませんか。
(Biiru o *nomi* ni ikimasen ka?)

noni のに〖助〗

¶あの人はこんなに暑いのに, セータ
ーを着ています。　(Ano hito wa
konna ni atsui *noni*, sētā o kite
imasu.)

¶今日は日曜日なのに, 学校へ行くの
ですか。　(Kyō wa nichiyōbi na
noni, gakkō e iku no desu ka?)

¶みんな遊んでいるのに, あの人だけ
勉強しています。　(Minna asonde
iru *noni*, ano hito dake benkyō
shite imasu.)

¶一生懸命に勉強したのに, 大学の
入学試験にとうとう受かりませんで
した。　(Isshōkenmei ni benkyō
shita *noni*, daigaku no nyūgaku-
shiken ni tōtō ukarimasen deshita.)

＊前件のことがらと後件のことがら
との相いれない関係を表す。予期する
ことがらと反対のことがらが起こるよ
うな場合に使う。後件には,「～う(よ
う)(～u [yō])」などの意志,「～なさ
い (～nasai)」などの命令,「～てく
ださい (～te kudasai)」などの依頼,
「～てもいい (～te mo ii)」などの許
可などの言い方は来ない。

nori のり〖名〗

nomu 〖v I〗　drink, swallow

drink water, **have a drink of** water
// **take** a drink; **drink** *sake* // **take**
medicine

¶ Won't you come and **have** some
beer with [us]?

noni 〖part〗　though, although, in
spite of

¶ [He] is wearing a sweater **even
though** it is so hot.

¶ Are you going to school today
even though it's Sunday?

¶ [He] alone is studying **while** everyone else is taking the day off.

¶ **In spite** of studying hard, in the
end [I] didn't pass [my] university entrance exams.

＊ Used when the first clause and the
second clause are not in conformity
with each other, such as when the
opposite of what would be expected
has happened. The second clause
does not end with an expression of
intent such as *-ō* 〖*-yō*〗, an order with
-nasai, a request with *-te kudasai*, or
a giving of permission such as *-te mo
ii*.

nori 〖n〗　paste, starch

のりではる (*nori* de haru)　のりを
つける (*nori* o tsukeru)
¶切手にのりをつけて封筒にはります。
(Kitte ni *nori* o tsukete fūtō ni
harimasu.)

norikae　乗り換え〚名〛
¶電車で行くと，乗り換えが多くてめ
んどうです。　(Densha de iku to,
norikae ga ookute mendō desu.)

norikaeru　乗り換える〚動Ⅱ〛
¶東京駅へ行くのには，どこで乗り換
えたらいいですか。　(Tōkyō-eki e
iku no ni wa, doko de *norikaetara*
ii desu ka?)
¶次の駅で乗り換えてください。
(Tsugi no eki de *norikaete* kudasai.)

norimono　乗り物〚名〛
¶乗り物には，汽車，電車，船，飛行機，
自動車などがあります。（*Norimono*
ni wa, kisha, densha, fune, hikōki,
jidōsha nado ga arimasu.)

nōritsu　能率〚名〛
能率がいい (*nōritsu* ga ii)　能率が
悪い (*nōritsu* ga warui)　能率が上
がる (*nōritsu* ga agaru)　能率が下
がる (*nōritsu* ga sagaru)
¶コンピューターのおかげで，事務の
能率がたいへん上がりました。
(Konpyūtā no okage de, jimu no
nōritsu ga taihen agarimashita.)

noru　乗る〚動Ⅰ〛
①〔人などが乗り物などで移動する〕
電車に乗る (densha ni *noru*)　自動

paste on, fasten with **paste** // apply
paste, paste together
¶[I] **paste** the stamp on the envelope.

norikae 〚n〛　**transfer, change** (of
train, plane, bus, etc.)
¶ The large number of **transfers** is a
nuisance when one goes there by
train.

norikaeru 〚v II〛　**to transfer,
change** (trains, planes, buses, etc.)
¶ Where **should I transfer** in order
to go to Tokyo Station?

¶ Please **transfer** at the next station.

norimono 〚n〛　**vehicle, con-
veyance**
¶ Types of **vehicles** include trains
〚steam and electric trains〛, ships, airplanes, automobiles, and the like.

nōritsu 〚n〛　**efficiency**
be efficient // be inefficient // become efficient // become inefficient

¶ Thanks to computers, [our] office
efficiency has been 〚was〛 greatly increased.

noru 〚v I〛　**ride, get on, board; step
on, mount**
① [ride, get on, board, take (a vehicle)]
ride a train; **board** a train // **ride** in

車に乗る (jidōsha ni *noru*) 馬に乗る (uma ni *noru*)

¶このバスは乗る時に料金を払います。 (Kono basu wa *noru* toki ni ryōkin o haraimasu.)

②[人や動物などが台などの上に上る]

¶いすの上に乗ってたなの物を取りました。 (Isu no ue ni *notte* tana no mono o torimashita.)

noru　載る〖動Ⅰ〗

①[何かの上に置いてある]

¶机の上に載っている辞書を取ってください。 (Tsukue no ue ni *notte* iru jisho o totte kudasai.)

②[新聞や本などに掲載される]

¶この言葉は辞書に載っていません。 (Kono kotoba wa jisho ni *notte* imasen.)

¶今朝の新聞にあなたの国のことが載っていました。 (Kesa no shinbun ni anata no kuni no koto ga *notte* imashita.)

nōryoku　能力〖名〗

能力がある (*nōryoku* ga aru) 能力がない (*nōryoku* ga nai)

¶あの人は，すばらしい計算の能力を持っています。(Ano hito wa, subarashii keisan no *nōryoku* o motte imasu.)

¶わたしの能力では，この仕事はできません。 (Watashi no *nōryoku* de wa, kono shigoto wa dekimasen.)

noseru　乗せる〖動Ⅱ〗

¶わたしはおばあさんをバスに乗せて

a car; **get in** a car // **ride** a horse; **mount** a horse

¶ With this type of bus, one pays when **getting on.**

② [step on, mount (a platform, etc.)]

¶ [I] **stepped** on top of a chair and took something off the shelf.

noru 〚v I〛 **lie on, be on top of; be recorded, be mentioned**

① [lie on, be on top of, rest on]

¶ Please hand me the dictionary **sitting** on the desk.

② [be recorded, be mentioned, appear, be published (in a newspaper, book, etc.)]

¶ This word **isn't in** the dictionary.

¶ There **was something** about your country **in** the newspaper this morning.

nōryoku 〚n〛 **ability, capability, capacity**

able, capable, competent // incapable, incompetent

¶ [He] has a marvelous **head** for figures.

¶ This job is beyond my **abilities.**

noseru 〚v II〛 **carry, take on board, place on board** (a train, bus, etc.)

あげました。 (Watashi wa obāsan o basu ni *nosete* agemashita.)

¶ I **helped** the old lady **onto** the bus.

noseru 載せる〖動Ⅱ〗

noseru 〚v Ⅱ〛 **place on; record, mention**

①[物を何かの上に置く]

① [place on, set on, lay on]

¶この箱の上には, 何も載せないでください。 (Kono hako no ue ni wa, nani mo *nosenaide* kudasai.)

¶ Please **don't put** anything **on** top of this box 〚case, casket, chest, etc.〛.

¶机の上に載せておいた万年筆を知りませんか。 (Tsukue no ue ni *nosete* oita mannenhitsu o shirimasen ka?)

¶ Do you know what happened to the fountain pen I left **on** the desk?

②[新聞や本などに掲載する]

② [record, mention, publish, carry]

¶この小説は何という雑誌に載せるのですか。 (Kono shōsetsu wa nan to iu zasshi ni *noseru* no desu ka?)

¶ What magazine is this novel going **to be published** in?

nōto ノート〖名〗

nōto 〚n〛 **notebook; notes**

①[ノートブック, 帳面]

① [notebook]

¶かばんの中には本やノートなどが入っています。 (Kaban no naka ni wa hon ya *nōto* nado ga haitte imasu.)

¶ The briefcase 〚bag, etc.〛 contains books, **notebooks,** etc.

②[書き留めること]

② [notes]

ノートをとる (*nōto* o toru)

take **notes**

nozoku 除く〖動Ⅰ〗

nozoku 〚v Ⅰ〛 **remove, eliminate; exclude, except, omit**

①[不必要なものなどを取り去る]

① [remove, eliminate, get rid of]

¶この中から腐ったみかんを除いて, いいみかんだけ残してください。 (Kono naka kara kusatta mikan o *nozoite* ii mikan dake nokoshite kudasai.)

¶ Please **take out** the spoiled mandarin oranges and leave just the good ones here.

②[ある範囲から外す]

② [exclude, except, omit]

¶その計画にはわたしを除いてみんなが賛成しました。 (Sono keikaku ni wa watashi o *nozoite* minna ga sansei shimashita.)

¶ All approved the plan **except for** me.

nozoku のぞく〖動Ⅰ〗

nozoku 〚v Ⅰ〛 **take a look; peek, take a peek**

①[窓やすき間などから向こうを見る]
¶窓から部屋の中を**のぞきました。**
(Mado kara heya no naka o *nozo-kimashita.*)
②[ちょっと見る，何かの一部分を見る]
¶試験のときには，隣の人の答えを**の
ぞいて**はいけません。 (Shiken no
toki ni wa, tonari no hito no kotae
o *nozoite* wa ikemasen.)

nugu 脱ぐ〖動Ⅰ〗
服を**脱ぐ** (fuku o *nugu*) ズボンを
脱ぐ (zubon o *nugu*) くつ下を**脱ぐ**
(kutsushita o *nugu*)
¶日本の家では，普通くつを**脱いで**部
屋に上がります。 (Nihon no ie
de wa, futsū kutsu o *nuide* heya
ni agarimasu.)
⇔**kiru** 着る **haku** はく

nukeru 抜ける〖動Ⅱ〗
①[離れて取れる]
髪の毛が**抜ける** (kaminoke ga *nu-keru*) 歯が**抜ける** (ha ga *nukeru*)
②[あるべきものが脱落する]
¶この本は1ページ**抜けて**います。
(Kono hon wa ippēji *nukete* imasu.)
③[もれる，なくなる]
¶タイヤの空気が**抜けて**います。
(Taiya no kūki ga *nukete* imasu.)

nuku 抜く〖動Ⅰ〗
くぎを**抜く** (kugi o *nuku*) 毛を**抜
く** (ke o *nuku*) 草を**抜く** (kusa o
nuku) 歯を**抜く** (ha o *nuku*)
¶もう一本ビールのせんを**抜きましょ**

① [take a look, look out, look in, peer at]
¶ **I looked** through the window into the room.
② [peek, take a peek, peep]

¶ One mustn't **look at** the answers of the person next to one during an exam.

nugu 〖v I〗 **take off** (an item of clothing)
undress // **take off** one's pants 〖trousers, slacks〗 // **take off** one's socks 〖stockings〗
¶ In Japan one usually **takes off** one's shoes at the door before going inside.

nukeru 〖v II〗 **come out, fall off; be missing, be omitted; escape, leak**
① [come out, fall off, become loose] one's hair **falls out,** one's hair **thins** // a tooth **comes out**
② [be missing, be omitted, be left out, be lacking]
¶ This book **is missing** a page.
③ [escape, leak, be gone]
¶ The air **is leaking** from the tire 〖The tire is flat〗.

nuku 〖v I〗 **pull out, extract, remove**
pull out a nail 〖spike, etc.〗 // **pull out** a hair // to weed, **pull out** weeds // **pull out** 〖**extract**〗 a tooth

うか｡ (Mō ippon biiru no sen o *nukimashō* ka?)

nuno 布〚名〛
布切れ (*nuno*gire) 布地 (*nuno*ji)
布製 (*nuno*sei)

nureru ぬれる〚動Ⅱ〛
¶かさを持って行かなかったので、雨にぬれてしまいました。 (Kasa o motte ikanakatta node, ame ni *nurete* shimaimashita.)
¶ぬれたシャツを着ていると、風邪を引きます。 (*Nureta* shatsu o kite iru to, kaze o hikimasu.)

nuru 塗る〚動Ⅰ〛
¶パンにバターを塗って食べます。 (Pan ni batā o *nutte* tabemasu.)
¶この腰掛けはペンキを塗ったばかりです。 (Kono koshikake wa penki o *nutta* bakari desu.)

nurui ぬるい〚形〛
¶早く飲まないと、コーヒーがぬるくなります。 (Hayaku nomanai to, kōhii ga *nuruku* narimasu.)

nusumu 盗む〚動Ⅰ〛
¶昨日店にどろぼうが入って、100万円盗んでいきました。 (Kinō mise ni dorobō ga haitte, hyakuman'en *nusunde* ikimashita.)
¶わたしは電車の中で財布を盗まれました。 (Watashi wa densha no naka de saifu o *nusumaremashita*.)

nuu 縫う〚動Ⅰ〛
¶わたしは自分で着物を縫います。 (Watashi wa jibun de kimono o

¶ Shall I open another bottle of beer (literally, **take** the cap **off**)?

nuno 〚n〛 **cloth**
a piece of **cloth** // **cloth, fabric** // **cloth,** made of **cloth**

nureru 〚v Ⅱ〛 **get wet, be wet, be damp**
¶ [I] didn't have an umbrella with [me] so [I] **got wet** in the rain.
¶ You will catch cold if you wear a **wet** shirt.

nuru 〚v Ⅰ〛 **to paint, varnish, plaster,** etc.
¶ [I] eat **buttered** bread 〚toast, rolls, etc.〛.
¶ This bench 〚seat, chair, stool, etc.〛 has just **been painted.**

nurui 〚adj〛 **tepid, lukewarm, not hot enough**
¶ [Your] coffee will **get cold** if [you] don't hurry up and drink it.

nusumu 〚v Ⅰ〛 **steal, rob**
¶ Burglars broke into my store 〚the store where I work〛 yesterday and **stole** a million yen.
¶ I **had** my wallet **stolen** on the train.

nuu 〚v Ⅰ〛 **sew, stitch**
¶ I **make** my own clothes.

nuimasu.)

nyū- 入-〖頭〗

入場 (*nyūjō*) 入場券 (*nyūjōken*)
入荷 (*nyūka*) 入港 (*nyūkō*) 入
国 (*nyūkoku*)

nyūgaku 入学〖名, ～する〗

入学式 (*nyūgakushiki*) 入学試験
(*nyūgaku*-shiken) 入学願書 (*nyūgaku*-gansho)

¶わたしの息子は今年小学校に入学
しました。(Watashi no musuko wa
kotoshi shōgakkō ni *nyūgaku* shimashita.)

⇔sotsugyō 卒業

nyūin 入院〖名, ～する〗

入院生活 (*nyūin*-seikatsu)

¶長い間入院していましたが, あした
やっと退院できるようになりました。
(Nagai aida *nyūin* shite imashita
ga, ashita yatto taiin dekiru yō ni
narimashita.)

¶田中さんはあした入院するそうで
す。(Tanaka san wa ashita *nyūin*
suru sō desu.)

⇔taiin 退院

nyūsu ニュース〖名〗

¶わたしは毎朝ラジオのニュースを聞
きます。(Watashi wa maiasa rajio
no *nyūsu* o kikimasu.)

¶山田さんが結婚したというニュース
を知っていますか。(Yamada san
ga kekkon shita to iu *nyūsu* o
shitte imasu ka?)

nyū- 〖pref〗 a prefix meaning entering

admission, entrance // a ticket of
admission, entry ticket // the **receipt** of goods // **entry** (into a port)
// **entry** into a country, immigration

nyūgaku 〖n, ～*suru*〗 **entrance or
admission into some sort of
school**

an **entrance** ceremony // a (school)
entrance exam // application for
admission (to a school)

¶ My son **entered** elementary school
this year.

nyūin 〖n, ～*suru*〗 **admission to a
hospital, hospitalization**
one's days **while in the hospital**

¶ [I] have **been in the hospital** for a
long time but tomorrow [I] can finally go home.

¶ I hear that [Mrs.] Tanaka is **going
into the hospital** tomorrow.

nyūsu 〖n〗 **news**

¶ I listen to **the news** on the radio
every morning.

¶ Did you hear **the news?** [Miss]
Yamada has gotten married.

O

o- お-〖頭〗

①［尊敬の気持ちを表す］

お考え (okangae) お元気 (ogenki)

¶お名前は何とおっしゃいますか。
(Onamae wa nan to osshaimasu
ka?)

¶このごろお忙しいようですね。(Ko-
no goro oisogashii yō desu ne.)

¶社長は，今新聞をお読みになってい
ます。(Shachō wa, ima shinbun o
oyomi ni natte imasu.)

¶あなたの手紙を読んで，ご家族の方
はお喜びなさるでしょう。(Anata no
tegami o yonde, gokazoku no kata
wa oyorokobi nasaru deshō.)

¶上田先生がわたしたちに英語をお教
えくださいました。(Ueda sensei ga
watashitachi ni Eigo o ooshie kudasaimashita.)

* 動詞の場合，「お(o)＋動詞（基幹の
形)＋になる (ni naru)」，「お (o)＋動
詞 (基幹の形)＋なさる (nasaru)」，
「お (o)＋動詞（基幹の形)＋くださる
(kudasaru)」などの形で使う。

②［謙譲の気持ちを表す］

¶あとでお電話するか，お手紙を差し
上げます。(Ato de odenwa suru ka,
otegami o sashiagemasu.)

¶その荷物をお持ちしましょう。(Sono
nimotsu o omochi shimashō.)

¶先生に旅行の写真をお見せいたしま

---

o- [[pref]] a prefix expressing respect,
humility, or politeness

① [used to express respect]

(your) idea, (your) thinking // (your)
being healthy

¶ What is your name?

¶ You seem to be busy these days.

¶ The company president is reading
the newspaper now.

¶ Your family will undoubtedly be
happy to receive your letter.

¶ Professor Ueda taught us English.

* *o-* expressing respect is used with
verbs in the patterns "*o-* + verb
(stem form) + *ni naru*," "*o-* + verb
(stem form) + *nasaru*," "*o-* + verb
(stem form) + *kudasaru*," etc.

② [used to express humility]

¶ I will call or write later.

¶ Shall I carry that package [bag,
etc.] for you?

¶ I showed my teacher [doctor]

した。(Sensei ni ryokō no shashin o *o*mise itashimashita.)

* 動詞の場合、「お (o)＋動詞（基幹の形）＋する (suru)」、「お (o)＋動詞（基幹の形)＋いたす (itasu)」などの形で使う。

③[丁寧の気持ちを表す]
お酒 (*o*sake) お寒い (*o*samui)
¶お茶とお菓子を買ってきました。(O-cha to *o*kashi o katte kimashita.)
* 外来語にはつきにくい。また、「応接間 (ōsetsuma)」などのように「お (o)」で始まる言葉にもつきにくい。
⇨go- 御-

o 　を〚助〛
①[動作の目的・対象などを表す]
¶わたしは小説を読むのが好きです。
(Watashi wa shōsetsu o yomu no ga suki desu.)
¶上田さんはセーターを着ています。
(Ueda san wa sētā o kite imasu.)
¶先生は学生に答えを言わせます。
(Sensei wa gakusei ni kotae o iwa-semasu.)
¶山田さんはときどき変な質問をして、先生を困らせます。(Yamada san wa tokidoki hen na shitsumon o shite, sensei o komarasemasu.)
②[移動の行われる場所や通過点などを表す]
公園を散歩する (kōen o sanpo suru)
¶道の真ん中を歩いてはいけません。
(Michi no mannaka o aruite wa ikemasen.)

photos from the trip.

* *o-* expressing humility is used with verbs in the patterns "*o-* + verb (stem form) + *suru*," "*o-* + verb (stem form) + *itasu*," etc.

③ [used to express politeness]
sake, liquor // cold, it's cold
¶ I bought (literally, bought and brought) some tea and sweets.
* *o-* is seldom added to borrowed words written in *katakana* or to words beginning in "o" such as *ōsetsuma* (parlor, reception room).

o 〚part〛 a particle used with a direct object, the place a movement takes place or passes through, etc.
① [indicates a direct object]
¶ I like reading novels 〚stories, fiction〛.
¶ [Miss] Ueda is wearing a sweater.
¶ The teacher calls on the students for their answers.
¶ [Mr.] Yamada sometimes pesters the teacher with odd questions.
② [indicates where a movement takes place or passes through]
stroll **in** the park, take a walk **in** the park
¶ One mustn't walk **in** the middle of the road.

¶その角を曲がると，郵便局があります。(Sono kado *o* magaru to, yūbin-kyoku ga arimasu.)

* 普通「行く (iku)」「通る (tooru)」「歩く (aruku)」「散歩する (sanpo suru)」などの移動を表す動詞といっしょに使う。

③［移動する動作の起点となる場所などを表す］

¶わたしは毎朝7時にうちを出て，学校へ行きます。(Watashi wa maiasa shichiji ni uchi *o* dete, gakkō e ikimasu.)

¶わたしは電車を降りて，バスで会社まで行きます。(Watashi wa densha *o* orite, basu de kaisha made iki-masu.)

oba おば〘名〙

¶わたしの**おば**は田舎にいます。(Watashi no *oba* wa inaka ni imasu.)

⇔**oji** おじ ⇒**obasan** おばさん

ōbā オーバー〘名〙

obasan おばさん〘名〙

①［他人のおばを尊敬しまたは自分のおばを親しんで言う言葉］

¶あなたの**おばさん**はどこに住んでいますか。(Anata no *obasan* wa doko ni sunde imasu ka?)

* 他人に自分のおばのことを話す場合には，普通「おばさん(obasan)」とは言わないで「おば (oba)」と言う。

→**oba** おば

②［よその中年の女の人］

¶ If you turn that corner, you will find a post office 〚There is a post office around that corner〛.

* Generally used with verbs expressing movement such as *iku* (go), *tooru* (pass through), *aruku* (walk), or *sanpo suru* (take a walk).

③ [indicates the starting point of a moving action]

¶ I leave the house at seven o'clock each morning and go to school.

¶ I get **off** the train and then take a bus to the office.

ō- ☞ **oo-**

-ō ☞ **-yō, u**

oba 〚n〛 **aunt**

¶ My **aunt** lives in the country.

ōbā 〚n〛 **overcoat**

obasan 〚n〛 **aunt; a middle-aged woman, a lady**

① [aunt; used to refer to another's aunt with respect or to one's own aunt with affection]

¶ Where does your **aunt** live?

* One usually uses *oba* rather than *obasan* when talking about one's aunt with someone outside of one's family.

② [a middle-aged woman, a lady]

¶八百屋のおばさんがわたしにりんごをくれました。(Yaoya no *obasan* ga watashi ni ringo o kuremashita.)

⇔ojisan おじさん

obāsan おばあさん〖名〗

①[他人の祖母を尊敬しまたは自分の祖母を親しんで言う言葉]

¶あなたのおばあさんは今年おいくつですか。 (Anata no *obāsan* wa kotoshi oikutsu desu ka?)

* 他人に自分の祖母のことを話す場合は, 普通「おばあさん (obāsan)」と言わないで「祖母 (sobo)」と言う。

→sobo 祖母

②[よその年寄りの女の人]

¶おばあさん, ここにお掛けなさい。(*Obāsan*, koko ni okakenasai.)

⇔ojiisan おじいさん

oboeru 覚える〖動Ⅱ〗

①[頭にとめておく]

¶あなたはわたしのことを覚えていますか。(Anata wa watashi no koto o *oboete* imasu ka?)

¶日本の歌をたくさん覚えていたのですが, もうだいぶ忘れました。(Nihon no uta o takusan *oboete* ita no desu ga, mō daibu wasuremashita.)

②[習得する]

¶早く仕事を覚えようとがんばっています。(Hayaku shigoto o *oboeyō* to ganbatte imasu.)

oboreru おぼれる〖動Ⅱ〗

¶台風で船が沈んで, 人がおおぜいおぼれました。(Taifū de fune ga shi-

¶ The vegetable and fruit store **lady** gave me an apple.

obāsan 〚n〛 grandmother; an elderly lady

① [grandmother; used to refer to someone else's grandmother with respect or to one's own grandmother with affection]

¶ How old is your **grandmother** this year?

* One usually uses *sobo* rather than *obāsan* when talking about one's grandmother with someone outside of one's family.

② [an elderly woman]

¶ **Ma'am,** please have this seat 〖Here's a seat for you, **ma'am**〗.

oboeru 〚v Ⅱ〛 memorize, remember, know; learn, master

① [memorize, remember, know]

¶ Do you **remember** me?

¶ I once **knew** many Japanese songs but I've forgotten most of them.

② [learn, master]

¶ I'm working hard **to master** the job as quickly as possible.

oboreru 〚v Ⅱ〛 drown, be drowned

¶ A ship went down in the typhoon and many lives **were lost.**

zunde, hito ga oozei *oboremashita*.)

¶わたしは川で泳いでいる時，おぼれそうになりました。 (Watashi wa kawa de oyoide iru toki, *oboresō* ni narimashita.)

ocha お茶〖名〗 ☞cha 茶

ochiru 落ちる〖動Ⅱ〗

①[あるものが上から下へ自然に移動する]

¶秋になると，木の葉が落ちます。(Aki ni naru to, ki no ha ga *ochimasu*.)

¶弟が階段から落ちてけがをしました。 (Otōto ga kaidan kara *ochite* kega o shimashita.)

②[程度が下がる，低くなる]

速度が落ちる (sokudo ga *ochiru*)

¶勉強しなかったので，成績が落ちました。 (Benkyō shinakatta node, seiseki ga *ochimashita*.)

③[落第する，試験に失敗する]

¶田中さんは大学の試験に落ちました。 (Tanaka san wa daigaku no shiken ni *ochimashita*.)

ochitsuku 落ち着く〖動Ⅰ〗

¶試験の結果が心配で落ち着きません。 (Shiken no kekka ga shinpai de *ochitsukimasen*.)

¶地震のときには，落ち着いて行動しなければなりません。 (Jishin no toki ni wa, *ochitsuite* kōdō shinakereba narimasen.)

odayaka 穏やか〖形動〗

①[静かな様子]

穏やかな気候 (*odayaka* na kikō)

ocha ☞ cha

ochiru 〖v Ⅱ〗 fall, drop; fall, go down; fail

① [fall, drop]

¶ Trees **shed** their leaves in the fall.

¶ My (younger) brother **fell down** the stairs and hurt himself.

② [fall, go down]

the speed **falls**

¶ [My] grades **fell** because [I] didn't study.

③ [fail]

¶ [Mr.] Tanaka **failed** [his] university entrance exams.

ochitsuku 〖v Ⅰ〗 calm down, become composed, settle down

¶ [I]'m so nervous about the exam results that [I] **can't settle down.**

¶ One must **keep one's head** during an earthquake.

odayaka 〖adj-v〗 quiet, peaceful; gentle, tranquil

① [quiet, peaceful, calm, mild]

a **mild** climate

¶ I **came close to drowning** while swimming in the river.

ōen

¶今日は風もなくて，海が穏やかです。(Kyō wa kaze mo nakute, umi ga *odayaka* desu.)

②[静かで落ち着いている様子]

¶中村さんは性格の穏やかな人です。(Nakamura san wa seikaku no *odayaka* na hito desu.)

odori 踊り〖名〗

¶わたしたちはみんなで日本の踊りを踊りました。(Watashitachi wa minna de Nihon no *odori* o odorimashita.)

odoroku 驚く〖動Ⅰ〗

①[びっくりする]

¶「火事だ。」という声を聞いて，驚いて外へ飛び出しました。("Kaji da!" to iu koe o kiite, *odoroite* soto e tobidashimashita.)

②[感心する]

¶あの人は歌がとても上手なので驚きました。(Ano hito wa uta ga totemo jōzu na node *odorokimashita*.)

odoru 踊る〖動Ⅰ〗

¶わたしと踊ってくださいませんか。(Watashi to *odotte* kudasaimasen ka?)

ōen 応援〖名，〜する〗

①[人手がなくて困っているときなどに助ける]

¶人が足りないそうですから，応援に行きましょう。(Hito ga tarinai sō desu kara, *ōen* ni ikimashō.)

②[声援する]

応援団 (*ōen*dan)

¶ There's no wind today and the sea **is calm.**

② [gentle, tranquil, mild]

¶ [Mr.] Nakamura is **mild-mannered.**

odori 〖n〗 dance, dancing

¶ We all did some Japanese **dances** together.

odoroku 〖v Ⅰ〗 be surprised; be amazed

① [be surprised, be startled]

¶ **Startled** by the cry of "Fire!" [I] ran outside.

② [be amazed, marvel at]

¶ [We] **marveled** at how good a singer [he] is.

odoru 〖v Ⅰ〗 to dance

¶ Could I please **have this dance?**

ōen 〖n, ~*suru*〗 aid, assistance; cheer on, support

① [aid, assistance]

¶ I hear they are shorthanded—let's go **help.**

② [cheer on, support, root for]

cheerleaders, a **cheering** section

563

¶昨日、野球の応援に行きました。
(Kinō, yakyū no ōen ni ikimashita.)

oeru 終える〖動Ⅱ〗

①[終了する]

¶これで今日の仕事を全部終えました。
(Kore de kyō no shigoto o zenbu oemashita.)

¶兄は来年、大学を終えます。(Ani wa rainen, daigaku o oemasu.)

②[ある動作が終了することを表す]

¶御飯を食べ終えたら、すぐ出かけましょう。(Gohan o tabeoetara, sugu dekakemashō.)

¶やっと論文を書き終えました。
(Yatto ronbun o kakioemashita.)

*「動詞（基幹の形）＋終える (oeru)」の形で使う。

⇔hajimeru 始める ⇒owaru 終わる

ōfuku 往復〖名, ～する〗

往復切符 (ōfuku-kippu) 往復はがき (ōfuku-hagaki)

¶ここから東京まで往復で 1200 円です。(Koko kara Tōkyō made ōfuku de sennihyakuen desu.)

⇔katamichi 片道

ogamu 拝む〖動Ⅰ〗

¶おおぜいの人がお寺の前で手を合わせて拝んでいました。(Oozei no hito ga otera no mae de te o awasete ogande imashita.)

ohayō お早う〖連〗

¶朝、人に会ったら、「お早うございます。」とあいさつします。(Asa, hito ni

¶ [I] went **to cheer on** our baseball team yesterday.

(-)oeru 〖v II〗 finish, complete; finish doing something

① [finish, complete, end]

¶ This **finishes** all the work for today.

¶ My older brother **completes** college next year.

② [finish doing something]

¶ Let's leave right after we **finish** eating.

¶ [I]'ve finally **finished** writing [my] thesis 〖I finally **finished** writing my thesis〗.

* Used in the pattern "verb (stem form) + -oeru."

ōfuku 〖n, ~suru〗 going and returning, coming and going, round trip

a **round-trip** ticket // a postcard with an attached **return** card

¶ The **round-trip** fare between here and Tokyo is 1,200 yen.

ogamu 〖v I〗 worship, pray

¶ A great number of people were standing in front of the temple with their hands pressed together **in prayer**.

ohayō 〖compd〗 Good morning

¶ One greets people in the morning by saying **ohayō** gozaimasu 〖**good** attara, "*Ohayō* gozaimasu." to aisatsu shimasu.)

＊ 丁寧に言う場合は「お早うございます (ohayō gozaimasu)」と言う。

oi おい〚名〛

⇔**mei** めい

oide おいで〚連, 名〛

1〚連〛

①[行く]

¶先生は先ほどあちらへ**おいで**になりました。 (Sensei wa sakihodo achira e *oide* ni narimashita.)

＊「行く (iku)」の尊敬語。

②[来る]

¶こちらへ**おいで**ください。 (Kochira e *oide* kudasai.)

¶先生が**おいで**になりました。 (Sensei ga *oide* ni narimashita.)

＊「来る (kuru)」の尊敬語。

③[いる]

¶お父さんは**おいで**ですか。 (Otōsan wa *oide* desu ka?)

＊「いる (iru)」の尊敬語。

＊ あとに「～になる (～ni naru)」「～ください (～kudasai)」「～です (～desu)」などが来る。

2〚名〛

¶先生の**おいで**をお待ちいたしております。 (Sensei no *oide* o omachi itashite orimasu.)

oishii おいしい〚形〛

¶このお菓子は**おいしい**です。 (Kono okashi wa *oishii* desu.)

¶テーブルの上に, **おいし**そうな料理

morning〛.

＊ One uses *ohayō gozaimasu* rather than *ohayō* when speaking politely.

oi 〚n〛 **nephew**

ōi ☞ **ooi**

oide 〚compd, n〛 **go; come; be, be present**

1 〚compd〛

① [go]

¶ The professor 〚doctor〛 **went** there a little while ago.

＊ The honorific form of *iku*.

② [come]

¶ Please **come** here.

¶ The professor 〚doctor〛 **has come.**

＊ The honorific form of *kuru*.

③ [be, be present]

¶ **Is** your father **there** 〚**home**〛?

＊ The honorific form of *iru*.

＊ Followed by *ni naru*, *kudasai*, *desu*, etc.

2 〚n〛 going, coming, being present

¶ I am waiting for the professor 〚doctor〛 **to come** 〚I am looking forward to **your visit,** sir〛.

oishii 〚adj〛 **good-tasting, delicious**

¶ This sweet **is very good.**

¶ There is a **good-looking** spread of

が並んでいます。(Tēburu no ue ni, *oishisō* na ryōri ga narande imasu.)

⇔**mazui** まずい ⇒**umai** うまい

oitsuku 追いつく〔動Ⅰ〕

¶急いで歩いたら，途中で山田さんに追いつきました。(Isoide aruitara, tochū de Yamada san ni *oitsuki-mashita*.)

¶病気で休んでいても，一生懸命勉強すれば，すぐみんなに追いつきます。(Byōki de yasunde ite mo, isshō-kenmei benkyō sureba, sugu minna ni *oitsukimasu*.)

oiwai お祝い〔名〕

¶わたしは春子さんの誕生日のお祝いに花を上げました。 (Watashi wa Haruko san no tanjōbi no *oiwai* ni hana o agemashita.)

⇒**iwau** 祝う

oji おじ〔名〕

¶わたしのおじは医者です。(Watashi no *oji* wa isha desu.)

⇔**oba** おば ⇒**ojisan** おじさん

ojigi おじぎ〔名，〜する〕

¶わたしは先生に「お早うございます。」と言っておじぎをしました。(Watashi wa sensei ni "Ohayō gozaimasu." to itte *ojigi* o shi-mashita.)

ojiisan おじいさん〔名〕

①〔他人の祖父を尊敬しまたは自分の祖父を親しんで言う言葉〕

¶あなたのおじいさんは今年おいくつですか。(Anata no *ojiisan* wa koto-

oitsuku 〔v I〕 **overtake, catch up with**

¶ Walking fast, **I caught up** with [Mrs.] Yamada on the way.

¶ Even if you did miss school when you were sick, you will soon **catch up** with everyone if you study hard.

oiwai 〔n〕 **congratulations, celebration**

¶ I gave Haruko flowers **for** her birthday.

oji 〔n〕 **uncle**

¶ My **uncle** is a doctor.

ojigi 〔n, ~*suru*〕 **bow, curtsy**

¶ I **bowed** to our teacher and said, "*Ohayō gozaimasu*."

ojiisan 〔n〕 **grandfather; an old man**

① [grandfather; used when referring to someone else's grandfather with respect or to one's own grandfather with affection]

¶ How old is your **grandfather** this

shi oikutsu desu ka?)

* 他人に自分の祖父のことを話す場合には，普通「おじいさん (ojiisan)」と言わないで「祖父 (sofu)」と言う。

→sofu 祖父

②[よその年寄りの男の人]

¶おじいさん，お元気ですね。(*Ojiisan*, ogenki desu ne.)

⇔obāsan おばあさん

ojisan　おじさん〘名〙

①[他人のおじを尊敬しまたは自分のおじを親しんで言う言葉]

¶あなたの**おじさん**は何をなさっていますか。(Anata no *ojisan* wa nani o nasatte imasu ka?)

* 他人に自分のおじのことを話す場合には，普通「おじさん (ojisan)」と言わないで「おじ (oji)」と言う。

→oji おじ

②[よその中年の男の人]

¶魚屋の**おじさん**はいつも元気です。(Sakanaya no *ojisan* wa itsu mo genki desu.)

⇔obasan おばさん

oka　丘〘名〙

okage　おかげ〘名〙

¶『お元気ですか。』(Ogenki desu ka?)「**おかげ**さまで，元気です。」(*Okage*-sama de, genki desu.)

¶一生懸命勉強した**おかげ**で成績が上がりました。(Isshōkenmei benkyō shita *okage* de seiseki ga agari-mashita.)

okāsan　お母さん〘名〙

year?

* When talking about one's grand-father with someone outside one's family, one usually uses *sofu* rather than *ojiisan*.

② [an old man]

¶ You seem very spry, **sir.**

ojisan 〚n〛　**uncle; a middle-aged man**

① [uncle; used to refer to someone else's uncle with respect or to one's own uncle with affection]

¶ What does your **uncle** do?

* When talking about one's own un-cle with someone outside one's fami-ly, one usually uses *oji* rather than *ojisan*.

② [a middle-aged man]

¶ The fish store **man** is always in good spirits.

oka 〚n〛　**hill, rise, hillock**

okage 〚n〛　**thanks to, owing to, by grace of**

¶ "How are you?"
　"Fine, **thank you.**"

¶ [My] grades improved **as a result of** hard study.

okāsan 〚n〛　**mother**

¶お母さんはうちにいらっしゃいますか。(*Okāsan* wa uchi ni irrasshaimasu ka?)

＊他人の母親について話す場合，または自分の母親に呼びかけたり，家族の者に母親のことを言う場合に使う。他人に自分の母親のことを話す場合には，普通「お母さん (okāsan)」と言わないで「母 (haha)」と言う。

⇔otōsan お父さん ⇨haha 母

okashii おかしい〖形〗

①[こっけいだ，おもしろい]

¶山田さんはおかしい話をして，みんなを笑わせました。(Yamada san wa *okashii* hanashi o shite, minna o warawasemashita.)

→omoshiroi おもしろい

②[普通でなくて変だ]

¶おかしいですね。約束したのに，中村さんはまだ来ません。(*Okashii* desu ne. Yakusoku shita noni, Nakamura san wa mada kimasen.)

＊「おかしな (okashina)」(連体) という言葉もある。「おかしな話 (okashina hanashi)」

-oki -おき〖尾〗

¶わたしは1日おきに事務所へ行きます。(Watashi wa ichinichi *oki* ni jimusho e ikimasu.)

¶5メートルおきに木を植えました。(Gomētoru *oki* ni ki o uemashita.)

okiru 起きる〖動Ⅱ〗

①[目を覚ます，寝床から出る]

¶あなたは朝何時ごろ起きますか。

¶ Is **your mother** at home?

＊ *Okāsan* is used when talking about someone else's mother, in direct address to one's own mother, and when talking about one's own mother with other family members. When talking about one's own mother with nonfamily members, one usually uses *haha* rather than *okāsan*.

okashii 〚adj〛 **funny, amusing; funny, strange**

① [funny, amusing, comic]

¶ [Mr.] Yamada told a **funny** story and made everyone laugh.

② [funny, strange, odd, queer]

¶ That's **odd.** [Miss] Nakamura hasn't come yet for [our] date 〚appointment〛.

＊ The form *okashina* is sometimes used as a modifier before a noun, as in *okashina hanashi* (a funny story, an odd story).

-oki 〚suf〛 **at intervals of ～, ～ apart**

¶ I go to the office **every other** day.

¶ [I] planted the trees **at intervals of** five meters 〚five meters **apart**〛.

ōkii ☞ **ookii**

okiru 〚v Ⅱ〛 **wake up, get up; be up, be awake; take place, occur**

① [wake up, get up]

¶ What time do you **get up** in the

(Anata wa asa nanji goro *okimasu ka?*)

¶赤ん坊が**起きる**から，静かにしてください。 (Akanbō ga *okiru* kara, shizuka ni shite kudasai.)

②[寝ないでいる]

¶上田さんは毎晩遅くまで**起きて**勉強しています。 (Ueda san wa maiban osoku made *okite* benkyō shite imasu.)

③[事件などが生じる]

事件が**起きる** (jiken ga *okiru*) 戦争が**起きる** (sensō ga *okiru*)

→okoru 起こる

okonau 行う〖動Ⅰ〗

¶これから今日の授業を**行い**ます。 (Kore kara kyō no jugyō o *okonaimasu.*)

¶その祭りは今でもこの地方に**行われ**ています。 (Sono matsuri wa ima demo kono chihō ni *okonawarete* imasu.)

okoru 怒る〖動Ⅰ〗

①[腹を立てる]

¶父が**怒った**顔をしています。 (Chichi ga *okotta* kao o shite imasu.)

¶山田さんは，あなたが約束を破ったことを**怒って**いますよ。 (Yamada san wa, anata ga yakusoku o yabutta koto o *okotte* imasu yo.)

②[しかる]

¶わたしは子供のころ，よく母に**怒られました**。 (Watashi wa kodomo no koro, yoku haha ni *okoraremashi-*

morning?

¶ Please be quiet—you'll **wake up** the baby (literally, the baby **will wake up**).

② [be up, be awake]

¶ [Miss] Ueda **stays up** late every night studying.

③ [take place, occur]

an incident **takes place** // war **breaks out**

okonau 〖v I〗 hold, perform, do, carry out

¶ Today's class **will start** now.

¶ That festival **is** still **observed** in this region even today.

okoru 〖v I〗 get angry, be angered; scold

① [get angry, be angered, lose one's temper]

¶ My father looks **angry.**

¶ [Mr.] Yamada **is angry** at you for not keeping your word.

② [scold]

¶ When I was a child I **was** often **scolded** by my mother.

ta.)

okoru 起こる〖動Ⅰ〗

¶昨日，ここで交通事故が起こりました。(Kinō, koko de kōtsū-jiko ga *okorimashita*.)

¶戦争が起こった時，わたしは外国にいました。 (Sensō ga *okotta* toki, watashi wa gaikoku ni imashita.)

⇨okiru 起きる

okosu 起こす〖動Ⅰ〗

①〔目を覚まさせる〕

¶あしたの朝，6時に起こしてください。(Ashita no asa, rokuji ni *okoshite* kudasai.)

②〔立たせる〕

¶子供が転んだので，起こしてやりました。(Kodomo ga koronda node, *okoshite* yarimashita.)

③〔生じさせる〕

¶上田さんは事故を起こして，警察で調べられています。 (Ueda san wa jiko o *okoshite*, keisatsu de shirabe-rarete imasu.)

oku 奥〖名〗

山の奥 (yama no *oku*)

¶大切な物は引き出しの奥にしまってあります。 (Taisetsu na mono wa hikidashi no *oku* ni shimatte arimasu.)

¶玄関では話ができませんから，どうぞ奥へお入りください。(Genkan de wa hanashi ga dekimasen kara, dōzo *oku* e ohairi kudasai.)

oku 億〖名〗

okoru 〖v I〗 **happen, occur, take place**

¶ A traffic accident **took place** here yesterday.

¶ I was abroad when war **broke out.**

okosu 〖v I〗 **wake up; raise, set up; give rise to, cause**

① [wake up, rouse]

¶ Please **wake me up** tomorrow morning at six o'clock.

② [raise, set up, set upright]

¶ **I helped up** the child who had fallen down.

③ [give rise to, cause]

¶ [Mr.] Ueda **caused** an accident and is being interrogated by the police.

oku 〖n〗 **interior, recesses, depths the heart** of a mountain, **deep** in the mountains

¶ The valuables are shut away towards **the back** of the drawer.

¶ Please come **inside;** we can't talk comfortably here in the entryway.

oku 〖n〗 **100 million**

1億 (ichi*oku*) 10億 (jū*oku*) 100億 (hyaku*oku*)

100,000,000 // 1,000,000,000; one billion // 10,000,000,000; ten billion

oku 置く〖動Ⅰ〗

oku 〚v Ⅰ〛 **put, place, lay, leave**

¶机の上に本を置きます。(Tsukue no ue ni hon o *okimasu*.)

¶[I] **will put** the book on the desk.

¶荷物はここに置いてください。(Nimotsu wa koko ni *oite* kudasai.)

¶ Please **put** [your] things 〚load, bags, packages, etc.〛 here.

(〜te) oku (〜て) おく〖連〗

(-te) oku 〚compd〛 an expression indicating something being left in a certain state or something being done in preparation

①[ある動作が終わったままの状態にする]

① [leave, let, keep; leave or keep something in a certain state]

¶わたしはいつも部屋のかぎを掛けておきます。(Watashi wa itsu mo heya no kagi o kakete *okimasu*.)

¶ I always **keep** my room locked.

¶ここに置いておいた辞書を知りませんか。(Koko ni oite *oita* jisho o shirimasen ka?)

¶ Do you know what happened to the dictionary **that was here?**

②[あらかじめ準備したりする]

② [make preparations, do in advance]

¶お客さんが来ますから，部屋を掃除しておきましょう。(Okyakusan ga kimasu kara, heya o sōji shite *okimashō*.)

¶ **Let's clean** the room—a guest is coming.

¶行く前に電話をかけておいたほうがいいですよ。(Iku mae ni denwa o kakete *oita* hō ga ii desu yo.)

¶ You had better **telephone** before you go there.

ōku ☞ **ooku**

okubyō おく病〖名，形動〗

okubyō 〚n, adj-v〛 **cowardice, timidity**

¶この子はおく病で，夜一人では歩けません。(Kono ko wa *okubyō* de, yoru hitori de wa arukemasen.)

¶ This child **is timid** and is afraid to walk alone at night.

¶一度失敗すると，次からはおく病になります。(Ichido shippai suru to, tsugi kara wa *okubyō* ni narimasu.)

¶ One **loses one's nerve** after failing once.

okujō 屋上〖名〗

okujō 〚n〛 **roof, housetop, rooftop the rooftop** of a building

ビルの屋上 (biru no *okujō*)

¶あのデパートの屋上には，子供のた

¶ There is a play area for children on

めの遊び場があります。(Ano depāto no *okujō* ni wa, kodomo no tame no asobiba ga arimasu.)

the roof of that department store.

okureru 遅れる〚動Ⅱ〛

¶早くしないと，学校に遅れますよ。(Hayaku shinai to, gakkō ni *okuremasu* yo.)

¶田中さんは約束の時間に30分も遅れてきました。(Tanaka san wa yakusoku no jikan ni sanjippun mo *okurete* kimashita.)

okureru 〚v Ⅱ〛 be late, be tardy

¶ If you don't hurry **you'll be late** for school.

¶ [Mr.] Tanaka **was** 30 minutes **late** for [our] appointment 〚date〛.

okureru 後れる〚動Ⅱ〛

¶3か月も学校を休んだので，勉強が後れてしまいました。(Sankagetsu mo gakkō o yasunda node, benkyō ga *okurete* shimaimashita.)

¶その時計は5分後れています。(Sono tokei wa gofun *okurete* imasu.)

okureru 〚v Ⅱ〛 be behind, fall back

¶ [I] was out of school for three months so [I] **am** 〚**was**〛 behind in [my] studies.

¶ That clock **is** five minutes **slow.**

okurimono 贈り物〚名〛

¶友達のうちに赤ちゃんが生まれたので，お祝いの贈り物を持って行きました。(Tomodachi no uchi ni akachan ga umareta node, oiwai no *okurimono* o motte ikimashita.)

⇨**purezento** プレゼント

okurimono 〚n〛 present, gift

¶ My friends had a baby so I took them **a present.**

okuru 送る〚動Ⅰ〛

①[物をある所から他の所まで届ける]
¶田舎の母がりんごを送ってくれました。(Inaka no haha ga ringo o *okutte* kuremashita.)

¶あなたは家から毎月いくらぐらいお金を送ってもらいますか。(Anata wa ie kara maitsuki ikura gurai okane o *okutte* moraimasu ka?)

okuru 〚v Ⅰ〛 send; see off, see home

① [send]

¶ My mother **sent me** some apples from the country.

¶ How much money does your family **send you** each month?

②[見送る，ある所までつき添っていく]

¶あした，わたしは飛行場へ友達を送りに行きます。(Ashita, watashi wa hikōjō e tomodachi o *okuri* ni ikimasu.)

¶道が暗いから，わたしが駅まで送りましょう。(Michi ga kurai kara, watashi ga eki made *okurimashō*.)

okuru 贈る〖動 I〗

¶わたしは田中さんにクリスマスのプレゼントを贈りました。(Watashi wa Tanaka san ni kurisumasu no purezento o *okurimashita*.)

okusama 奥様〖名〗☞ okusan 奥さん

okusan 奥さん〖名〗

¶中村さんの奥さんは英語の先生です。(Nakamura san no *okusan* wa Eigo no sensei desu.)

¶奥さん，このりんごはおいしいですよ。(*Okusan*, kono ringo wa oishii desu yo.)

＊他人の妻に直接呼びかけたり，他人の妻のことを話す場合に使う。丁寧に言う場合には「奥様 (okusama)」と言う。

⇨kanai 家内 tsuma 妻

omawarisan お巡りさん〖名〗

¶道がわからないので，交番のお巡りさんにききました。(Michi ga wakaranai node, kōban no *omawarisan* ni kikimashita.)

⇨keikan 警官

② [see off, see home]

¶ Tomorrow I'm going to the airport **to see off** a friend.

¶ I'll **walk with you** to the station as the streets are dark now.

okuru 〚v I〛 give as a present, present with

¶ I **gave** a Christmas present to [Miss] Tanaka.

okusama ☞ okusan

okusan 〚n〛 wife, married woman

¶ Mr. Nakamura's **wife** teaches English.

¶ These apples are good today, **ma'am.**

＊ Used in direct address to someone else's wife or when referring to someone else's wife. When speaking politely, *okusama* is used.

omawarisan 〚n〛 policeman

¶ [I] didn't know the way so [I] went to a police box and asked **the policeman** for directions.

omedetō おめでとう〖連〗

¶明けましておめでとうございます。
(Akemashite *omedetō* gozaimasu.)

¶誕生日おめでとう。(Tanjōbi *omedetō*.)

¶御結婚おめでとうございます。(Go-kekkon *omedetō* gozaimasu.)

＊丁寧に言う場合は,「おめでとうございます (omedetō gozaimasu)」と言う。

⇨medetai めでたい

omedetō 〚compd〛 **Congratulations**

¶ **Happy** New Year!

¶ **Happy** birthday!

¶ **Congratulations** on your marriage!

＊When speaking politely, *Omedetō gozaimasu* is used.

omo 主〖形動〗

¶日本の主な輸出品は工業製品です。
(Nihon no *omo* na yushutsuhin wa kōgyō-seihin desu.)

¶あの学校の留学生は東南アジアの学生が主です。(Ano gakkō no ryūgakusei wa Tōnan-ajia no gakusei ga *omo* desu.)

omo 〚adj-v〛 **chief, main, principal**

¶ The **principal** exports of Japan are manufactured goods.

¶ The foreign students at that school are **chiefly** from Southeast Asia.

omocha おもちゃ〖名〗

¶子供がおもちゃで遊んでいます。
(Kodomo ga *omocha* de asonde imasu.)

omocha 〚n〛 **toy**

¶ The children are playing with **toys.**

omoi 重い〖形〗

①[目方が多い]

¶この荷物は重くて,一人では持てません。(Kono nimotsu wa *omokute*, hitori de wa motemasen.)

②[程度がはなはだしい]

¶上田さんは重い病気で3か月も入院しています。(Ueda san wa *omoi* byōki de sankagetsu mo nyūin shite imasu.)

⇦karui 軽い

omoi 〚adj〛 **heavy; severe, grave**

① [heavy]

¶ This load 〖package, bag, etc.〗 **is too heavy** for a single person to carry.

② [severe, grave, serious]

¶ [Mrs.] Ueda is **seriously** ill and has been in the hospital for three months.

omoshiroi

omoidasu 思い出す〖動Ⅰ〗

¶わたしはときどき，小さいころのことを思い出します。(Watashi wa toki-doki, chiisai koro no koto o *omoi-dashimasu*.)

¶あの人の名前がどうしても思い出せません。(Ano hito no namae ga dōshite mo *omoidasemasen*.)

omoide 思い出〖名〗

¶だれでも皆，子供のころのいろいろな思い出を持っています。(Dare demo mina, kodomo no koro no iroiro na *omoide* o motte imasu.)

¶今日の会は日本でのいい思い出になるでしょう。(Kyō no kai wa Nihon de no ii *omoide* ni naru deshō.)

omoni 主に〖副〗

¶この会には主に学生が集まります。(Kono kai ni wa *omoni* gakusei ga atsumarimasu.)

¶夜は主にラジオの音楽番組を聞いています。(Yoru wa *omoni* rajio no ongaku-bangumi o kiite imasu.)

omosa 重さ〖名〗

¶この荷物の重さを量ってください。(Kono nimotsu no *omosa* o hakatte kudasai.)

¶その小包の重さはどのぐらいですか。(Sono kozutsumi no *omosa* wa dono gurai desu ka?)

⇨ -sa -さ

omoshiroi おもしろい〖形〗

①[おかしくて笑いたくなる様子]
¶中村さんはいつもおもしろい話をし

omoidasu 〖v Ⅰ〗 recall, remember

¶ Every now and then I **think back** to when I was small.

¶ I just **can't remember** [his] name for the life of me.

omoide 〖n〗 memory, recollection

¶ All of us have various **memories** of our childhood.

¶ I will fondly **remember** today's gathering as one of my best times in Japan.

omoni 〖adv〗 mainly, for the most part, generally

¶ These meetings **mainly** attract students.

¶ **For the most part** [I] listen to music on the radio in the evening.

omosa 〖n〗 weight

¶ Please **weigh** this package 〖load, bag, etc.〗.

¶ How much does that parcel **weigh?**

omoshiroi 〖adj〗 amusing, funny; pleasant, entertaining; interesting

① [amusing, funny]

て，みんなを笑わせます。(Nakamura
san wa itsu mo *omoshiroi* hanashi
o shite, minna o warawasemasu.)

→**okashii** おかしい

②[楽しい]

¶旅行はとても**おもしろかった**です。
(Ryokō wa totemo *omoshirokatta*
desu.)

③[興味深い]

¶この小説は**おもしろい**です。(Kono
shōsetsu wa *omoshiroi* desu.)

omote 表［名］

①[表面]

¶封筒の**表**に，相手の住所と名前を書
きます。(Fūtō no *omote* ni, aite no
jūsho to namae o kakimasu.)

↔**ura** 裏

②[家の外]

¶家の中にばかりいないで，**表**で遊び
なさい。 (Ie no naka ni bakari
inaide, *omote* de asobinasai.)

omou 思う［動 I］

①[考える]

¶あなたはこの計画をどう**思います**か。
(Anata wa kono keikaku o dō
omoimasu ka?)

②[推量する]

¶あの人は 40 歳ぐらいだと**思います**。
(Ano hito wa yonjissai gurai da to
omoimasu.)

③[信じる]

¶あなたはきっとその仕事に成功する
と**思います**。(Anata wa kitto sono
shigoto ni seikō suru to *omoimasu*.)

¶ [Mr.] Nakamura always makes
everyone laugh with [his] **funny** stories.

② [pleasant, entertaining, enjoyable]
¶ The trip **was** a lot of **fun.**

③ [interesting]
¶ This novel **is interesting.**

omote [[n]] face, surface; outside,
outdoors

① [face, surface, right side, front]
¶ One writes the name and address
of the recipient on **the front** of an
envelope.

② [outside, outdoors]
¶ Don't stay inside all the time—go
play **outside.**

omou [[v I]] think; suppose; believe; expect; feel; want; intend

① [think]
¶ What **do you think** of this plan?

② [suppose, guess, imagine]
¶ **I suppose** [he]'s around 40.

③ [believe]
¶ **I am sure** you will be a success at
that job.

④［予期する］
¶山田さんは8時には来ると思います。
(Yamada san wa hachiji ni wa kuru to *omoimasu*.)

⑤［感じる］
¶あなたの国より日本のほうが寒いと思いますか。 (Anata no kuni yori Nihon no hō ga samui to *omoimasu* ka?)

⑥［望む］
¶わたしはその映画を見に行きたいと思っています。 (Watashi wa sono eiga o mi ni ikitai to *omotte* imasu.)

⑦［あることをするつもりである］
¶わたしは2週間ぐらい日本にいようと思っています。(Watashi wa nishūkan gurai Nihon ni iyō to *omotte* imasu.)

onaji 同じ〖形動〗
¶どの品物も値段は皆同じです。(Dono shinamono mo nedan wa mina *onaji* desu.)
¶わたしもあなたと同じ30歳です。 (Watashi mo anata to *onaji* sanjissai desu.)
¶あの人はわたしと同じシャツを着ています。 (Ano hito wa watashi to *onaji* shatsu o kite imasu.)
＊名詞などを修飾する場合は,「同じ (onaji)」の形で使う。

onaka おなか〖名〗
おなかが痛い(*onaka* ga itai) おなかがすく (*onaka* ga suku)

④ [expect]
¶ **I expect** [Miss] Yamada will be here at eight o'clock.

⑤ [feel]
¶ **Do you find** that Japan is colder than your native country?

⑥ [want, desire, wish]
¶ **I would like** to go see that movie.

⑦ [intend to, plan to, think of]
¶ **I am planning** to stay in Japan for about two weeks.

onaji 〖adj-v〗 the same, alike
¶ All of the merchandise costs **the same.**
¶ I am also 30 years old, **the same** as you.
¶ He is wearing the **same** shirt as I am.
＊ Used in the form *onaji* when modifying a noun, etc.

onaka 〖n〗 stomach
have a **stomach**ache, have **stomach** pains // be hungry

¶もう，おなかがいっぱいです。(Mō, *onaka* ga ippai desu.)

⇨hara 腹

ondo 温度〖名〗

温度計 (*ondo*kei) 温度が上がる (*ondo* ga agaru) 温度が下がる (*ondo* ga sagaru) 温度が高い (*ondo* ga takai) 温度が低い (*ondo* ga hikui)

¶部屋の中の温度は，今20度ぐらいです。(Heya no naka no *ondo* wa, ima nijūdo gurai desu.)

onegai お願い〖名〗☞ negai 願い

onēsan お姉さん〖名〗

¶お姉さんはどこに勤めていらっしゃいますか。(*Onēsan* wa doko ni tsutomete irasshaimasu ka?)

＊他人に自分の姉のことを話す場合には，普通「お姉さん (onēsan)」と言わないで「姉 (ane)」と言う。

⇨ane 姉

ongaku 音楽〖名〗

音楽家 (*ongak*ka) 音楽会 (*ongak*-kai)

¶わたしは毎晩ラジオで音楽を聞きます。(Watashi wa maiban rajio de *ongaku* o kikimasu.)

¶あの人は中学の音楽の先生です。(Ano hito wa chūgaku no *ongaku* no sensei desu.)

oniisan お兄さん〖名〗

¶お兄さんは今年おいくつですか。(*Oniisan* wa kotoshi oikutsu desu ka?)

¶ I'm **full** now.

ondo 〚n〛 temperature, heat

a thermometer // **the temperature** rises // **the temperature** falls // **the temperature** is high // **the temperature** is low

¶ The room **temperature** is presently around 20 degrees.

onegai ☞ negai

onēsan 〚n〛 older sister

¶ Where does **your older sister** work?

＊ When talking with nonfamily members about one's own elder sister, one usually uses *ane* rather than *onēsan*.

ongaku 〚n〛 music

a musician // a concert, recital

¶ I listen to **music** on the radio every night.

¶ [He] is a junior high school **music** teacher.

oniisan 〚n〛 older brother

¶ How old is **your elder brother** this year?

＊他人に自分の兄のことを話す場合には，普通「お兄さん(oniisan)」と言わないで「兄(ani)」と言う。
⇨ani 兄

onna 女〖名〗
¶これは**女**の時計です。(Kore wa *onna* no tokei desu.)
¶部屋の中に**女**の人が二人います。
(Heya no naka ni *onna* no hito ga futari imasu.)
⇔**otoko** 男

onsen 温泉〖名〗
¶日本には**温泉**がたくさんあります。
(Nihon ni wa *onsen* ga takusan arimasu.)

oo- 大-〖頭〗
大雨(*oo*ame) 大通り(*oo*doori) 大急ぎ(*oo*isogi) 大騒ぎ(*oo*sawagi)

ooi 多い〖形〗
¶あなたのクラスは，どこの国の学生が**多い**ですか。 (Anata no kurasu wa, doko no kuni no gakusei ga *ooi* desu ka?)
¶このごろ，自動車の事故が**多く**なりました。(Konogoro, jidōsha no jiko ga *ooku* narimashita.)
⇔**sukunai** 少ない

ookii 大きい〖形〗
¶この**大きい**くつは山田さんのです。
(Kono *ookii* kutsu wa Yamada san no desu.)
¶中村さんはわたしよりずっと**大きい**です。 (Nakamura san wa watashi yori zutto *ookii* desu.)

＊ When talking with nonfamily members about one's own elder brother, one usually uses *ani* rather than *oniisan*.

onna 〖n〗 woman, female
¶ This is a **woman's** watch.

¶ There are two **women** in the room.

onsen 〖n〗 a hot spring, a spa
¶ There are many **hot springs** in Japan.

oo- 〖pref〗 large, great
a **heavy** rain, a downpour // a **main** thoroughfare // in **great** haste, urgent // a **great** commotion, an uproar

ooi 〖adj〗 many, numerous, much
¶ What nationalities are **heavily** represented in your class?
¶ The number of automobile accidents **has increased** recently.

ookii 〖adj〗 big, large, great
¶ These **large** shoes belong to [Mr.] Yamada.

¶ [Mr.] Nakamura is much **larger** than I am.

¶ラジオの音をあまり**大きく**しないでください。(Rajio no oto o amari *ookiku* shinaide kudasai.)

⇔**chiisai** 小さい ⇒**ookina** 大きな

ookina 大きな〚連体〛

大きな荷物 (*ookina* nimotsu) 大きな声 (*ookina* koe)

⇔**chiisana** 小さな ⇒**ookii** 大きい

ookisa 大きさ〚名〛

¶その木の実の**大きさ**は卵ぐらいです。(Sono ki no mi no *ookisa* wa tamago gurai desu.)

⇒**-sa** -さ

ooku 多く〚名〛

多くの人 (*ooku* no hito)

¶この学校には**多くの**国から留学生が勉強に来ています。(Kono gakkō ni wa *ooku* no kuni kara ryūgakusei ga benkyō ni kite imasu.)

oozei おおぜい〚名〛

¶東京には外人が**おおぜい**住んでいます。(Tōkyō ni wa gaijin ga *oozei* sunde imasu.)

¶**おおぜい**で旅行するのは，とても楽しいです。(*Oozei* de ryokō suru no wa, totemo tanoshii desu.)

＊動物や物などの場合には「おおぜい (oozei)」は使わない。

oreru 折れる〚動Ⅱ〛

¶チョークが**折れました**。(Chōku ga *oremashita*.)

¶風で木の枝が**折れそう**です。(Kaze de ki no eda ga *oresō* desu.)

orimono 織物〚名〛

¶ Please don't have the radio on too **loud.**

ookina 〚attrib〛 **big, large, great**

a **large** load 〚package, etc.〛 // a **loud** voice

ookisa 〚n〛 **size, dimensions, magnitude, volume**

¶ That fruit is about **the size** of an egg.

ooku 〚n〛 **many, a number of, much**

many people; **most** people

¶ This school has foreign students from **many different** countries.

oozei 〚n〛 **a great number of people, a crowd**

¶ **A great many** foreigners live in Tokyo.

¶ It is very pleasant to travel in **a large group.**

＊ *Oozei* is only used to refer to people.

oreru 〚v Ⅱ〛 **break, be broken**

¶ The chalk **broke in two.**

¶ The tree branch **is close to breaking off** in the wind.

orimono 〚n〛 **cloth, textile**

織物工場 (*orimono*-kōjō)

¶日本は昔から織物が盛んです。

(Nihon wa mukashi kara *orimono* ga sakan desu.)

oriru 降りる〔動Ⅱ〕

¶バスを降りて少し歩きました。(Basu o *orite* sukoshi arukimashita.)

oriru 下りる〔動Ⅱ〕

¶足が痛いので，階段をゆっくり下りました。(Ashi ga itai node, kaidan o yukkuri *orimashita*.)

orosu 降ろす〔動Ⅰ〕

¶次の交差点の所で降ろしてください。

(Tsugi no kōsaten no tokoro de *oroshite* kudasai.)

¶荷物をたなから降ろしてください。

(Nimotsu o tana kara *oroshite* kudasai.)

orosu 下ろす〔動Ⅰ〕

貯金を下ろす (chokin o *orosu*)

¶わたしは銀行へお金を下ろしに行きました。(Watashi wa ginkō e okane o *oroshi* ni ikimashita.)

oru 折る〔動Ⅰ〕

①〔曲げて取ったり傷めたりする〕

¶公園の木の枝を折ってはいけません。

(Kōen no ki no eda o *otte* wa ikemasen.)

¶転んで足の骨を折ってしまいました。

(Koronde ashi no hone o *otte* shimaimashita.)

②〔たたむ，曲げて重ねる〕

¶紙を二つに折れば，この封筒に入ります。(Kami o futatsu ni *oreba*,

a **textile** mill

¶ **Textiles** have flourished in Japan from ancient times.

oriru 〔v Ⅱ〕 **get off, disembark**

¶ [I] **got off** the bus and walked a little ways.

oriru 〔v Ⅱ〕 **come down, descend**

¶ As my leg 〖feet〗 hurt 〖was sore〗, I **went down** the stairs slowly.

orosu 〔v Ⅰ〕 **take down, lower; let off, unload**

¶ Please **let me off** at the next intersection.

¶ Please **lift** the packages 〖bags, etc.〗 **down off** the shelf.

orosu 〔v Ⅰ〕 **withdraw money from a bank account**

withdraw one's savings

¶ I went to the bank **to take out** some money.

oru 〔v Ⅰ〕 **break, break off; fold, bend**

① [break, break off, snap]

¶ One mustn't **break** branches **off** the trees in the park.

¶ [I] fell and **broke** [my] leg 〖a bone in my foot〗.

② [fold, bend]

¶ **If you fold** the paper in half it will fit into this envelope.

kono fūtō ni hairimasu.)

oru 織る〖動Ⅰ〗

¶この地方の人たちは布を織って生活しています。(Kono chihō no hitotachi wa nuno o *otte* seikatsu shite imasu.)

osaeru 押さえる〖動Ⅱ〗

¶手で紙を押さえて, 飛ばないようにしました。(Te de kami o *osaete*, tobanai yō ni shimashita.)

¶犬を押さえているから, こわがらなくてもいいです。(Inu o *osaete* iru kara, kowagaranakute mo ii desu.)

osameru 納める〖動Ⅱ〗

¶今月の末までに税金を納めなければなりません。(Kongetsu no sue made ni zeikin o *osamenakereba* narimasen.)

¶授業料はいつまでに納めればいいですか。(Jugyōryō wa itsu made ni *osamereba* ii desu ka?)

oshieru 教える〖動Ⅱ〗

①[知識や技術などを人に与える]
¶上田さんは中学で数学を教えています。(Ueda san wa chūgaku de sūgaku o *oshiete* imasu.)

②[知っていることを人に知らせる]
¶駅へ行く道を教えてください。(Eki e iku michi o *oshiete* kudasai.)

oshii 惜しい〖形〗

①[残念だ]
¶父に買ってもらった時計をなくして, 惜しいことをしました。(Chichi ni katte moratta tokei o nakushite,

oru 〖v I〗 **weave**

¶ The people in this region make their living from **weaving.**

osaeru 〖v II〗 **hold down, press down; suppress, control, restrain**

¶ [I] **held down** the paper with [my] hand(s) so that it wouldn't blow away.

¶ [I] **have hold** of the dog so you needn't be afraid.

osameru 〖v II〗 **settle, pay**

¶ Taxes **must be paid** by the end of this month.

¶ What is the final date **for paying** tuition?

oshieru 〖v II〗 **teach; tell, inform**

① [teach, instruct, show how]
¶ [Miss] Ueda **teaches** math in a junior high school.

② [tell, inform]
¶ Please **tell me** the way to the station.

oshii 〖adj〗 **disappointing, regrettable; a waste, a shame**

① [disappointing, regrettable]
¶ **I feel bad** that I lost the watch my father bought me.

oshii koto o shimashita.)

②[もったいない]

¶そのくつはまだはけます。捨てるのは惜しいですよ。 (Sono kutsu wa mada hakemasu. Suteru no wa *oshii* desu yo.)

osoi 遅い〖形〗

①[時刻が早くない]

¶山田さんはいつも夜遅く帰って来ます。 (Yamada san wa itsu mo yoru *osoku* kaette kimasu.)

¶遅いですね。中村さんはまだ来ませんか。 (*Osoi* desu ne. Nakamura san wa mada kimasen ka?)

↔hayai 早い

②[速度が速くない]

¶この汽車はずいぶん遅いですね。 (Kono kisha wa zuibun *osoi* desu ne.)

↔hayai 速い

osoraku 恐らく〖副〗

¶恐らく上田さんは今日は来ないでしょう。 (*Osoraku* Ueda san wa kyō wa konai deshō.)

¶恐らくあしたは雨でしょう。 (*Osoraku* ashita wa ame deshō.)

＊普通 あとに「だろう (darō)」「でしょう (deshō)」などの推量の言い方が来る。

osore おそれ〖名〗

¶台風が来ているので、大雨の**おそれ**があります。(Taifū ga kite iru node, ooame no *osore* ga arimasu.)

¶このテレビの番組は子供たちに悪い

② [a waste, a shame]

¶ Those shoes are still good. **It's a shame** to throw them away.

osoi 〖adj〗 **late; slow**

① [late]

¶ [Mr.] Yamada always returns home **late** at night.

¶ Hasn't [Miss] Nakamura come yet? [She]'s **so late!**

② [slow]

¶ This train is really **slow-moving**, isn't it?

osoraku 〖adv〗 **probably**

¶ [Mrs.] Ueda **probably** isn't coming today.

¶ It will **probably** rain tomorrow 〖**Chances are** it will rain tomorrow〗.
＊ Usually followed by an expression of conjecture such as *darō*, *deshō*, etc.

osore 〖n〗 **fear, concern, danger, risk, chance**

¶ There is **a threat** of heavy rains as a typhoon is on its way here.

¶ There is **concern** that this televi-

影響を与える**おそれ**があります。

(Kono terebi no bangumi wa kodomotachi ni warui eikyō o ataeru *osore* ga arimasu.)

sion program might have a bad influence on children.

osoreru 恐れる〚動Ⅱ〛

① [こわがる]

¶死を**恐れない**人はいません。 (Shi o *osorenai* hito wa imasen.)

② [心配する]

¶間違いを**恐れて**いては、日本語が上手になりません。 (Machigai o *osorete* ite wa, Nihongo ga jōzu ni narimasen.)

osoroshii 恐ろしい〚形〛

¶わたしはゆうべ**恐ろしい**夢を見ました。 (Watashi wa yūbe *osoroshii* yume o mimashita.)

¶**恐ろしくて**ひざが震えました。

(*Osoroshikute* hiza ga furuemashita.)

ossharu おっしゃる〚動Ⅰ〛

¶先生が「あした試験をする。」と**おっしゃいました。** (Sensei ga " Ashita shiken o suru." to *osshaimashita*.)

¶お名前は何と**おっしゃいます**か。

(Onamae wa nan to *osshaimasu* ka ?)

＊「言う (iu)」の尊敬語。「ますの形」は「おっしゃいます (osshaimasu)」となる。

osu 雄〚名〛

雄犬 (*osu*inu)　雄ねこ (*osu*neko)

＊動物について言い，人間には使わない。

⇔mesu 雌

osoreru 〚v Ⅱ〛 fear, be frightened; be apprehensive, be fearful

① [fear, be frightened, be afraid]

¶ Everyone **fears** death (literally, There is no one who **doesn't fear** death).

② [be apprehensive, be fearful, dread]

¶ You will not become good at Japanese if **you are afraid** of making mistakes.

osoroshii 〚adj〛 terrible, fearsome, horrible, dreadful

¶ I had a **terrible** nightmare last night.

¶ [I] **was so frightened** [my] knees were knocking.

ossharu 〚v I〛 say

¶ The teacher **said,** "There will be a test tomorrow."

¶ What **is** your name please? (very polite)

＊ *Ossharu* is the honorific form of *iu*. The -*masu* form is *osshaimasu*.

osu 〚n〛 male (animal)

a **male** dog // a **male** cat, a tomcat

＊ *Osu* is used only for animals.

osu 押す〖動Ⅰ〗
①［力を加えて物などを向こうへ動かす］
¶ドアを押して開けました。(Doa o *oshite* akemashita.)
¶危ないから，後ろから押さないでください。(Abunai kara, ushiro kara *osanaide* kudasai.)
↔**hiku** 引く
②［力を加えて印などをつける］
¶ここに判を押してください。(Koko ni han o *oshite* kudasai.)

oto 音〖名〗
音を立てる (*oto* o tateru)
¶庭の方で大きな音がしました。(Niwa no hō de ookina *oto* ga shimashita.)
¶ラジオの音をもう少し小さくしてください。(Rajio no *oto* o mō sukoshi chiisaku shite kudasai.)

otoko 男〖名〗
男の子 (*otoko* no ko) 男の人 (*otoko* no hito)
¶これは男のくつです。(Kore wa *otoko* no kutsu desu.)
¶このクラスには男の学生が少ないです。(Kono kurasu ni wa *otoko* no gakusei ga sukunai desu.)
⇔**onna** 女

otona 大人〖名〗
¶電車賃は大人100円，子供50円です。(Denshachin wa *otona* hyakuen, kodomo gojūen desu.)
¶その映画は大人だけしか見られません。(Sono eiga wa *otona* dake shika

osu 〖v Ⅰ〗 **push; stamp, seal**
① [push, shove, press]
¶ [I] **pushed** open the door.
¶ Please **don't push**—it's dangerous (said to people in a crowd, etc.).
② [stamp, seal, impress]
¶ Please **stamp** your personal seal here.

otagai ☞ **tagai**

oto 〖n〗 **sound, noise**
make **a sound,** make **a noise**
¶ There was a large **crash** 〖great **noise**〗 in the yard 〖garden〗.
¶ Please turn the radio down a little.

otoko 〖n〗 **man, male**
a boy // a man
¶ These are **men's** shoes.
¶ There are few **male** students in this class.

otona 〖n〗 **an adult, a grown-up**
¶ The train fare is a hundred yen **for adults** and fifty yen for children.
¶ Admission to that movie is restricted to **adults.**

miraremasen.)

⇔**kodomo** 子供

otonashii おとなしい〚形〛

¶山田さんはおとなしい人です。(Ya-mada san wa *otonashii* hito desu.)

¶「おとなしくしていれば，お菓子を上げます。」と，お母さんが子供に言いました。("*Otonashiku* shite ireba, okashi o agemasu." to, okāsan ga kodomo ni iimashita.)

otōsan お父さん〚名〛

¶あなたはお父さんに手紙を書きましたか。(Anata wa *otōsan* ni tegami o kakimashita ka?)

¶お父さん，お母さんが呼んでいますよ。(*Otōsan*, okāsan ga yonde imasu yo.)

＊ 他人の父親について話す場合，または自分の父親に呼びかけたり，家族の者に父親のことを言う場合に使う。他人に自分の父親のことを話す場合には，普通「お父さん (otōsan)」と言わないで「父 (chichi)」と言う。

⇔**okāsan** お母さん ⇒**chichi** 父

otosu 落とす〚動Ⅰ〛

①[落下させる]

¶コップを落として，割ってしまいました。(Koppu o *otoshite*, watte shimaimashita.)

②[なくす，失う]

¶電車の中でお金を落としました。(Densha no naka de okane o *oto-shimashita*.)

③[程度などを低い状態にする]

otonashii 〚adj〛 **gentle, docile, quiet, well-behaved, reserved, mild-mannered, even-tempered**

¶ [Mrs.] Yamada is **mild-mannered.**

¶ The mother said to her children, "**If you're good** I'll give you a sweet."

otōsan 〚n〛 **father**

¶ Have you written a letter to **your father?**

¶ **Dad,** Mom is calling you.

＊ *Otōsan* is used when talking about someone else's father, in direct address to one's own father, or when talking about one's father with other family members. When talking with nonfamily members about one's own father, one usually uses *chichi* rather than *otōsan*.

otosu 〚v Ⅰ〛 **drop; lose; decrease, lessen**

① [drop, let fall]

¶ [I] **dropped** the glass tumbler and it broke.

② [lose]

¶ [I] **lost** [my] money in the train.

③ [decrease, lessen, lower]

速度を落とす (sokudo o *otosu*)

otōto 弟〖名〗

¶わたしの弟は小学生です。(Watashi no *otōto* wa shōgakusei desu.)

¶あなたの弟さんはおいくつですか。(Anata no *otōto*san wa oikutsu desu ka?)

⇔ani 兄

ototoi おととい〖名〗

¶おとといは何日でしたか。(*Ototoi* wa nannichi deshita ka?)

¶おとといの晩，近所に火事がありました。(*Ototoi* no ban, kinjo ni kaji ga arimashita.)

ototoshi おととし〖名〗

¶わたしはおととしの2月に日本へ来ました。(Watashi wa *ototoshi* no nigatsu ni Nihon e kimashita.)

otto 夫〖名〗

¶妻は寝ないで夫の帰りを待っていました。(Tsuma wa nenaide *otto* no kaeri o matte imashita.)

＊結婚した男女の男のほうをさす言葉。自分の夫のことを他人に話す場合には普通「主人 (shujin)」と言う。

⇔tsuma 妻 ⇒shujin 主人

ou 追う〖動Ⅰ〗

①[追い払う]

¶手ではえを追いました。(Te de hae o *oimashita*.)

②[追いかける]

¶警官がどろぼうを追っていきました。(Keikan ga dorobō o *otte* ikimashita.)

reduce one's speed, slow down

otōto 〚n〛 **younger brother**

¶ My **younger brother** is an elementary school student.

¶ How old is your **younger brother?**

ototoi 〚n〛 **the day before yesterday**

¶ What was the date **the day before yesterday?**

¶ There was a fire in the neighborhood **the night before last.**

ototoshi 〚n〛 **the year before last**

¶ I came to Japan in February **the year before last** 〚**two years ago**〛.

otto 〚n〛 **husband**

¶ The wife waited up for **her husband.**

＊ *Otto* is used to indicate a male spouse. When talking with others about one's own husband, one usually uses *shujin*.

ou 〚v Ⅰ〛 **drive away; pursue, chase; be pressed, be driven**

① [drive away, shoo away]

¶ [He] **shooed away** a fly with [his] hand.

② [pursue, chase]

¶ The policeman **chased after** the thief.

③[急がされる]

¶仕事に追われて休む暇がありません。

(Shigoto ni *owarete* yasumu hima ga arimasen.)

owari 終わり〚名〛

¶夏休みも今週で終わりです。(Natsu-yasumi mo konshū de *owari* desu.)

¶今日の授業はこれで終わりです。

(Kyō no jugyō wa kore de *owari* desu.)

⇔hajime 始め

owaru 終わる〚動Ⅰ〛

①[終了する]

¶日本語の授業は9時に始まって4時に終わります。 (Nihongo no jugyō wa kuji ni hajimatte yoji ni *owarimasu*.)

¶もう仕事は終わりましたか。

(Mō shigoto wa *owarimashita* ka?)

¶これで今日の授業を終わります。

(Kore de kyō no jugyō o *owarimasu*.)

* 普通，自動詞として使うが，他動詞として使うこともある。

②[ある動作が終了することを表す]

¶その本はもう読み終わりました。(Sono hon wa mō yomi*owarimashita*.)

¶答えを書き終わったら，出してください。 (Kotae o kaki*owattara*, dashite kudasai.)

*「動詞(基幹の形)+終わる (owaru)」の形で使う。

⇔hajimaru 始まる ⇒oeru 終える

oya 親〚名〛

③ [be pressed, be driven, be over-tasked]

¶ [I] **have so much** work [I] have no time to rest.

owari 〚n〛 **end, close, conclusion**

¶ Summer vacation **ends** this week.

¶ This **concludes** class for today.

(-)owaru 〚v Ⅰ〛 **to end; to finish doing something**

① [end, finish, be finished]

¶ Japanese classes begin at nine o'clock and **end** at four o'clock.

¶ **Are you through** with work for today now ⟦**Is** the work **done** already⟧?

¶ This **concludes** class for today.

* *Owaru* is usually an intransitive verb, but it can also be used as a transitive verb.

② [finish doing something]

¶ [I]'ve already **finished** reading that book.

¶ Please hand in your answers when you're **finished.**

* Used in the pattern "verb (stem form) + -*owaru.*"

oya 〚n〛 **parents, a parent**

父親 (chichi*oya*) 母親 (haha*oya*)
¶この子はよく病気をして親に心配を
かけます。 (Kono ko wa yoku
byōki o shite *oya* ni shinpai o
kakemasu.)
⇔ko 子

oyako 親子〚名〛
¶あの人たちは親子のようによく似て
います。 (Ano hitotachi wa *oyako*
no yō ni yoku nite imasu.)

oyasumi nasai お休みなさい〚連〛
¶「お休みなさい」は，寝るときのあい
さつです。 (*"Oyasumi nasai"* wa,
neru toki no aisatsu desu.)

ōyō 応用〚名，～する〛
応用問題 (*ōyō*-mondai) 理論を実際
に応用する (riron o jissai ni *ōyō*
suru)

oyogu 泳ぐ〚動Ⅰ〛
¶あなたは泳ぐことができますか。
(Anata wa *oyogu* koto ga dekimasu
ka?)
¶池の中には魚がたくさん泳いでいま
す。 (Ike no naka ni wa sakana ga
takusan *oyoide* imasu.)
⇒suiei 水泳

a father // a mother
¶ This child is a worry to **its parents**
as it is frequently ill.

oyako 〚n〛 **parent and child**
¶ Those two resemble each other as
closely as if they were **parent and
child.**

oyasumi nasai 〚compd〛 **Good
night;** set expression exchanged
when parting for the last time that
evening or when retiring for the night
¶ *Oyasumi nasai* is the expression
used to someone at bedtime.

ōyō 〚n, ～*suru*〛 **practice, practical
application**
exercises (in a textbook), an **applied** question (on an exam) // put a
theory into actual **practice**

oyogu 〚v I〛 **swim**
¶ Do you know how **to swim?**
¶ There are many fish **swimming** in
the pond 〚pool〛.

ōzei ☞ **oozei**

P

painappuru パイナップル〖名〗

pan パン〖名〗
¶わたしは毎朝パンを食べてコーヒー
を飲みます。 (Watashi wa maiasa
pan o tabete kōhii o nomimasu.)

panku パンク〖名, ～する〗
¶自動車のタイヤがパンクしました。
(Jidōsha no taiya ga *panku* shimashita.)

-pāsento -パーセント〖尾〗
¶4分の1は 25 パーセントです。
(Yonbun no ichi wa nijūgo*pāsento*
desu.)
¶地震のときでもここにいれば，100パ
ーセント安全です。 (Jishin no toki
demo koko ni ireba, hyaku*pāsento*
anzen desu.)

pasupōto パスポート〖名〗
¶外国へ旅行するときには，パスポート
が必要です。(Gaikoku e ryokō suru
toki ni wa, *pasupōto* ga hitsuyō
desu.)

pātii パーティー〖名〗
¶昨日のパーティーはとても楽しかっ
たです。 (Kinō no *pātii* wa totemo
tanoshikatta desu.)
¶来週の日曜日に誕生日のパーティ
ーをしますから，ぜひおいでください。
(Raishū no nichiyōbi ni tanjōbi no
pātii o shimasu kara, zehi oide
kudasai.)

painappuru 〚n〛 pineapple

pan 〚n〛 **bread, toast, rolls, buns,**
etc.
¶ I have **bread** 〚**toast, croissants,
rolls,** etc.〛 and coffee every morning.

panku 〚n, ～*suru*〛 **a puncture, a
blowout**
¶ A tire **blew out** on the car.

-pāsento 〚suf〛 **percent**
¶ One-fourth is 25 **percent.**

¶ It is 100 **percent** safe here, even in
the case of an earthquake.

pasupōto 〚n〛 **passport**
¶ **A passport** is necessary when
traveling abroad.

pātii 〚n〛 **a party**
¶ **The party** yesterday was a lot of
fun.

¶ Please be sure to come to the birthday **party** next week Sunday.

-pēji　-ページ〖尾〗
¶10ページを開けてください。(Jip*pēji* o akete kudasai.)
¶わたしはこの本を50ページ読みました。(Watashi wa kono hon o gojip*pēji* yomimashita.)

pen　ペン〖名〗
¶わたしはペンを3本持っています。(Watashi wa *pen* o sanbon motte imasu.)

penki　ペンキ〖名〗
壁にペンキを塗る (kabe ni *penki* o nuru)

piano　ピアノ〖名〗
¶妹がピアノを弾いています。(Imōto ga *piano* o hiite imasu.)
¶山田さんはピアノが上手です。(Yamada san wa *piano* ga jōzu desu.)

pinpon　ピンポン〖名〗
¶友達とピンポンをしました。(Tomodachi to *pinpon* o shimashita.)

pittari　ぴったり〖副, ～する〗
①[すき間なくつく様子]
¶戸をぴったり閉めてください。(To o *pittari* shimete kudasai.)
②[よく合う様子]
¶この服はあなたにぴったりです。(Kono fuku wa anata ni *pittari* desu.)

poketto　ポケット〖名〗
ポケットに財布を入れる (*poketto* ni saifu o ireru)
¶ポケットの中に何が入っていますか。

-pēji 〖suf〗　**a page**
¶ Please open your books to **page** 10.
¶ I have read 50 **pages** of this book.

pen 〖n〗　**pen**
¶ I have three **pens.**

penki 〖n〗　(house) **paint**
to paint a wall

piano 〖n〗　**piano**
¶ My (younger) sister is playing **the piano.**
¶ [Mrs.] Yamada plays **the piano** well.

pinpon 〖n〗　**ping-pong, table tennis**
¶ [I] played **ping-pong** with a friend.

pittari 〖adv, ~*suru*〗　**tightly; exactly**
① [tightly]
¶ Please close the door **tightly.**
② [exactly, to a tee]
¶ This outfit is **exactly right** for you ⟦is **a perfect fit** on you⟧.

poketto 〖n〗　**pocket**
put one's wallet ⟦change purse⟧ in **one's pocket**
¶ What's in [your] **pocket**?

(*Poketto* no naka ni nani ga haitte
imasu ka?)

posuto　ポスト〖名〗
¶手紙をポストに入れました。
(Tegami o *posuto* ni iremashita.)

purezento　プレゼント〖名, ～する〗
¶クリスマスのプレゼントに何を上げ
ましょうか。(Kurisumasu no *purezento* ni nani o agemashō ka?)
⇨okurimono 贈り物

posuto 〖n〗　mailbox, postbox
¶ [I] dropped the letter in **the mailbox.**

purezento 〖n, ～*suru*〗　present, gift
¶ What shall [we] give [him] **for
Christmas?**

R

raigetsu 来月〖名〗

来月の中旬 (*raigetsu no chūjun*)

¶来月，アメリカから友達が来る予定です。(*Raigetsu, Amerika kara tomodachi ga kuru yotei desu.*)

rainen 来年〖名〗

来年の春 (*rainen no haru*)

¶上田さんは来年大学を卒業します。(*Ueda san wa rainen daigaku o sotsugyō shimasu.*)

raishū 来週〖名〗

¶来週の火曜日は何日ですか。(*Raishū no kayōbi wa nannichi desu ka?*)

¶来週，わたしは京都へ行くつもりです。(*Raishū, watashi wa Kyōto e iku tsumori desu.*)

raitā ライター〖名〗

ガスライター (*gasu-raitā*)

¶ライターでたばこに火をつけます。(*Raitā de tabako ni hi o tsukemasu.*)

rajio ラジオ〖名〗

ラジオをつける (*rajio o tsukeru*)

ラジオを消す (*rajio o kesu*)

¶毎朝，ラジオのニュースを聞いてから学校へ行きます。(*Maiasa, rajio no nyūsu o kiite kara gakkō e ikimasu.*)

raku 楽〖名，形動〗

①[体や心に苦しさを感じない様子，安らかな様子]

raigetsu 〖n〗 **next month**

the middle of **next month**

¶ A friend from the United States is scheduled to arrive **next month.**

rainen 〖n〗 **next year**

next spring, the spring of **next year**

¶ [Miss] Ueda graduates from college **next year.**

raishū 〖n〗 **next week**

¶ What date is Tuesday **next week?**

¶ I plan to go to Kyoto **next week.**

raitā 〖n〗 **lighter, cigarette lighter**

a butane **lighter**

¶ One uses **a lighter** to light cigarettes.

rajio 〖n〗 **radio**

turn on **the radio** // turn off **the radio**

¶ I listen to the **radio** news each morning before going to school.

raku 〖n, adj-v〗 **relief, at one's ease; comfortable, well-off; easy, simple**

① [relief, ease from pain, comfortable, at one's ease]

593

¶注射をしたので，痛みが楽になりました。(Chūsha o shita node, itami ga *raku* ni narimashita.)

②[経済的に余裕がある様子]
¶こんなに安い月給では，とても楽な生活はできません。(Konna ni yasui gekkyū de wa totemo *raku* na seikatsu wa dekimasen.)

¶物価が高いので，生活が楽ではありません。(Bukka ga takai node, seikatsu ga *raku* de wa arimasen.)

③[易しくて苦労しなくてもよい様子]
¶今度の試験は案外楽にできました。(Kondo no shiken wa angai *raku* ni dekimashita.)

¶外国語で毎日日記をつけるのは楽ではありません。(Gaikokugo de mainichi nikki o tsukeru no wa *raku* de wa arimasen.)

rāmen ラーメン〚名〛
¶食堂でラーメンを注文しました。(Shokudō de *rāmen* o chūmon shimashita.)

rareru られる〚助動〛
①[受け身の意味を表す]
¶その学生は質問に上手に答えたので，先生にほめられました。(Sono gakusei wa shitsumon ni jōzu ni kotaeta node, sensei ni home*raremashita*.)
¶わたしは大好きなお菓子を弟にみんな食べられてしまいました。
(Watashi wa daisuki na okashi o otōto ni minna tabe*rarete* shimaimashita.)

¶ The pain **was alleviated** by the shot.

② [comfortable, well-off]
¶ There is no way one can live **in comfort** on such cheap wages.

¶ Life **is not easy** with such high prices.

③ [easy, simple]
¶ The test this time was surprisingly **easy.**

¶ **It is no easy task** to keep a daily diary in a foreign language.

rāmen 〚n〛 Chinese noodle soup
¶ [I] ordered *rāmen* in a restaurant 〚the cafeteria〛.

-rareru 〚auxil〛 a verb ending expressing the passive, the potential, respect, etc.
① [expresses the passive and suffering passive]
¶ That student **was praised** by the teacher for answering the question well.
¶ My younger brother **ate up** all of my favorite cakes 〚candy, etc.〛 (the suffering passive).

¶あしたは試験があるので，今日友達に来られると困ります。 (Ashita wa shiken ga aru node, kyō tomodachi ni ko*rareru* to komarimasu.)

② [可能の意味を表す]

¶この肉は腐っているので，食べられません。 (Kono niku wa kusatte iru node, tabe*raremasen*.)

¶質問が難しかったので，わたしは答えられませんでした。 (Shitsumon ga muzukashikatta node, watashi wa kotae*raremasen* deshita.)

③ [尊敬の意味を表す]

¶いつごろ日本へ来られたのですか。 (Itsu goro Nihon e ko*rareta* no desu ka?)

¶先生は毎朝何時ごろお宅を出られますか。 (Sensei wa maiasa nanji goro otaku o de*raremasu* ka?)

④ [自発の意味を表す]

¶だんだん秋らしい様子が感じられるようになりました。 (Dandan akirashii yōsu ga kanji*rareru* yō ni narimashita.)

＊ Ⅱ型動詞とⅢ型動詞の「来る (kuru)」につく。Ⅰ型動詞とⅢ型動詞の「する (suru)」には「れる (reru)」がつく。

⇨reru れる

rashii　らしい〚助動〛

¶中村さんは留守らしいです。 (Nakamura san wa rusu *rashii* desu.)

¶どうも風邪を引いたらしく，頭が痛いです。 (Dōmo kaze o hiita *rashi-*

¶ As I have a test tomorrow it would be inconvenient if a friend **should come to visit me** today (the suffering passive).

② [expresses the potential]

¶ This meat **can't be eaten**—it's rotten.

¶ I **couldn't answer** as the question was very difficult.

③ [expresses respect]

¶ When **did you come** to Japan?

¶ What time **do you leave home** each morning, sir〚ma'am〛? (said to a teacher, doctor, etc.)

④ [expresses autonomous action]

¶ It has gradually **come to look** like autumn.

＊ *-rareru* is added to Type II verbs and to the Type III verb *kuru* (→ *korareru*); *-reru* is added to Type I verbs and to the Type III verb *suru* (→ *sareru*).

rashii〚auxil〛 **seem, appear, look like**

¶ **It seems** that [Mrs.] Nakamura isn't at home.

¶ [My] head aches—**it feels like**

ku, atama ga itai desu.)

¶今度の試験は難しいらしいですよ。

(Kondo no shiken wa muzukashii *rashii* desu yo.)

＊ 名詞，動詞，形容詞，形容動詞，ある種の助動詞などについて，ある根拠に基づいてものごとの状況や事態などを推定するという意味を表す。

-rashii -らしい〖尾〗

男らしい顔 (otoko*rashii* kao) 女らしい態度 (onna*rashii* taido)

¶今日は本当に春らしい天気です。

(Kyō wa hontō ni haru*rashii* tenki desu.)

rei 礼〖名〗

①〖おじぎ〗

¶先生が教室に入ってこられたので，学生は立って礼をしました。 (Sensei ga kyōshitsu ni haitte korareta node, gakusei wa tatte *rei* o shimashita.)

②〖謝意を表すこと〗

お礼をする (o*rei* o suru)

¶お世話になったお礼に何か差し上げたいのですが。 (Osewa ni natta o*rei* ni nani ka sashiagetai no desu ga.)

rei 例〖名〗

¶先生は例を挙げて，学生にわかりやすく説明しました。 (Sensei wa *rei* o agete, gakusei ni wakariyasuku setsumei shimashita.)

rei 零〖名〗

零下 10 度 (*rei*ka jūdo)

[I]'ve caught a cold.

¶ **It sounds like** the next exam will be a hard one.

＊ *Rashii* is used with nouns, verbs, adjectives, adjective-verbs, and certain auxiliaries. It expresses a supposition about a state or condition based on certain evidence.

-rashii 〖suf〗 **be like, be worthy of**

a man**ly** face // a lady**like** bearing, feminine deportment

¶ Today is a really spring**like** day.

＊ -*rashii* indicates that something or someone is acting like what it in fact is, i.e., *otokorashii* indicates a man being manly and not a woman being manlike, etc.

rei 〖n〗 **bow, salute; thanks**

① [bow, salute]

¶ The students stood and **bowed** when their teacher entered the classroom.

② [thanks, gratitude, appreciation]

give **a token of one's appreciation;** give **a reward**

¶ I want to give you something **in appreciation** for your kindness to me.

rei 〖n〗 **example**

¶ The teacher gave **an example** in order to explain in a way easy for the students to understand.

rei 〖n〗 **zero**

10 degrees below **zero,** minus 10 de-

¶昨日の試験で，零点を取ってしまいました。(Kinō no shiken de, *rei*ten o totte shimaimashita.)

reibō 冷房〖名，〜する〗
¶この建物には冷房があります。(Kono tatemono ni wa *reibō* ga arimasu.)
⇔**danbō** 暖房

reigai 例外 〖名〗
¶デパートはたいてい6時に閉まりますが，このデパートだけは例外で，7時まで開いています。 (Depāto wa taitei rokuji ni shimarimasu ga, kono depāto dake wa *reigai* de, shichiji made aite imasu.)
¶例外のない規則はないと言われています。 (*Reigai* no nai kisoku wa nai to iwarete imasu.)

reinkōto レインコート〖名〗
¶雨が降りそうだから，レインコートを着ていきなさい。(Ame ga furisō da kara, *reinkōto* o kite ikinasai.)

reizōko 冷蔵庫〖名〗
冷蔵庫にしまう (*reizōko* ni shimau)
¶牛乳が腐らないように冷蔵庫に入れておきます。 (Gyūnyū ga kusaranai yō ni *reizōko* ni irete okimasu.)

rekishi 歴史〖名〗
¶わたしは大学で日本の歴史を勉強しています。(Watashi wa daigaku de Nihon no *rekishi* o benkyō shite imasu.)
＊「日本の歴史 (Nihon no rekishi)」は「日本史 (Nihonshi)」，「世界の歴史 (sekai no rekishi)」は「世界史

grees

¶ [I] got **a zero** on yesterday's test.

reibō 〖n, ~*suru*〗 **air conditioning**
¶ This building has **air conditioning.**

reigai 〖n〗 **exception**
¶ Although department stores generally close at six o'clock, this one **is an exception** and stays open until seven.

¶ It is said that there is **an exception** to every rule (literally, that there is no rule without **an exception**).

reinkōto 〖n〗 **raincoat**
¶ Wear **a raincoat**—it looks like rain.

reizōko 〖n〗 **refrigerator, freezer**
put away in **the refrigerator** 〖**freezer**〗
¶ [We] keep the milk in **the refrigerator** so it won't spoil.

rekishi 〖n〗 **history**
¶ I am studying Japanese **history** at college.

＊ *Nihon no rekishi* (the history of Japan) is shortened to *Nihonshi*, *sekai no rekishi* (world history) to (sekaishi)」,「東洋の歴史 (tōyō no rekishi)」は「東洋史 (tōyōshi)」,「西洋の歴史 (seiyō no rekishi)」は「西洋史 (seiyōshi)」と言う。

sekaishi, *tōyō no rekishi* (Oriental history) to *tōyōshi*, *seiyō no rekishi* (Western history) to *seiyōshi*, etc.

rekōdo レコード〖名〗

レコードをかける (*rekōdo* o kakeru)
¶田中さんは, コーヒーを飲みながらレコードを聞いています。(Tanaka san wa, kōhii o nominagara *rekōdo* o kiite imasu.)

rekōdo 〖n〗 (musical) **record**

put on **a record,** play **a record**
¶ [Miss] Tanaka is drinking coffee and listening to **a record.**

ren'ai 恋愛〖名, ～する〗

恋愛小説 (*ren'ai*-shōsetsu) 恋愛結婚 (*ren'ai*-kekkon)
¶恋愛して結婚する若い人が増えています。(*Ren'ai* shite kekkon suru wakai hito ga fuete imasu.)
⇨koi 恋

ren'ai 〖n, ～*suru*〗 **love**

a **love** story, a romance // a **love** marriage (vs. an arranged marriage)
¶ The number of young people marrying in **love** matches is increasing.

renraku 連絡〖名, ～する〗

¶長い間連絡がないので, どうしたのかと心配していました。(Nagai aida *renraku* ga nai node, dō shita no ka to shinpai shite imashita.)
¶すぐ山田さんに電話で連絡してください。(Sugu Yamada san ni denwa de *renraku* shite kudasai.)

renraku 〖n, ～*suru*〗 **contact, communication, connection**

¶ I hadn't **heard anything** from you for a long time so I was worried about what had happened to you.

¶ Please **telephone** [Mr.] Yamada right away.

renshū 練習〖名, ～する〗

練習問題 (*renshū*-mondai)
¶春子さんは毎日3時間ピアノを練習しています。(Haruko san wa mainichi sanjikan piano o *renshū* shite imasu.)
¶難しい発音でも, 練習すれば上手になります。(Muzukashii hatsuon demo, *renshū* sureba jōzu ni nari-

renshū 〖n, ～*suru*〗 **practice, rehearsal**

exercises, **practice** problems
¶ Haruko **practices** the piano for three hours every day.

¶ **If you practice,** you can master even difficult pronunciations.

masu.)

repōto レポート〚名〛

¶宿題のレポートをあしたまでに出してください。(Shukudai no *repōto* o ashita made ni dashite kudasai.)

reru れる〚助動〛

①［受身の意味を表す］

¶上田さんは宿題を忘れたので，先生にしかられました。(Ueda san wa shukudai o wasureta node, sensei ni shikara*remashita*.)

¶わたしは犬に手をかまれました。(Watashi wa inu ni te o kama*remashita*.)

¶買い物に行く途中で，雨に降られて困りました。(Kaimono ni iku tochū de, ame ni fura*rete* komarimashita.)

¶委員会は2階の会議室で開かれています。(Iinkai wa nikai no kaigishitsu de hiraka*rete* imasu.)

②［可能の意味を表す］

¶昨日は病気で学校に行かれませんでした。(Kinō wa byōki de gakkō ni ika*remasen* deshita.)

¶ゆうべはコーヒーを飲みすぎて，なかなか眠られませんでした。(Yūbe wa kōhii o nomisugite, nakanaka nemura*remasen* deshita.)

* この場合はほとんどⅠ型動詞の可能の形，例えば「行ける (ikeru)」「眠れる (nemureru)」を使う。また，「自動車の運転をする (jidōsha no unten o suru)」の「する (suru)」，「自動車

repōto 〚n〛 **report, research paper, term paper**

¶ Please hand in **your papers** by tomorrow.

-reru 〚auxil〛 a verb ending expressing the passive, the potential, respect, etc.

① [expresses the passive and the suffering passive]

¶ [Miss] Ueda **was scolded** by [her] teacher for forgetting [her] homework.

¶ I **had** my hand **bitten** by a dog (the suffering passive).

¶ **I was caught** in the rain on my way shopping (the suffering passive).

¶ The committee 〚board〛 meeting **is being held** in the conference room on the second floor.

② [expresses the potential]

¶ Yesterday [I] was sick and **couldn't go** to school.

¶ Last night I drank too much coffee and **had a hard time getting to sleep.**

* The potential of almost all Type I verbs is formed in this way, as in *ikeru* (from *iku*) or *nemureru* (from *nemuru*). In the case of constructions with the Type III verb *suru*,

を運転する (jidōsha o unten suru)」の「運転する (unten suru)」などのⅢ型動詞の場合は、「自動車の運転ができる (jidōsha no unten ga dekiru)」、「自動車が運転できる (jidōsha ga unten dekiru)」などと「できる (dekiru)」を使う。

→dekiru できる

③[尊敬の意味を表す]

¶山田先生はもうお宅へ帰られましたか。(Yamada sensei wa mō otaku e kaeraremashita ka?)

¶いつ、そのニュースを聞かれたのですか。(Itsu, sono nyūsu o kikareta no desu ka?)

④[自発の意味を表す]

¶昔の写真を見ると、子供のころのことが思い出されます。(Mukashi no shashin o miru to, kodomo no koro no koto ga omoidasaremasu.)

＊Ⅰ型動詞とⅢ型動詞の「する (suru)」につく。Ⅱ型動詞とⅢ型動詞の「来る (kuru)」には「られる (rareru)」がつく。

⇨rareru られる

ressha 列車〚名〛

貨物列車 (kamotsu-*ressha*)

¶駅に列車がとまっています。(Eki ni *ressha* ga tomatte imasu.)

resutoran レストラン〚名〛

¶あの角のレストランで食事をしましょう。(Ano kado no *resutoran* de shokuji o shimashō.)

(-)retsu (-)列〚名, 尾〛

---

such as *jidōsha no unten o suru* (drive a car) or *jidōsha o unten suru* (drive a car), *dekiru* is used: *jidōsha no unten ga dekiru* (be able to drive a car), *jidōsha ga unten dekiru* (be able to drive a car).

③ [expresses respect]

¶ **Has** Professor 〚Doctor〛 Yamada already **left for home?**

¶ When **did you hear** that news?

④ [expresses autonomous action]

¶ Looking at old photos **reminds** [me] of [my] childhood.

＊ *-reru* is used with Type I verbs and the Type III verb *suru* (→ *sareru*); *-rareru* is used with Type II verbs and the Type III verb *kuru* (→ *korareru*).

ressha 〚n〛 **train**

a freight **train**

¶ **A train** is stopped at the station.

resutoran 〚n〛 **restaurant**

¶ Let's eat at that **restaurant** on the corner.

(-)retsu 〚n, suf〛 **line, queue; row, column**

1 〖名〗

¶駅はたいへんこんでいて，切符を買う人が列を作っていました。(Eki wa taihen konde ite, kippu o kau hito ga *retsu* o tsukutte imashita.)

2 〖尾〗

1列 (ichi*retsu*)　2列 (ni*retsu*)
前列 (zen*retsu*)　後列 (kō*retsu*)

rieki 利益〖名〗

①[もうけ]

¶この本を売ると，20パーセントの利益があります。(Kono hon o uru to, nijippāsento no *rieki* ga arimasu.)

②[ためになること，得になること]

¶将来，何か社会の利益になることをしたいと思います。(Shōrai, nani ka shakai no *rieki* ni naru koto o shitai to omoimasu.)

rikai 理解〖名，～する〗

¶新しい言葉は，辞書を引いて意味を正しく理解しなければいけません。(Atarashii kotoba wa, jisho o hiite imi o tadashiku *rikai* shinakereba ikemasen.)

¶あの人の言うことは，どうもよく理解できません。(Ano hito no iu koto wa, dōmo yoku *rikai* dekimasen.)

rikō りこう〖形動〗

¶この子はりこうな子供で，どの科目もよくできます。(Kono ko wa *rikō* na kodomo de, dono kamoku mo yoku dekimasu.)

¶危ない仕事は初めからしないほうがりこうです。(Abunai shigoto wa

---

1 〚n〛 line, queue

¶ The station was very crowded; people **were lined up** to buy tickets.

2 〚suf〛 row, column

one **row**, one **column** // two **rows**, two **columns** // the front **row** // the back 〚last〛 **row**

rieki 〚n〛 **profit; benefit, advantage**

① [profit]

¶ There is a 20 percent **profit** on the sale of this book.

② [benefit, advantage]

¶ My future plans are to work for the public **good.**

rihatsuten ☞ **tokoya**

rikai 〚n, ~*suru*〛 **understanding, comprehension**

¶ Words new to you should be looked up in the dictionary so you correctly **grasp** their meaning.

¶ I just don't **understand** what [he] says.

rikō 〚adj-v〛 **bright, intelligent, sensible, shrewd, smart**

¶ This child **is quite bright** and does well in every subject at school.

¶ **It is wiser** to refuse dangerous work from the outset.

601

hajime kara shinai hō ga *rikō* desu.)

riku 陸〖名〗

¶わたしは船を降りて陸に上がりました。(Watashi wa fune o orite *riku* ni agarimashita.)

¶海の広さは陸の広さの何倍ですか。(Umi no hirosa wa *riku* no hirosa no nanbai desu ka?)

rikutsu 理屈〖名〗

①[道理, ものごとがそうなるわけ]
理屈に合わない (*rikutsu* ni awanai)
¶あの人の言うことにも理屈はあります。(Ano hito no iu koto ni mo *rikutsu* wa arimasu.)

②[自分の考えを通すための理由づけ]
¶田中さんは理屈ばかり言って何もしません。(Tanaka san wa *rikutsu* bakari itte nani mo shimasen.)

ringo りんご〖名〗

¶このりんごは一ついくらですか。(Kono *ringo* wa hitotsu ikura desu ka?)

rinji 臨時〖名〗

①[定時でないこと]
臨時休業 (*rinji*-kyūgyō) 臨時列車 (*rinji*-ressha)
¶あしたは臨時に休みます。(Ashita wa *rinji* ni yasumimasu.)
¶臨時の収入がありました。(*Rinji* no shūnyū ga arimashita.)

②[一時的なこと, 間に合わせ]
¶今日は山田先生がお休みですから, 臨時にわたしが教えます。(Kyō wa

riku 〚n〛 land, shore

¶ I alighted from the boat 〚ship〛 and stepped onto **the shore.**

¶ How many times is the area of the world's oceans larger than that of **the land?**

rikutsu 〚n〛 logic, reason; pretext, excuse

① [logic, reason]
illogical, irrational
¶ **There's something to** what [he] says too.

② [pretext, excuse]
¶ [Mr.] Tanaka is **all talk** and no action.

ringo 〚n〛 apple

¶ How much are these **apples** apiece?

rinji 〚n〛 special, extraordinary; temporary, provisional

① [special, extraordinary, extra, unscheduled, emergency]
a **special** holiday; Closed Today // a **special** train
¶ [We] will be closed tomorrow.
¶ [I] had some **supplementary** income.

② [temporary, provisional, interim]
¶ I will be your **substitute** teacher today as Professor Yamada is absent.

Yamada sensei ga oyasumi desu kara, *rinji* ni watashi ga oshie-masu.)

rippa 立派〖形動〗

①[堂々として美しい]

¶山田さんの家はずいぶん**立派**ですね。 (Yamada san no ie wa zuibun *rippa* desu ne.)

¶会議で自分の意見を主張した時の中村さんの態度は**立派**でした。 (Kaigi de jibun no iken o shuchō shita toki no Nakamura san no taido wa *rippa* deshita.)

②[申し分ない様子]

立派な学者 (*rippa* na gakusha)

¶田中さんは大学を**立派**な成績で卒業しました。(Tanaka san wa daigaku o *rippa* na seiseki de sotsugyō shimashita.)

¶あの人はなかなか**立派**な英語を話します。(Ano hito wa nakanaka *rippa* na Eigo o hanashimasu.)

riron 理論〖名〗

¶上田さんは物理学の新しい**理論**を発表しました。(Ueda san wa butsuri-gaku no atarashii *riron* o happyō shimashita.)

¶**理論**は立派ですが，実際にうまくいくでしょうか。(*Riron* wa rippa desu ga, jissai ni umaku iku deshō ka?)

risō 理想〖名〗

高い**理想** (takai *risō*)

理想的な家庭 (*risō*teki na katei)

¶**理想**と現実とは違います。(*Risō* to

rippa 〚adj-v〛 **fine, handsome, splendid; fine, excellent, superb**

① [fine, handsome, splendid, commanding]

¶ [Mr.] Yamada has a really **fine** house.

¶ [Mr.] Nakamura **was very impressive** while upholding [his] opinions at the meeting.

② [fine, excellent, superb, brilliant, admirable]

¶ [Miss] Tanaka graduated from college with a **fine** record.

¶ [He] speaks English **exceptionally well**.

riron 〚n〛 **theory**

¶ [Mr.] Ueda has made public a new **theory** in physics 〚Mr. Ueda made public a new **theory** in physics〛.

¶ It sounds fine **in theory** but will it actually work well in practice?

risō 〚n〛 **an ideal**

lofty **ideals** // a **model** home 〚family〛

¶ There is a gap between **the ideal**

genjitsu to wa chigaimasu.)

-rittoru -リットル〘尾〙
1リットル (ichi*rittoru*) 4リットル (yon*rittoru*) 9リットル (kyū*rittoru*)

riyō 利用〘名, ～する〙
¶わたしは図書館を利用して, 勉強しています。(Watashi wa toshokan o *riyō* shite benkyō shite imasu.)
¶余ったきれを利用して, 人形の服を作りました。(Amatta kire o *riyō* shite, ningyō no fuku o tsukurimashita.)

riyū 理由〘名〙
¶あなたが学校をやめる理由は何ですか。(Anata ga gakkō o yameru *riyū* wa nan desu ka?)
¶上田さんは病気を理由に会社を休みました。(Ueda san wa byōki o *riyū* ni kaisha o yasumimashita.)

rōdō 労働〘名, ～する〙
労働者 (*rōdō*sha) 労働組合 (*rōdō*-kumiai) 重労働 (jū*rōdō*) 労働時間 (*rōdō*-jikan)
¶この工場では1日8時間労働です。(Kono kōjō de wa ichinichi hachi-jikan-*rōdō* desu.)

rōjin 老人〘名〙
老人ホーム (*rōjin*-hōmu)
¶電車やバスの中では, 老人に席を譲りましょう。(Densha ya basu no naka de wa, *rōjin* ni seki o yuzuri-mashō.)
⇒toshiyori 年寄り

rōka 廊下〘名〙

and actual reality.

-rittoru 〚suf〛 **liter(s)**
one **liter** // four **liters** // nine **liters**

riyō 〚n, ～*suru*〛 **use, utilize, make good use of, exploit**
¶ I **avail myself** of the library in my studies.

¶ I **used** the leftover cloth to make doll's clothes.

riyū 〚n〛 **reason, cause**
¶ What is your **reason** for quitting school?

¶ [Miss] Ueda stayed home from work **for reasons of** ill health.

rōdō 〚n, ～*suru*〛 **labor, manual labor**
a laborer, a worker // a labor union // heavy labor // working hours; man-hours
¶ This factory has an eight-hour workday.

rōjin 〚n〛 an old person, the aged, the elderly
a home for the aged, an old-age home
¶ All should cooperate in offering train and bus seats to the elderly.

rōka 〚n〛 corridor, hall

¶廊下で話をしている人がいます。
(*Rōka* de hanashi o shite iru hito
ga imasu.)

roketto ロケット〖名〗
¶ロケットで月に行けるようになりま
した。(*Roketto* de tsuki ni ikeru yō
ni narimashita.)

roku 六〖名〗

rokugatsu 六月〖名〗

rokuon 録音〖名, ～する〗
録音機 (*rokuon*ki)
¶自分の声をテープに録音して, 発音
の練習をします。 (Jibun no koe o
tēpu ni *rokuon* shite, hatsuon no
renshū o shimasu.)

rōmaji ローマ字〖名〗
¶平仮名は読めませんから, ローマ字
で書いてください。(Hiragana wa
yomemasen kara, *rōmaji* de kaite
kudasai.)

(-)ron (-)論〖名, 尾〗

1〖名〗
¶そのことについては, いろいろな論
があります。(Sono koto ni tsuite
wa, iroiro na *ron* ga arimasu.)

2〖尾〗
世論 (se*ron*) 人生論 (jinsei*ron*)
文学論 (bungaku*ron*) 教育論 (kyōiku*ron*)

ronbun 論文〖名〗
卒業論文 (sotsugyō-*ronbun*) 博士
論文 (hakushi-*ronbun*)
¶ 12 月の末までに論文を書かなけれ
ばなりません。(Jūnigatsu no sue

roketto 〖n〗 **rocket**
¶ It is now possible to go to the
moon by **rocket.**

roku 〖n〗 **six**

rokugatsu 〖n〗 **June**

rokuon 〖n, ～*suru*〗 **recording,
make a recording of**
a recorder, a tape **recorder,** a
transcribing machine
¶ [I] practice pronunciation by **tap-
ing** [my] own voice.

rōmaji 〖n〗 **roman letters,** *romaji*
(roman letters used to transcribe
Japanese)
¶ [I] can't read *hiragana* so please
write it in **roman letters.**

(-)ron 〖n, suf〗 **argument, debate,
controversy; theory, opinion, view**
1 〖n〗 argument, debate; theory,
opinion
¶ There are various **theories** concerning that ⟦Opinion is divided on
that question⟧.
2 〖suf〗 theory, view
public **opinion** // one's **philosophy**
of life // one's **views** on literature, a
literary **theory** // educational **theory**
⟦philosophy⟧
ronbun 〖n〗 **essay, thesis, paper**
a graduation **thesis** // a doctoral
thesis
¶ [I] must finish writing **[my] thesis**

made ni *ronbun* o kakanakereba narimasen.)

rōsoku ろうそく〚名〛

¶ろうそくに火をつけてください。

(*Rōsoku* ni hi o tsukete kudasai.)

rusu 留守〚名〛

¶友達を訪ねましたが、留守で会えませんでした。(Tomodachi o tazunemashita ga, *rusu* de aemasen deshita.)

¶旅行に出かけるので、二、三日家を留守にします。 (Ryokō ni dekakeru node, ni-sannichi ie o *rusu* ni shimasu.)

ryō 量〚名〛

¶砂糖の量はこのぐらいでいいですか。(Satō no *ryō* wa kono gurai de ii desu ka?)

¶忙しすぎるから、来月から仕事の量を少し減らすつもりです。(Isogashisugiru kara, raigetsu kara shigoto no *ryō* o sukoshi herasu tsumori desu.)

ryō 寮〚名〛

¶わたしは学校の寮にいます。(Watashi wa gakkō no *ryō* ni imasu.)

¶山田さんは会社の寮に入りました。(Yamada san wa kaisha no *ryō* ni hairimashita.)

ryō- 両-〚頭〛

両手 (*ryō*te) 両足 (*ryō*ashi) 両国 (*ryō*koku)

-ryō -料〚尾〛

入場料 (nyūjō*ryō*) 電話料 (denwa-

by the end of December.

rōsoku 〚n〛 candle

¶ Please light **the candle.**

rusu 〚n〛 absent, out

¶ [I] went to visit a friend but [he] **wasn't at home.**

¶ The house **will be empty** for two or three days because [I] am going away on a trip.

ryō 〚n〛 quantity, amount, volume

¶ Is this enough sugar?

¶ I'm too busy so I plan to cut back on my work **load** starting next month.

ryō 〚n〛 dormitory

¶ I am living in a school **dormitory.**

¶ [Mr.] Yamada has moved into a company **dormitory** 〚Mr. Yamada moved into a company **dormitory**〛.

ryō- 〚pref〛 both, two, a couple of

both hands, **both** arms // **both** feet, **both** legs // **both** countries

-ryō 〚suf〛 charge, rate, fee, allowance

an admission **fee** // the telephone

ryō)　使用料 (shiyōryō)　授業料 (jugyōryō)　受験料 (jukenryō)

charge // a rental **fee** // tuition // an examination **fee**

ryōgawa　両側〖名〗

¶道の両側に店が並んでいます。(Michi no *ryōgawa* ni mise ga narande imasu.)

ryōgawa 〚n〛 **both sides, either side**

¶ There are shops on **both sides** of the street.

ryōhō　両方〖名〗

¶山田さんは英語もフランス語も両方上手です。 (Yamada san wa Eigo mo Furansugo mo *ryōhō* jōzu desu.)

¶わたしは二つの学校の試験を受けて両方とも受かりました。 (Watashi wa futatsu no gakkō no shiken o ukete *ryōhō*tomo ukarimashita.)

ryōhō 〚n〛 **both, both sides, both parties**

¶ [Mrs.] Yamada is good at **both** English and French.

¶ I took the entrance exams for two schools and passed **both** of them.

ryōji　領事〖名〗

領事館 (*ryōji*kan)

ryōji 〚n〛 **consul, consular representative**

a consulate

ryokan　旅館〖名〗

¶旅行するときは，ホテルより旅館に泊まるほうがおもしろいですよ。 (Ryokō suru toki wa, hoteru yori *ryokan* ni tomaru hō ga omoshiroi desu yo.)

ryokan 〚n〛 **Japanese-style inn**

¶ When traveling in Japan it is more fun to stay at **a Japanese-style inn** than at a Western-style hotel.

ryōkin　料金〖名〗

電気料金 (denki-*ryōkin*)　ガス料金 (gasu-*ryōkin*)　タクシー料金 (taku-shii-*ryōkin*)

¶子供の料金は大人の半分です。(Kodomo no *ryōkin* wa otona no hanbun desu.)

＊普通，何かをしてもらったり，使ったり，利用したりするときに払う金のことをいう。

ryōkin 〚n〛 **charge, rate, fee, fare, toll**

an electricity **bill** // a gas **bill** // a taxi **fare**

¶ The child's **fare** ⟦admission **fee**⟧ is half that of adults.

＊ Usually refers to the money paid when one has something done for one, uses something, etc.

ryokō　旅行〖名，～する〗

ryokō 〚n, ～*suru*〛 **travel, journey, trip**

¶わたしは旅行が好きです。(Watashi wa *ryokō* ga suki desu.)

¶日本へ行ったら、ほうぼうを旅行したいです。(Nihon e ittara, hōbō o *ryokō* shitai desu.)

ryōri 料理〚名，〜する〛
日本料理 (Nihon-*ryōri*) 中華料理 (Chūka-*ryōri*) フランス料理 (Furansu-*ryōri*) 料理を作る (*ryōri* o tsukuru)

¶あなたはどんな料理が好きですか。(Anata wa donna *ryōri* ga suki desu ka?)

¶山田さんの奥さんはとても料理が上手です。(Yamada san no okusan wa totemo *ryōri* ga jōzu desu.)

ryōshin 両親〚名〛
¶机の上に両親の写真が置いてあります。(Tsukue no ue ni *ryōshin* no shashin ga oite arimasu.)

¶あの子は小さい時に両親を亡くしました。(Ano ko wa chiisai toki ni *ryōshin* o nakushimashita.)

ryōshūsho 領収書〚名〛
¶買い物をして，領収書をもらいました。(Kaimono o shite, *ryōshūsho* o moraimashita.)

ryūgaku 留学〚名，〜する〛
留学生 (*ryūgaku*sei)
¶来年，わたしは日本へ留学するつもりです。(Rainen, watashi wa Nihon e *ryūgaku* suru tsumori desu.)

ryūkō 流行〚名，〜する〛
¶これが今年流行のネクタイです。(Kotoshi-ryūkō...)

¶ I like **to travel.**

¶ If I go to Japan **I want to travel** extensively there.

ryōri 〚n, ~*suru*〛 cooking, cuisine, food, dish
Japanese **cooking,** Japanese **food //** Chinese **cooking,** Chinese **food //** French **cuisine,** French **food //** fix **a meal**

¶ What kind of **food** do you like?

¶ Mr. Yamada's wife is an excellent **cook.**

ryōshin 〚n〛 one's parents
¶ There is a photo of **[my] parents** on [my] desk.

¶ That child lost **its parents** at an early age.

ryōshūsho 〚n〛 receipt
¶ [I] did some shopping and received **a receipt.**

ryūgaku 〚n, ~*suru*〛 study abroad
a student **studying abroad,** an **exchange** student
¶ I plan **to study** in Japan next year.

ryūkō 〚n, ~*suru*〛 fashion, fad, popularity; prevalence
¶ This is the type of necktie **in**

(Kore ga kotoshi *ryūkō* no nekutai desu.)

¶悪い風邪が流行していますから，気をつけてください。(Warui kaze ga *ryūkō* shite imasu kara, ki o tsukete kudasai.)

vogue this year.

¶ Please be careful as a bad flu virus **is going around** now.

S

sa 差〖名〗

¶この辺りは、昼と夜とではかなり温度の差があります。(Kono atari wa, hiru to yoru to de wa kanari ondo no *sa* ga arimasu.)

¶昨日の試験では、1点の差で1番になれませんでした。(Kinō no shiken de wa, itten no *sa* de ichiban ni naremasen deshita.)

-sa -さ〖尾〗

暑さ (atsu*sa*) 寒さ (samu*sa*) 美しさ (utsukushi*sa*) 白さ (shiro*sa*) 苦しさ (kurushi*sa*) 明るさ (akaru*sa*) 重さ (omo*sa*) 長さ (naga*sa*) 速さ (haya*sa*) 深さ (fuka*sa*) 正確さ (seikaku*sa*) すなおさ (sunao*sa*)

＊ 形容詞・形容動詞の語幹に続いて名詞を作り、ものごとの性質・状態やその程度を表す。

sā さあ〖感〗

① [人を促すときに使う]

¶さあ、行きましょう。(*Sā*, ikimashō.)

② [ためらうときに使う]

¶「あの人はだれですか。」(Ano hito wa dare desu ka?)「さあ、知りません。」(*Sā*, shirimasen.)

sabaku 砂ばく〖名〗

¶砂ばくは雨が少なく、植物がほとんど生えません。(*Sabaku* wa ame ga sukunaku, shokubutsu ga hotondo haemasen.)

sa [[n]] **difference, disparity, margin**

¶ There are considerable **changes** of temperature between the day and night in this area.

¶ [I] was only one point **from being** first on yesterday's exam.

-sa [[suf]] a suffix for making adjectives and adjective-verbs into nouns

heat, warm**th** // cold**ness,** the cold // beauty // white**ness** // anguish, distress // bright**ness** // weight // length // quick**ness,** speed // depth // accura**cy,** precis**ion** // frank**ness,** lack of guile

＊ *-sa* is added to the stem of an adjective or adjective-verb to form a noun; it expresses nature, condition, degree, etc.

sā [[interj]] **come, come now; well, well now**

① [come, come now; used when urging some course of action]

¶ Let's be off now!

② [well, well now, let me see; used when one is hesitant or unsure about something]

¶ "Who is that person?"

　"**Well,** I don't really know."

sabaku [[n]] **desert**

¶ **Deserts** have little rain, and few plants grow there.

sabi さび〔名〕

¶ 長い間使わなかったので，はさみに赤いさびがついてしまいました。

(Nagai aida tsukawanakatta node, hasami ni akai *sabi* ga tsuite shimaimashita.)

sabiru さびる〔動Ⅱ〕

¶ このナイフはずいぶんさびていますね。(Kono naifu wa zuibun *sabite* imasu ne.)

sabishii 寂しい〔形〕

① [にぎやかでない様子]

¶ この辺は夜になると，急に寂しくなります。(Kono hen wa yoru ni naru to, kyū ni *sabishiku* narimasu.)

② [孤独な様子]

¶ 友達がいなくて，とても寂しいです。

(Tomodachi ga inakute, totemo *sabishii* desu.)

¶ 田中さんはいつも寂しそうな顔をしています。(Tanaka san wa itsu mo *sabishisō* na kao o shite imasu.)

sābisu サービス〔名，～する〕

① [世話をすること]

セルフサービス (serufu*sābisu*) サービスが悪い (*sābisu* ga warui)

¶ あのホテルはとてもサービスがいいですよ。(Ano hoteru wa totemo *sābisu* ga ii desu yo.)

② [値段を引くこと，おまけ]

¶ シャツを買ったら，サービスにハンカチをくれました。(Shatsu o kattara, *sābisu* ni hankachi o kuremashita.)

sae さえ〔助〕

sabi 〚n〛 **rust, tarnish**

¶ The scissors 〚clippers, shears〛 haven't been used for a long time and have gotten **rusty** 〚The scissors weren't used for a long time and got **rusty**〛.

sabiru 〚v Ⅱ〛 **to rust, to become rusty**

¶ This knife is quite **rusty,** isn't it?

sabishii 〚adj〛 **deserted, lonely; lonely, lonesome**

① [deserted, lonely, desolate (about a place)]

¶ At night this area quite suddenly becomes **deserted.**

② [lonely, lonesome (about one's feelings)]

¶ [I] **am** very **lonely** as [I] don't have any friends.

¶ [Miss] Tanaka always **looks sad and lonely.**

sābisu 〚n, ~*suru*〛 **service; special price, special service**

① [service]

self-**service** // **the service** is poor, have poor **service**

¶ You get excellent **service** at that hotel.

② [special price, special service, something included free of charge]

¶ When [I] bought a shirt they gave me a handkerchief **free of charge.**

sae 〚part〛 **even, besides, on top of; if only, so long as**

①[極端な例を挙げて他の場合はもちろんであるという意味を表す]

¶わたしの子供は漢字はもちろん、平仮名さえまだ読めません。(Watashi no kodomo wa kanji wa mochiron, hiragana *sae* mada yomemasen.)

¶そんな易しい問題は、小学生でさえできます。(Sonna yasashii mondai wa, shōgakusei de *sae* dekimasu.)

②[その条件だけでじゅうぶんであるという意味を表す]

¶少しぐらい天気が悪くても、大雨さえ降らなければ行きましょう。(Sukoshi gurai tenki ga warukute mo, ooame *sae* furanakereba ikimashō.)

¶食べ物さえあれば、ほかには何もいりません。(Tabemono *sae* areba, hoka ni wa nani mo irimasen.)

*「~さえ~ば (~sae ~ba)」「~さえ~たら (~sae ~tara)」などの形で使う。

sagaru 下がる〖動Ⅰ〗

①[低い方へ移る]

温度が下がる (ondo ga *sagaru*) 物価が下がる (bukka ga *sagaru*) 熱が下がる (netsu ga *sagaru*)

¶勉強しなかったので、成績が下がってしまいました。(Benkyō shinakatta node, seiseki ga *sagatte* shimaimashita.)

↔agaru 上がる

②[下の方へ垂れる]

¶窓に白いカーテンが下がっています。(Mado ni shiroi kāten ga *sagatte*

① [even, besides, on top of; used when giving an extreme example and indicating something else is a matter of course]

¶ My children ⟦child⟧ can't **even** read *hiragana* yet, much less *kanji*.

¶ **Even** an elementary school student could do such a simple problem.

② [if only, so long as; indicates that a certain condition is enough by itself]

¶ Let's go even if the weather isn't so good **as long as** it's not raining heavily.

¶ [I] don't need **anything but** food.

* Used in the patterns "~ *sae* ~ -ba," "~ *sae* ~ -tara," etc.

sagaru 〖v I〗 fall, drop, decline; hang, hang down; step back

① [fall, drop, decline, go down] the temperature **falls** // prices **drop** // a fever **goes down**

¶ [My] grades **fell** ⟦**have fallen**⟧ because [I] didn't study.

② [hang, hang down, be suspended]
¶ There **is** a white curtain at the window.

imasu.)

③ [後ろへ退く]

¶危ないですから，後ろへ下がってください。(Abunai desu kara, ushiro e *sagatte* kudasai.)

sagasu 捜す〖動Ⅰ〗

¶田中さんがあなたを捜していましたよ。(Tanaka san ga anata o *sagashite* imashita yo.)

¶いくら捜しても，時計が見つかりません。(Ikura *sagashite* mo, tokei ga mitsukarimasen.)

sagasu 探す〖動Ⅰ〗

仕事を探す (shigoto o *sagasu*)

¶わたしは安くて静かなアパートを探しています。(Watashi wa yasukute shizuka na apāto o *sagashite* imasu.)

sageru 下げる〖動Ⅱ〗

①[低い方へ移す]

温度を下げる (ondo o *sageru*) 熱を下げる (netsu o *sageru*)

¶山田さんは丁寧に頭を下げてお礼を言いました。(Yamada san wa teinei ni atama o *sagete* orei o iimashita.)

¶値段を下げれば，買う人もいるでしょう。(Nedan o *sagereba*, kau hito mo iru deshō.)

↔ageru 上げる

②[下の方へ垂らす]

¶肩からカメラを下げている人が中村さんです。(Kata kara kamera o *sagete* iru hito ga Nakamura san desu.)

③ [step back, draw back]

¶ Please **step back** as it's dangerous to stand right there.

sagasu 〖v I〗 search for, look for, try to locate

¶ [Mrs.] Tanaka **was looking for** you.

¶ [I] can't find [my] watch no matter how much [I] **search**.

sagasu 〖v I〗 search for, look for, try to obtain

look for a job

¶ I'm **hunting for** a cheap and quiet apartment.

sageru 〖v II〗 lower, let down, drop; hang, wear

① [lower, let down, drop]

lower the temperature // **bring down** a fever

¶ [Mr.] Yamada politely **lowered** [his] head and thanked [them].

¶ **If [we] lower** the price it will probably sell.

② [hang, wear]

¶ The person **with** the camera over [his] shoulder is [Mr.] Nakamura.

sai- 最-〖頭〗

最終 (*sai*shū) 最強 (*sai*kyō) 最古 (*sai*ko) 最上 (*sai*jō) 最小 (*sai*shō) 最低 (*sai*tei) 最善 (*sai*zen) 最愛 (*sai*ai) 最新式 (*sai*shinshiki) 最年長者 (*sai*nenchōsha)

-sai -歳〖尾〗

¶わたしは今月の10日で30歳になります。 (Watashi wa kongetsu no tooka de sanjis*sai* ni narimasu.)

saiban 裁判〖名, ～する〗

裁判官 (*saiban*kan) 裁判所 (*saiban*sho)

¶この事件の裁判は来月二日に行われます。 (Kono jiken no *saiban* wa raigetsu futsuka ni okonawaremasu.)

saidai 最大〖名〗

¶世界最大の都市はどこですか。 (Sekai *saidai* no toshi wa doko desu ka?)

¶健康であることは最大の幸福です。 (Kenkō de aru koto wa *saidai* no kōfuku desu.)

saifu 財布〖名〗

¶この財布には, あまりお金が入っていません。 (Kono *saifu* ni wa, amari okane ga haitte imasen.)

saigo 最後〖名〗

¶最後にこの部屋を出た人はだれですか。 (*Saigo* ni kono heya o deta hito wa dare desu ka?)

¶どんなに苦しくても, 最後までがんばってください。 (Donna ni kuru-

sai- 〚pref〛 **the most, the maximum, ultra-**

the last, the ultimate // the strong**est** // the old**est** // the best, the fin**est**, supreme // the small**est**, the minimum, the least // the low**est**, the minimum; the worst // one's best, the best // dear**est**, beloved // the lat**est** style // the old**est** person

-sai 〚suf〛 **age, years**

¶ I will be 30 **years old** on the tenth of this month.

saiban 〚n, ～*suru*〛 **trial, hearing, judgment**

a judge, the judiciary // a court of law; a courthouse

¶ **The trial** in this case will be held 〚This case will be brought **to trial**〛 on the second of next month.

saidai 〚n〛 **greatest, largest, maximum**

¶ What is the **largest** city in the world?

¶ The **greatest** blessing is to have one's health.

saifu 〚n〛 **wallet**

¶ There isn't much money in this **wallet.**

saigo 〚n〛 **last, final, ultimate**

¶ Who was the **last** person to leave this room?

¶ Please stick it out to **the end,** no matter how difficult it may be.

shikute mo, *saigo* made ganbatte kudasai.)

⇔saisho 最初

saijitsu 祭日〖名〗

¶3月 21 日は祭日なので,学校は休みです。(Sangatsu nijūichinichi wa *saijitsu* na node, gakkō wa yasumi desu.)

¶来週は日曜と祭日が続くから, 旅行する人が多いでしょう。(Raishū wa nichiyō to *saijitsu* ga tsuzuku kara, ryokō suru hito ga ooi deshō.)

saikin 最近〖名〗

¶最近,あの人は学校へ来ません。(*Saikin,* ano hito wa gakkō e kimasen.)

¶最近は物の値段が上がる一方です。(*Saikin* wa mono no nedan ga agaru ippō desu.)

saikō 最高〖名〗

最高裁判所 (*saikō*-saibansho) 最高記録 (*saikō*-kiroku) 最高点 (*saikō*-ten)

¶昨日の最高気温は 30 度でした。(Kinō no *saikō*-kion wa sanjūdo deshita.)

sain サイン〖名, ～する〗

①[合図]

¶手を振ってサインを送りました。(Te o futte *sain* o okurimashita.)

②[署名]

¶この書類にサインをしてください。(Kono shorui ni *sain* o shite kudasai.)

¶あの俳優のサインが欲しいです。

saijitsu 〚n〛 a national holiday

¶ There's no school on March 21 as it's **a national holiday.**

¶ Monday is **a holiday** (more literally, **a holiday** comes after Sunday) next week so probably many people will be traveling over the three-day weekend.

saikin 〚n〛 the latest, recent; recently, lately

¶ [He] hasn't been coming to school **lately.**

¶ **Recently** prices just keep going up and up.

saikō 〚n〛 highest, maximum, supreme; the greatest

the **Supreme** Court // the **best** record (for a sports event, etc.) // the **highest** mark scored

¶ Yesterday's **high** temperature was 30 degrees.

sain 〚n, ～*suru*〛 sign, signal; signature, autograph

① [sign, signal]

¶ [He] **signaled** by waving [his] hand.

② [signature, autograph]

¶ Please **sign** these papers.

¶ I'd like to have that actor's

(Ano haiyū no *sain* ga hoshii desu.)

sainō 才能〖名〗

¶この子は音楽の**才能**があります。

(Kono ko wa ongaku no *sainō* ga arimasu.)

¶**才能**がなくても，努力すればすぐ上手になります。(*Sainō* ga nakute mo, doryoku sureba sugu jōzu ni narimasu.)

saisho 最初〖名〗

¶授業の**最初**にいつも発音の練習をします。(Jugyō no *saisho* ni itsu mo hatsuon no renshū o shimasu.)

¶この本は**最初**はつまらなかったが，だんだんおもしろくなってきました。

(Kono hon wa *saisho* wa tsumaranakatta ga, dandan omoshiroku natte kimashita.)

⇔**saigo 最後**

saisoku 催促〖名，～する〗

¶学校から授業料の**催促**を受けました。 (Gakkō kara jugyōryō no *saisoku* o ukemashita.)

¶早く本を返してくれるように，友達に**催促**しました。(Hayaku hon o kaeshite kureru yō ni, tomodachi ni *saisoku* shimashita.)

saka 坂〖名〗

坂道 (*saka*michi) 上り坂 (nobori-*zaka*) 下り坂 (kudari*zaka*)

¶あの辺は**坂**が多いから，自転車で行くのはたいへんですよ。(Ano hen wa *saka* ga ooi kara, jitensha de iku no wa taihen desu yo.)

〚actress's〛 **autograph.**

sainō 〚n〛 **talent, ability, aptitude**

¶ This child has **a talent** for music.

¶ Even if you don't have **any aptitude** for it, you will soon become good at it if you work hard.

saisho 〚n〛 **the first, the beginning; at first, originally**

¶ At **the beginning** of class [we] always have pronunciation drill.

¶ **At first** this book was boring but it has gradually gotten more interesting.

saisoku 〚n, ～*suru*〛 **urging, demand**

¶ [I] got a letter from the school **requesting** payment of [my] tuition.

¶ [I] **urged** [my] friend to return the borrowed book soon.

saka 〚n〛 **slope, incline, hill**

an up**hill** road, a **sloping** road // an ascent, an up**hill** road, a rising **grade** // a descent, a down**hill** road, a downward **grade**

¶ There are many **hills** in that area so it is hard to go there on a bicycle.

¶この坂は急ですから，気をつけて下りてください。(Kono *saka* wa kyū desu kara, ki o tsukete orite kudasai.)

¶ This **slope** is steep so please be careful going down it.

sakai 境〖名〗

¶ここが隣の土地との境です。(Koko ga tonari no tochi to no *sakai* desu.)

¶この川を境に，向こうがA国です。(Kono kawa o *sakai* ni, mukō ga Ē-koku desu.)

sakai 〖n〗 border, boundary

¶ This is **the border line** with the neighboring land.

¶ This river forms **the boundary**— the other side is Country A.

sakan 盛ん〖形動〗

¶この国は工業が盛んです。(Kono kuni wa kōgyō ga *sakan* desu.)

¶この国ではサッカーが盛んです。(Kono kuni de wa sakkā ga *sakan* desu.)

¶火が盛んに燃えています。(Hi ga *sakan* ni moete imasu.)

¶首相は空港で盛んな出迎えを受けました。(Shushō wa kūkō de *sakan* na demukae o ukemashita.)

sakan 〖adj-v〗 prosperous, flourishing, thriving; vigorous, lively; enthusiastic, keen; popular

¶ This country is **highly** industrialized.

¶ Soccer **is popular** in this country.

¶ The fire is burning **briskly.**

¶ The prime minister received a **warm** reception at the airport.

sakana 魚〖名〗

魚を捕る (*sakana* o toru)　魚をつる (*sakana* o tsuru)

¶この池には魚がたくさんいます。(Kono ike ni wa *sakana* ga takusan imasu.)

¶この魚は焼いて食べましょう。(Kono *sakana* wa yaite tabemashō.)

sakana 〖n〗 fish

catch **a fish,** catch **fish** // to fish

¶ There are many **fish** in this pond 〚pool〛.

¶ Let's eat this **fish** grilled.

sake 酒〖名〗

①〔アルコール分を含んだ飲み物〕

¶あなたは酒を飲みますか。(Anata wa *sake* o nomimasu ka?)

sake 〖n〗 liquor, alcoholic beverage; *sake*, Japanese rice wine

① [liquor, alcoholic beverage]

¶ Do you drink **alcohol?**

②[日本酒]

¶酒は米から造ります。(*Sake* wa kome kara tsukurimasu.)

¶ビールにしますか，お酒にしますか。(Biiru ni shimasu ka, o*sake* ni shimasu ka?)

sakebu 叫ぶ〖動Ⅰ〗

①[大きな声を出す]

¶だれかが「助けて。」と叫んでいます。(Dare ka ga "Tasukete!" to *sakende* imasu.)

②[あることを実現させるため世間の人々に強く訴える]

¶あの人たちは戦争反対を叫んでいます。(Ano hitotachi wa sensō-hantai o *sakende* imasu.)

sakeru 避ける〖動Ⅱ〗

¶あの人はわたしと会うのを避けているようです。(Ano hito wa watashi to au no o *sakete* iru yō desu.)

¶暗い道は避けて，明るい道を帰ったほうがいいですよ。(Kurai michi wa *sakete*, akarui michi o kaetta hō ga ii desu yo.)

(-)saki (-)先〖名，尾〗

1〖名〗

①[先端]

¶この鉛筆の先は丸くなっています。(Kono enpitsu no *saki* wa maruku natte imasu.)

②[前方]

¶銀行はこの先にあります。(Ginkō wa kono *saki* ni arimasu.)

¶20ページの問題が終わったら，その

② [*sake*, Japanese rice wine]

¶ ***Sake*** is made from rice.

¶ Which will you have—beer or ***sake?***

sakebu 〚v I〛 **shout, yell, cry out; clamor for, advocate**

① [shout, yell, cry out]

¶ Someone **is crying out** for help.

② [clamor for, advocate]

¶ Those people **are active** in their antiwar stand.

sakeru 〚v II〛 **avoid, evade, shirk**

¶ It seems [he] **is avoiding** me.

¶ You had better **keep away** from dark streets and take well-lit ones on your way home.

(-)saki 〚n, suf〛 **point, tip; ahead, beyond; in front, the head, the first; earlier than, before; future, coming; objective, destination**

1 〚n〛

① [point, tip]

¶ **The point** of this pencil is blunt.

② [ahead, beyond]

¶ The bank is **straight ahead.**

¶ When you have finished the prob-

先に進んでください。(Nijippēji no mondai ga owattara, sono *saki* ni susunde kudasai.)

③［先頭］

¶山田さんは先に立って，みんなを案内しました。(Yamada san wa *saki* ni tatte, minna o annai shimashita.)

④［時間的に前，それ以前］

¶田中さんはわたしより先に来ていました。(Tanaka san wa watashi yori *saki* ni kite imashita.)

¶今日は用事があるので，お先に失礼します。(Kyō wa yōji ga aru node, o*saki* ni shitsurei shimasu.)

⑤［将来］

¶これから十年先，日本はどうなっているでしょう。(Kore kara jūnen *saki*, Nihon wa dō natte iru deshō.)

2［尾］

送り先 (okuri*saki*) 届け先 (todoke-*saki*) 連絡先 (renraku*saki*)

¶田中さんの行き先がわかりません。(Tanaka san no iki*saki* ga wakarimasen.)

sakka 作家［名］

流行作家 (ryūkō-*sakka*)

¶わたしはあの作家の書いた小説は，全部読みました。(Watashi wa ano *sakka* no kaita shōsetsu wa, zenbu yomimashita.)

sakki さっき［副］

¶わたしは田中さんとさっき会ったばかりです。(Watashi wa Tanaka san to *sakki* atta bakari desu.)

lems on page 20, please go on **from there**.

③ [in front, the head, the first]

¶ [Mrs.] Yamada stood **in front** and acted as guide.

④ [earlier than, before, previous, prior]

¶ [Miss] Tanaka came **before** me.

¶ As I have an errand to do 〚other business to attend to〛, I will have to take my leave **before [you]**.

⑤ [future, coming]

¶ I wonder what Japan will be like 10 years **from now**.

2 〚suf〛 objective, destination **the address, the destination** (of something being sent) // the receiver's **address, the destination** (of something being sent or delivered); **the person** or **place** to which a report is to be given // the contact **address, telephone, person,** etc.

¶ [I] don't know **where** [Mr.] Tanaka went.

sakka 〚n〛 **author, writer, novelist**

a best-selling **writer**

¶ I have read all of that **author's** books.

sakki 〚adv〛 **a little while ago, just now, some time ago**

¶ I met [Mrs.] Tanaka just **a little while ago**.

¶子供たちは**さっき**まで遊んでいたのに，もう寝てしまいました。(Kodomotachi wa *sakki* made asonde ita noni, mō nete shimaimashita.)

＊ 改まった場合には「さきほど (sakihodo)」と言う。

saku- 昨-〚頭〛
昨日 (*saku*jitsu)　昨晩 (*saku*ban)
昨夜 (*saku*ya)　昨年 (*saku*nen)

saku 咲く〚動Ⅰ〛
¶庭に花が**咲い**ています。(Niwa ni hana ga *saite* imasu.)
¶東京では，だいたい4月の初めに桜が**咲き**ます。(Tōkyō de wa, daitai shigatsu no hajime ni sakura ga *sakimasu*.)

sakubun 作文〚名〛
¶この時間は，「わたしの一日」という題で**作文**を書いてください。(Kono jikan wa, "Watashi no ichinichi" to iu dai de *sakubun* o kaite kudasai.)

sakuhin 作品〚名〛
文学**作品** (bungaku-*sakuhin*)　芸術**作品** (geijutsu-*sakuhin*)
¶生徒の**作品**の展覧会を開きました。(Seito no *sakuhin* no tenrankai o hirakimashita.)
¶この絵は山田さんの若いころの**作品**です。(Kono e wa Yamada san no wakai koro no *sakuhin* desu.)

sakura 桜〚名〛
¶**桜**が咲きました。(*Sakura* ga sakimashita.)

¶ The children were playing until **a little while ago** but they're sleeping now.

＊ When speaking formally, *sakihodo* is used in place of *sakki*.

saku- 〚pref〛 **last**
yesterday // **last** night, yesterday evening // **last** night, yesterday evening // **last** year

saku 〚v Ⅰ〛 to bloom, blossom, flower
¶ Flowers **are in bloom** in the garden.
¶ In Tokyo the cherry blossoms generally **come out** in early April.

sakubun 〚n〛 composition, writing; an essay, a theme
¶ This class hour please write **a composition** on the topic: "My day."

sakuhin 〚n〛 a work, a production, a creation
a literary **work, a piece** of literature // an art**work**
¶ An exhibition of student **works** opened 〖has opened〗.
¶ This picture is an early **work** of Yamada's.

sakura 〚n〛 a cherry tree, cherry blossoms
¶ **The cherry blossoms** are 〖were〗 in bloom.

¶桜の花を見ながらごちそうを食べることを、お花見と言います。(Sakura no hana o minagara gochisō o taberu koto o, ohanami to iimasu.)

sakusha 作者〖名〗
小説の作者 (shōsetsu no *sakusha*)
¶この絵は15世紀にかかれたものですが、作者はわかりません。(Kono e wa jūgoseiki ni kakareta mono desu ga, *sakusha* wa wakarimasen.)

-sama -様〖尾〗
①[尊敬の意味を表す]
王様 (ō*sama*) 神様 (kami*sama*)
お母様 (okā*sama*) 御主人様 (goshujin*sama*)
¶封筒の表に「山田太郎様」と書いてあります。(Fūtō no omote ni "Yamada Tarō *sama*" to kaite arimasu.)
②[丁寧の意味を表す]
御苦労さま (gokurō*sama*) ごちそうさま (gochisō*sama*)

samazama さまざま〖形動, ～の〗
¶意見がさまざまでまとまりません。(Iken ga *samazama* de matomarimasen.)
¶留学生はさまざまな国から来ています。(Ryūgakusei wa *samazama* na kuni kara kite imasu.)
⇒**iroiro** いろいろ

sameru 冷める〖動Ⅱ〗
¶御飯が冷めないうちに、早く食べてしまいなさい。(Gohan ga *samenai* uchi ni, hayaku tabete shimainasai.)

¶ Eating delicacies while viewing **the cherry blossoms** is called *ohanami*.

sakusha 〖n〗 **author, artist, composer,** etc.
the author of a novel
¶ This picture dates from the 15th century but **the artist** is unknown.

-sama 〖suf〗 **Mr., Mrs., Miss, Ms.;** an honorific suffix added to names, occupations, etc.
① [expresses respect]
a king // God, a deity // mother // (your) husband
¶ "Yamada Tarō-**sama**" is written on the front of the envelope (i.e., **Mr. Tarō Yamada**).
② [expresses politeness]
Thank you for your trouble (see also the entry for *gokurōsama*) // Thank you for the fine meal (see also the entry for *gochisōsama*)

samazama 〖adj-v, ～no〗 **various, varied, diverse**
¶ Opinion **is divided,** and no agreement has been reached.
¶ The foreign students are from **many different** countries.

sameru 〖v II〗 **cool off, get cold**
¶ Eat your food **before it gets cold.**

¶おふろのお湯が冷めてしまったから、もう一度沸かしましょう。 (Ofuro no oyu ga *samete* shimatta kara, mō ichido wakashimashō.)

¶ The bath water **has cooled;** let me heat it up again for you.

sameru 覚める〖動Ⅱ〗

¶わたしは毎朝6時ごろに目が覚めます。(Watashi wa maiasa rokuji goro ni me ga *samemasu*.)

¶大きな音で目が覚めました。(Ookina oto de me ga *samemashita*.)

sameru 〚v Ⅱ〛 **wake up, awake**

¶ I **wake up** around six o'clock every morning.

¶ [I] **was awakened** by a loud noise.

samui 寒い〖形〗

¶今日は寒いですね。(Kyō wa *samui* desu ne.)

¶部屋が寒いので、ストーブをつけました。(Heya ga *samui* node, sutōbu o tsukemashita.)

¶だいぶ寒くなりましたね。 (Daibu *samuku* narimashita ne.)

⇔atsui 暑い

samui 〚adj〛 **cold, chilly**

¶ **It's cold** today, isn't it?

¶ The room **was cold** so I turned on the heater.

¶ It's turned quite **cold,** hasn't it?

san 三〖名〗

三人 (*sannin*) 三月 (*sangatsu*) 三年 (*sannen*) 三円 (*san'en*) 三軒 (*sangen*)

san 〚n〛 **three**

three persons // March // **three** years // **three** yen // **three** houses

-san -さん〖尾〗

山田さん (Yamada *san*) お父さん (otō*san*) お医者さん (oisha*san*)

＊名前・職業などにつけて尊敬や親しみの意味を表す。より丁寧に言う場合には「-様 (sama)」を使う。

-san 〚suf〛 **Mr., Mrs., Miss, Ms.**

Mr. 〚**Mrs., Miss, Ms.**〛 Yamada // father // a doctor

＊ Added to names, professions, etc., to indicate respect and a certain degree of familiarity. When speaking more politely, *-sama* is used.

sanbutsu 産物〖名〗

¶この地方の主な産物はコーヒーです。 (Kono chihō no omo na *sanbutsu* wa kōhii desu.)

¶東京のデパートでも京都の産物を買

sanbutsu 〚n〛 **product, produce**

¶ The principal **product** of this region is coffee.

¶ One can buy Kyoto **products** in

うことができます。(Tōkyō no depāto de mo Kyōto no *sanbutsu* o kau koto ga dekimasu.)

sangatsu 三月〔名〕

sangyō 産業〔名〕
産業が発達する (*sangyō* ga hattatsu suru)
¶あなたの国の主な産業は何ですか。 (Anata no kuni no omo na *sangyō* wa nan desu ka?)

sanka 参加〔名, 〜する〕
参加者 (*sanka*sha) 参加国 (*sanka*-koku)
¶あなたもこの研究会に参加しません か。(Anata mo kono kenkyūkai ni *sanka* shimasen ka?)

sankaku 三角〔名〕
三角形 (*sankak*kei)

sankō 参考〔名〕
参考書 (*sankō*sho)
¶この本は, わたしの研究にとても参 考になります。 (Kono hon wa, watashi no kenkyū ni totemo *sankō* ni narimasu.)
¶あなたの意見を参考にして, この計 画を立てました。(Anata no iken o *sankō* ni shite, kono keikaku o tatemashita.)

sanpo 散歩〔名, 〜する〕
¶これから散歩に行きませんか。(Kore kara *sanpo* ni ikimasen ka?)
¶公園を散歩していたら, 友達に会い ました。(Kōen o *sanpo* shite itara, tomodachi ni aimashita.)

Tokyo department stores.

sangatsu [[n]] **March**
sangyō [[n]] **industry**
industry progresses

¶ What is the principal **industry** in your country?

sanka [[n, ~*suru*]] **participation**
a participant, a contestant // **a participating** nation
¶ Won't you **take part** in our study group?

sankaku [[n]] **triangle, triangular**
triangle, triangular
sankō [[n]] **reference, consultation**
a **reference** book
¶ This book will be very **helpful** in my research.

¶ [I] drew up this plan taking your views **into consideration.**

sanpo [[n, ~*suru*]] **walk, stroll**
¶ Won't you come **for a walk** now?

¶ While **walking** in the park, [I] ran across a friend.

sansei 賛成〚名, 〜する〛

¶わたしもあなたの意見に賛成です。
(Watashi mo anata no iken ni *sansei* desu.)

¶この計画に賛成した人はあまりいません。(Kono keikaku ni *sansei* shita hito wa amari imasen.)

⇔hantai 反対

sanso 酸素〚名〛

sappari さっぱり〚副, 〜する〛

①[さわやかで気持ちのいい様子]

¶おふろに入ってさっぱりしました。
(Ofuro ni haitte *sappari* shimashita.)

②[まったく, 全然]

¶試験は難しくて, さっぱりわかりませんでした。(Shiken wa muzukashikute, *sappari* wakarimasen deshita.)

¶このごろ山田さんから, さっぱり手紙が来ませんね。(Konogoro Yamada san kara, *sappari* tegami ga kimasen ne.)

* あとに打ち消しの言葉が来る。

sara さら〚名〛

¶おさらを1枚持って来てください。
(Osara o ichimai motte kite kudasai.)

sarada サラダ〚名〛

野菜サラダ (yasai-*sarada*)

¶晩御飯に肉やサラダを食べました。
(Bangohan ni niku ya *sarada* o tabemashita.)

sarani 更に〚副〛

sansei 〚n, ~*suru*〛 agreement, approval, support

¶ I **am in agreement** with your view.

¶ Few **have given their approval** to this plan.

sanso 〚n〛 oxygen

sappari 〚adv, ~*suru*〛 refreshing, refreshed; completely, entirely, not at all

① [refreshing, refreshed]

¶ Taking a bath **refreshed** me.

② [completely, entirely, not at all]

¶ The exam was very difficult; I couldn't make **head or tail** of it.

¶ Recently there hasn't been a **single** letter from [Mr.] Yamada, has there?

* Used with the negative.

sara 〚n〛 dish, plate, saucer, etc.

¶ Please fetch **a plate.**

sarada 〚n〛 salad

(vegetable) **salad**

¶ [I] had meat and **a salad** for dinner.

sarani 〚adv〛 still more, further; again; anew, afresh

①[もっと，いっそう]

¶上田さんの病気は**更に**悪くなったそうです。(Ueda san no byōki wa *sarani* waruku natta sō desu.)

②[その上]

¶学校で5時間勉強して，家へ帰ってから**更に**2時間勉強します。(Gakkō de gojikan benkyō shite, ie e kaette kara *sarani* nijikan benkyō shimasu.)

saru さる〖名〗

¶動物園へ行って**さる**を見ました。(Dōbutsuen e itte *saru* o mimashita.)

sasaeru 支える〖動Ⅱ〗

¶木が風で倒れないように，棒で**支えて**あります。(Ki ga kaze de taorenai yō ni, bō de *sasaete* arimasu.)

¶けが人は友達に**支えられながら**病院へ入っていきました。(Keganin wa tomodachi ni *sasaerarenagara* byōin e haitte ikimashita.)

saseru させる〖助動〗

①[他に対してある行為を実現するように仕向ける意味を表す]

¶先生が質問して，学生に答え**させます**。(Sensei ga shitsumon shite, gakusei ni kotae*sasemasu*.)

¶わたしが来られなければ，弟を来**させます**。(Watashi ga korarenakereba, otōto o ko*sasemasu*.)

②[他の人がある行為をするのを許容あるいは黙認する意味を表す]

¶子供にあんなに夜遅くまでテレビを

① [still more, further]

¶ I hear that [Mrs.] Ueda's illness **has worsened.**

② [again; anew, afresh]

¶ [I] study five hours at school and then return home and study two hours **more.**

saru 〚n〛 monkey, ape

¶ [I] went to the zoo and saw **the monkeys.**

sasaeru 〚v II〛 support, hold up, prop, maintain, sustain

¶ The tree **is reinforced** with poles 〚stakes, sticks, etc.〛 so it won't be blown over by the wind.

¶ The injured person walked into the hospital **supported** by a friend.

-saseru 〚auxil〛 a verb ending indicating the causative, etc.

① [make someone do something, have someone do something]

¶ The teacher asks questions for the students **to answer.**

¶ If I can't come, I'll **have** my (younger) brother come.

② [let someone do something, allow someone to do something]

¶ You shouldn't **let** the children

見させておいてはいけませんよ。
(Kodomo ni anna ni yoru osoku made terebi o mi*sasete* oite wa ikemasen yo.)

¶子供にお菓子をあんなにたくさん食べさせていいのですか。(Kodomo ni okashi o anna ni takusan tabe-*sasete* ii no desu ka?)

＊ Ⅱ型動詞とⅢ型動詞の「来る (kuru)」につく。

⇨**seru** せる

sashiageru 差し上げる〘動Ⅱ〙

①[持ち上げる]
¶中村さんは重い石を頭の上まで差し上げました。(Nakamura san wa omoi ishi o atama no ue made *sashiagemashita*.)

②[与える]
¶お客様にお茶を差し上げてください。(Okyakusama ni ocha o *sashiagete* kudasai.)

¶あなたにこの本を差し上げましょう。(Anata ni kono hon o *sashiagemashō*.)

＊「与える (ataeru)」「やる (yaru)」の謙譲語で、「上げる (ageru)」より更に丁寧な言い方である。「(〜て) さしあげる ([〜te] sashiageru)」という言い方もある。「先生のお荷物を持ってさしあげました。(Sensei no onimotsu o motte sashiagemashita.)」

⇨**ageru** 上げる　　(〜te) **ageru**
(〜て) **あげる**

watch television until so late at night.

¶ **Should** the children be eating so many sweets?

＊ *-saseru* is added to Type II verbs and the Type III verb *kuru* (→ *kosaseru*).

sashiageru 〚v II〛　**lift, raise; give**

① [lift, raise, hold up]
¶ [Mr.] Nakamura **lifted** a heavy rock **up** over [his] head.

② [give]
¶ Please **serve** some tea to [our] guest 〚customer〛.

¶ I'd like **to give** you this book.

＊ *Sashiageru* is the humble form of *ataeru* or *yaru*; it is more polite than *ageru*. It is also used in the form (*-te*) *sashiageru*, as in "*Sensei no onimotsu o motte sashiagemashita*" (I carried the professor's 〚doctor's〛 things 〚bags〛 for him 〚her〛).

sashimi さしみ〚名〛

¶さしみはまだ食べたことがありません。(*Sashimi* wa mada tabeta koto ga arimasen.)

sasou 誘う〚動Ⅰ〛

¶わたしは山田さんを誘って，映画を見に行きました。(Watashi wa Yamada san o *sasotte,* eiga o mi ni ikimashita.)

¶京都へ行こうと誘われましたが，断りました。(Kyōto e ikō to *sasowaremashita* ga, kotowarimashita.)

sassoku 早速〚副〛

¶買ってきたくつを早速はいて出かけました。(Katte kita kutsu o *sassoku* haite dekakemashita.)

¶手紙を出したら，早速返事が来ました。(Tegami o dashitara, *sassoku* henji ga kimashita.)

sasu 刺す〚動Ⅰ〛

①［突く，突き通す］

¶針で指を刺してしまいました。(Hari de yubi o *sashite* shimaimashita.)

②［虫がかんだり針を刺したりする］

はちに刺される (hachi ni *sasareru*)

¶わたしは虫に足を刺されました。(Watashi wa mushi ni ashi o *sasaremashita.*)

sasu 指す〚動Ⅰ〛

①［指などで示す］

¶先生は黒板に書いた字を一つ一つ指しながら，学生に読ませます。(Sensei wa kokuban ni kaita ji o hitotsu hitotsu *sashinagara,* gakusei ni

sashimi 〚n〛 *sashimi,* slices of raw fish

¶ I haven't eaten *sashimi* yet.

sasou 〚v I〛 invite, ask

¶ I **invited** [Mr.] Yamada and we went to see a movie together.

¶ I **was invited** to go to Kyoto but I declined.

sassoku 〚adv〛 at once, immediately, right away

¶ I put on the shoes I had just bought and went out.

¶ [I] received a **prompt** response to the letter [I] sent.

sasu 〚v I〛 pierce, stab; bite, sting

① [pierce, stab, prick]

¶ [I] **pricked** [my] finger on the needle.

② [bite, sting]

be stung by a bee

¶ I **was bitten** on the leg 〚foot〛 by an insect.

sasu 〚v I〛 point to, indicate; designate

① [point to, point at, indicate]

¶ The teacher **points** one by one **at** the characters written on the blackboard and has [her] students read them aloud.

yomasemasu.)

¶時計の針がちょうど12時を指しています。(Tokei no hari ga chōdo jūniji o *sashite* imasu.)

②[指名する]
¶急に先生に指されたので，答えられませんでした。(Kyū ni sensei ni *sasareta* node, kotaeraremasen deshita.)

sasu さす〖動Ⅰ〗

①[注ぐ]
目薬をさす (megusuri o *sasu*) やかんに水をさす (yakan ni mizu o *sasu*)
¶機械を掃除して，油をさしました。(Kikai o sōji shite, abura o *sashimashita*.)

②[かさなどを開いて持つ]
¶雨がやんだのに，あの人はかさをさしています。(Ame ga yanda noni, ano hito wa kasa o *sashite* imasu.)

sasuga さすが〖副，～に，～の〗

①[そうはいうもののやはり]
¶社長の命令なので，さすがに「いやだ。」とは言えませんでした。(Shachō no meirei na node, *sasuga* ni "Iya da." to wa iemasen deshita.)

②[予想どおり，やはり]
¶田中さんはイギリスに留学していたので，さすがに英語が上手です。(Tanaka san wa Igirisu ni ryūgaku shite ita node, *sasuga* ni Eigo ga jōzu desu.)

¶朝から何も食べていないので，さすが

¶ The hands of the clock **are standing** exactly at twelve 〚The clock **reads** exactly twelve o'clock〛.

② [designate, name]

¶ The teacher **called on** me suddenly, and I was not able to answer.

sasu 〖v I〗 **pour in, fill, insert; hold up an umbrella**

① [pour in, fill, insert]
put in eye drops // **fill** a kettle with water

¶ [I] cleaned the machine and **oiled** it.

② [hold up an umbrella, etc.]

¶ [She] **has** [her] umbrella **up** even though it has stopped raining.

sasuga 〖adv, ～*ni*, ～*no*〗 **after all; as might be expected, like the ～ it is**

① [after all]

¶ As it was, **after all,** the order of the company president, [I] could not say that [I] didn't want to do it.

② [as might be expected, like the ～ it is]

¶ [Mr.] Tanaka speaks English well, **as might be expected** of someone who has studied in England.

¶ **It is only natural** that [I] am hun-

におなかがすきました。 (Asa kara nani mo tabete inai node, *sasuga* ni onaka ga sukimashita.)

sate さて〔接, 感〕

1 〔接〕

①[前のことがらを受けて話を続け別の話題に移るときなどに使う]

¶経済の問題についてはこのぐらいにしまして, **さて,** 次に教育の問題に移りたいと思います。 (Keizai no mondai ni tsuite wa kono gurai ni shimashite, *sate,* tsugi ni kyōiku no mondai ni utsuritai to omoimasu.)

②[前のことがらを受けて本題などに移るときに使う]

¶朝晩かなり寒くなってきましたが, お変わりございませんか。 **さて,** このたび1年間の予定で日本へ留学することになりました。 (Asaban kanari samuku natte kimashita ga, okawari gozaimasen ka? *Sate,* kono tabi ichinenkan no yotei de Nihon e ryūgaku suru koto ni narimashita.)

* 手紙で時候のあいさつなど前置きのあとで本題に入る場合によく使う。

2 〔感〕

¶さて, 帰りましょうか。 (*Sate,* kaerimashō ka?)

¶さて, これからどこへ行きましょうか。 (*Sate,* kore kara doko e ikimashō ka?)

¶さて, 困ったなあ。どうしよう。 (*Sate,* komatta nā. Dō shiyō?)

gry as [I] haven't eaten anything all day.

sate 〚conj, interj〛 **well, now**

1 〚conj〛

① [used when changing the subject of a conversation or other discourse]

¶ That concludes my remarks about economic matters. **Now** I would like to move on to educational matters.

② [used when moving on to the main topic of a conversation, discourse, or text]

¶ It's quite cold now in the mornings and the evenings, and I hope you are well. **Well then**, my news is that I'm going to go to Japan to study for a year (from a letter).

* Often used in a letter when moving from comments on the weather and other preliminary remarks on to the main text.

2 〚interj〛

¶ **Well,** shall we leave now?

¶ **Well,** where shall we go now?

¶ **Well,** that's awkward. What's best to do?

＊これから何かをしようとして，相手に呼びかけたり自問したりするときに使う。

satō　砂糖〔名〕

¶砂糖は１キロいくらですか。(*Satō* wa ichikiro ikura desu ka?)

-satsu　-冊〔尾〕

４冊 (yon*satsu*)　８冊 (has*satsu*)

¶このノートは１冊100円です。(Kono nōto wa is*satsu* hyakuen desu.)

-satsu　-札〔尾〕

五百円札 (gohyakuen*satsu*)　一万円札 (ichiman'en*satsu*)

satsuei　撮影〔名，〜する〕

¶ここはよく映画の撮影に使われます。(Koko wa yoku eiga no *satsuei* ni tsukawaremasu.)

¶夜撮影するのは難しいです。(Yoru *satsuei* suru no wa muzukashii desu.)

satto　さっと〔副〕

¶その青年はさっと立って，老人に席を譲りました。(Sono seinen wa *satto* tatte, rōjin ni seki o yuzurimashita.)

¶そのねこはわたしの姿を見ると，さっとベッドの下に隠れました。(Sono neko wa watashi no sugata o miru to, *satto* beddo no shita ni kakuremashita.)

sawagu　騒ぐ〔動Ⅰ〕

¶教室の中で騒いではいけません。(Kyōshitsu no naka de *sawaide* wa ikemasen.)

¶あのお酒を飲んで騒いでいる人はだ

＊ Used to attract the attention of the listener or to question oneself when one is about to start doing something.

satō 〔n〕 **sugar**

¶ How much is **sugar** a kilo?

-satsu 〔suf〕 the counter for bound books, magazines, etc.

four **volumes,** four **copies** // eight **volumes,** eight **copies**

¶ These notebooks are a hundred yen **each.**

-satsu 〔suf〕 the counter for paper money

a five hundred yen **bill** // a ten thousand yen **bill**

satsuei 〔n, ~*suru*〕 **photographing, filming**

¶ This spot is often used **in films.**

¶ Night **filming** is difficult 〖It is hard **to take photographs** at night〗.

satto 〔adv〕 **quickly, suddenly, all of a sudden**

¶ That youth **quickly** got up and offered his seat to an elderly person.

¶ That cat **dashed** under the bed and hid as soon as it saw me.

sawagu 〔v I〕 **be noisy, make a disturbance, go on a spree**

¶ One mustn't **be rowdy** in the classroom.

¶ Who is that drunk **making a nui-**

れですか。(Ano osake o nonde *sawaide* iru hito wa dare desu ka?)

sawaru 触る〖動Ⅰ〗

¶そこに並べてある作品に触らないでください。(Soko ni narabete aru sakuhin ni *sawaranaide* kudasai.)

¶汚い手で着物に触ったら，しかられました。(Kitanai te de kimono ni *sawattara*, shikararemashita.)

sayō 作用〖名，〜する〗

電気の作用 (denki no *sayō*)

¶薬の作用で痛みが止まりました。(Kusuri no *sayō* de itami ga tomarimashita.)

sayōnara さようなら〖連〗

¶「さようなら。」と言って，駅前で山田さんと別れました。(*"Sayōnara."* to itte, ekimae de Yamada san to wakaremashita.)

se 背〖名〗

①〖背中〗

背にかごを負う (*se* ni kago o ou)

②〖身長，物の高さ〗

背が伸びる (*se* ga nobiru)

¶上田さんは背が高いですね。(Ueda san wa *se* ga takai desu ne.)

¶田中さんのほうが，わたしより5センチ背が低いです。(Tanaka san no hō ga, watashi yori gosenchi *se* ga hikui desu.)

¶門のそばに背の高い木が2本あります。(Mon no soba ni *se* no takai ki ga nihon arimasu.)

sance of [him]self?

sawaru 〖v I〗 touch, handle, feel

¶ Please **don't touch** the works of art on display there.

¶ I was scolded for **touching** the *kimono* with dirty hands.

sayō 〖n, ~*suru*〗 working, operation, effect, function

the working of electricity

¶ The pain was relieved **by** the medicine.

sayōnara 〖compd〗 good-bye, farewell

¶ I parted from [Miss] Yamada in front of the station saying "*Sayōnara* 〖**Good-bye**〗."

se 〖n〗 the back; height, stature

① [the back]

carry a basket on **one's back**

② [height, stature]

grow taller

¶ [Mr.] Ueda **is tall,** isn't [he]?

¶ [Miss] Tanaka is five centimeters **shorter** than I am.

¶ There are two **tall** trees near the gate.

sei

sei

* 「背 (sei)」とも言う。

→sei 背

sei 背〖名〗

背が低い人 (sei ga hikui hito)

¶このクラスでは、だれがいちばん背が高いですか。(Kono kurasu de wa, dare ga ichiban sei ga takai desu ka?)

¶あの背の高い木は何という名前ですか。(Ano sei no takai ki wa nan to iu namae desu ka?)

＊「背 (se)」とも言う。

⇒se 背

sei せい〖名〗

¶風邪を引いたせいか、頭が痛いです。(Kaze o hiita sei ka, atama ga itai desu.)

¶この事業に失敗したのは、山田さんのせいです。(Kono jigyō ni shippai shita no wa, Yamada san no sei desu.)

-sei -製〖尾〗

①[物が作られた国や会社などを表す]

¶わたしはアメリカ製の万年筆を持っています。(Watashi wa Amerikasei no mannenhitsu o motte imasu.)

¶A社製の時計はたいへんいいです。(Ē-shasei no tokei wa taihen ii desu.)

②[材料を表す]

¶ナイロン製のくつ下は、絹のくつ下より丈夫だそうです。(Naironsei no kutsushita wa, kinu no kutsushita yori jōbu da sō desu.)

---

* Variant: sei.

sei 〚n〛 **height, stature**

a **short** person

¶ Who is the **tallest** student in this class?

¶ What is the name of that **tall** tree?

＊ Variant: se.

sei 〚n〛 **be due to ~, because of ~, be the fault of ~**

¶ I have a headache, perhaps **from** a cold.

¶ [Mr.] Yamada **is to blame** for the failure of this project.

-sei 〚suf〛 **make, manufacture**

① [indicates the place of manufacture or the manufacturer]

¶ I own an American-**made** fountain pen.

¶ The watches 〚clocks〛 **made** by Company A are very good.

② [indicates the raw material]

¶ They say that **nylon** socks 〚stockings〛 are stronger than silk ones.

seibutsu 生物〖名〗

¶生物を大きく分けると、動物と植物になります。(*Seibutsu o ookiku wakeru to, dōbutsu to shokubutsu ni narimasu.*)

¶この地球には、数えられないくらい多くの生物がいます。(*Kono chikyū ni wa, kazoerarenai kurai ooku no seibutsu ga imasu.*)

seichō 生長〖名, ～する〗

¶暖かい所では、草や木の生長が速いです。(*Atatakai tokoro de wa, kusa ya ki no seichō ga hayai desu.*)

seichō 成長〖名, ～する〗

¶太郎君は立派に成長して医者になりました。(*Tarō kun wa rippa ni seichō shite isha ni narimashita.*)

¶この会社は戦後、急に成長したのです。(*Kono kaisha wa sengo, kyū ni seichō shita no desu.*)

seido 制度〖名〗

教育制度 (*kyōiku-seido*) 選挙制度 (*senkyo-seido*)

¶来年から新しい奨学金の制度が作られます。(*Rainen kara atarashii shōgakukin no seido ga tsukuraremasu.*)

seifu 政府〖名〗

日本政府 (*Nihon-seifu*)

¶政府は今年の予算を決めました。(*Seifu wa kotoshi no yosan o kimemashita.*)

seigen 制限〖名, ～する〗

制限時間 (*seigen-jikan*)

seibutsu 〚n〛 **a living creature, life**

¶ **Living creatures** can be broadly divided into plants and animals.

¶ The number of **living creatures** on earth is beyond count.

seichō 〚n, ~*suru*〛 **growth**

¶ Grasses and trees **grow** rapidly in warm climates.

seichō 〚n, ~*suru*〛 **growth**

¶ Tarō **has grown** into a fine man and is now a doctor 〖Tarō **grew** into a fine man and became a doctor〗.

¶ This company **grew** rapidly in the postwar period.

seido 〚n〛 **system**

a school **system** // an electoral **system**

¶ There will be a new **system** for scholarships starting next year.

seifu 〚n〛 **the government**

the Japanese **government**

¶ **The government** has decided this year's budget.

seigen 〚n, ~*suru*〛 **restriction, limitation, limit**

a time **limit**

633

¶この会の会員には，年齢の制限はありません。(Kono kai no kaiin ni wa, nenrei no *seigen* wa arimasen.)

¶飛行機に載せる荷物は，20キロに制限されています。(Hikōki ni noseru nimotsu wa, nijikkiro ni *seigen* sarete imasu.)

seihin 製品〖名〗

電気製品 (denki-*seihin*) 繊維製品 (sen'i-*seihin*) 外国製品 (gaikoku-*seihin*)

¶あなたの会社では，どういう製品を作っているのですか。(Anata no kaisha de wa, dōiu *seihin* o tsukutte iru no desu ka?)

seiji 政治〖名〗

政治家 (*seiji*ka) 政治運動 (*seiji*-undō)

¶この国の政治家は立派な政治を行っています。(Kono kuni no *seiji*ka wa rippa na *seiji* o okonatte imasu.)

seikaku 性格〖名〗

①〔人の性質〕

性格がいい (*seikaku* ga ii) 性格が似ている (*seikaku* ga nite iru)

¶あの二人は性格が合わないから，けんかばかりしています。(Ano futari wa *seikaku* ga awanai kara, kenka bakari shite imasu.)

¶明るい性格の人はみんなに好かれます。(Akarui *seikaku* no hito wa minna ni sukaremasu.)

②〔ものの性質〕

¶それとこれとは，問題の性格が違い

¶ There is no **minimum or maximum** age for members of this club 〚association, society〛.

¶ The luggage of air passengers **is restricted** to 20 kilos.

seihin 〚n〛 a product, manufactured goods

electrical **products** // textile **goods** // foreign-made **articles**

¶ What kind of **goods** does your company make?

seiji 〚n〛 politics, political affairs, government

a politician, a statesman // a **political** movement; a **political** campaign

¶ **The politicians** in this country are conducting **the affairs of state** well.

seikaku 〚n〛 character, personality; character, nature

① [(human) character, personality]

be a good person // have similar **personalities**

¶ Those two **are incompatible** and are always fighting.

¶ **Sunny** persons are liked by all.

② [character, nature (of things)]

¶ These two matters are completely

634

ます。(Sore to kore to wa, mondai no *seikaku* ga chigaimasu.) different **in nature.**

seikaku 正確〖形動〗

¶この時計は正確ですか。(Kono tokei wa *seikaku* desu ka?)

¶この言葉はなかなか正確に発音できません。(Kono kotoba wa nakanaka *seikaku* ni hatsuon dekimasen.)

seikaku 〖adj-v〗 **accurate, precise, exact, correct**

¶ Is this clock **right?**

¶ [I] just can't pronounce this word **right.**

seikatsu 生活〖名, 〜する〗

家庭生活 (katei-*seikatsu*) 生活費 (*seikatsu*hi)

¶月給が安くて, 生活が苦しいです。(Gekkyū ga yasukute, *seikatsu* ga kurushii desu.)

¶わたしは外国で生活したことがありません。(Watashi wa gaikoku de *seikatsu* shita koto ga arimasen.)

seikatsu 〖n, 〜*suru*〗 **life, existence, livelihood, living**

family **life,** domestic **life** // **living** expenses, the cost of **living**

¶ [My] wages are low and it's hard to make ends meet.

¶ I have never **lived** abroad.

seiketsu 清潔〖名, 形動〗

¶この食堂はとても清潔です。(Kono shokudō wa totemo *seiketsu* desu.)

¶中村さんはいつも清潔なシャツを着ています。(Nakamura san wa itsu mo *seiketsu* na shatsu o kite imasu.)

seiketsu 〖n, adj-v〗 **clean, neat, pure**

¶ This eating place is very **clean and neat.**

¶ [Mr.] Nakamura is always wearing a **clean** shirt.

-seiki -世紀〖尾〗

紀元前3世紀 (kigenzen san*seiki*) 20世紀 (nijis*seiki*)

-seiki 〖suf〗 **century**

the third **century** B.C. // the 20th **century**

seikō 成功〖名, 〜する〗

¶実験は大成功でした。(Jikken wa dai*seikō* deshita.)

¶御成功を祈ります。(Go*seikō* o inorimasu.)

¶人間はついに月へ行くことに成功しました。(Ningen wa tsuini tsuki e

seikō 〖n, 〜*suru*〗 **success**

¶ The experiment was a great **success.**

¶ I wish you **success.**

¶ Humanity finally **succeeded** in going to the moon.

iku koto ni *seikō* shimashita.)

⇔shippai 失敗

seikyū 請求〖名, 〜する〗
請求書 (*seikyū*sho) 請求を受ける
(*seikyū* o ukeru)
¶本屋から本代の請求が来ました。
(Hon'ya kara hondai no *seikyū* ga
kimashita.)
¶あの人に請求しても, お金がないの
ですから, 払えないと思いますよ。
(Ano hito ni *seikyū* shite mo, okane
ga nai no desu kara, haraenai to
omoimasu yo.)

seimei 生命〖名〗
生命保険 (*seimei*-hoken)
¶戦争で多くの生命が失われました。
(Sensō de ooku no *seimei* ga
ushinawaremashita.)

seinen 青年〖名〗
¶青年時代に, できるだけ多くの本を
読んでおいたほうがいいですよ。
(*Seinen*-jidai ni, dekiru dake ooku
no hon o yonde oita hō ga ii desu
yo.)
¶山田さんの息子さんは, もう立派な
青年になりました。(Yamada san no
musukosan wa, mō rippa na *seinen*
ni narimashita.)

seinengappi 生年月日〖名〗
¶名前と生年月日をここに書いてくだ
さい。(Namae to *seinengappi* o koko
ni kaite kudasai.)

seireki 西暦〖名〗
¶わたしは西暦 1 9 3 6 年に生

seikyū 〚n, 〜*suru*〛 **demand, request, claim, application**
a bill // receive **a bill,** be billed

¶ **A bill** came from the bookstore.

¶ **Even if you demand payment**
from [him], I don't think [he] has the
money to pay you.

seimei 〚n〛 **life, existence, the soul**
life insurance
¶ Much **life** was lost in the war.

seinen 〚n〛 **a youth, young people,
the younger generation, a young
man**
¶ It is best to read as many books as
possible during **one's youth.**

¶ [Mr.] Yamada's son has grown into
a fine **young man.**

seinengappi 〚n〛 **one's date of
birth**
¶ Please write your name and **date
of birth** here.

seireki 〚n〛 **the Christian era,** A.D.
¶ I was born in 1936.

まれました。 (Watashi wa *seireki* senkyūhyaku-sanjūrokunen ni umaremashita.)

seiri 整理〖名, 〜する〗

交通整理 (kōtsū-*seiri*)

¶お客が来るので, 部屋の中を整理しました。 (Okyaku ga kuru node, heya no naka o *seiri* shimashita.)

¶このノートはまだ整理してありませんから, 読みにくいかもしれませんよ。 (Kono nōto wa mada *seiri* shite arimasen kara, yominikui ka mo shiremasen yo.)

seisaku 政策〖名〗

外交政策 (gaikō-*seisaku*) 経済政策 (keizai-*seisaku*) 農業政策 (nōgyō-*seisaku*) 政策を立てる (*seisaku* o tateru)

¶この国の政府は, 外国製品の輸入について厳しい政策をとっています。 (Kono kuni no seifu wa, gaikoku-seihin no yunyū ni tsuite kibishii *seisaku* o totte imasu.)

seisaku 製作〖名, 〜する〗

製作費 (*seisaku*hi) 製作所 (*seisaku*-jo)

¶この工場では, 農業機械を製作しています。 (Kono kōjō de wa, nōgyō-kikai o *seisaku* shite imasu.)

¶この映画は, 日本文化を紹介するために製作されたものです。(Kono eiga wa, Nihon-bunka o shōkai suru tame ni *seisaku* sareta mono desu.)

seisan 生産〖名, 〜する〗

seiri 〚n, ~*suru*〛 arranging, adjustment, regulation, putting in order

traffic **control**

¶ [I] **straightened up** the room as a guest is 〚was〛 coming.

¶ These notes **aren't edited** yet so they may be hard to read.

seisaku 〚n〛 policy

foreign **policy** // economic **policy** // agricultural **policy** // formulate **a policy**

¶ The government of this country is taking a hard **line** on foreign imports.

seisaku 〚n, ~*suru*〛 manufacture, production

the **production** cost // a factory, a plant

¶ This factory **manufactures** farm machinery.

¶ This movie **was made** in order to introduce Japanese culture to others.

seisan 〚n, ~*suru*〛 production

生産高 (*seisan*daka)　生産者 (*seisan*-sha)　生産技術 (*seisan*-gijutsu)

¶この工場では、一日何台の自動車が生産されているのですか。(Kono kōjō de wa, ichinichi nandai no jidōsha ga *seisan* sarete iru no desu ka?)

¶静岡県はお茶の生産地として有名です。(Shizuoka-ken wa ocha no *seisan*chi to shite yūmei desu.)

the output, the yield // **a producer, a maker** // **manufacturing** techniques, **industrial** technology

¶ How many cars **are produced** a day at this plant?

¶ Shizuoka Prefecture is famous as a tea-**producing** center.

seiseki　成績〘名〙

成績が悪い (*seiseki* ga warui)　成績が上がる (*seiseki* ga agaru)

¶あまり勉強しなかったので、成績が下がりました。(Amari benkyō shinakatta node, *seiseki* ga sagarimashita.)

¶試験の成績がよかったので、先生にほめられました。(Shiken no *seiseki* ga yokatta node, sensei ni homeraremashita.)

seiseki 〘n〙 **result, record, showing, score**

do poorly at school, get poor **grades;** make a poor **showing** (in business, etc.) // show a better **record** (in school, business, etc.)

¶ **[My] grades** fell as [I] didn't study very much.

¶ My teacher praised me for my good **mark** on the exam.

seishiki　正式〘名, 形動〙

¶それは結婚式のときに着る正式な服ではありません。(Sore wa kekkonshiki no toki ni kiru *seishiki* na fuku de wa arimasen.)

¶田中さんが社長になるといううわさがあったが、今日正式に発表がありました。(Tanaka san ga shachō ni naru to iu uwasa ga atta ga, kyō *seishiki* ni happyō ga arimashita.)

seishiki 〘n, adj-v〙 **formal, official, regular, full-dress**

¶ That is not **proper** dress for a wedding.

¶ There had been a rumor that [Mr.] Tanaka would be the next company president, and that was **officially** announced today.

seishin　精神〘名〙

精神病 (*seishin*byō)　精神力 (*seishin*ryoku)　精神的 (*seishin*teki)

¶あの人は精神が異常のようです。

seishin 〘n〙 **mind, spirit, soul, will**

mental illness // **spiritual** strength; the power of **the mind** // **spiritual, mental, moral**

(Ano hito wa *seishin* ga ijō no yō desu.)

¶田中さんは，どんな苦しみにも負けない強い**精神**を持っています。

(Tanaka san wa, donna kurushimi ni mo makenai tsuyoi *seishin* o motte imasu.)

¶ [He] appears to be not in [his] right **mind.**

¶ [Mrs.] Tanaka has a strong **spirit** such that [she] is not defeated no matter what hardship [she] might meet.

seishitsu 性質〖名〗

①[人が生まれつき持っている感情や考え方]

¶「山田さんはどんな**性質**の人ですか。」

(Yamada san wa donna *seishitsu* no hito desu ka?)「山田さんはとてもおとなしい人です。」(Yamada san wa totemo otonashii hito desu.)

②[ものごとに本来備わっている特色]

¶木綿と絹とは**性質**が違います。

(Momen to kinu to wa *seishitsu* ga chigaimasu.)

¶このことは問題の**性質**上 みんなに知らせないほうがいいでしょう。(Kono koto wa mondai no *seishitsu*jō minna ni shirasenai hō ga ii deshō.)

seishitsu 〖n〗 nature, temperament; property, quality, character

① [nature, temperament, disposition]

¶ "What **is** [Mr.] Yamada **like?**"
  "[He]'s very mild-mannered."

② [property, quality, character, nature]

¶ Cotton and silk are different **in nature.**

¶ Because of **its nature,** this matter should probably be kept secret.

seisho 聖書〖名〗

旧約**聖書** (kyūyaku-*seisho*) 新約**聖書** (shin'yaku-*seisho*)

¶わたしが子供の時，母がよく**聖書**を読んでくれました。(Watashi ga kodomo no toki, haha ga yoku *seisho* o yonde kuremashita.)

seisho 〖n〗 the Bible, the Scriptures

the Old **Testament** // the New **Testament**

¶ When I was small my mother often read to me from **the Bible.**

seito 生徒〖名〗

小学校の**生徒** (shōgakkō no *seito*)

¶わたしは中学校の**生徒**に英語を教え

seito 〖n〗 student, pupil, schoolboy, schoolgirl

an elementary school **student**

¶ I am teaching English to junior

ています。(Watashi wa chūgakkō no *seito* ni Eigo o oshiete imasu.)

high school **students.**

seiyō 西洋〖名〗

西洋人 (*seiyō*jin) 西洋史 (*seiyō*shi)

¶この辺には西洋風の建物が並んでいます。(Kono hen ni wa *seiyō*fū no tatemono ga narande imasu.)

⇔**tōyō** 東洋

seiyō 〖n〗 **the West, the Occident a Westerner // Western** history

¶ There are many **Western**-style buildings (i.e., homes) around here.

sekai 世界〖名〗

世界一 (*sekai*ichi) 世界史 (*sekai*shi)

¶世界でいちばん高い山はエベレストです。(*Sekai* de ichiban takai yama wa Eberesuto desu.)

sekai 〖n〗 **the world, the earth, the globe**

the greatest in **the world // world** history

¶ The highest mountain in **the world** is Mount Everest.

seken 世間〖名〗

¶世間を騒がせたどろぼうも、ついに捕まりました。(*Seken* o sawagaseta dorobō mo, tsuini tsukamarimashita.)

¶わたしは世間を離れて、一人で山の中で暮らしたいです。(Watashi wa *seken* o hanarete, hitori de yama no naka de kurashitai desu.)

seken 〖n〗 **world, people, the public, society**

¶ The thief that **everyone** was talking about has finally been caught 〖was caught in the end〗.

¶ I would like to leave **the world** behind and go live alone in the mountains.

seki 席〖名〗

席を離れる (*seki* o hanareru) 席へもどる (*seki* e modoru) 席を立つ (*seki* o tatsu)

¶席に着いてください。(*Seki* ni tsuite kudasai.)

¶電車はこんでいて、席がありませんでした。(Densha wa konde ite, *seki* ga arimasen deshita.)

⇒**zaseki** 座席

seki 〖n〗 **seat, one's place**

leave **one's seat** 〖**desk**〗 // return to **one's seat** 〖**desk**〗 // get up from **one's seat**

¶ Please take **your seat(s).**

¶ The train was crowded; there were no empty **seats.**

seki せき〖名〗

¶よくせきをしますね。風邪を引いた

seki 〖n〗 **cough, coughing**

¶ You **are coughing** a lot. Have you

のですか。(Yoku *seki* o shimasu ne. Kaze o hiita no desu ka?)

¶ゆうべは一晩じゅう**せき**が出て、眠れませんでした。(Yūbe wa hitobanjū *seki* ga dete, nemuremasen deshita.)

caught a cold?

¶ I was up all last night **with a cough.**

sekidō 赤道〖名〗

¶**赤道**に近づくにしたがって，だんだん暑くなります。(*Sekidō* ni chikazuku ni shitagatte, dandan atsuku narimasu.)

sekidō 〚n〛 **the equator**

¶ It gets hotter and hotter as one nears **the equator.**

sekinin 責任〖名〗

責任者 (*sekinin*sha) **責任**を果たす (*sekinin* o hatasu) **責任**をとる (*sekinin* o toru)

¶この事業が失敗したのは，わたしの**責任**です。(Kono jigyō ga shippai shita no wa, watashi no *sekinin* desu.)

¶仕事を引き受けたら，**責任**を持ってやらなければなりません。(Shigoto o hikiuketara, *sekinin* o motte yaranakereba narimasen.)

sekinin 〚n〛 **responsibility, obligation, duty**

the person **in charge** // fulfill **one's responsibility**, do **one's duty** // take **responsibility** for

¶ I **am responsible** for the failure of this undertaking.

¶ If you accept a job you must take on **the responsibility** for it.

sekitan 石炭〖名〗
石炭産業 (*sekitan*-sangyō)

sekitan 〚n〛 **coal**
the **coal** industry

sekiyu 石油〖名〗
石油ストーブ (*sekiyu*-sutōbu)

¶今では，石炭より**石油**のほうが多く使われています。(Ima de wa, sekitan yori *sekiyu* no hō ga ooku tsukawarete imasu.)

sekiyu 〚n〛 **petroleum, kerosene**
a **kerosene** heater
¶ Nowadays **oil** is used more widely than coal.

sekkaku せっかく〖副，〜の〗
①[あることのためにわざわざ努力するという意味を表す]

sekkaku 〚adv, 〜*no*〛 **specially, on purpose, with much trouble; precious; kindly**
① [specially, on purpose, expressly, with much trouble, at great pains]

¶せっかく来たのに，田中さんは留守でした。(*Sekkaku* kita noni, Tanaka san wa rusu deshita.)

¶せっかく日本に来たのですから，もう一年日本で勉強したいと思います。(*Sekkaku* Nihon ni kita no desu kara, mō ichinen Nihon de benkyō shitai to omoimasu.)

¶せっかくの努力がむだになりました。(*Sekkaku* no doryoku ga muda ni narimashita.)

②[めったになくて貴重だという意味を表す]

¶せっかくの日曜日なのに，朝から用事ができてゆっくり休めませんでした。(*Sekkaku* no nichiyōbi na noni, asa kara yōji ga dekite yukkuri yasumemasen deshita.)

¶せっかくの旅行だから，みんな参加することにしましょう。(*Sekkaku* no ryokō da kara, minna sanka suru koto ni shimashō.)

③[相手の好意に感謝の気持ちを表しながらその意に添えないことを表す]

¶せっかくの御招待ですが，あいにく用事があって行けません。(*Sekkaku* no goshōtai desu ga, ainiku yōji ga atte ikemasen.)

¶せっかくですが，あしたの会には出席できません。(*Sekkaku* desu ga, ashita no kai ni wa shusseki dekimasen.)

sekken 石けん〘名〙

¶石けんで顔を洗います。(*Sekken* de

¶ Even though [I] **came all the way** to see [him], [Mr.] Tanaka wasn't at home.

¶ As I have **come all the way** to Japan, I would like to study here one more year.

¶ **All** [our] efforts were 〚have been〛 in vain.

② [precious, long-awaited]

¶ Even though it was Sunday, I had various things to do from morning on so I couldn't just relax and take it easy.

¶ Let's all be sure to go on the trip as **it's not something we can do every day**.

③ [kindly]

¶ **It's very kind** of you to invite me, but unfortunately I have another appointment and won't be able to go.

¶ **Thank you** for asking me, but I won't be able to attend tomorrow's meeting 〚gathering, get-together, etc.〛.

sekken 〚n〛 **soap**

¶ [I] wash [my] face with **soap**.

kao o araimasu.)

sekkyokuteki 積極的〔形動〕

積極的な人 (*sekkyokuteki* na hito)

¶積極的な御意見をどうぞお出しください。 (*Sekkyokuteki* na goiken o dōzo odashi kudasai.)

¶田中さんはこの仕事に積極的に参加しています。(Tanaka san wa kono shigoto ni *sekkyokuteki* ni sanka shite imasu.)

⇔**shōkyokuteki** 消極的

semai 狭い〔形〕

¶この部屋は狭いですね。(Kono heya wa *semai* desu ne.)

¶この道は狭くて自動車が通れません。 (Kono michi wa *semakute* jidōsha ga tooremasen.)

⇔**hiroi** 広い

semento セメント〔名〕

¶セメントに砂などを混ぜて水を加えると、コンクリートができます。(*Semento* ni suna nado o mazete mizu o kuwaeru to, konkuriito ga dekimasu.)

sen 千〔名〕

千円 (*sen*'en) 千人 (*sen*nin) 数千キロ (sū*sen*kiro)

(-)sen (-)線〔名, 尾〕

1〔名〕

①〔筋〕

¶鉛筆で紙に線を引きます。 (Enpitsu de kami ni *sen* o hikimasu.)

②〔細長いもの〕

電線 (den*sen*) 線路 (*sen*ro)

---

sekkyokuteki 〖adj-v〗 **positive, active, vigorous, aggressive**

an **aggressive** person

¶ Please **don't hesitate** to give your opinions.

¶ [Miss] Tanaka is taking an **active** part in this work.

semai 〖adj〗 **narrow, small, limited, restricted, cramped**

¶ This room **is small,** isn't it?

¶ This street is **too narrow** for cars.

semento 〖n〗 **cement**

¶ One makes concrete by mixing sand and the like with **cement** and then adding water.

sen 〖n〗 **a thousand**

a thousand yen // a thousand persons // **thousands** of kilometers; **thousands** of kilos

(-)sen 〖n, suf〗 **line; wire, line, track, route; (train or air) line**

1 〖n〗

① [line]

¶ [I] draw **a line** on paper with a pencil.

② [wire, line, track, route]

an electric **wire**, a telephone **line**, a telegraph **wire** // a railroad **track**

2〖尾〗

山の手線 (Yamanote*sen*)　中央線 (Chūō*sen*)　国際線 (kokusai*sen*) 国内線 (kokunai*sen*)

2〚suf〛　(train or air) line

the Yamanote **Line** // the Chuo **Line** // **a plane** going overseas // **a plane** flying within the country

senaka　背中〖名〗

¶おふろで中村さんに背中を洗ってもらいました。(Ofuro de Nakamura san ni *senaka* o aratte moraimashita.)

senaka　〚n〛　the back

¶ [Mr.] Nakamura washed **my back** at the public bath.

-senchi　-センチ〖尾〗

¶1メートルは100センチです。(Ichimētoru wa hyaku*senchi* desu.)

-senchi　〚suf〛　centimeter(s)

¶ One meter is 100 **centimeters.**

senden　宣伝〖名, ～する〗

¶あの会社は新しい製品の宣伝を盛んにしています。(Ano kaisha wa atarashii seihin no *senden* o sakan ni shite imasu.)

¶テレビで宣伝していたカメラはこれですか。(Terebi de *senden* shite ita kamera wa kore desu ka?)

senden　〚n, ～*suru*〛　publicity, advertisement, propaganda

¶ That company is extensively **advertising** its new products.

¶ Is this the camera **advertised** on television?

sengetsu　先月〖名〗

¶わたしの誕生日は先月の二十日でした。(Watashi no tanjōbi wa *sengetsu* no hatsuka deshita.)

¶わたしは先月日本に来ました。(Watashi wa *sengetsu* Nihon ni kimashita.)

sengetsu　〚n〛　last month

¶ My birthday was the twentieth of **last month.**

¶ I came to Japan **last month.**

sengo　戦後〖名〗

¶戦後, 東京の町は大きく変わりました。(*Sengo*, Tōkyō no machi wa ookiku kawarimashita.)

⇔senzen 戦前

sengo　〚n〛　postwar, after World War II

¶ Tokyo changed greatly **after the war 〖after World War II〗.**

senjitsu　先日〖名〗

¶先日, 田中さんに会いました。(*Sen-*

senjitsu　〚n〛　the other day, a few days ago, lately

¶ [I] met [Mrs.] Tanaka **the other**

jitsu, Tanaka san ni aimashita.)

¶先日は子供がたいへんお世話になり、ありがとうございました。 (*Senjitsu wa kodomo ga taihen osewa ni nari, arigatō gozaimashita.*)

⇒**konoaida** この間

senkō 専攻〖名, 〜する〗

¶山田さんの専攻は何ですか。(*Yamada san no senkō wa nan desu ka?*)

¶わたしは大学で日本文学を専攻しました。 (*Watashi wa daigaku de Nihon-bungaku o senkō shimashita.*)

senkyo 選挙〖名, 〜する〗

選挙権 (*senkyoken*) 選挙運動 (*senkyo*-undō)

¶上田さんは選挙でクラスの委員に選ばれました。 (*Ueda san wa senkyo de kurasu no iin ni erabaremashita.*)

¶大統領は選挙をして選びます。(*Daitōryō wa senkyo o shite erabimasu.*)

senmenjo 洗面所〖名〗

¶朝起きると、まず洗面所で顔を洗います。(*Asa okiru to, mazu senmenjo de kao o araimasu.*)

senmon 専門〖名〗

専門家 (*senmonka*)

¶あなたの専門は何ですか。(*Anata no senmon wa nan desu ka?*)

¶わたしは日本の歴史を専門に勉強しようと思っています。(*Watashi wa Nihon no rekishi o senmon ni benkyō shiyō to omotte imasu.*)

day.

¶ Thank you very much for your kindness to my child **the other day.**

senkō 〚n, ~*suru*〛 special study, one's academic speciality, one's major

¶ What is [Mr.] Yamada's **speciality** 〖**major**〗?

¶ I **majored** in Japanese literature in college.

senkyo 〚n, ~*suru*〛 election

the franchise, suffrage, the right **to vote** // an **election** campaign

¶ [Miss] Ueda **was elected** to be one of the class officers.

¶ The nation's president is chosen in **an election.**

senmenjo 〚n〛 lavatory, washroom

¶ After getting up in the morning [I] first of all wash my face in **the bathroom.**

senmon 〚n〛 speciality, special subject of study, profession

a **specialist,** an **expert,** a **professional**

¶ What is your **field of specialization?**

¶ I plan **to specialize** in Japanese history.

senpūki　扇風機〖名〗

¶暑いですね。扇風機をつけましょう。
(Atsui desu ne. *Senpūki* o tsuke-mashō.)

senro　線路〖名〗

¶汽車は線路を走ります。(Kisha wa *senro* o hashirimasu.)

sensei　先生〖名〗

①〔学校の教師, 学問や芸術など特別な知識・技能などを教える人〕
数学の先生 (sūgaku no *sensei*)
¶あの人は小学校の先生です。(Ano hito wa shōgakkō no *sensei* desu.)
¶山田さんの奥さんは生け花の先生です。(Yamada san no okusan wa ikebana no *sensei* desu.)

②〔教師・医者・芸術家・弁護士などに呼びかける場合に使う言葉〕
¶先生, この言葉の意味を説明していただけませんか。(Sensei, kono kotoba no imi o setsumei shite itadakemasen ka?)
¶先生, わたしはいつ退院できますか。(*Sensei*, watashi wa itsu taiin dekimasu ka?)

③〔教師・医者・芸術家・弁護士などの名前につけて尊敬の気持ちを表す〕
¶わたしは田中先生に日本語を習っています。(Watashi wa Tanaka *sensei* ni Nihongo o naratte imasu.)
¶山田先生は国立病院の内科の先生です。(Yamada *sensei* wa kokuritsu-byōin no naika no sensei desu.)

senshu　選手〖名〗

senpūki 〚n〛　electric fan

¶ It's hot, isn't it? Let's turn on **the fan.**

senro 〚n〛　railroad track, line, rails

¶ The train runs along **the track.**

sensei 〚n〛　a teacher; a term of address or respect for teachers, doctors, artists, lawyers, etc.

① [teacher at a school, a teacher of some scholarly or artistic knowledge or skill]
a mathematics **teacher**
¶ [He] is an elementary school **teacher.**
¶ Mr. Yamada's wife **teaches** *ikebana*.

② [term of address for teachers, doctors, artists, lawyers, etc.]
¶ **Sir** 〚**Ma'am**〛, could you please explain the meaning of this word?

¶ **Doctor,** when will I be able to go home from the hospital?

③ [term of respect added to the names of teachers, doctors, artists, lawyers, etc.]
¶ I am studying Japanese with **Professor** Tanaka.
¶ **Dr.** Yamada is a physician in the department of internal medicine at a national hospital.

senshu 〚n〛　player, athlete

¶中村さんはテニスの選手です。
(Nakamura san wa tenisu no *senshu* desu.)

¶田中さんはオリンピックの選手に選ばれました。(Tanaka san wa Orinpikku no *senshu* ni erabaremashita.)

senshū 先週〚名〛

¶先週の月曜日は何日でしたか。(*Senshū* no getsuyōbi wa nannichi deshita ka?)

¶先週, わたしは友達と旅行しました。(*Senshū*, watashi wa tomodachi to ryokō shimashita.)

sensō 戦争〚名, ～する〛

戦争が始まる (*sensō* ga hajimaru)

戦争に行く (*sensō* ni iku)

¶A国とB国は今戦争をしています。(Ē-koku to Bii-koku wa ima *sensō* o shite imasu.)

sentaku 洗たく〚名, ～する〛

洗たく機 (*sentaku*ki) 洗たく物 (*sentaku*mono)

¶今日は天気がいいので, 洗たくをしようと思います。(Kyō wa tenki ga ii node, *sentaku* o shiyō to omoimasu.)

¶この汚れは洗たくしてもきれいになりません。(Kono yogore wa *sentaku* shite mo kirei ni narimasen.)

senzen 戦前〚名〛

¶わたしは戦前からここに住んでいます。(Watashi wa *senzen* kara koko ni sunde imasu.)

¶ [Mr.] Nakamura **is on the** tennis **team.**

¶ [Miss] Tanaka was chosen **to compete** in the Olympics.

senshū 〚n〛 **last week**

¶ What date was Monday **last week?**

¶ I went on a trip with friends **last week.**

sensō 〚n, ～*suru*〛 **war, warfare, hostilities, a battle**

a war breaks out // go off to **war**

¶ Country A and Country B are presently **at war** with each other.

sentaku 〚n, ～*suru*〛 **wash, washing, laundry**

a **washing** machine // **a washing, the laundry**

¶ I think **I'll do the wash** today as the weather is so nice.

¶ This dirt 〚spot, stain〛 won't **wash out** completely.

senzen 〚n〛 **prewar, before World War II**

¶ I've been living here since **before the war.**

⇔**sengo** 戦後

senzo 先祖〔名〕

先祖代々 (*senzo*daidai)

¶わたしは先祖のお墓へお参りに行きました。 (Watashi wa *senzo* no ohaka e omairi ni ikimashita.)

⇔**shison** 子孫 ⇒祖先 **sosen**

seru せる〔助動〕

①〔他に対してある行為を実現するように仕向ける意味を表す〕

¶病気をして，両親を心配させました。(Byōki o shite, ryōshin o shinpai sa*semashita*.)

¶先生が学生に本を読ませます。(Sensei ga gakusei ni hon o yoma*semasu*.)

¶病気が治ったばかりですから，あまり無理な運動はさせないほうがいいです。 (Byōki ga naotta bakari desu kara, amari muri na undō wa sa*senai* hō ga ii desu.)

②〔他の人がある行為をするのを許容あるいは黙認する意味を表す〕

¶子供を夜遅くまで外で遊ばせておくのはよくないです。 (Kodomo o yoru osoku made soto de asoba*sete* oku no wa yoku nai desu.)

¶今年は，娘が希望していた海外旅行に行かせることにしました。(Kotoshi wa, musume ga kibō shite ita kaigai-ryokō ni ika*seru* koto ni shimashita.)

＊Ⅰ型動詞とⅢ型動詞の「する (suru)」につく。

senzo 〚n〛 **ancestor, forefather, ancestry**

(a home, business, etc.) in the family for generations

¶ I visited my **family** graves.

-seru 〚auxil〛 a verb ending expressing the causative, etc.

① [make do, cause to do, have do]

¶ [I] **caused** worry to [my] parents with [my] illness.

¶ The teacher **has** the students read the book.

¶ As [he] has just recovered from [his] illness, you **should not let** [him] exercise too strenuously.

② [let do, allow to do]

¶ You shouldn't **let** the children play outside until so late at night.

¶ [We]'ve decided **to let** [our] daughter travel abroad this year as she has been wanting to do.

＊ *-seru* is added to Type I verbs and the Type III verb *suru* (→ *saseru*).

⇨**saseru** させる

sētā セーター〖名〗

¶上田さんは黒いセーターを着ています。 (Ueda san wa kuroi *sētā* o kite imasu.)

¶寒ければ，セーターを着なさい。 (Samukereba, *sētā* o kinasai.)

setsubi 設備〖名，〜する〗

暖房設備 (danbō-*setsubi*) 冷房設備 (reibō-*setsubi*)

¶このホテルは設備がよくありません。 (Kono hoteru wa *setsubi* ga yoku arimasen.)

setsumei 説明〖名，〜する〗

¶田中先生の説明はとてもわかりやすいです。 (Tanaka sensei no *setsumei* wa totemo wakariyasui desu.)

¶その言葉の意味をもう一度説明してください。 (Sono kotoba no imi o mō ichido *setsumei* shite kudasai.)

sewa 世話〖名，〜する〗

¶お母さんは赤ちゃんの世話で忙しいです。 (Okāsan wa akachan no *sewa* de isogashii desu.)

¶わたしは今おじの世話になっています。 (Watashi wa ima oji no *sewa* ni natte imasu.)

¶田中さんのお世話で，この会社に勤めることになりました。 (Tanaka san no o*sewa* de, kono kaisha ni tsutomeru koto ni narimashita.)

shachō 社長〖名〗

¶山田さんはこの会社の社長です。 (Yamada san wa kono kaisha no

sētā 〖n〗 sweater

¶ [Miss] Ueda is wearing a black **sweater.**

¶ Put on **a sweater** if you're cold.

setsubi 〖n, ~*suru*〗 equipment, facilities, accommodations, arrangements

heating **facilities** // air conditioning

¶ **The accommodations** at this hotel are poor.

setsumei 〖n, ~*suru*〗 explanation, interpretation, elucidation

¶ Professor Tanaka's **explanations** are very easy to understand.

¶ Please **explain** again the meaning of that word.

sewa 〖n, ~*suru*〗 care; help, assistance; kind offices

¶ The mother is busy **taking care** of her baby.

¶ I am now **being looked after** by my uncle.

¶ I got my job at this company through **the kind offices** of [Mr.] Tanaka.

shachō 〖n〗 company president, head of a firm

¶ [Mr.] Yamada is **the president** of

shachō desu.)

shakai　社会〖名〗

社会生活 (*shakai*-seikatsu)　社会問題 (*shakai*-mondai)

¶わたしはみんなが幸せになれる社会をつくるために働きたいです。(Watashi wa minna ga shiawase ni nareru *shakai* o tsukuru tame ni hatarakitai desu.)

¶学校を卒業して社会に出たら, 社会人としての責任があります。(Gakkō o sotsugyō shite *shakai* ni detara, *shakai*jin to shite no sekinin ga arimasu.)

shakaishugi　社会主義〖名〗

shashin　写真〖名〗

写真機 (*shashin*ki)　カラー写真 (karā-*shashin*) 写真を写す (*shashin* o utsusu)　写真を撮る (*shashin* o toru)

¶わたしは田中さんに写真を写してもらいました。(Watashi wa Tanaka san ni *shashin* o utsushite moraimashita.)

¶この写真はとてもよく撮れていますね。(Kono *shashin* wa totemo yoku torete imasu ne.)

shashō　車掌〖名〗

¶最近は, 車掌のいないバスが多くなりました。(Saikin wa, *shashō* no inai basu ga ooku narimashita.)

¶電車に乗っていると, 車掌が切符を調べに来ました。(Densha ni notte iru to, *shashō* ga kippu o shirabe

---

this company.

shakai 〖n〗 **society; the world community** life, **social** life // a **social** problem

¶ I want to work for the creation of **a society** where all can be happy.

¶ When one graduates from school and goes out into **the world** one has the responsibilities of **an adult member of society.**

shakaishugi 〖n〗 **socialism**

shashin 〖n〗 **photograph**

a camera // a color **photo** // take **a photograph** // take **a photograph**

¶ I had [Miss] Tanaka take **my picture.**

¶ This **photo** came out well, didn't it?

shashō 〖n〗 **conductor**

¶ Recently buses without **conductors** have increased.

¶ While [I] was on the train, **the conductor** came looking at everyone's tickets.

ni kimashita.)

shatsu シャツ〖名〗

¶山田さんは赤いシャツを着ています。

(Yamada san wa akai *shatsu* o kite imasu.)

shi 四〖名〗

四月 (*shi*gatsu)　四角 (*shi*kaku)

四方 (*shi*hō)　四季 (*shi*ki)

⇒**yon** 四

shi 死〖名〗

¶父の手紙で母の死を知りました。

(Chichi no tegami de haha no *shi* o shirimashita.)

shi 詩〖名〗

詩人 (*shi*jin)

¶わたしは詩を作って，みんなの前で読みました。　(Watashi wa *shi* o tsukutte, minna no mae de yomi-mashita.)

shi し〖助〗

¶今日は天気もいいし，暖かいから，どこかへ遊びに行きましょう。　(Kyō wa tenki mo ii *shi*, atatakai kara, doko ka e asobi ni ikimashō.)

¶秋子さんは性格も明るいし，親切なので，みんなから好かれています。

(Akiko san wa seikaku mo akarui *shi*, shinsetsu na node, minna kara sukarete imasu.)

¶風もないし，波も静かだし，海水浴にはとてもいい日でした。(Kaze mo nai *shi*, nami mo shizuka da *shi*, kaisuiyoku ni wa totemo ii hi deshita.)

shatsu 〖n〗 **undershirt, shirt, T-shirt, knit shirt,** etc.

¶ Mr. Yamada is wearing a red **shirt.**

shi 〖n〗 **four**

April // square, a square // the **four** quarters; all directions // the **four** seasons

shi 〖n〗 **death**

¶ I learned of **the death** of my mother in a letter from my father.

shi 〖n〗 **poem, poetry**

a poet

¶ I wrote **a poem** and read it aloud in front of everyone.

shi 〖part〗 **and, moreover, besides**

¶ Let's go somewhere, as it's so nice **and** warm out today.

¶ Everyone likes Akiko, as she's so cheerful **and** kind.

¶ What with the lack of wind **and** the calm seas, it was a very good day for going swimming.

¶雨も降っているし, 行くのはやめましょう。 (Ame mo futte iru *shi*, iku no wa yamemashō.)

¶ And besides it's raining—let's not go.

＊普通, 二つ以上のことがらを対等の関係で並列して述べるときに使う。またあとのことがらに対して理由などを表すことが多い。

＊ *Shi* is usually used to list two or more items of equal standing. It often gives the reason, etc., for what follows.

shiai 試合〔名〕

¶今日の午後, ピンポンの試合があります。 (Kyō no gogo, pinpon no *shiai* ga arimasu.)

¶テニスの試合をして, 負けてしまいました。 (Tenisu no *shiai* o shite, makete shimaimashita.)

shiai [[n]] **match, game, tournament**

¶ There is a ping-pong **match** this afternoon.

¶ [I] lost [my] tennis **match**.

shiawase 幸せ〔名, 形動〕

幸せを願う (*shiawase* o negau)
幸せな家庭 (*shiawase* na katei)

¶あなたはよいお子さんを持って幸せですね。 (Anata wa yoi okosan o motte *shiawase* desu ne.)

¶上田さんは, いつもにこにこして幸せそうです。 (Ueda san wa, itsu mo nikoniko shite *shiawasesō* desu.)

shiawase [[n, adj-v]] **happiness, fortune, good luck, blessing**

wish someone **good luck** // a **happy** home

¶ You **are fortunate** in having such nice children.

¶ [Mrs.] Ueda **seems to be quite happy**—[she] is always smiling.

shibafu 芝生〔名〕

¶天気がよかったので, 公園の芝生の上に座って本を読みました。 (Tenki ga yokatta node, kōen no *shibafu* no ue ni suwatte hon o yomimashita.)

shibafu [[n]] **lawn, patch of grass**

¶ As it was a nice day [I] read a book sitting on **the grass** in the park.

shibai 芝居〔名〕

¶あした, 芝居を見に行きませんか。 (Ashita, *shibai* o mi ni ikimasen ka?)

shibai [[n]] **play, drama, theatrical performance**

¶ Would you like to go to **the theater** with [me] tomorrow?

shibaraku しばらく〔副〕

shibaraku [[adv]] **a little while, a moment; quite a while, for a long time**

①[少しの間]

¶この仕事が終わるまで，しばらくお待ちください。 (Kono shigoto ga owaru made, *shibaraku* omachi kudasai.)

¶山田さんはしばらくして帰ってきました。 (Yamada san wa *shibaraku* shite kaette kimashita.)

②[やや長い間]

¶父からしばらく手紙が来ません。 (Chichi kara *shibaraku* tegami ga kimasen.)

¶しばらく会わないうちにずいぶん大きくなりましたね。 (*Shibaraku* awanai uchi ni zuibun ookiku narimashita ne.)

¶昨日，山田さんにしばらくぶりに会いました。 (Kinō, Yamada san ni *shibaraku* buri ni aimashita.)

shibaru 縛る〖動Ⅰ〗

ひもで縛る (himo de *shibaru*)

shibashiba しばしば〖副〗

¶わたしは医者にたばこを吸わないようにしばしば注意されました。 (Watashi wa isha ni tabako o suwanai yō ni *shibashiba* chūi saremashita.)

¶会社を辞めようと思ったこともしばしばありました。 (Kaisha o yameyō to omotta koto mo *shibashiba* arimashita.)

shiboru 絞る〖動Ⅰ〗

¶手ぬぐいをよく絞ってから干してください。 (Tenugui o yoku *shibotte* kara hoshite kudasai.)

① [a little while, a moment]

¶ Please wait **a moment** while I finish up this job.

¶ [Miss] Yamada stayed there **a little while** and then came home.

② [quite a while, for a long time]

¶ There hasn't been a letter from my father **for quite a while.**

¶ **It's been a long time** since I've seen you—[you]'ve really grown a lot, haven't [you]?

¶ Yesterday [I] met [Miss] Yamada for the first time **in a long while.**

shibaru 〖v I〗 tie, bind, fasten

fasten with string 〖twine, cord, a strap, etc.〗

shibashiba 〖adv〗 often, frequently, many times

¶ I was **repeatedly** warned by my doctor not to smoke.

¶ I thought **several times** about quitting my job.

shiboru 〖v I〗 wring, squeeze, press

¶ Please **wring out** the (hand) towel thoroughly before hanging it up.

653

shiboru 搾る〚動Ⅰ〛
¶わたしは父に牛の乳の搾り方を教え
てもらいました。(Watashi wa chi-
chi ni ushi no chichi no *shibori*-
kata o oshiete moraimashita.)

shichi 七〚名〛
七人 (*shichi*nin)　七時間 (*shichi*jikan)

＊「なな (nana)」とも言う。

shichigatsu 七月〚名〛

shidai ni 次第に〚副〛
¶２学期になって，勉強が**次第に**難し
くなってきました。(Nigakki ni na-
tte, benkyō ga *shidai ni* muzukashiku natte kimashita.)
¶夜になってから，風は**次第に**強くな
りました。　(Yoru ni natte kara,
kaze wa *shidai ni* tsuyoku narimashita)

shidō 指導〚名，～する〛
指導者 (*shidō*sha)　技術指導 (giju-
tsu-*shidō*)
¶わたしは田中先生の**指導**を受けて，
この研究を完成しました。(Watashi
wa Tanaka sensei no *shidō* o ukete,
kono kenkyū o kansei shimashita.)
¶おおぜいの学生を**指導**するのは，た
いへんでしょうね。　(Oozei no ga-
kusei o *shidō* suru no wa, taihen
deshō ne.)

shigatsu 四月〚名〛

shigeki 刺激〚名，～する〛
①〔人間・生物の感覚に外から働きか
けて何かの変化を起こさせること〕

shiboru 〚v Ⅰ〛　milk (a cow, etc.)
¶ My father taught me how **to milk** a
cow.

shichi 〚n〛　seven
seven persons // **seven** hours

＊ Variant: *nana*.

shichigatsu 〚n〛　July

shidai ni 〚adv〛　gradually
¶ The coursework has **gradually** become 〚**gradually** became〛 more difficult in the second semester.

¶ The wind **gradually** increased from
nightfall.

shidō 〚n, ～*suru*〛　guidance, lead-
ership, direction, coaching
a leader, director, coach, adviser
// technical **guidance**
¶ I completed this research under **the
guidance** of Professor Tanaka.

¶ It must be hard **to be responsible
for** 〚**to teach**〛 so many students.

shigatsu 〚n〛　April

shigeki 〚n, ～*suru*〛　stimulus, irritant; stimulation, excitement
① [stimulus, impetus, irritant, incen-
tive, incitement]

刺激を与える (*shigeki* o ataeru) 刺激を受ける (*shigeki* o ukeru)

¶コーヒーは胃を刺激するから，あまりたくさん飲まないほうがいいです。 (Kōhii wa i o *shigeki* suru kara, amari takusan nomanai hō ga ii desu.)

②〔人間の心に働きかけて何かを感じさせること〕

¶わたしは刺激のない田舎の生活にあきました。 (Watashi wa *shigeki* no nai inaka no seikatsu ni akimashita.)

shigen 資源〔名〕

天然資源 (tennen-*shigen*) 石油資源 (sekiyu-*shigen*)

¶日本は資源の少ない国です。 (Nihon wa *shigen* no sukunai kuni desu.)

shigeru 茂る〔動Ⅰ〕

¶道の両側には木が茂っています。 (Michi no ryōgawa ni wa ki ga *shigette* imasu.)

shigoto 仕事〔名〕

①〔働くこと〕

¶仕事は5時に終わります。 (*Shigoto* wa goji ni owarimasu.)

¶昨日は夜10時まで仕事をしました。 (Kinō wa yoru jūji made *shigoto* o shimashita.)

②〔職業〕

¶あなたの仕事は何ですか。 (Anata no *shigoto* wa nan desu ka?)

③〔事業〕

¶このごろ，どうも仕事がうまくいき

give **a stimulus** // receive **a stimulus**

¶ Coffee is **a stimulant which irritates** the stomach so it's best not to drink too much of it.

② [stimulation, excitement]

¶ I got ⟦am⟧ tired of life in the country with its lack of **stimulation**.

shigen ⟦n⟧ **resources**

natural **resources** // oil **resources**

¶ Japan is a country poor in **natural resources.**

shigeru ⟦v I⟧ **grow thick, be luxuriant, be overgrown**

¶ Both sides of the road are **heavily** forested.

shigoto ⟦n⟧ **working, employment; job, occupation; work, a task, one's duties**

① [working, employment, labor]

¶ **Work** ends at five o'clock.

¶ [I] **worked** until ten o'clock last night.

② [job, occupation]

¶ What **do you do?**

③ [work, a task, one's duties]

¶ Things aren't going well **at work**

ません。 (Konogoro, dōmo *shigoto* ga umaku ikimasen.)

recently.

shihai 支配〖名, ～する〗
支配者 (*shihai*sha) 支配人 (*shihai*-nin)

¶この国は長い間，A国の支配を受けていました。 (Kono kuni wa nagai aida Ē-koku no *shihai* o ukete imashita.)

shihai 〚n, ~*suru*〛 **control, rule, government, domination, management**

a ruler, master, governor // a manager, an executive

¶ For a long time this country was under **the rule** of Country A.

shihon 資本〖名〗
資本家 (*shihon*ka)

¶その事業を始めるのには，大きな資本が要ります。 (Sono jigyō o hajimeru no ni wa, ookina *shihon* ga irimasu.)

¶この会社の資本金は 20 億円です。 (Kono kaisha no *shihon*kin wa nijūokuen desu.)

shihon 〚n〛 **capital, funds**
a capitalist, financier

¶ A large **capital** is needed to begin that enterprise.

¶ This company **is capitalized** at 2 billion yen.

shihonshugi 資本主義〖名〗

shihonshugi 〚n〛 **capitalism**

shiitsu シーツ〖名〗

¶寝るときには布団の上にシーツを敷いて寝ます。 (Neru toki ni wa futon no ue ni *shiitsu* o shiite nemasu.)

shiitsu 〚n〛 (bed) **sheet**

¶ [I] sleep with **a sheet** spread on top of [my] *futon*.

shijū しじゅう〖副〗

¶あの人はしじゅう何か食べていますね。 (Ano hito wa *shijū* nani ka tabete imasu ne.)

¶子供がしじゅう仕事の邪魔をして困ります。 (Kodomo ga *shijū* shigoto no jama o shite komarimasu.)

shijū 〚adv〛 **from start to finish, all the time, continually, very often, frequently**

¶ [He] is **always** eating something, isn't [he]?

¶ [I] am bothered by the children **continually** interrupting [my] work.

shika しか〖助〗

¶その部屋にはわたし一人しかいませんでした。(Sono heya ni wa watashi hitori *shika* imasen deshita.)

shika 〚part〛 **only, no more than**

¶ There was **no one but** me in that room.

¶食べ物はもうこれだけ**しか**ありません。(Tabemono wa mō kore dake *shika* arimasen.)

¶ This is **all there is** to eat.

＊ いつも打ち消しの言葉を伴って，それだけと限る意味を表す。「だけしか (dake shika)」 は特に強い限定を表す。

＊ *Shika* is always used with the negative; it indicates that that is all there is. For special stress *dake shika* is used.

⇒**dake** だけ

shikaku 資格〔名〕

①〔身分・地位など〕

¶上田さんは今度大使の**資格**でA国へ行きました。(Ueda san wa kondo taishi no *shikaku* de Ē-koku e ikimashita.)

②〔ある身分や地位を得るのに必要な条件〕

¶医者の**資格**を取るには，国の試験に合格しなければなりません。(Isha no *shikaku* o toru ni wa, kuni no shiken ni gōkaku shinakereba narimasen.)

¶こんなことも知らないのでは，先生としての**資格**はありませんね。(Konna koto mo shiranai no de wa, sensei to shite no *shikaku* wa arimasen ne.)

shikaku 四角〔名，形動〕

四角なテーブル (*shikaku* na tēburu)

真四角 (ma*shikaku*)

＊「四角い (shikakui)」（形）という言葉もある。

shikamo しかも〔接〕

¶この国は土地も狭く，しかも人口が多いです。(Kono kuni wa tochi mo

shikaku 〖n〗 **capacity, status; qualification, credential, competency**

① [capacity, status]

¶ This time [Mr.] Ueda went to Country A **in the capacity** of ambassador.

② [qualification, credential, competency]

¶ One must pass a national examination in order **to qualify** as a physician.

¶ Anyone not knowing this sort of thing has no **right** to call [him]self a teacher.

shikaku 〖n, adj-v〗 **a square, a rectangle**

a **four-cornered** table // **square**, a true **square**

＊ The adjectival form *shikakui* can also be used.

shikamo 〖conj〗 **moreover, furthermore; and yet, nevertheless**

¶ This country is not only small **but**

semaku, *shikamo* jinkō ga ooi desu.)

¶この料理は安くて，しかもおいしいです。 (Kono ryōri wa yasukute, *shikamo* oishii desu.)

¶一生懸命勉強して，しかも入学できないときは，あきらめるよりしかたがありません。(Isshōkenmei benkyō shite, *shikamo* nyūgaku dekinai toki wa, akirameru yori shikata ga arimasen.)

＊ 前のことがらを受けて，更にあとのことがらをつけ加えるときに使う。前のことがらとあとのことがらが同じようなときには，前のことがらだけではなく，そのうえにというような意味を表し，前のことがらとあとのことがらとが対比的な関係にあるときには，前のことがらにかかわらず，なおというような意味を表す。

shikaru しかる〖動Ⅰ〗

¶お母さんがいたずらした子供をしかっています。 (Okāsan ga itazura shita kodomo o *shikatte* imasu.)

¶宿題をやらなかったので，先生にしかられました。(Shukudai o yarana-katta node, sensei ni *shikarare-mashita*.)

shikashi しかし〖接〗

¶今日はいい天気です。しかし，あまり暖かくはありません。 (Kyō wa ii tenki desu. *Shikashi*, amari atata-kaku wa arimasen.)

¶あの学生は頭はいいのです。しかし，

also heavily populated.

¶ This food is cheap and good **too.**

¶ One has no choice but to accept it as hopeless when one studies hard **but nevertheless** fails one's school entrance exams.

＊ *Shikamo* is used when adding something to what has been said. When the two items are of the same nature the meaning is "moreover, in addition," but when they are in opposition the meaning is "in spite of, nevertheless."

shikaru 〖v I〗 **scold, reprimand, lecture**

¶ The child who played the trick **is being scolded** by its mother.

¶ My teacher **reprimanded** me for not doing my homework.

shikashi 〖conj〗 **however, but**

¶ It's a nice day today. **However,** it is on the cool side (literally, is not very warm).

¶ That student is quite bright **but**

努力が足りません。(Ano gakusei wa atama wa ii no desu. *Shikashi*, doryoku ga tarimasen.)

⇨**keredomo** けれども

shikata 仕方〖名〗

¶漢字の勉強の仕方を教えてくださ い。(Kanji no benkyō no *shikata* o oshiete kudasai.)

¶子供にあいさつの仕方を教えてやり ました。 (Kodomo ni aisatsu no *shikata* o oshiete yarimashita.)

shikata ga nai しかたがない〖連〗

①[どうすることもできない様子]

¶なくしてしまったものは**しかたがあ りません**。これからは注意してくださ い。(Nakushite shimatta mono wa *shikata ga arimasen*. Kore kara wa chūi shite kudasai.)

¶バスがなくなってしまいました。**し かたがない**から，タクシーで帰りまし ょう。(Basu ga nakunatte shimai- mashita. *Shikata ga nai* kara, ta- kushii de kaerimashō.)

→**yamu o enai** やむをえない

②[我慢できない様子]

¶暑くて**しかたがない**から，窓を開け ましょう。(Atsukute *shikata ga nai* kara, mado o akemashō.)

¶あの人は日本へ行ってみたくて**しか たがない**のです。(Ano hito wa Nihon e itte mitakute *shikata ga nai* no desu.)

*「〜てしかたがない (〜te shikata ga nai)」の形で使う。

---

lacks application.

shikata 〚n〛 **way, method, means**

¶ Please tell [me] **how** to study *kanji*.

¶ [I] taught the children **the way** to give greetings.

shikata ga nai 〚compd〛 **cannot be helped, have no choice, be inevi- table; cannot stand, be unbearable**

① [cannot be helped, have no choice, be inevitable, be no use to]

¶ **What's lost is lost.** Just be more careful in the future.

¶ There are no more buses. **We have no choice** but to take a taxi home.

② [cannot stand, be unbearable]

¶ Let's open a window—it's **unbear- ably** hot in here.

¶ [He] **is dying** to go to Japan.

* Used in the pattern "*-te shikata ga nai.*"

shiken 試験〖名, ～する〗

入学試験 (nyūgaku-*shiken*) 試験を
受ける (*shiken* o ukeru)

¶来週, 英語の試験があります。

(Raishū, Eigo no *shiken* ga arimasu.)

¶中村さんは試験に合格しました。

(Nakamura san wa *shiken* ni gōkaku shimashita.)

shiki 四季〖名〗

¶わたしは四季の中で, 春がいちばん
好きです。 (Watashi wa *shiki* no
naka de, haru ga ichiban suki
desu.)

(-)shiki (-)式〖名, 尾〗

1〖名〗

入学式 (nyūgaku*shiki*) 卒業式
(sotsugyō*shiki*)

¶「結婚式は何時から始まりますか。」

(Kekkon*shiki* wa nanji kara hajimarimasu ka?) 「式は10時から始ま
ります。」 (*Shiki* wa jūji kara hajimarimasu.)

2〖尾〗

ヘボン式ローマ字 (Hebon*shiki*-rōma-
ji)

¶あの人は何でも新式のものが好きで
す。(Ano hito wa nan demo shin-
shiki no mono ga suki desu.)

shikirini しきりに〖副〗

①[同じことが繰り返して起こる様子]

¶最近, この辺でしきりに事故が起きま
す。(Saikin, kono hen de *shikirini*
jiko ga okimasu.)

shiken 〚n, ~*suru*〛 examination,
test

a school entrance **examination** //
take **an exam**

¶ There is an English **test** next week.

¶ [Miss] Nakamura passed **the exam.**

shiki 〚n〛 the four seasons

¶ Of **the four seasons,** I like spring
the best.

(-)shiki 〚n, suf〛 ceremony;
method, style, type

1 〚n〛 ceremony

an entrance **ceremony, a ceremony**
for newly admitted students // a
graduation **ceremony,** commencement **exercises**

¶ "What time does **the wedding**
start?"
    "At ten o'clock."

2 〚suf〛 method, style, type

the Hepburn **system** of romanization

¶ [He] is always interested in **the
latest** things.

shikirini 〚adv〛 frequently, often;
constantly, incessantly; eagerly,
intently

① [frequently, often, repeatedly]

¶ Recently there have been **many**
traffic accidents around here.

②[同じことがずっと続いて起こる様子]

¶しきりに電話のベルがなっているのに，だれも出ません。 (*Shikirini* denwa no beru ga natte iru noni, dare mo demasen.)

③[熱心に繰り返す様子]

¶山田さんが**しきりに**勧めるので，この本を買いました。 (Yamada san ga *shikirini* susumeru node, kono hon o kaimashita.)

shikkari しっかり〚副，〜と，〜する〛

①[堅固な様子，強い様子]

¶この箱はずいぶん**しっかり**していますね。 (Kono hako wa zuibun *shikkari* shite imasu ne.)

¶**しっかり**と持っていないと，落としますよ。 (*Shikkari* to motte inai to, otoshimasu yo.)

②[気をひきしめる様子]

¶入学試験が近いですから，**しっかり**勉強してください。 (Nyūgaku-shiken ga chikai desu kara, *shikkari* benkyō shite kudasai.)

¶このくらいの傷はなんでもないです。**しっかり**しなさい。 (Kono kurai no kizu wa nan demo nai desu. *Shikkari* shinasai.)

③[人の性質や考え方が間違いなく信用できる様子]

¶田中さんの奥さんはとても**しっかり**した人です。 (Tanaka san no oku-san wa totemo *shikkari* shita hito

② [constantly, incessantly, in rapid succession]

¶ The telephone **keeps on** ringing but no one answers.

③ [eagerly, intently, earnestly, keenly]

¶ [I] bought this book because [Miss] Yamada **kept on** recommending it to [me].

shikkari 〚adv, ~to, ~suru〛 strong, solid, firm; be strong-minded, be stouthearted; reliable, sound

① [strong, solid, firm; firmly, tightly]

¶ This is a very **solid** box, isn't it?

¶ You will drop that if you don't take a **firm** grip on it.

② [be strong-minded, be stouthearted, keep up one's nerve, brace oneself]

¶ The entrance exam is coming soon so you'd better **buckle down** and study hard.

¶ This is hardly any injury at all. **Take a hold of yourself** ⟦Pull yourself together⟧.

③ [reliable, sound, of firm character]

¶ Mr. Tanaka's wife is a person **of firm character** ⟦has her feet firmly on the ground⟧.

desu.)

shiku 敷く〖動Ⅰ〗

①[じゅうたん・布団・小石などを平らに広げる]

¶この部屋には赤いじゅうたんが敷いてあります。(Kono heya ni wa akai jūtan ga *shiite* arimasu.)

¶もう遅いから，布団を敷いて寝ましょう。(Mō osoi kara, futon o *shiite* nemashō.)

②[鉄道などを敷設する]

¶来年はこの辺まで鉄道が敷かれるそうです。 (Rainen wa kono hen made tetsudō ga *shikareru* sō desu.)

shima 島〖名〗

島国 (*shima*guni)

¶小さな島の間を船が通っていきます。 (Chiisana *shima* no aida o fune ga tootte ikimasu.)

shimai 姉妹〖名〗

¶春子さんは三人姉妹のいちばん下です。(Haruko san wa sannin *shimai* no ichiban shita desu.)

⇨**kyōdai** 兄弟

shimaru 閉まる〖動Ⅰ〗

¶戸が閉まっています。(To ga *shimatte* imasu.)

¶あの店は7時に閉まります。 (Ano mise wa shichiji ni *shimarimasu*.)

⇔**aku** 開く

shimatsu 始末〖名，〜する〗

始末をつける (*shimatsu* o tsukeru)

¶自分が使った物は自分で始末しなさ

shiku 〚v I〛 **spread, lay out; lay** (a railroad), **pave**

① [spread, lay out]

¶ This room **has** red carpeting.

¶ It's late—let's **lay out** the *futon* and go to bed.

② [lay (a railroad), pave]

¶ They say the railroad **will be extended** up to here next year.

shima 〚n〛 **island**

an **island** nation

¶ A ship is passing between 〚among〛 the small **islands.**

shimai 〚n〛 **sisters**

¶ Haruko is the youngest of three **sisters.**

shimaru 〚v I〛 **shut, close**

¶ The door **is closed.**

¶ That shop **closes** at seven o'clock.

shimatsu 〚n, ~*suru*〛 **circumstances, state of affairs; manage, deal with, settle, look after**

settle a matter, wind something up

¶ **Put back** yourself what you have

い。 (Jibun ga tsukatta mono wa jibun de *shimatsu* shinasai.)

shimau しまう〖動Ⅰ〗

①[外にあるものを中に入れる]

¶これを机の引き出しにしまっておいてください。 (Kore o tsukue no hikidashi ni *shimatte* oite kudasai.)

②[かたづける]

¶辞書を使ったら、元の所へしまいなさい。 (Jisho o tsukattara, moto no tokoro e *shimainasai*.)

(〜**te**) **shimau** (〜て)しまう〖連〗

①[動作・作用が完了することを表す]

¶宿題の作文をやっと書いてしまいました。 (Shukudai no sakubun o yatto kaite *shimaimashita*.)

¶この本はゆうべ全部読んでしまいましたから、お返しします。 (Kono hon wa yūbe zenbu yonde *shimaimashita* kara, okaeshi shimasu.)

¶昨日買ったパンはもう全部食べてしまいました。 (Kinō katta pan wa mō zenbu tabete *shimaimashita*.)

¶残っている仕事を片づけてしまってから、うちへ帰るつもりです。 (Nokotte iru shigoto o katazukete *shimatte* kara, uchi e kaeru tsumori desu.)

②[自分の意志に反してある動作・作用が行われ残念だという気持ちなどを表す]

¶花びんを落として、割ってしまいました。 (Kabin o otoshite watte *shimaimashita*.)

used 〖Don't make others **straighten up** after you〗.

shimau 〖vⅠ〗 **put away; put back**

① [put away]

¶ Please **put** this **away** in the desk drawer.

② [put back]

¶ **Put** the dictionary **back** after using it.

(-te) **shimau** 〖compd〗 **finish, end, bring to a close; end up ~ing, go and ~**

① [finish, end, bring to a close]

¶ [I] finally **finished** writing the assigned composition.

¶ I'll give this book back to you now—I **finished** reading it last night.

¶ [I]'ve **eaten up** all the bread 〖rolls, etc.〗 [I] bought yesterday.

¶ [I] plan to go home after **finishing up** the remaining work.

② [end up ~ing, go and ~; expresses regret at something that happened against one's will]

¶ The vase **fell and broke.**

¶かわいがっていた鳥がとうとう死んでしまいました。　(Kawaigatte ita tori ga tōtō shinde *shimaimashita*.)

¶父に買ってもらった時計をなくしてしまいました。(Chichi ni katte moratta tokei o nakushite *shimaimashita*.)

¶台風で庭の木や草花が倒れてしまいました。(Taifū de niwa no ki ya kusabana ga taorete *shimaimashita*.)

＊「(〜て) しまう ([〜te] shimau)」は「〜ちゃう (〜chau)」、「(〜で) しまう ([〜de] shimau)」は「〜じゃう (〜jau)」とも言う。「(〜て) しまった ([〜te] shimatta)」は「〜ちゃった (chatta)」、「(〜で) しまった ([〜de] shimatta)」は「〜じゃった (jatta)」とも言う。「食べちゃう (tabechau)」「読んじゃう (yonjau)」「終わっちゃった (owatchatta)」「死んじゃった (shinjatta)」など。

shimei　氏名〖名〗

¶ここに氏名、年齢、住所を書いてください。　(Koko ni *shimei*, nenrei, jūsho o kaite kudasai.)

⇒namae 名前

shimeru　閉める〖動Ⅱ〗

¶窓を閉めてください。(Mado o *shimete* kudasai.)

¶夜9時に店を閉めます。 (Yoru kuji ni mise o *shimemasu*.)

⇔akeru 開ける

shimeru　締める〖動Ⅱ〗

¶ The bird [we] were so fond of **died.**

¶ **I lost** the watch my father bought for me.

¶ Trees and flowers in the garden 〚yard〛 **were blown over** in the typhoon.

＊ (-te) *shimau* is contracted to -chau and (-de) *shimau* to -jau; (-te) *shimatta* becomes -chatta and (-de) *shimatta* becomes -jatta. Thus one has the forms tabechau (from *tabete shimau*), *yonjau (yonde shimau), owatchatta (owatte shimatta), shinjatta (shinde shimatta)*, etc.

shimei 〚n〛　name, full name

¶ Please write **your name,** age, and address here.

shimeru 〚v II〛　shut, close

¶ Please **close** the window.

¶ [I] **close** the shop at 9 PM.

shimeru 〚v II〛　tie, fasten, tighten, put on

帯を締める (obi o *shimeru*)

¶田中さんは赤いネクタイを締めています。(Tanaka san wa akai nekutai o *shimete* imasu.)

shimeru 湿る〚動Ⅰ〛

¶三日も雨がやまないため，畳まで湿ってきました。(Mikka mo ame ga yamanai tame, tatami made *shimette* kimashita.)

¶マッチが湿っていて，火がつきません。(Matchi ga *shimette* ite, hi ga tsukimasen.)

shimesu 示す〚動Ⅰ〛

¶その場所を地図で示して教えてください。(Sono basho o chizu de *shimeshite* oshiete kudasai.)

¶口で言うだけでなく，態度で示してください。(Kuchi de iu dake de naku, taido de *shimeshite* kudasai.)

shimo 霜〚名〛

霜が降りる (shimo ga oriru)

¶屋根が霜で白くなっています。

(Yane ga *shimo* de shiroku natte imasu.)

shin- 新-〚頭〛

新年 (*shin*nen)　新製品 (*shin*seihin) 新婚 (*shin*kon)　新人 (*shin*jin)　新入生 (*shin*nyūsei)　新学期 (*shin*gakki)

shinamono 品物〚名〛

¶この店の品物には値段がついていませんね。(Kono mise no *shinamono* ni wa nedan ga tsuite imasen ne.)

---

put on an *obi*

¶ [Mr.] Tanaka **is wearing** a red necktie.

shimeru 〚v I〛 **become damp, dampen, moisten**

¶ As it hasn't stopped raining for three days, even the *tatami* mats **are damp.**

¶ The match **is damp** and won't light.

shimesu 〚v I〛 **show, indicate, express, point out**

¶ Please **show me** where it is on the map.

¶ Don't just say it, but **look like you mean it** too.

shimo 〚n〛 **frost**

frost falls

¶ The roof is white with **frost.**

shin- 〚pref〛 **new, modern**

the **New** Year, a **new** year // a **new** product, a **newly issued** product // **newly** wed // a **new**comer, a **new** face, a rookie // a **new** student, freshman // a **new** school term

shinamono 〚n〛 **article, goods, wares**

¶ There are no prices on **the merchandise** in this shop.

¶この店には安くてよい品物がたくさんあります。 (Kono mise ni wa yasukute yoi *shinamono* ga takusan arimasu.)

shinbun 新聞〚名〛
新聞社 (*shinbun*sha) 新聞記者 (*shinbun*-kisha) 新聞紙 (*shinbun*shi)
¶あなたは日本語の新聞が読めますか。 (Anata wa Nihongo no *shinbun* ga yomemasu ka?)
¶毎朝, 少年が新聞を配達してくれます。 (Maiasa, shōnen ga *shinbun* o haitatsu shite kuremasu.)

shinchō 身長〚名〛
¶わたしは身長が 170 センチあります。 (Watashi wa *shinchō* ga hyakunanajissenchi arimasu.)

shindai 寝台〚名〛
寝台車 (*shindai*sha)
¶寝台が堅くて, ゆうべはよく眠れませんでした。 (*Shindai* ga katakute, yūbe wa yoku nemuremasen deshita.)
⇒**beddo** ベッド

shingō 信号〚名〛
¶道を渡るときには, 信号をよく見て渡りましょう。 (Michi o wataru toki ni wa, *shingō* o yoku mite watarimashō.)
¶信号が赤ですから, 車をとめなさい。 (*Shingō* ga aka desu kara, kuruma o tomenasai.)

shinjiru 信じる〚動Ⅱ〛
①〔確信する〕

¶ This shop has many fine **articles** that are inexpensively priced.

shinbun 〚n〛 newspaper
a **newspaper** publisher, **newspaper** office // a **newspaper** reporter, journalist // a **newspaper**
¶ Can you read a **newspaper** written in Japanese?
¶ A paperboy brings **my paper** each morning.

shinchō 〚n〛 stature, height
¶ I am 170 centimeters **tall.**

shindai 〚n〛 bed, berth
a **sleeping** car (on a train)
¶ **The bed** was hard so I didn't sleep well last night.

shingō 〚n〛 signal, sign, traffic light
¶ Please be sure to look at **the light** when crossing the street.
¶ Stop the car! **The light** is red.

shinjiru 〚v Ⅱ〛 be sure, be confident of; believe, trust; have faith
① [be sure, be confident of]

¶わたしは田中さんの成功を信じています。(Watashi wa Tanaka san no seikō o *shinjite* imasu.)

¶ I **am sure** [Mr.] Tanaka will succeed.

②[信用する]

¶わたしは山田さんを信じています。(Watashi wa Yamada san o *shinjite* imasu.)

② [believe, trust]

¶ I **trust** [Mrs.] Yamada.

¶あの人の言うことは信じられません。(Ano hito no iu koto wa *shinjiraremasen*.)

¶ **You can't believe** what [he] says.

③[信仰する]

¶わたしは神を信じています。(Watashi wa kami o *shinjite* imasu.)

③ [believe in, have faith]

¶ I **believe in** God.

shinju 真珠〖名〗

¶わたしは母から真珠の指輪をもらいました。(Watashi wa haha kara *shinju* no yubiwa o moraimashita.)

shinju 〚n〛 pearl(s)

¶ My mother gave me a **pearl** ring.

shinkansen 新幹線〖名〗

¶東京から大阪まで新幹線で約3時間です。(Tōkyō kara Oosaka made *shinkansen* de yaku sanjikan desu.)

¶あなたは新幹線に乗ったことがありますか。(Anata wa *shinkansen* ni notta koto ga arimasu ka?)

shinkansen 〚n〛 the Shinkansen, the bullet train

¶ It takes approximately three hours from Tokyo to Osaka on **the Shinkansen**.

¶ Have you ever ridden on **the Shinkansen**?

shinkei 神経〖名〗

①[動物の体内にあって運動・知覚などをつかさどる器官]

¶彼は運動神経が発達していて、スポーツは何でも上手です。(Kare wa undō-*shinkei* ga hattatsu shite ite, supōtsu wa nan demo jōzu desu.)

¶神経を抜いたから、歯の痛みはなくなりました。(*Shinkei* o nuita kara,

shinkei 〚n〛 a nerve; nerves, sensitivity

① [a nerve]

¶ His **reflexes** are fast so he is good at all sports.

¶ **The nerve** was extracted so [my] tooth stopped 〚has stopped〛 hurting.

667

ha no itami wa nakunarimashita.)

②〔心の働き〕
神経が鋭い (*shinkei* ga surudoi) 神経が鈍い (*shinkei* ga nibui)

¶あの人は無神経な人だから，周りの人の気持ちなど気にしません。 (Ano hito wa mu*shinkei* na hito da kara, mawari no hito no kimochi nado ki ni shimasen.)

② [nerves, sensitivity]
sensitive, thin-skinned, nervous, jumpy // insensitive, thick-skinned, dull, stolid

¶ [He]'s **thick-skinned** and doesn't care about the feelings of other people.

shinpai 心配〖名，〜する〗

¶両親に**心配**をかけないようにしなさい。 (Ryōshin ni *shinpai* o kakenai yō ni shinasai.)

¶飛行機は安全ですから，**心配**はいりません。 (Hikōki wa anzen desu kara, *shinpai* wa irimasen.)

shinpai 〖n, ~*suru*〗 **worry, anxiety, concern, fear**

¶ Don't cause your parents **worry**.

¶ There's no need for **fear**—flying is safe.

shinpo 進歩〖名，〜する〗

進歩的な考え (*shinpo*teki na kangae)

¶最近，日本語がだいぶ**進歩**しましたね。 (Saikin, Nihongo ga daibu *shinpo* shimashita ne.)

¶20世紀になって，科学が非常に**進歩**しました。 (Nijisseiki ni natte, kagaku ga hijō ni *shinpo* shimashita.)

shinpo 〖n, ~*suru*〗 **progress, advancement**
a **progressive** idea

¶ [Your] Japanese **has** greatly **improved** recently.

¶ Science **has made** great **strides** in the 20th century.

shinrui 親類〖名〗

¶お正月には，**親類**の人たちがみんなうちに集まりました。 (Oshōgatsu ni wa, *shinrui* no hitotachi ga minna uchi ni atsumarimashita.)

shinrui 〖n〗 **a relative, a relation**

¶ **My relatives** gathered at my home over the New Year's holidays.

shinsatsu 診察〖名，〜する〗

¶この病院は9時から**診察**が始まります。 (Kono byōin wa kuji kara *shi-*

shinsatsu 〖n, ~*suru*〗 **medical examination**

¶ **Consultations** start at nine o'clock

nsatsu ga hajimarimasu.)

¶体のぐあいが悪いので，お医者さんに**診察**してもらいました。 (Karada no guai ga warui node, oishasan ni *shinsatsu* shite moraimashita.)

at this hospital.

¶ I was feeling poorly so I went **to see** a doctor.

shinsen 新鮮〖形動〗

¶これは今海で捕れたばかりの**新鮮**な魚です。 (Kore wa ima umi de toreta bakari no *shinsen* na sakana desu.)

¶山の**新鮮**な空気を胸いっぱい吸いました。(Yama no *shinsen* na kūki o mune ippai suimashita.)

shinsen 〚adj-v〛 **fresh, new**

¶ This fish is **fresh** from the sea.

¶ [I] took a deep breath of the **fresh** mountain air.

shinsetsu 親切〖名，形動〗

¶田中さんはとても**親切**な方です。 (Tanaka san wa totemo *shinsetsu* na kata desu.)

¶交番で道を尋ねたら，**親切**に教えてくれました。 (Kōban de michi o tazunetara, *shinsetsu* ni oshiete kuremashita.)

¶御**親切**を心から感謝します。 (Go*shinsetsu* o kokoro kara kansha shimasu.)

shinsetsu 〚n, adj-v〛 **kind, kindly, friendly**

¶ [Mrs.] Tanaka is very **kind.**

¶ When I stopped and asked at the police box, they **very obligingly** told me the way.

¶ Thank you very much for **your kindness.**

shintō 神道〖名〗

shinu 死ぬ〖動Ⅰ〗

交通事故で死ぬ (kōtsū-jiko de *shinu*)

¶母が**死ん**だのは，わたしが6歳の時でした。 (Haha ga *shinda* no wa, watashi ga rokusai no toki deshita.)

¶苦しくて何度も**死の**うと思ったことがあります。 (Kurushikute nando mo *shinō* to omotta koto ga arimasu.)

shintō 〚n〛 **Shinto, Shintoism**

shinu 〚v I〛 **die, pass away**

die in a traffic accident

¶ My mother **died** when I was six years old.

¶ There have been many times that I've suffered so much that **I've wanted to die.**

shin'yō 信用〖名, ～する〗

信用できる (*shin'yō* dekiru) 信用を得る (*shin'yō* o eru) 信用を失う (*shin'yō* o ushinau)

¶山田さんは社長に信用があります。 (Yamada san wa shachō ni *shin'yō* ga arimasu.)

¶あの人はよくうそをつくから、だれにも信用されません。 (Ano hito wa yoku uso o tsuku kara, dare ni mo *shin'yō* saremasen.)

shinzō 心臓〖名〗

心臓病 (*shinzō*byō)

¶心臓の手術はたいへん難しいそうです。 (*Shinzō* no shujutsu wa taihen muzukashii sō desu.)

¶入学試験の発表の時には, 心臓がどきどきしました。 (Nyūgaku-shiken no happyō no toki ni wa, *shinzō* ga dokidoki shimashita.)

shio 塩〖名〗

塩辛い (*shio*karai)

¶この料理は塩で味をつけます。 (Kono ryōri wa *shio* de aji o tsukemasu.)

shippai 失敗〖名, ～する〗

試験に失敗する (shiken ni *shippai* suru) 事業に失敗する (jigyō ni *shippai* suru)

¶同じ失敗を二度と繰り返さないように注意しなさい。 (Onaji *shippai* o nido to kurikaesanai yō ni chūi shinasai.)

¶この計画は完全に失敗しました。

shin'yō 〚n, ~*suru*〛 confidence, trust, reliance, faith, credit

trustworthy, reliable, reputable // win **someone's confidence** // lose **someone's confidence**

¶ [Mr.] Yamada enjoys **the confidence** of the company president.

¶ No one **trusts** [him] as [he] often lies.

shinzō 〚n〛 the heart

heart disease

¶ I understand that **heart** surgery is very difficult.

¶ **My heart** was pounding 〚was in my throat〛 when the school entrance exam results were announced.

shio 〚n〛 salt

salty, too salty

¶ This dish is seasoned with **salt.**

shippai 〚n, ~*suru*〛 failure, error, mistake

fail an exam // **fail** in a business undertaking

¶ Be careful not to make the same **mistake** twice.

¶ This project was 〚is〛 a complete

(Kono keikaku wa kanzen ni *shippai* shimashita.)

⇔**seikō** 成功

shiraberu 調べる〖動Ⅱ〗

¶わからない言葉は辞書で調べなさい。

(Wakaranai kotoba wa jisho de *shirabenasai*.)

¶日本の宗教について調べたいのですが, どんな本がいいでしょうか。

(Nihon no shūkyō ni tsuite *shirabetai* no desu ga, donna hon ga ii deshō ka?)

¶うちじゅう調べてみましたが, その本は見つかりませんでした。(Uchijū *shirabete* mimashita ga, sono hon wa mitsukarimasen deshita.)

¶どろぼうが警官に調べられています。

(Dorobō ga keikan ni *shiraberarete* imasu.)

shiriai 知り合い 〖名〗

¶あの方とはお知り合いですか。

(Ano kata to wa o*shiriai* desu ka?)

¶あの大学にはわたしの知り合いがおおぜいいます。(Ano daigaku ni wa watashi no *shiriai* ga oozei imasu.)

shiritsu 私立〖名〗

¶私立の学校は国立や公立より授業料が高いです。(*Shiritsu* no gakkō wa kokuritsu ya kōritsu yori jugyōryō ga takai desu.)

¶中村さんは私立大学を卒業しました。 (Nakamura san wa *shiritsu*-daigaku o sotsugyō shimashita.)

⇨**kokuritsu** 国立 **kōritsu** 公立

failure.

shiraberu 〖v Ⅱ〗 investigate, study, examine, check, search, look up

¶ **Look up** any words you don't know in the dictionary.

¶ **I want to study** about Japanese religion. What books should I use?

¶ **I looked** all over the house but couldn't find that book.

¶ The police **are interrogating** the thief.

shiriai 〖n〗 acquaintance

¶ Do you **know** [him]?

¶ I have many **acquaintances** at that university.

shiritsu 〖n〗 private, non-governmental

¶ Tuition is higher at **private** schools than at national and other public ones.

¶ [Miss] Nakamura graduated from a **private** university.

shiro　白〖名〗

白のシャツ (*shiro* no shatsu)　白黒
フィルム (*shiro*kuro-firumu)

shiroi　白い〖形〗

¶山田さんは白いシャツを着ています。
(Yamada san wa *shiroi* shatsu o
kite imasu.)

¶あなたの髪の毛もずいぶん白くなり
ましたね。　(Anata no kaminoke
mo zuibun *shiroku* narimashita
ne.)

shiru　知る〖動Ⅰ〗

①[わかる]

¶「あなたは日本語を知っていますか。」
(Anata wa Nihongo o *shitte* imasu
ka?)　「いいえ，知りません。」(Iie,
shirimasen.)

②[知り合いである]

¶わたしは田中さんをよく知っていま
す。　(Watashi wa Tanaka san o
yoku *shitte* imasu.)

③[気がつく]

¶あの人はお金を落としたのを知らず
に行ってしまいました。　(Ano hito
wa okane o otoshita no o *shirazu*
ni itte shimaimashita.)

shirushi　印〖名〗

○印 (maru*jirushi*)　×印 (batsu-
jirushi)　目印 (me*jirushi*)

¶わからない言葉に印をつけて，あと
で先生にききます。　(Wakaranai
kotoba ni *shirushi* o tsukete, ato de
sensei ni kikimasu.)

shiryō　資料〖名〗

shiro 〚n〛　**white**

a **white** shirt // black-and-**white** film

shiroi 〚adj〛　**white**

¶ Mr. Yamada is wearing a **white**
shirt.

¶ Your hair has turned quite **white**
〚**gray**〛 too.

shiru 〚v I〛　**know; be acquainted
with someone; notice, realize**

① [know, be informed of, find out]

¶ "Do you **know** Japanese?"
"No, **I don't.**"

② [be acquainted with someone,
know someone]

¶ I **know** [Mr.] Tanaka quite well.

③ [notice, realize, be aware of]

¶ [She] walked on **without noticing**
that [she] had dropped some money

shirushi 〚n〛　**mark, sign**

a circle (used to indicate that an item
is correct or chosen) // an *X*, a cross
(used to indicate that an item is
wrong or not chosen) // mark, sign,
landmark, earmark

¶ [I] **mark** the words [I] don't understand and ask the teacher about them
later.

shiryō 〚n〛　**material(s), data**

研究資料 (kenkyū-*shiryō*) 資料を集める (*shiryō* o atsumeru)

¶図書館に行けば，古い時代の資料がたくさんありますよ。(Toshokan ni ikeba, furui jidai no *shiryō* ga takusan arimasu yo.)

research **materials** // collect **data**, gather **material**

¶ If you go to the library, you will find much **material** on olden times.

shisei 姿勢〖名〗

姿勢がいい (*shisei* ga ii) 姿勢が悪い (*shisei* ga warui)

¶楽な姿勢で話を聞いてください。(Raku na *shisei* de hanashi o kiite kudasai.)

shisei 〖n〗 **posture, pose, attitude, stance, carriage**

have a fine **posture** // have a poor **posture**

¶ Please **make yourself comfortable** and listen to what I have to say.

shishutsu 支出〖名，〜する〗

¶今月は収入が10万円で支出が7万円でしたから，3万円残りました。(Kongetsu wa shūnyū ga jūman'en de *shishutsu* ga nanaman'en deshita kara, sanman'en nokorimashita.)

¶物価が上がって，支出が増えました。(Bukka ga agatte, *shishutsu* ga fuemashita.)

⇔shūnyū 収入

shishutsu 〖n, 〜*suru*〗 **expenditure, expenses, outlay, disbursement**

¶ My income for this month was 100 thousand yen and **my expenditures** 70 thousand yen so I have 30 thousand yen left.

¶ Prices have gone up so **[my] expenses** have increased.

shisō 思想〖名〗

思想家 (*shisō*ka) 社会主義思想 (shakaishugi-*shisō*)

¶この本は日本の近代思想について書いたものです。(Kono hon wa Nihon no kindai-*shisō* ni tsuite kaita mono desu.)

shisō 〖n〗 **thought, idea, ideology a thinker** // socialist **thought**

¶ This book is about modern Japanese **thought.**

shison 子孫〖名〗

¶わたしは子孫に財産を残すつもりはありません。(Watashi wa *shison* ni zaisan o nokosu tsumori wa arimasen.)

shison 〖n〗 **a descendant, offspring, posterity**

¶ I do not intend to leave an estate to **my offspring.**

⇔senzo 先祖
せんぞ

shita 下〖名〗
した

①[位置が低い所]

¶テーブルの下にねこがいます。
した

(Tēburu no *shita* ni neko ga imasu.)

②[物の内側]

¶あの人はセーターの下にシャツを3
ひと　　　　　　　　　した　　　　　さん
枚も着ています。(Ano hito wa sētā
まい　き
no *shita* ni shatsu o sanmai mo
kite imasu.)

③[年齢・地位・程度などが低いこと]

¶田中さんはわたしより三つ下です。
たなか　　　　　　　　　　　みっ　した

(Tanaka san wa watashi yori mittsu
shita desu.)

¶このクラスは難しすぎるので，下の
むずか　　　　　　　　　した
クラスに入れてください。　　(Kono
い
kurasu wa muzukashisugiru node,
shita no kurasu ni irete kudasai.)

⇔ue 上
うえ

shita 舌〖名〗
した

¶「舌を出してみなさい。」と，医者が
した　だ　　　　　　　　　　　いしゃ
言いました。(*"Shita* o dashite minasai." to, isha ga iimashita.)
い

shitagau 従う〖動Ⅰ〗
したが

①[ついて行く]

¶わたしたちは，案内の人に従って工
あんない　ひと　したが　こう
場を見学しました。　(Watashitachi
じょう　けんがく
wa, annai no hito ni *shitagatte* kōjō
o kengaku shimashita.)

②[命令・規則・意見などのとおりに
する]

¶あなたの意見に従って，この計画は
いけん　したが　　　　　　けいかく
やめることにしました。　(Anata no

shita 〚n〛 under, below; beneath, underneath; lower, below; the lower part, the bottom; down, downwards

① [under, below]

¶ There is a cat **under** the table.

② [beneath, underneath]

¶ [He] is wearing three shirts **under** [his] sweater.

③ [lower, below (in age, status, degree, etc.)]

¶ [Mr.] Tanaka is three years **younger** than I am.

¶ This class is too difficult; please put me in a **lower** one.

shita 〚n〛 tongue

¶ The doctor said, "Put out **your tongue,** please."

shitagau 〚v I〛 follow, accompany; obey, comply with, agree to; in proportion to, according to, as

① [follow, accompany]

¶ We toured the factory, **following** the guide.

② [obey, comply with, agree to, accept]

¶ **In accordance with** your views, [we] have decided against this proiken ni *shitagatte*, kono keikaku wa yameru koto ni shimashita.)

¶規則には従わなければなりません。(Kisoku ni wa *shitagawanakereba* narimasen.)

③[一つのことがらが進むにつれて他のことがらが起こることを表す]

¶収入が増えるにしたがって、税金も多くなります。(Shūnyū ga fueru ni *shitagatte*, zeikin mo ooku narimasu.)

¶台風が近づくにしたがって，風が強くなってきました。(Taifū ga chikazuku ni *shitagatte*, kaze ga tsuyoku natte kimashita.)

* 「〜にしたがって（〜ni shitagatte）」の形で使う。

shitagi 下着〖名〗

¶わたしは毎日下着を替えます。(Watashi wa mainichi *shitagi* o kaemasu.)

shitaku 支度〖名，〜する〗

¶食事の支度ができました。(Shokuji no *shitaku* ga dekimashita.)

¶今，出かける支度をしているところです。(Ima, dekakeru *shitaku* o shite iru tokoro desu.)

shitashii 親しい〖形〗

¶山田さんはわたしの親しい友達です。(Yamada san wa watashi no *shitashii* tomodachi desu.)

¶わたしはあの人とはあまり親しくしていません。(Watashi wa ano hito to wa amari *shitashiku* shite ima-

ject.

¶ One **must abide** by the rules.

③ [in proportion to, according to, as]

¶ Taxes go up **in proportion to** income.

¶ **As** the typhoon comes closer, the wind has become stronger ⟦**As** the typhoon came closer, the wind became stronger⟧.

* Used in the pattern "~ *ni shitagatte*."

shitagi 〖n〗 underwear, underclothes

¶ I put on fresh **underwear** every day.

shitaku 〖n, ~*suru*〗 preparations, arrangements

¶ Dinner ⟦lunch, breakfast⟧ **is ready.**

¶ Right now **I'm getting ready** to go out.

shitashii 〖adj〗 close, friendly, intimate

¶ [Miss] Yamada is a **close** friend of mine.

¶ I am not particularly **close** to [him].

sen.)

-shitsu -室〖尾〗
教室 (kyō*shitsu*) 病室 (byō*shitsu*)
寝室 (shin*shitsu*) 温室 (on*shitsu*)
図書室 (tosho*shitsu*) 地下室 (chika*shitsu*)

shitsumon 質問〖名, ～する〗
¶質問はありませんか。 (*Shitsumon* wa arimasen ka?)
¶次の質問に答えてください。 (Tsugi no *shitsumon* ni kotaete kudasai.)
¶質問してもよろしいですか。(*Shitsumon* shite mo yoroshii desu ka?)

shitsurei 失礼〖名, 形動, ～する〗
①[人の気持ちを不愉快にさせるようなことを言ったりしたりすること]
¶お客様に失礼なことをしてはいけませんよ。 (Okyakusama ni *shitsurei* na koto o shite wa ikemasen yo.)
¶人の手紙を黙って読むのは失礼です。 (Hito no tegami o damatte yomu no wa *shitsurei* desu.)
②[相手にすまないという気持ちを表す]
¶お名前を間違えて失礼しました。 (Onamae o machigaete *shitsurei* shimashita.)
③[人に何かを尋ねるときの言葉]
¶失礼ですが、どなた様でいらっしゃいますか。 (*Shitsurei* desu ga, donata sama de irasshaimasu ka?)
* 普通「失礼ですが、 …(Shitsurei desu ga, …)」の形で使う。
④[別れるときのあいさつの言葉]

-shitsu 〖suf〗 **room(s)**
a class**room** // a sick**room,** hospital **room,** ward, infirmary // a bed**room** // a green**house** // a library // a basement, an underground **room**

shitsumon 〖n, ～*suru*〗 **question, questioning**
¶ Are there **any questions?**
¶ Please answer the following **questions.**
¶ May I ask **a question?**

shitsurei 〖n, adj-v, ～*suru*〗 **rudeness, impoliteness, discourtesy**
① [rudeness, impoliteness, discourtesy]
¶ One shouldn't **be rude** to a guest 〖customer〗.
¶ **It's rude** to read someone else's letters without permission.
② [used to indicate one is sorry]
¶ **I'm very sorry** to have mistaken your name.
③ [used to preface a question to someone]
¶ **Excuse me,** but could I have your name please?
* Usually used in the pattern "*Shitsurei desu ga…*"
④ [used when parting from someone]

¶お先に、失礼します。 (Osaki ni, *shitsurei* shimasu.)

shiyō 使用〖名, 〜する〗

¶今、この部屋は使用できません。 (Ima, kono heya wa *shiyō* dekimasen.)

¶現在、新聞などで使用されている漢字はどのくらいありますか。 (Genzai, shinbun nado de *shiyō* sarete iru kanji wa dono kurai arimasu ka?)

shizen 自然〖名〗

¶日本人は自然を愛する気持ちが強いです。 (Nihonjin wa *shizen* o aisuru kimochi ga tsuyoi desu.)

¶夏休みには都会を離れ、自然の中で過ごすことにしています。 (Natsuyasumi ni wa tokai o hanare, *shizen* no naka de sugosu koto ni shite imasu.)

shizen ni 自然に〖副〗

¶薬をつけなくても、傷は自然に治りました。 (Kusuri o tsukenakute mo, kizu wa *shizen ni* naorimashita.)

¶日本に住んでいる間に、日本語が自然にわかるようになりました。 (Nihon ni sunde iru aida ni, Nihongo ga *shizen ni* wakaru yō ni narimashita.)

✻「自然と (shizen to)」という言い方もある。

shizuka 静か〖形動〗

①[うるさい音や声が聞こえない様子]
¶みんな寝てしまって、寮の中は静かになりました。 (Minna nete shi-

¶ Well, **I must be going** now 〚Goodbye〛 (literally, **Excuse me** for leaving before you).

shiyō 〚n, ~*suru*〛 use, employment, application

¶ This room is not available **for use** at the present time.

¶ About how many *kanji* are presently **in use** in the newspaper and the like?

shizen 〚n〛 nature; natural

¶ The Japanese have a strong love of **nature.**

¶ [I] make it a practice to leave the city and live in the midst of **nature** during [my] summer holidays.

shizen ni 〚adv〛 naturally, spontaneously, automatically, instinctively, of itself

¶ The injury 〚cut, bite, scrape, etc.〛 healed **by itself** without putting any medication on it.

¶ Comprehension of Japanese **just came to me** while I was living in Japan.

✻ Variant: *shizen to*.

shizuka 〚adj-v〛 quiet, still; calm, tranquil

① [quiet, still, silent]
¶ With everyone asleep, the dormi-

matte, ryō no naka wa *shizuka* ni narimashita.)

¶図書館では，静かに しなければなりません。(Toshokan de wa, *shizuka* ni shinakereba narimasen.)

→**urusai** うるさい

②[おだやかな様子]

¶今日は海が静かです。(Kyō wa umi ga *shizuka* desu.)

¶夕方になって，風が静かになりました。(Yūgata ni natte, kaze ga *shizuka* ni narimashita.)

shizumu 沈む〔動 I 〕

①[太陽・月などが地平線などに隠れる]

¶日が西に沈みました。(Hi ga nishi ni *shizumimashita*.)

②[物が水面などから下の方へ動いて見えなくなる]

¶台風で船が沈んでしまいました。(Taifū de fune ga *shizunde* shimaimashita.)

↔**uku** 浮く

shōbai 商売〔名，～する〕

①[利益を目的として物の売買をすること]

¶田中さんは商売が上手です。(Tanaka san wa *shōbai* ga jōzu desu.)

②[仕事，職業]

¶あの人の商売は何ですか。(Ano hito no *shōbai* wa nan desu ka?)

shōbu 勝負〔名，～する〕

¶その試合はなかなか勝負がつきませ

---

tory fell **silent.**

¶ One must **be quiet** in the library.

② [calm, tranquil, peaceful]

¶ The sea **is calm** today.

¶ The wind **died down** in the evening 〖The wind **has died down** from the evening〗.

shizumu 〖v I〗 **set, go down; sink, be submerged**

① [set, go down]

¶ The sun **set** in the west.

② [sink, be submerged]

¶ The ship **sank** in the typhoon.

shōbai 〖n, ～*suru*〗 **trade, business, commerce; occupation, calling, trade**

① [trade, business, commerce]

¶ [Mr.] Tanaka has a good head for **business.**

② [occupation, calling, trade]

¶ What **line of business** is [he] in?

shōbu 〖n, ～*suru*〗 **victory or defeat; match, game, contest**

¶ That game 〖match〗 could have

んでした。 (Sono shiai wa naka-naka *shōbu* ga tsukimasen deshita.)

gone either way until the very end.

shōchi 承知〚名, 〜する〛

①[よく知っていること]

¶そのことは承知しています。 (Sono koto wa *shōchi* shite imasu.)

②[他の人の依頼・要求・願いなどを引き受けたり聞き入れたりすること]

¶「この仕事をあしたまでにやってください。」 (Kono shigoto o ashita made ni yatte kudasai.) 「はい, 承知しました。」 (Hai, *shōchi* shima-shita.)

¶父がわたしたちの結婚を承知しないので, 困っています。 (Chichi ga watashitachi no kekkon o *shōchi* shinai node, komatte imasu.)

shōchi 〚n, 〜*suru*〛 **know, be aware of; consent, agree to, accept**

① [know, be aware of]

¶ [I] **am aware** of that.

② [consent, agree to, accept]

¶ "Please have this job done by tomorrow."

"**All right.**"

¶ We have a problem as my father **objects** to our marriage.

shōgakkō 小学校〚名〛

¶あの子供たちは小学校の生徒です。 (Ano kodomotachi wa *shōgakkō* no seito desu.)

¶小学校の何年生から漢字を習いますか。 (*Shōgakkō* no nannensei kara kanji o naraimasu ka?)

shōgakkō 〚n〛 **elementary school**

¶ Those children are **elementary school** students.

¶ In what grade of **elementary school** do students first study *kanji*?

shōgakusei 小学生〚名〛

¶うちの子はまだ小学生です。 (Uchi no ko wa mada *shōgakusei* desu.)

shōgakusei 〚n〛 **pupil in elementary school**

¶ Our child **is** still **in elementary school.**

shō ga nai ☞ **shikata ga nai**

shōgatsu 正月〚名〛

¶母と姉がお正月の料理を作っています。 (Haha to ane ga o*shōgatsu* no ryōri o tsukutte imasu.)

＊「1月 (ichigatsu)」の意味であるが, 特に1月1日から1月7日ごろまでをさす場合が多い。

shōgatsu 〚n〛 **the New Year, the New Year's holidays; January**

¶ My mother and (older) sister are fixing food for **the New Year's holidays.**

＊ *Shōgatsu* originally had the meaning of January but usually refers to the period of January 1–7.

---

shōgyō 商業〖名〗

商業学校 (*shōgyō*-gakkō)

¶大阪は昔から商業の盛んな所です。
(Oosaka wa mukashi kara *shōgyō* no sakan na tokoro desu.)

shōhin 商品〖名〗

商品見本 (*shōhin*-mihon)

¶この商品は外国から輸入したものです。(Kono *shōhin* wa gaikoku kara yunyū shita mono desu.)

shōjiki 正直〖名, 形動〗

¶山田さんは正直な人です。(Yamada san wa *shōjiki* na hito desu.)

¶うそをつかないで正直に話しなさい。(Uso o tsukanaide *shōjiki* ni hanashinasai.)

shōjo 少女〖名〗

¶わたしは少女時代を外国で過ごしました。(Watashi wa *shōjo*-jidai o gaikoku de sugoshimashita.)

⇔**shōnen** 少年

shōkai 紹介〖名, ～する〗

自己紹介 (jiko-*shōkai*)　紹介状 (*shōkai*jō)

¶山田さんは, わたしを田中さんに紹介してくれました。(Yamada san wa, watashi o Tanaka san ni *shōkai* shite kuremashita.)

¶みなさんに御紹介します。こちらが田中さんです。(Minasan ni go*shōkai* shimasu. Kochira ga Tanaka san desu.)

shōko 証拠〖名〗

¶あの人がお金を盗んだという証拠が

---

shōgyō 〚n〛 commerce, trade, business

a **commercial** school

¶ Osaka has been an active **commercial** center since ancient times.

shōhin 〚n〛 commodity, goods, wares, merchandise

a **trade** sample, sample **ware**

¶ This **merchandise** is imported.

shōjiki 〚n, adj-v〛 honest, upright; honestly, frankly

¶ [Miss] Yamada is an **honest** person.

¶ Tell **the truth** now without any lying.

shōjo 〚n〛 young girl, girl

¶ I lived abroad when I was **a young girl.**

shōkai 〚n, ～*suru*〛 introduction

a self-**introduction** // a letter of **introduction**

¶ [Mr.] Yamada **introduced** me to [Mr.] Tanaka.

¶ I'd like **to introduce someone** to all of you now. This is [Mrs.] Tanaka.

shōko 〚n〛 evidence, proof

¶ Is there **any proof** that [he] stole

680

ありますか。(Ano hito ga okane o nusunda to iu *shōko* ga arimasu ka?)

¶御飯が食べられないというのは，どこか体が悪い証拠です。(Gohan ga taberarenai to iu no wa, doko ka karada ga warui *shōko* desu.)

the money?

¶ Your not being able to eat is **an indication** that something is physically wrong with you.

shokubutsu 植物〚名〛

植物園 (*shokubutsu*en) 高山植物 (kōzan-*shokubutsu*)

¶この山にはいろいろな種類の植物が生えています。(Kono yama ni wa iroiro na shurui no *shokubutsu* ga haete imasu.)

shokubutsu 〚n〛 **plant, plant life, vegetation**

botanical garden(s) // alpine **plant(s)**

¶ Many different **plants** are growing on this mountain.

shokudō 食堂〚名〛

① [食事をする部屋]

¶台所の隣に食堂があります。(Daidokoro no tonari ni *shokudō* ga arimasu.)

② [食事をする店]

¶学校の近くにある食堂は，いつも学生でいっぱいです。(Gakkō no chikaku ni aru *shokudō* wa, itsu mo gakusei de ippai desu.)

shokudō 〚n〛 **dining hall; restaurant, eating place**

① [dining hall, dining room, cafeteria]

¶ **The dining room** is next to the kitchen.

② [restaurant, eating place, diner]

¶ **Eating places** near a school are always filled with students.

shokugyō 職業〚名〛

¶あの人の職業は何ですか。(Ano hito no *shokugyō* wa nan desu ka?)

＊「職業を探す (shokugyō o sagasu)」「職業を失う (shokugyō o ushinau)」は普通「職を探す (shoku o sagasu)」「職を失う (shoku o ushinau)」と言う。

shokugyō 〚n〛 **occupation, calling, trade**

¶ What **does** [he] **do?**

＊ *Shokugyō o sagasu* (look for a job, seek employment) and *shokugyō o ushinau* (lose one's job, be put out of work) are shortened to *shoku o sagasu* and *shoku o ushinau*.

shokuji 食事〚名，～する〛

shokuji 〚n, ～*suru*〛 **meal, dinner; have a meal, dine**

食事代 (*shokuji*dai)

¶わたしは毎朝7時に**食事**をします。
(Watashi wa maiasa shichiji ni *shokuji* o shimasu.)

¶今晩，わたしは**食事**に招かれています。(Konban, watashi wa *shokuji* ni manekarete imasu.)

shokuryō　食料〔名〕

食料品 (*shokuryō*hin)

¶いつも日曜日に1週間分の**食料**を買っておきます。(Itsu mo nichiyōbi ni isshūkanbun no *shokuryō* o katte okimasu.)

¶このデパートの**食料**品売り場は，いつも人でいっぱいです。(Kono depāto no *shokuryō*hin-uriba wa, itsu mo hito de ippai desu.)

shōkyokuteki　消極的〔形動〕

¶彼はたいへん**消極的**で，自分からはあまり意見を言いません。(Kare wa taihen *shōkyokuteki* de, jibun kara wa amari iken o iimasen.)

⇔sekkyokuteki **積極的**

shōmei　証明〔名，〜する〕

証明書 (*shōmei*sho)　**身分証明書** (mibun-*shōmei*sho)

¶わたしがそこにいなかったことは，山田さんが**証明**してくれます。
(Watashi ga soko ni inakatta koto wa, Yamada san ga *shōmei* shite kuremasu.)

shōmen　正面〔名〕

¶**正面**から撮ったあなたの写真を送ってください。(*Shōmen* kara totta

board, **eating** expenses

¶ I **eat breakfast** every morning at seven o'clock.

¶ I have been invited out **for dinner** tonight.

shokuryō 〚n〛 **food, foodstuffs, provisions**

food, an article of **food, groceries**

¶ I always buy a week's **groceries** on Sunday.

¶ The **food** floor of this department store is always crowded.

shōkyokuteki 〚adj-v〛 **negative, passive**

¶ He **is** very **passive** and rarely states a personal opinion.

shōmei 〚n, ~*suru*〛 **proof, evidence, corroboration**

a certificate, diploma // an identification card, identification papers

¶ [Mr.] Yamada **will confirm** that I wasn't there.

shōmen 〚n〛 **the front, the front part, face, facade**

¶ Please send a **full-face** photograph.

anata no shashin o okutte kudasai.)

¶正面に見える高い建物がわたしの会
社です。 (*Shōmen* ni mieru takai
tatemono ga watashi no kaisha
desu.)

¶ The tall building you can see **in front of you** is my office.

shōnen 少年〚名〛

¶わたしがまだ少年だったころ，よく
この川で魚を捕って遊びました。
(Watashi ga mada *shōnen* datta
koro, yoku kono kawa de sakana
o totte asobimashita.)
⇔shōjo 少女

shōnen 〚n〛 **a boy, a youth**

¶ When I was still **a boy,** [we] often went fishing in this river.

shōrai 将来〚名〛

¶あなたは将来何になるつもりです
か。(Anata wa *shōrai* nani ni naru
tsumori desu ka?)
¶わたしたちは将来の希望について話
し合いました。 (Watashitachi wa
shōrai no kibō ni tsuite hanashiaimashita.)

shōrai 〚n〛 **the future, in time, some time**

¶ What do you want to be **when you grow up?**

¶ We talked about our hopes for **the future.**

shorui 書類〚名〛

¶あしたの会議に必要な書類を作りま
した。(Ashita no kaigi ni hitsuyō
na *shorui* o tsukurimashita.)
¶机の上にある書類を整理しておいて
ください。 (Tsukue no ue ni aru
shorui o seiri shite oite kudasai.)

shorui 〚n〛 **document(s), paper(s)**

¶ [I] prepared **the papers** necessary for the meeting tomorrow.

¶ Please put **the papers** on the desk in order.

shōryaku 省略〚名，〜する〛

以下省略 (ika *shōryaku*)

¶どうしてそうなったかという説明は
省略して，結論だけ言います。
(Dōshite sō natta ka to iu setsumei
wa *shōryaku* shite, ketsuron dake

shōryaku 〚n, 〜*suru*〛 **abbreviation, omission, abridgment**

the rest **has been omitted**

¶ **I will pass over** an explanation of why it turned out that way and only state my conclusions.

iimasu.)

shōsetsu 小説〖名〗

長編小説 (chōhen-*shōsetsu*) 短編
小説 (tanpen-*shōsetsu*) 歴史小説
(rekishi-*shōsetsu*) 推理小説 (suiri-
shōsetsu) 小説家 (*shōsetsu*ka)

¶ゆうべは宿題をやらないで、小説を
読んでいました。(Yūbe wa shuku-
dai o yaranaide, *shōsetsu* o yonde
imashita.)

¶わたしは父の一生を小説に書きたい
と思っています。 (Watashi wa
chichi no isshō o *shōsetsu* ni kakitai
to omotte imasu.)

shōtai 招待〖名, ～する〗

招待状 (*shōtai*jō) 招待を受ける
(*shōtai* o ukeru)

¶今晩の食事に山田さんを招待しまし
ょう。(Konban no shokuji ni Yamada san o *shōtai* shimashō.)

¶わたしは田中さんの結婚式に招待さ
れました。(Watashi wa Tanaka san
no kekkonshiki ni *shōtai* saremashita.)

⇨maneku 招く

shōten 商店〖名〗

商店街 (*shōten*gai)

¶この通りは商店がたくさんあって、
いつもにぎやかです。 (Kono toori
wa *shōten* ga takusan atte, itsu mo
nigiyaka desu.)

¶この辺りの商店は毎週月曜日が休
みです。(Kono atari no *shōten* wa
maishū getsuyōbi ga yasumi desu.)

shōsetsu 〚n〛 **novel, story, fiction**

a full-length **novel** // a short **story** //
an historical **novel** // detective **fiction** // a novelist

¶ [I] didn't do [my] homework last
night but read **a novel** instead.

¶ I would like to write about my
father's life in **the form of a novel.**

shōtai 〚n, ～*suru*〛 **invitation**

(written) **invitation** // receive **an invitation**

¶ **Let's invite** [Miss] Yamada to dinner tonight.

¶ I received **an invitation** to [Mr.]
Tanaka's wedding.

shōten 〚n〛 **store, shop**

a **shopping** street, a **shopping** district

¶ This street has lots of **shops** and is
always bustling.

¶ **The shops** around here are closed
every Monday.

shōtotsu 衝突〚名, 〜する〛

①[車などが強くぶつかること]

¶バスとタクシーが衝突して，けが人が出ました。 (Basu to takushii ga *shōtotsu* shite, keganin ga demashita.)

②[立場・意見などが激しく対立すること]

¶親と意見が衝突して，田中さんは家を出ていきました。(Oya to iken ga *shōtotsu* shite, Tanaka san wa ie o dete ikimashita.)

shōwa 昭和〚名〛

¶昭和 50 年は西暦 １９７５ 年です。 (*Shōwa* gojūnen wa seireki senkyūhyaku-nanajūgonen desu.)

¶わたしは昭和 30 年に生まれました。 (Watashi wa *Shōwa* sanjūnen ni umaremashita.)

shōyu しょう油〚名〛

¶焼いた魚にしょう油をかけて食べました。 (Yaita sakana ni *shōyu* o kakete tabemashita.)

shuchō 主張〚名, 〜する〛

¶わたしの主張は間違っているでしょうか。 (Watashi no *shuchō* wa machigatte iru deshō ka?)

¶あの人は自分の考えばかりを主張して，ほかの人の意見を聞きません。 (Ano hito wa jibun no kangae bakari o *shuchō* shite, hoka no hito no iken o kikimasen.)

shūchū 集中〚名, 〜する〛

集中講義 (*shūchū*-kōgi)

shōtotsu 〚n, ~*suru*〛 **collision; conflict, clash**

① [collision]

¶ A bus and taxi **collided** and some persons were injured.

② [conflict, clash, discord]

¶ [Mr.] Tanaka **fought** with [his] parents and moved out.

shōwa 〚n〛 **Showa;** the name given to the era beginning in 1926

¶ **Showa** 50 equals 1975.

¶ I was born in **Showa** 30 (1955).

shōyu 〚n〛 **soy sauce**

¶ [I] put **soy sauce** on the grilled fish before eating it.

shuchō 〚n, ~*suru*〛 **one's opinion, one's point; insist, assert, claim, stress, advocate**

¶ Is my **view** on this wrong?

¶ [He] only **pushes forward** [his] own views without listening to those of anyone else.

shūchū 〚n, ~*suru*〛 **concentration; concentrated, intensive**

an **intensive** course

¶日本の人口の約10パーセントが東京に集中しています。 (Nihon no jinkō no yaku jippāsento ga Tōkyō ni *shūchū* shite imasu.)

¶ Approximately 10 percent of the population of Japan **is concentrated** in Tokyo.

shudan 手段〘名〙

¶目的はたいへんいいが，手段が問題です。 (Mokuteki wa taihen ii ga, *shudan* ga mondai desu.)

¶科学は平和を実現する手段として用いなければなりません。 (Kagaku wa heiwa o jitsugen suru *shudan* to shite mochiinakereba narimasen.)

shudan 〖n〗 way, means, measure

¶ It is a very worthy end but there is a problem with **the means** being used 〖that you plan to use〗.

¶ Science must be utilized as **a means** of achieving peace.

-shugi -主義〘尾〙

民主主義 (minshu*shugi*) 自由主義 (jiyū*shugi*) 共産主義 (kyōsan-*shugi*) 社会主義 (shakai*shugi*)

-shugi 〖suf〗 -ism, principle, doctrine

democra**cy** // liberal**ism** // commu-n**ism** // social**ism**

shūgō 集合〘名，～する〙

集合時間 (*shūgō*-jikan) 集合場所 (*shūgō*-basho)

¶あした，8時に駅に集合してください。 (Ashita, hachiji ni eki ni *shūgō* shite kudasai.)

shūgō 〖n, ~*suru*〗 gathering, meeting, assembly

rendezvous time // **rendezvous** point

¶ Please **assemble** at the station tomorrow at eight o'clock.

shūi 周囲〘名〙

¶この湖の周囲は約20キロあります。 (Kono mizuumi no *shūi* wa yaku nijikkiro arimasu.)

¶この村は周囲を山に囲まれています。 (Kono mura wa *shūi* o yama ni kakomarete imasu.)

shūi 〖n〗 circumference, surroundings, environs

¶ **The circumference** of this lake is about 20 kilometers.

¶ This village **is surrounded** by mountains 〖hills〗.

shujin 主人〘名〙

①〔夫〕

¶「御主人はいらっしゃいますか。」 (Go*shujin* wa irasshaimasu ka?)
「主人はちょっと出かけております。」

shujin 〖n〗 husband; master; proprietor, landlord, employer

① [husband]

¶ "Is **your husband** there?"
"No, **he**'s out right now."

(*Shujin* wa chotto dekakete orimasu.)

* 他人に話す場合，自分の夫のことを「主人 (shujin)」と言い，他人の夫のことを「御主人 (goshujin)」と言う。
→**otto** 夫

②［飼い主］
¶あの犬は，毎日駅まで主人を迎えに行きます。 (Ano inu wa, mainichi eki made *shujin* o mukae ni ikimasu.)

③［店主］
¶旅館の主人が玄関でわたしたちを迎えてくれました。 (Ryokan no *shujin* ga genkan de watashitachi o mukaete kuremashita.)

shujutsu 手術［名，～する］
¶去年，わたしは胃の手術を受けました。 (Kyonen, watashi wa i no *shujutsu* o ukemashita.)
¶この病気は手術しなければ治りません。 (Kono byōki wa *shujutsu* shinakereba naorimasen.)

shūkaku 収穫［名，～する］
¶今年の麦の収穫は予想以上でした。 (Kotoshi no mugi no *shūkaku* wa yosō ijō deshita.)
¶この国では1年に2度米が収穫できます。 (Kono kuni de wa ichinen ni nido kome ga *shūkaku* dekimasu.)

shūkan 習慣［名］
¶国によって習慣が違います。 (Kuni ni yotte *shūkan* ga chigaimasu.)

* When talking with others, one refers to one's own husband as *shujin* and to someone else's husband as *goshujin*.

② [master]
¶ That dog goes to the station every day to meet **its master.**

③ [proprietor, landlord, employer]
¶ **The proprietor** of the Japanese inn greeted us in the entryway.

shujutsu [[n, ~*suru*]] **operation, surgery**
¶ I had a stomach **operation** last year.
¶ This disorder requires **surgery**.

shūkaku [[n, ~*suru*]] **harvest, crop, yield**
¶ This year's wheat [barley] **crop** surpassed expectation.
¶ Rice yields two **crops** a year in this country.

shūkan [[n]] **custom, convention, habit, practice**
¶ **Customs** differ from country to country.

¶わたしは夜遅くまで起きているのが習慣になってしまいました。(Watashi wa yoru osoku made okite iru no ga *shūkan* ni natte shimaimashita.)

¶ I have gotten into **the habit** of staying up late at night.

-shūkan -週間〚尾〛

¶1週間は7日です。(Is*shūkan* wa nanoka desu.)

¶日本語の授業は1週間に何時間ありますか。(Nihongo no jugyō wa is*shūkan* ni nanjikan arimasu ka?)

-shūkan 〚suf〛 **a week**

¶ One **week** is seven days.

¶ How many hours **a week** is Japanese class?

shukanteki 主観的〚形動〛

主観的な見方 (*shukanteki* na mikata)

¶あの人の考えは主観的すぎます。(Ano hito no kangae wa *shukanteki*sugimasu.)

⇔kyakkanteki 客観的

shukanteki 〚adj-v〛 **subjective**

a **subjective** outlook

¶ [His] thinking is too **subjective.**

shukudai 宿題〚名〛

¶山田先生は毎日宿題を出します。(Yamada sensei wa mainichi *shukudai* o dashimasu.)

¶宿題をやってくるのを忘れました。(*Shukudai* o yatte kuru no o wasuremashita.)

shukudai 〚n〛 **homework, assignment**

¶ Professor Yamada assigns **homework** every day.

¶ [I] forgot to do **[my] homework.**

shūkyō 宗教〚名〛

宗教家 (*shūkyō*ka)

¶あなたが信じている宗教は何ですか。(Anata ga shinjite iru *shūkyō* wa nan desu ka?)

shūkyō 〚n〛 **religion**

a person **of the cloth** (a priest, nun, minister, etc.), **religious** leader, scholar of **religion**

¶ What **religion** do you belong to?

shumi 趣味〚名〛

¶あなたの趣味は何ですか。(Anata no *shumi* wa nan desu ka?)

¶わたしの趣味はレコードを聞くこと

shumi 〚n〛 **hobby, interest, liking, taste**

¶ What are your **hobbies?**

¶ My **hobby** is listening to records.

です。 (Watashi no *shumi* wa rekōdo o kiku koto desu.)

shūnyū 収入〖名〗
収入が多い (*shūnyū* ga ooi) 収入が少ない (*shūnyū* ga sukunai)
¶わたしの1か月の収入は10万円です。 (Watashi no ikkagetsu no *shūnyū* wa jūman'en desu.)
¶あなたはその収入で生活ができますか。 (Anata wa sono *shūnyū* de seikatsu ga dekimasu ka?)
⇔shishutsu 支出

shuppan 出版〖名, 〜する〗
出版社 (*shuppan*sha)
¶中村さんの書いた小説が出版されることになりました。 (Nakamura san no kaita shōsetsu ga *shuppan* sareru koto ni narimashita.)

shuppatsu 出発〖名, 〜する〗
¶出発の日は3月30日に決まりました。 (*Shuppatsu* no hi wa sangatsu sanjūnichi ni kimarimashita.)
¶6時に出発しますから，遅れないようにしてください。 (Rokuji ni *shuppatsu* shimasu kara, okurenai yō ni shite kudasai.)
⇔tōchaku 到着

shūri 修理〖名, 〜する〗
修理代 (*shūri*dai)
¶時計が壊れたので，修理に出しました。 (Tokei ga kowareta node, *shūri* ni dashimashita.)
¶これを修理するには，1週間ぐらいかかりますよ。 (Kore o *shūri* suru

shūnyū 〖n〗 income, earnings, revenue

have a large **income** // have a small **income**
¶ My monthly **income** is a hundred thousand yen.
¶ Can you live on that **income?**

shuppan 〖n, ~*suru*〗 publication, publishing

a **publishing** company
¶ [Mrs.] Nakamura's novel has been chosen **for publication.**

shuppatsu 〖n, ~*suru*〗 departure, starting out

¶ The **departure** date has been fixed at March 30.
¶ **[We]'re leaving** at six o'clock— please don't be late.

shūri 〖n, ~*suru*〗 repairs, mending
a **repair** charge
¶ As [my] watch 〖clock〗 was broken I took it **to be repaired.**

¶ It will take about a week **to repair** this.

ni wa, isshūkan gurai kakarimasu
yo.)

shurui 種類〖名〗

¶この山にはいろいろな種類の鳥がい
ます。(Kono yama ni wa iroiro na
shurui no tori ga imasu.)

¶りんごにも種類がたくさんあります。
(Ringo ni mo *shurui* ga takusan
arimasu.)

shushō 首相〖名〗

¶次の首相にはだれがなるでしょう。
(Tsugi no *shushō* ni wa dare ga
naru deshō?)

shūshoku 就職〖名, ～する〗

¶おじが就職の世話をしてくれまし
た。 (Oji ga *shūshoku* no sewa o
shite kuremashita.)

¶わたしは卒業したら, 銀行に就職す
るつもりです。 (Watashi wa sotsu-
gyō shitara, ginkō ni *shūshoku* suru
tsumori desu.)

shūshū 収集〖名, ～する〗

¶弟は珍しい切手の収集をしていま
す。(Otōto wa mezurashii kitte no
shūshū o shite imasu.)

¶海岸へ行って, いろいろな貝を収集
してきました。(Kaigan e itte, iroiro
na kai o *shūshū* shite kimashita.)

shusseki 出席〖名, ～する〗

出席者 (*shusseki*sha) 出席簿 (*shusseki*bo) 出席が悪い (*shusseki* ga
warui)

¶出席を取りますから, 返事をしてく
ださい。 (*Shusseki* o torimasu kara,

shurui 〚n〛 **kind, sort, type**

¶ There are many different **sorts** of
birds on this mountain.

¶ There are many different **kinds** of
apples, too.

shushō 〚n〛 **prime minister, premier**

¶ [I] wonder who the next **prime
minister** will be.

shūshoku 〚n, ~*suru*〛 **looking for
employment, finding employment**

¶ My uncle helped me **find a job.**

¶ I want **to work** in a bank after
graduation.

shūshū 〚n, ~*suru*〛 **collection, col-
lecting**

¶ My younger brother **collects** rare
stamps.

¶ [I] **gathered** various seashells at
the shore.

shusseki 〚n, ~*suru*〛 **attendance,
presence**

persons **attending,** those **present** //
a **roll** book // have a poor **attendance** record

¶ I'm going to take **the roll** now;

690

henji o shite kudasai.)

¶あしたの会議に出席しますか。

(Ashita no kaigi ni *shusseki* shimasu ka?)

⇔kesseki 欠席

shūten 終点〚名〛

¶わたしはこの電車で終点まで行きます。(Watashi wa kono densha de *shūten* made ikimasu.)

¶この線は東京が終点です。(Kono sen wa Tōkyō ga *shūten* desu.)

shuto 首都〚名〛

¶日本の首都は東京です。(Nippon no *shuto* wa Tōkyō desu.)

sō そう〚副〛

①[話し相手の行動の様子などをさし示す]

¶そう急いでも、汽車にはもう間に合いませんよ。(*Sō* isoide mo, kisha ni wa mō maniaimasen yo.)

¶そうあわてては、転びますよ。(*Sō* awatete wa, korobimasu yo.)

②[ものごとの状態について話し相手などが考えている程度をさし示す]

¶この小説はそうおもしろくないです。(Kono shōsetsu wa *sō* omoshiroku nai desu.)

¶今日はお金がそうないから、買い物はしないことにしましょう。(Kyō wa okane ga *sō* nai kara, kaimono wa shinai koto ni shimashō.)

* あとに打ち消しの言葉が来る。話し相手または広く人々が期待したり予想したりしている程度には達していない

please answer when I call your name.

¶ **Will you be attending** tomorrow's meeting?

shūten 〚n〛 terminus, end of the line

¶ I take this train to **the end of the line.**

¶ This line **ends** at Tokyo Station.

shuto 〚n〛 capital, capital city, metropolis

¶ **The capital** of Japan is Tokyo.

sō 〚adv〛 so, like that, that way

① [so, like that, that way; used concerning the actions of the listener]

¶ Even hurrying **like that,** you won't be able to catch the train.

¶ Don't rush around **so**—you'll fall down.

② [so, so much; used concerning the thinking of the listener]

¶ This novel isn't **all that** interesting.

¶ I don't have **all that** much money with me today; let's not go shopping.

* Followed by the negative. Used when expressing the idea that something isn't as much as the listener or

という意味を表すときに使う。

③[文脈の上で話し相手の言ったものごとをさし示したり前に述べて話し相手にわかっているものごとの状態をさし示したりする]

¶「失礼ですが、中村さんでいらっしゃいますか。」(Shitsurei desu ga, Nakamura san de irasshaimasu ka?)「はい、**そうです**。」(Hai, *sō* desu.)

¶「山田さんは病気だそうです。」(Yamada san wa byōki da sō desu.)「**そうですか**。」(*Sō* desu ka.)

¶「伊豆の海岸は水もきれいだし、波も静かです。」(Izu no kaigan wa mizu mo kirei da shi, nami mo shizuka desu.)「**そういう**海岸なら、わたしも行ってみたいです。」(*Sō*iu kaigan nara, watashi mo itte mitai desu.)

⇨**kō** こう **ā** ああ **dō** どう

soba そば〖名〗

¶机のそばに本箱があります。(Tsukue no *soba* ni honbako ga arimasu.)

¶わたしはいつも辞書をそばに置いて勉強しています。(Watashi wa itsu mo jisho o *soba* ni oite benkyō shite imasu.)

soba そば〖名〗

¶昼御飯はおそばにしました。(Hirugohan wa o*soba* ni shimashita.)

¶このそば屋でそばを食べましょう。(Kono *soba*ya de *soba* o tabemashō.)

sobo 祖母〖名〗

as people in general might think.

③ [so, that; indicates something that has been talked about by the listener or already mentioned and understood by the listener]

¶ "Pardon me, but would you be [Mr.] Nakamura?"

"Yes, **that's right.**"

¶ "I heard that [Miss] Yamada is ill."

"Is **that so?**"

¶ "The sea is calm and the water clean along the Izu coast."

"I'd like to go to **that sort** of place."

soba 〚n〛 **beside; near, in the vicinity**

¶ There is a bookcase **next to** the desk.

¶ I always study with a dictionary **at my side.**

soba 〚n〛 *soba,* **buckwheat noodles**

¶ [I] had *soba* for lunch.

¶ Let's have *soba* at this *soba* shop.

sobo 〚n〛 **one's grandmother**

692

あなたのおばあさんとわたしの祖母
は、昔同じ学校に行っていたのだそう
ですね。(Anata no obāsan to watashi no *sobo* wa, mukashi onaji
gakkō ni itte ita no da sō desu
ne.)

⇔**sofu** 祖父　⇨**obāsan** おばあさん

sochira そちら〖代〗

①［話し手にとって少し隔たりのある
関係にある方向をさし示す］

¶**そちら**を見ないで、こちらを見てく
ださい。(*Sochira* o minaide, kochira
o mite kudasai.)

¶もう少し**そちら**へおつめください。
(Mō sukoshi *sochira* e otsume kudasai.)

¶「エレベーターはどこにありますか。」
(Erebētā wa doko ni arimasu ka?)
「**そちら**の方でございます。」(*Sochira*
no hō de gozaimasu.)

* 話し手にとって少し隔たりのある関
係にある方向は、話し相手に対しては
身近な関係にある方向である場合が多
い。したがって、話し相手に身近な関
係にある方向をさす場合が多い。

②［話し相手に対して身近な関係にあ
る方向に存在する所などをさし示す］

¶こちらはもう桜が咲いていますが、
そちらはまだ寒いでしょうね。
(Kochira wa mō sakura ga saite
imasu ga, *sochira* wa mada samui
deshō ne.)

* 話し相手に対して身近な関係にある
方向は話し手にとっては少し隔たりの

---

sochira 〖pron〗 **there, over there;
your place; that person; that one,
the other one; you, your family**

① [there, over there; indicates a
place somewhat separated from the
speaker]

¶ Please look here, not **there.**

¶ Please move a little more in **that
direction.**

¶ "Where is the elevator?"
  "It is **over there.**"

* In many cases a place somewhat
separated from the speaker is close to
the listener. Therefore *sochira* frequently indicates a direction or place
close to the listener.

② [your place; refers to a place, etc.,
physically close to the listener]

¶ The cherry blossoms are already
out here but it must still be cold
there where you are.

* Used for a place or direction close
for the listener but somewhat far for

ある関係にある方向になる。例えば，東京にいる人が北海道にいる人に対して言う場合には北海道のことについては，「あちら (achira)」とは言わないで「そちら (sochira)」と言う。

③[話し相手に身近な関係にある方向にいる人をさし示す]

¶こちらは中村さんで，**そちら**が山田さんです。(Kochira wa Nakamura san de, *sochira* ga Yamada san desu.)

*「そちらの方 (sochira no kata)」とも言う。

④[話し相手に身近な関係にある方向に存在するものごとをさし示す]

¶わたしはこちらの万年筆より**そちら**のほうがいいです。(Watashi wa kochira no mannenhitsu yori *sochira* no hō ga ii desu.)

⑤[話し相手をさし示す]

¶このことについて，**そちら**の御意見はいかがでしょうか。(Kono koto ni tsuite, *sochira* no goiken wa ikaga deshō ka?)

*「そっち (sotchi)」とも言うが，「そちら (sochira)」のほうが丁寧な言葉である。

⇨**kochira** こちら　**achira** あちら　**dochira** どちら

sō da　そうだ〘助動〙

①[ほかの人などから聞いて知ったという意味を表す]

¶天気予報によると，あしたは雨が降るそうです。(Tenki-yohō ni yoru

the speaker. For example, someone in Tokyo speaking to someone in Hokkaido will refer to Hokkaido as *sochira* and not as *achira*.

③ [that person; used to refer to a person close to the listener]

¶ This is [Miss] Nakamura and **that** is [Miss] Yamada.

* Variant: *sochira no kata*.

④ [that one, the other one; indicates something close to the listener]

¶ I prefer **that fountain pen** to this one.

⑤ [you, your family, your side; indicates the listener and those associated with the listener]

¶ What is **your** opinion concerning this matter?

* *Sotchi* is also used but *sochira* is more polite.

sō da 〖auxil〗　**they say, I hear; seem, appear, look like; threaten to, be likely to**

① [they say, I hear]

¶ The weather report **says** we will have rain tomorrow.

694

to, ashita wa ame ga furu *sō desu*.)

¶息子がお世話になったそうで，ありがとうございます。　(Musuko ga osewa ni natta *sō de*, arigatō gozaimasu.)

¶上田さんは最近忙しいそうです。(Ueda san wa saikin isogashii *sō desu*.)

¶田中さんは病気だそうです。(Tanaka san wa byōki da *sō desu*.)

② [現在そのように見えるという意味を表す]

¶このお菓子はおいしそうですね。(Kono okashi wa oishi*sō desu* ne.)

¶心配そうな顔をしていますね。どうしたんですか。(Shinpai*sō na* kao o shite imasu ne. Dō shita n desu ka?)

¶このナイフはよく切れそうですね。(Kono naifu wa yoku kire*sō desu* ne.)

* 形容詞・形容動詞，状態を表す動詞などにつく。ただし形容詞「よい(yoi)」「ない (nai)」につく場合は，それぞれ「よさそうだ (yosasō da)」「なさそうだ (nasasō da)」の形になる。「このネクタイがよさそうですから，これを買いましょう。」(Kono nekutai ga yosasō desu kara, kore o kaimashō.)「その映画はあまりおもしろくなさそうです。」(Sono eiga wa amari omoshiroku nasasō desu.)

③ [今にもそのようになる様子だという意味を表す]

¶ **I understand** that you have done a lot for my son. Thank you very much.

¶ **I hear** that [Mr.] Ueda has been quite busy recently.

¶ **I hear** that [Mrs.] Tanaka is ill.

② [seem, appear, look like]

¶ These sweets 〚cakes, candies, etc.〛 **look** good, don't they?

¶ **You look** worried. Is something wrong?

¶ This knife **looks** sharp.

* Added to adjectives, adjective-verbs, verbs expressing conditions, etc. When added to the adjectives *yoi* and *nai*, the resulting forms are *yosasō da* and *nasasō da*, as in "*Kono nekutai ga yosasō desu kara, kore o kaimashō*" (This tie looks nice—let's buy it) and "*Sono eiga wa amari omoshiroku nasasō desu*" (That movie doesn't look very interesting).

③ [threaten to, be likely to]

¶雨が降りそうな天気ですね。 (Ame ga furi*sō na* tenki desu ne.)

¶わたしは病気で死にそうになったことがあります。 (Watashi wa byōki de shini*sō ni* natta koto ga arimasu.)

＊丁寧に言う場合 「そうです (sō desu)」となる。

sōdan 相談〔名, 〜する〕

¶あなたに相談があるんですが…。 (Anata ni *sōdan* ga aru n desu ga...)

¶父と相談してから、決めたいと思います。 (Chichi to *sōdan* shite kara, kimetai to omoimasu.)

sodateru 育てる〔動Ⅱ〕

¶母が一人でわたしたちを育ててくれました。 (Haha ga hitori de watashi-tachi o *sodatete* kuremashita.)

¶父は菊の花を大事に育てています。 (Chichi wa kiku no hana o daiji ni *sodatete* imasu.)

sodatsu 育つ〔動Ⅰ〕

¶わたしは東京で生まれ、東京で育ちました。 (Watashi wa Tōkyō de umare, Tōkyō de *sodachimashita*.)

¶寒い所では、みかんは育ちません。 (Samui tokoro de wa, mikan wa *sodachimasen*.)

sode そで〔名〕

半そで (han*sode*) 長そで (naga-*sode*)

¶手を洗っている時、シャツのそでがぬれてしまいました。 (Te o aratte

¶ **It looks like** rain, doesn't it?

¶ I was once so sick that I was **on the point of** death.

＊ *Sō desu* is used instead of *sō da* when speaking politely.

sōdan 〚n, 〜*suru*〛 consultation, conference, talk

¶ There is something I would like **to talk** with you about.

¶ I want **to consult** with my father before deciding.

sodateru 〚v Ⅱ〛 bring up, raise, rear

¶ My mother **brought** us **up** all by herself.

¶ My father carefully **tends to** his chrysanthemums.

sodatsu 〚v Ⅰ〛 grow up, be brought up, be raised

¶ I was born and **raised** in Tokyo.

¶ Mandarin oranges **can't be grown** in a cold climate.

sode 〚n〛 sleeve

short **sleeves**, short-**sleeved** // long **sleeves**, long-**sleeved**

¶ [My] shirt **sleeves** got wet when [I] washed [my] hands.

iru toki, shatsu no *sode* ga nurete
shimaimashita.)

soeru 添える〖動Ⅱ〗
¶手紙に写真を添えて送りました。
(Tegami ni shashin o *soete* okurimashita.)
¶贈り物に花を添えて, 秋子さんに上
げました。 (Okurimono ni hana o
soete, Akiko san ni agemashita.)

sofu 祖父〖名〗
¶わたしの祖父は今年８０歳ですが, 今
でもとても元気です。 (Watashi no
sofu wa kotoshi hachijissai desu
ga, ima demo totemo genki desu.)
⇔**sobo** 祖母 ⇒**ojiisan** おじいさん

sōgō 総合〖名, ～する〗
総合病院 (*sōgō*-byōin) 総合大学
(*sōgō*-daigaku) 総合雑誌 (*sōgō*-
zasshi)
¶今までに出た意見を総合して考える
と, どうなるでしょうか。(Ima made
ni deta iken o *sōgō* shite kangaeru
to, dō naru deshō ka?)
¶一つ一つの専門的な研究よりも, 総
合的な研究が必要です。 (Hitotsu
hitotsu no senmonteki na kenkyū
yori mo, *sōgō*teki na kenkyū ga
hitsuyō desu.)

sōji 掃除〖名, ～する〗
¶この公園はいつもきれいに掃除がし
てあって, 気持ちがいいですね。
(Kono kōen wa itsu mo kirei ni
sōji ga shite atte, kimochi ga ii
desu ne.)

soeru 〖v Ⅱ〗 add, attach, accompany
¶ [I] **enclosed** a photograph in [my]
letter.
¶ [I] gave flowers to Akiko **along
with** a present.

sofu 〖n〗 one's grandfather
¶ My **grandfather** is 80 years old this
year, but he's still quite vigorous.

sōgō 〖n, ～*suru*〗 all-around, overall,
comprehensive, synthetic
a **general** hospital // a university // a
general magazine
¶ So what do we have if **we put
together all** the opinions expressed
so far?
¶ Rather than individual, specialized
research, **comprehensive, cross-
disciplinary** work is needed.

sōji 〖n, ～*suru*〗 cleaning, sweeping
¶ This park **is kept** so **clean** and nice
that it is always a pleasure to be here.

¶わたしは毎日部屋を掃除しています。 (Watashi wa mainichi heya o *sōji* shite imasu.)

¶ I **clean** my room 〚apartment〛 every day.

sokkuri そっくり〖副〗

¶この魚は骨まで**そっくり**食べられます。(Kono sakana wa hone made *sokkuri* taberaremasu.)

¶持っているお金を**そっくり**田中さんに貸しました。(Motte iru okane o *sokkuri* Tanaka san ni kashimashita.)

sokkuri 〚adv〛 **wholly, entirely, altogether, all**

¶ **All** of this fish can be eaten, even the bones.

¶ I loaned **all** the money I had on me to 〚Mr.〛 Tanaka.

sokkuri そっくり〖形動, ～の〗

¶春子さんはお母さんに**そっくり**な顔をしています。 (Haruko san wa okāsan ni *sokkuri* na kao o shite imasu.)

¶山田さんはお兄さんと声が**そっくり**ですね。(Yamada san wa oniisan to koe ga *sokkuri* desu ne.)

sokkuri 〚adj-v, ～*no*〛 **be exactly like, be just like**

¶ Haruko's face is **an exact replica** of her mother's.

¶ Mr. Yamada's voice **is just like** his older brother's.

soko 底〖名〗

①[容器などの下の面]

びんの底 (bin no *soko*)　くつの底 (kutsu no *soko*)

¶割れやすい物は、箱の底のほうには入れないで、上のほうに入れてください。(Wareyasui mono wa, hako no *soko* no hō ni wa irenaide, ue no hō ni irete kudasai.)

②[地面や水面から下の深い所]

¶海の底に潜って、沈んだ船を調べました。 (Umi no *soko* ni mogutte, shizunda fune o shirabemashita.)

¶地の底で石炭を掘っています。(Chi no *soko* de sekitan o hotte imasu.)

soko 〚n〛 **bottom; depths**

① [bottom, sole, riverbed]
the bottom of a bottle // **the sole** of a shoe

¶ Please put easily broken items towards the top of the box, not **the bottom.**

② [depths, bowels]
¶ [They] dived **deep** into the sea and looked over the sunken ship.

¶ Coal is mined **deep** in the earth.

698

soko そこ〖代〗

①[話し手にとって少し隔たりのある関係にある所をさし示す]

¶「そこに鉛筆がありますか。」(*Soko* ni enpitsu ga arimasu ka?)「はい、ここに鉛筆があります。」(Hai, koko ni enpitsu ga arimasu.)

¶「テニスはどこでしましょうか。」(Tenisu wa doko de shimashō ka?)「そこの庭でしましょう。」(*Soko* no niwa de shimashō.)

* 話し手にとって少し隔たりのある関係にある所は話し相手に身近な所である場合が多い。なお、話し手からも話し相手からも少し隔たりのある所をさし示すこともある。

②[文脈の上で前に述べて話し相手にもよくわかっていると認める所をさし示す]

¶伊豆の海岸に別荘があります。そこからは富士山がとてもきれいに大きく見えます。(Izu no kaigan ni bessō ga arimasu. *Soko* kara wa Fujisan ga totemo kirei ni ookiku miemasu.)

* 文脈の上で前に述べてある所を話し相手に身近な関係にある所としてさし示すのに使う。つまり、その所を共通の話題の所として取り扱うものである。

③[文脈の上で前に述べて話し相手にもよくわかっていると認める場面などをさし示す]

¶お金を落として困っていると、そこ

soko 〖pron〗 **that place, there, that**

① [that place, there, that; indicates a place somewhat far from the speaker]

¶ "Is there a pencil **there?**"
"Yes, there's a pencil here."

¶ "Where shall we play tennis?"
"Let's play in **that** yard **there.**"

* Often this place somewhat far from the speaker is close to the listener. Sometimes it is somewhat distant from both of them.

② [there, that place; refers to a place which has been talked about and is known to the listener]

¶ [We] have a country place on the Izu coast. From **there** you get a very nice view of Mount Fuji—it looks very close and large.

* Used to refer to a place known to the listener which has already been talked about. That is, it is treated as a common topic of conversation between the speaker and the listener.

③ [indicates a time, situation, etc., already talked about and regarded as known to the listener]

¶ [I] had lost [my] money and didn't

へちょうど上田さんが来ました。

(Okane o otoshite komatte iru to, *soko* e chōdō Ueda san ga kimashita.)

④[文脈の上で前に述べて話し相手によくわかっていると認めることがらの問題とすべき点・状態などをさし示す]

¶「向こうに着いたら，すぐ旅館を探さなければなりません。」(Mukō ni tsuitara, sugu ryokan o sagasanakereba narimasen.) 「もしなかったらどうしましょうか。」(Moshi nakattara dō shimashō ka?) 「そこまではまだ考えていません。」(*Soko* made wa mada kangaete imasen.)

¶先生，今おっしゃった，そこのところをもっと詳しく説明してください。

(Sensei, ima osshata, *soko* no tokoro o motto kuwashiku setsumei shite kudasai.)

＊話し相手の述べたことがらの問題とすべき点なども受けてさし示す。

⇨koko ここ　asoko あそこ　doko どこ

sōko 倉庫〖名〗

¶倉庫にいっぱい米が入っています。

(*Sōko* ni ippai kome ga haitte imasu.)

¶あまり使わない物は，倉庫にしまっておきます。(Amari tsukawanai mono wa, *sōko* ni shimatte okimasu.)

-soku -足〖尾〗

3足 (san*zoku*)　8足 (has*soku*)　10

---

know what to do **when** [Mr.] Ueda happened to come by.

④ [that; indicates an item already talked about and points it out as a problem]

¶ "[We] will have to look for an inn after arriving there."

"What will [we] do if there aren't any free rooms?"

"[I] haven't thought **that far** yet."

¶ [Sir], please explain **that** in more detail (said to a professor or teacher).

＊ Treats as a problem a matter, condition, etc., talked about by the listener.

sōko 〖n〗　**warehouse, storehouse**

¶ **The warehouse** is filled with rice.

¶ Articles not often used are put away in **the storehouse.**

-soku 〖suf〗　**a pair** (of shoes, socks, etc.)

three **pair(s)** // eight **pair(s)** // ten

足 (jis*soku*.)

¶わたしはくつを2足買いました。

(Watashi wa kutsu o ni*soku* kaimashita.)

sokudo 速度〖名〗

速度が速い (*sokudo* ga hayai) 速度が遅い (*sokudo* ga osoi)

¶あそこから道が狭くなっていますから, 車の速度を落としてください。

(Asoko kara michi ga semaku natte imasu kara, kuruma no *sokudo* o otoshite kudasai.)

sokutatsu 速達〖名〗

手紙を速達にする (tegami o *sokutatsu* ni suru)

¶この手紙を速達で出してください。

(Kono tegami o *sokutatsu* de dashite kudasai.)

¶父から速達が届きました。 (Chichi kara *sokutatsu* ga todokimashita.)

somatsu 粗末〖形動〗

①〔材料や作り方が悪い様子〕

¶粗末な食事でも, みんなで食べればおいしいですね。 (*Somatsu* na shokuji demo, minna de tabereba oishii desu ne.)

¶粗末な物ですが, どうぞ…。

(*Somatsu* na mono desu ga, dōzo…)

②〔大切にしない様子, むだにする様子〕

¶物を粗末にしてはいけません。

(Mono o *somatsu* ni shite wa ikemasen.)

pair(s)

¶ I bought two **pairs** of shoes.

sokudo 〚n〛 **speed, velocity**

at high **speed** // at low **speed**

¶ The road narrows there so please **slow down** (said to the driver of a taxi or other car).

sokutatsu 〚n〛 **special delivery**

send a letter **special delivery**

¶ Please have this letter sent **special delivery.**

¶ A letter 〚parcel, etc.〛 came **special delivery** from my father.

somatsu 〚adj-v〛 **coarse, crude, inferior; careless, rough, wasteful**

① [coarse, crude, inferior]

¶ Even **plain** food tastes good when eaten together with others.

¶ It is **nothing fine** but please take it (said when giving someone a present).

② [careless, rough, wasteful]

¶ You shouldn't handle things **roughly** 〚You should handle things with due respect〛.

701

¶一円のお金でも粗末に使ってはいけません。 (Ichien no okane demo *somatsu* ni tsukatte wa ikemasen.)

¶ One shouldn't **waste** even a penny.

someru 染める〖動Ⅱ〗

someru 〚v Ⅱ〛 **dye, tint, color**

¶白い生地を青く染めました。 (Shiroi kiji o aoku *somemashita*.)

¶ [I] **dyed** the white cloth blue.

¶山田さんは髪の毛を染めています。 (Yamada san wa kaminoke o *somete* imasu.)

¶ [Mr.] Yamada **dyes** [his] hair.

son 損〖名, 形動, ～する〗
損害 (*songai*)

son 〚n, adj-v, ~*suru*〛 **loss, damage, disadvantage**
damage, a loss

¶事業に失敗して, 百万円の損をしました。 (Jigyō ni shippai shite, hyakuman'en no *son* o shimashita.)

¶ [I] had a business failure and **lost** a million yen.

¶わたしは話し方が下手だから, いつも損をしています。 (Watashi wa hanashikata ga heta da kara, itsu mo *son* o shite imasu.)

¶ I **suffer the handicap** of being a poor speaker.

¶そんなつまらない絵に高いお金を出すのは損ですよ。 (Sonna tsumaranai e ni takai okane o dasu no wa *son* desu yo.)

¶ **It will be your loss** if you pay so much for such a poor painting.

⇔toku 得

sonkei 尊敬〖名, ～する〗

sonkei 〚n, ~*suru*〛 **respect, esteem**

¶あなたがいちばん尊敬している人はだれですか。 (Anata ga ichiban *sonkei* shite iru hito wa dare desu ka?)

¶ Who is the person you **respect** the most?

¶山田先生は立派な方なので, 学生に尊敬されています。 (Yamada sensei wa rippa na kata na node, gakusei ni *sonkei* sarete imasu.)

¶ As Professor Yamada is such a fine person, [he] **is highly regarded** by all [his] students.

sonna そんな〖連体〗

sonna 〚attrib〛 **such, that sort of, like that, that**

①〔話し相手に身近な関係にあるもの

① [such, that sort of, like that; used

ごとの状態などをさし示す]

¶先生にそんな失礼な言い方をしてはいけません。(Sensei ni *sonna* shitsurei na iikata o shite wa ikemasen.)

¶そんなふうに乱暴に扱ってはいけません。(*Sonna* fū ni ranbō ni atsukatte wa ikemasen.)

* 話し相手の言動などの状態をさし示すのに使う。場面や文脈の上でその状態のわかっているときには，例えば「そんな失礼な言い方 (sonna shitsurei na iikata)」の代わりに，「失礼な (shitsurei na)」を省いて「そんな言い方 (sonna iikata)」と言う場合もある。

②[文脈の上で話し相手の言ったものごとやその状態などをさし示したり前に述べて話し相手にわかっているものごとやその状態などをさし示したりする]

¶「山田さんという人を知っていますか。」(Yamada san to iu hito o shitte imasu ka?)「いいえ，そんな人は知りません。」(Iie, *sonna* hito wa shirimasen.)

¶ときどき国の母に会いたいと思います。そんなときにはよく手紙を書きます。(Tokidoki kuni no haha ni aitai to omoimasu. *Sonna* toki ni wa yoku tegami o kakimasu.)

⇨**konna** こんな　　**anna** あんな
donna どんな

sonna ni そんなに〖副〗

to indicate the nature of something associated with the listener]

¶ You shouldn't speak **so** rudely to your teacher ⟦the doctor⟧.

¶ You shouldn't be **so** rough with it.

* Used to indicate the nature of the speech, behavior, etc., of the person addressed. When understood from the situation or context, the phrase might be shortened so that, for example, *sonna shitsurei na iikata* (such an impolite way of talking) becomes *sonna iikata* (such a way of talking).

② [that; indicates something previously mentioned and known to the listener, something the listener said earlier, etc.]

¶ "Do you know [Mr.] Yamada?"
"No, I don't know **[him]**" (literally, **such** a person).

¶ Sometimes I miss my mother back home. I often write letters at times **like that.**

sonna ni 〖adv〗　**so, so much, like that**; (not) **very**, (not) **so**

①[話し相手の言動に関係のあるもの
ごとの様子などをさし示す]

¶そんなに急いで，どこへ行くんです
か。(*Sonna ni* isoide, doko e iku n
desu ka?)

¶そんなにあわてなくても，じゅうぶ
ん間に合いますよ。(*Sonna ni* awa-
tenakute mo, jūbun maniaimasu
yo.)

¶上田さんはそんなに偉くなりました
か。(Ueda san wa *sonna ni* eraku
narimashita ka?)

②[ものごとの状態について話し相手
などが考えている程度をさし示す]

¶「富士山に登るのはたいへんですか。」
(Fujisan ni noboru no wa taihen
desu ka?)「途中までバスで行けま
すから，そんなにたいへんではありま
せん。」(Tochū made basu de ikemasu kara, *sonna ni* taihen de wa
arimasen.)

¶「バスの止まる所から駅まで遠いです
か。」(Basu no tomaru tokoro kara
eki made tooi desu ka?)「いいえ，
そんなに遠くないです。」(Iie, *sonna
ni* tooku nai desu.)

¶「あなたは背が高いですね。１８０セ
ンチぐらいありますか。」(Anata wa
sei ga takai desu ne. Hyaku-
hachijissenchi gurai arimasu ka?)
「いいえ，そんなに高くありません。
１７５センチです。」(Iie, *sonna
ni* takaku arimasen. Hyakunanajū-
gosenchi desu.)

① [so, so much, like that; indicates
something concerning the speech or
behavior of the person addressed,
etc.]

¶ Where are you going in **such** a
hurry?

¶ You will make it in plenty of time
without rushing around **so** ⟦getting in
such a panic⟧.

¶ Has [Mr.] Ueda become **such** a
big name?

② [(not) very, (not) so; indicates the
listener's opinion of some degree or
quantity]

¶ "Is it hard to climb Mount Fuji?"
  "No, one can go partway by bus so
it's not **all that** hard."

¶ "Is it far to the station from where
the bus stops?"
  ."No, it's not **so** far."

¶ "You're really tall. Are you 180
centimeters tall?"
  "No, I'm not **that** tall. I'm 175
centimeters tall."

* あとに打ち消しの言葉が来る。話し相手または広く人々が期待したり予想したりしているほどではないという意味を表すときに使う。

⇨**konna ni** こんなに **anna ni** あんなに **donna ni** どんなに

sono その〖連体〗

①［話し手とものごととの少し隔たりのある関係をさし示す］

その人 (sono hito) その方 (sono kata)

¶「この本はだれのですか。」 (Kono hon wa dare no desu ka?) 「その本はわたしのです。」 (Sono hon wa watashi no desu.)

¶あなたの前にあるそのはさみを取ってください。(Anata no mae ni aru sono hasami o totte kudasai.)

* 話し手とものごととの少し隔たりのある関係は，話し相手に対しては身近な関係になる場合が多い。したがって，話し相手とものごととの身近な関係をさし示すことが多い。

②［文脈の上で前に述べたものごとと話し相手との身近な関係をさし示す］

¶「ここを新宿へ行くバスが通りますか。」 (Koko o Shinjuku e iku basu ga toorimasu ka?) 「はい，通ります。」 (Hai, toorimasu.) 「そのバスは池袋駅の前に止まりますか。」 (Sono basu wa Ikebukuro-eki no mae ni tomarimasu ka?)

¶りんごは5月に花が咲きます。そのあとに小さい実がたくさんなります。

* Followed by the negative. Used when stating that something is not as much as the listener or people in general might think.

sono 〖attrib〗 **that; the one in question, the very**

① [that; indicates something somewhat far from the speaker]

that person **there** // **that** person **there** (more polite)

¶ "Whose book is this?"
  "**That** book is mine."

¶ Please hand me **those** scissors there in front of you.

* Often what is somewhat far from the speaker is close to the listener. Therefore *sono* often indicates something close to the listener.

② [that, the one in question, the very; indicates a matter already mentioned or associated with the listener]

¶ "Does the bus going to Shinjuku pass by here?"
  "Yes, it does."
  "Does **it** stop at Ikebukuro Station?"

¶ Apple trees blossom in May. After **that** lots of small apples appear.

(Ringo wa gogatsu ni hana ga sakimasu. *Sono* ato ni chiisai mi ga takusan narimasu.)

* 文脈の上で前に述べて話し相手にわかっているものごとは話し相手に身近な関係にあるので，その関係をさし示すのに使う。また話し相手の言ったり，関係したりしていることがらを受けて，それをさし示す場合にも使う。

⇨**kono** この　**ano** あの　**dono** どの

sonzai 存在〖名，〜する〗

¶あなたは神の**存在**を信じますか。

(Anata wa kami no *sonzai* o shinjimasu ka?)

¶そんな名前の町は東京には**存在**しませんよ。 (Sonna namae no machi wa Tōkyō ni wa *sonzai* shimasen yo.)

sora 空〖名〗

青空 (ao*zora*)

¶雨がやんで，空が晴れてきました。

(Ame ga yande, *sora* ga harete kimashita.)

sore それ〖代〗

①〔話し手にとって少し隔たりのある関係にあるものごとをさし示す〕

¶「**それ**は何ですか。」 (*Sore* wa nan desu ka?)「これは日本語の本です。」(Kore wa Nihongo no hon desu.)

¶「このりんごはおいしいですよ。」 (Kono ringo wa oishii desu yo.)「では，**それ**を五つください。」(Dewa, *sore* o itsutsu kudasai.)

* 話し手にとって少し隔たりのある関

* Since something mentioned previously and known by the listener is close to the listener, *sono* is used to indicate that relationship. It is also used to indicate something said by the listener or associated with him or her.

sonzai 〖n, ~*suru*〗 existence, being

¶ Do you believe in **the existence** of God?

¶ **There isn't** any town of that name in Tokyo.

sora 〖n〗 the sky, the heaven, the skies, the air

the blue **sky,** blue **skies**; open-**air**

¶ The rain has stopped and **the skies** have cleared ⟦The rain stopped and **the skies** cleared⟧.

sore 〖pron〗 that; it, the one in question; that time, then

① 〔that; indicates something somewhat distant from the speaker〕

¶ "What is **that?**"
　 "This is a Japanese book."

¶ "These apples are very good."
　 "Well, give me five of **them.**"

* Often what is somewhat distant

係にあるものごとは話し相手に対しては身近な関係にあるものごとである場合が多い。

②［文脈の上で前に述べたものごとを話し手にとって少し隔たりのある関係にあるものとしてさし示す］

¶わたしはこの間 新しいカメラを買いました。今度の旅行にはそれを持って行くつもりです。　(Watashi wa konoaida atarashii kamera o kaimashita. Kondo no ryokō ni wa *sore* o motte iku tsumori desu.)

¶「上田さん、顔色がよくありませんね。どうしたのですか。」(Ueda san, kaoiro ga yoku arimasen ne. Dō shita no desu ka?)「体のぐあいが悪いのです。」(Karada no guai ga warui no desu.)「それはいけませんね。」(*Sore* wa ikemasen ne.)

* 文脈の上で前に述べて話し相手によくわかっていると認めるものごとをさし示すのに使う。また，話し相手が言ったことや関係していることをさし示す。

③［文脈の上で前に述べた話し相手に関係のあることがらの成立した時をさし示す］

¶中村さんは今年の四月に東京に出てきました。それまで，両親から離れて暮らしたことはありませんでした。(Nakamura san wa kotoshi no shigatsu ni Tōkyō ni dete kimashita. *Sore* made, ryōshin kara hanarete kurashita koto wa ari-

from the speaker is close to the person addressed.

② [it, the one in question; points to something previously mentioned as something which is somewhat distant from the speaker]

¶ I have recently bought a new camera. I plan to take **it** with me on the coming trip.

¶ "You look pale, [Miss] Ueda. Is something the matter?"

"I don't feel well."

"**That**'s too bad."

* Used to refer to something previously mentioned and treated as well known to the listener. Also used to indicate things said by the listener or concerning him or her.

③ [that time, then; indicates the time of something mentioned earlier which has some connection with the listener]

¶ [Mr.] Nakamura came to Tokyo this April. Before **that** [he] had never lived away from [his] parents.

masen deshita.)

⇨**kore** これ　**are** あれ　**dore** どれ

sorede　それで〘接〙

①［前のことがらを受けて当然だと考えられる結果をあとに続けるときに使う］

¶中村さんは10年フランスに住んでいました。それで，フランス語が上手なのです。(Nakamura san wa jūnen Furansu ni sunde imashita. *Sorede*, Furansugo ga jōzu na no desu.)

¶お母さんが病気なのです。それで，あの子は元気がないのです。(Okāsan ga byōki na no desu. *Sorede*, ano ko wa genki ga nai no desu.)

* 普通あとに 「〜なさい（〜nasai）」などの命令，「〜てください（〜te kudasai）」などの依頼などの言い方は来ない。

②［相手の話を受けて更に先に話を促すときに言う言葉］

¶「昨日，田中さんを見舞いに行きました。」(Kinō, Tanaka san o mimai ni ikimashita.) 「それで，田中さんのぐあいはどうでしたか。」(*Sorede*, Tanaka san no guai wa dō deshita ka?)

¶「汽車に間に合いませんでした。」(Kisha ni maniaimasen deshita.) 「それで，あなたはどうしましたか。」(*Sorede*, anata wa dō shimashita ka?)

soredewa　それでは〘接〙

①［相手の話を受けて それを根拠とし

sorede 〖conj〗　**therefore, consequently, accordingly; and, and then**

① [therefore, consequently, accordingly]

¶ [Mrs.] Nakamura lived for 10 years in France. **Therefore** [she] speaks French well.

¶ [His] mother is ill. **That's why** that child is in low spirits.

* Usually not followed by commands with *-nasai*, requests with *-te kudasai*, etc.

② [and, and then, thereupon]

¶ "[I] paid a sick call on [Mr.] Tanaka yesterday."
　"**And** how was [he]?"

¶ "I missed the train."
　"What did you do **then**?"

soredewa 〖conj〗　**if so; well, well then**

① [if so, if that is the case, in that

て自分の考え・判断などを述べるとき
に使う〕

¶あなたも行くんですか。**それでは**,わ
たしも行きましょう。(Anata mo iku
n desu ka? *Soredewa*, watashi mo
ikimashō.)

¶「いいレストランを知っていますよ。」
(Ii resutoran o shitte imasu yo.)
「そうですか。**それでは**, いつか連れ
ていってください。」 (Sō desu ka.
Soredewa, itsu ka tsurete itte kudasai.)

②〔何かを始めたり終えたり別れたり
するときに使う〕

¶**それでは**,これから授業を始めます。
(*Soredewa*, kore kara jugyō o hajimemasu.)

¶**それでは**, これで終わります。
(*Soredewa*, kore de owarimasu.)

¶**それでは**, さようなら。また, あし
た…。 (*Soredewa*, sayōnara. Mata
ashita...)

＊「それじゃ (soreja)」とも言う。
⇨**dewa** では

sorekara それから〖接〗

①〔前のことがらに続いてあとに起こ
ることがらを述べるときに使う〕

¶わたしは買い物をして, **それから**, あ
なたのうちへ行きます。 (Watashi wa
kaimono o shite, *sorekara*, anata no
uchi e ikimasu.)

¶田中さんは10年も留学していまし
た。**それから**, 帰ってきて, 大学の先
生になったそうです。 (Tanaka san

case]

¶ Are you going? **Then** I'll go too.

¶ "I know a good restaurant."
  "Really? **If that's the case,** please
take me there some time."

② [well, well then]

¶ **Well,** let's start class now.

¶ **Well,** let's stop here (said in a class,
meeting, etc.).

¶ **Well,** good-bye. See you tomorrow.

＊ Variant: *soreja*.

sorekara 〖conj〗 **after that, and
then; and, and also**

① [after that, and then; used when
something happens after something
else]

¶ I will do some shopping **and then**
go to your home.

¶ [Mr.] Tanaka studied abroad for 10
years. **And then** [he] became a college professor after returning home,

wa jūnen mo ryūgaku shite imashita. *Sorekara*, kaette kite, daigaku no sensei ni natta sō desu.)

②[前のものごとと同じようなものご
とをあとにつけ加えるときに使う]

¶わたしの部屋にはラジオ, テレビ, **そ
れから**, 冷蔵庫もあります。(Watashi
no heya ni wa rajio, terebi, *sorekara*, reizōko mo arimasu.)

¶鉛筆を2本ください。**それから**, ノ
ートもください。(Enpitsu o nihon
kudasai. *Sorekara*, nōto mo kudasai.)

soreni それに〘接〙

¶今日は頭が痛いし, **それに**, せきも
出ます。(Kyō wa atama ga itai shi,
soreni, seki mo demasu.)

¶あしたは雨が降るでしょう。**それに**,
風も強いでしょう。(Ashita wa ame
ga furu deshō. *Soreni*, kaze mo
tsuyoi deshō.)

＊ 前のことがらを受けて, 更に同じ
ようなことがらをつけ加えるときに使
う。

soretomo それとも〘接〙

¶コーヒーにしますか。**それとも**, 紅
茶にしますか。(Kōhii ni shimasu
ka? *Soretomo*, kōcha ni shimasu
ka?)

¶あしたはテニスをしますか。**それと
も**, 勉強しますか。(Ashita wa tenisu o shimasu ka? *Soretomo*,
benkyō shimasu ka?)

＊ 前のことがらとあとに述べること

according to what I hear.

② [and, and also; used when adding
similar items to what has already
been said]

¶ There is a radio, television, **and
also** a refrigerator in my room
〚apartment〛.

¶ Two pencils please. **And** a notebook too.

soreni 〖conj〗 **on top of that, in
addition to that, what is more,
moreover, besides**

¶ I have a headache today and, **what
is more,** a cough.

¶ It will probably rain tomorrow.
And in addition to that there will
probably be strong winds.

＊ Used when adding something
similar to what has already been said.

soretomo 〖conj〗 **or, or else**

¶ Which would you like—coffee **or**
tea?

¶ Are you going to play tennis
tomorrow? **Or** are you going to
study?

＊ Used when presenting a choice of

sorosoro

がらのうち，どちらかを選ぶときに使
う。普通「〜か。それとも，〜か。
(〜ka? Soretomo, 〜ka?)」の形で使
う。

sorezore　それぞれ〖名，副〗

1〖名〗

¶人には，**それぞれ**の考えがあります。
(Hito ni wa, *sorezore* no kangae ga
arimasu.)

2〖副〗

¶兄弟でも，**それぞれ**性格が違いま
す。(Kyōdai demo, *sorezore* seikaku
ga chigaimasu.)

sōridaijin　総理大臣〖名〗

☞**shushō　首相**

soroeru　そろえる〖動Ⅱ〗

①［二つ以上のものを同じようにする，
合わせる］

¶服とハンドバッグの色を**そろえまし
た**。(Fuku to handobaggu no iro
o *soroemashita*.)

¶みんなで声を**そろえて**言ってくださ
い。(Minna de koe o *soroete* itte
kudasai.)

②［全部集める］

¶図書館には，日本語の教科書が全部
そろえてあります。(Toshokan ni
wa, Nihongo no kyōkasho ga
zenbu *soroete* arimasu.)

¶必要な物を言ってください。あした
までに**そろえて**おきます。(Hitsuyō
na mono o itte kudasai. Ashita
made ni *soroete* okimasu.)

sorosoro　そろそろ〖副〗

two items. Usually used in the pattern "~ *ka? Soretomo*, ~ *ka?*"

sorezore 〚n, adv〛　**each, severally,
respectively**

1〚n〛

¶ Different people have **different**
ways of thinking.

2〚adv〛

¶ Even brothers have **their own**
characters.

sōridaijin ☞ **shushō**

soroeru 〚v Ⅱ〛　**make uniform,
match up; get ready, put in order,
complete, collect**

① [make uniform, make even, match
up]

¶ [I] **matched** the color of [my]
handbag to [my] outfit.

¶ Please say it aloud **together.**

② [get ready, put in order, complete,
collect]

¶ **A complete set** of Japanese textbooks is in the library.

¶ Please tell me what you need. I'll
have it ready for you by tomorrow.

sorosoro 〚adv〛　**soon, by and by;
(move) slowly, leisurely**

711

①[もうすぐ何かが行われる様子]

¶4時ですね。**そろそろ**出かけましょう。 (Yoji desu ne. *Sorosoro* dekakemashō.)

¶**そろそろ**父が帰ってくるころです。 (*Sorosoro* chichi ga kaette kuru koro desu.)

②[動作をゆっくり静かにする様子]

¶山田さんは足にけがをしているので、**そろそろ**歩いています。 (Yamada san wa ashi ni kega o shite iru node, *sorosoro* aruite imasu.)

*「そろそろと (sorosoro to)」の形でも使う。

sorou　そろう〖動Ⅰ〗

①[二つ以上のものが同じになる, 合う]

¶歌の練習をしていますが, なかなかみんなの声が**そろいません**。 (Uta no renshū o shite imasu ga, nakanaka minna no koe ga *soroimasen*.)

②[必要なものが集まる]

¶この学校にはいい先生が**そろって**います。 (Kono gakkō ni wa ii sensei ga *sorotte* imasu.)

¶みんな**そろった**から, 会を始めましょう。 (Minna *sorotta* kara, kai o hajimemashō.)

soru　そる〖動Ⅰ〗

¶顔を洗ってから, ひげを**そります**。 (Kao o aratte kara, hige o *sorimasu*.)

sosen　祖先〖名〗

¶人間の**祖先**はさるだと言われてい

① [soon, by and by]

¶ It's four o'clock. Let's be going **soon.**

¶ **It's getting to be** the time my father returns home.

② [(move) slowly, leisurely]

¶ [Mr.] Yamada **is inching along** as [his] leg 〚foot〛 is hurt.

* Variant: *sorosoro to.*

sorou 〚v I〛 **be uniform, match; be all present, assemble, become complete**

① [be uniform, be even, match]

¶ We have practiced the song, but somehow **can't sing it in perfect harmony.**

② [be all present, assemble, become complete]

¶ This school **has gathered together** a fine set of teachers.

¶ Everyone **has arrived now** so let's start the meeting 〚party〛.

soru 〚v I〛 **shave, get a shave**

¶ [I] **shave** after washing [my] face.

sosen 〚n〛 **ancestor, forefather**

¶ It is said that human beings **are de-**

す。(Ningen no *sosen* wa saru da to iwarete imasu.)

¶日本人の祖先はどこから来たのですか。(Nihonjin no *sosen* wa doko kara kita no desu ka?)

⇒**senzo** 先祖

soshiki 組織〖名, 〜する〗

¶今度、会社の組織が少し変わりました。(Kondo, kaisha no *soshiki* ga sukoshi kawarimashita.)

¶この委員会は、10名で組織されています。(Kono iinkai wa, jūmei de *soshiki* sarete imasu.)

soshite そして〖接〗

①［前のことがらを受けて次に起こることをあとで述べるときに使う］

¶わたしは昨日デパートへ行きました。そして、これを買いました。(Watashi wa kinō depāto e ikimashita. *Soshite*, kore o kaimashita.)

¶わたしは昨日銀座へ買い物に行きました。そして、これを買いました。(Watashi wa kinō Ginza e kaimono ni ikimashita. *Soshite*, kore o kaimashita.)

②［ことがらを並べて言うときなどに使う］

¶昨日は天気もよく、そして、波も静かでした。(Kinō wa tenki mo yoku, *soshite*, nami mo shizuka deshita.)

¶兄は医者になりました。そして、弟は先生になりました。(Ani wa isha ni narimashita. *Soshite*, otōto wa sensei ni narimashita.)

scended from apes.

¶ Where did **the ancestors** of the Japanese come from?

soshiki 〖n, ~*suru*〗 **organization, structure, system**

¶ **The organizational structure** of the company has changed somewhat recently.

¶ This committee 〖commission, board, panel〗 **is made up** of 10 persons.

soshite 〖conj〗 **then, and then; and, and now**

① [then, and then]

¶ I went to a department store yesterday **and** bought this.

¶ I went to Ginza to shop yesterday **and** bought this.

② [and, and now]

¶ The weather was nice yesterday, **and** the sea 〖lake〗 was calm.

¶ My older brother is 〖became〗 a doctor. **And** my younger brother is 〖became〗 a teacher.

¶田中さんは毎晩遅くまで働きました。そして，病気になってしまいました。(Tanaka san wa maiban osoku made hatarakimashita. *Soshite*, byōki ni natte shimaimashita.)

¶ [Mr.] Tanaka worked until late every night **and** became 〔has now become〕 ill.

* 前のことがらと同じようなことがらや対比的なことがらを並べるとき，また前のことがらの結果を述べるときなどに使う。

* Used when stating something similar to, in contrast to, or the result of what was stated earlier.

sōsu　ソース〖名〗

sōsu 〖n〗　**sauce, Worcestershire sauce**

¶この料理はソースをかけて食べると，おいしいですよ。(Kono ryōri wa *sōsu* o kakete taberu to, oishii desu yo.)

¶ This dish is good with **a sauce.**

sotchi ☞ **sochira**

soto　外〖名〗

soto 〖n〗　**outside, the exterior, outdoors**

¶ドアの外にだれかいますよ。(Doa no *soto* ni dare ka imasu yo.)

¶ There's someone **at** the door!

¶外はとても寒いです。(*Soto* wa totemo samui desu.)

¶ It's very cold **outside.**

¶このみかんは外側は腐っていますが，中は大丈夫です。(Kono mikan wa *soto*gawa wa kusatte imasu ga, naka wa daijōbu desu.)

¶ **The outside** of this mandarin orange is rotten but the inside is all right.

⇔uchi　内　naka　中

sotsugyō　卒業〖名，～する〗

sotsugyō 〖n, ~*suru*〗　**graduation**

卒業式 (*sotsugyō*shiki)　卒業生 (*sōtsugyō*sei)

a **graduation** ceremony, **commencement** exercises // **a graduate, alumni**

¶わたしは今年の三月に大学を卒業します。(Watashi wa kotoshi no sangatsu ni daigaku o *sotsugyō* shimasu.)

¶ I **will graduate** from college this March.

¶卒業後は，新聞社に勤めたいと思っています。(*Sotsugyō*go wa, shinbunsha ni tsutometai to omotte

¶ I would like a newspaper job after **graduating.**

imasu.)

⇔**nyūgaku** 入学

sotto そっと〖副, ～する〗

①[静かに何かをする様子]

¶赤ちゃんが寝ているから, そっと歩きなさい。 (Akachan ga nete iru kara, *sotto* arukinasai.)

②[相手に気づかれずに何かをする様子]

¶犬が子を産んだから, そっと見てごらんなさい。(Inu ga ko o unda kara, *sotto* mite goran nasai.)

③[そのままにしておく様子]

¶寝ているなら, そっとしておきましょう。 (Nete iru nara, *sotto* shite okimashō.)

sou 沿う〖動Ⅰ〗

¶川に沿って歩いていきました。 (Kawa ni *sotte* aruite ikimashita.)

¶電車はしばらく海岸に沿って走りました。(Densha wa shibaraku kaigan ni *sotte* hashirimashita.)

* 普通「～に沿って (～ni sotte)」の形で使う。

sōzō 想像〖名, ～する〗

¶これは百年後の日本を想像してかいた絵です。 (Kore wa hyakunengo no Nihon o *sōzō* shite kaita e desu.)

¶朝の電車は, あなたが想像できないくらいこみます。 (Asa no densha wa, anata ga *sōzō* dekinai kurai komimasu.)

su 巣〖名〗

ねずみの巣 (nezumi no *su*) くもの

sotto 〖adv, ～*suru*〗 **quietly, softly; secretly, stealthily;** (leave) **as is**

① [quietly, softly, lightly]

¶ Walk **quietly** as the baby is asleep.

② [secretly, stealthily]

¶ The dog has had her puppies—**be careful** so she doesn't see us looking.

③ [(leave) as is]

¶ If [he]'s asleep, let's **leave [him] alone.**

sou 〖v Ⅰ〗 **along, by, parallel to**

¶ [I] walked **along** the river.

¶ The train ran for some distance **parallel to** the coast.

* Usually used in the pattern "～ *ni sotte.*"

sōzō 〖n, ～*suru*〗 **imagination, conjecture, guess**

¶ This is a picture **visualizing** what Japan will be like in a hundred years.

¶ The morning trains are **unimaginably** crowded.

su 〖n〗 **nest, beehive, cobweb,** etc.

a rat's **nest,** a mouse **nest** // a cob-

巣 (kumo no *su*) 巣を作る (*su* o tsukuru)

¶この木の上には鳥の巣があります。(Kono ki no ue ni wa tori no *su* ga arimasu.)

su 酢〖名〗

¶料理に酢を使いすぎたので，すっぱくなってしまいました。(Ryōri ni *su* o tsukaisugita node, suppaku natte shimaimashita.)

sū(-) 数(-) 〖名, 頭〗

1〖名〗

数字 (*sū*ji) 数学 (*sū*gaku)

¶この大学の学生数はどのくらいですか。(Kono daigaku no gakusei*sū* wa dono kurai desu ka?)

2〖頭〗

数日 (*sū*jitsu) 数時間 (*sū*jikan) 数千人 (*sū*sennin)

¶その会には外国人も数人来ていました。(Sono kai ni wa gaikokujin mo *sū*nin kite imashita.)

* 4，5，6 ぐらいの数をさすことが多い。

subarashii すばらしい〖形〗

¶今日はすばらしい天気で，富士山がよく見えます。(Kyō wa *subarashii* tenki de, Fujisan ga yoku miemasu.)

¶山田さんはすばらしい成績で学校を卒業しました。(Yamada san wa *subarashii* seiseki de gakkō o sotsugyō shimashita.)

suberu 滑る〖動Ⅰ〗

web // build **a nest,** to nest

¶ There's a bird's **nest** in the top of this tree.

su 〖n〗 **vinegar**

¶ [I] put too much **vinegar** in the dish so it is ⟦was⟧ on the sour side.

sū(-) 〖n, pref〗 **a number; several**

1 〖n〗 a number, a figure

a figure, a numeral // mathematics

¶ **How many** students are there at this university?

2 〖pref〗 several

a few days, **several** days // **a few** hours, **several** hours // **thousands** of people

¶ **Several** foreigners came to that party ⟦meeting⟧.

* *Sū-* usually indicates around four, five, or six.

subarashii 〖adj〗 **wonderful, splendid, grand, excellent**

¶ It's a **marvelous** day today—one can see Mount Fuji clearly.

¶ [Miss] Yamada graduated from school with a **brilliant** academic record.

suberu 〖v Ⅰ〗 **slip, slide**

¶駅の階段で滑ってけがをしました。
(Eki no kaidan de *subette* kega o shimashita.)

¶道が凍っていて滑りやすいから，気をつけてください。(Michi ga kootte ite *suberi*yasui kara, ki o tsukete kudasai.)

subete すべて〔名，副〕

1〔名〕

¶ここにあるすべてのおもちゃは外国製です。(Koko ni aru *subete* no omocha wa gaikokusei desu.)

¶あの人はすべての点でわたしより優れています。(Ano hito wa *subete* no ten de watashi yori sugurete imasu.)

2〔副〕

¶旅行の準備はすべて終わりました。(Ryokō no junbi wa *subete* owari-mashita.)

sudeni 既に〔副〕

¶わたしが訪ねた時には，既に田中さんは出かけたあとでした。(Watashi ga tazuneta toki ni wa, *sudeni* Tanaka san wa dekaketa ato deshita.)

¶山田さんはこのことを既に知っていました。(Yamada san wa kono koto o *sudeni* shitte imashita.)

sue 末〔名〕

①〔ある期間の終わりのころ〕
今月の末 (kongetsu no *sue*)
¶東京では，桜の花は三月の末か四月の初めに咲きます。(Tōkyō de wa,

¶ [I] **slipped** on the station stairs and hurt [my]self.

¶ Please be careful—the road is icy and **slippery.**

subete 〚n, adv〛 all, everything; entirely

1 〚n〛

¶ **All** of the toys here are foreign-made.

¶ [He] is in **every** way my superior.

2 〚adv〛

¶ The preparations for the journey are 〚were〛 **all** complete.

sudeni 〚adv〛 already, previously, before

¶ When I went to see [her], [Mrs.] Tanaka had **already** left.

¶ [Miss] Yamada **already** knew this.

sue 〚n〛 the end, the close; last child; result

① [the end, the close]

the end of this month, **late** this month

¶ In Tokyo the cherry blossoms come

717

sakura no hana wa sangatsu no *sue* ka shigatsu no hajime ni saki-masu.)

②[いちばん下の子]
末っ子 (*sue*kko)　末の娘 (*sue* no musume)

③[あることをしたあと・結果]
¶いろいろ考えた末，その仕事を引き受けることにしました。　(Iroiro kangaeta *sue*, sono shigoto o hiki-ukeru koto ni shimashita.)

sūgaku　数学〖名〗
数学者 (*sūgaku*sha)
¶わたしは将来，大学で数学を研究しようと思っています。　(Watashi wa shōrai, daigaku de *sūgaku* o kenkyū shiyō to omotte imasu.)

sugata　姿〖名〗
①[体や物の形・かっこう]
¶姉は自分の姿を鏡に映して見ています。　(Ane wa jibun no *sugata* o kagami ni utsushite mite imasu.)
②[見えたり見えなかったりする生物などの体]
¶会の終わるころ，田中さんはやっと姿を現しました。　(Kai no owaru koro, Tanaka san wa yatto *sugata* o arawashimashita.)
③[身なり，服装]
¶こんな姿では恥ずかしくて，みんなの前に出られません。(Konna *sugata* de wa hazukashikute, minna no mae ni deraremasen.)

-sugi　-過ぎ〖尾〗

out at **the end** of March or the be-ginning of April.

② [last child]
the **youngest** child (of a family) // the **youngest** daughter (in a family)
③ [result, the end of an action]
¶ **After** much thought [I] decided to accept that work.

sūgaku 〚n〛　**mathematics**
a mathematician
¶ I would like to do advanced studies in **mathematics** at the university sometime.

sugata 〚n〛　**figure, shape, form; (make one's) appearance, (show) oneself; personal appearance, dress, posture**
① [figure, shape, form]
¶ My older sister is regarding **her re-flection** in the mirror.
② [(make one's) appearance, (show) oneself]
¶ [Mr.] Tanaka finally **showed up** when the party 〚meeting〛 was almost over.
③ [personal appearance, guise, dress, pose, posture]
¶ I am embarrassed to go out in front of everyone **dressed like this.**

-sugi 〚suf〛　**after, past; over-**

①[ある時間・年齢などを超えていること]

二十歳過ぎの娘 (hatachi *sugi* no musume)

¶今，9時5分過ぎです。 (Ima, kuji gofun *sugi* desu.)

¶午前中は忙しいから，お昼過ぎに来てください。 (Gozenchū wa isogashii kara, ohiru *sugi* ni kite kudasai.)

②[ある動作・状態などのちょうどよい程度を超えること]

¶食べすぎは胃によくありません。 (Tabe*sugi* wa i ni yoku arimasen.)

¶健康のため，たばこの吸いすぎに注意しましょう。 (Kenkō no tame, tabako no sui*sugi* ni chūi shimashō.)

sugiru 過ぎる〖動Ⅱ〗

①[通過する]

¶京都はさっき過ぎました。 (Kyōto wa sakki *sugimashita*.)

¶急行列車が勢いよく走り過ぎていきました。 (Kyūkō-ressha ga ikioi yoku hashiri*sugite* ikimashita.)

②[時間などが経過する]

¶この研究を始めてから，もう3年過ぎました。 (Kono kenkyū o hajimete kara, mō sannen *sugimashita*.)

¶父が死んでから，半年過ぎました。 (Chichi ga shinde kara, hantoshi *sugimashita*.)

③[ある動作・状態などのちょうどよ

① [after, past]

a young lady **over** 20 years of age

¶ It is now five minutes **past** 9.

¶ [I]'ll be busy during the morning so please come in the afternoon.

② [over-]

¶ **Over**eating is bad for the stomach.

¶ For the sake of one's health one should beware of smoking **too much.**

(-)sugiru ⟦v II⟧ pass by, go past; pass, elapse; exceed, go too far, over-

① [pass by, go past]

¶ We **went through** Kyoto a little while ago.

¶ The express train **sped by.**

② [pass, elapse]

¶ Three years **have passed** since [I] started this research.

¶ Half a year **has ⟦had⟧ passed** since the death of my father.

③ [exceed, go too far, over-]

い程度を超える〕

¶これは高すぎます。もっと安いのはありませんか。(Kore wa taka*sugimasu*. Motto yasui no wa arimasen ka?)

¶勉強をしすぎて、頭が痛くなりました。(Benkyō o shi*sugite*, atama ga itaku narimashita.)

sugoi すごい〔形〕

¶ゆうべはすごい雨でしたね。(Yūbe wa *sugoi* ame deshita ne.)

¶電車はすごくこんでいました。(Densha wa *sugoku* konde imashita.)

sugosu 過ごす〔動Ⅰ〕

¶昨日は休みだったので、一日じゅう子供と遊んで過ごしました。(Kinō wa yasumi datta node, ichinichijū kodomo to asonde *sugoshimashita*.)

¶では、夏休みを楽しくお過ごしください。(Dewa, natsuyasumi o tanoshiku o*sugoshi* kudasai.)

sugu すぐ〔副〕

①〔時間のかからない様子、ただちに〕

¶田中さんに手紙を出したら、すぐ返事が来ました。(Tanaka san ni tegami o dashitara, *sugu* henji ga kimashita.)

¶待っているから、すぐ来てください。(Matte iru kara, *sugu* kite kudasai.)

*「すぐに (sugu ni)」の形でも使う。

②〔ものごとが簡単に行われる様子〕

¶交番できいたら、上田さんのうちはす

¶ This is **too** expensive. Don't you have anything cheaper?

¶ [I] got 〖have gotten〗 a headache from studying **too much.**

sugoi 〖adj〗 **terrible, dreadful, terrific, amazing, great, wonderful**

¶ That was **really some** rain last night, wasn't it?

¶ The train was **terribly** crowded.

sugosu 〖v I〗 **pass** (time), **spend** (time)

¶ [I] had the day off yesterday so [I] **spent** the whole day playing with [my] children.

¶ Well, be sure and **have** a pleasant summer vacation.

sugu 〖adv〗 **at once, immediately; easily, readily; right** (here)

① [at once, immediately]

¶ [I] received a **prompt** reply to [my] letter to [Mr.] Tanaka.

¶ Please come **right away**—I'll be waiting for you.

* Also used in the form *sugu ni*.

② [easily, readily]

¶ [I] found [Miss] Ueda's place **easi-**

ぐわかりました。(Kōban de kiitara, Ueda san no uchi wa *sugu* wakari-mashita.)

¶ 買ったばかりのおもちゃが，**すぐ**壊れてしまいました。(Katta bakari no omocha ga, *sugu* kowarete shimai-mashita.)

* 「すぐに (sugu ni)」の形でも使う。

③ [距離などのごく近い様子]

¶ 山田さんの家は駅の**すぐ**近くです。(Yamada san no ie wa eki no *sugu* chikaku desu.)

¶ うちの**すぐ**そばに公園があります。(Uchi no *sugu* soba ni kōen ga arimasu.)

sugureru 優れる〖動Ⅱ〗

¶ あの学生は成績がたいへん**優れて**います。(Ano gakusei wa seiseki ga taihen *sugurete* imasu.)

¶ あの人は非常に**優れた**技術を持っています。(Ano hito wa hijō ni *sugureta* gijutsu o motte imasu.)

suidō 水道〖名〗

¶ ここは電気も**水道**もない山奥です。(Koko wa denki mo *suidō* mo nai yamaoku desu.)

suiei 水泳〖名，～する〗

¶ 午後はプールで**水泳**をします。(Gogo wa pūru de *suiei* o shimasu.)

¶ わたしはスポーツの中では**水泳**が得意です。(Watashi wa supōtsu no naka de wa *suiei* ga tokui desu.)

⇨**oyogu** 泳ぐ

suihei 水平〖名，形動〗

ly after inquiring at the police box.

¶ The toy [I] had just bought **soon** broke 〖The toy I just bought has **already** broken〗.

* Also used in the form *sugu ni*.

③ [right (here), just (there)]

¶ [Mrs.] Yamada's house is **close by** the station.

¶ There is a park **nearby** my home.

sugureru 〖v Ⅱ〗 be excellent, be superior

¶ That student has **excellent** grades.

¶ [He] is **superbly** skilled at it.

suidō 〖n〗 water service, running water; waterway, channel

¶ Here deep in the mountains there is neither electricity nor **running water.**

suiei 〖n, ~*suru*〗 swimming, a swim

¶ [I] **will swim** in the pool in the afternoon.

¶ The sport I'm strongest at is **swimming.**

suihei 〖n, adj-v〗 horizontal, level

水平線 (*suihei*sen)

¶コップの中の水の表面は、いつも水平です。 (Koppu no naka no mizu no hyōmen wa, itsu mo *suihei* desu.)

¶はかりは水平に置かなければなりません。 (Hakari wa *suihei* ni okana-kereba narimasen.)

the horizon; a **horizontal** line

¶ The top of water in a glass is always **on the horizontal.**

¶ Scales should be placed **on a level.**

suisan 水産〘名〙
水産物 (*suisan*butsu) 水産大学 (*suisan*daigaku)

¶日本は海に囲まれているので、水産業が盛んです。 (Nihon wa umi ni kakomarete iru node, *suisan*gyō ga sakan desu.)

suisan 〚n〛 **marine, fisheries**

marine products // a **fisheries** college

¶ As Japan is surrounded by the sea, it has an active **fishing** industry.

suiso 水素〘名〙

suiyō(bi) 水曜(日)〘名〙

suji 筋〘名〙

①[筋肉の繊維・血管など]

¶この肉は筋が多くて、おいしくありません。 (Kono niku wa *suji* ga ookute, oishiku arimasen.)

②[細長い線の模様、しま]

¶その縦に青い筋の入っている布を見せてください。 (Sono tate ni aoi *suji* no haitte iru nuno o misete kudasai.)

③[話の組み立て]

¶その小説の筋を簡単に話してください。 (Sono shōsetsu no *suji* o kan-tan ni hanashite kudasai.)

suiso 〚n〛 **hydrogen**

suiyō(bi) 〚n〛 **Wednesday**

suji 〚n〛 **muscle; line, stripe; plot**

① [muscle, tendon, vein, fiber, string]

¶ This meat isn't very good—it's too **stringy.**

② [line, stripe]

¶ Please show me that cloth with the vertical blue **stripe.**

③ [plot, story]

¶ Please give a brief synopsis of **the plot** of that novel.

sūji 数字〘名〙

¶1から10までの数字が黒板に書いてあります。 (Ichi kara jū made no

sūji 〚n〛 **figure, numeral**

¶ **The numbers** from one to ten are written on the blackboard.

sūji ga kokuban ni kaite arimasu.)

sukāto　スカート〖名〗

¶秋子さんは赤い**スカート**をはいています。　(Akiko san wa akai *sukāto* o haite imasu.)

sukejūru　スケジュール〖名〗

¶旅行の**スケジュール**を作りました。　(Ryokō no *sukejūru* o tsukurimashita.)

¶来年の**スケジュール**はまだわかりません。　(Rainen no *sukejūru* wa mada wakarimasen.)

sukēto　スケート〖名〗

スケートをする (*sukēto* o suru)

¶山田さんはスキーより**スケート**のほうが上手です。　(Yamada san wa sukii yori *sukēto* no hō ga jōzu desu.)

suki　好き〖形動〗

¶わたしが**好き**な先生は山田先生です。(Watashi ga *suki* na sensei wa Yamada sensei desu.)

¶わたしはこのごろ肉より魚のほうが**好き**になりまた。(Watashi wa konogoro niku yori sakana no hō ga *suki* ni narimashita.)

¶わたしは旅行が大**好き**です。(Watashi wa ryokō ga dai*suki* desu.)

¶わたしはあなたが**好き**です。(Watashi wa anata ga *suki* desu.)

⇔**kirai**　きらい

sukii　スキー〖名〗

スキーをする (*sukii* o suru)

---

sukareru ☞ **suku**

sukāto 〖n〗　a skirt

¶ Akiko is wearing a red **skirt.**

sukejūru 〖n〗　schedule, program, plan

¶ [I] made out **an itinerary** for the trip.

¶ [We] don't know **the schedule** for next year yet.

sukēto 〖n〗　skating, skates
to skate

¶ [Miss] Yamada is better at **skating** than skiing.

suki 〖adj-v〗　like, be fond of

¶ My **favorite** teacher is [Mr.] Yamada.

¶ Recently I have come to **like** fish better than meat.

¶ I **love** to travel.

¶ I **love** you 〖I **like** you **very much**〗.

sukii 〖n〗　skiing, skis
to ski

¶冬のスポーツでは，わたしは**スキー**がいちばん好きです。 (Fuyu no supōtsu de wa, watashi wa *sukii* ga ichiban suki desu.)

¶ **Skiing** is my favorite winter sport.

sukiyaki すきやき〖名〗

¶友達が来たので，牛肉や野菜などを買ってきて，**すきやき**にして食べました。 (Tomodachi ga kita node, gyūniku ya yasai nado o katte kite, *sukiyaki* ni shite tabemashita.)

sukiyaki 〖n〗 *sukiyaki*

¶ Some friends came by so [we] bought beef and vegetables and made *sukiyaki* for dinner.

sukkari すっかり〖副〗

①［全部，残らず，すべて］

¶パーティーの準備は**すっかり**できています。(Pātii no junbi wa *sukkari* dekite imasu.)

¶雨に降られて，**すっかり**ぬれてしまいました。 (Ame ni furarete, *sukkari* nurete shimaimashita.)

②［完全に，全く］

¶わたしはあなたとの約束を**すっかり**忘れていました。 (Watashi wa anata to no yakusoku o *sukkari* wasurete imashita.)

¶一日休んだら，疲れが**すっかり**とれました。 (Ichinichi yasundara, tsukare ga *sukkari* toremashita.)

sukkari 〖adv〗 **all, entirely, wholly; quite, utterly, completely**

① [all, entirely, wholly]

¶ **All** the preparations for the party are done now.

¶ [I] got soaked **to the skin** in the rain.

② [quite, utterly, completely]

¶ I **completely** forgot about my appointment 〖date〗 with you.

¶ One day's rest has **completely** relieved [my] fatigue 〖One day's rest **completely** relieved my fatigue〗.

sukoshi 少し〖副〗

①［数量が少ない様子，程度が低い］

¶わたしは朝御飯は**少し**しか食べません。 (Watashi wa asagohan wa *sukoshi* shika tabemasen.)

¶今日は頭が**少し**痛いです。 (Kyō wa atama ga *sukoshi* itai desu.)

②［時間が短い様子］

sukoshi 〖adv〗 **a little, somewhat; a moment, a little while; a little way; (not) at all, (not) a bit**

① [a little, a few, a little bit, somewhat]

¶ I have only a **small** breakfast.

¶ I have a **slight** headache today 〖My head is a **little** sore today〗.

② [a moment, a little while]

724

¶それでは，少し休みましょう。
(Soredewa, *sukoshi* yasumimashō.)

¶ Well, let's take a **short** break.

¶もう少したったら，田中さんが来ると思います。 (Mō *sukoshi* tattara, Tanaka san ga kuru to omoimasu.)

¶ I think [Mr.] Tanaka will be here **shortly.**

③〔距離が短い様子〕
¶駅はこの道をもう少し行った所です。
(Eki wa kono michi o mō *sukoshi* itta tokoro desu.)

③ [a little way, a short distance]
¶ The station is **a little farther** down this street.

④〔全然，何も〕
¶あの人は少しも日本語が話せないようです。 (Ano hito wa *sukoshi* mo Nihongo ga hanasenai yō desu.)

④ [(not) at all, (not) a bit]
¶ It seems [he] can't speak Japanese **at all.**

¶わたしは山田さんが大阪へ行ったことを，少しも知りませんでした。
(Watashi wa Yamada san ga Oosaka e itta koto o, *sukoshi* mo shirimasen deshita.)

¶ I had no idea **whatsoever** that [Mr.] Yamada had gone to Osaka.

*「少しも～ない(sukoshi mo ～nai)」の形で使う。

* Used in the pattern "*sukoshi mo ～ (-)nai.*"

suku 好く〔動Ⅰ〕

suku [[v I]] like, be fond of

¶山田さんは性格がいいので，みんなから好かれています。 (Yamada san wa seikaku ga ii node, minna kara *sukarete* imasu.)

¶ As [Mr.] Yamada is such a nice person, [he] **is well liked** by everyone.

¶だれからも好かれるような人になりたいです。 (Dare kara mo *sukareru* yō na hito ni naritai desu.)

¶ I want to become a person **liked** by all.

*「好かれる (sukareru)」の形で使うことが多い。

* Generally used in the form *sukareru.*

suku すく〔動Ⅰ〕

suku [[v I]] become empty, vacant, less crowded

¶おなかがすきました。 (Onaka ga *sukimashita*.)

¶ [I] am [[was]] **hungry.**

¶このレストランはいつもすいています

¶ This restaurant **is never crowded.**

す。 (Kono resutoran wa itsu mo *suite* imasu.)

¶汽車はこんでいましたか，すいていましたか。 (Kisha wa konde imashita ka, *suite* imashita ka?)

sukunai　少ない〖形〗

¶このクラスは女の人が少ないですね。 (Kono kurasu wa onna no hito ga *sukunai* desu ne.)

¶今年は，去年より雨が少なかったです。(Kotoshi wa, kyonen yori ame ga *sukunakatta* desu.)

¶山田さんは家にいることが少ないようです。 (Yamada san wa ie ni iru koto ga *sukunai* yō desu.)

⇔ooi 多い

sukunakutomo　少なくとも〖副〗

¶あしたのパーティーには少なくとも100人は集まるでしょう。(Ashita no pātii ni wa *sukunakutomo* hyakunin wa atsumaru deshō.)

¶この仕事を完成するには，少なくとも1か月はかかります。 (Kono shigoto o kansei suru ni wa, *sukunakutomo* ikkagetsu wa kakarimasu.)

sukuu　救う〖動Ⅰ〗

¶田中さんは川に落ちた子供を救ったので，両親から感謝されました。(Tanaka san wa kawa ni ochita kodomo o *sukutta* node, ryōshin kara kansha saremashita.)

¶このお金は，気の毒な子供たちを救うために使われます。(Kono okane wa,

¶ Was the train crowded or **were there plenty of seats?**

sukunai 〖adj〗　few, little, limited, scarce

¶ There **are few** women in this class.

¶ There **was less** rain this year than last year.

¶ It seems that [Mr.] Yamada spends **little** time at home.

sukunakutomo 〖adv〗　at least, at the very least

¶ **No less** than a hundred persons should show up at the party tomorrow.

¶ It will take **at least** a month to finish this job.

sukuu 〖v I〗　rescue, save, help

¶ [Mr.] Tanaka **rescued** a child that had fallen into the river and received the gratitude of its parents.

¶ This money will be used **to help** unfortunate children.

kinodoku na kodomotachi o *sukuu* tame ni tsukawaremasu.)

sumi 炭〔名〕

¶炭で魚を焼きます。　(*Sumi* de sakana o yakimasu.)

sumi 〔n〕 **charcoal**

¶ [I] grill fish over **charcoal.**

sumi すみ〔名〕

¶切手は普通，封筒の左上のすみにはります。(Kitte wa futsū, fūtō no hidariue no *sumi* ni harimasu.)

¶部屋のすみからすみまで捜しましたが，かぎは見つかりませんでした。

(Heya no *sumi* kara *sumi* made sagashimashita ga, kagi wa mitsukarimasen deshita.)

sumi 〔n〕 **corner, nook**

¶ Stamps are usually placed at the top left **corner** of the envelope.

¶ [I] searched **every inch** of the room but couldn't find the keys.

sumimasen すみません〔連〕

¶お待たせして，本当にすみませんでした。　(Omatase shite, hontō ni *sumimasen* deshita.)

¶すみませんが，その荷物を取っていただけませんか。　(*Sumimasen* ga, sono nimotsu o totte itadakemasen ka?)

⇒**gomen nasai** ごめんなさい

sumimasen 〔compd〕 **Excuse me, pardon me, I'm sorry, thank you;** a phrase used when calling attention to oneself, asking something, apologizing, or expressing gratitude

¶ **I'm** very **sorry** to have kept you waiting.

¶ **I'm sorry to trouble you,** but could you please hand me that package 〚bag, etc.〛?

sumō 相撲〔名〕

相撲をとる (*sumō* o toru)

¶相撲は日本で人気のあるスポーツです。(*Sumō* wa Nihon de ninki no aru supōtsu desu.)

sumō 〔n〕 *sumo, sumo* **wrestling**

wrestle with

¶ *Sumo* is a popular sport in Japan.

sumu 住む〔動 I〕

¶田中さんは今，大阪に住んでいます。(Tanaka san wa ima, Oosaka ni *sunde* imasu.)

¶兄は両親といっしょに住んでいます。　(Ani wa ryōshin to issho ni

sumu 〔v I〕 **live, reside, dwell**

¶ [Mrs.] Tanaka **is** now **living** in Osaka.

¶ My (elder) brother **is living** with our parents.

sunde imasu.)

sumu 済む〖動Ⅰ〗

¶会議は4時に済みました。 (Kaigi wa yoji ni *sumimashita.*)

¶仕事が済んだら、コーヒーでも飲みに行きましょう。 (Shigoto ga *sundara*, kōhii demo nomi ni ikimashō.)

suna 砂〖名〗

¶目に砂が入って痛いです。 (Me ni *suna* ga haitte itai desu.)

¶子供たちが庭で砂遊びをしています。 (Kodomotachi ga niwa de *suna*-asobi o shite imasu.)

sunao すなお〖形動〗

¶あの子はすなおな子で、親や先生の言うことをよくききます。 (Ano ko wa *sunao* na ko de, oya ya sensei no iu koto o yoku kikimasu.)

¶悪いことをしたのだから、すなおに謝りなさい。 (Warui koto o shita no da kara, *sunao* ni ayamarinasai.)

sunawachi すなわち〖接〗

¶わたしの高校では、40パーセントの人、すなわち5人に2人の人が大学に行きます。 (Watashi no kōkō de wa, yonjippāsento no hito, *sunawachi* gonin ni futari no hito ga daigaku ni ikimasu.)

¶日本の人口の10パーセントが、首都すなわち東京に集中しています。 (Nihon no jinkō no jippāsento ga, shuto *sunawachi* Tōkyō ni shūchū shite imasu.)

sumu 〖v I〗 **end, be concluded**

¶ The meeting 〖conference〗 **ended** at four o'clock.

¶ Let's go have some coffee **after** work.

suna 〖n〗 **sand, grit**

¶ My eye hurts because I've gotten **sand** in it.

¶ The children are playing in **the sand** out in the yard.

sunao 〖adj-v〗 **mild, docile, honest, frank, guileless**

¶ That is an **obedient** child who minds [his] parents and teachers.

¶ You did wrong so apologize **with good grace.**

sunawachi 〖conj〗 **namely, that is**

¶ Forty percent, **that is,** two out of five, of the students at my high school go on to college.

¶ Ten percent of the population of Japan is concentrated in the capital, **that is,** in Tokyo.

* 前のことがらを更に別の言葉で説明したり言い換えたりするときに使う。

supiido　スピード〖名〗

スピードを出す (*supiido o dasu*)
¶この辺は道が狭いから，スピードを落として，注意しながら運転してください。 (Kono hen wa michi ga semai kara, *supiido* o otoshite, chūi shinagara unten shite kudasai.)

supōtsu　スポーツ〖名〗

¶わたしはスポーツではテニスとピンポンが好きです。 (Watashi wa *supōtsu* de wa tenisu to pinpon ga suki desu.)

suppai　すっぱい〖形〗

¶わたしはレモンのようなすっぱい果物は好きではありません。 (Watashi wa remon no yō na *suppai* kudamono wa suki de wa arimasen.)

sūpu　スープ〖名〗

¶スープが冷めないうちに飲んでください。 (*Sūpu* ga samenai uchi ni nonde kudasai.)

supūn　スプーン〖名〗

¶スプーンでスープを飲みます。 (*Supūn* de sūpu o nomimasu.)

suru　する〖動Ⅲ〗

①[動作を行う]
¶今日はすることがたくさんあります。 (Kyō wa *suru* koto ga takusan arimasu.)
¶あなたは日曜日にはいつも何をしていますか。 (Anata wa nichiyōbi ni

* Used when explaining or expressing in different words what came before.

supiido 〚n〛 **speed**

speed up, pick up **speed**
¶ The streets around here are narrow so please drive **slowly** and carefully.

supōtsu 〚n〛 **a sport, sports**
¶ My favorite **sports** are tennis and ping-pong.

suppai 〚adj〛 **sour, acid, tart**
¶ I don't like **sour** fruits like lemons.

sūpu 〚n〛 **soup**
¶ Please eat **your soup** before it gets cold.

supūn 〚n〛 **spoon**
¶ One eats soup with **a spoon.**

suru 〚v Ⅲ〛 **do; perform** (a job); **make; cost; pass, elapse**

① [do]
¶ [I] have many things **to do** today.

¶ What do you usually **do** on Sunday?

wa itsu mo nani o *shite* imasu ka?)

②[ある仕事などに従事する]

¶田中さんはタクシーの運転手をしています。 (Tanaka san wa takushii no untenshu o *shite* imasu.)

¶姉は小学校の先生をしています。 (Ane wa shōgakkō no sensei o *shite* imasu.)

③[人をあるものにならせる，ある地位につける]

¶中村さんは息子さんを将来医者にするつもりだそうです。 (Nakamura san wa musukosan o shōrai isha ni *suru* tsumori da sō desu.)

¶山田さんをクラスの委員にしましょう。 (Yamada san o kurasu no iin ni *shimashō*.)

④[物をほかの形に変える，ほかの用途に使う]

¶一万円札を千円札十枚にしてください。 (Ichiman'ensatsu o sen'ensatsu jūmai ni *shite* kudasai.)

¶あの人は本をまくらにして寝ています。 (Ano hito wa hon o makura ni *shite* nete imasu.)

⑤[何かを感じる]

¶この花はとてもいいにおいがします。 (Kono hana wa totemo ii nioi ga *shimasu*.)

¶二階で大きな音がしました。 (Nikai de ookina oto ga *shimashita*.)

*「〜がする (〜ga suru)」の形で使う。

⑥[ものごとをある状態にならせる]

② [perform (a job), engage in]

¶ [Mr.] Tanaka **is** a taxi driver.

¶ My (elder) sister **is** an elementary school teacher.

③ [make, make into]

¶ I hear that [Mr.] Nakamura plans for [his] son **to become** a doctor.

¶ **Let's make** [Miss] Yamada the class representative.

④ [make, change, convert]

¶ Please **give me** 10 one-thousand yen bills for this ten-thousand yen bill.

¶ [He] is sleeping **using** a book as a pillow.

⑤ [make, produce, have]

¶ This flower **is** very sweet-**smelling.**

¶ There **was a** loud **noise** on the second floor.

* Used in the pattern "~ *ga suru.*"

⑥ [make into a certain condition or state]

¶よく聞こえないから，ラジオの音をもう少し大きくしてください。(Yoku kikoenai kara, rajio no oto o mō sukoshi ookiku *shite* kudasai.)

¶ Please **turn** the radio **up** a little—it's too low to hear.

¶部屋をきれいにしましょう。(Heya o kirei ni *shimashō*.)

¶ **Let's clean up** the room 〖apartment〗.

⑦[ものごとがある状態である，ある性質を持っている]

⑦ [have, be in a certain condition or state]

円い形をしたテーブル (marui katachi o *shita* tēburu)

a round table

¶彼は大きな手をしています。(Kare wa ookina te o *shite* imasu.)

¶ He **has** big hands.

¶上田さんは怒った顔をして，部屋を出ていきました。(Ueda san wa okotta kao o *shite*, heya o dete ikimashita.)

¶ [Mrs.] Ueda left the room **with** an angry look on [her] face.

¶その果物はどんな色をしていますか。(Sono kudamono wa donna iro o *shite* imasu ka?)

¶ What color **is** that fruit?

⑧[人などに対してある態度をとる]

⑧ [do, be]

¶おとなしくしていれば，お菓子を上げます。(Otonashiku *shite* ireba, okashi o agemasu.)

¶ If you **behave** yourself, I'll give you a sweet.

¶お年寄りには親切にしてあげましょう。(Otoshiyori ni wa shinsetsu ni *shite* agemashō.)

¶ Everyone **should be** kind to the elderly.

¶わたしが病気の時，上田さんはとても優しくしてくれました。(Watashi ga byōki no toki, Ueda san wa totemo yasashiku *shite* kuremashita.)

¶ When I was ill [Miss] Ueda **was** very kind to me.

⑨[値段を表す]

⑨ [cost]

¶その時計はいくらしましたか。(Sono tokei wa ikura *shimashita*

¶ How much did that watch 〖clock〗 **cost?**

ka?)

¶この部屋は一泊二万円もするそうです。 (Kono heya wa ippaku niman'en mo *suru* sō desu.)

¶ They say that this room **costs** twenty thousand yen a day.

⑩ [時間が経過する]

¶もう少しすると，御飯ですよ。 (Mō sukoshi *suru* to, gohan desu yo.)

¶あと1か月すれば卒業です。 (Ato ikkagetsu *sureba* sotsugyō desu.)

*「すると (suru to)」「すれば (sureba)」「したら (shitara)」の形で，未来のことを言うときに使う。

⑪ [決める]

¶お飲み物は何にしますか。 (Onomimono wa nan ni *shimasu* ka?)

¶来月，京都へ旅行することにしました。 (Raigetsu, Kyōto e ryokō suru koto ni *shimashita*.)

*名詞の場合は「名詞+にする (ni suru)」，動詞の場合は「動詞(連体の形)+ことにする (koto ni suru)」の形で使う。

⑫ [これから動作を行う状態であることを表す]

¶うちを出ようとすると，雨が降ってきました。 (Uchi o deyō to *suru* to, ame ga futte kimashita.)

¶今，あなたに電話しようとしていたところです。 (Ima, anata ni denwa shiyō to *shite* ita tokoro desu.)

*「動詞 (う・ようの形)+とする (to suru)」の形で使う。

✻「する (suru)」はある名詞や副詞

⑩ [pass, elapse]

¶ Dinner 〚lunch, breakfast, etc.〛 will be ready **in** a little while.

¶ It's only a month **until** graduation.

* Used in the patterns "*suru to*," "*sureba*," and "*shitara*" to refer to a future happening.

⑪ [decide]

¶ What **will you have** to drink?

¶ [I] **have decided** to take a trip to Kyoto next month.

* For nouns, used in the pattern "noun + *ni suru*." For verbs, used in the pattern "verb (dictionary form) + *koto ni suru*."

⑫ [try to, be about to]

¶ As I was leaving the house it started to rain.

¶ I was just now trying to telephone you.

* Used in the pattern "verb (-*ō* 〚-*yō*〛 form) + *to suru*."

✻ *Suru* combines with certain nouns

について動詞を作る。「勉強（ben-kyō）」は「勉強する（benkyō suru）」、「ぼんやり（bon'yari）」は「ぼんやりする（bon'yari suru）」となる。

and adverbs to form a new verb. For example *benkyō* (study, studying) becomes *benkyō suru* (to study) and *bon'yari* (absentmindedness) becomes *bon'yari suru* (to act absentmindedly).

surudoi　鋭い〖形〗

①［とがっている，よく切れる］

¶書きやすいように鉛筆の先を鋭くしておきました。　(Kakiyasui yō ni enpitsu no saki o *surudoku* shite okimashita.)

¶このナイフは先が鋭いから，気をつけて使いなさい。　(Kono naifu wa saki ga *surudoi* kara, ki o tsukete tsukainasai.)

②［頭の働きが速い］

¶田中さんはとても頭の鋭い人です。 (Tanaka san wa totemo atama no *surudoi* hito desu.)

surudoi 〚adj〛　pointed, sharp; quick, smart

① [pointed, sharp]

¶ [I] **sharpened** the pencils so they would be easy to write with.

¶ Please be careful as this knife is **sharply pointed.**

② [quick, smart, shrewd, acute, keen]

¶ [Mr.] Tanaka is very **quick-witted** 〚has a **keen** intelligence〛.

suruto　すると〖接〗

①［前のことがらを受けてその時その場面で起こったことがらや気づいたことがらなどをあとに続けるときに使う］

¶電気が暗くなりました。すると，どこからか静かな音楽が流れてきました。(Denki ga kuraku narimashita. *Suruto*, doko kara ka shizuka na ongaku ga nagarete kimashita.)

¶ドアを開けました。すると，部屋に知らない人が立っていました。　(Doa o akemashita. *Suruto*, heya ni shiranai hito ga tatte imashita.)

* 普通，前の文も「すると（suruto）」のあとの文も動詞の過去・完了を表す

suruto 〚conj〛　thereupon, just then; then, if so

① [thereupon, just then, and then]

¶ The lights were lowered. **And then** soft music could be heard drifting on the air.

¶ I opened the door. **And** a stranger was standing there inside the room.

* Usually the verbs in both clauses are in the *-ta* form expressing past or completed action. The clause with

「た の形」が来る。また，あとに話し手
が自分の意志で決めることができるよ
うな内容の文は来ない。「ドアの前に
立ちました。すると，ドアが開きまし
た。(Doa no mae ni tachimashita.
Suruto, doa ga akimashita.)」はい
いが，「ドアの前に立ちました。する
と，ドアを開けました。(Doa no mae
ni tachimashita. Suruto, doa o
akemashita.)」とは言えない。

②[前のことがらを受けてそのことか
ら当然起こると考えられることなどを
言うときに使う]

¶「大きな台風が近づいているそうで
す。」(Ookina taifū ga chikazuite
iru sō desu.)「すると，あしたは出発
は無理ですね。」(Suruto, ashita wa
shuppatsu wa muri desu ne.)

sushi すし〖名〗

¶おなかがすいたので，すし屋でおす
しを食べました。 (Onaka ga suita
node, sushiya de osushi o tabemashita.)

susumeru 勧める〖動Ⅱ〗

¶わたしはみんなにその会に参加する
ように勧めています。 (Watashi wa
minna ni sono kai ni sanka suru
yō ni susumete imasu.)

¶山田さんに保険に入ることを勧めら
れました。 (Yamada san ni hoken
ni hairu koto o susumeraremashita.)

susumeru 進める〖動Ⅱ〗

①[前方に行かせる，正しい時刻より
前にする)]

suruto does not express something
decided by the will of the speaker.
Thus "*Doa no mae ni tachimashita.
Suruto, doa ga akimashita*" (I stood
in front of the door. And then the
door opened) is possible, but one
cannot say * "*Doa no mae ni tachimashita. Suruto, doa o akemashita*"
(I stood in front of the door. And
then I opened the door).

② [then, if so, in that case, if that's
the case]

¶ "I hear a large typhoon is
approaching."

"**If that's so,** [we] won't be able to
leave on [our] trip tomorrow."

sushi 〖n〗 *sushi*

¶ [I] was hungry so [I] had some
sushi at a ***sushi*** shop.

susumeru 〖v Ⅱ〗 **recommend,
advise**

¶ I **recommend** that everyone participate in that club.

¶ [Mr.] Yamada **recommended** that
I take out insurance.

susumeru 〖v Ⅱ〗 **advance, put forward; promote, further**

① [advance, put forward]

¶この時計は 15 分進めてあります。
(Kono tokei wa jūgofun *susumete* arimasu.)

② [はかどらせる，進行させる]
¶雨の日が多くて，工事が進められません。(Ame no hi ga ookute, kōji ga *susumeraremasen*.)

susumu 進む〖動Ⅰ〗

① [前へ行く]
¶もう少し前へ進みなさい。 (Mō sukoshi mae e *susuminasai*.)
¶この前の授業はどこまで進みましたか。(Kono mae no jugyō wa doko made *susumimashita* ka?)

② [進歩する，進行させる]
進んだ考え (*susunda* kangae) 進んだ文化 (*susunda* bunka)
¶この国の農業技術はたいへん進んでいます。 (Kono kuni no nōgyō-gijutsu wa taihen *susunde* imasu.)

③ [時計が正しい時刻より早くなる]
¶この時計は 1 日に 5 分進みます。
(Kono tokei wa ichinichi ni gofun *susumimasu*.)

suteru 捨てる〖動Ⅱ〗
¶道路にごみを捨てないでください。
(Dōro ni gomi o *sutenaide* kudasai.)
¶このねこはだれが捨てたのでしょうか。(Kono neko wa dare ga *suteta* no deshō ka?)
⇒hirou 拾う

sutōbu ストーブ〖名〗
電気ストーブ (denki-*sutōbu*) ガス

¶ This watch ⟦clock⟧ **is** 15 minutes **fast.**

② [promote, further, speed up]
¶ There have been many rainy days, **hindering the progress** of the construction.

susumu ⟦v I⟧ advance, go forward; progress, advance; be fast, gain time

① [advance, go forward]
¶ **Move** a little farther **forward.**
¶ How far **did we get** in our lesson last time?

② [progress, advance, improve]
an **advanced** way of thinking // an **advanced** culture
¶ Agricultural techniques **are** very **advanced** in this country.

③ [be fast, gain time]
¶ This watch ⟦clock⟧ **gains** five minutes a day.

suteru ⟦v II⟧ throw away, discard, abandon, desert
¶ Please **don't litter** in the street.

¶ I wonder who **abandoned** this cat.

sutōbu ⟦n⟧ heater, stove
an electric **heater** // a gas **heater**

ストーブ（gasu-*sutōbu*） 石油ストーブ（sekiyu-*sutōbu*）　// a kerosene **heater**

¶寒くなりましたから，ストーブをつけましょうか。　(Samuku narimashita kara, *sutōbu* o tsukemashō ka?)　¶ It's gotten cold in here—shall I turn on **the heater?**

¶暑ぎますね。ストーブの火を消しましょう。　(Atsusugimasu ne. *Sutōbu* no hi o keshimashō).　¶ It's too hot. Let's turn off **the heater.**

suu 吸う〖動Ⅰ〗　**suu** 〚v I〛 inhale, smoke, sip, suck take a breath, breathe in

息を吸う (iki o *suu*)

¶ここでたばこを吸ってもいいですか。(Koko de tabako o *sutte* mo ii desu ka?)　¶ May **I smoke** here?

suwaru 座る〖動Ⅰ〗　**suwaru** 〚v I〛 sit down, take a seat

¶どうぞ，ここに座ってください。(Dōzo, koko ni *suwatte* kudasai.)　¶ Please **sit down** here.

¶日本の旅館では，畳に座って御飯を食べます。(Nihon no ryokan de wa, tatami ni *suwatte* gohan o tabemasu.)　¶ In a Japanese-style inn one eats **sitting** on the *tatami*-mat floor.

suzushii 涼しい〖形〗　**suzushii** 〚adj〛 cool

¶昼間は暑かったが，夕方になって涼しくなりました。(Hiruma wa atsukatta ga, yūgata ni natte *suzushiku* narimashita.)　¶ It was hot during the day but **cooled off** in the evening ⟦**has cooled off** from the evening⟧.

¶ここは夏は涼しく冬は暖かい，とてもいい所です。(Koko wa natsu wa *suzushiku* fuyu wa atatakai, totemo ii tokoro desu.)　¶ The summers **are cool** here and the winters warm, making it a very pleasant area.

T

ta 田〔名〕

¶この辺は畑より田のほうが多いです。(Kono hen wa hatake yori *ta* no hō ga ooi desu.)

¶米は田で作ります。(Kome wa *ta* de tsukurimasu.)

ta た〔助動〕

①〔過去・経験・回想などを表す〕

¶「あなたは昨日新宿へ行きましたか。」(Anata wa kinō Shinjuku e ikimashi*ta* ka?)「はい，行きました。」(Hai, ikimashi*ta*.)

¶わたしはあの映画を5回も見ました。(Watashi wa ano eiga o gokai mo mimashi*ta*.)

¶ゆうべはたいへん暑かったですね。(Yūbe wa taihen atsukat*ta* desu ne.)

¶若いころの上田先生は，とても怖い先生でした。(Wakai koro no Ueda sensei wa, totemo kowai sensei deshi*ta*.)

②〔完了を表す〕

¶「もう，昼御飯を食べましたか。」(Mō hirugohan o tabemashi*ta* ka?)「いいえ，まだ食べていません。」(Iie, mada tabete imasen.)

¶今，授業が終わったところです。(Ima, jugyō ga owat*ta* tokoro desu.)

¶あした学校へ行った時，本をお返し

---

ta 〔n〕 rice field, rice paddy

¶ Around here there is more land in **rice paddies** than under dry cultivation.

¶ Rice is grown in **rice paddies**.

-ta 〔auxil〕 a verb ending expressing past action, completed action, etc.

① [expresses action in the past, an experience, a recollection, etc.]

¶ "**Did you go** to Shinjuku yesterday?"

"Yes, **I did.**"

¶ **I've seen** that movie five times.

¶ **It was** very hot last night, wasn't it?

¶ [Mr.] Ueda **was** a very forbidding teacher when [he] was young.

② [expresses completed action]

¶ "**Have you** already **eaten** lunch?"

"No, I haven't eaten yet."

¶ Class just **ended.**

¶ [I] will return the book when [I] **go**

します。 (Ashita gakkō e it*ta* toki, hon o okaeshi shimasu.)

③［期待したり予想したりしたことなどが実際に起こったことを表す］

¶財布はやっぱり引き出しの中にありました。 (Saifu wa yappari hiki-dashi no naka ni arimashi*ta*.)

¶あ、バスが来ましたよ。(A *!* basu ga kimashi*ta* yo.)

④［忘れたことを思い出したり不確かなことを確かめるとき言う］

¶あしたは数学の試験がありましたね。 (Ashita wa sūgaku no shiken ga arimashi*ta* ne.)

¶あなたは田中さんの息子さんでしたね。 (Anata wa Tanaka san no musukosan deshi*ta* ne.)

¶上田さんはあしたフランスへ行くんでしたね。 (Ueda san wa ashita Furansu e iku n deshi*ta* ne.)

＊動作などを表す動詞の場合は「動詞（連体の形）＋の（ん）でした (no [n] deshita)」の形になる。

⑤［ものごとの性質や状態を表す］

太った人 (futot*ta* hito)　とがった鉛筆 (togat*ta* enpitsu)　黒板にかいた絵 (kokuban ni kai*ta* e)　砂糖を入れたコーヒー (satō o ire*ta* kōhii)

¶あの眼鏡をかけた人はだれですか。 (Ano megane o kake*ta* hito wa dare desu ka?)

¶川に沿った道を歩いていきました。 (Kawa ni sot*ta* michi o aruite ikimashita.)

to school tomorrow.

③ [used when something one has been expecting or waiting for actually happens]

¶ The wallet **was** in the drawer after all.

¶ Oh, the bus **is here!**

④ [used when remembering something one has forgotten or when confirming something one is unsure about]

¶ **There's** a math exam tomorrow, isn't there?

¶ Now, **you're** [Mr.] Tanaka's son, aren't you?

¶ **Wasn't** [Miss] Ueda going to leave for France tomorrow?

＊ In the case of a verb expressing an action, etc., the pattern "verb (dictionary form) + *no* [*n*] *deshita*" is used.

⑤ [used to express the nature or state of something]

a **fat** person // a **sharpened** pencil // a picture **drawn** on the blackboard // coffee **sweetened** with sugar

¶ Who is that person **wearing** glasses?

¶ [I] walked along the road **running parallel** to the river.

* 名詞を修飾する形で使われ，「〜て
いる (〜te iru)」「〜てある (〜te
aru) と置き換えることができる。

⑥[条件を表す]

¶春になっ**たら**，旅行をしましょう。
(Haru ni nat*tara*, ryokō o shimashō.)

¶もし高かっ**たら**，買いません。(Moshi
takakat*tara*, kaimasen.)

¶雨だっ**たら**，行きません。(Ame dat-
tara, ikimasen.)

* いつも「〜たら(ば)(〜tara [ba])」
の形で使う。

→**tara** たら

tabako たばこ〖名〗

¶わたしはたばこを吸いません。
(Watashi wa *tabako* o suimasen.)

tabemono 食べ物〖名〗

¶あなたは食べ物ではどんなものが
好きですか。(Anata wa *tabemono*
de wa donna mono ga suki desu
ka?)

¶わたしはきらいな食べ物はありま
せん。(Watashi wa kirai na *tabemono* wa arimasen.)

⇨**nomimono** 飲み物

taberu 食べる〖動Ⅱ〗

¶あなたは朝御飯を何時ごろ食べます
か。(Anata wa asagohan o nanji
goro *tabemasu* ka?)

¶わたしは昨日さしみを食べました。
(Watashi wa kinō sashimi o *tabemashita*.)

tabi 旅〖名〗

* Used modifying a noun. Can be replaced by *-te iru* or *-te aru*.

⑥ [used to express some stipulation]

¶ Let's take a trip **in** the spring.

¶ **If** it's expensive [I] won't buy it.

¶ **If** it rains [I] won't go.

* Always used in the *-tara* 〖*-ba*〗
form.

tabako 〖n〗 tobacco, cigarettes,
cigars

¶ I don't **smoke.**

tabemono 〖n〗 food, a dish, food-
stuff, edibles

¶ What **foods** do you like?

¶ I have no dislikes in **food.**

taberu 〖v Ⅱ〗 eat

¶ What time **do you eat** breakfast?

¶ I **ate** *sashimi* yesterday.

tabi 〖n〗 traveling, travel, journey,
trip

汽車の旅 (kisha no *tabi*) 空の旅
(sora no *tabi*) 旅人 (*tabi*bito) 旅
をする (*tabi* o suru)
¶この仕事が終わったら，しばらく旅
に出るつもりです。 (Kono shigoto
ga owattara, shibaraku *tabi* ni deru
tsumori desu.)
⇒**ryokō** 旅行

tabi たび〖名〗
¶わたしはこの写真を見るたびに，
子供のころを思い出します。(Watashi
wa kono shashin o miru *tabi* ni,
kodomo no koro o omoidashimasu.)
¶定期券を買わないで，電車に乗るた
びに切符を買います。 (Teikiken o
kawanaide, densha ni noru *tabi* ni
kippu o kaimasu.)

tabitabi たびたび〖副〗
¶小学生のころ病気で学校をたびた
び休みました。(Shōgakusei no koro
byōki de gakkō o *tabitabi* yasumimashita.)
¶たびたびお邪魔して申し訳ありませ
ん。(*Tabitabi* ojama shite mōshiwake arimasen.)

tabun たぶん〖副〗
¶あしたはたぶんいい天気でしょう。
(Ashita wa *tabun* ii tenki deshō.)
¶山田さんはひどい風邪で，今日は
たぶん来ないでしょう。 (Yamada
san wa hidoi kaze de, kyō wa
tabun konai deshō.)
＊「〜でしょう (〜 deshō)」「〜だろ
う (〜 darō)」などがあとに来ること

a train **trip** // a plane **trip** // a travel-
er, **a tourist** // travel, make **a journey,** take **a trip**
¶ I plan to go **traveling** for some
time after this job is over.

tabi 〖n〗 time, occasion, whenever
¶ I remember my childhood days
whenever I look at this photo.

¶ [I] haven't bought a commuter's
pass; [I] buy a ticket **each time** [I]
take the train.

tabitabi 〖adv〗 **often, frequently,
time after time**
¶ [I] was **frequently** absent from
school due to illness when [I] was in
elementary school.

¶ I am sorry to bother you 〚interrupt
your work〛 **so often.**

tabun 〖adv〗 probably, most likely
¶ **Chances are** it will be a nice day
tomorrow.
¶ As [Mr.] Yamada has a bad cold,
[he] will **probably** not come today.

＊ Generally followed by 〜 *deshō*,
〜 *darō*, etc.

が多い。

-tachi　たち〚尾〛

わたしたち (watashi*tachi*)　子供たち
(kodomo*tachi*)　あなたたち (anata-
tachi)　あの人たち (ano hito*tachi*)
学生たち (gakusei*tachi*)
＊人などの複数を表す。

-tachi 〚suf〛　a suffix indicating the plural

us, we, our // child**ren** // you (plural) // those people // student**s**

＊ Indicates the plural; used for human beings and sometimes animals.

tachiagaru　立ち上がる〚動Ⅰ〛

いすから立ち上がる (isu kara *tachi-agaru*)

¶足がしびれて，立ち上がることがで
きませんでした。(Ashi ga shibirete,
tachiagaru koto ga dekimasen
deshita.)

tachiagaru 〚v Ⅰ〛　stand up, get to one's feet

to rise from one's seat

¶ My leg had gone to sleep so that I had difficulty **getting up.**

tachiba　立場〚名〛

¶自分のことばかり考えないで，相手
の立場も考えなさい。 (Jibun no
koto bakari kangaenaide, aite no
tachiba mo kangaenasai.)

tachiba 〚n〛　position, standpoint, point of view

¶ Don't just think of yourself—put yourself **in the place** of the other person as well.

tachimachi　たちまち〚副〛

¶客がおおぜいだったので，料理はた
ちまちなくなってしまいました。
(Kyaku ga oozei datta node, ryōri
wa *tachimachi* nakunatte shimaimashita.)

¶飛行機はたちまち雲の中に見えなく
なりました。(Hikōki wa *tachimachi*
kumo no naka ni mienaku narimashita.)

tachimachi 〚adv〛　in an instant, in a flash, at once, immediately

¶ As there were many guests the food **quickly** disappeared.

¶ The plane **suddenly** disappeared from view behind a cloud.

tada　ただ〚名〛

¶今晩の映画会はただです。(Konban
no eigakai wa *tada* desu.)

¶この入場券をただで上げます。
(Kono nyūjōken o *tada* de age-

tada 〚n〛　free, without charge

¶ The movie showing this evening **is free.**

¶ I'd like you to have this admission ticket (to a concert, play, exhibition, masu.)

⇒**muryō 無料**

tada　ただ〖副〗

¶母親は、毎日ただ息子の勉強のことばかり心配しています。　(Hahaoya wa, mainichi *tada* musuko no benkyō no koto bakari shinpai shite imasu.)

＊「だけ (dake)」「ばかり (bakari)」「しか (shika)」などといっしょに使うことが多い。

tadashii　正しい〖形〗

①[間違いがない様子]

正しい発音 (*tadashii* hatsuon)

¶正しい答えには○、間違っている答えには×をつけなさい。　(*Tadashii* kotae ni wa maru, machigatte iru kotae ni wa batsu o tsukenasai.)

②[守るべきことに外れない様子]

正しい人 (*tadashii* hito)　正しい行い (*tadashii* okonai)

¶小さな子供には、何が正しいことなのかわかりません。(Chiisana kodomo ni wa, nani ga *tadashii* koto na no ka wakarimasen.)

taezu　絶えず〖副〗

¶水道のせんがよく閉まらないので、絶えず水が流れています。(Suidō no sen ga yoku shimaranai node, *taezu* mizu ga nagarete imasu.)

¶うちの母は絶えず文句を言っています。　(Uchi no haha wa *taezu* monku o itte imasu.)

tagai　互い〖名〗

etc.) **free of charge.**

tada 〖adv〗 **merely, solely, only, alone**

¶ Every day the mother does **nothing but** worry about her son's studies.

＊ Often used with *dake*, *bakari*, *shika*, etc.

tadashii 〖adj〗 **right, correct; right, upright, just, honest**

① [right, correct, exact, accurate]

the **correct** pronunciation

¶ Mark **correct** answers with a circle and wrong ones with an *X*.

② [right, upright, just, honest, proper, lawful]

a **just** person // **right** conduct

¶ Small children don't know **right** from wrong.

taezu 〖adv〗 **constantly, continually, without interruption**

¶ The faucet doesn't close tightly so it's **perpetually** dripping.

¶ My mother is **always** complaining.

tagai 〖n〗 **mutual, reciprocal, each other's, one another's**

¶世界各国の人々がお互いを理解し合うのが平和にとって大切なことです。
(Sekai kakkoku no hitobito ga o*tagai* o rikai shiau no ga heiwa ni totte taisetsu na koto desu.)

¶いっしょに生活するためには，お互いが気をつけなければなりません。
(Issho ni seikatsu suru tame ni wa, o*tagai* ga ki o tsukenakereba narimasen.)

＊ 普通「お互い (otagai)」の形で使う。

tagai ni 互いに〚副〛

¶わたしたちはお互いに助け合って生活しています。(Watashitachi wa o*tagai ni* tasukeatte seikatsu shite imasu.)

¶二人は互いに自分の国の言葉を教え合いました。(Futari wa *tagai ni* jibun no kuni no kotoba o oshie-aimashita.)

tagaru たがる〚助動〛

¶田中さんはカメラを買いたがっています。(Tanaka san wa kamera o kai*tagatte* imasu.)

¶妹は日本へ行きたがっています。
(Imōto wa Nihon e iki*tagatte* imasu.)

¶犬が外へ出たがっています。(Inu ga soto e de*tagatte* imasu.)

＊ 普通，話し手・話し相手以外の者があることをしたいと希望していることを客観的な立場から観察して述べる場合に使う。「～たがっている (～ta-

¶ **Mutual** understanding among the peoples of the world is important for world peace.

¶ People living together must be considerate **of each other.**

＊ Usually used in the form *otagai*.

tagai ni 〚adv〛 **mutually, reciprocally**

¶ We live helping **one another.**

¶ The two taught **each other** their own respective language.

-tagaru 〚auxil〛 **want to, be eager to, be apt to**

¶ [Mr.] Tanaka **wants** to buy a camera.

¶ My younger sister **wants** to go to Japan.

¶ The dog **wants** to go outside.
＊ Usually expresses an objective judgment about what someone other than the speaker or the listener wants to do; it is not used about others when speaking politely. Generally

gatte iru)」の形で使うことが多い。しかし，過去のことについて自分の心情を回想的に述べる場合や，相手にも自分の希望していることがわかっていると判断する場合には，話し手のことについても使う。また，話し相手の心情がよくわかっている状態のときには，話し相手のことについても使われることがある。「わたしは子供のころ，よく学校を休みたがって親を困らせました。(Watashi wa kodomo no koro, yoku gakkō o yasumitagatte oya o komarasemashita.)」「わたしが行きたがっていることを知っていながら，中村さんは連れていってくれませんでした。(Watashi ga ikitagatte iru koto o shitte inagara, Nakamura san wa tsurete itte kuremasen deshita.)」「あなたが行きたがっていることはよくわかりますが，今度は無理です。(Anata ga ikitagatte iru koto wa yoku wakarimasu ga, kondo wa muri desu.)」

⇨ **tai** たい **-garu** -がる

tai 対〖名〗

¶日本対アメリカのバレーボールの試合はあした行われます。(Nihon *tai* Amerika no barēbōru no shiai wa ashita okonawaremasu.)

¶試合は4対3で，わたしたちのチームが勝ちました。(Shiai wa yon *tai* san de, watashitachi no chiimu ga kachimashita.)

tai たい〖助動〗

used in the pattern "*-tagatte iru.*" However, it can also be used about the speaker's own desires when recollecting how one felt in the past or when judging that another understands one's desires. It can also be used concerning the listener's desires when the speaker knows well how the listener is feeling. For example, "*Watashi wa kodomo no koro, yoku gakkō o yasumitagatte oya o komarasemashita*" (When I was young I often troubled my parents with my desire to stay home from school); "*Watashi ga ikitagatte iru koto o shitte inagara, Nakamura san wa tsurete itte kuremasen deshita*" (Even though [he] knew I wanted to go, [Mr.] Nakamura didn't take me along); or "*Anata ga ikitagatte iru koto wa yoku wakarimasu ga, kondo wa muri desu*" (I realize you want to go but it's impossible this time).

tai 〖n〗 **versus, against**

¶ The **Japan–U.S.** volleyball game is tomorrow.

¶ Our team won the game with a score of 4 **to** 3.

-tai 〖auxil〗 **want to, feel like ~ing**

¶水が飲み**たい**です。(Mizu ga nomi-*tai* desu.)

¶何も食べ**たく**ありません。(Nani mo tabe*taku* arimasen.)

¶芝居を見に行き**たかったら**,連れていってあげます。(Shibai o mi ni iki-*takattara*, tsurete itte agemasu.)

¶わたしは一度日本へ行ってみ**たい**です。(Watashi wa ichido Nihon e itte mi*tai* desu.)

＊ある行為や事態の実現を希望する意味を表す。普通は話し手の希望を表すが，質問する場合や相手の心情を推量する場合や相手がそういう希望を持っているということが判断できる場合には話し手以外の人の場合にも使う。「あなたも今度の旅行にはいっしょに行きたいでしょう。(Anata mo kondo no ryokō ni wa issho ni ikitai deshō?)」「今度の旅行に行きたい人はもういませんか。(Kondo no ryokō ni ikitai hito wa mō imasen ka?)」「芝居を見に行きたかったら，連れていってあげます。(Shibai o mi ni ikitakattara, tsurete itte agemasu.)」

⇒**tagaru** たがる

taido 態度〖名〗

¶田中さんは授業中の**態度**が悪かったので，先生にしかられました。(Tanaka san wa jugyōchū no *taido* ga warukatta node, sensei ni shikararemashita.)

¶賛成か反対か，**態度**をはっきりしなさい。(Sansei ka hantai ka, *taido*

¶ **I want** a drink of water.

¶ **I don't want** anything to eat.

¶ I'll take you **if you'd like** to go see a play.

¶ I **would like** to go to Japan at least once.

＊ Used to refer to wanting to do something. Generally -*tai* refers to the speaker's wishes but it can also be used for the desires of others when asking a question, when guessing the feelings of another, or when one can judge that another has certain feelings. For example, "*Anata mo kondo no ryokō ni wa issho ni ikitai deshō?*" (You want to come with us on the trip too, don't you?); "*Kondo no ryokō ni ikitai hito wa mō imasen ka?*" (Aren't there any others who want to come on the trip?); or "*Shibai o mi ni ikitakattara, tsurete itte agemasu*" (I'll take you if you'd like to go see a play).

taido 〖n〗 attitude, stance, manner

¶ The teacher reprimanded [Mr.] Tanaka for [his] poor **attitude** during class.

¶ Make clear **where you stand,** for it or against it.

o hakkiri shinasai.)

taifū 台風〖名〗

台風が来る (*taifū* ga kuru)

¶日本では，八月の下旬から九月の上旬にかけて台風が多いです。(Nihon de wa, hachigatsu no gejun kara kugatsu no jōjun ni kakete *taifū* ga ooi desu.)

¶台風でたくさんの家が壊れました。(*Taifū* de takusan no ie ga kowaremashita.)

taihen たいへん〖副，形動〗

1〖副〗

¶今日はたいへん疲れました。(Kyō wa *taihen* tsukaremashita.)

¶妹はバナナがたいへん好きです。(Imōto wa banana ga *taihen* suki desu.)

¶田中さんは試験の成績にたいへん満足しています。(Tanaka san wa shiken no seiseki ni *taihen* manzoku shite imasu.)

2〖形動〗

①［重大である様子，程度が普通ではない様子］

¶あっ，たいへんだ。隣が火事だ。(A'! *Taihen* da. Tonari ga kaji da.)

¶今，東京に大地震が来たらたいへんです。(Ima, Tōkyō ni oojishin ga kitara *taihen* desu.)

¶「会社のお金を落としてしまいました。」(Kaisha no okane o otoshite shimaimashita.)「それはたいへんなことをしましたね。」(Sore wa *taihen*

taifū 〖n〗 typhoon

a typhoon approaches; **a typhoon** strikes

¶ **Typhoons** are frequent in Japan in late August and early September.

¶ Many homes were destroyed in **the typhoon.**

taihen 〖adv, adj-v〗 **very, greatly; serious, grave; hard, difficult**

1 〖adv〗 very, greatly, awfully

¶ Today **really** tired me out.

¶ My younger sister is **very** fond of bananas.

¶ [Mr.] Tanaka is **fully** satisfied with [his] mark on the exam.

2 〖adj-v〗

① [serious, grave, horrible, terrible]

¶ **My God!** There's a fire next door!

¶ **It would be disastrous** if a major earthquake should strike present-day Tokyo.

¶ "I lost some company money." "Oh, **how terrible.**"

na koto o shimashita ne.)

②［何かをするのに非常な苦労をしたり努力をしたりする様子］

¶「富士山に登るのはたいへんですか。」(Fujisan ni noboru no wa *taihen* desu ka?)「いいえ，途中までバスで行けますから，そんなにたいへんではありません。」(Iie, tochū made basu de ikemasu kara, sonna ni *taihen* de wa arimasen.)

¶「会議の資料を作っていたので，ゆうべは寝ませんでした。」(Kaigi no shiryō o tsukutte ita node, yūbe wa nemasen deshita.)「それはたいへんでしたね。」(Sore wa *taihen* deshita ne.)

② [hard, difficult]

¶ "**Is it difficult** to climb Mount Fuji?"

"No, you can go partway by bus so **it's not** so **bad**."

¶ "I was up all last night preparing papers for the meeting 〚conference〛."

"That's **really hard** on you" (literally, That was **terrible**).

taiiku 体育〖名〗

体育の日 (*taiiku* no hi)

¶今日の体育の授業は体育館で行います。(Kyō no *taiiku* no jugyō wa *taiiku*kan de okonaimasu.)

taiiku 〚n〛 **physical training, physical education**

Sports Day

¶ Today's **gym** class will be in **the gym.**

taiin 退院〖名，～する〗

¶田中さんは昨日退院したそうです。(Tanaka san wa kinō *taiin* shita sō desu.)

¶病気が重いので，いつ退院できるかわかりません。(Byōki ga omoi node, itsu *taiin* dekiru ka wakarimasen.)

⇔nyūin 入院

taiin 〚n, ～*suru*〛 **leave the hospital, discharge from the hospital**

¶ I hear that [Mrs.] Tanaka **came home from the hospital** yesterday.

¶ As [his] illness is quite serious, it is unclear when [he] will be able **to leave the hospital.**

taijū 体重〖名〗

¶今，わたしの体重は50キロです。(Ima, watashi no *taijū* wa gojikkiro desu.)

¶病気をしたので，体重が軽くなり

taijū 〚n〛 **one's body weight**

¶ I presently **weigh** 50 kilos.

¶ [I] lost **weight** 〚have lost **weight**〛

ました。(Byōki o shita node, *taijū* ga karuku narimashita.)

taikai 大会〖名〗

全国大会 (zenkoku-*taikai*)

¶東京で人口問題についての世界大会が開かれました。(Tōkyō de jinkō-mondai ni tsuite no sekai-*taikai* ga hirakaremashita.)

taikaku 体格〖名〗

¶上田さんはとてもいい体格をしています。(Ueda san wa totemo ii *taikaku* o shite imasu.)

¶スポーツをすると,体格がよくなります。(Supōtsu o suru to, *taikaku* ga yoku narimasu.)

taikutsu 退屈〖名, 形動, ～する〗

退屈な話 (*taikutsu* na hanashi)

¶何もすることがないので退屈です。(Nani mo suru koto ga nai node *taikutsu* desu.)

¶話がおもしろくないので, みんな退屈そうな顔をしています。(Hanashi ga omoshiroku nai node, minna *taikutsusō* na kao o shite imasu.)

taipuraitā タイプライター〖名〗

和文タイプライター (wabun-*taipuraitā*) 英文タイプライター (eibun-*taipuraitā*) タイプライターを打つ (*taipuraitā* o utsu)

＊「タイプ (taipu)」とも言う。

taira 平ら〖形動〗

¶平らな道が遠くまで続いています。(*Taira* na michi ga tooku made tsuzuite imasu.)

due to illness.

taikai 〚n〛 **mass meeting, rally, general meeting; conference, convention; meet, tournament**

a national **convention**

¶ A world **conference** concerning the population problem opened 〚has opened〛 in Tokyo.

taikaku 〚n〛 **physique, physical constitution, (body) build**

¶ [Mr.] Ueda has a fine **build.**

¶ **One's constitution** improves if one participates in sports.

taikutsu 〚n, adj-v, ～*suru*〛 **tedious, dull, boring**

a **boring** talk

¶ [I] **am bored** as there is nothing to do.

¶ Everyone **looks bored** as the lecture isn't very interesting.

taipuraitā 〚n〛 **typewriter**

a Japanese-character **typewriter** // a roman-letter **typewriter** // to type

＊ Variant: *taipu*.

taira 〚adj-v〛 **flat, even, level**

¶ The **flat** road stretches out into the distance.

¶山をけずって平らにすれば，もっと家が建てられます。(Yama o kezutte *taira* ni sureba, motto ie ga tate-raremasu.)

¶ If the hill **were leveled,** more houses could be built.

tairiku 大陸〖名〗

¶日本はアジア大陸の東にあります。(Nihon wa Ajia-*tairiku* no higashi ni arimasu.)

tairiku 〖n〗 continent

¶ Japan lies to the east of the Asian **continent.**

¶北アメリカ大陸と南アメリカ大陸はつながっています。(Kitaamerika-*tairiku* to Minamiamerika-*tairiku* wa tsunagatte imasu.)

¶ **The continents** of North and South America are joined together.

tairitsu 対立〖名，〜する〗

¶意見の対立は，話し合いで解決したほうがいいです。(Iken no *tairitsu* wa, hanashiai de kaiketsu shita hō ga ii desu.)

tairitsu 〖n, 〜*suru*〗 opposition, confrontation

¶ It is best to resolve **differences** of opinion through discussion.

¶意見が激しく対立して，会議はなかなか終わりませんでした。(Iken ga hageshiku *tairitsu* shite, kaigi wa nakanaka owarimasen deshita.)

¶ The meeting dragged on due to **the clash** of opinion.

taisetsu 大切〖形動〗

①[大事な様子]

大切なもの (*taisetsu* na mono) 大切な人 (*taisetsu* na hito) 大切な問題 (*taisetsu* na mondai)

¶石油は現在，非常に大切なものになっています。(Sekiyu wa genzai, hijō ni *taisetsu* na mono ni natte imasu.)

¶外国語を話すときは，発音が大切です。(Gaikokugo o hanasu toki wa, hatsuon ga *taisetsu* desu.)

②[丁寧に扱う様子，大事にする様子]

taisetsu 〖adj-v〗 important, serious, valuable; to value, prize

① [important, serious, grave, valuable, precious]

treasure, valuables // an **important** person, a **beloved** person // a **serious** problem

¶ Oil is presently an extremely **valuable** commodity.

¶ Pronunciation **is important** when speaking a foreign language.

② [to value, prize]

¶体を大切にしてください。(Karada o *taisetsu* ni shite kudasai.)

¶資源は大切に使いましょう。(Shigen wa *taisetsu* ni tsukaimashō.)

taishi 大使〚名〛
大使館 (*taishi*kan) 駐日アメリカ大使 (chūnichi-Amerika*taishi*)

taishite 大して〚副〛

¶この料理は大しておいしくありません。(Kono ryōri wa *taishite* oishiku arimasen.)

¶今度の試験は大して難しくありませんでした。(Kondo no shiken wa *taishite* muzukashiku arimasen deshita.)

＊ あとに打ち消しの言葉が来る。

taishō 対象〚名〛

¶これは高校生を対象とした雑誌です。(Kore wa kōkōsei o *taishō* to shita zasshi desu.)

¶わたしは戦後の日本経済を研究の対象としています。(Watashi wa sengo no Nihon-keizai o kenkyū no *taishō* to shite imasu.)

taishō 大正〚名〛
大正時代 (*Taishō*-jidai)

taisō 体操〚名，～する〛
ラジオ体操 (rajio-*taisō*)

¶わたしは毎朝体操をしています。(Watashi wa maiasa *taisō* o shite imasu.)

taisuru 対する〚動Ⅲ〛

①[向かう，相手とする]
¶目上の人に対しては，丁寧な言葉を使

¶ Please **take good care of** yourself.

¶ We should **value** our natural resources **and use** them **carefully.**

taishi 〚n〛 **ambassador**
an embassy // the American **ambassador** to Japan

taishite 〚adv〛 (not) **very,** (not) **much**

¶ This food isn't **very** good.

¶ The last test wasn't **particularly** difficult.

＊ Used with the negative.

taishō 〚n〛 **object, subject, target**
¶ This magazine **is aimed** at high school students.

¶ **The subject** of my research is the postwar Japanese economy.

taishō 〚n〛 **Taisho;** the name of a Japanese emperor and of his reign from 1912 to 1926
the **Taisho** period

taisō 〚n, ～*suru*〛 **gymnastics, athletic exercises**
radio **calisthenics**
¶ I do **exercises** every morning.

taisuru 〚v Ⅲ〛 **toward, to, against; concerning, in regard to**
① [toward, to, against, as opposed to, in comparison with]

わなければなりません。　(Meue no hito ni *taishite* wa, teinei na kotoba o tsukawanakereba narimasen.)

¶最近，子供の親に**対する**態度が変わってきました。(Saikin, kodomo no oya ni *taisuru* taido ga kawatte kimashita.)

②[あるものごとに関する]

¶この問題に**対する**意見は，ほかにありませんか。(Kono mondai ni *taisuru* iken wa, hoka ni arimasen ka?)

¶わたしは日本文化に**対して**興味があります。(Watashi wa Nihon-bunka ni *taishite* kyōmi ga arimasu.)

✲ 普通「〜に対する (〜ni taisuru)」の形で使う。

taitei　たいてい〖副，〜の〗

①[ほとんどの場合]

¶日曜日は**たいてい**家にいます。(Nichiyōbi wa *taitei* ie ni imasu.)

¶あなたは**たいてい**何時ごろ起きますか。(Anata wa *taitei* nanji goro okimasu ka?)

②[大部分]

¶**たいてい**の学生は歩いて学校へ来ます。(*Taitei* no gakusei wa aruite gakkō e kimasu.)

¶ここにある本は**たいてい**読みました。(Koko ni aru hon wa *taitei* yomimashita.)

taiyō　太陽〖名〗

¶地球は**太陽**の周りを回っています。(Chikyū wa *taiyō* no mawari o

¶ One should use polite language **toward** one's superiors.

¶ In recent years there has been a change in the attitude of children **toward** their parents.

② [concerning, in regard to]

¶ Are there any other opinions **concerning** this matter?

¶ I have an interest **in** Japanese culture.

✲ Usually used in the pattern "~ *ni taisuru*."

taitei　〖adv, ~*no*〗 **usually, generally, mostly; almost all, most**

① [usually, generally, mostly]

¶ [I] am **generally** at home on Sunday.

¶ What time do you **usually** get up?

② [almost all, most]

¶ **The majority** of students walk to school.

¶ [I] have read **almost all** of the books here.

taiyō　〖n〗 **the sun**

¶ The earth revolves around **the sun.**

mawatte imasu.)

taizai 滞在〖名, 〜する〗

¶「いつまでこちらに御滞在ですか。」
(Itsu made kochira ni go*taizai* desu ka?)「1週間ぐらい滞在する予定です。」(Isshūkan gurai *taizai* suru yotei desu.)

¶滞在期間をもう1年延ばすつもりです。 (*Taizai*-kikan o mō ichinen nobasu tsumori desu.)

takai 高い〖形〗

①[下から上までの長さが大きい様子, ものの位置が上の方にあって地面などから離れている様子]

高い木 (*takai* ki) 背が高い (se ga *takai*)

¶あの高い建物は何ですか。 (Ano *takai* tatemono wa nan desu ka?)

¶世界でいちばん高い山はエベレストです。(Sekai de ichiban *takai* yama wa Eberesuto desu.)

¶日が高く昇っています。 (Hi ga *takaku* nobotte imasu.)

↔hikui 低い

②[買うのに金が多くかかる様子]

¶この紙は1枚50円ですか。高いですね。 (Kono kami wa ichimai go-jūen desu ka? *Takai* desu ne.)

¶あまり高ければ買いません。(Amari *takakereba* kaimasen.)

↔yasui 安い

③[声・音が大きく聞こえる様子, 音階が上である様子]

高い音 (*takai* oto)

taizai 〚n, ~*suru*〛 **stay, visit, sojourn**

¶ "How long **will you be staying** here?"

"I plan **to stay** about a week."

¶ I intend to extend **my stay** for an additional year.

takai 〚adj〛 **high, tall; expensive; loud, high-pitched; elevated; exalted**

① [high, tall]

a **tall** tree // (a person is) **tall**

¶ What is that **tall** building over there?

¶ The **highest** mountain in the world is Mount Everest.

¶ The sun is **high** in the sky.

② [expensive, high-priced]

¶ This paper is 50 yen a sheet? **It's expensive,** isn't it?

¶ [I] won't buy it **if it's** too **expensive.**

③ [loud, high-pitched]

a **loud** sound

¶隣の部屋から**高い**笑い声が聞こえてきます。 (Tonari no heya kara *takai* waraigoe ga kikoete kimasu.)

¶春子さんの声は**高い**です。 (Haruko san no koe wa *takai* desu.)

↔hikui 低い

④[温度・熱などの数値が大きい]
温度が**高い** (ondo ga *takai*) 気圧が**高い** (kiatsu ga *takai*)

¶山田さんは熱が**高くて**，学校を休みました。 (Yamada san wa netsu ga *takakute*, gakkō o yasumimashita.)

↔hikui 低い

⑤[身分などが上である様子]
地位が**高い** (chii ga *takai*)

↔hikui 低い

takasa 高さ〖名〗

①[上へのびている程度]
¶わたしは背の**高さ**が弟と同じくらいです。 (Watashi wa se no *takasa* ga otōto to onaji kurai desu.)

¶富士山の**高さ**はどのくらいですか。 (Fujisan no *takasa* wa dono kurai desu ka?)

②[金のかかる程度]
¶東京の物価の**高さ**には驚きました。 (Tōkyō no bukka no *takasa* ni wa odorokimashita.)

⇨-sa -さ

take 丈〖名〗
¶このズボンは**丈**が短すぎます。 (Kono zubon wa *take* ga mijika-sugimasu.)

take 竹〖名〗

¶ [I] can hear someone laughing **loudly** next door.

¶ Haruko's voice **is high-pitched.**

④ [high, elevated]
the temperature **is high** // the atmospheric pressure **is high**

¶ [Miss] Yamada stayed home from school with a **high** fever.

⑤ [high, exalted, superior]
have a **high** social standing; have a **high** position

takasa 〖n〗 height; expensiveness

① [height]
¶ I am roughly the same **height** as my younger brother.

¶ How **high** is Mount Fuji?

② [expensiveness]
¶ [I] was surprised at the **high** prices in Tokyo.

take 〖n〗 length, height, stature
¶ These trousers 〖pants, slacks〗 are too **short**.

take 〖n〗 bamboo

753

竹の子 (*takenoko*) 竹やぶ (*takeya-bu*) 竹細工 (*takezaiku*) 竹かご (*takekago*) 竹で編んだざる (*take de anda zaru*)

a **bamboo** shoot // a **bamboo** grove // **bamboo**ware // a **bamboo** basket // a **bamboo** sieve

taku 炊く〖動 I 〗
御飯を炊く (*gohan o taku*)

taku 〖v I〗 boil, cook
boil rice

takusan たくさん〖副, ～の〗
①〔数や量が多い〕
¶ここにりんごが**たくさん**あります。(Koko ni ringo ga *takusan* arimasu.)
¶この川には魚が**たくさん**います。(Kono kawa ni wa sakana ga *takusan* imasu.)
¶広場に**たくさん**の人が集まってきました。(Hiroba ni *takusan* no hito ga atsumatte kimashita.)
②〔じゅうぶんである，それ以上いらない〕
¶「もう少しいかがですか。」(Mō sukoshi ikaga desu ka?)「もう**たくさん**いただきました。」(Mō *takusan* itadakimashita.)

takusan 〖adv, ～*no*〗 much, plenty, a great many; enough, sufficient
① [much, plenty, a great many, a large quantity]
¶ There are **a lot** of apples here.
¶ This river **abounds** with fish.
¶ There is 〖was〗 **a throng** of people gathered in the plaza.
② [enough, sufficient]
¶ "Would you like a little more?" "No, thank you. I've had **plenty.**"

takushii タクシー〖名〗
タクシーで行く (*takushii de iku*)
¶わたしは駅から**タクシー**に乗って帰ります。(Watashi wa eki kara *takushii* ni notte kaerimasu.)

takushii 〖n〗 taxi
go by **taxi**
¶ I will take **a taxi** home from the station.

tama 玉〖名〗
目玉 (me*dama*) 眼鏡の玉 (megane no *tama*) 十円玉 (jūen*dama*)

tama 〖n〗 ball, bead, lens, drop, jewel, etc.
the eye**ball** // an eyeglass **lens** // a 10-yen **coin**

tama 球〖名〗
電気の球 (denki no *tama*) 野球の球 (yakyū no *tama*) 球を打つ (ta-

tama 〖n〗 ball, bulb, globe
an electric light **bulb** // **a ball** for baseball // hit 〖bat〗 **a ball**

tama 弾〖名〗

ピストルの弾 (pisutoru no *tama*)
鉄砲の弾 (teppō no *tama*)

tamago 卵〖名〗

生卵 (nama*tamago*) 卵焼き (*tama-goyaki*) ゆで卵 (yude*tamago*) 半熟卵 (hanjuku*tamago*) 卵を産む (*tamago* o umu) 卵がかえる (*tamago* ga kaeru)

tama ni たまに〖副〗

¶わたしは**たまに**映画を見に行きます。 (Watashi wa *tama ni* eiga o mi ni ikimasu.)
¶山田さんは**たまにしか**図書館へ行きません。 (Yamada san wa *tama ni* shika toshokan e ikimasen.)

tamaru たまる〖動Ⅰ〗

①[物が一つの所に少しずつ集まってたくさんになる]
¶大雨が降ったので，道路に水が**たま**ってしまいました。(Ooame ga futta node, dōro ni mizu ga *tamatte* shimaimashita.)
②[貯金などが多くなる]
¶お金が**たまったら**，旅行に行きたいと思っています。 (Okane ga *tamattara*, ryokō ni ikitai to omotte imasu.)
③[仕事や支払いなどがかたづかないで残る]
アパート代が**たまる** (apātodai ga *tamaru*)
¶病気で会社を休んだので，仕事が**た**

tama 〚n〛 bullet, shell, shot
a pistol **bullet** // a gun 〚rifle〛 **bullet**

tamago 〚n〛 egg
an raw **egg** // an omelet // a boiled **egg** // a soft-boiled **egg** // lay **an egg,** spawn // **an egg** hatches

tama ni 〚adv〛 occasionally, now and then, at times, once in a while
¶ I **occasionally** go to see a movie.

¶ [Mr.] Yamada **seldom** goes to the library.

tamaru 〚v I〛 gather, collect, accumulate; save, be saved; be in arrears, be overdue

① [gather, collect, accumulate]
¶ There **are** 〚were〛 **puddles** in the street after the heavy rains.

② [save, be saved]
¶ **When I have** enough money **saved** I want to go on a trip.

③ [be in arrears, be overdue]

be behind on the rent

¶ [I] **am behind** in [my] work as [I]

tame

まってしまいました。 (Byōki de kaisha o yasunda node, shigoto ga *tamatte* shimaimashita.)

tame　ため〖名〗

①〔目的を表す〕

¶わたしは日本文学を勉強するために日本語を習っています。(Watashi wa Nihon-bungaku o benkyō suru *tame* ni Nihongo o naratte imasu.)

¶山田さんは，家を建てるためにお金をためています。(Yamada san wa, ie o tateru *tame* ni okane o tamete imasu.)

②〔理由・原因を表す〕

¶病気のため学校を休みました。(Byōki no *tame* gakkō o yasumimashita.)

¶不注意のため試験に失敗しました。(Fuchūi no *tame* shiken ni shippai shimashita.)

¶バスが遅れたために遅刻しました。(Basu ga okureta *tame* ni chikoku shimashita.)

③〔役に立つこと・利益になることを表す〕

¶これはとてもためになる本です。(Kore wa totemo *tame* ni naru hon desu.)

¶上田さんは会社のために夜遅くまで働いています。(Ueda san wa kaisha no *tame* ni yoru osoku made hataraite imasu.)

tameru　ためる〖動Ⅱ〗

①〔物を一つの所に少しずつ集めてた

---

had to take time off sick.

tame 〚n〛 in order to, to; because of, owing to; good, benefit

① [in order to, to]

¶ I am learning Japanese **so that** I can study Japanese literature.

¶ [Mr.] Yamada is saving money **in order** to build a house.

② [because of, owing to, on account of]

¶ [I] stayed home from school **due to** illness.

¶ [I] failed the exam **because of** carelessness.

¶ [I] am 〚was〛 late **because** the bus was delayed.

③ [good, advantage, benefit, sake]

¶ This is a very **instructive** book.

¶ [Mr.] Ueda works late at night **for the benefit** of [his] company.

tameru 〚v Ⅱ〛 accumulate, amass; save, store up; run up (a bill), leave undone

① [accumulate, amass, collect,

756

くさんにする]

¶この地方では雨水をためておいて, それを飲んでいるそうです。(Kono chihō de wa amamizu o *tamete* oite, sore o nonde iru sō desu.)

②[貯金などを多くする]

¶お金をためて, テープレコーダーを買うつもりです。(Okane o *tamete*, tēpurekōda o kau tsumori desu.)

③[仕事や支払いなどをかたづけないで残す]

部屋代をためる (heyadai o *tameru*)

tamesu 試す〖動Ⅰ〗

¶機械が直ったかどうか試してみましょう。(Kikai ga naotta ka dō ka *tameshite* mimashō.)

¶漢字の力を試すためにテストしましょう。(Kanji no chikara o *tamesu* tame ni tesuto shimashō.)

tana たな〖名〗

本だな (hon*dana*)　たなから物を降ろす (*tana* kara mono o orosu)

¶この箱をたなに上げてください。(Kono hako o *tana* ni agete kudasai.)

tane 種〖名〗

¶庭に花の種をまきました。(Niwa ni hana no *tane* o makimashita.)

¶このぶどうには種がありません。(Kono budō ni wa *tane* ga arimasen.)

tango 単語〖名〗

¶わたしはまだ日本語の単語を少ししか知りません。(Watashi wa mada

gather]

¶ I hear that in this area **they save** rainwater and use it for drinking water.

② [save, store up]

¶ I intend **to save** my money and buy a tape recorder.

③ [run up (a bill), leave undone]

let one's rent **fall in arrears, owe** rent

tamesu 〖vⅠ〗 **try, attempt, test**

¶ Let's **try out** the machine 〖device, apparatus, mechanism〗 and see if it's all right now after being fixed.

¶ Let's have a test **to see** how strong you are in *kanji*.

tana 〖n〗 **shelf, shelves, rack**

a book**shelf**, a book**case** // take an article from **a shelf**

¶ Please put this box on **the shelf.**

tane 〖n〗 **seed, pit, stone**

¶ [I] sowed flower **seed** in the garden.

¶ These are **seed**less grapes.

tango 〖n〗 **word(s), vocabulary**

¶ My Japanese **vocabulary** is still very limited.

Nihongo no *tango* o sukoshi shika

shirimasen.)

¶単語帳を作って勉強しています。

(*Tango*chō o tsukutte benkyō shite

imasu.)

tan'i 単位〔名〕

¶日本では，長さの単位はメートルを，重さの単位はグラムを使っています。

(Nihon de wa, nagasa no *tan'i* wa

mētoru o, omosa no *tan'i* wa gura-

mu o tsukatte imasu.)

tanin 他人〔名〕

①〔ほかの人〕

¶他人の迷惑になるようなことはしないでください。(*Tanin* no meiwaku

ni naru yō na koto wa shinaide

kudasai.)

②〔血縁関係のない人〕

¶あの二人はとてもよく似ていますが，他人なのです。(Ano futari wa tote-

mo yoku nite imasu ga, *tanin*

na no desu.)

tanjōbi 誕生日〔名〕

¶わたしの誕生日は3月3日です。

(Watashi no *tanjōbi* wa sangatsu

mikka desu.)

¶今晩，山田さんの誕生日のお祝いをします。(Konban, Yamada san no

tanjōbi no oiwai o shimasu.)

tanomu 頼む〔動Ⅰ〕

¶田中さんに頼んで，お金を貸してもらいました。(Tanaka san ni *tanon-

de*, okane o kashite moraimashita.)

¶友達にノートを貸してくれと頼んだ

¶ [I] study keeping a notebook of new **vocabulary.**

tan'i 〚n〛 a unit, a denomination

¶ **The unit** of length in use in Japan is the meter and **the unit** of weight is the gram.

tanin 〚n〛 another person, others; unrelated persons

① [another person, others]

¶ Please don't do anything that will inconvenience **others.**

② [persons unrelated by blood]

¶ Although those two look a lot alike, **they are unrelated** to each other.

tanjōbi 〚n〛 one's birthday

¶ My **birthday** is March 3.

¶ Tonight [we]'re having a **birthday** celebration for [Miss] Yamada.

tanomu 〚v I〛 ask, request

¶ When **I asked [him]**, [Mr.] Tanaka loaned me some money.

¶ **I asked** a friend to loan me [her]

ら，断られました。(Tomodachi ni nōto o kashite kure to *tanondara*, kotowararemashita.)

notes, but [she] refused.

tanoshii 楽しい〖形〗

¶今日のパーティーはとても楽しかったです。(Kyō no pātii wa totemo *tanoshikatta* desu.)

¶これから歌を歌って，楽しく過ごしましょう。(Kore kara uta o utatte, *tanoshiku* sugoshimashō.)

tanoshii 〖adj〗 pleasant, happy, delightful, enjoyable

¶ Today's party was a lot of **fun.**

¶ Let's have **a good time** singing songs now.

tanoshimu 楽しむ〖動Ⅰ〗

¶上田さんは一人で音楽を聞いて楽しんでいます。(Ueda san wa hitori de ongaku o kiite *tanoshinde* imasu.)

¶夏休みには，山に登ったり海で泳いだりして楽しもうと思っています。(Natsuyasumi ni wa, yama ni nobottari umi de oyoidari shite *tanoshimō* to omotte imasu.)

tanoshimu 〖v I〗 enjoy oneself, take pleasure in

¶ [Mr.] Ueda **is having a good time** listening to music by [him]self.

¶ I plan **to enjoy** summer vacation climbing mountains, swimming at the shore, and so forth.

tansan-gasu 炭酸ガス〖名〗

tansho 短所〖名〗

¶人にはだれでも長所と短所があります。(Hito ni wa dare demo chōsho to *tansho* ga arimasu.)

⇔**chōsho** 長所 ⇒**ketten** 欠点

tansan-gasu 〖n〗 carbon dioxide

tansho 〖n〗 defect, fault, shortcoming, weak point

¶ Everyone has **weak** and strong **points.**

tansū 単数〖名〗

⇔**fukusū** 複数

tansū 〖n〗 singular number, the singular

taoreru 倒れる〖動Ⅱ〗

¶昨日の地震でたくさんの家が倒れました。(Kinō no jishin de takusan no ie ga *taoremashita*.)

¶山田さんは気を失って倒れました。(Yamada san wa ki o ushinatte *taoremashita*.)

taoreru 〖v II〗 fall, fall down, collapse

¶ Many houses **were destroyed** in the earthquake yesterday.

¶ [Mr.] Yamada lost consciousness and **fell to the floor** 〖ground〗.

taoru タオル〘名〙

タオルで顔をふく (*taoru* de kao o fuku)　湯上がり**タオル** (yuagari-*taoru*)

taosu 倒す〘動Ⅰ〙

¶掃除をしていて，花びんを**倒して**しまいました。(Sōji o shite ite, kabin o *taoshite* shimaimashita.)

¶台風でたくさんの木が**倒されました**。(Taifū de takusan no ki ga *taosare-mashita*.)

tara たら〘助動〙

①〔前件が成立した場合にはそれに伴って後件が成立するという関係を表す〕

¶春になっ**たら**，旅行するつもりです。(Haru ni nat*tara*, ryokō suru tsumori desu.)

¶安かっ**たら**買ってもいいですが，高かっ**たら**買いません。(Yasukat*tara* katte mo ii desu ga, takakat*tara* kaimasen.)

¶暑かっ**たら**，上着を脱いでもいいですよ。(Atsukat*tara*, uwagi o nuide mo ii desu yo.)

¶車だっ**たら**10分で行けます。(Kuruma dat*tara* jippun de ikemasu.)

¶「あした雨が降っ**たら**，旅行には行きませんか。」(Ashita ame ga fut*tara*, ryokō ni wa ikimasen ka?) 「いいえ，雨が降っても，行きます。」(Iie, ame ga futte mo, ikimasu.)

→ba ば

②〔前件がもし成立していた場合には

taoru 〖n〗　**towel, toweling**

wipe one's face with **a towel** // a bath **towel**

taosu 〖v I〗　**throw down, knock down**

¶ [I] **knocked over** a vase while cleaning.

¶ Many trees **were blown over** in the typhoon.

-tara 〖auxil〗　**when, if**; a verb ending expressing the conditional

① [indicates that the second clause will be realized if or when the first clause is realized]

¶ I plan to travel **in** the spring.

¶ [I] might buy it **if** it's inexpensive but [I] won't buy it **if** it's expensive.

¶ You may remove your jacket **if** you're hot.

¶ It takes 10 minutes **by** car.

¶ "**If** it rains tomorrow will you give up on your trip?"

"No, [I]'ll go even if it rains."

② [indicates that the second clause would have been realized if the first

後件も成立するという関係を表す]

¶もう少し背が高かった**ら**，バスケットボールをやっていたと思います。
(Mō sukoshi se ga takakat*tara*, basukettobōru o yatte ita to omoimasu.)

¶お医者さんがもう少し早く来てくれ**たら**，父は助かったのに。 (Oishasan ga mō sukoshi hayaku kite kure-*tara*, chichi wa tasukatta noni.)

* 前件には実際には成立しなかったことが来る。

→**ba** ば　**nara** なら

③[願望や示唆などの意味を表す]

¶学生の時にもっと勉強していた**ら**と思います。 (Gakusei no toki ni motto benkyō shite i*tara* to omoimasu.)

¶頭が痛いんでしょう。今日は学校を休んだ**ら**。 (Atama ga itai n deshō? Kyō wa gakkō o yasun*dara*?)

→**ba** ば

④[前件が行われた時に後件が成立したという関係を表す]

¶山田さんと話をしていた**ら**，上田さんが来ました。 (Yamada san to hanashi o shite i*tara*, Ueda san ga kimashita.)

¶銀座を歩いていた**ら**，偶然小学校の時の友達に会いました。 (Ginza o aruite i*tara*, gūzen shōgakkō no toki no tomodachi ni aimashita.)

* 後件には過去・完了を表す「たの形」が来る。

---

clause had been realized]

¶ I think [I] would have played basketball **if** [I] had been a little taller.

¶ My father's life could have been saved **if only** the doctor had come a little sooner.

* The first clause was not actually realized.

③ [expresses a wish or suggestion]

¶ **I wish I had** studied more when I was a student.

¶ You have a headache, don't you? **Why don't you** stay home from school today?

④ [indicates that the second clause is realized when the first clause takes place]

¶ [Mr.] Ueda came **while** I was talking with [Mrs.] Yamada.

¶ I ran into a friend from my elementary school days **when** I was walking along the Ginza.

* The *-ta* form expressing past or completed action is found in the second clause.

→to と

⑤［前件の成立をきっかけとして後件が成立するという関係を表す］

¶一人の赤ちゃんが泣きだし**たら**，ほかの赤ちゃんまで泣きだしました。
(Hitori no akachan ga nakidashi-*tara*, hoka no akachan made nakidashimashita.)

¶部屋の電気をつけ**たら**，窓からたくさんの虫が入ってきました。 (Heya no denki o tsuke*tara*, mado kara takusan no mushi ga haitte kimashita.)

* 前件と後件の主語は異なる。後件には過去・完了を表す「たの形」が来る。

→to と

⑥［前件の成立によって後件のことがらに気づくという関係を表す］

¶箱を開け**たら**，りんごが五つありました。(Hako o ake*tara*, ringo ga itsutsu arimashita.)

¶台風のあと庭へ出てみ**たら**，木や花が倒れていました。 (Taifū no ato niwa e dete mi*tara*, ki ya hana ga taorete imashita.)

¶山の頂上に着い**たら**，遠くに海が見えました。(Yama no chōjō ni tsui-*tara*, tooku ni umi ga miemashita.)

* 後件には「あった (atta)」「～ていた (～te ita)」「見えた (mieta)」などの状態・作用を表す言葉のほかに「音がした (oto ga shita)」「においがした (nioi ga shita)」などの感覚を表す言葉も使い，前件によって後件の

⑤ [indicates that the second clause takes place because of the first clause]

¶ **When** one baby started crying the others started crying too.

¶ **When** [I] turned on the lights inside the room lots of insects flew in through the window.

* The two clauses have different subjects. The *-ta* form expressing past or completed action is found in the second clause.

⑥ [indicates that what comes in the second clause is noticed when the first clause is realized]

¶ [I] opened the box **and** found five apples.

¶ **When** [I] went out into the yard 〚garden〛 after the typhoon, blown-over trees and flowers were lying on the ground.

¶ **When** [we] got to the top of the mountain, [we] were able to see the ocean in the distance.

* The relationship of one being aware of the second clause because of the first clause is expressed by the use in the second clause of words expressing condition or process like *atta*, *-te ita*, and *mieta*; words concerning the physical senses like *oto ga*

ことがらに気づくという関係を表す。前件の主語と後件の主語は異なる。

→to と

⑦〔話題とすることがらを提示するのに使う〕

¶「田中さんはどこにいますか。」(Tanaka san wa doko ni imasu ka?)「田中さんだったら、図書室にいますよ。」(Tanaka san dat*tara*, toshoshitsu ni imasu yo.)

¶「辞書はどこにあるか知りませんか。」(Jisho wa doko ni aru ka shirimasen ka?)「辞書だったら、あのテーブルの上にありますよ。」(Jisho dat*tara*, ano tēburu no ue ni arimasu yo.)

＊普通「名詞＋だったら (dattara)」の形で使う。

→nara なら

tari たり〖助〗

¶昨日は、映画を見たり買い物をしたりしました。(Kinō wa, eiga o mi*tari* kaimono o shi*tari* shimashita.)

¶海で泳いだり貝を拾ったりして遊びました。(Umi de oyoi*dari* kai o hirot*tari* shite asobimashita.)

＊普通「～たり ～たりする (～tari ～tari suru)」の形で使う。動作を例示的に述べて代表させ、その他の動作もあることを表す。「ぶ (bu)」「ぐ (gu)」「む (mu)」「ぬ (nu)」で終わるⅠ型動詞のあとに「たり (tari)」が来る場合には「だり (dari)」となる。

tariru 足りる〖動Ⅱ〗

¶時間が足りなくて、最後の問題はで

shita, *nioi ga shita*; and so on. The subjects of the two clauses are different.

⑦ [used to point out the topic]

¶ "Where is [Mr.] Tanaka?"

"**[Mr.] Tanaka?** Oh, [he]'s in the library."

¶ "Do you know where the dictionary is?"

"**It's** over there on the table."

＊ Generally used in the pattern "noun + *dattara*."

-tari 〖part〗 now ~ now ~; now ~ and then ~; sometimes ~ sometimes ~

¶ Yesterday I **saw** a movie, **went** shopping, **etc.**

¶ [I] relaxed at the shore, **sometimes** swimming **and sometimes** picking up shells.

＊ Usually used in the pattern "-*tari* ~ -*tari suru*." It cites actions as representative examples and implies there were other actions as well. -*tari* changes to -*dari* in the case of Type I verbs ending in -*bu*, -*gu*, -*mu*, or -*nu*.

tariru 〖v II〗 be enough, be sufficient, suffice

763

きませんでした。(Jikan ga *tarinakute*, saigo no mondai wa dekimasen deshita.)

¶生活費は1か月10万円では足りません。(Seikatsuhi wa ikkagetsu jūman'en de wa *tarimasen*.)

¶ [I] **ran out** of time and wasn't able to do the last question.

¶ One hundred thousand yen a month **is not enough** to live on.

tashika 確か〖副, 形動〗

1〖副〗

¶山田さんがうちへ来たのは, 確か先月でした。(Yamada san ga uchi e kita no wa, *tashika* sengetsu deshita.)

¶上田さんは確か先月会社を辞めたはずですよ。 (Ueda san wa *tashika* sengetsu kaisha o yameta hazu desu yo.)

2〖形動〗

¶あの人の言うことは確かです。(Ano hito no iu koto wa *tashika* desu.)

¶父が何時に帰ってくるか, 確かな時間はわかりません。(Chichi ga nanji ni kaette kuru ka, *tashika* na jikan wa wakarimasen.)

¶あの人は確かに上田さんです。
(Ano hito wa *tashika* ni Ueda san desu.)

tashika 〖adv, adj-v〗 **probably, I think; certain, certainly; accurate, exact; reliable, trustworthy**

1 〖adv〗 probably, I think, if I am correct

¶ **If I remember correctly,** it was last month that [Mr.] Yamada visited [our] home.

¶ **I think** that it was last month that [Miss] Ueda quit the company.

2 〖adj-v〗 certain; exact; reliable

¶ **You can believe** what [he] says.

¶ I don't know **exactly** what time my father will return home.

¶ **I'm certain** that is [Mrs.] Ueda.

tashikameru 確かめる〖動Ⅱ〗

¶これが正しいかどうか確かめてください。(Kore ga tadashii ka dō ka *tashikamete* kudasai.)

¶飛行機が到着する時間を電話で確かめました。(Hikōki ga tōchaku suru jikan o denwa de *tashikamemashita*.)

tashikameru 〖v Ⅱ〗 **make sure, check, verify**

¶ Please **check** whether this is correct or not.

¶ [I] **verified** the arrival time of the airplane on the telephone.

tassuru 達する〖動Ⅲ〗

tassuru 〖v Ⅲ〗 **reach, arrive at, attain, achieve**

¶5時間も登って、ようやく山の頂上に達しました。(Gojikan mo nobotte, yōyaku yama no chōjō ni *tasshimashita*.)

¶ [We] at last **reached** the top of the mountain after five hours of climbing.

¶先月は工場の生産が目標に達しませんでした。(Sengetsu wa kōjō no seisan ga mokuhyō ni *tasshimasen* deshita.)

¶ Factory production **failed to reach** the target figure last month.

tasu 足す〚動 I〛

¶1足す1は2です。(Ichi *tasu* ichi wa ni desu.)

tasu 〚v I〛 **add**

¶ One **plus** one is two.

¶味が薄いので、しょう油を足しました。(Aji ga usui node, shōyu o *tashimashita*.)

⇔hiku 引く

¶ The flavor was too weak so [I] **added** some soy sauce.

tasū 多数〚名〛

多数決 (*tasū*ketsu)

¶この考えに多数の人が賛成しました。(Kono kangae ni *tasū* no hito ga sansei shimashita.)

tasū 〚n〛 **a large number; a majority**

a **majority** decision, decision **by majority**

¶ **A majority** agreed with this view.

tasukeru 助ける〚動 II〛

①［救助する］

¶上田さんは川に落ちた子供を助けました。(Ueda san wa kawa ni ochita kodomo o *tasukemashita*.)

tasukeru 〚v II〛 **save, rescue; give relief to; help, aid**

① [save, rescue]

¶ [Mr.] Ueda **rescued** a child that had fallen in the river.

¶「助けてくれ。」という叫び声がしました。("*Tasukete* kure!" to iu sakebigoe ga shimashita.)

¶ There was a voice crying out, "**Help, help!**"

②［困っている人や苦しんでいる人などに力を貸してやる］

¶わたしは体の不自由な人を助けるために働きたいと思います。(Watashi wa karada no fujiyū na hito o *tasukeru* tame ni hatarakitai to

② [give relief to, help someone in trouble]

¶ I want to work **to help** the physically handicapped.

omoimasu.)

③[手伝う]

¶上田さんはお兄さんの仕事を助けて
います。 (Ueda san wa oniisan no
shigoto o *tasukete* imasu.)

tatakau 戦う〖動Ⅰ〗

①[試合をする]

¶AチームはBチームと戦って勝ちま
した。 (Ē-chiimu wa Bii-chiimu to
tatakatte kachimashita.)

②[戦争をする]

¶青年たちは民族の独立と自由のため
に戦いました。 (Seinentachi wa
minzoku no dokuritsu to jiyū no
tame ni *tatakaimashita*.)

tataku たたく〖動Ⅰ〗

手をたたく (te o *tataku*) 肩をたた
く (kata o *tataku*) ドアをたたく
(doa o *tataku*)

¶だれかが戸をたたいていますよ。
(Dare ka ga to o *tataite* imasu yo.)
¶子供は悪いことをして，お母さんに
おしりをたたかれました。 (Kodomo
wa warui koto o shite, okāsan ni
oshiri o *tatakaremashita*.)

tatamu 畳む〖動Ⅰ〗

ハンカチを畳む (hankachi o *tatamu*)
布団を畳む (futon o *tatamu*)
¶毛布をきちんと畳んでください。
(Mōfu o kichinto *tatande* kudasai.)
¶シーツや下着を畳んで，引き出しに
しまいました。 (Shiitsu ya shitagi o
tatande, hikidashi ni shimaimashita.)

③ [help, aid, support]

¶ [Mr.] Ueda **helps** [his] older
brother in his work.

tatakau 〖v I〗 contest, play; fight,
struggle against

① [contest, play]

¶ Team A **played** Team B and won.

② [fight, struggle against] ·

¶ The youths **fought** for liberty and
their country's independence.

tataku 〖v I〗 strike, hit, knock,
slap, etc.

clap one's hands // **tap** someone on
the shoulder; massage someone's
shoulders by **tapping** with one's fists
// **knock** on a door

¶ Someone **is knocking** at the door.
¶ The children did something bad
and **were spanked** by their mother.

tatamu 〖v I〗 fold, fold up

fold a handkerchief // **fold up** *futon*
bedding, **put away** the bedding
¶ Please **fold** the blankets **up** neatly.

¶ [I] **folded up** the sheets and underwear and put them away in the drawers.

tate 縦〖名〗

縦10センチ横5センチの紙 (*tate* jissenchi yoko gosenchi no kami)

¶日本語には，縦書きと横書きの二つの書き方があります。 (Nihongo ni wa, *tate*gaki to yokogaki no futatsu no kakikata ga arimasu.)

⇔yoko 横

tatemono 建物〖名〗

¶あの建物は何ですか。(Ano *tatemono* wa nan desu ka?)

¶外は暑いですが，この建物の中は涼しいです。 (Soto wa atsui desu ga, kono *tatemono* no naka wa suzushii desu.)

tateru 立てる〖動Ⅱ〗

①[横になっていた物や倒れていた物を起こす，縦にまっすぐな状態にする]

国旗を立てる (kokki o *tateru*)

¶「芝生に入らないでください。」という札が立ててあります。 ("Shibafu ni hairanaide kudasai." to iu fuda ga *tatete* arimasu.)

②[計画や予定を考えて作る]

案を立てる (an o *tateru*)　予定を立てる (yotei o *tateru*)

¶もう夏休みの旅行の計画を立てましたか。 (Mō natsuyasumi no ryokō no keikaku o *tatemashita* ka?)

③[声や音を出す]

声を立てる (koe o *tateru*)

¶赤ちゃんが寝ていますから，大きな音を立てないでください。 (Akachan ga nete imasu kara, ookina oto o

tate 〚n〛 length, height; vertical, lengthwise

paper 10 centimeters **long** and 5 centimeters wide`

¶ Japanese can be written two ways—**up and down** or left to right.

tatemono 〚n〛 a building

¶ What is that **building** over there?

¶ It's hot outside but cool inside this **building.**

tateru 〚v Ⅱ〛 erect, raise; form, establish

① [erect, raise, put up]

raise the national flag

¶ A sign **is up** reading "Keep off the grass."

② [form, establish, lay down]

frame a plan // **map out** a program

¶ **Have** [you] **planned** [your] summer vacation trip yet?

③ [raise (a voice), make (a noise)]

cry out, **raise** one's voice

¶ The baby is sleeping so please **don't make** any loud noises.

tatenaide kudasai.)

④［感情などをたかぶらせる］

¶山田さんは，田中さんが約束を守らなかったので，たいへん腹を立てています。(Yamada san wa, Tanaka san ga yakusoku o mamoranakatta node, taihen hara o *tatete* imasu.)

*普通「腹を立てる (hara o tateru)」の形で使う。

tateru 建てる〖動Ⅱ〗

¶田中さんは最近家を建てました。(Tanaka san wa saikin ie o *tatemashita*.)

¶このお寺は約500年前に建てられました。(Kono otera wa yaku gohyakunen mae ni *tateraremashita*.)

tatoe たとえ〖名〗

たとえ話 (*tatoe*banashi)

¶わかりにくいことでも，たとえを使うとわかりやすいです。(Wakarinikui koto demo, *tatoe* o tsukau to wakariyasui desu.)

tatoe たとえ〖副〗

¶たとえ両親に反対されても，わたしはあの人と結婚します。(*Tatoe* ryōshin ni hantai sarete mo, watashi wa ano hito to kekkon shimasu.)

¶たとえ雨が降っても，ハイキングには出かけます。(*Tatoe* ame ga futte mo, haikingu ni wa dekakemasu.)

＊普通「たとえ〜ても (tatoe〜te mo)」の形で使う。「たとい (tatoi)」とも言う。

④ [be angry, lose one's temper]

¶ [Mr.] Yamada **is** very **angry** because [Mr.] Tanaka broke [his] promise.

* Generally used in the pattern "*hara o tateru*."

tateru 〖v II〗 build, construct, erect

¶ [Mr.] Tanaka **has** recently **built** a house.

¶ This temple **was erected** approximately five hundred years ago.

tatoe 〖n〗 simile, metaphor, fable, parable, proverb, example, illustration

fable, allegory, parable

¶ Even something hard to understand is easier to understand if one uses **an example.**

tatoe 〖adv〗 if, even if, although, supposing that, granted that

¶ I would marry [him] **even if** my parents were opposed.

¶ [I] will go hiking **even if** it should rain.

＊ Usually used in the pattern "*tatoe ~ -te mo.*" The form *tatoi* is also used.

tatoeba 例えば〚副〛

¶わたしは、古い町、例えば京都のような所に住みたいです。 (Watashi wa, furui machi, *tatoeba* Kyōto no yō na tokoro ni sumitai desu.)

¶料理に味をつけるものにはいろいろあります。例えば、塩、砂糖、しょう油などです。(Ryōri ni aji o tsukeru mono ni wa iroiro arimasu. *Tatoeba*, shio, satō, shōyu nado desu.)

tatsu 建つ〚動Ⅰ〛

¶東京には高いビルが次々に建っています。(Tōkyō ni wa takai biru ga tsugitsugi ni *tatte* imasu.)

¶この家が建ってから、もう 30 年になります。 (Kono ie ga *tatte* kara, mō sanjūnen ni narimasu.)

tatsu 立つ〚動Ⅰ〛

①[縦にまっすぐになる，立ち上がる]

¶田中さん，ちょっと立ってください。(Tanaka san, chotto *tatte* kudasai.)

¶電車がこんでいたので、ずっと立っていました。(Densha ga konde ita node, zutto *tatte* imashita.)

¶「ここで泳いではいけません。」という立て札が立っています。("Koko de oyoide wa ikemasen." to iu tatefuda ga *tatte* imasu.)

②[感情などがたかぶる]

¶悪口を言われて、腹が立ちました。(Warukuchi o iwarete, hara ga *tachimashita*.)

* 普通「腹が立つ (hara ga tatsu)」の形で使う。

tatoeba 〚adv〛 **for example, for instance, such as**

¶ I would like to live in an old place **such as** Kyoto.

¶ There are various seasonings used in cooking. **For example,** salt, sugar, soy sauce, etc.

tatoi ☞ **tatoe**

tatsu 〚v I〛 **be built, stand**

¶ Tall buildings **are going up** one after the other in Tokyo.

¶ Thirty years have passed since this house **was erected.**

tatsu 〚v I〛 **stand, stand up; leave, depart**

① [stand, stand up, be put up]

¶ [Mr.] Tanaka, **stand up** a moment please!

¶ [I] **stood** all the way as the train was crowded.

¶ A sign **is up** reading "No swimming here."

② [get angry, lose one's temper]

¶ [I] was insulted and **got angry.**

* Usually used in the pattern "*hara ga tatsu*."

③〔出発する〕

¶東京を朝の7時に立って，正午にこちらに着きました。(Tōkyō o asa no shichiji ni *tatte*, shōgo ni kochira ni tsukimashita.)

tatsu たつ〖動Ⅰ〗

¶日本語を習い始めてから，もう1年たちました。(Nihongo o naraihajimete kara, mō ichinen *tachimashita*.)

tayori 便り〖名〗

¶兄からはこのごろ便りが全然ありません。(Ani kara wa konogoro *tayori* ga zenzen arimasen.)

¶息子さんから便りがありますか。(Musukosan kara *tayori* ga arimasu ka?)

⇒tegami 手紙

tayoru 頼る〖動Ⅰ〗

¶あの人は親に頼らないで，自分で働いて大学を卒業しました。(Ano hito wa oya ni *tayoranaide*, jibun de hataraite daigaku o sotsugyō shimashita.)

¶わたしは兄を頼って東京に来ました。(Watashi wa ani o *tayotte* Tōkyō ni kimashita.)

tazuneru 尋ねる〖動Ⅱ〗

¶交番で道を尋ねました。(Kōban de michi o *tazunemashita*.)

tazuneru 訪ねる〖動Ⅱ〗

¶あした，息子の家を訪ねようと思っています。(Ashita, musuko no ie o *tazuneyō* to omotte imasu.)

③ [leave, depart, start, set out]

¶ [We] **left** Tokyo at seven in the morning and arrived here at noon.

tatsu 〖v I〗 pass, pass by, elapse

¶ A year **has passed** since [I] started studying Japanese.

tayori 〖n〗 correspondence, a letter, word, news

¶ I haven't **heard anything** from my (older) brother lately.

¶ **Do you hear regularly** from your son?

tayoru 〖v I〗 depend on, rely on, trust to

¶ [He] worked [his] way through college **without leaning** on [his] parents.

¶ I came to Tokyo **counting on the assistance** of my older brother.

tazuneru 〖v II〗 ask, inquire

¶ [I] **asked** the way at a police box.

tazuneru 〖v II〗 call on, visit, pay a visit to

¶ I plan **to go visit** my son tomorrow.

¶昨日の夜，田中さんが訪ねてきました。(Kinō no yoru, Tanaka san ga *tazunete* kimashita.)

te 手〖名〗

右手 (migi*te*)　左手 (hidari*te*)　両手 (ryō*te*)　手を挙げる (*te* o ageru)　手を振る (*te* o furu)　手をたたく (*te* o tataku)

¶御飯を食べる前には，手を洗いましょう。(Gohan o taberu mae ni wa, *te* o araimashō.)

te て〖助〗

①[前のことがらとあとのことがらが並列の関係にあることを表す]

¶田中さんは背が高くて，目が大きくて，髪が長いです。(Tanaka san wa se ga takaku*te*, me ga ookiku*te*, kami ga nagai desu.)

¶あの白い服を着て眼鏡をかけた人はだれですか。(Ano shiroi fuku o ki*te* megane o kaketa hito wa dare desu ka?)

②[前のことがらとあとのことがらが対比の関係にあることを表す]

¶ここは夏は涼しくて，冬は暖かいです。(Koko wa natsu wa suzushiku*te*, fuyu wa atatakai desu.)

¶兄は太っていて，弟のほうはやせています。(Ani wa futotte i*te*, otōto no hō wa yasete imasu.)

③[ものごとが次々に成立するという関係を表す]

¶わたしは毎朝，7時に起きて，顔を洗って，御飯を食べて，8時に家を出

¶ [Miss] Tanaka **called on** [us] yesterday evening.

te 〖n〗 hand, arm

the right **hand,** to the right, right-**handed** // the left **hand,** to the left, left-**handed** // both **hands,** with both **hands;** both **arms** // raise **one's hand,** hold up **one's hands;** raise **one's hand** against someone; give up // wave **one's hand** // clap **one's hands**

¶ One should wash **one's hands** before eating.

-te 〖part〗 a particle used to form the -*te* form of the verb

① [indicates that items are in a parallel relationship]

¶ [Mr.] Tanaka **is tall, has** large eyes, **and** has long hair.

¶ Who is that person **dressed** in white **and** wearing glasses?

② [indicates that items are in opposition to each other]

¶ It **is cool** here in summer **but** warm in winter.

¶ My older brother **is fat but** my younger brother is thin.

③ [indicates that items follow each other in sequence]

¶ Every morning I **get up** at seven o'clock, **wash** my face, **eat** break-

ます。(Watashi wa maiasa, shichiji ni oki*te*, kao o arat*te*, gohan o tabe*te*, hachiji ni ie o demasu.)

¶この道をまっすぐ行って、右へ曲がると、駅の前に出ます。(Kono michi o massugu it*te*, migi e magaru to, eki no mae ni demasu.)

④［ものごとが時間的に前後しているという関係を表す］

¶あなたは日本へ来てから、もう何年になりますか。(Anata wa Nihon e ki*te* kara, mō nannen ni narimasu ka?)

¶わたしは朝新聞を読んでから、学校へ行きます。(Watashi wa asa shinbun o yon*de* kara, gakkō e ikimasu.)

¶北海道へは5年前に行って以来、行っていません。(Hokkaidō e wa go-nen mae ni it*te* irai, itte imasen.)

* 普通「から (kara)」「以来 (irai)」「以後 (igo)」などといっしょに使う。

⑤［二つの動作・作用が同時に行われるという関係を表す］

¶考えごとをして歩いていたら、自動車にひかれそうになりました。(Kangaegoto o shi*te* aruite itara, jidōsha ni hikaresō ni narimashita.)

¶選手は手を振って入場してきました。(Senshu wa te o fut*te* nyūjō shite kimashita.)

¶川の水は音を立てて流れています。(Kawa no mizu wa oto o tate*te* nagarete imasu.)

fast, **and leave** the house at eight o'clock.

¶ If you **go** straight along this street **and** then turn right, you will come out in front of the station.

④ [indicates chronological order]

¶ How many years have you been in Japan (literally, How many years has it been **since you came** to Japan)?

¶ I go to school in the morning **after reading** the newspaper.

¶ [I] haven't been to Hokkaido **since going** there five years ago.

* Usually used with *kara, irai, igo*, etc.

⑤ [indicates that two items occur simultaneously]

¶ **While** walking along **deep in thought**, [I] was almost hit by a car.

¶ The players came onto the field ⟦court, ice, etc.⟧ **waving** their hands.

¶ The water in the river is flowing along **burbling**.

* 動作・作用の主体は同じである。

→**nagara ながら**

⑥[原因と結果の関係を表す]

¶昨日は頭が痛くて、学校を休みました。 (Kinō wa atama ga itaku*te*, gakkō o yasumimashita.)

¶この荷物は重くて、わたしには持てません。 (Kono nimotsu wa omoku*te*, watashi ni wa motemasen.)

¶雨にぬれて、風邪を引いてしまいました。 (Ame ni nure*te*, kaze o hiite shimaimashita.)

* 普通、「て (te)」のあとには「〜う [よう] (〜u [yo])」などの意志、「〜なさい (〜nasai)」などの命令、「〜てもいい (te mo ii)」などの許可、「〜てください (〜te kudasai)」などの依頼などの言い方は来ない。

→**node ので kara から**

⑦[前のことがらがあとのことがらの手段・方法となっているという関係を表す]

¶遅くなったから、タクシーに乗って帰りました。 (Osoku natta kara, takushii ni not*te* kaerimashita.)

¶わからない言葉は辞書を引いて調べなさい。 (Wakaranai kotoba wa jisho o hii*te* shirabenasai.)

⑧[前のことがらがあとのことがらの行なわれる状態であることを表す]

¶中村さんは昨日赤いセーターを着て町を歩いていました。 (Nakamura san wa kinō akai sētā o ki*te* machi o aruite imashita.)

* The subject of the two clauses is the same.

⑥ [indicates a cause-and-effect relationship]

¶ [I] stayed home from school yesterday **with** a headache.

¶ This load 〚package, case, etc.〛 **is so heavy that** I can't carry it alone.

¶ [I] **got wet** in the rain **and** caught a cold.

* Generally this *-te* is not followed by statements of intention with *-ō* 〚*-yō*〛, orders with *-nasai*, statements of permission with *-te mo ii*, requests with *-te kudasai*, etc.

⑦ [used when the *-te* clause is the way or means of accomplishing the following clause]

¶ As it was late [I] **went** home **by** taxi (literally, **by riding** in a taxi).

¶ **Look** words you don't understand **up** in the dictionary (literally, Investigate words you don't understand **by looking them up** in the dictionary).

⑧ [used when the *-te* clause describes the condition or state in which the following clause occurs]

¶ Yesterday [Mr.] Nakamura was walking around town **wearing** a red sweater.

¶転びますから，そんな重い荷物を持って走らないでください。 (Korobimasu kara, sonna omoi nimotsu o mot*te* hashiranaide kudasai.)

¶ Please don't run **while carrying** such a heavy load 〖package, etc.〗— you'll fall.

⑨ [前のことがらがあとのことがらの判断のよりどころであることを表す]

⑨ [used when the -te clause forms the basis of the following clause]

¶今年は去年に比べて，だいぶ暑いです。 (Kotoshi wa kyonen ni kurabe*te*, daibu atsui desu.)

¶ This year is quite hot **compared** to last year.

¶電話の声から考えて，田中さんはたいへん心配しているようです。 (Denwa no koe kara kangae*te*, Tanaka san wa taihen shinpai shite iru yō desu.)

¶ **Judging** from [his] voice on the telephone, [Mr.] Tanaka is very worried.

→**to** と　**ba** ば

⑩ [前のことがらが成立するとあとのことがらも成立するという関係を表す]

⑩ [indicates the second clause is realized when the first clause is realized]

¶兄弟はわたしを入れて5人です。 (Kyōdai wa watashi o ire*te* gonin desu.)

¶ **Including** myself, there are five of us children.

¶3に2を足して，いくつになりますか。 (San ni ni o tashi*te*, ikutsu ni narimasu ka?)

¶ How much is two **plus** three (literally, three **plus** two)?

→**to** と　**ba** ば　**tara** たら

⑪ [あとのことがらが前のことがらから予期されることとは逆の結果であるという関係を表す]

⑪ [indicates the second clause is the opposite of what might be expected from the first clause]

¶隣に住んでいて，あの人とは話をしたこともありません。 (Tonari ni sunde i*te*, ano hito to wa hanashi o shita koto mo arimasen.)

¶ [I] **live** next door to [him], **but** [I]'ve never talked with [him].

¶そんなにたくさんのお金をもらっていて，まだ足りないのですか。 (Sonna

¶ **You're getting** all that money **and** it's still not enough?

ni takusan no okane o moratte i*te*,
mada tarinai no desu ka?)

→noni のに

＊ 二つのことがらを結び合わせる役
目をするが，前のことがらとあとのこ
とがらとの意味内容の関係によってい
ろいろの意味が生じてくる。

＊ 動詞の「ての形」のあとに補助動
詞「いる (iru)」「ある (aru)」「おく
(oku)」「みる (miru)」「しまう (shimau)」「いく (iku)」「くる (kuru)」
「あげる (ageru)」「もらう (morau)」
「くれる (kureru)」などを続けて，動
詞にいろいろな意味をつけ加える。

＊ 動詞の「終止の形」の語尾が「ぶ
(bu)」「ぐ (gu)」「む (mu)」「ぬ
(nu)」で終わる I 型動詞のあとに「て
(te)」が来る場合には「で (de)」と
なる。

＊ *-te* serves to join together two
items but has many different meanings depending on the context and
the meaning of those two items.

＊ When the *-te* form of a verb is followed by such helping verbs as *iru,
aru, oku, miru, shimau, iku, kuru,
ageru, morau,* or *kureru,* different
meanings result. (See also the individual entries for these helping
verbs.)

＊ *-te* becomes *-de* in the case of
Type I verbs ending in *-bu (yobu→
yonde), -gu (oyogu→oyoide), -mu
(yomu→ yonde),* or *-nu (shinu→
shinde).*

tearai 手洗い〚名〛

¶ちょっとお尋ねしますが，お手洗い
はどこですか。 (Chotto otazune
shimasu ga, *otearai* wa doko desu
ka?)

⇨benjo 便所 toire トイレ

tearai 〚n〛 lavatory, rest room,
Ladies' Room, Men's Room

¶ Excuse me, but could you please
tell me where **the rest rooms** are?

tebukuro 手袋〚名〛

手袋をする (*tebukuro* o suru) 手
袋をはめる (*tebukuro* o hameru)
革の手袋 (kawa no *tebukuro*)

tebukuro 〚n〛 gloves, mittens

wear **gloves** // put on **gloves** //
leather **gloves**

tēburu テーブル〚名〛

¶テーブルの上をかたづけてください。
(*Tēburu* no ue o katazukete kudasai.)

tēburu 〚n〛 a table

¶ Please clear off **the table.**

techō 手帳〚名〛

techō 〚n〛 notebook, memorandum
book

¶わたしは約束したことや予定などはいつも手帳に書いておきます。(Watashi wa yakusoku shita koto ya yotei nado wa itsu mo *techō* ni kaite okimasu.)

¶ I always note appointments, scheduled events, etc., in **a pocket schedule**.

tegami 手紙〖名〗

¶母に手紙を書きました。 (Haha ni *tegami* o kakimashita.)

¶この手紙を出してきてください。(Kono *tegami* o dashite kite kudasai.)

⇨**tayori 便り**

tegami 〖n〗 **a letter, mail**

¶ I wrote **a letter** to my mother.

¶ Please go and mail this **letter** for me.

tehon 手本〖名〗

¶先生が黒板に書いた字を手本にして,漢字を習います。 (Sensei ga kokuban ni kaita ji o *tehon* ni shite, kanji o naraimasu.)

¶お手本のとおりにきれいに書いてください。 (O*tehon* no toori ni kirei ni kaite kudasai.)

tehon 〖n〗 **model, example**

¶ We learn *kanji* using the ones our teacher writes on the blackboard for **our model**.

¶ Please write it carefully following **the sample**.

teido 程度〖名〗

①[他のものと比べた場合の度合い]

程度が違う (*teido* ga chigau) 程度が低い (*teido* ga hikui)

¶この問題は, 中学生には程度が高すぎませんか。 (Kono mondai wa, chūgakusei ni wa *teido* ga takasugimasen ka?)

②[だいたいの 距離・時間・量などを表す]

¶旅行の費用は5万円程度でしょう。(Ryokō no hiyō wa goman'en *teido* deshō.)

¶この問題について5枚程度のレポー

teido 〖n〗 **grade, standard, level; degree, extent**

① [grade, standard, level]

differ in **degree,** differ in **quality** // be of a low **standard**

¶ Isn't this problem **too difficult** for middle school students?

② [degree, extent]

¶ The expenses for the trip **shouldn't exceed** fifty thousand yen.

¶ Please write a report **of about** five

トを書いてください。(Kono mondai ni tsuite gomai *teido* no repōto o kaite kudasai.)

teikiken　定期券〚名〛

¶わたしはいつも6か月の定期券を買います。(Watashi wa itsu mo rokkagetsu no *teikiken* o kaimasu.)
＊「定期 (teiki)」とも言う。

teikō　抵抗〚名，〜する〛

抵抗を受ける (*teikō* o ukeru)
¶あの人たちは，外国の軍隊が来た時抵抗して戦った人たちです。(Ano hitotachi wa, gaikoku no guntai ga kita toki *teikō* shite tatakatta hitotachi desu.)

teinei　丁寧〚形動〛

①〔礼儀正しい〕
¶帽子をとって，丁寧にあいさつしました。(Bōshi o totte, *teinei* ni aisatsu shimashita.)
¶先生には丁寧な言葉を使います。(Sensei ni wa *teinei* na kotoba o tsukaimasu.)

②〔親切で行き届いている様子〕
¶上田先生はいつも丁寧に教えてくださいます。(Ueda sensei wa itsu mo *teinei* ni oshiete kudasaimasu.)

③〔注意してものごとをする様子〕
¶もっと字を丁寧に書きなさい。(Motto ji o *teinei* ni kakinasai.)

teiryūjo　停留所〚名〛

¶この辺りにバスの停留所はありませんか。(Kono atari ni basu no *teiryūjo* wa arimasen ka?)

pages about this matter.

teikiken 〚n〛 commuting pass, season pass

¶ I always buy a six-month **commuter's pass**.

＊ Variant: *teiki*.

teikō 〚n, ~*suru*〛 resistance, opposition

meet with **opposition**

¶ They **resisted** and fought when the foreign troops came.

teinei 〚adj-v〛 polite; conscientious; careful

① [polite, civil, courteous]

¶ [He] raised [his] hat and gave a **polite** greeting.

¶ [I] use **polite** language toward [my] teacher.

② [conscientious, thorough]

¶ Professor Ueda always teaches **conscientiously** ⟦explains **thoroughly**⟧.

③ [careful]

¶ Please write more **carefully** ⟦**clearly**⟧.

teiryūjo 〚n〛 stopping place, stop, station

¶ Is there a bus **stop** around here?

teki　敵〖名〗

敵と戦う (teki to tatakau)　敵を追う (teki o ou)

¶敵が来たので，村の人たちはみんな逃げました。 (Teki ga kita node, mura no hitotachi wa minna nigemashita.)

-teki　-的〖尾〗

¶わたしには科学的な知識がないから，この本を読んでも全然わからないでしょう。 (Watashi ni wa kagakuteki na chishiki ga nai kara, kono hon o yonde mo zenzen wakaranai deshō.)

¶富士山は男性的な山だと思いませんか。(Fujisan wa danseiteki na yama da to omoimasen ka?)

¶部屋の中を徹底的に調べてみましたが，わたしのお金は見つかりませんでした。 (Heya no naka o tetteiteki ni shirabete mimashita ga, watashi no okane wa mitsukarimasen deshita.)

¶教育的な立場から見れば，子供にまんがばかり見せるのはよくないと思います。(Kyōikuteki na tachiba kara mireba, kodomo ni manga bakari miseru no wa yoku nai to omoimasu.)

＊普通，名詞について形容動詞の語幹を作り，あるものについての，ある性質を持つ，ある状態にある，あることをする上での，などの意味を表す。

tekitō　適当〖形動〗

teki [[n]]　enemy, foe

fight with **the enemy** // pursue **the enemy**

¶ Everyone in the village fled because **the enemy** was coming.

-teki [[suf]]　-ic, -ical

¶ Since I don't know anything **about** science I probably couldn't understand this book even if I did try to read it.

¶ Don't you think Mount Fuji is a "mascu**line**" (i.e., sharp and rugged vs. gently rounded) mountain?

¶ I searched the room thorough**ly** but couldn't find my money.

¶ From an education**al** standpoint, I don't think it's good for children to only watch cartoons.

＊ -teki generally converts a noun to an adjective-verb and conveys the meaning of having a certain character, being in a certain state, etc.

tekitō [[adj-v]]　fit, suitable, proper, appropriate

¶適当な例を挙げて説明してください。
(Tekitō na rei o agete setsumei
shite kudasai.)

¶下宿したいのですが、なかなか適当
な部屋が見つかりません。(Geshuku
shitai no desu ga, nakanaka tekitō
na heya ga mitsukarimasen.)

tekkyō 鉄橋〖名〗

¶汽車が鉄橋を渡っています。(Kisha
ga tekkyō o watatte imasu.)

¶この川には鉄橋が架かっています。
(Kono kawa ni wa tekkyō ga kakatte imasu.)

te mo ても〖助〗

①〔前件とはかかわりなく後件が成立
するという関係を表す〕

¶あなたがいくら待っても、春子さん
は来ないでしょう。(Anata ga ikura
matte mo, Haruko san wa konai
deshō.)

¶「あしたは雨が降ったら、行きません
か。」 (Ashita wa ame ga futtara,
ikimasen ka?)「いいえ、雨が降って
も、行くつもりです。」(Iie, ame ga
futte mo, iku tsumori desu.)

¶勉強はつらくても、我慢しなければ
なりませんよ。 (Benkyō wa tsura-
kute mo, gaman shinakereba narimasen yo.)

*普通、後件には「～でしょう(～ de-
shō)」などの推量、「～う［よう］(～
u［yō］)」などの意志、「～なければ
ならない(～nakereba naranai)」な
どの義務などの言い方が来る。また、

tekkyō 〖n〗 iron bridge, railway bridge

¶ The train is passing over **a bridge.**

¶ This river is spanned by **an iron railway bridge.**

-te mo 〖part〗 no matter how, however, even if

① [indicates that the second clause is realized unrelated to the first clause]

¶ **No matter** how long you wait, Haruko probably won't be coming.

¶ "Will you put off going tomorrow if it rains?"

"No, I plan to go **even if** it rains."

¶ **Even if** studying is hard, you must keep at it.

* Usually followed in the second clause by suppositions with ~ deshō, statements of intent with -ō 〖-yō〗, of obligation with -nakereba naranai, etc. The -ta form of the verb express-

-te mo

後件には過去・完了を表す「たの形」は来ない。

→to と ba ば tara たら

② [前件から期待されることは逆の結果が後件で成立するという関係を表す]

¶この子はいくらしかっても勉強しません。(Kono ko wa ikura shikat*te mo* benkyō shimasen.)

¶田中さんは，わたしが呼んでも返事もしませんでした。(Tanaka san wa, watashi ga yon*de mo* henji mo shimasen deshita.)

* 既に成立したことがらを言い，そのことがらから当然期待される結果とは逆のことをあとに続ける場合に使う。

③ [前件は実際には成立しなかったことを述べてその成立とはかかわりなく後件が成立するという関係を表す]

¶上田さんがあの大学の入学試験を受けても，合格できなかったでしょう。(Ueda san ga ano daigaku no nyūgaku-shiken o uke*te mo*, gōkaku dekinakatta deshō.)

¶もし雨が降っても，昨日は出かけるつもりでした。(Moshi ame ga fut*te mo*, kinō wa dekakeru tsumori deshita.)

¶「お金があれば，車を買いましたか。」(Okane ga areba, kuruma o kaimashita ka?)「いいえ，お金があっても，車は買いませんでした。」(Iie, okane ga at*te mo*, kuruma wa kaimasen deshita.)

ing past or completed action is not found in the second clause.

② [indicates that the second clause is the opposite of what might be expected from the first clause]

¶ This child won't study **no matter** how much [he] is scolded.

¶ **Even though** I called to [him], [Mr.] Tanaka didn't answer.

* Used when stating something that has already happened in the first clause and following it with a result opposite to what is expected or natural.

③ [used when the first clause is something that didn't actually happen; indicates that the second clause is realized unrelated to it]

¶ **Even if** [Mr.] Ueda had taken the entrance exam for that university, [he] probably wouldn't have passed it.

¶ I planned to go out yesterday **even in the case of** rain.

¶ "Would you have bought a car if you had had the money for it?"

"No, I would not have bought a car **even if** I had had the money."

* 普通，後件には「～でしょう（～
deshō）」などの推量，「～う［よう］
（～u［yō］）などの意志などの言い方
が来る。また，過去・完了を表す「た
の形」を使う。
↔to と　ba ば　tara たら
④［許可の意味を表す］
¶あしたは休んでもいいです。(Ashita
wa yasun*de mo* ii desu.)
¶鉛筆で書いてもかまいません。(En-
pitsu de kai*te mo* kamaimasen.)
*「～てもいい（～te mo ii）」「～ても
かまわない（～te mo kamawanai）」
の形で使う。
↔(～**te wa**) ikenai（～ては）いけ
ない
→(～**te mo**) ii（～ても）いい（～te
mo）kamawanai（～ても）かまわ
ない
⑤［不必要の意味を表す］
¶そんなに急がなくてもいいです。
(Sonna ni isoganaku*te mo* ii desu.)
¶お金は今すぐ払わなくてもかまいま
せん。(Okane wa ima sugu hara-
wanaku*te mo* kamaimasen.)
*「～なくてもいい（～nakute mo
ii）」「～なくてもかまわない（～naku-
te mo kamawanai）」の形で使う。
↔(～**te wa**) ikenai（～ては）いけ
ない
→(～**te mo**) ii（～ても）いい（～te
mo）kamawanai（～ても）かまわ
ない
＊「～たって（～tatte）」「～だって

* Usually followed in the second
clause by suppositions with ~ *deshō*,
statements of intent with *-ō* 〚*-yō*〛,
etc. The *-ta* form of the verb expressing past or completed action is also
used.
④ [expresses permission]
¶ You **may** have tomorrow off.

¶ You **may** write it in pencil.

* Used in the patterns "*-te mo ii*,"
"*-te mo kamawanai*."

⑤ [indicates something is unneces-
sary]
¶ **There's no need** to be in such a
hurry.
¶ **You don't have** to pay right this
moment.
* Used in the patterns "*-nakute mo
ii*," "*-nakute mo kamawanai*."

* Variants: *-tatte*, *-datte*.

（〜datte)」とも言う。

ten 天〚名〛

天と地 (ten to chi)　天気 (tenki)
晴天 (seiten)　雨天 (uten)

(-)ten (-)点〚名, 尾〛

1〚名〛

①［小さい印や句読点など］
点と線 (ten to sen)
¶長い文は読みにくいので，文の区切りのところに点を打ちます。 (Nagai bun wa yominikui node, bun no kugiri no tokoro ni ten o uchimasu.)

②［成績，評価］
点がいい (ten ga ii)　点が悪い (ten ga warui)　点が甘い (ten ga amai)　点が辛い (ten ga karai)

③［特に問題になる部分・ところ］
問題点 (mondaiten)
¶この点について何か御質問はありませんか。 (Kono ten ni tsuite nani ka goshitsumon wa arimasen ka?)

2〚尾〛
¶「試験の成績は何点ぐらいでしたか。」 (Shiken no seiseki wa nanten gurai deshita ka?)「80点でした。」 (Hachijitten deshita.)

-ten -店〚尾〛
商店 (shōten)　書店 (shoten)　売店 (baiten)

tenisu テニス〚名〛
テニスの試合 (tenisu no shiai)
¶父は若い時にはよくテニスをしたそうです。 (Chichi wa wakai toki ni

ten 〚n〛 the heavens, the sky; Heaven

heaven and earth // the weather // the blue **sky** // rainy **weather**

(-)ten 〚n, suf〛 point, dot; marks, grades; point, respect, detail; points, score

1 〚n〛

① [point, dot]
points and lines
¶ As long sentences are hard to read, [we] punctuate them with **commas** at natural breaks.

② [marks, grades]
have good **marks** // have bad **marks** // be liberal in **marking** // be strict in **marking**

③ [point, respect, detail]
the problem **point, the point** at issue
¶ Are there any questions about this **point** ⟦in this **regard**⟧?

2 〚suf〛 points, score
¶ "What was **your mark** on the exam?"
 "I got an 80."

-ten 〚suf〛 shop, store
a shop, store // a book**store** // **a stand, stall, concession**

tenisu 〚n〛 tennis
a **tennis** match
¶ I hear that my father often played **tennis** when he was young.

wa yoku *tenisu* o shita sō desu.)

tenjō 天井〖名〗

¶この家は天井が高いので、広く感じ
ます。 (Kono ie wa *tenjō* ga takai
node, hiroku kanjimasu.)

tenki 天気〖名〗

①[晴れ・曇り・雨などの空模様]
天気予報 (*tenki*-yohō)
¶明日はいい天気になるでしょう。
(Asu wa ii *tenki* ni naru deshō.)
②[いい天気]
¶あした天気なら行きます。 (Ashita
tenki nara ikimasu.)

tennō 天皇〖名〗

tenpura てんぷら〖名〗

¶魚と野菜のてんぷらを食べました。
(Sakana to yasai no *tenpura* o
tabemashita.)

¶てんぷらはえびがいちばんおいしい
ですね。 (*Tenpura* wa ebi ga ichiban oishii desu ne.)

tenrankai 展覧会〖名〗

¶今度の日曜日に絵の展覧会に行きま
せんか。 (Kondo no nichiyōbi ni e
no *tenrankai* ni ikimasen ka?)

tenugui 手ぬぐい〖名〗

手ぬぐいで手をふく (*tenugui* de te o
fuku)

tēpu テープ〖名〗

カセットテープ (kasetto-*tēpu*)

tēpurekōdā テープレコーダー〖名〗

¶テープレコーダーは、音や声を何度
も繰り返して聞けるので便利です。
(*Tēpurekōdā* wa oto ya koe o nando

tenjō 〚n〛 ceiling

¶ This house has high **ceilings,** giving it a feeling of great space.

tenki 〚n〛 the weather; fine weather

① [the weather]

weather forecast

¶ **The weather** will probably be nice
tomorrow.

② [fine weather]

¶ If it is **a nice day** tomorrow [I] will
go.

tennō 〚n〛 the Emperor

tenpura 〚n〛 *tempura*

¶ [I] had fish and vegetable *tempura.*

¶ The shrimp *tempura* is best, isn't
it?

tenrankai 〚n〛 exhibition, show

¶ Would you like to go to **an exhibition** of paintings next Sunday?

tenugui 〚n〛 hand towel, wash-
cloth (usually refers to a cotton cloth
of traditional size and pattern)

wipe one's hands on **a hand towel**

tēpu 〚n〛 tape, magnetic tape; paper streamer

a cassette **tape**

tēpurekōdā 〚n〛 a tape recorder

¶ **Tape recorders** are handy because
they make it possible to listen to recorded sounds and voices over and

mo kurikaeshite kikeru node benri desu.)

tera 寺〖名〗

¶京都や奈良には，有名な古いお寺がたくさんあります。(Kyōto ya Nara ni wa, yūmei na furui otera ga takusan arimasu.)

terasu 照らす〖動Ⅰ〗

¶月の光が辺りを明るく照らして，とても美しい夜です。(Tsuki no hikari ga atari o akaruku terashite, totemo utsukushii yoru desu.)

¶車のライトを照らして，合図をしました。(Kuruma no raito o terashite, aizu o shimashita.)

terebi テレビ〖名〗

¶わたしは毎晩テレビを見ます。

(Watashi wa maiban terebi o mimasu.)

teru 照る〖動Ⅰ〗

¶雨がやんで，雲の間から日が照ってきました。(Ame ga yande, kumo no aida kara hi ga tette kimashita.)

tetsu 鉄〖名〗

鉄橋 (tekkyō) 鉄砲 (teppō) 鉄筋 (tekkin)

¶この機械は鉄でできています。

(Kono kikai wa tetsu de dekite imasu.)

tetsudai 手伝い〖名〗

¶今日はお客さんがいらっしゃるので，姉は台所で母の手伝いをしています。

(Kyō wa okyakusan ga irassharu node, ane wa daidokoro de haha

over again.

tera 〚n〛 Buddhist temple

¶There are many famous ancient **temples** in Kyoto and Nara.

terasu 〚v I〛 shine on, light up, illuminate

¶Brightly **lit** by the moonlight, this is a perfectly lovely evening.

¶[They] signaled by **turning on the** car **lights.**

terebi 〚n〛 television, television set

¶I watch **television** every night.

teru 〚v I〛 shine

¶The rain has stopped and the sun has started **shining** from behind the clouds.

tetsu 〚n〛 iron, steel

an **iron** bridge, a railway bridge // a gun, firearms // an **iron** reinforcing bar 〚rod〛.

¶This machine 〚device, mechanism〛 is made of **steel.**

tetsudai 〚n〛 help, assistance

¶My (older) sister **is helping** our mother in the kitchen as we expect guests today.

no *tetsudai* o shite imasu.)

tetsudau 手伝う〖動Ⅰ〗

¶山田さん，すみませんが，この仕事を**手伝って**ください。(Yamada san, sumimasen ga, kono shigoto o *tetsudatte* kudasai.)

¶お金の計算を中村さんに**手伝って**もらいました。 (Okane no keisan o Nakamura san ni *tetsudatte* morai-mashita.)

tetsudō 鉄道〖名〗

¶この町が発展したのは，50年前に**鉄道**が通ってからです。(Kono machi ga hatten shita no wa, gojūnen mae ni *tetsudō* ga tootte kara desu.)

tetsuzuki 手続き〖名，〜する〗

¶入学の**手続き**は3月20日までです。(Nyūgaku no *tetsuzuki* wa sangatsu hatsuka made desu.)

¶外国旅行の**手続き**は，全部旅行会社がやってくれました。(Gaikoku-ryokō no *tetsuzuki* wa, zenbu ryokō-gaisha ga yatte kuremashita.)

te wa ては〖助〗

①[ものごとが繰り返し行われることを表す]

¶川に落ちたボールは，浮かん**では**沈みながら流れていきました。(Kawa ni ochita bōru wa, ukan*de wa* shizuminagara nagarete ikimashita.)

¶父はよく新宿へ寄っ**ては**お菓子を買ってきてくれます。(Chichi wa yoku Shinjuku e yot*te wa* okashi o katte kite kuremasu.)

tetsudau 〖v I〗 **help, assist**

¶ I'm sorry to trouble you, [Mr.] Yamada, but could you please **help me** with this job?

¶ [Miss] Nakamura **helped me** with the monetary calculations.

tetsudō 〖n〗 **railroad, railway**

¶ The development of this city dates from when **the railroad** came to it 50 years ago.

tetsuzuki 〖n, 〜*suru*〗 **procedure, formalities, steps**

¶ The entrance **procedures** for the university are to be completed by March 20.

¶ The travel agency took care of all **the paperwork** for [my] trip abroad.

-te wa 〖part〗 a particle making a verbal phrase into the topic

① [used to indicate something happens repeatedly]

¶ The ball that fell in the river was carried away alternately **floating** and sinking.

¶ My father often **stops by** in Shinjuku and brings back sweets.

②〔仮定または既定の条件を表す〕

¶こんな所で泳いでは危ないですよ。
(Konna tokoro de oyoi*de wa* abunai desu yo.)

¶そんなに夜も寝ないで勉強しては，体をこわしますよ。 (Sonna ni yoru mo nenaide benkyō shi*te wa,* karada o kowashimasu yo.)

¶芝生の中に入ってはいけません。
(Shibafu no naka ni hait*te wa* ikemasen.)

¶危ないですから，走っている車の中から手を出してはだめです。 (Abunai desu kara, hashitte iru kuruma no naka kara te o dashi*te wa* dame desu.)

¶こう寒くては我慢ができません。
(Kō samuku*te wa* gaman dekimasen.)

＊否定すべきこと，禁止すべきことなどを提示する場合が多い。「～てはいけない (～te wa ikenai)」「～てはだめだ (～te wa dame da)」「～ては我慢できない (～te wa gaman dekinai)」などの形で使うことが多い。
→（～te wa）ikenai（～ては）いけない

＊「ては (te wa)」は「ちゃ (cha)」，「では (de wa)」は「じゃ (ja)」とも言う。

to　戸〖名〗
戸を開ける (*to* o akeru)　戸を閉める (*to* o shimeru)

¶玄関の戸が開いていますから，閉め

② [used when expressing denial or restriction]

¶ It's dangerous **to swim** in this sort of spot.

¶ You'll get sick **studying** like that going without sleep at night.

¶ It is forbidden **to walk** on the grass.

¶ **Don't stick** your hand or arm **out** of a moving car—it's dangerous.

¶ I can't stand it **when it's** this **cold.**

＊ Usually used when indicating that something is denied or forbidden. Frequently used in the patterns "*-te wa ikenai,*" "*-te wa dame da,*" "*-te wa gaman dekinai,*" etc.

＊ Sometimes *-te wa* becomes *-cha* and *-de wa* becomes *-ja*.

to 〖n〗 **door, sliding door, shutter**
open **a door** // close **a door**

¶ Please close the entryway **door.**

786

てください。(Genkan no *to* ga aite imasu kara, shimete kudasai.)

to と〖助〗

①[動作の相手を表す]

¶わたしは昨日駅で上田さんと会いました。(Watashi wa kinō eki de Ueda san *to* aimashita.)

¶妹は山田さんと結婚しました。(Imōto wa Yamada san *to* kekkon shimashita.)

*「と (to)」は相手を必要とする動作を表す動詞の前についてその相手を表し，動作を行う者とその相手との相互の行為であることを表す。「田中さんと話す (Tanaka san to hanasu)」はわたしが田中さんと話し合う意味である。これに対し，「に (ni)」は動作が相手に対して一方的に行われることを表し，「田中さんに話す (Tanaka san ni hanasu)」はわたしが田中さんに一方的に話す意味である。したがって，「会う (au)」「話す (hanasu)」「相談する (sōdan suru)」などは「と (to)」でも「に (ni)」でもその相手を表すことができるが，一方的働きかけの関係ではない「結婚する (kekkon suru)」「けんかする (kenka suru)」などの動詞には「と (to)」しか使えない。

→ni に

②[いっしょに動作をする相手を表す]

¶あした，母とデパートへ行きます。(Ashita haha *to* depāto e ikimasu.)

¶昨日，友達といっしょに映画を見に

to 〖part〗 **to, with; with, together with**

① [indicates the object of an action]

¶ I met [Mrs.] Ueda at the station yesterday.

¶ My (younger) sister married Mr. Yamada.

* This *to* is used with verbs where the action requires another person, and it indicates the mutual nature of that action. *"Tanaka san to hanasu"* (I speak with Mr. Tanaka) means that the speaker talks mutually with Mr. Tanaka. The use of *ni*, on the other hand, indicates the one-way nature of the action so that *"Tanaka san ni hanasu"* means "I speak to Mr. Tanaka." Consequently, for verbs such as *au* (meet), *hanasu* (talk), and *sōdan suru* (consult), either *to* or *ni* can be used; but with verbs expressing an action that must be done mutually, such as *kekkon suru* (marry) or *kenka suru* (quarrel), one can only use *to*.

② [indicates the person one does something with]

¶ I will go **with** my mother to a department store tomorrow.

¶ [I] went to see a movie **with** a

to

行きました。 (Kinō, tomodachi *to* issho ni eiga o mi ni ikimashita.)

③[比較・異同などの基準を表す]

¶今年の夏は去年と比べると、たいへん暑いです。 (Kotoshi no natsu wa kyonen *to* kuraberu to, taihen atsui desu.)

¶昔と違って，今はおおぜいの日本人が外国旅行をするようになりました。 (Mukashi *to* chigatte, ima wa oozei no Nihonjin ga gaikoku-ryokō o suru yō ni narimashita.)

④[ものごとの成り行き・変化などの結果を表す]

¶心配していたことが事実となりました。 (Shinpai shite ita koto ga jijitsu *to* narimashita.)

* いつも「〜となる (〜to naru)」の形で使う。

→ni に

⑤[言ったり考えたりすることの内容を表すときに使う]

¶あしたはいい天気だと思います。 (Ashita wa ii tenki da *to* omoimasu.)

¶「ありがとう」は，あなたの国の言葉で何と言いますか。 ("Arigatō" wa, anata no kuni no kotoba de nan *to* iimasu ka?)

* 「言う (iu)」「書く (kaku)」「思う (omou)」などの動詞の前につく。

⑥[立場・資格などを表す]

¶上田さんは大使としてアメリカへ行きました。 (Ueda san wa taishi *to*

friend yesterday.

③ [indicates the standard for a comparison, difference, etc.]

¶ It's very hot this summer compared **to** last summer.

¶ In a change **from** the past, many Japanese now travel abroad.

④ [indicates an outcome, result, etc.]

¶ What I was afraid would happen actually happened 〚has actually happened〛.

* Always used in the pattern "〜 *to naru*."

⑤ [used when reporting what is said or thought]

¶ I think it will be a nice day tomorrow.

¶ How do you say "Thank you" in your language?

* Used before the verbs *iu*, *kaku*, *omou*, etc.

⑥ [indicates a position, qualification, etc.]

¶ [Mr.] Ueda went to the United

shite Amerika e ikimashita.)

¶山田さんは医者としてよりも政治家として有名です。(Yamada san wa isha *to* shite yori mo seijika *to* shite yūmei desu.)

* いつも「〜として (〜to shite)」の形で使う。

⑦[ある動作・作用がこれから行われる状態にあることを表す]

¶うちを出ようとしたら，雨が降りだしました。(Uchi o deyō *to* shitara, ame ga furidashimashita.)

¶芝居が終わって幕が下りようとした時，大きな拍手が起こりました。(Shibai ga owatte maku ga oriyō *to* shita toki, ookina hakushu ga okorimashita.)

* いつも「動詞（う・ようの形)＋とする (to suru)」の形で使う。

→suru する

⑧[ものごとの様子を表すときに使う]

¶子供は母親の手をしっかりと握りました。(Kodomo wa hahaoya no te o shikkari *to* nigirimashita.)

¶急がずにゆっくりと歩いてください。(Isogazu ni yukkuri *to* aruite kudasai.)

* 副詞などにつけることが多い。

to　と〚助〛

¶朝御飯はパンと牛乳とサラダを食べました。(Asagohan wa pan *to* gyūnyū *to* sarada o tabemashita.)

¶かばんの中には本とノートしかありません。(Kaban no naka ni wa

States **as** ambassador.

¶ [Mr.] Yamada is better known **as** a politician than **as** a physician.

* Always used in the pattern "~ *to shite*."

⑦ [indicates that some action or operation is about to take place or was about to take place]

¶ It started to rain **as I was about** to go out.

¶ The audience burst into applause as the play ended and the curtain **was on the point** of coming down.

* Always used in the pattern "verb (*-ō* 〖*-yō*〗 form) + *to suru*."

⑧ [used to indicate a state or condition]

¶ The child **tightly** grasped [her] mother's hand.

¶ Please walk **slowly** without hurrying.

* Generally used with an adverb, etc.

to 〚part〛 **and**

¶ [I] had bread 〖toast, a roll, etc.〗, milk, **and** salad for breakfast.

¶ There is only a book **and** a notebook in the briefcase 〖bag, etc.〗.

to

hon *to* nōto shika arimasen.)

＊ いくつかのものごとのすべてを対
等の関係で並べて言うときに使う。

to と〖助〗

①［前件が成立するとそれに伴ってい
つも後件が成立するという関係を表
す］

¶春になると、花が咲きます。(Haru ni
naru *to*, hana ga sakimasu.)

¶5に4を足すと、9になります。(Go
ni yon o tasu *to*, kyū ni narimasu.)

¶この道を左に曲がると、駅の前に出
ます。(Kono michi o hidari ni
magaru *to*, eki no mae ni demasu.)

¶わたしはこの歌を聞くと、子供のこ
ろのことを思い出します。(Watashi
wa kono uta o kiku *to*, kodomo no
koro no koto o omoidashimasu.)

¶わたしは若い時はお酒を飲むと、気
持ちが悪くなりました。(Watashi wa
wakai toki wa osake o nomu *to*,
kimochi ga waruku narimashita.)

¶船に乗ると、気持ちが悪くなります
か。(Fune ni noru *to*, kimochi ga
waruku narimasu ka?)「いいえ、船
に乗っても、大丈夫です。」(Iie, fune
ni notte mo, daijōbu desu.)

＊ 真理や習慣的なことがらを表すとき
よく使い、後件が過去・完了を表す
「たの形」のときは過去の習慣を表す。
また後件には、「～う［よう］(～u
[yō])」などの意志、「～なさい(～na-
sai)」などの命令、「～てください
(～te kudasai)」などの依頼などの言

＊ Used when stating all relevant
items; the items are on the same
level. (See also the entry for *ya*.)

to 〖part〗 **when, whenever, if, even if**

① [indicates that the second clause is
always realized when the first clause
is realized]

¶ Flowers bloom **in** the spring.

¶ Four **plus** five (literally, five **plus**
four) is nine.

¶ **If** you turn left from this street, you
will come out in front of the station.

¶ I am reminded of my childhood
whenever I hear this song.

¶ When I was young I always felt sick
whenever I drank *sake*.

¶ "Do you get seasick **on board** a
ship?"

"No, I don't get seasick while I'm
on board a ship."

＊ Often used concerning something
factual or habitual; if it is followed
by a verb in the *-ta* form expressing
past or completed action, it expresses
habitual action in the past. In the
second clause one does not find statements of intent with *-ō* 〖*-yō*〗, orders

790

い方は来ない。

→ba ば tara たら te mo ても

②[前件に既に成立していることがら
を述べてその条件のもとで後件が成立
するという関係を表す]

¶そんなひどいことを言うと，許しま
せんよ。(Sonna hidoi koto o iu *to,*
yurushimasen yo.)

¶これから寒くなると思うと，いやに
なります。(Kore kara samuku naru
to omou *to,* iya ni narimasu.)

→tara たら

③[前件の動作に引き続いて後件の動
作を行うという関係を表す]

¶田中さんは部屋に入ると，電話をか
けました。(Tanaka san wa heya ni
hairu *to,* denwa o kakemashita.)

¶上田さんは手紙を書くと，すぐ出か
けました。(Ueda san wa tegami o
kaku *to,* sugu dekakemashita.)

＊ 前件と後件の主語は同じで，両方と
も意志的な動作であることが多い。ま
た，後件には過去・完了を表す「たの
形」が来る。

④[前件の動作・作用が行われた時ま
たはその直後に後件の動作・作用が行
われるという関係を表す]

¶電車が止まると，乗っている人が降
り始めました。(Densha ga tomaru
to, notte iru hito ga orihajime-
mashita.)

¶庭を散歩していると，母がわたしを
呼びました。(Niwa o sanpo shite
iru *to,* haha ga watashi o yobi-

with -*nasai,* requests with -*te kudasai,*
etc.

② [indicates that the first clause is
already realized and the second
clause is realized based on that]

¶ I can't forgive **your saying** such a
terrible thing.

¶ It's depressing **to think** about its
getting colder from now on.

③ [indicates that the action of the
second clause continues from that of
the first clause]

¶ [Mr.] Tanaka **came in** the room
and made a telephone call.

¶ [Miss] Ueda left soon **after writing**
a letter.

* Generally the subjects of the two
clauses are the same, and both
clauses express a voluntary or inten-
tional action. The verb in the second
clause is in the -*ta* form expressing
past or completed action.

④ [indicates that the action or operation in the second clause takes place
at the same time as or soon after that
of the first clause]

¶ The train **stopped and** passengers
started to get off.

¶ My mother called to me **as I was**
walking in the garden 〚yard〛.

mashita.)

¶家を出ようとすると，雨が降りだしました。(Ie o deyō to suru *to*, ame ga furidashimashita.)

* 前件と後件の主語は異なる。後件には過去・完了を表す「たの形」が来る。

→tara たら

⑤［前件の成立をきっかけとして後件が成立するという関係を表す］

¶「うるさい。」と言うと，山田さんはラジオの音を小さくしました。("Urusai!" to iu *to*, Yamada san wa rajio no oto o chiisaku shimashita.)

¶男の子が女の子を押すと，女の子は転んでしまいました。(Otoko no ko ga onna no ko o osu *to*, onna no ko wa koronde shimaimashita.)

* 普通，前件と後件の主語は異なる。後件には過去・完了を表す「たの形」が来る。

→tara たら

⑥［前件の成立によって後件のことがらに気づくという関係を表す］

¶ふと空を見上げると，飛行機が飛んでいました。(Futo sora o miageru *to*, hikōki ga tonde imashita.)

¶川のそばまで来ると，子供たちが泳いでいるのが見えました。(Kawa no soba made kuru *to*, kodomotachi ga oyoide iru no ga miemashita.)

¶長いトンネルを抜けると，雪国でした。(Nagai tonneru o nukeru *to*, yukiguni deshita.)

¶びんのふたを開けると，いやなにお

¶ It started to rain **just as** I was leaving the house.

* The two clauses have different subjects. The verb in the second clause is in the *-ta* form expressing past or completed action.

⑤ [indicates the second clause is realized based on the realization of the first clause]

¶ **When** [I] cried out that it was too noisy, [Mr.] Yamada turned down the radio.

¶ The boy **pushed** the girl **and** she fell.

* Generally the two clauses have different subjects. The verb in the second clause is in the *-ta* form expressing past or completed action.

⑥ [indicates that what comes in the second clause is noticed through the realization of the first clause]

¶ **When** [I] happened to look up at the sky, there was an airplane flying there.

¶ **When** [I] came up to the river, [I] could see children swimming there.

¶ **On** coming out of the long tunnel [we] were in snow country.

¶ **When** [I] opened the top of the

いがしました。(Bin no futa o akeru *to*, iya na nioi ga shimashita.)

* 後件には「あった (atta)」「〜ていた (〜te ita)」「見えた (mieta)」などの状態・作用を表す言葉のほかに「音がした (oto ga shita)」「においがした (nioi ga shita)」などの感覚を表す言葉も使い，前件によって後件のことがらに気づくという関係を表す。前件の主語と後件の主語は異なる。

→**tara たら**

⑦［評価などを導くことを表す］

¶この病気を治すには，まずたばこをやめるといいです。(Kono byōki o naosu ni wa, mazu tabako o yameru *to* ii desu.)

¶君も早く結婚しないといけませんね。(Kimi mo hayaku kekkon shinai *to* ikemasen ne.)

*「〜といい (〜to ii)」「〜といけない (〜to ikenai)」「〜とだめだ (〜to dame da)」などの形で使う。

→**ba ば**

⑧［前件が後件のことがらの出どころとなっているという関係を表す］

¶今朝の新聞によると，昨日北海道に地震があったそうです。(Kesa no shinbun ni yoru *to*, kinō Hokkaidō ni jishin ga atta sō desu.)

¶山田さんの話だと，秋子さんは来月結婚するそうです。(Yamada san no hanashi da *to*, Akiko san wa raigetsu kekkon suru sō desu.)

bottle, a terrible smell emerged.

* The relationship of what comes in the second clause being noticed by means of what comes in the first clause is expressed by using in the second clause words indicating a state or process such as *atta*, *-te ita*, or *mieta*, words concerning the physical senses such as *oto ga shita* or *nioi ga shita*, etc. The subjects of the two clauses are different.

⑦ [used to introduce a judgment, etc.]

¶ To get over this illness **you should** first of all stop smoking.

¶ **You should** hurry up and get married too.

* Used in the patterns "~ *to ii*," "~ *to ikenai*," "~ *to dame da*," etc.

⑧ [indicates that the first clause is the grounds for the second clause]

¶ **According to** the newspaper this morning, there was an earthquake in Hokkaido yesterday.

¶ **According to** [Mrs.] Yamada, Akiko is going to get married next month.

⑨[前件のことがらにかかわらず後件のことがらが成立するという関係を表す]

¶人が何と言おうと，わたしは平気です。(Hito ga nan to iō *to*, watashi wa heiki desu.)

¶行こうと行くまいとわたしの自由です。(Ikō *to* ikumai *to* watashi no jiyū desu.)

* 普通「〜う［よう］（〜u［yō]）」「〜まい（mai）」などの言葉に続く。

tobidasu 飛び出す〖動 I〗

¶子供が急に道路へ飛び出しました。(Kodomo ga kyū ni dōro e *tobidashimashita*.)

¶兄は会社に遅れそうになったので，あわてて家を飛び出していきました。(Ani wa kaisha ni okuresō ni natta node, awatete ie o *tobidashite* ikimashita.)

tobu 飛ぶ〖動 I〗

¶白い鳥が海の上を飛んでいます。(Shiroi tori ga umi no ue o *tonde* imasu.)

¶飛行機が西の方へ飛んでいきました。(Hikōki ga nishi no hō e *tonde* ikimashita.)

tōchaku 到着〖名，〜する〗

¶弟が乗った飛行機は，今夜8時に到着します。(Otōto ga notta hikōki wa, kon'ya hachiji ni *tōchaku* shimasu.)

¶11時に着く予定の列車は，事故のため1時間遅れて到着します。

---

⑨ [indicates that the second clause is realized unconnected to the first clause]

¶ I don't care what others **may say.**

¶ **Whether I go or not** is for me to decide.

* Usually used with -ō [-yō], -mai, etc.

tō ☞ **too**

tobidasu 〚v I〛 run out, rush out; jump out

¶ A child suddenly **ran out** [has suddenly **run out**] into the road.

¶ In danger of being late to work, my (older) brother hurriedly **rushed out** of the house.

tobu 〚v I〛 fly, take to the air

¶ White birds **are flying** over the ocean.

¶ The airplane **flew off** into the west.

tōchaku 〚n, ~suru〛 arrival; arrive, reach

¶ The plane my (younger) brother is on **will arrive** tonight at eight o'clock.

¶ The train scheduled to arrive at eleven o'clock will be delayed an

(Jūichiji ni tsuku yotei no ressha wa, jiko no tame ichijikan okurete *tōchaku* shimasu.) hour due to an accident.

⇔shuppatsu 出発

tochi 土地〖名〗

¶山田さんは学校のそばに土地を買って，家を建てました。 (Yamada san wa gakkō no soba ni *tochi* o katte, ie o tatemashita.)

tochi 〖n〗 land, piece of land

¶ [Mr.] Yamada bought **land** near the school and built a house there.

tochū 途中〖名〗

¶昨日，家へ帰る途中本屋に寄って，この本を買ってきました。 (Kinō, ie e kaeru *tochū* hon'ya ni yotte, kono hon o katte kimashita.)

¶郵便局は学校へ行く途中にあります。 (Yūbinkyoku wa gakkō e iku *tochū* ni arimasu.)

tochū 〖n〗 on the way, midway

¶ **On [my] way** home yesterday [I] stopped by at the bookstore and bought this book.

¶ There is a post office **on the way** to school.

todokeru 届ける〖動Ⅱ〗

¶あなたに頼まれた手紙は，昨日中村さんに届けました。 (Anata ni tanomareta tegami wa, kinō Nakamura san ni *todokemashita*.)

¶デパートで買った家具はあした届けてくれます。 (Depāto de katta kagu wa ashita *todokete* kuremasu.)

todokeru 〖v Ⅱ〗 deliver, send, forward

¶ You asked me to give [Mr.] Nakamura a letter. **I gave** it to [him] yesterday.

¶ The furniture [I] bought at the department store **will be delivered** tomorrow.

todoku 届く〖動Ⅰ〗

①[あるものがある場所に達する]

¶このたなは高すぎて手が届きません。 (Kono tana wa takasugite te ga *todokimasen*.)

¶どんなに大きな声を出しても，川の向こうまでは届かないでしょう。 (Donna ni ookina koe o dashite mo, kawa no mukō made wa *todo-*

todoku 〖v Ⅰ〗 reach, get to; arrive, be received

① [reach, get to, carry to]

¶ This shelf is too high for me **to reach**.

¶ No matter how loud one shouts, one's voice probably **won't carry** to the other side of the river.

kanai deshō.)

②〔品物などが送り先に着く〕

¶今朝、母から小包が届きました。
(Kesa, haha kara kozutsumi ga *todokimashita*.)

tōfu 豆腐〖名〗

¶豆腐は大豆から作ります。 (*Tōfu* wa daizu kara tsukurimasu.)

toi 問い〖名〗

問いを出す (*toi* o dasu)

¶次の問いに答えなさい。 (Tsugi no *toi* ni kotaenasai.)

toire トイレ〖名〗

¶このトイレは清潔で気持ちがいいです。 (Kono *toire* wa seiketsu de kimochi ga ii desu.)

⇒benjo 便所 tearai 手洗い

tōitsu 統一〖名、〜する〗

国を統一する (kuni o *tōitsu* suru)

¶クラスの意見を統一するのは難しいです。 (Kurasu no iken o *tōitsu* suru no wa muzukashii desu.)

tōji 当時〖名〗

¶わたしが小学生だった当時は、まだこの辺はとても静かでした。(Watashi ga shōgakusei datta *tōji* wa, mada kono hen wa totemo shizuka deshita.)

¶両親が結婚したのは戦後間もなくですが、その当時は食べ物もあまりなかったそうです。(Ryōshin ga kekkon shita no wa sengo mamonaku desu ga, sono *tōji* wa tabemono mo amari nakatta sō desu.)

② [arrive, be received]

¶ A package from my mother **came** this morning.

tōfu 〖n〗 *tofu*, bean curd

¶ *Tofu* is made from soybeans.

toi 〖n〗 question, inquiry

ask **a question**

¶ Answer the following **questions.**

tōi ☞ tooi

toire 〖n〗 toilet, rest room

¶ This **rest room** is nice and clean.

tōitsu 〖n, ~*suru*〗 unified, uniform, united, concerted; unify, unite

unify a country, **bring** a country **under a single rule**

¶ It is difficult to get a **unified** (school) class opinion.

tōji 〖n〗 at that time

¶ This was still a very quiet area **when** I was in elementary school.

¶ My parents got married soon after the war ended; I hear food was scarce **then.**

tojiru 閉じる〖動Ⅱ〗

目を閉じる (me o *tojiru*)

¶本を閉じて，黒板の方を見てください。
(Hon o *tojite*, kokuban no hō o mite kudasai.)

⇔akeru 開ける ⇒hiraku 開く

toka とか〖助〗

①［同じようなものごとや動作について例を挙げて言う場合に使う〕

¶タイとかビルマとかいう暑い国では，1年に2回米が取れるそうです。
(Tai *toka* Biruma *toka* iu atsui kuni de wa, ichinen ni nikai kome ga toreru sō desu.)

¶勉強ばかりしないで，テニスをするとかピンポンをするとか，運動もしなさい。 (Benkyō bakari shinaide, tenisu o suru *toka* pinpon o suru *toka*, undō mo shinasai.)

②［聞いたことや自分の記憶などが不確かなときに使う〕

¶さっき山田さんとかいう人から電話がありましたよ。 (Sakki Yamada san *toka* iu hito kara denwa ga arimashita yo.)

tokai 都会〖名〗

¶夏休みには都会を離れて，田舎へ行くつもりです。(Natsuyasumi ni wa *tokai* o hanarete, inaka e iku tsumori desu.)

⇒inaka 田舎

tokasu 溶かす〖動Ⅰ〗

¶金属を溶かすためには高い温度が必要です。(Kinzoku o *tokasu* tame

tojiru 〚v Ⅱ〛 shut, close

close one's eyes

¶ Please **close** your books and look at the blackboard.

toka 〚part〛 and ~ and the like

① [used when citing similar things as examples]

¶ I understand two rice crops a year are possible in hot countries **such as** Thailand, Burma, **and the like.**

¶ Don't spend all your time studying—play tennis **or** ping-pong **or** take **some other** physical exercise.

② [used when one is not sure of what one has heard, of one's memory, etc.]

¶ There was a telephone call a little while ago from someone called Yamada **or something like that.**

tōka ☞ **tooka**

tokai 〚n〛 city, the town

¶ During summer vacation I intend to get out of **the city** and go to the country.

tokasu 〚v Ⅰ〛 melt, dissolve, liquefy; melt down, smelt

¶ High temperatures are necessary to

ni wa takai ondo ga hitsuyō desu.)

tokei 時計〖名〗

腕時計 (ude*dokei*) 柱時計 (hashira-*dokei*) 置時計 (oki*dokei*) 目覚まし時計 (mezamashi-*dokei*)

¶この時計は５分進んでいますよ。

(Kono *tokei* wa gofun susunde imasu yo.)

tokeru 溶ける〖動Ⅱ〗

①[液体の中に他の物が入り全体が液体のようになる]

¶砂糖は水に溶けます。(Satō wa mizu ni *tokemasu*.)

②[金属が熱せられて液体のようになる]

¶鉄をつくる工場で溶けた鉄を初めて見ました。(Tetsu o tsukuru kōjō de *toketa* tetsu o hajimete mimashita.)

tokeru 解ける〖動Ⅱ〗

①[結んであったものがほどける]

¶靴のひもが解けないように, きつく結びました。(Kutsu no himo ga *tokenai* yō ni, kitsuku musubimashita.)

②[わからない筋道が明らかになり問題の答えが見つかる]

なぞが解ける (nazo ga *tokeru*)

③[固体が液体になる]

¶春になって, 雪が解けてきました。(Haru ni natte, yuki ga *tokete* kimashita.)

toki 時〖名〗

①[時間]

melt metals.

tokei 〚n〛 **clock, watch, timepiece**

wrist**watch** // wall **clock** // table **clock,** mantel **clock** // alarm **clock**

¶ This **clock** 〚**watch**〛 is five minutes fast.

tokeru 〚v Ⅱ〛 **dissolve; melt, fuse**

① [dissolve]

¶ Sugar **dissolves** in water.

② [melt, fuse]

¶ [I] first saw **molten** iron at a steel plant.

tokeru 〚v Ⅱ〛 **come loose, untied, undone; be solved, be resolved, work out; melt, thaw, run**

① [come loose, untied, undone]
¶ [I] tied [my] shoelaces tightly so they **wouldn't come undone.**

② [be solved, be resolved, work out]
a puzzle **is solved, find the answer to** a puzzle

③ [melt, thaw, run]
¶ The snow **has melted** with the coming of spring 〚The snow **melted** with the coming of spring〛.

toki 〚n〛 **time; the time**

① [time, hour]

¶小説がおもしろかったので，時がたつのを忘れて読んでいました。
(Shōsetsu ga omoshirokatta node, *toki* ga tatsu no o wasurete yonde imashita.)

¶ The novel was so interesting that I lost track of **time.**

②[何かが行われる時刻]
¶食事をしている時，友達が来ました。
(Shokuji o shite iru *toki*, tomodachi ga kimashita.)

② [the time, the moment, when]
¶ A friend came **while** [I] was eating.

¶ちょうど家に帰った時，田中さんから電話がかかってきました。(Chōdo ie ni kaetta *toki*, Tanaka san kara denwa ga kakatte kimashita.)

¶ [I] got a telephone call from [Miss] Tanaka **just as** [I] arrived home.

③[時期・季節・時代など]
¶この大きな木は，おじいさんが子供の時植えたのだそうです。(Kono ookina ki wa, ojiisan ga kodomo no *toki* ueta no da sō desu.)

③ [time, age, period, season]
¶ I understand this big tree was planted by my grandfather **when** he was a child.

¶暑い時は物が腐りやすいから，気をつけてください。(Atsui *toki* wa mono ga kusariyasui kara, ki o tsukete kudasai.)

¶ Things easily go bad **during** hot weather so please be careful.

④[場合]
¶非常のときはここから外に出てください。(Hijō no *toki* wa koko kara soto ni dete kudasai.)

④ [time, occasion, case]
¶ **In case of** emergency please exit from here.

¶わたしは困ったときにはいつも田中先生に相談します。(Watashi wa komatta *toki* ni wa itsu mo Tanaka sensei ni sōdan shimasu.)

¶ I always consult Professor Tanaka **when** I have a problem.

tokidoki ときどき〖副〗
¶わたしはときどき映画を見に行きます。(Watashi wa *tokidoki* eiga o mi ni ikimasu.)

tokidoki 〚adv〛 **sometimes, once in a while, occasionally, at times**
¶ I **sometimes** go to see a movie.

tokkyū

¶田舎にいる母がときどき訪ねてきてくれます。(Inaka ni iru haha ga *tokidoki* tazunete kite kuremasu.)

¶ **Once in a while** my mother comes from the country to visit me.

tokkyū 特急〖名〗

¶あの駅は急行はとまりますが，特急はとまりません。(Ano eki wa kyūkō wa tomarimasu ga, *tokkyū* wa tomarimasen.)

tokkyū 〖n〗 a limited express train

¶ The express stops at that station but **the limited express** doesn't.

tokoro 所〖名〗

①〔場所〕

¶どこか景色のいい所へ旅行に行きたいです。(Doko ka keshiki no ii *tokoro* e ryokō ni ikitai desu.)

¶眼鏡を置いた所を忘れてしまいました。(Megane o oita *tokoro* o wasurete shimaimashita.)

②〔ものの存在する場所，その近く〕

¶門の所で待っています。(Mon no *tokoro* de matte imasu.)

¶郵便局の所で待っていてください。(Yūbinkyoku no *tokoro* de matte ite kudasai.)

③〔人の存在する場所・家庭・その人のもと〕

¶昨日，山田さんは上田さんの所に泊まりました。(Kinō, Yamada san wa Ueda san no *tokoro* ni tomarimashita.)

¶授業が終わったら，先生の所へ行ってください。(Jugyō ga owattara, sensei no *tokoro* e itte kudasai.)

④〔住所〕

¶この紙にお所とお名前をお書きください。(Kono kami ni o*tokoro* to

tokoro 〖n〗 place, spot; one's home, where one is; one's address; point, section; time, moment

① [place, spot]

¶ I want to take a trip **somewhere** with good scenery.

¶ [I] have forgotten **where** [I] put [my] glasses.

② [where something is or near there]

¶ [He] is waiting **at** the gate.

¶ Please wait **at** the post office.

③ [one's home, where one is]

¶ [Mr.] Yamada stayed at [Mr.] Ueda's **place** last night.

¶ Please go see **your teacher** after class is over.

④ [one's address]

¶ Please write your name and **address** on this paper.

onamae o okaki kudasai.)

⑤[部分，点]

¶わからない**ところ**があったらきいてください。　(Wakaranai *tokoro* ga attara kiite kudasai.)

¶何でもすぐにあきてしまうのがあなたの悪い**ところ**です。　(Nan demo sugu ni akite shimau no ga anata no warui *tokoro* desu.)

⑥[ある動作・作用がこれから起こるという状態にあることを表す]

¶今，出かける**ところ**です。　(Ima, dekakeru *tokoro* desu.)

¶これから御飯を食べる**ところ**です。 (Korekara gohan o taberu *tokoro* desu.)

*「動詞（連体の形）+ところ（tokoro）」の形で使う。

⑦[ある動作・作用が行われた直後の状態であることを表す]

¶会議は今始まった**ところ**です。(Kaigi wa ima hajimatta *tokoro* desu.)

¶父は今家を出た**ところ**です。(Chichi wa ima ie o deta *tokoro* desu.)

*「動詞（たの形）+ところ（tokoro）」の形で使う。

⑧[ある動作・作用が継続中の状態であることを表す]

¶わたしは今日本語の勉強をしている**ところ**です。　(Watashi wa ima Nihongo no benkyō o shite iru *tokoro* desu.)

¶田中さんは先生の所に話しに行っている**ところ**です。　(Tanaka san wa

⑤ [point, section, part]

¶ Please ask if there's **something** you don't understand.

¶ Becoming quickly bored is a bad **point** of yours.

⑥ [indicates that something is on the point of happening]

¶ [I]'m **just about** to go out now.

¶ [We]'re **just about** to eat at the moment.

* Used in the pattern "verb (dictionary form) + *tokoro*."

⑦ [indicates that something has just happened]

¶ The meeting has **just now** begun.

¶ My father **just** left the house **a moment ago**.

* Used in the pattern "verb (-*ta* form) + *tokoro*."

⑧ [indicates that something is in the course of taking place]

¶ I'm studying my Japanese **just now**.

¶ [Mr.] Tanaka is **now** talking with [his] teacher (literally, has gone to sensei no tokoro ni hanashi ni itte iru *tokoro* desu.)

*「動詞（ての形）＋いる（iru）＋ところ（tokoro）」の形で使う。

tokorode　ところで〚接〛

¶ところで，最近田中さんに会いましたか。(*Tokorode*, saikin Tanaka san ni aimashita ka?)

¶毎日いいお天気ですね。ところで，奥さんの御病気はいかがですか。

(Mainichi ii otenki desu ne. *Tokorode*, okusan no gobyōki wa ikaga desu ka?)

* 話題を変えるときなどに使う。

tokoroga　ところが〚接〛

¶妹はすぐ帰ると言って出かけました。ところが，3時間もたつのにまだ帰りません。(Imōto wa sugu kaeru to itte dekakemashita. *Tokoroga*, sanjikan mo tatsu noni mada kaerimasen.)

¶このおもちゃはたいへん高かったです。ところが，少し使っただけでもう壊れてしまいました。(Kono omocha wa taihen takakatta desu. *Tokoroga*, sukoshi tsukatta dake de mō kowarete shimaimashita.)

* 前のことがらを受けて，そのことがらに反するようなことがらをあとに続けるときに使う。普通あとに「〜なさい（〜nasai）」などの命令，「〜てください（〜te kudasai）」などの依頼，「〜う（よう）（〜u [yō])」などの意志などの言い方は来ない。

talk with his teacher and is **now** talking with him).

* Used in the pattern "verb (-*te* form) + *iru* + *tokoro*."

tokorode 〚conj〛 by the way, incidentally

¶ **By the way,** have you seen [Mr.] Tanaka recently?

¶ We've been enjoying nice weather, haven't we? **And** how is your wife's illness?

* Used when changing the subject, etc.

tokoroga 〚conj〛 however, but, and yet, on the contrary

¶ When my (younger) sister went out, she said she'd be back soon. **However,** it's been three hours and she hasn't gotten back yet.

¶ This toy was very expensive. **Nevertheless** it broke after being used only a little while.

* Used when stating something opposed to what came earlier. Usually it is not followed by orders with -*nasai*, requests with -*te kudasai*, statements of intent with -*ō* 〚-*yō*〛, etc.

tokoya　床屋〖名〗

¶床屋へ行って髪を短く切ってもらいました。　(*Tokoya* e itte kami o mijikaku kitte moraimashita.)

＊「理髪店 (rihatsuten)」とも言う。

toku　得〖名, 形動, 〜する〗

¶100円の物を 80 円で買ったので, 20 円の得をしました。　(Hyakuen no mono o hachijūen de katta node, nijūen no *toku* o shimashita.)

¶これは安くていい品物ですから, 買ったほうが得ですよ。(Kore wa yasukute ii shinamono desu kara, katta hō ga *toku* desu yo.)

⇔son 損

toku　解く〖動 I〗

①[結んであったものをほどく]

¶ひもを解いて, 箱を開けてみました。(Himo o *toite*, hako o akete mimashita.)

②[わからなかった筋道を明らかにし疑問や問題の答えを見つける]

¶この問題を解いた人は手を挙げてください。(Kono mondai o *toita* hito wa te o agete kudasai.)

tokubetsu　特別〖形動, 〜の〗

¶二, 三日の旅行ですから, 特別な準備はいりません。　(Ni-sannichi no ryokō desu kara, *tokubetsu* na junbi wa irimasen.)

¶ここは特別の部屋ですから, 一般の人は使用できません。　(Koko wa *tokubetsu* no heya desu kara, ippan no hito wa shiyō dekimasen.)

tokoya 〖n〗 **barber, barbershop**

¶ I went to **the barber** and got a haircut.

＊ Another word for "barbershop" is *rihatsuten*.

toku 〖n, adj-v, 〜*suru*〗 **profit, gain, advantage, benefit**

¶ As I bought a 100-yen article for 80 yen, **I saved** 20 yen.

¶ Buying this merchandise **will be to your advantage** as it is inexpensive and of good quality.

toku 〖v I〗 **untie, undo, unfasten; solve, work out**

① [untie, undo, unfasten, loosen]

¶ [I] **unfastened** the string 〖twine, etc.〗 and opened up the box.

② [solve, work out, answer]

¶ Will those who **have answered** this question please raise their hands.

tōku ☞ **tooku**

tokubetsu 〖adj-v, 〜*no*〗 **special, extraordinary, uncommon, exceptional**

¶ It's only a two- or three-day trip so no **special** preparations are necessary.

¶ This is a **special** room not for use by the general public.

tokuchō 特徴〖名〗

¶あの人の字には**特徴**があるので，すぐわかります。(Ano hito no ji ni wa *tokuchō* ga aru node, sugu wakarimasu.)

¶彼の顔の**特徴**はよく覚えていませんが，確か目の大きい人だったと思います。 (Kare no kao no *tokuchō* wa yoku oboete imasen ga, tashika me no ookii hito datta to omoimasu.)

tokui 得意〖名，形動〗

①［自慢する様子］

¶山田さんは先日の試験の成績がよかったので，**得意**になっています。(Yamada san wa senjitsu no shiken no seiseki ga yokatta node, *tokui* ni natte imasu.)

②［上手にできる］

¶わたしは物理や化学より生物のほうが**得意**です。 (Watashi wa butsuri ya kagaku yori seibutsu no hō ga *tokui* desu.)

tokuni 特に〖副〗

¶田中さんはいろいろなスポーツができますが，**特に**テニスが上手です。(Tanaka san wa iroiro na supōtsu ga dekimasu ga, *tokuni* tenisu ga jōzu desu.)

¶わたしは果物の中で**特に**りんごが好きです。(Watashi wa kudamono no naka de *tokuni* ringo ga suki desu.)

tomaru 止まる〖動Ⅰ〗

①［動いたり進んだりしているものな

tokuchō 〖n〗 special feature, characteristic, trait

¶ [He] has a **distinctive** handwriting easily identifiable as [his].

¶ I don't remember **the particular features** of his face but I think he had large eyes.

tokui 〖n, adj-v〗 vanity, boasting; one's forte, one's strong point

① [vanity, boasting, pride]

¶ [Mr.] Yamada **is suffering a swelled head** over [his] good mark on the exam last week.

② [one's forte, strong point, specialty]

¶ **I'm better** at biology than physics or chemistry.

tokuni 〖adv〗 especially, particularly, in particular

¶ [Mr.] Tanaka can play several different sports but [he] is **especially** good at tennis.

¶ Among fruits, I **particularly** like apples.

tomaru 〖v I〗 stop, halt; stop, cease, be suspended; perch

① [stop, halt; something stops mov-

どが動かなくなる]

¶ 車 が山田さんの家の前で**止まりまし
た**。 (Kuruma ga Yamada san no
ie no mae de *tomarimashita*.)

¶ The automobile 〚taxi〛 **stopped** in
front of [Mr.] Yamada's house.

¶あの時計は**止**まっていますよ。(Ano
tokei wa *tomatte* imasu yo.)

¶ That clock 〚watch〛 **has stopped
running.**

②[続いている状態が終わりになった
り続くはずのものが一時続かなくなっ
たりする]

② [stop, cease, be suspended; a state
ends or something stops temporarily]

¶あしたの午後10時から水道の水が**止
まる**そうです。(Ashita no gogo jūji
kara suidō no mizu ga *tomaru* sō
desu.)

¶ I hear that water service **will be
suspended** from ten o'clock tomorrow night.

¶ 薬 をつけてしばらくすると、足の血
が**止まりました**。(Kusuri o tsukete
shibaraku suru to, ashi no chi ga
tomarimashita.)

¶ [My] leg 〚foot〛 **stopped** bleeding a
little while after [I] put the medication 〚ointment, etc.〛 on it.

③[鳥や虫が何かにつかまって休む]

③ [perch]

¶あの木に**止**まっている白い鳥は何と
いう鳥ですか。 (Ano ki ni *tomatte*
iru shiroi tori wa nan to iu tori
desu ka?)

¶ What is the name of the white bird
in that tree over there?

¶ちょうちょうが赤い花に**止**まってい
ます。(Chōchō ga akai hana ni
tomatte imasu.)

¶ A butterfly **is alight** on the red
flower.

tomaru 泊まる〚動 I〛

tomaru 〚v I〛 **stay the night, lodge;
lie at anchor**

①[宿をとる]

① [stay the night, lodge]

¶日本を旅行するときは、ホテルでは
なく旅館に**泊まる**ことにしています。
(Nihon o ryokō suru toki wa,
hoteru de wa naku ryokan ni
tomaru koto ni shite imasu.)

¶ When [I] am traveling in Japan I
make it a practice **to stay** in
Japanese-style inns rather than
hotels.

②[船が港に入っている]

② [lie at anchor]

¶ 港 には日本の船だけでなく外国の船

¶ There are foreign as well as

も泊まっています。 (Minato ni wa Nihon no fune dake de naku gaikoku no fune mo *tomatte* imasu.)

tomato　トマト〖名〗

トマトを作る (*tomato* o tsukuru)

トマトがなる (*tomato* ga naru)

tōmei　透明〖形動〗

¶この酒のびんは透明だから，色も飲んだ量もよくわかります。 (Kono sake no bin wa *tōmei* da kara, iro mo nonda ryō mo yoku wakarimasu.)

¶この湖の水は透明で，底の方もよく見えます。(Kono mizuumi no mizu wa *tōmei* de, soko no hō mo yoku miemasu.)

tomeru　止める〖動Ⅱ〗

①[動いたり進んだりしているものなどを動かなくする]

¶手を挙げて，タクシーを止めました。 (Te o agete, takushii o *tomemashita*.)

¶その機械を止めてください。 (Sono kikai o *tomete* kudasai.)

②[続いている状態などを終わりにさせたり続くはずのものを一時的に続かなくさせる]

¶歯の痛みを止める薬がありますか。 (Ha no itami o *tomeru* kusuri ga arimasu ka?)

¶あした，工事のために電気を一時止めます。 (Ashita, kōji no tame ni denki o ichiji *tomemasu*.)

③[何かをしていたりこれからしよう

Japanese ships **at anchor** in the harbor.

tomato 〚n〛 **a tomato**

grow **tomatoes** // **a tomato plant** bears fruit

tōmei 〚adj-v〛 **transparent, clear**

¶ Since this bottle is made of **clear** glass, one can clearly see the color of the liquor and tell how much one has drunk.

¶ The water of this lake **is so clear** that one can see the bottom.

tomeru 〚v II〛 **stop, bring to a stop; stop, be off; dissuade, hold back, stop, forbid**

① [stop, bring to a stop, turn off; stop something moving]

¶ [I] **stopped** a taxi by raising [my] hand.

¶ Please **stop** that machine.

② [stop, be off; bring a condition to a close or temporarily stop something]

¶ Do you have anything to take **to relieve** a toothache?

¶ The electricity **will be off** for a time tomorrow due to construction.

③ [dissuade, hold back, stop, forbid]

とするのをやめさせる]

¶医者にたばこを**止められました**。
(Isha ni tabako o *tomeraremashita*.)

¶ The doctor **forbid me to** smoke.

¶お母さんは子供のいたずらを**止めました**。(Okāsan wa kodomo no itazura o *tomemashita*.)

¶ The mother **stopped** her child from playing pranks.

¶酔った人が石を車に投げようとしたので，上田さんが**止めました**。(Yotta hito ga ishi o kuruma ni nageyō to shita node, Ueda san ga *tomemashita*.)

¶ [Mr.] Ueda **dissuaded** the drunk from throwing stones at cars.

tomeru 留める〖動Ⅱ〗

¶姉がシャツのボタンを**留めて**くれました。(Ane ga shatsu no botan o *tomete* kuremashita.)

¶その地図が壁から落ちないようにしっかり**留めて**おいてください。(Sono chizu ga kabe kara ochinai yō ni shikkari *tomete* oite kudasai.)

tomeru [[v II]] **fasten, put in place, fix**

¶ My (older) sister **buttoned** my shirt for me.

¶ Please **fix** that map firmly onto the wall so it won't fall down.

tomeru 泊める〖動Ⅱ〗

¶昨晩は雨がひどく降ったので，山田さんの家に**泊めて**もらいました。(Sakuban wa ame ga hidoku futta node, Yamada san no ie ni *tomete* moraimashita.)

tomeru [[v II]] **lodge, give shelter, put up for the night**

¶ As it was raining so hard last evening, **I stayed the night** at [Mr.] Yamada's.

tomo 友〖名〗
☞**tomodachi** 友達

tomo ☞ tomodachi

-tomo -とも〖尾〗

①[あるものが全部そうであることを表す]

¶わたしたち夫婦は二人**とも**甘いものが大好きです。(Watashitachi fūfu wa futari*tomo* amai mono ga daisuki desu.)

-tomo [[suf]] **both, all**

① [both, all, neither]

¶ My husband ‖wife‖ and I **both** have a sweet tooth.

¶わたしたちの学校はテニスの試合で男女とも優勝しました。(Watashi-tachi no gakkō wa tenisu no shiai de danjo*tomo* yūshō shimashita.)

②[だいたいの限界を表す]

¶昨日，ここに集まった人は少なくとも 30 名以上でした。(Kinō, koko ni atsumatta hito wa sukunaku-*tomo* sanjūmei ijō deshita.)

¶遅くとも 10 時までには帰るつもりです。(Osoku*tomo* jūji made ni wa kaeru tsumori desu.)

tomodachi　友達〖名〗

友達になる (*tomodachi* ni naru)

¶わたしと田中さんとは親しい友達です。(Watashi to Tanaka san to wa shitashii *tomodachi* desu.)

tomokaku　ともかく〖副〗

①[あることは一応別にして]

¶日本人ならともかく，外国人が日本語を間違えるのはあたりまえでしょう。(Nihonjin nara *tomokaku*, gaikoku-jin ga Nihongo o machigaeru no wa atarimae deshō.)

¶成功するかしないかはともかく，一生懸命努力してみなさい。(Seikō suru ka shinai ka wa *tomokaku*, isshōkenmei doryoku shite mina-sai.)

* 普通「〜はともかく（〜wa tomo-kaku）」「〜ならともかく（〜nara tomokaku)」の形で使う。

②[問題はいろいろあるがひとまず次のことはしようというような意味を表

¶ Our school won **both** the men's and women's tennis matches.

② [indicates broad limits]

¶ **At the very least** there were over 30 persons gathered here yesterday.

¶ I plan to return home by ten o'clock **at the latest.**

tomodachi 〚n〛 friend

become **a friend** of, make **friends** with

¶ [Mr.] Tanaka and I are close **friends.**

tomokaku 〚adv〛 **setting aside, apart from; at any rate, in any case**

① [setting aside, apart from]

¶ **Leaving** the Japanese themselves **out of the question,** it is only to be expected that foreigners should make mistakes in Japanese.

¶ **Don't worry about** whether you will succeed or not, but just do your best.

* Usually used in the patterns "~ *wa tomokaku*" and "~ *nara tomokaku*."

② [at any rate, in any case, anyway]

す]

¶山田さんは行かないかもしれませんが，ともかく旅行のことは知らせておきました。(Yamada san wa ikanai ka mo shiremasen ga, *tomokaku* ryokō no koto wa shirasete okimashita.)

→tonikaku とにかく

tonari 隣〚名〛

¶兄は今隣の部屋で本を読んでいます。(Ani wa ima *tonari* no heya de hon o yonde imasu.)

¶田中さんの隣にいる人はだれですか。(Tanaka san no *tonari* ni iru hito wa dare desu ka?)

tonikaku とにかく〚副〛

¶結果はどうなるかわかりませんが，とにかくがんばってやってみましょう。(Kekka wa dō naru ka wakarimasen ga, *tonikaku* ganbatte yatte mimashō.)

¶山田さんはうちにいないかもしれませんが，とにかく行ってみましょう。(Yamada san wa uchi ni inai ka mo shiremasen ga, *tonikaku* itte mimashō.)

⇨tomokaku ともかく

tonneru トンネル〚名〛

¶汽車はトンネルを出て，海のそばを走っていきました。(Kisha wa *tonneru* o dete, umi no soba o hashitte ikimashita.)

too 十〚名〛

①[10個]

¶ [Miss] Yamada might not be going but **at any rate** I told [her] about the trip.

tonari 〚n〛 next, next-door, neighboring

¶ My (older) brother is presently reading a book in the **next** room.

¶ Who is the person **next to** [Mr.] Tanaka?

tonikaku 〚adv〛 anyway, at any rate, in any case

¶ [I] don't know how it will turn out but **at any rate** [I]'ll take a try at it.

¶ [Miss] Yamada might not be home, but let's go and see if [she] is **anyway**.

tonneru 〚n〛 tunnel

¶ The train emerged from **the tunnel** and ran along beside the sea.

too 〚n〛 10; 10 years old

① [10, 10 items]

¶かごの中にりんごが十あります。

(Kago no naka ni ringo ga *too* arimasu.)

¶ There are **10** apples in the basket.

②[10歳]

¶息子は十で、娘は八つになりました。

(Musuko wa *too* de, musume wa yattsu ni narimashita.)

② [10 years old]

¶ My son **is 10** and my daughter has turned eight.

tooi 遠い〖形〗

¶わたしのうちは学校から遠いので、毎日自転車で通っています。(Watashi no uchi wa gakkō kara *tooi* node, mainichi jitensha de kayotte imasu.)

tooi 〖adj〗 **far, distant, remote**

¶ As the school **is far** from my home, I commute there every day by bicycle.

¶海岸はここからあまり遠くないです。

(Kaigan wa koko kara amari *tooku nai* desu.)

¶ The shore **isn't far** from here.

⇔chikai 近い

tooka 十日〖名〗

①[日付を表す]

十月十日 (jūgatsu *tooka*)

②[日数を表す]

十日間 (*tooka*kan) 十日前 (*tooka*mae) 十日後 (*tooka*go)

⇨-ka -日

tooka 〖n〗 **the tenth of the month; 10 days**

① [the tenth of the month]

October **10**

② [10 days]

for **10 days, 10-days'** time // **10 days** ago, **10 days** earlier // **10 days** from now, **10 days** later

tooku 遠く〖名〗

¶危ないから,遠くへ遊びに行ってはいけませんよ。(Abunai kara, *tooku* e asobi ni itte wa ikemasen yo.)

¶この船は魚を捕るために,遠くの海へ出かけていきます。 (Kono fune wa sakana o toru tame ni, *tooku* no umi e dekakete ikimasu.)

⇔chikaku 近く

tooku 〖n〗 **a distant place; far away, in the distance**

¶ You mustn't play **too far away**— it's dangerous.

¶ This ship sails to **distant** seas to fish.

toori 通り〖名〗

toori 〖n〗 **road, street; street traffic; way, as, like**

-toori

① [道路]
大**通り** (oo*doori*)
¶この**通り**をまっすぐ行くと，右側に
交番があります。 (Kono *toori* o
massugu iku to, migigawa ni kōban
ga arimasu.)

② [人・車の往来]
人**通り** (hito*doori*)
¶駅の前のこの道は，いつも車の**通り**
が多いです。 (Eki no mae no kono
michi wa, itsu mo kuruma no *toori*
ga ooi desu.)

③ [同じ状態]
¶わたしが初めに歌いますから，あと
でその**とおり**に歌ってください。
(Watashi ga hajime ni utaimasu
kara, ato de sono *toori* ni utatte
kudasai.)

¶わたしが言う**とおり**に発音してくだ
さい。 (Watashi ga iu *toori* ni
hatsuon shite kudasai.)

-toori　-とおり〖尾〗
① [種類などを表す]
¶この漢字には三**とおり**の読み方があ
ります。 (Kono kanji ni wa mi*toori*
no yomikata ga arimasu.)

② [だいたい，ざっと]
¶彼が会社を辞めた理由は，ひと**とおり**
聞いて知っています。 (Kare ga kai-
sha o yameta riyū wa, hito*toori*
kiite shitte imasu.)

¶桜はもう九分**どおり**咲いていました。
(Sakura wa mō kubu*doori* saite
imashita.)

① [road, street]
a main **road,** thoroughfare
¶ If you go straight down this **street,**
there will be a police box on the
right.

② [street traffic, coming and going]
pedestrian **traffic**
¶ **Traffic** is always heavy on this road
in front of the station.

③ [way, as, like]
¶ I'll sing it first—then you please
sing it the same **way.**

¶ Please listen and pronounce it **like**
I do.

-toori 〖suf〗 **kind, sort; approximately, roughly; that way, like
that**
① [kind, sort]
¶ There are three different **ways** of
reading this *kanji.*
② [approximately, roughly]
¶ I've heard **in a general way** his
reasons for quitting his job.

¶ The cherry blossoms are 〚were〛
almost in full bloom.

tooru

③[そのようであることを表す]
予想どおり (yosō *doori*)
¶仕事は計画どおりに進んでいます。
(Shigoto wa keikaku *doori* ni susunde imasu.)
* いつも「〜どおり（〜doori）」の形で使う。

tooru 通る〖動Ⅰ〗
①[道を過ぎていく]
¶どちらの道を通って帰りましょうか。
(Dochira no michi o *tootte* kaerimashō ka?)
¶このバスは新宿を通りますか。
(Kono basu wa Shinjuku o *toorimasu* ka?)
②[一方からもう一方へ抜けて出る]
¶風がよく通るのでここは涼しいです。
(Kaze ga yoku *tooru* node koko wa suzushii desu.)
¶針の穴が小さくて、糸が通りません。
(Hari no ana ga chiisakute, ito ga *toorimasen*.)
③[認められる，合格する]
意見が通る (iken ga *tooru*)
¶田中さんは試験に通らなかったようです。　(Tanaka san wa shiken ni *tooranakatta* yō desu.)

toosu 通す〖動Ⅰ〗
①[一方からもう一方へ通過させる]
¶すみませんが、ちょっと前を通してください。　(Sumimasen ga, chotto mae o *tooshite* kudasai.)
¶ガラスは光を通します。　(Garasu wa hikari o *tooshimasu*.)

③ [that way, like that]
as expected
¶ The work is proceeding **according to** schedule.

* Always used in the pattern "~ -*doori*."

tooru 〖vⅠ〗 **pass, go by; pass through; pass** (an exam), **prevail**
① [pass, go by]
¶ Which streets shall **we take** on our return?
¶ Does this bus **go through** Shinjuku?

② [pass through]
¶ It's cool here as there's a good breeze **passing through.**
¶ **I can't thread** this needle—its eye is too small.

③ [pass (an exam), prevail]
an opinion **wins out**
¶ It seems that [Mr.] Tanaka **did not pass** [his] exam.

toosu 〖vⅠ〗 **let pass, pass through; show in, usher; persist in, keep at**
① [let pass, pass through]
¶ Excuse me, I'd like **to be let by** please.
¶ Glass **admits** light.

②[部屋などへ案内する]

¶お客様を座敷にお通ししました。

(Okyakusama o zashiki ni otooshi shimashita.)

③[あることを初めから終わりまで続ける]

¶上田さんは小学校, 中学校, 高等学校をずっと1番で通しました。(Ueda san wa shōgakkō, chūgakkō, kōtōgakkō o zutto ichiban de tooshimashita.)

toreru 取れる〖動Ⅱ〗

①[自然にある物や栽培した物が得られる]

りんごが取れる (ringo ga toreru)

¶今年は米がたくさん取れて, 農家の人たちも喜んでいるそうです。 (Kotoshi wa kome ga takusan torete, nōka no hitotachi mo yorokonde iru sō desu.)

②[ある物から有用な成分を抽出できる]

¶海水から塩が取れます。 (Kaisui kara shio ga toremasu.)

¶この花の種から油が取れますか。 (Kono hana no tane kara abura ga toremasu ka?)

③[必要ないものなどがなくなる]

熱が取れる (netsu ga toreru) 疲れが取れる (tsukare ga toreru)

¶薬を飲んだら, 傷の痛みが取れました。(Kusuri o nondara, kizu no itami ga toremashita.)

④[理解できる, 解釈できる]

② [show in, usher]

¶ [I] **showed** our guest into the parlor 〚our customer into the Japanese-style room〛.

③ [persist in, keep at, continue, carry through]

¶ [Miss] Ueda **remained** first in the class throughout elementary, junior high, and high school.

toreru 〚v II〛 **be obtained, be yielded; be made from, yield; be relieved of; be interpreted; come off**

① [be obtained, be yielded]

have a crop of apples, apples **are grown**

¶ I hear that the farmers are happy this year because of the large rice **crop.**

② [be made from, yield]

¶ Salt **is obtained** from salt water.

¶ **Can** oil **be extracted** from the seeds of this flower?

③ [be relieved of]

one's fever **falls** // **be relieved of** one's fatigue

¶ The medicine [I] took **relieved** [me] of the pain from the wound.

④ [be interpreted, be taken]

¶田中さんの返事は，行きたいともとれるし行きたくないともとれます。
(Tanaka san no henji wa, ikitai to mo *toreru*shi ikitaku nai to mo *toremasu.*)

⑤[ある物についていた物が離れて落ちる]

¶シャツのボタンが**とれ**そうですよ。
(Shatsu no botan ga *toresō* desu yo.)

¶子供が引っぱったので，人形の手が**とれて**しまいました。 (Kodomo ga hippatta node, ningyō no te ga *torete* shimaimashita.)

toreru 撮れる〖動Ⅱ〗
¶この写真はきれいに**撮れて**いますね。
(Kono shashin wa kirei ni *torete* imasu ne.)

tori 鳥〖名〗
鳥が鳴く (*tori* ga naku)
¶鳥がたくさん山の方へ飛んでいきます。(*Tori* ga takusan yama no hō e tonde ikimasu.)

toriageru 取り上げる〖動Ⅱ〗
①[手に取って持ち上げる]
¶山田さんは机の上の新聞を**取り上げ**て読み始めました。(Yamada san wa tsukue no ue no shinbun o *toriagete* yomihajimemashita.)
②[意見・申し出を採用・受理する]
¶会議でわたしの意見は**取り上げられ**ませんでした。(Kaigi de watashi no iken wa *toriageraremasen* deshita.)
③[持っている物を奪い取る]

¶ [Mr.] Tanaka's answer **can be taken to mean** either that [he] wants to go or that [he] doesn't want to go.

⑤[come off]

¶ The shirt button **is about to come off.**

¶ The arm of the doll **came off** when the child pulled on it.

toreru 〖v Ⅱ〗 (a photograph) **is taken, come out**

¶ This photo **came out** well, didn't it?

tori 〖n〗 **bird, fowl; chicken, poultry**

a bird cries 〖peeps, honks, crows, etc.〗
¶ A flock of **birds** is flying toward the mountains.

tōri ☞ **toori**

toriageru 〖v Ⅱ〗 **take up, pick up; accept, adopt; take away, seize**
① [take up, pick up]
¶ [Mrs.] Yamada **picked up** the newspaper on the desk and started to read it.
② [accept, adopt, listen to]
¶ The meeting **rejected** my opinion.

③ [take away, seize, confiscate]

¶兄は妹の持っていたおもちゃを取り上げてしまいました。(Ani wa imōto no motte ita omocha o *toriagete* shimaimashita.)

toriatsukau 取り扱う〚動Ⅰ〛

¶外国へ送る小包は，大きな郵便局でなければ取り扱いません。(Gaikoku e okuru kozutsumi wa, ookina yūbinkyoku de nakereba *toriatsukaimasen*.)

¶郵便局では電報を取り扱っていますか。(Yūbinkyoku de wa denpō o *toriatsukatte* imasu ka?)

torikaeru 取り替える〚動Ⅱ〛

¶シャツが汚れたので，新しいのに取り替えました。(Shatsu ga yogoreta node, atarashii no ni *torikaemashita*.)

¶ラジオの部品が壊れたので，新しいのに取り替えました。(Rajio no buhin ga kowareta node, atarashii no ni *torikaemashita*.)

toru 取る〚動Ⅰ〛

①［手に持つ，握る，つかむ］
¶山田さんは机の上の本を取って読み始めました。(Yamada san wa tsukue no ue no hon o *totte* yomihajimemashita.)

¶すみませんが，そこの新聞を取ってくださいませんか。(Sumimasen ga, soko no shinbun o *totte* kudasaimasen ka?)

②［自然にある物や栽培した物を得る］
貝を取る (kai o *toru*)　果物を取る

¶ The boy **took** a toy **away** from his younger sister.

toriatsukau 〚v I〛 treat, handle, deal with

¶ Only larger post offices **handle** parcels being sent abroad.

¶ Does the post office **handle** telegrams?

torikaeru 〚v II〛 exchange, change
¶ [My] shirt was dirty so [I] **changed** into a clean one.

¶ The radio part was broken so I **replaced it** with a new one.

toru 〚v I〛 take, take hold of; get, gather; obtain, win; engage, reserve; pick up, fetch; rob, steal; charge, ask; take, eat; obtain, extract; remove, take away

① [take, hold, take hold of]
¶ [Mr.] Yamada **picked up** the book on the desk and started to read it.
¶ Excuse me, but could you please **hand me** that newspaper?

② [get, gather, pick]
gather shells, **dig out** shellfish //

(kudamono o *toru*)

¶今年は天気が悪くて，米はあまり取れませんでした。(Kotoshi wa tenki ga warukute, kome wa amari *toremasen* deshita.)

③[自分の努力によって何かを得る]

¶英語の試験で100点を取りました。(Eigo no shiken de hyakuten o *torimashita*.)

¶田中さんは働きながら勉強を続けて，先生の資格を取りました。(Tanaka san wa hatarakinagara benkyō o tsuzukete, sensei no shikaku o *torimashita*.)

④[席や部屋を予約して得る]

ホテルの部屋を取る (hoteru no heya o *toru*)

¶あしたの芝居の席は取りました。(Ashita no shibai no seki wa *torimashita*.)

⑤[預けた物などを引き取る]

¶これから駅に預けた荷物を取りに行きます。(Kore kara eki ni azuketa nimotsu o *tori* ni ikimasu.)

⑥[他人の物を盗む]

¶どろぼうにお金を取られてしまいました。(Dorobō ni okane o *torarete* shimaimashita.)

⑦[お金などを払わせる]

月謝を取る (gessha o *toru*)　税金を取る (zeikin o *toru*)

¶昨日パーティーへ行ったら，会費を千円取られました。(Kinō pātii e ittara, kaihi o sen'en *toraremashita*.)

pick fruit

¶ The rice **crop is poor** this year due to bad weather.

③ [obtain, win]

¶ [I] **got** a score of 100 on the English test.

¶ [Miss] Tanaka continued [her] studies while working and **earned** [her] teaching credentials.

④ [engage, reserve, book]

book a hotel room

¶ [I]'ve **reserved** a seat for the play tomorrow.

⑤ [pick up, fetch]

¶ [I]'m going to go now **to pick up** the package 〚bags, items, etc.〛 [I] checked at the station.

⑥ [rob, steal]

¶ A thief **took** my money.

⑦ [charge, ask]

charge monthly tuition // **impose** a tax

¶ [I] **had to pay** a thousand yen toward expenses at the party yesterday.

⑧[食物などを体にとり入れる]
栄養を取る (eiyō o *toru*)
¶おなかのぐあいが悪くて，昨日から食事を取っていません。(Onaka no guai ga warukute, kinō kara shokuji o *totte* imasen.)

⑨[ある物から有用な成分を抜き出す]
¶塩は海水から取っています。 (Shio wa kaisui kara *totte* imasu.)
¶これは何から取った油ですか。(Kore wa nani kara *totta* abura desu ka?)

⑩[必要ないものなどを取り除く]
痛みを取る (itami o *toru*)　熱を取る (netsu o *toru*)　疲れを取る (tsukare o *toru*)
¶寝るときには眼鏡を取ります。(Neru toki ni wa megane o *torimasu*.)
¶もうすぐ田の草を取らなければなりません。(Mō sugu ta no kusa o *toranakereba* narimasen.)

⑪[年齢などを重ねる]
¶だれでも一年に一つずつ年を取ります。 (Dare demo ichinen ni hitotsu zutsu toshi o *torimasu*.)

⑫[ノートしたりメモをつけたりする]
ノートをとる (nōto o *toru*)
¶メモをとりながら先生の話を聞きました。 (Memo o *torinagara* sensei no hanashi o kikimashita.)

toru 捕る〘動Ⅰ〙
生け捕る (ike*doru*)
¶昨日捕った魚は池に入れてあります。(Kinō *totta* sakana wa ike ni irete

⑧ [take, eat]
eat nourishing food
¶ [I] **haven't eaten** since yesterday because of stomach trouble.

⑨ [obtain, extract]
¶ Salt **is obtained** from salt water.

¶ What kind of oil is this (literally, From what has this oil **been extracted**)?

⑩ [remove, take away]
relieve pain // **drive off** a fever // **relieve** fatigue

¶ [I] **take off** [my] glasses when [I] go to bed.

¶ Soon [we] will have **to weed** the rice field.

⑪ [age]
¶ Everyone **gets** a year **older** each year.

⑫ [take (notes, etc.)]
take notes
¶ [I] listened to the professor and **took** notes on [his] talk.

toru 〘v I〙 **catch, take, seize**
capture alive
¶ The fish [we] **caught** yesterday are in the pond 〖pool〗.

arimasu.)

¶ねこがねずみを捕ってきました。

(Neko ga nezumi o *totte* kimashita.)

toru 撮る〖動Ⅰ〗

写真を撮る (shashin o *toru*)

¶あそこで映画を撮っているから、行ってみましょう。(Asoko de eiga o *totte* iru kara, itte mimashō.)

toshi 年〖名〗

①［1年］

年の初め (*toshi* no hajime)　年の暮れ (*toshi* no kure)　年が明ける (*toshi* ga akeru)

¶1月1日に新しい年を迎えます。

(Ichigatsu tsuitachi ni atarashii *toshi* o mukaemasu.)

②［年齢］

年を取る (*toshi* o toru)　年上 (*toshi*-ue)　年下 (*toshi*shita)

¶兄はわたしより三つ年が上です。

(Ani wa watashi yori mittsu *toshi* ga ue desu.)

toshiyori 年寄り〖名〗

¶年寄りには席を譲りましょう。

(*Toshiyori* ni wa seki o yuzurimashō.)

→**rōjin** 老人

toshokan 図書館〖名〗

¶授業のないときには、図書館へ行って勉強します。(Jugyō no nai toki ni wa, *toshokan* e itte benkyō shimasu.)

totemo とても〖副〗

¶ The cat brought back a mouse **it had caught.**

toru 〚v I〛　**take** (a picture), **film**

take a photograph

¶ **They're filming** a movie over there—let's go watch.

tōru ☞ **tooru**

toshi 〚n〛　**a year; age, years old**

① [a year]

the beginning of **the year** // the **year**-end // a new **year** begins

¶ [We] welcome the New **Year** on January 1.

② [age, years old]

to age, grow older // (someone) older // (someone) younger

¶ My (older) brother is three **years** older than me.

toshiyori 〚n〛　**an old person, the aged**

¶ One should offer one's seat to **the elderly.**

toshokan 〚n〛　**library**

¶ When [I] don't have class [I] go to **the library** and study.

tōsu ☞ **toosu**

totemo 〚adv〛　**very, extremely, terribly; by no means, utterly**

①[非常に]

¶この料理は**とても**おいしいですね。
(Kono ryōri wa *totemo* oishii desu ne.)

¶電車は**とても**こんでいました。(Densha wa *totemo* konde imashita.)

②[どんなにしても]

¶こんなに重い荷物は，**とても**一人では持てません。(Konna ni omoi nimotsu wa, *totemo* hitori de wa motemasen.)

¶山田さんは**とても**50歳には見えません。(Yamada san wa *totemo* gojissai ni wa miemasen.)

* あとに打ち消しの言葉や否定的な意味の言葉が来る。

tōtō　とうとう〖副〗

①[いろいろな過程を経て最後にある事態になるという意味を表すときに使う]

¶長い間の研究が**とうとう**完成しました。(Nagai aida no kenkyū ga *tōtō* kansei shimashita.)

¶田中さんはお酒ばかり飲んでいたので，**とうとう**病気になってしまいました。(Tanaka san wa osake bakari nonde ita node, *tōtō* byōki ni natte shimaimashita.)

¶夢中になって本を読んでいたら，**とうとう**夜が明けてしまいました。(Muchū ni natte hon o yonde itara, *tōtō* yo ga akete shimaimashita.)

* 普通 あとに過去・完了を表す「たの形」が来，喜び・あきらめ・驚きな

① [very, extremely, terribly]

¶ This dish is **very** good.

¶ The train was **terribly** crowded.

② [by no means, utterly]

¶ A heavy package 〚load〛 like this **can't possibly** be carried by one person 〚I **can't possibly** carry something so heavy by myself〛.

¶ [Mr.] Yamada doesn't look **at all** like he's 50 years old.

* Followed by words or expressions negative in form or sense.

tōtō 〚adv〛 at last, finally; in the end, after all

① [at last, finally, ultimately; used when something happens after various stages]

¶ The research of so many years 〚months〛 was 〚is〛 **finally** complete.

¶ [Mr.] Tanaka did nothing but drink and **ultimately** [he] became ill 〚**in the end** he has become ill〛.

¶ While [I] was absorbed in reading [my] book a new day dawned.

* Usually followed by a verb in the *-ta* form expressing past or completed action and often followed by an expression of emotion such as joy, res-

どの感情を表すことが多い。「ついに (tsuini)」が事態の成立に重点があるのに対し、事態が成立するまでの過程に重点がある。

②〔前と同じ状態が続いて新しい事態が起こらないことが確定したときに使う〕

¶一日じゅう待っていたのに、山田さんはとうとう来ませんでした。(Ichi-nichijū matte ita noni, Yamada san wa *tōtō* kimasen deshita.)

¶忙しくてとうとうその映画を見に行けませんでした。(Isogashikute *tōtō* sono eiga o mi ni ikemasen deshita.)

* 普通あとに「～ませんでした (～masen deshita)」の形か、否定的な意味の言葉の過去・完了を表す「た形」が来る。

⇨tsuini ついに

totsuzen　突然〔副〕

¶突然、大きな音がしたので、びっくりしました。(*Totsuzen*, ookina oto ga shita node, bikkuri shimashita.)

¶夜遅く突然友達が訪ねてきました。(Yoru osoku *totsuzen* tomodachi ga tazunete kimashita.)

totte　とって〔連〕

¶それはわたしにとって大事な問題です。(Sore wa watashi ni *totte* daiji na mondai desu.)

¶あなたにとって成功とはいったい何ですか。(Anata ni *totte* seikō to wa ittai nan desu ka?)

* いつも「～にとって (～ni totte)」

ignation, surprise, etc. In the case of *tōtō* the emphasis is on the process leading up to a particular event while for *tsuini* it falls on the event itself.

② [in the end, after all; used when a preexisting state continues and one sees that a new event didn't happen]

¶ Even though I waited all day, **in the end** [Mr.] Yamada never showed up.

¶ [I] was busy and wasn't able to go see that film **after all.**

* Usually followed by a verb in the -*masen deshita* form or a verb in the -*ta* form expressing past or completed action and expressing a negative meaning.

totsuzen 〚adv〛 **suddenly, all at once, unexpectedly**

¶ [I] was startled by the **sudden** loud noise.

¶ Late at night a friend paid [me] a **surprise** visit.

totte 〚compd〛 **for, to, with**

¶ That is an important matter **to** me.

¶ What is success **for** you 〚What is your idea of success〛?

* Always used in the pattern "～ *ni totte*."

の形で使う。

tōyō 東洋〖名〗
東洋史 (*tōyōshi*) 　 東洋人 (*tōyōjin*)
¶東洋の文化は，西洋の文化とはいろ
いろな点で違います。(*Tōyō no bun-
ka wa, seiyō no bunka to wa iroiro
na ten de chigaimasu.*)
⇔seiyō 西洋

tōyō 〖n〗　the East, the Orient
Oriental history // an Oriental
¶ **Oriental** culture differs from West-
ern culture in various respects.

tozan 登山〖名，〜する〗
¶山田さんの趣味は登山です。
(*Yamada san no shumi wa tozan
desu.*)
¶天気の悪いときに登山するのは危険
です。(*Tenki no warui toki ni tozan
suru no wa kiken deshita.*)

tozan 〖n, 〜*suru*〗　mountain climbing, an ascent of a mountain
¶ [Mr.] Yamada's hobby is **mountain
climbing.**
¶ It is dangerous **to go mountain
climbing** in bad weather.

tōzen 当然〖副，形動，〜の〗
¶大学生なら，当然これくらいのこと
は知っていなければなりません。
(*Daigakusei nara, tōzen kore kurai
no koto wa shitte inakereba narimasen.*)
¶夜遅く寝れば，朝眠いのは当然です。
(*Yoru osoku nereba, asa nemui no
wa tōzen desu.*)
⇒atarimae あたりまえ

tōzen 〖adv, adj-v, 〜*no*〗　naturally,
as a matter of course, of course,
necessarily, in the nature of things
¶ As a university student, [you]
should **of course** be familiar with
something like this.
¶ If you go to bed late, **of course**
you will be sleepy in the morning.

(-)tsubu (-)粒〖名，尾〗

1〖名〗
米粒 (kome*tsubu*)
¶煙突から出る煙は炭のような粒が集
まったものです。(*Entotsu kara deru
kemuri wa sumi no yō na tsubu
ga atsumatta mono desu.*)

2〖尾〗
¶この薬を食事のあとで二粒ずつ飲

(-)tsubu 〖n, suf〗　a grain, a drop,
etc.

1 〖n〗
a grain of rice
¶ The smoke coming from the
smokestack is like a conglomeration
of charcoal **particles.**

2 〖suf〗
¶ Please take two **drops** of this

んでください。　(Kono kusuri o shokuji no ato de futa*tsubu* zutsu nonde kudasai.)

¶この花の種は二，三粒いっしょにまきます。　(Kono hana no tane wa ni-san*tsubu* issho ni makimasu.)

tsubureru　つぶれる〘動Ⅱ〙

¶かごを落としたので，卵がつぶれてしまいました。　(Kago o otoshita node, tamago ga *tsuburete* shimaimashita.)

¶地震でたくさんの家がつぶれました。(Jishin de takusan no ie ga *tsuburemashita*.)

tsubusu　つぶす〘動Ⅰ〙

¶じゃがいもをつぶして，サラダを作りました。　(Jagaimo o *tsubushite*, sarada o tsukurimashita.)

tsuchi　土〘名〙

¶土を掘って木を植えました。(*Tsuchi* o hotte ki o uemashita.)

tsūchi　通知〘名，〜する〙

¶来週の会議の通知はもう届きましたか。(Raishū no kaigi no *tsūchi* wa mō todokimashita ka?)

¶あしたの会が延期になったことをみんなに通知してください。　(Ashita no kai ga enki ni natta koto o minna ni *tsūchi* shite kudasai.)

tsugi　次〘名〙

¶この次の日曜日にテニスをしませんか。(Kono *tsugi* no nichiyōbi ni tenisu o shimasen ka?)

¶わたしは次の駅で降ります。(Wata-

medicine after each meal.

¶ The seeds of this flower are planted in **twos** and **threes**.

tsubureru 〚v II〛　**be crushed, smashed, destroyed**

¶ The eggs **smashed** when [I] dropped the basket.

¶ Many houses **were destroyed** in the earthquake.

tsubusu 〚v I〛　**crush, smash, mash, break**

¶ [I] **mashed** potatoes and made a salad.

tsuchi 〚n〛　**earth, soil, the ground**

¶ [I] dug a hole in **the ground** and planted a tree.

tsūchi 〚n, ~*suru*〛　**notice, notification, communication**

¶ Have you been **notified** of the meeting next week?

¶ Please **inform** everyone that tomorrow's meeting has been postponed.

tsugi 〚n〛　**next, following, coming**

¶ Would you like to play tennis this **coming** Sunday?

¶ I am getting off at the **next** station.

shi wa *tsugi* no eki de orimasu.)

¶わたしが今いちばん欲しいものはカメラで、その次に欲しいものは時計です。(Watashi ga ima ichiban hoshii mono wa kamera de, sono *tsugi* ni hoshii mono wa tokei desu.)

¶ The thing I want most right now is a camera and, **after that,** a watch.

tsugō　都合〖名〗

都合がいい (*tsugō* ga ii)　都合が悪い (*tsugō* ga warui)

¶今日の午後，御都合はどうでしょうか。(Kyō no gogo go*tsugō* wa dō deshō ka?)

¶都合が悪くて，その会には出席できません。(*Tsugō* ga warukute, sono kai ni wa shusseki dekimasen.)

tsugō 〖n〗 **convenience; circumstances**

be convenient // be inconvenient

¶ Would this afternoon **be convenient** for you?

¶ That meeting 〚gathering, etc.〛 is **at a bad time** for [me] so [I] won't be able to attend.

tsui　つい〖副〗

①[時間や距離などがほんのちょっとである様子]

¶山田さんには，つい先日学校で会ったばかりです。(Yamada san ni wa, *tsui* senjitsu gakkō de atta bakari desu.)

¶わたしのうちは，ついそこです。(Watashi no uchi wa, *tsui* soko desu.)

②[うっかり何かをする様子]

¶わたしは甘い物が好きなので，つい食べすぎてしまいます。(Watashi wa amai mono ga suki na node, *tsui* tabesugite shimaimasu.)

¶あまり忙しかったので，友達に電話するのをつい忘れてしまいました。(Amari isogashikatta node, tomodachi ni denwa suru no o *tsui*

tsui 〖adv〗 **only, just; inadvertently, unintentionally**

① [only, just]

¶ I met [Mr.] Yamada at school **just** the other day.

¶ My home is **just** over there.

② [inadvertently, unintentionally, by chance]

¶ Because of my sweet tooth I always eat too many of them 〚too much of it〛 **before I know it.**

¶ I was so busy that I forgot to call my friend.

wasurete shimaimashita.)

tsuide ni ついでに〖副〗

¶銀行へ行ったついでに，郵便局へ寄って切手を買って来ました。 (Ginkō e itta *tsuide ni*, yūbinkyoku e yotte kitte o katte kimashita.)

tsuini ついに〖副〗

①[いろいろな過程を経て最後にある事態になるという意味を表すときに使う]

¶何時間も急な山道を登って，ついに頂上に着きました。 (Nanjikan mo kyū na yamamichi o nobotte, *tsuini* chōjō ni tsukimashita.)

¶実験はついに成功しました。 (Jikken wa *tsuini* seikō shimashita.)

¶丈夫だった上田さんもついに病気で入院したそうです。 (Jōbu datta Ueda san mo *tsuini* byōki de nyūin shita sō desu.)

* 普通あとに過去・完了を表す「たの形」が来，喜び・失望・あきらめなどの感情を表すことが多い。「とうとう (tōtō)」が事態が成立するまでの過程に重点があるのに対し，事態の成立そのものに重点がある。

②[前と同じ状態が続いて新しい事態が起こらないことが確定したときに使う]

¶1時間待ったが，田中さんはついに来ませんでした。 (Ichijikan matta ga, Tanaka san wa *tsuini* kimasen deshita.)

¶時計がなくなったので，一生懸命捜

tsuide ni 〖adv〗 **while, in passing, at the same time**

¶ **On the way** to the bank [I] stopped off at the post office and bought some stamps.

tsuini 〖adv〗 **at last, finally; in the end, after all**

① [at last, finally, ultimately; used when an event takes place after various stages]

¶ After hours of climbing up the steep mountain trail, [we] **at last** reached the summit.

¶ The experiment **finally** succeeded 〖has **finally** succeeded〗.

¶ I hear that even the hardy [Mr.] Ueda was **ultimately** sick and in the hospital 〖has **in the end** become sick and is in the hospital〗.

* Usually followed by a verb in the *-ta* form expressing past or completed action and often used with expressions of emotion such as joy, disappointment, resignation, etc. In the case of *tōtō* the emphasis is on the process leading up to the event but for *tsuini* it is on the event itself.

② [in the end, after all; used when the preexisting state continues and one sees that some new event has not taken place]

¶ [I] waited an hour but **in the event** [Mr.] Tanaka didn't come.

しましたが，ついに見つかりませんでした。(Tokei ga nakunatta node, isshōkenmei sagashimashita ga, *tsuini* mitsukarimasen deshita.)

* 普通あとに「〜ませんでした（〜masen deshita）」の形か，否定的な意味の言葉の過去・完了を表す「たの形」が来る。

⇨**tōtō** とうとう

tsuitachi 一日〖名〗

¶今日は三月一日です。(Kyō wa sangatsu *tsuitachi* desu.)

⇨**-ka** -日

tsuite ついて〖連〗

¶あなたは日本で何について勉強するつもりですか。(Anata wa Nihon de nani ni *tsuite* benkyō suru tsumori desu ka?)

¶今日は，あなたがたの国について作文を書いてください。(Kyō wa, anatagata no kuni ni *tsuite* sakubun o kaite kudasai.)

* いつも「〜について（〜ni tsuite）」の形で使う。

tsūjiru 通じる〖動Ⅱ〗

①〔道などがある場所に続く〕

¶この道は学校の前に通じています。(Kono michi wa gakkō no mae ni *tsūjite* imasu.)

②〔交通や通信などがある所などとつながる〕

鉄道が通じる (tetsudō ga *tsūjiru*)

¶電話が通じません。どうしたのでしょう。(Denwa ga *tsūjimasen*. Dō

¶ [I] searched all over for [my] missing watch but it **never** turned up.

* Usually followed by a verb in the *-masen deshita* form or a verb in the *-ta* form expressing past or completed action and expressing a negative meaning.

tsuitachi 〖n〗 **the first day of the month**

¶ Today is March **1**.

tsuite 〖compd〗 **about, on, concerning, in regard to**

¶ **What** do you plan to study in Japan?

¶ Today please write a composition **about** your native countries.

* Always used in the pattern "~ *ni tsuite*."

tsūjiru 〖v Ⅱ〗 **pass, run; lead to, connect with; be understood, be comprehended; via, through the medium of**

① [pass, run]

¶ This street **passes** in front of the school.

② [lead to, connect with]

have train **service**

¶ The phone **is dead.** I wonder what happened.

shita no deshō?)

③[相手にわかってもらえる]

¶わたしの下手な英語では，とてもアメリカでは通じないでしょう。

(Watashi no heta na Eigo de wa, totemo Amerika de wa *tsūjinai* deshō.)

¶あの人には冗談を言っても通じません。 (Ano hito ni wa jōdan o itte mo *tsūjimasen*.)

④[全体にわたってという意味を表す]

¶一年を通じて今月がいちばん雨が多いです。 (Ichinen o *tsūjite* kongetsu ga ichiban ame ga ooi desu.)

* いつも「〜を通じて (〜o tsūjite)」の形で使う。

⑤[あるものを媒介としてという意味を表す]

¶そのニュースはラジオを通じて全国に放送されました。 (Sono nyūsu wa rajio o *tsūjite* zenkoku ni hōsō saremashita.)

* いつも「〜を通じて (〜o tsūjite)」の形で使う。

③ [be understood, be comprehended]

¶ With my poor command of English I probably **wouldn't be able to make myself understood** at all in the United States.

¶ [He] doesn't have any sense of humor—[he] **never understands the point** of a joke (literally, Even if you tell him a joke he **won't understand** it).

④ [throughout]

¶ **Of all** the year, this month has the most rainfall.

* Always used in the pattern "〜 *o tsūjite*."

⑤ [via, through the medium of]

¶ That news was broadcast to the whole country **on** the radio.

* Always used in the pattern "〜 *o tsūjite*."

tsukamaeru 捕まえる〖動Ⅱ〗

¶警官がどろぼうを捕まえました。

(Keikan ga dorobō o *tsukamaemashita*.)

¶子供たちが川で魚を捕まえています。 (Kodomotachi ga kawa de sakana o *tsukamaete* imasu.)

tsukamu つかむ〖動Ⅰ〗

①[指で強く持つ]

¶田中さんはわたしの腕をつかんで離

tsukamaeru 〖v Ⅱ〗 **capture, arrest; catch, grab**

¶ The police **arrested** the thief.

¶ The children **are catching** fish at the river (with a net or in their hands).

tsukamu 〖v Ⅰ〗 **grab, grip, hold; grasp, have a firm hold of; grasp, apprehend**

① [grab, grip, hold]

しませんでした。 (Tanaka san wa watashi no ude o *tsukande* hanashi-masen deshita.)

¶このひもの端をしっかり**つかん**でいてください。 (Kono himo no hashi o shikkari *tsukande* ite kudasai.)

②[確実にとらえて自分のものにする]

機会を**つかむ** (kikai o *tsukamu*) 幸福を**つかむ** (kōfuku o *tsukamu*)

③[要点・意味などを把握する]

¶わたしはこの文の意味を**つかむ**ことができません。 (Watashi wa kono bun no imi o *tsukamu* koto ga dekimasen.)

¶ [Mr.] Tanaka **took hold** of my arm and wouldn't let go of it.

¶ Please **take a** firm **hold** on the end of this string 〚twine, cord, etc.〛.

② [grasp, have a firm hold on]

seize an opportunity // **don't let** happiness **slip** through one's fingers

③ [grasp, apprehend]

¶ I can't **grasp** the meaning of this passage.

tsukareru 疲れる〚動Ⅱ〛

¶今日は仕事が忙しくて，たいへん疲れました。 (Kyō wa shigoto ga iso-gashikute, taihen *tsukaremashita*.)

¶疲れたら，少し休んでください。

(*Tsukaretara*, sukoshi yasunde ku-dasai.)

tsukareru 〚v Ⅱ〛 be tired, become tired

¶ [I]'m very **tired** as it was quite busy at work today.

¶ Please rest a bit **if you're tired**.

tsukau 使う〚動Ⅰ〛

¶この紙は何に**使います**か。 (Kono kami wa nan ni *tsukaimasu* ka?)

¶塩を**使って**，料理に味をつけます。 (Shio o *tsukatte*, ryōri ni aji o tsu-kemasu.)

¶英語を**使わないで**，日本語で話してください。 (Eigo o *tsukawanaide*, Nihongo de hanashite kudasai)

¶お金をむだに**使って**はいけません。 (Okane o muda ni *tsukatte* wa ikemasen.)

⇒mochiiru 用いる

tsukau 〚v Ⅰ〛 use, make use of, employ

¶ What is this paper **used for?**

¶ Salt **is used** to flavor food.

¶ Please **don't use** English—speak in Japanese.

¶ One shouldn't **waste** money.

tsukeru つける〖動Ⅱ〗

①〔あるものを何かの表面に付着させる〕

¶パンにバターを**つけて**食べます。

(Pan ni batā o *tsukete* tabemasu.)

¶けがをしたので，足に薬を**つけました**。(Kega o shita node, ashi ni kusuri o *tsukemashita*.)

②〔あるものを何かに添えたり加えたりする，留めて離れない状態にする〕

¶次の漢字に仮名を**つけ**なさい。

(Tsugi no kanji ni kana o *tsuke-nasai*.)

¶ボタンが取れたから**つけて**ください。

(Botan ga toreta kara *tsukete* kudasai.)

③〔決める，定める〕

値段を**つける** (nedan o *tsukeru*)

点数を**つける** (tensū o *tsukeru*)

¶赤ん坊が生まれたので，父に名前を**つけて**もらいました。 (Akanbō ga umareta node, chichi ni namae o *tsukete* moraimashita.)

④〔スイッチなどを入れる，点火する〕

電燈を**つける** (dentō o *tsukeru*)

ラジオを**つける** (rajio o *tsukeru*)

テレビを**つける** (terebi o *tsukeru*)

¶マッチでたばこに火を**つけました**。

(Matchi de tabako ni hi o *tsuke-mashita*.)

⑤〔注意する〕

¶道を歩くときは車に気を**つけましょ**う。(Michi o aruku toki wa kuruma ni ki o *tsukemashō*.)

tsukeru 〚v Ⅱ〛 **apply, put on; add, attach; set, price, assign; turn on, light; enter, put down**

① [apply, put on]

¶ I **butter** bread 〚toast, rolls, etc.〛 and eat it.

¶ [I] hurt [my] leg 〚foot〛 so [I] **put** some medication 〚ointment, etc.〛 on it.

② [add, attach, append]

¶ **Write** *kana* **alongside** the following *kanji*.

¶ Please **sew on** this button which has come off.

③ [set, price, assign, give]

put a price **on** something // **assign** a mark

¶ We had a baby and asked my father **to think of** a good name **for it**.

④ [turn on, light]

turn on the light, **turn on** an electric light // **turn on** the radio // **turn on** the television

¶ [I] **lighted** the cigarette with a match.

⑤ [be careful, pay attention to]

¶ **One must watch out** for cars when walking along the road.

* いつも「気をつける(ki o tsukeru)」の形で使う。

⑥[書く]
〇印をつける (marujirushi o tsu-keru)

¶わたしは毎日日記をつけています。(Watashi wa mainichi nikki o tsukete imasu.)

tsuki 月〖名〗

①[１年を12に分けたその一つ]
¶一年じゅうでいちばん寒い月は何月ですか。(Ichinenjū de ichiban samui tsuki wa nangatsu desu ka?)

②[衛星]
¶空に円いきれいな月が出ています。(Sora ni marui kirei na tsuki ga dete imasu.)

tsuku 着く〖動Ⅰ〗

①[目的の場所に達する]
¶１週間前にそちらに送った小包はもう着きましたか。 (Isshūkan mae ni sochira ni okutta kozutsumi wa mō tsukimashita ka?)
¶日本に着いたら，すぐあなたに手紙を書きます。 (Nihon ni tsuitara, sugu anata ni tegami o kakimasu.)

②[ある位置に身を置く]
¶席に着いてください。(Seki ni tsuite kudasai.)

tsuku つく〖動Ⅰ〗

①[あるものが何かの表面に付着する]
¶この切手の裏にはのりがついています。(Kono kitte no ura ni wa nori ga tsuite imasu.)

* Always used in the pattern "*ki o tsukeru.*"

⑥ [enter, put down, keep]
mark with a circle

¶ I **make** a diary entry every day.

tsuki 〚n〛 a month; the moon

① [a month]
¶ What is the coldest **month** of the year?

② [the moon]
¶ There's a lovely full **moon** up in the sky.

tsuku 〚v I〛 arrive, get to; take, occupy

① [arrive, get to, reach]
¶ Has the parcel [I] mailed you a week ago **arrived** yet?

¶ [I] will write you a letter soon after **[my] arrival** in Japan.

② [take, occupy, take one's position]
¶ Please **take** your seats.

tsuku 〚v I〛 stick to, be stained; be attached to, belong to; follow, accompany; be established, take root; be lighted, come on

① [stick to, be stained]
¶ This stamp **has** glue on the back.

829

¶手にインクが**ついて**しまいました。
(Te ni inku ga *tsuite* shimaimashita.)

¶ [My] hand **got stained** with ink.

②[あるものが何かに加わる]
¶この日本語の教科書の後ろには，日本の地図と漢字の表が**ついて**います。
(Kono Nihongo no kyōkasho no ushiro ni wa, Nihon no chizu to kanji no hyō ga *tsuite* imasu.)

② [be attached to, belong to]
¶ This Japanese textbook **has** a map of Japan and a table of *kanji* in the back.

¶わたしのかばんにはかぎが**ついて**いません。(Watashi no kaban ni wa kagi ga *tsuite* imasen.)

¶ My suitcase ⟦briefcase, bag, etc.⟧ **doesn't have** a lock on it.

③[何かがあるもののそばにいて離れない]
¶この犬は駅からずっとわたしに**ついて**きました。(Kono inu wa eki kara zutto watashi ni *tsuite* kimashita.)

③ [follow, accompany]

¶ This dog **has followed me** all the way from the station.

¶旅行の時は上田さんが**ついて**案内してくれるそうです。(Ryokō no toki wa Ueda san ga *tsuite* annai shite kureru sō desu.)

¶ I hear that [Mr.] Ueda **will accompany us** on the trip and act as guide.

④[決まる，定まる]
話が**つく** (hanashi ga *tsuku*) 解決が**つく** (kaiketsu ga *tsuku*)
¶1年間考えましたが，やっと会社をやめる決心が**つきました**。(Ichinenkan kangaemashita ga, yatto kaisha o yameru kesshin ga *tsukimashita*.)

④ [be established, take root]
come to an understanding, **reach** an agreement // settle a matter, **reach** a solution
¶ I thought it over for a year and finally **made up my mind** to quit my job.

⑤[感覚器官に感じられる]
¶看板は人の目に**つく**ような所に出さなければだめです。(Kanban wa hito no me ni *tsuku* yō na tokoro ni dasanakereba dame desu.)

⑤ [be sensed]
¶ Signboards must be placed where they **will catch the eye.**

⑥[スイッチなどが入る, 点火する]
火がつく (hi ga *tsuku*)

¶部屋に電燈がついています。 (Heya ni dentō ga *tsuite* imasu.)

⑦[注意が行き届く, あることがらを意識する]

¶山田さんはよく気がつく人です。 (Yamada san wa yoku ki ga *tsuku* hito desu.)

¶学校へ行く途中本を忘れたことに気がつきました。 (Gakkō e iku tochū hon o wasureta koto ni ki ga *tsukimashita*.)

* いつも「気がつく (ki ga tsuku)」の形で使う。

⑧[言う]

¶うそをつかないで本当のことを言いなさい。 (Uso o *tsukanaide* hontō no koto o iinasai.)

* 普通「うそをつく (uso o tsuku)」の形で使う。

tsukue 机〚名〛

¶机の上に本と鉛筆があります。 (*Tsukue* no ue ni hon to enpitsu ga arimasu.)

tsukuru 作る〚動Ⅰ〛

①[材料を使って物をこしらえる]

¶紙で人形を作ります。 (Kami de ningyō o *tsukurimasu*.)

¶わたしは料理を作るのが好きです。 (Watashi wa ryōri o *tsukuru* no ga suki desu.)

②[栽培する]
野菜を作る (yasai o *tsukuru*)

⑥ [be lighted, come on]
catch fire

¶ The lights **are on** in the room.

⑦ [notice]

¶ [Mr.] Yamada **is** very **considerate.**

¶ When [I] was partway to school [I] **realized** that [I] had forgotten the book.

* Always used in the pattern "*ki ga tsuku.*"

⑧ [say, speak]
¶ **No lies** now—tell the truth.

* Usually used in the pattern "*uso o tsuku*" (tell a lie).

tsukue 〚n〛 desk

¶ There are books and pencils on **the desk.**

tsukuru 〚v Ⅰ〛 make; raise, grow; make, create, compose; form, establish

① [make, prepare]
¶ [I] **will make** a doll out of paper.
¶ I like **to cook.**

② [raise, grow]
raise vegetables

¶この村では，米を作る人より花を作る人のほうが多いです。(Kono mura de wa, kome o *tsukuru* hito yori hana o *tsukuru* hito no hō ga ooi desu.)

③［芸術作品などを産み出す］
文を作る (bun o *tsukuru*)
¶上田さんの作った詩を見せてもらいました。(Ueda san no *tsukutta* shi o misete moraimashita.)

④［今まで無かったものを新しく考えだしたりこしらえたりする］
記録をつくる (kiroku o *tsukuru*)
規則をつくる (kisoku o *tsukuru*)
¶田中さんは友達と日本文学の研究会をつくるつもりです。(Tanaka san wa tomodachi to Nihon-bungaku no kenkyūkai o *tsukuru* tsumori desu.)

tsukuru 造る〖動Ⅰ〗
船を造る (fune o *tsukuru*) 酒を造る (sake o *tsukuru*)
¶山田さんは自分の家に大きな庭を造りました。(Yamada san wa jibun no ie ni ookina niwa o *tsukurimashita*.)

tsukusu 尽くす〖動Ⅰ〗
全力を尽くす (zenryoku o *tsukusu*)
¶食べ物は全部食べ尽くしてしまいました。(Tabemono wa zenbu tabe-*tsukushite* shimaimashita.)

¶わたしの言いたいことはもう言い尽くしました。(Watashi no iitai koto wa mō ii*tsukushimashita*.)

¶ In this village more people **raise** flowers than **grow** rice.

③ [make, create, compose]
write a text, **compose** a sentence
¶ [Miss] Ueda showed me the poem [she] **wrote** ⟦I was shown the poem Miss Ueda **wrote**⟧.

④ [form, establish, found]

set a new record // **set up** rules

¶ [Mr.] Tanaka plans **to found** a group of [his] friends to study Japanese literature.

tsukuru ⟦v I⟧ **make, manufacture, construct**
build a ship // **brew** *sake*

¶ [Mr.] Yamada **laid out** a large garden at [his] home.

(-)tsukusu ⟦v I⟧ **exhaust, use up; exert oneself, make efforts**
exert all one's powers
¶ [We] **ate up** ⟦**have eaten up**⟧ all the food.

¶ I've **said everything** I have to say (literally, want to say) ⟦I **said everything** I had to say⟧.

tsuma 妻〖名〗

¶わたしは妻と子供を連れて旅行に出ました。 (Watashi wa *tsuma* to kodomo o tsurete ryokō ni demashita.)

＊ 結婚した男女の女のほうをさす言葉。自分の妻のことを他人に話す場合には，普通「家内 (kanai)」と言う。⇔**otto** 夫 ⇒**kanai** 家内 **okusan** 奥さん

tsuma 〚n〛 a wife

¶ I went on a trip with **my wife** and children.

＊ Indicates the female spouse in a married couple. When speaking of one's own wife to others, one usually uses *kanai* instead.

tsumaranai つまらない〖形〗

①[おもしろくない]

¶あの映画はつまらなかったです。 (Ano eiga wa *tsumaranakatta* desu.)

¶話がつまらないので，眠くなりました。 (Hanashi ga *tsumaranai* node, nemuku narimashita.)

②[価値がない]

¶これはわたしがかいたつまらない絵ですが，どうぞ部屋に掛けてください。 (Kore wa watashi ga kaita *tsumaranai* e desu ga, dōzo heya ni kakete kudasai.)

tsumaranai 〚adj〛 uninteresting, dull; trifling, worthless

① [uninteresting, dull, monotonous, boring]

¶ That movie **was boring.**

¶ The speech **was uninteresting** so [I] became sleepy.

② [trifling, worthless]

¶ This is **just something** I painted myself but please hang it in your room if you'd like.

tsumari つまり〖副〗

¶山田さんが言いたいのは，つまり萩子さんと結婚したいということです。 (Yamada san ga iitai no wa, *tsumari* Akiko san to kekkon shitai to iu koto desu.)

¶お花見というのは，つまり桜の花を見ながらお酒を飲んだり，ごちそうを食べたりすることです。 (Ohanami to iu no wa, *tsumari* sakura no hana o minagara osake o nondari, go-

tsumari 〚adv〛 in brief, in other words

¶ **In short,** what Mr. Yamada is trying to say is that he wants to marry Akiko.

¶ **In other words,** *ohanami* refers to eating and drinking while viewing the cherry blossoms.

chisō o tabetari suru koto desu.)

tsumaru 詰まる〚動Ⅰ〛

①[ある空間にものがいっぱいになる]
¶かばんに本がいっぱい詰まっています。 (Kaban ni hon ga ippai *tsumatte* imasu.)

②[ふさがって通じなくなる]
¶風邪をひいて，鼻が詰まりました。
(Kaze o hiite, hana ga *tsumarimashita*.)

tsume つめ〚名〛

つめを切る (*tsume* o kiru)　つめが伸びる (*tsume* ga nobiru)

tsumeru 詰める〚動Ⅱ〛

¶お菓子をその箱に詰めてください。
(Okashi o sono hako ni *tsumete* kudasai.)
¶あとの人が乗れませんから，もう少し奥に詰めてください。 (Ato no hito ga noremasen kara, mō sukoshi oku ni *tsumete* kudasai.)

tsumetai 冷たい〚形〛

¶冷たい水を飲みました。 (*Tsumetai* mizu o nomimashita.)
¶このビールは冷蔵庫から出したばかりですから，冷たいですよ。 (Kono biiru wa reizōko kara dashita bakari desu kara, *tsumetai* desu yo.)
⇔atsui 熱い

tsumi 罪〚名〛

¶人を殺すと重い罪になります。(Hito o korosu to omoi *tsumi* ni narimasu.)

tsumori つもり〚名〛

tsumaru 〚v I〛　be full, be crammed; be stopped up, be obstructed

① [be full, be crammed, be stuffed]
¶ The bag 〚briefcase, etc.〛 **is crammed** full of books.

② [be stopped up, be obstructed, be clogged]
¶ [I] caught a cold and now [my] nose **is all stuffed up.**

tsume 〚n〛　a nail, a claw

trim **one's nails** // **one's nails** grow out

tsumeru 〚v II〛　stuff, cram, move closer

¶ Please **put** the candy 〚cake, sweets〛 in that box.

¶ Please **move** to the rear so there will be room for those getting on (said by the driver on a bus, etc.).

tsumetai 〚adj〛　cold, cool

¶ [I] drank some **cold** water.

¶ This beer **is chilled**—it's right out of the refrigerator.

tsumi 〚n〛　crime, sin, offense, guilt, blame, punishment

¶ Murder brings a severe **punishment.**

tsumori 〚n〛　intention, purpose, motive

¶あなたは夏休みに何を**する**つもりで
すか。 (Anata wa natsuyasumi ni
nani o suru *tsumori* desu ka?)
¶わたしは日本へ行って経済学を勉強
するつもりです。(Watashi wa Nihon
e itte keizaigaku o benkyō suru
tsumori desu.)

tsumoru 積もる〖動 I 〗
¶昨日降った雪が庭に**積**もっています。
(Kinō futta yuki ga niwa ni *tsu-
motte* imasu.)

tsumu 積む〖動 I 〗
①[重ねる]
¶机の上に本が**積**んであります。
(Tsukue no ue ni hon ga *tsunde*
arimasu.)
②[荷を載せる]
¶荷物を車に**積**みました。 (Nimotsu
o kuruma ni *tsumimashita*.)

tsuna 綱〖名〗
綱を引く (*tsuna* o hiku)　太い綱
(futoi *tsuna*)

tsunagu つなぐ〖動 I 〗
①[ある物を綱やひもで結んで離れな
いようにする]
¶犬を**つな**いでおいてください。 (Inu
o *tsunaide* oite kudasai.)
¶ボートが岸に**つな**いであります。
(Bōto ga kishi ni *tsunaide* arimasu.)
②[離れているものを一つに結ぶ]
¶わたしは妹と手を**つな**いで公園を散
歩しました。(Watashi wa imōto to
te o *tsunaide* kōen o sanpo shimashita.)

¶ What do you **intend** to do during
summer vacation 〖your summer
holidays〗?
¶ **I plan** to go to Japan and study
economics.

tsumoru 〖v I〗 **accumulate, pile up**
¶ The snow that fell yesterday **is
lying deep** on the ground in the
yard.

tsumu 〖v I〗 **pile up, stack; load,
take on board**
① [pile up, stack]
¶ Books **are piled up** on the desk.

② [load, take on board]
¶ [I] **loaded up** the car.

tsuna 〖n〗 **rope, line, cord, cable**
pull **a rope** // a thick **rope**

tsunagu 〖v I〗 **tie, fasten; connect,
link**
① [tie, fasten, chain, tether]
¶ Please keep the dog **tied up.**

¶ The boat **is moored** to the bank.

② [connect, link, join]
¶ My (younger) sister and I walked
in the park **hand in hand.**

¶この電話を社長室につないでください。 (Kono denwa o shachōshitsu ni *tsunaide* kudasai.)

tsune ni 常に〖副〗

¶わたしは病気をしないように常に注意しています。(Watashi wa byōki o shinai yō ni *tsune ni* chūi shite imasu.)

¶あの人は常にわたしの意見に反対します。(Ano hito wa *tsune ni* watashi no iken ni hantai shimasu.)

tsurai つらい〖形〗

¶あなたと別れるのは，とてもつらいことです。 (Anata to wakareru no wa, totemo *tsurai* koto desu.)

¶ゆうべ遅く寝たので，今朝は起きるのがつらかったです。 (Yūbe osoku neta node, kesa wa okiru no ga *tsurakatta* desu.)

tsureru 連れる〖動Ⅱ〗

¶わたしは毎朝犬を連れて散歩をします。 (Watashi wa maiasa inu o *tsurete* sanpo shimasu.)

¶先週の日曜日，弟を連れて映画を見に行きました。(Senshū no nichiyōbi, otōto o *tsurete* eiga o mi ni ikimashita.)

＊ 自分より目下の者や動物といっしょに行く場合に使う。

tsuri つり〖名〗

つり糸 (*tsuri*ito)

¶中村さんの趣味はつりです。(Nakamura san no shumi wa *tsuri* desu.)

tsuri つり〖名〗

¶ Please **put** this call **through** to the director's office.

tsune ni 〖adv〗 **always, ordinarily, customarily, usually**

¶ I **habitually** take care not to become ill.

¶ [He] **always** opposes my views.

tsurai 〖adj〗 **hard, trying, painful**

¶ **It is** very **painful** to say goodbye to you.

¶ Since [I] went to bed late last night **it was hard** to get up this morning.

tsureru 〖v Ⅱ〗 **bring, take, be accompanied by**

¶ I go for a walk **with** the dog every morning.

¶ **I took** my younger brother to a movie last Sunday.

＊ Used when one goes somewhere with an animal or a person lower in status than oneself.

tsuri 〖n〗 **fishing**

fishing line

¶ [Mr.] Nakamura's hobby is **fishing.**

tsuri 〖n〗 **change** (from a purchase)

¶細かいお金がないから，すみませんが一万円でおつりをください。

(Komakai okane ga nai kara, sumimasen ga, ichiman'en de *otsuri* o kudasai.)

tsuru　つる〖動Ⅰ〗

¶海でつってきた魚を料理して食べました。(Umi de *tsutte* kita sakana o ryōri shite tabemashita.)

tsūshin　通信〖名，〜する〗

通信社 (*tsūshin*sha)

¶最近，科学の進歩によって通信の方法が発達しました。(Saikin, kagaku no shinpo ni yotte *tsūshin* no hōhō ga hattatsu shimashita.)

¶台風のため，九州地方との通信ができなくなりました。(Taifū no tame, Kyūshū-chihō to no *tsūshin* ga dekinaku narimashita.)

tsutaeru　伝える〖動Ⅱ〗

①[伝言する]

¶「あしたは学校が休みです。」と山田さんに伝えてください。("Ashita wa gakkō ga yasumi desu." to Yamada san ni *tsutaete* kudasai.)

¶奥さんにどうぞよろしくお伝えください。(Okusan ni dōzo yoroshiku o*tsutae* kudasai.)

②[昔から今まで受け継いできている]

¶この話はこの地方に昔から伝えられているものです。(Kono hanashi wa kono chihō ni mukashi kara *tsutaerarete* iru mono desu.)

③[学問・芸術・宗教・制度などを外

¶ I'm sorry but I don't have anything smaller than this ten-thousand yen bill to pay with (literally, please give me **the change** out of ten thousand yen).

tsuru〖v I〗**fish, catch**

¶ [I] cooked and ate the fish [I] **caught** at the ocean.

tsūshin〖n, 〜*suru*〗**communication(s), news, information**

a **news** agency, a **wire** service

¶ The advance of science in recent years has resulted in improved means of **communication.**

¶ **Communications** with the Kyushu region were 〖are〗 cut off due to the typhoon.

tsutaeru〖v II〗**convey, tell; hand down, bequeath; introduce; transmit, conduct**

① [convey, tell, report]

¶ Please **tell** [Miss] Yamada that there will be no school tomorrow.

¶ Please **convey** my best regards to your wife.

② [hand down, bequeath, leave]

¶ This tale **has been handed down** in this region from long-ago generations.

③ [introduce]

国から持って来る〕

¶漢字は中国から日本に**伝えられた**ものです。 (Kanji wa Chūgoku kara Nihon ni *tsutaerareta* mono desu.)

④〔電気・音・熱などをほかに移す〕
熱を**伝える** (netsu o *tsutaeru*)

¶銅は電気をよく**伝えます**。 (Dō wa denki o yoku *tsutaemasu*.)

tsutawaru 伝わる〔動Ⅰ〕

①〔人を通してあることが広がる〕
ニュースが**伝わる** (nyūsu ga *tsutawaru*)

¶そのうわさは，たちまち町じゅうに**伝わりました**。 (Sono uwasa wa, tachimachi machijū ni *tsutawarimashita*.)

②〔昔から今に受け継がれてきている〕
¶古くからこの地方に**伝わる**話を集めて本を作りました。 (Furuku kara kono chihō ni *tsutawaru* hanashi o atsumete hon o tsukurimashita.)

③〔電気・音・熱などが移る〕
電気が**伝わる** (denki ga *tsutawaru*)
¶隣のうちのピアノの音がここまで**伝わってきます**。 (Tonari no uchi no piano no oto ga koko made *tsutawatte* kimasu.)

④〔一方から他方へあるものに沿って移る〕
¶どろぼうは窓を**伝わって**部屋に入ったらしいです。 (Dorobō wa mado o *tsutawatte* heya ni haitta rashii desu.)

tsutomeru 勤める〔動Ⅱ〕

¶ *Kanji* **were introduced** into Japan from China.

④ [transmit, conduct]
conduct heat

¶ Copper is a good **conductor** of electricity.

tsutawaru 〚v I〛 **spread, circulate; be handed down, come down; be transmitted, be conveyed; come across, go along**

① [spread, circulate]
news **travels**

¶ That rumor **spread** quickly throughout the village.

② [be handed down, come down]
¶ [I] collected tales **handed down** from olden times in this region and made them into a book.

③ [be transmitted, be conveyed, be carried]
electricity **is conducted**

¶ The sound of the piano next door **carries over** to here.

④ [come across, go along]

¶ It appears that the thief entered the room 〚apartment〛 **by** the window.

tsutomeru 〚v II〛 **be employed, hold a post, work for**

¶兄は会社に勤めています。 (Ani wa kaisha ni *tsutomete* imasu.)

¶わたしは卒業したら，銀行に勤めたいと思っています。 (Watashi wa sotsugyō shitara, ginkō ni *tsutometai* to omotte imasu.)

tsutomeru 努める〚動Ⅱ〛

¶できるだけ勉強するように努めなさい。 (Dekiru dake benkyō suru yō ni *tsutomenasai*.)

¶みんながこの問題の解決に努めています。 (Minna ga kono mondai no kaiketsu ni *tsutomete* imasu.)

tsutsumu 包む〚動Ⅰ〛

¶デパートで買い物をすると，きれいな紙に包んでくれます。 (Depāto de kaimono o suru to, kirei na kami ni *tsutsunde* kuremasu.)

tsūyaku 通訳〚名，～する〛

同時通訳 (dōji-*tsūyaku*)

¶彼女の職業は通訳です。 (Kanojo no shokugyō wa *tsūyaku* desu.)

tsuyoi 強い〚形〛

①[力・技などが優れている様子]

¶山田さんはたいへん力が強いから，この重い荷物を持ってもらいましょう。 (Yamada san wa taihen chikara ga *tsuyoi* kara, kono omoi nimotsu o motte moraimashō.)

¶わたしの学校は野球が強いです。 (Watashi no gakkō wa yakyū ga *tsuyoi* desu.)

②[激しい様子，程度がはなはだしい様子]

¶ My older brother **has an office job.**

¶ **I would like a position** at a bank after graduating.

tsutomeru 〚v II〛 **strive, endeavor, try hard, make an effort**

¶ **Try** to study as much as possible.

¶ All **are striving** to solve this problem.

tsutsumu 〚v I〛 **wrap, do up** (a parcel), **cover, envelop in**

¶ When one buys an article at a department store, they **wrap it up** in attractive paper.

tsūyaku 〚n, ~*suru*〛 **interpretation, an interpreter**

simultaneous **interpretation**

¶ She is a professional **interpreter.**

tsuyoi 〚adj〛 **strong, powerful; violent, strong; stout, healthy; be good at; resistant, tolerant**

① [strong, powerful]

¶ [Mr.] Yamada **is** very **strong**— let's have [him] carry this heavy load 〚bag, etc.〛.

¶ My school **is strong** in baseball.

② [violent, strong, intense, sharp]

強い雨 (*tsuyoi* ame)

¶山の方から突然風が強く吹いてきました。 (Yama no hō kara totsuzen kaze ga *tsuyoku* fuite kimashita.)

③[体などが丈夫な様子]

足が強い (ashi ga *tsuyoi*)

¶スポーツをして，強い体を作りましょう。 (Supōtsu o shite, *tsuyoi* karada o tsukurimashō.)

④[得意である様子]

数学に強い (sūgaku ni *tsuyoi*)

¶上田さんは英語に強いです。 (Ueda san wa Eigo ni *tsuyoi* desu.)

＊ いつも「〜に強い (〜ni tsuyoi)」の形で使う。

⑤[ものごとに耐える力がある様子]

¶ナイロンは水には強いですが，火には弱いです。 (Nairon wa mizu ni wa *tsuyoi* desu ga, hi ni wa yowai desu.)

¶わたしは暑さには強いですから，夏は好きです。 (Watashi wa atsusa ni wa *tsuyoi* desu kara, natsu wa suki desu.)

＊ いつも「〜に強い (〜 ni tsuyoi)」の形で使う。

⇔yowai 弱い

tsuyu 梅雨〖名〗

¶日本では，6月から7月の中ごろまで梅雨の季節です。 (Nihon de wa, rokugatsu kara shichigatsu no nakagoro made *tsuyu* no kisetsu desu.)

tsuzukeru 続ける〖動Ⅱ〗

a **heavy** rain

¶ A **sharp** wind suddenly started 〖has suddenly started〗 blowing in from the mountains.

③ [stout, healthy, robust]

be a **good** walker

¶ Let's all build **strong** constitutions by participating in sports.

④ [be good at]

be good at mathematics

¶ [Miss] Ueda **is very good** at English.

＊ Always used in the pattern "〜 *ni tsuyoi*."

⑤ [resistant, tolerant]

¶ Nylon **stands up** against water but is highly combustible.

¶ As I **don't feel** the heat, I like summer.

＊ Always used in the pattern "〜 *ni tsuyoi*."

tsuyu 〖n〗 the rainy season

¶ **The rainy season** in Japan falls from June to mid-July.

tsuzukeru 〖v Ⅱ〗 continue, keep up, go on

¶休まないで仕事を続けてください。
(Yasumanaide shigoto o *tsuzukete* kudasai.)

¶ Please **continue** working without taking a break.

¶山田先生は休まずに, 2時間続けて授業をしました。(Yamada sensei wa yasumazu ni, nijikan *tsuzukete* jugyō o shimashita.)

¶ Professor Yamada **went on** teaching for two hours without a break.

tsuzuku 続く〖動Ⅰ〗

¶天気のよい日が1か月も続いています。(Tenki no yoi hi ga ikkagetsu mo *tsuzuite* imasu.)

¶高い山がどこまでも続いています。(Takai yama ga doko made mo *tsuzuite* imasu.)

tsuzuku 〖vⅠ〗 continue, go on, last

¶ The fine weather **has continued** for a month now.

¶ The tall mountains **extend** as far as the eye can see.

U

u う〖助動〗

① [意志を表す]

¶君にこのお菓子をやろう。 (Kimi ni kono okashi o yarō.)

¶来年、日本へ行こうと思っています。 (Rainen, Nihon e ikō to omotte imasu.)

¶どんなテレビを買おうとお思いですか。 (Donna terebi o kaō to oomoi desu ka?)

¶上田さんは来年日本へ帰ろうと考えているそうです。 (Ueda san wa rainen Nihon e kaerō to kangaete iru sō desu.

* 「~と思う (~to omou)」「~と考える (to kangaeru)」などといっしょに使うことが多い。

② [勧誘を表す]

¶仕事が終わったから帰ろう。 (Shigoto ga owatta kara kaerō.)

¶勉強が終わったら, 映画を見に行こう。 (Benkyō ga owattara, eiga o mi ni ikō.)

③ [ある動作・作用がこれから行われるという意味を表す]

¶手紙を書こうとしたら, 電話がかかってきました。 (Tegami o kakō to shitara, denwa ga kakatte kimashita.)

¶エレベーターが閉まろうとしたので, 急いで乗りました。 (Erebētā ga shi-

-u 〚auxil〛 a verb ending indicating intent, urging, etc.

① [expresses intent]

¶ Here, **have** this candy 〚sweet, cake, etc.〛 (literally, **I will give** you this candy).

¶ **I am thinking of going** to Japan next year.

¶ What sort of television **are you thinking of buying**?

¶ I hear that [Mr.] Ueda **is thinking of returning** to Japan next year.

* Generally used together with ~ *to omou*, ~ *to kangaeru*, etc.

② [expresses urging]

¶ We've finished the job so **let's go home.**

¶ **Let's go see** a movie after studying.

③ [indicates that some action or process is about to occur]

¶ The phone rang **just as I was about to write** a letter.

¶ [I] hurriedly got in the elevator **just as the doors were about to**

842

marō to shita node, isoide norimashita.)

*「〜うとする (〜u to suru)」の形
で使うことが多い。

✳「う (u)」は I 型動詞につき，その
他の動詞には「よう (yō)」がつく。

⇨**yō よう**

uchi 内『名』

①[何かで区切られた中側]
内側 (*uchi*gawa)
¶電気が消えて，内も外も真っ暗です。
(Denki ga kiete, *uchi* mo soto mo
makkura desu.)
¶ドアには内からかぎが掛かっていて
開きません。(Doa ni wa *uchi* kara
kagi ga kakatte ite akimasen.)
↔**soto 外**

②[自分の所属しているところ]
¶うちの会社は駅の近くにあります。
(*Uchi* no kaisha wa eki no chikaku
ni arimasu.)
¶うちの父は小学校の先生です。
(*Uchi* no chichi wa shōgakkō no
sensei desu.)

③[ある一定の時間の間]
¶暗くならないうちに帰りましょう。
(Kuraku naranai *uchi* ni kaerimashō.)
¶この本は，読んでいるうちにだんだ
んおもしろくなってきました。(Kono
hon wa, yonde iru *uchi* ni dandan
omoshiroku natte kimashita.)

* 普通「〜うちに (〜uchi ni)」の形
で使う。

close.

* Generally used in the pattern "-ō
to suru."

✳ When added to Type I verbs -ō is
used, but for other verbs -yō is used.

uchi 〖n〗 inside, the interior; one's home, one's family; within, while; between, among

① [inside, the interior]
the inside, the **inner** part; within, inside
¶ The lights went out so it is now
pitch black both **inside** and out.
¶ The door won't open as it is locked
from **inside.**

② [one's home, family, etc.]
¶ **My** office is near the station.

¶ **My** father is an elementary school
teacher.

③ [within, while, in the course of,
before; during a set period of time]
¶ Let's start for home **before** it gets
dark.
¶ This book gradually became more
interesting **as** I read more of it 〖This
book has gradually become more interesting **as** I have read more of it〗.
* Usually used in the pattern
"~ *uchi ni.*"

④[ある範囲を表す]

¶試験問題十のうち半分しか答えられませんでした。(Shiken-mondai too no *uchi* hanbun shika kotaeraremasen deshita.)

¶5人のうちで、わたしがいちばん背が低いです。(Gonin no *uchi* de, watashi ga ichiban se ga hikui desu.)

uchi うち〖名〗

①[住居]

¶田中さんは最近うちを建てました。(Tanaka san wa saikin *uchi* o tatemashita.)

¶この辺には、大きくて立派なうちがたくさんあります。(Kono hen ni wa, ookikute rippa na *uchi* ga takusan arimasu.)

②[家庭]

¶あなたのうちは、何人家族ですか。(Anata no *uchi* wa, nannin kazoku desu ka?)

¶わたしのうちでは父も母も働いています。(Watashi no *uchi* de wa chichi mo haha mo hataraite imasu.)

⇒ie 家

uchiawaseru 打ち合わせる〖動Ⅱ〗

¶田中さんと電話で仕事について打ち合わせました。(Tanaka san to denwa de shigoto ni tsuite *uchiawasemashita*.)

¶旅行のことで友達とこれから打ち合わせなければなりません。(Ryokō no

④ [between, among, out of, of]

¶ [I] could only answer half **of** the 10 test questions.

¶ I am the shortest **of** the five of us.

uchi 〚n〛 a house; a household

① [a house]

¶ [Mr.] Tanaka built **a house** recently.

¶ There are many fine, large **homes** around here.

② [a household]

¶ How many are there in **your** family?

¶ Both **my** mother and father work.

uchiawaseru 〚v Ⅱ〛 make arrangements with, work out in advance

¶ [Mr.] Tanaka and I **decided** on the phone **how to do** the work.

¶ I must go now to **work out the details** of the trip with my friends.

844

koto de tomodachi to kore kara
uchiawasenakereba narimasen.)

ude 腕〖名〗

腕時計 (*ude*dokei) 腕を組む (*ude* o
kumu)

¶重い物を持っていたので、腕が痛い
です。 (Omoi mono o motte ita
node, *ude* ga itai desu.)

udon うどん〖名〗

¶御飯よりうどんのほうが好きです。
(Gohan yori *udon* no hō ga suki
desu.)

ue 上〖名〗

①［位置が高い所］

¶富士山の頂上は雲の上にあります。
(Fujisan no chōjō wa kumo no *ue*
ni arimasu.)

¶3ページの上から7行めを見てくだ
さい。 (Sanpēji no *ue* kara nana-
gyōme o mite kudasai.)

②［物の表面］

¶テーブルの上をふいてください。
(Tēburu no *ue* o fuite kudasai.)

¶床の上に紙くずが落ちています。
(Yuka no *ue* ni kamikuzu ga ochite
imasu.)

③［年齢・地位・程度などが高いこと］

¶いちばん上の姉は結婚しています。
(Ichiban *ue* no ane wa kekkon
shite imasu.)

¶英語を話す力は、山田さんのほうが
わたしより上です。 (Eigo o hanasu
chikara wa, Yamada san no hō ga
watashi yori *ue* desu.)

ude 〚n〛 **arm**

a **wrist**watch // fold **one's arms** in
front of one; link **one's arm** through
another's

¶ **My arms** are sore from holding
something heavy.

udon 〚n〛 *udon, udon* **noodles**

¶ I like *udon* better than rice.

ue 〚n〛 **up, upward, above; top;
higher, superior, older**

① [up, upward, above; the upper
part]

¶ The top of Mount Fuji is **above**
the clouds.

¶ Please look at the seventh line
from **the top** on page 3.

② [top]

¶ Please wipe off the table.

¶ Some paper scraps have fallen
onto the floor.

③ [higher, superior, older, more
than]

¶ My **oldest** sister is married.

¶ [Miss] Yamada can speak English
better than I can.

⇔shita 下

ueru 植える〖動Ⅱ〗

¶庭に木を植えました。 (Niwa ni ki o *uemashita*.)

ugokasu 動かす〖動Ⅰ〗

①[ある物の位置を移す]

¶重い石を一人で動かしました。

(Omoi ishi o hitori de *ugokashimashita*.)

②[機械などを働かせる]

¶この機械を動かすのは難しいですよ。

(Kono kikai o *ugokasu* no wa muzukashii desu yo.)

ugoki 動き〖名〗

①[運動・動作・行動など]

¶寒くなると、体の動きが鈍くなります。 (Samuku naru to, karada no *ugoki* ga nibuku narimasu.)

②[ものごとの移り変わり]

¶テレビやラジオのおかげで、世界の動きがよくわかるようになりました。

(Terebi ya rajio no okage de, sekai no *ugoki* ga yoku wakaru yō ni narimashita.)

ugoku 動く〖動Ⅰ〗

①[あるものの位置が移る]

¶写真を撮りますから、動かないでください。 (Shashin o torimasu kara, *ugokanaide* kudasai.)

②[機械などが働く]

¶この時計は動いていません。 (Kono tokei wa *ugoite* imasen.)

¶大雪で電車が動かなくなりました。

(Ooyuki de densha ga *ugokanaku*

ueru 〖v Ⅱ〗 plant, raise, grow

¶ [I] **planted** a tree in the yard.

ugokasu 〖v Ⅰ〗 move, change the position of; set in motion, operate

① [move, change the position of, shift]

¶ [I] **moved** the heavy rock all by [my]self.

② [set in motion, operate].

¶ It is difficult **to operate** this machine 〖apparatus, etc.〗.

ugoki 〖n〗 movement, motion; trend, movement

① [movement, motion, activity]

¶ [We] are loath **to move** when it is cold.

② [trend, movement]

¶ World **trends** have become easy to follow thanks to television and radio.

ugoku 〖v Ⅰ〗 move, stir; work, run, go

① [move, stir]

¶ **Don't move**—I'm going to take the photo now!

② [work, run, go]

¶ This clock 〖watch〗 **isn't running.**

¶ The trains have been 〖were〗 **brought to a standstill** by the heavy narimashita.)

uisukii ウイスキー〖名〗

¶わたしはウイスキーもビールも飲みます。(Watashi wa *uisukii* mo biiru mo nomimasu.)

ukabu 浮かぶ〖動Ⅰ〗

①[水面・空中などに物がとどまっている]

¶木の葉が水に浮かんでいます。(Ko-noha ga mizu ni *ukande* imasu.)

¶この海は, 油が浮かんでいて汚いですね。(Kono umi wa, abura ga *ukande* ite kitanai desu ne.)

¶青い空に白い雲が浮かんでいます。(Aoi sora ni shiroi kumo ga *ukande* imasu.)

→uku 浮く

②[あるものがものの表面に現れる]

¶悲しくて目に涙が浮かんできました。(Kanashikute me ni namida ga *ukande* kimashita.)

③[考えなどが頭などの中に現れる]

¶いい考えが頭に浮かびました。(Ii kangae ga atama ni *ukabi-mashita.*)

ukagau 伺う〖動Ⅰ〗

①[きく, 尋ねる]

¶すみません。ちょっと伺いますが…。(Sumimasen. Chotto *ukagaimasu* ga…)

¶田中さんの御意見を伺いたいのですが…。(Tanaka san no goiken o *ukagaitai* no desu ga…)

* 「きく (kiku)」「尋ねる (tazuneru)」

snows.

uisukii 〚n〛 whiskey

¶ I drink both **whiskey** and beer.

ukabu 〚v I〛 float; rise to the surface, appear; occur to one

① [float]

¶ Leaves **are floating** on top of the water.

¶ The water in this sea **is oily** and dirty.

¶ White clouds **are floating** in a blue sky.

② [rise to the surface, appear]

¶ [I] was so sad tears **came to** [my] eyes.

③ [occur to one, strike one]

¶ A good idea **came** to me 〖**popped** into my mind〗.

ukagau 〚v I〛 ask, inquire; hear; visit, call on

① [ask, inquire]

¶ Excuse me. Could you tell me ~?

¶ Could you give [us] your view, [Mr.] Tanaka?

* This *ukagau* is the humble form of

の謙譲語。

②[聞く，耳にする]

¶先生のおうわさはたびたび伺っております。 (Sensei no ouwasa wa tabitabi *ukagatte* orimasu.)

¶中村さんは来月アメリカへ行かれると伺っております。 (Nakamura san wa raigetsu Amerika e ikareru to *ukagatte* orimasu.)

*「聞く (kiku)」の謙譲語。

③[訪問する]

¶あした，先生のお宅へ伺ってもよろしいでしょうか。 (Ashita, sensei no otaku e *ukagatte* mo yoroshii deshō ka?)

¶何時ごろ伺ったらよろしいでしょうか。 (Nanji goro *ukagattara* yoroshii deshō ka?)

*「訪問する (hōmon suru)」の謙譲語。

ukeru 受ける〘動Ⅱ〙

①[自分の方に向かってくるものを支え止める]

¶山田さんは飛んできたボールを左手で受けました。 (Yamada san wa tonde kita bōru o hidarite de *ukemashita*.)

¶滝の水を手で受けて飲みました。 (Taki no mizu o te de *ukete* nomimashita.)

②[他からの働きかけに対して応じたり認めたりする]

質問を受ける (shitsumon o *ukeru*)

手術を受ける (shujutsu o *ukeru*)

kiku and of *tazuneru*.

② [hear]

¶ **I have heard** a lot about you, sir 〚ma'am〛 (said to one's teacher, doctor, etc.).

¶ **I hear** that [Mr.] Nakamura is going to the United States next month.

* This *ukagau* is the humble form of *kiku*.

③ [visit, call on]

¶ **May I call** on you at home tomorrow (said to one's teacher, doctor, etc.)?

¶ About what time **should I come?**

* This *ukagau* is the humble form of *hōmon suru*.

ukeru 〚v Ⅱ〛 catch, take; receive, accept, undergo; suffer, be subjected to; be given

① [catch, take]

¶ [Mr.] Yamada **caught** the ball in [his] left hand.

¶ [I] **took** water from the waterfall in [my] cupped hand(s) and drank it.

② [receive, accept, undergo]

take a question, **answer** a question // **undergo** a surgical operation, be operated upon

¶わたしは来年，大学の入学試験を受けます。　(Watashi wa rainen, daigaku no nyūgaku-shiken o *ukemasu*.)

¶ I **will take** university entrance exams next year.

¶わたしは山田さんから結婚について相談を受けました。　(Watashi wa Yamada san kara kekkon ni tsuite sōdan o *ukemashita*.)

¶ [Miss] Yamada **consulted me** about getting married.

③[ほかからの働きかけがあるものに及ぶ]

③ [suffer, be subjected to]

傷を受ける (kizu o *ukeru*)　影響を受ける (eikyō o *ukeru*)

be wounded, be injured // be influenced

¶この地方は台風で大きな被害を受けました。　(Kono chihō wa taifū de ookina higai o *ukemashita*.)

¶ This region **suffered** extensive damage in the typhoon.

④[ほかから何かを与えられる]

④ [be given]

許可を受ける (kyoka o *ukeru*)

obtain permission, be authorized

uketori　受取〖名〗

uketori 〚n〛　receipt

¶買い物をしたら，受取をもらってください。(Kaimono o shitara, *uketori* o moratte kudasai.)

¶ Please ask for **a receipt** when you buy something.

uketoru　受け取る〖動Ⅰ〗

uketoru 〚v I〛　receive, take delivery of

¶今日，母からの手紙を受け取りました。(Kyō, haha kara no tegami o *uketorimashita*.)

¶ **I received** a letter from my mother today.

¶お金を払って，品物を受け取るのを忘れました。(Okane o haratte, shinamono o *uketoru* no o wasuremashita.)

¶ [I] paid but forgot **to take** my purchase with [me].

uketsuke　受付〖名〗

uketsuke 〚n〛　acceptance, receipt; reception desk; receptionist, usher

¶御用の方は受付へおいでください。(Goyō no kata wa *uketsuke* e oide kudasai.)

¶ Visitors are directed to **the reception desk** (a written sign).

¶受付時間は午前9時から午後5時ま

¶ **Reception** 〔**office**〕 hours are from

でです。(*Uketsuke*-jikan wa gozen kuji kara gogo goji made desu.)

9 AM to 5 PM.

uketsukeru 受け付ける〖動Ⅱ〗

¶入学の申し込みは，今月の十日まで受け付けています。 (Nyūgaku no mōshikomi wa, kongetsu no tooka made *uketsukete* imasu.)

¶会員になりたい人はここで受け付けていますから，申し込んでください。(Kaiin ni naritai hito wa koko de *uketsukete* imasu kara, mōshikonde kudasai.)

uketsukeru 〖v Ⅱ〗 **accept, receive**

¶ Applications for admittance to this school **will be accepted** until the tenth of this month.

¶ Will those who wish to become members please apply here.

uku 浮く〖動Ⅰ〗

¶木の葉が水に浮いたり沈んだりして流れていきます。(Konoha ga mizu ni *uitari* shizundari shite nagarete ikimasu.)

¶湖には死んだ魚がたくさん浮いていました。(Mizuumi ni wa shinda sakana ga takusan *uite* imashita.)

⇔shizumu 沈む

uku 〖v Ⅰ〗 **float, rise to the surface**

¶ Leaves are being carried along by the current, now **rising** and now sinking below the surface.

¶ Numerous dead fish **were floating** on the lake.

uma 馬〖名〗

¶馬に乗ってこの広い野原を走ってみたいです。(*Uma* ni notte kono hiroi nohara o hashitte mitai desu.)

uma 〖n〗 **a horse**

¶ I would like to go **horseback** riding on this wide plain 〖in this large field〗.

umai うまい〖形〗

①〖上手，いい〗

¶あの女の人は歌がうまいですね。(Ano onna no hito wa uta ga *umai* desu ne.)

¶この言葉は発音が難しくてうまく言えません。(Kono kotoba wa hatsuon ga muzukashikute *umaku* iemasen.)

umai 〖adj〗 **skillful, good at; delicious**

① 〖skillful, expert, good at〗

¶ She is a **good** singer.

¶ This word is hard to say—〖I〗 can't pronounce it **well**.

850

↔**mazui** まずい →**jōzu** 上手

②［おいしい］

¶あの店の料理はとてもうまいよ。

(Ano mise no ryōri wa totemo *umai* yo.)

¶やはり新鮮な果物はうまいね。

(Yahari shinsen na kudamono wa *umai* ne.)

* 女性は「うまい (umai)」のかわりに「おいしい (oishii)」のほうをよく使う。

↔**mazui** まずい →**oishii** おいしい

umare 生まれ〖名〗

¶彼は大阪の生まれです。 (Kare wa Oosaka no *umare* desu.)

¶上田さんは生まれは東京ですが，育ったのは北海道だそうです。 (Ueda san wa *umare* wa Tōkyō desu ga, sodatta no wa Hokkaidō da sō desu.)

umareru 生まれる〖動Ⅱ〗

¶わたしは京都で生まれました。

(Watashi wa Kyōto de *umaremashita*.)

¶わたしが生まれたのは１９５０年です。 (Watashi ga *umareta* no wa senkyūhyaku-gojūnen desu.)

umeru 埋める〖動Ⅱ〗

¶うちで飼っていた鳥が死んだので，庭に穴を掘って埋めてやりました。

(Uchi de katte ita tori ga shinda node, niwa ni ana o hotte *umete* yarimashita.)

¶この辺は海を埋めて造った土地だそうです。(Kono hen wa umi o *umete*

② [delicious, good]

¶ The food is very **good** there 〚in that restaurant, coffee shop, etc.〛.

¶ When all is said and done, fresh fruit **does taste the best,** doesn't it?

* Women usually use *oishii* rather than *umai*.

umare 〚n〛 birth, origin, birthplace

¶ He's **a native** of Osaka.

¶ I hear that [Mr.] Ueda **was born in** Tokyo but raised in Hokkaido.

umareru 〚v Ⅱ〛 be born, come into existence

¶ I **was born** in Kyoto.

¶ I **was born** in 1950.

umeru 〚v Ⅱ〛 bury; fill up, plug up

¶ [Our] pet bird died so [we] dug a hole in the yard 〚garden〛 and **buried** it.

¶ I hear that the land around here **has been reclaimed** from the sea.

tsukutta tochi da sō desu.)

umi 海〖名〗

¶わたしの家は海の近くにあるので，夏には毎日海で泳ぎます。(Watashi no ie wa *umi* no chikaku ni aru node, natsu ni wa mainichi *umi* de oyogimasu.)

umu 産む〖動Ⅰ〗

¶妹が男の赤ちゃんを産みました。(Imōto ga otoko no akachan o *umimashita*.)

¶この鶏は毎日卵を産みます。(Kono niwatori wa mainichi tamago o *umimasu*.)

un 運〖名〗

運がいい (*un* ga ii) 運が悪い (*un* ga warui)

¶昨日，わたしが乗っていたタクシーが交通事故を起こしたのですが，わたしは運よくけがもしませんでした。(Kinō, watashi ga notte ita takushii ga kōtsū-jiko o okoshita no desu ga, watashi wa *un* yoku kega mo shimasen deshita.)

un うん〖感〗

¶わたしが「いっしょに行こう。」と誘ったら，彼は「うん。」と言ってうなずきました。(Watashi ga ''Issho ni ikō.'' to sasottara, kare wa ''*Un*.'' to itte unazukimashita.)

¶「みんなといっしょに話そうよ。」(Minna to issho ni hanasō yo.)「うん，そうしよう。」(*Un*, sō shiyō.)

＊「はい (hai)」「ええ (ee)」と同じ

umi 〚n〛 sea, ocean

¶ Since my home is near **the sea,** I go swimming every day in the summer.

umu 〚v I〛 give birth to; produce

¶ My younger sister **gave birth** to a boy.

¶ This chicken **lays** eggs every day.

un 〚n〛 destiny, fate, chance, fortune, luck

be lucky, be fortunate // be unlucky, be unfortunate

¶ The taxi I took yesterday caused an accident, but **fortunately** I escaped injury.

un 〚interj〛 yes, yeah

¶ When I invited him to go with us, he nodded and said **OK.**

¶ "Let's go talk with everyone."
　"**Yes,** let's."

＊ *Un* has the same meaning as *hai* or *ee*, but since it is not polite language

意味であるが，丁寧な言葉ではないから，目上の人などにはあまり使わない。

it is rarely used toward persons of higher status.

unazuku　うなずく〖動Ⅰ〗

¶彼女に結婚を申し込んだ時，彼女はぼくの顔をじっと見て，**うなずいて**くれました。(Kanojo ni kekkon o mōshikonda toki, kanojo wa boku no kao o jitto mite, *unazuite* kuremashita.)

¶あの人は，電話で話しながら何度も**うなずいて**いました。(Ano hito wa, denwa de hanashinagara nando mo *unazuite* imashita.)

unazuku 〖v Ⅰ〗　**nod, nod assent**

¶ When I asked her to marry me, she looked at me intently and then **nodded yes.**

¶ [He] **nodded** several times while talking on the telephone.

undō　運動〖名，～する〗

①［健康のために体を動かすこと］

運動会 (*undō*kai)　**運動**選手 (*undō*-senshu)

¶あなたは何か**運動**をしていますか。(Anata wa nani ka *undō* o shite imasu ka?)

¶最近は**運動**不足のため体の調子があまりよくないです。(Saikin wa *undō*-busoku no tame karada no chōshi ga amari yoku nai desu.)

②［ある目的のために人々に働きかけること］

政治**運動**(seiji-*undō*)　選挙**運動**(sen-kyo-*undō*)

¶彼は学生時代から世界を平和にしようという**運動**に参加しています。(Kare wa gakusei-jidai kara sekai o heiwa ni shiyō to iu *undō* ni sanka shite imasu.)

undō 〖n, ～*suru*〗　**motion, movement, exercise, sports; a movement, a campaign**

① [motion, movement, exercise, sports]

an **athletic** meet, a **field** meet // **an athlete, a sportsman**

¶ Do you take any **exercise** [Do you play some **sport**]?

¶ Recently I've been feeling a little off due to a lack of **exercise.**

② [a movement, campaign, drive]

a political **movement** // an election **campaign**

¶ He has been a participant in **the movement** for world peace since his student days.

unten　運転〖名，～する〗

unten 〖n, ～*suru*〗　**driving** (a car), **operating** (a machine)

運転手（*unten*shu）

¶あなたは自動車の運転ができますか。
(Anata wa jidōsha no *unten* ga dekimasu ka?)

¶雨の日は道が滑りやすいので，運転に気をつけなければなりません。
(Ame no hi wa michi ga suberi-yasui node, *unten* ni ki o tsukena-kereba narimasen.)

driver, operator

¶ Can you **drive** a car?

¶ The roads are slippery on rainy days so one must be particularly care-ful when **driving** then.

---

ura 裏〖名〗

①［表面の反対側］

足の裏 (ashi no *ura*)　裏側 (*ura*-gawa)

¶質問は表だけでなく裏にも書いてあります。 (Shitsumon wa omote dake de naku *ura* ni mo kaite arimasu.)

②［家などのうしろの場所・入口］

裏門 (*ura*mon)

¶子供たちは裏の空き地で遊んでいます。 (Kodomotachi wa *ura* no akichi de asonde imasu.)

¶表はかぎが掛かっていますから，裏から入ってください。 (Omote wa kagi ga kakatte imasu kara, *ura* kara haitte kudasai.)

⇔omote 表

ura 〖n〗 **the reverse, wrong side; the back, the rear**

① [the reverse, the wrong side, the back side, the other side]

the sole of the foot // the **back** side

¶ The questions are written on **the back** of the paper as well as the front.

② [the back, the rear (of a house, etc.)]

the **back** gate

¶ The children are playing in the vacant lot at **the back.**

¶ The front is locked so please enter at **the rear.**

---

urayamashii うらやましい〖形〗

¶わたしはあの人の成功がうらやましいです。 (Watashi wa ano hito no seikō ga *urayamashii* desu.)

¶あなたはお金も暇もたくさんあって，うらやましいですね。 (Anata wa okane mo hima mo takusan atte, *urayamashii* desu ne.)

urayamashii 〖adj〗 **be envious**

¶ **I envy** [his] success.

¶ **I envy you** for having so much money and free time.

ureshii　うれしい〖形〗

¶うれしそうですね。何かいいことがあったんですか。(*Ureshisō* desu ne. Nani ka ii koto ga atta n desu ka?)

¶試験の成績がよかったので，うれしかったです。(Shiken no seiseki ga yokatta node, *ureshikatta* desu.)

⇔kanashii　悲しい

uriba　売り場〖名〗

¶ネクタイ売り場はどこですか。(Nekutai-*uriba* wa doko desu ka?)

uru　売る〖動Ⅰ〗

¶これはデパートで売っていますか。(Kore wa depāto de *utte* imasu ka?)

¶あの店で売っているお菓子は，あまりおいしくありません。(Ano mise de *utte* iru okashi wa, amari oishiku arimasen.)

⇔kau　買う

urusai　うるさい〖形〗

¶ラジオの音がうるさくて，勉強ができません。(Rajio no oto ga *urusakute*, benkyō ga dekimasen.)

¶隣の部屋に病人がいるから，うるさくしないでください。(Tonari no heya ni byōnin ga iru kara, *urusaku* shinaide kudasai.)

⇒shizuka　静か

ushi　牛〖名〗

牛小屋 (*ushi*goya)

ushinau　失う〖動Ⅰ〗

¶田中さんは職を失って，生活に困

ureshii 〖adj〗 **be happy, glad, pleased, joyful**

¶ **You look happy.** Has something good happened?

¶ [I] **was happy** because [I] got a good mark on the exam.

uriba 〖n〗 **sales counter, store**

¶ Where is the necktie **counter?**

uru 〖v I〗 **sell**

¶ **Is** this **sold** at department stores 〚Can one buy this at a department store〛?

¶ The sweets 〚candy, cakes, etc.〛 **sold** at that store aren't very good.

urusai 〖adj〗 **noisy**

¶ The radio **is so noisy** [I] can't study.

¶ Please **be quiet** as there is someone sick in the next room.

ushi 〖n〗 **cow, cattle**

a **cow**shed, a **cattle** barn

ushinau 〖v I〗 **lose, be deprived of**

¶ [Mr.] Tanaka **has lost** [his] job

っています。(Tanaka san wa shoku o *ushinatte*, seikatsu ni komatte imasu.)

¶山田さんはついに外国へ行く機会を失ってしまいました。(Yamada san wa tsuini gaikoku e iku kikai o *ushinatte* shimaimashita.)

ushiro 後ろ〖名〗

¶先生の後ろに黒板があります。(Sensei no *ushiro* ni kokuban ga arimasu.)

¶道を歩いていたら，後ろから犬がついてきました。(Michi o aruite itara, *ushiro* kara inu ga tsuite kimashita.)

⇨**mae** 前

uso うそ〖名〗

うそをつく (*uso* o tsuku)

¶あの人が言ったことはうそです。(Ano hito ga itta koto wa *uso* desu.)

¶うそを言わないで，本当のことを言いなさい。(*Uso* o iwanaide, hontō no koto o iinasai.)

⇨**hontō** 本当

usui 薄い〖形〗

①［厚くない］

¶夏には薄いシャツを着ます。(Natsu ni wa *usui* shatsu o kimasu.)

¶辞書には薄い紙が使ってあります。(Jisho ni wa *usui* kami ga tsukatte arimasu.)

↔**atsui** 厚い

②［程度などが少ない］

---

and is having a hard time making ends meet.

¶ In the end [Mr.] Yamada **missed out** on the chance to go abroad.

ushiro 〚n〛 the back, the rear; behind, in back of

¶ There is a blackboard **in back** of the teacher.

¶ As [I] walked down the street a dog started following [me].

uso 〚n〛 a lie, falsehood

tell **a lie**

¶ What [he] said **isn't true.**

¶ Don't **lie** now, tell the truth.

usui 〚adj〛 thin; weak

① [thin, not thick]

¶ [We] wear **thin** shirts in summer.

¶ **Thin** paper is used in dictionaries.

② [weak, thin, light, scanty]

¶コーヒーは，薄いのと濃いのとどちらがいいですか。(Kōhii wa, *usui* no to koi no to dochira ga ii desu ka?)

↔**koi** 濃い

uta 歌〚名〛
歌を歌う (*uta* o utau)
¶春子さんは歌が上手です。(Haruko san wa *uta* ga jōzu desu.)

utagau 疑う〚動Ⅰ〛
¶山田さんは，わたしがうそをついているのではないかと疑っています。
(Yamada san wa, watashi ga uso o tsuite iru no de wa nai ka to *utagatte* imasu.)

⇔**shinjiru** 信じる

utau 歌う〚動Ⅰ〛
¶さあ，みんなで歌いましょう。(Sā, minna de *utaimashō*.)
¶子供が歌を歌っています。(Kodomo ga uta o *utatte* imasu.)

utsu 打つ〚動Ⅰ〛
①[ある物を他の物に瞬間的に強く当てる]
ボールをラケットで打つ (bōru o raketto de *utsu*) くぎを打つ (kugi o *utsu*)
¶田中さんは転んで，頭を強く打ちました。(Tanaka san wa koronde, atama o tsuyoku *uchimashita*.)
¶中村さんはそのニュースを聞いて，手を打って喜びました。(Nakamura san wa sono nyūsu o kiite, te o *utte* yorokobimashita.)
②[たたくような動作で何かをする]

¶ How do you like your coffee— **weak** or strong?

uta 〚n〛 a song, singing
sing **a song**
¶ Haruko is a good **singer.**

utagau 〚vⅠ〛 doubt, be doubtful; suspect, be suspicious
¶ [Mr.] Yamada **thinks** I might be lying.

utau 〚vⅠ〛 sing
¶ Well, **let's** all **sing** now.

¶ The children **are singing.**

utsu 〚vⅠ〛 strike, hit
① [strike, hit, beat, knock]

hit a ball with a racket // **strike** a nail

¶ [Mrs.] Tanaka fell and **got a** bad **knock** on the head.

¶ [Miss] Nakamura **clapped** [her] hands in joy at hearing the news.

② [strike, tap, touch, do]

電報を打つ (denpō o *utsu*)

send a telegram

¶わたしはタイプを打ったことがあり
ません。 (Watashi wa taipu o *utta*
koto ga arimasen.)

¶ I have never **typed** anything.

③[たたいて鳴らす]

③ [strike, beat, ring, sound]

鐘を打つ (kane o *utsu*)

ring a bell

¶時計が3時を打ちました。 (Tokei
ga sanji o *uchimashita*.)

¶ The clock **struck** three o'clock.

utsu 撃つ〖動Ⅰ〗

utsu 〖v I〗 **fire, shoot**

¶鉄砲で鳥を撃ちました。 (Teppō de
tori o *uchimashita*.)

¶ [I] **shot** a bird with a gun.

utsukushii 美しい〖形〗

utsukushii 〖adj〗 **beautiful, lovely, pretty**

¶この辺がいちばん景色の美しい所で
す。 (Kono hen ga ichiban keshiki
no *utsukushii* tokoro desu.)

¶ The scenery **is at its best** around
here.

¶会場は花で美しく飾られていまし
た。 (Kaijō wa hana de *utsukushiku*
kazararete imashita.)

¶ The hall was **prettily** decorated
with flowers.

utsuru 移る〖動Ⅰ〗

utsuru 〖v I〗 **move**

¶わたしは昨日から二階の部屋へ移り
ました。 (Watashi wa kinō kara
nikai no heya e *utsurimashita*.)

¶ I **moved** to a room 〖apartment〗 on
the second floor yesterday.

¶その会社は1か月前、東京から大阪
に移りました。 (Sono kaisha wa
ikkagetsu mae, Tōkyō kara Oosaka
ni *utsurimashita*.)

¶ That company **moved** from Tokyo
to Osaka a month ago.

utsuru 映る〖動Ⅰ〗

utsuru 〖v I〗 **be reflected**

¶湖に白い雲が映っています。
(Mizuumi ni shiroi kumo ga *utsutte*
imasu.)

¶ One can see a white cloud **reflected** in the lake.

¶鏡に外の景色が映っています。
(Kagami ni soto no keshiki ga
utsutte imasu.)

¶ **There is a reflection** of the scene
outside in the mirror.

utsuru 写る〖動Ⅰ〗

utsuru 〖v I〗 **be taken** (a photo,
etc.), **come out**

¶このカメラはとてもよく写ります。
(Kono kamera wa totemo yoku *utsurimasu*.)

¶部屋が暗いから，写真がよく写らないと思います。(Heya ga kurai kara, shashin ga yoku *utsuranai* to omoimasu.)

¶ This camera **takes** good **pictures**.

¶ This room is dark so I **don't think pictures will come out** well.

utsusu 移す〖動Ⅰ〗
¶本箱を机のそばへ移しました。
(Honbako o tsukue no soba e *utsushimashita*.)

¶卵をかごから冷蔵庫の中へ移しました。(Tamago o kago kara reizōko no naka e *utsushimashita*.)

utsusu 〖v I〗 **move, transfer**
¶ [I] **moved** the bookcase to beside the desk.

¶ [I] **transferred** the eggs from the basket to the refrigerator.

utsusu 映す〖動Ⅰ〗
¶先生が映画を映して見せてくださいました。(Sensei ga eiga o *utsushite* misete kudasaimashita.)

¶姉は自分の姿を鏡に映して見ています。(Ane wa jibun no sugata o kagami ni *utsushite* mite imasu.)

utsusu 〖v I〗 **reflect, project**
¶ The teacher **showed** us a film.

¶ My (older) sister is looking at **her reflection** in the mirror.

utsusu 写す〖動Ⅰ〗
¶写真を写しますから，集まってください。(Shashin o *utsushimasu* kara, atsumatte kudasai.)

¶先生が黒板に書いた字を学生がノートに写しています。(Sensei ga kokuban ni kaita ji o gakusei ga nōto ni *utsushite* imasu.)

utsusu 〖v I〗 **take** (a photograph), **film; copy**
¶ Please move together so [I] **can take** your picture.

¶ The students **are copying** in their notebooks the characters that their teacher wrote on the blackboard.

uwagi 上着〖名〗
¶暑いので，上着を脱ぎました。(Atsui node, *uwagi* o nugimashita.)

uwagi 〖n〗 **coat, suit jacket, upper garment, outerwear**
¶ As it was hot [I] took off **[my] jacket**.

uwasa うわさ〖名，〜する〗
¶山田さんが結婚するといううわさは

uwasa 〖n, ~*suru*〗 **rumor, gossip, report, talk, hearsay**

本当ですか。 (Yamada san ga kekkon suru to iu *uwasa* wa hontō desu ka?)

¶ うわさによると，今度山田さんは会社を辞めるそうです。 (*Uwasa* ni yoru to, kondo Yamada san wa kaisha o yameru sō desu.)

¶ Is **the rumor** that [Mr.] Yamada is going to get married true?

¶ **Rumor** has it that [Mr.] Yamada is going to quit [his] job soon.

W

wa 輪〖名〗

①[円形または円形のもの]

指輪 (yubi*wa*)

¶わたしたちは，先生の周りに輪になって座りました。(Watashitachi wa, sensei no mawari ni *wa* ni natte suwarimashita.)

②[車輪]

車の輪 (kuruma no *wa*)

wa は〖助〗

①[ものごとを特定的に取り上げて それについて述べるときに使う]

¶わたしは学生です。(Watashi *wa* gakusei desu.)

¶バスの停留所はどこですか。(Basu no teiryūjo *wa* doko desu ka?)

¶日本は地震が多いです。(Nihon *wa* jishin ga ooi desu.)

¶この本は，昨日駅前の本屋で買いました。(Kono hon *wa*, kinō ekimae no hon'ya de kaimashita.)

¶昨日はいい天気でしたね。(Kinō *wa* ii tenki deshita ne.)

* 「だれ (dare)」「どれ (dore)」「何 (nani)」などの疑問の言葉のあとにはつかない。「どなたは田中さんですか。(Donata wa Tanaka san desu ka?)」とは言わないで，「田中さんはどなたですか。(Tanaka san wa donata desu ka?)」と言う。

②[ものごとを対比的に または区別し

wa 〖n〗 circle, ring, link; wheel

① [circle, ring, link, loop]

a ring (jewelry)

¶ We sat in **a circle** around our teacher.

② [wheel]

a car **wheel**

wa 〖part〗 a particle indicating the topic of a sentence, etc.

① [used to indicate the topic]

¶ I am a student.

¶ Where is **the bus stop?**

¶ There are a lot of earthquakes **in Japan.**

¶ [I] bought **this book** yesterday at the bookstore in front of the station.

¶ It was a nice day **yesterday,** wasn't it?

* *Wa* is not used after interrogatives such as *dare, dore,* or *nani.* One says "*Tanaka san wa donata desu ka*" (Which one of you is Mr. Tanaka?) and not * "*Donata wa Tanaka san desu ka.*"

② [used when contrasting or distin-

て取り上げて述べるときに使う]

¶わたしはりんごは好きですが，みかんはきらいです。(Watashi wa ringo *wa* suki desu ga, mikan *wa* kirai desu.)

¶風は吹いていますが，雨は降っていません。(Kaze *wa* fuite imasu ga, ame *wa* futte imasen.)

¶あの山には登らないでください。(Ano yama ni *wa* noboranaide kudasai.)

¶田中さんはテレビは見ないそうです。(Tanaka san *wa* terebi wa minai sō desu.)

＊「あの山には (Ano yama ni wa)」や「田中さんは (Tanaka san wa)」の文では，文中に直接対比されているものはないが，ほかの山には登ってもよいがあの山だけはという気持ち，テレビは見なくてもラジオは聞くというような対比の気持ちが感じられる。また，一般的に否定の文には「は (wa)」が使われることが多い。述語が名詞・形容動詞の否定の文は「～ではありません (～de wa arimasen)」となる。「暑くはありません。(Atsuku wa arimasen.)」「行こうとは思いません。(Ikō to wa omoimasen.)」「学校へは行きません。(Gakkō e wa ikimasen.)」・「まだ，話してはいません。(Mada, hanashite wa imasen.)」「いい天気ではありません。(Ii tenki de wa arimasen.)」「あまり元気ではありません。(Amari genki de wa arima-

guishing items]

¶ I like **apples** but dislike **mandarin oranges.**

¶ **The wind** is blowing but it is not **raining.**

¶ Please don't climb **that mountain.**

¶ I hear that **[Mr.] Tanaka** doesn't watch television.

＊ In the case of *ano yama ni wa* and *Tanaka san wa* in the sentences above, a contrast is implied such that one may climb other mountains but not that particular one or that even though Mr. Tanaka doesn't watch television he listens to the radio. Also, in general *wa* is the particle used in negative sentences; the predicate for the negative of a noun or adjective-verb is *~ de wa arimasen.* Other examples of negative sentences with *wa* are "*Atsuku wa arimasen*" (It's not hot), "*Ikō to wa omoimasen*" (I don't have any intention of going), "*Gakkō e wa ikimasen*" (I'm not going to school), "*Mada hanashite wa imasen*" (I haven't talked with them about it yet), "*Ii tenki de wa arimasen*" (It's not very nice weather), and "*Amari genki de wa arimasen*" (He's sen.)」

wa　わ〖助〗

①〔独り言のような言い方で詠嘆・感動などを表す〕

¶困った**わ**。財布を落としたらしいの。(Komatta *wa*. Saifu o otoshita rashii no.)

¶重い**わ**，この荷物。(Omoi *wa,* kono nimotsu.)

¶あそこに おまわりさんがいる**わ**。道をきいてみましょう。(Asoko ni omawari san ga iru *wa*. Michi o kiite mimashō.)

②〔話し手の主張や決意を表す〕

¶あなたはさっき確かに そう言いました**わ**。(Anata wa sakki tashika ni sō iimashita *wa*.)

¶もうやめる**わ**，こんな仕事。(Mō yameru *wa,* konna shigoto.)

¶もう休みます**わ**，疲れましたから。(Mō yasumimasu *wa,* tsukaremashita kara.)

＊一般に女性が使う。

wagamama　わがまま〖名，形動〗

¶あの人はいつも わがままを言って，みんなを困らせます。(Ano hito wa itsu mo *wagamama* o itte, minna o komarasemasu.)

¶独りっ子はどうしても わがままになりやすいです。(Hitorikko wa dōshite mo *wagamama* ni nariyasui desu.)

¶わがままな人はみんなにきらわれます。(*Wagamama* na hito wa minna ni kirawaremasu.)

somewhat downcast).

wa 〚part〛 a sentence-final particle used for emphasis, etc.

① [used to express emotion when talking to oneself]

¶ Oh, what shall I do? It looks like I've lost my wallet.

¶ My, this bag 〚parcel, etc.〛 is heavy.

¶ Oh, there's a policeman. I'll ask him for directions.

② [used to indicate the speaker's determination or to stress what is being said]

¶ I'm sure that's what you said a little while ago.

¶ That's it! I'm not going to do this work any more!

¶ I'm tired. I'm going to take a break now.

＊ This *wa* is generally used by women.

wagamama 〚n, adj-v〛 **selfish, self-centered, self-indulgent, willful**

¶ [He] is always inconveniencing others with [his] **self-centered** remarks.

¶ It is easy for an only child to become **spoiled.**

¶ **Selfish** persons are universally disliked.

wakai 若い〖形〗

¶山田さんの奥さんは若くてきれいです。 (Yamada san no okusan wa *wakakute* kirei desu.)

¶田中さんは年より若く見えますね。 (Tanaka san wa toshi yori *wakaku* miemasu ne.)

¶上田さんは，あなたよりいくつ若いんですか。 (Ueda san wa, anata yori ikutsu *wakai* n desu ka?)

wakareru 別れる〖動Ⅱ〗

¶わたしたちは「さようなら。」と言って別れました。 (Watashitachi wa "Sayōnara." to itte *wakaremashita*.)

¶わたしは家族と別れて，独りで東京にいます。 (Watashi wa kazoku to *wakarete*, hitori de Tōkyō ni imasu.)

⇒au 会う

wakareru 分かれる〖動Ⅱ〗

¶男と女に分かれて，ゲームをしました。 (Otoko to onna ni *wakarete*, gēmu o shimashita.)

¶ここをまっすぐ行くと，道が二つに分かれています。 (Koko o massugu iku to, michi ga futatsu ni *wakarete* imasu.)

¶意見が分かれて，今日は結論が出ませんでした。 (Iken ga *wakarete*, kyō wa ketsuron ga demasen deshita.)

wakaru わかる〖動Ⅰ〗

①［理解することができる，意味などが明らかになる］

¶あなたは日本語がわかりますか。 (Anata wa Nihongo ga *wakarimasu*

wakai 〖adj〗 **young, younger**

¶ Mr. Yamada's wife is **young** and pretty.

¶ [Mrs.] Tanaka doesn't look [her] age 〖looks **younger** than she actually is〗.

¶ How many years **younger** than you is [Mr.] Ueda?

wakareru 〖v II〗 **part, separate from, divorce, split up, bid farewell, leave**

¶ We **parted**, saying "Good-bye."

¶ I **left** home and came to live alone in Tokyo.

wakareru 〖v II〗 **split, be divided**

¶ [We] **split up** by sex and played games.

¶ If you go straight here the road **divides** in two.

¶ Opinion **was divided** and no conclusion was reached today.

wakaru 〖v I〗 **understand; know**

① [understand, comprehend, grasp]

¶ **Do you understand** Japanese?

ka?)

¶わからない言葉は、辞書で調べてください。(*Wakaranai* kotoba wa, jisho de shirabete kudasai.)

¶ Please look up in the dictionary any words **you don't understand.**

②[知りたいと思うことなどを知ることができる、見たり聞いたりして知ることができる]

② [know, learn, be known, be identified]

¶いつ試験があるか、まだわかりません。(Itsu shiken ga aru ka, mada *wakarimasen.*)

¶ [We] **don't know** yet when there will be a test.

¶田中さんの電話番号がわかりますか。(Tanaka san no denwa-bangō ga *wakarimasu* ka?)

¶ **Do you know** [Miss] Tanaka's phone number?

wakasu 沸かす〖動Ⅰ〗
¶お湯を沸かして、コーヒーをいれましょう。(Oyu o *wakashite*, kōhii o iremashō.)

wakasu 〖vⅠ〗 boil, heat
¶ **I'm going to boil** water and fix some coffee.

wake わけ〖名〗
①[ことがらや言葉などの意味・内容を表す]
¶この言葉のわけを字引で調べてみましたが、わかりませんでした。(Kono kotoba no *wake* o jibiki de shirabete mimashita ga, wakarimasen deshita.)

wake 〖n〗 meaning, sense; reason, cause; circumstances, case
① [meaning, sense]
¶ [I] looked up this word in the dictionary but in the end didn't learn **its meaning.**

¶この文は何を言おうとしているのか、さっぱりわけがわかりません。(Kono bun wa nani o iō to shite iru no ka, sappari *wake* ga wakarimasen.)

¶ [I] can't make **head or tail** of this sentence.

②[理由・原因を表す]
¶あんなに仲のよかった夫婦が、どういうわけで離婚してしまったのでしょう。(Anna ni naka no yokatta fūfu ga, dōiu *wake* de rikon shite

② [reason, cause, grounds]
¶ I wonder **how** that couple came to be divorced when they seemed to get along so well together.

shimatta no deshō?)

¶なぜ学校をやめるのか，その**わけ**を話してください。 (Naze gakkō o yameru no ka, sono *wake* o hanashite kudasai.)

③[当然のこととして納得できるという意味を表す]

¶「田中さんは試験に失敗したそうです。」 (Tanaka san wa shiken ni shippai shita sō desu.)「やはりそうでしたか。全然勉強しなかったんですから，落ちる**わけ**です。」 (Yahari sō deshita ka. Zenzen benkyō shinakatta n desu kara, ochiru *wake* desu.)

¶田中さんはいつも人の悪口ばかり言っています。みんなにきらわれる**わけ**です。 (Tanaka san wa itsu mo hito no warukuchi bakari itte imasu. Minna ni kirawareru *wake* desu.)

④[事情やいきさつなどを説明するときに使う]

¶わたしはお金がなくて大学へ行けなかった**わけ**ですが，息子には行かせたいと思います。 (Watashi wa okane ga nakute daigaku e ikenakatta *wake* desu ga, musuko ni wa ikasetai to omoimasu.)

¶月末には必ず返すと言うので，田中さんに5万円貸した**わけ**です。ところが，もう2か月にもなるのに，まだ返してくれません。 (Getsumatsu ni wa kanarazu kaesu to iu node,

¶ Please give me **your reasons** for wanting to quit school.

③ [used to indicate that something is natural or reasonable]

¶ "I hear that [Mr.] Tanaka failed the test."

"I thought [he] might. **It stands to reason** that one will fail if one doesn't study at all ⟦**No wonder** he failed—he didn't study at all⟧."

¶ [Mr.] Tanaka is always speaking ill of others. **That's why** [he]'s universally disliked.

④ [used when explaining the circumstances, etc.]

¶ I couldn't go to college myself **because of** insufficient funds, but I'd like to have my son go.

¶ I lent fifty thousand yen to [Mr.] Tanaka **because** [he] said [he] would pay it back without fail at the end of the month. However, two months have gone by and [he] still hasn't

Tanaka san ni goman'en kashita *wake* desu. Tokoroga, mō nikagetsu ni mo naru noni, mada kaeshite kuremasen.)

paid it back.

⑤［簡単なこと・すぐできることなどの意味を表す］

¶一日に漢字を五つ覚えるのは，**わけ**ないことです。(Ichinichi ni kanji o itsutsu oboeru no wa, *wake* nai koto desu.)

⑤ [used to indicate that something is easy or simple]

¶ **It's a simple matter** to memorize five *kanji* a day.

¶機械でやれば，そんなことは**わけ**なくできます。(Kikai de yareba, sonna koto wa *wake* naku dekimasu.)

¶ If you do it by machine it will be done **in no time at all.**

＊「わけない (wake nai)」「わけはない (wake wa nai)」の形で使う。

＊ Used in the patterns "*wake nai*" and "*wake wa nai*."

⑥［不可能であるという意味を表す］

¶いくら困っても，人の物を盗む**わけ**にはいきません。(Ikura komatte mo, hito no mono o nusumu *wake* ni wa ikimasen.)

⑥ [used to indicate that something is impossible]

¶ **There is no excuse** for stealing no matter how difficult one's situation might be.

¶お金がないので，あまり高い物を買う**わけ**にはいきません。(Okane ga nai node, amari takai mono o kau *wake* ni wa ikimasen.)

¶ [I] don't have much money so [I] **can't possibly** buy anything expensive.

＊いつも「わけにはいかない (wake ni wa ikanai)」の形で使う。

＊ Always used in the pattern "*wake ni wa ikanai*."

⑦［常識的に考えてとてもそういうことはありえないことを表す］

¶山田さんはあんなによく勉強したんですから，試験に落ちる**わけ**がありません。(Yamada san wa anna ni yoku benkyō shita n desu kara, shiken ni ochiru *wake* ga ari-

⑦ [used to indicate that something is unreasonable or contrary to common sense]

¶ [Miss] Yamada **cannot possibly** fail the exam after studying so hard.

867

masen.)

¶山田さんはいつも人に親切ですから，みんなにきらわれる**わけ**がありません。(Yamada san wa itsu mo hito ni shinsetsu desu kara, minna ni kirawareru *wake* ga arimasen.)

* いつも 「わけがない「(wake ga nai)」の形で使う。

⑧[特にそのようなことはないという意味を表す]

¶漢字が できない といっても，全然読めない**わけ**ではありません。 (Kanji ga dekinai to itte mo, zenzen yomenai *wake* de wa arimasen.)

¶わたしは魚はきらいですが，全然食べない**わけ**ではありません。(Watashi wa sakana wa kirai desu ga, zenzen tabenai *wake* de wa arimasen.)

* いつも 「わけではない (wake de wa nai)」の形で使い，部分否定を表す。

wakeru 分ける〖動Ⅱ〗

①[全体をいくつかの部分にする]
¶人数が多いので，二組に分けました。(Ninzū ga ooi node, futakumi ni *wakemashita*.)

②[分類する]
¶りんごを大きさによって3種類に分けました。(Ringo o ookisa ni yotte sanshurui ni *wakemashita*.)

③[全体をいくつかにして人に与える]
¶りんごをたくさんいただいたので，隣の家にも分けてあげました。

(Ringo o takusan itadaita node,

¶ [Mr.] Yamada is always kind to others so **it cannot be** that [he] is unpopular.

* Always used in the pattern "*wake ga nai*."

⑧ [used to indicate that something is not the case]

¶ [I] don't have a good knowledge of *kanji*, but **that isn't to say** that [I] can't read them at all 〚but I can read them a little bit〛.

¶ I don't like fish, but **it's not the case** that I never eat it 〚but I do eat it sometimes〛.

* Always used in the pattern "*wake de wa nai*"; it forms a partial negative.

wakeru 〖v Ⅱ〗 divide; separate, sort; distribute, allot

① [divide, part, split]
¶ As there were so many people [we] **were split up** into two groups 〚teams〛.

② [separate, sort, classify]
¶ [I] **sorted** the apples into three groups by size.

③ [distribute, allot, share]
¶ Someone gave [me] lots of apples so [I] **gave some** to [my] next-door neighbors.

tonari no ie ni mo *wakete* agemashita.)

¶一本のたばこを二人で分けました。

(Ippon no tabako o futari de
wakemashita.)

waki わき〖名〗

①〖腕のつけねの下の所〗
¶山田さんがたくさんの本をわきに抱
えて，こちらへ来ます。(Yamada san
ga takusan no hon o *waki* ni kakaete, kochira e kimasu.)

②〖すぐ近くの所，そば〗
¶わたしの家は，学校のすぐわきにあ
ります。(Watashi no ie wa, gakkō
no sugu *waki* ni arimasu.)

waku 沸く〖動Ⅰ〗
¶お湯が沸きました。お茶にしましょ
う。(Oyu ga *wakimashita*. Ocha ni
shimashō.)

¶おふろが沸きましたから，お入りく
ださい。 (Ofuro ga *wakimashita*
kara, ohairi kudasai.)

＊「水が沸く (mizu ga waku)」とは
言わないで，「お湯が沸く (oyu ga
waku)」と言う。

warai 笑い〖名〗
笑い話 (*warai*banashi)
¶あまりおかしくて，笑いが止まりま
せんでした。 (Amari okashikute,
warai ga tomarimasen deshita.)

warau 笑う〖動Ⅰ〗
¶山田先生がおもしろいことを言った
ので，みんな大声で笑いました。

(Yamada sensei ga omoshiroi koto

¶ The two **split** a cigarette.

waki 〚n〛 **armpit, under one's
arm(s); beside, very close**

① [armpit, under one's arm(s)]
¶ [Mr.] Yamada is coming this way
carrying many books **under [his]
arm.**

② [beside, very close]
¶ My house is **very near** to the
school.

waku 〚v I〛 **boil, grow hot**
¶ The water **is boiling.** Let's have
some (green) tea.

¶ The bath **is ready now.** Please go
ahead and have a bath.

＊ The expression * *mizu ga waku* is
not used; instead one says *oyu ga
waku*.

warai 〚n〛 **laugh, laughter, smile,
smiling**
a **funny** story
¶ It was so funny [I] couldn't stop
laughing.

warau 〚v I〛 **laugh, smile**
¶ Professor Yamada said something
amusing and everyone **laughed**
loudly.

o itta node, minna oogoe de *warai-mashita*.)

wareru 割れる〖動Ⅱ〗

¶ボールが当たって、窓ガラスが**割れ**てしまいました。 (Bōru ga atatte, madogarasu ga *warete* shimaimashita.)

¶スケートをしていたら、氷が**割れて**池の中へ落ちてしまいました。

(Sukēto o shite itara, koori ga *warete* ike no naka e ochite shimaimashita.)

wareware われわれ〖代〗

¶**われわれ**学生にとって最も重要なことは勉強することです。 (*Wareware* gakusei ni totte mottomo jūyō na koto wa benkyō suru koto desu.)

＊「わたしたち (watashitachi)」より少しかたい感じの言葉。一体感を強めて言う場合に使う。女性は普通使わない。

-wari -割〖尾〗

3割 (san *wari*) 10割 (jū *wari*)

wariai 割合〖名〗

¶あの学校の入学試験を受けて合格する人の**割合**は、30パーセントぐらいでしょう。 (Ano gakkō no nyūgaku-shiken o ukete gōkaku suru hito no *wariai* wa, sanjippāsento gurai deshō.)

wariai ni 割合に〖副〗

¶このお菓子は**割合**においしいですね。 (Kono okashi wa *wariai ni* oishii desu ne.)

wareru 〖v Ⅱ〗 **split, break**

¶ The window **broke** when the ball hit it.

¶ When [I] was skating, the ice **cracked** and [I] fell into the pond.

wareware 〖pron〗 **we, us, our**

¶ Studying is the most important thing for **us** students.

＊ *Wareware* is a little more formal than *watashitachi*. It is used when stressing a sense of solidarity. It is not usually used by women.

-wari 〖suf〗 **percentage** (1 *wari* = 10%)

30 percent // 100 percent

wariai 〖n〗 **rate, percentage, proportion, ratio**

¶ **The percentage** of persons passing the exam for entrance to that school is around 30 percent.

wariai ni 〖adv〗 **comparatively, relatively**

¶ This sweet 〖candy, cake〗 is **quite** good.

¶あの<ruby>学生<rt>がくせい</rt></ruby>は<ruby>割合<rt>わりあい</rt></ruby>によく<ruby>勉強<rt>べんきょう</rt></ruby>します。
(Ano gakusei wa *wariai ni* yoku benkyō shimasu.)

*「<ruby>割合<rt>わりあい</rt></ruby> (wariai)」「わりに (warini)」とも言う。

⇨**warini わりに**

warini わりに〖副〗

¶<ruby>小<rt>ちい</rt></ruby>さな<ruby>店<rt>みせ</rt></ruby>ですが，<ruby>味<rt>あじ</rt></ruby>は**わりに**いいですよ。 (Chiisana mise desu ga, aji wa *warini* ii desu yo.)

¶<ruby>田中<rt>たなか</rt></ruby>さんの<ruby>家<rt>いえ</rt></ruby>は<ruby>駅<rt>えき</rt></ruby>から**わりに**<ruby>近<rt>ちか</rt></ruby>いです。 (Tanaka san no ie wa eki kara *warini* chikai desu.)

*「わりと (warito)」「<ruby>割合<rt>わりあい</rt></ruby>に (wariai ni)」とも言う。

⇨**wariai ni <ruby>割合<rt>わりあい</rt></ruby>に**

wari ni <ruby>割<rt>わり</rt></ruby>に〖連〗

¶この<ruby>店<rt>みせ</rt></ruby>の<ruby>料理<rt>りょうり</rt></ruby>は，<ruby>安<rt>やす</rt></ruby>い<ruby>割<rt>わり</rt></ruby>においしいです。 (Kono mise no ryōri wa yasui *wari ni* oishii desu.)

¶あの<ruby>学生<rt>がくせい</rt></ruby>は，<ruby>勉強<rt>べんきょう</rt></ruby>する<ruby>割<rt>わり</rt></ruby>には<ruby>成績<rt>せいせき</rt></ruby>がよくないです。 (Ano gakusei wa, benkyō suru *wari ni* wa seiseki ga yoku nai desu.)

¶<ruby>山田<rt>やまだ</rt></ruby>さんは<ruby>50歳<rt>ごじっさい</rt></ruby>の<ruby>割<rt>わり</rt></ruby>には<ruby>若<rt>わか</rt></ruby>く<ruby>見<rt>み</rt></ruby>えます。 (Yamada san wa gojissai no *wari ni* wa wakaku miemasu.)

*「<ruby>動詞<rt></rt></ruby>・<ruby>形容詞<rt></rt></ruby>・<ruby>形容動詞<rt></rt></ruby>（<ruby>連体<rt></rt></ruby>の<ruby>形<rt></rt></ruby>）＋<ruby>割<rt>わり</rt></ruby>に (wari ni)」「<ruby>名詞<rt></rt></ruby>＋の (no)＋<ruby>割<rt>わり</rt></ruby>に (wari ni)」の<ruby>形<rt></rt></ruby>で<ruby>使<rt></rt></ruby>う。

waru <ruby>割<rt>わ</rt></ruby>る〖動 I 〗

①[まとまっているものをいくつかの部分にする]

¶ナイフでりんごを<ruby>半分<rt>はんぶん</rt></ruby>に<ruby>割<rt>わ</rt></ruby>って，<ruby>二人<rt>ふたり</rt></ruby>

¶ That student studies **relatively** hard.

* Variants: *wariai, warini*.

warini 〖adv〗 **comparatively, rather**

¶ It's just a small place, but the food is **quite** good.

¶ [Mr.] Tanaka's house is **relatively** close to the station.

* Variants: *warito, wariai ni*.

wari ni 〖compd〗 **for, considering, relative to, in proportion to**

¶ The food here is quite good **considering** how cheap it is.

¶ That student's marks aren't so good **considering** how much [he] studies.

¶ [Mr.] Yamada looks younger than [his] 50 years.

* Used in the patterns "verb, adjective, or adjective-verb (dictionary form) + *wari ni*" and "noun + *no* + *wari ni*."

waru 〖v I〗 **divide; break; divide by**
① [divide, cut, halve]

¶ [We] **cut** the apple in half with a knife and split it between the two

で食べました。(Naifu de ringo o hanbun ni *watte*, futari de tabemashita.)

②[固い物を壊す]

コップを割る (koppu o *waru*) 窓ガラスを割る (madogarasu o *waru*)

¶花びんを落として割ってしまいました。(Kabin o otoshite *watte* shimaimashita.)

③[割り算をする]

¶4割る2は2です。(Yon *waru* ni wa ni desu.)

warui 悪い〖形〗

①[道徳的・法律的に正しくない様子]

¶人の物を盗むのは悪いことです。

(Hito no mono o nusumu no wa *warui* koto desu.)

¶花びんを壊したのはしかたがないが，悪いのはうそをついたことです。

(Kabin o kowashita no wa shikata ga nai ga, *warui* no wa uso o tsuita koto desu.)

↔ii いい **yoi** よい

②[性質が善良でない様子]

¶世の中にはいい人もいるが悪い人もいるから，気をつけなければなりません。(Yononaka ni wa ii hito mo iru ga *warui* hito mo iru kara, ki o tsukenakereba narimasen.)

↔ii いい **yoi** よい

③[人間関係がよくない様子]

¶山田さんと田中さんは仲が悪いそうです。(Yamada san to Tanaka san wa naka ga *warui* sō desu.)

of [us].

② [break, crack, smash]

break a glass tumbler // **break** a window

¶ [I] dropped the vase and **it broke.**

③ [divide]

¶ Four **divided by** two is two.

warui 〚adj〛 **bad, wrong; evil; inferior; in poor condition**

① [bad, wrong, evil]

¶ **It is wrong** to steal something belonging to another.

¶ Breaking the vase couldn't have been helped, but **it was wrong** to lie about it.

② [bad, evil, wicked]

¶ There are **bad** people as well as good people in the world so one must be careful.

③ [be on bad terms with]

¶ I hear that [Mr.] Yamada and [Mr.] Tanaka **don't get along well** with each other.

* 普通「仲が悪い (naka ga warui)」
の形で使う。

↔ii いい　yoi よい

④［ものごとが劣っている様子］
悪い品物 (*warui* shinamono) 頭が
悪い (atama ga *warui*)
¶上田さんは3学期の成績がたいへん
悪かったそうです。 (Ueda san wa
sangakki no seiseki ga taihen
warukatta sō desu.)

↔ii いい　yoi よい

⑤［状態などの好ましくない様子，気
持ちのよくない様子］
気分が悪い (kibun ga *warui*)
¶天気が悪い日には散歩はしません。
(Tenki ga *warui* hi ni wa sanpo
wa shimasen.)
¶雨が降って，道が悪くなりました。
(Ame ga futte, michi ga *waruku*
narimashita.)
¶お酒を飲んだら，気持が悪くなりま
した。 (Osake o nondara, kimochi
ga *waruku* narimashita.)

↔ii いい　yoi よい

⑥［気の毒である，申し訳ない］
¶みんなを待たせると悪いから，急い
で行きましょう。(Minna o mataseru
to *warui* kara, isoide ikimashō.)
¶忙しい時に来て悪かったですね。
(Isogashii toki ni kite *warukatta*
desu ne.)
* 会話の文の中で自分の行為が相手に
迷惑をかけたり不都合な影響を及ぼし
たりするときに使う。

* Usually used in the pattern "*naka
ga warui*."

④ [bad, inferior, poor]
inferior goods // be **slow,** be **slow**-
witted
¶ I hear that [Miss] Ueda's marks for
the third term were very **poor.**

⑤ [be in poor condition]

feel **ill**
¶ [I] don't go for a walk on days
when the weather **is poor.**

¶ The roads **were [are] bad** because
of the rain.

¶ [I] felt [feel] **sick** after doing some
drinking.

⑥ [be wrong, be at fault]
¶ Let's hurry as we **shouldn't** keep
everyone waiting.

¶ [I]'m **sorry** to have disturbed you
when you are so busy.

* Used in conversation when one's
actions have bothered or inconvenienced another.

wasureru 忘れる〖動Ⅱ〗

①[覚えたことなどが思い出せない]

¶学生時代に習った外国語は，もうみんな**忘れて**しまいました。(Gakusei-jidai ni naratta gaikokugo wa, mō minna *wasurete* shimaimashita.)

②[うっかりして物をどこかに置いてきてしまう]

¶教室に日本語の本を**忘れて**きてしまいました。(Kyōshitsu ni Nihongo no hon o *wasurete* kite shimaimashita.)

wata 綿〖名〗

¶寒い所では冬は**綿**の入った着物を着ます。(Samui tokoro de wa fuyu wa *wata* no haitta kimono o kimasu.)

¶空には白い**綿**のような雲が浮かんでいます。(Sora ni wa shiroi *wata* no yō na kumo ga ukande imasu.)

watakushi 私〖代〗

¶**私**は皆様の御親切を決して忘れません。(*Watakushi* wa minasama no goshinsetsu o kesshite wasuremasen.)

＊「**私**(watakushi)」は，「わたし(watashi)」の丁寧な言い方で，改まったときに使う。

wataru 渡る〖動Ⅰ〗

川を**渡る** (kawa o *wataru*)　橋を**渡る** (hashi o *wataru*)

¶本屋は交差点を**渡った**ところにあります。(Hon'ya wa kōsaten o *watatta* tokoro ni arimasu.)

wasureru 〚v II〛 **forget, escape one's memory; forget, leave behind**

① [forget, escape one's memory]

¶ [I]'ve completely **forgotten** the foreign languages [I] learned in [my] student days.

② [forget, leave behind]

¶ [I] **accidentally left** my Japanese book in the classroom.

wata 〚n〛 **cotton, cotton wool**

¶ In cold areas they wear clothing padded with **cotton** in the winter.

¶ **Fleecy** white clouds are floating in the sky.

watakushi 〚pron〛 **I, myself, me, mine**

¶ **I** will never forget how kind all of you have been to me.

＊ *Watakushi* is the polite form of *watashi;* it is used on more formal occasions.

wataru 〚v I〛 **cross, go across**

cross a river // **cross** a bridge

¶ The bookstore is **on the other side** of the intersection.

¶冬になると，北からいろいろな渡り鳥が日本に**渡って**きます。 (Fuyu ni naru to, kita kara iroiro na watari-dori ga Nihon ni *watatte* kimasu.)

watashi　わたし〖代〗

¶**わたし**は山田です。 (*Watashi* wa Yamada desu.)

watasu　渡す〖動Ⅰ〗

①［人から人へある物を移す］

¶田中さんが来たら，この手紙を**渡して**ください。 (Tanaka san ga kitara, kono tegami o *watashite* kudasai.)

②［こちら側から向こう側へあるものを送る］

¶ここには橋がないので，人々を船で向こう岸に**渡して**います。 (Koko ni wa hashi ga nai node, hitobito o fune de mukōgishi ni *watashite* imasu.)

wazawaza　わざわざ〖副〗

①［あることのために特別に苦労などして何かを行う様子］

¶この**セーター**は**わざわざ**わたしのために編んでくださったのですか。 (Kono sētā wa *wazawaza* watashi no tame ni ande kudasatta no desu ka?)

¶わたしが北海道へ行った時，上田さんは忙しいのに，**わざわざ**ホテルまで会いに来てくれました。 (Watashi ga Hokkaidō e itta toki, Ueda san wa isogashii noni, *wazawaza* hoteru made ai ni kite kuremashita.)

②［そのことをする必要がないのにそ

¶ In the winter various migratory birds **cross** the sea to Japan from the north.

watashi 〖pron〗 **I, myself, me, mine**

¶ I'm [Mr.] Yamada.

watasu 〖v I〗 **hand over; carry across**

① [hand over, deliver, give to]

¶ Please **give** this letter to [Mrs.] Tanaka when [she] comes.

② [carry across, take over]

¶ There is no bridge here so people **are ferried** to the other side by boat.

wazawaza 〖adv〗 **purposely, expressly; take the trouble to**

① [purposely, expressly, specially]

¶ Did you knit this sweater **just for me?**

¶ When I went to Hokkaido, [Mr.] Ueda **took the time** from [his] busy schedule to come see me at my hotel.

② [take the trouble to, go ou

うと知りながら何かを行う様子]

¶近くの店で買えるのに，どうして**わ
ざわざ**遠くの店まで買いに行ったので
すか。(Chikaku no mise de kaeru
noni, dōshite *wazawaza* tooku no
mise made kai ni itta no desu ka?)

wazuka　わずか 〚副，形動，〜の〛
¶うちから学校までは，**わずか**5分で
す。 (Uchi kara gakkō made wa,
wazuka gofun desu.)

¶父が亡くなったのは，わたしが**わず
か**三つの時でした。 (Chichi ga
nakunatta no wa, watashi ga *wazuka* mittsu no toki deshita.)

¶夜遅くまで働いたのに，**わずか**のお
金しかもらえませんでした。(Yoru
osoku made hataraita noni, *wazuka*
no okane shika moraemasen deshita.)

one's way to]

¶ Why did you **make a special trip**
to a more distant shop when you
could have bought it nearby?

wazuka 〚adv, adj-v, ～*no*〛 **only a
few, only a little, scanty, mere**

¶ It's **only** five minutes to school
from my home.

¶ My father died when I was **only**
three years old.

¶ Even though [I] worked until late
at night on it, [I] only received a
trifling payment for it.

Y

ya　や〚助〛

¶机の上には，本やノートや鉛筆などがあります。(Tsukue no ue ni wa, hon *ya* nōto *ya* enpitsu nado ga arimasu.)

¶このクラスの学生はアメリカやフランスやタイなどいろいろな国から来ています。 (Kono kurasu no gakusei wa Amerika *ya* Furansu *ya* Tai nado iroiro na kuni kara kite imasu.)

＊ いくつかあるものの中から，その一部を列挙する場合に使う。

⇒to と

-ya　-屋〚尾〛

八百屋 (yao*ya*)　魚屋 (sakana*ya*)
菓子屋 (kashi*ya*)　本屋 (hon'*ya*)　酒屋 (saka*ya*)　文房具屋 (bunbōgu-*ya*)

yā　やあ〚感〛

¶やあ，しばらく。お元気ですか。
(*Yā*, shibaraku. Ogenki desu ka?)

yabureru　破れる〚動Ⅱ〛

¶この紙はすぐ破れます。(Kono kami wa sugu *yaburemasu.*)

¶このシャツは少し破れていますが，まだ着られます。 (Kono shatsu wa sukoshi *yaburete* imasu ga, mada kiraremasu.)

yabureru　敗れる〚動Ⅱ〛

戦争に敗れる (sensō ni *yabureru*)

ya 〚part〛 **and, or**

¶ There are books, notebooks, pencils, **and** the like on the desk.

¶ The students in this class are from many different countries such as the United States, France, **and** Thailand.

＊ *Ya* is used when citing only part of a set of items.

-ya 〚suf〛 a suffix indicating a store, shop, dealer, etc.

a vegetable **store,** a grocer // a fish **shop,** a fish **dealer** // a confectionery **store,** a candy **shop,** a confectioner // a book**store,** a book**seller** // a liquor **store,** a wine **dealer,** a *sake* **brewery** // a stationery **store,** a stationer

yā 〚interj〛 **hi, hello**

¶ **Hello there!** How are you doing?

＊ *Yā* is used by men only.

yabureru 〚v Ⅱ〛 **be torn, rip, be broken, wear out, become threadbare**

¶ This paper **tears** easily.

¶ This shirt **is** a little **worn** but it's still good (literally, can still be worn).

yabureru 〚v Ⅱ〛 **be defeated, lose lose** a war

¶テニスの試合で，田中さんは山田さんに敗れました。 (Tenisu no shiai de, Tanaka san wa Yamada san ni *yaburemashita*.)

¶ [Mr.] Tanaka **lost** the tennis match to [Mr.] Yamada.

⇨makeru 負ける

yaburu 破る〖動Ⅰ〗

①［紙・布などを引き裂いたりする〕
¶山田さんは怒って，手紙を破って捨てました。 (Yamada san wa okotte, tegami o *yabutte* sutemashita.)

②［約束や決まりなどを守らない〕
¶田中さんはわたしとの約束を破って，ついに来ませんでした。(Tanaka san wa watashi to no yakusoku o *yabutte*, tsuini kimasen deshita.)

③［試合や勝負などで相手を負かす〕
¶テニスの試合で，ＡチームはＢチームを破りました。 (Tenisu no shiai de, Ē-chiimu wa Bii-chiimu o *yaburimashita*.)

yaburu 〖v I〗 **tear, rip; break, violate; beat, defeat**

① [tear, rip]
¶ [Miss] Yamada angrily **tore up** the letter and threw it away.

② [break, violate]
¶ [Mr.] Tanaka never showed up for [his] appointment with me.

③ [beat, defeat]
¶ Team A **beat** Team B at tennis.

yado 宿〖名〗

¶1時間も歩いて，やっと宿を見つけました。 (Ichijikan mo aruite, yatto *yado* o mitsukemashita.)

¶今晩はどこに宿をとりましょうか。 (Konban wa doko ni *yado* o torimashō ka?)

yado 〖n〗 **lodging, inn, a room**

¶ After walking for a hour [we] finally found **a room** for the night.

¶ Where shall we seek **lodging** tonight?

yagate やがて〖副〗

¶山田さんも，やがて来るでしょう。 (Yamada san mo, *yagate* kuru deshō.)

¶田中さんが外国へ行ってから，やがて1年になります。 (Tanaka san ga gaikoku e itte kara, *yagate* ichinen

yagate 〖adv〗 **soon, shortly, nearly, after all**

¶ [Mrs.] Yamada should be here **shortly.**

¶ **Nearly** one year has passed since [Mr.] Tanaka went abroad.

ni narimasu.)

yahari やはり〚副〛

①[ほかの場合と同じように]

¶この言葉の意味がわからないので，山田さんにきいてみましたが，**やはり**わかりませんでした。(Kono kotoba no imi ga wakaranai node, Yamada san ni kiite mimashita ga, *yahari* wakarimasen deshita.)

¶山田さんは医者ですが，息子さんも**やはり**医者になりたいそうです。

(Yamada san wa isha desu ga, musukosan mo *yahari* isha ni naritai sō desu.)

②[前の場合と同じように]

¶上田さんは今でも**やはり**小学校の先生をしていらっしゃいますか。(Ueda san wa ima demo *yahari* shōgakkō no sensei o shite irasshaimasu ka?)

¶去年の夏も暑かったですが，今年も**やはり**暑いですね。(Kyonen no natsu mo atsukatta desu ga, kotoshi mo *yahari* atsui desu ne.)

③[予想していたとおりに]

¶わたしが思っていたとおり，**やはり**あの人はうそをついていました。

(Watashi ga omotte ita toori, *yahari* ano hito wa uso o tsuite imashita.)

¶中村さんは試験に合格しないだろうと思っていましたが，**やはり**だめでした。(Nakamura san wa shiken ni gōkaku shinai darō to omotte imashita ga, *yahari* dame deshita.)

yahari 〚adv〛 **too, also, likewise; still, just the same; after all, as expected**

① [too, also, likewise]

¶ I didn't understand the meaning of this word so I asked [Mr.] Yamada but he didn't understand **either.**

¶ [Mrs.] Yamada is a doctor and I hear [her] son wants to become a doctor **too.**

② [still, just the same]

¶ Is [Miss] Ueda **still** teaching in elementary school?

¶ It was hot last summer and it's hot **again** this year **too.**

③ [after all, as expected]

¶ It's just as I thought—[he] *was* lying.

¶ I thought [Mr.] Nakamura would fail the exam and that's **just** what happened.

＊「やっぱり (yappari)」とも言う。

＊ Variant: *yappari*.

yakamashii やかましい〖形〗

¶隣の部屋がやかましくて,勉強ができません。 (Tonari no heya ga *yakamashikute*, benkyō ga dekimasen.)

¶やかましい。静かにしろ。 (*Yakamashii*. Shizuka ni shiro.)

yakamashii 〚adj〛 **noisy**

¶ It's so noisy in the room next door that [I] can't study.

¶ Quiet! Stop making **such a racket!** (literally, **You're too loud.** Be quiet!)

yakeru 焼ける〖動Ⅱ〗

①[火で燃える]

¶火事で家が何軒も焼けました。 (Kaji de ie ga nangen mo *yakemashita*.)

②[食べ物などが熱を加えられて食べるのに適するようになる]

¶肉が焼けましたよ。どうぞ,おあがりください。 (Niku ga *yakemashita* yo. Dōzo, oagari kudasai.)

③[日光などにあたって色が変わる]

¶泳ぎに行って,顔が真っ黒に焼けました。 (Oyogi ni itte, kao ga makkuro ni *yakemashita*.)

yakeru 〚v Ⅱ〛 **burn, be burnt; be roasted; be sunburned, be suntanned**

① [burn, be burnt]

¶ Many houses **burned down** in the fire.

② [be roasted, grilled, broiled, baked, toasted]

¶ The meat is done 〖**grilled, roasted,** etc.〗. Please have some.

③ [be sunburned, be suntanned]

¶ [His] face **got browned** in the sun when [he] went swimming.

yaku 焼く〖動Ⅰ〗

①[火をつけて燃やす]

ごみを焼く (gomi o *yaku*)

¶この手紙はもう要らないから,焼いてください。 (Kono tegami wa mō iranai kara, *yaite* kudasai.)

②[食べ物などに熱を加えて食べるのに適するようにする]

魚を焼く (sakana o *yaku*)

¶パンを焼いて,バターをつけて食べました。 (Pan o *yaite*, batā o tsukete tabemashita.)

yaku 〚v Ⅰ〛 **burn, set on fire; roast**

① [burn, set on fire]

burn the trash

¶ [I] don't need this letter any more. Please **burn it.**

② [roast, broil, grill, bake, toast]

grill 〖**roast, broil**〗 fish

¶ [I] ate the bread 〖roll, muffin, etc.〗 **toasted** and buttered.

yaku 役〖名〗

①［務め，仕事上の地位〗
上役 (uwa*yaku*)　役目 (*yaku*me)
¶田中さんは，その委員会でどんな役をしているのですか。(Tanaka san wa, sono iinkai de donna *yaku* o shite iru no desu ka?)

②［劇などに出てくる人物などの役割〗
役者 (*yaku*sha)　主役 (shu*yaku*)
¶この劇の主人公の役は，だれがやるのですか。(Kono geki no shujinkō no *yaku* wa, dare ga yaru no desu ka?)

③［割り当てられた仕事，引き受けた仕事〗
¶京都の案内役は，わたしが引き受けます。(Kyōto no annai*yaku* wa, watashi ga hikiukemasu.)

④［はたらき，有用であること〗
役に立つ (*yaku* ni tatsu)　役立つ (*yaku*datsu)
¶この道具は全然役に立ちません。(Kono dōgu wa zenzen *yaku* ni tachimasen.)
¶この辞書は，日本語を勉強するのにとても役立ちます。(Kono jisho wa, Nihongo o benkyō suru no ni totemo *yaku*dachimasu.)
＊ いつも「役に立つ (yaku ni tatsu)」「役立つ (yakudatsu)」の形で使う。

yaku 約〖連体〗
¶駅からうちまで，歩いて約 15 分です。(Eki kara uchi made, aruite *yaku* jūgofun desu.)

yaku 〖n〗 office, post; role, part; duty, function

① [office, post, position]
a senior **official,** one's superior // duty, function
¶ What is [Mr.] Tanaka's **position** on that committee 〖commission, board〗?

② [role, part]
an actor, actress // the lead, leading **role**
¶ Who is playing **the lead** in this play?

③ [duty, function]
¶ I will undertake **to act as** guide in Kyoto.

④ [use, service]
be **useful,** be of **use** // be **useful,** be of **use**
¶ This tool 〖utensil, apparatus, appliance〗 is of no **use** whatsoever.
¶ This dictionary is very **useful** for studying Japanese.
＊ Always used in the patterns "*yaku ni tatsu*" and "*yakudatsu*."

yaku 〖attrib〗 about, nearly, approximately
¶ It is **roughly** a 15-minute walk from the station to my house.

¶これで仕事も約半分終わりました。
(Kore de shigoto mo *yaku* hanbun owarimashita.)

yakusho 役所〚名〛
市役所 (shi*yakusho*)
¶わたしの兄は役所に勤めています。
(Watashi no ani wa *yakusho* ni tsutomete imasu.)
¶外国へ行く手続きは，どこの役所でするのですか。(Gaikoku e iku tetsuzuki wa, doko no *yakusho* de suru no desu ka?)

yakusoku 約束〚名，〜する〛
約束を守る (*yakusoku* o mamoru)
約束を破る (*yakusoku* o yaburu)
¶わたしは今晩友達と食事をする約束があります。 (Watashi wa konban tomodachi to shokuji o suru *yakusoku* ga arimasu.)
¶山田さんと約束して，日曜日に映画を見に行くことにしました。(Yamada san to *yakusoku* shite, nichiyōbi ni eiga o mi ni iku koto ni shimashita.)

yakusu 訳す〚動Ⅰ〛
①[ある国の言葉を別の国の言葉に直す]
¶山田さんは日本の現代小説を英語に訳しています。 (Yamada san wa Nihon no gendai-shōsetsu o Eigo ni *yakushite* imasu.)
②[古い言葉や難しい言葉をわかりやすい言葉に直す]
¶中村さんは源氏物語を現代語に訳し

yakusho 〚n〛 **a government office** a city **hall**
¶ My elder brother is in **government** service.

¶ What **office** handles the paperwork for going abroad?

yakusoku 〚n, ~*suru*〛 **promise, agreement, appointment, engagement, date**
keep **a promise;** keep **an appointment** // break **a promise;** miss **an appointment**
¶ I have **a date** to have dinner with a friend tonight.
¶ **I promised** to go to a movie with [Mr.] Yamada on Sunday.

yakusu 〚v Ⅰ〛 **translate**
① [translate from one language to another]
¶ [Miss] Yamada **translates** contemporary Japanese novels into English.

② [render something in older or difficult language into language easier to understand]

¶ This marks **more or less** the half-way point of the work.

ました。(Nakamura san wa Genji-monogatari o gendaigo ni *yakushi-mashita*.)

¶ [Mr.] Nakamura **put** *The Tale of Genji* **into** modern Japanese.

yama 山〘名〙

¶富士山は日本でいちばん高い山です。(Fujisan wa Nihon de ichiban takai *yama* desu.)

¶夏休みには山に登るつもりです。(Natsuyasumi ni wa *yama* ni noboru tsumori desu.)

yama 〚n〛 **mountain, peak, hill**

¶ Mount Fuji is the highest **mountain** in Japan.

¶ I plan to go **mountain** climbing during summer vacation.

yameru 辞める〘動Ⅱ〙

¶中村さんは先月会社を辞めました。(Nakamura san wa sengetsu kaisha o *yamemashita*.)

yameru 〚v Ⅱ〛 **quit, resign**

¶ [Mr.] Nakamura **quit** [his] job last month.

yameru やめる〘動Ⅱ〙

①[続けてきたことを終わりにする]

¶今日の勉強は、これでやめることにしましょう。(Kyō no benkyō wa, kore de *yameru* koto ni shimashō.)

¶たばこをやめようと思っているのですが、なかなかやめることができません。(Tabako o *yameyō* to omotte iru no desu ga, nakanaka *yameru* koto ga dekimasen.)

②[する予定でいたことをしないことにする]

¶風邪を引いたので、旅行に行くのをやめました。(Kaze o hiita node, ryokō ni iku no o *yamemashita*.)

yameru 〚v Ⅱ〛 **stop, end; give up, quit**

① [stop, end]

¶ Let's **end** our lesson here today.

¶ **I'm trying to stop** smoking but it's hard to do.

② [give up, quit]

¶ [I] **gave up** on going on the trip because [I] caught a cold.

yamu やむ〘動Ⅰ〙

¶雨がやみました。(Ame ga *yami-mashita*.)

¶風がやんで、辺りが静かになりました。(Kaze ga *yande*, atari ga shizuka

yamu 〚v Ⅰ〛 **stop, cease**

¶ The rain **has stopped.**

¶ It became 〚has become〛 quiet with **the dying away** of the wind.

ni narimashita.)

yamuoenai　やむをえない〚連〛

¶あしたの会議には，やむをえない用事で欠席させていただきます。（Ashita no kaigi ni wa, *yamuoenai* yōji de kesseki sasete itadakimasu.）

¶用事があって来られなければ，やむをえません。（Yōji ga atte korarenakereba, *yamuoemasen*.）

⇨shikata ga nai　しかたがない

yamuoezu　やむをえず〚副〛

¶乗り物がなくなってしまったので，やむをえず歩いてうちに帰りました。（Norimono ga nakunatte shimatta node, *yamuoezu* aruite uchi ni kaerimashita.）

yane　屋根〚名〛

¶あの赤い屋根の建物が郵便局です。（Ano akai *yane* no tatemono ga yūbinkyoku desu.）

yaoya　八百屋〚名〛

¶八百屋で野菜を買ってきてください。（*Yaoya* de yasai o katte kite kudasai.）

yaru　やる〚動Ⅰ〛

①［人や動植物などに物を与える］

¶わたしは弟に万年筆をやりました。（Watashi wa otōto ni mannenhitsu o *yarimashita*.）

¶犬にえさをやってください。（Inu ni esa o *yatte* kudasai.）

¶夕方，植木に水をやりました。（Yūgata, ueki ni mizu o *yarimashita*.）

* 普通，ある人が同等または目下の人，

yamuoenai 〚compd〛 **unavoidable, inevitable, cannot be helped, beyond one's control**

¶ I will have to be absent from tomorrow's meeting due to **unavoidable** circumstances.

¶ **It can't be helped** if [you] have some business that prevents [you] from coming.

yamuoezu 〚adv〛 **unavoidably, inevitably, of necessity**

¶ [I] **was forced** to walk home as nothing was running 〚as the trains and buses had stopped running for the night〛.

yane 〚n〛 **roof**

¶ That building with a red **roof** is the post office.

yaoya 〚n〛 **vegetable store, grocer**

¶ Please go buy some vegetables at **the vegetable store.**

yappari ☞ **yahari**

yaru 〚vⅠ〛 **give; do; work; make do, live on**

① [give]

¶ **I gave** my younger brother a fountain pen.

¶ Please **feed** the dog.

¶ [I] **watered** the plants in the evening.

* *Yaru* usually expresses the meaning

動植物などにある物を与えるという意味を表す。与える人の側に立って言うときに使う。

→**ageru** 上げる

②[ものごとをする，行う]

¶テニスを**やりません**か。 (Tenisu o *yarimasen* ka?)

¶おもしろい映画を**やって**いるから，見に行きませんか。(Omoshiroi eiga o *yatte* iru kara, mi ni ikimasen ka?)

¶来週，田中先生の送別会を**やる**予定です。(Raishū, Tanaka sensei no sōbetsukai o *yaru* yotei desu.)

③[ある職業に就く，仕事をする]

¶わたしの兄は本屋を**やって**います。(Watashi no ani wa hon'ya o *yatte* imasu.)

④[収入などを得て生活する]

¶あなたは1か月10万円で**やって**いけますか。 (Anata wa ikkagetsu jūman'en de *yatte* ikemasu ka?)

(〜**te**) **yaru** (〜て) **やる**〖連〗

¶子供を動物園へ連れていって**やりま**した。(Kodomo o dōbutsuen e tsurete itte *yarimashita*.)

¶わたしは妹にくつを買って**やりまし**た。(Watashi wa imōto ni kutsu o katte *yarimashita*.)

＊ 一般的に，相手のためにある動作をするという意味を表す。動作をする人の側に立って言うときに使う。普通，同等または目下の人などのためにある動作をするときに使う。

of a person giving something to someone of equal or lower status or to an animal or plant. Used from the standpoint of the giver.

② [do, hold]

¶ **Won't you play** tennis?

¶ **There's** an interesting movie **on.** Won't you come with [me] to see it?

¶ A farewell party for Professor 〚Doctor〛 Tanaka is scheduled for next week.

③ [work, perform]

¶ My elder brother **runs** a bookstore.

④ [make do, live on]

¶ Can you **live on** a hundred thousand yen a month?

(-te) **yaru** 〚compd〛 **do something for someone**

¶ **I took** the children to the zoo.

¶ **I bought** shoes for my younger sister.

＊ Generally indicates an act done for another person. Used from the standpoint of the performer of the act. Usually used for an act done for someone of equal or lower status.

⇨(～**te**) **ageru** （～て）あげる

yasai 野菜〖名〗

¶わたしは畑でじゃがいもやキャベツやトマトなどの野菜を作っています。
(Watashi wa hatake de jagaimo ya kyabetsu ya tomato nado no *yasai* o tsukutte imasu.)

yasashii 優しい〖形〗

¶田中さんは心の優しい人です。
(Tanaka san wa kokoro no *yasashii* hito desu.)

¶入学試験に落ちてがっかりしていたら、山田さんが優しく慰めてくれました。(Nyūgaku-shiken ni ochite gakkari shite itara, Yamada san ga *yasashiku* nagusamete kuremashita.)

yasashii 易しい〖形〗

¶日本語は易しいですか。難しいですか。(Nihongo wa *yasashii* desu ka? Muzukashii desu ka?)

¶問題が易しかったので、すぐできました。(Mondai ga *yasashikatta* node, sugu dekimashita.)

⇔**muzukashii** 難しい

yaseru やせる〖動Ⅱ〗

¶中村さんはわたしよりやせています。
(Nakamura san wa watashi yori *yasete* imasu.)

¶わたしは病気をしてやせてしまいました。 (Watashi wa byōki o shite *yasete* shimaimashita.)

⇔**futoru** 太る

yasui 安い〖形〗

---

yasai 〖n〗 **vegetable(s)**

¶ I grow **vegetables**—potatoes, cabbage, tomatoes, etc.—in a field.

yasashii 〖adj〗 **gentle, tender, kindly, considerate**

¶ [Mr.] Tanaka is a **kindhearted** person.

¶ When [I] was downhearted at failing [my] college entrance exams, [Miss] Yamada **gently** comforted [me].

yasashii 〖adj〗 **easy, simple**

¶ **Is** Japanese **easy?** Or is it hard?

¶ The (test) problem **was easy** so [I] finished it quickly.

yaseru 〖v II〗 **become thin, lose weight**

¶ [Mr.] Nakamura **is thinner** than I am.

¶ I **lost weight** due to my illness.

yasui 〖adj〗 **cheap, inexpensive**

¶もっと安いのを見せてください。
(Motto *yasui* no o misete kudasai.)
¶安ければ買いますが，高ければ買いません。 (*Yasukereba* kaimasu ga, takakereba kaimasen.)
⇔takai 高い

-yasui -やすい〖尾〗
¶田中さんの手紙は，字がきれいで読みやすいです。 (Tanaka san no tegami wa, ji ga kirei de yomi*yasui* desu.)
¶夏は食べ物が腐りやすいです。
(Natsu wa tabemono ga kusari-*yasui* desu.)
⇔-nikui -にくい

yasumi 休み〖名〗
休み時間 (*yasumi*jikan)　昼休み (hiru*yasumi*)
¶あしたは学校が休みです。 (Ashita wa gakkō ga *yasumi* desu.)
¶今日，山田先生は風邪でお休みです。 (Kyō, Yamada sensei wa kaze de o*yasumi* desu.)

yasumu 休む〖動Ⅰ〗
①[休息する，心や体を楽にする]
¶それでは，10分間休みましょう。
(Soredewa, jippunkan *yasumimashō*.)
②[学校や会社などに行くことをやめる]
¶体のぐあいが悪いので，会社を休みました。(Karada no guai ga warui node, kaisha o *yasumimashita*.)

yatou 雇う〖動Ⅰ〗

¶ Please show me a **cheaper** one.

¶ [I] will buy it **if it's cheap** but not if it's expensive.

-yasui 〖suf〗 **be easy to ~, be apt to ~**
¶ [Miss] Tanaka's letters are written in an attractive and **easy**-to-read handwriting.
¶ Food goes bad **easily** in the summer.

yasumi 〖n〗 **a rest, a break; a holiday, vacation, time off**
work-**breaks**, the time **between classes** // the lunch **break**
¶ There is **no school** tomorrow.
¶ Professor Yamada **is out** today with a cold 〖the flu〗.

yasumu 〖vⅠ〗 **rest, take a break; be absent from work, school**, etc.
① [rest, take a break]
¶ Well, **let's have a** 10-minute **break** now.
② [be absent from work, school, etc.]
¶ [I] **stayed home** from work as [I] don't 〖didn't〗 feel well.

yatou 〖vⅠ〗 **employ, hire**

¶あそこの家は金持ちで，お手伝いさんを3人も雇っています。　(Asoko no ie wa kanemochi de, otetsudaisan o sannin mo *yatotte* imasu.)

¶ That family is rich—**they have** three maids.

yatto　やっと〖副〗

①[困難な状況に耐えたりその状態を打開するための努力などをしてある事態が実現することを表す]

¶1時間並んで，やっと汽車の切符を買うことができました。　(Ichijikan narande, *yatto* kisha no kippu o kau koto ga dekimashita.)

¶一生懸命走って，やっと電車に間に合いました。(Isshōkenmei hashitte, *yatto* densha ni maniaimashita.)

¶長い厳しい冬が終わって，やっと暖かい春になりました。(Nagai kibishii fuyu ga owatte, *yatto* atatakai haru ni narimashita.)

* 普通，待ち望んでいた結果が実現したときに使う。あとに過去・完了を表す「たの形」が来ることが多い。「やっとのことで (yatto no koto de)」の形でも使う。

→yōyaku ようやく

②[あることがらが可能ではあるがじゅうぶんではないという意味を表す]

¶あの部屋は狭くて，5人がやっと入れる広さです。(Ano heya wa semakute, gonin ga *yatto* haireru hirosa desu.)

*「〜がやっとです (〜ga yatto desu)」の形でも使う。「月給が安いので，自分一人が生活するのがやっと

yatto 〖adv〗　**at last, finally; barely, narrowly, just**

① [at last, finally, with much effort]

¶ After standing in line for an hour [I] was **at last** able to buy a train ticket.

¶ [I] ran as hard as [I] could and **managed** to catch the train.

¶ Spring has **finally** come 〚**finally** came〛 after the long, hard winter.

* Usually used when some desired result has been achieved. Generally followed by the *-ta* form expressing past or completed action. Also used in the pattern "*yatto no koto de.*"

② [barely, narrowly, just]

¶ The room is small—it **barely** holds five persons.

* Also used in the pattern "*~ ga yatto desu.*" For example, "*Gekkyū ga yasui node, jibun hitori ga seikatsu*

yo

です。(Gekkyū ga yasui node, jibun hitori ga seikatsu suru no ga yatto desu.)」

suru no ga yatto desu" (My wages are barely enough for one person to live on).

yattsu 八つ〖名〗

①[8個]
¶ここに卵が八つあります。 (Koko ni tamago ga *yattsu* arimasu.)

②[8歳]
¶今年, この子は八つになりました。 (Kotoshi, kono ko wa *yattsu* ni narimashita.)

yattsu 〖n〗 **eight; eight years old**

① [eight, eight items]
¶ There are **eight** eggs here.

② [eight years old]
¶ This child turned **eight** this year.

yawaraka 柔らか〖形動〗
柔らかな手 (*yawaraka* na te) 柔らかな布団 (*yawaraka* na futon)
→**yawarakai 柔らかい**

yawaraka 〖adj-v〗 **soft, gentle, tender**
a **soft** hand // **soft** *futon* bedding

yawarakai 柔らかい〖形〗
¶このパンは今焼いたばかりですから柔らかいですよ。(Kono pan wa ima yaita bakari desu kara *yawarakai* desu yo.)
¶ゆうべは柔らかい布団でぐっすり眠りました。 (Yūbe wa *yawarakai* futon de gussuri nemurimashita.)
→**yawaraka 柔らか**

yawarakai 〖adj〗 **soft, gentle, tender**
¶ This bread **is nice and moist** because it's freshly baked.

¶ [I] slept well last night on the **soft** *futon* bedding.

yo よ〖助〗
①[意志や感情や判断などを相手に印象づけて表したり念を押したりする場合に使う]
¶急ぎますから,わたしはもう帰りますよ。 (Isogimasu kara, watashi wa mō kaerimasu *yo*.)
¶早くしないと遅れますよ。 (Hayaku shinai to okuremasu *yo*.)
¶あの映画はとてもおもしろいですよ。

yo 〖part〗 a sentence-final particle used for stress, etc.
① [used for emphasizing to the listener the force of one's intent, emotion, judgment, etc.]
¶ I'm leaving now as I'm in a hurry.

¶ You'll be late if you don't hurry!

¶ That movie is really interesting.

(Ano eiga wa totemo omoshiroi desu *yo*.)

②[命令・依頼・勧誘などの気持ちを相手に訴える場合に使う]

¶そんなことをしてはいけませんよ。(Sonna koto o shite wa ikemasen *yo*.)

¶あした必ず来てくださいよ。(Ashita kanarazu kite kudasai *yo*.)

¶疲れたから, 少し休みましょうよ。(Tsukareta kara, sukoshi yasumimashō *yo*.)

＊一般に丁寧に言う場合は男性も女性も「〜ですよ (〜desu yo)」「〜ますよ (〜masu yo)」の形を使う。名詞, 形容動詞の語幹, 助詞に直接「よ (yo)」が続く形は, 女性だけが使う。「これはあなたの本よ。(Kore wa anata no hon yo.)」「この花きれいよ。(Kono hana kirei yo.)」「あした休みなのよ。(Ashita yasumi na no yo.)」 男性は「だ (da)」をつけて使う。「これは君の本だよ。(Kore wa kimi no hon da yo.)」「この花きれいだよ。(Kono hana kirei da yo.)」「あした休みなんだよ。(Ashita yasumi na n da yo.)」 形容詞に直接「よ (yo)」のつく形は, 一般に男性が使う。「この本おもしろいよ。(Kono hon omoshiroi yo.)」 女性の場合は「この本おもしろいわよ (Kono hon omoshiroi wa yo.)」などと言う。

② [used to appeal to the listener as in an order, request, urging, etc.]

¶ You shouldn't do that!

¶ Now be sure to come tomorrow.

¶ I'm tired—let's take a break!

＊ When speaking politely generally used in the forms "~ *desu yo*," "-*masu yo*" by both men and women. *Yo* directly follows a noun, adjective-verb, or particle only in women's language. Examples are "*Kore wa anata no hon yo*" (This is *your* book), "*Kono hana kirei yo*" (What a pretty flower!), and "*Ashita yasumi na no yo*" (Tomorrow is a holiday; It's closed tomorrow). In men's language *da* is used before *yo*: "*Kore wa kimi no hon da yo*"; "*Kono hana kirei da yo*"; and "*Ashita yasumi na n da yo*." Using *yo* directly after an adjective is also generally done by men, as in "*Kono hon omoshiroi yo*" (This is really an interesting book). Women will say something like "*Kono hon omoshiroi wa yo*" instead.

yō 用〖名〗

用が済む (*yō* ga sumu) 用を済ませ

yō 〚n〛 **business, engagement, errand, things to do**

one's business is completed // fin-

-yō

る (*yō o sumaseru*) ... ish **one's business**

¶用があるから，ちょっと来てください。(*Yō ga aru kara, chotto kite kudasai.*)
¶ Please come here a minute—there's **something I want to see you about.**

¶何か御用でしょうか。(*Nani ka goyō deshō ka?*)
¶ Is there **something I can do for you?**

⇨**yōji** 用事

-yō　-用〖尾〗
子供用自転車 (*kodomoyō-jitensha*)
非常用の階段 (*hijōyō no kaidan*)

-yō 〚suf〛 use, service, for ~
a **child's** bicycle // a **fire** escape

yō　よう〖助動〗
①[意志を表す]
¶その荷物を持ってあげよう。(*Sono nimotsu o motte ageyō.*)
¶わたしはA大学の入学試験を受けようと思っています。(*Watashi wa Ē-daigaku no nyūgaku-shiken o ukeyō to omotte imasu.*)
¶あなたはどんな勉強をしようとお考えですか。(*Anata wa donna benkyō o shiyō to okangae desu ka?*)
¶上田さんは早くから東京へ来ようと思っていたそうです。(*Ueda san wa hayaku kara Tōkyō e koyō to omotte ita sō desu.*)
*「～と思う (~to omou)」「～と考える (~to kangaeru)」などといっしょに使うことが多い。
②[勧誘を表す]
¶みんなでいっしょに御飯を食べようよ。(*Minna de issho ni gohan o tabeyō yo.*)
③[ある動作・作用がこれから行われるという意味を表す]

-yō 〚auxil〛 a verb ending indicating intent, urging, etc.
① [indicates intent]
¶ **Let me carry** that package 〚bag, etc.〛 for you.
¶ **I plan to take** the entrance exam for University A.
¶ What **do you plan** to study?
¶ I hear that [Mr.] Ueda **had wanted to come** to Tokyo for some time.
* Often used with ~ *to omou*, ~ *to kangaeru*, etc.
② [indicates urging]
¶ **Let's** all **eat** together.
③ [indicates that some action or operation is about to take place]

891

¶出かけ**よう**としているところへ友達が訪ねて来ました。　(Dekake*yō* to shite iru tokoro e tomodachi ga tazunete kimashita.)

¶夜が明け**よう**とするころ，わたしたちは出発しました。(Yo ga ake*yō* to suru koro, watashitachi wa shuppatsu shimashita.)

* 「〜ようとする（〜*yō* to suru）」の形で使う。

＊ 「よう（*yō*）」はＩ型動詞以外の動詞につく。

⇨**u　う**

yobō　予防〖名，〜する〗

予防注射（*yobō*-chūsha）

¶毎日歯をみがいて，虫歯を**予防**しましょう。(Mainichi ha o migaite, mushiba o *yobō* shimashō.)

¶ダムを作ったり山に木を植えたりして，水害を**予防**します。　(Damu o tsukuttari yama ni ki o uetari shite, suigai o *yobō* shimasu.)

yobu　呼ぶ〖動Ⅰ〗

①[大声で声をかける]

¶山田さんが「おおい。」とわたしを**呼**びました。　(Yamada san ga "Ōi." to watashi o *yobimashita*.)

②[声をかけてそばに来させる]

¶母に**呼**ばれたので，急いで行きました。(Haha ni *yobareta* node, isoide ikimashita.)

③[使いや手紙などをやって来させる]

¶すぐ医者を**呼**んでください。(Sugu isha o *yonde* kudasai.)

¶ A friend came to visit [me] **just as [I] was about to go out.**

¶ We set out **as** the sun **was coming up.**

* Used in the pattern "-*yō* to suru."

＊ -*yō* is added to verbs other than Type I verbs.

yobō 〚n, ~*suru*〛 **prevention, protection; preventive**

an innoculation, vaccination, immunization

¶ Everyone should brush their teeth every day **to ward off** cavities.

¶ Flood **control** is done by building dams, planting trees on hillsides, and so on.

yobu 〚v Ⅰ〛 **call, call out; call over, draw over; summon, send for**

① [call, call out, hail]

¶ Mr. Yamada **called out** to me, saying "Hey!"

② [call over, draw over]

¶ [I] went to her quickly when [my] mother **called.**

③ [summon, send for, call for]

¶ Please **send for** a doctor right away.

yō da ようだ〚助動〛

①[あるものごとがほかのものごとに似ていることを表す]

¶あの雲は人の顔のようですね。(Ano kumo wa hito no kao no *yō desu* ne.)

¶あの人は日本語を日本人のように上手に話します。(Ano hito wa Nihongo o Nihonjin no *yō ni* jōzu ni hanashimasu.)

②[あるものごとを例として示すことを表す]

¶わたしは、東京のようなにぎやかな町より京都のような静かな町が好きです。(Watashi wa, Tōkyō no *yō na* nigiyaka na machi yori Kyōto no *yō na* shizuka na machi ga suki desu.)

¶わたしは上田さんのような立派な医者になりたいです。(Watashi wa Ueda san no *yō na* rippa na isha ni naritai desu.)

③[推量・不確かな判断などを表す]

¶あしたは雨のようですよ。(Ashita wa ame no *yō desu* yo.)

¶山田さんは来月アメリカへ行くようです。(Yamada san wa raigetsu Amerika e iku *yō desu*.)

④[あるものごとの内容が同じであることを表す]

¶中村さんの言うようにしてください。(Nakamura san no iu *yō ni* shite kudasai.)

¶以上のようなわけで、わたしは会社

yō da 〚auxil〛 like, as; seem like, look like

① [like]

¶ That cloud **is like** a person's face.

¶ [He] speaks Japanese **like** a native speaker.

② [like, such as]

¶ I like quiet cities **like** Kyoto better than lively ones **like** Tokyo.

¶ I want to become a good doctor **like** Dr. Ueda.

③ [look like, seem like, appear]

¶ **It looks like** rain tomorrow.

¶ **It seems that** [Miss] Yamada is going to the United States next month.

④ [like, as]

¶ Please do **what** [Mr.] Nakamura tells you to.

¶ I plan to quit my job for the above

を辞めるつもりです。 (Ijō no yō *na* wake de, watashi wa kaisha o yameru tsumori desu.)

⑤［方法などを表す］

¶あなたのうちは駅からどのように行くのですか。 (Anata no uchi wa eki kara dono yō *ni* iku no desu ka?)

¶「この言葉は漢字でどのように書きますか。」 (Kono kotoba wa kanji de dono yō *ni* kakimasu ka?)「このように書きます。」 (Kono yō *ni* kakimasu.)

＊ 普通「どのように (dono yō ni)」「このように (kono yō ni)」「そのように (sono yō ni)」「あのように (ano yō ni)」の形で使う。

⑥［あることを意識的に心がけて行うことを表す］

¶病気になってからは、毎日牛乳を飲むようにしています。 (Byōki ni natte kara wa, mainichi gyūnyū o nomu yō *ni* shite imasu.)

¶いつも日本語だけで話すようにしています。(Itsu mo Nihongo dake de hanasu yō *ni* shite imasu.)

¶毎日，予習と復習をするようにしてください。 (Mainichi, yoshū to fukushū o suru yō *ni* shite kudasai.)

＊ 普通「～ようにする (～yō ni suru)」の形で使う。

⑦［目標や目的などを表す］

¶汽車の時間に間に合うように急いでください。 (Kisha no jikan ni maniau yō *ni* isoide kudasai.)

reasons.

⑤ [way, manner]

¶ **How** do [I] get from the station to your home?

¶ "**How** is this word written in *kanji*?"

  "It is written **like** this."

＊ Usually used in the patterns "*dono yō ni,*" "*kono yō ni,*" "*sono yō ni,*" and "*ano yō ni.*"

⑥ [make it a practice to]

¶ Since becoming ill [I] **make it a practice** to drink milk every day.

¶ [I] **make it a practice** to speak only Japanese.

¶ Please **try** to prepare your lessons and to review every day.

＊ Usually used in the pattern "～ *yō ni suru.*"

⑦ [in order to, so as to]

¶ Please hurry **so** you'll be in time for the train.

¶肉が腐らない**ように**冷蔵庫に入れておいてください。 (Niku ga kusaranai *yō ni* reizōko ni irete oite kudasai.)

¶ Please put the meat in the refrigerator **so** it won't spoil.

* 「ように (yō ni)」の前には動詞の「ないの形」か無意志性の動詞が来ることが多い。

* This *yō ni* is generally preceded by a verb in the *-nai* form or by a verb expressing uncontrollable action.

⑧[ある状態の変化の結果を表す]

⑧ [an effect]

¶日本へ来てから，日本語が上手に話せる**ようになりました**。 (Nihon e kite kara, Nihongo ga jōzu ni hanaseru *yō ni* narimashita.)

¶ [I] **have become** good at Japanese since coming to Japan.

¶早く100メートル泳ぐことができる**ようになりたい**です。 (Hayaku hyakumētoru oyogu koto ga dekiru *yō ni* naritai desu.)

¶ I want **to become** able to swim a hundred meters as soon as possible.

¶弟は高等学校に入ってから，一生懸命勉強する**ようになりました**。

(Otōto wa kōtōgakkō ni haitte kara, isshōkenmei benkyō suru *yō ni* narimashita.)

¶ My younger brother **has started** to study hard since entering high school 〖My younger brother **started** to study hard after entering high school〗.

* 普通「～ようになる (～yō ni naru)」の形で使う。

* Usually used in the pattern "~ *yō ni naru*."

⑨[願望・要求・勧めなどの内容を表すときに使う]

⑨ [used when expressing a desire, request, recommendation, etc.]

¶早くよくなる**ように**お祈りしております。 (Hayaku yoku naru *yō ni* oinori shite orimasu.)

¶ I hope [you] will be better soon (very polite).

¶山田さんにあしたわたしのうちへ来る**ように**言ってください。 (Yamada san ni ashita watashi no uchi e kuru *yō ni* itte kudasai.)

¶ Please ask [Mr.] Yamada to come to my place tomorrow.

¶田中さんに本を返してくれる**ように**頼みました。 (Tanaka san ni hon o

¶ I asked [Miss] Tanaka to please return the book.

kaeshite kureru *yō ni* tanomima-
shita.)

* あとに「言う (iu)」「話す (ha-
nasu)」「頼む (tanomu)」「命令する
(meirei suru)」「勧める (susumeru)」
「祈る (inoru)」などの動詞が来る。

✻ 丁寧に言う場合「ようです (yō
desu)」となる。

* Followed by verbs like *iu, hanasu,
tanomu, meirei suru, susumeru, inoru,* etc.

✻ When speaking politely, *yō desu* is
used rather than *yō da.*

yofukashi 夜更かし〖名, 〜する〗
¶夜更かしをした次の日は, なかなか
起きられません。(*Yofukashi* o shita
tsugi no hi wa, nakanaka okiraremasen.)

¶夜更かしするのは, 体によくありま
せん。 (*Yofukashi* suru no wa,
karada ni yoku arimasen.)

yofukashi 〖n, ~*suru*〗 **stay up late
at night, keep late hours**

¶ [I] have a hard time getting up the
next day after **staying up late.**

¶ **Late hours** are bad for the health.

yōfuku 洋服〖名〗
洋服だんす (*yōfuku*-dansu)
¶田中さんはいつも茶色の洋服を着て
います。(Tanaka san wa itsu mo
chairo no *yōfuku* o kite imasu.)

yōfuku 〖n〗 **Western clothes, a
suit, a dress,** etc.

a wardrobe, a **clothes**press
¶ [Mr.] Tanaka **is** always **dressed** in
brown.

yogoreru 汚れる〖動Ⅱ〗
¶シャツが汚れたので, 洗たくしまし
た。(Shatsu ga *yogoreta* node, sentaku shimashita.)

¶どろ道を走ったので, 車が汚れてし
まいました。(Doromichi o hashitta
node, kuruma ga *yogorete* shimaimashita.)

yogoreru 〖v Ⅱ〗 **become dirty, be
soiled**

¶ [I] washed the shirt as it **was dirty.**

¶ The car **got dirty** on the muddy
roads.

yogosu 汚す〖動Ⅰ〗
¶スープをこぼして, 洋服を汚してし
まいました。 (Sūpu o koboshite,
yōfuku o *yogoshite* shimaimashita.)

¶きれいな着物を着たのですから, 汚

yogosu 〖v Ⅰ〗 **make dirty, stain,
soil, deface**

¶ [I] spilled some soup and **stained**
[my] clothes.

¶ Please be careful **not to dirty** that

さないように気をつけなさい。(Kirei
na kimono o kita no desu kara,
yogosanai yō ni ki o tsukenasai.)

pretty *kimono* you're wearing.

yohō 予報〖名, 〜する〗

¶天気予報によると、明日は雨が降る
そうです。(Tenki-*yohō* ni yoru to,
asu wa ame ga furu sō desu.)

yohō 〖n, 〜*suru*〗 forecast, prediction

¶ According to the weather **forecast,**
there will be rain tomorrow.

yohodo よほど〖副〗

¶ゆうべはよほど寒かったのでしょう。
水道が凍っています。(Yūbe wa
yohodo samukatta no deshō. Suidō
ga kootte imasu.)
¶息子は一度に五杯も御飯を食べまし
た。よほどおなかがすいていたのでし
ょう。(Musuko wa ichido ni gohai
mo gohan o tabemashita. *Yohodo*
onaka ga suite ita no deshō.)

yohodo 〖adv〗 very, much, greatly

¶ It must have gotten **exceptionally**
cold last night. The water pipes have
frozen.

¶ My son ate five bowls of rice at
one sitting. He must have been
famished.

yoi よい〖形〗

①[正しい立派な様子]
¶よいと思ったことは、勇気を持って
実行しなさい。(*Yoi* to omotta koto
wa, yūki o motte jikkō shinasai.)
¶人の物を取るのはよくないことです。
(Hito no mono o toru no wa *yoku*
nai koto desu.)
↔**warui** 悪い

②[善良である様子]
¶山田さんはとてもよい人ですね。
(Yamada san wa totemo *yoi* hito
desu ne.)
↔**warui** 悪い

③[親しい様子]
¶春子さんと秋子さんはたいへん仲の
よい友達です。(Haruko san to

yoi 〖adj〗 good, right; nice; fine; all right

① [good, right]

¶ You should be brave and do what
you think **is right.**

¶ Taking things that belong to others
is not right.

② [good, nice]
¶ [Mr.] Yamada is a **fine** person.

③ [good, close]
¶ Haruko and Akiko are **good**
friends.

Akiko san wa taihen naka no *yoi* tomodachi desu.)

*普通「仲がよい (naka ga yoi)」の形で使う。

* Usually used in the pattern "*naka ga yoi.*"

↔**warui** 悪い

④[ものごとの優れている様子]

¶上田さんは成績がたいへん**よい**そうです。 (Ueda san wa seiseki ga taihen *yoi* sō desu.)

④ [good, fine, excellent]

¶ They say that [Miss] Ueda's record 〚grade(s)〛 is **excellent.**

¶この万年筆はあまり**よく**ないです。 (Kono mannenhitsu wa amari *yoku* nai desu.)

¶ This fountain pen **isn't** very **good.**

⑤[状態の好ましい様子，気持ちのよい様子]

⑤ [good, nice, pleasant]

病気が**よく**なる (byōki ga *yoku* naru)

one's illness gets **better**

¶天気が**よい**日には散歩をします。 (Tenki ga *yoi* hi ni wa sanpo o shimasu.)

¶ [I] go for a walk on **nice** days.

¶あの店は感じの**よい**店ですね。 (Ano mise wa kanji no *yoi* mise desu ne.)

¶ That restaurant 〚coffee shop, shop, etc.〛 has a **good** atmosphere, doesn't it?

¶お酒を飲んだら**よい**気持ちになって，ゆうべは早く寝てしまいました。 (Osake o nondara *yoi* kimochi ni natte, yūbe wa hayaku nete shimai-mashita.)

¶ Last night I was feeling **good** after having something to drink and I went to bed early.

↔**warui** 悪い

⑥[じゅうぶんである様子]

¶「ここから駅までどのくらいかかりますか。」 (Koko kara eki made dono kurai kakarimasu ka?) 「10分もあれば**よい**と思います。」 (Jippun mo areba *yoi* to omoimasu.)

⑥ [all right, enough]

¶ "How long does it take to get to the station from here?"

  "It shouldn't take more than 10 minutes (literally, I think 10 minutes **will be enough**)."

¶今度の旅行には五千円も持って行けばよいでしょう。 (Kondo no ryokō ni wa gosen'en mo motte ikeba *yoi* deshō.)

⑦[同意や許可などの意味を表す]
¶時間はありますから，急がなくてもよいでしょう。 (Jikan wa arimasu kara, isoganakute mo *yoi* deshō.)
¶たばこを吸ってもよいですか。
(Tabako o sutte mo *yoi* desu ka.)
*「～てもよい (～te mo yoi)」の形で使う。

→(～te mo) ii (～ても) いい
＊「終止の形」「連体の形」のときには「いい (ii)」も使われる。

⇨ii いい

yōi 用意〖名，～する〗
¶食事の用意ができました。(Shokuji no *yōi* ga dekimashita.)
¶旅行に行くのに，いくらぐらい用意したらいいでしょうか。 (Ryokō ni iku no ni, ikura gurai *yōi* shitara ii deshō ka?)

yōji 用事〖名〗
用事がない (*yōji* ga nai) 用事を済ませる (*yōji* o sumaseru)
¶用事がありますので，お先に失礼します。 (Yōji ga arimasu node, osaki ni shitsurei shimasu.)
¶用事が済んだら，お茶を飲みに行きましょう。 (Yōji ga sundara, ocha o nomi ni ikimashō.)

⇨yō 用

yōjin 用心〖名，～する〗

¶ Five thousand yen **should be enough** for the coming trip.

⑦ [all right, may]
¶ There's still time so you **don't have to** hurry.

¶ **Do you mind** if I smoke?

* Used in the pattern "-*te mo yoi.*"

＊ In the dictionary or plain form, the form *ii* is also used.

yōi 〖n, ~*suru*〗 preparation, arrangements, provisions
¶ Dinner 〖lunch, breakfast〗 **is ready.**
¶ How much money **will [we] need** for the trip?

yōji 〖n〗 business, errand, engagement, things to do
have nothing **that needs to be attended to,** be free // settle **one's business,** finish **an errand**
¶ I'm sorry to leave early but I have **some other business** to see to.
¶ Let's go have some tea after you've finished up **your business.**

yōjin 〖n, ~*suru*〗 care, caution

用心深い (*yōjin*bukai)

¶風邪を引かないように用心してください。(Kaze o hikanai yō ni *yōjin* shite kudasai.)

¶電車の中でお金を取られないように用心したほうがいいですよ。(Densha no naka de okane o torarenai yō ni *yōjin* shita hō ga ii desu yo.)

yōka 八日〔名〕

①［日付を表す］
五月八日 (gogatsu *yōka*)

②［日数を表す］
八日前 (*yōka*mae)　八日後 (*yōka*go)

⇨-ka -日

yokeru よける〔動Ⅱ〕

¶自動車が来たから，よけないと危ないですよ。(Jidōsha ga kita kara, *yokenai* to abunai desu yo.)

yokka 四日〔名〕

①［日付を表す］
一月四日 (Ichigatsu *yokka*)

②［日数を表す］
四日前 (*yokka*mae)　四日後 (*yokka*-go)

⇨-ka -日

yoko 横〔名〕

①［物に向かって左右の方向］
¶あなたの横に座っている人は，横を向いて写っていますね。(Anata no *yoko* ni suwatte iru hito wa, *yoko* o muite utsutte imasu ne.)

②［四角形で水平方向の辺，またその長さ］
¶この紙を縦10センチ，横 15 センチ

careful, cautious, prudent

¶ Please **be careful** not to catch a cold.

¶ It is advisable **to be on one's guard** against pickpockets while riding the train (literally, **be careful** one's money is not stolen).

yōka 〚n〛 the eighth of the month; eight days

① [the eighth of the month]
May **8**

② [eight days]
8 days ago, **8 days** earlier // **8 days** from now, **8 days** later

yokeru 〚v II〛 avoid, keep away from, dodge

¶ **Look out** for that car! (literally, A car is coming and it will be dangerous **if you don't move away** from its path)

yokka 〚n〛 the fourth of the month; four days

① [the fourth of the month]
January **4**

② [four days]
four days ago, **four days** earlier // **four days** from now, **four days** later

yoko 〚n〛 side; width; sideways, horizontally

① [side, flank]
¶ The person sitting **next** to you in the photo has **the side** of [her] face towards the camera.

② [width, breadth]

の大きさに切ってください。 (Kono kami o tate jissenchi, *yoko* jūgo-senchi no ookisa ni kitte kudasai.)

↔**tate** 縦

yoku 欲〖名〗

¶あの人はとても欲が深いです。(Ano hito wa totemo *yoku* ga fukai desu.)

¶あの人くらい欲のない人はいませんね。 (Ano hito kurai *yoku* no nai hito wa imasen ne.)

yoku よく〖副〗

①[じゅうぶんに]

¶疲れていたので，ゆうべはよく眠りました。(Tsukarete ita node, yūbe wa *yoku* nemurimashita.)

¶交差点を渡るときは，よく注意してください。 (Kōsaten o wataru toki wa, *yoku* chūi shite kudasai.)

②[しばしば，たびたび]

¶山田さんはよく図書館へ行きます。 (Yamada san wa *yoku* toshokan e ikimasu.)

¶子供のころは，よくけんかをしたものです。(Kodomo no koro wa, *yoku* kenka o shita mono desu.)

③[程度がはなはだしい様子]

¶春子さんはお姉さんと顔がよく似ています。(Haruko san wa onēsan to kao ga *yoku* nite imasu.)

¶このナイフはよく切れますね。 (Kono naifu wa *yoku* kiremasu ne.)

④[相手をほめたりねぎらったりするときに使う]

¶ Please cut this paper so it's 10 centimeters long and 15 centimeters **wide.**

yoku 〖n〗 **greed, desire, want, passion**

¶ [He] is very **greedy.**

¶ [He] is a [man] of few **wants** (more literally, There are few people with as few **wants** as him).

yoku 〖adv〗 **well, fully; often; much**

① [well, fully, thoroughly, carefully]

¶ I was tired so I slept **well** last night.

¶ Please be **very** careful when crossing the street.

② [often, frequently]

¶ [Miss] Yamada **often** goes to the library.

¶ [I] was in **a number of** fights during [my] childhood.

③ [much, a good deal]

¶ Haruko looks **a lot** like her older sister.

¶ This knife is **quite** sharp, isn't it?

④ [used when praising or thanking someone, etc.]

¶よくがんばりましたね。(*Yoku* ganbarimashita ne.)

¶ You did **well** not to get discouraged.

¶よくいらっしゃいました。 (*Yoku* irasshaimashita.)

¶ Welcome 〚I'm glad you could come〛.

yokujitsu 翌日〚名〛

¶土曜日に旅行に出かけて，翌日の日曜日に帰ってきました。 (Doyōbi ni ryokō ni dekakete, *yokujitsu* no nichiyōbi ni kaette kimashita.)

yokujitsu 〚n〛 **the next day**

¶ I left on the trip on Saturday and came back the **following** Sunday.

yōkyū 要求〚名，～する〛

¶あなたがたの要求には応じられません。 (Anatagata no *yōkyū* ni wa ōjiraremasen.)

¶社長に月給を上げてくれるように要求しました。 (Shachō ni gekkyū o agete kureru yō ni *yōkyū* shimashita.)

yōkyū 〚n, ~*suru*〛 **demand, request, claim**

¶ [I] can't agree to your **demands.**

¶ [I] **asked** the company president for a raise in salary.

yome 嫁〚名〛

嫁にもらう (*yome* ni morau) 嫁にやる (*yome* ni yaru) 息子の嫁 (musuko no *yome*) 花嫁 (hana*yome*)

¶春子さんは，お金持ちのところへお嫁に行ったそうですね。(Haruko san wa, okanemochi no tokoro e o*yome* ni itta sō desu ne.)

yome 〚n〛 **bride, wife, daughter-in-law**

marry (a woman) // give (one's daughter) in marriage // one's son's **wife,** one's daughter-in-law // **bride**

¶ I hear that Haruko **married** into a wealthy family.

yomu 読む〚動Ⅰ〛

¶聞こえませんから，もっと大きな声で読んでください。 (Kikoemasen kara, motto ookina koe de *yonde* kudasai.)

¶あなたは今，どんな本を読んでいますか。 (Anata wa ima, donna hon o *yonde* imasu ka?)

yomu 〚v I〛 **read**

¶ [I] can't hear you—please **read it** in a louder voice.

¶ What books **are you reading** now?

yon 四〖名〗

四個 (*yon*ko) 四匹 (*yon*hiki)

＊人数のときは「四人 (yonin)」，時刻のときは「四時 (yoji)」と言う。

⇨shi 四

yonaka 夜中〖名〗

¶ゆうべ，夜中に近所で火事がありました。(Yūbe, *yonaka* ni kinjo de kaji ga arimashita.)

⇨yoru 夜

yononaka 世の中〖名〗

①[世間，社会]

¶あの人は幸せに育って，世の中の苦労を知らないようです。(Ano hito wa shiawase ni sodatte, *yononaka* no kurō o shiranai yō desu.)

②[時代]

¶今は昔と違って，世界のどこへでもすぐ行ける世の中です。(Ima wa mukashi to chigatte, sekai no doko e demo sugu ikeru *yononaka* desu.)

yori より〖助〗

¶山田さんは中村さんより背が高いです。(Yamada san wa Nakamura san *yori* se ga takai desu.)

¶わたしはりんごよりみかんのほうが好きです。(Watashi wa ringo *yori* mikan no hō ga suki desu.)

yorokobu 喜ぶ〖動Ⅰ〗

¶山田さんは試験に合格して喜んでいます。(Yamada san wa shiken ni gōkaku shite *yorokonde* imasu.)

¶秋子さんは，誕生日の贈り物をもらってとても喜んでいます。(Akiko

yon 〚n〛 four

four items // **four** animals (dogs, cats, cows, goldfish, etc.)

＊ Four persons is *yonin* and four o'clock is *yoji*.

yonaka 〚n〛 at midnight, in the middle of the night

¶ There was a fire in [my] neighborhood **late** last night.

yononaka 〚n〛 the world, society; the times, the age

① [the world, society, life]

¶ It seems that [he] had a happy childhood and has not yet experienced the grim realities **of life.**

② [the times, the age]

¶ The present age differs from the past in that one can soon go anywhere in the world.

yori 〚part〛 than; from

¶ [Mr.] Yamada is taller **than** [Mr.] Nakamura.

¶ I like mandarin oranges better **than** apples.

yorokobu 〚v I〛 be glad, rejoice

¶ [Miss] Yamada **is happy** because [she] passed the exam.

¶ Akiko **is very pleased** with her birthday presents.

san wa, tanjōbi no okurimono o moratte totemo *yorokonde* imasu.)

¶その会には 喜んで 出席いたします。
(Sono kai ni wa *yorokonde* shusseki itashimasu.)

¶ [I] **will take great pleasure** in attending that gathering ⟦meeting⟧.

---

yoroshii　よろしい〖形〗

¶もう 帰ってもよろしいでしょうか。
(Mō kaette mo *yoroshii* deshō ka?)

¶よろしかったら, 今日うちへいらっしゃいませんか。　(*Yoroshikattara*, kyō uchi e irasshaimasen ka?)

＊「よい (yoi)」「いい (ii)」の改まった言い方。

yoroshii 〖adj〗　**good, all right**

¶ **May I** leave now?

¶ **If it's convenient,** won't you come visit me today?

＊ *Yoroshii* is the formal form of *yoi*, *ii*.

---

yoroshiku　よろしく〖副〗

①［今後の交際などを願うときのあいさつの言葉］

¶わたしは山田です。どうぞよろしく。
(Watashi wa Yamada desu. Dōzo *yoroshiku*.)

＊ 普通「どうぞよろしく。(Dōzo yoroshiku.)」または 「どうぞよろしくお願いします。　(Dōzo yoroshiku onegai shimasu.)」の形で使う。

②［好意を伝えるときに使う］

¶それでは, これで失礼します。奥様によろしくお伝えください。(Soredewa, kore de shitsurei shimasu. Okusama ni *yoroshiku* otsutae kudasai.)

yoroshiku 〖adv〗　**well, as one thinks fit; one's regards**

① [well, as one thinks fit, at one's own discretion; used to express hopes for friendly relations or kind treatment into the future]

¶ My name is Yamada. **I'm pleased to meet you** (more literally, Please treat me **kindly**).

＊ Usually used in the patterns "*Dōzo yoroshiku*," "*Dōzo yoroshiku onegai shimasu*."

② [one's regards, one's best wishes]

¶ Well, I'll be going now. Please **remember me** to your wife.

---

yoru　夜〖名〗

¶あなたは夜何時ごろ寝ますか。
(Anata wa *yoru* nanji goro nemasu ka?)

¶父は毎日, 夜遅くまで 働いています。
(Chichi wa mainichi, *yoru* osoku

yoru 〖n〗　**night, evening, nighttime**

¶ What time do you go to bed **at night**?

¶ Every day my father works far into **the night**.

made hataraite imasu.)

⇔hiru 昼　hiruma 昼間

yoru 寄る〖動Ⅰ〗

①[近づく]

¶もっとそばに**寄って**，よく見てください。 (Motto soba ni *yotte*, yoku mite kudasai.)

②[立ち寄る，目的の所へ行く途中ついでにほかの所へ行く]

¶帰りにデパートに**寄って**，買い物をしてきました。 (Kaeri ni depāto ni *yotte*, kaimono o shite kimashita.)

yoru　よる〖動Ⅰ〗

①[基づく]

¶天気予報に**よる**と，あしたもいい天気だそうです。 (Tenki-yohō ni *yoru* to, ashita mo ii tenki da sō desu.)

¶山田さんの話に**よる**と，中村さんは入院したそうです。 (Yamada san no hanashi ni *yoru* to, Nakamura san wa nyūin shita sō desu.)

②[ものごとのそれぞれの性質・事情などに応じてという意味を表す]

¶国に**よって**習慣や考え方が違います。 (Kuni ni *yotte* shūkan ya kangaekata ga chigaimasu.)

¶場合に**よって**は，あしたは休むかもしれません。 (Baai ni *yotte* wa, ashita wa yasumu ka mo shiremasen.)

③[あるものを手段とすることを表す]

¶わたしたちは，毎日のいろいろなできごとを新聞やテレビに**よって**知ります。 (Watashitachi wa, mainichi no

yoru 〖v Ⅰ〗 **approach, come near; drop by, stop off at**

① [approach, come near]

¶ Please **move closer** and take a better look.

② [drop by, stop off at]

¶ [I] **stopped off** at a department store on [my] way home and did some shopping.

yoru 〖v Ⅰ〗 **based on, according to; depending on; by; due to**

① [based on, according to]

¶ **According to** the weather forecast, it will be a nice day tomorrow too.

¶ **According to** [Mr.] Yamada, [Miss] Nakamura has entered the hospital.

② [depending on]

¶ Customs and ways of thinking differ **from** country **to** country.

¶ **Depending on** circumstances, [I] may take the day off 〖stay home〗 tomorrow.

③ [by, according to]

¶ We are informed of what takes place each day **by** the newspaper and television.

iroiro na dekigoto o shinbun ya terebi ni *yotte* shirimasu.)

④〔あるものごとに原因があるということを表す〕

¶親の不注意によって，子供がけがをしたのです。(Oya no fuchūi ni *yotte*, kodomo ga kega o shita no desu.)
¶たばこの火の不始末によって，大火事になりました。(Tabako no hi no fushimatsu ni *yotte*, ookaji ni narimashita.)

＊いつも「～による (～ni yoru)」の形で使う。

④ [due to, owing to]

¶ The child's injury was **due to** its parents' carelessness.

¶ The large fire **resulted from** the careless disposal of a cigarette butt.

＊ Always used in the patterns "～ *ni yoru*" and "～ *ni yotte*."

yosan　予算〖名〗

①〔必要な費用を見積もること，また見積もった金額〕

¶家を買いたいのですが，予算が足りません。(Ie o kaitai no desu ga, *yosan* ga tarimasen.)
¶旅行にいくらかかるか，予算を立ててみましょう。(Ryokō ni ikura kakaru ka, *yosan* o tatete mimashō.)

②〔国家や地方公共団体などが1年間の収入と支出を見積もること〕

¶来年度の予算はいつ決まりますか。(Rainendo no *yosan* wa itsu kimarimasu ka?)

yosan 〖n〗 estimate, estimated cost; budget

① [estimate, estimated cost, personal budget]

¶ [I] want to buy a house, but **[my] budget** doesn't permit it.

¶ Let's draw up **an estimate** of what the trip will cost.

② [budget (for a government, etc.)]

¶ When will next year's **budget** be decided?

yoseru　寄せる〖動Ⅱ〗

¶机やいすを教室のすみに寄せてください。(Tsukue ya isu o kyōshitsu no sumi ni *yosete* kudasai.)
¶花びんをもう少し右へ寄せてみてください。(Kabin o mō sukoshi migi e *yosete* mite kudasai.)

yoseru 〖v Ⅱ〗 move aside, put aside, bring something near

¶ Please **move** the desks and chairs to the corner(s) of the classroom.

¶ Please **move** the vase a little to the right.

yoshū 予習〖名, 〜する〗

¶あしたの予習はもう済みましたか。
(Ashita no *yoshū* wa mō sumimashita ka?)

¶予習していったので, 先生の話がよくわかりました。 (*Yoshū* shite itta node, sensei no hanashi ga yoku wakarimashita.)

⇔**fukushū** 復習

yosō 予想〖名, 〜する〗

予想が当たる (*yosō* ga ataru) 予想が外れる (*yosō* ga hazureru)

¶この試合は, 最後までどちらが勝つか予想できませんでした。 (Kono shiai wa, saigo made dochira ga katsu ka *yosō* dekimasen deshita.)

¶わたしの予想どおり, 山田さんは秋子さんと結婚しました。 (Watashi no *yosō* doori, Yamada san wa Akiko san to kekkon shimashita.)

yōsu 様子〖名〗

①[ものごとの有様・状態]

¶病人の様子はどうでしたか。 (Byōnin no *yōsu* wa dō deshita ka?)

¶わたしはまだ日本の様子がよくわかりません。 (Watashi wa mada Nihon no *yōsu* ga yoku wakarimasen.)

②[ものごとの情況などから判断される状態]

¶わたしがその話をしたら, 田中さんは驚いた様子でした。 (Watashi ga sono hanashi o shitara, Tanaka san wa odoroita *yōsu* deshita.)

yoshū 〚n, ~*suru*〛 **preparation of lessons**

¶ Have you finished **preparing** for tomorrow's class(es) yet?

¶ [I] understood what the teacher was talking about because [I] **had prepared** beforehand.

yosō 〚n, ~*suru*〛 **expectation, forecast, estimate, supposition**

one's expectations come true, fulfill **one's expectations** // be disappointed in **one's expectations**

¶ The outcome of this match **was unpredictable** until the very end.

¶ **As I expected,** Mr. Yamada married Akiko.

yōsu 〚n〛 **state, circumstances; appearance, looks**

① [state, circumstances]

¶ How was the patient?

¶ I still don't understand Japan fully.

② [appearance, looks]

¶ [Mr.] Tanaka **seemed** surprised when I mentioned that.

¶空が曇ってきて，今にも雨が降りそうな様子でした。(Sora ga kumotte kite, ima ni mo ame ga furisō na *yōsu* deshita.)

yotei 予定〖名，～する〗

¶わたしは30日に東京へ行く予定です。 (Watashi wa sanjūnichi ni Tōkyō e iku *yotei* desu.)

¶今日の午後は何か予定がありますか。 (Kyō no gogo wa nani ka *yotei* ga arimasu ka?)

¶汽車は予定どおりに上野に着きました。(Kisha wa *yotei* doori ni Ueno ni tsukimashita.)

yottsu 四つ〖名〗

① [4個]

¶ここにみかんが四つあります。(Koko ni mikan ga *yottsu* arimasu.)

② [4歳]

¶この子は四つです。 (Kono ko wa *yottsu* desu.)

you 酔う〖動Ⅰ〗

① [酒などを飲んで心や体が正常でなくなる]

¶ゆうべはお酒を飲みすぎて，すっかり酔ってしまいました。 (Yūbe wa osake o nomisugite, sukkari *yotte* shimaimashita.)

② [乗り物に乗って気持ちが悪くなる]

¶わたしは車に弱くてすぐに酔ってしまうので，本当に困ります。(Watashi wa kuruma ni yowakute sugu ni *yotte* shimau node, hontō ni komarimasu.)

yotei 〚n, ~*suru*〛 **program, plan, schedule, prearrangement, expectation**

¶ **I plan** to go to Tokyo on the thirtieth.

¶ Do you have any **plans** for this afternoon?

¶ The train arrived at Ueno **on schedule.**

yottsu 〚n〛 **four; four years old**

① [four, four items]

¶ There are **four** mandarin oranges here.

② [four years of age]

¶ This child is **four years old.**

you 〚v I〛 **get drunk; be seasick, carsick,** etc.

① [get drunk, be intoxicated]

¶ Last night [I] drank too much and **got drunk.**

② [be seasick, carsick, airsick, etc.]

¶ **I get carsick** very easily (more literally, I am susceptible to carsickness and **get carsick** very easily). It's really a nuisance.

¶海が荒れたので，すっかり船に酔ってしまいました。 (Umi ga areta node, sukkari fune ni *yotte* shimaimashita.)

¶ The sea was rough and [I] **got** very **seasick.**

yowai 弱い〖形〗

yowai 〚adj〛 **weak; frail; unskilled**

①[力・技などが劣っている様子]
¶弱い者をいじめてはいけません。
(*Yowai* mono o ijimete wa ikemasen.)

① [weak in strength, technique, etc.]
¶ One shouldn't tease 〚bully〛 those **weaker** than oneself.

¶わたしの学校はテニスは強いですが，バスケットボールは弱いです。 (Watashi no gakkō wa tenisu wa tsuyoi desu ga, basukettobōru wa *yowai* desu.)

¶ My school is strong in tennis but **weak** in basketball.

②[程度が低い様子]
¶風がだいぶ弱くなってきましたね。
(Kaze ga daibu *yowaku* natte kimashita ne.)

② [weak, faint]
¶ The wind has become a lot **weaker.**

¶電気の光が弱いので，新聞の字がよく読めません。 (Denki no hikari ga *yowai* node, shinbun no ji ga yoku yomemasen.)

¶ The electric light **is so weak** that it is hard to read the newspaper.

③[体などが丈夫でない様子]
足が弱い (ashi ga *yowai*)
¶田中さんは体が弱くて，よく病気をします。 (Tanaka san wa karada ga *yowakute,* yoku byōki o shimasu.)

③ [weak, frail]
be a walker **who tires easily**
¶ [Mr.] Tanaka **is quite delicate** and is frequently ill.

④[不得意・苦手である様子]
数学に弱い (sūgaku ni *yowai*)
¶わたしは漢字に弱いです。 (Watashi wa kanji ni *yowai* desu.)

④ [weak, poor, unskilled]
be poor at mathematics
¶ **I am poor** at *kanji.*

* いつも「～に弱い (～ni yowai)」の形で使う。

* Always used in the pattern "~ *ni yowai.*"

⑤[ものごとに対して抵抗力が少ない様子]

地震に弱い建物 (jishin ni *yowai* tatemono)

¶この生地は熱に弱いです。 (Kono kiji wa netsu ni *yowai* desu.)

¶わたしは船に弱いので，なるべく乗らないようにしています。 (Watashi wa fune ni *yowai* node, narubeku noranai yō ni shite imasu.)

* いつも 「〜に弱い (〜ni yowai)」の形で使う。

⇔tsuyoi 強い

yoyaku 予約〖名，〜する〗

席を予約する (seki o *yoyaku* suru)

¶京都はこんでいますから，宿を予約していらっしゃるほうがいいですよ。 (Kyōto wa konde imasu kara, yado o *yoyaku* shite irassharu hō ga ii desu yo.)

yōyaku ようやく〖副〗

¶夕方になって，ようやく涼しい風が吹き始めました。 (Yūgata ni natte, *yōyaku* suzushii kaze ga fukihajimemashita.)

¶上田さんは3度めの試験でようやく合格しました。 (Ueda san wa sandome no shiken de *yōyaku* gōkaku shimashita.)

¶わたしは3年日本語を勉強して，ようやく新聞が読めるようになりました。 (Watashi wa sannen Nihongo o benkyō shite, *yōyaku* shinbun ga yomeru yō ni narimashita.)

⑤ [weak, have a low tolerance]

a building **easily damaged** by earthquake

¶ This cloth **has little resistance** against heat.

¶ I **get seasick easily** so I avoid being on board boats.

* Always used in the pattern "~ *ni yowai*."

yoyaku 〚n, ~*suru*〛 **reservation, advance order**

book a seat

¶ Kyoto is crowded so it would be best **to reserve** a room in advance.

yōyaku 〚adv〛 **at last, finally, at length**

¶ A cool breeze **finally** came up after it got dark 〚A cool breeze has **finally** come up since it has gotten dark〛.

¶ [Mr.] Ueda **finally** passed the exam on [his] third try.

¶ After studying the language for three years, I can now **at last** 〚I **at last** became able to〛 read the newspaper in Japanese.

＊なかなか実現しない事態が，一定の時間を経過した後，実現するという意味を表す。普通，待ち望んでいた結果が実現したときに使う。

＊あとに過去・完了を表す「たの形」が来ることが多い。「ようやくのことで（yōyaku no koto de）」の形でも使う。

⇨**yatto** やっと

yoyū 余裕〖名〗

¶時間の余裕がありません。早くしてください。(Jikan no *yoyū* ga arimasen. Hayaku shite kudasai.)

¶うちは貧乏ですから，そんな高い物を買う余裕はありません。(Uchi wa binbō desu kara, sonna takai mono o kau *yoyū* wa arimasen.)

yu 湯〖名〗

①［水に熱を加えて熱くしたもの］

¶お湯を沸かして，お茶を入れましょう。(O*yu* o wakashite, ocha o iremashō.)

②［ふろ］

¶わたしは1日おきにお湯に入ります。(Watashi wa ichinichi oki ni o*yu* ni hairimasu.)

yū- 夕-〖頭〗

夕飯（*yū*han） 夕方（*yū*gata） 夕暮れ（*yū*gure） 夕焼け（*yū*yake）

yūbe ゆうべ 〖名〗

¶ゆうべは8時ごろ寝ました。(*Yūbe* wa hachiji goro nemashita.)

¶ゆうべ，うちの近くに火事がありました。(*Yūbe*, uchi no chikaku ni

＊ *Yōyaku* indicates that something difficult to achieve has at last been realized after the passage of a certain period of time; this is usually a desired result.

＊ Often followed by the *-ta* form expressing past or completed action. Also used in the pattern "*yōyaku no koto de.*"

yoyū 〖n〗 **margin, leeway**

¶ There is no time **to spare.** Please hurry up ⟦Please do it quickly⟧.

¶ We are poor so we **cannot afford** to buy anything that expensive.

yu 〖n〗 **hot water; a bath, a public bath**

① [hot water]

¶ I'm going to heat **some water** and fix (green) tea.

② [a bath, a public bath]

¶ I take **a bath** every other day.

yū- 〖pref〗 **evening**

evening meal, dinner // **evening** // dusk, twilight // sunset, **evening** glow

yūbe 〖n〗 **last night, yesterday evening**

¶ [I] went to bed at around eight o'clock **last night.**

¶ There was a fire near my home **last night.**

kaji ga arimashita.)

yubi 指〖名〗
親指 (oya*yubi*)　人指し指 (hitosa-
shi*yubi*)　中指 (naka*yubi*)　薬指
(kusuri*yubi*)　小指 (ko*yubi*)　指輪
(*yubi*wa)

¶足の指にけがをしました。(Ashi no
yubi ni kega o shimashita.)

yūbin 郵便〖名〗
郵便局 (*yūbin*kyoku)　航空郵便
(kōkū-*yūbin*)　郵便配達 (*yūbin*-
haitatsu)

¶郵便局へ行って，手紙を出しました。
(*Yūbin*kyoku e itte, tegami o dashimashita.)

¶この辺では，1日に2回郵便が配達
されます。(Kono hen de wa, ichinichi ni nikai *yūbin* ga haitatsu
saremasu.)

yudan 油断〖名，～する〗
¶油断してかぎを掛けなかったら，ど
ろぼうに入られました。(*Yudan* shite
kagi o kakenakattara, dorobō ni
hairaremashita.)

¶試験は易しいと思って油断していた
ら，難しくて全然できませんでした。
(Shiken wa yasashii to omotte *yudan* shite itara, muzukashikute
zenzen dekimasen deshita.)

yūgata 夕方〖名〗
¶今日は，朝から夕方まで本を読んで
いました。(Kyō wa, asa kara *yūgata*
made hon o yonde imashita.)

yuka 床〖名〗

yubi 〖n〗 **a finger, a toe**
the thumb; the big **toe** // the index
finger // the middle **finger** // the
third **finger**, the ring **finger** // the little **finger**; the little **toe** // a ring
(jewelry)

¶ [I] have injured **[my] toe(s)** 〚I injured **my toe(s)**〛.

yūbin 〖n〗 **mail, postal service**
the **post** office // air**mail** // **mail** delivery; **mail**man

¶ [I] went to the **post** office and
mailed a letter.

¶ There are two **mail** deliveries a day
in this area.

yudan 〖n, ～*suru*〗 **carelessness,
inattention, negligence**
¶ [I] **carelessly** left the door un-
locked and [we] were robbed.

¶ I thought the test would be easy
and **was caught unprepared** when
it was difficult—I couldn't answer
anything at all.

yūgata 〖n〗 **evening, nightfall**
¶ [I] read books from morning to
night (that is, until **dark**) today.

yuka 〖n〗 **the floor**

¶川があふれて，床の上まで水が来ました。(Kawa ga afurete, *yuka* no ue made mizu ga kimashita.)

¶ The river overflowed and the water came up over **the floor.**

yukai 愉快〖形動〗

¶昨日のクラス会はたいへん愉快でした。(Kinō no kurasukai wa taihen *yukai* deshita.)

¶田中さんは愉快な人で，いつも冗談ばかり言っています。 (Tanaka san wa *yukai* na hito de, itsu mo jōdan bakari itte imasu.)

yukai 〖adj-v〗 **pleasant, happy, delightful**

¶ The class party 〚reunion〛 yesterday **was** a lot of **fun.**

¶ [Mr.] Tanaka is a **cheerful** person—[he] is always cracking jokes.

yuki 雪〖名〗

雪が積もる (*yuki* ga tsumoru) 雪が解ける (*yuki* ga tokeru)

¶雪が降って，1メートルも積もりました。 (*Yuki* ga futte, ichimētoru mo tsumorimashita.)

yuki 〖n〗 **snow**

snow piles up on the ground // **snow** melts

¶ **The snow** fell to a depth of one meter.

yuki 行き〖名〗

行き先 (*yuki*saki) 東京行きの電車 (Tōkyō *yuki* no densha)

¶この汽車は大阪行きです。(Kono kisha wa Oosaka *yuki* desu.)

⇒iki 行き

yuki 〖n〗 **going, bound for**

destination // a Tokyo train, a train **bound for** Tokyo

¶ This train **is going to** Osaka.

yūki 勇気〖名〗

勇気がある (*yūki* ga aru)

¶正しいことは，勇気を持って行いなさい。(Tadashii koto wa, *yūki* o motte okonainasai.)

¶彼は勇気を出して，独りで敵に向かっていきました。 (Kare wa *yūki* o dashite, hitori de teki ni mukatte ikimashita.)

yūki 〖n〗 **courage, bravery**

brave, courageous, bold

¶ **Be brave** and do what is right!

¶ He screwed up **his courage** and went to face the enemy single-handedly.

yukkuri ゆっくり〖副〗

①〔急がない様子，速くない様子〕

yukkuri 〖adv〗 **slowly; at one's leisure**

① [slowly]

¶あまり速くてわかりませんから，もっと**ゆっくり**話してください。(Amari hayakute wakarimasen kara, motto *yukkuri* hanashite kudasai.)

¶おばあさんが**ゆっくり**坂を上ってきます。(Obāsan ga *yukkuri* saka o nobotte kimasu.)

②[心や体がくつろぐ様子]

¶今日は，一日**ゆっくり**休みたいと思っています。(Kyō wa, ichinichi *yukkuri* yasumitai to omotte imasu.)

¶久しぶりに会ったのですから，今晩は**ゆっくり**話をしましょう。(Hisashiburi ni atta no desu kara, konban wa *yukkuri* hanashi o shimashō.)

yume 夢〖名〗

¶わたしはゆうべおもしろい**夢**を見ました。(Watashi wa yūbe omoshiroi *yume* o mimashita.)

yūmei 有名〖形動〗

¶あの山が**有名**な富士山ですか。(Ano yama ga *yūmei* na Fujisan desu ka?)

¶京都は古いお寺がたくさんあるので**有名**です。(Kyōto wa furui otera ga takusan aru node *yūmei* desu.)

yunyū 輸入〖名，～する〗

輸入品 (*yunyū*hin)

¶日本はA国から石油を**輸入**しています。(Nihon wa Ē-koku kara sekiyu o *yunyū* shite imasu.)

⇔**yushutsu** 輸出

¶ Please speak a little more **slowly** as I can't understand it when you speak so quickly.

¶ The old woman is **slowly** climbing up the hill toward [us].

② [at one's leisure, unhurriedly]

¶ I want to **take it easy** and not do anything at all today.

¶ As we haven't met in such a long time let's have a **nice, long** talk tonight.

yuku ☞ **iku**

yume 〚n〛 dream

¶ I had an interesting **dream** last night.

yūmei 〚adj-v〛 **famous, well-known, celebrated**

¶ Is that mountain the **famous** Mount Fuji?

¶ Kyoto **is known for** its large number of ancient temples.

yunyū 〚n, ～*suru*〛 **importing, importation**

imports, **imported** goods

¶ Japan **imports** oil from Country A.

yureru 揺れる〖動Ⅱ〗
¶地震で家が激しく揺れました。
(Jishin de ie ga hageshiku *yure-mashita*.)
¶この先はバスが揺れますから，御注意ください。 (Kono saki wa basu ga *yuremasu* kara, gochūi kudasai.)

yurusu 許す〖動Ⅰ〗
①［願いなどを許可する］
¶両親が許してくれたので，日本へ留学することに決めました。 (Ryōshin ga *yurushite* kureta node, Nihon e ryūgaku suru koto ni kimemashita.)
②［罪や間違いなどをとがめない］
¶わたしが悪かったのです。許してください。 (Watashi ga warukatta no desu. *Yurushite* kudasai.)
¶あんなに謝っているのですから，今度だけは許してあげましょう。 (Anna ni ayamatte iru no desu kara, kondo dake wa *yurushite* agemashō.)

yūryō 有料〖名〗
有料道路 (*yūryō*-dōro)　有料駐車場 (*yūryō*-chūshajō)
¶この駐車場は有料です。 (Kono chūshajō wa *yūryō* desu.)
⇔**muryō** 無料

yūshō 優勝〖名，〜する〗
優勝旗 (*yūshō*ki)　優勝カップ (*yūshō*-kappu)
¶山田さんはテニスの試合で優勝しました。 (Yamada san wa tenisu no shiai de *yūshō* shimashita.)

yureru 〖v II�〗　shake, tremble, sway
¶ The house **shook** violently in the earthquake.

¶ Please be prepared for the coming **pitching** 〖**jolting, swaying,** etc.〗 of the bus (said by the driver, etc.).

yurusu 〖v I〗　permit, approve; forgive, pardon
① [permit, approve, allow]
¶ I decided to study in Japan since my parents **had given me their permission**.

② [forgive, pardon, excuse]
¶ It was my fault. Please **forgive me.**

¶ **Let's forgive [him]** this one time as [he] has apologized so profusely.

yūryō 〖n〗　toll ~, pay ~
a **toll** road // a **pay** parking lot, a **pay** parking garage
¶ **You have to pay** to park here.

yūshō 〖n, ~*suru*〗　victory, championship
a **championship** flag 〖banner, pennant〗 // a **championship** cup, a trophy
¶ [Mr.] Yamada **won** the tennis match.

915

yushutsu 輸出〖名, ～する〗

輸出品 (*yushutsu*hin)

¶日本は自動車やテレビをたくさん輸出しています。 (Nihon wa jidōsha ya terebi o takusan *yushutsu* shite imasu.)

⇔**yunyū** 輸入

yuzuru 譲る〖動Ⅰ〗

¶わたしは年寄りにはいつも席を譲ってあげます。(Watashi wa toshiyori ni wa itsu mo seki o *yuzutte* agemasu.)

yushutsu 〚n, ～*suru*〛 exporting, exportation

an export, **exported** goods

¶ Japan **exports** a large number of automobiles and television sets.

yuzuru 〚v I〛 give way, make room; hand over, transfer

¶ I always **give up** my seat to elderly persons.

Z

zaimoku 材木〘名〙

¶この家にはいい材木が使われています。(Kono ie ni wa ii *zaimoku* ga tsukawarete imasu.)

¶山道を歩いていたら，材木をたくさん積んだ車に出会いました。(Yamamichi o aruite itara, *zaimoku* o takusan tsunda kuruma ni deaimashita.)

zairyō 材料〘名〙

¶この料理の材料は，肉と野菜と豆腐です。(Kono ryōri no *zairyō* wa, niku to yasai to tōfu desu.)

¶いい材料を使わないと，こんな立派な家具はできませんね。(Ii *zairyō* o tsukawanai to, konna rippa na kagu wa dekimasen ne.)

zaisan 財産〘名〙

¶山田さんは土地や建物などずいぶん財産を持っているようです。(Yamada san wa tochi ya tatemono nado zuibun *zaisan* o motte iru yō desu.)

zannen 残念〘形動〙

¶もう少し早く来れば秋子さんに会えたのに，残念でしたね。(Mō sukoshi hayaku kureba Akiko san ni aeta noni, *zannen* deshita ne.)

¶残念ながら，今日の会には出席できません。(*Zannen* nagara, kyō no kai ni wa shusseki dekimasen.)

zaseki 座席〘名〙

zaimok 〚n〛 **wood, lumber, timber**

¶ High-quality **lumber** has been used in this house.

¶ While I was walking along a mountain road, a truck loaded up with **timber** came toward me.

zairyō 〚n〛 **material, raw materials, ingredients, data**

¶ **The ingredients** of this dish are meat, vegetables, and *tōfu*.

¶ Good **materials** are necessary to produce fine furniture like this.

zaisan 〚n〛 **estate, assets, property, fortune**

¶ It seems that [Mr.] Yamada owns much **property**—land, buildings, etc.

zannen 〚adj-v〛 **regrettable, disappointing**

¶ **It's a pity** you didn't arrive a little earlier—you could have met Akiko.

¶ **Regrettably,** I won't be able to attend today's meeting.

zaseki 〚n〛 **a seat, seating**

917

座席に着く (*zaseki* ni tsuku)

¶山田さんが，わたしの座席を取っておいてくれました。(Yamada san ga, watashi no *zaseki* o totte oite kuremashita.)

⇨seki 席

zashiki 座敷〘名〙

¶お客様を奥の座敷に御案内してください。(Okyakusama o oku no *zashiki* ni goannai shite kudasai.)

zasshi 雑誌〘名〙

週刊雑誌 (shūkan-*zasshi*)

¶この雑誌は毎月 15 日に発行されます。(Kono *zasshi* wa maitsuki jūgonichi ni hakkō saremasu.)

zehi ぜひ〘副〙

¶ぜひ，わたしのうちへ遊びに来てください。(*Zehi*, watashi no uchi e asobi ni kite kudasai.)

¶日本へ行ったら，ぜひ京都へ行ってみたいと思っています。(Nihon e ittara, *zehi* Kyōto e itte mitai to omotte imasu.)

zeikin 税金〘名〙

¶父は税務署へ税金を納めに行きました。(Chichi wa zeimusho e *zeikin* o osame ni ikimashita.)

zen- 全-〘頭〙

①[すべての]

全財産 (*zen*-zaisan)　全国民 (*zen*-kokumin)

②[あるもののすべて]

全国 (*zenkoku*)　全校 (*zenkō*)　全世界 (*zen*-sekai)

take **a seat**, be seated

¶ [Miss] Yamada saved **a seat** for me.

zashiki 〚n〛 **room, reception room, parlor;** usually a *tatami*, Japanese-style room

¶ Please show our customer 〚guest〛 to **the room** in the back.

zasshi 〚n〛 **magazine, periodical**

a weekly, a weekly **magazine**

¶ This **magazine** comes out each month on the fifteenth.

zehi 〚adv〛 **without fail, by all means**

¶ **Do** come and visit me at home some time.

¶ If I go to Japan, I want **by all means** to visit Kyoto.

zeikin 〚n〛 **a tax**

¶ My father has gone to the tax office to pay **our taxes.**

zen- 〚pref〛 **whole, entire; all; complete**

① [whole, entire]

total assets // the **whole** nation, **all** the people

② [all (of a certain thing)]

the **whole** country, nation**wide,** national // **all** the school // the **whole** world, **throughout** the world

③〔全部で〕

全10巻の百科事典 (*zen*-jikkan no hyakka-jiten)

zenbu 全部〘名〙

¶男の子が5人，女の子が3人，子供は全部で8人います。 (Otoko no ko ga gonin, onna no ko ga sannin, kodomo wa *zenbu* de hachinin imasu.)

¶この家は古いから，一部だけではなく全部直さなければなりません。

(Kono ie wa furui kara, ichibu dake de wa naku *zenbu* naosana-kereba narimasen.)

⇨ichibu 一部

zenkoku 全国〘名〙

¶この放送は日本全国どこでも聞けます。 (Kono hōsō wa Nihon-*zenkoku* doko demo kikemasu.)

¶東京へは全国から学生が集まってきます。 (Tōkyō e wa *zenkoku* kara gakusei ga atsumatte kimasu.)

zentai 全体〘名〙

¶この問題については，あしたクラス全体の意見をまとめて先生に報告します。 (Kono mondai ni tsuite wa, ashita kurasu *zentai* no iken o matomete sensei ni hōkoku shi-masu.)

¶自分のことだけでなく，社会全体のことも考えなければいけません。

(Jibun no koto dake de naku, shakai *zentai* no koto mo kangae-nakereba ikemasen.)

③ [complete]

an encyclopedia **complete** in 10 volumes

zenbu 〖n〗 all, whole, entire, total

¶ There are eight children **in all**—five boys and three girls.

¶ As this house is old it will have to **all** be rebuilt, not just a part of it.

zenkoku 〖n〗 the whole country, national

¶ This broadcast can be heard **any-where** in Japan.

¶ Students flock to Tokyo from **all over the country.**

zentai 〖n〗 whole, entire, general

¶ Tomorrow I will get the opinion of the **whole** class concerning this mat-ter and report it to the teacher.

¶ One must think not of oneself alone, but of **the whole** of society.

zenzen 全然〘副〙

¶初めて日本へ来た時には、日本語が全然わかりませんでした。(Hajimete Nihon e kita toki ni wa, Nihongo ga *zenzen* wakarimasen deshita.)

¶山田さんが病気だったことは全然知りませんでした。(Yamada san ga byōki datta koto wa *zenzen* shirimasen deshita.)

¶たばこをやめようとしましたが、全然だめでした。(Tabako o yameyō to shimashita ga, *zenzen* dame deshita.)

＊ あとに打ち消しの言葉や否定的な意味の言葉が来る。

zero ゼロ〘名〙 ☞rei 零

zettai 絶対〘副〙

¶このことは絶対にほかの人に話さないでくださいね。(Kono koto wa *zettai* ni hoka no hito ni hanasanaide kudasai ne.)

¶わたしはその意見には絶対反対です。(Watashi wa sono iken ni wa *zettai* hantai desu.)

＊「絶対に (zettai ni)」の形でも使う。

zōka 増加〘名、〜する〙

¶車の増加が空気を汚す原因の一つになっています。(Kuruma no *zōka* ga kūki o yogosu gen'in no hitotsu ni natte imasu.)

¶このごろ，日本語を習う外国人の数が増加してきました。(Konogoro, Nihongo o narau gaikokujin no

zenzen 〘adv〙 wholly, entirely; not at all

¶ When I first came to Japan I didn't know **any** Japanese **at all**.

¶ **I had no idea** that [Mrs.] Yamada was ill.

¶ I tried to stop smoking but it was a **complete** failure.

＊ Followed by words or expressions negative in form or sense.

zero ☞ rei

zettai 〘adv〙 absolutely, unconditionally, positively

¶ Please be **absolutely sure** not to speak of this to anyone.

¶ I am **unconditionally** opposed to that position.

＊ Also used in the form *zettai ni.*

zōka 〘n, ~*suru*〙 increase, gain, rise

¶ **The increase** in the number of automobiles is one cause of air pollution.

¶ The number of foreigners studying Japanese **has increased** recently.

kazu ga *zōka* shite kimashita.)

⇔**genshō** 減少 ⇨**fueru** 増える

zu 図〖名〗

①［物の形や状態を絵やグラフなどで表したもの］

天気図 (tenki*zu*)

¶先生が黒板に図をかいて，発音の説明をしてくださいました。(Sensei ga kokuban ni *zu* o kaite, hatsuon no setsumei o shite kudasaimashita.)

②［土地の様子などを言葉によらないでわかりやすくかいたもの］

地図 (chi*zu*)　案内図 (annai*zu*)

¶交番で道を尋ねたら，図をかいて教えてくれました。(Kōban de michi o tazunetara, *zu* o kaite oshiete kuremashita.)

zu ず〖助動〗

¶昨日は，どこへも行かずに家で本を読んでいました。(Kinō wa, doko e mo ika*zu* ni ie de hon o yonde imashita.)

¶勉強もせずに，どこへ行っていたんですか。(Benkyō mo se*zu* ni, doko e itte ita n desu ka?)

＊「する (suru)」を「ない (nai)」で打ち消す場合には「しない (shinai)」となるが，「ず (zu)」で打ち消す場合には「せず (sezu)」となる。

zubon ズボン〖名〗

ズボンを脱ぐ (*zubon* o nugu)

¶田中さんはいつも茶色のズボンをはいています。(Tanaka san wa itsu mo chairo no *zubon* o haite imasu.)

zu 〖n〗 drawing, diagram; map, plan

① [drawing, diagram, figure, graph]

a weather **map,** a weather **chart**

¶ The teacher draw **a diagram** on the board and explained the pronunciation.

② [map, plan]

a map // a guide **map, a map** for visitors

¶ When I asked the way at a police box they drew **a map** for me.

-zu 〖auxil〗　a negative verb ending

¶ Yesterday [I] **didn't go** anywhere but stayed home and read books.

¶ Where did you go **before finishing** your studying?

＊ The negative of *suru* formed with *-nai* is *shinai* but the negative formed with *-zu* is *sezu*.

zubon 〖n〗 trousers, pants

take off **one's trousers**

¶ Mr. Tanaka always wears brown **trousers.**

zuibun ずいぶん〖副〗

¶このお菓子_かはずいぶん甘_{あま}いですね。
(Kono okashi wa *zuibun* amai desu ne.)

¶あの人_{ひと}は若_{わか}い時_{とき}ずいぶん苦労_{くろう}をしたそうです。 (Ano hito wa wakai toki *zuibun* kurō o shita sō desu.)

-zume -詰め〖尾〗

かん詰_づめ (kan*zume*) びん詰_づめ (bin-*zume*) 四百字詰_{よんひゃくじづ}めの原稿用紙_{げんこうようし} (yon-hyakuji*zume* no genkōyōshi)

¶友達_{ともだち}が箱詰_{はこづ}めのみかんを送_{おく}ってくれました。(Tomodachi ga hako*zume* no mikan o okutte kuremashita.)

zutsu ずつ〖助〗

①[それぞれが同じ数量であるという意味を表す]

¶りんごが一_{ひと}つしか残_{のこ}っていなかったので，二人_{ふたり}で半分_{はんぶん}ずつ食_たべました。
(Ringo ga hitotsu shika nokotte inakatta node, futari de hanbun *zutsu* tabemashita.)

¶3人_{さんにん}の子供_{こども}に1000円_{せんえん}ずつ小遣_{こづか}いをやりました。(Sannin no kodomo ni sen'en *zutsu* kozukai o yarimashita.)

②[同程度の数量が繰り返されるという意味を表す]

¶わたしは日本語_{にほんご}を毎日_{まいにち}5時間_{じかん}ずつ1年間勉強_{ねんかんべんきょう}しました。 (Watashi wa Nihongo o mainichi gojikan *zutsu* ichinenkan benkyō shimashita.)

¶わたしは今_{いま}2週間_{しゅうかん}に1回_{いっかい}ずつ病院_{びょういん}に通_{かよ}っています。(Watashi wa ima nishūkan ni ikkai *zutsu* byōin ni

zuibun 〖adv〗 **fairly, quite, very**

¶ This cake ⟦confection, etc.⟧ is **quite** sweet, isn't it?

¶ I hear [he] underwent **much** hardship in [his] youth.

-zume 〖suf〗 a suffix indicating being packed in or filled up

canned goods, canning, canned // bottled goods, bottling, bottled // 400-character writing paper (for writing Japanese)

¶ My friend sent me some **boxed** mandarin oranges.

zutsu 〖part〗 **each, respectively**

① [indicates each is the same amount]

¶ As there was only one apple left, [we] **each** ate half of it.

¶ [I] gave **each** of the three children a thousand yen allowance.

② [indicates a repetition of the same amount]

¶ I studied Japanese five hours a day for a year.

¶ I am receiving treatment at the hospital every other week.

kayotte imasu.)

¶最近，少しずつ太ってきて困っています。(Saikin, sukoshi *zutsu* futtote kite komatte imasu.)

＊数や量を表す言葉につく。

zutto ずっと〖副〗

①［比べてみて大きな違いのある様子］

¶今日は昨日より**ずっと**暖かいですね。(Kyō wa kinō yori *zutto* atatakai desu ne.)

¶駅へ行くには，この道のほうが**ずっと**近いですよ。(Eki e iku ni wa, kono michi no hō ga *zutto* chikai desu yo.)

②［時間の隔たりがある様子］

ずっと昔のこと（*zutto* mukashi no koto)

¶わたしがそのことを知ったのは，**ずっと**あとのことでした。(Watashi ga sono koto o shitta no wa, *zutto* ato no koto deshita.)

③［初めから終わりまで続いている様子］

¶わたしは東京に来てから，**ずっと**おじの家にいます。(Watashi wa Tōkyō ni kite kara, *zutto* oji no ie ni imasu.)

¶数年間，**ずっと**この辞書の仕事をしてきたので，たいへん疲れました。(Sūnenkan, *zutto* kono jisho no shigoto o shite kita node, taihen tsukaremashita.)

¶ Lately I have been putting on weight **little by little** and don't know what to do about it.

＊ Added to words expressing number or amount.

zutto 〖adv〗 by far, much more; long, far; all the time, throughout, all along; direct, straight, all the way

① [by far, much more]

¶ It's **much** warmer today than yesterday, isn't it?

¶ This road is **much** shorter for going to the station.

② [long, far]

something **far** in the past

¶ I learned that **long** afterwards.

③ [all the time, throughout, all along]

¶ I've been living at my uncle's **ever since** I came to Tokyo.

¶ [I] am very tired after working on this dictionary for several years.

AN INTRODUCTION

TO JAPANESE GRAMMAR*

Compiled by Nobuko MIZUTANI

VI. VERBS

VII. KEIGO (POLITE LANGUAGE)

---

* This is intended to provide a practical overview of Japanese grammar for foreign students of Japanese. Further example sentences and usage notes can be found under the appropriate entries in the dictionary itself. For more detail, readers should consult reference works on the subject.

I. THE STRUCTURE OF JAPANESE SENTENCES

1. Sentences

1-1 A sentence usually consists of (1) a noun phrase, (2) a verb phrase, or (3) an adjective phrase.

    (1) *Nichiyōbi desu.*   (It is Sunday.)

    (2) *Kimashita.*   (I/You/He/She/It/We/They came.)

    (3) *Akai desu.*   (It is/They are red.)

1-2 When the subject needs to be mentioned, the particle **ga** is added to the noun or pronoun.

    *Tanaka san **ga** kimashita.*   (Mr./Mrs./Miss Tanaka came.)

1-3 When the topic needs to be mentioned, the particle **wa** is added to the noun or pronoun.

    *Kyō **wa** nichiyōbi desu.*   (Today is Sunday.)

    *Kono hana **wa** akai desu.*   (This flower is red.)

1-4 A verb phrase is often preceded by (1) an object or (2) an adverbial phrase.

    (1) **Hon o** *yomimashita.*   (I/You/He/She/We/They read **a book.**)

    (2) **Sanji ni** *kite kudasai.*   (Please come **at three o'clock.**)

2. Omission

2-1 Any of (1) the topic, (2) a verb phrase, (3) an object, and (4) an adverbial phrase are left out when they can be understood from the context.

    (1) Speaker A: *Kyō wa naniyōbi desu ka?* (What day of the week is it today?)

           Speaker B: *Nichiyōbi desu.* (It's Sunday.)

    (2) Speaker A: *Nanji goro ikimasu ka?* (What time are you going?)

           Speaker B: *Sanji goro.* (At around three.)

    (3) Speaker A: *Ano hon o kaimasu ka?* (Are you going to buy that book?)

           Speaker B: *Ee, kaimasu.* (Yes, I'm going to buy it.)

3. Word order

3-1 Modifiers precede what is modified.

akai *hana*	(a **red** flower, **red** flowers)
saite iru *hana*	(flowers **in bloom)**
watashi ga mita *hana*	(flowers **that I saw**)

3-2 Particles are always added to other words and phrases.

ame **ga**	(**the** rain)
sen'en **shika**	(**only** a thousand yen)

3-3 Phrases can be reversed in order in conversation.

Kimashita yo, Yamada san ga.	(Mr. Yamada came!)
Kirei desu ne, kono hana.	(This flower is beautiful!)

4. *Desu* (the copula)

4-1 **Desu,** or the copula, is used either to form a phrase or to make an adjective phrase more polite.

noun phrase: *Nichiyōbi* **desu.** (**It's** Sunday.)
adjective phrase: *Akai* **desu.** (**It's** red.)

4-2 The negative form of *desu* is **ja arimasen** (informal).

Kyō wa nichiyōbi **ja arimasen.** (Today **is not** Sunday.)

4-3 The past form of *desu* is **deshita,** and the past negative form is **ja arimasen deshita** (informal).

Nichiyōbi **deshita.** (**It was** Sunday.)
Nichiyōbi **ja arimasen deshita.** (**It wasn't** Sunday.)

4-4 **Deshō** is used to mean "it probably is" or "it probably will be."

Ashita wa ame **deshō.** (Tomorrow **probably will** be rainy.)

The negative form of *deshō* is **ja nai deshō** (informal).

Ashita wa ame **ja nai deshō.** (Tomorrow **probably will not** be rainy.)

4-5 **Da** is used instead of *desu* in familiar speech; it has the following forms.

da (present affirmative)	*Nichiyōbi **da**.*	(**It is** Sunday.)
ja nai (present negative)	*Nichiyōbi **ja nai**.*	(**It isn't** Sunday.)
datta (past affirmative)	*Nichiyōbi **datta**.*	(**It was** Sunday.)
ja nakatta (past negative)	*Nichiyōbi **ja nakatta**.*	(**It wasn't** Sunday.)
darō (probability)	*Nichiyōbi **darō**.*	(**It probably will be** Sunday.)

5. Particles

5-1 Particles are used to indicate relations between words, phrases, and clauses; they also express the speaker's feelings.

5-2 Particles are divided into (1) case particles, (2) modifying particles, (3) connecting particles, and (4) sentence particles.

(1) **Case particles:** These are added to nouns and pronouns.

ga (subject)	*Ame **ga** futte imasu.* (It is raining.)
o (object)	*Hon **o** yomimashita.* (I read a book.)
ni (at, in, on)	*Tōkyō **ni** sunde imasu.* (I live **in** Tokyo.)
e (to, toward)	*Kaisha **e** ikimasu.* (I'm going **to** the office.)
no (of)	*Yamada san **no** hon desu.* (It's Mr. Yamada's book.)
to (and)	*Sore **to** kore o kudasai.* (Please give me this **and** that.)
de (by, with)	*Naifu **de** kirimashita.* (I cut it **with** a knife.)
kara (from)	*Uchi **kara** ichijikan kakarimasu.* (It takes an hour to go there **from** my house.)
yori (than)	*Kore wa are **yori** yasui desu.* (This is cheaper **than** that.)
ya (and)	*Tokei **ya** megane o kaimashita.* (I bought a watch, glasses, **and other things.**)
ka (or)	*Tanaka san **ka** Yoshida san ni tanomimasu.* (I will ask Mr. Tanaka **or** Mr. Yoshida to do it.)

(2) **Modifying particles:** These are used as modifiers.

wa (as for)	*Watashi **wa** sushi da.* (Give me *sushi.*)
mo (also, too)	*Biiru **mo** kudasai.* (Please give me some beer, **too.**)
demo (or something)	*Ocha **demo** nomimashō ka?* (Shall we have tea **or something?**)
shika (only)	*Sen'en **shika** arimasen.* (I have **only** a thousand yen.)

(3) **Connecting particles:** These are used to connect phrases and clauses.

ga (but, and)	*Sumimasen **ga,** chotto matte kudasaimasen ka?* (I am sorry, **but** would you wait a moment?)
kara (because, so)	*Jikan ga arimasen **kara,** yomemasen.* (I cannot read it **because** I have no time.)
ke(re)do(mo) (but)	*Takai **keredo,** kaimasu.* (It is expensive, **but** I will buy it.)
shi (and what's more)	*Hiroi **shi** shizuka desu.* (It's spacious **and** quiet.)
-tari (do A and B)	*Uta o utat**tari** odot**tari** shimashita.* (We sang songs **and** danced.)
-te, -de (used for making the *-te* form)	*Mado ga ai**te** imasu.* (The window **is open.**)
-te mo, -de mo (even if)	*Ame ga fut**te mo** ikimasu.* (I will go **even if** it rains.)
to (when)	*Yūgata ni naru **to** samuku narimasu.* (It becomes cold in the evening— literally, **when** it becomes evening.)
-nagara (while)	*Ocha o nomi**nagara** hanashimashita.* (We talked **while** having tea.)
node (so)	*Kuraku natta **node** shigoto o yamemashita.* (It became dark, **so** we stopped working.)
noni (although)	*Renshū shita **noni** umaku dekimasen deshita.* (**Although** I practiced hard, I couldn't do it well.)

(4) **Sentence particles:** These are added at the end of a sentence.

ka (question)	*Yamada san desu **ka?*** (Are you Mr. Yamada?)
ne (agreement)	*Ii otenki desu **ne.*** (Lovely day, isn't it?)
yo (emphasis)	*Kamaimasen **yo.*** (That's all right.)
na (monologue)	*Ii otenki da **na.*** (It's a lovely day.)
tomo (emphasis)	*Kekkō desu **tomo.*** (That's fine.)
no (question, familiar)	*Doko e iku **no?*** · (Where are you going?)

II. NOUNS

1. Number

Most nouns are not distinguished as to number. However, some suffixes can be added to indicate the plural in the case of human beings.

-tachi	*kodomo**tachi*** (child**ren**)
-ra	*kodomo**ra*** (child**ren**)
-gata (honorific)	*sensei**gata*** (professor**s**)

2. Case

The case of nouns is usually indicated with particles (see I-5-2).

3. Gender

Nouns have no gender.

4. Form nouns

There are several nouns which have no concrete meaning and are always used in a phrase, preceded by modifiers. These are called form nouns; the most important ones are: ***koto, tame, mono, wake, hō, tokoro, toki, mae, ato,*** etc.

koto	*Mada tabeta **koto** ga arimasen.* (I have never tasted it.)
tame	*Daigaku ni hairu **tame** ni benkyō shite imasu.* (I am studying **in order** to enter college.)
mono	*Sonna koto o iu **mono** ja arimasen.* (You should not say such a thing.)

See also the entries for each of the form nouns in the dictionary.

III. PRONOUNS

1. List of pronouns

1-1 The following is a list of the most commonly used pronouns.

	singular	plural
1st person	*watashi*	*watashitachi*
		watashidomo (humble)
	boku (male, informal)	*bokutachi, bokura*
	atashi (female, informal)	*atashitachi*
2nd person	*anata*	*anatatachi*
		anatagata (honorific)
	kimi (male, informal)	*kimitachi, kimira*
3rd person	*ano hito*	*ano hitotachi*
	kare (he, informal)	*karera* (informal)
	kanojo (she, informal)	*kanojotachi* (informal)
	ano kata (honorific)	*ano katagata* (honorific)

1-2 There are several other pronouns used in polite or vulgar speech.

1-3 Pronouns are not used as frequently in Japanese as in English. They are left out when understood from the context.

> Speaker A: *Yamada san, kimashita ka?* (Did Mr. Yamada come?)
> Speaker B: *Ee, kimashita.* (Yes, he did.)

2. Other terms used as pronouns

2-1 Personal names are often used instead of pronouns.

> **Yamamoto san** *mo ikimasu ka?*
>   (Are you going, too?—said to Yamamoto san.)
> *Kore,* **Yoshiko san** *no deshō?* (Isn't this yours?—said to Yoshiko, familiar.)

2-2 Nouns indicating position or status are also used instead of pronouns.

> **Okusan** *mo ikimasu ka?*
>   (Are you going, too?—said to someone's wife.)

Shachō *wa dochira ni osumai desu ka?* (Where do you live?—said to a director of a company.)

2-3 Kinship terms are also used instead of pronouns.

Otōsan *mo iku?* (Are you going, too?—said to one's father.)

IV. DEMONSTRATIVES

1. *Ko/so/a/do*

There are four groups of demonstratives, or words used to point to someone or something: (1) the *ko-* group, (2) the *so-* group, (3) the *a-* group, and (4) the *do-* group.

the *ko-* group	the *so-* group	the *a-* group	the *do-* group
kore (this one)	*sore* (that one)	*are* (that one over there)	*dore* (which one)
kono (of this)	*sono* (of that)	*ano* (of that over there)	*dono* (which)
koko (this place)	*soko* (there)	*asoko* (over there)	*doko* (where)
kochira (this way)	*sochira* (that way)	*achira* (that way over there)	*dochira* (which way)
kotchi (this way)	*sotchi* (that way)	*atchi* (that way over there)	*dotchi* (which way)
kō (in this way)	*sō* (in that way)	*ā* (in that way there)	*dō* (in which way)
konna (like this)	*sonna* (like that)	*anna* (like that over there)	*donna* (what kind of)

2. The *ko-* group

The **ko-** group words are used for indicating something near the speaker.

Kore *wa ikura desu ka?* (How much is **this?**)
Kono *kasa, ikura desu ka?* (How much is **this** umbrella?)

3. The *so-* group

3-1 The ***so-*** group words are used for indicating something closer to the listener than to the speaker.

> ***Soko*** *ni aru hon o totte kudasai.* (Would you get me the book **near you?**)
>
> ***Sochira*** *no hō ga ookii desu ne.* (**That one** is bigger, isn't it?)

3-2 The ***so-*** group words are also used to refer to what has already been talked about or what the speaker has just heard.

> *Kinjo no kissaten e ikimashita.* ***Soko*** *de kōhii o nomimashita.* (I went to a nearby coffee shop. I had some coffee **there.**)

> Speaker A: *Kodomo ga netsu o dashimashita.* (My child has a fever.)
>
> Speaker B: ***Sore*** *wa ikemasen ne.* (**That**'s too bad.)

4. The *a-* group

4-1 The ***a-*** group words are used to refer to something at a distance from both the speaker and the listener.

> Speaker A: ***Are*** *wa nan deshō.* (I wonder what **that** is.)
>
> Speaker B: *A,* ***are*** *wa byōin desu.* (Oh, **that**'s a hospital.)

4-2 The ***a-*** group words are also used to refer to something that both the speaker and the listener have knowledge of.

> Speaker A: *Akutagawa no "Hana" o yomimashita.* (I read "Hana" by Akutagawa.)
>
> Speaker B: *A,* ***are*** *wa omoshiroi desu ne.* (Oh, **that** is a very interesting story, isn't it?)

5. The *do-* group

The ***do-*** group words are used to ask questions.

> *Kore wa* ***dō*** *sureba ii deshō.* (**How** should I handle this?)
>
> ***Donna*** *ongaku ga suki desu ka?* (**What types of** music do you like?)

V. ADJECTIVES

1. Types of adjectives

There are two types of adjectives: (1) true adjectives and (2) adjective-verbs.

2. True adjectives

2-1 The true adjectives, or *-i* **adjectives,** have the following forms.

dictionary form	*akai* (red)	*omoshiroi* (interesting)
-ku form	*akaku*	*omoshiroku*
-eba form	*akakereba*	*omoshirokereba*
plain past, affirmative	*akakatta*	*omoshirokatta*
plain past, negative	*akaku nakatta*	*omoshiroku nakatta*

2-2 In polite speech, **desu** is added to the dictionary form to form an adjective phrase.

Akai **desu.** (**It is** red.)
Omoshiroi **desu.** (**It is** interesting.)

2-3 The **-ku** form is used to make the negative form and the past negative form.

Akaku *(wa) arimasen.* (It is not **red.**)
Akaku *(wa) arimasen deshita.* (It was not **red.**)

2-4 The **-ku** form is used adverbially.

Akaku *narimashita.* (It became **red.**)
Hayaku *kite kudasai.* (Please come **quickly.**)

2-5 The **-ku** form followed by **-te** is used to connect adjective phrases with other phrases.

Akakute *kirei desu.* (It is **red and** beautiful.)
Samukute *komarimashita.* (It was **so cold that** we had a difficult time.)

2-6 The **-eba** form is used to indicate the conditional.

akakereba	(if it is red)
omoshirokereba	(if it is interesting)

2-7 The plain past form is used as is in familiar conversation, and **desu** is added in polite speech.

Akakatta.	(It was red—familiar)
Akakatta desu.	(It was red—polite)

2-8 Among the true adjectives, those describing feelings are usually used to refer to the feelings of the speaker.

Ureshii desu. (I am happy.)

*Sono toki totemo **kanashikatta desu**. (**I was** very **sad** at that time.)*

When describing feelings in the second or the third person, one refers to the appearance, rather than the feeling itself; thus, (1) **-sō** (look like) or (2) **yō** (seem) is used.

(1) **Ureshisō** *desu ne.* (You **look happy**.)
*Tanaka san wa totemo **kanashisō** deshita.*
(Miss Tanaka **looked** very **sad**.)
(2) *Tanaka san wa **sabishii yō** desu.*
(Miss Tanaka **seems to be lonely**.)

Or else, verbs rather than adjectives are used.

*Tanaka san wa **kanashinde imasu**. (Miss Tanaka **is sad**.)*
*Tanaka san wa **sabishigatte imashita**. (Miss Tanaka **was lonely**.)*

3. Adjective-verbs

3-1 The adjective-verbs, or **na adjectives,** have the following forms.

dictionary form	*shizuka* (quiet)	*genki* (healthy)
na form	*shizuka na*	*genki na*
de form	*shizuka de*	*genki de*
ni form	*shizuka ni*	*genki ni*

3-2 In polite speech, **desu** is added to the dictionary form to form an adjective phrase.

*Shizuka **desu**.*　　　　(**It is** quiet.)

3-3 The *na* form is used when modifying a noun.

> **shizuka na** *heya* (a **quiet** room)
>
> **genki na** *kodomo* (a **healthy** child)

3-4 The *de* form is used to connect two adjective phrases.

> **Shizuka de** *hiroi heya deshita.* (It was a **quiet and** spacious room.)
>
> **genki de** *akarui shōnen* (a **healthy and** cheerful boy)

3-5 The *ni* form is used adverbially.

> **Shizuka ni** *heya o dete ikimashita.* (She went out of the room **quietly.**)
>
> *Kodomo wa sugu* **genki ni** *narimashita.* (The child soon recovered—literally, became **healthy.**)

3-6 For the polite negative, polite past affirmative, polite past negative, plain past affirmative, and plain past negative, see *desu* (I.4).

VI. VERBS

1. Verbs and auxiliary verbs

Verbs are usually used with **jodōshi,** auxiliary verbs. In traditional Japanese grammar, *ikimashita* is explained as the combination of the verb *iku* and the auxiliary verbs -*masu* and -*ta*. But to make the explanation simpler, auxiliary verbs are included in with verbs in this discussion.

2. Conjugation

2-1 Verbs are divided into three classes, depending on how they are conjugated; these are (1) Type I verbs, (2) Type II verbs, and (3) Type III verbs.

2-2 Type I verbs, or **godan** verbs or -*u* verbs: This class includes verbs which end in -*u,* preceded either by one of the consonants *k, s, t, n, m, g,* and *b,* or by a vowel other than *e.*

> | | |
> |---|---|
> | *yomu* | (read) |
> | *kaku* | (write) |
> | *kiru* | (cut) |
> | *au* | (meet) |

The verb stem for the -*masu* form is made by changing the final **-u** of the dictionary form into **-i.**

yomu	*yomi-*	*yomimasu*
kaku	*kaki-*	*kakimasu*
kiru	*kiri-*	*kirimasu*
au	*ai-*	*aimasu*

2-3 Type II or **-*ru* verbs:** The dictionary forms of verbs in this group end in **-*ru*** preceded by **e** or **i.**

taberu	(eat)
miru	(see)
hajimeru	(begin)
kiru	(wear)

The verb stem for the -*masu* form is made by dropping the final **-*ru.***

taberu	*tabe-*	*tabemasu*
miru	*mi-*	*mimasu*
hajimeru	*hajime-*	*hajimemasu*
kiru	*ki-*	*kimasu*

2-4 Type III verbs: There are two **Type III verbs, *kuru*** and ***suru*.**

kuru (come)	*ki-*	*kimasu*
suru (do)	*shi-*	*shimasu*

2-5 The following five verbs belong to **Type I,** but the final **-*ru*** of the dictionary form is changed into **-*i*** when making the **-*masu*** form.

kudasaru (give)	*kudasai-*	*kudasaimasu*
ossharu (say)	*osshai-*	*osshaimasu*
irassharu (be, go, come)	*irasshai-*	*irasshaimasu*
nasaru (do)	*nasai-*	*nasaimasu*
gozaru (copula)	*gozai-*	*gozaimasu*

3. Polite and plain speech

3-1 Verbs are used in different forms depending on the level of speech. In polite speech -*masu* is added to the stem of verbs to indicate non-past (present and future), while verbs are used in their dictionary form in familiar speech. These two styles are called "polite" and "plain."

Yomimasu.	(I (will) read it—polite)
Yomu.	(I (will) read it—plain)

3-2 Verbs are used in their dictionary form when used as a modifier.

kore kara **yomu** *hon*	(a book that **I am going to read**)
watashi ga **yonda** *hon*	(a book that **I have read**)

4. The negative

4-1 To change verbs in the *-masu* form into the negative, change the **-masu** to **-masen.**

Ikimasu.	(I will go.)		*Ikimasen.*	(I will not go.)
Tabemasu.	(I will eat it.)		*Tabemasen.*	(I will not eat it.)

4-2 To change verbs in the plain form into the negative:

(1) Type I verbs: Replace the final vowel by **-anai.**

iku	*ikanai*
yomu	*yomanai*

For Type I verbs ending in a vowel plus **-u,** replace the final vowel by **-wanai.**

au (meet)	*awanai*
iu (say)	*iwanai*

For Type I verbs ending in *-tsu,* replace the **-tsu** by **-tanai.**

matsu (wait)	*matanai*

(2) Type II verbs: Replace the final **-ru** by **-nai.**

taberu	*tabenai*

(3) Type III verbs, *kudasaru,* etc.: Replace the final **-ru** by **-anai.** The plain negative form of **kuru** is **konai,** and that of **suru** is **shinai.**

(4) The plain negative form of the verb **aru** (to be) is **nai.**

5. The *-te* form

5-1 Verbs in the **-te** (or **-de**) form, or gerund, are used together with other verbs such as *iru, kuru,* and *kudasaru.*

Kaite *imasu.*	(I am **writing** it.)
Kaite *kudasai.*	(Please **write** it.)

5-2   Verbs in the *-te* form are also used to connect clauses.

> *Onaka ga* ***suite***, *hatarakemasen.* (**I am so hungry that** I cannot work.)
> ***Okite***, *shokuji o* ***shite***, *dekakemashita.* (**I got up, had a meal, and** went out.)

5-3   The *-te* form is formed in the following way:

(1) Type I verbs: Change the dictionary form as follows.

-u	to	*-tte*	*kau*	(buy)	*katte*
-tsu	to	*-tte*	*matsu*	(wait)	*matte*
-ru	to	*-tte*	*agaru*	(go up)	*agatte*
-su	to	*-shite*	*hanasu*	(talk)	*hanashite*
-ku	to	*-ite*	*kiku*	(hear)	*kiite*
-gu	to	*-ide*	*isogu*	(hurry)	*isoide*
-bu	to	*-nde*	*yobu*	(call)	*yonde*
-mu	to	*-nde*	*yomu*	(read)	*yonde*
-nu	to	*-nde*	*shinu*	(die)	*shinde*
exception			*iku*	(go)	*itte*

(2) Type II verbs: Change the final *-ru* to *-te*.

taberu	*tabete*
miru	*mite*

(3) Type III verbs: For *kudasaru*, etc., change the final *-ru* to *-tte*.

kudasaru	*kudasatte*

For *kuru* and *suru*, change *kuru* to ***kite*** and *suru* to ***shite***.

6. The *-ta* form

6-1   Verbs in the *-ta* (or *-da*) form are used to indicate either (1) that the action took place in the past or (2) that it has/had been completed.

(1) *Kinō wa ame ga* ***furimashita.*** (**It rained** yesterday.)
   Sono kamera wa itsu ***kaimashita*** *ka?* (When **did you buy** that camera?)

(2) *Ima* ***kita*** *bakari desu.* (I have just **arrived**.)

*Kai ni **itta** toki mō urikirete imashita.* (When I **went** to buy it, it was sold out.)

6-2 To change verbs in the *-masu* form into the *-ta* form, change **-masu** to **-mashita** and **-masen** to **-masen deshita.**

ikimasu — ikimashita ikimasen — ikimasen deshita
tabemasu — tabemashita tabemasen — tabemasen deshita

6-3 To change verbs in the plain form into the *-ta* form, change the final **-e** of the *-te* form into **-a.**

iku itte itta
taberu tabete tabeta

6-4 To change verbs in the plain negative form into the *-ta* form, change the final **-nai** into **-nakatta.**

iku ikanai ikanakatta
taberu tabenai tabenakatta

7. Transitive and intransitive verbs

7-1 Verbs which are usually preceded by an object plus the particle **o** are called transitive, and verbs which never so occur are called intransitive.

*mado **o** akeru* (open the window—transitive)
*mado **ga** aku* (the window opens—intransitive)
*Kitte **o** atsumemashita.* (I collected stamps—transitive)
*Kitte **ga** atsumarimashita.* (Stamps have been collected—intransitive)

7-2 The following is a table of the most important sets of transitive and intransitive verbs.

	transitive	intransitive	
(1) *-eru/-aru (-waru)*	shimeru	shimaru	(shut)
	kakeru	kakaru	(hang)
	kaeru	kawaru	(change)
(2) *-eru/-u*	akeru	aku	(open)
	tsukeru	tsuku	(attach)
(3) *-asu/-u*	dasu	deru	(put out)
	wakasu	waku	(boil)

(4) *-su/-ru*	*naosu*	*naoru*	(repair)
	toosu	*tooru*	(pass)
(5) *-u/-eru*	*kesu*	*kieru*	(extinguish)
	mosu	*moeru*	(burn)

7-3   Intransitive verbs are used with a noun plus **o** when referring to an action which takes place through, along, or from, a certain place.

> *tooru*   *Kono basu wa doko **o toorimasu** ka?* (What course does this bus **take**—literally, Where does this bus **go through?**)
>
> *deru*   *Kuji ni uchi **o demashita**.* (**I left** home at nine—literally, **I went out** of the house at nine.)

7-4   Transitive verbs in the **-te** form followed by **aru** express a state that has resulted from an action.

> *tsukeru*   *Dentō ga **tsukete arimasu**.* (The light **is on**—literally, The light **has been turned on**.)
>
> *shimeru*   *To ga **shimete arimasu**.* (The door **is closed**—literally, The door **has been closed**.)

8. The potential

8-1   The potential form is used to indicate that one can do something or that something can be done.

> *Nama no sakana wa **taberaremasen**.* (**I cannot eat** raw fish.)

8-2   The potential form is constructed as follows:

(1) Type I verbs: The final **-u** is replaced by **-eru.**

> *yomu*   *yomeru* (can read)
> *kaku*   *kakeru* (can write)

(2) Type II verbs: The final **-ru** is replaced by **-rareru.**

> *taberu*   *taberareru* (can eat)
> *miru*   *mirareru* (can see)

(3) Type III verbs such as *kudasaru*: The final **-u** is replaced by **-eru,** but these verbs are seldom used in the potential form. The potential form of **kuru** is **korareru,** and that of **suru** is **dekiru.**

8-3 To change the plain potential form into the *-masu* form, replace the final **-ru** by **-masu.**

yomu	*yomeru*	*yomemasu*
taberu	*taberareru*	*taberaremasu*

8-4 In sentences employing the potential form, an object is usually followed by **ga** rather than **o.**

> *Sakana **o** taberu.* — Sakana **ga** taberareru.
> *Hon **o** yomu.* — Hon **ga** yomeru.

In the negative, **ga** often changes into **wa.**

> *Sakana **ga** taberareru.* — Sakana **wa** taberarenai.
> *Hon **ga** yomemasu.* — Hon **wa** yomemasen.

9. The passive

9-1 Passive sentences are constructed by using a verb in the passive form, with the performer of the action indicated by the particle **ni.**

> *Haha **ni shikararemashita.*** **(I was scolded by** my mother.)

9-2 The passive form is constructed in the following way:

(1) Type I verbs: The final **-u** is replaced by **-areru.**

yomu	*yomareru* (to be read)
kaku	*kakareru* (to be written)

(2) Type II verbs: The final **-ru** is replaced by **-rareru** (identical to the potential form).

taberu	*taberareru* (to be eaten)
miru	*mirareru* (to be seen)

(3) The passive of **kuru** is **korareru,** and that of **suru** is **sareru.** The irregular verbs like *kudasaru* are not usually used in the passive.

9-3 There are two kinds of passive sentences: those in the suffering passive and those in the non-suffering passive.

9-4 Sentences in the suffering passive imply that the speaker is unfavorably affected by the action described by the verb. The subject of these sentences is usually the speaker, whether explicitly indicated or not. When the subject needs to be stated, a phrase plus *wa* is used.

Ani ni nagararemashita.　　　(I **was hit** by my brother.)

Kodomo wa tomodachi ni nagararemashita. (My child **was hit** by his friend.

When an action is described with a verb plus object, the object is followed by **o.**

> *Densha no naka de ashi o fumaremashita.* (**Someone stepped on** my foot in the train—literally, I **had** my foot **stepped on.**)

9-5　In the case of the suffering passive, intransitive verbs can also be used in the passive form.

> *Kaeri ni ame ni furaremashita.* (**It rained** on my way home— literally, I **was rained** on.)
>
> *Kodomo no toki chichi ni shinaremashita.* (My father **died** when I was a child.)

9-6　Sentences in the non-suffering passive are similar to passive sentences in English; they are usually used to report a fact without referring to an agent.

> *Shiken no kekka ga happyō saremashita.* (The results of the examination **were announced.**)
>
> *Sono hon wa raigetsu shuppan saremasu.* (That book **will be published** next month.)

10. The causative

10-1　The causative form is used to mean "someone makes or lets someone do something."

10-2　The causative form is constructed as follows:

(1) Type I verbs: The final **-u** is replaced by **-aseru.**

> *yomu*　　　　　　*yomaseru* (cause someone to read)
> *kaku*　　　　　　*kakaseru* (cause someone to write)

If the Type I verb ends in two vowels, the final **-u** is replaced by **-waseru.**

> *kau*　　　　　　*kawaseru* (cause someone to buy)

(2) Type II verbs: The final **-ru** is replaced by **-saseru.**

taberu	*tabesaseru* (cause someone to eat)
miru	*misaseru* (cause someone to see)

(3) The causative form of **kuru** is **kosaseru** and that of **suru** is **saseru.** Irregular verbs like *kudasaru* are not used in the causative form.

10-3 Causative sentences are constructed in the following way.

(1) When an intransitive verb is used to describe an action, the person caused to do that action is indicated with the particle **o.**

*Kodomo **o** gakkō e **ikasemashita.*** (I **made** my child **go** to school.)

(2) When a transitive verb is used to describe an action, the person caused to do that action is indicated with **ni,** and the object of the action with **o.**

*Kodomo **ni** hon **o** yomasemashita.* (I **made** my child **read** a book.)

10-4 The causative form usually refers to making someone do something by force; it cannot be used when politely asking someone to do something.

10-5 The causative form followed by **-te kudasai** is used to mean "let me do something" or "allow me to do something."

*Kono denwa o **tsukawasete kudasai.** (**Please let me use** this telephone.)

10-6 The causative form followed by the passive ending **-rareru** indicates that someone is forced to do something.

yomu	*yomaseru*	*yomaserareru*

*Hon o **yomaseraremashita.*** (I **was forced to read** a book.)

11. The conditional

11-1 The conditional is expressed by (1) the **-eba** form of a verb, (2) the **-tara** form of a verb, and (3) by adding the particle **to** to the dictionary form of a verb. These three roughly correspond to the English "if" or "when"; in some cases they can be used interchangeably but not in others.

11-2 The three conditional forms are constructed in the following way:

(1) The *-eba* form is made by replacing the final *-u* of the verb by **-eba.**
For adjectives the final *-i* is replaced by **-kereba.**

yomu	*yomeba*
taberu	*tabereba*
akai	*akakereba*

(2) The *-tara* form is made by adding **-ra** to the plain past form of both
verbs and adjectives.

yomu	*yonda*	*yondara*
taberu	*tabeta*	*tabetara*
akai	*akakatta*	*akakattara*

(3) The *to* form is made by adding the particle **to** to the dictionary form of
both verbs and adjectives.

yomu	*yomu to*
taberu	*taberu to*
akai	*akai to*

11-3 These three forms cannot be used interchangeably in the following cases:

(1) The **-eba** and **to** forms are not usually followed by a verb, phrase, or
clause indicating past action.

wrong: * *Yomeba wakarimashita.*

wrong: * *Yomu to wakarimashita.*

Instead, the **-tara** form is used.

right: **Yondara** (or *Yonde **mitara***) *wakarimashita.*
(When I read it, I understood.)

(2) The **to** form cannot be followed by verbs indicating a request or invitation.

wrong: * *Jikan ga aru to tetsudatte kudasai.*

wrong: * *Jikan ga aru to issho ni ikimashō.*

wrong: * *Yasui to kaimasen ka?*

Instead, **-tara** is usually used.

right: *Jikan ga **attara** tetsudatte kudasai.* (Please help me **if
you have** time.)

right: *Jikan ga **attara** issho ni ikimashō.* (Let's go together **if
you have** time.)

right: **Yasukattara** *kaimasen ka?* (Would you want to buy it **if
it were inexpensive?**)

945

(3) **To** and **-eba** indicate a general condition, while **-tara** is used for referring to a particular condition or circumstance.

> *Jikan ga* **aru to** *dekimasu.* (One can do it **if one has** time.)
> *Jikan ga* **areba** *dekimasu.* (One can do it **if one has** time.)
> *Ashita jikan ga* **attara** *yarimasu.* (I will do it tomorrow **if I have**
> time.)

12. Commands

12-1   Commands are expressed either with the plain imperative form or with
the **-nasai** form.

12-2   The plain imperative form is constructed in the following way:

(1) Type I verbs: Replace the final **-u** by **-e.**

yomu	*yome*
iku	*ike*

(2) Type II verbs: Replace the final **-ru** by **-ro.**

taberu	*tabero*
miru	*miro*

(3) The plain imperative form of **kuru** is **koi,** and that of **suru** is **shiro.**

12-3   The plain imperative form is not used in polite speech, except in indirect
speech conveying someone's command.

> *Sensei ga* **yome** *to osshaimashita.* (The professor told me **to read it.**)

12-4   To form the *-nasai* form, add **-nasai** to the stem of the verb.

yomu	*yominasai*
taberu	*tabenasai*
kuru	*kinasai*

12-5   The **-nasai** form is used when giving an order.

> *Sā, mō* **okinasai.**   (Now you **get up!**)

12-6   For expressing a request, **kudasai** is added to the **-te** form of the verb.

yomu	*yonde*	*yonde kudasai*
taberu	*tabete*	*tabete kudasai*

The negative request is constructed by adding **-de kudasai** to the plain negative form of the verb.

yomu	*yomanai*	*yomanaide kudasai*
taberu	*tabenai*	*tabenaide kudasai*

13. Desideratives

13-1   To mean "want to," **-tai** is added to the verb stem. This usually expresses the desires of the speaker.

> *Gakkō e **ikitai** desu.*   (**I want to go** to school.)

13-2   When the verb used with *-tai* is a transitive verb, the object is indicated with **ga** rather than o.

> *Ocha **ga nomitai** desu.*   (**I want to drink** some tea.)

13-3   Verbs ending in **-tai** are conjugated in the same way as true adjectives (IV.2).

Ikitaku wa arimasen.	(I don't want to go—polite)
Ikitaku wa nai.	(I don't want to go—plain)
Ikitakatta desu.	(I wanted to go—polite)
Ikitakatta.	(I wanted to go—plain)

13-4   To refer to wishes in the third person, **-tagaru** is added to the stem of the verb.

> *Kodomo wa gakkō e **ikitagatte** imasu.* (My child **wants to go** to school.)

13-5   Verbs ending in **-tagaru** are conjugated in the same way as Type I verbs.

> *Kodomo wa gakkō e **ikitagarimasen.*** (My child does **not want to go** to school—polite)
>
> *Kodomo wa gakkō e **ikitagaranai.*** (My child does **not want to go** to school—plain)

13-6   When **-tagaru** is used with a transitive verb, the object is indicated with the particle **o.**

> *Kodomo wa mizu **o nomitagatte** imasu.* (The child **wants to drink** some water.)

13-7 To refer to wishes in the second or third person, indirect expressions such as (1) *-sō* (look like), (2) *yō* (seem), and (3) *to iu* (say that ...) are used. This is the same as the expression of emotion with adjectives (V.2-8).

    (1) *-sō*:

        *Ikita**sō** desu ne.* (You **look like** you want to go.)

        *Tanaka san mo ikita**sō** deshita.* (Miss Tanaka also **looked like** she wanted to go.)

    (2) *yō*:

        *Tanaka san mo ikitai **yō** desu.* (**It seems** that Miss Tanaka wants to go, too.)

    (3) *to iu*:

        *Tanaka san mo ikitai **to iimashita**.* (Miss Tanaka **said that** she wants to go, too.)

13-8 To politely refer to wishes in the second or third person, *-tai* and *-tagaru* are usually replaced by completely different expressions. For example, "*Irasshaimasu ka?*" (Would you like to go?—literally, Are you going?) is used rather than * *Ikitai desu ka?*; and "*Shachō ga oyobi desu*" (The director would like to see you—literally, The director is calling you) is used rather than * *Shachō ga aitagatte imasu.*

14. The volitional

14-1 To refer to one's intentions, the volitional form is used; this corresponds to the English "I will" or "I shall."

14-2 The volitional form is constructed in the following way:

    (1) Type I verbs: The final *-u* is replaced by *-ō*.

        iku   *ikō*

        yomu   *yomō*

    -tsu is replaced by *-tō*.

        matsu   *matō*

    (2) Type II verbs: The final *-ru* is replaced by *-yō*.

        taberu   *tabeyō*

        miru   *miyō*

(3) The volitional form of **kuru** is **koyō** and that of **suru** is **shiyō**.

14-3 In polite speech the volitional form is followed by **to omoimasu,** while in familiar speech it is used as is.

> *Ashita eiga o **miyō to omoimasu**.* (**I think I will go** to the movies tomorrow.)
> *Ashita eiga o **miyō**.* (**I think I will go** to the movies tomorrow.)

14-4 The volitional form is used for invitations in familiar speech.
> *Issho ni **ikō**.*   (**Let's go** together.)

In polite speech, **-mashō** is used instead.
> *Issho ni **ikimashō**.*

14-5 The volitional form followed by **to suru** refers to an action which is about to take place.

> ***Kaerō to shita** toki ame ga furidashimashita.* (When **I was about to go back,** it started to rain.)

14-6 The volitional form followed by **to suru** is also used to mean "try to."

> ***Tabeyō to shimashita** ga, taberaremasen deshita.* (**I tried to eat it,** but I couldn't.)

15. Expressing appearance

15-1 To refer to appearance, (1) *rashii*, (2) *yō da*, and (3) *mitai da* are added to words, phrases, and clauses.

(1) **Rashii** is added to phrases and sentences; it is also added to verb phrases indicating the past tense.

> *Tanaka san mo iku **rashii desu**.* (**It seems that** Miss Tanaka also is going.)
> *Tanaka san mo itta **rashii desu**.* (**It seems that** Miss Tanaka also went.)

When **rashii** is added to a noun, it usually forms an adjective meaning "really like ..."

onna	*onna**rashii*** (woman**ly**, lady**like**)
kodomo	*kodomo**rashii*** (**just like** a child, innocent, lively, etc.)

949

(2) **Yō da** is also added to phrases and clauses; it is used as **yō desu** in polite speech.

> *Kekka ga happyō sareta* **yō desu.** (**It seems that** the results have been announced.)

Yō is conjugated in the same way as the adjective-verbs; **yō na** is used as a modifier, and **yō ni** is used as an adverb.

> *Wakatta* **yō na** *ki ga shimasu.* (**I feel that** I understand.)
> *Keikaku wa shippai shita* **yō ni** *miemasu.* (**It seems that** the plan has ended in failure.)

Yō da, preceded by the particle **no,** is used to describe a noun.

> *haru* **no yō**   (**like** spring)
> *Haru* **no yō desu.**   (**It is like** spring.)
> *Haru* **no yō na** *hi deshita.*   (It was **like** a day in spring.)

(3) **Mitai da** is also added to phrases and clauses; it is conjugated in the same way as the adjective-verbs.

> *Kyō wa haru* **mitai da.**   (**It is like** spring today.)
> *Kyō wa haru* **mitai na** *hi da.*   (Today is **like** a spring day.)
> *Kyō wa haru* **mitai ni** *atatakai.* (It is warm **like** spring today.)

15-2   The above three are similar in meaning, but *yō da* sounds more formal, and *mitai da* sounds more familiar. For further differences, see the respective entries in the dictionary.

16. Helping verbs

16-1   Verbs are often added to the *-te* form of other verbs; verbs used in this way can be called "helping verbs."

16-2   *-te iru:*

A verb in the **-te** form plus **iru** refers either (1) to an action that goes on over a period of time, or (2) to the state resulting from an action.

> (1) *Ima hon o* **yonde imasu.** (I **am** now **reading** a book.)
>   *Sono toki ocha o* **nonde imashita.** (I **was drinking** tea at that time.)

(2) *Dentō ga* **tsuite imasu.** (The light **is on.**)

Futari wa **kekkon shite imasu.** (The two **are married.**)

16-3 *-te aru:*

A transitive verb in the **-te** form plus **aru** refers to the state that has resulted from an action (See 7-4).

16-4 *-te shimau:*

A verb in the **-te** form plus **shimau** indicates either (1) that an action has been completed, or (2) that the speaker has regrets about the completion of the action.

(1) *Zenbu* **yonde shimaimashita** *kara, toshokan ni kaeshimasu.* (Since I **have finished reading** them all, I am going to return them to the library.)

(2) *Kabin o* **otoshite shimaimashita.** (I **dropped** the vase—and I **regret** it.)

Osoku **natte shimatte,** *sumimasen.* (I am sorry I **am so** late.)

16-5 *-te oku:*

A verb in the **-te** form plus **oku** refers to doing something for future use.

Mado o **akete okimashita.** (I **left** the window **open**—so that the air would circulate.)

Yoku **shirabete oite** *kudasai.* (Please **make** a thorough **investigation beforehand.**)

16-6 *-te miru:*

A verb in the **-te** form plus **miru** means "to try and see."

Oishii ka dō ka **tabete mimashō.** (I **will taste it** to see if it is good or not.)

Atte minakereba *wakarimasen.* (I cannot tell [what he is like] **unless I see** him in person.)

16-7 *-te iku:*

A verb in the **-te** form plus **iku** refers to a change taking place from the present into the future.

Dandan samuku **natte iku** *deshō.* (It **will become** colder and colder.)

16-8   *-te kuru:*

A verb in the *-te* form plus **kuru** indicates either (1) that a change has been taking place up to the present, or (2) that an action is done in the direction of the speaker.

> (1) *Dandan samuku* **natte kimashita.** (It **has been getting** colder and colder.)
>
> > *Kono kaisha ni nijūnenkan* **tsutomete kimashita.** (I **have been working** for this company for 20 years.)
>
> (2) *Mukō kara ookina kuruma ga* **chikazuite kimashita.** (A large car **came from** the opposite direction.)
>
> > *Haha ga sētā o* **okutte kimashita.** (My mother **sent** me a sweater.)

17. Narration

17-1   To quote someone's speech, **to iu** is used; what is quoted is described in plain form even in polite speech.

> *Yamada san wa iku* **to itte** *imasu.* (Mr. Yamada **says that** he is going to go there.)
>
> *Tanaka san wa ongaku ga suki da* **to itte** *imasu.* (Miss Tanaka **says that** she likes music.)

17-2   To change the sentence into the past tense, only the main verb is changed into the past.

> *Yamada san wa iku* **to iimashita.** (Mr. Yamada **said that** he was going to go there.)

17-3   If the verb in the quoted clause is in the past, as well as the main verb, the action took place prior to the time of the statement.

> *Yamada san wa itta* **to iimashita.** (Mr. Yamada **said that** he had gone there.)

17-4   To relate what the speaker thinks, **to omou** is used; the rules of 17-1 to 17-3 apply in this case also.

> *Yamada san wa iku* **to omoimasu.** (**I think that** Mr. Yamada is going to go there.)

Yamada san wa iku **to omoimashita.** (**I thought that** Mr. Yamada was going to go there.)

Yamada san wa itta **to omoimashita.** (**I thought that** Mr. Yamada had gone there.)

17-5   When the quoted part includes an interrogative, **ka** is added at the end of the quoted part.

Doko e iku ka *iimasen deshita.* (He didn't tell me **where he was going.**)

Nani ga hoshii ka *itte kudasai.* (Please tell me **what you want.**)

17-6   The rule of 17-5 also applies when such verbs as **shiru, wakaru, oshieru,** and **shiraseru** are used as the main verb.

Naze sonna koto o shita ka *wakarimasen.* (I don't know **why he did such a thing.**)

Itsu dekiru ka *shitte imasu ka?* (Do you know **when it will be completed?**)

18. Giving and receiving

18-1   The verbs describing the action of giving and receiving things—*ageru, sashiageru, yaru, morau, itadaku, kureru, kudasaru*—are used depending on the relations between the giver and the receiver.

18-2   **Giving:** Verbs referring to giving are used as follows:

ageru	give something to one's equals or inferiors
sashiageru	give something to one's superiors
yaru	give something to one's inferiors or animals

Tomodachi ni shashin o **agemashita.** (**I gave** a picture to my friend.)

Sensei ni shashin o **sashiagemashita.** (**I gave** a picture to the professor.)

Otōto ni shashin o **yarimashita.** (**I gave** a picture to my brother.)

18-3   **Receiving:** Verbs referring to receiving are used as follows:

morau	receive something from one's equals or inferiors
itadaku	receive something from one's superiors

*Tomodachi ni/kara shashin o **moraimashita.** (**I received** a picture from my friend.)*

*Otōto ni/kara shashin o **moraimashita.** (**I received** a picture from my brother.)*

*Sensei ni/kara shashin o **itadakimashita.** (**I received** a picture from the professor.)*

18-4   Giving something to the speaker: The following verbs are used only when the speaker or someone who can be identified with the speaker is given something.

> *kudasaru*   one's superiors give something to the speaker
> *kureru*   one's equals or inferiors give something to the speaker

*Sensei ga shashin o **kudasaimashita.** (The professor **gave me** a picture.)*

*Tomodachi ga shashin o **kuremashita.** (My friend **gave me** a picture.)*

*Otōto ga shashin o **kuremashita.** (My brother **gave me** a picture.)*

18-5   When these verbs are used as helping verbs, they refer to doing and receiving a favor in the same way as when they are used for giving and receiving physical objects.

*Tomodachi no shigoto o **tetsudatte agemashita.** (**I helped** my friend with his work.)*

*Otōto no shigoto o **tetsudatte yarimashita.** (**I helped** my brother with his work.)*

*Tomodachi ni shigoto o **tetsudatte moraimashita.** (My friend **helped me** with my work—literally, **I received help** from my friend.)*

*Sensei ni shigoto o **tetsudatte itadakimashita.** (The professor **helped me** with my work.)*

*Sensei ga shigoto o **tetsudatte kudasaimashita.** (The professor **helped me** with my work.)*

*Tomodachi ga shigoto o **tetsudatte kuremashita.** (My friend **helped me** with my work.)*

In the case of *sashiageru*, the humble form "*o- ~suru*" is preferred.

Sensei no shigoto o **otetsudai shimashita. (I helped** the professor with his work.)

VII. KEIGO (POLITE LANGUAGE)

The Japanese language is used in different ways depending on to whom it is spoken and to whom one refers. **Keigo,** or polite language, refers to a linguistic style in Japanese used when speaking to and about someone politely. It is usually divided into three types: (1) honorific, (2) humble, and (3) polite.

1. Honorific language

1-1 Honorific language is used to refer to someone with respect; special prefixes, suffixes, verbs, and verb forms are used for this purpose.

1-2 Prefixes: The honorific prefixes **o-** and **go-** are used when referring to someone's belongings with respect.

otaku	(your house, his/her/their house)
oshigoto	(your work, his/her/their work)
gokenkyū	(your research, his/her/their research)

1-3 Suffixes: The honorific suffixes **sama, san,** and the like are used when referring to someone with respect.

goshujin **sama**	(someone's husband)
kodomo **san**	(someone's child(ren))

1-4 Verbs: Special verbs are used to refer to someone's actions with respect.

irassharu	(be, go, come)
ossharu	(say)
nasaru	(do)
meshiagaru	(eat, drink)
goran ni naru	(see)

1-5 Verb forms: Special verb forms are used to refer to someone's actions with respect.

(1) **o-** + verb stem + **ni naru**
oyomi **ni naru** (someone reads)
ooshie **ni naru** (someone teaches)

(2) The passive form of a verb is also used to show respect.

yom**areru**	(someone reads)
oshie**rareru**	(someone teaches)

2. Humble language

2-1 Special verbs are used to refer to the actions of oneself and one's family members in order to express a humble attitude.

oru	(be)
mairu	(go, come)
itadaku	(receive, eat, drink)
haiken suru	(see something)
ome ni kakaru	(see someone)
mōshiageru	(tell someone)
ojama suru	(visit)
ukagau	(ask, hear, visit)

2-2 Special verb forms are used to refer to one's own actions; namely, **o-** + verb stem + **suru.**

oyobi **suru**	(I call someone)
omachi **suru**	(I wait for someone to come)

2-3 The special helping verbs **itasu** and **mōshiageru** are also used.

oyobi **itasu**	(I call someone)
ohanashi **mōshiageru**	(I tell it to someone)

3. Polite language

Polite forms are used in formal speech and conversation between persons who are not on familiar terms or when talking to one's superiors; the plain forms are used in conversation between family members, to good friends, and to one's inferiors.

Staff

Senior Editors (Japanese text)

MOCHIZUKI Kōitsu
KUMAZAWA Seiji
YOSHIOKA Hideyuki
SANADA Kazuko

Associate Editors (Japanese text)

SHIBATA Shunzō
IMADA Shigeko
NITOGURI Akira

Editorial Supervisor (English text)

MIZUTANI Nobuko

Translator (English text)

Janet M. ASHBY

Proofreaders (English text)

Janet M. ASHBY
Keith D. LEARMONTH

THE JAPAN FOUNDATION
BASIC
JAPANESE-ENGLISH
DICTIONARY

基礎日本語学習辞典（英語版）

1986年12月10日　初版第1刷発行　　　　　　定価 2,500円
1987年4月20日　初版第2刷発行

著作権者　国際交流基金
　　　　　〒102 東京都千代田区紀尾井町3－6

発 行 者　田中久光

発 行 所　株式会社　凡人社
　　　　　〒102 東京都千代田区麹町6－2
　　　　　電 話 販売 (03) 472－2 2 4 0
　　　　　　　　編集 (03) 353－4 2 1 1

印刷製本　細川活版所

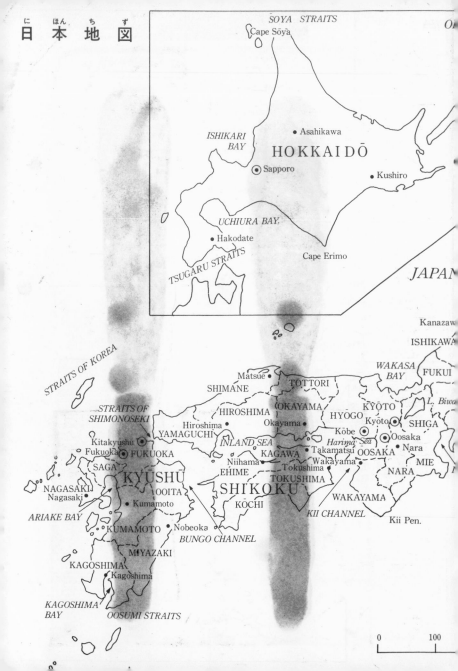

日 本 地 図
に ほん ち ず

SOYA STRAITS

Cape Sōya

ISHIKARI BAY

HOKKAIDŌ

• Asahikawa

◉ Sapporo

• Kushiro

UCHIURA BAY

• Hakodate

Cape Erimo

TSUGARU STRAITS

JAPAN

Kanazaw

ISHIKAWA

WAKASA BAY

FUKUI

Matsue •

TOTTORI

SHIMANE

OKAYAMA

KYŌTO

L. Biwa

HIROSHIMA

HYOGO

SHIGA

STRAITS OF KOREA

STRAITS OF SHIMONOSEKI

Okayama •

Kōbe ◉

Kyōto ◉

Oosaka ◉

Hiroshima •

YAMAGUCHI

Harima Sea

Nara •

Kitakyūshū ◉

INLAND SEA

KAGAWA

OOSAKA

Fukuoka ◉ FUKUOKA

Takamatsu •

Wakayama •

SAGA

Niihama •

Tokushima

MIE

KYŪSHŪ

EHIME

TOKUSHIMA

NARA

NAGASAKI

OOITA

SHIKOKU

WAKAYAMA

Nagasaki •

• Kumamoto

KŌCHI

ARIAKE BAY

KII CHANNEL

Kii Pen.

KUMAMOTO

• Nobeoka

BUNGO CHANNEL

MIYAZAKI

KAGOSHIMA

Kagoshima

KAGOSHIMA BAY

OOSUMI STRAITS

0   100

You're Reading in the Wrong Direction!!

Whoops! Guess what? You're starting at the wrong end of the comic!

...It's true! In keeping with the original Japanese format, **One Piece** is meant to be read from right to left, starting in the upper-right corner.

Unlike English, which is read from left to right, Japanese is read from right to left, meaning that action, sound effects and word-balloon order are completely reversed...something which can make readers unfamiliar with Japanese feel pretty backwards themselves. For this reason, manga or Japanese comics published in the U.S. in English have sometimes been published "flopped"—that is, printed in exact reverse order, as though seen from the other side of a mirror.

By flopping pages, U.S. publishers can avoid confusing readers, but the compromise is not without its downside. For one thing, a character in a flopped manga series who once wore in the original Japanese version a T-shirt emblazoned with "M A Y" (as in "the merry month of") now wears one which reads "Y A M"! Additionally, many manga creators in Japan are themselves unhappy with the process, as some feel the mirror-imaging of their art skews their original intentions.

We are proud to bring you Eiichiro Oda's **One Piece** in the original unflopped format. For now, though, turn to the other side of the book and let the journey begin...!

—Editor

Drum Island is really turning out to be quite the fiasco! Luffy and Sanji are caught in an avalanche while still being hunted by the Lapins! Plus, Wapol is hot on their trail. Not one to give up easily, Luffy is determined to climb the highest peak in the island to reach the eccentric doctor living there. But will he make it to the top, and if he does what kind of reception can he hope to find?

ON SALE NOW!

INSTEAD OF CARING FOR YOUR PEOPLE, YOU HELD THE SICK OF THE NATION HOSTAGE!!

THAT IS A CRIME!!!

WITH EVERY DOCTOR IN THE WHOLE COUNTRY IN YOUR CASTLE...

...THE SICK HAD TO BEG YOU FOR MEDICAL TREATMENT!

KILL HIM, MEN! KILL YOUR FORMER COMMANDER!!!

YOU DON'T HEED YOUR WORDS AT ALL, DO YOU!!?

I'D HOPED THAT ONE DAY YOU'D COME TO YOUR SENSES, BUT YOU NEVER WILL!!!

RMB

RMB

YOU ARE THE SON OF THE FORMER KING TO WHOM I AM INDEBTED.

HE WAS THE COMMANDER OF THE DRUM KINGDOM MILITIA. *BWA HA HA HA...*

HE SHOULD HAVE DIED THEN!!

HMPH...

I'M SURPRISED HE MANAGED TO SURVIVE WITHOUT ANY DOCTOR AROUND.

BUT LITTLE DID THEY KNOW...

OUTSIDERS...

...THAT THERE WERE ONLY 20 DOCTORS HERE, AND THEY ALL WORKED IN THE CASTLE RESEARCH LABORATORY! ALL THE OTHER DOCTORS WERE EXPELLED FROM THE COUNTRY.

...USED TO THINK OF THIS AS A LAND OF ADVANCED MEDICAL SCIENCE.

THAT'S BAD GOVERNANCE!!!

COULDN'T BE HELPED. THAT'S POLITICS.

TA—DAH!!

HUH?

KING WAPOL, WAIT!! WE HAVEN'T REATTACHED YOUR HEAD!!

PHEW! I REALLY THOUGHT I WAS GOING TO DIE.

DA-DOOM!!

KING!!!

YOU WILL ADDRESS ME AS KING WAPOL!!!

WAPOL?

YOU ARE MY VASSAL, DALTON!

WAPOL, LET'S GO!!

WE DON'T BELONG HERE ANYMORE.

HE RISKED HIS LIFE! HE ALMOST DIED!!!

HE'S THE ONLY ONE OF YOUR MINISTERS WHO STAYED TO DEFEND THIS COUNTRY!!!

DALTON'S NOT YOUR VASSAL ANYMORE!!!

THEY'RE HEADED FOR DRUM CASTLE.

I HAVE A REPORT, KING WAPOL!! ABOUT THOSE IMPUDENT STRAW HATS...

WELL, IT SEEMS THE TRAITOR...

...DR. KUREHA, HAD THE AUDACITY TO OCCUPY YOUR CASTLE.

WHAT !!? WHY !!?

THAT OLD HAG IS IN MY CASTLE !!!?

PLO INK!!

WHAT !!?

Chapter 136:
A MAN NAMED DALTON

STAY ON GUARD! WE'RE GONNA FIGHT!! USOPP'S PIRATE GALLERY!!!

NOW IT'S THE MONSTER'S BROTHER!!

CONGRATULATIONS!

EMILY, 14

A BABY PIRATE KING!

ELOISA, 13

GOOD SET OF CHOPPERS!

BRUCE

HOLD THAT POSE!

SARA, 17

SWEET PANTS, DUDE.

MIKAEL, 14

ARLONG'S GOT THE BLING!

JOHN, 8

SHE LEFT TOWN!!?

HUH!!?

COCOA-WEED

IT'S AN EMERGENCY. DO YOU KNOW WHICH WAY SHE WENT!?

ARE YOU LOOKING FOR THE DOCTOR, DALTON?

SHE MADE ME BETTER A LITTLE WHILE AGO.

NO WAY! WE JUST MISSED HER?

WHERE'S THAT?

GYASTA?

I HEARD SOMEONE SAY SHE WAS HEADING FOR GYASTA.

188

NOD NOD

UMF

OVER THERE ON THE RIVER-BANK!!!

IT'S THE SHIP OF THOSE PIRATES WE MET YESTER-DAY!

WHAT!!?

DOOM!

WHAT IS IT!?

KING WAPOL! I HAVE NEWS!!

B-BUT... THERE'S NO ONE ON BOARD!!!

KILL THEM ALL!!!

WE DON'T KNOW WHERE THEY ARE!

I WON'T FORGET WHAT THEY DID TO ME!! HOW I SUFFERED!!!

THOSE STRAW HATS ARE IN MY KING-DOM!!?

BWA HA HA HA HA !!

IT HASN'T CHANGED, YOUR MAJESTY.

BWA HA HA HA HA

I'M NO LONGER A PIRATE!! I AM A KING ONCE AGAIN!!

THEN ON TO THE CASTLE!! MY DEAR CASTLE!!!

UMF?

WELL STOP MOPING! THIS IS A GLORIOUS OCCASION!!!

...BECAUSE I KILLED YOUR BROTHERS !!?

!! THERE, THERE... ARE YOU STILL UPSET...

ONWARD, ROBSON !!

ROBSON WHITE WALKY (ALIAS WOOLY HIPPO)

SNORT

GRUNT

YES, REALLY.

TA-DOON!!

HMPH... THESE GUARDS WERE TOO SLOW.

UMF

TMP

WHAT WERE THEY THINKING, SHOOTING AT US?

CHESS! IS MY CASTLE INTACT?

UNCHANGING, EVER-BEAUTIFUL NATURE!!!

183

176

IF THE DOCTOR'S HERE IN COCOAWEED...

...WE'LL JUST HAVE TO ASK HER TO RETURN TO HER CASTLE.

LET'S HOPE SHE'LL DO IT!

...

THERE'S NO NEED TO APOLOGIZE, DALTON!

KLOP KLOP KLOP KLOP KLOP

IF ONLY THIS COUNTRY HAD MORE DOCTORS.

...

HUH?

I'M SORRY.

LET'S HURRY!

KLOP KLOP KLOP KLOP KLOP KLOP

COCOAWEED

BIGHORN

SLOOSH

FORGIVE ME.

I MADE A MISTAKE!!

...SO I DIDN'T THINK SHE'D COME AGAIN SO SOON!!

BUT I WAS WRONG!!

I GOT WORD THAT THE DOCTOR HAD COME DOWN FROM THE MOUNTAIN YESTERDAY...

IT'S NOT GONNA BE EASY TO CATCH UP WITH THEM!

THOSE TWO TOOK OFF IN SUCH A HURRY!

IT'S OKAY! IT WASN'T YOUR FAULT!!

Chapter 135:
LAPINS

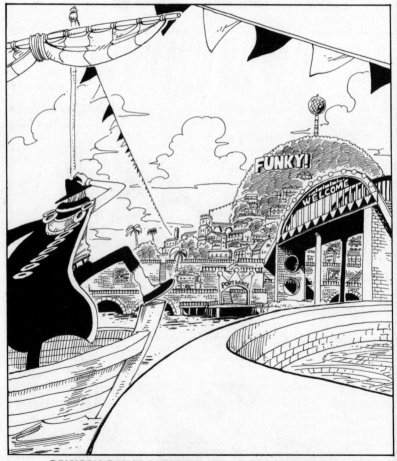

DJANGO'S DANCE PARADISE, VOL. 8: THE EAST BLUE'S MOST POPULAR DESTINATION, MIRROR-BALL ISLAND

GRAB YOUR BRUSH!! LET'S FIGHT!! USOPP'S PIRATE GALLERY !!!

HUH!? A BABY MONSTER !!

WHAT'S HE WHISTLING?

NATALIE, 14

ONE FIST, COMING RIGHT UP!

STEPHEN, 16

IT'S ON!

GARTH, 26

SAY CHEESE!

CYNTHIA, 14

I'M GONNA GRAB YA!

AUSTIN, 12

WHO'S HE RUNNING FROM?

DANIEL, 15

ONE PIECE

172

KAK KAK KAK KAK!!

WHAT A SWEET TIP.

K-LAK!!

!

KAK KAK KAK KAK...

OH, GOODY !!

I'LL PAY YOU. THANK YOU!

I'LL ONLY TAKE 49% NOW.

DON'T EVER FORGET IT!!!

DA-DOOM!!

WHAT I DID JUST NOW!!!

YOU TAKE ADVANTAGE OF PEOPLE'S WEAK-NESSES!!!

GRAH GRAH

...

YOU SENILE OLD WOMAN!!!

ISN'T THAT RIGHT!!? WELL!!?

GRANDMA...

...

THEY'RE JUST PRATTLING CHILDREN. CHOPPER, DOWN BOY.

VEEN!!

AGA

!!

DOOM!!

HEE HEE

THANK YOU!!

IT FEELS MUCH BETTER...

fire STOO

JUST KEEP THE LEG BANDAGED FOR A WHILE.

THERE, ALL DONE. MY MEDICINE IS VERY EFFECTIVE.

FWUMP

IF IT GETS STIFF, PUT ICE ON IT. UNDERSTAND?

HUH?

A A A G H!!

OKAY, NOW FOR THE INJECTION. GET READY.

AAAAH!!

WHAP!!

DON'T BE SO ROUGH!!!

I'M GOING TO MAKE A SMALL INCISION NOW.

AAGH!!

HEY, CAN'T YOU AT LEAST GIVE HIM A PAIN-KILLER!

...AND RUM AND I'LL TAKE WHATEVER FOOD YOU HAVE. OH, AND I'LL TAKE HALF OF THIS SHOP'S ASSETS.

KLAK!!

OOOO

AND FOR PAYMENT, LET ME SEE... I'M RUNNIN LOW ON GARBAGE BAGS AND TOILET PAPER...

ALMOST DIED? WHAT A LAUGH! HE WAS JUST CRYING BECAUSE HE FELL DOWN!!

DON'T FALL FOR THAT, SHOPKEEPER!! SHE'S CHEATING YOU!!!

RGAH

SHE ONLY PRETENDED TO CURE HIM!!!

GRAH

I CAN'T GIVE YOU HALF OF MY ASSETS!!?

WHAT!?

LOAD THE SLEIGH.

NOD

CHOPP...

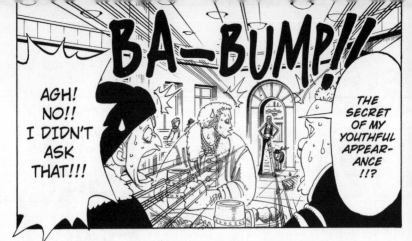

BA-BUMP!!

AGH! NO!! I DIDN'T ASK THAT!!!

THE SECRET OF MY YOUTHFUL APPEARANCE !!?

THIS CHILD ISN'T SICK!!

HUH!!? CURE HIM OF WHAT?

WAHH!

SHALL I CURE HIM?

I'M ONLY 139 YEARS OLD!!!

I CAN'T BELIEVE THAT OLD BIDDY IS REALLY 140 YEARS OLD.

EEEK!

LET'S GO, CHOPPER.

T-TURN

HEY! WAIT!!!

...

GULP

fire STOOL

ARE YOU A DOCTOR ?

YACK

YACK

WE'VE GOT A BAD FATHER HERE.

GLANCE

GLANCE

STAND BACK.

THIS IS THE SHOP.

I'M COMING IN!!

!!!?

THE NEIGHBORING TOWN OF COCOAWEED

SHUT THAT KID UP!! I CAN'T TAKE IT!!!

HEY, SHOP-KEEPER! GIVE ME A BREAK!!

WAAAAAH !!!

I'M SORRY.

STOOL

IF YOU DON'T STOP CRYING, I'LL LOCK YOU OUTSIDE!!

TAMA!! WHAT'S WRONG!!

WAAAAAAAH !!!

IF YOU KEEP CRYING, I CAN'T UNDERSTAND YOU. AND YOU'RE BOTHERING THE CUSTOMERS!

WHAT'S WRONG, TAMA!? WHERE DOES IT HURT!?

WAAAAAH

WAAAAAAH

A CHILD THAT WON'T STOP CRYING HAS SOMETHING WRONG WITH ITS BODY.

KRUNCH

KRUNCH

KAK KAK KAK KAK...

OH DEAR, DID YOU HEAR THAT, CHOPPER?

BUT NOW WAPOL'S EVIL REIGN IS OVER.

YOU'RE RIGHT.

UNTIL WE'RE ABLE TO REBUILD OUR COUNTRY...

...THE RESTORATION OF THE MONARCHY IS THE THING TO BE FEARED MOST.

WHICH IS WHY WE FEAR WAPOL'S RETURN MORE THAN ANYTHING.

THIS ISLAND BELONGS TO THOSE OF US WHO REMAIN!! THE TOWNS AND VILLAGES ARE BEGINNING TO RECOVER.

RIGHT NOW, WE'RE UNITED AND TRYING TO BUILD A NEW NATION.

...PEACEFUL NATION.

WE WANT TO BUILD A NEW...

BELIEVE IT OR NOT, WHEN THEY SAW THE PIRATES' STRENGTH...

...THEY ABANDONED THE NATION TO ITS FATE!! THEY FLED LIKE RATS FROM A SINKING SHIP!!

WAPOL ESCAPED TO THE SEA.

KRK!!!

HOW COULD A KING DO SUCH A THING!!?

AND THE COUNTRY LOST HOPE!! THAT THEIR OWN KING WOULD--

...

IT'S DESPICABLE FOR A KING TO ABANDON HIS PEOPLE!!

VIVI...

THE PIRATE PART IS A COVER.

WAPOL IS SCOURING THE SEAS IN SEARCH OF THIS ISLAND.

WHAT'S GOING ON HERE?

THIS COUNTRY WAS DEFEATED, BUT THE KING'S NOT ONLY ALIVE, HE'S TURNED PIRATE!!

THAT'S A LAUGH!!!

DEFEATED!?

THEN THOSE MEN ON THE SHIP WERE SOLDIERS THAT THE PIRATES DEFEATED...

...AND DROVE OFF THE ISLAND?

HUH?

...DIDN'T EVEN ATTEMPT TO FIGHT!!!

WHEN THE PIRATES ARRIVED, WAPOL'S ARMY...

YOU KNOW WAPOL !!?

WHAT !!?

WHEN I WAS A CHILD, MY FATHER TOOK ME...

YES. I REMEMBER HIM CLEARLY NOW.

...TO A MEETING OF KINGS AND I MET HIM THERE.

ACTUALLY, I REMEMBER HIM SAYING SOMETHING ABOUT THE DRUM KINGDOM...

BUT I CHASED HIM OFF.

DO WE EVER! THAT'S THE PIRATE THAT ATTACKED OUR SHIP!!

!! IS THAT SO!?

...

IT WAS YESTERDAY ON OUR WAY HERE...

ANYWAY!!! I MET THIS WAPOL!!

OH NO! I MEAN...

A MEETING OF KINGS!? JUST WHO ARE--

154

Chapter 134:
DR. KUREHA

**DJANGO'S DANCE PARADISE, OUTSIDE ISSUE, REPORT:
KAYA IS NOW A DOCTOR'S APPRENTICE AND DOING FINE**

ONE PIECE STORYBOARD PRESENTATION!! #17

*FROM VOL. 16 PAGE 57 - ED.

...DEFEATED BY PIRATES!!!

ONLY A FEW MONTHS AGO, THIS COUNTRY WAS...

YES. THE MERE MENTION OF PIRATES STILL MAKES US UNEASY.

NO WONDER EVERYONE WAS SO NERVOUS WHEN WE SHOWED UP.

IT WAS!!?

HUH?

FIVE PIRATES!? YOU MUST BE KIDDING!!?

BLACK-BEARD!?

THEY WERE IMMENSELY POWERFUL. WE NEVER HAD A CHANCE. THEY DEFEATED US BEFORE WE KNEW WHAT HIT US.

THE CAPTAIN CALLED HIMSELF BLACK-BEARD.

THERE WERE ONLY FIVE PIRATES.

SHIVER

ME TOO.

SHIVER

THAT'S ALL RIGHT. I'LL STAY OUT HERE FOR A WHILE.

THEN I'LL KEEP YOU COMPANY.

FWUMF

I SEE.

...

...

HUH?

DOCTORS. BUT CIRCUMSTANCES CAUSED THEM ALL TO LEAVE.

LONG AGO, WE DID HAVE THEM.

UH-HUH...

ME TOO!!!

DOOM!!

THAT SHOULD DO.

I'LL BE WAITING HERE! I'D ONLY BE A BURDEN IF I CAME ALONG.

WAIT! DON'T MOVE!! IT HAS TO BE TIED TIGHT!

TUG

AWRIGHT! HANG ON TIGHT, NAMI!!

THERE ARE LAPINS ON THIS SIDE. THEY'RE VICIOUS FLESH-EATING RABBITS. IF YOU ENCOUNTER A PACK OF THEM, IT'S CERTAIN DEATH!!

IF YOU'RE SERIOUS ABOUT THIS, I WON'T STOP YOU, BUT AT LEAST START THE CLIMB FROM THE OTHER SIDE.

YEAH.

RIGHT?

RABBITS? WE'RE IN A HURRY. WE CAN HANDLE THEM.

I'LL KICK 'EM!!!

KAK KAK KAK KAK KAK...

IT SOUNDS STRANGE, BUT I'VE HEARD THAT ON MOONLIT NIGHTS, SHE RIDES A SLEIGH THROUGH THE SKY...

...AND COMES DOWN THE MOUNTAIN. SOME PEOPLE EVEN CLAIM TO HAVE SEEN IT.

THAT'S WHY THEY CALL HER A WITCH.

I KNEW HE'D BE HERE!! A WITCH AND A SNOW MONSTER!!!

ARGH!! I KNEW IT!! IT'S HERE! SEE!? IT'S THE ABOMINABLE SNOWMAN!!! AFTER ALL, THIS IS A SNOW-COVERED MOUNTAIN!!!

AAAGH

OTHERS SAY SHE COMES WITH A STRANGE BEAST UNLIKE ANYTHING THEY'VE SEEN BEFORE.

OH PLEASE, DON'T LET ME MEET UP WITH THEM!!!

...ONE DOCTOR FOR AN ENTIRE COUNTRY MAKES NO SENSE!!!

YOU KNOW...

IT'S BEST TO JUST WAIT HERE UNTIL SHE COMES DOWN THE MOUNTAIN.

SHE'S OUR ONLY DOCTOR...

BUT...

...BUT WE DON'T LIKE TO GET INVOLVED WITH HER IF WE CAN HELP IT.

WHAT!?

AND SHE CALLS HERSELF A DOCTOR!? WHAT KIND OF WOMAN IS SHE!?

I'D LIKE TO, BUT WE HAVE NO WAY OF CONTACTING HER.

WHY WOULD SHE WANT TO LIVE WAY UP THERE?

ANYWAY, CALL HER DOWN HERE!! IT'S AN EMERGENCY!!

WHAT DO THE PEOPLE HERE DO WHEN THEY GET SICK OR INJURED!?

AND... LET'S SEE... SHE LIKES PICKLED PLUMS.

DO-OOM

WHAT? 140!? AND SHE'S STILL KICKING!?

HER SKILLS AS A DOCTOR ARE INDISPUTABLE. BUT SHE'S...

...RATHER ECCENTRIC. SHE'S NEARLY 140 YEARS OLD.

SIP

BUT HOW DOES A WOMAN THAT OLD GET DOWN THE MOUNTAIN?

HEY, SHE'S JUST LIKE A PIRATE!!

SOUNDS LIKE A NASTY OLD LADY.

SIP SIP SIP SIP

...TAKES WHATEVER SHE WANTS IN COMPENSATION, AND GOES HOME.

THEN SHE LOOKS FOR PATIENTS, TREATS THEM...

SHE COMES DOWN THE MOUNTAIN WHENEVER SHE FEELS LIKE IT.

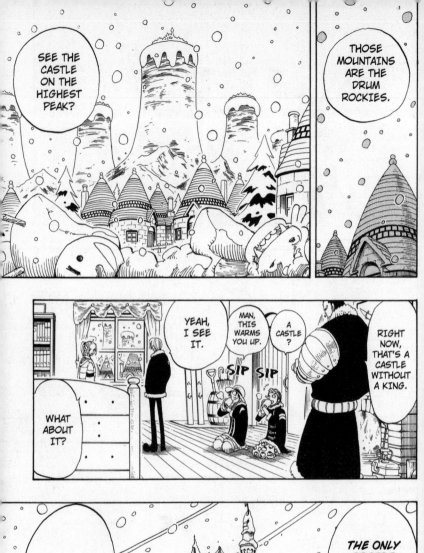

SEE THE CASTLE ON THE HIGHEST PEAK?

THOSE MOUNTAINS ARE THE DRUM ROCKIES.

YEAH, I SEE IT.

MAN, THIS WARMS YOU UP.

SIP SIP

A CASTLE?

RIGHT NOW, THAT'S A CASTLE WITHOUT A KING.

WHAT ABOUT IT?

...LIVES THERE.

THE ONLY DOCTOR IN THIS COUNTRY, DR. KUREHA, WHOM PEOPLE CALL "THE WITCH"...

WHAT!?

YOU SEE THOSE MOUNTAINS OUT THE WINDOW!?

THE WITCH...

DOOM

WHOA! IT'S BIG.

!

YOU GUYS ARE GONNA GET IT!!!

IT'S THE SNOW MONSTER SHIRORA!!!

IT'S A SUPER SNOWMAN!!!

YEAH!

SHWAK

KRAK

KRAK

KRAK

HER FEVER'S BEEN RISING STEADILY FOR THREE DAYS.

WEEZ

WEEZ

HER TEMPERATURE IS... 107.6 DEGREES!!?

LOOK, WE JUST NEED A DOCTOR. ANY DOCTOR! WHERE'S THIS WITCH!!?

YES. BUT WE DON'T KNOW THE CAUSE OF HER ILLNESS OR HOW TO TREAT IT.

IF IT GOES ANY HIGHER, SHE'LL DIE.

THEY'RE ALL CIVILIANS.

THEY'RE NOT REAL SOLDIERS?

PLEASE, COME TO MY HOUSE FOR NOW.

I DON'T THINK THEY MEAN US ANY HARM.

TRUST ME. I FEEL IT IN MY GUT.

WILL YOU BE ALL RIGHT ALONE, DALTON? THEY'RE PIRATES.

EXCEPT FOR THOSE ON GUARD DUTY, YOU CAN ALL GO BACK TO WORK.

THANK YOU, EVERY-ONE.

YES, EVERYTHING'S FINE. DON'T WORRY.

ARE YOU ALL RIGHT?

DALTON, I HEARD THERE WERE PIRATES HERE!

AGAIN!?

HUH!? LOOK, LUFFY!! THE HIKING BEAR!

I'M NOT WORTHY!!!

OH NO!! NOT ME!!!

EVERY-ONE SAYS THEY'RE VOTING FOR YOU.

KRUNCH KRUNCH

DALTON, I'M LOOKING FORWARD TO THE ELECTION IN TWO DAYS.

...HAS NO NAME.

THIS COUNTRY...

AAAAH

EVERY-BODY PLAY DEAD!!

WAAAH!!! A BEAR!!!

I'VE NEVER HEARD OF SUCH A THING.

A COUNTRY WITHOUT A NAME?

IT'S NOT DANGEROUS. DON'T FORGET TO BOW-- IT'S A MOUNTAINEER TRADITION.

THAT'S JUST THE HIKING BEAR.

...

KRUNCH

KRUNCH Chapter 133: ADVENTURE IN A NAMELESS COUNTRY

Q: When I saw the SBS in Volume 13, it was like lightning had struck me. That's because I'd always thought that SBS stood for *sugoi bakamitaina sekushon*, or "Terribly Stupid Section." And I told about five of my friends that it meant that. Now what am I supposed to do? Huh?

A: Well, actually, 90% of the questions we receive for the SBS are ~~stupid silly~~ gags. Not that I mind.

Q: I want to say one thing to Mr. 8!! You don't know anything about saxophones!! I mean, look at the way you hold your instrument!! And that embouchure!! At least use a strap!! Get it right!! Now go!!
--Head of the Wind Instruments Department

A: Right, right! I know! He's way off, that guy! That em-embouchure thing too!! And the strip--I mean, strap--too. He looks down on the sax!! You tell him!! (upset) Please teach me, All-knowing Himeko.

Q: Oda Sensei, I really, really loooooooooooove you!! Pleeeeeeeeeeease marry me. If you won't, then will you answer my questions, pleeeeeeeease? Number 1, Gold Roger and "Red-Haired" Shanks look pretty tough, but what exactly are the bounties on their heads? And Question Number 2 is…will you pleeeeease marry me after all?

A: Oda Flying Cross Chop!!! Krash!! This is the end of the Question Corner!! We'll meet again in the next volume!! Hyah!!!

COME WITH ME.

I'LL TAKE YOU... TO THE VILLAGE.

YEAH.

YOU SURE ARE SMART.

SEE?

HE UNDER-STANDS US.

HUH?

THERE'S ONLY ONE DOCTOR IN THIS COUNTRY... AND SHE'S A WITCH.

BUT I SHOULD WARN YOU...

PLEASE CALL A DOCTOR.

TUMP!!

PLEASE HELP OUR FRIEND.

WEEZ

WEEZ

IMPULSIVENESS DOESN'T SOLVE ANYTHING!!

LUFFY, YOU'RE A FAILURE AS A CAPTAIN.

VIVI!?

PLIP

PLIP

...WHAT WILL HAPPEN TO NAMI?

IF YOU GET US ALL KILLED...

...

I WAS WRONG !!!

YOU'RE RIGHT. FORGIVE ME!

DON'T TRY YOUR TRICKS ON US, YOU DIRTY PIRATES!

WE HAVE A SICK PERSON ABOARD!!

WE CAME HERE TO FIND A DOCTOR!!

OR WE'LL BLAST YOUR SHIP FROM THE WATER!!!

NOW RAISE YOUR ANCHOR AND GO!!!

THIS IS OUR COUNTRY!! WE'LL LET NO PIRATE SET FOOT HERE!!!

THEY REALLY DON'T LIKE US. AND WE ONLY JUST MET.

...YOU PIRATES.

STOP RIGHT THERE...

!!

THEY LOOK PRETTY NASTY.

···!

HEY, THERE'S PEOPLE.

...AND LEAVE. NOW!

TURN YOUR VESSEL AROUND...

AN ISLAND!!!

WAAH!!!

JUST REMEMBER, LUFFY!! WE'RE NOT HERE FOR AN ADVENTURE THIS TIME.

WE'RE GOING TO FIND A DOCTOR FOR NAMI, THEN WE'RE LEAVING IMMEDIATELY.

IT'S SO WHITE!!

IT'S SNOW! A SNOW ISLAND!

PREPARE TO MAKE LANDFALL!

SNOW'S SO NICE AND WHITE.

OH NO! MY "DON'T-GO-ON-THE-ISLAND" DISEASE IS COMING BACK!!

WAIT! ARE YOU SURE IT'S SAFE? IF THERE'S SNOW HERE, COULDN'T THERE BE A SNOW MONSTER!?

DO WE EVEN KNOW IF THERE ARE PEOPLE THERE?

SNOW IS GREAT...

IT'S NO USE. HE'S NOT LISTENING.

THROB THROB

SUMMER
SPRING
AUTUMN
WINTER

SUMMER
SPRING
AUTUMN
WINTER

SUMMER
SPRING
AUTUMN
WINTER

SUMMER
SPRING
AUTUMN
WINTER

SUMMER ISLAND

SPRING ISLAND

AUTUMN ISLAND

WINTER ISLAND

...YOU WILL HAVE TO ENDURE 16 SEASONS...

...BEGINNING WITH SUMMER ON SUMMER ISLAND AND ENDING WITH WINTER ON WINTER ISLAND.

IN OTHER WORDS...

WHEN YOU SAIL THE GRAND LINE, AT THE VERY LEAST...

...IT'S NO WONDER THE SEAS BETWEEN THEM ARE SO TURBULENT.

I SEE. IF THERE ARE CLUSTERS OF ISLANDS LIKE THAT...

WHAK WHAK

OF COURSE THERE ARE EXCEPTIONS TO THIS, AS WELL AS UNKNOWN WEATHER PATTERNS.

YOU'RE RIGHT!

I SEE IT!!

THAT'S WHY STABLE WEATHER MEANS THERE'S AN ISLAND NEARBY!

EXACTLY.

THIS SEA...

YEAH. IT'S NOT EVEN DEPENDABLY UNPREDICTABLE HERE.

TAK TAK

THE WEATHER'S BEEN UNUSUALLY STABLE LATELY. STABLE BUT COLD.

TAK–TAK TAK–TAK W

NEVER MIND THEM...

A WINTER ISLAND?

WE MUST BE APPROACHING A WINTER ISLAND.

WHAK!!

OUCH!

VIVI...

SANJI, KEEP A SHARP LOOKOUT.

IT'S A SIGN THAT THERE'S LAND NEARBY.

AND EACH OF THESE ISLANDS GENERALLY HAS FOUR SEASONS.

SUMMER ISLANDS, SPRING ISLANDS, AUTUMN ISLANDS AND WINTER ISLANDS.

CLIMATICALLY, THE ISLANDS OF THE GRAND LINE CAN BE DIVIDED UP INTO FOUR TYPES--

THE MOON'LL BE FULL SOON.

BRRR... C-COLD... S-SO COLD...

WON'T THAT COOL HER DOWN?

WHAT IF WE THROW SOME WATER ON HER?

DOOM!!

WHAM!

OOF...

THWAK!!

ARE YOU CRAZY!!?

WITHOUT NAMI TO NAVIGATE, WE CAN'T SAIL AT NIGHT.

I KNOW. WE HAVE TO DROP ANCHOR SOMEWHERE.

KLUNK!

THUD

THIS IS BAD. THE SUN'S GOING DOWN, VIVI.

Chapter 132: SEE?

Q: How about an elephant-sized radish?
(I caught it myself!!) --An Ultra-Canadian Man

A: Hmm, looks delicious. Thank you. Krunch krunch munch munch... Oh!! Huh? Oh! Krunch krunch munch munch...

Q: Hello, Mr. Oda, how are you? Listen, I was assigned to write about my aspirations, so I asked my teacher if my topic could be that my second wish is to become a pirate, and my teacher said, "Get serious!" I **am** serious! --Saori

A: Of course you're serious. Who'd joke about a thing like that? You ask that teacher of yours, "What's wrong with being a plunderer!?" Okay?

Q: I was watching the *One Piece* anime the other day, (the adaptation of volume 7, chapter 57: "If You Have a Dream," where Zeff loses his leg). It said that Zeff lost his leg in a shipwreck. Was that changed for the sake of the little kids who watch the show?

A: Exactly. An episode titled "Eat Your Own Leg" might be too much for small children. Television audiences can number in the millions, and special precautions have to be taken. Kudos to the animators who create such wonderful works while being careful about things like that. If you want to show them your appreciation, send them a letter. It will cheer them up.

MY MOUTH HURTS JUST WATCHING HIM!!!

KRUNK YECH!

MUNCH MUNCH

KRUNCH KREK

WHO IS THAT GUY?

HE JUST ATE THAT KNIFE.

DO YOU HAVE AN ETERNAL POSE OR A LOG POSE!?

POP

WE WANT TO GO TO THE *DRUM KINGDOM.*

IT'S NOT GOOD TO RUSH THROUGH LIFE. IF YOU DON'T HAVE EITHER OF THOSE ITEMS, WE'LL TAKE YOUR TREASURE AND YOUR SHIP INSTEAD.

SO, IF YOU'RE DONE, GO AWAY!

WHAT!?

KRUNCH MUNCH MUNCH

NOPE.

AND WE'VE NEVER HEARD OF THAT PLACE EITHER.

...FROM THE LOOKS OF IT.

I THOUGHT IT WAS SOMETHING LIKE THAT...

HEY, WE'RE IN A HURRY.

DOOM!!!

MUNCH

MUNCH

MUNCH

FOUR OF YOU...

HMM...

CAN'T BE JUST THE FOUR OF YOU...

GAA...

WE DON'T HAVE TIME FOR THIS.

WOW...

A PIRATE SHIP!!?

GOSH DARN IT!!!

SHOOM!!

HEY, WHAT'S GOING ON!?

OKAY.

TMP TMP.!!

VIVI, TAKE OVER HERE!!

THAT SHIP ATTACKED US.

HMM...

FWIK

WHAT HAPPENED?

SO...?

PUFF

REALLY?

UH-HUH, IT'S COLD ALL RIGHT.

YEAH, SURE IS.

...

OOOOO

!!

BOY, SURE IS COLD TODAY.

TWITCH!!

92

Chapter 131:
WAPOL OF TIN

DJANGO'S DANCE PARADISE, VOL. 5: GETAWAY DANCE

Q: Mr. Eiichiro Oda, please… **Give me something.**
(a personal possession of yours)

A: I don't think so.

Q: Oda Sensei, hello, how do you do? In school right now, there's a rumor going around…that you're a dog. A poodle actually!! Is that true?

A: Bow wow. Bow wow. Bow wow wow wow. (Translation: How could I be a dog?) Bow wow. (Okay, next.)

Q: Where do they sell men's spirits? By the way, I already bought a woman's spirit from a second-hand shop.

A: Really?

Q: Oda Sensei!! I've been wondering about something for a long time. What are Luffy, Zolo, Nami, Usopp, and Sanji's birthdays? Please tell me!!

A: I get this question a lot, so I guess I should answer it.
Luffy--May 5; Zolo--November 11; Nami--July 3;
Usopp--April 1; Sanji--March 2 Happy Birthday!!
Was that too easygoing of me? All those who think
I was too easygoing, raise your hands.
Wow…a million people.
Ah, well, what's done is done. I don't hear any
complaints. Go tell their parents.

Q: Do you believe in kappa (water sprites)?

A: Of course. They're all over the place. Really.

HWOOO

AND SO, IGNORING THE ETERNAL POSE THAT POINTED THE WAY TO ALABASTA, THEY SAILED THE MERRY GO IN SEARCH OF A DOCTOR...

...AND THE VERY NEXT DAY...

YOU EXPECT US TO FIND A DOCTOR OUT HERE?!

HEY...

SEE ANY DOC-TORS?

SANJI, KAROO!! BE QUIET!!

VIVI, WHAT'LL WE DO? NAMI'S FEVER ISN'T GOING DOWN!!

SHO

IS THAT SOMEBODY STANDING OUT THERE?

HEY, GUYS, TAKE A LOOK...

WHAT A CLOSE CALL!! WE BARELY MISSED IT!!!

IF WE'D CONTINUED ON THAT COURSE, WE'D HAVE SAILED STRAIGHT INTO IT!!!

THAT'S THE DIRECTION WE WERE SAILING IN BEFORE WE TURNED...

W-WAIT A MINUTE! THAT DIREC-TION...

IT'S AS THOUGH SHE FEELS IT IN HER BONES!!!

WEEZ

THIS GIRL DOESN'T JUST USE...

...THE WIND AND SKY TO PREDICT THE WEATHER.

AMAZING... THEY SAY THE CYCLONES ON THE GRAND LINE HAPPEN WITHOUT WARNING, AND YET...!!

AYE-AYE!!!

WE'RE GONNA HEAD SOUTH!! WE GOTTA FIND A DOCTOR!!!

AWRIGHT, LET'S HURRY!!

I'VE NEVER SEEN A SEAFARER LIKE HER...

I'M SURE! THAT'S WHY WE NEED TO MAKE NAMI WELL QUICKLY.

ARE YOU SURE ABOUT THIS? WHAT ABOUT THOSE MILLION PEOPLE OF YOURS?

· · ·

THIS SHIP CAN'T GO ANY FASTER THAN THAT!!

ABSOLUTELY!!

· · ·

YOU'VE GOT A BIG HEART.

I LIKE YOU!!!

WELL SAID, VIVI!!!

AAH!! WHAT THE HECK IS THAT!!?

...!! SORRY, VIVI... I THINK...

WEEZ

WEEZ

...I'M NOT COMPLETELY WELL YET...

BUT, NAMI, DON'T PUSH YOURSELF SO HARD!!

THANK YOU FOR YOUR CONCERN!!

OF COURSE! WE PROMISED YOU WE WOULD!!

SO LET'S LOOK FOR AN ISLAND WITH A DOCTOR AS SOON AS POSSIBLE.

...WE NEED TO GET NAMI WELL...

IF WE WANT TO GET TO ALABASTA...

...SO WE CAN GET THERE FASTER!

...BUT MY COUNTRY IS IN GRAVE PERIL, AND I'VE GOT TO GET BACK RIGHT AWAY!

I KNOW THIS IS SELFISH OF ME, AFTER ALL YOU'VE DONE ALREADY...

EVERYONE, I NEED TO ASK A FAVOR OF YOU.

...

THERE'S NOT A MOMENT TO SPARE!!

SO...

...AND HEAD STRAIGHT FOR ALABASTA!!

...

SO I WANT YOU TO SAIL THIS SHIP AT MAXIMUM SPEED...

UNH...

WEEZ

WEEZ

JUST HURRY UP AND TURN THIS SHIP!!

HEY, NAMI, YOU'D BETTER...

I SAID I'M FINE.

...I KNOW YOU WANT TO HELP VIVI, BUT IF YOU OVEREXERT YOURSELF...

NAMI...

IT DOESN'T... SOUND LIKE THE WIND...

SHWOO

WEEZ

WEEZ

WHAT'S THAT?

CRACKLE

...

...GET BACK TO ALABASTA AS SOON AS POSSIBLE.

I HAVE TO...

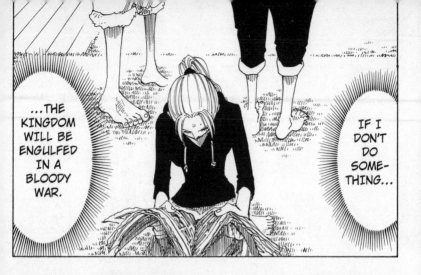

...THE KINGDOM WILL BE ENGULFED IN A BLOODY WAR.

IF I DON'T DO SOMETHING...

...OF ALABASTA!!! CROCODILE WILL TAKE OVER!

I HAVE TO PREVENT THAT AT ALL COSTS... OR IT WILL MEAN THE END...

VIVI, YOU HAVE A HEAVY WEIGHT ON YOUR SHOULDERS.

A MILLION PEOPLE !!?

I'VE GOT TO GET HOME OR A MILLION OF MY PEOPLE WILL KILL EACH OTHER IN A SENSELESS WAR.

SWUP!!

I DON'T JUST HAVE TO GET HOME ALIVE, BUT AS SOON AS POSSIBLE!

80

IT WAS PROBABLY JUST SUN STROKE.

I DON'T NEED TO SEE A DOCTOR.

YOU NEED TO SEE A DOCTOR, NAMI.

I'M FIN

THAT THERMOMETE MUST BE BROKEN. IT' IMPOSSIBLE TO HAVE A TEMPERATUR OF 104.

...AND HEAD STRAIGHT FOR ALABASTA.

BLINK

BLINK

WE HAVE TO STICK TO THE PLAN...

SHE ALWAYS HAS TO BE SO STRONG.

IS SHE REALLY BETTER?

HEY...

BLINK

BLINK

THANKS FOR WORRYING ABOUT ME.

RUSTLE !!!

300,000 SOLDIERS HAVE DEFECTED FROM THE ROYAL ARMY AND JOINED THE REBELS!?

THIS IS TERRIBLE!!!

NOW THE VIOLENCE IN ALABASTA WILL INTENSIFY...

WEEZ

THIS... CHANGES EVERYTHING!!!

THE ROYAL ARMY USED TO HAVE 600,000 MEN AND THE REBEL ARMY HAD 400,000.

IT IS. I'M GLAD TO SEE YOU'RE ACTUALLY TAKING THIS SERIOUSLY.

I GET THE FEELING IT'S PRETTY BAD.

DO YOU UNDERSTAND, LUFFY?

I'M SORRY. LETTING YOU SEE THAT WOULDN'T MAKE THE SHIP GO FASTER...

...AND I DIDN'T WANT YOU TO WORRY, SO I HID IT FROM YOU.

THAT NEWSPAPER'S FROM THREE DAYS AGO...

SKREE

SKREE

SPLASH

SPLASH

KLAZK

KLAZK

SMOOTH SAILING... AHEAD...

HMM...

KLAZK

KLAZK

IS IT ABOUT ALABASTA, VIVI!!?

WHAT'S WRONG?

IT CAN'T BE...

ISN'T THERE ANYONE ON BOARD WHO KNOWS A LITTLE MEDICINE?

WEEZ

EVEN A LITTLE COLD CAN KILL YOU IF YOU'RE NOT CAREFUL.

WEEZ

SOB!!

THAT'S BASIC CARE YOU'D GIVE ANY SICK PERSON.

WELL, I'LL COOK UP SOMETHING SHE CAN EAT.

RIGHT, SANJI!!?

SHE JUST NEEDS TO EAT SOME MEAT!! THAT'LL CURE HER.

BUT IT WON'T NECES-SARILY MAKE HER WELL.

Chapter 130:
MAXIMUM SPEED

DJANGO'S DANCE PARADISE, VOL. 4: PURSUIT!! USOPP'S SECURITY FORCE

Q: I have a question. In Volume 12, page 31, what are they doing with that barrel? -- Vivi Fan No. 017

A: They kicked open the lid of a beer barrel to celebrate reaching the Grand Line. It's sort of a One Piece sailing ceremony. I wanted to show more, but this was the end of the 100th chapter, "The Legend Begins," and I didn't have much time. But isn't it kind of cool anyway?

◎ First, there's an opening ceremony before the shipbuilding begins.

◎ Then there's the completion ceremony when the ship is finished.

◎ And finally, there's a huge celebration and a christening when the ship is launched.

So the most exciting ceremony is the ship's birthday or christening. One of the rituals is the striking of a champagne bottle against the bow of the ship. If the bottle doesn't break, it's a bad omen. So the person throwing the bottle has to be very serious about it. I've heard that Viking sailing ceremonies included the spilling of sacrificial blood on the ship.

THE SWANDA IS READY.

SPLASH

MR. 2 BON CLAY!!

SANDY ISLAND HARBOR (THE KINGDOM OF ALABASTA)

NO WAY!! EVEN IF WE ATTACKED ALL AT ONCE, HE'D SLAUGHTER US!!

WHY ALL THE FUSS?! CAN'T YOU KILL MR. 3 BY YOUR-SELVES?!

ALL RIGHT, ALL RIGHT, ALL RIGHT!! QUIET!!

WEAKLINGS! WHAT A PAIN!!

おかま道

HMPH.

PLEASE HELP US!! IT'S THE BOSS'S ORDERS!!

RUB

RUB

DOOM!!

PRINCESS VIVI, DO YOU HAVE THE RESOLVE TO STAY ALIVE?

WHATEVER SACRIFICES MUST BE MADE, EVEN IF YOU MUST BETRAY OTHERS, YOU MUST LIVE!!! NO MATTER WHAT!!!

NO NEED TO WORRY, VIVI.

T M P

...AND RETURN TO ALABASTA!!!

I WILL LIVE...

AND THERE'S A CHOICE OF COFFEE OR TEA.

PETIT FOUR? THEY'RE MY TREAT OF THE DAY.

SANJI...

YOU HAVE ME!!!

TA-DAH!!

NOW FINALLY...

YOU CAN GO HOME.

...AND SAVE MY KING- DOM...

YES. I'VE GOT TO GET HOME.

IF WE DON'T RUN INTO TROUBLE...

...BETWEEN HERE AND ALABASTA, THAT IS.

YOUR FATHER, THE KING, IS POWERLESS NOW!!

YOU'RE THE ONLY ONE, PRINCESS!!

YOU MUST LIVE!!!

...OR THIS VIOLENCE WILL NOT END!!!

THE PEOPLE MUST HEAR THE TRUTH FROM YOUR LIPS...

...SAILED PEACEFULLY OVER THE OCEAN.

SKREE

YOU GUYS!! SOMEDAY, I SWEAR!!

MEANWHILE, THE MERRY GO...

SKREE

I'M GOING TO ELBAPH!! TO THE VILLAGE OF WARRIORS !!!

SPLASH

EL--BAPH-BAPH--♪ EL--BAPH-BAPH--??♪ EVERYONE IS HUGE--♪ 'CAUSE THEY'RE GIANTS--

THEY'RE SURE IN A GOOD MOOD.

LET'S GO TO THE LAND OF THE GIANTS !!

ALL RIGHT, USOPP!! LET'S DO IT!!

NOD NOD

......

VIVI, CAN YOU KEEP AN EYE ON THE LOG POSE?

SWMUP

SWUP

I'M STILL EXHAUSTED FROM THAT ADVENTURE.

NOD NOD

...

64

BOOM!!

THERE'S THE SIGNAL.

OH...

HMM... SAME HERE.

THERE'S SOMETHING I CAN'T REMEMBER.

BY THE WAY, BROGGY...

RIGHT! WE'LL WORK IT OUT LATER!!!

OH, NEVER MIND!! LET'S JUST SETTLE THIS!!!

BUT THAT WAS...

...A LONG TIME AGO.

KLANG!!!

HO HO HO HO HO HO HO!!!

GWAH HA HA HA HA HA!!!

LONG AGO...

...A GROUP OF RUFFIANS CALLING THEMSELVES THE PIRATE GIANTS...

...TERROR-IZED THE SEAS.

...BROGGY THE RED AND DORRY THE BLUE, WERE WARRIORS OF UNIMAGINABLE STRENGTH.

THE TWO LEADERS OF THESE PIRATES...

Chapter 129:
STRAIGHT AHEAD!!!

DJANGO'S DANCE PARADISE, VOL. 3: THE ONION APPEARS!!

⊹ COLORING CORNER ⊹

HAVE FAITH IN US, AND SAIL STRAIGHT AHEAD!!! NO MATTER WHAT HAPPENS, SAIL STRAIGHT AHEAD!!!

...WE WILL ALLOW NO ENEMY TO TRAMPLE ON OUR FRIENDS' PRIDE!!!

IT'S TIME TO SAY GOODBYE.

WE'LL SAIL STRAIGHT AHEAD !!!

WHAT'RE THEY TALKING ABOUT?

OKAY !!!

LOOK!! UP AHEAD !!!

WHUP

YES, I HOPE SO TOO.

I HOPE WE MEET AGAIN.

...THAT'LL TAKE US TO THE EAST OF THE ISLAND.

IF WE SAIL STRAIGHT AHEAD...

HEY, CAN'T WE CARRY ANY MORE MEAT?

DO YOU WANT TO SINK US?

THAT'S ALL THE SHIP WILL HOLD!

THEY CAME TO SEE US OFF.

HEY, LOOK!! THE GIANTS!

43

OUR FRIENDS ARE ABOUT TO SET SAIL ON THE EASTERN SEA.

WE CAN'T LET THEM GO BY THEMSELVES WITH THAT MONSTER OUT THERE.

OF COURSE. THIS AXE HAS BEEN MY PARTNER IN BATTLE FOR OVER A HUNDRED YEARS, BUT...

HAVE YOU ANY REGRETS?

WHUP

MY AXE AND YOUR SWORD HAVE HAD GOOD LIVES.

WHUP

I'LL LIVE.

DORRY?

HOW'S YOUR WOUND...

THEN IT'S SETTLED.

TOMP

...IF IT'S TO HELP THOSE PEOPLE...

...IT'S WELL WORTH IT!!!

IT'S SAD TO SEE YOU GO, BUT I WON'T STOP YOU!!

I HOPE YOU'RE ABLE TO SAVE YOUR KINGDOM.

OH... YOU SEEM TO BE IN A HURRY.

THANK YOU.

GOODBYE, MASTERS! ONE DAY, I SHALL GO TO ELBAPH!!!

QUACK!

WE'LL SEE.

JUST WAIT. MINE'S DEFINITELY BIGGER.

DON'T KILL EACH OTHER, GIANTS!

...

...

...A LITTLE WHILE AGO...

YOU MEAN...

THAT'S WHAT I TOLD HIM.

AND YOU TOLD HIM WE WERE ALL DEAD!?

HE THOUGHT I WAS MR. 3.

THAT'S RIGHT.

...YOU SPOKE WITH MR. ZERO?

GRR!!

BAROQUE WORKS IS OFF OUR TRAIL, BUT WE'RE STILL STUCK ON THIS ISLAND!

DO !!!!? !!!!!

WHAT?

HUH!?

WE'RE STUCK? WHAT'S TO KEEP US HERE...

...NOW THAT WE HAVE THIS?

NO ONE'S MAD AT YOU.

WHERE'D YOU GET THOSE?

WANT A RICE CRACKER?

SHE'S RIGHT, VIVI. DON'T WORRY ABOUT IT.

KRUNCH

KRUNCH

KRUNCH

DOOM

HA HA HA HA!! GEE, USOPP, YOUR EYES ARE ABOUT TO POP OUT!!

WHAK!

A HA HA H

IDIOT...

AGAIN! DO IT AGAIN!!

BLUSH BLUSH

HEY, NAMI, DANCE FOR US!!

ALL RIGHT!! LET'S HAVE A RICE CRACKER PARTY!

...

HA HA!!

ARE YOU KIDDING? EVEN WE CAN'T CONTROL A LOG POSE.

IS THERE ANYTHING YOU CAN DO, GIANTS?

I'LL SAY! WE'RE IN REAL TROUBLE.

IT TAKES A YEAR FOR THE LOG POSE TO RESET HERE. THAT'S NO GOOD.

OH HO HO HO!!

LITTLE GARDEN, ISLAND OF GIANTS

WE COMPLETELY FORGOT THERE WAS A PRICE ON OUR HEADS!!

HAR HAR HAR HAR HAR!!

WE WANT TO REPAY YOU.

YOU LITTLE PEOPLE SAVED OUR LIVES.

DON'T SAY THAT.

TWEEK

OUCH!

THEY...

...BE-CAUSE OF ME.

...ONLY CAME TO THIS ISLAND...

ALABASTA IS A KINGDOM IN THE GRIP OF A REBELLION.

DO YOU THINK A CRIMINAL ORGANIZATION AND THE STRAW HAT PIRATES ARE SOMEHOW INVOLVED?

SHE'S THE MISSING PRINCESS OF ALABASTA.

PRINCESS VIVI...

CONTACT HEADQUARTERS AND GET AN ETERNAL POSE.

AYE.

THEN ARE WE...?

YES, SIR.

I DON'T KNOW, BUT THIS IS OUR FIRST CLUE TO THE STRAW HATS' WHEREABOUTS.

...THE DESERT KINGDOM OF ALABASTA.

SET A COURSE FOR...

(SPLISH)

...HE COULD BE GETTING DIRECT ORDERS...

...FROM SOME CRIMINAL ORGANIZATION.

MAYBE. IF 11 IS HIS CODENAME...

...CONNECTED TO MR. 11, THAT DUBIOUS SWORDSMAN WE CAPTURED IN LUNESS RECENTLY?

IS THIS MR. ZERO...

...

WH-WHAT!!? I-I WAS SURE I BURNED THEM!

GULP!!

HUH!? ER... THAT WAS... UM...

THEN EXPLAIN THOSE **ORDERS** WE FOUND IN YOUR POCKET!

YOU'RE WAY OFF THE MARK.

HEH HEH... MR. ZERO!? A CRIMINAL ORGANIZATION!? THAT'S ABSURD!

DA-DOOM!

MR. 11 BAROQUE WORKS (FRONTIER AGENT)

...!!!

THERE WAS NOTHING IN YOUR POCKETS.

GOTCHA!!

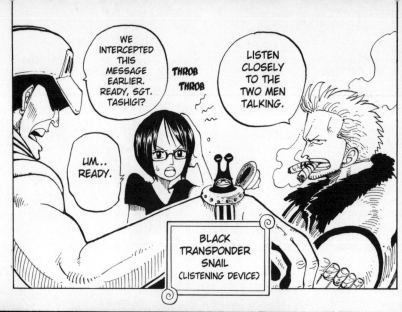

WE INTERCEPTED THIS MESSAGE EARLIER. READY, SGT. TASHIGI?

THROB THROB

LISTEN CLOSELY TO THE TWO MEN TALKING.

UM... READY.

BLACK TRANSPONDER SNAIL (LISTENING DEVICE)

KRRK

ZZK

ZZT... YES.

MISSION ACCOMP-- ...BZZT

DID YOU... PRINCESS VIVI AND...

STRAW HATS?

KRRK...

ZZK...

"ORDERS DIRECTLY."

"MR. ZERO."

"STRAW HATS."

"PRINCESS VIVI."

YES. THE TRANSMISSION IS GARBLED, BUT WE CAN MAKE OUT FOUR KEYWORDS FROM THIS CONVERSATION.

STRAW...!! THE STRAW HATS!!!

POP
ZZT
ZZK

Chapter 128: PIRATE PRIDE

PLAY IT AGAIN.

AYE, CAP'N.

TASHIGI!! COME HERE AND LISTEN TO THIS.

ONLY ON THE GRAND LINE CAN YOU FIND A FINE-GRADE SWORD SO EASILY!

THE FINE-GRADE SWORD KASHU!!

SHAAA

WHAT BEAUTIFUL WORKMANSHIP.

AYE-AYE!!! HUH?!

BOOM!!

WHAT IS IT, CAPTAIN SMOKER? COFFEE?!

KLANK BANG

TASHIGI!!! ARE YOU DEAF, YOU SWORD-CRAZY FOOL?!!

Reader: And now, everyone! Instead of Oda Sensei, Ms. Valentine will begin the Question Corner!!

Welcome, Ms. Valentine!!

Valentine: Kya ha ha ha ha! Let the Question Corner begin! ♥

Oda: Sure…

Q: Ei-chan!! Here's the secret of tempura. It was originally a Portuguese word, but it has no real meaning. Long ago, the Japanese just wrote down what the Portuguese said phonetically. It's a loanword. If there's anything else you don't understand, just ask me. ♥ Eh-heh ♥♥
All-knowing Himeko from Yamaguchi

A: Wow. Amazing. All-knowing Himeko really knows all!! Here's a question for All-knowing Himeko. In the panel below from page 51 of volume 1, why are the three scars missing? And why, even though many readers have pointed it out, have I never corrected it? There must be some deep significance to it, right? I know!! It's a message to young boys and girls to be so cheerful that even their scars go away!! Right? Nah. Sorry. I just forgot…

HO RAY RAISE THE SAILS! WE'RE OFF WITH THE TIDE!! WEIGH THE ANCHOR! → HO RAY RAISE THE SAILS! WE'RE OFF WITH THE TIDE!! WEIGH THE ANCHOR!

Now then, everyone!! It's time to pick up a pen and do some revisions! Everybody's entitled to a few mistakes, but not this kind.

JUST WHO WERE THESE GUYS?

THIS IS...

KLUNK

ALABASTA.

HMM...

THE GRAND LINE

CAP'N SMOKER!! WE JUST INTERCEPTED A VERY INTERESTING TRANSMISSION!!

CAP'N!!!

WHAT!?

SKREE

SKREE

SMOKER MARINE

MARINE

SPLASH

...HAVE MR. 3 DISPOSED OF.

SOMEWHERE BETWEEN LITTLE GARDEN AND ALABASTA...

HE HUNG UP.

...SIR CROCODILE.

YOU'RE SO RUTHLESS...

NO, NO... I'LL DO AS YOU SAY. NO PROBLEM.

MINIONS ARE REPLACEABLE. ARE YOU TALKING BACK TO ME?

KLIK KLIK

YOU'RE TO GO STRAIGHT TO ALABASTA.

ANYWAY...

SO THERE'S NO NEED TO SEND ANYONE ELSE AFTER THEM.

BUT I FINISHED THEM FOR GOOD THIS TIME.

UM, WELL... YOU MAKE IT SOUND BAD.

OKAY?

HEREAFTER, YOU'LL RECEIVE YOUR ORDERS DIRECTLY, AS IN THE PAST.

THAT IS ALL. I WISH YOU SUCCESS, MR. 3.

AND THIS WILL BE OUR LAST ELECTRONIC COMMUNICATION.

WE CAN'T HAVE THE NAVY CATCHING ON TO US.

DISPATCH MR. 2 TO LITTLE GARDEN.

YES?

MS. ALL SUNDAY.

KLAK

KLINK

STILL ALIVE...

......

...YOU SAY?

sss

KLINK KLINK

KLINK

sss

KLINK

SNAP!!

...THE MISSION WAS ACCOMPLISHED?

DIDN'T YOU JUST TELL ME...

FWuP

IN OTHER WORDS...

...YOU GAVE ME A FALSE REPORT.

BUT THEY WEREN'T AS DEAD AS I THOUGHT.

ER, YES. I THOUGHT IT WAS...

POW POW POW POW !!!

NOW...

...JUST A..

FWIP!!

...DARN MINUTE...

WOMP!!

...YOU OVER-GROWN CHICKEN!

...

TURNS OUT THE STRAW HATS WERE STILL ALIVE.

REALLY.

OH, UM.. NOTHING. *HUFF...*

BUT IT'S OKAY, I FINISHED THEM. REALLY.

FWUMP!

TUP

Mr 3

WHAT'S GOING ON?

WHO ARE THESE GUYS?

ER... NOTHING...

WHAT'S THE MATTER?

...TO CONFIRM THAT THE JOB IS DONE...

...AND DELIVER SOMETHING.

I SEE. GOOD WORK.

THE UNLUCKIES ARE ON THEIR WAY THERE NOW...

...TO ALABASTA.

THE ETERNAL POSE...

KLINK

DELIVER SOMETHING?

UNLUCKIES?

GO TO ALABASTA...

...AND AWAIT FURTHER ORDERS.

I WANT YOU TO HEAD FOR ALABASTA WITH MS. GOLDEN WEEK.

THE TIME HAS COME TO BEGIN THE MOST CRUCIAL PART OF OUR PLAN.

WHY DO YOU HESITATE?

BLUP BLUP

BLUP

I HOPE THE OTHERS ARE OKAY!!!

WHAT A SPOT. WE'RE STILL BEING HUNTED.

CRAP...

HAVE YOU ELIMINATED PRINCESS VIVI AND THE STRAW HATS?

I ASKED YOU A QUESTION.

EVERYONE WHO KNEW YOUR SECRET...

OH, YEAH... MISSION ACCOMPLISHED.

...HAS BEEN ELIMINATED. SO YOU CAN CALL OFF THE HUNT.

...

FWOO

ONE OF THE SEVEN WARLORDS OF THE SEA!!!?

. . . . .

MR. 3?! SO THIS IS HIS SNAIL-O-PHONE...

HAVE YOU ACCOMPLISHED YOUR MISSION, MR. 3?

YOU'VE BEEN GONE A LONG TIME.

. . . . .

THIS IS THE ENEMY'S CAMP. THE GUY WHO WANTS TO KILL VIVI, MR. 3, IS ON THIS ISLAND!

NOW I GET IT.

WOOOOOOO

MR....

...ZERO?

...THE LEADER OF VIVI'S ENEMIES?

ISN'T MR. ZERO...

TAP TAP

THEN THE GUY ON THE OTHER END OF THIS SNAIL-O-PHONE IS...

14

Chapter 127:
SNAIL-O-PHONE

DJANGO'S DANCE PARADISE, VOL. 2: FIRST, KNOW YOUR PLACE

Vol. 15
STRAIGHT AHEAD!!!

CONTENTS

THE STORY OF Volume 15
ONE PIECE

Dorry

Roronoa Zolo
A former bounty hunter and master of the "three-sword" style. He plans to be the world's greatest swordsman.

Sanji
The kind-hearted cook (and ladies' man) whose dream is to find the legendary sea, the "All Blue."

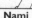

Nami
A thief who specializes in robbing pirates. Nami hates pirates, but Luffy convinced her to be his navigator.

"Red-Haired" Shanks
A pirate that Luffy idolizes. Shanks gave Luffy his trademark straw hat.

Princess Vivi

Broggy

Usopp
A village boy with a talent for telling tall tales. His father, Yasopp, is a member of Shanks's crew.

Monkey D. Luffy
Boundlessly optimistic and able to stretch like rubber, he is determined to become the King of the Pirates.

Monkey D. Luffy started out as just a kid with a dream—and that dream was to become the greatest pirate in history! Stirred by the tales of pirate "Red-Haired" Shanks, Luffy vowed to become a pirate himself. That was before the enchanted Devil Fruit gave Luffy the power to stretch like rubber, at the cost of being unable to swim—a serious handicap for an aspiring sea dog. Undeterred, Luffy set out to sea and recruited some crewmates: master swordsman Zolo, treasure-hunting thief Nami, lying sharpshooter Usopp, and Sanji, the high-kicking chef.

Luffy and the crew of the *Merry Go* finally reach the Grand Line and are soon up to their necks in intrigue! Having saved Princess Vivi from the super-secretive criminals of Baroque Works, they vow to return her to her kingdom so that she can defuse a rebellion instigated by the mysterious Mr. Zero. But when the Princess accidentally reveals Mr. Zero's secret identity, the Straw Hat pirates suddenly find themselves at the top of Baroque Works' hit list.

Their first stop en route to Alabasta is the strange island of Little Garden. There they find two giant warriors locked in a century-long battle of honor. But the battle is cut short by the machinations of Baroque Works agents who want to collect a huge reward for the Brobdingnagian combatants. Infuriated by this dastardly act, Luffy and crew clobber the criminals. But can the Straw Hats survive on Little Garden until their Log Pose resets—a whole year from now?!

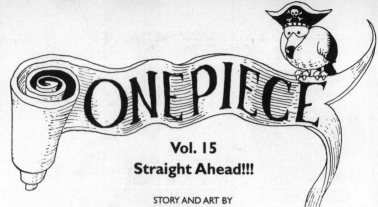

ONEPIECE

Vol. 15
Straight Ahead!!!

STORY AND ART BY
EIICHIRO ODA

ONE PIECE VOL. 15
BAROQUE WORKS PART 4

SHONEN JUMP Manga Edition

This volume contains material that was originally
published in English in **SHONEN JUMP** #51–55.

STORY AND ART BY EIICHIRO ODA

English Adaptation/Lance Caselman
Translation/JN Productions
Touch-up Art & Lettering/Vanessa Satone
Additional Touch-up/Josh Simpson
Design/Sean Lee
Editor/Urian Brown

Printed in the U.S.A.

Published by VIZ Media, LLC
P.O. Box 77010
San Francisco, CA 94107

10 9 8 7
First printing, August 2007
Seventh printing, April 2013

www.viz.com

THE WORLD'S
MOST POPULAR MANGA
SHONEN JUMP
www.shonenjump.com

尾田栄一郎

Eiichiro Oda

--Continued from the previous volume--
"Kah!!" shouted the ninja. "Batan!!" And the older students collapsed in a heap. It was the famous kanashibari jutsu technique!!
After that, he stunned us by stopping someone's heart from beating and showing photos from his years of training. We were in total awe. Then the ninja said, "Actually, I could stand upside down on the ceiling of this hall for five hours, but we don't have time today."
I saw the ninja. He wasn't kidding.

-Eiichiro Oda, 2000

iichiro Oda began his manga career at the age of 17, when his one-shot cowboy manga **Wanted!** won second place in the coveted Tezuka manga awards. Oda went on to work as an assistant to some of the biggest manga artists in the industry, including Nobuhiro Watsuki, before winning the Hop Step Award for new artists. His pirate adventure **One Piece**, which debuted in **Weekly Shonen Jump** in 1997, quickly became one of the most popular manga in Japan.